A Companion to Moral Anthropology

The *Blackwell Companions to Anthropology* offers a series of comprehensive syntheses of the traditional subdisciplines, primary subjects, and geographic areas of inquiry for the field. Taken together, the series represents both a contemporary survey of anthropology and a cutting edge guide to the emerging research and intellectual trends in the field as a whole.

1. *A Companion to Linguistic Anthropology*, edited by Alessandro Duranti
2. *A Companion to the Anthropology of Politics*, edited by David Nugent and Joan Vincent
3. *A Companion to the Anthropology of American Indians*, edited by Thomas Biolsi
4. *A Companion to Psychological Anthropology*, edited by Conerly Casey and Robert B. Edgerton
5. *A Companion to the Anthropology of Japan*, edited by Jennifer Robertson
6. *A Companion to Latin American Anthropology*, edited by Deborah Poole
7. *A Companion to Biological Anthropology*, edited by Clark Larsen (hardback only)
8. *A Companion to the Anthropology of India*, edited by Isabelle Clark-Decès
9. *A Companion to Medical Anthropology*, edited by Merrill Singer and Pamela I. Erickson
10. *A Companion to Cognitive Anthropology*, edited by David B, Kronenfeld, Giovanni Bennardo, Victor de Munck, and Michael D. Fischer
11. *A Companion to Cultural Resource Management*, edited by Thomas King
12. *A Companion to the Anthropology of Education*, edited by Bradley A.U. Levinson and Mica Pollack
13. *A Companion to the Anthropology of the Body and Embodiment*, edited by Frances E. Mascia-Lees
14. *A Companion to Paleopathology*, edited by Anne L. Grauer
15. *A Companion to Folklore*, edited by Regina F. Bendix and Galit Hasan-Rokem
16. *A Companion to Forensic Anthropology*, edited by Dennis Dirkmaat
17. *A Companion to the Anthropology of Europe*, edited by Ullrich Kockel, Máiréad Nic Craith, and Jonas Frykman
18. *A Companion to Border Studies*, edited by Thomas M. Wilson and Hastings Donnan
19. *A Companion to Rock Art*, edited by Jo McDonald and Peter Veth
20. *A Companion to Moral Anthropology*, edited by Didier Fassin
21. *A Companion to Gender Prehistory*, edited by Diane Bolger
22. *A Companion to Organizational Anthropology*, edited by D. Douglas Caulkins and Ann T. Jordan
23. *A Companion to Paleoanthropology*, edited by David R. Begun
24. *A Companion to Chinese Archaeology*, edited by Anne P. Underhill
25. *A Companion to the Anthropology of Religion*, edited by Janice Boddy and Michael Lambek
26. *A Companion to Urban Anthropology*, edited by Donald M. Nonini

A Companion to Moral Anthropology

Edited by
Didier Fassin

WILEY Blackwell

This paperback edition first published 2015

Edition history: John Wiley & Sons, Inc (hardback, 2012)

Registered Office
John Wiley & Sons, Ltd, The Atrium, Southern Gate, Chichester, West Sussex, PO19 8SQ, UK

Editorial Offices
350 Main Street, Malden, MA 02148-5020, USA
9600 Garsington Road, Oxford, OX4 2DQ, UK
The Atrium, Southern Gate, Chichester, West Sussex, PO19 8SQ, UK

For details of our global editorial offices, for customer services, and for information about how to apply for permission to reuse the copyright material in this book please see our website at www.wiley.com/wiley-blackwell.

Library of Congress Cataloging-in-Publication Data

A companion to moral anthropology/edited by Didier Fassin.
pages cm
Includes bibliographical references and index.
ISBN 978-0-470-65645-7 (hardback) – ISBN 978-1-118-95950-3 (paperback)
1. Anthropology–Moral and ethical aspects–Handbooks, manuals, etc. I. Fassin, Didier, editor of compilation.
GN27.C647 2012
306–dc23

2012015861

A catalogue record for this book is available from the British Library.

Cover image: From top: Hell, fragment of a triptych depicting the Last Judgment by Hieronymus Bosch, © 1500 (Private collection); Gauguin, Sisters of Charity (detail), 1902 (McNay Art Museum, San Antonio, Texas. Bequest of Marion Koogler McNay, Acc.n: 1950.47. © 2001 McNay Art Museum / Art Resource, New York / Scala, Florence); Goya, The Third of May 1808 (detail), 1814 (Prado, Madrid. Photo © Fine Art Images / Superstock).

Set in 10/12.5pt Galliard by SPi Publisher Services, Pondicherry, India

Printed in Singapore by C.O.S. Printers Pte Ltd

1 2015

Contents

Notes on Contributors

Kwame Anthony Appiah is Laurance S. Rockefeller University Professor of Philosophy and the University Center for Human Values at Princeton University. He grew up in Ghana and was educated at the University of Cambridge, where he took undergraduate and doctoral degrees in philosophy. He has written widely in philosophy of mind and language, ethics and political philosophy, and the philosophy of art, of culture, and of the social sciences; as well as in literary studies, where his focus has been on African and African American literature. His current research focuses on questions about the connection between theory and practice in moral life. He is the editor, with Henry Louis Gates Jr., of the five-volume *Africana: The Encyclopedia of the African and African-American Experience* (Oxford University Press, 2005). His recent publications include *The Ethics of Identity* (Princeton University Press, 2005); *Cosmopolitanism: Ethics in a World of Strangers* (Norton, 2006), which has been translated into more than a dozen languages; *Che cos'è l'Occidente?* (Fondazione San Carlo di Modena, 2008); *Experiments in Ethics* (Harvard University Press, 2009); and *The Honor Code: How Moral Revolutions Happen* (Norton, 2010).

Nicolas Baumard is a Postdoctoral Fellow at the University of Pennsylvania. After an education in natural sciences (biology and cognitive sciences) and in human sciences (social sciences and philosophy), he completed his PhD at the Institut Jean-Nicod in Paris before joining the Institute of Cognitive and Evolutionary Anthropology in Oxford. Inspired by contractualist theories, his work is based on the idea that morality aims at sharing the costs and benefits of social interactions in a mutually advantageous way. This theory has led to a book, *Comment nous sommes devenus moraux: une histoire naturelle du bien et du mal* (Odile Jacob, 2010) and a series of articles in evolutionary biology, experimental psychology, and cognitive anthropology.

Jonathan Benthall is an Honorary Research Fellow in the Department of Anthropology, University College London, and an Associate Fellow with the Humanitarian and Conflict Research Institute, University of Manchester. He was formerly Director of the

Royal Anthropological Institute and Founder Editor of *Anthropology Today*, as well as Chair of the International NGO Training and Research Centre, Oxford. In 1993 he received the American Anthropological Association's Anthropology in Media Award. Since 2005 he has advised on projects sponsored by the Swiss Federal Department of Foreign Affairs relating to Islamic charities. His publications include *Disasters, Relief and the Media* (I. B. Tauris, 1993; new edn. 2010), *The Best of "Anthropology Today"* (as editor; Routledge, 2002), *The Charitable Crescent: Politics of Aid in the Muslim World* (with Jérôme Bellion-Jourdan; I. B. Tauris, 2003; new paperback edn. 2008), and *Returning to Religion: Why a Secular Age is Haunted by Faith* (I. B. Tauris, 2008). He reviews regularly for the *Times Literary Supplement*.

João Biehl is the Susan Dod Brown Professor of Anthropology and Faculty Associate at the Woodrow Wilson School of Public and International Affairs at Princeton University. He is also the co-director of Princeton's Program in Global Heath and Health Policy. He is the author of the award-winning books *Vita: Life in a Zone of Social Abandonment* (University of California Press, 2005) and *Will to Live: AIDS Therapies and the Politics of Survival* (Princeton University Press, 2007). He is also the coeditor of the book *Subjectivity: Ethnographic Investigations* (University of California Press, 2007). He is currently writing the history of a religious war – the Mucker war – that took place among German immigrants in nineteenth-century Brazil. He is also coediting *When People Come First*, a book on evidence, theory, and advocacy in global health. His current research explores the social impact of large-scale treatment programs in resource-poor settings and the role of the judiciary in administering public health.

Veena Das is Krieger–Eisenhower Professor of Anthropology and Professor of Humanities at Johns Hopkins University. She is the author and editor of several books, including *Life and Words: Violence and the Descent into the Ordinary* (University of California Press, 2007) and *Anthropology and Sociology of Economic Life: The Moral Embedding of Economic Action* (with Ranendra Das; Oxford University Press, 2010). Her forthcoming books include *Speaking of Violence: Essays on Language, Gender, and Narrative* and *Estranged Intimacies: To Be a Muslim in Contemporary India*. She is a Fellow of the American Academy of Arts and Sciences, and Fellow of the Academy of Scientists from Developing Countries. She received an honorary doctorate from the University of Chicago in 2000.

James Dungan is a graduate student, pursuing a PhD in social psychology at Boston College under the direction of Liane Young. He received his BS in brain and cognitive sciences from the Massachusetts Institute of Technology in 2011. His current research attempts to characterize distinct moral domains by investigating their cognitive and neural basis. To this end, he uses common social psychology methods to explore the behavioral and emotional signatures of different moral violations, as well as the tools of cognitive neuroscience, such as functional magnetic resonance imaging (fMRI), to explore their neural underpinnings.

Marc Edelman is Professor of Anthropology at Hunter College and the Graduate Center of the City University of New York. He has also taught or been a visiting researcher at Yale, Fordham, Princeton, Columbia, the Institute for Advanced Study, and the universities of Illinois, Tashkent and Costa Rica. He has a longstanding concern with understanding changing forms of capitalism and with the politics of controlling markets, whether through welfare states, civil society pressure, or global trade rules. His current research is on the campaign of transnational agrarian movements to have the United Nations approve a declaration, and eventually a convention, on the rights of peasants. He is the author of *The Logic of the Latifundio* (Stanford, 1992) and *Peasants against Globalization* (Stanford, 1999); coauthor of *Social Democracy in the Global Periphery* (Cambridge University Press, 2007); and coeditor of *The Anthropology of Development and Globalization* (Blackwell, 2005) and *Transnational Agrarian Movements Confronting Globalization* (Wiley-Blackwell, 2009).

Harri Englund is Reader in Social Anthropology at the University of Cambridge. He is also Research Associate in Social Anthropology at the University of Cape Town and Docent of African Studies at the University of Helsinki. He has carried out research among Chichewa/Nyanja speakers in south-central Africa for over two decades. He has written and edited several books on rights discourses, Christianity, war and displacement, mass media, and democratization. His current research explores arguments about freedom and belonging in Africa's vernacular media in both colonial and contemporary contexts. His book *Prisoners of Freedom: Human Rights and the African Poor* (University of California Press, 2006) was awarded the Amaury Talbot Prize of the Royal Anthropological Institute. His most recent books are *Human Rights and African Airwaves: Mediating Equality on the Chichewa Radio* (Indiana University Press, 2011) and the edited volume *Christianity and Public Culture in Africa* (Ohio University Press, 2011).

Didier Fassin is James D. Wolfensohn Professor of Social Science at the Institute for Advanced Study of Princeton and Director of Studies at the École des Hautes Études en Sciences Sociales in Paris. He was the Founding Director of IRIS (Interdisciplinary Research Institute for Social Sciences). His domain of interest is political and moral anthropology. Laureate of the Advanced Grant "Ideas" of the European Research Council, he is currently conducting an ethnography of the state, exploring how institutions such as police, justice, and prison treat immigrants and minorities in France. His recent publications include, as editor, *De la question sociale à la question raciale?* (with Eric Fassin; La Découverte, 2006), *Les politiques de l'enquête* (with Alban Bensa; La Découverte, 2008), and *Contemporary States of Emergency* (with Mariella Pandolfi; Zone, 2010); and, as author, *When Bodies Remember: Experiences and Politics of AIDS in South Africa* (University of California Press, 2007), *The Empire of Trauma: An Inquiry into the Condition of Victimhood* (with Richard Rechtman; Princeton University Press, 2009), *Humanitarian Reason: A Moral History of the Present* (University of California Press, 2011) and *La force de l'ordre: une anthropologie de la police des quartiers* (Seuil, 2011).

James D. Faubion is Professor and Director of Graduate Studies in the Department of Anthropology at Rice University. His work addresses reformism and radicalism, religion and politics, the temporal imagination, kinship, classical and contemporary social thought, and the sociocultural dynamics of the variations and the limits of the formation, the maintenance, and the transformations of the ethical subject. He is the author of *Modern Greek Lessons: A Primer in Historical Constructivism* (Princeton University Press, 1993), *The Shadows and Lights of Waco: Millennialism Today* (Princeton University Press, 2001), and *An Anthropology of Ethics* (Cambridge University Press, 2011). He is the editor of *Rethinking the Subject: An Anthology of Contemporary European Social Thought* (Westview, 1995), *The Ethics of Kinship: Ethnographic Inquiries* (Rowman & Littlefield, 2002), two of the three volumes of *Essential Works of Michel Foucault* (New Press, 1999, 2001), and the forthcoming *Critical Thinkers Now: Michel Foucault*; and coeditor of *Fieldwork Is Not What It Used to Be: Learning Anthropology's Method in a Time of Transition* (Cornell University Press, 2009).

Michael M. J. Fischer is Andrew W. Mellon Professor in the Humanities and Professor of Anthropology and Science and Technology Studies at MIT. A past director of the Center for Cultural Studies at Rice University, and the Program in Science, Technology, and Society at MIT, his domains of interest are anthropological methods for the contemporary world with special attention to the interfaces with science and technology; the anthropology of the biosciences and biotechnologies; and the anthropology of media circuits with special attention to Iran and south Asia. He is currently conducting an ethnography of the Genome Institute of Singapore and the Human Genome Organization. His publications include *Iran from Religious Dispute to Revolution* (Harvard University Press, 1980), *Anthropology as Cultural Critique* (with George E. Marcus; University of Chicago Press, 1986), *Debating Muslims: Cultural Dialogues in Postmodernity and Tradition* (with Mehdi Abedi; University of Wisconsin Press, 1990), *Emergent Forms of Life and the Anthropological Voice* (Duke University Press, 2003), *Mute Dreams, Blind Owls, and Dispersed Knowledges: Persian Poesis in the Transnational Circuitry* (Duke University Press, 2004), *Anthropological Futures* (Duke University Press, 2009), and *A Reader in Medical Anthropology: Theoretical Trajectories, Emergent Realities* (coedited; Wiley-Blackwell, 2010). He edits (with Joe Dumit) the Duke University Press series "Experimental Futures: Technological Lives, Scientific Arts, Anthropological Voices."

Carolyn Fluehr-Lobban, PhD, is a Professor Emerita of Anthropology and African Studies at Rhode Island College. She has spent six years since 1970 living and conducting research in three different African countries, including the Sudan, Egypt, and Tunisia, and has traveled extensively, including two trips around the world teaching anthropology with the University of Pittsburgh Semester at Sea program. Her research subjects have covered such topics as Islamic law and Islamic society, women's social and legal status in Muslim societies, ethics and anthropological research, human rights and cultural relativism, and comparative studies in law and society. She is the author or editor of 11 books, including the following works on anthropology and ethics: *Ethics and the Profession of Anthropology* (AltaMira, 1990, 2003) and a forthcoming textbook *Anthropology and Ethics: Ideas and Practice*; and works on the Sudan: *Shari'a and Islamism in Sudan: Conflict, Law and Social Transformation* (I. B. Tauris, 2011), *Islamic Law and Society in the Sudan* (Routledge, 1987; Arabic translation 2004), *Historical Dictionary of the Sudan* (coauthored, Scarecrow, 1992, 2002), and *Race and Identity in the Nile Valley* (Red Sea, 2004). She has authored three textbooks: *Race, and Racism: An Introduction* (AltaMira, 2005),

Female Well-Being (Zed, 2005), and *Islamic Society in Practice* (University Press of Florida, 1994, 2004).

Mark Goodale is an anthropologist, sociolegal scholar, and social theorist. He is currently Associate Professor of Conflict Analysis and Anthropology at George Mason University and Series Editor of Stanford Studies in Human Rights. He was formerly the first Marjorie Shostak Distinguished Lecturer in Anthropology at Emory University. He is currently working on an ethnographic study of revolution, folk cosmopolitanism, and neo-Burkeanism in Bolivia based on several years of research funded by the National Science Foundation and the Wenner-Gren Foundation for Anthropological Research. He is the author or editor of six books, including *Mirrors of Justice* (with K. Clarke; Cambridge University Press, 2010), *Surrendering to Utopia* (Stanford University Press, 2009), *Human Rights: An Anthropological Reader* (Wiley-Blackwell, 2009), *Dilemmas of Modernity* (Stanford University Press, 2008), and *The Practice of Human Rights* (with S. E. Merry; Cambridge University Press, 2007). Forthcoming books include *Human Rights at the Crossroads* (edited; Oxford University Press) and *The Bolivia Reader* (with Sinclair Thomson et al.; Duke University Press). His writings have appeared in *Current Anthropology*, *American Anthropologist*, *American Ethnologist*, *Law & Society Review*, *Law & Social Inquiry*, *Social & Legal Studies*, *Anthropologie et Sociétés*, and *Ethnohistory*, among others.

Carol J. Greenhouse is Professor of Anthropology and Department Chair at Princeton University. She is a sociocultural anthropologist specializing in the ethnography of law. She is president elect of the American Ethnological Society and past president of the Law and Society Association and the Association for Political and Legal Anthropology; she is also past editor of the journal *American Ethnologist*. She has taught at Indiana University Bloomington and Cornell University, and at the École des Hautes Études en Sciences Sociales (Paris) as Visiting Chair in American Civilization. She is a member of the American Philosophical Society, and has been awarded the Law and Society Association's Kalven Prize for distinguished research contributions to sociolegal studies. Her main publications include *The Paradox of Relevance: Ethnography and Citizenship in the United States* (University of Pennsylvania Press, 2011), *A Moment's Notice: Time Politics across Cultures, Law and Community in Three American Towns* (with David Engel and Barbara Yngvesson; Cornell University Press, 1996), and *Praying for Justice* (Cornell University Press, 1989), as well as edited volumes *Ethnographies of Neoliberalism* (University of Pennsylvania Press, 2009), *Ethnography in Unstable Places* (with Elizabeth Mertz and Kay Warren; Duke University Press, 2002), and *Democracy and Ethnography: Constructing Identities in Multicultural Liberal States* (SUNY Press, 1998).

Josiah M. Heyman is Professor of Anthropology and Chair of Sociology and Anthropology at the University of Texas at El Paso. Among his publications are *States and Illegal Practices* (Berg, 1999), *Finding a Moral Heart for U.S. Immigration Policy: An Anthropological Perspective* (American Anthropological Association, 1998), and *Life and Labor on the Border: Working People of Northeastern Sonora, Mexico 1886–1986* (University of Arizona Press, 1991), as well as over 60 scholarly articles and book chapters. His research interests include migration and border control; states, bureaucracies, and power; and engaged social science.

Alexander Hinton is Founding Director of the Center for the Study of Genocide, Conflict Resolution, and Human Rights and Professor of Anthropology and Global Affairs at Rutgers University, Newark. He is the author of the award-winning *Why Did They Kill? Cambodia in the Shadow of Genocide* (University of California Press, 2005) and six edited or coedited collections, *Transitional Justice: Global Mechanisms and Local Realities after Genocide and Mass Violence* (Rutgers University Press, 2010), *Genocide: Truth, Memory, and Representation* (Duke University Press, 2009), *Night of the Khmer Rouge: Genocide and Democracy in Cambodia* (Paul Robeson Gallery, 2007), *Annihilating Difference: The Anthropology of Genocide* (University of California Press, 2002), *Genocide: An Anthropological Reader* (Blackwell, 2002), and *Biocultural Approaches to the Emotions* (Cambridge University Press, 1999). He is currently working on several other book projects, including an edited volume, *Mass Violence: Memory, Symptom, and Response*, and a book on the Khmer Rouge Tribunal. In recognition of his work on genocide, the American Anthropological Association selected Hinton as the recipient of the 2009 Robert B. Textor and Family Prize for Excellence in Anticipatory Anthropology. He was recently listed as one of *Fifty Key Thinkers on the Holocaust and Genocide* (Routledge, 2011). He is also currently President of the International Association of Genocide Scholars (2011–13) and a Member at the Institute for Advanced Study of Princeton (2011–12).

Karen Ho is an Associate Professor of Anthropology at the University of Minnesota, Twin Cities. Her research centers on the problematic of understanding and representing financial markets, sites that are resistant to cultural analysis and disavow various attempts to locate or particularize them. Her domain of interest is the anthropology of economy, broadly conceived, with specific foci on finance capital, capitalism, globalization, corporations, inequality, dominant discourses, comparative studies of race and ethnicity, and feminist epistemologies. Her ethnography, *Liquidated: An Ethnography of Wall Street* (Duke University Press, 2009), based on three years of fieldwork among investment bankers and major financial institutions, has won two honorable mentions from the Society for Cultural Anthropology and the Society for the Anthropology of North America. Recent publications include "Disciplining Investment Bankers, Disciplining the Economy" (*American Anthropology*, 2009), "Finance" (*Encyclopedia of Social and Cultural Anthropology*, 2010), and "Outsmarting Risk: From Bonuses to Bailouts" (*Anthropology Now*, 2010). Her latest book project attempts to excavate an alternative cultural history of financial risk.

Caroline Humphrey has worked in the USSR/Russia, Mongolia, Inner Mongolia, Nepal, and India. Her research interests include the anthropology of socialist and postsocialist economies; religion, ritual, and morality; and the contemporary transformations of cities. She is currently Director of the Mongolia and Inner Asia Studies Unit in the Department of Social Anthropology at the University of Cambridge. Recently she completed a book on the maintenance of tradition in a Buddhist monastery in Inner Mongolia (China) and an edited volume on migration and urban life in the Black Sea region. Currently she is carrying out research on the north Asian border between Russia and China. Major publications include: *Karl Marx Collective: Economy, Society and Religion in a Siberian Collective Farm* (Cambridge University Press, 1983), *The Archetypal Actions of Ritual: Illustrated by the Jain Rite of Worship* (with James Laidlaw; Clarendon, 1994), *Shamans and Elders: Experience, Knowledge and Power among the Daur Mongols* (with Urgunge Onon; Clarendon, 1996), *The End of Nomadism? Society, the State and the Environment in Inner Asia* (with David Sneath; Duke University Press/White Horse, 1999), *The Unmaking of Soviet Life: Everyday Economies after Socialism* (Cornell University Press, 2002), *Urban Life in Post-Soviet Central Asia* (coedited with Catherine Alexander and Victor Buchli; UCL Press, 2007).

Isabelle Kalinowski is a CNRS Researcher at the Laboratoire Pays Germaniques, École Normale Supérieure, Paris. Her major field of interest is Max Weber's sociology and anthropology, especially his texts on religion, which she has commented on and translated into French: *L'Ethique protestante et l'esprit du capitalisme* (Champs Flammarion, 2000); *Hindouisme et bouddhisme* (Champs Flammarion, 2003); *Sociologie de la religion* (Champs Flammarion, 2006); *Le Judaïsme antique* (Champs Flammarion, 2010). She has published many articles on Weber in French and German, and a book, *Leçons wébériennes sur la science et la propagande* (Agone, 2005). She is currently working on a second book on Weber's theory of charisma (*Le charisme: autour de Max Weber*). In relation to that religious topic, she also studies the theories on the agency of sacred and primitive arts elaborated by early twentieth-century anthropologists and art specialists, in particular Franz Boas and Carl Einstein (she coedited, with Maria Stavrinaki, a special issue of *Gradhiva* on "Carl Einstein et les primitivismes," November 2011).

Bruno Karsenti is Directeur d'Études at the École des Hautes Études en Sciences Sociales of Paris, and Director of the Marcel Mauss Institute. He has taught political philosophy and the epistemology of the social sciences at the Universities of Lyon and Paris-Sorbonne. His latest publications are *L'homme total: sociologie, anthropologie et philosophie chez Marcel Mauss* (Presses Universitaires de France, 2011), *Politique de l'esprit: Auguste Comte et la naissance de la science sociale* (Hermann, 2006), and *La société en personnes: Études durkheimiennes* (Économica, 2006). He is editor of two book series "Pratiques théoriques" (Presses Universitaires de France) and "Raisons pratiques" (Editions de l'EHESS).

Michael Lambek is Professor of Anthropology and Canada Research Chair in the Anthropology of Ethical Life at the University of Toronto and has also taught at the London School of Economics. He explores questions of action, person, historicity, and religion, especially with respect to the western Indian Ocean (Mayotte, northwest Madagascar) and Switzerland. Single-authored books are *Human Spirits: A Cultural Account of Trance in Mayotte* (Cambridge University Press, 1981), *Knowledge and Practice in Mayotte: Local Discourses of Islam, Sorcery, and Spirit Possession* (University of Toronto Press, 1993), and *The Weight of the Past: Living with History in Mahajanga, Madagascar* (Palgrave Macmillan, 2002). Edited books include *Tense Past: Cultural Essays in Trauma and Memory* (with Paul Antze; Routledge, 1996), *Bodies and Persons: Comparative Perspectives from Africa and Melanesia* (with Andrew Strathern;

Cambridge University Press, 1998), *A Reader in the Anthropology of Religion* (Blackwell, 2002; 2nd edn. 2008), *Illness and Irony: On the Ambiguity of Suffering in Culture* (with Paul Antze; Berghahn, 2003), and *Ordinary Ethics: Anthropology, Language and Action* (Fordham University Press, 2010).

Roger Lancaster is Professor of Anthropology and Cultural Studies at George Mason University, where he directs the Cultural Studies PhD Program. His research tries to understand how sexual mores, racial hierarchies, and class predicaments interact with political economy in a volatile world. He is currently conducting research on gay life in Mexico under neoliberal globalization. His most recent book is *Sex Panic and the Punitive State* (University of California Press, 2011), which won the Ruth Benedict Prize. Other books include *The Trouble with Nature: Sex in Science and Popular Culture* (University of California Press, 2003), *The Gender/Sexuality Reader: Culture, History, Political Economy* (coedited with Micaela di Leonardo; Routledge, 1997), and *Life is Hard: Machismo, Danger, and the Intimacy of Power* (University of California Press, 1992), which won the C. Wright Mills Award and the Ruth Benedict Prize.

Catherine Lutz is the Thomas J. Watson Jr. Family Professor of Anthropology and International Studies at the Watson Institute for International Studies and Chair of the Department of Anthropology at Brown University. She is the author of *Carjacked* (with A. Fernandez-Carol; Palgrave Macmillan, 2010), *Breaking Ranks* (with M. Gutmann; University of California Press, 2010), *The Bases of Empire* (as editor; New York University Press, 2009), *Local Democracy Under Siege* (with D. Holland et al.; New York University Press, 2007), *Homefront* (Beacon, 2001), *Reading National Geographic* (with J. Collins; University of Chicago Press, 1993), and *Unnatural Emotions* (University of Chicago Press, 1988). She is the recipient of the Distinguished Career Award from the Society for the Anthropology of North America and former President of the American Ethnological Society. Her books have received the Leeds Prize, the Victor Turner Prize for Ethnographic Writing, and the Delmos Jones and Jagna Sharff Memorial Prize for the Critical Study of North America. She has conducted some of her research in conjunction with activist organizations, including a domestic violence shelter, the American Friends Service Committee, and Cultural Survival.

Saba Mahmood teaches anthropology at the University of California at Berkeley. She is the author of *Politics of Piety: The Islamic Revival and the Feminist Subject* (Princeton University Press, 2005), and coauthor of *Is Critique Secular? Blasphemy, Injury, and Free Speech* (University of California Press, 2009). She is the recipient of the Carnegie Corporation's Islamic Scholar's award (2007–8), and the Frederick Burkhardt Fellowship from the American Council of Learned Societies (2009–10). She is currently working on a book project entitled *Politics of Religious Freedom: Geopolitics, Sexuality, and the Minority Question* which focuses on the Middle East and Europe. In 2010 she received a three-year grant from the Henry R. Luce Initiative on Religion and International Affairs for a comparative study of the right to religious liberty in a global perspective. Her broader work centers on issues of secularism, religion, ethics and politics, and gender in postcolonial Muslim societies.

Kathleen Millar is a Postdoctoral Fellow in Duke University's Thompson Writing Program where she teaches a seminar called "Writing Poverty: Ethnography and the Politics of Representation." Her interests include moral anthropology, urban poverty and social inequality, environmental suffering, and the politics of labor within neoliberal capitalism. She is currently writing an ethnography that explores the subjectivities and political practices of over 2,000 laboring poor who collect recyclables on the largest garbage dump in Latin America, located on the outskirts of Rio de Janeiro. Her research has appeared in *The Anthropology of Work Review* and in several edited volumes including *Cooperation in Economy and Society* (ed. Robert C. Marshall; AltaMira, 2010) and *Recycling Economies* (ed. Catherine Alexander and Joshua Reno; Zed, forthcoming).

Adriana Petryna is Edmund J. and Louise W. Kahn Term Professor in Anthropology at the University of Pennsylvania. In her anthropological work, she has probed the cultural and political dimensions of science and medicine in eastern Europe and in the United States (with a focus on the Chernobyl nuclear disaster and on clinical research and pharmaceutical globalization). Her research has focused on public and private scientific knowledge production and on the role of science and technology in public policy (particularly in contexts of crisis, inequality, and political transition). She is currently carrying out an ethnography of the legal and economic aspects of patienthood and recovery in transnational medicine. She is the author of *Life Exposed: Biological Citizens after Chernobyl* (Princeton University Press, 2002), and the coauthor of *Global Pharmaceuticals: Ethics, Markets, Practices* (Duke University Press, 2006). Her recent book *When Experiments Travel: Clinical Trials and the Global Search for Human Subjects* (Princeton University Press, 2009) explores patient protections in globalizing clinical research. She is coeditor (with João Biehl) of the forthcoming edited volume, *Evidence, Actuality, and Theory in Global Health.*

Stacy Leigh Pigg is Professor of Anthropology at Simon Fraser University and former editor of the journal *Medical Anthropology: Cross-Cultural Studies of Health and Illness.* Her research in Nepal has generated writings on the cultural politics of international development and on the production of public knowledge about AIDS. She is currently looking at the internationalization of contraceptive technologies. With Vincanne Adams, she edited the book *Sex in Development: Science, Sexuality, and Morality in Global Perspective* (Duke University Press, 2005).

Peter Redfield is Associate Professor of Anthropology at the University of North Carolina at Chapel Hill. Trained as a cultural anthropologist sympathetic to history, he concentrates on circulations of science and technology in colonial and postcolonial contexts, and currently focuses on humanitarian inspired design. The author of *Space in the Tropics: From Convicts to Rockets in French Guiana* (University of California Press, 2000) and *Life in Crisis: The Ethical Journey of Doctors Without Borders* (University of California Press, forthcoming), he is also the coeditor, with Erica Bornstein, of *Forces of Compassion: Humanitarianism between Ethics and Politics* (SAR Press, 2011).

Massimo Reichlin is Professor of Moral Philosophy at the Faculty of Philosophy of the Università Vita-Salute San Raffaele in Milan, Italy. His interests are in the history of moral philosophy and in contemporary ethical theory, with particular reference to bioethics. He is the author of several books on issues such as euthanasia and assisted suicide, the ethics of abortion, the ethics of artificial reproduction and embryo experimentation, and the main theoretical approaches in practical ethics. He has just completed a book on the history of utilitarianism and is presently writing another on moral issues in contemporary neuroscience. His most recently published books in Italian are *Etica della vita: nuovi paradigmi morali* (Bruno Mondadori, 2008) and *Aborto: la morale oltre il diritto* (Carocci, 2007). His recent articles in English include "The Role of Solidarity in Social Responsibility for Health" (*Medicine, Philosophy and Health Care*, 2011), "Life Extension and Personal Identity" (with G. Barazzetti, in *Enhancing Human Capacities* (ed. J. Savulescu et al.; Wiley-Blackwell, 2011), "Ordinary Moral Knowledge and Philosophical Ethics in Sidgwick and Kant" (*Etica & Politica/Ethics & Politics*, 2008), and "The Challenges of Neuroethics" (*Functional Neurology*, 2007).

Joel Robbins is Professor of Anthropology at the University of California, San Diego. Much of his work has focused on issues of morality, the anthropology of Christianity, and other topics in the anthropology of religion. He is the author of *Becoming Sinners: Christianity and Moral Torment in a Papua New Guinea Society* (University of California Press, 2004). He has recently coedited a special issue of the journal *South Atlantic Quarterly* entitled "Global Christianity, Global Critique." He is also coeditor of the journal *Anthropological Theory*.

Richard A. Shweder is a cultural anthropologist and the William Claude Reavis Distinguished Service Professor of Human Development in the Department of Comparative Human Development at the University of Chicago. He is author of *Thinking through Cultures: Expeditions in Cultural Psychology* (Harvard University Press, 1991) and *Why Do Men Barbecue? Recipes for Cultural Psychology* (Harvard University Press, 2003). He is editor or coeditor of many books in the areas of cultural psychology, psychological anthropology, and comparative ethics. His recent research examines the scopes and limits of pluralism and the multicultural challenge in Western liberal democracies. He examines the norm conflicts that arise when people migrate from Africa, Asia, and Latin America to countries in the "North." He has coedited two books on this topic (with Martha Minow and Hazel Markus) entitled *Engaging Cultural Differences: The Multicultural Challenge in Liberal Democracies* (Russell Sage Foundation, 2004) and *Just Schools: Pursuing Equality in Societies of Difference* (Russell Sage Foundation, 2008).

Dan Sperber is a French social and cognitive scientist. He is Emeritus Researcher at the Institut Jean Nicod in Paris and Professor in the Departments of Cognitive Science and of Philosophy of the Central European University in Budapest. He is the author of numerous articles in anthropology, linguistics, philosophy, and psychology, and of three books: *Rethinking Symbolism* (Cambridge University Press, 1975), *On Anthropological Knowledge* (Cambridge University Press, 1985), and *Explaining Culture* (Blackwell, 1996). In these books he has developed a naturalistic approach to culture under the name of "epidemiology of representations." With Deirdre Wilson, he has developed a cognitive approach to communication known as "relevance theory" and coauthored *Relevance: Communication and Cognition* (Blackwell, 1986) and *Meaning and Relevance* (Cambridge University Press, 2012). Both the epidemiology of representations and relevance theory have been influential and also controversial. Dan Sperber has edited *Metarepresentations: A Multidisciplinary Perspective* (Oxford University Press, 2000) and coedited two books: *Causal Cognition: A Multidisciplinary Debate* (with David Premack and Ann James Premack; Oxford University Press, 1995), and *Experimental Pragmatics* (with Ira Noveck; Palgrave Macmillan, 2004).

Karen M. Sykes is Professor of Anthropology at the University of Manchester. Her research career began in 1991 with an extended period of fieldwork investigating the lives of secondary school leavers in New Ireland, Papua New Guinea, where she has lived for nearly four years since that first trip. Between 1999 and 2001, she carried out research into the character of intellectual property in New Ireland as the Senior Research Associate on an ESRC-funded project, "Property Transactions Creations: New Economic Relations in Melanesia," which was directed by Marilyn Strathern (Cambridge) and Eric Hirsch (Brunel). At present she is directing a project funded by the ESRC between 2011 and 2015, entitled "The Domestic Moral Economy: An Ethnographic Study of Value in the Asia Pacific," which involves scholars working at the Australian National University, Queens University Belfast, and the University of Manchester. She is the author of *Arguing with Anthropology: An Introduction to Critical Theories of the Gift* (Routledge, 2005), and *Ethnographies of Moral Reasoning: Living Paradoxes of a Global Age* (Palgrave Macmillan, 2008), as well as the editor of "Interrogating Individuals: The Theory of Possessive Individualism in the Western Pacific," a special issue of *Anthropological Forum* (2007).

John Symons is Associate Professor and Chair of Philosophy at the University of Texas at El Paso. His recent publications include *The Routledge Companion to Philosophy of Psychology* (Routledge, 2009), *Otto Neurath and the Unity of Science* (Springer, 2010), and *The Unity of Science and the Special Sciences* (Springer, 2011). He is currently studying computational models and the problem of emergence in science and metaphysics.

C. Jason Throop is an Associate Professor in the Department of Anthropology at UCLA. He has conducted extensive ethnographic fieldwork on pain, empathy, suffering, and morality on the island of Yap in the Western Caroline Islands of Micronesia. He is the author of *Suffering and Sentiment: Exploring the Vicissitudes of Experience and Pain in Yap* (University of California Press, 2010) and coeditor of *Toward an Anthropology of the Will* (with Keith M. Murphy; Stanford University Press, 2010) and *The Anthropology of Empathy: Experiencing the Lives of Others in Pacific Societies* (with Douglas Hollan; Berghahn, 2011).

Thomas Widlok is Professor of Anthropology at the Department of Cultural Anthropology and Development Studies at Radboud University Nijmegen, the Netherlands, and Research Fellow at the University of Cologne in Germany. He holds a PhD from the London School of Economics and Political Science and has taught anthropology at London, Cologne, Heidelberg, Durham, and Zurich. His fields of interest are hunter-gatherer studies (with long-term field research in southern Africa and Australia), cognition and language, religion, and economics. He has published on a wide range of anthropological topics including property relations (*Property and Equality*, with W. Tadesse; New York University Press, 2005), morality and virtue theory ("Sharing by Default? Outline of an Anthropology of Virtue," *Anthropological Theory*, 2004). His recent publications include work on religion and on economic anthropology.

Liane Young is an Assistant Professor of Psychology at Boston College, where she is Director of the Morality Lab. She received her BA in philosophy from Harvard University in 2004, her PhD in psychology from Harvard University in 2008, and her postdoctoral training in the Department of Brain and Cognitive Sciences at MIT. Her research focuses on the cognitive and neural basis of human moral judgment and behavior. Her current research focuses on the role of theory of mind and emotions in moral cognition. To explore these topics, she uses the methods of social psychology and cognitive neuroscience, including functional magnetic resonance imaging (fMRI), and examination of patient populations with specific cognitive deficits.

Everett Yuehong Zhang is an Assistant Professor of Anthropology in the Department of East Asian Studies at Princeton University. He was born in China, and worked for the Chinese Academy of Social Sciences before coming to the United States. His previous project on the body is being published under the title *Impotence in China: An Illness of Chinese Modernity* (forthcoming). His current project compares two major earthquakes in contemporary China – the Tangshan quake in 1976 in the era of Mao, and the Sichuan quake in 2008, three decades into reform – to tell the story of 30 years of change in the governance of life in China and the moral experience of destruction and reconstruction of material as well as psychic life. He is an editor (with Arthur Kleinman and Tu Weiming) of *Governance of Life in Chinese Moral Experience: A Quest for an Adequate Life* (Routledge, 2011).

Jarrett Zigon is an Assistant Professor in the Department of Anthropology and Sociology at the University of Amsterdam. His research interests include morality, subjectivity, and institutional spaces of disciplinary practice. These interests are taken up from the perspective of an anthropology strongly influenced by post-Heideggerian phenomenology and critical theory. He has completed two research projects in Russia: one on the relationship between personal experience and moral conceptions, and a second on Russian Orthodox Church drug rehabilitation programs as spaces for moral training. His current research focuses on human rights as a transnational moral discourse. His articles can be found in *Anthropological Theory*, *Ethnos*, and *Ethos*, among other journals. His books include *Morality: An Anthropological Perspective* (Berg, 2008), *Making the New Post-Soviet Person: Narratives of Moral Experience in Contemporary Moscow* (Brill, 2010), and *HIV is God's Blessing: Rehabilitating Morality in Neoliberal Russia* (University of California Press, 2011).

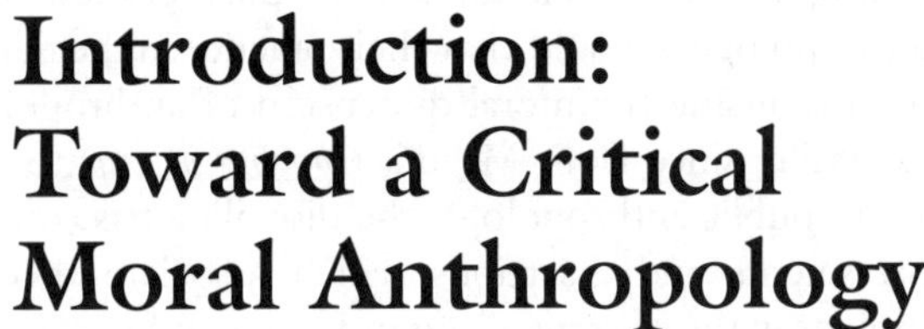

Introduction: Toward a Critical Moral Anthropology

Didier Fassin

> *To deal usefully with the relationship between morality and the social sciences one must first realize that modern social science arose to a considerable extent in the process of emancipating itself from the traditional moral teachings.*
>
> Albert Hirschman, "Morality and the Social Sciences: A Durable Tension," 1981

> *If the moral domain corresponds to what people treat as the ultimate terms of their existence, of their lives together, of their fates, then moral concerns are concerns with the integrity of cultural life, with the nature, significance, potential, and viability of the life that culture makes possible and makes necessary.*
>
> Steven Parish, *Moral Knowing in a Hindu Sacred City*, 1994

The attempt to coin the expression "moral anthropology" seems immediately and irremediably doomed from the start by its Kantian paternity. Indeed, it is often considered that the author of the *Metaphysics of Morals* invented this phrase to define his project of "applied moral philosophy" as an empirical counterpoint to his theoretical *metaphysica pura*: "Moral anthropology, he writes, is morality applied to human beings" (Louden 2003: 7). Although Kant never formulated a comprehensive description of this part of his practical philosophy – "the second part of morals," as he designates it – one can understand, through the lectures he gave, that it is definitely a normative enterprise which aims at contributing to the fulfillment of the moral laws he has characterized. In this sense, anthropology is a tool for the implementation of morals in relation to human beings. But it does not deal with individuals or cultures, as one would expect; rather, it concerns the "human species" as a whole and its accomplishment through moral progress. It is universalistic in essence.

A Companion to Moral Anthropology, First Edition. Edited by Didier Fassin.

Understood in this way, Kant's anthropology has little to do with Boas's relativist anthropology, and one can assume that very few of those who think of themselves as anthropologists would view their practice in the filiation of the master of Koenisgberg. Yet, dismissing the moral dimension of anthropology in its Kantian sense might be less facile, since from Mead's *Coming of Age* to Lévi-Strauss's *Race et Histoire*, to recent public anthropology, the discipline has constantly been involved in producing assessments and assertions which associate theoretical knowledge and empirical findings with concerns about judging conducts, reforming society, and improving the human condition – even when these normative postures were not explicitly formulated. The Kantian legacy is indeed more deeply enshrined in the discipline than most of its members would probably admit.

However, when proposing the expression "moral anthropology," what I have in mind is a radically different project – if not an anti-Kantian, at least a non-Kantian one. It could rather be regarded as a Durkheimian or Weberian scientific program – despite how different these authors may seem in this respect. In the preface to the first edition of *The Division of Labor in Society*, Émile Durkheim, presenting his general intention to study "moral life according to the methods of the positive sciences," pleads for a descriptive rather than the usual prescriptive approach: "We do not wish to deduce morality from science, but to constitute the science of morality, which is very different. Moral facts are phenomena like any others" (1984 [1893]: xxv). Indeed, the French sociologist, who died before completing his great book on *La Morale*, had a view about the "rules for action" and the "laws that explain them" which we may not share, but we can probably still adhere to his idea that morality is an object that can be regarded as any other. In his essay on *Objectivity in Social Science and Social Policy*, Max Weber (1949 [1904]: 52), describing the intellectual ambition of the new journal he was launching, establishes even more clearly the distinction between the normative approach in the social science, which he rejects, and the analytical approach of values and evaluations, which he claims. "It can never be the task of an empirical science to provide binding norms and ideals from which directives for immediate practical activity can be derived," he affirms, adding a clarification: "What is the implication of this proposition? It is certainly not that value-judgments are to be withdrawn from scientific discussion because in the last analysis they rest on certain ideals and are therefore 'subjective' in origin." For the author of *The Protestant Ethic*, assessing the validity of values is merely "a matter of faith," whereas making sense of judgments is fully an object of science. "Criticism is not to be suspended in the presence of value-judgments, insists Weber. The problem is rather: what is the meaning and purpose of the scientific criticism of ideals and value-judgments?" It is the project of this volume to deploy this distinction by studying morals through issues, themes, regions of the world, and periods of history from a critical perspective.

The Trouble with Morals

A moral anthropology, in this sense, does not support particular values or promote certain judgments more than political anthropology would favor a given partisan position or recommend a specific public policy. It does not defend the rights of peoples to define and implement their particular values or, conversely, the overarching authority of universal human rights. It neither condemns so-called genital mutilation and forced marriage nor denounces as imperialist the efforts deployed by feminists to combat them. It takes these moral tensions and debates as its objects of study and considers seriously the moral positions of all sides. A moral anthropology has no moralizing project. This preliminary statement may seem perfectly superfluous or, even worse, irremediably naive. After all, is it not the foundational principle of any social science to analyze rather than evaluate, to understand instead of judging? And at the same time, do we not know that perfect objectivity is illusory and that its claim is destined to be immediately refuted by a thorough epistemological analysis? Yet, it is worth reasserting and discussing this apparently obvious position, since the expression "moral anthropology" is problematic in two different ways.

The first problem is semantic. It concerns the meaning and connotation of the adjective "moral," which is ineluctably and inextricably descriptive and prescriptive, in common sense as well as in scholarly use. It is as if the phrase "moral anthropology" implied not only an anthropology of the good but also a do-gooder's anthropology, not only an endeavor to analyze moral issues but also a moral engagement in the world with the ultimate intention to make it better. This is certainly worth noticing: the adjective "moral" is in itself distinctively and overwhelmingly normative, an ambiguity which makes it unique. Medical or linguistic anthropologies do not pose similar difficulties of interpretation and everyone understands that the former deals with bodies, ailments, and medicines, and the latter concerns communication, codes, and languages – although neither of them is completely impervious to normative positions. By contrast, it is much more difficult to comprehend and accept that moral anthropology is simply the study of moral sentiments, judgments, and practices. Probably the legacy of moral philosophy, which is definitely normative in its endeavor to answer questions such as what a virtuous act is, what a good life should be, what one should do under certain circumstances, weighs heavily in this regard. By its genealogical – and indeed moral – proximity with philosophy, anthropology tends to be viewed, even by its members, as a discipline dedicated to ameliorating the human condition.

The second problem is historical. It is not simply that anthropology is regarded as morally committed: it is that anthropologists have often acted as moral agents. They have adopted moral views and defended moral causes. This is true from a theoretical perspective, as well as from a practical outlook. Going back to the origins of the discipline, contradictory as they are, evolutionism and culturalism share the same postulate that anthropology has a moral message to convey, respectively, about the hierarchy or, conversely, the incommensurability of values. Considering the relationships anthropologists had with colonization in the case of Europe or with imperialism in the case of the United States, as well as, symmetrically and more recently, their stance against the oppression of peoples or in favor of human rights, suggests that their axiological neutrality has often been an ideal or even an illusion rather than a faithful representation of their activity. Histories of the discipline often retain the scandals that have marked its development, such as involvement with the military or the intelligence, which is often represented as the "dark side" of anthropology, but they have been less attentive to its "bright side," that of the denunciation of evil in the world and of the defense of the wretched and the dominated, which is no less revealing of their taking sides on moral grounds and no less problematic precisely because they generally remain unquestioned.

For these semantic as well as historical reasons, one would certainly be tempted to renounce the formulation "moral anthropology." After all, would it not be preferable to speak of anthropology of moralities in the same way as one refers to the anthropology of religion or the anthropology of science? This is for that matter a designation proposed by most authors, such as John Barker (2007) or Monica Heinz (2009), echoing previous similar appellations by Signe Howell (1997), these various collections of papers having in common the consideration of moralities as local moral worlds (Zigon 2008) to use the expression coined by Arthur Kleinman (2006) with a somewhat distinct intention. I consider most disputes over appellations to be futile and would not want to involve myself in a quarrel on terminology: in the end, everyone would certainly agree that no formulation is entirely satisfactory and perhaps even that, far from being an obstacle, this dissatisfaction has the merit to leave interrogations and potentialities open. Still, I would like to defend in this introduction and to illustrate in this volume the payoff of speaking of moral anthropology rather than of the anthropology of moralities. The distinction I suggest here is not lexical – labels are not important – but theoretical: meanings are what count. There are two major reasons, in my view, to use the adjective rather than the noun. One has to do with the delimitation of the object, the other one with the reflexivity of the discipline.

First, what the word "morality" designates is too narrow for the object of our inquiry. There is no necessity to confine moral anthropology to local configurations of norms, values, and emotions: the domain under study and the issues that are raised go far beyond local moralities; they include but exceed them. And there is no need to limit its scope to moralities as discrete entities separated from the other spheres of human activities: moral questions are embedded in the substance of the social; it is not sufficient to analyze moral codes or ethical dilemmas as if they could be isolated from political, religious, economic, or social issues. Moral anthropology deals with how moral questions are posed and addressed or, symmetrically, how nonmoral questions are rephrased as moral. It explores the moral categories via which we apprehend the world and identifies the moral communities that we construe, examines the moral signification of action and the moral labor of agents, analyzes moral issues and moral debates at an individual or collective level. It concerns the creation of moral vocabularies, the circulation of moral values, the production of moral subjects and the regulation of society through moral injunctions. The object of a moral anthropology is the moral making of the world. This definition has a practical consequence, to which this book attests. Most authors convened in the present conversation around a moral anthropology would not qualify themselves as anthropologists of moralities or describe their domain of interest as anthropology of moralities. They would rather assert that they work on moral questions, which they might sometimes prefer to characterize as ethical, just as they do on political, religious, medical, scientific issues, and therefore would not restrict themselves to the particular realm of morality. Actually, I must confess this also happens to be my own relationship with moral objects. It is my conviction that this outsiders' perspective, which is often a side view, shifting our usual vision of moral facts and questioning what we take for granted about them, is crucial for the development of a moral anthropology.

Second, considering "morality" as the object of anthropology may lead to the anthropologist as subject being obscured or neglected. Moral anthropology encompasses the delicate topic of the moral implication of the social scientist: it is reflexive as much as descriptive. If the social sciences have an epistemological uniqueness, since the fact that human beings study other human beings implies that complete detachment is unattainable and that some involvement is necessarily present, it is even more accurate when we tackle moral questions. All human activities are grounded on moral assumptions – often so much taken for granted that they are not perceived as such any more – and research on human activities is no exception. Although they profess cultural relativism, anthropologists have not been exempt from various forms of moral universalism, whether they criticize racial discrimination here or female circumcision there, capitalist exploitation or male domination, inequality or torture. We are not neutral agents when we deal with social problems. Whether we recognize it or not, there is always a moral positioning in the objects we choose, the place we occupy in the field, the way we interpret facts, the form of writing we elaborate. Our investigations of Walmart or Wall Street, our framework of cultural anthropology or evolutionary biology, our choice of addressing academic or public audiences involve moral commitments, which go far beyond their formal presentations as deontological prescriptions verified by institutional review boards. Being aware of it and working on it is therefore an epistemological necessity. Indeed, the reflexive posture I plead for should include a broader questioning of our recent interest in moral issues. Two or three decades ago, anthropologists did not work on violence and suffering, trauma and mourning, prisons and camps, victims of wars and disasters, humanitarianism and human rights. These realities existed but received little attention from the discipline. Other objects, whether kinship or myths, witchcraft or rituals, peasantry or development, were seen as more relevant for the understanding of human societies. This transformation of our gaze and of our lexicon has been accompanied by frequently more engaged positioning. Such a remarkable evolution raises the question of why we were unaware of or indifferent to the tragic of the world before and, symmetrically, why we became so passionately involved in it in recent years. It also elicits an interrogation about what was gained, and what was lost, in this evolution, or, to say it differently, about how our apprehension of the human condition was reconfigured. The moral turn of anthropology is thus an object of reflection per se for a moral anthropology.

Up to this point, I have used the words "moral" and "moralities" as if they could be taken for granted, and I have occasionally referred to "ethical" and "ethics" as if these pairs of terms were interchangeable. Prima facie, affirming the obvious signification of the words "moral" and "moralities" and their equivalence with the terms "ethical" and "ethics" may seem arguable. It is not unfounded, though.

On the one hand, most people immediately understand what morality means and what a moral act is without needing definitions. Adapting ordinary language theory, we could therefore acknowledge that the adjective "moral" designates what is viewed as good, or right, or just, or altruistic, and although the qualifications in this series represent distinct values, they are frequently not distinguished by common sense. Indeed, whereas, during the past 25 centuries, moral philosophers have attempted to circumscribe "morality" in general or, alternatively, in relation to specific contents, to discuss whether the category of "good" should not be replaced by more precise categories such as "generous" or "truthful," and to stress the differences between "norms" viewed as conventions and "values" regarded as principles, social scientists generally avoid starting with these a priori assumptions and explore instead what people do and say in everyday action and ordinary language to make sense of it a posteriori (Das 2010). Rather than defining what is "morality" and verifying whether people's deeds and judgments correspond to the definition, they tend to apprehend morality in acts and discourses, to understand what men and women do which they consider to be moral or good or right or generous (Lambek 2010). Actually, such a position can be found in certain contemporary philosophies, notably pragmatism. I take this approach to be a common ground for most anthropologists interested in moral questions, including in the present volume. Consequently, I will not provide a definition of what is meant by "morality" and "moral," not just because philosophers are still disputing it, but because for social scientists there is a benefit from proceeding in this inductive way.

On the other hand, the distinction between morality and ethics is far from being universally or univocally accepted. Whereas philosophers traditionally affirm that morality refers to culturally bound values and ethics designates a branch of their discipline, thus implicitly assuming a hierarchy between the two concepts, many recent philosophical works do not establish any difference, using the two words indistinctly. Similarly, social scientists do not share a common language and, for instance, speak of Christian morality as well as of Protestant ethic, without making the difference explicit. Anthropologists themselves diverge on this point, depending on the philosophical tradition in which they are inscribed, some insisting on the distinction between the two concepts, others attaching no importance to it. Rather than choosing between these positions myself, which would ultimately proceed from an arbitrary decision, whatever justification I would supply, it seems more interesting to understand what is at stake in this choice. Morality has increasingly been an object of inquiry for the social sciences during the past quarter of a century, and anthropologists have focused their attention on moral norms and values that govern collective and individual behavior, thus following Abraham Edel's insistent proposition (1962) and D. F. Pocock's reiterated invitation (1986). Authors who have recently called for an anthropology of ethics have distanced themselves from this approach by emphasizing ethical practices resulting from social agency. By doing so, they make two distinct although related claims. The first one concerns the recognition of ethical subjectivities in societies often viewed as traditional precisely on the assumption that they are dominated by moral norms which determine conducts, therefore leaving no initiative to individuals (Laidlaw 2002). The second one deals with the processes of ethical subjectivation engaged by social agents through technologies of the self since classical antiquity (Faubion 2011). In these two claims, postulates are the same, but stakes differ somewhat: the former revalorizes other societies (presenting their members as free ethical agents) while the latter requalifies more familiar horizons (convening a genealogy of ethics). Thus, depending on the intellectual project, morals and ethics, or morality and ethic, are declared commutable or regarded as distinct. Of these divergences, the present volume wittingly keeps the trace. By conjoining these various perspectives, I intend to leave this trace visible as a testimony to the diversity of the domain but also to the strategic uses of these terms.

Philosophical Affinities

Indeed the field of morality and ethics is not a theoretically homogeneous realm. Not surprisingly, it is divided along theoretical lines corresponding to philosophical traditions, which have already begun to become apparent in the previous discussion. At the risk of simplifying a rich literature, two main bodies of research may be identified.

The first approach – chronologically – derives from Durkheim. It is based on the three principles defined in his lecture on "The Determination of Moral Facts": "all morality appears to us as a system of rules of conduct"; "moral rules are invested with a special authority by virtue of which they are obeyed simply because they command"; "to become the agents of an act it must interest our sensibility to a certain extent and appear to us as, in some way, desirable" (1974 [1906]: 35–36). In other words, morality is duty plus desire: we are not only obliged to do the good, we are also inclined to do it. Either explicitly or implicitly, this perspective has long been dominant in most of the studies of morality, especially in so-called traditional societies. In his "essay in comparative ethics," K. E. Read draws a parallel between Christian morality and the morality of the Gahuku-Gama of Papua New Guinea, presented as a "particular ethical pattern amenable to logical and systematic explanation" (1955: 233–234). In his tentative "descriptive ethics," John Ladd proposes a philosophical analysis of the "moral code" of the Navajo Indians, which corresponds to the "collection of moral rules and principles relating to what ought or ought not to be done" (1957: 1, 9). Remarkably, ethics and morality both refer to the system of norms and obligations that underlie judgments and regulate conducts in a given society.

The second approach – more recent – finds its inspiration in Michel Foucault. It is expressed in the profound distinction established between the moral and the ethical, in particular in the introduction of *The Use of Pleasure* where three dimensions of morality are discussed: it is a "set of values and rules of action that are recommended to individuals through the intermediate of prescriptive agencies such as the family, educational institutions, churches"; it is also "the real behaviors of individuals in relation to the rules and values that are recommended to them"; it is finally "the manner in which one ought to form oneself as an ethical subject acting in reference to the prescriptive elements that make up the code" (1990 [1984]: 25–26). What Foucault is interested in is not the first two dimensions, the "moral code" or the "moral behavior," but the last one, the "ethical conduct" and the process he calls, paraphrasing Durkheim, "the determination of the ethical substance." This ethical subjectivation has nourished an important current of research, most notably around Talal Asad's work on the genealogy of religions (1993). Instead of viewing religion as a cultural system somewhat exterior to individuals, these authors explore it through the disciplinary exercises and reflexive practices which produce ethical subjects, as Saba Mahmood (2005) does with Muslim piety movements in Egypt.

The two anthropological paradigms I have briefly characterized can easily be related to two philosophical genealogies: the Durkheimian lineage has a Kantian genealogy, that of the deontological ethics, recently revisited by Thomas Nagel and Thomas Scanlon; the Foucauldian lineage has an Aristotelian genealogy, that of virtue ethics, rediscovered in the past half-century by Elizabeth Anscombe, Bernard Williams, and Alasdair MacIntyre. According to the former, an action is judged in relation to the respect of rules or principles to which the agent can refer. According to the latter, an action is assessed in function of the virtuous disposition that underlies the appropriate psychology of the agent. Anthropologists inscribed in the first paradigm view morality as the set of values and norms that determine what agents are supposed to do and not to do. Ethnographers adopting the second paradigm regard ethics as the subjective work produced by agents to conduct themselves in accordance with their inquiry about what a good life is. The former tend to see morality as exterior to individuals and imposed on them as a social superego: it is a given. The latter are inclined to analyze ethics as an inner state nourished by virtue and nourishing action: it is a process. Hence the differentiated empirical approaches, in search of moral codes analyzed in general terms, or of ethical debates apprehended through particular situations.

This tension is expressed by Joel Robbins (2007) as the opposition between the reproduction of a moral order and the recognition of an ethical freedom: are human beings doomed to conform themselves to rules or are they able to determine the right action by themselves? During the past decade, a shift in focus has been patent in anthropology, from the previously dominant approach of moral codes toward the analysis of the formation of ethical subjects, sometimes with explicit discussion of "virtues" (Widlok 2004) or, in a different perspective, of "care" (Garcia 2010). Far from being univocal, these works use various concepts, such as the "moral breakdown" of Orthodox Muscovites (Zigon 2007), the "moral selfhood" of Indonesian Muslims (Simon 2009), the "moral reasoning" of the inhabitants of New Ireland (Sykes 2009), or the "moral sentiments" of the Yap of Micronesia (Throop 2010) – a further evidence, in passing, of the lack of empirical significance of the distinction between ethics and morality, for most authors, who use the adjective "moral" even when they tend to adopt the paradigm of the "ethical" subject.

The reference to the philosophical affinities of these anthropological works on morality and ethics should not, however, be misinterpreted or overemphasized. By describing intellectual landscapes and drawing conceptual lines I do not want to give the impression that ethnographers working on morality or ethics pledge allegiance to particular schools of thought. Actually many of these studies do not discuss or even mention Durkheim or Foucault, Kant or Aristotle. This should not be a surprise. After all, it is the strength – and sometimes also the weakness – of the inductive method deployed by anthropologists to be more attentive to the complexity and subtlety of local arrangements of the social than scrupulously faithful to any grand theory that would possibly account for it. The richness of their monographs and the intricacy of the corresponding empirical material generally dismiss or even refute any simple inscription of their theoretical interpretation into a particular philosophy, as if human action and social life resisted being defined by one theory or another. This is certainly a lesson to be remembered.

Moral philosophy is often represented as a trilogy of paradigms. To the deontological ethics and virtue ethics upon which I have already commented, one adds the consequentialist ethics, which assesses conducts according to their consequences rather than their conformity with preexisting rules or their resulting from a specific disposition of the agent. However, in "real world" situations that anthropologists examine, when they attempt to comprehend the moral arguments expressed by individuals to justify their actions or the ethical practices performed by them in the course of their everyday life, it is seldom possible to sort out the deontological, virtuous, and consequentialist threads. For instance, in the case of the disputed and courageous decision made by Doctors Without Borders to remain in Baghdad at the onset of the 2003 war against Iraq (Fassin 2007), the three were intimately entangled, revealing the multiple logics at work among humanitarian workers: they regard themselves as defending superior secularized moral values, such as the sacredness of life and the exaltation of compassion; yet, their activity involves an ethical sense of commitment and solidarity, which leads them to confront their own limits in terms of acceptance of risk as well as of their relations to others; finally, although their decisions seem to be mainly the result of general principles and personal dispositions, they also appear to be motivated by more or less rigorous assessment of the effects produced by their intervention. The heated tensions during the debates within the organization implicitly referred to the three paradigms even if the position of each member was never entirely stabilized on any of them. Indeed, they were moral as well as political.

To account for these proximities between the moral and the political, one can have recourse to another lexicon, more familiar to social scientists. The confrontation of different positions in a process of decision may be interpreted in Weber's terms as the conflict between an ethics of conviction – exemplified by the attitude of the Christian who "does the right thing and leaves the outcome in the hands of God" – and an ethics of responsibility – corresponding to the affirmation that "one must answer for the foreseeable consequences of one's action" (2008 [1919]: 198). The former, which is grounded on principles or dispositions, is therefore related to deontological or virtue ethics. The latter, which acknowledges the complications necessarily involved in the exercise of power, clearly adopts a consequentialist approach. It is noteworthy, though, that the recent blossoming of anthropological works on morality and ethics has apparently overlooked this third philosophical thread, thus neglecting the articulation of the moral and the political. Yet, the question "Should one do the right thing or act in function of the foreseeable consequences?" is crucial to the practice of politics, whether it concerns remote societies or closer horizons.

In an attempt to constitute their objects, the analyses of local moralities and of ethical subjectivities seem to have specified the moral and the ethical to the point that they often became somewhat separated from the political, as if norms and values could be isolated from power relations, or sensibilities and emotions from collective histories. Recently, this dualism and its consequences – the distinction of morality and ethics, the shift from the former to the latter, and the relative neglect of politics – have been criticized on two convergent grounds. First, as Harri Englund (2008) discusses in the case of poverty alleviation programs in Malawi, the study of global inequalities and international solidarity as well as of local configurations and village expectations shows that morality should not be restricted to a set of rules, and that obligations and dependencies should not be replaced by ethical dilemmas and individual decisions. Second, as Paul Anderson (2011) argues about the piety movement in Egypt, self-formation does not account entirely for the meaning of these practices, which are also oriented toward the achievement of a nonsecular sociality in opposition to the commodity economy. These critiques converge in questioning the contours of morality and ethics and inquiring into their connections with the ideological and the political. In fact, this should not be viewed as a contradiction since, using the terminology of Foucault's last lectures (2010 [2008]), one has to admit that the moral impulse is part of the governing of others, as the ethical formation is crucial to the governing of the self, therefore calling more attention to the political.

The starting point of the reflection in this respect is the remarkable emergence of moral and ethical issues in the public sphere over the past decades: not only humanitarianism, as previously evoked, but also bioethics, business ethics, the moralization of finance, care for the poor, the deployment of transitional justice, the expansion of human rights, the introduction of the responsibility to protect, and, symmetrically, the denunciation of inequality, exclusion, violence, corruption, greed, intolerance, oppression. All these terms and the corresponding realities have become part of our political language – of our way of interpreting the world and justifying our private or public actions through moral judgments and moral sentiments. The presence of a moral vocabulary in political discourses is definitely not new and one could even argue that politics, especially in democracies, has always included moral arguments about good government and public good, fairness and trust, as well as moral condemnations of all sorts of evils. Yet, the current moralization of politics as a global phenomenon imposing its moral obviousness should be regarded as an object of inquiry in its own right. The study of the production, circulation, and appropriation of norms and values, sensibilities, and emotions in contemporary societies – what one can designate as their moral economies (Fassin 2009) – is all the more important for a moral anthropology since it concerns what we most easily take for granted, sometimes even viewing it in terms of moral progress. These changing moral configurations deserve particular thought, especially when they combine opposite and even contradictory judgments and sentiments: it is thus remarkable that approaches to social problems as diverse as asylum, immigration, poverty, epidemics, addictions, prostitution, and orphanhood associate the moral languages of order and care, of coercion and empathy (Fassin 2011). That this dialectic of repression and compassion lie at the heart of contemporary politics must elicit questioning from a moral anthropological outlook.

Opening Territories

Research in the anthropology of moralities and ethics has been outstandingly productive in recent years and this volume should be viewed as a tribute to this dynamism. But it is also conceived as an endeavor to expand the domain beyond its current frontiers by integrating objects and reflections not usually regarded as being part of it. That the contributors may have accepted this intellectual venture is remarkable.

The first part, "Legacies," includes thinkers and topics that have profoundly shaped the anthropological apprehension of moral and ethical issues. It may seem surprising that the four authors presented are two sociologists (Durkheim and Weber), a philosopher (Foucault), and a historian (E. P. Thompson) – with no anthropologist. There is always an element of arbitrariness in the choice of founding fathers and one could have proposed, among others, Westermarck for his monumental *The Origins and Development of the Moral Ideas* (1917), or Malinowski for his short *Crime and Custom in Savage Society* (1926), but in spite of their innovative character, these works have not significantly influenced the way we think about morality and ethics in the social sciences. As previously indicated, Durkheim and Foucault have respectively defined what is viewed as moral facts and ethical subjects, whereas Weber's discussion of values, ethos, and ethics has shaped our understanding of morals. The addition of E. P. Thompson's moral economy may seem more arguable, but it represents an exploration of the borders of morality and its articulation with politics, as it became clear in the way the concept was used by anthropologists working on structural inequalities and social movements. Two points seem crucial to what moral anthropology has inherited. The first one concerns the long-lasting debate between relativism and universalism, which has haunted the discipline and rendered its members suspicious to many critics: to account for this dispute, one should differentiate not only cultural and moral relativism, but also the contextualization of values and sensibilities observed in other societies and their justification; for lack of these two clarifications, many confusions have been made possible. The second one deals with the history of ethical and moral questions faced by anthropologists in their relations with the authorities as well as with the natives: ignored for decades, these questions have become more prevalent within the discipline, as a result of controversies about activities described as compromising, of criticisms pronounced by the subjects under study, and of the increasing pressure of institutional review boards; a moral anthropology must definitely encompass an ethics of anthropology.

The second part, "Approaches," proposes a series of outlooks on moralities and ethics through various analytical tools. Despite their centrality to any description of morality, values have probably received less attention from anthropologists than from philosophers; yet they pose important theoretical questions, in terms of the interpretation of the role of culture in the shaping of moral values and, reciprocally, the role of morality in the making of cultural values, as well as in terms of conflicts between values inherited from various cultures, and therefore the hierarchies and compromises to which they give rise. In opposition to what has been often regarded as a temptation by most philosophers to prefer simple, abstract, formal, and sometimes highly improbable situations and dilemmas, ordinary ethics has been claimed by some anthropologists as the site of expression of ethical issues in everyday life and through common sense; ethical discourses and ethical practices are constitutive elements of human existence and should therefore be acknowledged as such. A major interrogation for moral philosophers has long concerned the precedence of emotion or reason in the production of moral action: are we moved by pure compassion or do we decide after an internal deliberation? While the theory of moral sentiments provides one answer, highlighting the importance of empathy in the engendering of a moral sense, the concept of moral reasoning suggests an alternative, with the deployment of debates and contradictions. It is noteworthy that anthropologists have shifted this discussion on emotion and reason, which is typical of modern philosophy, to so-called traditional societies. This inquiry into subjectivity and agency has recent developments, both conceptual, with the focus on virtues, and methodological, with the emphasis on narratives, although this distinction should be questioned since the former often emanate from the latter.

The third part, "Localities," comprises studies of various topics that are deeply morally invested and inscribes them in the social context which makes them meaningful. Piety can be viewed as a religious category but it is also a moral one, or rather, if we consider it not from the perspective of religious morality, which would be imposed on individuals, but from the perspective of ethical subjectivation, which agents would deliberately make their own, it can be regarded as a category of practice: certain Egyptian Muslim groups have made it essential to their being in the world; understanding the signification they give it provides a completely different view on Islam. Care has been claimed, initially by feminists, as a concept that could serve as an alternative to that of justice, which they viewed as a dominantly masculine outlook on society; this sort of intimate attention and compassionate dedication to others is gendered, which does not imply of course that it should be seen as a feminine attribute and restricted to women; it can be contrasted with the much less studied disposition to disregard, which is compellingly illustrated in the case of persons abandoned by their families in Brazil. Mourning corresponds to a psychological state resulting from loss; however, ethnography demonstrates that it is simultaneously social and moral; not only is its bodily or ritualized expression culturally shaped, but also its signification varies according to the context; thus in China, it assumed a definitely political and moral dimension when grieving of certain deaths became repressed by the regime and appeared to be, symmetrically, a form of protest against it. Poverty has long been an object of moral concern, classically translated in the practice of philanthropy; the novelty of the contemporary world is precisely that it is also contemporaneous, in the sense that at a global level there is a coeval presence of the wealthy and the poor, which therefore poses moral questions of obligation of the former toward the latter at the same time as questions of expectations of the second toward the first, as shown in the case of Malawi's programs against poverty. Inequality is obviously a related issue, yet it poses potentially different moral questions, which do not have to do with compassion or even solidarity, but of justice and fairness; its approach raises a theoretical point, however, since inequality supposes an agreement about criteria to recognize and measure it, which does not exist in societies where certain goods or groups are considered incommensurable; in parallel, an empirical problem is difficult to solve when contradictory practices of justice and drives toward inequity coexist; contemporary Russia is exemplary of these theoretical and empirical complications. Sexuality appears to be a distinctive object since it is generally invested both morally and ethically; on the one hand, the moralization of sexuality is an enduring social concern embedded in religious prescriptions; on the other hand, the subjectivation of sexuality has more recently been apprehended as an important element of the ethical formation of the self; the case of Nepal offers an unexpected and sometimes paradoxical illustration of this duality and its consequences.

The fourth part, "Worlds," explores various domains of activity, with relations more or less visible to morality and ethics. Religion is certainly the realm most obviously in the proximity of morality, but the articulation of the two is complex, variable in time and space, claimed and controversial at the same time; depending on the sociological tradition one is inscribed in, one may insist on the role of ritual practices or value formation. Charity also offers an interesting case for cross-cultural comparison of practices of giving, the present participle introducing a substantial difference with the classical anthropological approach of the gift; it is an act of generosity with no counter-gift, except precisely in terms of the moral satisfaction it brings to the donor; this asymmetry has ethical as well as political consequences, especially in international relations. Medicine is not solely a technical activity based on biological and biochemical knowledge; it also implies a moral intervention grounded on values and expressing sensibilities, with claims of altruism by professionals and expectations about the role the sick should play in the management of their illness; and it simultaneously raises ethical issues, as controversies about clinical trials in the developing world or about global organ trafficking have recently shown. Science itself involves values and sensibilities, and even apparently purely cognitive activities carried on in a laboratory such as objectification or quantification are invested with moral intentions historically construed as ways to attain truth; ethical issues definitely become crucial when knowledge leaves the protected space of experimentation to be applied in the real world, whether it is for drugs, weapons, or industrial innovations. Finance has long been socially invisible, but the multiplication of increasingly serious crises, the tragic human consequences of inconsistent choices, the accusations of greediness against bankers, traders, and company executives and their lack of accountability have generated strong public moral condemnation and repeated demands for ethical rules; however, the financial realm is governed by specific rules, norms, and values which can be analyzed like any moral economy. Law, finally, appears to be so closely related to morality that some have affirmed that it was the formal translation into codes of informal norms and values; actually, the relation between law and morality is more complex; ethnographical accounts reveal in particular how legal texts and procedures may be used as resources for moral claims or, on the contrary, violated when the use of force becomes a way to annihilate moral expectations of rights.

The fifth part, "Politics," explores the interface between morality and politics and, more precisely, the issues raised and problems posed by the growing articulation of the moral and the political. Humanitarianism is the example that comes to mind and rather than considering it as separate from politics, as some argue, it seems more accurate to analyze how politics is reformulated through humanitarianism; the place occupied by humanitarian organizations in the global public sphere and the appropriation of their language by states and even the military to qualify wars as humanitarian attests to the success of the moral enterprise as well as its ambiguity, which often engenders discomfort among concerned agents. Human rights may appear as a parallel path followed by the moral stance in the political domain; although it has a long genealogy, its history as a driving force in politics is more recent; moreover, its contestation as either imperialist or double standard, in other words in excess or by default, has come to be the central scientific and ideological site of the debate between universalism and relativism. Indeed both humanitarianism and human rights are inscribed in a common moral Western tradition, but whereas the former mainly relies on moral sentiments, moral principles primarily underlie the latter. By contrast with these politics of the good, war and violence are often assimilated with the side of evil. Yet, closer analysis demonstrates that such a Manichaean view is difficult to hold. Warfare, long ignored by anthropologists, has received much more attention in the past decades and its moral dimension has been approached through questions of the legitimization of military intervention as just, the disqualification of certain practices, such as the use of child soldiers, the demonization of certain resistance movements, designated as terrorism; in each case, moral arguments were produced; noticeably social scientists themselves have participated in this moral discourse via their critique of war. Violence, in a similar way, has been the object of recent interest of anthropologists, again giving rise to normative stances, more frequently when it is committed by agents easily characterized as dominants than when it occurs among those regarded as the dominated; not only does the qualification of an act as violent always engage a form of moral reprobation, but also the issues of the expansion of the object, such as with the reformulation of poverty and inequality as structural violence, and of the homogeneity of its expression, as implied in the idea of a continuum of violence from sexual abuse to genocide, involve profound moral interrogations. Punishment offers a moral counterpoint, since it is assumed that it represents the justice dispensed for violations of the social norm; however, the limits with vengeance are not clear and the psychic economy of pulsions associated with chastisement is far from transparent; indeed the civilizing of punishment, with the disappearing of its spectacle, generally associated with modernity, is often contradicted by actual facts in societies that appear to be increasingly intolerant and punitive. Borders are often exclusively thought of as delimitations of territories; yet, with the growing anxieties about immigration and identities, they have become sites of intense moralization, both symbolically in the public sphere and concretely in the work of border officers, awakening the debate between cosmopolitanism and nationalism.

The sixth and final part, "Dialogues," results from an endeavor to arouse interest in and to facilitate conversations with neighboring disciplines. Moral philosophy comes first, of course, since, as has been argued earlier, the moral questioning of anthropologists has been nourished by concepts and theories inherited from moral philosophers. Yet, its current reorientation via the philosophy of language brings new interrogations, in connection with the recent developments of evolutionary biology, cognitive anthropology, moral psychology, neuroethics, and neuroimaging. The two larger fields of the sciences of society and the sciences of the mind have long deployed their paradigms – one mostly grounded in observation, the other principally in experimentation – on parallel paths, largely ignoring and occasionally discrediting each other. Although these paradigms are objectively competing interpretations of what human beings think and do, it seems timely to engage a dialogue based on a better understanding of what is assumed in each field. The recent development of new approaches of morality and ethics in anthropology and sociology, on the one hand, and in cognitive and evolutionary disciplines, on the other hand, invite one to exchanges and debates. A critical discussion of some of the premises of the sciences of the mind, such as the hard-wired structure of morality, the universality of moral grammars, the moral progress of mankind as a result of evolution or the precedence of moral emotions over reasoning – some of them disputed within these disciplines – can be engaged only on the basis of in-depth comprehension and mutual recognition.

Conclusion

Moral anthropology does not exist as such. Should it? Inviting this diverse range of authors to assemble their texts in a collective volume is obviously the beginning of an answer. But is it worth it? The only response to this question is that the proof is in the pudding or the evidence in the volume itself. Actually it is not my intention – nor is it that of the authors of the 34 chapters, as far as I know – to claim a new field or subfield in anthropology. It is more modestly to pose new questions on human life and to allow new possibilities of answering them. The success of the enterprise can be assessed only in function of its heuristics. For those who have already been involved in it for some time, as well as for those who temporarily joined it on the occasion of this book, it practically signifies exploring new territories. It is our intuition that questioning moral and ethical issues in contemporary societies and in our own scientific practice may be as significant for our discipline as has been, in recent decades, questioning political, racial, or gender issues, that is, unveiling invisible stakes and seeing the world differently.

But this endeavor implies a critical approach to morality and ethics, as would be the case for any object studied by the social sciences. Critique is not criticism. What it means here is four things, corresponding respectively to theoretical, methodological, epistemological, and political dimensions. First, critique signifies not taking for granted the moral values and ethical principles that constitute our common sense of morality and ethics. Not only do we know they are not always shared across societies or groups, but we also recognize they have not even always been ours. Actually the very idea of morality and ethics is culturally and historically inscribed. The point is not so much the sense of relativity to which this awareness leads as the new interrogations it authorizes. In particular, when we become conscious of the fact that the moral and ethical order we consider obvious, or natural, or simply good, could have been different, then we can start asking ourselves what has been gained and what has been lost in this process of making it what it is. Of course, this game language is a simplification and rather than mere additions and subtractions we generally have more complex reconfigurations, as for example with the major shift that has occurred concerning the value of life, from what can be sacrificed for a cause to what should be protected as sacred. Second, critique implies that in the social world morality and ethics are generally not given a priori but interpreted a posteriori by the agents as well as the anthropologist. Certainly they can be found explicitly and formally in religious doctrines or in the philosophical corpus or even as sets of rules that specific authorities pronounce, and people may even refer to them. Yet, from a pragmatic perspective, the moral and the ethical are revealed in the course of action rather than on the occasion of formal dilemmas. Hence the futility of providing a definition of morality and ethics and of attempting to verify its adequacy with actual discourses and practices. To the question concerning what he or she means by moral and ethical, the ethnographer answers through his or her interpretation of the way in which the agents make sense of their actions. Indeed the very categories of morality and ethics are seldom mobilized by individuals even when their conduct seems governed by what they think of as being good, virtuous, fair, or right in a specific situation and context. A major consequence of this comprehension of morality and ethics is the recognition that they are not pure objects discernible in the social world but are most of the time intricately linked with other domains, in particular the political. Third, critique involves the anthropologist as subject, that is, as an individual actively engaged in moral commitments and ethical positions, which he or she does not necessarily acknowledge. One should not forget that the social sciences were born in an effort to distance the intellectual gaze from normative positioning. Epistemological rigor remains therefore indispensable, especially since moral engagement is sometimes obvious, but at other times not. In both cases, reflexivity is neither an exercise of ego analysis for its own sake nor a dismissal of the possibility of a grounded analysis, but on the contrary the condition of an objective analysis of moral and ethical issues. Fourth, critique supposes an interrogation about the reasons, justifications, and consequences of the deployment of morality and ethics as a language to describe, interpret, and act in the contemporary world. Certainly this language is not entirely new, but its recent deployment questions the signification of this ethical turn. It is necessary to apprehend the economic and social issues it reformulates or eclipses, particularly in terms of inequality and power, and the alternative perspectives it delegitimizes, whether they invoke justice or conflict. There is always, ultimately, a politics of morality.

Acknowledgments

The conception and realization of this volume have been made possible thanks to an Advanced Grant of the European Research Council entitled "Towards a Critical Moral Anthropology." The introduction has benefited from numerous discussions with the researchers of the group I constituted in Paris within the framework of this program, as well as with my colleagues at the Institute for Advanced Study and the fellows invited as part of the theme I developed on this topic in Princeton. I am grateful to all of them for their generous exchange of ideas and critiques, as well as to Jacqueline Harvey for her careful copy-editing, Nancy Cotterman and Laura McCune for their attentive proofreading, and Linda Garat for her helpful assistance in the whole process of preparing this volume.

REFERENCES

Anderson, Paul (2011) "The Piety of the Gift": Selfhood and Sociality in the Egyptian Mosque Movement. *Anthropological Theory* 11(1): 3–21.

Asad, Talal (1993) *Genealogies of Religion: Discipline and Reasons of Power in Christianity and Islam.* Baltimore: Johns Hopkins University Press.

Barker, John ed. (2007) *The Anthropology of Morality in Melanesia and Beyond.* Aldershot: Ashgate.

Das, Veena (2010) Engaging the Life of the Other: Love and Everyday Life. In Michael Lambek (ed.), *Ordinary Ethics: Anthropology, Language, and Action.* New York: Fordham University Press, pp. 376–399.

Durkheim, Émile (1974 [1906]) The Determination of Moral Facts. In *Sociology and Philosophy.* New York: Free Press, pp. 35–62.

Durkheim, Émile (1984 [1893]) *The Division of Labor in Society.* New York: Macmillan.

Edel, Abraham (1962) Anthropology and Ethics in Common Focus. *Journal of the Royal Anthropological Institute of Great Britain and Ireland* 92(1): 55–72.

Englund, Harri (2008) Extreme Poverty and Existential Obligations: Beyond Morality in the Anthropoogy of Africa. *Social Analysis* 52(3): 33–50.

Fassin, Didier (2007) Humanitarianism as a Politics of Life. *Public Culture* 19(3): 499–520.

Fassin, Didier (2009) Les Économies Morales Revisitées. *Annales. Histoire, Sciences Sociales* 64(6): 1237–1266.

Fassin, Didier (2011) *Humanitarian Reason: A Moral History of the Present.* Berkeley: University of California Press.

Faubion, James (2011) *An Anthropology of Ethics.* Cambridge: Cambridge University Press.

Foucault, Michel (1990 [1984]*) The Use of Pleasure.* New York: Vintage Books.

Foucault, Michel (2010 [2008]) *The Government of the Self and Others: Lectures at the Collège de France 1982–1983.* New York: Palgrave Macmillan.

Garcia, Angela (2010) *The Pastoral Clinic: Addiction and Dispossession along the Rio Grande.* Berkeley: University of California Press.

Heinz, Monica (ed.) (2009) *The Anthropology of Moralities.* New York: Berghahn.

Hirschman, Albert (1981) Morality and the Social Sciences. In *Essays in Trespassing: Economics to Politics and Beyond.* Cambridge: Cambridge University Press, pp. 294–305.

Howell, Signe (ed.) (1997) *The Ethnography of Moralities.* London: Routledge.

Kleinman, Arthur (2006) *What Really Matters: Living a Moral Life amidst Uncertainty and Danger.* Oxford: Oxford University Press.

Ladd, John (1957) *The Structure of a Moral Code: A Philosophical Analysis of Ethical Discourse Applied to the Ethics of the Navaho Indians.* Cambridge, MA: Harvard University Press.

Laidlaw, James (2002) For an Anthropology of Ethics and Freedom. *Journal of the Royal Anthropological Institute* 8(2): 311–332.

Lambek, Michael (2010) Toward an Ethic of the Act. In Michael Lambek (ed.), *Ordinary Ethics: Anthropology, Language, and Action.* New York: Fordham University Press, pp. 39–63.

Louden, Robert (2003). The Second Part of Morals. In Brian Jacobs and Patrick Kain (eds.), *Essays on Kant's Anthropology.* Cambridge: Cambridge University Press, pp. 60–84.

Mahmood, Saba (2005) *Politics of Piety: The Islamic Revival and the Feminist Subject.* Princeton: Princeton University Press.

Malinowski, Bronislaw (1926) *Crime and Custom in Savage Society.* London: Routledge & Kegan Paul.

Parish, Steven (1994) *Moral Knowing in a Hindu Sacred City: An Exploration of Mind, Emotion and Self.* New York: Columbia University Press.

Pocock, D. F. (1986) The Ethnography of Morals. *International Journal of Moral and Social Studies* 1(1): 3–20.

Read, K. E. (1955) Morality and the Concept of the Person among the Gahuku-Gama. *Oceania* 25(4): 233–282.

Robbins, Joel (2007) Between Reproduction and Freedom: Morality, Value, and Radical Cultural Change. *Ethnos* 72(3): 293–314.

Simon, Gregory (2009) The Soul Freed of Cares? Islamic Prayer, Subjectivity, and the Contradictions of Moral Selfhood in Minangkabau, Indonesia. *American Ethnologist* 36(2): 258–275.

Sykes, Karen (ed.) (2009) *The Ethnographies of Moral Reasoning: Living Paradoxes in a Global Age.* New York: Palgrave Macmillan.

Throop, Jason (2010) *Suffering and Sentiment: Exploring the Vicissitudes of Experience and Pain in Yap.* Berkeley: University of California Press.

Weber, Max (1949 [1904]) Objectivity in Social Science and Social Policy. In Edward Shils and Henry Finch (eds.), *Methodology of Social Sciences.* Glencoe, IL: Free Press, pp. 49–112.

Weber, Max (2008 [1919]) Politics as a Vocation. In *Max Weber's Complete Writing on Academic and Political Vocations.* New York: Algora, pp. 155–207.

Westermarck, Edward (1917) *The Origins and Development of the Moral Ideas.* New York: Macmillan.

Widlok, Thomas (2004) Sharing by Default? Outline of an Anthropology of Virtue. *Anthropological Theory* 4(1): 53–70.

Zigon, Jarrett (2007) Moral Breakdown and the Ethical Demand: A Theoretical Framework to an Anthropology of Moralities. *Anthropological Theory* 7(2): 131–150.

Zigon, Jarrett (2008) *Morality: An Anthropological Perspective.* Oxford: Berg.

PART I Legacies

CHAPTER 1

Durkheim and the Moral Fact

Bruno Karsenti

Trans. Amy Jacobs

In being constituted as a science, sociology produced the equivalent of an earthquake in philosophy, attacking as it did the very idea of "theoretical morality" and any undertaking to identify a foundation for morality. Not only would moral philosophy never be the same, but it became questionable whether the discipline had the least relevance any longer. Durkheim had formulated his critique early on, during his 1886 trip to Germany – well before writing *The Division of Labor in Society.* He meant not only to make the point that mores varied by particular society but also to reap the implications of the idea that "moral facts" were conditioned by the "state of society" in which they appeared. To understand "morality," then, required not an approach in which it was simply conceived as an essence illustrated by historical-social forms but a social science of moral facts. This could be achieved only if the concept of "moral fact" could be made to acquire stable contours in accordance with the terms of the new social science. In sum, the moral fact had to be determined. Durkheim set out to accomplish this in 1906, in a lecture to the Société Française de Philosophie. That his argument was made to and for philosophers is certainly not indifferent. He meant to demonstrate in the very locus of the discipline from which sociology was emancipating itself the validity of the view the new discipline had managed to acquire of philosophy's own preferred object of study. Durkheim laid the grounds at that time for an approach that has fueled much lively thinking – some of it quite recent – on whether or not moral sociology can cohere as an independent discipline – independent, that is, from philosophy.

But returning to Durkheim has always raised objections. The positivist approach implied in Durkheim's very notion of moral fact has seemed to suggest it can only really serve in descriptive studies of the mores and social constraints they manifest, and that it is incapable of relating that material to the properly subjective pole of

A Companion to Moral Anthropology, First Edition. Edited by Didier Fassin.

morality, marked by the subject's relation to values and reflected not so much in externally observable moral facts as in moral acts and judgments that can be understood only by reconstituting their internal structure. The point is particularly paradoxical since at a different level Durkheim was at pains to point out the normative character of sociological knowledge as such, often going so far as to adopt the tone of a moralist able to discern the tendencies underlying and working to shape society's present state and likewise able to define, within that obscure, often conflictual, present state, what direction society should now take. In this respect, the emergence of sociology, and more importantly the figure of the sociologist, clearly brought about not only a change in the space of knowledge – that is, an epistemological change – but also in the way a society could intervene morally and even religiously in its own ongoing existence (Bellah 1974). Given that the ambiguity between descriptive and normative viewpoints was constitutive of the new discipline, that ambiguity is probably most visible in the moral sociology sector. Indeed, at the very moment this kind of approach is used to apprehend the object of study as specifically *social*, that object seems to escape its grasp, slipping into the subjective dimension where moral experience is made and takes shape as practical judgments and convictions. It is as if, of all observable social facts and precisely because of its normative texture, the moral fact necessarily overflowed the bounds of externalist factual determination. This in turn seems to suggest that sociology must resign itself either to switching perspectives – for example, adopting the Weberian perspective of value-oriented social action – or letting other disciplines take over. Durkheim's moral sociology may even appear split in two, composed on one hand of a sort of sociological morality, that of the moralist or prophet that the sociologist sometimes seems to represent in the society he speaks in, and on the other a resolutely descriptive approach ultimately destined to become – in direct contradiction to Durkheim's own presuppositions – a kind of moral psychology or philosophy. As we shall see, it was precisely by twisting the definition of morality that Durkheim managed to guard against such a scission.

Determination by "Sanction"

What exactly did Durkheim mean by "moral fact"? In the first (1893) edition of *La division du travail social*, he proclaimed the institution of "a science that, after it had classified moral phenomena, would seek to identify the conditions of each type and determine its role – that is, a positive science of morality" (Durkheim 1975b: 271). But for such a science to be possible, a stable criterion had to be found that would define what was to be included in the taxonomy. Clearly by 1893 Durkheim had already formulated the problem of "determining the moral fact" or "moral reality," his understanding being that such reality was complex and heterogeneous, and had to be typologically organized in a way that would clarify its structure. He resolved this problem as follows. Every moral fact consists in a diffusely sanctioned rule of behavior. "Sanction," understood as a predetermined social reaction to rule violation, is presented as the fundamental criterion for objectifying moral facts. Morality and law, explains Durkheim, are species of a single genus, distinguished only by the mode in which sanctions are administered: "diffuse" in the former, "organized" in the latter. Clearly this criterion makes the relationship between rule and instituted fact more problematic in matters of morality than in law, precisely because the question of subjectively distributed moral judgment cannot be raised in the same terms for morality as for a clearly outlined, circumscribed, judgment-making institution.

Durkheim granted priority to sanction because sanction alone allows for distinguishing moral rules from purely technical ones within the general domain of rules. In other words, an action is sanctioned not only when it has violated a rule but inasmuch as it has violated a rule. Rather than being a consequence of the act and so analytically contained in the concept of that act, the sanction is a consequence of the relationship between the act and the rule as rule. If there were no such relationship, no sanction-type consequence could attach to the act. This, according to Durkheim's liberal interpretation of Kant's distinction between precept and imperative, is because the sanction-to-act relationship is a synthetic one (Durkheim 2004 [1925]: 61). Intrinsically, there is nothing in the act that leaves it open to sanction. Rather, a synthesis is produced – and as we shall see, it can only be produced socially – between act and sanction, and it is this synthesis that enables me to say not that I am being punished because I have done such-and-such but inasmuch as I have done such-and-such, that is, as a consequence of my relationship to the rule.

However, there is a difficulty implied in using the notion of sanction to meet the requirement of fact objectification. Durkheim's aim was to provide sociology with the means of envisaging and organizing moral facts in their plurality, and he meant to achieve this by turning away from classic philosophical analysis of the concept of moral act. But trying to grasp moral facts from without meant concentrating on the effects of violation, the consequences of acts that go against morality. Sanction, as Durkheim put it, is a reagent; the way it achieves objectification is by pointing to a rule as that which has been disregarded or negated. But might not the reagent notion imply an unacceptable restriction here? It would seem to fail to take into account acts that express respect for obligations whose transgression does not incur sanction (Pharo 2004: 99).

To correctly measure the impact of this objection, we have to return to the conceptual economy of the relationship between obligation and sanction, as that is the form Durkheim's argument actually takes. For him it was beside the point to determine whether a transgression actually carried a risk of sanction or even whether that risk was clearly perceived by the agent. All repressive sanctions aim to diminish the agent and therefore consist quite literally in a *peine* (punishment). That the sanction is aimed at the agent this way has a considerable effect on how Durkheim understood obligation. Penal law – from which, once again, morality as he understood it differs not in nature but only in the way that punishment is administered – "does not first state, as does civil law: This is the duty; but states immediately: This is the punishment" (Durkheim 1996 [1893]: 41; English edn. 1974: 35). One implication of this is that the obligation itself is ever-already known. Moral obligation, then, is characterized by a specific cognitive situation and indicated by a certain type of sanction. Another implication is that not only does this understanding in terms of sanction not preclude evaluation of the type "moral judgment," but it actually implies such evaluation from the outset, as the point is to discover what serves as a foundation for obligations characteristic of repressive sanction, regardless of whether such sanctions are organized or diffuse.

How Durkheim's Thinking is Related to Kant's

What is the source of sanctions characteristic of moral rules? Durkheim only provided a full answer to this question in the above-mentioned 1906 lecture, entitled *Determination du fait moral*, and he obtained that answer by shifting the emphasis of the classic Kantian argument he was using. A brief review of the terms of the philosophical debate is in order. Durkheim claimed that, in contrast to Kantian thought, utilitarianism, particularly Spencer's, "betrays a complete ignorance of the nature of obligation" (2004: 63; English edn. 1974: 44) in that utilitarian thinkers could understand the consequence of violating an obligation in analytic terms only as the "mechanical consequence of an act." This amounted to a failure to understand the very concept of sanction, for sanction involved a synthetic tie between act and rule. The objective perspective of sanction, on the other hand – quite different from the perspective a Kantian would adopt in that, as Durkheim recognizes and indeed claims for his own argument, it implies "rigorously empirical analysis" – leads to the conclusion that what makes an obligation an obligation pertains not to the nature of what is commanded but rather to the *fact* of being commanded. Behind sanctioned rules of conduct, that is, those rules in which moral obligations are incarnated, we must therefore discover a "special authority," in accordance with which rules "are obeyed simply because they command" (Durkheim 2004: 50; English edn. 1974: 36). This provided a solution to the problem raised by repressive sanctions: A moral obligation need not be formulated; rather it can be assumed to be "ever-already known," precisely because it is not known in terms of its content, as the only thing that need be known about a moral obligation is that it obligates, and that knowledge is implied in its very form, that of moral commandment.

This amounts to claiming that duty is or carries within it its own foundation. Indeed, that is what gives duty primacy over good. Here Durkheim seems to align himself with Kant: morality must be founded not on an objectively qualified good but rather on duty as "objective necessity" for action – precisely Kant's words. For Kant, the commandment specific to moral law must be formally characterized as an imperative that determines "will as will," not as a means to attain a desired effect. It is neither subjective like maxims nor conditioned like precepts, which are merely hypothetical imperatives. It is instead categorical – Kant's word for defining the order of strictly practical necessity.

It is by means of the classic form of commandment that Durkheim seeks to determine what makes the moral fact absolutely distinctive. However, he then immediately subverts its meaning by laying down a principle that is not in the least Kantian and at first seems irreconcilable with the definition of formal obligation recalled above. The notion of duty, writes Durkheim, is in itself insufficient, and pure formalism is untenable, because it is "impossible for us to carry out an act simply because we are ordered to do so and without consideration of its content" (2004: 50; English edn. 1974: 36). The classic rigoristic solution, then, was in Durkheim's view only partially right; to it must be added a material element that actually contravenes its formalist dimension. In other words, the only legitimate way to affirm the primacy of duty over good – good being, for Kant, the "material but only objective determining ground of objects of action" (1983 [1788]: 79; English edn. 1997: 43) – is to perceive good in duty itself and thus to furnish content for what Kant considered the purely formal principle of moral commandment. Durkheim's move was to demonstrate that the correct understanding of the notion of obligation and the correct analysis of duty could not do without the notion of good. Thus, contrary to all expectations, the bases for a nonformal theory of morality were to be found within rigorism.

Durkheim's combined critique of Kantian formalism and return to morality understood in terms of duty by universalizing the action maxim was no novelty; it was a commonplace of republican French philosophy, the philosophical thinking that had come to the fore in the second half of the nineteenth century and been presented by such authors as Barni, Renouvier, Fouillée, and Paul Janet. Nascent sociology resparked that debate at the turn of the century and took up one of its main concerns: finding a motive for action that could inscribe the categorical imperative within feeling, feeling of a kind that went beyond mere respect for the law – "a feeling that is positive in its intellectual cause" (Kant 1983: 83; English edn. 1997: 68) – since respect for the law would not suffice as subjective determination to act, that is, precisely the type of determination that republican morality was seeking to reactivate through appropriate educational techniques. The universal could not be reduced in practice to an abstraction, ran this argument, and even less to the content of a commandment whose form alone was enough to guarantee its validity. Frédéric Rauh summed up the republican thinkers' aim in 1890 in a work that proved decisive for the position of the morality issue in this period: "We must surpass Kant's logicism by justifying feeling as reconciled with the idea" (1890: 4).[1]

However, within this general framework, where the point was to show that the purpose of the universal was situated at the very heart of feeling and therefore at a level that Kantian thinking rejected as pathological, the uniqueness of Durkheim's position is immediately apparent, first of all in his aforementioned refusal to remain on the same grounds of discussion. His point was to determine moral facts, and this meant examining moral reality not through the internal experience of the moral subject – that is, the individual's representation of what is moral – but from the outside. As Durkheim saw it, the attempts by moralists (Kant, Renouvier, Janet, but also the English utilitarian thinkers) to provide a foundation or a new foundation for morality could not succeed because they were introspective and individualistic. But this was not all: for Durkheim the point was not to amend rigorism but to bolster it. He meant to establish an internal tie, unsuspected by either Kant or his critics, between duty and good, obligation and desire. Moral things, or what Durkheim called *the moral* (substantivizing the adjective primarily for the purpose of objectification and thus, in accordance with the first "rule of sociological method," to apprehend a thing as posited outside the subject), were desirable in themselves. This objective desirability brought the notion of good back to the fore and required a more complex analysis of duty. The paradox – a paradox that sociology alone could render acceptable – was that desirability was simply one aspect of duty itself: "something of the nature of duty" (Durkheim 2004: 51; English edn. 1974: 36).

"We feel a *sui generis* pleasure in performing our duty simply because it is our duty" (Durkheim 2004: 64; English edn. 1974: 45). "*Sui generis* pleasure" must be understood as a pleasure that cannot be reduced to that obtained from ends pursued elsewhere than in the moral realm: a pleasure engendered by duty itself and specific to the fact of obeying a moral commandment as such. This was the pleasure of "attachment," a crucial term in Durkheim's analyses and one that must be interpreted by taking into account its two meanings, one physical and the other pertaining to feeling. Indeed, we are "attached to" our duty (feeling) in that we are "attached or bound *by*" it (physical condition). The pleasure we take in the feeling of attachment cannot be dissociated from the pleasure of being attached or bound – that is, literally, obligated.

In this particular understanding of pleasure, eudemonism not only coexists with rigorism but becomes incorporated into it – while remaining its opposite: "Eudemonism and its contrary pervade moral life" (Durkheim 2004: 64; English edn. 1974: 45). Durkheim is fully aware that this is a contradiction, since obligation revealed by sanction as just analyzed always implies *peine* (pain) and a diminishing of the agent. In fact, the challenge is to understand such diminishment as elevation and to create a link between that elevation and authentic pleasure, an utterly unique type of pleasure. In other words, though the contradiction between the diminishment and elevation of the agent is blatant, it is absolutely constitutive of the moral fact itself. Therefore, according to Durkheim, we must not rush to remove it dialectically but rather work to understand it by further probing and analyzing empirical realities: facts.

Durkheim was careful to point out that a contradiction of this kind in no way indicated a disconnect within the subject, a split between reason and feeling conceived as two heterogeneous facets of subjectivity. Kant's great error, according to Durkheim, was to have understood dualism in those terms. On the contrary, because good is within duty and duty within good, feeling and reason, though remaining distinct, must be understood to connect with each other – at an intersection point that remained to be identified. The crucial fact was the interpenetration of the two elements. And this in turn meant that in studying morality we had to rid ourselves of any and all foundationalist notions or intentions. If it was true that "the notion of good enters into those of duty and obligation just as they in turn enter into the notion of good" – in sum, if those opposites were indeed part of each other – then neither one could be granted exclusive founding privileges. No order of priority could be postulated (Durkheim 2004: 67; English edn. 1974: 45), and the two notions had to be situated on one and the same plane. Nor should we conclude that they were enough to account for moral reality in its entirety. Empirical analysis would undoubtedly clarify other characteristics of moral life, for morality was by definition varied. Nonetheless, "moral Daltonism" – the unique coloring of morality that resulted from the two opposed colors of duty and good combined in infinitely variable proportions – not only did not dissolve phenomenal reality into a relativism devoid of any unifying principle but actually justified sociological investigation into variations in those proportions, investigation that was to be conducted on the basis of a single interpretive schema. Replacing the "foundation" thesis with the claim that good and duty were actually interpenetrated amounted to attacking the foundation perspective as such. The aim of the 1906 lecture was both philosophical and sociological: to determine a type of fact and therefore to position oneself to be able to read and analyze all instances of that type of fact, the goal being not to determine a foundation for morality but to make morality the research object of a necessarily *social* science.

The Sacred

To determine the moral fact, then, was to grasp the structuring nature of the contradiction contained in such facts. According to Durkheim, their terms formed a bipolar arrangement within which moral judgments and acts were formulated and carried out. But this only made the religious underpinnings of morality more visible. Grasping the moral fact in terms of its intrinsic contradiction reconnected it with "the sacred," the touchstone of Durkheim's definition of religion. The sacred, which Durkheim said was "revealed" to him while reading *The Religion of the Semites* by Robertson Smith (Durkheim 1975a: 404), is a quality attributed to certain beings that gives them equal powers to attract and repel, rendering them objects of both desire and prohibition. What characterized the sacred, then, was its ambivalence. And it was defined negatively: the sacred is what is not profane, what must be distanced from and in no case confused with the profane but also what attracts the profane, what the profane inclines toward without ever being able to touch. If it is true that all social existence presupposes an experience of the sacred (religious facts being fully subsumed by this defining core), then at a certain level of our social experience, good and duty are exactly the same thing – they meld into one and the same thing. The sacred is desirable; it is the object of a *sui generis* desire that cannot be reduced to any other form of sense-related desire though it is still incontrovertibly rooted in feeling. In other words, to use Kantian language, the superior faculty of desiring, though aimed at a particular object, is still a matter of feeling. But the sacred is also forbidden, and forbidden in that it is sacred: the sacred is what is "set apart" in absolute terms. It represses inasmuch as it elevates, and elevates inasmuch as it constrains. The sacred is decidedly an object of respect, but that respect has nothing in common with what Kant conceived as nonpathological, purely practical feeling. Durkheim's notion of respect, with its dual aspects of desire and subservience, is fully reintegrated into the realm of sensibility through the intercession of our feeling of the sacred.

Nonetheless, explains Durkheim, the sacred too is a fact, less an elucidation than an illustration – the empirical manifestation – of the coexistence of opposites. Through the sacred, the two opposed terms of "good" and "duty" achieve what must be called a contradictory unity rather than a resolution of that contradiction. That contradiction is attested to, rather than overcome, through an experience of unity that ineluctably reconnects morality to religion. Durkheim's radicalization of the analysis leads us to the conclusion that the foundation of morality is a fundamental, ineradicable religiosity. Morality could of course be secularized, lose its theological foundation, claim to be human and only human; nonetheless, it necessarily implied the sacred, and in this sense it remained religious, regardless of what beings it endowed with sacredness. Durkheim's contribution to the idea of "secular faith" advocated in the Third Republic – namely by Ferdinand Buisson, his predecessor at the Sorbonne – thus becomes clear. The point was less to move beyond religion than to shift the position religion occupied within a moral sphere now understood to fulfill the function of "making sacred," a function without which there could be no collective existence.

What distinguished modern manifestations of the sacred, and thus determined the unique combination of good and duty to be found in societies defined in *The Division of Labor in Society* by the concept of organic solidarity, was the locus of sacredness, the fact that in modern societies sacredness was entirely immanent in the existence of social subjects. No longer projected outside the subject as theological transcendence or deified nature, sacredness had come to lodge in the individual himself or better yet the *person*, a relatively new product of the historical individuation process that Durkheim (1970), in some texts, was willing to call "individualism". It is on the individual that our most intense and fully determined social feelings have come to be concentrated; attacking those feelings necessarily provokes a moral or penal reaction.

But this also means that the entity to which we are most rigorously obligated – obligated, that is, by way of a commandment – is precisely the entity that is closest to us, so close that it has become ourselves. This in turn means that what is "set apart," separate – the sacred – is also the eminent focus of our "sympathy" (Durkheim 2004: 68; English edn. 1974: 48), the focal point of our most immediate desire.

We should not be misled by Durkheim's use of the classic category of sympathy; it in no way signaled a return to the Anglo-Scottish tradition in which the concept was first delimited. While sympathy is a figure of sensibility or feeling in Durkheim's thought, the reference is once again to the *sui generis* form he was able to identify by analyzing desire for the law as a desire internal to law itself. It is not sympathy for another person perceived as unique, nor even sympathy of the sort that conceals an attitude toward oneself and that therefore takes – or has been assigned – an indirect path, but rather desire in the direction of the person as such, the form of the individual, incarnated equally in each of us. In sum, while pulling closer than ever to the subject here, the sacred remained of a separate order. The personal or human turn that morality had taken in modern societies should therefore be interpreted by means of the previously identified schema. In the notion of the individual or the person, a remarkable balance between duty and good – indeed, the right proportions – was realized: when considered in connection with the personal or human, the focus of duty more clearly illuminated the fact that it was itself a good: a good *for us*. The question then became what meaning should be attributed to "us." And asking that question amounted to taking the analysis of the interpenetration of opposites – without which "the moral" would lose all consistency – one step further. In sum, it implied moving away from the sacred, which only reveals a reality without explaining it, and focusing on the structure of moral judgment itself.

The Individual, the Ideal of the Person

A point to which Durkheim returns incessantly throughout his work is that the individual is what has the greatest moral value for us in modern societies. However, it is important to understand – and herein lies the incontrovertible difference between Durkheim's thinking and that of the liberals – that it was not the individual herself who was responsible for that extraordinary value; rather she had gradually acquired it through a socially determined individuation process, a process that is not merely affected by certain social conditions but entirely governed by a social dynamic, a process at the conclusion of which it could be said that "the social ideal is a particular form of the ideal of humanity"(Durkheim 2004: 76; English edn. 1974: 53), a process in which, consequently, value for the group and value for me had become directly related. From this unique relation was born the concept of the person, a concept that modern societies have the privilege of promoting consciously, as an ideal, in their practical thinking.

How can this dynamic be perceived? We recall the change described in *The Division of Labor in Society*. Because of the relatively simple structure of primitive groups, collective representations were in control in those groups because they could be in control: the society could be represented as a whole while the individual could be conceived of – and could conceive of himself – only in relation to that whole (to the extent that an individual could conceive of society). In such societies, collective consciousness accounted for individual consciousness in its entirety; there were no points where the latter did not perfectly correspond or conform to the former. Indeed, individual consciousness did not amount to much compared to collective consciousness precisely because the group itself could be represented as an individual entity. Conversely, "the more we advance in time, the more complex and immense does our civilization become, and consequently, the more does it transcend the individual consciousness and the smaller does the individual feel" (Durkheim 2004: 78; English edn. 1974: 54). That situation corresponds first and foremost to functional differentiation, by which each subject gets assigned a specialty whose meaning depends on a higher purpose that she can no longer directly perceive. But such differentiation nonetheless reflects a certain type of cohesion – organicity – and this is because somewhere within us, in the manner of an echo and above all in a way that differs from sovereign collective representations, society remains present. The form that society's presence takes in members of modern societies is individuality, a social production in the dual sense that it was produced by society and that it enables society to produce itself continuously as a coherent whole despite its being fragmented into individual consciousnesses.

It is crucial to grasp this paradox: society is present in us in the form of the individual – that is, as what, at first glance, would seem nonsocial (see Isambert 1992: 364–365, who perfectly recapitulates this paradox). But it is present only if we are careful not to confuse the individual with our own individuality, in other words, to the extent that we understand our individuality as internally dual. This means that the sociological perspective is not so much a redefinition of relations between the individual and society as the difficult apprehension of a concept of the individual that is different from that of the traditional individualist approach. It is through the individual understood as a dual being that society exists in its differentiated, complex unity, with the understanding that individual consciousness and collective consciousness are necessarily distinct from each other. Durkheim thus arrives at a quite singular type of dualism: not individual/group, but a dualism hollowed out within individuality itself between the presence of the social in the individual, a presence attested to by the rise of the category of the person, and the purely empirical self-presence of particular individuality (Durkheim 1990 [1912]: 386; Karsenti 2004).[2]

The coexistence of opposites, or rather the structuring nature of contradiction in morality – the fact that neither of its two constitutive terms, "duty" and "good," prevails over the other and no unifying synthesis is permissible – highlights Durkheim's particular interpretation of the notion of ideal. His typical "ideal" has nothing to do with Weber's ideal type. It is not a theoretical construction by means of which the sociologist, equipped against intrusion from value judgments, situates and arranges concrete facts by measuring differences between them. On the contrary, Durkheim's typical ideal is a normative concept; it is what society produces in the way of a purpose, that which is morally desirable to the individual, a surpassing of self that coincides with self-realization. We are attached to the ideal by an affective tie that can only exist thanks to moral good. But through the ideal we are also partially detached from ourselves, from our empirical sense-based individuality. With this in mind, the fact that society produces the ideal takes on a specific meaning: society, while playing the role of normative commanding authority, produces representations that act as a magnet within individual consciousnesses. That we are worthy of the ideal we share as members of the same group is reflected in the existence of our desire for that ideal, a desire that cannot be dissociated from obligation. Clearly, the notion of the ideal implies a certain notion of value, while providing a response to the current objection that Durkheim's objectivism cannot free morality from conformism since in his thinking morality necessarily depends on currently existing social factors incarnated in external norms that operate exclusively through sanction. That response is as follows: society as it exists at a given moment, with its particular morphological conditions, group structure, means of communication, the ways in which its internal social "milieu" is determined, is not a realization of the ideal; rather, the ideal inheres in a society that, on the basis of the composite substratum just mentioned (particular morphological conditions, group structure, etc.), seeks to exist through our very actions, precisely in that those actions are susceptible, at their own level, of moral regulation. The internal correlation between good and duty culminates in the realization that in desiring the ideal, we are consenting to society's will to be through us, which is also its will to be transformed by us. The "true nature of society," as Durkheim (2004: 95; English edn. 1974: 65) put it in his response to Darlu, can very well inhere in revolt against whatever rules are currently in effect – a certain state of the rules – if those rules are no longer linked to the particular ideal in accordance with which society wishes to *be*. In such a case, revolt, not conformity, is moral. This is due to a necessity that can be understood only at the level of action, as action is the real mode by which society produces itself.

Value Judgments

We begin to see how to overcome the difficulties arising from Durkheim's apparently positivist understanding of morality. If we cannot move beyond the idea of an opposition between external norms and the subject, if we insist on reducing the moral issue to that of subject's incorporation of external norms, then indeed Durkheim's perspective is a narrow one. But that would be to neglect his work on the concept that forms the basis of his theory: individuality. The way Durkheim both identified his thinking with Kant's and circumvented Kant's position through his main thesis on interpenetrated opposites in the moral sphere, and the use of that idea in his concept of the ideal, cast a different light on his sociology, freeing it from the objectivism or conformism for which it is commonly criticized.

The traits of this other Durkheim are clearest in his handling of "value judgments" in a paper delivered in 1911 to the International Congress of Philosophy in Bologna (Durkheim 2004: 117–141; Gurvitch 1937: 68–70).[3] Here again, the way the problem is formulated is Kantian: How are value judgments possible? In the framework of classical judgment analysis, the question of value raises a serious difficulty. Whereas judgments of reality say no more than what things are, value judgments say what things are worth "in relation with a particular sensibility" (Durkheim 2004: 117; English edn. 1974: 80–81). How are we to understand this reference to subjectivity, which seems to affirm that morality has a subjective foundation, when Durkheim has elsewhere claimed that value can be objectified and that value judgments themselves are therefore characterized by a kind of objectivity?

In itself, a sensibility-generated judgment – what the subject feels – is actually nothing more than a type of judgment of reality. Judgments related to tastes or what Durkheim calls preferences fall into this category. Value judgments, on the other hand, are objective in character (Durkheim 2004: 118) as they pertain to the value of the thing in question. Subjective sensibility of the sort that generates a preference thus does not produce a moral judgment. Does this mean that our sensibility goes no further than noting the properties of a thing, recognizing something that exists outside of ourselves and imposes its being on us? More fundamentally, what does the word "thing" mean when the thing in question gets endowed with value? Durkheim's answer involves an analysis of the process of appraising a thing's value – evaluating it (which he distinguishes from the process of formulating a preference). In evaluating something, the subject seems to note a dimension of the object that is independent of the way she perceives that object with her senses. However, while the object's value is not part of the relationship obtaining between it and the evaluating subject, that value does imply, by definition, the existence of such a relationship. Value does exist outside of myself, but only "in a way" (Durkheim 2004: 119). Durkheim's restriction is decisive. A value judgment is not a judgment of reality because value does not exist the way a thing does; nonetheless, value does exist outside the subject, objectively. Between the thing and its state of being a thing runs a line – a border – that Durkheim tries to stabilize. Value does inhere in the thing. Its objectivity is reflected in the intrinsic communicability of a value judgment and in its justifiability, the fact that such a judgment can be legitimately affirmed only if it is demonstrated on the basis of impersonal reasons. In operations of justification – and here Durkheim strikingly anticipates the major problematic of contemporary sociology of action, at least if we make an effort not to think of him as prisoner to his "dilemma" (Boltanski and Thévenot 1991 is the primary reference here) – the subject is implicated impersonally.

Durkheim's probing leads to the following question: How are we to explain that a thing's value is independent of both subjective, sense-based determinations and the relationship between it and the evaluating subject, a relationship that necessarily implies a kind of subjectivity? As Durkheim put it, "Can a state of feeling be independent of the subject that feels it?" (2004: 119; English edn. 1974: 82). Not only does that question point to the existence of a little-known dimension of internal experience, one that cannot be explained by subjective resources alone and imposes itself on the subject in a way that nonetheless remains attached to that subject – that is, feeling; it also offers a new way of looking at *things*, namely, in terms of the "feeling" that gets mixed into and "enriches" them.[4] In this respect, "the state of feeling" is the value itself, situated outside the person and in the thing it increases. What is at issue here is quite literally the *auctoritas* of certain things, an attribute that inheres in their being as things (Durkheim 1987 [1895]; 1990: 298).[5]

Interpreting the question of how value judgments are possible by way of the activity of evaluation shifts the center of gravity of the morality question. The point is to enlarge the focus from moral evaluation in the sense of judgments of actions to judgments of things-that-are-more-than-things, that is, that belong to the order of *social things* that Durkheim was seeking to circumscribe: things whose reality in the strict sense of that word – their status as *res* – encompasses the perception the subject has of them in the same way that the thing imposes itself on that subject's perception. Describing the process by which such things are constituted presupposes first that we part ways with cursory objectivism, which can only lead to a reductive understanding of value as a "state of fact" (*état de chose*) caused within the subject by the intrinsic properties of a certain type of object. Making a value judgment would then involve nothing more than the subject's noting the effect a certain objective reality has on her; the path would then run from without to within through a causal process. This, Durkheim explains, is a misguided view that amounts to endowing things with properties that could themselves *cause* a subjective state, a state favorable or unfavorable to the thing causing it, and in turn trigger a positive or negative judgment of it. The existence of objective good(s) would thereby be accredited, but only at the cost of absolutizing both the properties of valued things and certain aspects of the evaluating subject affected by those properties. The subject could be conceived in two ways. Either we say that the foundation of the subject is the individual, in which case we are back to a psychological theory of values, or we attribute primacy to the group as such and conceive *it* as a subject endowed with certain stable characteristics, regardless of the various forms in which it is historically incarnated. Clearly neither of these was a satisfactory solution.

The particularity of Durkheim's perspective lies first and foremost in his rejection of the second solution. Can an evaluation be called objective only "by being a collective one" (Durkheim 2004: 122; English edn. 1974: 84)? It all depends on what is meant by collective. The difficulty here is likely to be the same as in psychology-driven individualist theory: we still do not have a means to understand how it is that value varies, and varies constitutively – by definition, as it were. If value is reduced to a single evaluating or valuing "pole" assumed to correspond to some essential feature of the subject in whose eyes that value obtains, then the reality of values, their plurality, disappears. With regard to individualism, Durkheim emphasizes that it is impossible to think of all subjective perceptions as being of the same type; that is to say, what prevails in all subjective perceptions is the extremely abstract determination of valuing "life" in the biological sense of that term (Durkheim 2004: 121). At the collective level, Durkheim's point is to show that it is impossible to find an essential principle of evaluation to which all values could ultimately be referred back in a society thought of as one big subject that cannot be reduced to the individual subjects of which it is composed. In vain would we evoke the requirements of something on the order of "social life," for that determination is too vague to constitute a value susceptible of unifying the entire set of social values, at least as long as no undertaking has been made to define the notion.

Durkheim's move away from biological vitalism is an essential feature of his argument. The collective subject is not one big organism whose functions define a vital order that all activities must comply with and that could thus be evaluated by how well they did so comply or conform. The notion of social utility, of maintaining or fostering the life of the group as group, cannot be used to define a one and only evaluation criterion. This is attested first by the pluralism of social values, their heterogeneity and incommensurability – economic value, moral value, aesthetic value, scientific value – but above all by the impossibility of asserting the utility criterion over all others in each of the spheres of activity defined by social values (Durkheim 2004: 125; Mauss 1966):

> Life as man at all times has conceived it is not simply a precise arrangement of the budget of the individual or social organism, the reaction with the least possible expense to the

> outside stimulus, the careful balance between debit and credit. To live is above all things to act, to act without counting the cost and for the pleasure of acting.[6] (Durkheim 2004: 128; English edn. 1974: 86)

This definition brings to light the wellspring of Durkheim's notion of values and makes it clear that his distance from the vitalist position based on an organic–functional understanding of the group is related to his view of action. Social life is action. It is many differentiated actions that cannot possibly be reduced to a single purpose or aim. Of course society seeks to maintain itself. But for society, maintaining itself does not mean uniformly reproducing itself or continuously insuring vital functions. Self-maintenance for society is change, movement. If such movement were merely repetition it would be the equivalent of collapse. Action by individuals, the many paths such action takes, is the only content that can be given to the notion of "social life" (Durkheim 2004: 132). Social life is not the life of the social body conceived as a higher-order organism, but rather the set of individual actions through which society truly lives, ever recreating itself and therefore changing. The only principle with which the concept of value, irreducibly differentiated as it is, can be equated is action. And this principle precludes the possibility of attributing inherent value to things, value they would supposedly have by virtue of their intrinsic properties. Such quality or value is necessarily added to things by the way the subject, in acting, relates to them.

Society in Actuality and Society in Action

We still need to understand the nature of this addition, this augmenting of things that occurs through action. That is, how does practice relate to the value attributed to a thing? If value is not *in* things such that those things themselves have qualities capable of making the subject recognize them as valuable, must we say that the experience of value does not exist as experience but rather as something like purely intellectual apprehension of a reality situated outside all possible experience – a noumenal reality? We catch a glimpse of the Kantian pair of alternatives here. However, Durkheim rejects those alternatives for a reason that follows from his earlier definition of the ideal and its intrinsic relation to action. Kant's vision led to a rigid, hypostatized sense of the ideal, incompatible with the variability it has been seen to possess (Durkheim 2004: 129; English edn. 1974: 89). The point here is not merely that the ideal varies historically and socially; it is not merely to state the plurality of valuing processes as demonstrated by sociohistorical analysis. It is instead to show that variation is part of "the nature of things" and thus to integrate the ideal into natural phenomena as the force that moves them. At this level Durkheim's understanding of the importance of action comes to the fore. To set ideals outside nature is to detach them from action, whereas it is through action that the specific life of subjects who organize their behavior as a function of values is determined. In other words, to understand value judgments we can neither reduce them to judgments of reality nor cut them off from reality as it unfolds in time and space. We cannot locate or anchor value judgments anywhere but within phenomenal reality, reality composed of the subjective actions that weave the fabric of social life.

The ideal is not "mere possibility" (Durkheim 2004: 130; English edn. 1974: 89); it is not merely conceived, but desired. This fact is once again the sign of active attachment. The ideal possesses an intense power of attraction, and this power constitutes a certain phenomenal reality – namely the tension it confers on action itself. The ideal is willed in that it is borne "into action" by subjects who desire it. In this sense it is indeed a "living reality" (Durkheim 2004: 130; English edn. 1974: 89): it has its own life. This might lead us to grant it a detached existence, but in fact the life of the ideal is not really distinct from the life of subjects attached to it, who bear it forward in the same movement by which they are captured by its power to attract.

The importance of Durkheim's move to naturalize the ideal cannot be overemphasized, for the properly sociological meaning of his concept of ideal depends on it, as does his establishing of a method for making the ideal knowable. A force physics is implied here, whose criterium is intensity of attachment. The value question is more profoundly one of social valuing processes, processes to be measured and compared in terms of variations in intensity. It is never only values themselves – their content – that vary, but always also the currents of feeling and will – attachment, with the double meaning identified above – underlying those values. In sum, Durkheim accredits a certain view of social physics, not at all in connection with morphology but in the matter of representations themselves: Representations possess a measurable, analyzable normative dimension. While sociology must recognize "the field of ideals" as its own particular field (Durkheim 2004: 141; English edn. 1974: 96), the positive character of social phenomena means that sociology's task, rather than to record the ideal as if it were an objective fact, is to describe "social things," that term to be defined as an augmentation process through which nature "surpass[es] itself" (Durkheim 2004: 141; English edn. 1974: 97).

The core of Durkheim's argument is that values are located within *social* things, that is, the natural things by means of which nature surpasses itself. Precisely because such surpassing is *self*-surpassing, we do not move outside nature when we study it. From this follows Durkheim's position on value judgments: on the one hand, they cannot be reduced to judgments of reality; on the other, they cannot be radically separated from such judgments. Though the two are distinct, they proceed out of one and the same faculty of judgment, applied in both cases to natural realities. It is only the way in which the given is given that distinguishes the ideal from a simple fact. In the case of the ideal, the surpassing or transfiguration of the given is itself the object of judgment, a judgment that now moves beyond observing what is, evaluating instead a reality of a new sort – an "enriched" reality, endowed with value, value that is nothing other than the process by which it comes to surpass itself within nature.

While surrendering nothing of his realism – indeed, deepening it – Durkheim opened up perspectives in sociology that the objectivism of *The Rules of Sociological Method*, *Division of Labor in Society*, and *Suicide* gave no cause to anticipate. He did so by concentrating on social things that make their power felt as values in certain of our judgments. He did so by relating the concept of society to "social life" understood as the life in which individuals' lives are truly engaged and which, though irreducible to the lives of its individual components, can be accomplished only through those individuals, their ability to fuel society through constant innervation, a process attested to by value judgments and the moral acts commanded by those judgments. Durkheim's moral sociology is a sociology of moral facts, facts intrinsically linked to other types of facts, judgments, and acts, facts in which social subjects are actively implicated. If his sociology appears externalist, that is because he undertook to redefine the subjective status of social subjects, inscribing a split within the subject that is not resolved by that subject's integrating of moral norms, a split according to which a kind of being-outside-self becomes the very wellspring of internal moral tension, determined by the ever continuous, ever timely coexistence of good and duty in the structuring contradiction of their coexistence. Living socially does of course mean submitting to an external order. But the externality of that order, all the difficulty it involves, is to be found first within the subject, as one of the subject's own dimensions.

Durkheim's resistance to pure objectivism was ultimately expressed in his rejection of the utilitarian position, wherein the sovereign value is the life of the social body. To present society as "a system of organs and functions, maintaining itself against outside forces of destruction" (Durkheim 2004: 132; English edn. 1974: 91) was to reduce what is called the life of the group to an appropriate response to outside stimuli. That vision completely eclipsed an element without which the very concept of life as applied to society lost all meaning: the internal moral life (2004: 132). Despite its spiritualist echoes, the expression should not mislead us. That life, composed as it is of ideals and values, can be an object of scientific inquiry precisely because ideals and values are natural realities that can be grasped as things. Clearly the ambiguity lies in the way that last word is interpreted. There can be no moral life, no life of judgments and moral acts carried out by social subjects, unless values become tangible, that is, unless they are reflected and objectified in instituted phenomena. By insisting on this aspect of moral reality, Durkheim gave greater salience to its realness, and externalist determinism may seem to win the day. But the notion of "social thing" demands fuller attention. Once value objectivity is subordinated to the ever ongoing creation of ideals generated by the internal moral life, social things have to move and change. This is because their value inheres in an addition, a real increase, and therefore a transformation of sense-perceived givens – a transformation that Durkheim sought to circumscribe by means of several categories, whose epicenter may be considered the sacred.

In moral reality – which we can investigate only by considering the subjective investments that are its incompressible dimension – this transformation process can be seen as it occurs. Internal moral life cannot be reduced to a purely physical system because that life is what makes society visible at a certain level of itself, like a body in movement propelled by ideals that by definition overflow or exceed the current reality they undertake to transform. Contrary to what we might have thought, it is from the perspective of moral sociology, precisely by way of what cannot be resolved into objectivism, that we can most clearly see the social in the process of creating itself, social things in the process of becoming. Not, of course, as fruits of free, unregulated creation, but as changes in reality at the level at which reality unfolds as actions and judgments of actions. In other words, it is through actions understood as *social* that nature comes to surpass itself.

NOTES

1 Rauh discussed Durkheim's arguments in fine detail in his 1903 work, *L'expérience morale.*

2 On this point, which led Durkheim to make a stricter conceptual distinction between individual and person, see Durkheim 1990 and my commentary (Karsenti 2004).

3 Text republished in Durkheim 2004; English edn. 1974. For a resituating of Durkheim's position in the context of contemporary thinking on values, see Gurvitch 1937.
4 Durkheim's strategic verb "enrich" was a primary focus of pragmatist critiques in 1914.
5 In an important note, Durkheim (1990) identified the problem of authority as sociology's problem par excellence, more fundamental than the problem of constraint to which he had given priority in *The Rules of Sociological Method.*
6 As early as 1911 Durkheim concentrated his argument on the phenomenon of human energy-*spending*, of disinterested activity involving an extravagant use of energy, thereby developing an anti-utilitarian argument that foreshadows some of Mauss's arguments (1966). Particularly striking in this connection is Durkheim's statement that "economic life itself does not always follow closely the rules of economics" (2004; English edn. 1974: 86).

REFERENCES

Bellah, Robert N. (1974) Introduction. In *Emile Durkheim on Morality and Society: Selected Writings*, ed. Robert N. Bellah. Chicago: University of Chicago Press.
Boltanski, Luc and Thévenot, Laurent (1991) *De la justification: Les économies de la grandeur.* Paris: Gallimard.
Durkheim, Emile (1970 [1898]) L'individualisme et les intellectuels. In *La science sociale et l'action.* Paris: Presses Universitaires de France, pp. 261–278.
Durkheim, Emile (1975a) *Textes I.* Paris: Editions de Minuit.
Durkheim, Emile (1975b) *Textes II.* Paris: Editions de Minuit.
Durkheim, Emile (1987 [1895]) *Règles de la méthode sociologique.* Paris: Presses Universitaires de France/Quadrige.
Durkheim, Emile (1990 [1912]) *Les formes élémentaires de la vie religieuse.* Paris: Presses Universitaires de France/Quadrige.
Durkheim, Emile (1996 [1893]) *La division du travail social.* Paris: Presses Universitaires de France/Quadrige. Published in English as *The Division of Labor in Society*, trans. W. D. Halls, New York: Free Press, 1974.
Durkheim, Emile (2004 [1925]) *Sociologie et philosophie.* Paris: Presses Universitaires de France/ Quadrige. Published in English as *Sociology and Philosophy*, trans. D. F. Pocock, New York: Free Press, 1974.
Gurvitch, Georges (1937) *Morale théorique et sciences des mœurs.* Paris: Presses Universitaires de France.
Isambert, François-André (1992) Les avatars du fait moral. In *De la religion à l'éthique.* Paris: Éditions du Cerf, pp. 357–393.
Kant, Immanuel (1983 [1788]) *Critique de la raison pratique*, trans. Picavet. Paris: Presses Universitaires de France/Quadrige. Published in English as *Critique of Practical Reason*, ed. and trans. Mary Gregor, Cambridge: Cambridge University Press, 1997.
Karsenti, Bruno (2004) La sociologie à l'épreuve du pragmatisme: Réaction durkheimienne. In B. Karsenti and L. Quéré (eds.), *La croyance et l'enquête: Aux sources du pragmatisme*, Paris: Ecole des Hautes Etudes en Sciences Sociales, Raisons Pratiques, pp. 319–349.
Mauss, Marcel (1966 [1924]) *Essai sur le don.* In *Sociologie et anthropologie.* Paris: Presses Universitaires de France, pp. 145–279.
Pharo, Patrick (2004) *Morale et sociologie.* Paris: Gallimard.
Rauh, Frédéric (1890) *Essai sur le fondement métaphysique de la morale.* Paris: Alcan.
Rauh, Frédéric (1903) *L'expérience morale.* Paris: Alcan.

CHAPTER 2

Weber and Practical Ethics

Isabelle Kalinowski

Trans. Matthew Carey

The core of Max Weber's published works is a series of major studies that explicitly link (in their very titles) the notion of an "ethic" and religion or a religion: *The Protestant Ethic and the Spirit of Capitalism* (1958a [1904–5]; hereafter PE) and *The Economic Ethics of World Religions* (which includes *Hinduism and Buddhism*, *Confucianism and Taoism* and *Ancient Judaism* (1952 [1917, 1920]; hereafter AJ), all of which were published in the 1910s). In this essay, I propose to explore the nature of the link between these two concepts. Weber's reputation as a theorist of "secularization" probably does more to obscure than to clarify this relationship, as the movement from religion to an ethic should not be seen as a simple process of succession or organic continuity. For Weber, religion is not some immovable foundation upon which an ethic is constructed until it can finally stand alone. Rather, Weber argues that ethics are indissociable from religion in general and, more specifically, from *a* particular religion, which determines a particular ethics in opposition to those born of other religions. Religions and ethics are both necessarily plural, with the historical plurality of religions leading to a situation of ethical plurality. Ethics are simultaneously anchored in the Absolute of a religion and in the contingency of history. The question is how to understand the relationship between these two dimensions of their existence.

Ethical Science and the Science of Ethics

In "The 'Objectivity' of Knowledge in Social Science and Social Policy" (1949 [1904]; hereafter O), published in 1904 in the journal *Archiv für Sozialwissenschaft*, which he co-founded and edited with Werner Sombart and Edgar Jaffé, Weber

A Companion to Moral Anthropology, First Edition. Edited by Didier Fassin.

outlines the journal's approach to the social sciences, arguing for a radically "nonethical" and "nonobjective" science. These two terms work together to describe those spheres that, Weber believed, could be addressed only through renunciation. And he gives a similarly restrictive definition of science in his 1917 lecture, *Science as a Vocation* (1958b [1919]; hereafter SV). The domain of science has been drastically reduced, and Weber lists its lost territories: morality, values, the existence of God, the definition of beauty, the meaning of life, the meaning of death, etc. These are all domains from which science has been forced to retreat and renounce its jurisdiction. Modern science must abandon all claims to authority with regard to those principles that are held up as absolute values. Weber asserts the impossibility of grounding these in reason – that is he argues that they are fundamentally irrational. This does not mean, as we shall see, that the logic of value lies outside rationality, or that it cannot be taken as a valid scientific object. It is simply that their ultimate foundation is indemonstrable and that adherence to them requires what Weber describes as an act of faith. As he bluntly states in his article on "Objectivity" (a term that he always surrounds with scare quotes), "undoubtedly, all evaluative ideas are 'subjective'" (O, 83).

The argument that underpins this claim is extremely simple: the plurality of such values necessarily implies that none can definitively impose its truth upon the others. Or, more exactly, their plurality is evidence of irreducible difference and so incompatibility. This is a central tenet of Weberian thought: the fact that these values have become "subjective" does not mean that they have lost their absolute quality. In defending one value, one attacks another and even inaction involves taking sides. For Weber, the different values cannot be reduced to a "lowest common denominator" (O, 57). And the claim that science is able to answer ethical questions by identifying particular standards that are more or less consensual at a given point in history (though not eternally) is "far worse" a thing than mere "naïve objectivism." This "combination of ethical evolutionism and historical relativism" is for Weber an aberration: the sociologist must renounce, once and for all, the idea of constructing an "ethical science" by means of hypothetical averages and statistics (O, 52). There is no such thing as "ethical science."

In the same way, the fact that values are "henceforth subjective" does not imply that they can be repressed or neutralized: such values are invariably present and even though he may ignore them, they still actively influence the scientist's stance. Weber's frequent reminders of the need for *Wertfreiheit*, unhappily translated into English as "axiological neutrality," does not mean that values can be "neutralized." Rather, it stresses the indemonstrability of values and the fallacy of attempts to justify them scientifically. Values will out, even unbeknownst to he who holds them, and in affirming themselves, they also oppose others. Though in the final instance they are indemonstrable, they nonetheless imply a series of rational consequences, which are not always made explicit and may remain unconscious, but which still imply a form of absolute logical consistency (*Konsequenz*). These logically necessary consequences explain why values are mutually incompatible and oblige us to move beyond the conciliatory ground of relativism. The Weberian notions of "polytheism of values" and of the "unceasing struggle of these gods with one another" (SV, 149) force us to recognize that science cannot attain value "objectivity."

Though there is no such thing as "ethical science," is it yet possible to conceive of a "science of ethics"? And what is the object of such a science? Weber answers this question in magisterial fashion in *The Protestant Ethic and the Spirit of Capitalism*. The sociologist should not take value as a starting point, but instead endeavor to reconstruct the implacable logic of value through analysis of social phenomena that appear to be fundamentally divorced from or even inimical to such values. It is highly likely that the first of Weber's religious studies, *The Protestant Ethic*, was intended not only as an analysis of the conditions of emergence of capitalism, but also as a demonstration of a method. The heuristic value of the text reposes on the apparent chasm separating the economic fact of capitalist accumulation and an act of faith, to wit the belief in predestination. Weber takes a perfectly immoral economic system (capitalism), and reconstructs its moral foundation, discovering a form of morality that we would doubtless today describe as fundamentalist.

His purpose is not to argue in favor of this morality, or to argue for the wider "morality" of capitalism or for the need for it to be "moralized." His study of this particular economic model is not intended to contribute to an "ethical science"; he merely sketches out the origins of the model by tracing back a series of inductive (rather than deductive) links. It must, however, be stressed that such reconstructions are necessarily partial: this process of "causal regression" can never be "exhaustive" (O, 78). The sociologist reconstructs a causal chain that is perforce limited and that ought to be the opposite of a generalizable law. In contrast to the universality of "natural laws," those pertaining to historical phenomena are necessarily circumstantial: "meaningfulness naturally does not coincide with laws as such, and the more general the law the less the coincidence" (O, 76). It is only when the scholar has identified a particular "constellation" or a "historical individual" that his work is done (O, 72). Weber's "science of reality" aims to analyze social phenomena by identifying and exploring "the causes of their being historically *so* and not *otherwise*" (O, 72). The "historical individual" is not an isolated event, but a specific phenomenon that simultaneously embodies certain historical conditions and determinants, and *undermines* them to create something new. All of Weber's different analyses of the relationship between ethical values and economic practice, at various historical and cultural junctures, were intended as proof of the irreducible singularity of ethico-practical configurations. The social sciences cannot identify their foundations, but they can shed light on their specific logics, because once a given value is established, it ramifies in a rationally coherent manner. This ramification is not necessarily explicit, but it can be teased out and contextualized.

For the same reason, as Weber makes clear in his article on "Objectivity" and in *Science as a Vocation*, the social sciences are not restricted to analysis of the past, but can also engage with the present. Their role is also consultative: they do not say what "ought" to be, but draw out the implications of a given set of values (notably their negative impact on other sets of values). As Weber puts it: "you serve this god and offend the other god when you decide to adhere to this position" (SV, 148). And, contrariwise, they can identify the values that underpin particular stances even when the relationship in question remains "unconscious." In general terms, then, the role of the social sciences is not to defend or to promote certain values, but to "raise awareness" of the fact that particular values are at work in social practices and judgments.

> It can, insofar as it sets itself this goal, aid the acting willing person in obtaining self-clarification concerning the final axioms from which his desired ends are derived. It can

> assist him in becoming aware of the ultimate standards of value which he does not make explicit to himself or, which he must presuppose in order to be logical. The elevation of these ultimate standards, which are manifested in concrete value-judgments, to the level of explicitness is the utmost that the scientific treatment of value-judgments can do without entering into the realm of speculation. (O, 54)

This implies a stark contrast between the shadow of unknowability into which the scientist must cast the origins and foundation of particular values, and the light he seeks to shed, in almost authoritarian fashion, on their implications. As he puts it: "we can force the individual, or at least we can help him, to give himself an *account of the ultimate meaning of his own conduct*" (SV, 150).

The Social Sciences and Theology

In his demonstrations of the importance of ethico-religious values for understanding social action, Weber makes use of concepts and methodological tools that are not in any simple relationship of exteriority to their object. To the contrary, a great many of his analytical tools are theological in origin. His aim is not to blur the boundary between sociologist and theologian, nor to suggest that the former adopt the latter's religious perspective. Weber was quite clear on this point, stating he was not antireligious, but lacked faith, and he unambiguously declared in *Science as a Vocation* that modern science needs must occupy a position of exteriority vis-à-vis religious values. The sociologist's reasons for employing theological concepts are quite different: for Weber, the wealth and insight of religious models of human action makes them indispensable. The sociologist must heed the outpourings of a style of thought that has, over millennia of history and in an infinity of cultures, ceaselessly explored the issues surrounding human behavior.

We can then read the entirety of Weber's vast religious sociology, which addresses several major world religions, as an attempt to describe both these religions' associated social configurations and to sound them out for explanatory models of social action that might contribute to the wider project of sociology. For Weber, scholarly forms of religious thought (i.e., theology) are not part of the prehistory of rationality as Enlightenment thinkers and their successors would have it, but are instead the very crucible of rationality and scientific thought. He even maintains that religious thought has produced the most sophisticated forms of religious critique, which were first elaborated and developed by theologians and religious reformers before being taken up by "secular" theorists. For the sociologist, religions are not merely an object of study, but a virtuoso training ground for thought. And science offered the very same things: "methods of thinking, tools and the training for thought" (SV, 150). For Weber, sociology and theology share a similar modus operandi that gives them their remarkable theoretical vitality: their conceptual models are never divorced from practice, from either the expectations of the faithful or from social behavior. Weber illustrates this feedback loop between theological thought and the needs of the faithful with reference to the practice of "pastoral care." Priests must answer for the practical applicability of dogma, and the constant back-and-forth between scholarly models and pastoral requirements gives theological thought its distinctive color and force.

It was Weber's interest in the interstitial space between theory and practice that drew him to sociology rather than to a more speculative discipline. And he placed similar emphasis on the power of texts (both religious and otherwise) born of the pendular movement between writing and orality – for example, the Indian Vedas or the Old Testament's Deuteronomy (AJ, 333). These types of production fascinated Weber because their existence depended upon a transgression of social boundaries and was marked by their dual origin.

In Weber's work, the notion of ethos intervenes at the point where a body of religious doctrine meets a set of practices. As Weber states in *The Protestant Ethic and the Spirit of Capitalism*, "it is not the ethical *doctrine* of a religion, but that form of ethical conduct upon which *premiums* are placed that matters. Such premiums operate through the form and the condition of the respective goods of salvation. And such conduct constitutes 'one's' specific 'ethos' in the sociological sense of the word" (PE, 321). Ethos must not be confused with the religious ethic that gives rise to and delivers it. It is neither a doctrine, nor a series of "life maxims," but a form of "conduct of life" which endows the economic activity of the faithful with internal consistency and regularity. An ethos is forged through education and rolls out an ethic in pre-reflexive and spontaneous, but above all constant fashion. An ethic tends to decisively influence the economy – by methodically altering its constituent activities – when it aims to insure "continuity of the religious mood" (SR, 161). Ethos is to be found at the juncture of religious content and forms of economic organization and management that, Weber claims, cannot themselves produce a rupture such as the advent of "rational capitalism." The emergence of this latter is less the product of a shift in economic structures and techniques (which could, in fact, remain relatively stable), than of the gradual assertion of a new ethos.

Ethic and ethos, then, remain distinct and are not manifest at the same level of social reality. The opposition between them, however, is not one of relative versus absolute. As Weber shows, notably toward the end of *Politics as a Vocation* (1958c [1919]; hereafter PV), it is within the domain of ethics itself that we can observe the conflict between the fundamentalism of an "ethic of ultimate ends" (*Gesinnungsethik*) and the relativism of an "ethic of responsibility" (*Verantwortungsethik*) (PV, 120). The former – exemplified by the Sermon on the Mount, in the pacifism of Tolstoy or of the Pennsylvanian Quakers, and in the Grand Inquisitor of Dostoyevsky – "cannot stand up under the ethical irrationality of the world," preferring instead a form of "cosmic-ethical rationalis[m]" (PV, 122). Weber describes this mystical position as "not of this world" (calling it "acosmic") and insists that it must not be seen as a form of "religious" ethic that we might counterpose to its "profane" equivalent. Not all religions preached an "ethic of ultimate ends"; indeed, many of them have theologically defended (in the form of "theodicy") an "ethic of responsibility." He illustrates this with the Indian example of differentiated dharma and caste, which legitimizes the violence of the warrior caste (Kshatriya), while condemning it for all others. He shows particular interest in those religions that have leaned toward an ethic of responsibility, drawing parallels between the moral doctrines they propound and an epistemological position that accepts the need to renounce the possibility of absolute truth.

Weber's reflections on the limits of knowledge in the social sciences owe much to neo-Kantian epistemology, notably the work of his friend Heinrich Rickert, but they are also heavily marked by separation theology. What concerns us here is less the (evident) influence of theology on Weberian sociology, and more the parallels between two forms of radical separation from the Absolute: that of God and that of Knowledge. Weber's famous idea of "disenchantment of the world" (*Entzauberung der Welt*), which he argues first emerged within Judaism, signals a rupture between man and the realm of the gods. Whereas mythical religions establish a form of magical continuity between men and gods (who can mutually constrain one another), the invention of absolute transcendence in Jewish monotheism consummates a definitive separation between the two. God is no longer a mere Baal, a local divinity. Yahweh is an external God whose face may not be seen. He lies beyond human magic. This separation is epitomized in the aniconism of Judaism. Unlike in idolatry, God cannot be seen as a thing; and realism is proscribed.

In *Ancient Judaism*, Weber explains that this theological separation between men and God establishes a new regime of relationality – that of *interpretation*. Of course, magical action also requires the constant production of interpretations, not only regarding the will of the gods, but also the relevance of particular rituals. However, these hermeneutic activities are respectively rewarded or invalidated by the success or failure of rituals, whereas men's interpretations of the will of God are deprived of this final moment of elucidation, where interpretation may be revealed as truth. The Old Testament prophets discussed in *Ancient Judaism* have visions of God and they hear his voice, but the status of these revelations is problematic. They are neither transparent nor straightforward, but must be interpreted and verified. Such revelations cannot pretend to objectivity because God neither confirms nor denies them. He never brings the process of interpretation to an end, even when expressing himself in signs and epiphanies. Sociology, from the point of view of Weber, is the same: much as the ancient prophets did, the sociologist hears and sees things and his approach to social practice is definitively interpretive. The social sciences seek to identify the meaning of these practices, but they cannot hope to fully circumscribe this meaning and the authority of their interpretations is perforce partial.

The story of Job, for which Weber shows a certain predilection, perfectly illustrates the link between theological commentary and sociological analysis. The tribulations that befall this previously fortunate man raise an acute problem of interpretation: they are the object of moral judgments and are seen by some of his peers as a mark of his sin. Does sorrow not afflict the sinner? Job knows himself to be innocent and loudly protests, but even he asks God the reason for his tribulations. But God remains silent; he justifies nothing. "Characteristically, when Job requests God to answer for the unjust order of man's condition and when God makes his appearance in the storm, he argues with not a single word the wisdom of his order of human relations, as, for instance, the Confucian would presuppose. Instead Yahweh exclusively argues his sovereign might and greatness in the events of nature" (AJ, 132–133). This passage allows us to grasp a capital point: the transcendence that rids God of the need to "account" for his action, and places his commands in the realm of a form of free will uncoupled from reason, does indeed imply a radical separation between human and divine intelligibility, but this in no way impedes the human labor of rational explanation. On the contrary, the less intelligible divine action is, the greater man's efforts to explain it rationally. Job and his friends Eliphaz the Temanite, Bildad the Shuhite, and Zophar the Naamathite discuss the matter for seven days and seven nights. In Weber's reading, the story of Job is testament to this increased call for rational speculation. This reaches new heights in Puritanism (which Weber describes as a radicalized Judaism), where God is no longer merely enigmatic as regards his intentions, as he had been in ancient Judaism, but definitively silent, invisible, and absent. The parallel with the social sciences is easy to discern: for them too, the loss of objectivity has not led to a collapse into irrationality, but rather to a renewed and intensified emphasis on rational logic.

Ethics and *Ethos*: The "Rationality" of Action

One of Weber's most striking sociological revelations is the paradoxical relationship between knowledge and action. This is the polar opposite of the rather crude theory of "instrumental action" so often attributed to him (and so at odds with his habitual style of thought), with its "rational actor" mechanically performing his calculations in a manipulable world. Instead, at key points in his varied *oeuvre*, Weber highlights the disconnect between the plane of knowledge and that of action. The radically limited nature of knowledge does not imply that action is similarly limited. On the contrary, it is precisely this painful confrontation with the limits of knowledge and with a form of negativity that produces an irrepressible dynamic of worldly action. This argument is at the heart of *The Protestant Ethic and the Spirit of Capitalism*, whose starting point is a context of absolute frustration of knowledge. The Puritan who admits the dogma of predestination is thereby deprived of direct access to God's decrees: he can never know with certainty whether he is of the elect or whether he is damned. And this uncertainty also applies to his fellows. The egalitarianism and "democratic" sensibility of Puritan culture are the product of this pure negativity: men are equal before God in the possibility of their damnation. However, according to Weber, it is precisely this state of absolute unknowability that leads to a dynamic of *action*. Puritans create the most intensive form of worldly action while simultaneously cultivating the most extreme suspicion of the world. Capitalist action is born of the unknowability of personal salvation: efforts to calculate and predict the world, to organize and manage in capitalist fashion are not the product of a positive project of rational accumulation, but rather of this epistemological negativity.

In *The Protestant Ethic*, Weber analyzes a system where the meaning of action and its fruits are irrevocably divorced. The accumulation of wealth is not the goal of capitalism, but its by-product. Its primary aim is instead the pure asceticism of action and work; wealth is derived from the "injunction to save." Weber remarks that if asceticism were not the primary goal of action, but rather a hypocritical facade for the accumulation of wealth, then it could never have attained the prodigious proportions it assumes in modern capitalism. In the second edition of *The Protestant Ethic* (revised in 1920, 15 years after the first), Weber quotes a text by John Wesley that also stresses the simultaneously tense and collaborative relationship that exists between asceticism and wealth: "For religion must necessarily produce both industry and frugality, and these cannot but produce riches. But as riches increase, so will pride, anger, and love of the world in all its branches" (PE, 175) Asceticism necessarily encourages the accumulation of wealth, which then threatens the original asceticism. Asceticism is then both itself and its contrary. This "Wesley's Law," as I call it, implies an inevitable process of routinization, but above all it defines an irreversible causal chain that leads from asceticism and "pure religiosity" to wealth. The unprecedented accumulation of profit that emerges with modern capitalism is, according to Weber, not the result of a positive project, but the product of a process set in train by an original negativity, a renouncement of the world. It is only this sort of dynamic, born of worldly renunciation, that can explain the explosive force of the economic model and its unprecedented productivity and profitability.

How can we understand this inversion? In truth, Weber himself does not describe it very clearly. Even in *The Protestant Ethic*, certain passages seem to suggest that we are dealing with a psychological compensation reaction: the uncertainty of salvation is so unbearable an ordeal that Puritans must seek "confirmation" in wealth. Weber recognizes this existential need at several points. But that is not the core of his argument. His idea is rather that, faced with the phenomenon of modern capitalism, the sociologist must analyze the causal chain leading to its emergence in inductive fashion and assume, because it cannot be proven, that its origins lie in a particular religious or moral instant which is the first cause of everything that follows. The causal chain described by Wesley identifies precisely this process that leads to the accumulation of wealth. At the other end of the chain, we must assume that there is a religious value whose reality cannot be grasped as an "objective" fact. This is a boundary that sociological investigation cannot cross. But the sociologist can make the assumption that there is a value underlying the concatenation of events. An instant of belief and sincerity that is first, but indemonstrable, and that is the contrary of those motivations habitually invoked to explain the emergence of capitalism: rational interest and cynicism.

In his essay "The Protestant Sects and the Spirit of Capitalism," Weber describes an adult baptism he witnessed during a trip to the United States (1905), using it to explain his sociological method. He attended a baptism ceremony of Baptist adults "on a beautiful clear Sunday afternoon," in North Carolina, "in a pool fed by a brook which descended from the Blue Ridge Mountains, visible in the distance." The weather was quite cold and freezing; farmers' families were standing around the pool where "about ten persons of both sexes in their Sunday-best stepped into the pond, one after another," and immersed completely with the help of the preacher. Weber was accompanied by a relative, "unchurchly in accordance with German traditions," who observed the scene a little "disdainfully." According to the cousin, the baptism of one of the young men immersed in the pool was motivated only by the wish to "open a bank in M." "Once being baptized he will get the patronage of the whole region and he will outcompete everybody." Weber asked him why and the cousin answered that admission to the local Baptist congregation "follows only upon the most careful 'probation' and after closest inquiries into conduct going back to early childhood" (PE, 304–305).

In the same way as early anthropologists stressed the physical violence of primitive religion, Weber here highlights the most troubling aspect of the religious practice in question: immersion in the frozen waters of a pond. The details he gives concerning the weather, the participants' sneezing, and so forth, all serve to underscore the contradiction between the "irrationality" of religious belief and the extreme "rationality" of the interests it sets in play. Weber achieves this by playing on the notion of "credit": religious credit, which is the collective corollary of private belief, is sanctioned by adult baptism, and simultaneously endows the latter with social credit because the sect is known for rigorously selecting its members. In turn, social credit is the manifest sign of economic credit, which is concretely manifest in material success and the elimination of rivals.

Weber conceives of this tripartite notion of "credit" (religious, social, and economic) as an ensemble and argues for its coherence and rationality. This is not to say that he sees religious credit as nothing more than a mask for more material interests. Instead, he attributes this "cynical" interpretation of the religious rite to his American cousin, distancing himself from it in the process. For Weber, the spectacular nature of the baptism is better seen as a tangible illustration of the intensity of properly religious motivations. The causal chain he identifies leads back to a religious instant whose existence cannot be proven, but which must be assumed in order to account for its observable consequences in social practice.

The Religion of India: The Sociology of Hinduism and Buddhism (1958d [1917]; hereafter H&B) applies a similar form of sociological method to the founding fathers of ancient Buddhism. Far from constituting an established church, early Buddhism lacked any clear institutional organization. It was spread by itinerant monks who traveled from village to village begging for alms.

> As shown, ancient Buddhas, using the firmly given differential qualification for salvation as a basic fact and point of departure, imposed almost no other duties upon the laity than the support of the monks. Originally, it knew no contributors to the community, … [but] only gifts to individual monks.
>
> Gradually this changed in the direction of the usual monastic organization. Doubtless, the *avasika*, that is, the no longer migratory monks who are in residence in the monastery not only during the rainy season but permanently, represent … steps in the course of the development towards monastic landlordism. (H&B, 230)

This transformation, which Weber describes as a "process of 'prebendalism'" (H&B, 229), tended to fix monks in a particular locale and attach them to a lay community, which then became a "clientele" over which they sought to maintain a "monopoly." The monks' interest in the management of these prebends gradually displaces their initial missionary ardor until, much as with the Puritans, the accumulation of wealth poses a threat to the founding spirit of their ascetic activity. Just as with the Puritans, however, this process of routinization should not obscure the fact that material interest is not the initial motor that sets prebendalism in train. Only later does it become the dominant factor; in the early period, it is precisely the monks' disinterested behavior that leads lay villagers to shower them with alms and gifts. As a causal sequence this is strikingly similar to "Wesley's Law." The accumulation of wealth by Buddhist monks is first and foremost the result of a state of mind that insures their "credit" among lay villagers, and only later does it come to provoke their moral decline. Weber notes these effects and assumes the presence of a religious "ethic" that cannot be objectively proven to exist. In each case, we can, following Pierre Bourdieu in *Practical Reason*, speak of the "interest in disinterestedness," but everything functions as if disinterestedness were not exclusively interested. Interest and disinterestedness are not mutually exclusive, but imply one another.

The scholar's subject position does not allow him fully to explain the enigma of this "ethical" instant: he can never analyze it directly. Rather, he explores a tripartite system wherein "ethical" action is refracted through the perception of third parties who feel its effects and reciprocally influence it. The sociological gaze is turned toward this relationship, rather than toward the action itself. The same is true of the Weberian concept of charisma. The sociologist cannot pass judgment on the existence or otherwise of a thing called "charisma"; he can only note that belief in an individual's charisma produces certain social effects. But the scholar's critical gaze does not analytically encompass this relationship: his aim is not to denounce it as illusory, as if he could situate himself outside his subjective perspective. The sociologist can neither prove the existence or the inexistence of ethical acts or charisma.

Ethics, Causality, and Culpability

In the chapter of *Economy and Society* (1978 [1972]) devoted to religious sociology, Weber combines his reflections on the adequate apprehension of sociological causality with an analysis of the religious origins of the notion of causality. For Weber, the idea that human action is both meaningful and causally entangled with other, equivalent actions is the product of a particular process of social evolution in which certain religions, at certain historical junctures, gave rise to a novel form of representation – one which seeks to attribute a unified "meaning" to human behavior. He claims that this religious instant only occurs in highly intellectual forms of religion and is accompanied by the emergence of a concept of evil. Theories of causality emerge out of intellectual reflection on the origin of sin. The idea that the appropriate unit of analysis of sociological causality is the "conduct of life" (*Lebensführung*) – an ensemble of dispositions shared by a given social group and individually realized in more or less coherent social action – is one that Weber is at pains to describe as "constructed," partial, and historically specific. It does not emerge in all religions, or even in all intellectual religions. More precisely, Weber argues that there is a close link between his conception of sociological causality, which focuses on units of socially constructed practice (i.e., different forms of "conduct of life") and the religious history of Christianity up until the emergence of Puritan ascetic thought. Puritanism, he suggests, breaks with previous Christian perspectives, including post-Reformational ones, and for the first time stresses the importance of quotidian social practice. Thus the whole range of professional and domestic practice becomes the relevant unit of analysis, and its coherence and legitimacy the object of religious judgment. This signifies a change of scale: it is no longer isolated acts (be they good or evil) that are seen as decisive, but the wider range of daily behavior – the "conduct of life."

In *The Sociology of Religion* (1963; hereafter SR), Weber explores at length the potential scope of representations of evil and identifies the specific range which gives rise to sociological representations of causality (or at least to his own). Within this conceptual system, the various possible axes of evil are arranged according to different sets of variables, such as the human or superhuman (natural, divine, diabolical) nature of "evil," the personal or impersonal quality of guilt, the association of evil with one-off acts or with more unified sets of "behavior," and the question of temporality. It is, for instance, quite possible to think of sin (or of causality) as pertaining to temporal schemata that stretch beyond the lifespan of an individual, and to attach them to families, social groups, or even entire nations. "The suffering of the present generation, it was believed, was the consequence of the sins of the ancestors, for which god holds the descendants responsible, just as someone carrying out blood revenge may hold an entire tribe accountable, and as pope Gregory VII excommunicated descendants down to the seventh generation" (SR, 139). In India, the doctrine of *karman* epitomizes this idea of a form of temporal continuity that stretches beyond the lifespan of an individual, by developing the notion of the transmigration of souls, which projects the individual both into the past and into the future.

> The world is viewed as a completely connected and self-contained cosmos of ethical retribution. Guilt and merit within this world are unfailingly compensated by fate in the successive lives of the soul ... What may appear from the viewpoint of a theory of compensation as unjust suffering the terrestrial life of a person should be regarded as atonement for sin in a previous existence. Each individual forges his own destiny exclusively, and in the strictest sense of the word.
>
> The belief in the transmigration of souls ... [epitomizes] a universal mechanism of retribution, for which no act that is *ethically relevant* can ever be lost. (SR, 145–146)

The idea of *karman* interests Weber in that it offers a coherent formulation of the problem of individual responsibility in the genesis of evil. It refers the individual both back to himself and to something that lies beyond him. An individual is responsible for his own sins (which are then "sins" in the true sense of the word), but because the concept of the transmigration of souls radically extends the boundaries of individuality, it circumvents the theoretical problem posed by the notion of the individual's absolute, instantaneous, and total responsibility for his actions. It is never possible unambiguously to determine fault, just as one can never be certain of the cause of any given social phenomenon. Human actions do not belong to the same regime of causality as natural phenomena, and do not conform to unequivocal or potentially unequivocal laws such as those of physics.

The vast overview of different doctrines of evil sketched out in the *Sociology of Religion* allows Weber to refine sociological conceptions of the relationship between individual responsibility and collective constraints. Unlike the Indian concept of *karman*, Weber's notion of sociological causality not only anchors the individual in a diachronic form of continuity (one of reincarnations, which we can assimilate to traditional forms of filiation), but also unambiguously locates him in a synchronic space of professional and religious practices. And these practices pertain not to the individual, but to the wider group, and so severely constrain him. Rather than singularizing, different forms of "conduct of life" represent conformity to a *stand*. Here, Weber is thinking of the Puritan worker or entrepreneur, who simultaneously represents absolute individuality (by virtue of the dogma of predestination, which singles out each of God's creatures for personal election or damnation) and embodies the ultimate social agent, obsessed by his quest for ethical conformity and constantly subject to the judgment of his fellow believers. In this model, individualization and social constraint are not antithetical, but complementary. As Weber argues in *The Protestant Ethic*, the individual's investment in his vocation can segue into a radical representation of individual "responsibility" and so into a desperate quest to conform to the collective norm. Weber seeks to fix the sociological gaze on a particular object: the practices of social agents who believe in these practices, even if they cannot necessarily explain the "reasons" why they perform them. These agents live their individualization as a tormentuous tragedy: they are tortured by the quest for their *own* conformity, and are personally responsible if they stray from the path. Weber sees a continuity between religious ideas of damnation (or the fear of damnation) and this purely negative form of ethical individualization.

Conclusion

It is clear that for Weber, a particular ethic is first and foremost defined by religious factors. He admits the possibility of alternative approaches to ethical dispositions, based for instance on social class (the "petty bourgeois *ethos*," or "aristocratic *ethos*"), but in his work, religion always determines ethics both more intensively and more decisively than other factors, be they class, nationality, ethnic identity, or type of political regime. And yet Weber vigorously rejects the inextirpable temptation to appeal to "monistic" explanations (O, 69). Should we then see this as a contradiction? Not, I would suggest, if we consider the religious factor to be both a nonobjectifiable value and a dimension of history entangled with other sociological factors specific to a particular place and time. As Weber humorously notes toward the end of *Politics as a Vocation*, the attempt to situate an ethic historically should in no way be seen as an act of relativism: "The same holds for this ethic as has been said of causality in science: it is not a cab, which one can have stopped at one's pleasure; it is all or nothing" (PV, 119).

REFERENCES

Weber, Max (1949) The "Objectivity" of Knowledge in Social Science and Social Policy. In *The Methodology of the Social Sciences*, trans. Edward A. Shils and Henry A. Finch. Glencoe, IL: Free Press. ("Die "Objektivität" sozialwissenschaftlicher und sozialpolitischer Erkenntnis," 1904.) (O)

Weber, Max (1952) *Ancient Judaism*. Glencoe, IL: Free Press. (*Das antike Judentum*, 1917.) (AJ)

Weber, Max (1958a) *The Protestant Ethic and the Spirit of Capitalism*, trans. Talcott Parsons. New York: Charles Scribner's Sons. (*Die protestantische Ethik und der "Geist" des Kapitalismus*, 1904–5.) (PE)

Weber, Max (1958b) Science as a Vocation. In *From Max Weber: Essays in Sociology*, trans. H. H. Gerth and C. Wright Mills. Oxford: Oxford University Press. (*Wissenschaft als Beruf*, 1919.) (SV)

Weber, Max (1958c) Politics as a Vocation. In *From Max Weber: Essays in Sociology*, trans. H. H. Gerth and C. Wright Mills. Oxford: Oxford University Press. (*Politik als Beruf*, 1919.) (PV)

Weber, Max (1958d) *The Religion of India: The Sociology of Hinduism and Buddhism*, trans. Hans H. Gerth and Don Martindale. New York: Macmillan. (*Hinduismus und Buddhismus*, 1917.) (H&B)

Weber, Max (1963) *The Sociology of Religion*, trans. Ephraim Fischoff; intro. Talcott Parsons. Boston: Beacon. ("Religionssoziologie" in *Wirtschaft und Gesellschaft*, 5th edn., 1972.) (SR)

Weber, Max (1978) *Economy and Society*, 2 vols., ed. G. Roth and C. Wittich. Berkeley: University of California Press. (*Wirtschaft und Gesellschaft*, 5th edn., 1972.)

CHAPTER 3

E. P. Thompson and Moral Economies

Marc Edelman

British cultural historian Edward Palmer Thompson (1924–93) might well have been a revered ancestor for today's anthropologists, but instead he is like a specter whose traces are ubiquitous but who remains almost invisible. Thompson was a social constructionist before social constructionism, a fervent antistructuralist before the poststructuralist turn, an early proponent of the importance of "agency" and "experience" in social analysis, and a tenacious polemicist and militant intellectual before anthropology embraced activism. Yet while Thompson's ideas pervade contemporary anthropology, his direct influence – in acknowledgments, citations, explicit recognition – is surprisingly slight. A search (in June 2011), of the American Anthropological Association's online AnthroSource database, which indexes over 30 journals and professional newsletters, turns up scant mentions of E. P. Thompson. Just one of the 10 contributions in Jonathan Parry and Maurice Bloch's *Money and the Morality of Exchange* (1989) mentions Thompson (and that in a footnote). Adam Kuper's *Culture* (1999), similarly, quotes Thompson once, but only in a larger discussion of Raymond Williams. Renato Rosaldo's important essay "Celebrating Thompson's Heroes: Social Analysis in History and Anthropology" (1990) was cited a mere eight times in the two decades after it was published (according to Google Scholar). Of the 11 essays in Katherine Browne and Lynne Milgram's *Economics and Morality: Anthropological Approaches*, only two cite work by Thompson and only one considers it in any depth (Little 2009). Jarrett Zigon, in *Morality: An Anthropological Perspective* (2008: 70–72), devotes a few paragraphs to Thompson, but misreads him as being concerned with "peasant food riots" when the "crowds" that Thompson (1971) analyzed in his famous "Moral Economy" article (1971) actually consisted of tinners, colliers, weavers, hosiery workers, and "labouring people," many if not most of them urban.

Joan Vincent's massive tome *Anthropology and Politics* (1990: 403) described Thompson as "extremely influential" in peasant studies and suggested that his notion

A Companion to Moral Anthropology, First Edition. Edited by Didier Fassin.

of moral economy was "immensely attractive to political anthropologists," although she acknowledged obliquely that much of this "attraction" actually centered less on Thompson than on James Scott's *The Moral Economy of the Peasant* (1976). Vincent also viewed Thompson as a foundational figure in legal anthropology (particularly his *Whigs and Hunters*, 1975) and in efforts to question "the consensus model of law" (1990: 422–423). Several anthropologists in the broad movement to bring history "back in" (e.g., Gerald Sider, Jean and John Comaroff) refer to Thompson in passing, but mainly to invoke his name as legitimation for their own intellectual projects. Thompson collaborated briefly with Jack Goody (Goody et al. 1978), one of the few anthropologists on the editorial board of the progressive journal *Past & Present*, but on an anthology that almost exclusively involved European social historians. Benjamin Orlove's (1997) analysis of an early twentieth-century urban food riot in Chile employed a Thompsonian moral economy framework, but this was unusual for the anthropological literature in its explicit, extensive adoption of Thompson's model. William Roseberry (1989), almost alone among anglophone anthropologists, dealt at length and appreciatively – albeit critically – with Thompson's theoretical legacy, but even he was more enamored of Raymond Williams, whom Thompson lambasted in a blistering 1961 attack in *New Left Review*.

This essay points first to interrelations between Thompson's biography, thinking, and methods that help to explain his theoretical orientation and scholarly practice, as well as anthropologists' relative neglect of his work. It then examines the origins and subsequent trajectories of the concept of moral economy, arguably the contribution by Thompson that has had and continues to have the most impact in anthropology and allied fields. The essay also attempts to further unpack the profoundly political content of Thompson's concept of "moral" and argues that his research agenda and scholarly concerns were inextricably bound up with his life as an activist – so much so that it is impossible and indeed misleading to speak about one and not the other.

Early Life on the Left

Readers who were not reared in left-wing families between the 1930s and the 1960s or who were not otherwise immersed in the sectarian politics of that period may find it difficult to comprehend the source of the passionate, acerbic, polemical style of argumentation that permeates E. P. Thompson's writing. Thompson was a man and an intellectual of the Left before he became a historian and he never ceased being a militant and activist. This simple reality is the necessary starting point for analyzing Thompson, even if it is ignored or downplayed in the numerous social scientific exegeses that abstract from politics his contributions to the "agency" versus "structure" debate, to understandings of law or to discussions of moral economy. As Bryan Palmer indicates,

> his blasts of intervention were powered by rage as well as by love. Even when he was whispering for effect his voice was loud, his presentation dramatic, his every word and gesture theatrically explosive. When Thompson set his sights on an evil, it was with a cannon, and he would never let it slip by... His place of choice... was one of opposition, a tone of unfulfilled political engagement registered in refusals that were as consistently powerful as they were unfailingly impolite. (1994: 8)

Thompson read history at Cambridge, but he never did graduate work. He joined the Communist Party of Great Britain (CPGB) at age 18, in 1942, before entering the military. He saw combat as a tank commander and fondly recalled the warm welcome and the wine he received in small villages in liberated Italy when he would identify himself as a "comrade." Following the war he participated in volunteer construction brigades in Yugoslavia and Bulgaria, where his elder brother had died while fighting with communist partisans against the Nazis. His formation as a historian owed at least as much to experiences like these and to the CPGB Historians' Group (which included such luminaries as Maurice Dobb, Eric Hobsbawm, and Rodney Hilton) as it did to Cambridge and the elite spheres of English academia, about which he frequently expressed ambivalence and even contempt (Thompson 1978b: 38; 1991: 274–275, 350–351; Kaye 1995). It was this group that nurtured his curiosity about the links between England's Romantic poets and early socialists, a fascination which culminated in his epic literary-political biography of William Morris (1955). His first academic position was in adult education in the University of Leeds' Extra-Mural Department, a post he chose "precisely because it offered the Morris-like possibility of 'making socialists' at the same time as it opened out into new avenues of learning for himself" (Palmer 1994: 65). The work that cemented Thompson's scholarly reputation, *The Making of the English Working Class* (1963), began as a project to write a textbook on the British labor movement for extramural students.

Thompson abandoned the CPGB in 1956 after Khrushchev's revelations about Stalinist repression and the Soviet intervention in Hungary, along with some 8,000–10,000 other militants. "I commenced to reason in my thirty-third year," he later wrote, "and, despite my best efforts, I have never been able to shake the habit off" (1978b: i).

Together with other ex-party members and independent leftists, Thompson helped to found *New Left Review*, a project that was initially more than a journal. *NLR* readers' clubs sprang up across Britain and became a significant current in the 1960s New Left, which prided itself on its "socialist humanism" and eventually developed ties to new left intellectuals and youth and anticolonial rebellions elsewhere. In 1963 Perry Anderson, the newly appointed editor, sacked *NLR*'s founders, including Thompson, from the editorial board and opened the journal and its publishing house to a (sometimes critical) engagement with French structural Marxism (Anderson 1980: 114–115; Trimberger 1984: 217).

In 1965, not long after the publication of *The Making of the English Working Class*, Thompson moved to the University of Warwick to direct the Centre for the Study of Social History (though in 1970 he resigned to devote himself to writing and to a series of visiting appointments at other institutions). Thompson's *Making* was, on the one hand, part of a broader trend by British Marxist historians toward studying social struggles that included Christopher Hill's (1997 [1958]) work on the English Revolution, Eric Hobsbawm's books on primitive rebels and bandits (1959, 1969), and Rodney Hilton's (1973) analyses of medieval peasants. On the other hand, *Making* marked the beginning of Thompson's prolonged frontal attack on two influential approaches to social-historical analysis. The first was "serial" quantitative economic history, with prominent proponents in Cambridge and Chicago and among the Annales group in Paris. The second was the structural Marxism of Louis Althusser and his followers (Althusser 1969; Althusser and Balibar 1971).

Thompson's indignation about Louis Althusser and his epigones was rooted not just in misgivings about their schematic, ahistorical view of social change or their scorn for "socialist humanism," but in differences between their respective political trajectories. While Thompson left the CPGB after the 1956 events, Althusser had joined the French Communist Party (PCF) in 1948 and eventually became its official philosopher, charged with developing a scholastic philosophical system that, after 1956 and especially after 1968 (when the PCF allowed him a certain leeway to flirt with Maoism), would keep leftist intellectuals loyal to the party. Althusser, in Thompson's view, not only missed the PCF's heroic involvement in the Resistance; his theory of modes of production was a pseudo-sophisticated version of Stalin's pamphlets on *Marxism and Linguistics* and on *Dialectical and Historical Materialism*, which had been sacred writ in the international communist movement. "When the illusions were finally dispelled, in 1956," Thompson declared, "it was Althusser's business to sew up people's eyes and block their ears, to put the whole corrupt structure of falsehood back in a more sophisticated form" (1978b: 132).[1]

Thompson's "Anthropologies" and Anthropologists' Neglect

Thompson was researching and writing his most influential historical works at a time when Althusser-influenced structural Marxists were ascendant in French (Maurice Godelier, Claude Meillassoux, Pierre-Philippe Rey, Emmanuel Terray), British (Barry Hindess, Paul Hirst) and US (Marshall Sahlins, Jonathan Friedman) anthropology (and in Latin American – especially Mexican – anthropology as well, although Thompson was likely unaware of that). Renato Rosaldo suggests that Thompson's "disagreements with anthropology resemble his attacks on Louis Althusser's structuralism and his critique of Raymond Williams' notion of culture as consensus" (1990: 105). I would suggest instead that Thompson never really engaged seriously with the diversity of views and approaches within anthropology. Indeed, he confessed that his knowledge of the discipline was "intermittent and eclectic" (1978a: 247); that he oversimplified Raymond Williams' work in the interests of winning an argument; and that his polemic against Althusser aroused him much more than his rather tepid disagreements with anthropologists, as Rosaldo acknowledges in a footnote and as anyone who compares Thompson's 1978 essays on "Folklore, Anthropology and Social History" and "The Poverty of Theory" will immediately appreciate.

While Thompson looked askance at the ahistorical proclivities of British social anthropology in its structural-functionalist phase, he was not averse to using it as a foil against economistic interpretations that purported to explain working-class collective action with graphs of price movements and that failed to take account of popular experience and expectations. These, he commented, were a manifestation of

> the schizoid intellectual climate, which permits this quantitative historiography to co-exist (in the same places and sometimes in the same minds) with a social anthropology which derives from Durkheim, Weber, or Malinowski. We know all about the delicate tissue of social norms and reciprocities which regulates the life of Trobriand islanders, and the psychic energies involved in the cargo cults of Melanesia; but at some point this infinitely complex social creature, Melanesian man, becomes (in our histories) the

> eighteenth-century English collier who claps his hand spasmodically upon his stomach, and responds to elementary economic stimuli. (1971: 78)

This momentary invocation of Durkheim and Malinowski, however, was little more than an adroit rhetorical device. Thompson saw no place for his interest in social conflict and class-specific cultures in the antihistorical social science of Durkheim, Radcliffe-Brown, Parsons, and Levi-Strauss, all of whom in varying ways emphasized equilibrium, stasis, and the generic characteristics of particular groups or even of all of humanity (Thompson 1978a).[2] History for Thompson was, above all, the discipline of "context" and "process." This meant studying evidence within its "whole historical context," since "each fact can be given meaning only within an ensemble of other meanings." "Context" was a form of "discipline" against "abstract typological air" and, Thompson believed, would almost always render the latter worthless (1972, 1978a). "Just as the historian who is innocent of anthropological discipline may impose 20th-century categories upon 17th-century material," he wrote, "so the anthropologically trained may be in danger of imposing categories from a wholly different social culture … The increasing tendency to abstract some anthropological or sociological finding from its context, and to flourish it around as if it was possessed of some intrinsic value as a typological fact about all human societies is actively injurious to history" (1972: 43).

This emphasis on "context" also implied extreme caution about cross-cultural or transhistorical comparisons and claims:

> The principles which can be taken across from one society to the other are few, although large in significance; for example, the notion that if a community believes that magic works, it will, within limits, work (the man who is cursed will become ill, the thief who knows that the wizard is searching him out will, for fear of discovery, return the stolen goods …). (1972: 47)

The historian, Thompson maintained, had to understand evidence in close relationship to the cultural setting in which it was produced. Concretely, this involved amassing other, similar evidence from the same period and nearby locales; interrogating the facts in relation to other knowledge about the ways of life, the language, and the subjectivity of the people who produced them; and accounting for "the conditions of recording and preservation of the fact" (Calhoun 1994: 230). This was "historical logic" and the core of Thompson's method, and he saw it as something wholly distinct from and often opposed to anthropological practice and thinking.[3]

Even worse for Thompson was that anthropologists did not seem to get it. In "The Poverty of Theory," Thompson recalled being

> in Cambridge as a guest at a seminar of distinguished anthropologists, when I was asked to justify a proposition, I replied that it was validated by "historical logic." My courteous hosts dissolved into undisguised laughter. I shared in the amusement, of course; but I was also led to reflect upon the "anthropological" significance of the exchange. For it is customary within the rituals of the academy for the practitioners of different disciplines to profess respect, not so much for the findings of each other's discipline, as for the authentic credentials of that discipline itself. And if a seminar of historians were to laugh at a philosopher's or anthropologist's very *credentials*, (that is, the logic or discipline

> central to their practice) this would be regarded as an occasion for offence. And the significance of this exchange was that it was very generally supposed that "history" was an exception to this rule; that the discipline central to its practice was an occasion for laughter; and that, so far from taking offence, I, as a practitioner, would join in the laughter myself. (1978b: 37; emphasis original)

Anthropologists' relative neglect of Thompson cannot be simply explained as reciprocity or retaliation for his less than friendly attitude toward them or, as Rosaldo suggests, because the people they write about "have cultural traditions whose antagonisms differ from our own" (1990: 119). Thompson's epistemology and form of argument are challenging for anthropologists.[4] He rarely made his theoretical premises explicit, but rather sought to construct arguments by adducing more and more cases and an unassailably massive accretion of detail until he had built a conclusive argument.[5] His exposition was recursive and nonlinear, interwoven with fiery diatribes against adversaries large and small, past and present. Like Marx, his language is often ambiguous and, surprisingly and to the disappointment of some critics, he displayed an "apparent lack of interest in the economic workings of capitalism" (Wood 1990: 136). Moreover, his adversarial stance vis-à-vis political and scholarly opponents was doubtless troublesome for the discipline's remaining positivists, who masked their partialities in the supposedly value-free, neutral language that Thompson eschewed and abhorred.

Thompson also wrote culture-bound, very English works that pose challenges to readers outside England. At over 800 pages, his magisterial book on *The Making of the English Working Class* is an intricate, beautifully and passionately written work. It assumes not only considerable background about its most famous protagonists (William Cobbett and William Godwin, among others), but also a fine-grained knowledge of English regions and social types. Commenting on contrasts between Irish emigrants from different regions of Ireland, for example, Thompson explains that they "differed as greatly from each other as Cornish labourers and Manchester cotton-spinners" (1963: 430–431), an allusion not necessarily accessible to those unschooled in the minutiae of English history and geography. This "English" predisposition is every bit as intense in subsequent writings as in the *Making*. In a 1972 essay he questioned why a colleague's list of mob attacks on "arsonists, witches, and scolds" included an action "against 'a skimmington'" (1972: 50) and, in yet another work, he mentioned that local authorities acted against petty offenders who included "badgers, forestallers and regrators" (1991: 263), expressions that surely sent more than one reader running for a dictionary. Thompson himself was aware of this difficulty, admitting that "there is, perhaps, too much sensibility mixed up with my thought – a relapse into an 'English idiom' which may confuse international exchanges" (1978b: iii).

The Moral Economy

In his 1978 essay on "Folklore, Anthropology and Social History," Thompson quoted Marc Bloch's *The Historian's Craft* (1953), noting that "to the great despair of historians, men fail to change their vocabulary every time they change their customs." Any investigation of moral economy, the aspect of Thompson's work with the greatest resonance outside England and beyond the discipline of history, would do well to heed Bloch's admonition. This section examines Thompson's use of moral economy, beginning with his *William Morris*, passing through *The Making of the English Working Class* and his celebrated 1971 article on "The Moral Economy of the English Crowd in the Eighteenth Century," and culminating with his retrospective essay "The Moral Economy Reviewed" (1991). Following this discussion, I turn to the appropriation and transformation of the concept by several other scholars.

Thompson's use of "moral" in moral economy conflated two interrelated meanings of the word (sometimes with more emphasis on one than the other). The first is "moral" in relation to "mores" or customs, with both understood as historical products thoroughly interwoven in a social fabric (Thompson was partial to weaving metaphors, possibly a manifestation of his sympathy with his Luddite subjects). The second meaning of "moral" relates to a principled stance vis-à-vis society, the world, and especially the common good, with the latter defined both in terms of customary rights *and* utopian aspirations. I highlight the latter, future-oriented utopian aspect both because it is an insufficiently recognized dimension of Thompson's conception of "the moral" – often viewed as resting only on longstanding custom and tradition – and because it provides a connecting thread that links his historical research with his commitment to the peace movement in the 1980s (see below).

Thompson's notion of "the moral" was already evident in his first book, on poet and socialist activist William Morris (1955), both as a category of analysis and as a virtue attributed to his protagonist. In describing the early nineteenth-century context, he wrote that

> The terrible prophetic vision of Blake was becoming realized. All values were becoming … tainted with the property-values of the market, all life being bought and sold. The great aspirations at the source of the Romantic Revolt – for the freeing of mankind from a corrupt oppression, for the liberation of man's senses, affections, and reason, for equality between men and between the sexes – were being destroyed by each new advance of industrial capitalism. (Thompson 1955: 43)

According to Thompson, Morris's inspiration derived not just from this contemporary crisis of values, but from "the utopian aspirations of the peasants of medieval England and the far-sighted moral indignation of Sir Thomas More" (1955: 842). His contributions to poetry, the decorative arts, political organizing, political theorizing, and art criticism were, Thompson laments, all "muddled" at best. Instead,

> Morris' claim to greatness must be founded, not on any single contribution to English culture, in one field alone, but on the quality which unites and informs every aspect of his life and work. This quality might best be described as "moral realism": it is the practical moral example of his life which wins admiration, the profound moral insight of his political and artistic writings which gives them life … Morris never sought to disguise the leading part which moral considerations played in the formation of his outlook, and in guiding his actions. (1955: 828).

This individual quality was, however, inseparable, from broader historical processes and social struggles. Morris's

> moral criteria were derived from his understanding of the unfolding aspirations of men in history, and his direct perception of "real living men" in the present. Every time he cut through all the casuistries and sophistries to the underlying moral realities, the naked antagonism of classes, the real misery of the exploited peoples, the actual denial of life in capitalist society. (1955: 835)

The Making of the English Working Class (1963) contains a far more developed, if still somewhat inchoate, notion of moral economy. The context and period – the industrial revolution – are essentially the same as the early part of *William Morris*, but the Romantic poets recede and popular complaints and voices take center stage. Thompson enumerates "the grievances felt by working people as to changes in the character of capitalist exploitation":

> the rise of a master-class without traditional authority or obligations; the growing distance between master and man; the transparency of the exploitation at the source of their new wealth and power; the loss of status and above all of independence for the worker, his reduction to total dependence on the master's instruments of production; the partiality of the law; the disruption of the traditional family economy; the discipline, monotony, hours and conditions of work; loss of leisure and amenities; [and] the reduction of the man to the status of an "instrument." (1963: 202–203)

This tension between working people's historical experience, customary practices, and moral expectations, on the one hand, and the cruel exigencies of the new industrial capitalist order, on the other, is the central explanatory principle in Thompson's analysis of early nineteenth-century working-class politics. All the elements of what later became his more articulated theory of moral economy are there, though the phrase itself makes only a few appearances in the entire text (1963: 67, 550). One of these is in connection with Thompson's discussion of the Luddite weavers and stockingers, whom pundits, politicians, and historians (bourgeois and Marxist) to this day caricature as archaic reactionaries because of their attacks on factories and machinery. Thompson, instead, situates the Luddites in a setting where paternalist protective legislation had been abrogated, where new cotton mills confined child laborers and beat down wages, and where pride in craft ceded to pitiless exploitation, and erstwhile artisans were reduced to a "dependent" state. The sense of generalized outrage and violation this generated "gave a sanction to the Luddites and afforded them protection" in the communities in which they lived:

> The "free" factory-owner or large hosier or cotton-manufacturer, who built his fortune by these means, was regarded not only with jealousy but as a man engaging in *immoral* and *illegal* practices. The tradition of the just price and the fair wage lived longer among "the lower orders" than is sometimes supposed. They saw *laissez faire*, not as freedom, but as "foul Imposition." They could see no "natural law" by which one man, or a few men, could engage in practices which brought manifest injury to their fellows. (1963: 549; emphasis original)

Moreover, Luddite direct action was not an atavism or a manifestation of apolitical or "pre-political" spontaneity.[6] It had, Thompson maintained, future-oriented, profoundly democratic elements and was both spontaneous *and* highly organized, depending on the moment and the locality.

> On the one hand, it looked backward to old customs and paternalist legislation which could never be revived; on the other hand, it tried to revive ancient rights in order to establish new precedents. At different times their demands included a legal minimum wage; the control of the "sweating" of women or juveniles; arbitration; the engagement by the masters to find work for skilled men made redundant by machinery; the prohibition of shoddy work; the right to open trade union combination. All these demands looked forwards, as much as backwards; and they contained within them a shadowy image, not so much of a paternalist, but of a democratic community, in which industrial growth should be regulated according to ethical priorities and the pursuit of profit be subordinated to human needs. (1963: 551–552)

Thompson began the research reported in "The Moral Economy of the English Crowd in the Eighteenth Century" (1971) while he was awaiting the page proofs of *The Making of the English Working Class*. Remarkably, considering the usual academic practice of rushing into print, this 60-page article was thus almost a decade in the making. Originally conceived as a comparison of late eighteenth-century English and French grain riots, in collaboration with Richard Cobb and Gwyn Williams, the joint project fell through for reasons Thompson professed not to remember and each author ultimately published results separately.[7] In looking backward at the eighteenth century, Thompson sought to elucidate both the proximate roots of the popular *mentalités* he had documented in *Making* and to scrutinize the supposedly quiescent period between England's "revolutionary" seventeenth century and the radical effervescence of its nineteenth century. "The Moral Economy of the English Crowd," more than any other of Thompson's works, presents an explicit theoretical argument and examines a question (When do grievances or distress result in collective action?) that have made it of enduring interest for social scientists.

The source of social unrest in Thompson's "English Crowd" lay in the tension between two models of economy, the moral economy of artisans, colliers, and the poor and what late eighteenth-century Chartists and other critics of laissez-faire capitalism called the "political economy" espoused by "quacks" (1991: 336–337). This friction involved the prolonged demise of a set of paternalist, regulatory practices and their associated assumptions in the face of creeping liberalization of the grain markets. In the eighteenth century the English population and the poor in particular subsisted largely on breads made from wheat, rye, corn, barley, oats, and peas. These grains (and legumes) and the breads made from them formed part of a dietary status hierarchy that marked class, region, and taste. Refined white wheat breads were most esteemed and "coarser," darker mixtures, especially of oats and peas, which cost less and could more easily conceal adulterants, were the sustenance of the poor. Moreover, Thompson notes that demand for corn or bread is highly inelastic: "When bread is costly, the poor (as one highly placed observer was once reminded) do not go over to cake" (1971: 91). Indeed, in such times they may eat more bread to make up for the loss of other, more expensive foods.

Law and custom in eighteenth-century England dictated that grain could be sold only in the public market, at controlled prices, and with regulated weights and measures. Farmers were not permitted to sell their output before it was harvested, to withhold their stocks from the market in the hope that prices might rise, to deal with intermediaries, or to sell small "samples" of grain on their farms. Local people and the poor were permitted to make their purchases first, before the larger dealers or "factors," whose operations were "hedged around with many restrictions." Millers and bakers, similarly, were required to make sufficient supplies of the "coarser, household" flours and breads and were considered "servants of the community, working not for a profit but for a fair allowance" (1971: 83).

In the eighteenth century this traditional framework for production and provision came under increasing pressure as farmers, dealers, millers, and bakers took advantage of a modernizing agriculture and a rapidly liberalizing economy to circumvent the rules and to press for what today might be called further deregulation. The violations of widely held expectations and of law, however, provoked the frequent ire of the poor, especially in times of dearth, giving rise to seizures of bread, grain and flour, crowds' insistence on "setting the price," attacks on mills, and thinly veiled threats that those who sold "samples" at inflated prices, who benefited from export "bounties," or who otherwise transgressed longstanding expectations would suffer dire consequences. Thompson demonstrates that in times of plenty the authorities tended to reduce their enforcement efforts, but "the moral economy," "the old model remained in men's minds as a source of resentment" (1971: 85). In scarcity years, when crowds formed and riots broke out, the authorities attempted to reimpose traditional practices, though with diminishing effectiveness over the course of the eighteenth century. "The crowd," Thompson wrote, "derived its sense of legitimation … from the paternalist model … [but] in one respect the moral economy of the crowd broke decisively with that of the paternalists: for the popular ethic sanctioned direct action by the crowd, whereas the values of order underpinning the paternalist model emphatically did not" (1971: 95, 98).

One of Thompson's signal contributions was to highlight the extent to which "markets" are political constructions and outcomes of class struggle. He provides copious examples of how "crowd pressure" resulted in price reductions, ad hoc local subsidy and charity programs, and "prudential self-restraint" on the part of farmers and dealers who hoped to preclude more injurious popular actions. The latter sectors sought a medium "between a soaring 'economic' price in the market, and a traditional 'moral' price set by the crowd" (1971: 126). This occurred, however, in "a smaller and more integrated community" (1971: 131), in a localized market, a place not only where "working people most often felt their exposure to exploitation" but also where "they could most easily become organized" (1971: 134).

> The market remained a social as well as an economic nexus. It was the place where one-hundred-and-one social and personal transactions went on; where news was passed, rumour and gossip flew around, politics was (if ever) discussed in the inns or wine-shops round the market square. The market was the place where the people, because they were numerous, felt for a moment that they were strong. (1971: 135)

"Dare one suggest," Thompson later asked, "that market day could actually be fun?" (1991: 319). That too is why the marketplace became a nexus of conflict and struggle.

In the eighteenth century the concept of market or marketplace thus evoked a concrete location, and one rife with social relations of all kinds. Only later, with the demise of the moral economy, did the term "market" assume the metaphorical and deterritorialized qualities that increasingly adhere to it. The political sleight of hand that accompanied this semantic shift involved making the institutions and political forces that actually shaped markets invisible, as well as creating the appearance of a separate and autonomous economic domain disembedded from society. The great achievement of Adam Smith, David Ricardo, Thomas Malthus, and other classical political economists was, as Michael Perelman (2000) demonstrates, to promote the extension to new domains of "free" markets; meanwhile they simultaneously obscured the brutal dispossession that accompanied the spread of such markets and promoted interventionist measures, which thoroughly contradicted laissez-faire doctrine, to force the poor to work.

The "Migration" of Moral Economy

The concept of moral economy, as Didier Fassin suggests, is a "beautiful example of transdisciplinary migration ..., invented by a historian and imported by a political scientist into anthropology, where it knew its greatest success" (2009: 1246). While it might be an exaggeration to maintain that moral economy was invented by a historian, it is doubtless true that without Thompson it would never have attained such widespread acceptance. This migration, however, has also inevitably involved shifts in meaning. Today, moral economy has become a polysemic category with multiple genealogical strands and contemporary interpretations.[8]

In "The Moral Economy Reviewed" Thompson located the first mentions of "moral economy" in the late eighteenth and early nineteenth centuries (1991: 336–337). Nonetheless, there and elsewhere he also pointed to several antecedents that go much further back, to early modern and even ancient times (1955: 842; 1991: 271). These include the "moral" component of Aristotle's *oikonomike* as a precursor of contemporary theories of moral economy or "natural" economy (Taussig 1980; Booth 1994) and the medieval notion of the "just price" developed by Thomas Aquinas (Zigon 2008; Lind 2010).

Importantly, as well, many recent moral economy studies derive not so much from Thompson as from others who have adopted his terminology and conceptual apparatus, particularly political scientist James Scott (and to a lesser extent Raymond Williams and Stuart Hall, who collaborated with Thompson on *New Left Review* and later in the 1980s peace movement). There is, moreover, a proliferation of "moral economy" analyses in medical anthropology and elsewhere that employ the term in ways that escape the intentions of Thompson and Scott and that at times end up eviscerating the category of most of its political and particularly its class content (see Conclusion below).

In *The Moral Economy of the Peasant* (1976), James Scott hews closely to Thompson's understanding of "moral economy," though with less emphasis on consumers' involvement in local food markets and more on producers' values or mores. These included peasants' notions of "just prices" (including "just" rents and taxes), as well as other sorts of entitlements, such as access to land, gleaning and fishing rights, rights of way across landowner properties, and redistributive mechanisms and forms of reciprocity that linked peasants with elites and with each other. Scott's approach is also more concerned with developing a "phenomenological theory of exploitation" (1976: 161). Most peasants in Vietnam and Burma, according to Scott, held deeply rooted views about patron–client relations and the right to "subsistence security"

(1976: 35). They manifested a generalized aversion to risks that might threaten this security and an utter dread of those "thresholds" past which a household could plummet downward to hunger and misery (1976: 110).These subjective elements or *mentalités* in turn become key determinants of where, in any given conjuncture, peasants ended up on the continuum between seeming quiescence and open rebellion.

Scott's treatment of values was an integral part of a larger framework that situated moral economy within a system of conflictual class relations. Even though his book barely mentions or cites Thompson, Scott shared with him a fundamental concern with class conflict and class-based collective action. Years later, in his "Moral Economy Revisited" essay, Thompson both praised Scott and warned that the equation of values with moral economy in other scholars' works could be a slippery slope if it were separated from class analysis. "If values, on their own, make a moral *economy*," he declared, "then we will be turning up moral economies everywhere. My own notion of the moral economy of the crowd in the food market includes ideal models or ideology (just as political economy does), which assigns economic roles and which endorses customary practices (an 'alternative' economics), in a particular balance of class or social forces" (1991: 340; emphasis original).

This insistence on the class dimension of moral economy has not prevented the concept from evolving or from moving away from a narrow focus on class-specific cultures situated in fields of conflictual class relations. One of the most extensive initial efforts of this sort was John Lonsdale's richly eloquent study "The Moral Economy of Mau Mau" (1992), which delves into Kenyan history in order to develop a concept of "moral ethnicity." With nary a nod to either Thompson or Scott, Lonsdale posits that ethnicity is both a universal and a highly contingent condition. It is universal in providing "the identity that makes social behavior possible" and it is contingent inasmuch as "all ethnicities are inwardly disputed" and instruct "by moral exclusion" (1992: 328). The "inward disputes" among the diverse peoples considered Kikuyu revolved around contested origin stories, histories of migration and incorporation, and sneering "at each other's barbarities of speech" (Lonsdale 1992: 335). Ethnicity and class reinforced each other, but the former was vastly more complex and contested than the latter, ending up on both extremes of the class divide while at the same time serving as an available idiom for the politics of each side (1992: 403).

Moral economy, in this account of Kikuyu subjectivity, continues to be informed by the expectations that accompany highly developed patron–client relations and a "vital contrast between reciprocal duty and one-sided oppression" (Lonsdale 1992: 352). Moral ethnicity is not entirely coterminous with moral economy, however, and it is hardly primordialist. On the contrary, Lonsdale stresses the fluidity of group boundaries and the importance of locality and of strategic alliances – in business, marriage, politics – that cross ethnic lines. He suggests that group differences usually enter little into everyday life, becoming salient only in particularly charged, infrequent conjunctures. Moreover, African ethnicity, according to Lonsdale, is integrally bound up with the growth of the state, colonial administrative imperatives, and the rise of a "competitive tribalism" that seeks access to public-sector goods. Echoing earlier anthropological theorists of state formation (e.g., Fried 1975), he asserts that "tribe was not so much inherited as invented" (1992: 329). The key point here is that in Lonsdale's hands moral economy – and the associated violence it partly explains – includes a "native" understanding of wealth as a reward for virtue and hard work along with the social obligations that come with having obtained riches. As Angelique Haugerud points out in an analysis of moral economy in Kenya that is a useful complement to Lonsdale's, "the putative virtue of wealth was a convenient weapon to justify or naturalize economic inequality [and] to guard one's privileges by limiting numbers of or assistance to dependents" (1995: 147).

In Lonsdale's analysis, the popular outrage at ill-gotten gains that was so central to Thompson's examination of the English crowd is manifested, if at all, in a different register, less concerned with the source of wealth or its legitimacy than with whether it is shared with clients and family members, less focused on class per se, except perhaps in times of dearth, and susceptible at any moment to expression in both ethnic and anticolonial idioms. As in eighteenth-century England, however, in Kenya "the moral lessons of social inequality had in any case never been unquestioned. The wealthy may have been glad of the blessing of God and the ancestors, but the poor were always challenged to think critically about human responsibility" (Lonsdale 1992: 337).

Lorraine Daston's "The Moral Economy of Science" (1995) took the discussion in yet another direction. For Daston,

> a moral economy is a web of affect-saturated values that stand and function in well-defined relationship to one another. In this usage, "moral" carries its full complement of eighteenth- and nineteenth-century resonances: it refers at once to the psychological and the normative … Here *economy* also has a deliberately old-fashioned ring: it refers not to money, markets, labor, production, and distribution of material resources, but rather to an organized system that displays certain regularities, regularities that are explicable but not always predictable in their details. A moral economy is a balanced system of emotional forces, with equilibrium points and constraints. (1995: 4)

Daston's main concern is to explain the rise of normative systems of scientific rigor and quantification since the seventeenth century as "forms of moral obligation and discipline" (1995: 10). "Moral obligation," she suggests, exists in the scientist's relation to a community of scientists, while "discipline" involves the removal of the person of the scientist from the procedure, the reining in of judgment, and the submission to rules that make accurate quantification and replicable experiments possible. Both involve the creation of the codes of honor and communities of trust that are fundamental to scientific work. "Moral economies of science," Daston maintains, "derive both their forms and their emotional force from the culture in which they are embedded – gentlemanly honor, Protestant introspection, bourgeois punctiliousness" (1995: 24).

While Daston's splendid account of the emergence of empirically based science has much to recommend it, her use of moral economy marks a major departure from Thompson's and Scott's approaches. The most notable divergence is the transformation of moral economy from a principle that explains class conflict to an element of a functionalist "balanced system" with "equilibrium points" that produces "stability and integrity" (1995: 4). In Daston's work an affirmation that moral economy has a Durkheimian and Mertonian genealogy makes an uneasy appearance, implicitly arguing for coexistence under the same umbrella with the Marxism of Thompson and the Thompsonian (and other) influences on Scott. In effect, Daston attempts to "migrate" the category from the realm of conflict to the realm of equilibrium.

In 1999 Jean-Pierre Olivier de Sardan published a provocative article on "A Moral Economy of Corruption in Africa?" The idea that practices commonly viewed as corruption could be the products of and governed by a moral economy (even if the essay's title ends with a question mark) constitutes a striking contrast to Daston's use of the term to denote a community of scientists governed by norms of professional integrity. The distance between Daston and Olivier de Sardan is not, however, as great as it might appear at first. According to Olivier de Sardan, the practices typically glossed as "corruption" include many that are part of or at least close to "customary social norms and attitudes" which are widely recognized as legitimate (1999: 27). Hence, for example, the custom of giving small gifts to family members, friends' children, neighbors, coworkers, and acquaintances extends seamlessly, he says, to customs officials, driver's license examiners, and other functionaries who promise to deliver needed services or documents. Not to participate in this gift economy, which despite employing the language of "favors" has become increasingly monetized, is to invite reproach, ostracism, and shame, as well as future bureaucratic complications. Those who accede to high-level positions are expected to profit and to spread the benefits within their extended families and social networks. Such opportunities are supported by "positive social values …, such as generosity, largesse and gratitude to all those who in the past, when you were unimportant, weak, in need, provided help, encouragement and support" (1999: 43).

"Corruption" is thus "simultaneously a functional necessity (conditioning the effectiveness of all administrative undertakings), and a normative necessity (the foundation of all forms of sociability)" (Olivier de Sardan 1999: 41). "Networks of solidarity" in villages and among the technocratic elite both encourage corruption and allow impunity to flourish (1999: 30–31). The "logics" of corruption (a term the author prefers to "cultural" explanations) are "normative configurations" or "shared social codes" that shape actors' strategies and that contribute to making corrupt practices routine, banal, pervasive, and nearly impossible to uproot. These "codes," furthermore, simultaneously justify corruption and allow both parties to any corrupt transaction to deny that it is such. Olivier de Sardan's "moral economy of corruption," for all its brilliant deciphering of the processes though which corruption is legitimized, is – like Daston's "moral economy of science" – essentially an equilibrium-based rather than a conflict-based theory. Moreover, its consensus model of culture, with its implicit assumptions about unanimity of beliefs and universality of norms and behavior, may be especially problematical in the Kenyan case, where, for example, Eric Wainaina's 2001 hit song "Nchi ya Kitu Kidogo" (Country of Bribes) caused a political sensation and brought its author domestic and international acclaim (Lacey 2001).

Moral economy theory has clearly drifted in the direction of Mauss's (1967) emphasis on the obligation to give and the obligation to receive and away from the concern with class tensions and rebellion that characterized its inception. This Maussian emphasis on steady-state reciprocity can exist alongside a class analysis not framed in moral economic terms. Philippe Bourgois and Jeff Schonberg's powerful ethnography *Righteous Dopefiend* (2009), for example, locates homeless heroin addicts in San Francisco in a US lumpenproletariat conceived in conventional Marxist terms as a socially excluded, "residual class" created as a byproduct of late twentieth-century neoliberal economic policies. The homeless addicts' expectations of elite largesse are minimal, but their horizontal relations and drug-sharing practices are permeated with webs of reciprocity and mutual obligation. In the homeless encampments dope is shared to ward off withdrawal symptoms, to make claims on future favors, to buy love, and for myriad other reasons. The "moral economy of heroin sharing" (Bourgois and Schonberg 2009: 82) is every bit as much a survival mechanism as other moral economies that made claims on superordinate groups or colonial powers, but its "logics" are entirely internal to a marginalized population and unrecognized outside of that group.

Conclusion

"I have no right to patent the term," E. P. Thompson observed in his essay on "The Moral Economy Reviewed" (1991: 340). This somewhat grudging recognition, however, accompanied an insistence on its centrality to the concept of class, morality, and economy and a caution that depoliticizing moral economy would render it analytically useless. The proliferation of moral economy frameworks and the "banalization" (Fassin 2009) or broadening of the term into an overly capacious, catchall category run the danger of rendering it simultaneously clever and meaningless. What, then, is to be done?

A first step might be to point out that Thompson's use of "moral" reflected a profound political sensibility and commitment that are sometimes less apparent in those who subsequently appropriated and transformed his language. Although Thompson occasionally cautioned historians about imposing their own analytical categories on their material, his identification with his subjects – whether William Morris, nineteenth-century radical laborers, or eighteenth-century "mob" participants – was so profound that it is nearly impossible to disentangle their notions of the moral universe from his. This, indeed, is one of the criticisms most frequently leveled at Thompson (Anderson 1980; Rosaldo 1990). It reflects the centrality of moral criteria to his politics (as was the case with William Morris's), especially in the period after 1956 when he "began to reason."

In the 1980s Thompson threw himself into peace movement activism with his characteristic passion and nearly ceased historical research (Wood 1990: 149). While his involvement in peace activities had stretched back decades, the announcement in late 1979 that some 160 NATO nuclear-tipped cruise missiles would be sited in Britain, and the Soviet invasion of Afghanistan at the same time, convinced him that the cold war posed an imminent threat to human survival. He published a pamphlet, *Protest and Survive*, which called attention to the absurdities of nuclear war fighting doctrine and he drafted the European Nuclear Disarmament Appeal (END), which contributed to mobilizing millions of people throughout Europe. Importantly, his analysis of the dangers of the moment went beyond the nuclear danger to question the entire, self-perpetuating logic of the cold war and was as critical of the Soviet Union as it was of NATO. The peace movement was, he hoped, "a détente of peoples rather than of states," which had the possibility of inextricably linking the causes of peace and of freedom, in both the East and the West (Thompson 1982: 50).

Thompson, however, was not only a movement theoretician and strategist. He made speeches, appeared on radio and television, organized working groups, was "lugged around" by police during a sit-down strike in Oxford, and drove a car in support of the 40,000 women who surrounded the cruise missile base at Greenham

Common (Palmer 1994: 142), a site whose very name suggests its erstwhile status as the kind of nonprivate property that he had written about in *Whigs and Hunters*. In the early to mid-1980s, public opinion polls ranked him among the most admired and most trusted public figures in England, second only to the "first women" of the nation, Margaret Thatcher, Queen Elizabeth, and the Queen Mother (Calhoun 1994: 223; Palmer 1994: 126–127).

Thompson's peace movement writings, while not published in academic journals, echo his scholarly work and the voices of his eighteenth- and nineteenth-century laborers and weavers in their insistence on the moral responsibility of the individual to his or her fellows and to the planet, as well as the rootedness of this obligation in a common culture:

> We have, if not a duty, then a need, deeply engraved within our culture, to pass the place on no worse than we found it. Those of us who do not expect an afterlife may see in this our only immortality: to pass on the succession of life, the succession of culture. It may even be that we are happier when we are engaged in matters larger than our own wants, larger than ourselves. (1982: 51)

Thompson did popularize the notion of moral economy, but others who appropriated it did so much more. It is unremarkable that concepts such as this evolve. Indeed, the genealogy of moral economy constitutes a fine example of what Thompson himself warned against when he invoked Marc Bloch's remark about historians' frustration in the face of "men" who fail to alter their vocabularies when their customs change. The first job of any historian or social scientist is to indicate the sense in which she or he is employing a particular term, a specification that often involves genealogical scrutiny of the category itself. Analytical concepts, in other words, have histories, and these are relevant to how we employ them. They also have moral and political content. Given this, it is a pity that Thompson's signal contribution to theories of moral economy has of late so often been obscured.

NOTES

1 Anderson (1980) provides a detailed critical discussion of Thompson's battle with Althusser and a partial defense of the latter. Anderson also asks a very reasonable "moral" question: Why were Thompson's illusions about Stalinism dispelled only in 1956 and not before, especially given the existence of an extensive anti-Stalinist Marxist literature by Trotskyists, Mensheviks, and left social democrats.

2 Elsewhere, however, he refers to Evans-Pritchard's *The Nuer* in arguing that the sense of time is culturally and historically specific, and that "clock time" and "work-discipline" disrupted preexisting notions and became foci of contention (Thompson 1967).

3 One manifestation of this distance from anthropology is that Thompson paid no attention at all to earlier works in the anthropological canon that had great resonance with his work, most notably Mauss's *The Gift* (1967 [1925]) and Polanyi's *The Great Transformation* (2001 [1944]). The neglect of Polanyi is perhaps most surprising, since his book covers much of the same territory as *The Making of the English Working Class* and *Whigs and Hunters*, and he had taught in the Workers' Educational Association, as Thompson later did at Leeds.

4 The situation in sociology is similar. As Trimberger remarks, "however much they might admire him as a social historian and a compelling literary stylist, most historical sociologists do not see theoretical relevance in Thompson's work. A perceived lack of theoretical generalization and explicit methodology in Thompson's social history has been used to

account for his meager impact on sociologists, despite his influence among historians" (1984: 211).

5 Twenty years after his "Crowd" essay, Thompson remarked, "My files bulge with material collected on mills and marketing and meal mobs, etc., but since much of this repeats the evidence adduced in my article, it need not now be deployed. But a lot of work underlay my findings, and I may be forgiven if I am impatient with trivial objections" (1991: 260).

6 The contrast here with the analysis in Hobsbawm's *Primitive Rebels* (1959) is particularly notable.

7 Presumably this collaboration would have addressed directly some of the "serial" historians' controversial claims about food prices and the causes of the French Revolution, a debate that is outlined in Edelman (2005).

8 "Maybe the trouble lies with the word 'moral,'" Thompson declared in his 1991 retrospective essay on moral economy. "'Moral' is a signal which brings on a rush of polemical blood to the academic head. Nothing has made my critics angrier than the notion that a food rioter might have been more 'moral' than a disciple of Dr Adam Smith" (1991: 271).

REFERENCES

Althusser, Louis (1969) *For Marx*. New York: Pantheon.

Althusser, Louis and Balibar, Étienne (1971) *Reading Capital*. New York: Pantheon.

Anderson, Perry (1980) *Arguments within English Marxism*. London: Verso.

Bloch, Marc (1953) *The Historian's Craft*. New York: Vintage.

Booth, William James (1994) On the Idea of Moral Economy. *American Political Science Review* 88(3): 663–667.

Bourgois, Philippe and Schonberg, Jeff (2009) *Righteous Dopefiend*. Berkeley: University of California Press.

Calhoun, Craig (1994) E. P. Thompson and the Discipline of Historical Context. *Social Research* 61(2): 223–243.

Daston, Lorraine (1995) The Moral Economy of Science. *Osiris* 10: 2–24.

Edelman, Marc (2005) Bringing the Moral Economy Back in … to the Study of 21st-Century Transnational Peasant Movements. *American Anthropologist* 107(3): 331–345.

Fassin, Didier (2009) Les économies morales revisitées. *Annales Histoire, Sciences Sociales* 6: 1237–1266.

Fried, Morton (1975) *The Notion of Tribe*. Menlo Park, CA: Cummings.

Goody, Jack, Thirsk, Joan, and Thompson, E. P. (eds.) (1978) *Family and Inheritance: Rural Society in Western Europe, 1200–1800*. Cambridge: Cambridge University Press.

Haugerud, Angelique (1995) *The Culture of Politics in Modern Kenya*. Cambridge: Cambridge University Press.

Hill, Christopher (1997) *Puritanism and Revolution: Studies in Interpretation of the English Revolution of the Seventeenth Century*. New York: St. Martin's Press.

Hilton, Rodney (1973) *Bond Men Made Free: Medieval Peasant Movements and the English Rising of 1381*. London: Temple Smith.

Hobsbawm, Eric J. (1959) *Primitive Rebels: Studies in Archaic Forms of Social Movement in the 19th and 20th Centuries*. Manchester: Manchester University Press.

Hobsbawm, Eric J. (1969) *Bandits*. London: Weidenfeld & Nicolson.

Kaye, Harvey (1995) *The British Marxist Historians: An Introductory Analysis*. New York: St. Martin's Press.

Kuper, Adam (1999) *Culture: The Anthropologists' Account*. Cambridge, MA: Harvard University Press.

Lacey, Marc (2001) Nairobi Journal: A Song about Corruption Takes Kenya by Storm. New York Times (Sept. 6.) At http://www.nytimes.com/2001/09/06/world/nairobi-journal-a-song-about-corruption-takes-kenya-by-storm.html?emc=eta1, accessed Feb. 13, 2012.

Lind, Christopher (2010) *Rumours of a Moral Economy*. Halifax, NS: Fernwood.

Little, Walter E. (2009) Maya Daykeepers: New Spiritual Clients and the Morality of Making Money. In Katherine Browne and B. Lynne Milgram (eds.), *Economics and Morality: Anthropological Approaches.* Lanham, MD: AltaMira Press, pp. 77–97.

Lonsdale, John (1992) The Moral Economy of Mau Mau: Wealth, Poverty & Civic Virtue in Kikuyu Political Thought. In Bruce Berman and John Lonsdale (eds.), *Unhappy Valley: Conflict in Kenya and Africa.* London: James Currey, pp. 315–505.

Mauss, Marcel (1967) *The Gift: Forms and Functions of Exchange in Archaic Societies.* New York: Norton.

Olivier de Sardan, J. P. (1999) A Moral Economy of Corruption in Africa? *Journal of Modern African Studies* 37(1): 25–52.

Orlove, Benjamin S. (1997) Meat and Strength: The Moral Economy of a Chilean Food Riot. *Cultural Anthropology* 12(2): 234–268.

Palmer, Bryan D. (1994) *E. P. Thompson: Objections and Oppositions.* London: Verso.

Parry, Jonathan and Bloch, Maurice (eds.) (1989) *Money and the Morality of Exchange.* Cambridge: Cambridge University Press.

Perelman, Michael (2000) *The Invention of Capitalism: Classical Political Economy and the Secret History of Primitive Accumulation.* Durham, NC: Duke University Press.

Polanyi, Karl (2001) *The Great Transformation: The Political and Economic Origins of Our Time*, 2nd edn. Boston: Beacon.

Rosaldo, Renato (1990) Celebrating Thompson's Heroes: Social Analysis in History and Anthropology. In Harvey J. Kaye and Keith McClelland (eds.), *E. P. Thompson: Critical Perspectives.* Philadelphia: Temple University Press, pp. 103–124.

Roseberry, William (1989) *Anthropologies and Histories: Essays in Culture, History, and Political Economy.* New Brunswick, NJ: Rutgers University Press.

Scott, James C. (1976) *The Moral Economy of the Peasant: Rebellion and Subsistence in Southeast Asia.* New Haven: Yale University Press.

Taussig, Michael (1980) *The Devil and Commodity Fetishism in South America.* Chapel Hill, NC: University of North Carolina Press.

Thompson, E. P. (1955) *William Morris: Romantic to Revolutionary.* London: Lawrence & Wishart.

Thompson, E. P. (1963) *The Making of the English Working Class.* New York: Random House.

Thompson, E. P. (1967) Time, Work-Discipline, and Industrial Capitalism. *Past & Present* 38: 56–97.

Thompson, E. P. (1971) The Moral Economy of the English Crowd in the Eighteenth Century. *Past & Present* 50: 76–136.

Thompson, E. P. (1972) Anthropology and the Discipline of Historical Context. *Midland History* 1(3): 41–55.

Thompson, E. P. (1975) *Whigs and Hunters: The Origin of the Black Act.* New York: Pantheon.

Thompson, E. P. (1978a) Folklore, Anthropology, and Social History. *Indian Historical Review* 3(2): 247–266.

Thompson, E. P. (1978b) *The Poverty of Theory and Other Essays.* New York: Monthly Review Press.

Thompson, E. P. (1982) East, West – Is There a Third Way? *The Nation* (July 10), 33: 48–51.

Thompson, E. P. (1991) The Moral Economy Reviewed. In *Customs in Common.* Pontypool: Merlin, pp. 259–351.

Trimberger, Ellen Kay (1984) E. P. Thompson: Understanding the Process of History. In Theda Skocpol (ed.), *Vision and Method in Historical Sociology.* Cambridge: Cambridge University Press, pp. 211–243.

Vincent, Joan (1990) *Anthropology and Politics: Visions, Traditions, and Trends.* Tucson: University of Arizona Press.

Wood, Ellen Meiksins (1990) Falling through the Cracks: E. P. Thompson and the Debate on Base and Superstructure. In Harvey Kaye and Keith McClelland (eds.), *E. P. Thompson: Critical Perspectives.* Philadelphia: Temple University Press, pp. 125–152.

Zigon, Jarrett (2008) *Morality: An Anthropological Perspective.* Oxford: Berg.

CHAPTER 4

Foucault and the Genealogy of Ethics

James D. Faubion

Foucault develops his genealogy of ethics in the second and third volumes of *The History of Sexuality*, in a concomitant series of interviews and set pieces, and in the last three years of lectures that he delivered at the Collège de France. He dwells at greatest length on the distant past: archaic, classical, and Hellenistic Greece; the Roman republic and empire; early Christianity. Only in the final year of his lectures at the Collège does he arrive at the nineteenth century, and then only schematically, and in terms quite different from those that the program inaugurated in the first volume of *The History of Sexuality* might have led readers to expect. His investigations are in any event roughly linear in their historical unfolding. They are far from random in their attention. On the contrary, they reveal an increasing, increasingly urgent, and self-reflexive preoccupation with what the second volume of the *History* first identified as the ethics of *le souci de soi*, the care of or concern for the self. They testify further to an increasingly crystallized triangulation of focus: on the relation between the ethics of the care of the self as a mode of self-governance and the stewardship, the governance, of others; of the relation between the governance of others and the philosophical practice of parrhesia, of a particular mode of truth-telling; and of the relation between and the ethics of the care of the self (Foucault 2005, 2008, 2009; Faubion 2011: 26). Foucault himself neatly summarizes the triangle – a quasi-philosophical triangle – by resort to a triad of Greek terms: *alêtheia* (truth), *politeia* (polity), *êthos* (character, habitus, habitat).

It goes without saying that matters of eros and sex are at the forefront of the second and third volumes of the *History of Sexuality* (1985, 1986). They barely figure at all, however, in the final two years of his lectures – delivered at the very same time that those volumes were being prepared for press. If they belong within the parameters of the Foucauldian triangle, if they are at the center of a genealogy of sexuality, they are far less central to the genealogy of the ethics of the parrhesiastic way of life with which

A Companion to Moral Anthropology, First Edition. Edited by Didier Fassin.

the final two years of lectures are chiefly concerned. They both have their place – but the place each occupies is ultimately relative to the priorities of what Foucault characterizes as a distinctly modern "philosophical ethos" – and his own ethos – whose realization and dynamics consist of "a critique of what we are saying, thinking, and doing, through a historical ontology of ourselves" (1997e: 315). The critique is "genealogical" in its design; it does not "deduce from the form of what we are what it is impossible for us to do and to know," but rather separates out, "from the contingency that has made us what we are, the possibility of no longer being, doing, or thinking as we are, do, or think" (1997e: 315–316). It is "archeological" in its method; it does not "seek to identify universal structures of all knowledge or of all possible moral action," but instead seeks "to treat the instances of discourse that articulate what we think, say, and do as so many historical events" (1997e: 315). Truth turns out to trump sex in Foucault's quest. That it does so is somewhat at odds with his quest in the first volume of *The History of Sexuality* to discover how it is that "desire" has become "the truth of our being" (1978: 5). It is clear as the last of his lectures comes to a close that the truth of our being extends beyond desire. Yet, as will be seen, in just what else that truth resides, just how one might know the truth and so speak it frankly – all this remains unresolved, and Foucault's triangle and the genealogy of the ethics of along with it. The lack of resolution has its poignancy, not least because Foucault died before he had any chance of addressing it further. But then, the genealogy of ourselves could never permit of closure, unless all of our possible, all of our potential options of being other than we are were somehow to run entirely dry.

Toward Ethics

In Foucault's first sustained articulation of it, genealogy is a "gray" enterprise (Foucault 1999b: 369). It aims at exposing of the historical contingency of the presumptively necessary, of the heterogeneity of the presumptively elemental, of the dirty underbelly of the presumptively lofty. In the majority of scholarly commentaries – my own included (Faubion 1999) – it is the hallmark of the second Foucault. That Foucault leaves behind the stratigraphy, the site-mappings, the systemic and periodizing matrices of his earlier, archaeological investigations for a method that grants a fundamental privilege to the event, to its particularity and to its potentially radical inauguration of systemic change. Sorry to say (sorry for myself among others), that isn't quite accurate, and on two fronts. On one of them: in a magisterial rereading of *The History of Madness*, Lynne Huffer (2010) convincingly identifies a genealogical procedure that anticipates nearly in its entirety the organization of the analytical trajectory of *Discipline and Punish* (1977) and the first volume of *The History of Sexuality*. Huffer is entirely correct to underscore the return in those works of the gray, the critical, the enterprise of unmasking. Foucault assesses the continuity of his work in just these terms (1999a). What indeed remains constant from *The History of Madness* through the first and, indeed, the second and third volumes of *The History of Sexuality* is the project of the historicization of the subject, and especially as the subject has been conceived in the Western philosophical and, more broadly, epistemological tradition. On the other front: Foucault makes no explicit mention of archaeology, either in *Discipline and Punish* or in the first volume of *The History of Sexuality*, but the periodizations that his archaeology of the human sciences establishes, not merely in *The History of Madness* but also in *The Order of Things* and *The Birth of the Clinic*, are preserved without revision in *Discipline and Punish* and, if with truncation, in the first volume of *The History of Sexuality*. Hence, we should take Foucault at his word, however retrospective, in "What is Enlightenment?" He pursued a historical ontology of ourselves archaeological in its method and genealogical in its design all along.

Ethics is for its part late to register in Foucault's analytical consciousness. It is nowhere in the uniformly ethically bleak chapters of *Discipline and Punish*. It is nowhere in the equally bleak chapters of the first volume of the *History*. It does not appear as an explicit analytical category in his monographs before the second volume of the *History*. Foucault's inquiry into the history of liberalism, which began after the completion of the first volume of the *History*, accounts in part at least for its emergence. Only in the aftermath of that inquiry did he begin with any analytical or – it would appear – personal confidence to consider that the Western configurations of the relationship between the powers that be and the subjects over and through whom those powers were and are exercised could be anything other than a relationship of the suzerainty of the former over the latter. The genealogy of ethics is the apparent outcome of that confidence. The tyrannies of the powers that be continue to attract his scrutiny – but they come to be cast as only one side of "governmentality" (2000). Archaeological method and genealogical design perdure, but tragic irony gives way to a troubled optimism that follows from his coming to recognize that at least some of us have the possibility, if always historically conditioned, of constituting ourselves as the "moral subjects of our own actions" (1997e: 318). The domain of such possibilities is the other side of governmentality – and is the structurally objective domain of ethics as Foucault conceives of it.

Toward Athens

Nothing in the first volume of *The History of Sexuality* (1978) foreshadowed that Foucault would dwell so long – or indeed at all – in antiquity. As he first conceived it, the genealogy of the ethico-medical and biopolitical inscription of sexual desire as and at the heart of our modern being was largely an affair of the nineteenth century. If it reached back further, it reached only to the late seventeenth-century roots of an ascendant bourgeoisie's polemics against the "peculiarity" of aristocratic blood in favor of its own vitality and fecundity (1978: 126; Faubion 2011: 25). Its thematic nexus, which Foucault planned to develop in six projected volumes, was the concomitant naturalization and normalization of the divide between the characterologically normal and abnormal. Its administrators included psychiatrists, sexologists, statisticians, and physical anthropologists. The administered included populations and races; children, women, and (among women) mothers and hysterics; criminals; perverts of all persuasions. In its original design, the project would have served to render transparent the historical specificity of "sexuality" as an experience. As Foucault recounts in the introduction to the second volume of *The History of Sexuality*, it would have been able to render explicit its three constitutive axes: "the formation of knowledges (*savoirs*) that refer to it; the systems of power that regulate its practice; the forms in which individuals can and must recognize themselves as subjects of sexuality" (1985: 10). It proved, however, too narrow to allow him adequately to address "the modes in which individuals are brought to recognize themselves as sexual subjects" (1985: 11). In order to do that, he realized that he would have to add to the genealogy – the successive configurations of the subject of desire – an investigation of "how individuals have been brought to exercise on themselves, and on others, a hermeneutics of desire" of far deeper historical roots than those of sexuality alone and of which "their sexual comportment was the occasion, but not the exclusive domain" (1985: 11). He realized further that such an investigation would extend beyond the confines of the legislations of sexual comportment into the terrain of those "reflexive and voluntary practices by which human beings not only determine for themselves the rules of their conduct but also seek to transform themselves, to modify themselves in the singularity of their being" (1985: 16). It would extend, in short, into that other side of governmentality, into ethical terrain, the terrain of "arts of existence" and "techniques of the self" (1985: 17). In the writings of the classical Greek philosophers, he found "one of the first chapters" of the history of just such arts, just such techniques.

What he famously did not find, in either the philosophical or the broader ancient corpus, was any notion of sexuality *à la moderne*. Contrary to what some of his readers have presumed (e.g., Cohen 1991: 171–172), he does not conflate the absence of that notion with the absence of the notion of something like "sexual orientation." Though he has been, Foucault should not be misunderstood to be contending that the ancients lacked any conception of something like "sexual orientation," even of an orientation defined in accord with whether it is directed to an object of the same or of the opposite sex. Having read Kenneth Dover's *Greek Homosexuality* (1978) and incorporating it thoroughly into his scholarly apparatus, Foucault is aware that there are several loci in the ancient corpus that strongly suggest that such a conception was available (Faubion 2011: 27–28). As Dover himself argues, the ethical evaluation of sexual conduct did not rest per se on the appropriateness or inappropriateness of the object to which it was directed, but rather on the manner in which it was expressed and consummated (1978: 40–109). Nor does ancient medicine leave us with any reason to presume that the orientation of sexual conduct was conceived as belonging to pathology. Like Dover and many others before him, Foucault further recognizes that the praise or blame that a Greek man might garner for his sexual practices does not, again, fundamentally hinge on what we would understand as his orientation – and it is this precisely that is the linchpin of Foucault's judgment that ancient sexology (if I may) was not the sexology of sexualities that we still tend to take for granted (1985: 187–189).

Citizens were the marked men – and strictly speaking, citizens were always and only men – of ancient sexology. Again with Dover, Foucault identifies the divide between active and passive conduct (a divide that still functions in the classification of participants in homosexual intercourse) as an ethical master-dichotomy and the nexus of approbation and disapprobation (Foucault 1985: 47). Reviewing the philosophical discourse on *ta afrodisia*, on "carnal pleasures" more generally, however, he discerns a broader ethical regime of which that dichotomy is only a part. In doing so, he comes to the person the Greeks deemed *sôfrôn* and so in full possession of *sôfrosunê*. *Sôfrosunê* might be ascribed to either sex (Dover 1974: 66–69), but is the diacritical virtue of the free man (Dover 1974: 116; after Pohlenz 1966: 67–71). It has often been glossed into English as "temperance," but the gloss is misleading in suggesting an unmitigated self-reserve more typical of the Calvinist than of the ancient (or modern) Athenian. *Sôfrosunê* is the virtue of a man who can enjoy his sex and his food and drink, but who knows when to cease indulging in sex and eating and drinking and who can and does cease doing so when he knows he should. It is, moreover, the virtue of the man who need not exercise what one would usually call "self-control" over appetites and passions that call out still to be indulged even after he has already indulged them enough. The *sôfrôn* or "self-controlling" man is a man whose appetites and passions have already been brought under control, have been so cultivated that they do not linger beyond what his best interest warrants. Foucault is correct in glossing *sôfrosunê* the virtue of self-governance and to join many others before him in recognizing it to be at the very core of the ethical imagination of the civic era of ancient Greece, the virtue that complements and completes all others and with which all others synergistically make a Greek man *agathos*, "good." The regime links the carnal asceticism of Plato's Socrates with the wisdom of Ischomachus, the leading actor of Xenophon's *Oeconomicus* (1923) and an exemplar of the ideal management of the *oikos*, the ancient "estate." It encompasses a dietetics. It encompasses an economics. It encompasses the credentials that a man must have to participate as a good citizen in the city-state itself. In its full range, it comprises the classical arts of existence.

The Grounds and Parameters of the Ethical Domain

Informing Foucault's approach to those arts – as to their successors – is an analytical apparatus that rests on what are likely two variable phrasings of the same presumption. One of them – the domain of ethics – is a domain of the development of one or another competent and conscious exercise of the practice of freedom. The other is a domain of the development of the potential occupant into the actual occupant of a subject position of collectively acknowledged legitimacy in and from which the conscious practice of freedom is exercised. For Foucault, every ethical subject position – or ethical subject, more briefly put – is socially, culturally, and historically specific. It is thus far removed from subject of Aristotle's ethics, the *sôfrôn* citizen of a polity presumed to be the singular consummation of human civilization. It is even further removed from the universal subject of Kant's Second Critique (2002) and the subjects of the later idealist philosophical tradition.

Foucault's subjects differ as well from the subjects of Pierre Bourdieu's theory of practice (1977). Foucault's like Bourdieu's subjects are always socially and culturally specific, but they are also subjects capable of knowledge – at the very least, of knowledge of themselves. Subjects occupy "positions" – but the spatial phraseology that Foucault so often deploys belies a genealogy of ethics that is fundamentally concerned with processes of becoming, of ethical visions but also of ethical revisions. Bourdieu's theory of practice is, in contrast, a theory of sociocultural reproduction, and specifically of the reproduction of domination. As a consequence and as a matter of its logical composition, it can only treat the causes of structural change of whatever sort as structurally exogenous. The severe restrictions of Bourdieusian subjects' capacities of self-comprehension follow accordingly. As Michel de Certeau recognized, the Bourdieusian theory of practice limits the concrete actor exclusively to his or her role in structural reproduction and so is unable to address actors or actions that intervene refractively or fractiously into the given constraints and possibilities of structural reproduction (de Certeau 1984: 55–56). As de Certeau also recognized – before the second volume of *The History of Sexuality* had been published, or perhaps even conceived – Foucault's own approach to practice is thus not merely an addendum to Bourdieu's theorization but a potential correction of it. This said, it does not forge an entirely separate path. Whatever might be thought of de Certeau's odd detection of Marxism in Foucault, his approach is in any event fully consistent with Bourdieu's own conviction that structural constraints and structural inertia are in the long run far more likely than not to trump whatever reformist or revolutionary ambitions concrete actors jointly or severally might have. Genealogists of ethics cannot be burdened with the Bourdieusian problematic of reproduction, but genealogists of a Foucauldian stripe must not overestimate the scope of what everyone now seems fond of calling "agency" (Faubion 2011: 138). Hence, if Foucault's ethical subjects are by definition free, they are so only in some measure. If they are not free in any measure at all, then they are the equivalent of the slave, and the slave – whom Foucault ideal-typically conceives as a subject wholly under the power of his master – has and can have "no ethics" (1997a: 286).

Beyond this, Foucault offers in the second volume of *The History of Sexuality* an analytics of the ethical domain, a general conceptual outline of what he takes to be its four basic parameters (see Rabinow 1997). A discussion of them best begins with "ethical substance." In French and in English, the term is a familiar translation of *Sittlichkeit* as it appears in Hegel's *Philosophy of Right* (1952). *Sittlichkeit* is not the merely "negative" freedom that Kant ascribed to actors uninhibitedly satisfying their desires. Nor is it merely the "positive" freedom that he ascribed to actors obedient to rational moral law. It is rather the condition of those who assimilate moral law into the very tissue of their being and convert morality into ethics – a relation of the moral subject to itself – in doing so (see Gros 2002). Foucault's conceptualization of ethical substance is clearly linked to Hegel's treatment, but it is not the same. For Foucault, ethical substance is whatever stuff – cognitive, emotional, physical, or what-not – it is; that is, the object at once of conscious consideration and of those labors required to realize a systematic ethical end, which is to say the being of a subject of a certain qualitative kind. Ethical substances are ethically neutral or, better put, conceived neither as irredeemably evil nor as always already and incorruptibly good. Not so for Hegel, the universalist philosopher of right. Second, the ethical substances proper to a genealogy of ethics are one or another of the primary materials understood to be constitutive of or a part or aspect of the very being of the subject to whose ethical realization it might serve as resource or roadblock or both. In Greece, Foucault thus focuses on *ta afrodisia*. Finally, Foucault's treatment of ethical substance as an aspect of the subject that must be put under ethical review and targeted for ethical labor contrasts sharply with Hegel's *Sittlichkeit* as a condition of ethical completion, for which whatever review and labor were necessary in bringing it into being are things of the past. Foucault's concept of ethical substance encourages the diagnostic highlighting of such review and such labor in a manner that Hegel's concept of *Sittlichkeit* does not. One can, I think, fairly speak of Foucault's appropriation of the concept – but an appropriation that is also a genealogical undoing of philosophical essentialism (Faubion 2011: 42).

The concept of the ethical subject – a concept of something that is at once particular and the same in each case – becomes in Foucault liable to an indefinite variation in both form and substance. Hegel's unitary concept of ethical embodiment arguably becomes in Foucault a concept divided in two. On the one hand, it appears as ethical substance in what might be thought of as its initial state, its crude givenness. On the other hand, it appears as another of Foucault's basic parameters of the ethical field: precisely the systematic end, the telos of the ethical subject (1985: 27–28). In the Greek case, that telos was *sôfrosunê* and the other cardinal virtues. Whether the telos of the Foucauldian apparatus must be understood in general as the consummation of an existential "project," which a scholastic cottage industry of Heideggerian bent seems to take entirely for granted, will not detain me here. It need not be so conceived. At the very least, not every ethical telos permits of being resolved into the culmination of a specific goal or purpose. An ethics of loving, for example, has its telos, but a telos whose purposes and goals may well be resolutely indeterminate, beyond defining.

Between the ethical substance and the telos of any given subject lie the two parameters of Foucault's fourfold that give his diagnostics its specific difference, its distinctively Foucauldian twist. One especially – that of ethical *askêsis* – has also borne notable analytical fruit in other hands. Foucault borrows *askêsis* directly from the Greek, and whatever his precise intention might have been in doing so, it has a marked citational and rhetorical effect. It at once evokes and demurs from the critical regard not merely of Nietzsche's *Genealogy of Morals* (1956) but of Nietzsche's broader insinuation that the flesh-denying Christianity that he so despised was the ultimate issue of the ugly Socrates' cruel rationalism (Nietzsche 1954: 473–479). Foucault does not explicitly reject the family tree that Nietzsche sketches. Indeed, in his last lectures, he largely affirms it and, with that affirmation, a Nietzschean current that long carries his reflections on ethics. Yet he takes considerable pains to demonstrate that Greek *sôfrosunê* was not in its realization an asceticism of the sort that Weber does not quite identify as the democratization of the practices of the spiritual virtuosi of Catholic monasticism, but that Calvinist and many denominations of post-Calvinist Protestantism in any event imposed on every believer. The *sôfrôn* was far from a flesh-denying subject; his *sôfrosunê* was not the basis of an ascetics that rejected pleasures carnal or intellectual but of a strategics that put them to best use. (Consequentialism reigns.) The Greek *askêsis* neither denotes nor connotes what its linguistic derivatives do. Nietzsche's satire of the triumph of the ascetic *ressentiment* of the slave and the commoner over the robust self-affirmation of the ancient aristocracy (1956: 170–173) fades in Foucault into a more balanced assessment of a civic elite's cultivation of an art of existence resting in the virtues of self-governance.

Every art of existence requires in turn its techniques (or "technologies") of the self (1997d: 223–251). Such technologies include any number of plans, regimes, methods, and devices that subjects might employ, follow, or perform in the pursuit of their ethical formation. Foucault notes at various junctures in his investigations several tools of the examination of the self that antiquity leaves to posterity: the physical exercises that the Greeks pursued in the interest of sustaining their personal vigor and military skill (1997d: 239–240); the Stoic collection of *hupomnêmata*, "notebooks" or "jottings" through which one might "make one's recollection of the fragmentary logos transmitted through teaching, listening, or reading a means of establishing a relationship of oneself with oneself, a relationship as adequate and accomplished as possible" (1997c: 211); meditative disciplines from the Greek *meletê* to the Stoic *praemeditatio malorum* or "pondering of future ills," intended to prepare the self to face with dispassion any misfortune that might befall it (1997d: 239–240); the *paraskeuê* or cognitive-practical "equipment" of the Stoics and Cynics (2005: 320–327; see also Rabinow et al. 2011a); interpretation of dreams (1997d: 241–242; 1986: 4–36); the writing and exchange of personal letters (1997c: 218–220); Christian *exomologêsis*, the "recognition of truth" or, as it comes to be known, "confession" (1997d: 243). Though with less generality, Weber had already recognized the importance of technologies of the self in his treatment of both Calvinist and yogic "methodism" (1958a: 117–127; 1958b: 163–165).

Analytically, Foucault's delimitation of technologies of the self as instruments of the self's work on itself, hence as reflexive instruments, and very often as instruments of reflection as well, is entirely of a piece with his characterization of ethics broadly as the reflexive practice of freedom. It also amounts to an important corrective of Aristotle's ethics, for which the ethical subject is a practitioner and so cannot be a maker, least of all a maker of himself. Reflection in Aristotle's ethics is a matter of judgment, of judging what to do. In Foucault's apparatus, it might also be a matter of self-intervention, of autopoiesis, of the self's production of itself. In his approach to the Greek case as to later cases, however, Foucault lingers over technologies of the self not merely to bring to light the "poetic" aspect of ethics but at least as much to emphasize what he calls the "practice-oriented" nature of ancient ethics (1985: 30).

Weber's treatment of the Calvinists may well have benefited from a more active concept of technologies of the self, but because Calvinist ethics was quite as ascetic as it was, his conception of ethics as a code of practical conduct was at least roughly commensurate with that of his historical subjects. Ancient *askêsis* reveals an ethics of considerably greater complexity than one in which the ethical status of any action hinges on its conformity or lack of conformity with a statutory canon of imperatives or laws or commandments more or less insensitive to the particularities of context. What captures Foucault's interest is not primarily that ancient Greece and Rome, well stocked with ritual specialists but lacking doctrinal doctors, had no clear sociocultural topos for a clergy of either the doctrinal or the ethical sort. Nor does his interest rest primarily in the ancient tendency to conceive of what is right as relative to what is good rather than the modern tendency to the contrary.

As his lectures on the "hermeneutics of the subject" (2005) suggest all the more forcibly in the at best tenuous consistency of their argument, his interest and fascination rather rest with the distinctive personalism of ancient ethics, a personalism that accommodated general conceptions of virtue but left little fertile ground for the taxonomization of ethical genera and species for which later disciplinary and biopolitical regimes provide such rich nourishment. Nor did ancient personalism press nearly as much toward the substantive standardization of the ethical subject as modern philosophies of right from Hegel forward have done. In its personalism precisely, ancient ethics preserves a hiatus between prescription (and proscription) and action within which the relation between ethics and reflexivity is not merely analytically available but over the course of several centuries also provides the analyst with a rich sampler of its variations.

Foucault renders that hiatus analytically formal not only with *askêsis* but even more primarily with his remaining parameter of the ethical domain, "the mode of subjectivation" (1985: 27). The term is a gloss of *le mode d'assujetissement*, whose more standard translation – which *The Use of Pleasures* preserves – would be "the mode of subjection" or "subjugation." The trouble with that translation is that it misleadingly aligns the lineaments of the ethical subject with the condition of the slave – himself a subject of *assujettissement*. In order to avoid equivocation, subsequent English translations – and Foucault gradually along with them – reserve subjectivation for ethics and leave the slave in his subjugation. Foucault characterizes the mode of subjectivation, then, as "the way in which an individual establishes his relation to the rule and recognizes himself as obligated to put it into practice" (1985: 27). At another juncture, he characterizes it slightly differently as "the way in which people are invited or incited to recognize their moral obligations" (1997b: 264). If the way in question is merely that of brutal imposition, then subjectivation falls into subjection and so falls outside the ethical domain – into "slavery." This at least is clear enough. It is also clear that Foucault intends the parameter of the mode of subjectivation to be an index of the "deontological" – precisely that aspect of the ethical domain that has to do with obligation or duty (1985: 37). Moreover, the ambiguity that arises in shifting from the active voice of the subject who "establishes his relation to the rule" to the passive voice of people who "are invited or incited" to recognize their obligations is tolerable, even instructive. As a self-reflexive practice, ethical practice proceeds after all in the middle voice, actively and passively, often at one and the same time (Faubion 2001: 94; 2011: 50; see also Tyler 1998).

Further ambiguities find their way into Foucault's treatment of the mode of subjectivation, however, and they are of less service. First, one can hardly do justice to the deontological with simple reference to "the rule," a term which, as Bourdieu has pointed out, is subject to multiple interpretations (1977: 22–30). Even more oddly, an apparatus that stipulates that the telos of the ethical domain is generally that of the occupation of a given subject position or the becoming of a certain subject surely must include more within the purview of the mode of subjectivation than the subject's mode of recognizing himself or being recognized to be the subject of one or another moral obligation. There is more to the ethical conditioning of a subject than its relation to duty, to which the ethical relevance of exemplars especially (known in much contemporary ethical discourse under the pale rubric of the "role model") cannot be reduced (Humphrey 1997). One's duties are one matter; one's values and the ideals to which one might aspire are often quite another. Foucault's concentration on the personalism of ancient ethics and particularly of its ethics of carnal pleasures may have diverted him from assigning as formal and constitutive a place to what might be thought of as the exemplary function within the ethical domain as the Greeks themselves thought it due. What more likely diverted him was his classification of the exemplary figures celebrated in Homer or Pindar precisely as figures of an "aesthetics of existence" and so distinguishable in principle if perhaps not in fact in the archaic Greek past from figures *stricto sensu* of an ethical sort (2009: 149–150). Personalism, the aesthetics of heroic self-formation, but above all his increasingly exclusive concern with the parrhesiastic ethics of the care of the self seems to have diverted him further from developing as thoroughly as he might have the ethical standing or distinction of a subject position of which the ethical exemplar is an occupant.

The Care of the Self

Foucault devotes attention to parrhesia in his final lectures at the Collège, but he anticipates it in the second volume of the *History* in his attention to the Delphic imperative *gnôthi seauton*, "know thyself." Oracular, the imperative is also an ancient philosophical commonplace. Foucault is at pains to demonstrate – and does so convincingly – that it should not be read simply as an imperative to look inward, to dwell on the self as the be-all and end-all of the classical arts of existence. On the contrary: a fundamentally ecological conception of the ethical domain is constant throughout the ancient period. Self-knowledge, however important, is rather only one step toward the cultivation of the *sôfrosunê* that at once enables and licenses the *sôfrôn* to act as a steward and leader. Foucault makes the point very well, if within the bounds of his triangle:

> The care of the self is ethical in itself; but it implies complex relationships with others insofar as … [the] êthos of freedom is also a way of caring for others. This is why it is important for a free man who conducts himself as he should to be able to govern his wife, his children, his household; it is also the art of governing. Êthos also implies a relationship with others, insofar as the care of the self enables one to occupy his rightful place, the community, or interpersonal relationships, whether as a magistrate or a friend. And the care of the self also implies a relationship with the other as proper care of the self requires listening to the lessons of a master. One needs a guide, a counselor, a friend, someone who will be truthful with you. Thus, the problem of relationships with others is present throughout the development of the care of the self. (1997a: 287; see also 2008: 35)

Foucault emphasizes here the *askêsis* that informs the practice of the care of the self, but also its external expression, its enactment over and with others, who themselves demand care, consideration, acknowledgment, direction perhaps, deference sometimes, across all the domains in which the ethical agent acts and must act as a condition of the full realization of his care of himself. Greek ethics is indeed personal, but unlike an ethics grounded in a metaphysics of autonomy, of a radical and absolute freedom, it places ethical practice in the encompassing web of the house and the polis, both of which are also topoi of friendship (at least for Xenophon and Aristotle). Ethics and its domestic and political environment are thus entirely of a piece. The Foucault who pronounces that "the freedom of the subject and its relationship to others" is "the very stuff of ethics" (1997a: 300) is in this respect a loyal follower of ancient precedent (see Gros 2002).

Precisely because the *sôfrôn* is responsible for others, pederasty begins to attract a philosophical anxiety that is present even in Diotima's identification of the boy beloved as the initial portal into the ancient dialectic of enlightenment in *The Symposium* (Plato 1961: 561 [210a–b]). Foucault recognizes that the philosophers' worries arise because the boy whose *leitourgia* or "service" the pederast would win greatest honor (or envy) in securing was no mere ethical other. The most desirable boy beloved was free-born and elite and so a future citizen socially qualified to hold the highest political and religious offices that the polis had to fill. The philosophers' worries were twofold. The more explicit – no doubt because it was not beyond the bounds of publicity, at least among philosophical friends – was that the very practice of the relationship, of which the beloved's acceptance of the lover's gifts was a sign and intercrural (not anal: see Dover 1978: 98–100) intercourse the permissible consummation, demoted the boy in many respects to the position of a subordinate, which was incompatible with his future standing. Their less explicit and indeed barely mentionable worry was that the boy would come to savor his social and sexual subordination and continue to do so into his adulthood (Foucault 1985: 211, 222) as an inveterate *kinaidos*, "catamite," but more generally a social failure.

In ancient Greece especially, the pederastic lover was no mere *sôfrôn*, either – or had better not merely be. The fathers of the boys caught up in the "hunt" and "chase" (as the Greek metaphors had it: Dover 1978: 81–91) of pederastic romance by all accounts policed their doings carefully, and above all spent considerable time and trouble collecting information about the character of their sons' would-be lovers. Pederasty was coded as romance. Its legitimacy, however, rested in the lover's assumption of his beloved as a pedagogical charge, not in the narrow sense of tutoring him in letters or the harp but always in the sense of offering him an ethical example, the best of citizen manhood (Marrou 1956: 29–32). Thus incorporated into the broader scenes of instruction of the elite sectors of the polis, pederasty can be understood as the domestication of a relationship that in its first Greek expressions belonged more strictly to the pedagogy of the warrior (see Marrou 1956: 36). It highlights in any case that the relationship between the future ethical subject and his pedagogue or pedagogues is not merely a potentially delicate one. It is central to ancient philosophical reflection on ethics from Plato to the present (Faubion 2011: 54).

Such pedagogues are one of the ethical masters, if not the only one, that Foucault has in mind in delimiting the range of the ecology of the ancient arts of existence. Already in his address of Socrates in the second volume of *The History of Sexuality* but especially in his later treatment of the relationship – erotic, pedagogical, and epistolary – between the young Marcus Aurelius and Cornelius Fronto, he is at pains to point out that the ethical subject in training does not merely benefit from but is directionless without a master, without a figure of already established ethical authority, a figure worthy of emulation and capable of serving at once as existential guide, psychological critic, and practical adviser (1997d: 233–234). Here, indeed, an exemplar of an explicitly ethical sort makes an appearance in Foucault's investigations – if an exemplar of a very special sort. He functions as something of a footnote to Socrates: he amounts to a positive response to Socrates' questioning whether or not virtue could be taught. He supports as well Aristotle's response to that questioning, which is emphatically in the affirmative. Here again Foucault shows every sign of following classical footsteps.

The problematization of pederasty was thus a problematization of the paradoxical status of and potential corruption of the boy beloved, but also of the character and legitimate privileges of his master. It was a problematization of the relationship between eros, *êthos*, and truth, but also of the erotics and *êthos* of hierarchy. (Once again: *êthos*, *alêtheia*, *politiea*.) For Foucault the genealogist, problematization is in fact the inaugural intellectual moment and the fulcrum of the history of thought in general (1986: 27). It should never be confused with any merely academic exercise. Its causes are collective; its impact is also collective. Otherwise, it would not *stricto sensu* be an instance of problematization at all. In classical Athens, the trouble with the boy beloved arose among an aristocratic elite whose customary occupation of virtually all high political and all high religious offices even in a formally democratic polity was coming under the increasing pressure of what Plato disparagingly called "sophists" and the ambitious young citizen men whom they undertook to train in the arts of political persuasion. The trouble with the boy beloved was that he was in danger of becoming an aristocrat without any proper ethical portfolio, incapable of the self-governance that the city-state demanded as a prerequisite of the governance of others. The trouble with him is that he might just allow the upstarts to have their way. The troubles were not the same for the citizens of the Hellenistic and Roman empires, in which the potential for tyranny weighed more heavily on the consciences of the elite and the *noblesse de robe* alike. The Stoic cultivation of dispassion and trust in Providence would emerge as a response in both cases. The erosion of aristocratic hegemony in the later Roman empire brought ethical visions and revisions of its own. The result, though the philosophers could not have anticipated it, was early Christianity's radical rejection not merely of pederasty but of pagan *sôfrosunê* and the equally radical valorization of the anerotic life as among the constituents of the pinnacle of human aspiration.

We thus move from the second to the third volumes of *The History of Sexuality* – the latter aptly titled *The Care of the Self*. That volume preserves the fourfold analytical framework of its predecessor. It continues to investigate the ethics of pleasure-taking long before sexuality appeared on the ethico-epistemic horizon. Historically, it extends from the second to the third centuries CE, from Artemidorus' treatise on the interpretation of dreams to Plutarch and the pseudo-Lucian. It does not arrive at early Christianity – the period at issue in a fourth volume of the *History* on which Foucault was still working at the time of his death and only fragments of which have been or are likely ever to be in print. It has had its critics, historians of philosophy among them. But then, Foucault was never a historian of philosophy – or of anything else – of any conventional, academically consecrated sort. He was a genealogist, and as a genealogist confined himself to selecting from the intellectually and practically more diverse currents of distinct historical periods (whose circumscription he was happy to leave to the judgment of academic historians) those he deemed most important to the descent of the subject of desire. The third volume of the *History* is no doubt highly selective in its sources. It aspires even so to chart the philosophical course that led – without ever altogether abandoning its original channels – from the valorization to the erotics of the beautiful boy to the elevation of the woman not merely as his erotic equal in the inspiration of virtue but also as the only person in relation to whom pleasures and their proper fruition might be truly reciprocal (1986: 203–225). The matrimonial relationship to which the Christian fathers will come to confine the only permissible engagement in erotic pleasure is not yet the philosophical order of the day. It is nevertheless on the horizon. Looming with it, perhaps over it, is the ever more salient, ever more dominant suspicion that indulgence in carnal pleasures and responsible care of the self are in fact at odds (1986: 123).

Foucault's last three years of lectures at the Collège are crucial supplements to the volumes of *The History of Sexuality* – the incomplete volume included. Likely because they are supplements, they dispense with the analytical fourfold – of genealogical design and purpose – that informs those volumes (and let me express my gratitude here to Paul Rabinow and Anthony Stavrianakis for bringing me to this point – or rather, speculation). The triangulation of the governance of the self, the governance of others, and parrhesia dominates those lectures. So, too, does a certain isoscelean bias. Foucault frequently visits the most expansive of the structural provocations of ethical transformation in *The Hermeneutics of the Subject.* He does not neglect them in the two volumes of *The Governance of the Self and Others.* The care of the self and its wide and historically variable techniques are everywhere in the lectures. In *The Hermeneutics of the Subject*, however, the angle formed at the intersection between self-governance and parrhesia expands and the relation of both to the governance of others contracts (2005: 192); "theorized" as the relation between "the practice of the subject" and "veridiction" (2005: 229; see Rabinow et al. 2011b), it reaches to encompass and to educe the overarching thematics of the nexuses at which ancient modes – early Christian modes here included – link the care of the self to the knowledge of the self.

The lectures that constitute *The Hermeneutics of the Subject* are wide-ranging. They oscillate back and forth from the fourth century BCE to the fourth century CE. Unsurprisingly, they are more a thinking through of the shifts and turns of self-care and self-knowledge than a definitive synopsis of them (see Gros 2005: 518). I cannot do them justice here. Instead, I can only note three of their analytical leitmotifs. The first of these is the establishment of the indissoluble ancient link between the imperative to know oneself and the *epimelia heautou*, the care of the self as such. The second is the establishment of the ethical centrality of what Foucault insists is not a concept but rather the "practical schema" of "conversion" to and of the self (2005: 209–223). Just this practical schema is the genealogical matrix that enables Foucault to trace the descent but also the differences between the hermeneutics of self from Plato and the Platonists, through the Stoics and Epicureans, to the Christian fathers. For Plato, conversion was a reversion, an *epistrefê* or return to the self, to its elemental past, to its original dwelling in Being and so to its fundamental reality; it was an epistemological process and epistemological terminus (2005: 210). For the Stoics, in contrast, it was an exercise that aimed at a "fleeing of the self" (2005: 211), and above all a flight from the passions that chained the self to its desires, its pleasures, but also its hopes and dreams, and so from its past, its present, and its future. The Stoic *praemeditatio malorum*, which in Foucault's opinion could never even have been countenanced by the Greeks, was thus part and parcel of its ethical liberation. For the Christians, yet again in contrast, it was and long remained (and in some Christian quarters still remains) a renunciation of the self, a death and rebirth into "a different self" that "no longer has anything to do with an earlier self in its being, its mode of being, in its habits or its êthos" (2005: 211). But conversion it was, in every case. Finally, the lectures depart from and preserve in their entirety a divide between an ancient tradition of ethics that consistently conceived of the knowledge of Being as having its crux in the fusion of self-knowledge and the care of the self and a modern philosophical and tradition that – from its "Cartesian moment" forward – came to conceive of the knowledge of Being as grounded solely "in knowledge (*connaissance*) and knowledge alone" (2005: 17). The arguments of *The History of Madness*, *The Birth of the Clinic*, *Discipline and Punish*, and the first volume of *The History of Sexuality* inform Foucault's judgment of the depth – if not an entirely unbridgeable depth – of that divide. The arguments of the two installments of Foucault's lectures at the Collège reaffirm that judgment, if in somewhat different terms.

Parrhesia and the Governance of Others

In the two volumes of *The Government of the Self and Others*, an isoscelean bias of the Foucauldian triangle is once again evident, but its angle is not the same. The care of the self remains salient, but Foucault's concerns lead to a broadening of the angle formed by the intersection of parrhesia and the governance of others – but at length also to the weakening of the bond that ties the two vectors of the intersection together. Though already identified in the lectures that preceded them, the ancient philosopher emerges full-fledged in the last two years of lectures as the parrhesiast par excellence. He seeks to speak the truth of himself to himself, but his ultimate work as parrhesiast has a collective and a specifically political target: those who rule. The parrhesiast thus comes to light in Foucault's final lectures as the literal *locus classicus* of the figure who speaks truth to power.

In Greek – ancient and modern – parrhesia denotes frankness, candor, but not necessarily the speaking of the truth. Foucault's parrhesiast, however, is presumptively a truth-teller and – again adding something to ancient semantics – he speaks the truth not of being as such, nor of art or craft, nor of destiny, but instead of *êthos* (2009: 25). He thus stands in contrast to the sage, the technical instructor, and the prophet (2009: 17). That he stands in contrast to the latter must account in part for Foucault's leaving aside the longstanding interest in parrhesia among Christologists – though in the end, it is difficult to view the Christ merely as a visionary of things to come. In any event, the early doctors of Christian ethics stand in his place.

Before the doctors and even before their pagan predecessors, however, Foucault attends – and at startling length – to Euripides' *Ion*. The *Ion* is not regarded as one of Euripides' most distinguished achievements, but it is the *locus classicus* of parrhesia – the term itself. English translators of the play largely agree – and I agree with them – that parrhesia in that locus and in its multiple occurrences denotes freedom of speech. Foucault, however, reads the play as an apologia for Athenian democracy or, more precisely, for a democracy in which the frank speaking of the truth and nothing but the truth prevails over flattery, and legitimate counsel and persuasion over manipulative demagoguery. He concludes that parrhesia in its original, its Euripidean, expression is thus a distinctly governmental practice, a practice integral to the justification of the democratic *hegemôn* and democracy alike. It is the marker, in short, of a genuinely ethical democracy. It is also the source of two problems, both of which will occupy the greatest of the philosophical minds shortly to come – and Foucault's mind in train. The first and most fundamental of these is the question of the circumstances in which parrhesia might indeed prevail over flattery, enlightened hegemony over dark despotism. The second is the correlative question of whether such circumstances must include what Foucault characterizes as the "ethical differentiation" of those fit to be parrhesiasts from those fit only to benefit from their guidance.

As most do, Foucault reads Plato as arguing forcibly for the latter, not the former, alternative. He reads him as a skeptic of democracy. It is nevertheless worth pausing at Foucault's interrogation of Plato's development of his argument for two reasons. First, the interrogation results in a compelling elaboration of one strand of the usual story. Addressing *The Seventh Letter*, Foucault highlights Plato's (or "Plato's": the authenticity of the letter is somewhat in doubt) admission that his acceptance of the tyrant Dionysius II's invitation to come to Sicily to counsel him rested importantly in his not wanting merely to be the voice of *logos*, of reason, but instead to show that he was "capable of participation, of putting his hand to the *ergon*" (2008: 261; translations from the French here and *infra* are my own). Just what *ergon* – task or work – is at issue preoccupies Foucault for another 60 pages of text. As we might expect, his initial conclusion is that philosophical work is the work of parrhesia (2008: 201–211). Hence, "the test by which philosophy will manifest itself is not logos itself ... [but] the fact that it addresses itself, that it can address itself, that it has the courage to address itself to whoever exercises power" (2008: 210). In just what such an address consists is still unclear. Not as much explicating *The Seventh Letter* as putting it to his own use, Foucault concludes that philosophical rationality is not political rationality (2008: 266). It is not "the rationalization of," the apology for, any particular course or systematization of political action (2008: 198). The reality and the work of philosophy is instead the sustained practice of "the articulation of the *problem* of the government of the self and of the government of others" (2008: 236).

Philosophical practice so conceived has its preconditions. Some are circumstantial – among them, that the philosopher cannot realize himself (or herself) as parrhesiast if, in doing so, he or she literally risks his or her life. Parrhesia is risky, but it demands that risk have its limits. Other preconditions are inherent. *The Seventh Letter* identifies to Foucault's mind the most fundamental of them. The *pragmata*, the "affairs" of philosophy, are not at base contemplative, but rather have the character of "a long and painful labor," an everyday practice "at the interior of which the subject should show himself to be *eumathês* (capable of learning), *mnêmôn* (capable of remembering), *logizesthai dunatos* (capable of reasoning). Foucault educes several consequences from this characterization. Posing the question of the import that such a practice might have, he infers that it is "quite simply the subject himself":

> It is in the relation to self, in the work of the self on itself, in the labor upon oneself, in this mode of activity of the self on itself that the reality of philosophy will in effect be manifested and attested. Philosophy encounters its reality in the practice of philosophy, understood as the ensemble of practices by which the subject has relation to himself, elaborates himself, labors on himself. The labor of the self on itself – that is the reality of philosophy. (2008: 224)

Here precisely, the bond between the philosophical ethics of parrhesia and the governance of others comes apart.

It further comes apart in his genealogical leap forward to modernity just more than midway through the last year of his lectures. In modernity, he says, the case is very different. Our parrhesiastic masters are now "the doctor, the psychiatrist, the psychologist, the psychoanalyst" (2009: 7). From the author of *The History of Madness*, the claim sounds ironic – though an irony more tragic than comic. It echoes Foucault's seeming conviction that the philosophical life as the parrhesiastic life is dead, perhaps long dead. Yet it would seem that in Foucault's judgment the parrhesiastic life itself is not entirely dead. Surveying the modern landscape for heirs to the most scandalous of the parrhesiastic currents of the philosophical tradition, that of the Cynics, Foucault finds more than one plausible representative. One is the political militant and the political revolutionary (2009: 169–171). Another is the modern artist (2009: 172–173).

The modern artist: here, surely, the link between parrhesia and the governance of others comes entirely undone. We do not – whether in the West or elsewhere – live under the governance nor within the governmentality of artist-kings. Beyond this, for all its breadth and depth, Foucault's genealogy of parrhesia leaves entirely unresolved the issue of the difference between candor and the speaking of what is indeed the truth.

Coda: A Genealogy of the Ethics of the Future

As an anthropologist of ethics, I have primarily been interested in expanding and supplementing Foucault's analytical apparatus of the ethical domain – an apparatus that I think singularly intellectually productive – in order to render it of a more comprehensive anthropological reach. As someone – anthropologist and inescapably modern – who conceives of anthropology at its best as a secular wisdom literature, I cannot overlook Foucault's considered assertion that a genealogically designed ontology of us is at the core of a modern ethos whose realization and whose *ergon* rest with bringing to light how we might be different subjects from the subjects that we currently find ourselves being and presumptively restricted or consigned to being. Though not in a genealogical mode, the American tradition of cultural anthropology has shared Foucault's critical ambitions from its Boasian outset. The question that remains – and I pose it precisely as a question – is what sort of *êthos* such an ambition requires. The West – whatever it is – knows three prevailing ethical philosophies (and I am grateful to Didier Fassin for enabling me to express them so concisely): an ethics of good consequences; an ethics of duty and principle; and an ethics of virtue, which might be conceived either as an ethics of good consequences (the classical resolution) or as an ethics of obedience to principle (the Kantian and liberal resolutions), or as an ethics of both. Foucault's formulation of his own secular wisdom does not, I think, cleave to one over another of these alternatives. It is rather a melding of all of them, but a melding that has a particular twist. Very much at odds with the *longue durée* of the tradition of the philosophy of ethics that precedes and is contemporary with him, but equally at odds with Nietzsche's revolutionary ethics of the transvaluation of all values and the quasi-ethics of the will to power, the modern philosophical ethics that Foucault proposes in "What is Enlightenment?" is neither aprioristic nor a throwing off of the past. It has its ground rather in an ethos whose activity is devoted to the assessment of the historical limits and the emergent possibilities of living in ways that we have not yet been able to live, of forms of life that we have not yet been able to realize. Foucault's inquiry into the genealogy of the putatively scientific codification of sexuality was in its end – though an abrupt and incomplete end – the prelude to and argument for an intellectual imagining and a practical realization of what as yet had no place in the present that he knew. The anthropologist as writer of wisdom literature may or may not follow him, but at the very least cannot ignore his intellectual call to arms – a call to an ethos dedicated not to the utopian vision of either negative or positive freedom, and neither of those nor even *Sittlichkeit*, but instead a constant monitoring and preparedness to alter as circumstances demand the provisional axioms of any particular moment or period of the pragmatics at once of one's ethical judgments and of one's interventions – politically, in the strict sense of the term, or more broadly political – as a consequence. It's not that everything is up for grabs. Instead, it's that at least some things allow of reconsidering, in light of socially, culturally, and historically specific circumstances, of being. Nothing might come of that reconsideration. Then again, something might – a distinctively modern philosophical way of being in the present world. The ultimate Foucauldian point is that the modern critical ethos cannot presume fully to comprehend the present in which finds itself nor anticipate a future to come. For Foucault, the past of ethics is in fact a *magistra vitae*, a teacher of life, and what it teaches is that ethics has a history and is not the same in its course from the past to the present, even within the presumptive boundaries of the Western tradition. For the anthropologist of ethics, this is merely a point of departure. For the anthropologist who conceives of the best of anthropology as Wisdom Literature, it is of the essence. It is an ethical telos. A project, of definitive resolution, of definition? No.

REFERENCES

Bourdieu, Pierre (1977) *Outline of a Theory of Practice*, trans. Richard Nice. Cambridge: Cambridge University Press.

Cohen, David (1991) *Law, Sexuality and Society in Ancient Greece: The Enforcement of Morals in Classical Athens*. Cambridge: Cambridge University Press.

de Certeau, Michel (1984) *The Practice of Everyday Life*, trans. Stephen Rendall. Berkeley: University of California Press.

Dover, Kenneth J. (1974) *Greek Popular Morality in the Time of Plato and Aristotle*. Berkeley: University of California Press.

Dover, Kenneth J. (1978) *Greek Homosexuality*. New York: Vintage.

Faubion, James D. (1999) Introduction. In *The Essential Works of Michel Foucault*, vol. 2: *Aesthetics, Method, Epistemology*, ed. James D. Faubion. New York: New Press, pp. xiii–xliv.

Faubion, James D. (2001) Toward an Anthropology of Ethics: Foucault and the Pedagogies of Autopoiesis. *Representations* 74: 83–104.

Faubion, James D. (2011) *An Anthropology of Ethics*. Cambridge: Cambridge University Press.

Foucault, Michel (1977) *Discipline and Punish: The Birth of the Prison*, trans. Alan Sheridan. New York: Vintage.

Foucault, Michel (1978) *The History of Sexuality*, vol. 1: *An Introduction*, trans. Robert Hurley. New York: Pantheon.

Foucault, Michel (1985) *The History of Sexuality*, vol. 2: *The Use of Pleasure*, trans. Robert Hurley. New York: Pantheon.

Foucault, Michel (1986) *The History of Sexuality*, vol. 3: *The Care of the Self*, trans. Robert Hurley. New York: Pantheon.

Foucault, Michel (1997a) The Ethics of the Concern of the Self as a Practice of Freedom. In *The Essential Works of Michel Foucault, 1954–1984*, vol. 1: *Ethics: Subjectivity and Truth*, ed. Paul Rabinow, trans. Robert Hurley et al. New York: New Press, pp. 281–302.

Foucault, Michel (1997b) On the Genealogy of Ethics: An Overview of a Work in Progress. In *The Essential Works of Michel Foucault, 1954–1984*, vol. 1: *Ethics: Subjectivity and Truth*, ed. Paul Rabinow, trans. Robert Hurley et al. New York: New Press, pp. 253–280.

Foucault, Michel (1997c) Self-Writing. In *The Essential Works of Michel Foucault, 1954–1984*, vol. 1: *Ethics: Subjectivity and Truth*, ed. Paul Rabinow, trans. Robert Hurley et al. New York: New Press, pp. 207–222.

Foucault, Michel (1997d) Technologies of the Self. In *The Essential Works of Michel Foucault, 1954–1984*, vol. 1: *Ethics: Subjectivity and Truth*, ed. Paul Rabinow, trans. Robert Hurley et al. New York: New Press, pp. 223–252.

Foucault, Michel (1997e) What is Enlightenment? In *The Essential Works of Michel Foucault, 1954–1984*, vol. 1: *Ethics: Subjectivity and Truth*, ed. Paul Rabinow, trans. Robert Hurley et al. New York: New Press, pp. 303–319.

Foucault, Michel (1999a) Foucault. In *The Essential Works of Michel Foucault, 1954–1984*, vol. 2: *Aesthetics, Method, Epistemology*, ed. James D. Faubion. New York: New Press, pp. 459–464.

Foucault, Michel (1999b) Nietzsche, Genealogy, History. In *The Essential Works of Michel Foucault, 1954–1984*, vol. 2: *Aesthetics, Method, Epistemology*, ed. James D. Faubion. New York: New Press, pp. 369–392.

Foucault, Michel (2000) Governmentality. In *The Essential Works of Michel Foucault, 1954–1984*, vol. 3: *Power*, ed. James D. Faubion. New York: New Press, pp. 32–50.

Foucault, Michel (2005) *The Hermeneutics of the Subject*, trans. Graham Burchell. New York: Palgrave Macmillan.

Foucault, Michel (2008) *Le gouvernement de soi et des autres*. Paris: Seuil/Gallimard.

Foucault, Michel (2009) *Le courage de la vérité: le gouvernement de soi et des autres II*. Paris: Seuil/Gallimard.

Gros, Frédéric (2002) Sujet moral et soi éthique chez Foucault. *Archives de Philosophie* 65(2): 229–237.

Gros, Frédéric (2005) Course Context. In *Michel Foucault, The Hermeneutics of the Subject*, ed. Frédéric Gros. New York: Palgrave Macmillan, pp. 507–550.

Hegel, G. W. F. (1952) *The Philosophy of Right*, trans. T. M. Knox. Chicago: Encyclopaedia Britannica.

Huffer, Lynne (2010) *Mad for Foucault: Rethinking the Foundations of Queer Theory*. Durham, NC: Duke University Press.

Humphrey, Caroline (1997) Exemplars and Rules: Aspects of the Discourse of Morality in Mongolia. In Signe Howell (ed.), *The Ethnography of Moralities*. London: Routledge, pp. 25–48.

Kant, Immanuel (2002) *Critique of Practical Reason*, trans. Werner S. Pluhar. Indianapolis: Hackett.

Marrou, Henri (1956) *A History of Education in Antiquity*, trans. George Lamb. New York: Sheed & Ward.

Nietzsche, Friedrich (1954) *The Portable Nietzsche*, trans. Walter Kauffmann. New York: Viking.

Nietzsche, Friedrich (1956) *The Birth of Tragedy and the Genealogy of Morals*, trans. Francis Golffing. Garden City, NY: Doubleday Anchor.

Plato (1961) Symposium. In *Plato: The Collected Dialogues*, ed. Edith Hamilton and Huntington Cairns; trans. Michael Joyce. Princeton: Princeton University Press.

Pohlenz, Max (1966) *Freedom in Greek Life and Thought. The History of an Ideal*, trans. Carl Lofmark. New York: Humanities Press.

Rabinow, Paul (1997) Introduction: The History of Systems of Thought. In *The Essential Works of Michel Foucault*, vol. 1: *Ethics: Subjectivity and Truth*, ed. Paul Rabinow. New York: New Press, pp. xi–xlii.

Rabinow, Paul, Bennett, Gaymon, and Stavrianakis, Anthony (2011a) Anthropological Research on the Contemporary: Studio 1. At http://anthropos-lab.net/studio/episode/01, accessed Feb. 14, 2012.

Rabinow, Paul, Bennett, Gaymon, and Stavrianakis, Anthony (2011b) Anthropological Research on the Contemporary. Bios Technika: Concepts. At http://bios-technika.net/concepts.php#veridiction, accessed Feb. 14, 2012.

Tyler, Stephen (1998) Them Others – Voices without Mirrors. *Paideuma* 44: 31–50.

Weber, Max (1958a) *The Protestant Ethic and the Spirit of Capitalism*, trans. Talcott Parsons. Oxford: Oxford University Press.

Weber, Max (1958b) *The Religion of India: The Sociology of Hinduism and Buddhism*, ed. and trans. Hans Gerth and Don Martindale. New York: Free Press.

Xenophon (1923) *Memorabilia, Oeconomicus, Symposium, Apology*, trans. E. C. Merchant and O. J. Todd. Cambridge, MA: Harvard University Press.

CHAPTER 5 Relativism and Universalism

Richard A. Shweder

As the moral philosopher David Wong has noted: "The standard characterizations of [moral] relativism make it an easy target and seldom reveal what really motivates people who are attracted to it. Introductory textbooks in ethics frequently portray the view as an extreme variety of subjectivism (or conventionalism) in which anything goes – a person's (or group's) accepting that something is right makes it right for that person (or group)" (2006: xi). This variety of moral relativism pictures human subjectivity in terms of human reactions of both acceptance (feelings of approbation) and rejection (feelings of opprobrium). Its central principle states that approving of some act or customary practice makes it right (good, virtuous, moral) and disapproving of the very same act or customary practice makes it wrong (bad, vicious, immoral); and this is so for any conceivable act or customary practice whether it is eating pork, terminating a pregnancy, drinking alcohol, spanking a child, banning a book, marrying a member of your own sex, marrying more than one member of the opposite sex, walking bare-breasted on a public beach, covering yourself with a burka[1] in the public square, conducting a brith,[2] surgically reshaping the genitals of all the children in one's family regardless of their gender, assisting someone in committing suicide, or immolating oneself on the funeral pyre of one's husband. Writing more or less in this vein, the anthropologist Ruth Benedict once defined morality as "a convenient term for socially approved habits" (1934: 73).

It is not too surprising that this variety of moral relativism is viewed as extreme by many moral philosophers, if for no other reason than that moral relativism of this variety rejects the most basic principle of moral reasoning presupposed by each of the parties in any genuine moral dispute, namely the presupposition that if I am right in judging a particular course of action to be wrong, bad, vicious, or immoral then you cannot be equally right in thinking it right, good, virtuous, or moral (see, for example, Rashdall 1914; also Cook 1999). One implication of moral relativism so portrayed is

A Companion to Moral Anthropology, First Edition. Edited by Didier Fassin.

that the very same act or customary practice becomes right *and* wrong, good *and* bad, virtuous *and* vicious, moral *and* immoral, to the very extent that two people (or groups) *disagree* about whether it is right or wrong, good or bad, virtuous or vicious, moral or immoral. This is because the extreme variety of moral relativism (as subjectivism or conventionalism) asserts that in fact there is nothing objective (impersonal, impartial) to be right or wrong about (no such thing as "natural" or "inalienable" rights, for example[3]) when one person (or group) calls an action or custom or law right and another person (or group) calls it wrong. Instead, according to moral relativism so portrayed, when one person (or group) says such-and-such is right (good, virtuous, moral) and another person (or group) says the opposite they are merely expressing their feelings (for example, of pleasure or displeasure) or registering a difference in subjective preferences (desires, likes), in personal opinions, habits, or intuitions or in past collective choices as explicitly expressed through legal enactments or implicitly made manifest in inherited traditions and local social norms.

According to moral relativism so portrayed those feelings, preferences, tastes, opinions, habits, intuitions, enactments, traditions, and social norms are the only moral standards in town. They are constitutive of what is right and wrong. But their definitions of right and wrong are also subject-relative. Thus each moral standard applies only to the person (or group) in question and has no universal validity. Germany has its own moral standards concerning the separation of church and state in public schools and they are different from the standards in the United States; hence according to moral relativism (so portrayed) teaching religion in public schools is right in Germany and wrong in the United States and there is nothing more to be said. Saudi Arabia has its own moral standards concerning sex differences and they are different from the standards in the United States; hence according to moral relativism (so portrayed) a ban on issuing driver's licenses to women is right in Saudi Arabia and wrong in the United States and there is nothing more to be said. If the extreme doctrine of moral relativism as subjectivism or conventionalism is true, then genuine moral disputes can never even arise let alone be resolved through the intelligent use of evidence and reason.

This variety of relativism has become a frequent target in ethics textbooks largely because moral philosophy is about the proper use of the human intellect to resolve genuine moral disputes and because moral relativism (so portrayed) denies that it is possible to ever have a genuine moral dispute in moral philosophy, in public policy arenas, in courtrooms, in everyday life, or anywhere else. "It is all subjective and political, stupid!" is the eventual message of this variety of moral relativism. That message strikes many moral philosophers as the ultimate expression of irrationalism.

Moral Universalism: The Standard Characterization

A point similar to the one made by David Wong might be made about standard characterizations of universalism, where moral universalism is sometimes portrayed in anthropological texts as an extreme variety of objectivism (or absolutism) in which only one thing goes. The easy target in that case is the view that there exists a single true and detailed moral charter for the organization of the ideal universal civilization. That detailed moral charter is a uniformly applicable set of authoritative prescriptions for kinship, marriage, parent–child relations, sex roles, politics, economics, religion, and even cuisine which can and should be used as the global standard for judging the validity of diverse ways of life and ranking them in terms of their moral worth (for example, on a developmental scale from savage to civilized or backward to advanced).

Moral universalism, so characterized, is a doctrine postulating the objective reality of concrete touchstones for judging what is right and wrong. Its posited moral charter is concrete in the sense that it sets forth clear and determinate instructions, principles, or commands for the actual behavior of individuals and members of groups (do and don'ts such as "thou shall not bow down before carved images," or "thou shall never use physical punishment to discipline a child," or "thou shall always permit widows to remarry if they want to, but never require them to do so"). Those concrete touchstones of the moral charter are then said to be objective in the sense that (according to the doctrine) their requirements (obligations, duties, rights, prohibitions) are, and always have been, binding on all persons (or groups) without exception, and are universally obligatory regardless of a person's or people's subjective or conventional acceptances, actual cultural practices, or historical circumstances.

At least since the early twentieth century most (although certainly not all) anthropologists have rejected extreme versions of moral universalism. Many anthropologists associate moral universalism with either religious missionary efforts or with secular colonial interventions (military occupation and/or direct or indirect political rule) justified on the basis of cultural superiority, the "white man's burden" and "the civilizing project." The suspicion was also in full evidence in 1947 when the Executive Board of the American Anthropological Association (whose membership included the avowed cultural relativist Melville Herskovits) refused to endorse the United Nations Declaration on the Rights of Man on the ground that it was an ethnocentric document. The members of the Executive Board asked: "How can the proposed Declaration be applicable to all human beings, and not be a statement of rights conceived only in terms of the values prevalent only in the countries of Western Europe and America?" (AAA Executive Board 1947; see also Engle 2002).

Indeed that distrust was so widespread and deep that one suspects if extreme versions of moral relativism have ever appealed to cultural anthropologists it is largely because the doctrine initially seems to offer an effective counter to this or that despised version of moral universalism (or absolutism). Moral relativism as conventionalism or subjectivism does provide one way to oppose on philosophical grounds the imperial and globetrotting project of using an imagined one true moral charter to draw a moral map of the peoples and cultures of the world. This is frequently a map according to which the customary practices of the peoples and cultures studied by anthropologists (in Africa and Asia, for example) were, and still are, designated as morally backward or even barbaric (for example, with respect to their customary treatment of women and children), and as ripe for moral uplift by activists and interventionists who view themselves as altruistic, compassionate, righteous reformers of morally defective ways of life.

The counter offered by extreme versions of moral relativism runs as follows: If, for each and every person or group, the mere belief or acceptance that something is right (or good) is all that it takes to make it right (or good) then the very idea of the one true (objective and absolute) morality is itself really nothing other than a projection of the subjective preferences (likes and dislikes made manifest in habits and customs) of particular agents. The rub of course is that some of those proselytizing universalizers may also have the wealth, influence, or power to successfully project or spread their subjective preferences widely, even among local elites in other societies.

It should be acknowledged, however, that since the advent of global feminism and the international human rights movement, the scene within the discipline of anthropology has become more complex. Some anthropologists have even begun to look more favorably on doctrines of moral universalism, especially versions of the doctrine formulated in the language of "natural rights" or as part of a moral critique of patriarchy aimed at liberating women (and children) and cleansing the world of so-called oppressive or harmful cultural practices: bride-price, polygamy, female genital surgery, child labor, arranged marriage, the sexual division of labor in the family, and "veiling" might be examples of customs disfavored by contemporary versions of moral universalism within the profession of cultural anthropology. Nevertheless that historical distrust evidenced by the 1947 AAA Executive Board Statement is not just a thing of the past. A similar view was forcefully expressed in 1995 by Roy D'Andrade in his critical response to various re-emergent moral universalisms in anthropology when he remarked:

> Finally, the current moral model [in the discipline of anthropology] is ethnocentric. It is strong for equality (the escape from inequality) and freedom (the release from oppression). In my opinion these are not bad values but they are very American. These are not the predominant values of modern Japan, India, China, the Middle East or Southeast Asia, but they are the predominant values in the United States and much of Europe. It is ironic that these moralists should be so colonialist in their assumptions about what is evil. (D'Andrade 1995: 408; see also Menon and Shweder 1998; Menon 2003)

Fortunately, those extreme characterizations of moral relativism and moral universalism are not the end of the story. Many so-called moral relativists in anthropology will recoil at extreme characterizations of their doctrine. They will recoil because in their own minds their primary aim is not to subvert the entire process of genuine moral debate by denying the existence of moral truths. By their lights their primary aims are to caution against haste (rapid, habitual, affect-laden, or spontaneous information-processing) and parochialism (assimilating all new experiences to readily available local frames of reference) and to lend credence to the general caution that one should be slow to make moral judgments about the customary practices of little-known others.

Many who embrace moral universalism in anthropology will recoil at extreme characterizations of their doctrine as well. They will recoil because in their own minds the primary aim of their objectivism (and invocation of moral absolutes) is not to congratulate themselves that their own way of life is the best or only way to live a moral life but rather to provide insiders and outsiders, minority groups and majority groups (in other words everyone), with a common frame of reference for engaging in genuine moral debates and for judging what is right and what is wrong in one's own society, and in other societies as well.

In the remainder of this essay I try to honor the aims of both camps by sketching a conception of relativism as "universalism without the uniformity." This is an approach to the anthropological study of morality inspired by Michel de Montaigne (and many others) in which one tries to credibly advance one particular type of answer to the central question posed by the global diversity of concrete moral judgments. That central question, of course, is why the many peoples of the world disagree with each other so much in their concrete moral judgments and why those judgments don't possess the universality that is characteristic of the idea of truth.[4]

Descriptive Work in Moral Anthropology: A Summary of Findings and Limits

Here it may be useful in clarifying the doctrines of moral relativism and moral universalism to mention a few of the more robust findings from descriptive work in anthropology on the human experience of moral value. Descriptive fieldwork on a worldwide scale (including reports found in the writings of Montaigne and other early ethnographers) has of course demonstrated that moral judgments are ubiquitous in human groups. A moral judgment is the expressed or (more typically) implied judgment that person P *ought to* do X under such-and-such circumstances, where the doing of X under those circumstances is thought to be the right thing to do because it is presumed to be productive of some objective good. When it comes to the human perception of value, moral judgments are experienced as though they are judgments about the true nature of some posited objective moral charter (see, for example, Shweder 1982; Shweder et al. 1987; Shweder with Much 1991; Haidt et al. 1993; Beldo 2011).

This truth-seeking (or "cognitive") feature of everyday moral judgments has been noted by the philosopher Arthur Lovejoy. He points out that when someone says "It is wrong to oppress the helpless" or "The conduct of Adolph Hitler was wicked," they "do not in fact conceive of themselves merely to be reporting on the state of their own emotions" and mean to be saying something more than "I am very unpleasantly affected when I think of it" (Lovejoy 1961: 253, 255). On a worldwide scale it appears that when folk make a moral judgment (for example, "Male circumcision is an outrage," "Abortion is evil") they themselves believe there are matters of objective fact to which their judgment refers and that they are making a truthful claim about some impersonal or independently existing domain of moral reality.

Lovejoy's observation is consistent with several classic ethnographically based research findings on moral norms and moral reasoning, including the work of Malinowski (1926), Read (1955), Fortes (1987 [1959]), Ladd (2004 [1957]), and Firth (2011[1951]). Raymond Firth's pithy remark about the people of Tikopia is typical of these ethnographers' accounts of the objectivism characteristic of local understandings of the moral charter whether in New Guinea, West Africa, Melanesia, or among Native American populations in the USA: "The spirits, just as men, respond to a norm of conduct of an external character. The moral law exists in the absolute, independent of the Gods" (quoted in Nadel 1969: 270–271).

That observation is not meant to gainsay the fact that moral judgments (that's good, that's wrong, that's sinful) around the world are also felt (see, for example, Rozin et al. 1999). They are often experienced as aesthetic and emotional reactions (that's ugly, that's odious, that disgusts me, "I am very unpleasantly affected when I think of it") and not solely as objective representations of moral truths. Indeed, moral judgments are motivators of action in significant measure because they are affect-laden and produce in people powerful feelings of arousal, distress, pollution, repugnance, guilt, indignation, pride, or shame. Characteristically, however, the moral judgments of the peoples of the world studied by anthropologists are truth-seeking judgments about some moral charter assumed to be "of an external character."

At the same time, fieldwork by anthropologists has also documented that as a matter of fact many concrete moral judgments about actions and customs do not seem to spontaneously converge across autonomous or even semi-autonomous cultural groups.[5] Actions and cultural practices that are a source of moral approbation in one community (for example, polygamy or female genital surgeries) are frequently the source of moral opprobrium in another, and moral disagreements can persist over generations, if not centuries. Indeed, the history of moral anthropology as an empirical undertaking is in some significant measure the history of the discovery of astonishing cultural variations in human judgments about the proper moral charter for an ideal way of life.

Nevertheless, the import of ethnographic findings of variability in concrete moral judgments for the doctrine of moral relativism is far from obvious. In and of itself the mere existence of diversity in moral judgments across (and within) cultural groups is not necessarily incompatible with the normative doctrine of moral universalism. From a strictly descriptive point of view Clifford Geertz (2000: 44) may have been on firm ground when he remarked that the encounter with anthropological evidence on other societies has *seemed* like "a massive argument against absolutism in thought, morals and esthetic judgment" and that the message anthropologists *have been thought to have* is this one: "that, as they see things differently and do them otherwise in Alaska or the D'Entrecastreaux, our confidence in our own seeings and doings and our resolve to bring others around to sharing them are rather poorly based" (44). Nevertheless, from a strictly normative point of view both the argument and the message are far from compelling and are themselves rather poorly based. This is because according to the doctrine of moral universalism diversity in moral opinions is not necessarily a surprise and any failure of either individuals or groups to actually recognize the one true morality (or to abide by the moral charter once its requirements have been understood) is simply viewed as an index of the lower (or arrested) stage of moral development of that individual or group.

Among the most influential moral development stage theories in the history of social science research are those proposed by Leonard T. Hobhouse in his book *Morals in Evolution: A Study in Comparative Ethics* (1915) and by Lawrence Kohlberg in his collection of essays *The Philosophy of Moral Development: Moral Stages and the Idea of Justice* (1981). Both Hobhouse and Kohlberg subscribed to a doctrine of moral universalism. Both believed that liberal enlightenment thinking had come closest to discovering the terms of the one true moral charter. Both viewed tribalism (in-group favoritism) and hierarchy (which they viewed as incompatible with autonomy) as lower forms of social organization. Both argued that the moral consciousness of human beings had not only evolved over the course of cultural history but should be encouraged to continue to develop in what they viewed as the progressive liberated and liberal direction. Kohlberg went so far with his universalism as to suggest that the history of the cultures of the world (and the history of childhood in all societies) is (and ideally ought to be) a history of the discovery of the moral principles underlying the American Revolution, as expressed in the Bill of Rights of the Constitution of the United States (also see Rawls 1971; Turiel 2008).

Echoes of this liberal version of the doctrine of moral universalism can be readily found in contemporary public policy forums and throughout the academy in North America and Europe. Consider, for example, this resonant formulation by the former United States president George W. Bush, which he voiced in his first State of the Union Address to Congress after the terrorist attacks of September 11, 2001:

> America will lead by defending liberty and justice because they are right and true and unchanging for all people everywhere. No nation owns these aspirations and no nation is exempt from them. We have no intention of imposing our culture, but America will always stand firm for the non-negotiable demands of human dignity, the rule of law, limits on the power of the state, respect for women, private property, free speech, equal justice and religious tolerance. (January 29, 2002)

Those were weighty and portentous words expressing the foreign policy doctrine that American wealth and power should be used to make the world a better place by upholding what many American activists and interventionists (both on the Left and on the Right) view as an incontestable universal framework for promoting moral development and social progress on a global scale.

Thus the anthropological documentation of cultural variability in moral judgments is not an argument-ending discovery. At best it is just the beginning of a conversation, precisely because when "red state" evangelical Christians condemn gay marriage and "blue state" secular liberals condone it the difference in their judgments might just be a sign of the deficient moral development of one of the parties to the disagreement. Even self-evident moral truths might not be evident to those who live and think at a lower level of moral consciousness. That idea of an uneven or patchy moral development of the peoples of the world (or of the members of different factions within a society) is readily adduced by adherents of the doctrine of moral universalism as a compelling (and even compassionate) ground for supporting global moral education campaigns, cultural reform movements, and even (under special circumstances) forceful interventions into foreign lands.

Edward Westermarck, who is arguably the deepest and most philosophically sophisticated moral relativist (and subjectivist) in the history of anthropology and whose book-length critique of moral universalism titled *Ethical Relativism* (first published in 1932) should be mandatory reading in any curriculum on moral anthropology, describes the core idea of moral universalism as follows:

> objectivity presupposes universality. As truth is one it has to be the same for anyone who knows it, and if[6] morality is a matter of truth and falsity, in the normative sense of the terms, the same must be the case with moral truth. If a certain course of conduct *is* good or bad, right or wrong, it is so universally, and cannot be both good and bad, right and wrong. (Westermarck 1932: 183)

With regard to the doctrine of moral universalism Westermarck in fact concedes that "The universality of truth does not mean, of course, that everybody knows what is true and false. It has constantly been argued against ethical subjectivism that the variety of moral judgments no more justifies the denial of moral objectivity than the diversity in judgments about the course of things disproves the objectivity of truth" (Westermarck 1932: 183).

Back to Montaigne: On Being Slow to Judge Little-Known Others

If one wants to accurately understand the appeal of so-called moral relativism for many of those anthropologists who have in one way or another been attracted to some variety of it, it is not a bad idea to go back to the late sixteenth century, to the famous essay by Michel de Montaigne (1948) titled "Of Cannibals" (or "On the Cannibals"). In that essay Montaigne, who was an early ethnographer of sorts, tried to come to terms with the recently discovered cultural practices of the native peoples of La France Antartique (today known as the Caribs of Brazil). He describes and morally evaluates the beliefs, values, and customs of a people who believed that hosting a captive of war and then killing, roasting, and making a common meal of him, and "sending chunks of his flesh to absent friends" was right and good. That particular practice seemed shocking and repulsive to Portuguese and French moral sensibilities in the sixteenth century, just as many customary practices of peoples in the Southern and Eastern worlds of Africa, Asia, and the Americas south of the border seem barbaric, odious, and detestable to many peoples of the Northern and Western worlds today. Nevertheless, Montaigne dared to offer a critical (and ironical) response to the Portuguese and French opprobrium directed at the so-called cannibals of La France Antartique.

It is noteworthy that early in his essay Montaigne cautions the reader to step back and be reflective about his or her own spontaneous aversive response to stories about Carib practices: "we should beware of clinging to vulgar opinions and judge things by reason's way, not by popular say" (1948: 150). It is also noteworthy that there are many references throughout to the universal virtues and duties readily detectible by any human being open to being informed about the details of the Carib way of life: "their whole ethical science contains only these two articles: resoluteness in war and affection for their wives" (154) – which he also describes as "valor against the enemy and love for their wives" (158). Writing as an ironist, a skeptic, and a detached observer of human behavior, Montaigne was prepared to complicate the European colonial encounter with alien societies. He was not inclined to let the righteous elite moralists of the metropoles of the Western world make the world safe for condescension and for an imperial European rule justified under the banner of cultural superiority. Indeed, by means of various cultural comparisons, he invited his readers to see the dark side of their own way of life. He writes:

> But there never was any opinion so disordered as to excuse treachery, disloyalty, tyranny and cruelty, which are our ordinary vices. So we may well call these people barbarians, in respect to the rules of reason, but not in respect to ourselves, who surpass them in every kind of barbarity. Their warfare is wholly noble and generous, and as excusable and beautiful as this human disease can be; its only basis among them is their rivalry in valor. They are not fighting for the conquest of new lands … they have no wish to enlarge their boundaries. (Montaigne 1948: 156)

Commenting on the customary practice of polygamy by the Carib he remarks favorably on the lack of jealousy among the women of the society and notes: "Being more concerned for their husbands' honor than for anything else, they strive and scheme to have as many companions as they can, since that is a sign of their husbands' valor" (158). And, perhaps most remarkably, he goes on to rebut the anticipated counterclaims (which are still commonplace today) that "all this is done through a simple and servile bondage to usage and through the pressure of the authority of their ancient customs, without reasoning or judgment, and because their minds are so stupid that they cannot take any other course" (158). In other words, for Montaigne the "cannibals" did not lack either agency or virtue, and by his lights their exercise of their agency was quite compatible with the embrace of their cultural tradition. The essay was written between 1578 and 1580!

Somewhat more recently, on the occasion of the 1984 Distinguished Lecture at the American Anthropological Association Meeting, the eminent cultural anthropologist Clifford Geertz delivered an oration titled "Anti Anti-Relativism" in which he featured the following provocative (and often misunderstood) quotation from Montaigne's essay: "Each man calls barbarism whatever is not his own practice … for we have no other criterion of reason than the example and idea of the opinions and customs of the country we live in." Geertz went on to say, "What the relativists, so-called, want us to worry about is provincialism – the danger that our perceptions will be dulled, our intellects constricted, and our sympathies narrowed by the overlearned and overvalued acceptances of our own society" (2000: 45).

But what precisely is that expressed notion of Montaigne's and how should cultural anthropology make use of it to sharpen our perceptions, expand our intellects, and widen our sympathies? Donald Frame's translation of Montaigne's essay renders the key passage this way:

> Now, to return to my subject [namely the question, how should we go about thoughtfully evaluating our intuitive or spontaneous moral judgments about other peoples' customs?], I think there is nothing barbarous and savage in that nation, from what I have been told, except that each man calls barbarism whatever is not his own practice; for it seems we have no other test of truth and reason than the example and pattern of the opinions and customs of the country we live in. *There* [in the country we live in] is always the perfect religion, the perfect government, the perfect and accomplished manners in all things. (Montaigne 1948: 185)

Even more recently Montaigne's essay (and that passage in particular) has been a subject for interpretation by the moral philosopher David Wiggins (2005: n. 15). Wiggins points to the obvious ironical tone in the quoted material. He then persuasively dismisses the interpretation that Montaigne was a relativist of the subjectivist or conventionalist variety. According to Wiggins, the overriding message of "On the Cannibals" is to caution us about a very general human liability. That liability is our unfortunate inclination to rush to judgment about others, especially when confronted with cultural differences that instantly flood and arouse us with unpleasant feelings. Hence, Wiggins avers, we are vulnerable to "mistakes and misapprehensions in findings of barbarity" (2005: 17). There in those particular ironic sentences, he concludes, "Montaigne is only reporting that he has the same difficulty as everyone else in fighting free of parochial misconceptions" (17).

Montaigne's essay not only remains a leading example of an admirable attempt to correct spontaneous misunderstandings when engaging cultural differences. His sixteenth-century critique of parochial misconstruing sets the agenda for all subsequent discussions (including this one) of the scope and limits of moral relativism in cultural anthropology. Toward that end the remainder of this essay seeks to identify a hybrid variety of moral relativism (more accurately described as "moral universalism without the uniformity") that is appealing precisely because it embraces and puts to work that basic principle of all moral reasoning, namely that the very same act or custom cannot be both right (good, virtuous, moral) and wrong (bad, vicious, immoral) at the same time. That basic principle holds true even when the very same act or custom initially or habitually elicits pleasure from one person and disgust from another; that is to say, prior to thoughtful reflection upon the full and true nature of the act in question and before the correction of factual mistakes and/or parochial misapprehensions. And it is that basic principle that assists many thoughtful anthropologists in their own confrontations with cultural differences, because that principle cautions anthropologists to bracket or set aside their own initial or spontaneous reactions of aversion to alien customs, to seek a fuller and more objective understanding of the true nature of the act in question, and to press on, as Michel de Montaigne did, in their search for some universally recognizable moral goods promoted by the unfamiliar customs of little-known others.

Why do the many peoples of the world disagree with each other so much in their concrete moral judgments and why don't those judgments possess the universality that is characteristic of the idea of truth? The challenge for cultural anthropologists who are inspired by Montaigne is to answer that question (1) without suggesting that objective reality is devoid of moral truths; (2) without suggesting that those who disagree with our own judgments of right and wrong are either moral cretins or barbarians who fail to understand the requirements of the one true morality or demonic others who willfully seek to promote vice over virtue; and (3) without assuming in advance that one's own way of life is the only possible flowering of the ideals of an objective moral charter. How might one proceed in meeting that challenge? Allow me to proceed by example.

Moral Judgment in Two Temple Towns

Consider the following illustration of global diversity in concrete moral judgments drawn from my own collaborative research in the Hindu temple town (the so-called "Old Town") of Bhubaneswar in Orissa, India and in the Hyde Park community surrounding the secular temple known as the University of Chicago (see, for example, Shweder et al. 1987, 2003a, 2003b). Reflect on the following four courses of action and rank them in terms of your personal judgment of the seriousness of moral breach or ethical failure in each instance:

1. A poor man went to the hospital after being seriously hurt in an accident. At the hospital they refused to treat him because he could not afford to pay. (The reader is likely to judge this to be a very serious moral failure.)
2. In a family the firstborn son slept with his mother or grandmother until he was 10 years old. During these 10 years he never slept in a separate bed. (The reader is likely to judge this to be a moral breach, although perhaps only as a minor violation of the moral order, as moral attitudes toward cross-generational and even cross-gender co-sleeping may be changing in the reader's cultural group.)

3 The day after his father's death the eldest son had a haircut and ate chicken. (The reader will not judge this to be a moral breach.)
4 A widow in your community eats fish two or three times a week. (The reader will not judge this to be a moral breach.)

The following is the way most Oriya Hindu Brahmans, women and men, in the temple town of Bhubaneswar would rank these courses of action, with the most serious moral breach listed first.

1 The day after his father's death the eldest son had a haircut and ate chicken. (This would be judged a very serious moral breach, indeed one of the most serious moral failures imaginable.)
2 A widow in your community eats fish two or three times a week. (This would be judged a very serious moral breach.)
3 A poor man went to the hospital after being seriously hurt in an accident. At the hospital they refused to treat him because he could not afford to pay. (This would be judged a serious moral breach but not quite as serious as the other two.)
4 In a family the firstborn son slept with his mother or grandmother until he was 10 years old. During these 10 years he never slept in a separate bed. (This would not be judged a moral breach and might even be viewed as morally desirable.)

David Wong, the moral philosopher mentioned at the start of this essay, points to one possible way to rise to the challenge (answering the question why different peoples disagree in their concrete moral judgments) when he reminds his readers that it is not incoherent to "be a universalist and a 'situational' ethicist at the same time," holding that what is right, good, virtuous or moral "varies with context in such a way that anyone reasoning correctly [by which he means logically and consistently] and with all the relevant facts would judge in the same way, regardless of one's society or culture" (Wong 2006: xii). And David Wiggins, the moral philosopher inspired by Montaigne, provides a provisional account of situational ethics (he calls it "contextualism") in which he writes: "No act or practice can be assessed as right or wrong, good or bad, etc. without the full specification of circumstances and context (context embracing, in some versions, the identity of agents). An act or a practice is a response in some situation to something somehow discriminable in that situation or a framework that contains that situation." Wiggins cautions his readers that "properly to situate an act or a practice or an instance of a practice is the necessary preliminary to passing judgment on that act, that practice, or that instance. *Unless we do this, we shall scarcely know what we are passing judgment upon*" (2005: n. 17; emphasis added).

Indeed, what *are* we passing judgment on when we learn that a typical Oriya Brahman, female or male, in an Indian temple town in the late twentieth century judges that it is a greater evil for the firstborn son to get a haircut and eat chicken the day after his father's death than for doctors in a hospital to refuse to treat an accident victim because he is too poor to pay? And what type of judgment should we make about the moral development of those Oriya Brahman adults? A primary task for a moral anthropology of the sort imagined (universalism without the uniformity) is to provision us with a "full specification of circumstances and context" in such a way "that anyone reasoning correctly and with all the relevant facts would judge in the same way, regardless of one's society or culture." How might one proceed to do that in the instance of the firstborn son who eats chicken and gets a haircut the day after his father dies?[7]

Here is a brief sketch of the intellectual framework (the goals, values, and pictures of the world) that contains the relevant situation and leads to the local moral condemnation reported above. Oriya Brahmans who live in the temple town generally believe that every person has an immortal reincarnating soul. They believe that when a person dies his or her soul strongly desires to detach itself from his or her corpse and go on its transmigratory journey. Nevertheless, the soul of the person finds itself initially trapped or attached to the corpse and held back by the so-called death pollution that emanates from the dead body and from its subsequently processed physical remains. As an act of beneficence, care, and reciprocity (all of which are assumed to be objective moral goods), relatives of the deceased (and especially the firstborn son, for whom this is a major and widely acknowledged moral duty and perhaps the most profound moment in the relationship of a son with his father) undertake the project of assisting the soul of the dead person to get free of its ties to the physical form it once occupied. Thus, some of the kinsmen of the dead person turn their own living bodies into what I as an outside observer have sometimes referred to as "death pollution collection sites." They essentially suck up the death pollution associated with the corpse (and its cremation and disposal) into themselves. They believe that the most effective way to do this is by keeping all other types of pollutions away from their living bodies, thus providing maximal space for the personal intake of the death pollution. Among the most commonplace competing types of pollutions that might interfere with their project are sexual activities and the ingestion of "hot foods" (for example, fish and meat – the relevant social fact here is that chicken is a "hot food"). Thus for 12 days they stay at home fasting (maintaining a very restricted diet of "cool" foods) and practicing abstinence. They believe that on the twelfth day the soul of the deceased will have been released from its bondage to its bygone material form and is therefore free to proceed on its journey to the world of transmigrating spirits. On that day they cleanse themselves of the death pollution which they have absorbed into their own bodies and which has accumulated there. They believe that the pollution migrates to the extremities of the body and is especially concentrated in their hair and under their fingernails. On that twelfth day of abstinence and fasting the family barber cuts off all their hair and the barber's wife cuts their fingernails. Then they take a ceremonial bath and go back to the workaday world, having fulfilled their moral obligation to the soul of the deceased.

"The day after his father's death the firstborn son had a haircut and ate chicken." To any Oriya Hindu Brahman in the temple town, this conduct signals a willful and horrifying renunciation of the entire project of assisting the soul of his father and places the father's spiritual transmigration in deep jeopardy. No wonder they are morally distraught at the very idea of such behavior, and judge it more severely than nontreatment of the accident victim at the hospital who is too poor to pay. Wouldn't you judge things that way too if that was your picture of the essential parts of the person (including the idea of an immortal reincarnating soul), of connections between means and ends (cause and effect with respect to death pollution and its absorption) and the objective moral charter for particular kinship relationships (the values ideally made manifest in father–son and other kinship obligations)? And doesn't David Wiggins make the decisive point – without such a specification of the local framework we (as innocent and untutored outsiders) in fact did not know what we were passing judgment on when we initially heard that a firstborn son in an Oriya Brahman temple town got a haircut and ate chicken the day after his father's death.

The main point I wish to make with respect to this illustration is that the imaginative framework used by Oriya Brahmans in discriminating aspects of the situation and judging the son to have behaved immorally is a framework that provides reasons that would justify anyone drawing that same conclusion if they adopted that Oriya worldview. The framework of interpretation is, of course, contingent in this instance and rests on a set of metaphysical, causal, and means–ends beliefs. The point, however, is that if *we* don't draw that conclusion (that the firstborn son committed a very serious moral breach) it is because we don't employ that framework of interpretation (and hence don't situate or even identify the course of action in the same way) and not because either Oriya Brahmans or we ourselves fall short in our recognition of existing universal values? Many cultural anthropologists who are attracted to cultural relativism ultimately trace the source of cross-cultural diversity in concrete moral judgments to differences in worldviews or beliefs and to the particular subset of universal goods privileged in any particular cultural or historical tradition of values.

Moral Pluralism as Universalism without the Uniformity (in Brief)

An alternative name for this version of relativism is moral pluralism. It is the doctrine that human reason at some point reaches a limit that allows for discretion as to which values or goods to privilege and how they should properly be applied in the light of local beliefs, interests, and social facts. Indeed, it is out of respect for our rationality that moral pluralists hold that there is no single and complete rational ordering of morally relevant goods (see Gray 1996, 2000; Galston 2002 for a discussion of Isaiah Berlin and his theory of the inherent multiplicity and irreducibility of the objective domain of moral goods or values). And it is also out of respect for the limits of our rationality that moral pluralists recognize that many universal existential and metaphysical questions relevant to the organization of a social life are cognitively undecidable and leave room for morally sensitive and reasonable truth-seeking members of different cultural traditions to disagree about which interpretive framework to employ in situating a course of action.

Writing as a moral pluralist I once referred to those universal existential and metaphysical questions as social existence themes (Shweder 1982). The variations in concrete moral judgments of the many peoples of the world can be viewed, in part, as expressions of the many answers that are possible to those universal questions or social existence themes. Questions such as these: What is me and what is not me (the question of personal boundaries)? What is male and what is female (the question of gender identity)? Who is one of my kind and who (or what) is not one of my kind (the question of in-group versus out-group identity)? Who is up and who is down (the question of hierarchy)? How should the burdens and benefits of life be distributed (the question of justice)? And others.

Those in the social sciences who have over the decades engaged in descriptive research in the cultural psychology of morality investigate local answers to those unavoidable and hence universal existential and metaphysical questions. And, as noted throughout this essay, what they have discovered is that many of those answers have local authority because of their perceived connection to an imagined objective moral charter mediated by local beliefs or worldviews.[8] What they have discovered is that moral judgments around the world are ubiquitous, passionate, motivating, truth-asserting, and divergent, and that in all cultures there is some sense of natural moral law and the development of some kind of normative language of rights, duties, obligations, or values for regulating and justifying action (see, for example, Kroeber 1952; Kluckhohn & Strodtbeck 1961; D'Andrade 2008).

Conclusion

In conclusion, human beings are not typically extreme relativists of the subjectivist variety. Values or moral goods are universally viewed as such undeniably good reasons for engaging in a course of action that once a moral end is the perceived result of a course of action nothing more needs to be said by way of its justification. Nevertheless, at the same time, the imagined moral truths or goods asserted in deliberative moral judgments around the world are many, not one. Researchers who study moral discourse and the reflective application of human intelligence to evaluate spontaneous or intuitive moral judgments have discovered that the objective moral character of an action or practice (e.g., voluntarily ending a pregnancy) is typically established by connecting that action through a chain of factual, means–ends, and causal reasoning to some argument-ending terminal good, for example personal freedom, family privacy, or the avoidance of physical or psychological harm On a worldwide scale the argument-ending terminal goods of deliberative moral judgments privileged in this or that cultural community are rich and diverse, and include such moral ends as autonomy, justice, harm avoidance, loyalty, benevolence, piety, duty, respect, gratitude, sympathy, chastity, purity, sanctity, and others. Several proposals have been advanced in the social sciences for classifying these goods into a smaller set, such as the "Big Three" ethics of autonomy, community, and divinity proposed by this author and his colleagues and the four-dimensional classification of types of interpersonal relationships and associated duties and moral responsibilities proposed by Alan Fiske (1993) and his colleagues.

Universalism without the uniformity is one way to describe the variety of relativism characteristic of all these proposals. The "Big Three," for example, propose that the human self or subject can be represented and experienced as either an autonomous preference structure seeking to maximize the satisfaction of its wants, or as an office-holder or social status bearer in a bounded community (a family for example) defined by role-based and often hierarchically interdependent duties and responsibilities, or as a free will or spirit whose capacity to initiate action and experience things of value derives from some kind of elevating connection to something that is inherently higher, dignified, pure, or divine. These pictures of the self are probably present to some degree in all cultural groups but they are emphasized to different degrees and made manifest or institutionalized in different ways. So too the values associated with them: the moral goods favored by the ethics of autonomy and by many liberal societies (harm, rights, justice, self-governance, and equality, for example) are not those favored by the ethics of community (duty, hierarchy, loyalty, interdependence, personal sacrifice) or by the ethics of divinity (sanctity, pollution avoidance, purity, cleanliness). Many descriptions of cultural and subcultural differences in moral orientation and judgment utilizing this framework or similar frameworks (for example, the "Big Five" proposed by Jon Haidt and his colleagues) are available in the moral anthropology and moral psychology literature (see Shweder et al. 1987, 2003a; Haidt et al. 1993; Miller 1994, 1997a, 1997b; Jensen 1997, 1998, 2008; Menon 2003; Haidt & Joseph 2004; Haidt & Graham 2007; Beldo 2011; and Hickman 2011; for an influential discussion of culture and the self, see Markus & Kitayama 1991). The development and defense of this type of moral pluralism is an ongoing process and will face many challenges. But perhaps its most basic principle (and its Montaigne-like caution for researchers in moral anthropology) is that the illiberality of a cultural practice is not necessarily an index of its immorality.

NOTES

1 The enveloping outer garment and face cover worn by women in public spaces in some Islamic traditions.
2 The Jewish ritual in which the foreskin of a male infant is surgically removed eight days after his birth.
3 For a useful historical and critical discussion of debates about the "natural" or objective status of human rights see Moyn (2010).
4 For a useful sampling of answers to this question see the collections edited by Wilson (1970) and Hollis and Lukes (1992). For a sample of key readings in the history of moral anthropology and contemporary discussions of moral relativism see Herskovits 1960; MacIntyre (1984); Levy-Bruhl (1985); Fischer (1989); Shweder with Bourne (1991); Shweder and Haidt (1993); Mead (2001 [1935]); Shweder et al. (2003b); Sumner (2007); Lukes (2008); Shweder (2008); and Boas (2010 [1911]).
5 Those concrete moral judgments are not typically uniform within cultural groups either and the challenge of factions, sections, interest groups, or "wings" for the organization of a viable society is a classic issue in the social sciences dating from at least the brilliant treatment of the topic by James Madison in the Federalist Papers (Federalist 10). See, for example, Jensen (1997, 1998) and Haidt and Graham (2007).
6 Westermarck of course believed this was a big "if" and he contested it.
7 This is a situation, a framework and a moral judgment I have discussed in other writings.
8 It should be noted, of course, that there is considerable cross-cultural and intracultural variation in the extent or degree to which all social norms are moralized and viewed as manifestations of an objective, external, or sacred charter (see, for example, Shweder et al. 1981, 1987; Turiel 1983; Haidt et al. 1993).

REFERENCES

American Anthropological Association (AAA), Executive Board (1947) Statement on Human Rights. *American Anthropologist* 49: 539–543.

Beldo, Les (2011) A Special Kind of "Ought": Toward a New Theoretical Model for the Anthropology of Morality. Unpublished manuscript available from the author.

Benedict, Ruth (1934) Anthropology and the Abnormal. *Journal of General Psychology* 10: 59–82.

Boas, Franz (2010 [1911]) *The Mind of Primitive Man*. New York: Macmillan.

Cook, John W. (1999) *Morality and Cultural Differences*. Oxford: Oxford University Press.

D'Andrade, Roy G. (1995) Moral Models in Anthropology. *Current Anthropology* 36: 399–408.

D'Andrade, Roy G. (2008) *A Study of Personal and Cultural Values: American, Japanese and Vietnamese*. New York: Palgrave Macmillan.

Engle, Karen (2002) From Skepticism to Embrace: Human Rights and the American Anthropological Association from 1947 to 1999. In Richard A. Shweder et al. (eds.), *Engaging Cultural Differences: The Multicultural Challenge in Liberal Democracies*. New York: Russell Sage Foundation, pp. 344–362.

Firth, Raymond (2011 [1967]) *Tikopia Ritual and Belief*. London: Routledge.

Fischer, David Hackett (1989) *Albion's Seed: Four British Folkways in America*. Oxford: Oxford University Press.

Fiske, Alan P. (1993) *Structures of Social Life*. New York: Free Press.

Fortes, Meyer (ed.) (1987) *Religion, Morality and Person: Essays on Tallensi Religion*. Cambridge: Cambridge University Press.

Galston, William (2002) *Liberal Pluralism: The Implications of Value Pluralism for Political Theory and Practice*. New York: Cambridge University Press.

Geertz, Clifford (2000) Anti Anti-Relativism. In *Available Light: Anthropological Reflections on Philosophical Topics*. Princeton: Princeton University Press.

Gray, John (1996) *Isaiah Berlin*. Princeton: Princeton University Press.

Gray, John (2000) *Two Faces of Liberalism*. New York: New Press.

Haidt, Jonathan and Graham, J. (2007) When Morality Opposes Justice: Conservatives Have Moral Intuitions that Liberals May Not Recognize. *Social Justice Research* 20: 98–116.

Haidt, Jonathan and Joseph, Craig (2004) Intuitive Ethics: How Innately Prepared Intuitions Generate Culturally Variable Virtues. *Daedalus* 133: 55–66.

Haidt, Jonathan, Koller, Sylvia, and Dias, Maria (1993) Affect, Culture and Morality, or Is It Wrong to Eat Your Dog? *Journal of Personality and Social Psychology* 65: 613–628.

Herskovits, Melville (1960) *Man and His Works: The Science of Cultural Anthropology*. New York: Knopf.

Hickman, Jacob (2011) Morality and Personhood in the Hmong Diaspora: A Person-Centered Ethnography of Migration and Resettlement. PhD thesis, Department of Comparative Human Development, University of Chicago.

Hobhouse Leonard T. (1915) *Morals in Evolution: A Study in Comparative Ethics*. New York: Henry Holt.

Hollis, Martin and Lukes, Steven (eds.) (1992) *Rationality and Relativism*. Cambridge, MA: MIT Press.

Jensen, Lene (1997) Different World Views, Different Morals: America's Culture War Divide. *Human Development* 40: 325–344.

Jensen, Lene (1998) Moral Divisions within Countries between Orthodoxy and Progressivism: India and the United States. *Journal for the Scientific Study of Religion* 37: 90–107.

Jensen, Lene (2008) Through Two Lenses: A Cultural-Developmental Approach to Moral Reasoning. *Developmental Review* 28: 289–315.

Kluckhohn, Florence and Strodtbeck, Fred (1961) *Variations in Value Orientation*. Evanston, IL: Row Peterson.

Kohlberg, Lawrence (1981) *The Philosophy of Moral Development: Moral Stages and the Idea of Justice*. San Francisco: Harper & Row.

Kroeber, Alfred L. (1952) Value as a Subject of Natural Science Inquiry. In *The Nature of Culture*. Chicago: University of Chicago Press, pp. 136–138.

Ladd, John (2004) *The Structure of a Moral Code: Navajo Ethics*. Eugene, OR: Wipf & Stock.

Levy-Bruhl, Lucien (1985) *How Natives Think*. Princeton: Princeton University Press.

Lovejoy, Arthur (1961) *Reflections on Human Nature*. Baltimore: Johns Hopkins University Press.

Lukes, Steven (2008) *Moral Relativism*. New York: Picador.

MacIntyre, Alasdair (1984) *After Virtue: A Study in Moral Theory*. Notre Dame, IN: University of Notre Dame Press.

Malinowski, Bronislaw (1926) *Crime and Custom in Savage Society*. Totowa, NJ: Littlefield, Adams.

Markus, Hazel R. and Kitayama, Shinobu (1991) Culture and the Self: Implications for Cognition, Emotion and Motivation. *Psychological Review* 98: 224–253.

Mead, Margaret (2001 [1935]) *Sex and Temperament in Three Primitive Societies*. New York: HarperCollins.

Menon, Usha (2003) Neither Victim nor Rebel: Feminism and the Morality of Gender and Family Life in a Hindu Temple Town. In Richard A. Shweder et al. (eds.), *Engaging Cultural Differences: The Multicultural Challenge in Liberal Democracies*. New York: Russell Sage Foundation, pp. 288–308.

Menon, Usha and Shweder, Richard A. (1998) The Return of the "White Man's Burden": The Moral Discourse of Anthropology and the Domestic Life of Hindu Women. In Richard A. Shweder (ed.), *Welcome to Middle Age (And Other Cultural Fictions)*. Chicago: University of Chicago Press.

Miller, Joan G. (1994) Cultural Diversity in the Morality of Caring: Individually Oriented versus Duty-Based Interpersonal Moral Codes. *Cross Cultural Research* 28: 3–39.

Miller, Joan G. (1997a) Cultural Conceptions of Duty: Implications for Morality and Motivation. In J. Schumaker et al. (eds.), *Motivation and Culture*. New York: Routledge, pp. 178–193.

Miller, Joan G. (1997b) Understanding the Role of World Views in Morality. *Human Development* 40: 350–354.

Montaigne, Michel de (1948) *The Complete Works*, trans. Donald M. Frame. New York: Knopf.

Moyn, Samuel (2010) *The Last Utopia: Human Rights in History*. Cambridge, MA: Harvard University Press.

Nadel, S. F. (1969) *A Theory of Social Structure*. London: Cohen & West.

Rashdall, Hastings (1914) *Is Conscience an Emotion? Three Lectures on Recent Ethical Theories*. New York: Houghton Mifflin.

Rawls, John (1971) *A Theory of Justice*. Cambridge, MA: Belknap Press of Harvard University Press.

Read, Kenneth E. (1955) Morality and the Concept of the Person among the Gahuku-Gama. *Oceania* 25: 233–282.

Rozin, Paul, Lowery, L., Imada, S., and Haidt, Jonathan (1999) The CAD Triad Hypothesis: A Mapping between Three Moral Emotions (Contempt, Anger, Disgust) and Three Moral Codes (Community, Autonomy, Divinity). *Journal of Personality and Social Psychology* 76: 574–586.

Shweder, Richard A. (1982) Beyond Self-Constructed Knowledge: The Study of Culture and Morality. *Merrill-Palmer Quarterly* 28: 41–69.

Shweder, Richard A. (2008) After Just Schools: The Equality–Difference Paradox and Conflicting Varieties of Liberal Hope. In Martha Minow et al. (eds.), *Just Schools: Pursuing Equality in Societies of Difference*. New York: Russell Sage Foundation, pp. 254–290.

Shweder, Richard A. with Bourne, Edward (1991) Does the Concept of the Person Vary Cross-Culturally? In Richard A. Shweder, *Thinking through Cultures: Expeditions in Cultural Psychology*. Cambridge, MA: Harvard University Press, pp. 113–155.

Shweder, Richard A. and Haidt, Jonathan (1993) The Future of Moral Psychology: Truth, Intuition and the Pluralist Way. *Psychological Science* 4: 360–365.

Shweder, Richard A. with Much, Nancy C. (1992) Determinations of Meaning: Discourse and Moral Socialization. In *Thinking through Cultures: Expeditions in Cultural Psychology*. Cambridge, MA: Harvard University Press, pp. 186–240.

Shweder, Richard A., Turiel, Elliot, and Much, Nancy C. (1981) The Moral Intuitions of the Child. In John Flavell and Lee Ross (eds.), *Social Cognitive Development*. New York: Cambridge University Press, pp. 288–305.

Shweder, Richard A., Mahapatra, Manamohan, and Miller, Joan G. (1987) Culture and Moral Development. In Jerome Kagan and Sharon Lamb (eds.), *The Emergence of Morality in Young Children*. Chicago: University of Chicago Press, pp. 1–82.

Shweder, Richard A., Much, Nancy C., Mahapatra, Manamohan, and Park, Lawrence (2003a) The "Big Three" of Morality (Autonomy, Community, Divinity) and the Big Three Explanations of Suffering. In Richard A. Shweder, *Why Do Men Barbecue? Recipes for Cultural Psychology*. Cambridge, MA: Harvard University Press, pp. 74–133.

Shweder, Richard A., Jensen, Lene, and Goldstein, William (2003b) Sleeps by whom Revisited: Extracting the Moral Goods Implicit in Practice. In Richard A. Shweder (ed.), *Why Do Men Barbecue? Recipes for Cultural Psychology*. Cambridge, MA: Harvard University Press, pp. 46–73.

Sumner, William Graham (2007 [1906]) *Folkways: A Study of Mores, Manners, Customs and Morals*. New York: Cosimo.

Turiel, Elliot (1983) *The Development of Social Knowledge: Morality and Convention*. New York: Cambridge University Press.

Turiel, Elliot (2008) *The Culture of Morality: Social Development, Context and Conflict*. New York: Cambridge University Press.

Vasquez, Kristin, Keltner, Dacher, Ebenbach, David H., and Banaszynski, Tracy L. (2001) Cultural Variation and Similarity in Moral Rhetorics: Voices from the Philippines and the United States. *Journal of Cross-Cultural Psychology* 32: 93–120.

Westermarck, Edward (1932) *Ethical Relativity*. New York: Harcourt, Brace.

Wiggins, David (2005) Objectivity in Ethics; Two Difficulties, Two Responses. *Ratio* 18: 1–26.

Wilson, Bryon R. (ed.) (1970) *Rationality*. New York: Harper & Row.

Wong, David B. (2006) *Natural Moralities: A Defense of Pluralistic Relativism*. Oxford: Oxford University Press.

CHAPTER 6

Anthropology and Ethics

Carolyn Fluehr-Lobban

Ethics and morality can be confused in everyday life and language and this confusion has been transferred to discourse in anthropology. Morality as a culturally defined set of ideals and rules is more ambiguous than ethics, normally discussed as specific professional responsibilities. Philosopher Bernard Gert has defined morality as "an informal public system applying to all rational persons, governing behavior that affects others, and which has the minimization of evil as its end" (1988: 6). Ethical codes are most often statements of conduct that reflect informal public systems that are not enforced, such as the anthropology codes. Codes are enforced if they are tied to licensing standards and grievance models. Since anthropology has not set up a system with a recognized authority to determine what counts as morally acceptable professional behavior, any public moral system for anthropology remains an informal one where, within limits, anthropologists can disagree with each other on what behavior counts as morally acceptable professional behavior. This means that, except for mandatory review by institutional review boards (IRBs), each anthropologist determines for himself/herself what is morally acceptable behavior. Thus, any imagined public moral system in anthropology exists mostly as a self-imposed, self-regulated set of ideas of ethics.

Morality is also defined as actions having the effect of lessening of evil or harm, including rules prohibiting killing, the causing of pain, deception, and the breaking of promises (Rawls 1971; Gert 2004: 29–53), and in this respect "do no harm" can be extrapolated to an ethical position to "do less harm" (Fluehr-Lobban 2009).

Do No Harm

Anthropology evokes and is uniquely capable of addressing human moral and ethical dilemmas. Avoidance of harm is an example of an overriding moral evocative. It is likewise a cornerstone of every professional code of ethics irrespective of discipline or

A Companion to Moral Anthropology, First Edition. Edited by Didier Fassin.

field of work. However, it is often evoked without being unpacked. Widespread agreement exists among humans that harm occurs when death, pain, disability, loss of freedom or pleasure results from an act by one human upon another (Gert 2004: 12). It may be assumed that rational, moral humans understand what "do no harm" means, but when its presumed intent is applied to professional ethics it may not be so clear (Fluehr-Lobban 2008).

A primary moral emphasis would concentrate on avoidance of harm to the most vulnerable segments of the population – for example, women, children, the aged, and targeted ethnic minorities. The application of specialized cultural knowledge that anthropologists possess is an obvious priority. But for whom and for which intended purposes is this knowledge deployed? Therein lies the contentious rub, and all manner of government and nongovernmental organizations have been called to account for their actions and use of anthropological information. Could it be asserted, for example, that the only moral and ethical engagement for anthropologists operating in zones of chronic conflict and humanitarian crisis is to work with/for missions whose intent is to reduce, ameliorate, or prevent harm or further harm?

I propose a distinction between primary and secondary harm. Primary harm is that which affects "the people studied," including both direct, traditional fieldwork projects and those removed from direct fieldwork contact. Primary harm results when a researcher intentionally deceives the people studied about the real intent of research, for example, taking blood samples from an indigenous people for pharmacological or cell-line sale and use when the research was explained as a kinship and ancestry study. Secondary harm addresses harm to professionals, in this instance anthropologists. Alleging harm to the scholarly or personal reputation of an anthropologist who has been accused of professional or fieldwork-related misconduct is one example of a secondary harm. In a moral system for anthropology primary harm is that to which anthropologists first turn in consideration of the consequences of engagement with the people studied. Secondary harm addresses the professional standing of an anthropologist who, for example, placed herself at odds with a powerful agent that impeded or halted her research or applied project for its own motives.

The complexities of harm in a variety of culturally relative contexts are in the early stages of discussion by anthropologists, led by concerns with universal human rights. An entire spectrum of harmful human practices – from culturally legitimated homicide, to domestic and family violence, to female circumcision, and more – could be profitably debated. A line of distinction has been drawn between anthropologists who see human rights advocacy as a moral and professional responsibility and those who see such advocacy as a moral choice but not an ethical obligation (Graham, in Turner et al. 2009). At this point the ambiguity between obligation and choice is not viewed as a case of moral right and wrong but is a matter of reasonable persons who happen to be anthropologists disagreeing. Anthropologists have asserted but not debated sufficiently "good" or "bad" cultural practices, not to mention the appropriate interventions that might be advocated or applied. By contrast, human rights advocacy groups have made clear moral choices, such as Western feminist campaigns against female circumcision that were unilaterally labeled "female genital mutilation," later modified by indigenous activists as "genital cutting" or "female circumcision.'

The several codes of ethics that the Anthropological Association of America (AAA) has adopted since 1971 (Principles of Professional Responsibility, 1971; Code of

Ethics, 1998) have been often viewed as inadequate tools for education, deliberation, and decision-making in regard to ethical practice in anthropology. The latest effort, driven by the moral challenge of the potential recruitment of anthropologists for US military Human Terrain Teams (HTT) resulted in a four-year effort to sort out the ethical, moral, and decidedly political issues embedded in this latest challenge. The demand to "do something" was in large measure generated by a front-page feature story in the *New York Times* which described the work of "Tracy," one of the first recruits to the HTT in Afghanistan (Rohde 2007). The program was credited with a 60 percent reduction in casualties by Colonel Martin Schweitzer, commander of the 82nd Airborne Division, working with the anthropologists. Although it was never a program for anthropologists only, other social sciences whose professionals had also been intended for recruitment to the HTT program did not take the interest in it that anthropologists did. The very public debate spawned interest outside of anthropology and drew attention to the problematic relationship of anthropology with the military that is well summarized by George R. Lucas's *Anthropologists in Arms: The Ethics of Military Anthropology* (2009).

A Commission on the Engagement of Anthropology with the US Security and Intelligence Communities (CEAUSSIC) was formed in 2007 and continued its work over two two-year terms until 2010. Although it was given a broad mandate, the four-year work of the Commission was preoccupied with the issue of Human Terrain Teams and a "boots on the ground" anthropology. Other forms of engagement by anthropologists – for example, providing training as regional experts or in cultural knowledge – as "subject matter experts" (SMEs) for military or USAID projects or those working in development or archaeology salvage operations – were noted but not interrogated. In the end, the Final Report of the Commission proved the general tenet that ethics discourse in anthropology is mostly reactive to the professional needs of the moment – in this case what to do about the HTT (Fluehr-Lobban 1991, 2003). Arguments for the use of guiding principles over detailed codes (Fluehr-Lobban 2009) have prevailed and the current draft code works through a series of ethical principles that may prove more efficacious in ethics education in anthropology.

Fragments of History

During the first half of the twentieth century professional anthropology and the name of Franz Boas were inextricably tied. Boas had a distinguished record as a pacifist during World War I, despite the virulent nationalism that swept the United States at the time. It was Boas's expressed outrage against the wartime activities of four anthropologists who had combined intelligence-gathering with their research in his published letter to *The Nation* in 1919 that is the subject of the first clear-cut case of the issue of unprofessional behavior being raised within the organizational framework of the AAA. Boas wrote:

> I wish to enter a vigorous protest … that a number of men who follow science as their profession, men whom I refuse to designate any longer as scientists, have prostituted science by using it as a cover for their activities as spies … In consequence of their acts every nation will look with distrust upon the visiting foreign investigator who wants to

> do honest work, suspecting sinister designs. Such action has raised a new barrier against the development of international friendly cooperation. (1919: 729)

These words have resonated with nearly every anthropological crisis over ethics since they were penned. Although a founder of the AAA in 1900 and a scholar with a recognized reputation for accuracy and detail, Boas was censured by a vote of the Executive Council of the Anthropology Society of Washington, voting 20 to 10. His censure was rescinded only in 2005 by a resolution to that effect at the AAA and he is currently nominated for an award for Exemplary Service to the discipline.

And in 2000, 81 years later and using the same headline as in 1919, "Anthropologists as Spies," David Price revealed that the AAA itself had collaborated with the CIA during the cold war by providing, without their knowledge or consent, names of anthropological scholars working abroad. The issue of the relationship of science to government had not been clarified and anthropologists concerned with social issues such as racism or world peace found few outlets within the organizational framework of the AAA to express these concerns.

In Great Britain social anthropology developed as an unselfconscious field closely tied to British colonialism. Classic designations in political anthropology, such as "acephalous" and "cephalous" societies, were created as analytical tools for use in colonial administration and indirect rule. French social anthropology during colonialism mirrored this reality with neither expressing much substantive or critical reservation based on ethics or morality. European intellectuals in the wake of postcolonial independence of their former colonies have taken up the multiple, complex legacies of colonialism and have filled in the gaps left by the absence of the perspective of the ethnographic other during the decades of colonialism that lasted from the late nineteenth through the mid-twentieth centuries.

The first code of ethics in the United States was that by the Society for Applied Anthropology in 1949, in the postwar, post-European Holocaust awakening of the need for greater scientific responsibility and the United Nations Universal Declaration of Human Rights. It took the deep moral questioning of the Vietnam War for the American Anthropological Association to offer its first professional code of ethics, the Principles of Professional Responsibility, in 1971 (AAA 1971). It was generated out of a crisis of political-moral controversy over alleged clandestine counterinsurgency research carried out by anthropologists in Thailand, relating to the war in southeast Asia. A grievance model was adopted but not used in this or any other case relating to ethical malpractice. Indeed, the grievance model was dropped in 1998 as it had been solicited only in cases involving alleged plagiarism or conflicts between colleagues.

The most severe test of the old grievance model and the new education mandate came with the controversies surrounding allegations of wrongdoing by anthropologist Napoleon Chagnon and geneticist James Neel for their decades of research among the Yanomami made by Patrick Tierney in his 2000 book *Darkness in El Dorado: How Scientists and Journalists Devastated the Amazon*. Primary harm to the Yanomami was alleged not only by Tierney but by anthropologist Terence Turner (2001) and others with direct fieldwork experience, especially with Chagnon's characterization of the Yanamamo as "the fierce people" in his bestselling ethnography. The depiction of this indigenous South American people as "savage" was seen as an essential backdrop to the admitted deceit practiced by ethnographer Chagnon and the lack of informed consent in carrying out biological and social anthropological research. An investigative task force filed a report which concluded that mild breaches of ethics may have taken place, but that the major allegation of the scientists – of physical harm to the Yanomami caused by a failure to control a deadly measles epidemic, or, as was alleged, a desire to scientifically observe its "natural" course – was not demonstrated. After the report was made public, two of Chagnon's supporters introduced a resolution that largely retracted the report and instead condemned the harm done to the reputations of the scientists. This resolution passed by a wide margin in an AAA mail ballot (Borofsky & Albert 2005). The case ended up being more about the secondary harm done to the anthropologist than the concerns over primary harm affecting the people studied.

Debates about Codes

Peter Pels (1999) argued that in anthropological codes of ethics there is an inherent tension with Western ethics discourse and with the epistemology of anthropology as the study of the "other." This "duplexity," in his terms, creates an unintentional double standard in professional practice, a discourse for the West and another for the Rest. In the legalistic and litigious United States, the elimination of codes of ethics is unlikely to be a banner raised. Instead the debate is about the application and use of codes rather than their inherent worth. Pels noted in 1994 that codes are not uniform in their most basic ethical stands: "It might be that one code says the interests of the research participants should be paramount (US AAA and British ASA codes) while another says that the prime responsibility is towards 'science' (as in the Dutch code for sociologists and anthropologists)" (1994: 9).

The debate in anthropology over accountability for ethical research methods moved from an initial grievance/censure model, adopted in 1971 in the heated period of the Vietnam War to an "education mandate." This move to replace the stick with the carrot offered a model whereby the code of ethics itself was to be taught, debated, and modified, if necessary, through a vigorous discourse in undergraduate and graduate education and among AAA professionals. It is an understatement to say that the promise of the education mandate has not been fulfilled in the years since the code was ratified in 1998. It is still true that few programs of anthropology have systematic training in ethics, and the old maxim that anthropological ethics gain attention in their breach remains true. At such times, and only at such times, are the conference halls filled with eager "students" of ethics. And the discourse is reactive, personal, and often far from the principles of professional practice that need to be addressed in these "teachable moments."

Diverse and evolving views regarding the efficacy of codes of ethics, their interpretation and use, persist. Codes in the United States have been driven by federal regulation of research and the "Common Rule," general standards for ethical research, although AAA history also reflects American politics, as already implied. There has been a historic reluctance on the part of anthropologists to deny the utility of federal and institutional regulation of research, especially the federally mandated Institutional Review Boards, to which most anthropologists and all researchers must now apply and receive approval for their research proposal, if there is any connection to federal funding, which is virtually ubiquitous.

Charles Bosk (2007) notes a "chorus of complaints" from anthropologists about IRB protocols, which are critical of IRBs' lack of full appreciation of what ethnography entails and how it does not sit easily with IRB protocols. There is a failure of both complexity and reflexivity on the question of ethnographic ethics, including "ethics creep" emanating from the IRB to the anthropologist's research mission and design. This is beyond the bounds of the IRB, Bosk argues. It seems there is certainly much room for negotiation between anthropologists and ethnographers and the IRB.

Canadian sociologist Kevin Haggerty (2004) references "ethics creep" in the regulation of social science research. He also complains of IRB overregulation, especially with somewhat mechanical concepts of "harm" (any act which "might cause serious or lasting harm to a participant"). He argues that social science harm is less than medical harm (primary and secondary harm?) and argues further that journalists are able to do what anthropologists are constrained from doing in terms of informed consent. He suggests that each anthropologist imagines her or his own relationship to "subjects" speaking *for* the underprivileged. IRBs are cautious and conservative and university and university lawyers are driving the process.

Lederman (2007) asks with whom ethnographers might find common cause and what the disciplinary boundaries are among the social sciences. Anthropological research is not psychology. She argues that anthropological research is not process improvement, and consistency is desperately needed. In terms of the sociology of knowledge, she asks the fundamental question of how much of it is imagined reality and how much (clearly) documented reality mediated through the ethnographer.

Indigenous Colleagues, Often Overlooked

Despite its universalist mission, anthropology has been predominantly a Western enterprise since its origins in colonial America and imperial Europe. Only a few of the colonized – whether Indians in America or Africans and Asians colonized by Europe – became anthropologists. Japanese American anthropologist Peter Suzuki (2009) has taken on the anthropological establishment through its main vehicle, the AAA, in criticizing the activities of anthropologists during World War II as collaborators in the Japanese American internment camps.

Since the end of this era anthropology has been decolonizing, but the numbers of indigenous anthropologists remains small. Their presence at the anthropologists' table is particularly valuable for their "native" perspective on knowledge, practical applied development projects, human rights, and anthropological ethics. Imagine an anthropological code of ethics drafted by a pan-Indian research council. Indeed, in practical terms research among indigenous peoples of America is subject to Tribal Research Board approval and is strictly regulated, which is indicative of a trend in decolonizing research and its implications for ethics.

Sudanese anthropologists have differed from Western views on the subject of female circumcision, yet their voices have been marginalized, as is common with indigenous anthropologists (El Dareer 1983; Abdel Halim 2006; Abu Sharaf 2006). In the end, the practice of female circumcision is changing, perhaps as a result of pressure from human rights and feminist critics, but also from an evolving diverse urban society that is loosening its attachment to all manner of "traditional" customs. Infibulation rates are declining and various symbolic forms of light cutting or nicking of the clitoris or of circumcision are replacing it.

Anthropologists are public persons in fieldwork and contract work. Indigenous anthropologists are often university contract workers hired by international NGOs whose local knowledge and linguistic skills are valued. They may also have a personal commitment to human rights, peace, and nation-building in their countries, but their work rarely attracts scholarly attention. Partnership between Western anthropologists and indigenous anthropologists is becoming more common, but equality and full agency between the partners may be asymmetrical. Setting the agenda for research and collaborative work may also be driven by asymmetrical funding or by the agendas of powerful international funding bodies or NGOs. Collaborative publication is a high form of ethical engagement.

Collaborative Research: From Research "Subjects" to "Participants"

Participatory-collaborative research is acknowledged as having been derived from feminist research that developed modified or nonhierarchical methods for their research. The premises for this approach to research include consultation with and incorporation of the research population into the research design, methodology, and outcomes of research. A new anthropology journal *Collaborative Anthropology* has been launched by Eric Luke Lassiter. Some anthropologists following this method do not publish their work until it has been read and critiqued by the research participants. Taken to its logical end, the lines between researcher and researched are ideally minimized and perhaps morally justified.

It is important to point out that researchers are overwhelmingly relatively powerful people originating from the wealthier nations. Although many of those who work in non-Western and in comparative research or practice with NGOs do not usually see themselves in this light, it can at least be acknowledged that they are perceived as powerful individuals representing powerful and wealthy institutions, governmental or nongovernmental. Relatively powerful individuals may not need to make morality a priority.

The term "subject" is a profound statement of the research relationship. The collaborative, participatory research model is beginning to displace the old paradigm of conducting research *on subjects* (who are still typically called "informants"). This decisive shift parallels and reflects national and global changes that witnessed decolonization, the end of the cold war with its politicized discourse on human rights, and the search for international standards of human rights irrespective of nation or culture.

Thus, research *with* rather than *on* peoples takes the discourse on ethics, research, and practice into potentially historic new directions that may be described as moral. Extending the classic "do no harm" – that evolved from the Nuremberg trials to the various biomedical and later social science professional codes of ethics – collaborative researchers may seek to "do some good" in the government or nongovernmental organizations with which they work and in the research topics they select. The moral connection in this shift is obvious.

The collaborative model of research involves the people studied in an active way – as individuals or as a group – with a vested interest in participating in the study. Jointly directed and jointly authored projects begin to replace the older model of research "from above," planned, executed, and published by the anthropologist alone. Community or individual involvement in the progress of research, thus designed, becomes a condition for its success, not simply a fortuitous by-product of work with communities. The new model presumes a literate, conscious community of participants who not only participate in, but may read and critique, drafts of the published work.

Collaborative research is not only more ethically conscious and proactive, but capable of providing a moral compass in research through its continuous process of engagement with those studied.

Informed Consent as a Process of Moral Engagement with Participants

Informed consent as a formal legal-ethical construct grew out of a 1972 US Supreme Court case *Canterbury v. Spence*, which articulated the principle for medical research. As is well known, the principle evolved to become the gold standard for the conduct, not only of medical and biological research, but also for most of behavioral science research as well. However, informed consent may be viewed as a way of morally engaging with the research participants with whom anthropologists work. As openness and nondeception are expected in research, it follows the general moral prerogative to tell the truth and not to deceive.

The language of informed consent holds a central place in the codes of ethics of the American associations of psychologists and of sociologists, and finally in anthropology, the last among the social sciences (Fluehr-Lobban 1994). All research involving humans, regardless of funding source, is subject to regulation by Institutional Review Boards (IRBs) in the United States. It is worth noting that a number of other disciplines and professions employ methods similar to, if not the same as, anthropology – particularly the methods of long-term participant observation, building relations of trust with the research population, as well as conducting surveys and interviews with research participants. These include many in the fields of non-Western and comparative studies, whether in history, political science, or religion – and in the field of educational studies, in the United States at least.

Initial resistance by anthropologists to IRBs as the main ethical standard of informed consent has given way to acceptance and also to an active engagement with what it means to "do anthropology" and apply informed consent standards to the sometimes unique populations that we study (Lederman 2007). The new discourse has extended to newly recognized vulnerable populations, such as indigenous peoples; ethnic, racial, gender, class, and other social and political minorities; and victims of human rights abuses.

Collective informed consent – for example, among indigenous communities – or studies of human relations in hierarchical communities where gender, minority status, class, or other status that disempowers the individual, may be a higher form of moral engagement. The application of special proactive measures designed to protect vulnerable populations in regard to consent to participation in research may be for a higher good, as in the case of victims of human rights abuses. The researcher is cautioned to be aware of his or her potential paternalism or maternalism in knowing what is "best" for the people studied and justifying it in the name of morality.

Is Secret or Clandestine Research Immoral?

The 1971 Principles of Professional Responsibility were clear that there should be "no secret research" and warned against anthropologists working for any government, whether one's own or that of the fieldwork site. Further, researchers should disseminate their findings in timely and appropriate ways (AAA 1971: III). Although it is never explicitly stated, the long-term and widely accepted disapproval of secret or clandestine research approaches a statement on moral behavior in anthropology. However, an exception was originally made for anthropologists whose ethnographic research was to be kept secret as a promise to the people studied (e.g., secret societies), but then the moral complexity of differentiating this kind of secrecy from that of national security research made it imperative that it be ruled the two are no different. The politics of morality in this case are notable. Documented cases of anthropologists conducting clandestine research are rare, although more are alleged. The case of "Project Camelot" in the 1960s involved Latin American anthropologists in alleged counterinsurgency research in South America. The anthropologists involved in comparable research in Vietnam were not named, nor were they subjected to the AAA grievance procedure when it came into effect after 1971.

The 2011 revised code of ethics restates the fundamental view that any research that by its design does not allow the anthropologist to know the full scope of a project (i.e., parts of large government projects known as "compartmentalized research") is ethically problematic, since by definition the researcher cannot communicate transparently with participants. Also singled out as problematic is the use of the old language of "secret or clandestine research" that deceives research participants about the sponsorship, purpose, or implications of the research. This is organically tied to informed consent as the basic requirements of openness, honesty, and transparency are not met (AAA 2011).

The issue of secrecy is relevant to the field of human rights research and advocacy where a strong case can be made for the use of secrecy in order to protect victims of harm and abuse. A philosopher's fresh perspective on this quasi-sacred language (Lucas 2009) notes that there is a certain American obsession with "secrecy" and "clandestine research" when in fact the justification for the actual use of these terms is weak in the real (rather than imagined) history of American anthropology. Philosopher George Lucas's characterization of anthropology's obsession with some nonissues and its historic neglect of real issues, like informed consent, offers a refreshing view. Lucas sees anthropology's history of ethics as an exercise in a "litany of shame" over alleged secrecy in research and ethical malpractice, while critical standards, such as informed consent and "do no harm," were historically ignored. Recall that language on informed consent was not introduced into a code of ethics until 1998. Perhaps more than any other issue, that of "secret," "clandestine" research reveals more about anthropology's historic preoccupation with professional rather than disciplinary issues of ethics.

A Public Moral System for Anthropology: Cultural Relativism and Universal Rights

The idea of a public moral system for anthropology would have as its ideal a universal morality recognized by all rational anthropologists. While an informal standard, it still can refer to the general public system for morally acceptable behavior. However, even an informal public moral system for anthropology, which should be accepted by all anthropologists, would likely be challenged by some anthropological relativists as imperfectly universal for enunciating a set of ethical standards. Absolute cultural relativism has been questioned by many anthropologists.

The closest thing to a universal philosophical, moral, and ethical norm is the "do no harm" principle, which the new AAA code has proposed as a core principle. The question of the ways in which harmful cultural practices, such as female circumcision or various forms of domestic and family violence, can be viewed as universally morally reprehensible or justified in cultural terms has been debated. Shweder (2002) has argued that Western moralists and anthropologists do not have the right to instruct African women, the historic conservators of the practice of what the West calls "female genital mutilation," as to what is right or wrong in their culture. I have argued against absolute cultural relativism from the perspective of nearly four decades of anthropological fieldwork in northern Sudan where the most severe form of the practice, infibulation, has been practiced. The pain and suffering, that is the harm, done to the girl-child (circumcision is typically carried out on preadolescent females, as is the less drastic operation on preadolescent males) and to the married, birthing woman is, in my view, a culturally harmful practice that is not justified on moral grounds or those of universal human rights. In the future, multiple subjects of questionable cultural practices may be judged as harmful to a transnational, gendered anthropology but the relativist tradition is strong and in general it serves both the pedagogy and practice of anthropology very well.

The AAA (1998) Code of Ethics states that "anthropologists may choose to move beyond disseminating research results to a position of advocacy, but that making this choice is not an ethical responsibility" (III.C.2). Advocacy is, of course, subject to an anthropologist's views regarding a particular issue. It is therefore personal and subjective. In human rights discourse, as elsewhere, there can be a range of views that could be oppositional, such as the debates over "choice" or the "right to life" in US discourse on abortion. Both sides of this bitter debate argue from fundamental moral, human rights perspectives opposing the rights of the unborn to that of the woman-mother. Thus, advocacy might be best employed as a personal choice that anthropologists may exercise in their lives as citizens of their respective states, but when they use their anthropological knowledge and expertise to influence policy or affect the course of events in the lives of individuals and/or groups whom they study, does this constitute a professional or a moral responsibility? I argue that it is the latter and not the former.

Likewise, not all human rights groups – nor those describing themselves as human rights groups – are equal. International human rights movements have broad, highly differentiated moral and political agendas. Many anthropologists would find themselves in broad agreement with advocacy groups such as Amnesty International or

Human Rights Watch. Indeed, such groups have gained both high international credibility and legitimacy, and are often seen as necessary supra-state watchdog groups for violations of human rights by individual states that do not respond to pressure. It is noteworthy that various political and human rights groups were not unanimous in their use of the term "genocide" to describe the conflict in Darfur, and it might be argued that the politics of genocide made the human rights response more complicated as a result. Christian-based human rights groups such as Save the Children have a clear religious as well as humanitarian agenda, further complicating moral-ethical choices.

Conclusion

Anthropology as the study of humanity in all of time and space has such breadth, depth, and complexity that discussions of ethics and morality within its scope can be daunting. Nonetheless, ethics, and by extension morality, is central to our work, our discipline, and our legitimacy as a profession. Lucas has observed that anthropology's moral narrative has been a "strange reflective" without critical substance apart from its "litany of shame." Its major organizations have acted like professional organizations to protect the professional anthropologist, rather than crafted a disciplinary narrative for anthropology and ethics. Lucas further remarks that if this distorted focus continues, it will have "decided negative consequences for the moral self-consciousness of the discipline" (2009: 89). As anthropology has made its stock and trade the study of the other, it is well advised to listen to the diverse voices of its own as well as voices from outside the boundaries of the profession.

REFERENCES

Abdel Halim, Osman (2006) *Sudanese Women in the United States: The Double Problem of Gender and Culture*. Lewiston, NY: Edwin Mellen.

Abu Sharaf, Rogaia (ed.) (2006) *Female Circumcision: Multicultural Perspectives*. Philadelphia: University of Pennsylvania Press.

American Anthropological Association (AAA) (1971) Statements on Ethics: Principles of Professional Responsibility. At http://www.aaanet.org/stmts/ethstmnt.htm, accessed Mar. 2, 2012.

American Anthropological Association (AAA) (1998) Code of Ethics of the American Anthropological Association. At http://www.aaanet.org/committees/ethics/ethcode.htm, accessed Mar. 2, 2012.

American Anthropological Association (AAA) (2011) Draft Code of Ethics. At http://www.aaanet.org/coe/2011/preamble_and_principles_9_10_11.pdf, accessed Mar. 2, 2012.

Boas, Franz (1919) Correspondence: Scientists as Spies. *Nation* 109: 729.

Borofsky, Robert and Albert, Bruce (2005) *Yanomami: The Fierce Controversy and What We Can Learn from It*. Berkeley: University of California Press.

Bosk, Charles L. (2007) The New Bureaucracies of Virtue, or, When Form Fails to Follow Function. *PoLAR: Political and Legal Anthropology Review* 30: 192–209.

El Dareer, Asma (1983) *Woman, Why Do You Weep? Circumcision and its Consequences*. London: Zed.

Fluehr-Lobban, Carolyn (1991) *Ethics and the Profession of Anthropology: Dialogue for a New Era*. Philadelphia: University of Pennsylvania Press.

Fluehr-Lobban, Carolyn (1994) Informed Consent in Anthropological Research: We are Not Exempt. *Human Organization* 53(1): 1–10.

Fluehr-Lobban, Carolyn (ed.) (2003) *Ethics and the Profession of Anthropology: Dialogue for Ethically Conscious Practice*, 2nd edn. Walnut Creek, CA: AltaMira.

Fluehr-Lobban, Carolyn (2008) New Ethical Challenges for Anthropologists. *Chronicle Review* (Nov. 14), B11–B12.

Fluehr-Lobban, Carolyn (2009) Guiding Principles over Detailed Codes. *Anthropology News* (Sept.), 8–9.

Gert, Bernard (1988) *Morality: A New Justification of the Moral Rules*. New York: Oxford University Press.

Gert, Bernard (2004) *Common Morality*. New York: Oxford University Press.

Haggerty, Kevin D. (2004) Ethics Creep: Governing Social Science Research in the Name of Ethics. *Qualitative Sociology* 27: 391–414.

Lederman, Rena (2007) Comparative "Research": A Modest Proposal Concerning the Object of Ethics Regulation. *PoLAR: Political and Legal Anthropology Review* 30(2): 305–327.

Lucas, George (2009) *Anthropologists in Arms: The Ethics of Military Anthropology*. Lanham, MD: Rowman & Littlefield.

Pels, Peter (1994) National Codes of Ethics and European Anthropology: A Call for Cooperation and Sharing. *EASA Newsletter* (Sept.), 9–10.

Pels, Peter (1999) Professions of Duplexity: A Prehistory of Ethical Codes in Anthropology. *Current Anthropology* 40(2): 101–136.

Price, David (2000) Anthropologists as Spies. *The Nation* (Nov. 20), 24–27.

Rawls, John (1971) *A Theory of Justice*. Cambridge, MA: Harvard University Press.

Rohde, David (2007) Army Enlists Anthropology in War Zones. *New York Times* (Oct. 5). At http://query.nytimes.com/gst/fullpage.html?res=9d04e3d81130f936a35753c1a9619c8b63&pagewanted=all, accessed Feb. 29, 2012.

Shweder, Richard A. (2002) What about Female Genital Mutilation and Why Understanding Culture Matters in the First Place. In Richard A. Shweder et al. (eds.), *Engaging Cultural Differences: The Multicultural Challenge in Liberal Democracies*. New York: Russell Sage Foundation, pp. 216–238.

Silverstein, Leni (2004) Uncensuring Boas. *Anthropology News* (Nov.), 5–6.

Suzuki, Peter (2009) The Activities of Anthropologists during WWII in the Japanese American Internment Camps. *Paper presented at the session* "Partially Out of the Closet: Taking Cognizance of the Unethical Activities of the Internment-Camp Anthropologists," 108th Annual Meeting of the American Anthropological Association, Philadelphia.

Tierney, Patrick (2000) *Darkness in El Dorado: How Scientists and Journalists Devastated the Amazon*. New York: Norton.

Tierney, John (2007) "Circumcision" or "Mutilation"? And Other Questions about a Rite in Africa. *New York Times* (Dec. 5). At http://tierneylab.blogs.nytimes.com/2007/12/05/circumcision-or-mutilation-and-other-questions-about-a-rite-in-africa/, accessed Feb. 29, 2012.

Turner, Terence (2001) The Yanomami and the Ethics of Anthropological Practice. *Public Anthropology/Engaging Ideas* (May 27).

Turner, Terry, Graham, Laura R., Fluehr-Lobban, Carolyn, and Cowan, Jane K. (2009) Anthropology and Human Rights: Do Anthropologists have an Ethical Obligation to Promote Human Rights? In Mark Goodale (ed.), *Human Rights: An Anthropological Reader*. Oxford: Wiley-Blackwell, pp. 198–206.

Ulrich, George (1999) Comment to Peter Pels "Professions of Duplexity." *Current Anthropology* 40(2): 126–127.

PART II Approaches

CHAPTER 7 Cultural Values

Joel Robbins

The argument I will develop is that the study of cultural values can make important contributions to the anthropological study of morality. Perhaps this does not sound like a particularly challenging argument to make. After all, many people would likely be prepared to accept the idea that some notion of value is at least implicitly if not explicitly at the heart of any discussion of morality. If the good is defined as that which is valuable, or if a value is defined, as the anthropologist Kluckhohn (1962 [1951]: 395) in part defined it, as a cultural "conception" of that which is "desirable" (in contrast to that which is simply desired), then it is difficult to imagine a discussion of morality that does not make some reference to values. And it is easy enough to find philosophers who make this point. Thus, for example, the political philosopher Galston writes that "Moral reflection is the effort to bring different dimensions of value to bear on specific occasions of judgment and to determine how they are best balanced or ordered, given the facts of the case" (2002: 6). Yet it is also true that in these early days of the anthropology of morality, value has not emerged as any more or less central to the developing discussion than any other object of study. Like such terms of art as "self," "care," "breakdown," "reason," "freedom," "virtue," and other notions currently in play, value remains just one brushstroke in a picture whose main outlines have yet to become wholly clear. Given this, my aim in this essay is to suggest some aspects of the social life of morality that the study of cultural values is particularly helpful in illuminating, rather than to support a claim that this area of study exhausts what can be accomplished by the anthropology of morality.

The central claim I aim to support here is that an approach to morality that recognizes its grounding in cultural values helps us to comprehend a certain Janus-faced quality of morality that has challenged previous social scientific attempts to define it comprehensively as a field of study. The challenge has been to develop an approach to morality that illuminates both the fact that in all societies morality

A Companion to Moral Anthropology, First Edition. Edited by Didier Fassin.

encompasses the demand that people adhere to shared models of action and the fact that people sometimes confront situations in which no single model of action is clearly best and must make moral choices between a number of models of how to proceed. Can there be an account of morality that helps us understand both of these kinds of moral situations on a single basis, or do we simply have to do here with two different aspects of social life, only one of which should be the focus of the anthropology of morality? Before answering this question, let me lay out a bit more clearly what I mean by the two faces of morality.

One face of morality suggests that people treat all routine action – action that conforms to cultural expectations and meets the demands of cultural norms – as moral, and that actors must account for their deviations from even the most banal cultural expectations or risk being judged morally suspect by others. Among the Urapmin of Papua New Guinea, with whom I carried out fieldwork in the early 1990s, one is expected to shake hands with everyone one encounters each day on the first occasion of coming into contact with them. One day I was walking with a friend on the main path that connects the villages that make up the Urapmin community when we got caught in a torrential downpour. We began to run for shelter and at one point passed another man we both knew running with equal determination in the other direction. We did not stop to shake hands. As soon as we got ourselves into a house, my friend agitatedly insisted that once the storm passed we would need to go find the man we ran by, shake his hand, and explain that it was because of the rain that we did not stop to shake his hand when we first saw him. If we did not do this, my friend pointed out, we would be in the wrong and the man we ran past could take us to the village court for failing to shake his hand. The reason the failure to shake hands can be treated as an actionable moral and legal breach among the Urapmin is not that people there invest hand-shaking with some kind of supernatural significance or consider it one of the most important things a person does each day. It is rather that hand-shaking is culturally expected in situations of meeting, and this shared expectation is enough to make shaking hands a moral accomplishment and the failure to shake hands a moral breach.

This kind of morality of adhering to routine expectations, or what I have elsewhere called the morality of reproduction because it is a kind of moral action that reproduces already existing patterns of behavior, is at the heart of Durkheimian approaches to the moral (Robbins 2007). It is because Durkheim focuses on this kind of morality that he is seen to equate the moral with the social. Durkheim's approach has received important confirmation in work coming from the ethnomethodological tradition, from Garfinkel's (1967) breaching experiments, which showed how high the moral stakes are for violations of even the most minute interactional expectations, through more recent work on the ways social actors are always prepared to give accounts of why they have done what they have done, and are particularly quick to do so when they know they have already violated or are about to violate the routine expectations of others (Buttny 1993). The fact that most people meet cultural expectations most of the time explains why the morality of reproduction is often invisible on the surface of social life and in people's everyday conversations. It is also the existence of this kind of morality and people's fairly consistent success in meeting its demands that, I would contend, allows most people in most places to think of themselves as tolerably morally successful persons most of the time.

In contrast to the morality of reproduction, the other face of morality is one that is characterized by a sense on the part of social actors that they need to make moral choices, often between competing goods, and that it can be difficult to do this well. Because the possibility of and need for choice is so foregrounded in this kind of moral experience, I refer to this as the morality of freedom. I can again return to the Urapmin to illustrate this point. Since the late 1970s, Urapmin has been a completely Christian community. Urapmin Christian morality strongly interdicts anger, both as a feeling and in verbal expression. Yet the Urapmin also understand the demand for bridewealth, a central aspect of the formalization of all marriages, which is to be driven by the anger the bride's family feel in losing her to another household. For this reason, they expect bridewealth negotiations to be carried out in angry tones. It is adult men who negotiate bridewealth, but during the current Christian period some men withdraw from negotiations, even over their own daughters' bridewealth, because they find the feelings and displays of anger the practice requires to be too great a moral threat to what they call their "Christian lives." Others recognize the moral danger of bridewealth negotiation and try as much as possible to tone down the anger involved, but they determine that the moral force of the bridewealth institution as a key to marriage is too strong for them to resist, and they do engage in the practice. Bridewealth negotiation, then, is an area in which the Urapmin feel themselves to have the freedom to decide what to do, and one in which they feel their decisions are fraught with moral import. In this case, there is no question of simply adhering to routines because the appropriateness of the routines is itself in question.

We can now return to the matter of whether we should work to develop an anthropology of morality that aims to explore both the morality of reproduction and that of freedom, or whether we should we perhaps define only one of these as our proper domain of study. Some of the earliest work in the new wave of writing on the anthropology of morality has suggested that if the field is to grow we will need to set aside the Durkheimian interest in the morality of reproduction and focus our attention firmly on the morality of freedom (e.g., Laidlaw 2002, from whom I have drawn on heavily in developing the approach I am laying out here; Zigon 2007; and, more cautiously, Lambek 2010). There are reasons for making this suggestion, most notably the concern rooted in the history of anthropological practice until recently that once one identifies all routine social action with moral performance, it becomes hard to attend to morality as an object of study in its own right. But I want to suggest that we should not have to make a choice between highlighting the morality of reproduction and the morality of freedom. Instead, we can acknowledge that both kinds of morality go into shaping social life everywhere. If we accept this point, then two key questions arise. First, can we offer a single account of the source of moral concern in both kinds of moral framework in any given society? Second, can we account in any given society for what parts of social life tend to be governed by the morality of reproduction and what parts by that of freedom? Can we explain why, for example, shaking hands in Urapmin is not a matter about which one regularly makes conscious moral choices, whereas abstaining from or joining in bridewealth negotiations does require such deliberation? What I argue in this essay is that an approach to both kinds of morality that sees them as rooted in cultural values, but as situated in relation to cultural values in different ways, can allow us to develop productive answers to precisely these kinds of questions.

Cultural Values and Morality

I take cultural values to be cultural conceptions of the good or desirable. More than this, I also take them to be those cultural conceptions that arrange other cultural elements (such as cultural ideas about persons, kinds of actions, things, etc.) into hierarchies of better and worse or more and less desirable. Often, one can learn about cultural values by attending to relatively fixed statements people make about what is good and bad. In the broad North American culture I inhabit, for example, people regularly say such things as "Peace is better than war," "To be rich is better than to be poor," "It is better to be healthy than sick," "One should rely on oneself rather than be dependent on others," and "It is better to be happy than sad." These kinds of bald hierarchical statements are in turn often organized into further hierarchies by virtue of the relative rank of the values they express. Thus one often hears North Americans, at least those from the middle class, assert that it is better to be healthy and happy than rich. Or, in a case for which there is no standard slogan, it is appropriate to be dependent on others when one is a patient in a hospital setting because one can rely on oneself only if one is healthy – a position that ultimately puts temporary dependence in medical contexts in the service of the higher value of health, while health itself is in the service of the even higher value of independence (this ranking of independence above health is why the issue of how to think about people who require constant medical care that permanently compromises their independence is so agonizing in the North American context). To switch locales to Urapmin, we can make the same point about the ranking of values by noting that one of the things Urapmin people very frequently express is that the most important thing any person can do is be ready when Jesus returns to take the saved to heaven. They also say that it is important to have a "calm" heart – that is, to have a heart (the seat of all thought and feeling) not marred by anger or envy or strong desires. If you ask why that is the case, you learn that to have a "bad" heart is to be in sin and thus unprepared for Jesus' return. Thus, the strong value placed on having a calm heart is subordinated to the value of attaining salvation, which is the highest value in Urapmin culture.

The organization of values into hierarchies of their own is what lends cultures a good deal of their complexity – the kind of complexity that allows observers sometimes to see cultural life as so ridden with contradictions that it appears to be shaped by no consistent values at all, and this despite the fact that those living in any given culture rarely seem bothered at all by such apparent inconsistencies. Among the Urapmin, for example, in spite of all the assertions that anger is bad, and in spite of the fact that in many circumstances people do work hard to avoid feeling and expressing anger, there is one quite common context in which people routinely talk quite heatedly, almost angrily, to others and in which this kind of "strong" or "clear" talk is valued. This is when one is exhorting others to avoid sin and work toward salvation. When one harangues others about sin, one forgoes realizing a lower-level value of emotional and interactional peacefulness in order to realize a higher one of aiding in one's own and others' salvation. For this reason, it is morally appropriate to speak heatedly when giving Christian moral instruction in ways it is not appropriate, from a Christian point of view, to do so in bridewealth negotiations, since these do not contribute to realizing the value of salvation. Cultural life is full of cases like this in which a practice that is highly valued in some contexts (e.g., emotional control among the Urapmin) can be set aside in a different context in which one is aiming toward a more highly valued goal. For those living within a culture, these shifts are not generally thought of as courting contradiction or moral failure.[1]

When looking at the relation between values as we have just been doing, the most salient fact about them is that they are ranked in relation to one another. But when considering a value on its own, its most important cultural effect is that it organizes one or more kinds of action that work toward realizing the goals it sets. The most important values in a culture tend to organize not only single actions, but also strings of concatenated actions that aim at their realization. Some of the constituent actions that make up these strings also realize other, lower-order values, but their most important feature is their contribution to the ultimate realization of a higher-order value. We can say that these higher-order values organize entire spheres of action. Within a given sphere, the rank of any specific constituent action is tied to its contribution to the realization of the value that organizes it.

I borrow this notion of spheres of value from Weber (1946, 1949). In his most well-known formulation, he analyzes modern society as possessing an economic sphere, a political sphere, an aesthetic sphere, an erotic sphere, and an intellectual sphere (Weber 1946). Each sphere, Weber argues, is governed by a different value and each possesses its own "inherent laws" or "inherent logic" on the basis of which it defines the series of constituent actions necessary to realize that value (Weber 1946: 123; Bruun 2008: 102). In capitalist societies, on this model, action within the economic sphere is organized so as to realize the value of the creation and individual accumulation of wealth. In Weber's terms, economic action has been "rationalized" to meet those goals. Action in the other spheres, aimed at realizing other values, is rationalized to meet different goals.

The language of value spheres is not native to anthropology and often seems not to fit well intuitively with the ways anthropologists imagine the organization of social life (see, for example, Zigon 2009a). I want to pause here in the development of my overall argument to make two points that may help address this problem. The first is that, as Bruun (2008) has pointed out, Weber's notion of value spheres is not so different from that of "fields" as developed, for example, by Bourdieu, or of "systems," as developed by Luhmann. To this list of concepts that are in important respects similar to that of value spheres, I would add from anthropology the once widely deployed idea of "domains" and Dumont's notions of contexts and levels (Barnes et. al. 1985). What all these concepts share is a conception of social life as unfolding in a number of distinct zones of activity, or as organized around relatively distinct collections of practices, each of which is governed by its own rules and formulated in such a way as to meet distinctive goals. Among this congeries of similar concepts, the distinctive feature of Weber's conception of value spheres is its foregrounding of the claim that they are organized by values. This is the reason I stick with that term here, even as "domain," "field," or "context" might sound more familiar to the anthropological ear.

A second point I want to make in order to ease the reception among anthropologists of an argument about value spheres addresses the fact that Weber himself only discussed the spheres he saw as constitutive of modernity – the economic, political, aesthetic, erotic, and intellectual ones – and also concerns the way that Weber's model of spheres is important to the theoretical position that modernity is characterized by the increasing differentiation of such discrete spheres of social activity. In response to the fact that Weber wrote only about the value spheres that give modernity its shape, it is enough to note that, while this is true, nothing in his work suggests that other societies might not also be characterized by spheres, albeit ones shaped by different values than those at the heart of modernity (Robbins 2007: 298; Bruun 2008: 101). The second concern is a bit more pointed, for it suggests that spheres may not exist at all in societies that are in one way or another nonmodern. Following Mauss (1990), anthropologists have long argued that in nonmodern societies, rather than finding actions assigned to specific spheres, one often finds that they are "total social facts" that touch on all or many of the kinds of concerns that modern societies separate from one another and relegate to different spheres. Major exchange rituals, to take Mauss's key example, often have political and religious as well as economic significance. I do not want to contest this founding insight of modern anthropology, but I do contend that it leaves open the possibility that nonmodern societies might also be shaped by value spheres, but by ones that are different from the modern ones, so often conflated in those activities that stand as total social facts. I only assert this point here, but in the next section I will give an example of different value spheres in a nonmodern society from Papua New Guinea.

Returning to my main argument, I have noted that, taken singly, values organize their own spheres aimed at their realization and in doing so create hierarchies of elements within each sphere, while between values there are also hierarchical relations. It remains to note that the ranking of values means that value spheres themselves are often ranked in relation to one another, and more highly ranked value spheres are more likely to organize the structure of less important ones than vice versa. In North America, the economy is the most highly valued sphere. The sphere of the family is also valued, but not as highly. For this reason, the sphere of the family serves the realization of the goals of the economic sphere (by, for example, operating to produce independent individuals capable both of working and consuming effectively) more often than the economic sphere contributes to the realization of the values of the family (Birken 1988). Examples such as this indicate that the study of a culture organized around values must take account of the hierarchical organization of value spheres in relation to one another, as well as attending to the organization of elements within each individual sphere. Just how thoroughly "rationalized" or "integrated" the relation between spheres is in any given culture I take to be an open question, though near the end of this chapter I will suggest that different ways of answering it pose important questions for future research.

At this point, I have laid out a sketch of a way to look at cultures as organized by values. My next task is to relate this sketch to the anthropological study of morality. The basis of this relationship is the claim that most cultural practices or actions aim to realize one or more values. At its simplest, moral action consists in carrying out a practice correctly in the right context such that appropriate values are realized. This is true both for actions that unfold under the sign of the morality of reproduction and those that result from choices made from within the morality of freedom.

I will illustrate this point about the link between values and morality by returning to some Urapmin materials I have already introduced. We can begin with handshaking. A value that I have elsewhere called that of relationalism is salient in many contexts of Urapmin life (Robbins 2004). Actions governed by the value of relationalism work toward the creation or maintenance of relations between people. Hand-shaking upon meeting each day is for the Urapmin a way of affirming and thereby maintaining the relation that holds between the parties who perform it. There are more elaborate and important ways of affirming and creating relationships in Urapmin, including various kinds of gift-giving. The value of relationalism organizes these practices into ideal chains that normatively structure the social sphere in Urapmin, such that those who shake hands also often exchange gifts and engage in other relation-maintaining actions. But I focus on hand-shaking here to follow up on my earlier discussion. When I first mentioned Urapmin hand-shaking, I used it to illustrate the moral weight of routine actions. I can now expand that account by pointing out that the moral weight of hand-shaking is grounded not only in its routine quality, but also in its fittingness to realize the value of relationalism. Indeed, its routine quality follows from its moral tie to the paramount value of relationalism. It is its link to a key Urapmin value that ultimately gives hand-shaking its moral relevance, and such links are characteristic of all routine actions.

It is important to note, however, that hand-shaking is routine not only by virtue of its tie to the value of relationalism. Its routine quality is further rooted in the fact that there are no competing practices Urapmin might choose to use to do the work hand-shaking does and, more importantly, there are few situations of meeting someone in Urapmin where one would not want the interaction to unfold in the value sphere governed by relationalism. In Urapmin, people who are in dispute work hard to avoid one another. They often retreat to live in relatively isolated garden houses in the bush until matters are settled and thereby avoid meeting each other and having to decide whether to shake hands and engage in other actions that realize the value of relationalism. This means that one generally meets for the first time each day only those with whom one wants to engage in the relational value sphere, and one is therefore willing to affirm with them at least the minimal relation signaled by hand-shaking. It is both because hand-shaking realizes a key value that organizes a widely relevant value sphere and because it is rarely called for in situations in which people are attracted to replacing it with other kinds of practices that Urapmin take it largely for granted, treating it as a practice that is supported by the morality of reproduction.

In all cultures there are many situations like that of meeting for the first time during a day in Urapmin in which the value sphere in which action should unfold is evident and routine governs its performance. We can think of these as situations that take place predominantly within a single value sphere. These are the kinds of value contexts in which the morality of reproduction holds sway. In what kinds of value situations, then, do we find the morality of freedom taking hold? My suggestion is that this kind of morality comes into play when it is not clear in which value sphere an interaction should take place. In such situations, people experience having a choice of which value to realize. Urapmin men facing the choice of whether or not to engage in bridewealth negotiations are in this position. Traditional norms of bridewealth negotiation are focused on the creation of new relationships, and they recognize anger and struggle as playing legitimate roles in this process. From the point of view of these norms, anger and struggle are moral practices when put in service of the value of creating relationships. But Urapmin Christian morality values individual salvation over the creation of relationships and sees anger and struggle as always damaging the realization of its preeminent goal. Men thus have to choose to realize one or the other value, and to act appropriately in the sphere of whichever value they choose. Both kinds of action are moral because they both realize important values, but it is not clear in every situation which value most demands to be served. Situations in which it is not evident which value should govern interaction are those in which the morality of freedom comes to the fore.

At this point, I have addressed the concerns with which I started. I have shown how a single analysis of morality as rooted in values can account for the existence of both the morality of reproduction and that of freedom, and I have shown how this analysis also provides an account of the different kinds of situations in which each kind of morality appears in social life. In concluding this section, I need to make a final theoretical point. The approach to value and morality I have been developing here is a *cultural* one. My aim has been to consider how values shape culture and define what counts as moral action in matters both of reproduction and of freedom. Social scientific discussions of values often treat them as matters of individual preference, but that is not what I am doing here. I am arguing that one can identify the key values in a culture by looking at the common patterns of its social life and exploring the logic of its enduring conceptions (Robbins 2004, 2007). The study of individual experiences of moral choice and moral action is a different matter, and one I will not focus on here. I would suggest that cultural values provide the conditions of possibility for individual moral experience, even if they do not exhaustively explain it. But the effort to study individual moral experience is separate from that of providing a cultural analysis of morality and may well require theoretical materials beyond those I have offered here (for more on this, see my exchange with Zigon: Zigon 2009a, Robbins 2009; Zigon 2009b).

I have already provided some brief examples of the kind of cultural analysis this approach to morality supports, but in what follows I want to offer some slightly more sustained ethnographic sketches of the role of cultural values in constructing moral worlds. Because I have elsewhere presented a case in which the morality of freedom is to the fore (Robbins 2007), I focus in the next section on showing how one can use this approach to study the morality of reproduction in novel ethnographic terms.

Ethnographies of Value and the Morality of Reproduction

Ayala Fader's (2009) ethnography *Mitzvah Girls: Bringing Up the Next Generation of Hasidic Jews in Brooklyn* is a superb study of the socialization of girls and young women into a "nonliberal" cultural world in the contemporary United States. Marked by a keen sensitivity to the way girls and the women who socialize them understand their moral lives, and alert to the extent to which key values organize Hasidic culture, Fader's book provides us with an opportunity to consider in some detail how values shape the morality of reproduction. The linguistic situation of the Hasidic people Fader studies is particularly complex, with at least three languages routinely in play. One of the great accomplishments of the book is to allow us to see how values at once organize and moralize the way these languages are used.

The Bobover and unaffiliated Hasidim Fader studies take their place among a number of highly orthodox groups of Jews living in Brooklyn, New York. They insist on the strict observance of religious rules aimed at bringing about the highest value their culture promotes: the redemption of the Jewish people (Fader 2009: 87). Men work toward this value in the religious sphere, devoting their youth and young adulthood solely to religious study and worship. While adult men are expected to work for a living after marriage, an ultimate goal even during this period is to make enough money to retire and again devote oneself full-time to study (230). Women also participate in worship, but another way they support the attainment of Jewish redemption is by navigating the secular world to meet the needs of their families. It is their responsibility, for example, to interact with "pediatricians, social service agencies, and the electric company" (22). By carrying out such tasks, women protect the men of their families from the possible corruptions of the secular world and allow them to devote themselves more fully to sacred tasks. As Fader puts it, "women must be fluent enough in the secular world so they can protect Torah-studying males from its distractions" (120). Yet even as they enter the secular world, women must also mark their difference from it. It is crucial that they retain their identities as Jews at all times, even to the extent of "hyperbolizing their distinctiveness" from non-Jews (Gentiles) (14). This maintenance of a distinctive identity is what allows them to act in the secular world – to realize to some extent its values – but to do so for their own purposes and therefore without ceasing to work toward the realization of the ultimate sacred values of their community.

The value system I have just described extensively structures the linguistic situation in the Hasidic community. As noted above, three languages are in use. *Loshn-koydesh* ("holy language") is the language of the Torah, prayers, and the early rabbinic literature (Fader 2009: 87). A mixture of ancient Hebrew and Aramaic, this is the most sacred of the three languages and is used primarily by men in study and worship, though also by women in prayer. The everyday vernacular of men is Yiddish. Their use of this language, and their relative lack of fluency in English, is a marker of their commitment to the realization of sacred values. It distinguishes them absolutely from Gentiles and, as we shall see, also from women. When men or women speaking Yiddish need to borrow English words, they are encouraged to pronounce them with a Yiddish accent. This allows speakers to "religiously uplift the English words they need" while continuing to keep their code distinct from that of the Gentiles (94). Speaking Yiddish as one's main vernacular language, and speaking it in such a way as to assimilate borrowed English words to its form, is a routine moral practice for men, and one that is closely tied to the realization of their highest value.

Women, who must engage the secular world, speak much less Yiddish. Their primary vernacular is English, the language of that secular world. But their English is distinctive in ways that reflect their need to balance the value of managing the secular world to achieve their own Hasidic ends with the need always to keep in mind higher sacred values and to maintain Jewish distinctiveness as part of the effort to realize them. Most importantly, Hasidic women's English borrows Yiddish intonation and phonology, and is also peppered with Yiddish words and phrases (101–103). In this way, "they adapt and redeem" English by making it "sound … Hasidic" (116). As with men's use of Yiddish, women's use of a form of English that is distinctive in the way it sounds and in its lexicon is a routine moral practice closely tied to the realization of the community's most important religious values.

In many societies, speaking is much of the time a routine activity, and the value-defined moral system of Hasidic language use I have just described reads in Fader's ethnography as one that is largely given over to the morality of reproduction. Yet there are hints in her account of some issues that threaten to unsettle the easy moral reproduction of this linguistic system. In order to appreciate this, we must recognize that the languages of this Hasidic world are themselves ranked in value, with *loshn-koydesh* at the top followed by Yiddish, and then English, which, even in its heavily modified form, is at the bottom. With a recent push in the community for even greater religious stringency, men have begun to ask that women make Yiddish their vernacular, reserving English only for contexts in which it is absolutely necessary. To this point, the campaign to increase Yiddish use among women has not been successful. All women, along with men, speak a Yiddish baby-talk register to their children, insuring that everyone's first language is a relatively sacred one (Fader 2009: 124). But women continue to speak their Hasidic form of English to their older children and among themselves, as well as to Gentiles. Nor do women seem particularly morally troubled by their failure to increase their use of Yiddish. Fader gives some reasons for this. These include the fact that the generation of women who are now mothers did not, for historical reasons, learn much Yiddish and so simply cannot speak it, and these are the women after whom younger girls pattern themselves. To this argument, I would add that from Fader's work it appears that women's use of English fits the value system too well to become deeply problematic. Not only must women learn English to be able to engage the secular world for their families, but it also serves to differentiate them from Hasidic men, a process that makes its own contribution to realizing the sacred values of the community. So the pattern of women speaking English remains dominant and morally comfortable in the community. For some women, however, one senses that the male push to increase Yiddish usage may be opening up room for the exercise of moral freedom in choosing whether to use Yiddish or English in many contexts. Exploring this kind of development of new areas of moral freedom is one of the avenues of research toward which the anthropological study of value and morality is well positioned to direct us.

From the point of view of the theory of values and morality I have been laying out, the Hasidic case is a complex but ultimately quite orderly one. The value of attaining redemption for the Jewish people is clearly the most important one in the community, and all activities must orient to or accommodate that value to a greater or lesser extent. The other ethnographic case I want to present, drawn from the literature on Papua New Guinea, is one in which the ranking between values is harder to determine and the discrepancies between actions carried out in different spheres are more to the fore.

Avatip is a Sepik River community located in Papua New Guinea's East Sepik Province (Harrison 1985b: 413). Harrison (1985a, 1985b) has written a pair of now classic articles exploring the opposed values that organize what he calls the "ritual" and the "secular" domains in Avatip. In the terms I have been deploying throughout this essay, these domains are distinctive values spheres. The Avatip case is instructive for how differently moral action is defined in each sphere, and for the way in which the moral import of these differences is recognized in the local conception of personhood.

As was at least formerly the case in many Sepik societies, Avatip ritual life is centered around a male initiation cult. As Harrison puts it, "the central concerns of the men's cult are with the maintenance of the cosmic order by men, and with their assertion of their individual and collective strength in warfare" (1985b: 417). The key value that organizes their efforts in this direction he calls "ritual hierarchy." All important practices of the men's cult represent the cosmos and the social world as hierarchical, and they place Avatip adult men at the top of the human portion of this hierarchy, above Avatip women and younger men, and above their enemy neighbors. This emphasis on hierarchy is reflected, for example, in the organization of the cult into a number of different initiatory levels. As they move through these levels, boys are taught sacred knowledge they must keep secret from women and younger boys, thus asserting their ritual priority over them. As befits Avatip ritual's general commitment to the realization of the value of hierarchy, actions in the ritual sphere are often aggressive and self-assertive. They draw on and develop a part of the person the Avatip call the "Spirit" (*kaiyik*) (Harrison 1985a: 117). A person's Spirit is the basis of growth, self-will, and, when cultivated, power over others. It is that part of a person that allows him or her to take, even if only temporarily, a hierarchical position above others. It is thus well suited to drive action in the ritual sphere.

By contrast to the ritual domain, the secular sphere in Avatip is structured by the value of equality. Everyday life, governed by this value, is marked by sensitivity to others and an interest in achieving equivalence through reciprocity in "marriage negotiations, exchanges of agricultural labor, the productive cooperation of spouses, and so forth" (Harrison 1985b: 419). Relations between the sexes in marriage are notably supportive, with both men and women seen as contributing strongly to the maintenance of the household (416). Just as actions taken toward the realization of ritual hierarchy are grounded in Avatip ideas about Spirit as an aspect of personhood, so too do the Avatip see secular equality as flowing from a distinct part of the person: his or her "Understanding" (*mawul*) (Harrison 1985a: 118–119). Recognized as the seat of thought and feeling, the Understanding is responsible for people's "sociability, compassion" and sense of "respect" for others (117). Assertions of hierarchical dominance are foreign to the Understanding, and they have little place in secular everyday life in the Avatip community.

One of Harrison's most original claims in these articles is that we should not see ritual hierarchy as a male value and secular equality as a female value. Instead, they are distinctive spheres of action the legitimacy and values of which both men and women recognize (see M. Strathern 1988). When acting in the secular sphere, both men and women usually draw on their Understanding to realize the value of equality. Similarly, women support men's cultivation and hierarchical expression of their Spirit in the ritual sphere, and in some contexts also express the power of their own Spirits (Harrison 1985a: 121). From the point of view of my argument in this essay, the ritual and the secular spheres shape moral behavior for everyone around two quite distinctive values. Within each sphere, the morality of reproduction expects very different kinds of action from people. The bifurcation of the self into two distinct components reflects the extent of this difference, almost as if every Avatip person possessed two kinds of moral personhood, each aimed at the realization of a different value.[2]

For the most part, the two spheres seem quite discrete in Avatip, which would perhaps lead to few situations involving the values of hierarchy and equality in which the morality of reproduction might give way to the morality of freedom. The ethnography Harrison reports supports this interpretation. But it is worth noting that he does observe that the "conflicting demands of these different spheres ... lie at the root of a moral or existential tension which, I think, many men keenly if inarticulately feel, between the ideals of Spirit and Understanding" (1985a: 126). Without more information than this passing remark, we cannot go further in exploring where the morality of freedom might find a place in Avatip society. But it is worth noting that in another Sepik society, post-contact changes led one group, in which men felt this kind of conflict between ritual hierarchy and secular equality, to abandon the male cult system entirely in favor of a Christian revival movement that supported more egalitarian values, leading to a period in which the morality of reproduction lost much of its grip on their lives (Tuzin 1982, 1997). Another important project for the anthropology of morality and value would thus be learning to identify where tensions that give the morality of freedom room to operate may exist even in societies in which value spheres appear to be neatly segregated and not obviously in conflict. Such considerations verge on questions of value integration and pluralism that I want to take up in the next section.

On Value Integration, Pluralism, and Morality

One feature of the Avatip case that distinguishes it sharply from the Hasidic one is that in Avatip it appears that neither hierarchy nor equality is ranked above the other, while in the Hasidic community Fader studied the religious value of attaining redemption stands squarely at the top of the hierarchy of values and organizes when and how other, lower-ranked values (for example, the value women pursue of successfully negotiating the secular world) can express themselves. The difference between these two cases bears on the most prominent discussion of cultural values in the Western academy today. This discussion is not being carried out by anthropologists. It is instead a philosophical one that turns on the question of whether in terms of values most societies are or should be organized like Avatip or like the Hasidic Jews of Brooklyn. In this discussion, Avatip would stand as a representative of the pluralist position, while the Hasidic community offers a case of what the philosophers call monism. Weber and Berlin are well-known pluralists (Lassman 2004). They assert that values are always in competition and that there are no cases, or at least no legitimate ones, in which a stable hierarchy holds between all the value spheres of a society. As Weber has famously put it, the "various value spheres of the world stand in irreconcilable conflict with each other" (1946: 147). In Berlin's equally influential phrasing: "If, as I believe, the ends of men are many, and not all of them are in principle compatible with each other, then the possibility of conflict – and of tragedy – can never be wholly eliminated from human life, either personal or social. The necessity of choosing between absolute claims is then an inescapable characteristic of the human condition" (1998: 239). For those who hold the monist position, values do not inevitably conflict it this way. There is no conflict either, because, as Galston expresses this position, there is "a comprehensive hierarchy or ordering among goods" (2002: 6), or, as in Dworkin's (2011) major recent formulation, each important value supports the realization of all others.[3]

For political philosophers, debates about whether pluralism or monism is the best way to understand value can be both normative and ontological (in the strong philosophical sense of determining which things exist regardless of whether any given culture defines them as existing or not). They can be, that is to say, about how societies should be organized in relation to value and about the truth of which values exist in the world and how they are in reality related to one another (Dworkin [2011] vigorously reviews many of these debates). Anthropologists are not in a position to enter these debates on the terms political philosophers set, but I want to suggest that the broad questions these philosophers pose about how cultural values are organized do present at least two issues anthropologists of value and morality might productively take up.

The first of these issues is that of whether actually existing cultures tend to be pluralist or monist in composition, or if there is no distinct tendency and societies are equally likely to take either shape. The most important anthropological theorist of value, Dumont (1977, 1980, 1986), is well known for his claim that societies are organized by paramount values and for at least implying that cultures (or what he called "ideologies") can be exhaustively studied from the point of view of the way their paramount values organize the relations between all other values. The exception to this rule in Dumont's program would be in cases in which a culture is changing and an older paramount value is fading or is under pressure from a new one (Dumont 1994; see also Robbins 2004). Although such cases would be pluralist ones, theoretically they would tend to move toward a situation in which either the old or the new value eventually establishes paramountcy and monism again becomes the norm.

With the general anthropological abandonment of strong theories of culture from the late 1980s forward, Dumont's monist approach to value fell from favor. Scholars have since then had trouble imagining a culture organized around a single paramount value. They see social life as marked by too much conflict, and as too much shaped by individual variation in thought and practice, to be susceptible to such an analysis. What replaced Dumont's monism, however, was not a well-worked-out theory of value pluralism. Instead, it was a general disinterest in cultural values complemented when necessary by a model much closer to neoclassical economic ones that define value as a matter of individual preference (a shift Dumont would ironically have little trouble explaining in terms of his monist analysis of Western culture). Given this situation, I see the development of a sophisticated anthropology of value pluralism as a cultural phenomenon as a key goal for future research. Only with this in hand can we hope to answer questions about whether monism or pluralism is a more common form of cultural organization, or whether both are found with equal frequency.

If anthropologists were to pursue this agenda, I would add that I think it would be unwise for them to assume for theoretical reasons that monism is in fact rare. The individualist drift of contemporary anthropological theory would lead thought in that direction, but precisely because the assumption of pluralism is so in keeping with Western cultural values, we would do well to not accept it without interrogating its fit to the world. Working quickly to illustrate my point with materials readers are likely to know, I would note that many Western academics would likely see the values of the intellectual sphere in which they participate as in strong conflict with those of the economic sphere. And indeed they often are. But as is abundantly clear at present, the intellectual sphere in the West is organized so as ultimately to support the dominant economic sphere and the individualist values it promotes. Regardless of what academics write and teach in the classroom, the system they act in provides human and ideational materials for the economic sphere. Looking at individual preferences and self-understandings among academics, there appears to be a good deal of pluralistic value conflict between the intellectual and the economic spheres. But from the point of view of cultural analysis, the hierarchy between these two spheres is evident and not currently under threat. It would of course take a much fuller analysis of all the modern value spheres to demonstrate that full-fledged monism is at work in any given modern culture, but I hope to have at least pointed to the kinds of data that make it hard to rule out the possibility that this claim is correct. One reason to keep the distinctiveness of cultural analysis in mind when considering the distribution of monism and pluralism throughout the cultures of the world is that it allows us to think beyond our own understanding of our personal experience in just this way.

The second issue the philosophical debate between pluralists and monists raises for us is whether moral life differs in societies marked by each of these kinds of organization. Having already noted that we do not yet have a well-developed anthropology of pluralism, I cannot report established findings here. But I do want to suggest the importance of the question. On theoretical grounds, one would expect that truly monist cultures would present their members with relatively fewer situations in which the morality of freedom is in play, whereas pluralist ones would likely offer fewer opportunities for the morality of reproduction. To be sure, those living in monist cultures might still at times wrestle with their own desires not to honor the demands of the morality of reproduction, and there might be instances in which they are unclear about how to apply the morality of reproduction in a situation that nonetheless seems to them obviously to demand it (Robbins 2009), but one imagines that they less often face the truly "tragic" (borrowing Berlin's term) moments of moral freedom in which they feel compelled to sacrifice one value in the name of another that seems to be its equal rather than its superior. Ethnographies like Fader's give us a feel for this kind of monist moral life and describe people who appear to exhibit a strong sense of moral purpose and moral accomplishment. By contrast, ethnographies of situations of strong pluralist conflict between values, such as my own study of how the Urapmin live in the wake of radical cultural change, present a picture of the dominance of the morality of freedom as leading to a great deal of moral worry – a worry that can show up even in quite mundane situations (Robbins 2004, 2007). Further ethnographic work on the cultural organization of values and the ways different kinds of organization shape moral life can help us to develop further comparative work along these lines.

Conclusion

The excitement around the anthropology of morality at the moment follows in part from people's sense that it is a wide open field, rich in possibilities. I have tried in this essay to make the case for exploring the connection between cultural values and morality as one important path through this field. Although the study of cultural values is a relatively minor topic in anthropology in general at the moment, I hope to have made the point that the anthropology of morality will have to reckon with the issues raised by the study of cultural values if it is to give a well-rounded account of the materials with which it is concerned. In particular, I have suggested that an analysis of the role of cultural values in shaping moral life enables us to encompass the morality of reproduction and that of freedom within a single framework. Accounting for both kinds of morality in some way is a task we will have to accomplish if we hope to have ethnographies of morality that correspond to what we already know to be the diverse nature of people's moral lives. I have also argued that a focus on values will allow us to contribute to the study of issues of pluralism that are at the center of political philosophical debate today. I hope these suggestions might be enough to keep the topic of cultural values near the forefront of the rapidly developing conversation around the anthropology of morality.

NOTES

1 In this part of my discussion of cultural values I am drawing heavily, though sometimes loosely, on the work of Dumont (in this paragraph, particularly Dumont 1986, but for my discussion as a whole see Dumont 1977 and 1980 as well). In other places, I have laid out my debts to Dumont more thoroughly and have developed aspects of my own position I do not address explicitly in this discussion (Robbins 1994, 2004, 2007).

2 I should note that in one of the two articles under discussion, Harrison (1985a: 117) writes that men aim to realize "'aesthetic' values" in the ritual sphere while people in general aim to realize "moral ones" in the secular sphere. This distinction is not central to his argument, and my own discussion of both spheres as moral does not in any way clash with his overall account. In any case, given my definition of moral action here as action tied to the realization of cultural values, it is clear that both spheres are moral ones – a point Harrison implicitly affirms by talking about a "moral … tension" that arises as people attempt to cope with the differences between them (1985a: 126; and see my discussion further in the main text).

3 Galston suggests a third kind of monism, which "reduces goods to a common measure" (2002: 6). I do not mention this one in the text because, from the point of view of the cultural organization of values, I do not see how this differs from having a comprehensive hierarchy of goods, since in such a hierarchy each value would be ranked on a single scale on the basis of the strength of its contribution to whatever value provides the substance of the common measure.

REFERENCES

Barnes, R. H., De Coppet, Daniel, and Parkin, R. J. (eds.) (1985) *Contexts and Levels: Anthropological Essays on Hierarchy*. Oxford: JASO.

Berlin, Isaiah (1998) *The Proper Study of Mankind: An Anthology of Essays*. New York: Farrar, Straus & Giroux.

Birken, Lawrence (1988) *Consuming Desire: Sexual Science and the Emergence of a Culture of Abundance, 1871–1914*. Ithaca, NY: Cornell University Press.

Bruun, Hans Henrik (2008) Objectivity, Value Spheres, and "Inherent Laws": On Some Suggestive Isomorphisms between Weber, Bourdieu, and Luhmann. *Philosophy of the Social Sciences* 38(1): 97–120.

Buttny, Richard (1993) *Social Accountability in Communication*. London: Sage.

Dumont, Louis (1977) *From Mandeville to Marx: The Genesis and Triumph of Economic Ideology*. Chicago: University of Chicago Press.

Dumont, Louis (1980) *Homo Hierarchicus: The Caste System and its Implications*, rev. edn., trans. Mark Sainsbury, Louis Dumont, and Basia Gulati. Chicago: University of Chicago Press.

Dumont, Louis (1986) *Essays on Individualism: Modern Ideology in Anthropological Perspective*. Chicago: University of Chicago Press.

Dumont, Louis (1994) *German Ideology: From France to Germany and Back*. Chicago: University of Chicago Press.

Dworkin, Ronald (2011) *Justice for Hedgehogs*. Cambridge, MA: Harvard University Press.

Fader, Ayala (2009) *Mitzvah Girls: Bringing Up the Next Generation of Hasidic Jews in Brooklyn*. Princeton: Princeton University Press.

Galston, William A. (2002) *Liberal Pluralism: The Implications of Value Pluralism for Political Theory and Practice*. Cambridge: Cambridge University Press.

Garfinkel, Harold (1967) *Studies in Ethnomethodology*. Englewood Cliffs, NJ: Prentice Hall.

Harrison, Simon (1985a) Concepts of the Person in Avatip Religious Thought. *Man* 20(1): 115–130.

Harrison, Simon (1985b) Ritual Hierarchy and Secular Equality in a Sepik River Village. *American Ethnologist* 12(3): 413–426.

Kluckhohn, Clyde (1962 [1951]) Values and Value-Orientations in the Theory of Action: An Exploration in Definition and Classification. In T. Parsons and E.A. Shils (eds.), *Toward a General Theory of Action: Theoretical Foundations for the Social Sciences*. New York: Harper & Row, pp. 388–433.

Laidlaw, James (2002) For an Anthropology of Ethics and Freedom. *Journal of the Royal Anthropological Institute* 8(2): 311–332.

Lambek, Michael (2010) Introduction. In M. Lambek (ed.), *Ordinary Ethics: Anthropology, Language, and Action*. New York: Fordham University Press, pp. 1–36.

Lassman, Peter (2004) Political Theory in an Age of Disenchantment: The Problem of Value Pluralism: Weber, Berlin, Rawls. *Max Weber Studies* 4(2): 253–271.

Mauss, Marcel (1990 [1925]) *The Gift: The Form and Reason for Exchange in Archaic Societies*, trans. W. D. Halls. London: Routledge.

Robbins, Joel (1994) Equality as a Value: Ideology in Dumont, Melanesia and the West. *Social Analysis* 36: 21–70.

Robbins, Joel (2004) *Becoming Sinners: Christianity and Moral Torment in a Papua New Guinea Society*. Berkeley: University of California Press.

Robbins, Joel (2007) Between Reproduction and Freedom: Morality, Value, and Radical Cultural Change. *Ethnos* 72(3): 293–314.

Robbins, Joel (2009) Value, Structure, and the Range of Possibilities: A Response to Zigon. *Ethnos* 74(2): 277–285.

Strathern, Marilyn (1988) *The Gender of the Gift: Problems with Women and Problems with Society in Melanesia*. Berkeley: University of California Press.

Tuzin, Donald (1982) Ritual Violence among the Ilahita Arapesh: The Dynamics of Moral and Religious Uncertainty. In G. H. Herdt (ed.), *Rituals of Manhood: Male Initiation in Papua New Guinea*. Berkeley: University of California Press, pp. 321–355.

Tuzin, Donald (1997) *The Cassowary's Revenge: The Life and Death of Masculinity in a New Guinea Society*. Chicago: University of Chicago Press.

Weber, Max (1946) *From Max Weber: Essays in Sociology*, trans. H. H. Gerth and C. W. Mills. New York: Oxford University Press.

Weber, Max (1949) *The Methodology of the Social Sciences*, trans. E. A. Shils and H. A. Finch. New York: Free Press.

Zigon, Jarrett (2007) Moral Breakdown and the Ethical Demand: A Theoretical Framework for an Anthropology of Moralities. *Anthropological Theory* 7(2): 131–150.

Zigon, Jarrett (2009a) Phenomenological Anthropology and Morality: A Reply to Robbins. *Ethnos* 74(2): 286–288.

Zigon, Jarrett (2009b) Within a Range of Possibilities: Morality and Ethics in Social Life. *Ethnos* 74(2): 251–276.

CHAPTER **8**

Ordinary Ethics

Veena Das

The idea of ordinary ethics that I put forward in this essay takes its inspiration from a strand in philosophy found in the works of J. L. Austin and Stanley Cavell that traces the vulnerability of everyday life to the facts of our being both, embodied creatures and beings who have a life in language. My attraction to the work of Austin and Cavell comes from my intuition that in both these philosophers we find an aspiration to think of philosophical problems as *human* problems in that they arise in the lives of actual people and not only in the hallowed halls of philosophy. Cavell, for instance, repeatedly draws examples from what he calls the humble use of philosophically famous words whether in fiction or in Hollywood movies to think of the philosophical problems of inhabiting the everyday that is shadowed by skepticism (see Das 2011b). Austin draws on such regions of everyday life as the offering of excuses and pretending as crucial to his ability to challenge the profundities of arguments about the relation between language and the world which ultimately rests on a copy theory of truth (Austin 1969a, 1969b). On their side, anthropologists have argued that ethics is simply part of our life with others – it is not a domain that is set apart. As Michael Lambek recently noted:

> human beings cannot avoid being subject to ethics, speaking and acting with ethical consequences, evaluating our actions and those of others, acknowledging and refusing acknowledgement, caring and taking care, but also being aware of our failure to do so consistently. As a species, given our consciousness, our socialization and sociality, and our use of language, we are fundamentally ethical. (2010: 1)

But here lies the paradox – within this framework of thought how are we to account for the fact that human beings also act unethically, judge their own or others' action to be wrong and as Austin's (1962, 1969a, 1969b) work shows, our "natural language" itself expresses the minute distinctions we make when our actions misfire or when we become implicated in concealments of all kinds.[1]

A Companion to Moral Anthropology, First Edition. Edited by Didier Fassin.

One way to think of the issue of ethics is with the help of a vocabulary of rules and their infringement – assuming that the normative rules of our society give us the guidelines of how to act ethically. This view, however, has to confront the worry that these rules could themselves be subjected to moral critique both from within and outside our social worlds. Many scholars have tried to address this issue by making distinctions between morality and ethics referring to socially embedded rules that are particularistic versus more abstract rules that are more generally applied; others find such distinctions to be of little use since it is hard to keep ethics and morality, however defined, apart in the actual flux of life (Taylor 1996; Kleinman 2006; Lambek 2010; Faubion 2011). As Cora Diamond (1996: 102) reflects, describing events, real or imagined, is itself a moral activity and when moral life is tied too closely to notions of choice and of freedom exercised in the capacity to choose, other forms of moral activity become invisible.

Much discussion on ethics accords a centrality to judgments based on reasoning. It is assumed by many that objective, universal measures are needed to overcome the subjective dispositions that obscure a clear view of the moral landscape (for a critique of this view, see Crary 2007). I will argue for a shift in perspective from thinking of ethics as made up of judgments we arrive at when we stand away from our ordinary practices to that of thinking of the ethical as a dimension of everyday life in which we are not aspiring to escape the ordinary but rather to descend into it as a way of becoming moral subjects. Such a descent into the ordinary does not mean that no attempt is made to work on this ordinary in the sense of cultivating critical attitudes toward one's culture as it stands, and also working to improve one's conditions of life but that such work is done not by orienting oneself to transcendental, objectively agreed-upon values but rather through the cultivation of sensibilities *within* the everyday. One way to put this is in terms of the labor of bringing about an eventual everyday from within the actual everyday. In order to give flesh to this argument, I will offer examples from ethnographies (my own and that of others) to show how we might think of what is moral striving in the everyday from this perspective. I would like to think of these ethnographic descriptions as scenes, somewhat like Wittgenstein's (2001 [1953]) scenes of instruction. With the help of these ethnographic examples, I want to reflect on the following three issues: (1) how rule-following is different from the notion of a moral life in the everyday; (2) what it takes to allow life to be renewed, to achieve the everyday, under conditions of grinding poverty or catastrophic violence that erode the very possibility of the ordinary; and (3) what form moral strivings take in the work performed to give birth to the eventual everyday from within the actual everyday. The following sections are not organized to correspond to each of these questions – rather the questions are addressed throughout the essay. I hope that this discussion will help to show that the notions of ethics and morality on the register of the ordinary are more like threads woven into the weave of life rather than notions that stand out and call attention to themselves through dramatic enactments and heroic struggles of good versus evil.[2]

Moral Life, Rules, Customs, and Habits

In discussing certain virtues in Theravada Buddhism, through which one learns to be attentive to how one inhabits the world with others, Charles Hallisey (2010) offers a discussion of two conceptions of the ethical from the modern West in the light of which we might consider how to think of ordinary ethics. In response to the ancient question of how one ought to live one's life, one view associated with theorists such as Paul Ricoeur (1994) postulates that ethics are primarily about how one lives well *with* others or *for* others. The second view, articulated in Foucault's work on the care of the self, offers the thought that this same question involves practices that involve the self's relation to the self – concrete practices of self-fashioning that he calls "technologies of the self" (Foucault 1997, 2005). However, before we think that these are opposed practices, we must heed Hallisey's advice that we not set aside one of these conceptions too quickly in favor of the other,

> if only because the desire to live well with others frequently provides motive and guidance to those undertaking a wide range of practices of self-fashioning in any particular moral culture or ethical tradition. This is especially the case whenever the practices of self-fashioning entail a critique of the self and a desire to become other than what one discovers oneself to be. (Hallisey 2010: 143)

For Foucault (1997, 2005) too the self's relation to the self is no simple matter – the mode of subjectivation involves an inquiry into how the subject is invited or incited to become a moral subject. Simply stated, one might say that the mode of subjectivation necessarily involves the work one must do on oneself to bring oneself into accord with or in alignment with a moral tradition that lies outside of oneself (Mahmood 2005), but this mode of subjectivation is not the same as simply learning to obey explicitly formulated rules. Sylvain Perdigon (2011), in his recent work on Palestinian refugees, presents this idea through the Islamic notion of *al-iman* as the state of veridiction in which there is an accord between what one knows in one's heart, what one says with one's tongue, and what one does with one's limbs in everyday practices of kinship (see especially Murata and Chittick 1994). Let us also recall my earlier discussion of Austin and Cavell that such notions of work on the self and with others has to be undertaken in the context of the recognition of the vulnerability and fragility of everyday life particularly noticeable in the contexts of the fragile conditions in which vulnerable populations such as refugees or poor migrants are compelled to make their everyday life (Das 2011a).

In the low-income neighborhoods in Delhi in which much of my recent work is situated, I came to recognize the delicacy of maintaining regard for others through the minutest of gestures (Das 2010a, 2010b). Thus, for instance, women would refrain from sweeping the floor right after a guest had left because that might suggest that "We think that guest is just trash." In the two decades of the 1970s and 1980s, when I was conducting fieldwork among Punjabi families in the crowded localities of Old Delhi (Das 1976, 2007), I would watch with some amusement the verbal barbs women directed at each other over quotidian fights – who threw that bucket of dirty water after doing laundry from the rooftop into the street? Which child had hit one's child? How dare a neighbor engage in crooked speech (*ulti seedhi batein*) and spread rumors about another? Nevertheless, the quarrels would stop when it was time for the men to return home in the evening, though sometimes a woman might place an upturned *mooda* (a bamboo stool) on the threshold as a sign that she intended to resume the arguments next day.[3] It did not seem right to many women to confront a tired man who had braved the heat and dust of the streets to be confronted with an atmosphere of discord. One might read this as the patriarchal ideology of a serene home that women were expected to create for men – such gestures surely expressed this idea and sometimes, by the same token, the inability to maintain a serene home could lead to acts of domestic violence (Price 2002; Kelly 2003). Thus, the possibility of speaking of ordinary ethics allows us also to think of the unethical as growing within the forms of life that people inhabit – it is, thus, not a matter of eliciting opinions about what behavior is considered ethical or unethical, or of cataloguing cultural practices on which we can bring judgment from an objective, distant position but rather of seeing how forms of life grow particular dispositions. Such an argument has some important methodological implications.

Some authors such as Leela Prasad have argued that modes of narration, especially of painful events, may themselves be regarded as ethical or unethical. For instance, doing something enjoyable when recounting a tragedy in the past would constitute an ethical breach for some of her respondents (Prasad 2010). For me it was not simply a matter of how one narrates an event but rather how the everyday words and gestures were folded into ways of acknowledging or withholding acknowledgment to the concrete others within a web of other practices. This raises the delicate question of why and under what conditions one is led to articulate something like a general statement in the form of a norm, or when it is that explicit formulation of a rule or a justification is called for – a point that I will attend to in the later part of this essay.

For many of the women and men I came to know in my ethnographic work, words and gestures expressed how one is with others. Going beyond an etiquette of narration, language might be seen, then, to uncover the nature of the world and the self – hence language becomes much more than a system of communication: it expresses ethical commitments that have become completely embedded in everyday life. For many of my respondents, what was important was not simply the content of communication but also the manner – so that the self-respect, dignity, and honor of the participants in a communication was not harmed. An even more subtle issue was to protect, what people said, is the "heart" of the other person, *dil rakhna*. The modality of ordinary ethics traverses the lines of public and private in important ways as one moves from considerations pertaining to maintaining the "face" of the other in public situations to "keeping his or her heart" in private, intimate contexts.

It was well recognized by everyone in the neighborhoods I studied that any hint of an insult offered within the public domain could be read, and was sometimes meant, to be an assault on the honor and respectability (*maan-izzat*) of the person who was thus insulted. Such insults were dealt with according to the resources that a family could command. Bourdieu (1990) and Gilsenan (1996) have given fine ethnographic analyses of the timeliness or otherwise of a response in both exchange of gifts and exchange of insults so that the calibration of time was of utmost importance. Return a gift too soon and it could become an insult – wait too long to strike back after an insult and it loses all force. Steven Caton's (1986, 2005) exemplary work shows how much the maintenance of face is a matter of being able to wield the right kind of language in interpersonal exchanges, and in the way different tribes in Yemen are able to hold their own in the competitive staging of poetry. In short, it seems that an agreement is maintained between various social actors in a given situation by which the fragile balance between enhancing one's own honor and prestige and being mindful of the honor that has to be shown to others is not disturbed. This delicacy of communication is preserved not only in publicly performed actions of greetings and gift exchanges but also in the minutest shifts in words and tones. The agreements that

I speak of here are, however, neither contractual agreements nor agreements in opinions – they grow out of the forms of life. Hence they are also subject to things going wrong from one moment to the next, letting loose a whole series of events that I tried to capture elsewhere by the notion of the social as the domain of unfinished stories that can lie undisturbed for many years and then suddenly come alive in moments of tremendous violence (Das 2007). I will give one last example and then proceed to examine why one might invest the notion of the moral in the quotidian efforts that go to maintain these forms of life and why one might regard them as more than mere fulfillment of social obligations demanded by rules and regulations.

My final example for this set of issues is drawn from Khare's (1976) fine ethnography of classification of food and the remarkable way in which the materiality of food provides the ground for expression of closeness and difference in social life in India and elsewhere (see also Prasad 2007). Khare, for example, shows that in a wedding feast kin who are relatively less endowed with material wealth can be given offense by such invitations as *aaiye aap bhi bhojan kar lijiye* ("please come – you too partake of the feast") rather than *aaiye bhojan kar lijiye* ("please come and partake of the feast"). Notice that in both cases the honorific "you" has been used but the addition of a single word – "too" next to the pronoun "you" manages to offer a subtle insult that will be remembered and perhaps repaid at an appropriate time, or it might simply be swallowed if the addressee is a dependent relative of the host.

If it is easy to use language to insult by these subtle means, it is also possible to use forms of greeting or affirmation to cover up situations that might be fraught with the risk of loss of face for a vulnerable relative or a neighbor. The best examples of this form of behavior arise when the distinctions between gift, charity, and debt have to be signaled without being put into words. I recall going with Manjit, a woman I have described at some length in my earlier work (Das 2007) who was quite well-off, to visit her cousin (mother's brother's daughter), Manpreet, who lived in very strained circumstances in a one-room quarter with her adult son and his wife. Manjit knew that her cousin did not have access to much cash and also that her position within her joint family was somewhat precarious as her son's wife was not looking after her well. It was winter and Manjit would have loved to gift Manpreet with a warm shawl. This was, however, a situation she could not negotiate very easily. She could have bought shawls for her sister and the daughter-in-law but since there was no ritual occasion to warrant such a gift and since Manjit is the younger of the two, that would have been seen as flaunting her wealth. A gift only for the sister would be seen as if the sister had been complaining to her relatives about the treatment she received. So, instead Manjit thought she might just find a way of leaving some money with her cousin. When we went to her house, her cousin insisted on sending a grandchild to get some *pakoras* (a savory) from the market. We prevailed on her not to get bottles of Coca-Cola (at an astronomical price) on the grounds that I suffered from diabetes but there was no avoiding the money spent on the *pakoras*, as Manpreet said to me *Manjit de ghar do to roz khande ho – aaj garib bahen de ghar vich wi kuch kha lao* ("You eat everyday in Manjit's house – today have something in the house of this poor sister too"). I responded – *dil amir hona chahida hai – paize te haath di mail hai* ("The heart should be flowing with wealth – money is just the dirt of the hand"). The reference to money being the dirt of the hand does not imply any opprobrium attaching to money but rather to its ephemeral character – money disappears as easily as the dirt of the hand.[4] I also suggest that such forms of speech, noted for the absence of the specific signature of a speaker or hearer but rather addressed to one and all, do not take the imperative form. Thus they are distinguished from rules but offer opportunities to express bits of moral wisdom that can be deployed in particular circumstances to do a variety of actions – admonish, console, or help to cover up an embarrassing situation.

As we were leaving, Manjit found a moment to tuck a wad of currency notes in her cousin's blouse (a common place where women tuck a pouch for small amounts of cash), away from the daughter-in-law's eyes. I do not say that this form of interaction is the only one available between more well-off relatives and poorer ones – sometimes the richer relative will accept responsibility for specific tasks, for example, fostering a child for a specific period, fixing a monthly allowance for a specific item of need such as medicine, taking responsibility for meeting the expenses of a daughter's wedding, or agreeing to pay back a high-interest debt through the fiction that the poor relative is only borrowing money for a short period of time though it is known that despite the best of intentions the loan will not be paid back. There are different fictions maintained to save face in some cases, for example, the child stands in a special relation to an aunt or an uncle; in other cases the facts of dependency are openly acknowledged. A common expression for such ruses is to say *dil rkkhan vaste udhaar keh ditta* ("In order to keep the heart I said it was a debt"). Han (2011) similarly describes how neighbors and kin of a family facing a financial crisis in her field site in Chile try to help with gifts of food or by staging a "party" so that they can give the family help in a manner whereby their dignity is not compromised.

As can be imagined, maintaining these kinship obligations is not always easy, especially when the economic difference between the two sides is not all that pronounced. I have described elsewhere the case of a man called Billu who is haunted by his failure to save his brother's life because he does not have enough resources for his treatment (Das 2010c). Often such events lead to lasting bitterness between parents and children, two brothers, or even neighbors and become the subject of moral reflections on the declining moral quality of "our times." Yet, despite the fact that families in need are often left wanting more help than they can get, ethnographic and economic evidence shows that interest-free loans and gifts from kin play an important part in helping poor families to meet expenditures for catastrophic events such as a medical emergency or for fulfilling other social obligations such as the marriage of a daughter (Collins et al. 2009).

In what way might one think of the performance of these quotidian acts as constituting an "ordinary ethics"? Are the sorts of descriptions of everyday life I offer not *too* quotidian to qualify as forms of ethical behavior? I offer some reflections on the imagination of human action and on the moral as a dimension of everyday life rather than as a separate domain to defend my metaphor of a descent into the ordinary. I attempt to do so by recasting habit as a kind of moral action and by showing how dramatic enactments of ethical value, as in publicly performed rituals or in legal pronouncements on rules, are grounded within the normative practices of everyday life.

Many philosophers and social theorists think of ethical commitment in terms of a leap away from everyday life even when they are sympathetic to the notion of the ethical as a mode of living rather than simply evaluating their own or others' actions. Thus, for instance, Pierre Hadot (1995, 2009) offers the concept of "spiritual exercises" to distinguish practices embedded in ancient Greek philosophy in order to distinguish them from religious practices. All ancient philosophy, he says, has its aim not just to inform but to form. For the ancients (whether masters or disciples), to engage in philosophy is a spiritual exercise "because it is a mode of life, a form of life, a choice of life" (Hadot 2009: 94). Hadot gives moving descriptions of what it is to cultivate a philosophical vision in the practice of one's life – yet there is also a sense of the banality of ordinary existence. Thus, for instance, in speaking of what he learned from Heidegger, Hadot says:

> It remains that de Waelhen's book allowed me to understand what I consider the essential of Heidegger – at least what is very important in what Heidegger brought me, especially the distinction between what we call the everyday, … and authentic existence … In Heidegger this becomes the opposition between the everyday, the banal, and a state in which one is conscious of being doomed to death … thus conscious of one's finitude. At this moment, existence takes on an entirely different aspect, which moreover generates anxiety – perhaps because of death, but also because of the enigma represented by the fact of existing. (2009: 128–129)

It was in an implicit contrast with this and similar views that I had concluded my last book, somewhat scandalously, with the following words:

> My sense of indebtedness to the work of Cavell in these matters comes from a confidence that perhaps Manjit did not utter anything that we would recognize as philosophical in the kind of environments in which philosophy is done … but Cavell's work shows us that there is no real distance between the spiritual exercises she undertakes in her world and the spiritual exercises we can see in every word he has ever written. To hold these types of words together and to sense the connection of these lives has been my anthropological kind of devotion to the world. (Das 2007: 221)

I say "scandalously" because the kind of philosophical formation that Hadot is thinking of is about scaling heights, whereas I am trying to wrest the very expression of spiritual exercises away from the profundity of philosophy to the small disciplines that ordinary people perform in their everyday life to hold life as the natural expression of ethics. While I must reserve my reflections on the impulse in philosophy to violence against the everyday for another occasion, my notion of both ethics and subjectivity takes me far away from the sensibilities of philosophers such as Alain Badiou (1994, 2001) who emphasize the importance of the exceptional event that forces a break from the everyday course of knowledge and brings into being a "subject" who was formerly "just a human animal, a mere inhabitant of a given situation" (Hughes 2007).[5] As we shall see in the last section, I too take up events that shatter the ordinary modes of living, but I locate the ethical there in precisely the small acts that allow life to be knitted together pair by pair.

So how should we think of habits and customs that form the texture of everyday life? Because of the strong emphasis on intentionality and agency in our contemplation of ethics, habitual actions are often reduced to "mere behavior." Even philosophers and social theorists who are sympathetic to the role of habit see its value primarily as the enormous flywheel of society. At best, then, habits are considered important at the acquisition stage as means of cultivating good practices in children (Erasmus 1560); while at a later stage they are said to become a ground for securing everyday life as a site of routine (Dewey 1922).

While I do not dispute such characterizations of habitual action, I claim that we can give a different slant to this discussion if we shift from considerations of individual agency and intentionality to the place where we see the individual within the flux of collective life. Here I offer two different considerations. First, I contend that even though we might feel that the values that a society holds dear become most visible at the moment of dramatic enactments – those which Austin (1962) was fond of thinking as having illocutionary force – a moment's reflection would tell us that we get the feel of the rightness of certain actions or pronouncements only when we can take these dramatic moments back and integrate them into the flux of everyday life.

The philosopher John McDowell (1996) expresses this region of thought extremely well. He argues that our sense of what is right cannot be determined by something else that stands above that action such as a rule or a reason for doing it this way, since our inquiry is precisely to ask what makes it right to do it *this* way. Wittgenstein (2001) famously argued that following a rule is a custom by which he meant that it is the entanglement of habits and customs that make following a rule one way rather than another seem right to us. Thus, unlike both Kant and Frege, whose intellectual Platonist conception of norms leads us to think that to assess the correctness of an action we must always be able to make at least an implicit reference to a rule or a principle that must be evoked and made explicit, for Wittgenstein it is the quality of practice that makes it evident that performance of explicit rules does not form an autonomous stratum that could exist without the support of other expressions of norms that he called customs and habits. As Brandom states this, "Norms that are *explicit* in the form of rules presuppose norms that are *implicit* in practice" (2008: 20).

Does this critique of rules as embodying norms reduce the phenomena of habit to mere mechanical actions, which would not be subject to considerations of correctness at all? While no one would deny that habituation involves the dulling of the senses to some extent (I do not have to think every step of the process when I cook our daily meals), it also involves heightened awareness and attentiveness to other aspects. For instance, during my fieldwork I came to appreciate the fact that a woman would remember in such a small gesture as serving tea to the family that I did not take sugar in my tea, that one of her sons liked lots of sugar, another liked to have *malai* (clotted cream on top of the milk) to float on his tea rather than mixed in it, and that her husband preferred to drink tea in a glass rather than a cup (see also Prasad 2007 for some nice examples of the expressions of care through the materiality of food).

Detecting the Human

The rightness or otherwise of certain habitual actions, I claim, is judged by the cultivation of a moral sensibility that is able to detect the "human" within actions that might otherwise be termed as the work of autonomation. Our uneasy relationship with the possibility of the mechanical (as distinct from the animal) was signaled for Henri Bergson through our attention to the comic. Thus, in his book on laughter, Bergson comments on how laughter is drawn out of us, for instance, when we see a runner stumble on a stone and fall or by the victim of a practical joke. The laughable element in both cases, he says, consists of a certain inelasticity, just where one would expect to find a wide, waking adaptability and living pliability of a human being

(Bergson 1911: 10). While the comic is, indeed, an important register for expressing the thought that the human can sometimes be seen as a machine – and I can think of numerous occasions when the involuntary bursting of the mechanical or the animal interrupted the solemn performance of a ritual and elicited uncontrolled laughter – the attempts to defeat the mechanical aspect of being human that I was most impressed by was in the region of concealment, as if whatever else a machine can do it cannot possess a body that can learn the language of pretending, of concealing the intentions behind its actions. Here we find the ethical within the habitual or the routine where we least expect it to be, namely, in acts of concealment and pretending through which one's knowledge of the constrained circumstances of the other is hidden when offering a larger than usual gift, or in the use of words to recast a debt as a gift. Thus while gift-giving can be explained as the "normal" or "routine" gesture one performs when visiting a relative or a friend as well as on ritual occasions, its mode of performance draws on a register of normativity other than simply fulfilling a social obligation.

I argued earlier that gift-giving as a form of reciprocity is fraught with dangers that one might undermine another but also with possibilities of offering help and demonstrating care that is oriented to the specific needs of another. This double nature of reciprocity is recognized by Michael Jackson who points out that:

> When Marcel Mauss invoked the Maori spirit (*hau*) of the gift to elucidate the threefold character of reciprocity … he glossed over the fact that the Maori word for reciprocity – appropriately a palindrome, *utu* – refers *both* to the gift-giving that sustains social solidarity and the violent act of seizure, revenge and repossession that are provoked when one party denies or diminishes the integrity (*mana*) of another. (2005: 42)

It is interesting to observe that for the families I have worked with in Delhi who engage in endless discussions on the modalities of giving and receiving, what is often at stake is the reading of the body language of the giver and the receiver. In his classic essay on pretending, Austin (1969b) points out that at the heart of pretending is a certain kind of concealment – but that I conceal sometimes to deceive the other and sometimes to conceal my knowledge that, if expressed, will turn out to have grievous consequences for the other. Cavell writes in his masterful description of the act of concealing:

> Whatever in me I have to conceal I may betray exactly by the way in which I conceal it. Just *that* is what is concealed: the concealment of what it is up to me to express is a perfect expression of it – the slight edge of my denials, the over-casualness of my manner, the hint of autonomanity in my smile or gait or position, each of which I may succeed in concealing … there are those who know how to read such concealments. The concealment of what there is to express is an exacting art, like camouflage. You might call it a language: the language of the body. About human beings there are only open secrets or open questions. (1979: 459)

These open secrets or questions, though, are the stuff of both tragedy and comedy, leading one to acknowledge that our human form of life has elements of other lives – of stones, of machines, of animals, of gods – and that habits performed in the dark of reason (Pollard 2008, 2010) do much more than act as flywheels of society: they remind us that in the face of the precariousness of life the mundane rituals we evolve, the way we conceal knowledge that might hurt, the way we continue to secure routine, is what allows our lives with others to be regarded as ethical or unethical.

Finally, I want to make the point that the sensibility by which we recognize the ethical in the small acts of everyday life also alerts us to the lethal ways in which our capacity to hurt others might also be expressed in completely quotidian ways. Pooja Sattyogi, a graduate student working on cases of domestic cruelty in Delhi, was surprised to find that many women reporting cases of domestic cruelty would provide narrations which in themselves might appear to be rather trivial but which took on the force of cruelty for them because of the circumstances in which they were embedded (personal communication). For instance, one woman who felt completely suffocated in her conjugal family gave the example that, just as she would be getting ready to leave for work, her mother-in-law might ask her to perform a task that would make it impossible for her to reach her office in time. The task – let us say, of peeling a bunch of pea shells with the injunction that the smaller pods be separated and kept in a separate container from the larger ones – performed on a lazy winter afternoon with a group of women working in companionable rhythms might not seem cruel at all, but to a harassed young daughter-in-law who has barely managed to serve everyone breakfast and then got dressed to catch a bus to go to the office, it is an act through which her very existence as a responsible working woman might be put into complete jeopardy. It is thus that the hurts and insults of everyday life sometimes corrode the possibility of building a life together. Whether such hurts and everyday insults are the grounds on which larger spectacular forms of violence that we witness in publicly enacted riots or during warfare are built is a question that I do not know how to answer yet. However, the opposite move of sensing how the quotidian asserts itself within scenes of violence of a more massive scale is worth tracking. It offers a picture of healing that is also located in unremarkable everyday acts.

Then, What about Good and Evil?

I have emphasized the importance of habit as the site on which the working of ordinary ethics can be traced. A critic is entitled to ask, though, that in the light of the atrocities that assail our normal sensibilities and of which we are made increasingly aware by a variety of media – news reports, testimonial literature, images on print and electronic media – is it enough to speak of ethics on the register of the ordinary? Though I have addressed some aspects of this question in my earlier work (Das 1995, 2007) I will briefly put forward some further thoughts on this important issue.

In a recent paper on Abu Ghraib and the problem of evil, Steven Caton (2010) states that though he does not wish to exonerate any of the powerful institutions for the atrocities committed against prisoners, what he finds compelling is that such ordinary people were capable of committing what he calls "evil." Caton is not comfortable with naming the kinds of acts committed at Abu Ghraib as simply "unethical" and proposes instead the category of "situational evil" to get out of the universalism versus relativism quandary. Nor does he find Kant's transcendental view of evil satisfactory. As he says, "What is missing in these transcendental views of good and evil is the possibility that ethical conduct is not simply assured by following an ethical code, but that such conduct *emerges* in a given situation" (Caton 2010: 174; emphasis original). Caton then turns to the question of responsibility. He finds Hannah Arendt's (1963) thesis on the banality of evil particularly helpful, in that it takes account of both the bureaucratic machine within which such evil takes place and the individual responsibility of those who claim immunity on the grounds that they were simply cogs in the machine. Arendt, as we know, did recognize that Eichmann was no Macbeth or Iago – Caton too recognizes that the evil committed by the perpetrators of Abu Ghraib stuns us by its banality rather than the larger-than-life character of the persons involved. Yet, in the final analysis, Caton would place responsibility on the individual: "Finally, there is no way to determine in advance which individuals will act ethically or even evilly in given situations; in the sense that this is 'spontaneous' the individual as Kant insisted, is free to choose" (2010: 182). I will reserve comment on Caton's conclusion though I recognize how difficult and tortuous it is to come on one side or another, either that of individual responsibility or that of institutional evil. I have proposed in my own work that shifting the question elsewhere to the work of time gives us a different kind of insight into the moral issues at stake, for then the focus shifts from the commitment of dramatic acts of evil to that of how such acts are lived in the course of daily life (Das 2007).

If the problem of evil makes us stutter, so does the problem of extraordinary courage. In recent years a number of extremely courageous accounts by women who survived terrifying violence have emerged in the public domain (Amy 2010; Talebi 2011; see also Rechtman 2006 and, for the widespread use of torture in democracies, Rejali 2007). These accounts constitute the most remarkable testimonies of both the utter cruelty and evil their authors confronted and their ability to survive in defiance of the powers of annihilation that were let loose upon them. There is clearly no standard template that one can deduce from these accounts – each is remarkable for its singularity. Out of this compelling literature I want to take one recent, stunning account by Shahla Talebi (2011) of her life as a political prisoner in Iran, first, under the regime of the Shah when she was just 18 years old, and later under the Islamic republic. In prison for nearly a decade, where she was repeatedly tortured, along with her husband who was later executed, Telebi draws a picture of life in prison that Stefnia Pandolfo, in her blurb on the book, describes as a creation at the limits of life. But what I want to do here is to ask what the questions are that puzzle Talebi both in prison and out of it. To follow her puzzlement, I feel, is the best way to follow what moral issues might be at stake when we are silenced by the enormity of the violence and the determination to combat this evil on the one hand, and the irruptions of everyday life in her account on the other.

I will not attempt to give a depiction of the cruelty and torture, but Talebi's descriptions are the clearest indication that many prisoners did not let themselves be reduced to "bare life." As one example, here is her description of how they "celebrated" the Iranian New Year:

> Prior to every Iranian New Year, we took days to clean up our cells as if they were our homes – we embraced the risk of stealing soil and seeds on our way to the clinic, for interrogation, to our family meetings, so that we could plant our New Year *sabzeh*, the green plants we grow for the New Year as a symbol of growth. (Talebi 2011: 69)

Yet the "we" here is somewhat deceptive, for it hides deep moral divisions that were created in the prison. I take one example. As in most prisons and camps, the administrators relied on collaborators, men and women who either could not bear the torture any more or sought some advantage for themselves or their families through collaboration. It is not difficult to understand that prisoners who had been able to withstand torture and who refused to recant became the harshest critics of such collaborators. When one stands with such prisoners one understands that they must have attributed some responsibility for the unbearable pain and torture inflicted on them in the prison to the collaborators. Yet one can also stand with the collaborators and see that it is only our exaggerated ideas of agency that makes us feel that we can say with Kant that in the final analysis the individual is free to choose, since some people were able to hold up against the torturers even while others succumbed. When we read such accounts, our moral sensibilities intuitively cry out to distinguish the perpetrators from the victims and for juridical purposes it is necessary to do so – but our moral intuitions can fail us badly in some cases, or so it seems to me when I read the following paragraph in Talebi on a woman who had collaborated with the prison officials.

> Fozi's collaboration with the interrogators reached such an ugly and disgusting level that her infamy spread to all the wards and even to the outside world. Her husband, who was able to flee the country and was exiled in Europe, sent her a message of repudiation and abrogated his marriage to her. Her parents stopped coming to visit her for months until she became mentally ill. (2011: 83)

Then, after describing the madness into which Fozi fell, Talebi puzzles:

> Fozi went to sleep [having been forcibly administered an injection by the guards to keep her quiet] while many of us restlessly contemplated the incredible capacity human beings have of becoming so different from one another. Why is it that there are people who risk their lives to ease others' pain, although their own suffering may be even greater, while there are others willing to rescue themselves by walking on the injured shoulders of others? (86–87)

Surely in face of this puzzle we must see that matters here touch on things far beyond agency, choice, exhortations to duty, and so on through which moral philosophy moves on its accustomed paths. Surely we must see that while women in the prison might have the standing to pass judgment on each other – even as we acknowledge the courage of some, we must despair that Fozi's husband and her parents found it fit to pass judgment on her.

And finally, there is the puzzlement of Talebi who finds herself falling in love years later when she is in the United States:

> It was 1999, and I was extremely heartbroken following a failed romantic relationship for which my inexperienced heart had no preparation. My only previous experience of romantic love was with Hamid, whom I had lost so violently. And here I was with no regime to take away my love, yet I had lost him without knowing how to make sense of this loss. (2011: 129)

The scandal of the survivor is not that she cannot go on but that she does go on and this is what appears to shock Talebi, that she can still fall in love, that everyday life can be recovered. In my earlier work I have shown that for one of my respondents, Asha, it was that life could be re-engaged again, and that her own body would betray her by feeling such desire that made her voice deeply divided – re-engaging life and yet turning her own voice against herself.

I suggested that moral philosophy here is taken on paths to which it is not accustomed. Let me go further and state that, just as in the ordinary course of life we might find the presence of moral and ethical formations within everyday habitual acts, so in the cases of the kind of violence described by the testimonial literature the ethical may be found in the impersonal rhythms of the social that allow life to be knitted together again. One of the best descriptions of the kind of process I have in mind is the description given by Heonik Kwon (2008, 2010) of how, in the region of Quang Nam in Vietnam that he studied, villagers began to revive ancestral shrines in the mid-1990s, after a long period of suspicion of religious activities by the Communist regime. Kwon also discovered that, along with rehabilitating ancestors, villagers began to build parallel shrines for the unknown dead in the Vietnam War and the thousands of displaced people who had died in strange places. What does such a gesture of recognition of one's former enemies mean? Kwon places these acts within an ethics of memory and makes the delicate point that such attempts meant that the law of hospitality and the law of kinship – one addressing the stranger and the second one's kinsmen – ran on parallel courses in the life of the community. However, while on the surface one might attribute different meanings to the ways of honoring kinsmen versus finding a place for strangers in the ritual life of the community, in a deeper sense the villagers were also trying to find a way to bring back one's errant ancestors – those who fell on the wrong side of the Vietnam War – to inhabit again the space of the domestic. These errant ancestors, who were expelled from the domestic community, were invited back just as the strangers – American soldiers whose ghosts pressed on the consciousness of the villagers since they too had died away from home – were accommodated in the ritual life. Kwon's work reminds us that deep political divides also fray the sphere of the family. Other anthropologists have shown how such impersonal forces as a god or a jin might become the bridge by which those divided within one threshold of life by conflicts that cannot be resolved might find a shared symbolic space within another threshold of life (Singh 2009). It seems that the "ordinary ethics" evident in such gestures have the potential to generate an eventual everyday from the ruins of the actual everyday by putting together the rubbles and ruins and learning to live in that very space of devastation yet once again.

In my own work on the Partition of India in 1947 and the horrendous violence to which women were submitted I tried to portray precisely what it meant to inhabit that very space of devastation once again (Das 2007). Women not only used such powerful metaphors as "drinking the pain" and "digesting the pain" but also, in their everyday acts of endurance, they protected the children against knowledge they thought would be too hard for them to bear; they allowed life to be lived as best as they knew. Similarly, in Didier Fassin's (2010) work on the lives of terminally ill patients suffering from AIDS in South Africa, the ethical is encountered in the way in which survival itself becomes ethical as life is redefined to include the traces that one strives to leave for the living. I have argued that it is in the flux of everyday life that we can recognize the moral as a dimension of everyday life and that attention to the apparatuses of everyday life – habits, excuses, pretenses, concealments, as well as endurance, acknowledgment (Jackson 2005; Reader 2007, 2010) – all these are critical for understanding how everyday life might provide the therapy for the very violation to which it has suffered. In laying this theory of ordinary ethics I have privileged the voices of women. I hope this gesture will appeal to those who are willing to think from the feminine regions of the self as a way of inhabiting the world with others.

Acknowledgments

I am grateful to Andrew Bush, Sylvain Perdigon, and Bhrigupati Singh for their comments on this paper and for the opportunity to learn from their work on related themes. Didier Fassin's thoughtful comments helped me greatly in weeding out unnecessary distractions in the paper and in sharpening my thoughts on the idea of the ordinary. I am very thankful for the opportunity to think with Didier on these issues, though none of these thoughtful interlocutors are responsible for the frailties of the arguments here.

NOTES

1 There is some criticism from scholars of metapragmatics that although all of Austin's examples are taken from English he draws universal conclusions from these examples. Such criticisms ignore the role of example in his philosophy since his argument does not require that the same linguistic expressions be found in all languages but rather that we find some expressions that convey the fragility of human action corresponding to the region of excuses or other ways of acknowledging that we can become victims of language. For example, in theories of sacrifice in the Sanskritic tradition, the fragility of speech was figured through the notion of *vani* (speech) as running away from the sacrificial arena and hence having to be ritually bound. This aspect was contrasted with *akshara* (word) as that which remains steadfastly the same.

2 I will revisit the question of the everyday and the subtle differences between theorists who are committed to finding ethical life in the everyday but from the perspective of a leap that takes us from a limited perspective to a universal one and the idea I am putting forward of the work one does on the actual everyday to generate the eventual everyday through a descent into the ordinary.

3 I have not observed this gesture among the slum populations that I now study.

4 In a classic paper on money Jonathan Parry (1989) has argued that the suspicion of money as a sign of modernity that many have assumed to be widespread in traditional societies does not hold fast for India where it is the gift that is imbued with ambiguity.

5 I am making a limited point with regard to Badiou's notion of the ethical as a leap away from the everyday – the full development of the argument would need much more space than is available here.

REFERENCES

Amy, Lori E (2010) *The Wars We Inherit: Military Life, Gender Violence and Memory.* Philadelphia: Temple University Press.

Arendt, Hannah (1963) *Eichmann in Jerusalem: A Report on the Banality of Evil.* New York: Penguin.

Austin, J. L. (1962) *How to do Things with Words.* Cambridge, MA: Harvard University Press.

Austin, J. L. (1969a) A Pleas for Excuses. In *Philosophical Papers*, ed. J. O. Urmson and G. J. Warnock. Oxford: Oxford University Press, pp. 175–205.

Austin, J. L. (1969b) Pretending. In *Philosophical Papers*, ed. J. O. Urmson and G. J. Warnock. Oxford: Oxford University Press, pp. 253–272.

Badiou, Alain (1994) Being by Numbers: Lauren Sedofsky Talks with Alain Badiou. *Artforum* (Oct.), 84–87, 118, 123–124.

Badiou, Alain (2001) *Ethics: An Essay on the Understanding of Evil*, trans. Peter Hallward. London: Verso.

Bergson, Henri (1911) *Laughter: An Essay on the Meaning of the Comic*. London: Macmillan.

Bourdieu, Pierre (1990) *The Logic of Practice*. Cambridge: Polity.

Brandom, Robert (2008) *Making It Explicit: Reasoning, Representing and Discursive Commitment*. Cambridge, MA: Harvard University Press.

Caton, Steven (1986) "Salam Tahiyah": Greetings from the Highlands of Yemen. *American Ethnologist* 13(2): 290–308.

Caton, Steven (2005) *Yemen Chronicle: An Anthropology of War and Mediation*. New York: Hill & Wang.

Caton, Steven (2010) Abu Ghraib and the Problem of Evil. In Michael Lambek (ed.), *Ordinary Ethics: Anthropology, Language and Action*. New York: Fordham University Press, pp. 165–187.

Cavell, Stanley (1979) *The Claim of Reason: Wittgenstein, Skepticism, Morality and Tragedy*. New York: Oxford University Press.

Collins, Daryl, Murduch, Jonathan, Rutherford, Stuart, and Ruthven, Orlanda (2009) *Portfolios of the Poor: How the World's Poor Live on $2 a Day*. Princeton: Princeton University Press.

Crary, Alice (2007) *Beyond Moral Judgment*. Cambridge, MA: Harvard University Press.

Das, Veena (1976) Masks and Faces: An Essay on Punjabi Kinship. *Contributions to Indian Sociology* 10(1): 1–30.

Das, Veena (1995) *Critical Events: An Anthropological Perspective on Contemporary India*. New Delhi: Oxford University Press.

Das, Veena (1998) Wittgenstein and Anthropology. *Annual Review of Anthropology* 27: 171–195.

Das, Veena (2007) *Life and Words: Violence and the Descent into the Ordinary*. Berkeley: University of California Press.

Das, Veena (2008) Violence, Gender and Subjectivity. *Annual Review of Anthropology* 37: 283–299.

Das, Veena (2010a) Moral and Spiritual Striving in the Everyday: To Be a Muslim in Contemporary India. In Anand Pandian and Daud Ali (eds.), *Ethical Life in South Asia*. Bloomington: Indiana University Press, pp. 232–253.

Das, Veena (2010b) Engaging the Life of the Other: Love and Everyday Life. In Michael Lambek (ed.), *Ordinary Ethics: Anthropology, Language and Action*. New York: Fordham University Press, pp. 376–400.

Das, Veena (2010c) The Life of Humans and the Life of Roaming Spirits. In Michelle Molina and Donald K. Swearer (eds.), *Rethinking the Human*. Cambridge, MA: Harvard University Press, pp. 31–51.

Das, Veena (2011a) State, Citizenship and the Urban Poor. *Citizenship Studies* 15(3–4): 319–333.

Das, Veena (2011b) Time is a Trickster and Other Fleeting Thoughts on Cavell, his Life, his Work. *MLN* 126(5): 943–953.

Dewey, J. (1922) *Human Nature and Conduct*. New York: Henry Holt.

Diamond, Cora (1996) "We are Perpetually Moralists": Iris Murdoch, Fact and Value in Moral Philosophy. In Maria Antonaccio and William Schweiker (eds.), *Iris Murdoch and the Search for Human Goodness*. Chicago: University of Chicago Press, pp. 79–110.

Emerson, Ralph W. (1969) Experience. In *Essays: Second Series: Facsimile of First Editions*. Columbus, OH: Charles E. Merrill, pp. 49–86.

Erasmus (1560) *The Civility of Childhood*. London. (Translation from Latin of *De cilitate morum puerilium.*)
Fassin, Didier (2010) Ethics of Survival: A Democratic Approach to the Politics of Life. *Humanity: An International Journal of Human Rights* 1(1): 81–95.
Faubion, James D. (2011) *An Anthropology of Ethics*. Cambridge: Cambridge University Press.
Foucault, Michel (1997) *Ethics, Subjectivity and Truth*, ed. Paul Rabinow. New York: New Press.
Foucault, Michel (2005) *The Hermeneutics of the Subject: Lectures at the College de France, 1981–1982*, trans. Frédéric Gros; intro. A. I. Davidson. New York: Picador.
Gilsenan, Michael (1996) *Lords of the Lebanese Marches: Violence and Narrative in an Arab Society*. Berkeley: University of California Press.
Hadot, Pierre (1995) *Philosophy as a Way of Life*, ed. Arnold I. Davidson. Oxford: Blackwell.
Hadot, Pierre (2009) *The Present Alone is Our Happiness: Conversations with Jeannie Carlier and Arnold I. Davidson*. Stanford: Stanford University Press.
Hallisey, Charles (2010) Between Intuition and Judgment: Moral Creativity in Theravada Buddhist Ethics. In Anand Pandian and Daud Ali (eds.), *Ethical Life in South Asia*. Bloomington: Indiana University Press, pp. 141–153.
Han, Clara (2011) Symptoms of Another Life: Time, Possibility and Domestic Relations in Chile's Credit Economy. *Cultural Anthropology* 26(1): 7–32.
Hughes, Robert (2007) Riven: Badiou's Ethical Subject and the Event of Art as Trauma. *Postmodern Culture* 27(3): 1–36.
Jackson, Michael (2005) *Existential Anthropology: Events, Exigencies and Effects*. New York: Berghahn, chs. 3, 6, 9.
Kelly, K. A. (2003) *Domestic Violence and the Politics of Privacy*. Ithaca, NY: Cornell University Press.
Khare, Ravindra S. (1976) *The Hindu Hearth and Home*. Durham, NC: Carolina Academic Press.
Kleinman, Arthur (2006) *What Really Matters: Living a Moral Life amidst Uncertainty and Danger*. New York: Oxford University Press.
Kwon, Heonik (2008) *Ghosts of War in Vietnam*. Cambridge: Cambridge University Press.
Kwon, Heonik (2010) The Ghosts of War and the Ethics of Memory. In Michael Lambek (ed.), *Ordinary Ethics: Anthropology, Language and Action*. New York: Fordham University Press, pp. 400–415.
Lambek, Michael (2010) Toward an Ethics of the Act. In Michael Lambek (ed.), *Ordinary Ethics: Anthropology, Language and Action*. New York: Fordham University Press, pp. 1–39.
Mahmood, Saba (2005) *Politics of Piety: The Islamic Revival and the Feminist Subject*. Princeton: Princeton University Press.
McDowell, John (1996) *Mind and World*. Cambridge, MA: Harvard University Press.
Murata, Sachiko and Chittick, William C. (1994) *The Vision of Islam*. New York: Paragon.
Parry, Jonathan (1989) On the Moral Perils of Exchange. In J. Parry and M. Bloch (eds.), *Money and the Morality of Exchange*. Cambridge: Cambridge University Press, pp. 64–94.
Perdigon, Sylvain (2011) *Between the Womb and the Hour: Ethics and Semiotics of Relatedness amongst Palestinian Refugees in Tyre*, Lebanon. PhD dissertation, Johns Hopkins University, Baltimore.
Pollard, Bill (2008) *Habits in Action: A Corrective to the Neglect of Habits in Contemporary Philosophy of Action*. Saarbrücken: Dr. Muller.
Pollard, Bill (2010) Habitual Actions. In Timothy O'Connor and Constantine Sandis (eds.), *A Companion to Philosophy of Action*. Oxford: Wiley-Blackwell, pp. 74–81.
Prasad, Leela (2007) *Poetics of Conduct: Oral Narrative and Moral Being in a South Indian Town*. New York: Columbia University Press.
Prasad, Leela (2010) Ethical Subjects: Time, Timing and Telalbility. In Anand Pandian and Daud Ali (eds.), *Ethical Life in South Asia*. Bloomington: Indiana University Press, pp. 174–192.

Price, J. M. (2002) The Apotheosis of Home and Maintenance of Spaces of Violence. *Hypatia* 17(4): 39–70.

Reader, Soran (2007) The Other Side of Agency. *Philosophy* 82(4): 579–604.

Reader, Soran (2010) Agency, Patency and Personhood. Timothy O'Connor and Constantine Sandis (eds.), *A Companion to Philosophy of Action*. Oxford: Wiley-Blackwell, pp. 200–207.

Rechtman, Richard (2006) The Survivor's Paradox: Psychological Consequences of the Khmer Rouge Rhetoric of Extermination. *Anthropology and Medicine* 13(1): 1–11.

Rejali, Daius (2007) *Torture and Democracy*. Princeton: Princeton University Press.

Ricoeur, Paul (1994) *Oneself as Another*. Chicago: University of Chicago Press.

Talebi, Shahla (2011) *Ghosts of Revolution: Rekindled Memories of Imprisonment in Iran*. Stanford: Stanford University Press.

Taylor, Charles (1996) Iris Murdoch and Moral Philosophy. In Maria Antonaccio and William Schweiker (eds.), *Iris Mudoch and the Search for Human Goodness*. Chicago: University of Chicago Press, pp. 1–39.

Wittgenstein, Ludwig (2001 [1953]) *Philosophical Investigations*, trans. G. E. M. Anscombe. Oxford: Blackwell.

CHAPTER 9 Moral Sentiments

C. Jason Throop

Sentiments, emotions, affects, feelings, and moods have been at the center of a number of influential moral theories in philosophy. They have also figured prominently in many anthropological engagements with morality, although rarely in an explicit effort to articulate a specific moral theory. When anthropologists have focused their attention on the moral side of sentiments they have tended to ethnographically examine the role that particular moral emotions, such as love, compassion, anger, guilt, or shame, play in defining an individual's or a community's ethical life (Rosaldo 1980; Shweder 1997; Lutz 1998). They have also at times emphasized how sentiments can be understood as the direct embodiment of particular moral orders that are significantly culturally defined (Geertz 1973; Csordas 1994; Parish 1994; Robbins 2004). In still other cases, anthropologists have sought to understand what may be deemed morally problematic or ambivalent emotions, passions, and desires as a means to expand or challenge our taken-for-granted assumptions about the various forms of life and the potential range of practices that may have bearing, positive or negative, for moral assessments of our own self-experience and the experience of others (Briggs 1995; Scheper-Hughes 1995; Biehl 2005; Garcia 2010; Zigon 2011).

In this essay, I will seek to advance a perspective on moral sentiments grounded in a cultural phenomenological approach to moral experience that I have been developing over the past few years (Throop 2009a, 2009b, 2010a, 2010b). To begin, I will briefly review some of the key moral theories of sentiment in philosophy, as well as some of the major anthropological contributions. While not meant to be comprehensive, this brief review will provide some contextual and historical background from which to critically examine the merits of undertaking a cultural phenomenological approach to moral experience. It is precisely such an approach, I argue, that can generatively shed important light on the place of sentiments in defining distinctive moral modes of being in particular communities of practice.

In outlining my approach, I will, however, shift the emphasis away from the realm of sentiment per se to what I take to be the more expansive category of

A Companion to Moral Anthropology, First Edition. Edited by Didier Fassin.

sensibility (see also Desjarlais 1992; Geurts 2002; Hirschkind 2006). Such a cultural phenomenological orientation to moral sensibilities provide, I argue, a means to account for the diverse range of embodied experiences that may be implicated in the culturally constituted emplacement of sentiments in the articulation of local moral worlds (Kleinman 2006). Additionally, it foregrounds the complex temporal dynamics of such moral modes of being in the context of concrete everyday engagements in which existential asymmetries, and what Jarrett Zigon (2007) has termed elsewhere moments of "moral breakdown," are necessarily implicated in the cultivation, contestation, and transformation of our moral lives.

Finally, to demonstrate the philosophical and anthropological relevance of such a perspective, I will briefly draw from my longstanding ethnographic research in Yapese communities that has over the years explored a number of topics that coalesce around issues of pain, suffering, and morality. In so doing, I will examine the place of sentiment in Yapese moral life, as well as the place of moral sentiments and sensibilities in the context of a particular ethnographic encounter in which a young girl's pain and suffering evidences a moment of moral breakdown.

Moral Sentiments and Moral Sense Theory in Philosophy

In the history of moral theory in philosophy, sentiments, emotions, affects, and desires have all too often played a background role in defining moral modes of being. If sentiments or emotions do figure in philosophical moral theories they are often understood to be in direct conflict with moral reasoning and the development of those modes of being that are held to define the good life and right conduct in particular communities. As Martha Nussbaum explains, in the history of philosophy the emotions have all too often been "sidelined in accounts of ethical judgment" (2001: 1). Even despite this striking lacuna, however, there are still a few important exceptions to the rule. Most notably, moral sentiments and emotions do figure prominently in both Aristotelian and classical Stoic accounts of virtue ethics.

For Aristotle, Alasdair MacIntyre instructs, "Virtues are dispositions not only to act in particular ways, but also to feel in particular ways" (2002: 149). To undertake an education of the sentiments, to cultivate certain sentiments over others, to learn to deal with conflicting desires and mutually incompatible goods, to cope with the complexities of our emotions, to work to modulate certain intensities of emotional life, and to make an effort to understand the vulnerabilities and values that give rise to particular emotional experiences are all concerns that are centrally implicated in Aristotle's account of the virtues (Nussbaum 2001). Both the generative source and end of such ethical efforts at cultivating morally appropriate orientations to sentiments were, for Aristotle, also significantly tied to the cultivation of practical wisdom or *phronesis* (Aristotle 1976). Given this Aristotelian emphasis on moral sentiments, it is interesting to note that his virtue ethics has recently influenced a number of prominent anthropological accounts of morality (see Mattingly 1998; Lambek 2010).

An interest in the life of sentiment in relation to virtue was also at the heart of Stoic approaches to morality. A significant question for the Stoics was "How should a human being live?" As Nussbaum explains, the Stoics believed that the "answer to that question is the person's conception of *eudaimonia*, or human flourishing, a complete human life" (2001: 32). From this perspective, human flourishing was tied directly to the cultivation of certain virtues, which were in turn often directly linked to both particular sentiments and an individual's abilities to refine and control the intensities and qualities of such sentiments.

Next to Aristotelian and Stoic accounts of moral sentiment, it is arguably the work of the Scottish moral sense theorists Lord Shaftesbury and Francis Hutcheson, as well as the moral theories that owe the greatest debt to them, namely those of David Hume and Adam Smith, who have developed the most explicit moral theories based upon sentiments. While it is true that Plato, Spinoza, Schopenhauer, and numerous others have sought to think through the place of emotions, in particular the emotions of compassion and love, in the cultivation of moral modes of being (see Nussbaum 2001: 482–511), it is the Scottish moral sense theorists who have most explicitly framed their ethical theories around the life of sentiments.

According to the Scottish moral sense theorists, morality was significantly tied to the disinterested operation of a *sensus communis*, or common sensibility, that oriented actors with sympathy toward the needs, trials, pains, and suffering of others. As opposed to self-love and self-preservation, which were advanced as primary motives in the cynical moral theories of Hobbes and Mandelbaum, the moral sense theorists held that individuals, through benevolence, were oriented beyond their own self-centered aims and desires to others' predicaments and concerns. Moral sentiments of sympathy, benevolence, and pity were thus held to be at the center of a moral theory that sought to challenge the assumption that human passions were necessarily self-interested, animalistic, and callously unconcerned with the plight of others. For Shaftesbury and Hutcheson, such a moral sense was thought to be an intrinsic feature of the human mind. It could be cultivated, most certainly. But moral sense was understood as a "natural" aspect of what it means to be human.

Influenced by, and yet still critical of, Shaftesbury and Hutcheson, David Hume proposed a view of morality based on the idea that it is the passions that propel reason, and not the other way around. If it is the passions that drive us to act, and if moral judgments are meant to guide our actions, then moral judgments must be oriented to, and concerned with, the passions that motivate action (Hume 2005). Accordingly, Hume argued that "Morality, therefore, is more properly felt than judged of" (cited in MacIntyre 1966). By distinguishing between "artificial virtues" which are based solely in conventional rules and expectations, and so-called "natural virtues" which are predicated upon our natural inclinations, Hume attempted to show how both self-enhancing and other-oriented actions could be morally patterned. In particular, he wished to highlight how the intermingling of the passions and the imagination could result in sympathy for others' predicaments and situations. For Hume, the cultivation of sympathy importantly served to balance and correct passions and inclinations based upon self-interest.

Refining Hume's account of sympathy as a basis for moral action, as well as his notion of an "imaginary spectator of our actions, who provides the standard by which they are to be judged" (MacIntyre 1966: 176), Adam Smith's *The Theory of Moral Sentiments* is arguably one of the most influential contributors to the Scottish school of moral sense philosophy. Smith's account of moral sentiments centers around three core sentiments: pity, compassion, and sympathy. Whereas Smith takes pity and compassion to be specific applications of sympathy as "our fellow-feeling for the misery of others" (2002: 12), sympathy is taken to be a more general imaginative tendency to experience "fellow-feeling" with any range of passions whatsoever. Seeing sympathy as oriented not only toward the acts and experiences of others, but, also reflexively back toward how those same others view the actions and experiences of the self, Smith views the mutuality of the sympathetic imagination as located at the heart of moral experience. It is also from such mutuality that Smith derives the notion of the ideal impartial spectator. As Haakonssen explains, in the midst of moral conflict (i.e., those moments in which the mutuality of sympathetic alignment breaks down) we "tend to imagine how a spectator would judge us and our behavior if he or she was not limited by prejudice, partiality, ignorance, poor imagination and lack of ordinary good will in the way in which the actual spectators of us, including ourselves, are limited" (2002: xv).

Such a rendering of sympathy critically displaces any simplistic notion of sentiment as a purely individualistic emotional response to moral problems. The intersubjective constitution of such sentiments is also, as we will see, at the basis for the phenomenological approach to ethical modalities of being that I will outline below. Entailing what seems to be a significant intersubjective orientation, Smith's notion of sympathy is thus necessarily a social affair, although one that always expects there to remain important asymmetries of experience between individuals who work to coordinate their actions and reactions with one another through time.

On Being Internally Divided

Quite distinct from the virtue ethical or Scottish traditions, and speaking in quite a different register, Fredrick Nietzsche (1989) is another important contributor to understandings of moral sentiments in philosophy. Shifting the emphasis to the historical sedimentation and genealogy of moral sentiments, Nietzsche radically destabilized the view that moral life flows unproblematically from natural inclinations. The importance of Nietzsche in light of contemporary anthropological orientations to moral sentiments is tied directly to his impact on two very different and influential theoretical orientations to moral experience, namely those of Sigmund Freud (1989) and Michel Foucault (1985, 2005). Nietzsche's significance is also tied, however, to his attempts to complicate our understanding of moral life by focusing on the experience of being internally divided. In this respect, a key problem for Nietzsche concerns the paradoxical fact that the idea of a conscience entails postulating a being that is capable of being voluntarily at odds with itself. How, Nietzsche asks, is it possible for a being to feel painful emotions of guilt, shame, and regret for actions, desires, and wishes that stem from its own inclinations?

The sentiments that Nietzsche is most attuned to in the development of his account of the historical formation of a being who is "voluntarily" at odds with itself are those of suffering, guilt, regret, fear, shame, and pain. Tracing a particular genealogy of moral sentiments to the pains inflicted on those who failed to follow through on their previous promises to repay their debts, Nietzsche outlines the deep history of cruelty that lies at the basis of the historical sedimentation of the "instinct of conscience." According to Nietzsche, the instinct of conscience arises out of the memory and binding power of a promise that is born directly from the fear and threat of pain.

As Nietzsche observes, there is a paradox here inasmuch as the self who promises to repay a given debt must subject itself to the threat of painful punishment before the possibility to claim mastery over what is otherwise servitude to "momentary affect and desire" can arise (Nietzsche 1989: 61). It is this paradoxical subjection of the subject to a power greater than itself as a means to realize power over itself and its world that also serves for Nietzsche as foundational to the development of a view of punishment in which the moral offender "could have acted differently" (63).

Nietzsche's account of the historical crafting of a subject who becomes voluntarily at odds with itself through the internalization of sentiments like guilt and fear played a significant role in shaping later Freudian, psychodynamic, and in turn anthropological accounts of moral sentiments. For Freud (1989), the internalization of social moral norms, while necessary for the functioning of society, is characterized as at odds with individual desires. As such, for Freud, as for Nietzsche, civilization itself is an unavoidable source of our suffering. Echoing Nietzsche, Freud argues that there are multiple forms of subjection and violence that are brought to bear in the formation of a subject who becomes internally dived against itself. It is out of such violence and subjection, Freud theorized, that the subject is decentered through its organization into discrete and at times mutually antagonistic aspects that function according to a pleasure principle (Id), a reality principle (Ego), and an ethical principle (Superego). In this view, the life of sentiment registers the fault lines of conflict between cultural values, social responsibilities, and individual desires.

At the heart of Freud's metapsychology is a postulated antagonistic and deeply ambivalent relationship between individual and society as mediated through desires, drives, and particular moral sentiments like shame, regret, and guilt. And yet, those selfsame moral sentiments are also implicated for Freud in mitigating those forms of social suffering that emplace an individual's fragile existence between the dangers of nature and the potential dangers of the "situation among his fellow men" (Ricoeur 1970: 250; Freud 1989). The fact that the very same emotions that restrict the fulfillment of an individual's desires also provide protection against others' desires makes the life of sentiment a space of ever present moral ambivalence and conflict for Freud and his followers.

Engaging similar Nietzcheian thematics but in a very different voice, Michel Foucault sought to detail the subtle dynamics and histories of power that bring into being particular ethical subjectivities. In contrast to Freud, however, Foucault's genealogical account of historically distinct sedimentations of particular forms of subjectivation and codes of conduct reflects of a view of moral life as arising from disciplined "inclination" (see Asad 1993; Mahmood 2001). Given Foucault's astute analysis of the micro-dynamics of power relations that lie at the base of such formations, it should also be noted, however, that Foucault's "hermeneutics of suspicion" (Ricoeur 1970; see Throop 2012) seriously destabilizes any naive view that the inclinational side of morality is in any way necessarily coterminous with the "good."

In the spirit of Nietzsche, Foucault views the crafting of particular ethical subjectivities as realized through the deployment of particular historically defined technologies and hermeneutics of self that delimit specific realms of self-experience as relevant to moral assessment, concern, and practice. In Foucault's account, historically, particular technologies and hermeneutics of self were necessarily connected to a determination of a particular ethical substance to be cultivated, resisted, or transformed, a reliance upon particular modes of subjection to moral precepts, as well as a defined moral goal or telos that such practices were held to generatively produce (Foucault 1985: 28; see also Foucault 2005). For contemporary anthropological accounts of moral sentiments Nietzsche's legacy in the form of both Freudian and Foucauldian schools of thought is very much alive and well today.

Anthropology and Moral Sentiments

Perhaps due to the fact that the anthropology of moralities has only recently coalesced into a defined field of study, anthropological assessments of ethical understandings and uses of sentiments have seldom resulted in a direct engagement with, critique, or extension of the philosophical accounts of moral sentiments described above (see Howell 1997; Robbins 2004; Zigon 2008; Hertz 2009). That said, there has still been a long, if often underrecognized, ethnographic focus upon moral sentiments in anthropology. Perhaps not surprisingly, when it is read alongside philosophical contributions, what stands out most about anthropological work on moral sentiments is the extent to which such sentiments are shown to be configured by political, economic, historical, linguistic, and cultural concerns (see Fassin 2012).

Anthropological interest in moral sentiments has a long history in the discipline that can be traced back to the Boasian tradition and the configurationalist writings of Ruth Benedict (1989) Margaret Mead, (2001), and Gregory Bateson (1958). Drawing from Gestalt psychology and Boas's neo-Kantian approach to the unconscious habitual configuration of perceptual, emotional, and sensory registers of experience, the configurationalists sought to explore the ways that sentiment and emotion were selected as more or less desired in the ethical and normative frameworks that defined the contours of locally valued ideal "personality" types. Such moral sentiments and emotions were similarly central to the more psychodynamically based theory of basic personality that was advanced by Abram Kardiner (1939), Cora DuBois (1960), and others.

While caricatures of "Apollonian Pueblo Indians" and "Dionysian Plains Indians" have perhaps irrevocably tainted a serious contemporary revisiting of so-called "culture and personality" approaches to moral sentiments, the notion of "ethos" as advanced in some of Gregory Bateson's (1958) early writings is still a potentially generative source for thinking through the significance of moral sentiments from an anthropological frame of reference. In attempting to highlight the "emotional tone" and "feel" of a given community or culture, Bateson set out to position sentiments centrally in anthropologically motivated attempts at understanding the norms, values, and motives patterning those particular cares and concerns that arise in the everyday lives of people who live in a given community.

Highlighting the contemporary relevance of Bateson's ideas, Linda Garro has recently suggested that "As a conceptual tool, ethos provided Bateson with a way of talking about how 'culture standardizes emotional reactions of individuals, and modifies the organization of their sentiments' … and an avenue for exploring the social and cultural mediation of 'specific tones of behavior' in situated and interactive contexts" (2011: 303). In an attempt to foreground the situated and interactive specificities of such culturally patterned sentiments, Garro suggests that Bateson's insights speak to possibilities not only for defining a generalized ethos that is variously shared within a community, but also for detailing specific "enactments of ethos" for interlocutors who are engaged in particular interactive contexts.

Aside from Bateson, arguably one of the most influential accounts of moral sentiments advanced under the guise of the concept of ethos is found in Clifford Geertz's (1973) discussion of religious perspectives and the moods and motives that serve to define them. Geertz argued that religious systems shape social actors' lifeworlds by directly impacting the motivations and moods those social actors habitually take up. Seeing ethos as divided between these two differing affective registers, Geertz characterized motivations as focused, goal-oriented, and discrete dispositions to feel and act in particular ways, according to specific ends, in particular circumstances. Moods, in contrast, were defined by Geertz as diffusely dispersed, objectless, context-defining, and totalistic in their encompassment (see also Throop 2009b). Both forms of sentiment, while existentially distinct, were for Geertz each centrally implicated in the visceral articulation of a particular religious worldview or perspective.

Around the same time that Geertz was first reflecting on the significance of motivations and moods in constituting religious perspectives, two pioneering ethnographic contributions to the anthropology of emotion were being developed. Published in 1970 and 1973 respectively, Jean Briggs's *Never in Anger* and Robert Levy's *Tahitians* each set out to illustrate the central place of emotions in cultural life, while also dealing with the ways that moral concerns are deeply intertwined with the experience and expression of them. The legacy of Briggs's and Levy's insights can be seen in the efflorescence of interest in the emotions that occurred in anthropology in the 1970s, 1980s, and early 1990s. This included significant contributions by Edward Schieffelin (1976), Michele Rosaldo (1980), Catherine Lutz (1988), Jane Wellenkamp (1988), Elinor Ochs and Bambi Schieffelin (1989), Douglas Hollan (1992), Renato Rosaldo (1989), and Steven Parish (1994). While they do not always explicitly emphasize the moral side of emotional life, a close reading of each of these works reveals a significant intertwining of moral and emotional experience.

In more recent years, this interest in the moral side of sentiments has been most compellingly articulated in ethnographies that have sought to examine issues of mourning and loss (Seremetakis 1990; Desjarlais 2003), love and attachment (Scheper-Hughes 1992; Garcia 2010), care and suffering (Good 1994; Mattingly 1998; Kleinman 2006, Throop 2010b), empathy (Hollan and Throop 2008; Throop 2010a), as well as those forms of life that arise in the midst of moral struggle and social abandonment (Biehl 2005; E. C. James 2010; Zigon 2010; Fassin 2012). While all of these scholars have contributed much to exploring the moral significance of sentiments, as well as their ideological, political, and economic entailments, they have not always explicitly set out to theorize the place of sentiments in the ongoing flux of moral and ethical life. It is precisely toward such a theoretical framing that I will now turn in outlining a phenomenological approach to moral sentiments.

Toward a Cultural Phenomenology of Moral Experience

A cultural phenomenological approach to morality is rooted in the basic phenomenologically grounded insight that perception, as Thomas Csordas argues, does not begin, but rather, "ends in objects" (1990: 9; 1994). That is, social actors are never simply passively registering a predetermined world of experience. Instead, the world individuals experience is, at least in part, shaped by their active engagements with it. In this respect there are always numerous sensory, imaginal, emotional, existential, and embodied processes that underlie the constitution of any given object of experience. Moreover, the specific organization of such multidimensional processes shifts through time. As Edmund Husserl (1962) taught, in the dynamic flux of subjective life individuals are continuously shifting their attention to differing aspects of their lived experience, whether morally articulated or otherwise. In so doing, they take up and attune to particular aspects of what is always a complex and shifting reality that coalesces for moments into discernible objects of attention and interest before yet another aspect of that reality, including their own and others' experience of it, calls forth their attention and captivates them.

In addition to the capacity to alter our modes of attention to differing aspects of experience whether imagined, felt, recollected, or perceived, Husserl further argued that individuals are able to shift between differing "attitudes" – from a "natural attitude" to a "theoretical attitude" for instance – by engaging in acts of phenomenological modification (Husserl 1962; see also Duranti 2009, 2010; Throop 2008, 2009a, 2010a, 2010b). Individuals are, in other words, able to step out from the ongoing flow of their everyday habitual engagements to examine their actions and experiences reflexively. For instance, an individual may at times participate in unexamined engagements with other social actors as "beings like me" – as meaning-endowing, feeling, knowing, and willing subjects who may experience suffering and joy the "same" way that he or she does (see also Stein 1989; Husserl 1993; Throop 2010a). Alternatively, he or she may confront the actions and reactions of others that do not make immediate sense, that call forth in their wake a need to reflect upon what might be unique and distinctive about other individuals' particular perspectives on the world. The very same individual may also at times modify his or her attention to those selfsame others by orienting to them as objects, as physical entities, as corporeal bodies that have been divested of such subjective entailments, just as physicians might do in conducting physical examinations of their patients (see Good 1994). There could, of course, be important moral and ethical concerns implicated in each of these various acts of phenomenological modification and the attitudes they are entailed by, and entail.

There have been diverse attempts within phenomenologically oriented anthropology to examine how insights such as these articulate with cultural processes. I have undertaken a more detailed examination of this literature elsewhere (see Throop 2003, 2005, 2008, 2010b; Duranti 2009, 2010; Desjarlais and Throop 2011). One particularly generative contribution to our understanding of this linkage is found in Csordas's notion of "somatic modes of attention." Drawing on Schutz's (1970) and Merleau-Ponty's (1999) phenomenological insights, Csordas defines somatic modes of attention as those "culturally elaborated ways of attending to and with one's body in surroundings that include the embodied presence of others" (1993: 138). By grounding attention directly in the existential structure of our bodily ways of being-in-the-world, Csordas wishes to highlight the various ways that culture can serve to pattern one's attention to bodily sensations in relation to perception, sociality, and motility. Significantly, the cultural patterning of attentional modalities in relation to embodied experience includes the organization of moral sensibilities (Geurts 2002).

From this perspective we can understand moral sensibilities, sentiments, and values as residues of collectively structured modes of selective attention (see W. James 1890). Borrowing from the language of Michel Foucault (1985, 2005), we can say that the organization of attention as mediated through our sensorium can be directly affected by differing hermeneutics and technologies of self. That is, the cultural organization of attention is often implicated in the ethical work "that one performs on oneself, not only in order to bring one's conduct into compliance with a given rule, but to attempt to transform oneself into the ethical subject of one's behavior" (Foucault 1985: 27; see also Robbins 2004; Zigon 2010; Faubion 2011).

Possibilities for ethical self-transformation arise not only with the habitual instillation of practical embodied dispositions, interpretive tendencies, and sensory attunements, however. They also arise in moments where one's taken-for-granted mode of being-in-the world, one's "natural attitude" as Husserl termed it, is challenged (see Throop 2010b). The shift that occurs in one's self-understanding in the face of such destabilization gives rise to possibilities for rearticulating one's orientation to existence, whether such an orientation is deemed practical, theoretical, aesthetic, religious, scientific, or otherwise (see Geertz 1973; Throop 2003, 2009b, 2010a, 2010b; Duranti 2009, 2010). Significantly, such moments of destabilization are also moments that may be definitively marked by the experience of particular sentiments, moods, emotions, and feelings (see also Desjarlais 1992; Geurts 2002; Hirschkind 2006).

In a recent article, Jarrett Zigon (2007) has explored some comparable insights in detailing the significance of a Heideggerian-inspired approach to the problem of morality. Most useful for my purposes in this essay is Zigon's attempt to employ Heideggerian philosophy to distinguish between moral and ethical modalities of existence. Where moral modalities of existence are tied to our practical, embodied, and unrecognized ways of being-in-the-world that are familiar to the point of being taken for granted as natural, ethical modalities of existence arise in contrast at heightened moments of self-reflection (see also Kleinman 1999). Following Heidegger (and to a somewhat lesser extent Foucault), Zigon points out that such ethical moments of reflection often occur at points in which our taken-for-granted moral engagements with the world are somehow breached, or in Husserlian terms destabilized (see Throop 2010b). It is in the face of such moments of "moral breakdown," as Zigon terms it, that possibilities for reassessing, transforming, and then reclaiming aspects of one's previously unnoticed moral engagements with the world become possible.

In an effort to generatively extend Zigon's insights, I suggest that it is crucial to recall the role that sentiments and sensibilities play in everyday moral experience and in moments of moral breakdown. Potential moments for heightened self-reflexivity and self-transformation afforded through experiences of moral breakdown, as well as the habitual modes of being from which they stem and toward which they aim, are equally mediated by various sensory, emotional, and embodied modalities of being. Moral experiences are, therefore, through and through, sentiment-based affairs. This holds true, although perhaps still in distinctive ways, for both unscrutinized moral experiences and more highly reflective ethical concerns.

From this perspective then, the ways that we are conditioned to move, balance, see, touch, hear, taste, and smell, to feel particular emotions, sentiments, motives, and moods, may all be registers of our existence that are potentially configured by, and configure, particular moral or ethical assumptions (see also Geurts 2002; Howes

2003). And yet, the cultural elaboration of particular varieties and intensities of feeling, emotion, sentiment, and sensibility are not the only ways that such existential registers are articulated with particular moral assumptions and orientations, however. As I have argued in a recent article on empathy, mourning, and loss, such feelings, emotions, sentiments, and sensibilities can also guide our attention to salient aspects of a particular situation or interaction that may then be taken to have relevance for our moral modes of being-in-the-world (2010a). Seeing sentiments and sensibilities as not only the sedimented dispositional results of efforts after moral cultivation, but also active and online modes of attuning our attention to morally salient aspects of our own and others' ways of being, is also implicated in the asymmetries of experience that come to characterize our moral life in time (something we saw as also salient to Smith's early writings on sympathy). Such a sentiment-based organization of attention in response to particular personal, interpersonal, and contextual cues may thus also play an important role in engendering a stance of ethical reflection (Zigon 2007). Again, I would argue that moments of moral breakdown and ensuing moments of ethical reflection are equally prone to being interlaced with, as well as being themselves at times generated by, sensible and affective valences as everyday habitual moral sensibilities are.

Moral Sensibilities in Yap

As a means to illustrate the analytic purchase provided by taking up such a phenomenological approach to moral experience, I will now briefly turn to my research on pain, suffering, and morality in Yap. While I do not have the space to discuss the various and complex ways that moral sentiments and sensibilities are centrally implicated in everyday life in Yapese communities (see Throop 2010b), I will provide a brief sketch of two significant moral orientations to sentiments that are at times in tension for particular individuals as they struggle to make sense of their own and others' suffering and pain. Having done that, I will turn to a specific encounter I had with the suffering of another as a means to more concretely ground the temporal dynamics and complexities of how moral sentiments articulate with particular phenomenological modifications, resulting shifts in attitude, and moments of moral breakdown.

A central dynamic in Yapese understandings of morality concerns the interplay of two sentiments, suffering and compassion. The Yapese term for suffering is *gaafgow* and it is a concept that is pivotal to understanding local configurations of social relationships, personhood, and morality. The term, which is heard repeatedly in everyday conversations and in innumerable different contexts, as one well-respected elder explained to me, is one of the central "teachings of Yap." It is out of suffering, she noted, that a number of other important virtuous qualities of a moral person are cultivated, qualities such as patience (*nuwaen'*), endurance (*athamagil*), temperance (*kadaen'*), respect (*liyoer*), care (*taa fan, ayuw*), and humility (*sobutaen'*). It is never *mere suffering* that is construed to be a virtue in Yap, however. Yapese people, like all people, do not see value in simply suffering for suffering's sake. It is instead *suffering for others* in the form of self-sacrifice that is construed to be a virtue. Suffering for your children, suffering for your family, suffering for your estate, suffering for your community, or suffering for your chiefs is held to be one of the central virtues underpinning local moral modes of being (see Throop 2008, 2010b). It is precisely in this way that embodied experiences of pain and suffering become linked to other sensory modalities, sentiments, and forms of emotional connection that are deemed central to experiences of social belonging.

The culturally appropriate response to the perception of suffering, or perhaps more accurately endurance in the face of suffering, is to feel compassion, or *runguy*. As a form of compassion, *runguy* is arguably itself a type of suffering, a suffering for the suffering of another (see Levinas 1998). Relations of power are also intimately connected to such sentiments, however, as it is always a higher-status individual who is ideally to feel compassion for a lower-status individual's plight. This is not to say that lower-status individuals (e.g., children, those of low caste, young men, and women) may not feel compassion for a higher-status person who is undergoing difficulties or hardship. It is only to say that directly expressing such a sentiment could, depending upon the circumstance, be deemed as an attempt to humiliate or challenge the authority of the higher-status sufferer. Individuals who express compassion for another's suffering are thus often placed in a position of authority over them. In even the most ideal-typical of cases the flow of power is seldom unidirectional, however. There are also subtle, and on occasion not so subtle, power dynamics implicated in the act of expressing one's suffering to another. The expression of suffering places an ethical demand upon those who witness it. This demand requires individuals to help in whatever way possible to alleviate the conditions producing a given sufferer's pain, hardship, and struggle. In this way a dynamic of power is differentially arrayed between compassionate witnesses and those who voice suffering alike.

The interplay of suffering and sentiment, while always delicately calibrated according to perceived status differentials (as well as attempts to subtly and at times not so subtly alter them) are further complicated by what can be seen as an at times competing moral orientation to sentiments in Yapese communities. Ideally speaking, a socially competent person in Yap is understood to be a person who is able to sacrifice his or her individual desires, wants, wishes, feelings, opinions, and thoughts to family, village, and broader community dictates (see Throop 2010b). The virtues of self-abnegation and self-restraint as realized through careful reflection and deliberation are essential to the cultivation of those qualities that inhere in a virtuous person, a person who acts thoughtfully, with self-control, humility, and concern for others. A person who is not able to cultivate these qualities, who acts impulsively, who transparently expresses his or her personal feelings and emotions, who speaks without thinking or acts without regard to the concerns of others is a person thought to have a "weak mind," not unlike a child. Accordingly, the capacity to master the ability to monitor and selectively share one's emotions, feelings, thoughts, and opinions in the service of wider familial and community goals is one of the essential existential bases of local ethical modalities of being.

The virtue of self-governance is closely tethered to the valuation of privacy, secrecy, and concealment. Not sharing, not expressing, and not acting upon one's "true" feelings, opinions, or thoughts – a pattern also widely noted in the context of other Polynesian and Micronesian cultures (Robbins and Rumsey 2008; Hollan and Throop 2011) – is one of the core cultural values at the basis of Yapese social life. Such a virtuous cultivation of mental opacity ideally emphasizes a fundamental disconnect between individual expressivity and an individual's inner life. In Yapese communities, an individual's inner states, defined in terms of personal wants, desires, opinions, feelings, emotions, sensations, and thought-objects, are often held to have ideally, in many contexts, a nondirect, nontransparent connection to action and expression. While individuals are morally attuned to the ongoing dynamics of compassion and suffering in everyday encounters, they also recurrently run up against individuals' morally motivated efforts to conceal their subjective life from the scrutiny of others. To better understand the complexities of how such at times competing orientations to moral experience play out in concrete situations, it will be helpful to examine a specific interactional moment in which such moral sentiments and sensibilities are variously at play.

An Encounter with Suffering

On a humid afternoon in the fall of 2002 I had the opportunity to attend, for the first time, a healing session that was being conducted by a local healer specializing in traditional massage and bone-setting. On this particular day the healer, Lani, was treating a young Yapese girl named Tinag. As the session got going Lani applied a bit of coconut oil to her hands, gently took Tinag's arm, and began to feel with her fingers and her thumb the length of her forearm. Trying to conceal her fear and pain, Tinag, only 10 years old, sat still and rigid, all the time looking down at her arm in order to avoid eye contact with the girl. Lani asked Tinag to try turning her arm so that it was flat (i.e., with the palm of the hand directed to the ground). Tinag was in terrible pain and was moving her shoulders and her torso instead of her forearm to try to get her arm in the desired position. Seeing her struggle, Lani gently tried to help turn the arm, while Tinag looked away, grunted, and winced. With the arm in position, Lani began to press up and down Tinag's forearm and asked whenever she moved to a new location on her arm if there was pain (*Baaq amiith?*). She finally centered on the area where the break had occurred, before stopping.

Lani suggested that Tinag's father come and hold her so that they could try resetting the arm. Her father positioned himself behind Tinag and began rubbing her head and back. Lani explained that it was going to be very painful as she tried to put the bones back into position but that once it was all over, the pain would fade quickly and she would feel much better. She pointed out that the reason Tinag was having such a hard time moving her forearm was because the "small bone" in her forearm was misaligned. If they did not reset the bone today, while it was still moving, she cautioned, it would be much harder later as the bone began to heal. Just before the resetting of the arm began, her father whispered in Tinag's ear that there was going to be very strong pain (*Ra yib rib geel amiith*) but that she would persevere (*Maachnea ga ra athamagil*). He also told her that after the bone had been reset the pain would quickly weaken (*Ra waer, ra waer*).

Lani took hold of Tinag's good arm and showed both Tinag and her father what she was going to do. She said that she needed Tinag's father to hold the elbow in place as she pulled the arm toward her and attempted to reset the bones. As Tinag watched, Lani and her father practiced with her good arm. Seeing this, she started to whimper and shake her head. Lani asked her if she didn't want to go through with the procedure, and Tinag replied that she could not (*Daabiyog*). At this point I noticed that Tinag's father was beginning to tear up (as was I). When Lani noticed this she said to Tinag that her father was old and weak and that was why he was crying but that she was strong and she would be fine. Her father then repeated to Tinag *M'athamagil* ("You endure"). And then, despite her cries and screams, the bone-setting began.

As I sat there witnessing the intensity of Tinag's pain as she screamed, cried, struggled, and pleaded with her father and the healer to stop the procedure, I could not help but embody her suffering in the form of quiet tears. At that moment, watching her father bravely try to comfort his suffering daughter, sitting still, with tear-filled eyes, I had a crisis of faith. What was I doing here? Why should I attempt to document such private suffering and pain? Was my presence not just making things worse for everyone involved? What right did I have to witness such hurt and such fear? Just as these questions were rushing through my mind I noticed Lani, who also had tears in her eyes look over at me. Our eyes met for what could not have been longer than a split second, but apparently it was long enough for her to register my response to the situation.

After the bone was finally reset Lani told Tinag to rest for a minute. Tinag slumped back into her father's lap, who then massaged her head and good arm. Lani wiped the tears from her own eyes and called to her daughter to prepare the medicine. Lani began telling us that she had been treating a boy for the last three weeks who had a much worse break than Tinag and that he was now feeling good enough to be running around without a brace. Lani then added that the boy in question had screamed and cried a lot during the resetting of the bone but that Tinag was strong and barely cried at all. Her father then added with a hint of pride that Tinag did not even cry when she had originally broken her arm after the fall.

As Lani spoke, I could not help but feel uncomfortable and embarrassed, worried that my own tears had been somehow problematic. From what I already knew of Yapese expectations concerning the expression of emotion I knew that I was failing miserably in living up to local ideals of expressive opacity and emotional quietude that are expected of everyone, but especially of men. At the end of the session, however, Lani came over to talk to me. She said softly, "I saw you crying over there," and smiled, tears still fresh in her own eyes. I nodded and may have apologized. She put her hand on my shoulder and told me that I could stop by anytime.

Moral Breakdown, Sentiments, and Ethics of Suffering

As this brief encounter attests, emotions of fear, worry, anxiety, sadness, embarrassment, compassion, and pride are interlaced throughout Tinag's struggles to endure the horrible intensities of pain associated with traditional bone-setting without analgesics. Such sentiments were also intersubjectively distributed between Tinag, Lani, her father, and me. Sentiments, moral and otherwise, were in constant flux and closely tied to ongoing shifting interactional dynamics and anticipated actions. Such sentiments also served to variously pattern our attention to salient aspects of the encounter, including Tinag's attempts to focus away from anticipated pain, her father's gentle attention to comforting his terrified daughter, Lani's struggles to go on with the procedure despite her distress witnessing Tinag's hurt, and my own moment of moral breakdown, which led me to wonder what right I had to be there at all. That breakdown, a private ethically reflective moment, or at least that is how it seemed to me at the time of its occurrence, was intimately associated with tears, however, that caught Lani's attention and led her to feel a compassionate concern for my own suffering.

Elsewhere I have attempted to argue that a phenomenology of moral experience is generatively enhanced by thinking of how particular phenomenological modifications, shifting attitudes and perspectives, and temporally configured modes of selective attention articulate with Emmanuel Levinas's reflections on ethics and suffering (Throop 2010b). For Levinas, it is possible to situate moral experience in those interhuman spaces in which efforts at typification are stilled, even if only momentarily. Cultivating an openness to the other, working to avoid reducing the plenitude of another's existence to the self-sameness of our own being, is a definitive ethical stance in Levinas's view. The extent to which particular sentiments may potentiate or foreclose such orientations is certainly a topic that needs more careful attention. Given that I do not have the space to consider such questions in much detail in this essay, let me focus specifically on the temporal dynamics of moral sentiments and the phenomenological modifications associated with them, as a means to trace the contours of the intersubjectively generated moment of moral breakdown that I experienced in witnessing Tinag's pain. This breakdown was situated in what was simultaneously a space of existential asymmetry and social attunement.

Again, Levinas is helpful here. From a Levinasian perspective, my present thoughts, feelings, emotions, and moods are held to arise for me in a moment that can only be recognized by *you* in the modality of an after. That is, the expressions you take up as indications of my subjective state are already at that moment retentions or past recollections for *me* of my previously experienced intentions, goals, plans, and desires. My anticipatory horizons, while attentive to your responses, are also feeding forward to the horizons of my own desires, wishes, and hopes for what is to come next. That the synchronization of our two beings in even the most intimate of "we-relationships" (see Schutz 1967) is one of a delayed asymmetry constituting an interhuman time that is neither precisely mine nor yours is, Levinas (1987) argues, a basic fact of human existence revealing the necessary "excess of being."

There is another side to such intersubjective asymmetries that is not captured in Levinas's account, however. It is found instead in Schutz's (1967) discussion of the "we-relationship." According to Schutz, in dynamic moments of face-to-face attunement that characterize the co-presence of a "we-relationship," there are moments of possibility in which another may perceive aspects of my own self-experience that I am not yet aware of myself. In this case, the Levinasian asymmetry is reversed. The dynamic flux of my field of expressions is palpably available to *you* in a way that is not available to *me*. Indeed, it is immediately present for you, while for me it may be made available only through my ability to notice and track your expressive responses to my expressions. As Schutz explains, in the face-to-face situation my

> observations keep pace with each moment of his stream of consciousness as it transpires. The result is that I am incomparably better attuned to him than I am to myself. I may indeed be more aware of my own past … than I am of my partner's. Yet I have never been

> face to face with myself as I am with him now; hence I have never caught myself in the act of actually living through an experience. (1967: 169)

Again, a temporal delay, or a space of disjuncture is centrally placed in even the most closely attuned of human encounters. It is within this space of temporal disjuncture that ongoing phenomenological modifications to our own and others' existence are triggered not only by our mutual expressive fields but also by the sentiments that arise within them. As Schutz explains:

> If I know that you and I are in a face-to-face relationship, I also know something about the manner in which each of us is attuned to his conscious experiences, in other words, the "attentional modifications" of each of us. This means that the way we attend to our conscious experiences is actually modified by our relationship to each other. (1967: 171)

In this light, sentiments may not only be considered morally valenced in and of themselves but may also generatively serve to trigger phenomenological modifications that are morally configured. Moments of moral breakdown are, indeed, often sparked by sentiments that make thematic previously unrecognized moral assumptions that arise as we attune to new aspects of our own and others' existential dilemmas, cares, and concerns.

Returning to my own moment of moral breakdown and the sentiments and sensibilities that were associated with it, it was precisely in those moments where I was made to existentially question my own very presence as a witness, to confront my own interests and plans (interests and plans that led me to participate in the suffering of another that could never be my own) that I was faced with the true integrity of Tinag's being – a being that is not assumable to the self-sameness of my own being. The intensity and viscerality of Tinag's pain, her suffering, her cries, tears, and screams compelled a shift in my orientation to her. In those moments, she could no longer ever simply be a subject of my research, a token of a type of person who suffers pain, even if at times virtuously from a Yapese perspective. Tinag's uniqueness, irreplaceability, and singularity would always outstrip my attempts at understanding her, whether in terms of my own theoretical commitments or in terms of our shared interactional history together. My own tears, my own suffering for Tinag's suffering, in short my own experience of sentiment, was also a point of connection, however, with Lani. The tears which I was only vaguely aware of as I sat reflecting upon my positionality and presence in this most painful and vulnerable of moments for Tinag, were noticed by Lani, whose very noticing also then made them thematic for me. My suffering, my sadness, which could never be Lani's suffering or sadness, may have also destabilized, however briefly, the typifications she used in understanding my presence there. At that moment she came to see me as more than a strange outsider, a researcher, an anthropologist, a student, or what have you. I was in that moment uniquely human, vulnerable, and unassumable in my own right.

Conclusion

As I hope to have shown with this brief example, the space of sentiments in a phenomenological account of moral experience is quite differently positioned from the space that is provided for them in the traditional philosophical accounts of moral sentiments in virtue ethics, moral sense theory, and Nietzschean genealogical perspectives. It is also rather distinct from either strictly Freudian or Foucauldian accounts. Looking at the history of anthropological engagements with moral sentiments, the phenomenological approach I have advocated in this essay certainly relies similarly upon a close attention to the various ways that sentiments, emotions, feelings, and moods are made ethically significant in particular communities of practice and in the lives of particular individuals. It moves beyond these assessments, however, by exploring the ways such sentiments, always locally understood and configured, impact dynamic shifts in our attention, in particular phenomenological modifications, and in traceable transformations in perspective, that are always intersubjectively distributed and temporally arrayed. It is precisely within such dynamic shifts that those aspects of persons, encounters, events, and interactions that are implicated in moving us from less-examined orientations to moral experience to more explicitly thematic and reflexive varieties occur (Zigon 2007, 2010). It is also within this space that particular moral sensibilities are sedimented through time as habitual modes of anticipating, remembering, and attuning to/with such sensibilities occur through time.

Acknowledgments

I would like to thank Didier Fassin and Jarrett Zigon for providing a number of insightful suggestions that helped to significantly improve the quality of this essay.

REFERENCES

Aristotle (1976) *Ethics.* New York: Penguin.

Asad, Talal (1993) *Genealogies of Religion: Discipline and Reasons of Power in Christianity and Islam.* Baltimore: Johns Hopkins University Press.

Bateson, Gregory (1958) *Naven: A Survey of the Problems Suggested by a Composite Picture of the Culture of a New Guinea Tribe drawn from Three Points of View.* Stanford: Stanford University Press.

Benedict, Ruth (1989) *Patterns of Culture.* Boston: Houghton Mifflin.

Biehl, João (2005) *Vita: Life in a Zone of Social Abandonment.* Berkeley: University of California Press.

Briggs, Jean (1970) *Never in Anger: Portrait of an Eskimo Family.* Cambridge, MA: Harvard University Press.

Briggs, Jean (1995) *Inuit Morality Play: The Emotional Education of a Three-Year-Old.* New Haven: Yale University Press.

Csordas, Thomas (1990) Embodiment as a Paradigm for Anthropology. *Ethos* 18(1): 5–47.

Csordas, Thomas (1993) Somatic Modes of Attention. *Cultural Anthropology* 8(1): 135–156.

Csordas, Thomas (1994) *The Sacred Self: A Cultural Phenomenology of Charismatic Healing.* Berkeley: University of California Press.

Desjarlais, Robert (1992) *Body and Emotion: The Aesthetics of Illness and Healing in the Nepal Himalayas.* Philadelphia: University of Pennsylvania Press.

Desjarlais, Robert (2003) *Sensory Biographies.* Berkeley: University of California Press.

Desjarlais, Robert and Throop, C. Jason (2011) Phenomenological Approaches in Anthropology. *Annual Review of Anthropology* 40: 87–102.

DuBois, Cora (1960) *The People of Alor.* Cambridge, MA: Harvard University Press.

Duranti, Alessandro (2009) The Relevance of Husserl's Theory to Language Socialization. *Journal of Linguistic Anthropology* 19(2): 205–226.

Duranti, Alessandro (2010) Husserl, Intersubjectivity, and Anthropology. *Anthropological Theory* 10(1): 1–20.

Fassin, Didier (2012) *Humanitarian Reason: A Moral History of the Present.* Berkeley: University of California Press.

Faubion, James D. (2011) *An Anthropology of Ethics.* Cambridge: Cambridge University Press.

Foucault, Michel (1985) *The Use of Pleasure*, trans. Robert Hurley. New York: Pantheon.

Foucault, Michel (2005) *The Hermeneutics of the Subject: Lectures at the Collège de France, 1981–1982.* New York: Palgrave Macmillan.

Freud, Sigmund (1989) *Civilization and its Discontents*, trans. and ed. James Strachey. New York: Norton.

Garcia, Angela (2010) *The Pastoral Clinic: Addiction and Dispossession along the Rio Grande.* Berkeley: University of California Press.

Garro, Linda (2011) Enacting Ethos, Enacting Health: Realizing Health in the Everyday Life of a California Family of Mexican Descent. *Ethos* 39(3): 300–330.

Geertz, Clifford (1973) *The Interpretation of Cultures.* New York. Basic Books.

Geurts, Kathryn Linn (2002) *Culture and the Senses: Bodily Ways of Knowing in an African Community.* Berkeley: University of California Press.

Good, Byron (1994) *Medicine, Rationality, and Experience: An Anthropological Perspective.* Cambridge: Cambridge University Press.

Haakonssen, Knud (2002) Introduction. In Adam Smith, *The Theory of Moral Sentiments.* Cambridge: Cambridge University Press, pp. vii–xiv.

Hertz, Monica (ed.) (2009) *The Anthropology of Moralities.* New York: Berghahn.

Hirschkind, Charles (2006) *The Ethical Soundscape: Cassette Sermons and Islamic Counterpublics.* New York: Columbia University Press.

Hollan, Douglas (1992) Emotion Work and the Value of Emotional Equanimity among the Toraja. *American Ethnologist* 31(1): 45–56.

Hollan, Douglas W. and Throop, C. Jason (2008) Whatever Happened to Empathy? Introduction. *Ethos* 36(4): 385–401.

Hollan, Douglas W. and Throop, C. Jason (eds.) (2011) *The Anthropology of Empathy: Experiencing the Lives of Others in Pacific Societies.* New York: Berghahn.

Howell, Signe (1997) *The Ethnography of Moralities.* London: Routledge.

Howes, David (2003) *Sensual Relations: Engaging the Senses in Culture and Social Theory.* Ann Arbor: University of Michigan Press.

Hume, David (2005) *A Treatise of Human Nature.* New York: Barnes & Noble.

Husserl, Edmund (1962) *Ideas: General Introduction to Pure Phenomenology.* New York: Collier.

Husserl, Edmund (1993) *Cartesian Meditations.* London: Kluwer.

James, Erica Caple (2010) *Democratic Insecurities: Violence, Trauma, and Intervention in Haiti.* Berkeley: University of California Press.

James, William (1890) *The Principles of Psychology.* New York: Henry Holt.

Kardiner, Abram (1939) *The Individual and his Society.* New York: Columbia University Press.

Kleinman, Arthur (1999) Experience and its Moral Modes: Culture, Human Conditions, and Disorder. In G. B. Peterson (ed.), *Tanner Lectures on Human Values*, vol. 20. Salt Lake City: University of Utah Press, pp. 357–420.

Kleinman, Arthur (2006) *What Really Matters: Living a Moral Life amidst Uncertainty and Danger.* Oxford: Oxford University Press.

Lambek, Michael (ed.) (2010) *Ordinary Ethics: Anthropology, Language, and Ethics.* New York: Fordham University Press.

Levinas, Emmanuel (1987) *Time and the Other*, trans. Richard A. Cohen. Pittsburgh: Duquesne University Press.

Levinas, Emmanuel (1998) *Entre Nous: On Thinking-of-the-Other*, trans. Michael B. Smith and Barbara Harshav. New York: Columbia University Press.

Levy, Robert (1973) *Tahitians.* Chicago: University of Chicago Press.

Lutz, Catherine (1988) *Unnatural Emotions*. Chicago: University of Chicago Press.
MacIntyre, Alasdair (1966) *A Short History of Ethics: A History of Moral Philosophy from the Homeric Age to the Twentieth Century*. New York: Macmillan.
MacIntyre, Alasdair (2002) *After Virtue: A Study in Moral Theory*, 3rd edn. Notre Dame, IN: University of Notre Dame Press.
Mahmood, Saba (2001) Feminist Theory, Embodiment and the Docile Agent: Some Reflections on the Egyptian Islamic Revival. *Cultural Anthropology* 16(2): 202–236.
Mattingly, Cheryl (1998) *Healing Dramas and Clinical Plot: The Narrative Structure of Experience*. Cambridge: University of Cambridge Press.
Mead, Margaret (2001) *Sex and Temperament in Three Primitive Societies*. New York: HarperCollins.
Merleau-Ponty, Maurice (1999) *Phenomenology of Perception*. London: Routledge.
Nietzsche, Friedrich (1989) *On the Genealogy of Morals and Ecce Homo*, trans. Walter Kaufmann and R. J. Hollingdale. New York: Random House.
Nussbaum, Martha (2001) *Upheavals of Thought: The Intelligence of Emotions*. Cambridge: Cambridge University Press.
Ochs, Elinor and Schieffelin, Bambi (1989) Language has a Heart. *Text* 9(1): 7–25.
Parish, Steven M. (1994) *Moral Knowing in a Hindu Sacred City: An Exploration of Mind, Emotion, and Self*. New York: Columbia University Press.
Ricoeur, Paul (1970) *Freud and Philosophy: An Essay in Interpretation*, trans. Danis Savage. New Haven: Yale University Press.
Robbins, Joel (2004) *Becoming Sinners*. Berkeley: University of California Press.
Robbins, Joel, and Rumsey, Alan (2008) Introduction: Cultural and Linguistic Anthropology and the Opacity of Other Minds. *Anthropological Quarterly* 81(2): 407–420.
Rosaldo, Michele (1980) *Knowledge and Passion: Illongot Notions of Self and Social Life*. Cambridge: Cambridge University Press.
Rosaldo, Renato (1989) Grief and a Headhunter's Rage: On the Cultural Force of Emotions. In *Culture and Truth: The Remaking of Social Analysis*. Boston: Beacon.
Scheper-Hughes, Nancy (1992) *Death without Weeping*. Berkeley: University of California Press.
Scheper-Hughes, Nancy (1995) The Primacy of the Ethical: Propositions for a Militant Anthropology. *Current Anthropology* 36(3): 409–420.
Schieffelin, Edward L. (1976) *The Sorrow of the Lonely and the Burning of the Dancers*. New York: St. Martin's.
Schutz, Alfred (1967) *The Phenomenology of the Social World*. Evanston, IL: Northwestern University Press.
Schutz, Alfred (1970) *On Phenomenology and Social Relations*, ed. Helmut R. Wagner. Chicago: University of Chicago Press.
Seremetakis, Nadia (1990) The Ethics of Antiphony: The Social Construction of Pain, Gender and Power in the Southern Peloponnese. *Ethos* 18(4): 481–512.
Shweder, Richard (1997) *Why do Men Barbecue? Recipes for Cultural Psychology*. Cambridge, MA: Harvard University Press.
Smith, Adam (2002) *The Theory of Moral Sentiments*. Cambridge: Cambridge University Press.
Stein, Edith (1989) *On the Problem of Empathy*. Washington, DC: ICS.
Throop, C. Jason (2003) Articulating Experience. *Anthropological Theory* 3(2): 219–241.
Throop, C. Jason (2005) "Hypocognition, a "Sense of the Uncanny," and the Anthropology of Ambiguity: Reflections on Robert I. Levy's Contribution to Theories of "Experience" in Anthropology. *Ethos* 33(4): 499–511.
Throop, C. Jason (2008) From Pain to Virtue: Dysphoric Sensations and Moral Sensibilities in Yap (Waqab), Federated States of Micronesia. *Journal of Transcultural Psychiatry* 45(2): 253–286.
Throop, C. Jason (2009a) "Becoming Beautiful in the Dance": On the Formation of Ethical Modes of Being in Yap (Waqab), Federated States of Micronesia. *Oceania* 79(2): 179–201.

Throop, C. Jason (2009b) Interpretation and the Limits of Interpretability: On Rethinking Clifford Geertz' Semiotics of Religious Experience. *Journal of North African Studies* 14(3): 369–384.

Throop, C. Jason (2010a) Latitudes of Loss: On the Vicissitudes of Empathy. *American Ethnologist* 37(4): 771–782.

Throop, C. Jason (2010b) *Suffering and Sentiment: Exploring the Vicissitudes of Experience and Pain in Yap*. Berkeley: University of California Press.

Throop, C. Jason (2012) On Inaccessibility and Vulnerability: Some Horizons of Compatibility between Phenomenology and Psychoanalysis. *Ethos* 40(1): 75–96.

Wellenkamp, Jane (1988) Notions of Grief and Catharsis among the Toraja. *American Ethnologist* 15(3): 486–500.

Zigon, Jarrett (2007) Moral Breakdown and Ethical Demand. *Anthropological Theory* 7(2): 131–150.

Zigon, Jarrett (2008) *Morality: An Anthropological Perspective*. London: Berg.

Zigon, Jarrett (2010) *Making the New Post-Soviet Person: Narratives of Moral Experience in Contemporary Moscow*. Leiden: Brill.

Zigon, Jarrett (2011) *"HIV is God's Blessing": Rehabilitating Morality in Neoliberal Russia*. Berkeley: University of California Press.

CHAPTER 10 Moral Reasoning

Karen M. Sykes

> *Ongka explains that if money looks after white people then pigs look after them [the Kawelka]. "You have to have pigs for whatever you want to do. Pigs are our strong thing, you must have pigs for everything. Pigs are everything. You must have pigs for moka, to pay for troubles, to get wives. If you don't have pigs, you are rubbish, you are nothing. There are a lot of men who don't realize this."*
>
> Ongka, *The Kawelka: Ongka's Big Moka*, 1976

"If you don't have pigs, you are rubbish, you are nothing. There are a lot of men who don't realize this." These words are the conclusion of a two-minute meditation in which Ongka, a Papuan leader, explains how to create a good life. He deliberates the moral contradictions that lie between managing material wealth and upholding the social good. Known as a Big-man, normally a prestigious or a good leader, Ongka must always be ready to present his friends, enemies, and competitors alike with pigs for their enjoyment and use. Ongka reasons that a powerful and good man is a man who can give away his personal wealth lavishly, and show his friends and enemies alike that his wealth is so abundant that he can easily present more than enough pigs to satisfy all who come to the feast. This seeming personal capacity to convince some people to invest their pigs in a complex system of exchange with others' pigs enables his village to flourish. The paradoxes faced by Papua New Guinea (PNG) Big-men might be similar to those known to financial investors whose passionate concern with prestige and flourishing communities of exchange outstrips all measures of economic rationality (Martin 2009). In this essay, I analyze the nature of the moral reasoning that embraces both sentiment and rationality, as do Ongka, his fans, and the financial investors of recent years. In addition, I consider Ongka's growing concern that he has lost respect in the new political order of the independent PNG. Ongka questions his morals: "Is rubbishness eating me?" Does self-interest overtake generosity? Is Ongka like others who recognize that both personal reputation and successful public work is a legacy of their moral deliberations, as they find reason confounded by sentiments?

A Companion to Moral Anthropology, First Edition. Edited by Didier Fassin.

Ongka's meditation on pigs is rapidly and intensely spoken, as if the Big-man felt his earnest message would otherwise miss his uninformed viewers. His disquisition can be accessed through YouTube (a media-sharing website) because the film has been cut and divided into seven short videos. Viewers of YouTube have heard and documented their replies to Ongka's speech; long lists of praise can be found underneath the film clips. "Ongka rocks," writes one of the viewers about the YouTube segment one, which is the most popular. Other student responses to the video echo the same sentiment. They are not simply responding to exotic economics; they express real pleasure at finding the opportunity to revisit now what they have enjoyed in their university classrooms. In addition, some document their thoughts about the economy of financial greed. The feast is a social form which is surprisingly familiar to these viewers who are interested in the same questions as Ongka: What is greedy or generous behavior toward others? When is economic rationality not an obvious measure of good judgment? How is respect won and shown?

Not all anthropologists who come upon the YouTube video-casts will know that *Moka* is a Papuan word from the central highlands of PNG, which refers to the material good that is returned to the giver of wealth. Writing of *moka* in the region, Andrew Strathern (1971) compares it to interest on the debt, a return on an investment. Thus, the concept, although untranslated, is not so strange to the viewers, who have quickly established that the social form which is familiar to the Papua New Guinean highlands is also a social form that is meaningful in explaining the contemporary Anglo-American investors' economy of the early twenty-first century. Although interest is a concept that deserves further interrogation (Sahlins 1972, 1976; Gregory 2011; Lederman 1986; Hirschman 1993; Sykes 2004), the measure of interest shown in the making of a *moka* feast might also be described as the measure of morality of investment in each location; yet that standard of measure is elusive to observers and participants alike. Ongka stops to wonder if his "rubbishness," his greed, is eating him, and he therefore cannot achieve the success he desires, to become a Big-man, renowned for generosity with his food and wealth. Those scholars already familiar with the film might also find it intriguing that viewers tune in to Ongka's speech in an era of market volatility, in a period of the free fall of trading standards. It is well known that in Ongka's lifetime, as in the viewers', the measure of the worth of material goods was being eroded by the collapse of the ranked standards of value in that region of the newly independent nation of PNG (Gregory 1986). Thereafter, pigs, like the white man's money, became "everything," and economic bubble and older "currencies" – kina shells, bird feathers, oils, and cowries – became valueless. Pigs are essential to *moka*; they are the embodiment of value as evidence of the social good. Furthermore, the character of the investor, of the market trader, has been scrutinized more narrowly, and found lacking because the trader knows no restraint on his greed. In the contemporary Anglo-American economy, and in the PNG economy on the eve of independence, something, or someone, had to give.

At the point that I am writing this, the first video segment, "Ongka's Big Moka," has been viewed over 32,000 times and the second, "Ongka's Meditation on Pigs," has been viewed over 18,000 times within the two or three years since they were first uploaded to YouTube. Although they are things of a different order, it is interesting to compare the number of citations registered by Google Scholar in 2012 for other significant texts in economic anthropology: *Stone Age Economics* (Sahlins 1972) registers over 4,300 citations, and *Gifts and Commodites* (Gregory 1982) lodged 900 on the same index, whereas Marcel Mauss's *The Gift* (1990) received nearly 9,000 citations. The actual ethnography of the *moka* (A. Strathern 1971) registers 229 citations. Significant books by anthropologists, such as *The Interpretation of Cultures* (Geertz 1973b) which received more than 25,000 citations, have competed favorably with the fame of Ongka's film, but are not quite so widely renowned. Perhaps the high scores for the impact of the film are a measure of the form of presentation: Ongka's famous film first appeared on family television screens in 1976, broadcast by Granada Television, and later became a staple of the undergraduate curriculum. However, if virtual and visual forms of intellectual work make a difference to the regeneration of the intellectual community, then work in related mediums, the economic anthropology blogs, the knowledge "commons," the social networking sites such as the Open Anthropology Cooperative, with 5,900 members at the time of writing, cannot compete with this video distribution of Ongka's words. Can we say that Ongka has succeeded in winning a respectable place in the ranks of the current academic standards of value, ranks that reflect the timely fascination with quantitative measures of the worth of scholarship, and measures that award distinction to concrete evidence of citation and use? In the contemporary university the validity of scholarship is increasingly measured by impact and accounting evidence of the number of citations. I am concerned about the narrowness of this window on measures of scholarly validity, one by which the example of Ongka's celebrity, his status as a commentator on the nature of economic behavior, his ability to address issues of key importance to his viewers' understanding of the contemporary economic collapse, and the scholarly rigor of his argument converge into one scale of value. From this view, we might raise some final important questions for social scientists, especially anthropologists, about living with such contradictions in the moral economy of the contemporary university.

Living with the paradoxes of the contemporary situation wherein the Anglo-American economy appears to be suffering a free fall in the value of its currencies, economic anthropologists might author a better understanding of moral reasoning about wealth and the social good, namely one that reckons with the collapse of value standards or the volatility of a moral economy which relies on one standard – such as pigs, money, or citations – as its rule. Taking a cue from his YouTube celebrity, I suggest that for such times as these Ongka is the man to follow. For the present, at least, it would seem that anthropologists Maurer (2009) and Hart and Ortiz (2008) were right in ways they did not anticipate when they argued that the study of "non-Western" society, a cold war era concept which presumed a division between the western world and the rest of the world, and between late capitalist and non-capitalist societies, no longer provides models for the study of economic reason. The case has been made convincingly that people live in a joined-up world: what scholars of Melanesia can report from recent studies (Errington and Gewertz 2004; Kirsch 2006; Bashkow 2008), and differently from earlier research (A. Strathern 1971; M. Strathern 1981), is that far from being exemplars of "non-Western" society, many studies of PNG societies – such as the Kawelka in which Ongka lives – reveal how people live lives that are profoundly joined up to the Australian and the Anglo-American economy, and further, that the production, use, and distribution of ethnographic studies, replete with compelling images, are themselves most surely part of it. Ongka's experience in a period of social and economic change on the cusp of full political independence in PNG, is part of Western society, and shares more with the Anglo-American economy of the present, when new forms of economic governance feature in interpersonal business transactions, and new political governance emerges in the form of the corporate state. Ongka's meditation on wealth and the social good is an account of the living paradoxes of his times, a period that feels familiar to his viewers. Ongka's reasoning follows from his experience of the confusion of long-established value standards, and speaks to the enduring question of just what the social good is. In such a global world, in which models of collapsing value standards from the PNG highlands of the pre-independence period pertain to plummeting Anglo-American market values, anthropologists have new questions to ask about that. This essay examines the nature of moral reasoning about the social good, and the questions Ongka's meditation raises for understanding the living paradoxes of a global age.

A few things can be said about the film and its importance in both the wider public and the university. *Ongka's Big Moka* is the subtitle of a film, *The Kawelka*. Not a new film, it was produced in 1976 by Granada Studios in the famous *Disappearing World* series that brought the lives of people in other societies through the medium of ethnographic film to the television screens of viewers who had already warmed to the nature documentary. However, far from being a series that explored human emotions as if they were part of animal behavior, the series of films made for *Disappearing World* used the well-established capacity of the screen image to convey the emotions of its subjects to the viewer, and in turn to create a sense of the place and peoples by drawing on the empathy of those who were watching the films (Loizos 1980). Viewers who watch the full-length film are introduced to Ongka, who is planning a *moka*. Viewers see Ongka first in his home in the central highlands of PNG, where he is organizing the feast at which valuable goods will be redistributed widely to his clansmen as well as to long-term trading partners from distant valleys. The consulting anthropologist for the film, Andrew Strathern, explains to the viewers that Ongka's prestige relies on the success of the feast, not so much as a money-making venture, but more as a vehicle for showing he is a good man. His prestige is proven at the *moka* by virtue of the large number of other prestigious people who bring goods to it: pigs, pearl shells, bird of paradise plumage, as well as intangible goods, such as magic, dance, and music. Ongka explains how to make a *moka* in a detailed fashion, which is shared with the viewers in a long, rapidly spoken disquisition about pigs. The film shows the work of making arrangements for the feast, the work of preparing to give away the valuables, the rearing of pigs, the amassing of shells, the centrality of persuasive rhetoric in soliciting donations, and the necessity of magic to ward off inclement weather on the day. In the film we learn that this ritual exchange is the central social and economic event, if not the only salient one for the establishment of political standing in the region. Making *moka* is a good thing to do, and all involved in it feel this is true. This film is a fine example of the careful deliberations of moral reasoning about the complexity of the meaning of the social good. In it Ongka shows that his passion to do good , for his kinsmen and for his exchange partners, is satisfied by the reasoning about the redistributions of goods. Ongka meditates on relationships between pigs as wealth and the various meanings of the social good in human society in order to enlighten viewers as to the significance of what they see on the screen.

I have taught the film *The Kawelka* to undergraduate classes in 2009 and 2010, and have noticed how compelling it is to this new generation of students who believe they face a difficult economic future, when they hear the forecast for a decade of hard times ahead. However, watching Ongka organize his big *moka* throughout the film enlivens most students; it is a film ripe with sexual metaphors to explain economic motivation in the *moka*, coloring their understanding of both the hopes and disappointments of making financial "arrangements." It is, nonetheless, more than a provocation: they see that Ongka struggles with problems they might recognize now and will meet later in life. Informed viewers who use the film in economic anthropology classes know that *Ongka's Big Moka* is used as a "textbook example" that resonates with those of Malinowski, whose study of the exchange of valuables in a system linking renowned traders and chiefs in the Trobriand Islands of the South Pacific emphasized the problematic relationship between utility and the social good. The goodness of the trader is not a matter of expertise alone, but is a trait of his powerful and effective character. His ability to manage the exchange of goods depends upon the persuasiveness of his rhetoric and the success of his social actions in soliciting participation in his feast.

I use the film to show how Ongka, in his meditation on the good, navigates the uncharted waters that lie between "worth" and "wealth." Because the film is popular, and Ongka's power to make a *moka* depends on his ability to persuade through expert use of oratory and rhetoric, the film usually becomes an object lesson in the definition of prestige. However, more importantly, to put it in other academic terms, Ongka knows how those intractable qualities known and felt as value must be concretized first as an object, in the form of a good, before he exchanges that good as a valuable pig in ceremonial exchange or in everyday life. Gregory (1997, 2008) argues that we can use ethnographic case studies to explain how "value" is materialized, such that the invisible chain that links people to things, to other people, and to the institutions and social relationships between people and things can be realized and manipulated to specific ends. Ethnographic film is especially well adapted to doing the job of illuminating the social good, especially when it makes invisible relations of the social good visible by documenting transactions of material goods.

Perhaps Ongka discusses an important and uncharted problem of contemporary wealth. Ethnographies and biographies of politicians, bankers, and appraisers expose how moral sentiments create a tenuous link between economic rationality and the social good that is embedded in most accounts of their work (Schroeder 2008; Ho 2009; Tett 2009). Ongka, by contrast, believes he can tell his viewer how to establish a firm relationship between what is good to do and the value of goods. However, the pathway of his reason is not always unilinear; his narrative is about how wealth comes and goes in the form of pigs, assets which a Big-man acquires and disposes in transactions made along many "roads." His moral reasoning, through the contrary and contradictory value standards of the good, raises important questions about what a good life is. Elsewhere I have argued that anthropology's habit has been to explain difficult and contradictory behavior among the subjects of our research by reference to either the deep structure of their rationality or the relativism of their cultural knowledge (Sykes 2008). I have argued that in order to adequately address the moral sentiments of others whom we know through conducting our fieldwork, the anthropologist must advance a new kind of explanation, one that records the paradoxes and contradictions felt by others, in a close ethnographic description of moral reasoning as a social act.

Expert commentators in both eras, the times shown in *Ongka's Big Moka* and the current period of widely felt distress over economic instability in the global markets, are disposed to reason about the morality of the relationship between the good and the social good, between pigs and neighborliness, or between money and well-being. Media pundits comment on the morality of various investment strategies, the reliability of banks, and the responsibility of political governance over these things during the free fall of the currency markets; Ongka comments on the relationship between moral reason and the good in a rapidly changing world when the value of pigs and shells for bridewealth could not be predicted. The film explores the world of ceremonial exchange in the highlands of PNG, in the era when new political independence from the colonial rule of Australia gave the Papuan residents reason to think that relations between political stature and economic wealth were anything but straightforward. Ongka is a strong and charming leader who is facing the end of a world of ceremonial exchange, of polygamy, of prestige. This world of the Big-man as a "good" man was nearly over. The film projects a sentiment to the viewer that is not unlike what may be the felt experience of European or American youth during times of dramatic economic change in the developed world. The students who respond to the seven clips that make up YouTube's version of *Ongka's Big Moka* live in a time when access to wealth and its use present specific kinds of moral problems. The worth of the good rests more firmly on our trust that bankers, politicians, assessors, and insurers have the expertise to clarify the standards they use to determine the value of tangible and intangible goods. Commonly agreed and established prices for goods were once based on stable economies that insured the costs of living were mostly constant over time. Although one commentator wonders about the cost of a medium-sized pig, a fair price for a pig is not the only problem that Ongka has to address. Ongka, as most student viewers realize, has worked out an answer to life's bigger questions about how we know we are human.

Moral Reasoning about the Social Good: Anthropology's Black Box

> *We must first of all draw up as large as possible a catalogue of categories, beginning with all those which can be discovered which mankind has ever employed. It will then be seen there have been, and that there still are, many dead moons, and others pale or obscure in the firmament of reason.*
>
> Marcel Mauss, *Sociologie et anthropologie*, 1950 (p. 309)

Visual media, both its apparatuses and the images in which it trades, operates like a "black box" in the discipline of anthropology. A black box does work that is not transparent to others, even while its processes are central to the field of research. Introducing the concept to the sociology of scientific scholarship, Latour reminds us that in the field of engineering, a black box transforms energy or transmits information without the engineer programming it as part of his wider field of research, locating it within the wider system, or linking it to broader knowledge. The conceptual work of a black box is also akin to Mauss's concept of a pale or a dead moon, by which he means a class of knowledge that is both within and outside of the field of study. The quote from Mauss seems highly appropriate for the current juncture when moral reasoning about the social good requires a refiguring of the work of the discipline, in order to create a moral anthropology that can grapple with the good as an elusive category.

It cannot be denied that the challenge of understanding moral reasoning about the social good is as old as the discipline, if one considers how often anthropologists regularly confront the problem of the untranslatability of most key concepts from their fieldwork. Here I discuss moral reasoning about the social good as it is used in the famous case study of the the *moka*, but correlated concepts included *hau*, potlatch, totem, and taboo, all of which find a place in the discussion in the related disciplines of philosophy, psychology, sociology, history, and modern literatures wherein similar concerns with the character of moral reasoning arise. However, anthropologists have judged their scientific rigor in dealing with such obdurately untranslatable concepts by charting the place of rationality in their work and measuring their success in communicating their understandings against the ethnocentrism by which non-Western societies were seen as irrational. As I will show, this approach also became a meta-level debate about the nature of anthropologic reason that ran for a full generation or more. Others sought to use the poetics of anthropological scholarship to create a meaningful place for the voicing of allegedly "non-Western" ideas, concepts, and beliefs. I take a step back from my somewhat provocative discussion of a specific black box, namely the ethnographic video of Ongka's fame. In the first part of this essay, I showed how it spread throughout the community of viewers on YouTube, in order to introduce the role of moral reason in grappling with an elusive form, the social good. In this section, I examine the role of moral reasoning about the social good in constructing a new field of scholarship named "moral anthropology."

It is fair to say that the way anthropologists approach the nature of moral reason has changed from Durkheim's day, when the study of normative social behavior presented a challenge to a society struggling to understand the rise of secular belief and the decline of religion. Scholars today are concerned not only with social scientific reasoning about the normative moral order, but also with the diversity of moral reasoning about the social (for example, Heintz 2009; Zigon 2009). In an extended discussion of the changing nature of bridewealth exchanges, I argued that ordinary folk and community leaders alike work through the paradoxes of everyday existence, as they deliberate how to make a good marriage or a good life (Sykes 2008). In this section, I subject that example of moral reasoning to examination, in the way of Latour (1979, 1990), who has studied conceptual objects such as scientific reason as if they are black boxes, or tools to create specific ends. Instead of taking up Latour's interest in scientific reason, I began this essay with a discussion of an example of moral reasoning, Ongka's long meditation on pigs. I note that Ongka's monologue ends on a wry note about pigs as both a mark of personal wealth and a social good. Can they be both? He says that a lot of men do not realize the importance of exchanging pigs, and such moral reasoning must be better understood if everyone is to benefit from it. Taking this cue, in the following pages, I shall examine the emergence of moral reasoning as a black box in the social sciences against the background of wide-ranging national debates on both sides of the Atlantic about the status of rationality and scientific reason in anthropology. Whereas philosophers in the Kantian tradition advocate theories of the moral agent as a rational actor, whose reasoning does not tolerate contradiction and paradox as a part of it, an anthropologist allows space for paradox and ambiguity in reason. I compare moral reason in anthropology as a means to examine ways to know the good, as akin to the inductive reason of the philosophy of David Hume in his search for the good as it is known within human action. The ethnographer describes the process of moral deliberation as a social act, wherein people reason about how to act toward each other so that their interpersonal relationships may flourish. Throughout this chapter, I hold to a caveat: An anthropologist is neither an ethicist nor a philosopher. He or she can examine the range of answers that others offer to the question of what is the good, and then discuss why one should be convinced by those answers. The ethnographer describes the process of moral deliberation as a social act, wherein people reason about how to act toward each other so that their interpersonal relationships may flourish.

When I open the black box marked "moral reasoning," I can unpack several anthropological debates that envelop the ethicist's question of how one should live. From a historical perspective, the debate about the relationships between moral reason and social difference has had three successive incarnations. In the late nineteenth and the early twentieth centuries, anthropology defined social science as the discipline that was fundamentally concerned with the symbolic capacities of human societies to constitute and communicate about moral relationships. In the new social science, cultural difference emerged out of variations in the distinctive relationship between the moral order and the social order (Durkheim and Mauss 1963). In the first half of the twentieth century some anthropologists questioned the grounds of the new science of society. It had become common for anthropologists to examine the intricacies of fieldwork as a way of underlining that the explanations which informants share are reasonable, but not strictly scientific (Evans-Pritchard 1976 [1937]). In the decades after World War II Lévi-Strauss (1968) elaborated a theory of anthropology that focused on the symbolic nature of otherwise inaccessible forms of human knowledge, returning to Mauss's and Durkheim's earlier insights that classificatory logic was the key to forging a rational social science. Even until the last decade of the twentieth century, anthropologists normally insisted that the complex stories and explanations that others recount to anthropologists during fieldwork are distinctive forms of reason that challenged social scientists to confront the limits of rationality, and should therefore be explained in their own terms, as if valuable in their own right (Wagner 1986, 2001; Sahlins 1994; M. Strathern 1999). The twentieth century appears to have swung between explanations that human cohesion and social variation were founded on the principle of a universal capacity for rational thought (structuralists), and descriptions that exposed human commonality and difference in the poetics of interpretation and translation (interpretivists). Was this all one debate, the irreconcilability of the "other minds" of anthropologists' informants with the Western "scientific" rationality of the discipline?

Although the wider epistemological debate between "interpretivists" and "structuralists" in the twentieth century coincided with the discussion within British social anthropology about the nature of reason and "other minds," the different debates do not address the same concerns. A closer examination of the status of moral reasoning in the two arenas of intense discussion shows very different claims about how to answer the ethicist's question. Structural and interpretive anthropology each debated how scholarship created the identity of the anthropological object as a representation of lived experience, but each school differed as to how this was so: on the one hand were the structuralists who believed the identity of the anthropological object could be reached through the principles of rational logic, and on the other the interpretivists who believed that the identity of the object lay in its meaning as it was elicited through poetic interpretation (Lévi-Strauss 1968; Boon 1972, 1982; Geertz 1973a, 1973b). Because each of the two different approaches to the identity of the anthropological object was concerned with the function of description, the debate floundered when cognitive and linguistic anthropologists showed that the symbolic functions of reason did not make sense (Tyler 1979, 1986). In what later was called the crisis of representation (Marcus and Fischer 1986), anthropologists reflected upon the epistemic bases of their discipline (Fabian 2002 [1983]) and called for a new understanding of moral reason.

A different debate between anthropologists and philosophers of language echoed in the halls of British social anthropology, one which has greater implications for the groundwork of a moral anthropology. In the 1984 meetings of the Association of Social Anthropology which addressed the theme "Rationality and Rationales," those present agreed that the work of reason falls like a shadow between fieldwork and writing (Overing 1985). In the decades leading up to the meetings, anthropological examples had become a resource for philosophers of language, but philosophers' attention ultimately challenged the legitimacy of anthropologists' work. At the meetings, flags were flown in support of the opposing teams, those of Evans-Pritchard and Winch, who differed on the nature of "other minds." Evans-Pritchard argued that, where explanation might seem irrational, ultimately the reason used by others was meaningful in their society, in which case reason's social context was more potent than reason itself. By comparison, Winch was concerned with the truthfulness of others' claims as they are made in language games, emphasizing the efficacy of communication as a human universal. I will not be recovering the details of the debates in this essay, but impressive collections exist for the reader who wants to examine them in detail (Wilson 1970; Hollis and Lukes 1982). By the end of the twentieth century the society of anthropologists had come to agree, at least implicitly, with Evans-Pritchard's assertion that many of his informants' beliefs were not only completely reasonable but empirically correct by their own measures, even if they seemed irrational (Overing 1985). And they conceded, as did Evans-Pritchard (1976), that the privileged place of scientific rationality was in question, not that of reason. A famously quoted example from colonial Africa helps to establish this. Evans-Pritchard discussed the example of the termite-infested veranda which ultimately fell to the ground. The causes of the accident were empirically clear, but scientific explanations for why it buckled at that point in time were very different from the accounts of the moral infractions that led ultimately to its collapse and to the concrete damage felt by the humans endangered by it. Without drawing out the differences between the moral and scientific reasons, as Evans-Pritchard did, the philosopher Peter Winch (1990 [1958]) argued that people normally do not worry about whether their statements are rational or not. Instead, most people understand each other because they play a "language game" which involves judging the effect of their words on another person. He showed that effective communication is the best measure of "rationality," "logic," or "reason." While Winch did not assuage the anthropologists' concern with the legitimacy or illegitimacy of the "truth" of social science, he did allow them to newly engage with their informants as "moral agents," as people who seek an answer to the question of how one should live.

Some anthropologists in recent years have turned to Kant (1998) in order to find inspiration for anthropology as a kind of practical ethics, as if anthropology's deep reconciliation with the discipline of philosophy would resolve both of anthropology's national debates in the United States and Britain. However, Kant's anthropology cannot subsume the two debates without succumbing to nationalistic intellectual traditions. A better Kantian "anthropology as practical ethics" of the grassroots, or the subaltern peoples would be welcomed by many anthropologists and philosophers alike. As a step toward that, I am concerned here with the role played by people whom anthropologists meet in their fieldwork, men such as Ongka, whose moral reasoning about the nature of the social good has influenced the thought of many anthropologists, students, and educated viewers alike. The questions raised by Ongka and other individuals in conversations with anthropologists are often challenging. Friends, acquaintances, and informants in the field question the kind of reasoning which gives shape to the moral economy of the Western European world, and its relationship to the different pace of economic development in the rest of the world. Anthropologists have charted these questions about the moral economy, and how they answer them is giving rise to a new anthropology of the moral economy in which "reasoning" takes center stage.

How moral reason navigates contradiction and paradox inflects the new moral economy that has emerged in the period after decolonization and the end of the cold war. In his afterword to *Savage Money* (1997), Gregory argues that any progress toward a "radical critical ethnography" must also reason through the nature of the commonplace contradictions that the subjects of our anthropological research navigate in such a complex society. Ongka had wanted to make a *moka*, to give pigs to the first parliamentarian in PNG, and thereby outdo and overshadow the prestige of the new leader by "giving so much." However, Ongka also questions the sincerity of his own altruism in making *moka*, and wonders if his competitiveness with the parliamentarian is self-interested. He ponders his "rubbishness" in moments when he believes he is more interested in his own wants than he is in the best interests of others. Ongka manages the contradiction between his desire to be known as a truly Big-man and his wish to be generous toward others, but not by resolving or eliminating the paradox. It is not that Ongka is simply competitive and seeks fame under a guise of generosity. He shows us that he is a human being who is capable of both self-interest and altruism, and that these are complexly interwoven. As he says of the possibility that his feast will fail, "It is possible that I will lose my investment, but I will never lose the glory of giving it." Such altruism can coexist with self-interest, and one value (altruism) does not exclude the existence of others (self-interest). Although it is the case that some more axiomatic contradictions, those emerging from relationships of mutual negation, are resolved one way or the other. (For example, can a relationship founded in antipathy be at the same time a bond of empathy? Or can a relationship of gamesmanship recognize both players winners?) However, as a moral reasoner, Ongka meets the commonplace paradoxes of living and finds them to be both irresolvable and unavoidable, and so he proceeds with daily life by reasoning through the morality of his actions.

Whereas late twentieth-century anthropologists argued that legitimate social science relied on the separation of reason from emotion as a way of insuring scientific objectivity about economic decision-making, at the beginning of the twenty-first century much older concerns with the relations between moral economy and moral reason have returned to center stage. New scholarship (Sen 2010) has re-examined the arguments of Adam Smith in *The Theory of the Moral Sentiments* (2010 [1759]), and of David Hume in *A Treatise on Human Nature* (2000) (O'Neill 2011).

Commonplace Contradictions: Moral Reason, Moral Economy, and the Good

The problem of knowledge is posed in new terms.
Durkheim, *Elementary Forms of the Religious Life*, 27

The most important lesson to be taken from Ongka's meditation is not the spread of his fame through the YouTube community. Rather, at the time of writing, he has challenged 32,000 viewers to reflect on the nature of his moral reason. If moral anthropology is timely, or rather more than timely, it is because the field builds on the recognition that there has been a shift in how anthropologists have addressed moral reason. It is a shift that also grasps the change in the nature of the moral economy. The aim of the new moral anthropology is less to judge the morality of the people we study, although this has long been a debatable aim (but see D'Andrade 1995; Scheper-Hughes 1995), and more to grasp the changing terrain of contemporary human experience of the moral dilemmas of a global age. A fresh debate about the nature of moral reason in a global economy has been flagged by some anthropologists as the forward flank of the pragmatists' project in establishing the human economy (Gregory 1997, 2009; Hahn and Hart 2009). The appeal of Aristotle's moral philosophy to anthropologists and social scientists is strong because efficacious reason often succeeds; its outcomes are the good, a conceptual object that is both a description of what is and a prescription of what ought to be. In anthropology, pragmatic reason, as a legacy from the ancient philosophers, remains different from scientific reason, which holds the distinction between fact and value as a legacy of the modern enlightenment. In the last decades, other anthropologists have argued in very different ways (for example, Dumont 1970; Fabian 2002 [1983]; Laidlaw 2004) that the fact/value distinction collapses in anthropology when scholars become most concerned with the effects of ethnography in social life and the role of scholarship in the constitution of the good. The burgeoning debate about the moral economy of the twenty-first century and the forms that the good might take has involved anthropologists in fresh discussions.

Clearly not only a feature of anthropological scholarship, the commonplace contradiction features in the moral reasoning of men and women like Ongka who must live every day with the mundane paradoxes of a global age. Although it is as old as Milton's logic and grammar, Gregory (1997) identified this form of reason as central to the work of a radical critical ethnography for a postcolonial anthropology, which recognizes that the development of the discipline shared the history of the people it studied while not sharing the same values and norms. A fine example of a commonplace contradiction is that of the good, and the distinction drawn between gifts and commodities as a way of reflecting upon and measuring out experiences of transacting the good. The commonplace contradiction between the gift and the commodity does not absolutely negate the other (as it would if one were informed by rational logic and the other irrational belief); instead, the identity of each form of good is created by and complements the other (as with reason and sentiment). Ongka knows very well how everyday life rests on paradoxes; his own experience confirms it, following the collapse of multiple currencies in the central highlands, following the inflationary bubble in pearl shells that had emerged in the new nation on the eve of independence in what Anglo-American economies might call a renegotiation of trading standards (A. Strathern 1971; Gregory 1997).

There have been many paths of anthropological inquiry into the moral economy of the good. With Ongka as a guide, the economic anthropology of Melanesia becomes an educational journey. It is primarily interested in the motivations of the people at the grass roots, who might either avoid or assail the dominant values of the economic elites in the course of daily life. PNG has long been recognized as one of the birthplaces of economic anthropology, and the publication of Malinowski's (1922) first monograph grappled with the nature of economic reason. It was followed by a critical rejoinder addressing the theory of the gift (Mauss 1990). Contemporary anthropologists (Kirsch 2006; Bashkow 2008) have recently shown that Melanesians still pose some of the most compelling questions about the workings of the contemporary global economy and about their moral agency in it (Robbins 2004; Sykes 2007). For example, the Melanesian leader Yali famously asks what it is about Western economic practice that insures the success of development there and its failure elsewhere (Diamond 1997; Errington and Gewertz 2004). In short, new studies of the moral economy in Melanesia draws neither on culture nor politics as the bottom line for its truth, but takes the moral paradoxes of social life as endemic in life there.

For those contemporary anthropologists who wish to unpack the good from the black box of moral reason, the key issue is to know *who* is asking *what* and *of whom*. The observation that "reasoners" create reasons and "valuers" create value (Gregory 2008) might seem obvious at first, but these are basic insights that have been overlooked in the literature which has been dominated largely by philosophical inquiry into the logical consistency of moral reason, as if rationality were its own justification of and for moral reason. Anthropologists are not so concerned with rationality or with the quality of philosophical argument. They use different intellectual skills when they describe the social process by which moral agents as reasoners create reasons, and thereby establish both expert and inexpert modes of reasoning. Anthropologists have at their disposal a means of explaining the efficacy of moral reasoning in alienating concepts, moral values, and social worth as goods. If an anthropologist explains the good as an outcome of a particular form of moral reasoning, then a careful description of his or her informants' actions can distinguish the good as a gift or as a commodity, depending upon the existing motives to alienate the value of the good from the social relationships in which it is transacted (Gregory 1982). Reflecting on his earlier work, Gregory (1997, 2009) shows that just who raises the questions about whether or not one should give or receive the gift matters a great deal to its status (or not) as an inalienable object. It is through a process of moral reasoning that a person can alienate the good as an object for commodity exchange or enchain others with obligations to reciprocate it. In the new moral economy, the material good, whether as a gift or as a commodity, is the outcome of the act of moral reasoning, in which a practical ethic informs the selection of one form of reason rather than another.

David Hume, one of the fathers of the modern study of the moral economy, and also of the epistemology of inductive reason, argued that pragmatic reason was a form of moral reasoning because the objects of its study were convention and justice. Still, moral claims for Hume were imaginative ones, reasoned inductively from the basis of empirical fact. That there was a moral economy at all depended on the possibility that a person could imagine the needs of another, based on the earlier record of their own need. For example, a person might make a series of observations over years about the needs of his own household for food in harsh times, as when the food stored for winter has been used up according to a pattern that the householder recognizes over years. That pattern allows him to infer that there is a relationship between the amount of food kept for the household and its well-being during periods of more general scarcity of food. From intellectual experiments such as ones like this, Hume argues that the institution known as private property was not grounded only in the nature of self-interest, as when a person calculates his rights to hold property in relation to his needs for his own household and the necessity of fulfilling them. Rather, private property is a complex moral institution grounded on justice. The ability of a person to imagine the food necessary to fulfill the needs of another household is a moral claim grounded in convention and justice; the personal experience of want of food alone is insufficient to ground human knowledge of private property. Hume reasoned that it was necessary to link the want for wealth with its use, yet there was nothing in lived experience that insured the existence of a causal link between the necessity of having food in the household and satiation of the household's needs. That linkage required speculation, whether by custom or using the human imagination. Accordingly, Hume pointed out that knowledge of private property as a moral institution relied on its negative correlate, the concept of theft. He reckoned that a person did not take the food of the household without reasoning about that household's needs, and to take food from a household without concern for their needs would be a theft from it. Theft of food from the household provisions, according to Hume, is conceived of as a moral infraction committed against a household. The logic is based on the imagination that the other household's needs were like the thieves' experience of their own household necessities and on the customary wisdom that each household must plan to provide for its members.

Hume famously said that "reason is, and ought only to be, the slave of the passions" (2000 [1739–40]: 2.3.3.4) and then put his efforts to the test using the empiricist approach, whereby humans know the world through experiencing it via their senses rather than through rational categories. By "passions" Hume meant several things: the senses, the felt goods, received wisdom or custom, and also the means of induction, by which he came to create an epistemology of inductive reason as the very ground for human knowledge. Many later commentators on Hume argue that he believed that human knowledge, not humankind's ability to understand, was limited by inductive reason. When I consider his definition of the concept of property, I think that they are right. Hume certainly claims to know things about the human world through invoking notions such as "custom" or "the imagination," but he thought these claims could best be used speculatively to raise doubts about what could be known rather than to assert new truths or to declare certainty of insight about the conditions of being in the world. It seems reasonable then to conclude, as did Kenyon and Craig (1985), that inductive reason is not a pathway to truth about the quality of relations in the natural world, but a way of raising doubts about the rigidity of conventional wisdom and the status of widely shared beliefs.

Hume's is a useful way to reach a better understanding of moral reasoning which is neither simply rational self-interest nor altruistic. His assumptions require a small critical revision for a moral anthropology. As Mauss has urged us to see in *The Gift* (1990), the *hau*, the spirit of the gift, is known in the moment, in the act of valuing or judging the good; the *hau* is unknowable prior to the act of giving. He brings to his study of the moral economy many long years of reading about the role of giving in different societies in order to better understand a classic question about the social and moral nature of economy. For Mauss, as for many other scholars, moral economy was a deceptively simple term that described the moral and social relations that people called up as they struggled with the old question of what is the just price for the good. Some contemporary uses of the term "moral economy" mean enjoining reciprocal relationships with family, neighbors, friends, and colleagues in cooperative resistance, as in E. P. Thompson's (1971) study of the moral economy of how the English crowd took over the price-setting rules in the open markets in the towns of the early industrial revolution. "Moral economy" later was used to describe the moral grounds of agrarian resistance in the context of subsistence (Scott 1976), whereas the general sense of the term, as Mauss understood it, is part of classical scholarship.

It is fair to say that Mauss's own studies and education were sufficient to make him familiar with the thought of classical philosophers, and hence with the concept of the just price. Mauss started a new anthropological discussion about the qualities of the good, wherein the concept of the just price refers to the sense of what is good about the exchange of things. The just measure of equivalence of goods can be felt in the sense that this transaction insures a fair exchange of goods. It is also fair to say that Mauss understood gift-giving as a universal phenomenon which manifested itself in many different forms. When understood in this way, the moral grounds of social life were more malleable and less fixed, long-lasting rather than ephemeral, and mutual rather than individual. The universality of the gift was evidence of the felt sense that the bonds between people were the substance of social life itself and these were not to be taken simply as the product of one individual's actions toward another. Ongka is wise too about his own social circumstances; his wealth is inextricable from his social life. He measures his work and pronounces, "It is possible that I will lose my investment [the pigs], but I will never lose the glory of giving it."

Conclusion

Anthropologists have sometimes felt challenged to bring their disciplinary expertise to bear on the task of analyzing the moral economy, but without also rethinking the nature of moral reason. In order to rectify that, this essay has made moral reasoning the object of study, first in a discussion of how to value the video clip referred to as "Ongka's meditation on pigs," then in an analysis of the debates over reason and sentiment and the disputes about symbolic thought. Finally, I examined moral reasoning as a navigation of commonplace contradictions of daily life and as a keystone of the contemporary study of moral economy. For example, I have shown that reasoning about the exchange of goods is never simply a discussion of whether these are gifts or commodities, or goods with spiritual values. What is at stake is a better understanding of the process of moral reasoning, and its work in advancing decisions about the social good. If that is so, then it is possible to say that Ongka's meditation on pigs enlightens us as to the moral economy of PNG on the eve of independence, and a fuller study of the moral economy can in turn shape a better understanding of the nature of investor behavior in the morning after the collapse of the standards of value for world currency trading. In either case, the study of the commonplace contradictions and living paradoxes of moral reasoning can be a significant point of entry for a study of the good in the new moral economy of a global age.

To my mind, moral reason is the keystone of the arch that supports the moral economy: I wonder how apposite that seems to members of the university when value standards of scholarship are in disarray, and when the validity of scholarship in the present has come to rely on concretizations of its value in citation indexes, as if these had become, like pigs, everything and excluded all other goods from use. I suggest this new focus on the materializations of the value of anthropological knowledge has replaced a century-old debate about the status of reason in anthropological argument, and its relationship to what can be known through the moral imagination, sentiments, and empathetic investigations. One might hope that anthropology was a form of moral reasoning. Through engaging in a study of moral reasoning, anthropologists learn just how the subjects of their research have negotiated the complex terrain of intercultural exchange, where multiple and changing standards of value are commonplace. This essay argues that moral reasoning does not require expert skill. Rather, it is an exercise which anyone can pursue, and which can fully engross each person.

REFERENCES

Bashkow, Ira (2008) *The Meaning of White Men*. Chicago: University of Chicago Press.

Boon, James A. (1972) *From Symbolism to Structuralism: Lévi-Strauss in a Literary Tradition*. Oxford: Blackwell.

Boon, James A. (1982) *Other Tribes, Other Scribes*. Cambridge: Cambridge University Press.

D'Andrade, Roy (1995) Moral Models in Anthropology. *Current Anthropology* 36(3): 399–408.

Diamond, Jared (1997) *Guns, Germs, and Steel: The Fates of Human Societies*. New York: Norton.

Dumont, Louis (1970) *Homo Hierachicus*. Chicago: University of Chicago Press.

Durkheim, Emile (1965) *Elementary Forms of the Religious Life*. New York: Free Press.

Durkheim, Emile and Mauss, Marcel (1963) *Primitive Classification*. Chicago: University of Chicago Press.

Errington, Frederick and Gewertz, Deborah (2004) *Yali's Question: Sugar, Culture, and History*. Chicago: University of Chicago Press.

Evans Pritchard, E. E. (1976 [1937]) *Witchcraft, Oracles, and Magic among the Azande*. Oxford: Clarendon.

Fabian, Johannes (2002 [1983]) *Time and the Other*. New York: Columbia University Press.

Geertz, Clifford (1973a) The Cerebral Savage. In Geertz (1973c), pp. 345–359.

Geertz, Clifford (1973b) The Impact of the Concept of Culture on the Concept of Man. In Geertz (1973c), pp. 33–54.

Geertz, Clifford (1973c) *The Interpretation of Cultures*. New York: Basic Books.

Gregory, Chris A. (1982) *Gifts and Commodities*. London: Academic Press.

Gregory, Chris A. (1986) Cowries and Conquest: Towards a Subalternate Quality Theory of Money. *Comparative Studies in Society and History* 38(2): 195–216.

Gregory, Chris A. (1997) *Savage Money: The Politics and Anthropology of Commodity Exchange.* Amsterdam: Harwood.

Gregory, Chris A. (2008) Afterwords. In Sykes (2008), pp. 189–201.

Gregory, Chris A. (2009) Whatever Happened to Economic Anthropology? *Australian Journal of Anthropology* 20(3): 285–300.

Gregory, Chris A. (2011) On Money, Debt and Morality. Plenary lecture given at conference on "Debt: Interdisciplinary Considerations of an Enduring Human Passion." Centre for Research in the Arts, Social Sciences and Humanities, May 12.

Hann, Chris and Hart, Keith (2009) *Market and Society: The Great Transformation Today.* Cambridge: Cambridge University Press.

Hart, Keith and Ortiz, Horacio (2008) Anthropology in the Financial Crisis. *Anthropology Today* 24(6): 1–3.

Heintz, Monica (2009) *The Anthropology of Moralities.* New York: Berghahn.

Hirschman, A. (1993) *The Passions and the Interests: Political Arguments against Capitalism before its Triumph.* Princeton: Princeton University Press.

Ho, Karen Zouwen (2009) *Liquidated: An Ethnography of Wall Street.* Durham, NC: Duke University Press.

Hollis, Martin and Lukes, Steven (eds.) (1982) *Rationality and Relativism.* Cambridge, MA: MIT Press.

Hume, David (2000[1739–40]) *A Treatise on Human Nature: Being an Attempt to Introduce the Experimental Method of Reasoning into Moral Subjects*, ed. David F. Norton and Mary Norton. Oxford: Oxford University Press.

Kant, Immanuel (1998) *Groundwork for the Metaphysics of Morals.* Cambridge: Cambridge University Press.

Kenyon, John D. & Craig, Edward (1985) Doubts about the Concept of Reason. *Proceedings of the Aristotelian Society Supplementary Volume* 59: 249–267.

Kirsch, Stuart (2006) *Reverse Anthropology.* Palo Alto, CA: Stanford University Press.

Laidlaw, James (2004) For an Anthropology of Ethics and Freedom. Malinowski Lecture of 2001. *JRAI* 8(2): 311–332.

Latour, Bruno (1979) *Science in Action.* Cambridge, MA: Harvard University Press.

Latour, Bruno (1999) *Pandora's Hope.* New York: Columbia University Press.

Lederman, Rena (1986) *What Gifts Engender.* Cambridge: Cambridge University Press.

Lévi-Strauss, Claude (1968) *The Savage Mind.* Chicago: University of Chicago Press.

Loizos, Peter (1980) Television Production: Granada Television's Disappearing World Series: An Appraisal. *American Anthropologist* 82(3): 573–594.

Malinowski, Bronislaw (1922) *Argonauts of the Western Pacific.* London: Routledge & Kegan Paul.

Marcus, George E. and Fischer, Michael M. J. (1986) *Anthropology as Cultural Critique.* Chicago: University of Chicago Press.

Martin, Keir (2009) Magic and the Myth of the Rational Market. *Financial Times* (Aug. 24), 5.

Maurer, Bill (2009) Moral Economies, Economic Moralities: Consider the Possibilities! In Katherine E. Browne and B. Lynne Milgram (eds.), *Economics and Morality: Anthropological Approaches.* AltaMira, pp. 257–269.

Mauss, Marcel (1950) *Sociologie et anthropologie.* Paris: Presses Universitaires de France.

Mauss, Marcel (1990[1954]) *The Gift: Forms of Exchange in Archaic Societies.* London: Routledge.

O'Neill, John (2011) On Moral Economy. Working paper. The Value Question Today series, University of Manchester.

Ongka (1976) *The Kawelka: Ongka's Big Moka* [film], dir. Charlie Nairn. *Disappearing World.* London and Manchester: Granada Television.

Overing, Joanna (1985) *Reason and Morality.* London: Routledge.

Robbins, Joel (2004) *Becoming Sinners: Christianity and Moral Torment in a Papua New Guinean Society.* Berkeley: University of California Press.

Sahlins, Marshall David (1972) *Stone Age Economics*. Chicago: Aldine, Atherton.
Sahlins, Marshall David (1976) *Culture and Practical Reason*. Chicago: University of Chicago Press.
Sahlins, Marshall David (1994) *How Natives Think*. Chicago: University of Chicago Press.
Scheper-Hughes, Nancy (1995) The Primacy of the Ethical. *Current Anthropology* 36(3): 409–419.
Schroeder, Alice (2008) *The Snowball: Warren Buffett and the Business of Life*. London: Bloomsbury.
Scott, James C. (1976) *The Moral Economy of the Peasant*. New Haven: Yale University Press.
Sen, Amartya (2010) Introduction. In Smith (2010), pp. 1–178.
Smith, Adam (2010[1759]) *The Theory of the Moral Sentiments*, ed. Ryan Hanley. Harmondsworth: Penguin.
Strathern, Andrew (1971) *The Rope of Moka*. Cambridge: Cambridge University Press.
Strathern, Marilyn (1981) *No Money on Our Skins: Hagen Migrants in Port Moresby*. Port Moresby and Canberra: Government of Australia Printers.
Strathern, Marilyn (1999) *Property, Substance and Effect: Anthropological Essays on Persons and Things*. Linton: Athlone.
Sykes, Karen (2004) Negotiating Interests in Culture. In Eric Hirsch and Marilyn Strathern (eds.), *Transactions and Creations: Property Debates and the Stimulus of Melanesia*. New York: Berghahn, pp. 153–172.
Sykes, Karen (ed.) (2007) Interrogating Individuals: The Theory of Possessive Individualism in the Western Pacific [special issue]. *Anthropological Forum* 17(3).
Sykes, Karen (2008) *Ethnographies of Moral Reasoning: Living Paradoxes of a Global Age*. New York: Palgrave Macmillan.
Tett, Gillian (2009) *Fool's Gold: How Unrestrained Greed Corrupted a Dream, Shattered Global Markets and Unleashed a Catastrophe*. London: Little, Brown
Thompson, E. P. (1971) The Moral Economy of the English Crowd in the 18th Century. *Past & Present* 50(1): 76–136.
Tyler, Stephen A. (1979) *Mind, Meaning, Culture*. New York: Academic Press.
Tyler, Stephen A. (1986) Post-Modern Ethnography: From Document of the Occult to Occult Document. In James Clifford and George E. Marcus (eds.), *Writing Culture: The Poetics and Politics of Ethnography*. Berkeley: University of California Press, pp. 122–140.
Wagner, Roy (1986) *Symbols that Stand for Themselves*. Chicago: University of Chicago Press.
Wagner, Roy (2001) *The Anthropology of the Subject*. Berkeley: University of California Press.
Wilson, Bryan R. (ed.) (1970) *Rationality*. Oxford: Blackwell.
Winch, Peter (1990[1958]) *The Idea of a Social Science and its Relation to Philosophy*. London: Routledge.
Zigon, Jarrett (2009) *Morality: An Anthropological Perspective*. Oxford: Berg.

CHAPTER 11 Virtue

Thomas Widlok

What are virtues? Why do many anthropologists find it difficult to contribute to an ethics of virtues? What would a critical and informed anthropological research program about virtues look like? What are the preliminary results of such research and what is its theoretical relevance?

OCM 577 seems an obvious place to start looking for virtues. Subject no. 577, entitled "Ethics," of the Outline of Cultural Materials (OCM) is the place that cross-cultural anthropology has allocated for "virtue" as a keyword in the Human Relations Area Files (HRAF), the discipline's attempt to compile relevant paragraphs according to subjects in its most comprehensive ethnographic database.[1] The description for OCM 577 reads as follows:

> Abstract ethical ideals (e.g., truth, righteousness, justice); ideals of individual virtue (e.g., honesty, loyalty, industry, courage, temperance, tolerance, filial piety); notions of right and wrong; conception of conscience and character; incidence and causes of, and attitudes toward breaches of ethics (e.g., lying, cowardice, flouting of kinship obligations); conflicts between ideal values and practical considerations; gender-typed attitudes and values; etc. (HRAF, n.d.)

Outlining the category "virtue" in such a broad way in the HRAF seems to suggest that ethnographers routinely ask for lists of individual virtues so that cross-cultural anthropology could correlate these findings with other aspects of individual and social life across cultures. However, a basic search produces a fairly meager 279 paragraphs (in 170 documents) covering 90 cultures (out of 230) in which the term "virtue" itself is used. There are slightly more hits than for "ethics" but fewer than for "morality" and considerably fewer than for many other key anthropological terms such as, for instance, "mobility." More is to be gained if we search for all entries relating to virtue as a coded concept rather than for the term itself (namely 9,239

A Companion to Moral Anthropology, First Edition. Edited by Didier Fassin.

paragraphs in 1,270 documents covering 206 cultures). However, virtues are not a typical index word that anthropologists would use to organize their field data. One still has to search far afield in the anthropological record to actually find an ethnographic account that explicitly deals with virtues. This is also true for the ethnographic area that I know best: Khoisan southern Africa. Here, we need to venture beyond the HRAF for an explicit account on virtue and it is to be found in writings from the 1940s by Heinrich Vedder, a missionary with rather mixed credentials as a lay ethnographer. Just as many other indigenous people outside Europe, the "Bushmen" of Vedder's time were largely treated as "vermin" by both European settlers and by the African majority in the region. Given this historical context, Vedder concedes an impressive list of virtues to the "Bushmen," namely gratitude, devotion, friendship, respect for property, thriftiness, religious sentiments, compassion, vindictiveness, honor/shame, and orderliness/cleanliness (Vedder 1942: 83). It is telling that it is primarily the nonprofessional lay ethnographers like Vedder who feel that their (nonanthropological) audience should be told about virtues in the context of an ethnographic description.

Vedder probably did his best to emphasize, against the odds of the time, that the "Bushmen" had, indeed, a system of "ethical sentiments" and that it would even match that of the European colonists. Along these lines he also provides a list of "the ten commandments of the Bushman" (1922: 19–20) which today read like a well-intended policy paper to soften tensions between "Bushmen" and settlers while being anthropologically rather uninformed, decontextualized, and biased. Whatever Vedder knew about the "Bushman" moral system, it was made to fit the expectations of his colonial Christian audience in form and function, namely as a set of principles in close parallel to the Ten Commandments.[2] Moreover, there is also an element of arrogance and ridicule in that he filled up the list with what to Europeans must appear to be an impoverished version of truly important values: faithfulness and not stealing are juxtaposed with the command not to "point to a grave with your finger" and to bury one's blood "so that the dogs don't lick it" (for a critique see Widlok 2009: 22–23). This example of a culturally biased rendering of an ethical system in terms of Christian virtues (of the nineteenth and twentieth centuries) may illustrate why there is a widespread reluctance among anthropologists to explicitly deal with virtues in their ethnographies. However, while it is easy to reject a synthetic account of this sort from a current anthropological perspective, we may still ask: What would a more appropriate description of virtues look like? And is there an ethnographic gap if we do not find (or provide) any account of virtues in our descriptions and in anthropological analysis?

A Practice Approach to the Anthropology of Virtue

Unfortunately, the HRAF does not provide any definition of "virtue" (beyond the list of examples given above) that would allow us to clearly recognize a virtue if we encountered one in the field. Even worse, it suggests that virtues are idealized ideas rather than observable practices. Elsewhere I have argued that a more appropriate and productive concept of virtues considers them to be practices relating to the realization of fundamental goods intrinsic to these practices (Widlok 2004). This echoes Alasdair MacIntyre's definition of virtue as "an acquired human quality the possession and exercise of which tends to enable us to achieve those goods which are internal to practices and the lack of which effectively prevents us from achieving any such goods" (2007: 191). The main point of this definition is that it allows us to distinguish the intrinsic goods entailed in virtuous practice from "classified" or specific goals (which MacIntyre calls "external goods"). Typical examples for the latter are money, status, and power which can be achieved by various means. A more pedestrian example (given by MacIntyre 2007: 188) for such an external good is the sweet that a child aims for as a reward for winning a game of chess – either through playing well or through cheating – whereas the excellence of playing chess well (which may or may not produce an extra reward) would be considered an inherent good of chess-playing. My own ethnographic example relates to virtue as a human quality observable in the practice of sharing in contradistinction to systems of exchange (Widlok 2004, 2010). For a long time these two forms of transfer were not appropriately distinguished, partly due to the adaptation of Sahlins's confusing terminology that list various types of "reciprocities" even when there is no reciprocal flow in two directions. In fact, sharing is often not only unbalanced but it is typically a one-directional flow. However, to call sharing a "one-way transfer" and exchange a "two-way transfer" (Hunt 2000) and to highlight that they are represented as morally distinct from one another (Woodburn 1998) does not entirely solve the problem because such a boundary easily becomes fuzzy. Depending on where the observer draws the (largely arbitrary) boundary with regard to the time-depth or the extension of a social network involved, one-way transfers may eventually and broadly become two- or multidirectional (Widlok 2004: 61). Moreover, even emic representations do not always help because in practice transfers that are expected to even out often do not. While a consequentialist perspective fails, an anthropology of virtue, by contrast, allows us to distinguish exchange – for "external" and strategic benefits such as having a network of partners, creating obligations for the future, etc. – from sharing that entails the intrinsic goods of receiving a share (sharing out) and of being accepted as a member of the community of humans with recognized needs (sharing in). We have an extensive record of social institutions regulating exchange systems such as *kula* in Melanesia, potlatch on the Pacific northwest coast and *hxaro* in Khoisan southern Africa, where transfers are typically geared toward external goods, usually those that become specific properties of specific groups or persons. Typically, institutionalized forms regulate how external goods are realized, often in a competitive mode. The goals are often, but necessarily, in tension with the shared good of a larger community (or humanity at large). From this perspective, sharing has often been considered to be the "unregulated" default that is found when institutionalized exchange is absent. It is supposedly governed by either ecological need and pressure or a diffuse notion of generosity and altruism. However, the ethnographic record shows that sharing takes place not only under conditions of scarcity, and that it typically takes the form of demand sharing rather than apparently generous gift-giving. In fact, as I have suggested elsewhere (Widlok 2010), a number of cultural conditions have to be in place for sharing to work. Unlike the case of the abovementioned exchange systems, these conditions are not formally institutionalized normative systems but, instead, complex systems of habitual practice. In the ethnographic cases under consideration here, sharing works because people have a shared history of mutual involvements as kin, because they master numerous ways of initiating sharing through implicature and other forms of talk, and finally because they recognize the presence of others as the (often silent) demand that it constitutes toward those who have and who are in a position to give. Or to put it differently in terms of my own ethnography of southern African foragers, sharing works through kin talk drawing another person closer, through constantly nagging or through simply hanging around when resources are brought into camp. Typically, sharing takes place when others are physically present, whereas not being co-present on the scene dramatically reduces the chance of receiving a share. The practices of accepting classificatory and "fictive" kin relations, responding appropriately to speech acts and recognizing the presence of others in the context of sharing are moral skills that we may safely term "virtues." Although they may not be marked by explicit generosity, they rely on receiver and giver cooperatively realizing an intrinsic good, which is in contrast to the often competitive gift-giving in exchange systems. While the *goods* shared may be limited, or even scarcer than the objects of exchange systems, the *good* of recognizing others and their needs is an intrinsic one that is not limited in the sense that the excellent practice of one person would decrease the amount of that good available to another individual.[3]

The ethnography of exchange systems and of sharing practices underline the fact that there are major differences between the two. Exchanges, especially ceremonial gift-exchange, are characterized not only by a sphere of personal competition (and probably play a major role in the emergence of inequality: see Hayden 1994). These exchanges also create long-term obligations; require keeping a record of the biography of things; are instrumental for systematic intergenerational and interregional dependencies; and allow the forging of large-scale alliances, the reassurance of allegiances, and the building of followership and patronage. Not surprisingly, therefore, these exchanges are often couched in ceremonies, surrounded by taboos, detailed norms and rules. We find very little, if anything, of that with regard to sharing. Sharing is typically unceremonial. Instead of a formal handing over, we find arrangements whereby recipients are the initiators ("demand sharing"), they are allowed to take ("tolerated theft"), they may be critical rather than grateful ("insulting the meat," "accusing the hunter"), and often the transfer is mediated by sending a child to deliver the food or whatever is shared. Often sharing goes without saying except that it is often accompanied by more or less explicit words (and gestures) of demand instead of words of offer. What I have found in my ethnography of the ≠Akhoe Hai//om San of northern Namibia is echoed by many accounts of sharing, in particular in hunting and gathering contexts. Both giver and recipient de-emphasize the position of giver and receiver, thereby making it hard for the giver to bank on the giving and to create the obligations that are so central for exchange systems for realizing external goods.

Moreover, there are institutional frameworks that allow individuals to train and habitualize the necessary skills involved, for instance in the context of the healing ritual, where participation can be conceptualized as "demand cooperation" in parallel to the "demand sharing" with regard to food and objects (Widlok 1999: 256). Sharing, I suggest, is done for the sake of shared enjoyment of whatever it is that is being shared – it is ethically and logically an act for its own sake – while exchange aims at something else, an obligation into the future or a compensation from the past. To say that it is a habitual skill is not to suggest that no attempts are being made to depart from the expected course of things. Among hunter-gatherers, too, we see attempts to divert resources from sharing to purposes of exchange. ≠Akhoe Hai//om try to hide some of their resources, for instance keeping a separate full pouch of tobacco apart from the almost empty one that everyone can see. They try to make deals with members of other ethnic groups, for instance when distilling liquor, but often they fail (Widlok 1999: 103). In both cases a particular effort has to be made if one wants to depart from entrenched sharing practices. In effect, the only way to avoid established sharing is to alter the situation that would otherwise lead to sharing. The logic cuts both ways: the most promising way of inducing sharing is by creating a situation that allows for the habitual practices to unfold their force. In another ethnographic example I have shown how a particular wild fruit is made subject to sharing after it had initially been the possession of an individual young man who had put it into ground holes where the fruit was left to ripen (see Widlok 2004: 63). As soon as the fruit was brought into the camp, where the open settlement structure leaves no room for hiding, it was once again subject to indiscriminate sharing. The element of choice is not so much in whether to give or not to give a share but rather whether to enter or to avoid a situation that by virtue of its constellation would require sharing. Consequently, the recipients are typically not passive but they gear their movements toward a sharing situation. They do not rely on a sense of duty instilled in others but they clearly signal in forceful and clear ways that the current situation is one that requires sharing. Demand sharing is therefore no contradiction in terms but is in fact the likely default form of sharing. Sharing is likely to have evolved not out of any innate altruism but as a side product of a combination of socially approved modes of interaction that provoke and enable it. As I have argued elsewhere, sharing breaks down, often to the outspoken detriment of social agents, when the practices of relating, conversing, and interacting in spaces that are conducive to it are discontinued (Widlok 2010: 98). If sharing works in a social network like liquid flowing through communicating tubes, then it is not the external situations of scarcity or affluence that keep the system working but the maintenance of connections from within, by keeping the flow free of obstacles. Whether these moves are successful or not depends on the skillful mastery of kin relatedness, of conversation and co-presence that are individually trained and socially framed. I suggest that these skills are best conceptualized as virtues and that our analysis of ethics would be incomplete if we limited ourselves to explicit and institutionalized moral norms and rules, such as those that govern many exchange systems.

Clearing the Ground: Conceptual Obstacles

If we were to simply drop the notion of virtue because of the cultural baggage implicit in the term (see below), we would produce a one-sided account, highlighting the institutionalized morality that protects vested interests and the external goods that are subject to competition. Our account of ethics would be restricted to the ways in which people talk normatively about classified goals and external goods. This would introduce a cultural bias toward moral norms and it would caricature ethics in terms of one of its opposites, namely ubiquitous moralism, the use of morality for ulterior aims and purposes (see Løgstrup 1989: xiii). An account of virtues, by contrast, not only fills a gap in the ethnographic record but it can also strengthen an anthropological analysis that seeks to establish how ethics are related to moral(izing) and how virtues are related to institutionalized practices in any particular setting, a relation that constitutes an important dimension of the dynamics of human agency. There is no reason to believe that the relation (or the proportion) of intrinsic vis-à-vis external goods is fixed across time and space. Rather, we would expect a comparative perspective always to include both and to look at their changing articulations. Moreover, I would argue that a great amount of personal problem-solving, decisions, reflections, assessment, and social conflict surround the tensions between the pursuit of practices with intrinsic goods on the one hand and the expectation and need to also realize extrinsic/external goods on the other hand. Furthermore, many individual and collective conflicts that are now conceptualized in a culturally specific opposition of good versus evil may become understandable in terms of a tension between the simultaneous realization of different and at times conflicting goods.

In terms of anthropological theory, research on virtues (or a corresponding concept possibly labeled differently) opens the door to a study of how humans place themselves in relation to what they envision to be a good life. Social agents typically do not position themselves with reference to abstract questions of good and bad or to philosophical questions of what constitutes "the good life." However, an anthropology of virtue can reconnect these questions with the ethnographic record on how humans habitually practice ways of realizing intrinsic (and extrinsic) goods that are intertwined in any particular real-life situation. This allows us to go beyond the question of how isolated, singular goods are ranked or weighted against one another, as found in much of economic and psychological research. Instead, we aim to describe and understand the experience of complex life situations and to explain the process whereby human agents derive singular classified goods from these complex, and at time diffuse, shared situations in the first place. As I will point out below, this allows anthropology to get closer to the actual experience of situations that constitutes human life – including its ethical aspects. It helps us not to mistake post-fact reflections, moral justifications, and formal decisions for the situational foundation from which these rationalizations are derived in the first place.

What I have done in these opening remarks is to point at important advantages for maintaining a notion of virtue in ethnography and comparative anthropology. What needs to be done before we move on to an actual program of anthropological research on virtue is to deal with the weaknesses of some interpretations of the term "virtue" that puts off many anthropologists today (for example, Zigon 2008: 24). We need to free the concept of its unwanted "baggage" and then to reconstruct it on a sound theoretical and empirical basis. The main part of this article aims to do exactly that: first, to clear the ground of unwanted (and in my view unnecessary) obstacles for using the term and, second, to programmatically outline what a productive use of the term in a future anthropology of morality could look like.

Consider the following analogy. Imagine a situation in which a major technological disaster strikes (say a leaking nuclear power plant or some other likely event), with the result that humans turn their back on the natural sciences which are effectively threatening to make the larger part of the planet inhospitable. People stop teaching science at school and burn science books; centuries later, all that is left are bits and pieces of scientific terms and ideas but without the founding theories that give sense to these terms and ideas. This scenario, MacIntyre (2007: 1–5) argues, is exactly what has happened to our theories of ethics and virtue. We still use terms such as "morality" and "virtue" but in very different ways than in previous times, with very different social functions and, most importantly, without a framework that provides a clear place for these terms and concepts. At the same time, the prevalent frameworks of moral theory remain problematic if they cannot critically integrate notions of virtue. As Gertrude Anscombe (1958) argued, the major strands in moral theory, namely utilitarianism, Kantian deontological ethics, and social contract ethics have come to use terms such as "ought" and "right and wrong" in a secular legalistic framework at the cost of any substantial content in ethics. Within modern moral philosophy the work of Anscombe and MacIntyre and others has continued to fuel an alternative account to which anthropology can relate well because the ethnography of ethics is not limited to systems of legalistic rules but rather presents bodies of knowledge about substantial issues involving moral implications of particular actions. One of the key contributions of anthropology to a wider moral theory is therefore that of further opening up venues for alternatives, as envisaged by Anscombe and MacIntyre, by putting notions such as virtue on a broader and cross-culturally valid basis.

The meaning of the key terms of moral theory, like all cultural terms, change over the centuries and partially overlap with changes in social and economic organization, to which they are dynamically related. This is also the case for virtue and for most of the terms covered in this volume (such as "value," "narrative," "sentiments," "ordinary," or "reason"). The contents of the so-called "tables of virtues," ranked lists of virtues, can be shown to have changed across social formations (from the Greek *polis* to the Prussian state). Different thinkers (from Aristotle to Benjamin Franklin) have come up with their distinct lists of primary and secondary virtues (see MacIntyre 2007 for details on these historical changes). Whereas manly virtues, such as courage, dominated in the middle ages (and helped to coin the Latin term *virtus*), the much more recent, almost exclusive identification of virtue with restrained sexuality, in particular female chastity, has been a feature of the eighteenth century when the emphasis on property was linked to the importance of knowing your legitimate heir in early modern Europe. However, what has also changed is the concept of virtue itself and the role that it has played in the social and philosophical narratives of which it formed a part. As already indicated, the Greek (Aristotelian) view of virtue as the realization of goods that are internal to actions and that lead humankind to a happy life (*eudaimonia*) implied that the internal good was considered to be the same for individuals and for humanity at large. The more restrictive notion of "morality" as that which we need in order to curb the egoistic drives of individuals to realize their own independent goals is a much more recent idea and one that would place virtue on the side of a sense of moral and social duty against the interests of individuals. The discussion about an apparent tradeoff or complementarity between private vice and public virtue (Carrier and Miller 1999) emerges in a rather specific situation of the capitalist system and is not universally conceived in this way. Defined in this modern sense, there appear to be different sets of virtues, arguably one for every (sub)culture or even for every thinker, religion, culture, time period, occupational group, political movement, and so forth. Although some philosophers are at pains to point out that there are overlaps and shared properties at a more abstract level between these manifestations (Moody-Adams 1997) the main point to note in this context is that the reality of different sets of virtues in the late capitalist sense does not invalidate the more fundamental claim that virtues are constituted by intrinsic goods enshrined in practices.

Similarly, virtue has only recently become identified with the abiding of rules and with the notion of principled behavior in the context of very specific branches of European thought, which created a narrow version of virtue that was made compatible with the deontologically conceived moralities of fulfilling one's duty (Robbins 2007). These branches of European thought gave up establishing what the intrinsic shared goods of human life would be and instead focused on the duties of following rules and obligations (as in the Kantian tradition) or on the appropriate choice of the right principles for a maximal number of beneficiaries (as in the utilitarian tradition). In other words, in the context of other terms and concepts that we associate with morality as a domain, the notion of virtue has changed and become marginalized in the framework of emerging modernist thinking (Anscombe 1958). Since anthropology aims to include the wider human spectrum, beyond the confines of modernism, this suggests that we may be well advised to rehabilitate a notion of virtue. However, given the long history, briefly sketched above, of redefining not just the contents of tables of virtues but the notion of virtue itself in the larger set of terms, we may still wonder whether we should not replace virtue with a different terminology. Could we not, for instance, simply speak of "evidence for moral experience and for human moral sense empirically found in everyday behavior"? While I concede that a research program formulated this way may also deliver interesting insights, I think there is now good evidence that this would not constitute an analysis that is less culturally biased and has less of a convoluted conceptual history load than our study of virtues. "Empirical," "evidence," "experience" and "sense" – these keywords are exactly those that the recent cross-linguistic research of Anna Wierzbicka (2010) has shown to carry considerable cultural baggage, an Anglo bias, as she calls it. The long and changing history of such terms leaves little doubt that these are not culture-free and neutral terms but that we may buy into particular preconceived ideas and cultural traditions when using them. While I agree with Wierzbicka that this cultural embeddedness of our key terms is not sufficiently reflected in English-speaking academic work I do not think we need to drop terms like these in favor of a very restrictive set of basic vocabulary (seemingly "natural" semantic metalanguage).[4] Rather, I think there is something to be said for relying on key concepts such as virtue, for which this history of changing cultural embedding is well documented (as exemplified by MacIntyre's study of virtue) instead of relying on other terms where the impression of "not being culturally contaminated" is only covering up little-known and therefore little-controlled biases that are built into them.

In what follows I provide further arguments why and how it makes sense to maintain a notion of virtue, if not necessarily the term "virtue" itself, in the light of the complexities sketched above. I propose that the notion could be turned into a point of departure for exploring the domain of ethics and morality more generally if we anchor it firmly in anthropological theory and ethnography. The three sources of my arguments are (1) new developments in the theory of social-cultural anthropology, (2) ideas from philosophical anthropology, and (3) empirical evidence from ethnography.

Virtue in Terms of Artful Agency and Skill

Although much is to be said for interdisciplinary debate and joint effort when attempting to further develop the anthropology of morality, far too often this has led to a rather facile division of labor whereby philosophy and, increasingly, developmental psychology, provided theories and concepts and anthropology limited itself to providing cross-cultural data. When discussing issues of morality from a genuine anthropological perspective, I argue, anthropologists can do better than simply importing a more or less haphazard selection of theoretical ideas from other disciplines and exposing them to non-Western settings. Rather, there is something to be said for anthropology exploring the domain of ethics through key theoretical ideas that have already been developed and successfully elaborated in other domains of anthropological inquiry. The potential for using this strategy is greater by far than what is currently being realized. Given the link between being virtuous and being virtuoso, as outlined above, it is not far-fetched to look more closely at cutting-edge anthropological theories dealing in particular with the arts and skill. As I have suggested elsewhere (Widlok 2004), two promising points of departure in this respect are Alfred Gell's (1998) ideas surrounding art as agency and Tim Ingold's (2000) work on technology as embodied skill.

With regard to the anthropology of art there are striking similarities between the study of non-Western moralities and that of what used to be called "primitive art." The traditional division of labor suggested that in both aesthetics and morality, anthropological theory had to account for the practices and attitudes that fell outside the sociocultural systems that characterized "the West" and then came to dominate "the rest." The most common pattern was for anthropology to relativistically criticize the theories of aesthetics that were developed in the West and to show that they would not hold for any particular ethnographic case outside the West (in the abstract). Gell (1998) suggested that we should not be satisfied with anthropological studies that confirm the incompatibility of different aesthetic systems, but that we should rather look at art objects as manifestations of "actions, intended to change the world rather than encode symbolic propositions about it" (1998: 6). Anthropology can achieve this by providing a particular "biographical" depth of focus while at the same time expanding concepts such as "style" from that of individuals expressing their identity to the virtuosity of artworks that instantiate what is collectively considered to be excellent (1998: 158).

Similarly, I would suggest, we should not necessarily expect to find a cross-cultural domain of "morality" and we should not be satisfied with confirming the incompatibility of different moral systems, elucidating their culture-specific rules, or with considering morality as a matter of individuals enacting general moral principles (Widlok 2009). Neither should we limit ourselves to studying the "external" functions of morality as a stabilizer of social order, or fear that including morals or virtue would necessarily lead to a "moralistic" analysis. Rather, an anthropological analysis of morality is likely to be most productive when we look at virtues as actions intended to change the world rather than as ideas encoding a particular moral ideology. A sociological analysis of the "supra-biographical" effects of (a)moral behavior tends toward utilitarian consequentialism, and cognitive scientists may "infra-biographically" seek to establish how individuals follow duties, and thereby tend toward deontologism (compare Gell 1998: 10). By contrast, the anthropological frame is that of the agent's life context, which by definition includes the presence of others and the relations with them, and it leads us to an anthropology of virtue and shared good, instead of consequences and duties. In other words, looking at art as agency can help to frame our anthropological contribution to the study of morality in terms of social agency, namely in the context of individual lives embedded in what is excellent in the realization of good action and thinking.

The second domain of anthropological inquiry from which we may derive a theoretical lead is the study of technology, or more precisely that of connecting artworks with artifacts. In this context, I have already referred to the work of Tim Ingold (Widlok 2004: 59). Just as Gell's emphasis of the art object – externalized from its creator turning into a social agent itself – included the artistic agency of pure doing (as in installation art), so Ingold's study of making objects includes "doing things" (well) more generally. This is relevant insofar as the difference of skill being primarily a matter of making and virtue being primarily a matter of doing in these frameworks is a difference of degree rather than a categorical distinction.

Skill, according to Ingold, is not only involved in the making of objects and it is not the technical execution of a plan (2000: 289–290). The distinction that is commonly made between design and construction seems at least exaggerated – if not seriously misleading – for those many cases in which "the pattern of regular movement" is that which determines the resulting forms and not a preexisting design conceived independently of its practice (291). The bias of conventional analysis tends to overemphasize formal instruction as it suggests that knowledge about how to make things (for instance, doing knots in handicraft) is typically handed on "as a package of rules and representations, independently and in advance of their practical application" (358). Rather, practitioners can become skilled producers of artifacts without having privileged access to professional knowledge encoded by specialists simply by perfecting their own movements in practice.[5]

Again, there are striking similarities between skill in this sense and with what is usually discussed under the notion of "virtue." Virtue is not the strict enforcement of a moral rule or duty and it is not to be confused with rule-abiding behavior. The distinction that is commonly made between knowing a rule and knowing how to apply rules to particular situations is, again, exaggerated if not misleading. In many cases the patterns of regularly responding to ethical demands (Løgstrup 1997) and to situations that demand moral decisions constitute what is considered to be virtuous – and not following any particular code of conduct. The bias of conventional analysis of morality tends to overemphasize formal encoding and suggests that moral knowledge about how to do things right (for instance, resolving the knots of interpersonal conflict) is typically handed on as a package of rules and representations, independently and in advance of their practical application. By contrast, moral agents can be considered virtuous without having privileged access to the specialist knowledge of moral codes simply by perfecting their own practice. This puts the focus of moral analysis back on the individual and on situated actions while still recognizing that virtue is not determined by isolated individuals but is generated in reference to a field of social relations that constitute a shared good. The new anthropology of virtue, I suggest, includes many more instances of moral behavior from the anthropological record than a more restrictive notion predicated on ethical systems and moral codices.

Philosophical Considerations

In the previous section I have highlighted the importance of developing key concepts of our analysis from within the discipline, by adapting approaches and ideas that have successfully been applied in neighboring domains of anthropological inquiry, namely art and skill. I shall now second this move by expanding the argument into another neighboring field that is also adjacent but typically falls under the label of another discipline, namely philosophical anthropology. It appears that anthropologists who feel that they can do without the notion of virtue (or an equivalent different term) follow the majority of analytical philosophers who when discussing morality focus on the ability and complexity of making correct moral choices. Simplifying one of the most complex discussions surrounding human "free will," one may say that there are two camps: naturalists who claim that basically humans are determined in their behavior and only have the illusion of a free will, and idealists who claim the opposite, that human choice is indeterminate. While the latter have been dominant during a long period in the history of ideas, current brain research tends to tilt the scale heavily toward the determinist side. Anthropologists (for instance, Robbins 2009; Zigon 2009) have tried to steer a way through this bifurcated intellectual landscape by suggesting that there are two broad modes of morality, one in which humans routinely follow moral norms (that is, when their behavior is determined by these norms) and one in which they experience a moment of reflection and choice (that is, when they are confronted with the need and the possibility to choose). Both approaches focus on the ranking of values (if at different moments) and they disregard the possibility that there may be an inherent and continuous link between features of human existence and human ethics.

However, there is a relevant minority position in philosophical anthropology that maintains that responding ethically to situational demands is a general feature of the human condition and that moral responsibility is not limited to moments of normative decisions or of reflected choice. Hermann Schmitz suggests that there is constant independent initiative based on a freedom of ethical conviction (*Gesinnungsfreiheit*) rather than on a freedom of will (*Willensfreiheit*) (2009: 128). According to Knut Løgstrup (1997) any everyday situation, and not more or less rare moments of willful decision, carries a "silent moral demand," to which we respond in action and attitude. In contrast to the dominant "choice between values" approach, the notion of virtue suggests that if there is a distinction to be made between "types of morality" it is not a temporal alternation between reproduction and reflection, periods of normality and moral crisis. Rather, the scenario is one of constantly attuning one's attitude in reference to the ethical demands of changing situations and the possibility of deriving moral reflections from this engagement, potentially at all times but not necessarily at any time. Virtue, in this sense, is not a derivative from moral decisions and reflections, but it is the largely unreflected foundation for any other moral activity and therefore of particular relevance.

THE UNIVERSALITY OF VIRTUE AND THE PARTICULARS OF ETHNOGRAPHY

The third pillar with which I want to substantiate my claim that virtue can be made a productive notion for anthropological inquiry is the ethnographic record itself. The evidence that I present is highly selective in the sense that it is based on very specific field research experiences. As Bauman has pointed out, "People tend to weave their images of the world out of the yarn of their experience" (2007: 244–245). But ultimately the same applies to the selection of anthropological and philosophical theoretical arguments. The ethnography of southern African hunter-gatherers that I have elaborated on in various ways (1999, 2004, 2007, 2010) is clearly different from that of globalized consumerism, with its tendency toward suspicion and mistrust, mutual exploitation and abuse, and with a mediatized outlook on life that makes the "old" virtues appear disadvantageous or suicidal (Bauman 2007). However, the ethnographic situation that I know best is also far from idyllic, and in many ways it is undergoing a process of unintended dilapidation (Widlok 2010). Nevertheless, it suggests that across ethnographic contexts we find the shared positive evaluation of certain goods and a fair possibility of realizing the intrinsic good in practices such as sharing – not as a philosophical postulate but as an ethnographic reality (see Widlok 2004: 64). While we cannot and should not generalize any particular situation, I maintain that what is generalizable across very different cases is the fact that in ethnography we typically encounter people concerned with ethical concerns based on a link between ethical actions and intrinsic goods and with the virtuousness of the people around them.

It is not that the "just plain folks" of our field sites would lack the philosophical concepts needed to reflect about morality and ethics in abstract ways. To take ≠Akhoe Hai//om, the southern African Khoisan language that I know best, as an example: The derivative morphemes of that language would make it easy to turn any particular behavior that one observes not only into a noun or a compound noun or a noun indicating passivity, reflexivity, reciprocity, purpose, direction, application, and so forth, but also into an abstract noun (using a special derivative morpheme *si*, which indicates "abstractness"). In the ≠Akhoe Hai//om language one can formulate who and what is "right" (*≠hanu*) but also create abstract notions such as *≠hanu≠hanuda!haros* ("affirmative action": see Haacke and Eizeb 2002: 400). Talking of "righteousness" or even something like "right-less-able-ness-acity" would not be problematic because several derivative morphemes can be combined and grammatical constructions of irrealis, of skeptical reflection, of triadic reciprocity integrated in complex pragmatics are all possible (see Widlok et al. 2008). The point is that none of these available linguistic and conceptual strategies are commonly used to solve moral problems. Instead, the most common term used with regard to ethics is simply *≠hanu* (straight) as an adjective linked to agents and actions. Even more common is a characterization of humans and their actions that goes completely without saying, a simple gesture that points straight (*≠hanu*, "right") forward, extending from one's face versus a gesture or gaze that indicates a bent ("crooked"). Gestures and interjections, evocative speech rather than propositions, are the most common linguistic tools not only of moral judgment but also of moral behavior in the form of speech acts. Turning toward someone, or turning away from a person, is recognition (or lack of recognition) of their "silent demands," be it a demand to receive a share of food, recognition as a visitor or as being included in a host of social activities (Widlok 2004, 2010). There is no specialized vocabulary or register for "morality talk" but there are underlying regularities of reasoning that emerge, for instance, through moral scenario elicitation (Widlok 2009). When presenting open-ended moral scenarios to small groups of≠Akhoe Hai//om speakers who are then asked to discuss how they think the situations are likely to develop further, some remarkable features emerge: Scenarios that philosophy treats as dilemmas (such as having to make a choice between the life of an unborn and already born children), were not accepted as dilemmas and were instead converted into problems. ≠Akhoe Hai//om when responding to scenarios of possible infanticide (in a situation of food shortage), dishonesty (in emergencies), or disloyalty (for the greater good) did not accept these scenarios as constituting dilemmas, choices of inescapable costs, but rather as problems that needed further working out by getting to know the details of the situation (Widlok 2009).

For instance, the "infanticide dilemma" was presented as a problematic situation for which solutions existed. The problem was one of making an extra effort to find sufficient food that would allow all children to live and that would make infanticide unnecessary. The problem of judging behavior ethically was one of knowing the relevant facts of the situation. Conversely, some choices that we as researchers did not consider to be of moral concern (for instance, taking a long route versus taking a short route with a danger, a snake, on it) readily received a moral dimension (as, for instance, when asking about the motivation and reliability of those who had reported the snake on the road). In both instances the scenarios were not propelled *up* onto the plain of abstract rules or conventions but instead boiled *down* to the particulars of situations that would allow for appropriate action and proper ethical judgment. More generally, the prevalent solution to resolve difficult situations depicted in the scenario was to go deeper into the situation instead of abstracting from it. The way in which this was achieved was by (1) retelling the story, often adding more details to it than were contained in the original, sparse version; (2) posing questions about further details of the situation; (3) impersonation of characters in the story (using direct speech); (4) replacing the third-person perspective of the original scenario with personal first- and second-person pronouns.

The responses elicited with ≠Akhoe Hai//om show that the persons asked were not solving moral problems by reducing the situations to mere "cases" or "instances" to be solved on grounds of principle. To the contrary, the dominant strategy and pattern of moral reasoning observed was one of discussants getting a feel for the situation and making sense of it by embedding the possible actions into a dense social picture and by immersing themselves into the scenario so that they could reconstruct what the personalized, and maybe even spontaneous reaction, was. Solving ethical tasks appeared to rely in the first instance on practice, on having gained experience by working through situations with complex ethical issues (in experience or in discourse), on special skills that we may call "virtues."

How can we know whether any of these results are simply culturally specific for≠Akhoe Hai//om or whether they are indicative of a more general feature of human ethics? The advantage of such elicitation tasks is that they can be used comparatively. Although the cross-cultural application of this research has only just started, there are some striking results (Widlok 2009). Those of us who grew up with moral dilemma scenarios as prompts for philosophical and political debates had to learn that, in places such as the Trobriand Islands or northern Namibia, the scenarios do not provoke intensive debate, verbal dispute, and confrontational argument. Rather, there is a much broader spectrum of prevalent strategies ranging from presupposed and prospective consensus (on Trobriand: Gunter Senft, personal communication) to autonomous heterodoxy (in Namibia where ≠Akhoe Hai//om accepted individual variations in group responses). In both instances the impression we get from these transcripts is that the group discussions are not so much a dialogue for exchanging opinions or for marking and justifying moral positions against one another. Rather, the participants seem to work on the situations that were put in front of them in a similar way as they generally work their way through the situations that they master together in everyday life. Employing the same elicitation in Italy Maya Turolla (personal communication) has shown that Europeans, at least in some instances, tend to use moral dilemma scenarios for distinguishing themselves and for primarily clarifying the responsibility for themselves instead of taking responsibility for the situation at large. In contradistinction to this rather peculiar approach, the "particularizing" strategy of the ≠Akhoe Hai//om may point at a more universal feature of human moral agency, namely working through particular shared situations (Schmitz 2008: 145). It may also support the notion that moral responsibility can be universal without being general, particular without being singular (Løgstrup 1989; see also Widlok 2004). In any case, it appears that this strategy is not limited to an extraordinary cultural model. It is more likely that the "generalizing" strategy that takes recourse in principles is the odd cultural model out in the wider cultural spectrum. Thinking in terms of moral rules and principles and duties rather than laterally across situations seems another instance of a modernistic bias of WEIRD (Western Educated Industrial Rich Democratic) people that dominates the results of cross-cultural research up to this point (Henrich et al. 2010).[6] Ethical behavior may be conspicuously absent in much of today's globalized consumerist settings, with their weak rules and frail bonds. But this does not invalidate the claim that ethical behavior originates in habitual practice, precisely because ethical behavior is *not* based on the processes of distancing reflection and choice idealized in the modern situation (Baumann 2007: 250). Any attempt to establish moral universalism is likely to fail if it does not engage with this interpersonal basis of ethical demands and the responses to situations (see Zimmermann 2009 and comments). Based on the suggestive ethnographic evidence, the dominant research focus on individual choices and the ranking of values appears to be another feature of a modernist bias for which the anthropology of virtue may provide some counterweight.

In the framework of a theory of virtue even the diversity of ethical standards that constitutes a headache for normative attempts to create a binding "world ethos" could be considered a blessing in disguise for the ethnographer. If we assume that virtues are a critical foundation for the narratives of what constitutes a good life and ultimately on the telos of human existence then, by implication, investigating virtues is a very good way of learning about these different (and partially overlapping) narratives, their gaps and contradictions, as much as the sense of continuity and orientation that they provide. Research on virtue is therefore not the final goal of anthropological inquiry, but it promises to be an entry point for understanding the narratives and worldviews that inform our ethical behavior. Ultimately, I would argue, this is also the basis for criticizing these narratives and for developing new alternative ones, in other words, the basis for any applied extension of the anthropological research project. It satisfies the demand for a critical stance and it builds on the kind of knowledge that anthropologists are particularly good, if not irreplaceable, at providing (Fassin 2008: 339).

Conclusion

At the beginning of this contribution I defined virtues as practices relating to the realization of fundamental goods intrinsic to these practices and I pointed to "sharing" as an appropriate ethnographic illustration. I outlined why a narrow notion of virtue as "morally principled behavior" is offputting for the anthropological quest to reduce cultural biases. At the same time I underlined that a notion of virtue informed by a current anthropology of agency and skill brings us closer to the ethical dimension of experience with regard to the situations in which humans find themselves. Using examples from ethnographic elicitation with moral scenarios, I suggested that ethnographic case studies point at a key feature of human ethical agency, namely that of working through shared situations. The anthropological contribution to ethical debates that emerges from this account is one of broadening the spectrum of ideas and practices that relate to ethics. More specifically, an anthropology of virtue can provide a critical corrective against social science research on ethical values and decision-making because it no longer reduces ethical agency to strategies of individual choice in culturally codified systems of abstractions. Instead, it provides opportunities to derive narratives of what constitutes a good life and a good in personal lives, from a rich record of interpersonal agency in complex situations.

Ethnography, I suggest, indicates that often we may have been looking for empirical clues for moral agency in the wrong place. When thinking of virtues the social sciences have been wrongly focusing on abstractly codified personal virtues rather than on how these emerge from particular narratives of what constitutes a good life and a good in personal lives. If it is peculiar to the Enlightenment that it cannot provide a new narrative of goods but even tends to destroy existing narratives, as MacIntyre (2007) suggested, we may be better advised to look for the ways in which social agents in different quarters of the modernized world attempt to rescue or recreate a coherent narrative of intrinsic goods and the good life that they are meant to achieve. Anthropology, with its good access to the non-WEIRD lifeworlds, has a particular opportunity to reinvigorate critical research in the field of ethics. In this field we reach an impasse when we restrict ourselves to the empirical reality or the ideals of the dominant modern worldview. If we consider virtues in the light of the narratives and objectives about what constitutes a good (in) life, there appears to be much more information in the ethnography (also as contained in the HRAF) than what a conventional restricted notion of virtue as rule-abiding duty would suggest. The virtues listed as examples by the HRAF are neither merely codes and conventions (a third-person perspective) nor merely subjectively ranked goals (a first-person perspective) but they can readily be analyzed in terms of expectations, initiatives, and responses in social relations and situations (the second-person perspective). In fact, it would be hard to define any of these virtues if we did not do it with regard to the way they manifest themselves in interpersonal agency across recurring situations. At this point, OCM 577 may no longer be the most obvious place to look for virtues ethnographically but we will have to cast a much wider net. At the same time, the claim that theoretically informed ethnography continues to be a privileged place for investigating ethical issues is supported by an analysis that takes virtue as a point of departure.

NOTES

1 The HRAF is housed at Yale University, now also available online to subscribers as eHRAF at http://www.yale.edu/hraf/about.htm. It constitutes the most comprehensive ethnographic database for which ethnographic texts have been cut and coded into a list of more than 800 subjects (or index categories) with the aim to faciliate cross-cultural research across ethnographic case studies.

2 Vedder's "Ten Commandments of the Bushman" read as follows: "Be faithful to your parents; Be faithful to your spouse; Do brideservice; Avoid your mother-in-law; Don't eat meat prohibited to you; Don't threaten an elder; Don't steal from another Bushman; Hide your cut-off hair from sorcerers; Bury your blood so that the dogs don't lick it; Don't point to a grave with your finger" (Vedder 1922: 19; my translation).

3 This does not preclude that practices can be in conflict with one another, creating tradeoffs, and that choices have to be made (see further in the essay).

4 While this is not the place to provide a Wierzbickian-type study of the way in which the term "virtue" is used cross-culturally (or was used in the past), a quick look at two etymologies may suffice. The English "virtue" (like French *vertu*), for instance, keeps a link between "virtuous" (particularly moral) and "virtuoso" (particularly skilled) which we do not find in Germanic languages. When Max Weber (1985 [1922]) wrote of the "religious virtuoso" (religious experts with their own ethics who are virtuosos in dealing with religious rules), he may have tried to reestablish this link. By contrast, German *Tugend* (or Dutch *deugd* for that matter) refer back to the root *taugen/deugen* ("to be of good use") which underlines a notion of virtue as defined by an intrinsic good (ethically good for something) that is also there in the Aristotelian notion of virtues. It suggests an alternative to the Latinized learned discourse of the Enlightenment philosophers that has been instrumental in creating the theoretical underexposure of much of our terminology for dealing with things moral.

5 This new anthropology of skill not only provides a theory that covers a much broader spectrum of skillful agency than more restrictive notions of technology, notably by including the many diverse examples from the anthropological record. It can also do away with strict and artificial separation between the "natural" skills (for instance, of birds making their nests) developed in evolution and the "cultural" skills (for instance, of making string bags or building houses) developed in history, and thereby open up to a more comprehensive account. In parallel, research on virtues could open up some new exciting links between the social and natural sciences, for example between sharing among animals and sharing among humans, between apparently "natural" ills (for instance, personal drives for egoistic benefits) developed in evolution and apparently "cultural" wills (for instance, altruism).

6 The debate triggered by Henrich et al. (2010) focuses on economic experiments, some of which, however, do have moral implications insofar as they are meant to measure trustworthiness by asking for subjects to allocate shares. One researcher who has employed these experiments in Namibia reports that "people repeatedly did not understand what was meant when they were asked "*in general* do you trust …" (Bjorn Vollan, personal communication). Interestingly this observation was not included in the published account (Vollan 2007: 256), which suggests that they were unwilling to solve the apparently moral task without recourse to the particulars of a situation.

REFERENCES

Anscombe, Gertrude Elizabeth (1958) Modern Moral Philosophy. *Philosophy* 33: 1–19.

Bauman, Zygmunt (2007) Lévinas and Logstrup in the Globalized World of Consumers. In David Brugge and Peter Aaboe Sorensen. (eds.), *Livtag med den etiske fordring*. Aarhus: Klim, pp. 231–261.

Carrier, James and Miller, Daniel (1999) From Private Virtue to Public Vice. In Henrietta Moore (ed.), *Anthropological Theory Today*. Cambridge: Polity Press, pp. 24–47.

Fassin, Didier (2008) Beyond Good and Evil? Questioning the Anthropological Discomfort with Morals. *Anthropological Theory* 8(4): 333–344.

Gell, Alfred (1998) *Art and Agency: An Anthropological Theory*. Oxford: Clarendon.

Haacke, Wilfrid and Eizeb, Eliphas (2002) *A Khoekhoegowab Dictionary with an English–Khoekhoegowab Index*. Windhoek: Gamsberg Macmillan.

Hayden, Brian (1994) Competition, Labor, and Complex Hunter-Gatherers. In E. Burch and L. Ellanna (eds.), *Key Issues in Hunter-Gatherer Research*. Oxford: Berg, pp. 223–239.

Henrich, Joseph, Heine, Steven, and Norenzayan, Ara (2010) The Weirdest People in the World? *Behaviour and Brain Sciences* 33(2–3): 61–83.

HRAF (n.d.) Human Relations Area Files. At http://www.yale.edu/hraf/outline.htm accessed Mar. 5, 2012.

Hunt, Robert (2000) Forager Food Sharing Economy: Transfers and Exchanges. In G. Wenzel et al. (eds.), *The Social Economy of Sharing: Resource Allocation and Modern Hunter-Gatherers*. Osaka: National Museum of Ethnology, pp. 7–26.

Ingold, Tim (2000) *The Perception of the Environment: Essays on Livelihood, Dwelling and Skill*. London: Routledge.

Løgstrup, Knut (1989) *Norm und Spontanität: Ethik und Politik zwischen Technik und Dilettantokratie*. Tübingen: Mohr.

Løgstrup, Knut (1997) *The Ethical Demand*. Notre Dame, IN: University of Notre Dame Press.

MacIntyre, Alasdair C. (2007) *After Virtue: A Study in Moral Theory*. Notre Dame, IN: University of Notre Dame Press.

Moody-Adams, Michele (1997) *Fieldwork in Familiar Places: Morality, Culture and Philosophy*. Cambridge, MA: Harvard University Press.

Robbins, Joel (2007) Between Reproduction and Freedom: Morality, Value, and Radical Cultural Change. *Ethnos: Journal of Anthropology* 72(3): 293–314.

Robbins, Joel (2009) Value, Structure, and the Range of Possibilities: A Response to Zigon. *Ethnos: Journal of Anthropology* 74(2): 277–285.

Schmitz, Hermann (2008) *Logische Untersuchungen*. Freiburg: Alber.

Schmitz, Hermann (2009) *Kurze Einführung in die neue Phänomenologie*. Freiburg: Alber.

Vedder, Heinrich (1922) *Von den Buschmännern*. Barmen: Missionshaus.

Vedder, Heinrich (1942) *Am Lagerfeuer der anderen*. Windhoek: Meinert.

Vollan, Bjorn (2007) What Reciprocity? The Impact of Culture and Socio-Political Background on Trust Games in Namibia and South Africa. In Elinor Ostrom and Achim Schlüter (eds.), *Challenge of Self-Governance in Complex, Globalizing Economies: Collection of Revised Papers of a PhD Seminar, 17th to the 26th of April 2007 in Freiburg*. Freiburg: Institut für Forstökonomie, pp. 241–270. At http://www.ife.uni-freiburg.de/dateien/pdf-dateien/ab47, accessed Feb. 20, 2012.

Weber, Max (1985 [1922]) *Wirtschaft und Gesellschaft*. Tübingen: Mohr.

Widlok, Thomas (1999) *Living on Mangetti: "Bushman" Autonomy and Namibian Independence*. Oxford: Oxford University Press.

Widlok, Thomas (2004) Sharing by Default? Outline of an Anthropology of Virtue. *Anthropological Theory* 4(1): 53–70.

Widlok, Thomas (2007) From Individual Act to Social Agency in San Trance Rituals. In Mirjam de Bruijn, Rijk van Dijk, and Jan-Bart Gewald (eds.), *Strength beyond Structure: Social and Historical Trajectories of Agency in Africa*. Leiden: Brill, pp. 163–188.

Widlok, Thomas (2009) Norm and Spontaneity: Elicitation with Moral Dilemma Scenarios. In Monica Heintz (ed.), *The Anthropology of Moralities.* New York: Berghahn, pp. 20–45.

Widlok, Thomas (2010) Sharing as a Cultural Innovation. In Marion Benz, (ed.), *The Principle of Sharing Segregation and Construction of Social Identities at the Transition from Foraging to Farming.* Berlin: Ex Oriente, pp. 91–104.

Widlok, Thomas, Rapold, Christian, and Hoymann, Gertie (2008) Kinship, Interrogatives and Reciprocals in ≠Akhoe Hai//om. In David Keith Harrison et al. (eds.), *Lessons from Documented Endangered Languages.* Amsterdam: Benjamins, pp. 355–370.

Wierzbicka, Anna (2010) *Experience, Evidence, and Sense: The Hidden Cultural Legacy of English.* Oxford: Oxford University Press.

Woodburn, James (1998) "Sharing is Not a Form of Exchange": An Analysis of Property Sharing in Inmmediate-Return Hunter-Gatherer Societies. In C. Hann (ed.), *Property Relations: Renewing the Anthropological Tradition.* Cambridge: Cambridge University Press, pp. 48–63.

Zigon, Jarrett (2008) *Morality: An Anthropological Perspective.* Oxford: Berghahn.

Zigon, Jarrett (2009) Within a Range of Possibilities: Morality and Ethics in Social Life. *Ethnos: Journal of Anthropology* 74(2): 251–276.

Zimmermann, Rolf (2009) Moralischer Universalismus als geschichtliches Projekt. *Deliberation–Knowledge–Ethics* 20(3): 415–496.

CHAPTER 12 Narratives

Jarrett Zigon

Narrative is an emerging concept and analytical focus within the anthropological study of moralities. This is so because narratives are widely seen as a way in which persons make, remake, articulate, interpret, and come to understand meaning in their lives, and as such the analysis of narratives has become central to many anthropological attempts to understand social life in general and moral life in particular. Although narrative analysis began with a focus on stories, since the 1980s what has come to count as narrative has increasingly broadened. Thus, for example, Paul Ricoeur (1992) has argued that identity itself is produced through narrativizing, Alasdair MacIntyre (1981) has argued that "the good" can be realized only within the narrative of one's own life as it is lived within the greater narrative of a particular tradition, and Jerome Bruner (1990) has argued that narratives provide a way for creating meaning in what might otherwise be discordant and chaotic experiences. Thus, narrative as an analytical concept, and particularly so in anthropological analyses, often goes beyond a mere story and encompasses all sorts of verbal and nonverbal interactions.

Although I consider narratives essential to anthropological analyses of moral and ethical assemblages, and have used them extensively in my own work, I have become skeptical of some of the capacities attributed to narrative. In particular, I have come to seriously question the way in which meaning, mutual understanding, and at times coherence are often highlighted as the most significant outcome of narrative articulations and analysis. Although in my past work I have tried to emphasize the incoherence of narrative "logic" by paying particular attention to the assumptions, contradictions, and veiled references of the narratives of my interlocutors, I have also been attracted to the analytic assumption of the meaning-endowing capacity of narrative (e.g., Zigon 2009, 2010). In this essay I reconsider this assumption and hope to show that narratives and their analysis can bear the most fruit for the study of moralities when we move away from reading them as meaning-making articulations – and particularly as providing mutual understanding

A Companion to Moral Anthropology, First Edition. Edited by Didier Fassin.

of these meanings – and instead read them as articulations of the embodied struggle to morally be with oneself and others in the social world.

In this essay, then, I will argue that the analysis of narratives, broadly taken, is important for an anthropology of moralities for two reasons. First, and as I have already suggested, narratives do not for the most part reveal a process of coming to mutual meaningful understanding – although they can do this sometimes as well – but rather reveal the intersubjective struggle to live through a moral breakdown together; or as I have put it elsewhere – borrowing from the philosopher Alain Badiou (2001) – to "keep going!" (Zigon 2007). As such, what narratives most often show is the ethical process by which individuals intersubjectively work to reattune their embodied ways of being-with-oneself and those others living in their shared social world. Similar to the way in which Jason Throop (2010a) discusses the vicissitudes of empathic experience, so too this process becomes manifest in diverse forms depending on the personal, intersubjective, and social context of its enactment. No matter the context, however, this ethical process is more fruitfully considered as a process of coming to an embodied "agreement" on how to live together rather than of coming to a mutual meaningful understanding. While words and utterances may be essential to this process it is not because they carry meaningful propositions or representations, but because they are themselves social acts and gestures by which individuals can come to once again live in the world together sanely (see Desjarlais 2011).

This leads to the second reason narratives can be an important part of an anthropology of moralities, because often times this "being with" is best achieved by means of acts of charity rather than in terms of shared or mutual meaningful understanding. As I will explain below, to understand and live with another charitably is not to share meaning with others, but to assume one can live with others despite the uncertainty of any such sharedness. Therefore, in contrast to the contention that narratives primarily reveal or facilitate meaning, in this essay I will contend that narratives are better understood as the articulation of the ethical process of attempting to regain moral comfort in the world by charitably negotiating moral breakdowns. What is articulated, then, is not a concern for meaning or mutual understanding, but rather the embodied struggle once again to be with others comfortably in their mutually inhabited world. In order to make this argument, however, I will first consider the predominant approaches to anthropological analyses of narrative and how these have recently been utilized in the emerging anthropology of moralities.

Narrative – From Meaning to Being Together With

For those anthropologists who take narratives as a key source for analyzing sociality, self, and increasingly morality, narrative is considered a social form of speech. This is so not only because narrative is often done with others, but also because it is considered ripe with shared values and meanings (Ries 1997: 3–4). As Cheryl Mattingly and Linda Garro (2000: 10) argue in their seminal volume on the uses of narrative analysis in anthropological studies, narrative is "a fundamental human way of giving meaning to experience," and as such serves to connect experience with the "inner" and "outer" worlds of persons engaged in intersubjective relations, thus linking "motive, act, and consequences." Because of this, narrative is considered essential to meaningful understanding between those involved in such intersubjective relations. That is to say, narratives – whether as stories or as narrative interactions – are considered a primary means by which meaning and moral values are publicly articulated, transmitted, adopted, and reworked (for examples of explicit analysis of narratives for moral values see Villenas 2001; Cole 2003; Kleinman 2006; Ladwig 2009; Mattingly 2010; Throop 2010b; Zigon 2009, 2010). This is so according to Ochs and Capps (2001) because narratives offer two ways in which meaning is made in the world: first by creating coherence between often incoherent events, acts, and so on, and second by working through the uncertainties that remain despite this tendency in everyday life to find meaningful coherence. Thus, while not all of those anthropologists working with narratives would agree on all points, narratives are for the most part seen as a way in which meaningful, coherent, and mutual understanding can be made and communicated in everyday interactions.

Sociality, however, is not a simple sharing. Rather, it is a dialogue within a range of possibilities of understanding. It is often through narrative that individuals negotiate this understanding, in doing so they navigate the potentially dangerous waters of difference and similarity, ambiguity and coherence, unfamiliarity and recognizability that is their social world. When individuals articulate their moral worlds narratively or negotiate a moral breakdown narratively, they do so in ways that are both personal and socially recognizable. Indeed, narrative is a means by which individuals negotiate this tension between personal and shared experiences of living through a particular sociohistoric-cultural world (Mattingly et al. 2009; Zigon 2010). This allows them, in turn, to conceive of and to articulate morality in a way that may not be entirely unique, but also may not be entirely shared. In this sense, narrative articulations of individual moral worlds are best considered as articulations of what I call elsewhere their personal articulated public discourse of morality (Zigon 2011). That is to say, they are primarily the self-reflected articulation of their own embodied moralities, their own understanding of institutional and other public discourses of moralities, and the ethical practices they perform. In this sense, narrative articulations of moral worlds may best be read as ideal representations or conceptions of moral subjectivity, rather than as an accurate account of actual behavior (see Parish 1991). The analysis of narrative articulations, then, provides a description of the ways in which our interlocutors *conceive of their own* lives and experiences (Desjarlais 2003: 5–6).

Similarly, Ochs and Capps have argued that narratives "do not present objective, comprehensive accounts of events but rather perspectives on events" (2001: 45). An important aspect of this perspective is what they call a moral stance. By this Ochs and Capps contend that through their narratives individuals often recount what they interpret as moral transgressions, and in so doing clarify, reinforce, or revise what they morally believe and value (46). In my own research I have found that this narrative work is certainly an important part of my interlocutors' moral lives (Zigon 2010). The narrative articulations of my interlocutors not only recount the moments that were vital to the cultivation of their current moral stance and subjectivity, but also provide an opportunity for revisiting, and perhaps refining, the ethical work done in moments of moral breakdown. Narratives themselves, then, can instigate a second breakdown in which further ethical work can be done. As Kathleen Stewart has put it in her ethnography of West Virginia coalminers, narratives not only express "local epistemology," but also help create a "positioned subject" (1996: 30–31). And as James Faubion has argued, narratives "function as technologies of deliberation and decision, of practical reasoning" (2001: 49). In other words, as Ricoeur (1992) has convincingly argued, narratives not only articulate the moral world of a person, but also help constitute her very identity as a moral subject. Although the argument I make below similarly considers narrative interactions as a key ethical practice for moral subjectivity and an existential ground for being together with others, I differ from Ricoeur in the importance the evaluative aspect of narratives carry. While narratives may often explicitly evaluate events, actions, and characters, I will argue below that what is most morally significant about narrative interactions is not this evaluation, but rather the very act of speaking with an other.

Cheryl Mattingly (e.g., 1998a, 1998b, 2010) is a key figure in the narrative turn in anthropology and has contributed significantly to anthropological and social scientific interest in narrative. Not only has Mattingly argued that narrative articulations are essential for understanding self and the processes of meaning-making within a social world, she has also argued persuasively for considering human action as having a narrative structure, which in part implies that action is best understood in terms of its dramatic unfolding, its temporality, and as the locus for meaning in the world (Mattingly 1998a). Here again Ricoeur's influence is clear. According to Ricoeur (1983) temporality is inherent in the structure of narrative, and thus through the temporalizing capacity of narrative, diverse events and actions are ordered into a coherent experience and story from which motives, consequences, and ultimately meanings may be discerned (see also Throop 2010b: 258–263). Thus Mattingly, through the influence of Ricoeur, as well as the psychologist Jerome Bruner, has played a key role in bringing to anthropology a perspective on narrative that goes well beyond narrative as a story, but broadens this concept to include diverse kinds of everyday verbal and nonverbal interactions, as well as the very structure of action and identity.

Mattingly has also argued, and increasingly so in her most recent work, that a narrative approach – both in terms of analyzing narrative articulations and viewing action as narrative – is vital for understanding morality. In Mattingly's view, narrative interactions tell stories – though these need not be explicit stories as such – "featuring human adventures and suffering," and connect "motives, acts and consequences in causal chains"[1] (1998b: 275). In this way narratives are essential for understanding moral ways of being in the world. Mattingly clearly shows this with her notion of narrative reasoning (1998b: 284). For her, narrative reasoning emphasizes motives as causes, embeds these motives within a particular social world, and as such is able to explore and assert "the good" of a particular situation in that world. Because narrative reasoning recognizes both the subjective and the social nature of all singular situations, it allows for conclusions to be drawn about the best course of action, considering the particular subjective and social context of any singularity.

In her more recent work, which increasingly focuses on an anthropology of moralities, Mattingly has sought to merge her narrative approach with a MacIntyrian virtue ethics. In *After Virtue* MacIntyre (1981) seeks to revive virtue ethics, utilizing a narrative approach that is not unlike Mattingly's. MacIntyre's argument, in short, goes something like this: moral virtues can be debated, transmitted, and embodied only within traditions, and a tradition, as well as the individuals who participate in it, should be conceived as a narrative unity. As he puts it:

> unless there is a telos which transcends the limited goods of practices by constituting the good of a whole human life, the good of a human life conceived as a unity, it will both be the case that a certain subversive arbitrariness will invade the moral life and that we shall be unable to specify the context of certain virtues adequately. (MacIntyre 1981: 189)

MacIntyre's work is increasingly influential in the anthropology of moralities, and one reason for this is because it has been interpreted as presupposing "that actions are embedded in an ongoing social narrative [and that it] is only within the context of such a narrative that actions acquire a meaning" (Mattingly et al. 2009: 17). As I argued earlier in this section, the view that narratives play a central role in the meaning-making process has made their analysis attractive to anthropologists. It is this same capacity that seems to be ushering it into the anthropological study of moralities. To the best of my knowledge, however, an explicit theory of meaning has not yet been elucidated by those anthropologists who utilize narrative analysis. It seems clear, however, that some form of a foundational theory of meaning is quite common. The foundational theory of meaning "attempts to specify the facts in virtue of which expressions of natural languages come to have the semantic properties that they have" (Speaks 2010), and the form of this theory most common within anthropology would appear to be some mix of a mentalist theory, concerned with intentions and motivations, and a social normative theory, concerned with elucidating the public resources by which meaning-making is available to members of a particular social community (see Robbins 2007: 14–15). Narrative genres, for example, would be one such public resource considered available to members of a certain social community for coming to mutual meaningful understanding of one another's motivations, intentions, and beliefs, and the process by which some narrative analysts have said this is done is by narrative mind reading (Mattingly 2010; see also Bruner 1990). Thus, the narrative tradition within anthropology posits that narratives are essential for individuals coming to mutually understand what others believe and intend, and to discern the sources of their motivation, that is, to come to mutually understand what others mean. I suggest that beyond the narrative tradition, and thanks in large part to the influence of Clifford Geertz, some version of this view of mutual meaningful understanding is prevalent within the discipline even if only implicitly.

Finally I should add that in some ways the argument I will make in this chapter is similar to what Michael Lambek calls ordinary ethics and his explication of this ethics in relation to what linguists call ordinary language (Lambek 2010a: 2). Drawing from theories of ordinary language influenced by the likes of Austin and Wittgenstein, Lambek argues that ethics is an action much in the sense that speaking is also an act. That is, neither is grounded in abstract principles or rules, belief or meaning, and both are done largely nonconsciously. Just as one is able to speak "intuitively," without reference or reflection on how to do so, Lambek argues, ethics is similarly grounded in the very ways in which we speak, interact with, and are with others. As Wittgenstein argued that criteria is largely a matter of public agreement and therefore rarely needs to be publicly enunciated, so too for Lambek ethics is a matter of such agreement and "naturally" internal to a particular form of life (2010b: 43–44).

The relationship between language and morality that I am arguing for in this essay, however, differs in large part on this last issue of criteria. It seems to me that the significance of the ordinary language perspective is that such criteria are for the most part nonconsciously enacted and, therefore, remain largely in the background of everyday life. Although Lambek is certainly attracted to this and it appears to be the basis for drawing a parallel between ordinary language and ordinary ethics, if I read him correctly, he appears to slip away from this position when he writes that at least a part of ethics, what he calls practice, is "understood as the ongoing exercise of judgment" (2010b: 63). Unless this "ongoing exercise of judgment" is exercised nonconsciously – which I suppose it could be but then we should be told that – then Lambek loses the theoretically most significant aspect of the ordinary language approach. If ethics is, at least partly, about ongoing judgments, then it shifts from a largely nonconscious and embodied practice, which I take is what Lambek is mostly arguing for, to a fully aware evaluator of how acts measure against criteria. In this way Lambek, while arguing against just the kind of rationalistic/mentalistic/mind-based approach that lingers in much of anthropology despite claims otherwise, appears to fall back to such a position.

This is perhaps foreshadowed in his translation of Aristotle's notion of *phronesis* as "practical judgment" (Lambek 2010b: 62). But the more common translation as "practical wisdom," while also overly emphasizing the self-aware reflection aspect of *phronesis*, is a bit closer to Aristotle's argument, which is that the virtuous person, the person of practical wisdom, need not consciously make judgments, for she has already fully embodied them in such a way that actions are simply done rightly. To speak of judgments here, as in ordinary language theory, is perhaps misplaced. The point I am trying to make is that while I agree with Lambek that language is essential to morally being-in-the-world, and is so because of the very capacity of having and using language, we differ to a great extent as to what this capacity is. For Lambek, influenced largely by analytic philosophy of language, language is key because it is where criteria are embedded. For me – influenced largely by continental philosophy and always intrigued by Wittgenstein, Davidson, and other analytics who speak to this tradition – language is not a carrier of criteria, but a bridge of being, a means of connecting with others, a way of showing that one is here, now, with the other. In other words, language is not the grounds of criteria, as if a hidden rulebook, but instead the very ground of human existence, the auditory expression that communicates the fact that "I am here with you now," regardless of what might actually be said.

Ultimately, then, in this essay I will argue that narratives reveal the primacy of morally being-in-the-world in an embodied intersubjective manner, rather than as a matter of shared meaningful understandings. This perspective on narrative suggests that words and utterances need not always, or even primarily, act to convey meaningful propositions or representations, but instead are better understood as a means by which individuals attempt to intersubjectively live in and live through their world together. That is to say, I will argue that words and utterances are first and foremost an existential ground for being-in-the-world with others (see Jackson 2002: 15–16).

I do not want to be misunderstood. There is no doubt that at times the articulation of narratives act as a process of meaning-making and that part of this process is the attempt by the speaker to achieve some form of mutual understanding with her interlocutors. But I would argue that this is most common in moments when narratives are elicited or other kinds of verbal interactions framed by a desire of rhetorical persuasion or quasi-rational explication. I would contend, however, that most *morally* intersubjective engagements are not best characterized in these ways. Rather, such engagements are perhaps best described as embodied struggles to "deal" with the various questions, dilemmas, and obstacles encountered in moments of moral breakdown and not as a process of finding or making or even remaking meaning. Rather, this may be better understood as a process of ethically working to once again live sanely (Asad 2003: 73) or feel comfortable in the new form of life into which she has been thrown (Zigon 2011). Because such breakdowns commonly happen to a person unexpectedly, this is an imposed ethical process that necessitates finding ways to once again be with oneself and others. These are more moments of risk, anxiety, and hope than moments of meaning and understanding. This necessitates not only struggling and coming to control and deal with – to some extent – the dilemma one now confronts, but in fact to come to inhabit a new, embodied way of being in which such struggles and dilemmas no longer – or less often – arise. Understanding and meaning may eventually be derived *after* one has finally, and once again, found a way to comfortably be in the world, and narrative may at times be a vital means for deriving this self-reflection, but, I contend, these are neither the aim nor the most significant outcome of such an ethical process.

Understanding as Charitable Living Through

There is a Russian phrase I have always thought interesting not so much for what it says but for when it is used: "to kill with a word" (*ubit' slovom*). The most common explanation of it is that one can "kill" another with words of disrespect, offense, and insult. But when is it used? Or, more appropriately, what situations can it be used to describe? Normally the term describes a situation in which an individual, and most usually a stranger or someone who is not very close, makes little attempt to engage in what Russians would call "normal relations" with the one who is "killed." One of my interlocutors simply put it like this: "A word can have the same power as a physical act." But in what way is this true? How can we conceive of words as having the same moral value for maintaining social relations as physical acts? This is the question that will guide me through the rest of this essay. To do so I will consider how both the ideal of mutual understanding and its failure to be manifested in social relations was evoked in various narrative articulations of my Muscovite interlocutors. In doing so, I will raise serious questions about commonly held anthropological views of understanding, agreement, and shared forms of life.

Recently Cheryl Mattingly (2010) has addressed the centrality of misunderstanding in intersubjective relations. Drawing from both Aristotle's observation that because each situation is to some extent unique, pre-understandings must by necessity be misunderstandings, and Schleiermacher's claim that understanding entails misunderstanding, she recognizes that an "ongoing confrontation with *misunderstanding* is an essential aspect of practical know-how" (Mattingly 2010: 121–122; emphasis original). In her ethnographic engagement with this observation, Mattingly focuses on those moments she calls the "borderland," or a moment of conflict or friction between "familiar strangers," that highlight such misunderstanding. But misunderstanding does not only come to the fore in such border moments between individuals who are strangers, for misunderstanding can also be central to very intimate relations between individuals who are the closest of friends. My first example will show just this. What follows is a narrative interaction I had with two of my Muscovite interlocutors during research on moral experience in a post-Soviet global city.[2] This narrative is central to the point I hope to make in this essay because, although it begins as an elicited ideal portrait of moral relations and mutual understanding between friends in response to my interview question, it ends by revealing the centrality of misunderstanding to the maintenance of this friendship, when the narrative interaction reaches a moment of breakdown as my two interlocutors work through a dilemma. This narrative, then, is particularly important because it raises serious concerns over the dual assumption that narratives, words, and utterances reveal or facilitate mutual meaningful understanding and that intersubjective relations ultimately rely on some form of such understanding.

Olya and Larisa, in their late twenties, are best friends who met at university. Both were born, raised, and at the time of this narrative interaction lived in Moscow. Interestingly, they maintain their friendship despite holding very different worldviews. The most striking difference is in terms of religion – Olya is a dedicated member of the Orthodox Church and Larisa is not. These differences, however, do not negatively affect the friendship. We could say that Olya and Larisa have agreed, whether explicitly or tacitly, to disregard the differences. Yet, when they talk about their relationship they often do so in terms of a mutual understanding. That is to say, each claims to understand the other in all her difference. This raises the question, however, of what they mean by understanding – how it is achieved and what it allows not only in terms of evaluating difference, but more importantly in terms of acknowledging difference.

This issue arose once during a conversation we had in a cafe in central Moscow about various themes that had repeatedly come up in my research. One such theme was friendship and understanding. Olya and Larisa agreed that they have higher expectations of their friends or other people with whom they are close, for example family members like Olya's brother, than of strangers. These expectations tend to center around, on the one hand, the predictability of behavior and, on the other hand, a small probability for transgression, especially transgression toward "me as friend." Both of these expectations were widely communicated to me by my other interlocutors.

But what I find more interesting is the second expectation, that transgression among friends will be few and far between. Many of my interlocutors agreed that there is a deep-seated trust between friends – it is expected that, no matter what, a friend will not "hurt" or betray me. This is, after all, what a friend is. The expectations that a friend will not transgress or betray one, and that a friend's behavior is predictable, are founded on the assumption that friends know or understand one another in the most intimate and profound way. As one of my interlocutors put it, "with close friends it is somewhat different, meaning that you can expect to relax with them, you don't need to worry about anything with them, you can open up to them and say anything, and you can open up so they can look into your soul." This openness allows for both the ideal notion of mutual understanding as well as the low expectation of transgression. But is this always the case? Let's look at the conversation I had with Olya and Larisa and see how the conversation turns to the ways in which friends actually can and do transgress against one another. When I asked if they felt like they could "get away with more with friends than with strangers," this is what they told me:

LARISA: Yes, certainly.
JARRETT: Why? Can you give an example?
OLYA: For example I can be late to meet a friend and …
LARISA: Yes, do you know that Olya was 30 minutes late today because she was doing her hair?
OLYA: Yes, and she is very good, her heart is very good – she will never kill me for this! But with a stranger of course I will do my best not to be late.
LARISA: That is what I'm always irritated about, people always think this is my friend and he will put up with this, but this is a stranger, I must not treat him badly. I think friends require more attention than strangers, of course. But as for moral boundaries, I'm more open with friends … With friends we can be nastier, and so on.
JARRETT: And why can you be nastier with your friends?
LARISA: Because I know for sure that my friends accept me for who I am with all my faults, deficiencies, and bad qualities.
JARRETT: Could you give an example of nasty and bad?
OLYA: If I'm interested in something I could ask Larisa about it. And if she doesn't reply I can ask her about it again the next time we speak. But, for example, if I ask another person and she doesn't answer, I will not ask it again because I understand that she doesn't want to reply. Things are different, though, if it is with a close friend – I will ask her every time until she answers me. I will get what I want no matter the cost!
LARISA: About my bad behavior with friends, I don't know, some minor offenses such as forgetting birthdays or sometimes I can be very blunt.
JARRETT: What do you say when you are blunt?
LARISA: Oh, for example, today I told Olya when she wanted to tell me a story that I wasn't interested in it. I became ashamed about me saying this at the very moment I said it.

We can see here that despite the initial claim of a low expectation of friends transgressing against one another, a shift has occurred in that both now admit that they feel they have looser boundaries in terms of what they can and cannot do with friends. The question should be raised here: is this a matter of transgression or simply that friendship allows for a broader conception of moral boundaries? That is, are there different moral bounds between friends than between strangers? The answer seems to be that there are indeed different bounds or expectations between friends with strangers and that with friends they are broader, that is, less strict. With a friend, more is allowed. If this is so, how does one know where these bounds are, and why do friends let each other broaden these limits? Here we come to the climax of the conversation. I asked Olya what her response to Larisa was:

OLYA: I just understood her because of course she wouldn't be very interested in what I had to tell her. I understand her and I just said never mind.
JARRETT: How did you understand her?
OLYA: I know that I had already talked a lot about this subject and she doesn't need to know more. She spent a lot of time with me and V. [an exchange student from France] going to the park and to different places and maybe she is bored …

LARISA: [interjecting while quickly leaning forward in her chair toward Olya]: No, I'm not!
OLYA: … of this person and doesn't want to hear more about it.

By this point the narrative conversation has shifted to a moment of moral breakdown in that it is no longer about responding to elicited questions per se but rather narrative attempts by Olya and Larisa to overcome a dilemma that has arisen in their embodied capacities to be together. Olya claims not to be morally offended by Larisa's transgression because she claims to *understand* why Larisa would act the way she did. But Larisa disagrees and adamantly interjects "No," exclaiming that this is not the reason she had not wanted to hear the story. After finishing her sentence that Larisa had responded to with such a bodily rejection, Olya shifts the conversation to another topic.

Here we see that Larisa's "No" not only denies the validity of Olya's claim to understand why Larisa acted the way she did, but also sufficiently puts an end to any possibility of coming to a mutual understanding of the slight, if not mundane, transgression. What are we left with in considering Olya's claim to understand Larisa's act? After a closer look at these last utterances it becomes clear that Olya is in fact using the notion of understanding (*ponimanie*) in two different ways. In the first utterance, which is a response to my question of how she responded to Larisa, Olya seems to be making a more general claim of understanding Larisa as a person and how she might generally act in such situations (this was confirmed by both of them in a later discussion we had about this interaction). This is suggested in her use of "of course," which appears to refer to a more general characteristic of Larisa rather than to the particular situation under discussion. This interpretation is supported by Olya's earlier claim that she knows the "character traits" of her friends very well and that because of this she knows what to expect from them. In this case, because she knows Larisa very well, because of the years of friendship and the understanding established between them, Olya understands that "of course" Larisa would not be interested in this particular topic.

But in the course of the interview I misread Olya's claim to understand Larisa at this more general level and instead asked her how she understood Larisa's particular action in the situation. It is only after my situational misinterpretation of Olya's words that she attempts to hypothesize why Larisa acted as she did. It is this attempt that Larisa disagrees with in her adamant "No." And Larisa may be right in her response that Olya has misunderstood her reason for acting as she did. But that is not the point Olya was originally trying to make when she spoke of understanding Larisa, and it is perhaps for this reason that Olya changes the topic of conversation. For she does not consider it important enough to continue to discover or to know the *exact reason* why Larisa acted as she did in the moment, since at the more general level Olya already understands Larisa well enough *as a person* to not even count her actions as a transgression despite Larisa having felt badly about it.

So what are we left with in considering the notion of mutual understanding? The answer to this depends on how we consider the concept of understanding. If we consider it in the sense that it is normally utilized in anthropological analyses, and particularly those focused on narrative and the mutual understandability of meaning such narratives are said to reveal, then we must conclude that there is no understanding in this sense. Indeed, it could even be said that there is a false understanding. Once I push Olya to articulate her understanding of what particular reason in this instance led Larisa to this slight transgression – I did this, of course, because I made that very common anthropological assumption about understanding – Larisa in fact reports that this is a false understanding and therefore not the particular reason for her transgressive act. But this matters little to Olya, for in fact it is not this kind of meaning-laden sense of understanding that matters in her relations with Larisa. It is for this reason, I suggest, that Olya shifts the conversation at this point. For what is important for Olya is not a mutual understanding of meaningful reasons for acting, but rather an embodied understanding of Larisa and the kind of person she is – an embodied understanding of Larisa as a person who can at times act in this way. It is this kind of understanding, which is not an understanding of meaning as intention, motivation, or belief, but rather an attuned disposition toward Larisa as a singular and unique person, that allows Olya to accept that this is simply how Larisa *can* be. Their friendship, then, is based on a mutual embodied acceptance of one another spoken of as understanding.

And perhaps acceptance is a more precise way to speak of what Olya and Larisa are doing. For intersubjectivity, which I take to be the existential foundation for all possible sociality, neither necessitates nor necessarily leads to mutual meaningful understanding, but is perhaps better understood as the capacity for being able to be together (Jackson 1998: 4; Duranti 2010). Mutuality in this sense might be better understood as similar to Gadamer's notion of a fusion of horizons through which agreement or acceptance becomes possible without sharedness (2004: 305). It is in this way that we can best understand Olya and Larisa's articulation of understanding as the basis of their friendship. For, over time, Olya and Larisa have come to acquire embodied dispositions specifically attuned toward one another that allow them to accept each other along with their respective faults and in so doing to be able to be together as friends. It is this process of an intersubjective and embodied, rather than a logical or propositional, negotiation of reattuning their dispositional way of being-with one another that Olya and Larisa describe in their narrative articulation, and it is only after the assuming anthropologist leads the conversation in the wrong direction that this negotiation breaks down.

While this may be the case between such good friends as Olya and Larisa, what of those individuals Mattingly focuses on who are not as close or who are strangers? If we accept the view of moral intersubjectivity I have so far outlined even between these latter, then this would leave us with a very different view of both social and moral relationships. It would leave us with the fluidity of normal social and moral relations based not on mutual meaningful understanding, but on enacted attempts to reattune embodied dispositions so as to allow individuals to live-through-the-moment-together-safely and to return once again to comfortably being-in-the-world-together. The point I am trying to make is that perhaps what is most central to moral and social relations is not meaningful understanding, but comfortably being-with-others in an embodied way despite the lack of such understanding. This would suggest that an anthropology of moralities would be more concerned with emphasizing something like the ethical process of anxiety reduction over that of meaning-making.

Such a view was articulated to me by Zhenia, a 30-year-old writer living in Moscow and an active member of a harm-reduction organization for drug users. The following is how Zhenia described her expectations of and interactions with strangers or individuals whom she does not know well:

ZHENIA: Understanding and listening to each other. Very often people don't understand each other because they have different views, but at least they need to be able to listen to each other. You know there is a saying that we should be able to listen to other people's opinions. That doesn't mean that you necessarily have to understand it, but you have to listen to it … It is more about listening to people, not so much understanding … If I don't know anything about the other person before we met, I don't know what he has done and what he thinks. And he sees me for the first time and he doesn't know what my experiences are either. Obviously none of us know what the starting point will be for our relationship. It is easy for me to start with something that is not very important. So far as we stick to these things it will be ok. But I always try to control the interaction so as to see when the aggression will begin … most people have their own principles and most people will not take my principles as their own. Of course those who are close to me will accept my principles as my own, but I don't expect them to take them as their own. So I would begin by trying to find out what the other person's principles are and try to realize them for myself. If his point of view is unpleasant, I will probably try to avoid contact with him. But if the situation is that I have to communicate with him, then I will try to find something in his principles that is neutral from which we begin, or even something positive since every coin has two sides. And at the same time I would try to softly present my views.

JARRETT: And try to convince the other person?

ZHENIA: No, I would try to *survive* with that person if I have to communicate with him, and in a way that would not cause aggression. Because if we understand initially that we hold contradictory or opposite views, then that means we have to remain on neutral terms.

For Zhenia, then, interactions with others can be a matter of, as she puts it, survival. The word Zhenia used was *vyzhit'*, which means to survive but can also be translated as "to live through" or "to pull through." It is on this latter sense of "to live through" that I would like to focus my attention. When Zhenia interacts with those she does not know and with whom she does not share what she calls principles, she considers the goal to be not mutual understanding but living through the situation. How does she do this? As she puts it, when the ideal notion of mutual understanding is not possible, all that is left is to listen. To listen is not to understand; to listen is not to agree with the other; to listen is not to attempt to convince the other of one's own principles. To listen, however, *is* to accept that difference exists and that its insurmountability should not hinder the social and human need to live-through-the-moment-at-hand.

To listen to the other is not to accept her view or principles, but rather to allow for the negotiation through the moment of difficulty. To speak here of negotiation is to use its double meaning. First, in terms of negotiating agreement, is agreement on how to live through mutually, even if such agreement constitutes a lack of shared understanding or, for that matter, no attempt at such understanding at all (see Duranti 2010: 21). This, then, is agreement on how *to be* together and not on how to have meaning together. Second, negotiation is in terms of negotiating one's movement through difficult terrain, that is, negotiating the situation tactfully so as to move on. These two senses of negotiation suggest that a moment of moral breakdown is not a set context in which a certain mode of argumentation, set of values, or even narrative genres can always be applied. Rather, they suggest that the moment of moral breakdown faced by two or more individuals is worked through together in a similar way to what some linguistic anthropologists have called "contextualization." These anthropologists "argue that communicative contexts are not dictated by the social and physical environment but emerge in negotiations between participants in social interaction … Contextualization involves an active process of negotiation in which participants reflexively examine the discourse as it is emerging, embedding assessments of its structure and significance in the speech itself" (Bauman and Briggs 1990: 68–69). In other words, through the negotiation process, a significant part of which is listening, the participants in the moment of moral breakdown contextualize the situation, that is, make it a manageable moment, so that they can move through it together better. John Gumperz (1992) has shown this to be a delicate process that does not always lead to mutual understanding but remains, nevertheless, an important aspect of moments of contention and ethical dilemmas. Similarly, I suggest that the contextualization process of negotiating agreement to move through together the moment of moral breakdown, or to "keep going," is a common practice utilized by individuals to leave behind this moment and return safely to the unreflective state of being in the world (Zigon 2007).

When these two meanings of negotiation are brought together in the way just suggested, it is what some of my interlocutors meant by respect. For example, Anna, a poet in her late twenties, told me the following:

> ANNA: Respect is not to try to destroy everything that you do not like; because all people are different, you are like this, he likes that, but you cannot destroy that which you don't like.
>
> JARRETT: Can you give me an example of when you exercise respect with someone?
>
> ANNA: I think every day we do this because life cannot be the way that you desire, but you should always remember to respect others.

Here Anna makes the point explicitly. To respect another is to acknowledge that she is other than oneself and therefore has another perspective, point of view, and perhaps a different set of values from oneself. To respect another is not to destroy or to disregard the other as other. But then the question must be asked: if we respect the other enough to allow her to stand opposed to us in all her difference, and if this standing opposed often leads to the inability to reach mutual understanding, then how do individuals manage to live through safely together or to move on through together the situation that presents itself as a moment of moral breakdown?

This question was answered for me by Anna: "Sometimes it's just impossible to reach mutual understanding, because no matter what happens sometimes people remain with their own ideas. The only thing left to do is to just accept this and go on, either that or separate for good." Since sometimes "separating for good" is not an option, the only thing left to do is to "accept this [difference] and go on." The moment of the breakdown is often a moment that *must* be lived through together. It is a moment that necessitates agreement, agreement not *in* understanding, but agreement to move on even if with a lack of meaningful understanding. That is to say, to agree does not necessitate sharing anything other than the desire to live through safely together the moment at hand.

And it is here, I suggest, that the phenomenological tradition provides an important starting point for both narrative analysis and an anthropology of moralities. For as

Alessandro Duranti (2010) has pointed out, one of phenomenology's central concepts, that is, intersubjectivity in its original Husserlian sense, neither necessitates nor entails mutual meaningful understanding. I agree entirely with Duranti's assessment and read much of the phenomenological tradition as an attempt to move away from concerns with meaning as the basis of sociality. Based on this reading, then, a phenomenological approach to morality would consider intersubjective moral relations in terms of an embodied desire to live through safely a moment of moral breakdown, or to "keep going," and once again return to comfortably or sanely being in one's social world. Thus, morality necessitates neither shared meanings nor mutual understanding; nevertheless, in this ethical process it may very well help to assume or to claim that such understanding has in fact been reached, for when interacting with those who are not as close as Larisa is with Olya, an adamant "No" is unlikely to help either person live through safely together.

If this is the case, then the claimed understanding most likely to occur in such breakdowns would be similar to what Donald Davidson (1984) calls radical interpretation and charity. By this Davidson means that in listening to others speak we must charitably assume two things: (1) that the speaker holds to be true what it is she says; and (2) that the speaker does indeed believe and mean by the words she uses what I the listener mean and believe by those same words. Thus, to charitably understand and live with another is not necessarily to share meaning with others, but to assume that one can live with others despite any uncertainty that such sharedness exists. Only in this radical attitude of charity can we legitimately claim that as conversants, or as a community of speakers, we understand one another when we make utterances. This includes utterances that are made up of such words as, for example, "morality," "good," or "right." This is so because we can never know for sure that we share meanings, concepts, beliefs, or intentions with others. Similarly, from a phenomenological perspective we can never assume that we can read others' minds, nor, as Duranti has pointed out, would this be necessary for intersubjectively being-in-the-world with others (2010: 20). Rather, in intersubjective relations with those who are not as close to us as Olya and Larisa are to one another, and toward whom we do not already have a previously attuned embodied disposition, the best we can do is to have a properly attuned *attitude* of charity to those with whom we engage. At times such an attitude may lead to mutual meaningful understanding, but this is not necessary for working through breakdowns and returning to the everydayness of morally being in the world together. What is necessary, however, is charitably living through the moral breakdown with the other, one aspect of which may be to listen and respect in the ways that Zhenia and Anna suggested. It is this attitude of charity, then, and not mutual meaningful understanding that for the most part allows us to morally be together.[3]

Davidson's work encourages us to second-guess our anthropological assumptions about the sharedness of the social world and allows us to consider how it is that the individuals with whom I spoke are able, in certain moments, to charitably agree to "understand" the other even when such understanding is reportedly not accomplished. Sharedness, then, would not be a matter of mutually held meaningful propositions or representations, but rather the charitable ability to comfortably be together in the world despite difference (see Wikan 1992). Indeed this notion of charity not only would hold in those moments of breakdown or interaction with strangers or those with whom we are not very close, but is also a way in which we could describe the attuned embodied understanding that individuals such as Olya and Larisa have with one another. It should further be noted that this view of intersubjective morality and its related ethical processes does not fall into the dangers of solipsism, for solipsism is a danger only when the starting assumption is that sociality and the primary way in which individuals share a social world is through meaningful propositions and representations. But when this assumption is set aside, a space for conceiving of sociality as described in this essay begins to open, that is, a sociality in which, for example, acts, gestures, emotions, words, and utterances are not only or primarily mediums of meaning but rather enter into the world as bridges of being serving not to collapse difference into unity but to connect difference by means of their very enactment.

Conclusion

My point in this essay is simply this: in speaking and listening to the other, Zhenia and my other Muscovite interlocutors participate in an ethical moment that does not necessarily lead to mutual meaningful understanding, but instead is best conceived as an ethical attempt to charitably be together comfortably in the world and to live through safely together the moment of moral breakdown. Without this possibility individuals are left with the ability to either turn away from one another – and in so doing destroy the possibility of any *mutual* return to the unreflective state of social being – or to injure one another – and in so doing risk the possibility that one or none of the participants will ever again return to that state of unreflective social being. Thus, conversation, which includes narrative interactions, as both speaking and listening can, echoing Heidegger, "support our existence" (1949: 278). Because we can never look into or read another's mind, the speaking and listening of conversation is indeed an ontological-moral necessity, for it allows for those moments of "feeling as one" that Vincent Crapanzano (2006) beautifully describes as characteristic of that intersubjective modality he calls "the scene," and Olya and Larisa might call "understanding." And yet, as I have been trying to make clear throughout this essay, even when engaged in such morally necessary conversation, individuals do not always reach mutual meaningful understanding, even when, as sometimes occurs, they believe and say they have done so.

NOTES

1 It should be noted that Mattingly would say that this ordering does not necessarily result in coherence (personal communication, Apr. 26, 2011). While this may be true, I would argue that in many everyday interactions it is in fact one of the goals of narrating.

2 I have analyzed this narrative interaction elsewhere in a slightly different manner (Zigon 2010).

3 Much of what I am arguing for in this essay is very similar to some of the key concepts of ethnomethodology and conversation analysis. Due to constraints of space, however, I am unable to address such concepts as repair, the "as if," and the et cetera principle. For further reading see, for example, Garfinkel 1967 and Sacks et al. 1974. For a recent example of conversation analysis in the anthropology of moralities, see Sidnell 2010. I would like to thank Elinor Ochs for pointing this out to me.

REFERENCES

Asad, Talal (2003) *Formations of the Secular: Christianity, Islam, Modernity.* Stanford: Stanford University Press.

Badiou, Alain (2001) *Ethics.* London: Verso.

Bauman, Richard and Briggs, Charles L. (1990) Poetics and Performance as Critical Perspectives on Language and Social Life. *Annual Review of Anthropology* 19: 59–88.

Bruner, Jerome (1990) *Acts of Meaning.* Cambridge, MA: Harvard University Press.

Cole, Jennifer (2003) Narratives and Moral Projects: Generational Memories of the Malagasy 1947 Rebellion. *Ethos* 31(1): 95–126.

Crapanzano, Vincent (2006) The Scene. *Anthropological Theory* 6(4): 387–405.

Davidson, Donald (1984) *Inquiries into Truth and Interpretation.* Oxford: Clarendon.

Desjarlais, Robert (2003) *Sensory Biographies: Lives and Deaths among Nepal's Yolmo Buddhists.* Berkeley: University of California Press.

Desjarlais, Robert (2011) Attendant Rhythms: An Ethics of Mourning and Consolation among Nepal's Yolmo Buddhists. Paper presented at the Biennial Meeting of the Society of Psychological Anthropology, Santa Monica, Apr. 1.

Duranti, Alessandro (2010) Husserl, Intersubjectivity and Anthropology. *Anthropological Theory* 10(1–2): 16–35.

Faubion, James D. (2001) *The Shadows and Lights of Waco: Millennialism Today.* Princeton: Princeton University Press.

Gadamer, Hans Georg (2004) *Truth and Method.* London: Continuum.

Garfinkel, Harold (1967) *Studies in Ethnomethodology.* Englewood Cliffs, NJ: Prentice Hall.

Gumperz, John J. (1992) Contextualization and Understanding. In Alessandro Duranti and Charles Goodwin (eds.), *Rethinking Context: Language as an Interactive Phenomenon.* Cambridge: Cambridge University Press, pp. 229–252.

Heidegger, Martin (1949) Hölderlin and the Essence of Poetry. In *Existence and Being.* Chicago: Henry Regnery, pp. 270–291.

Jackson, Michael (1998) *Minima Ethnographica: Intersubjectivity and the Anthropological Project.* Chicago: University of Chicago Press.

Jackson, Michael (2002) *The Politics of Storytelling: Violence, Transgression and Intersubjectivity.* Copenhagen: Museum Tusculanum.

Kleinman, Arthur (2006) *What Really Matters: Living a Moral Life amidst Uncertainty and Danger.* Oxford: Oxford University Press.

Ladwig, Patrice (2009 Narrative Ethics: The Excess of Giving and Moral Ambiguity in the Lao Vessantara-Jataka. In Monica Heintz (ed.), *The Anthropology of Moralities.* New York: Berghahn, pp. 136–160.

Lambek, Michael (2010a) Introduction. In Michael Lambek (ed.), *Ordinary Ethics: Anthropology, Language, and Action.* New York: Fordham University Press, pp. 1–36.

Lambek, Michael (2010b) Toward an Ethics of the Act. In Michael Lambek (ed.), *Ordinary Ethics: Anthropology, Language, and Action.* New York: Fordham University Press, pp. 39–63.

MacIntyre, Alasdair (1981) *After Virtue: A Study in Moral Theory.* Notre Dame, IN: University of Notre Dame Press.

Mattingly, Cheryl (1998a) *Healing Dramas and Clinical Plots: The Narrative Structure of Experience.* Cambridge: Cambridge University Press.

Mattingly, Cheryl (1998b) In Search of the Good: Narrative Reasoning in Clinical Practice. *Medical Anthropology Quarterly* 12(3): 273–297.

Mattingly, Cheryl (2010) *The Paradox of Hope: Journeys through a Clinical Borderland.* Berkeley: University of California Press.

Mattingly, Cheryl and Garro, Linda C. (eds.) (2000) *Narrative and the Cultural Construction of Illness and Healing.* Berkeley: University of California Press.

Mattingly, Cheryl, Jensen, Uffe Juul, and Throop, C. Jason (2009) Narrative, Self and Social Practice. In Cheryl Mattingly and Uffe Juul Jensen (eds.), *Narrative, Self and Social Practice*. Aarhus: Philosophia, pp. 5–36.

Ochs, Elinor and Capps, Lisa (2001) *Living Narrative: Creating Lives in Everyday Storytelling*. Cambridge, MA: Harvard University Press.

Parish, Steven M. (1991) The Sacred Mind: Newar Cultural Representations of Mental Life and the Production of Moral Consciousness. *Ethos* 19(3): 313–351.

Ricoeur, Paul (1983) *Time and Narrative*, vol. 1. Chicago: University of Chicago Press.

Ricoeur, Paul (1992) *Oneself as Another*. Chicago: University of Chicago Press.

Ries, Nancy (1997) *Russian Talk: Culture and Conversation during Perestroika*. Ithaca, NY: Cornell University Press.

Robbins, Joel (2007) Continuity Thinking and the Problem of Christian Culture: Belief, Time, and the Anthropology of Christianity. *Current Anthropology* 48(1): 5–38.

Sacks, Harvey, Schegloff, Emanuel A., and Jefferson, Gail (1974) A Simplest Systematics for the Organization of Turn-Taking for Conversation. *Language* 50: 696–735.

Sidnell, Jack (2010) The Ordinary Ethics of Everyday Talk. In Michael Lambek (ed.), *Ordinary Ethics: Anthropology, Language, and Action*. New York: Fordham University Press, pp. 123–139.

Speaks, Jeff (2010) Theories of Meaning. In Edward N. Zalta (ed.), *Stanford Encyclopedia of Philosophy* (Winter 2010 edn.). At http://plato.stanford.edu/archives/ win2010/entries/ meaning/, accessed Feb. 25, 2012.

Stewart, Kathleen (1996) *A Space on the Side of the Road: Cultural Poetics in an "Other" America*. Princeton: Princeton University Press.

Throop, C. Jason (2010a) Latitudes of Loss: On the Vicissitudes of Empathy. *American Ethnologist* 37(4): 771–782.

Throop, C. Jason (2010b) *Suffering and Sentiment: Exploring the Vicissitudes of Experience and Pain in Yap*. Berkeley: University of California Press.

Villenas, Sofia (2001) Latina Mothers and Small-Town Racisms: Creating Narratives of Dignity and Moral Education in North Carolina. *Anthropology and Education Quarterly* 31(1): 3–28.

Wikan, Unni (1992) Beyond the Words: The Power of Resonance. *American Ethnologist* 19(3): 460– 82.

Zigon, Jarrett (2007) Moral Breakdown and the Ethical Demand: A Theoretical Framework for an Anthropology of Moralities. *Anthropological Theory* 7(2): 131–150.

Zigon, Jarrett (2009) Morality and Personal Experience: The Moral Conceptions of a Muscovite Man. *Ethos* 37(1): 78–101.

Zigon, Jarrett (2010) *Making the New Post-Soviet Person: Moral Experience in Contemporary Moscow*. Leiden: Brill.

Zigon, Jarrett (2011) *HIV is God's Blessing: Rehabilitating Morality in Neoliberal Russia*. Berkeley: University of California Press.

PART III Localities

CHAPTER 13 Ethics and Piety

Saba Mahmood

There is a long philosophical tradition, at least since Aristotle, that draws a distinction between ethics and morality wherein the former is said to pertain to individual conduct and the latter to a system of collective rules, norms, and codes. The genealogy of this tradition is varied and contoured. Various philosophers and religious traditions have adopted this distinction while critiquing and discarding other aspects of the Aristotelian theory of ethics. Among contemporary philosophers who are heir to this distinction is Michel Foucault, particularly in his later work on ethics and technologies of the self. Like Aristotle, Foucault distinguishes ethical practices from "morals," reserving the latter to refer to sets of norms, rules, values, and injunctions. Not unlike Aristotle, for Foucault ethics is not so much a question of knowledge or meaning but has to do with modifications of the soul, feelings, faculties, and dispositions oriented toward the goal of living well – what Aristotle called *eudomenia* and what Foucault glossed as a state of happiness or truth (Martin, et al. 1988; Foucault 1990, 1997a, 1997b, 1997c; Davidson 1994; Rabinow 1997).

Unlike scholars writing in the tradition of "virtue ethics," Foucault's use of Aristotelian ethics is not aimed at asserting its universal validity or recuperating its various elements for solving contemporary moral problems – such as reclaiming the idea of telos or a collective notion of the good life (Foot 1978; Anscombe 1981; MacIntyre 1984; Taylor 1995; Lovibond 2002).[1] What Foucault retains is the Aristotelian emphasis on ethics as a set of practical activities[2] whose value resides not so much in what they mean but in what they do or achieve. Claire Colebrook aptly calls this a "positive conception of ethics" that extends the domain of ethics "beyond notions of norms, justification, legitimation, and meaning to include the consideration of the practices, selves, bodies, and desires that determine (and are codetermined by) ethics" (1998: 50).

Foucault was criticized by some scholars for casting Aristotle's conception of ethics as an individualistic enterprise freed from the grammar of authority, telos, and exemplarity

A Companion to Moral Anthropology, First Edition. Edited by Didier Fassin.

within which it was embedded. Pierre Hadot, the preeminent historian of ancient Greece whose work informed Foucault's own ruminations on the subject, argued:

> What I am afraid of is that by focusing his interpretation too exclusively on the culture of the self, the care of the self, and conversion toward the self – more generally by defining his ethical model as an aesthetics of existence – Foucault is propounding a culture of the self which is too aesthetic. In other words this may be a new form of Dandyism in late twentieth century style. (Hadot 1995: 211)

Others contend that, despite his focus on practices of the self, the subject of Foucault's analysis is not a voluntaristic, autonomous subject who fashions herself in a protean manner. Rather, the subject is formed within the limits of a historically specific set of practices and injunctions that are delimited in advance – what Foucault characterizes as "modes of subjectivation" (Butler 1997; Rose 1998; Butler and Connolly 2000). In other words, Foucault treats subjectivity not as a private space of self-cultivation, but as an effect of power operationalized through a set of moral codes that summon a subject to constitute herself in accordance with its precepts. For Foucault, ethics is therefore a modality of power that "permits individuals to effect by their own means or with the help of others, a certain number of operations on their own bodies and souls, thoughts, conduct, and way of being" in order to transform themselves into the willing subjects of a particular discourse (Foucault 1997c: 225).

In this essay I reflect on the relevance of this debate to the anthropology of religion and how its insights have been engaged and extended by the scholarship produced in the last two decades. In order to address this issue it is important first to reflect on how ethics, morality, and religion have been traditionally viewed in the discipline. Michael Lambek provides an influential account of this history in this volume (see Chapter 19). Notably, at the beginning of his essay Lambek states that he makes no distinction between ethics and morality – a position I suspect many anthropologists would share. In doing so, Lambek breaks not only with the Aristotelian tradition I have outlined above but also with a dominant view in post-Enlightenment philosophy that regards ethics as a systematic study of people's reasoning when they are said to act morally. In fact, philosophers in this tradition (such as A. J. Ayer) insist on making a hard distinction between systemic ethical reasoning and people's actions – with philosophical ethics firmly located in the former. On this view, insomuch as ethical philosophy is neutral in regard to people's actual conduct, it considers ethics to be a study of abstract reason, ideas, and principles (see MacIntyre 1966, esp. ch. 1). I suspect Lambek's indifference to the distinction between morality and ethics is a result of the recognition among anthropologists that moral systems are inherently multiplicitous, and the task of the ethnographer lies in faithfully describing this diversity and how the members of each moral system live by its codes. Anthropology's preoccupation with how people live the structures they inherit, in other words, might account for why anthropologists like Lambek avoid making a distinction between morality and ethics. It is worth pointing out that, despite these differences, Lambek shares the Aristotelian tradition's preoccupation with everyday ordinary conduct (rather than conceive of ethics as a system of abstract norms, ideas, and rules).

In what follows I would like to consider a different tradition within anthropology whose concerns are at times shared with the tradition Lambek describes and at times quite distinct from it. This tradition is indebted to Talal Asad's (1993) seminal critique of the modern concept of religion which has had an important impact in the human sciences. This critique is well known and I do not want to rehearse it here other than to give its most elementary features so as to return to the question I raised earlier: What is the significance of Foucault's rearticulation of Aristotelian ethics in contemporary debates in the anthropology of religion?

In a widely cited article, Asad critiqued a dominant conception of religion in anthropology – of which Clifford Geertz was the most influential proponent – as a system of beliefs in a set of propositions to which an individual gives assent. Asad argued that insomuch as this privatized and individualized concept of religion is rooted in a Protestant genealogy, it is inadequate not only for understanding premodern Christianity and other religious traditions but, more importantly, it obfuscates how secular modern power constructs religion as a distinct domain of action and belief, with a certain essence, which can be systematically compared across time, place, and societies. Asad's critique is distinct from that of Wilfred Cantwell Smith who argued that the modern concept of religion reifies belief at the expense of the phenomenological and lived experience of the divine or the transcendent (Smith 1991). Asad's argument is that universal definitions of religion assume an essential singularity – religion as faith, belief, transcendence, or experience – thereby diverting us from asking what a historically or culturally particular definition of religion includes and excludes, by whom, under what conditions, and for what purposes. Asad's argument, however, is not simply that religion is always historically particular – to do so would be to assume that there are a group of activities and assumptions across time and space that can be provisionally or comparatively termed "religion." Rather, Asad's most important intervention lies in arguing that "religion" itself is a modern concept – not so much because it reifies belief over experience (as Smith would have it) but because it is conceptually and practically tied to the emergence of "the secular" as a domain from which it is supposed to be normatively independent but to which it is indelibly linked. As a result, Asad argues that "religion has been part of the restructuration of practical times and spaces, a rearticulation of practical knowledges and powers, of subjective behaviors, sensibilities, needs, and expectations in modernity. But … [this] applies equally to secularism, whose function has been to try to guide that rearticulation and to define 'religions' in the plural as a species of (non-rational) belief" (2001: 221).

The impact of this critique has been variously absorbed within a variety of disciplines including anthropology. In my view, one of the most powerful aspects of Asad's work is the kind of questions it has opened up in the study of religion (and by extension secularism, ethics, and morality) for a generation of scholars. A cluster of these questions are focused around the concept of practice – practice understood not so much as an instantiation of an ideology or structure (Bourdieu 1977; Ortner 1984) but as a set of embodied capacities and dispositions that one acquires through labor in order to become the willing subject of a tradition. This framing forces us to think of religion as a discourse ensconced in a broader set of questions about how one becomes the subject of a certain tradition – one that might include a tradition in which belief is salient but extends to other traditions as well (whether religious or secular).

According to Asad, by defining religion as a matter of belief or faith, a tradition comes to be treated as "a cognitive framework, not as a practical mode of living, not as techniques for teaching the body and mind to cultivate specific virtues and abilities that have been authorized, passed on, and reformulated down the generations." By focusing on religion as experience or belief, Asad suggests, one often occludes the materiality of religious practices, that is religious traditions in terms of sounds, visual imagery, as "language uttered and inscribed (on paper, wood, stone, or film) or recorded in electronic media" or "as ways in which the body learns to paint and see, to sing and hear, and to dance and observe; as masters who can teach pupils how to do these things well; and as practitioners who can excel in what they have been taught (or fail to do so)" (Asad 2001: 216). In drawing attention to these elements, Asad's point is to emphasize how religious and secular experiences cannot be so easily separated in the modern world, given the shared set of material disciplinary practices through which they are mutually produced. For Asad, therefore, instead of considering "religion as faith that is essentially individual and otherworldly," anthropology has to account for "the ways in which 'indigenous psychologies' orient traditional practices in different religions at different times and in different places in order to examine some of the preconditions for religious experience and attitude – including [those identified] as faith." This implies that one should "abandon the idea of religion as always and essentially the same, and as dependent on faith that is independent of practical traditions because and to the extent that it is transcendental" (220). By treating religion as a matter of (belief in) transcendence, we fail to account for how religious and secular practices are mutually constitutive both at the practical level and at the level of political and state regulation in modern societies.

Despite Asad's emphasis on bodily practices, it is important to note that it differs from other phenomenological approaches to religion (e.g., Csordas 1994; Jackson 2009) in his insistence that the body be treated not so much as the substrate on which culture or religion inscribes its meaning but as the "developable means" through which one comes to acquire particular capacities to think, act, and feel in this world. In his emphasis on the intertwining of the religious and the secular, Asad's argument is also distinct from the school of "political theology" that, following the work of Carl Schmitt (2006), proposes that many modern political concepts (such as sovereignty) are secularized versions of earlier Christian ones. This way of thinking is problematic for Asad in that it presupposes a religious essence that is supposed to animate the past and the present in structurally analogous ways. Insomuch as there is no religious essence that cuts across history, Asad argues that modern secular power is unique in its continuous regulation of religious forms of knowledge and life through various technologies of governance, a regulation that transforms the normative, ideational, and epistemological basis of religious truth as well as its practices and experience. Given Asad's emphasis on the subject, embodied capacities, and pedagogy, it is not difficult to see the affinities between his work and Aristotelian and Foucauldian framings of ethics.

Religion and Subjectivity

In order to elaborate some of the themes discussed above, let me turn to my own ethnographic work with a women's piety movement in Cairo, Egypt. Between 1995 and 1997, I conducted fieldwork with an informally organized grassroots movement in which women from a variety of socioeconomic backgrounds provide lessons to each other focused on the teaching and studying of Islamic scriptures, social practices, and forms of bodily comportment considered germane to the cultivation of the ideal virtuous self (Mahmood 2005). The aim of the movement is to inculcate orthodox religious sensibilities among the participants as a means to counter what they describe as the "secularization" of Egyptian society which has reduced Islamic knowledge (both as a mode of conduct and as a set of principles) to an abstract system of beliefs that has no direct bearing on how one lives one's daily life. The women's piety movement seeks to educate ordinary Muslims in those virtues, ethical capacities, and forms of reasoning which the participants perceive to have become either unavailable or irrelevant to the lives of ordinary Muslims. Practically, this means instructing Muslims not only in the proper performance of religious duties and acts of worship but, more importantly, in how to organize their daily conduct in accord with principles of Islamic piety and virtuous behavior. An important feature of this movement is its focus on the minutiae of religious practices (rituals, rites, liturgies, pious behavior) as a necessary condition for the acquisition and expression of piety.

As I will elaborate below, the piety movement is often dismissed by liberal Muslims who regard such attention to Islamic rituals as a fetishization of these forms over the principles they are supposed to embody. This critique is indebted to a secular conception of religiosity that presupposes a distinction between a privatized interiority (the proper locus of belief) and a public exteriority (the expression of this belief). On this view, while rituals and bodily practices might represent belief they are not essential to its acquisition or expression. This understanding of Islam (often glossed as "liberal Islam") concords with the view of many scholars of religion who seek to establish an analytical distinction between the "true" nature of belief in divinity (abstract, universal, acontextual) and the fickle world of religious signs whose meanings are this-worldly and only contingently (but not necessarily) related to the abstractions they signify.[3]

In contrast to such an understanding of religion, the piety movement posits a very different relationship between outward bodily acts (rituals, liturgies, and worship) and inward belief (state of the soul). Not only are the two inseparable in their conception but, more importantly, belief does not precede (or is the cause of) these outward devotional practices but is the product of their apt performance. Why is this difference consequential? Because, far from being an ideational or intellectual stance, it affects the way people live and order their lives, their sense of self and personhood, their understanding of authority and its proper relationship to individual desires and capacities, and distinct conceptions of human flourishing. This topography of the self has profound consequences not only for religion but also for how politics is imagined and lived. As a result, battles between orthodox and liberal interpretations of Islam often enfold contrastive conceptions of the subject and politics – the importance of which is often overlooked by students of religion and politics alike.[4]

This scholarly treatment of rituals and rites in the analysis of religion may be traced back at least to Kant (1998), for whom morality proper was primarily a rational matter that entailed the exercise of the faculty of reason, shorn of the specific context (of social virtues, habit, character formation, and so on) in which the act unfolded. The Kantian legacy becomes particularly important in light of the Aristotelian tradition it displaced, in which ethics was both realized through, and manifest in, outward behavioral forms. Against this tradition, Kant argued that a moral act could be moral only to the extent that it was not a result of habituated practice but a product of the critical faculty of reason.[5] The latter requires that one act morally in spite of one's inclinations, habits, and disposition. Kant's telescoping of moral action to the movements of the will stands in contrast to the value ascribed to the particular form a moral act took in the Aristotelian worldview.[6] The question of motivation, deliberation, and choice in the Aristotelian tradition was important too, of course, but only from the standpoint of actual practices.

One consequence of the Kantian tradition is an overall demotion of the role of ethical practices in relation to the enactment of moral law. (For Kant, while "ethical gymnastics" might aid in taming appetites and inclinations, they should not serve as the basis of the exercise of moral reason.) This Kantian legacy continues to shape contemporary theorizations of embodiment and habitus. As Jeffrey Minson (1993: 31) points out, even a scholar like Bourdieu, whose work focuses on what he calls "the practical mnemonics" of a culture, considers them interesting only insofar as a rational evaluation reveals them to be the signs and symbols of a much deeper and more fundamental reality of social structures and cultural logics. I understand Minson to be saying that when Bourdieu analyzes the variety of practices that characterize a particular social group (such as their styles of eating, socializing, and entertainment), he is primarily concerned with how these practices embody and symbolize the *doxa* and ethos of the group such that the ideologies the members inhabit come to be congealed in their social or class habitus (see, for example, Bourdieu 1977, 1990). However, if we follow Foucault, it may be argued that the significance of an embodied practice is not exhausted by its ability to function as an index of social and class status or a group's ideological habitus. The specificity of a bodily practice is also interesting for the kind of relationship it presupposes to the act it constitutes wherein an analysis of the particular form that the body takes might transform our conceptual understanding of the act itself. Furthermore, bodily behavior does not simply stand in a relationship of significance to self and society, but it also endows the self with certain kinds of capacities that provide the substance from which the world is acted upon.

Interiority and Exteriority

Let me elaborate on this understanding of bodily practice through an ethnographic vignette from my work with the Egyptian piety movement. The women I worked with described the condition of piety as the quality of "being close to God": a manner of being and acting that suffuses all of one's acts, both religious and worldly in character. Although the consummation of a pious comportment entails a complex disciplinary program, at a fundamental level it requires that the individual perform those acts of worship made incumbent upon Muslims by God (*al-fara'id*),[7] as well as Islamic virtues (*fada'il*) and acts of beneficence that secure God's pleasure (*al-a'ma, al-saliha*). The attitude with which these acts are performed is as important as their prescribed form: sincerity (*al-ikhlas*), humility (*khushu'*), and feelings of virtuous fear and awe (*khashiya*, *taqwa*) are all emotions by which excellence and virtuosity in piety are measured and marked. Many of the mosque attendees noted that though they had always been aware of these basic Islamic duties, it was only through attending mosque lessons that they had acquired the necessary skills to perform them regularly and with diligence.

According to the participants of the piety movement, one of the minimal requirements critical to the formation of a virtuous Muslim is the act of praying five times a day. The performance of ritual prayer (sing. *salat*, pl. *salawat*) is considered to be so central in Islam that the question of whether someone who does not pray regularly qualifies as a Muslim has been a subject of intense debate among theologians. The correct execution of *salat* depends on the following elements: (1) an intention to dedicate the prayer to God; (2) a prescribed sequence of gestures and words; (3) a physical condition of purity; and (4) proper attire. While fulfilling these four conditions renders prayer acceptable (*maqbul*), I was told it is also desirable that *salat* be performed with all the feelings, concentration, and tenderness of the heart appropriate to the state of being in the presence of God – a state called *khushu'*.

While it is understandable that an ideal such as *khushu'* would have to be learned through intense devotion and training, it was surprising to me that the women pietists considered the desire to pray five times a day (with its minimal conditions of performance) an object of pedagogy. Many of the participants acknowledged that they did not pray diligently and seemed to lack the requisite will to accomplish what was required of them. They often held the general social and cultural ethos in which they lived to be responsible for the erosion of such a will, claiming that it fostered instead desires and aspirations that were quite inimical to the demands of piety. Because such states of will were not assumed to be natural by the teachers, or by their followers, women took extra care to teach one another the means by which the desire to pray could be cultivated and strengthened in the course of performing the sort of routine, mundane actions that occupied most women during the day.

The complicated relationship between the performance of *salat* and one's daily activities was revealed to me in a conversation that I observed among three women, all of whom I had come to regard as experienced in the cultivation of piety. My measure for coming to such a judgment was none other than the one used by the mosque participants: they not only carried out their religious duties (*al-fara'id*) diligently, but also attested to their faith (*iman*) by continuously doing good deeds (*al-a'mal al-saliha*)[8] and practicing virtues (*al-fada'il*). As the following exchange makes clear, these women pursued the process of honing and nurturing the desire to pray through the performance of seemingly unrelated deeds during the day (whether cooking, cleaning, or running an errand) until that desire became a part of their condition of being.

The setting for this conversation was a mosque in downtown Cairo, where their discussions sometimes attracted other women. In this instance, a young woman in her early twenties had been sitting and listening intently when she suddenly interrupted the discussion to ask a question about one of the five basic prayers required of Muslims, a prayer known as *al-fajr*. This prayer is performed right after dawn breaks, before sunrise. Many Muslims consider it the most demanding and difficult of prayers because it is hard to leave the comfort of sleep to wash and pray, and also because the period within which it must be performed is very short. This young woman expressed the difficulty she encountered in getting up for the morning prayer and asked the group what she should do about it.

Mona, a member of the group in her mid-thirties, turned to the young woman with a concerned expression on her face and asked, "Do you mean to say that you are unable to get up for the morning prayer habitually and consistently?" The young woman nodded yes. Bearing the same concerned expression on her face, Mona said, "You mean to say that you forbid yourself the reward [*sawab*] of the morning prayer? This surely is an indication of *ghafla* on your part?" The young woman looked somewhat perturbed and guilty, but persisted and asked, "What does *ghafla* mean?" Mona replied that it refers to what you do in the day: if your mind is mostly occupied with things that are not related to God, then you are in a state of *ghafla* (carelessness, negligence). According to Mona, such a condition of negligence results in an inability to say the morning prayer.

Looking puzzled, the young woman asked, "What do you mean what I do in the day? What does my saying of the prayer [*salat*] have to do with what I do in the day?" Mona answered:

> It means what your day-to-day deeds are. For example, what do you look at in the day? Do you look at things that are prohibited to us by God, such as immodest images of women and men? What do you say to people in the day? Do you insult people when you get angry and use abusive language? How do you feel when you see someone doing acts of disobedience [*m'asi*]? Do you get sad? Does it hurt you when you see someone committing a sin or does it not affect you? These are the things that have an effect on your heart, and they hinder or impede your ability to get up and say the morning prayer. [The constant] guarding against disobedience and sins wakes you up for the morning prayer. *Salat* is not just what you say with your mouth and what you do with your limbs. It is a state of your heart. So when you do things in a day for God and avoid other things because of Him, it means you're thinking about Him, and therefore it becomes easy for you to strive for Him against yourself and your desires. If you correct these issues, you will be able to rise up for the morning prayer as well.

Perhaps responding to the young woman's look of concentration, Mona asked her, "What is it that annoys you the most in your life?" The young woman answered that her sister fought with her a lot, and this bothered her and made her angry most days. Mona replied:

> You, for example, can think of God when your sister fights with you and not fight back with her because He commands us to control our anger and be patient. For if you do get angry, you know that you will just gather more sins [*dhunub*], but if you are quiet then you are beginning to organize your affairs on account of God and not in accord with your temperament. And then you will realize that your sister will lose the ability to make you angry, and you will become more desirous [*raghiba*] of God. You will begin to notice that if you say the morning prayer, it will also make your daily affairs easier, and if you don't pray it will make them hard.

Mona looked at the young woman, who had been listening attentively, and asked: "Do you get angry and upset when you don't say your morning prayer?" The young woman answered yes. Mona continued:

> But you don't get upset enough that you don't miss the next morning prayer. Performing the morning prayer should be like the things you can't live without: for when you don't

> eat, or you don't clean your house, you get the feeling that you must do this. It is this feeling I am talking about: there is something inside you that makes you want to pray and gets you up early in the morning to pray. And you're angry with yourself when you don't do this or fail to do this.

The young woman looked on and listened, not saying much. At this point, we moved back to our previous discussion, and she stayed with us until the end.

The answer Mona gave this young woman was not a customary answer, such as invoking the fear of God's retribution for habitually failing to perform one's daily prayers. Mona's response reflects the sophistication and elaboration of someone who has spent considerable time and effort familiarizing herself with an Islamic interpretive tradition of moral discipline. I would like to draw your attention here to the economy of discipline at work in Mona's advice to the young woman, particularly the ways in which ordinary tasks in daily life are made to attach to the performance of consummate worship. Notably, when Mona links the ability to pray to the vigilance with which one conducts the practical chores of daily living, all mundane activities – such as getting angry with one's sister, the things one hears and looks at, the way one speaks – become a place for securing and honing particular moral capacities. As is evident from the preceding discussion, the issue of punctuality clearly entails more than the simple use of an alarm clock; it encompasses an entire attitude one cultivates in order to create the desire to pray. Of significance is the fact that Mona does not assume that the desire to pray is natural, but that it must be created through a set of disciplinary acts. That is to say, desire in this model is not the antecedent to, or cause of, moral action, but its product.[9] The techniques through which pious desires are cultivated include practices such as avoiding seeing, hearing, or speaking about things that make faith (*iman*) weaker, and engaging in acts that strengthen the ability to enact obedience to God's will. The repeated practice of orienting all acts toward securing God's pleasure is a cumulative process, the net result of which is, on one level, the ability to pray regularly and, on another level, the creation of a pious self.

Mona's discussion of ritual prayer problematizes two longstanding distinctions anthropologists have made: between ritual and conventional behavior, and between the spontaneous expression of emotion and its theatrical performance (see Radcliffe-Brown 1964; Evans-Pritchard 1965; Turner 1969; Bloch 1975; Obeyesekere 1981; Tambiah 1985). Based on these two distinctions, anthropologists have suggested that ritual is a space of "conventional" and not "genuine" (that is, personal or individual) emotions (Bloch 1975; Kapferer 1979; Tambiah 1985).[10] Ritual, in these views, is either understood to be the space where individual psychic drives are channeled into conventional patterns of expression, or where they are temporarily suspended so that a conventional social script may be enacted. Common to both these positions is the understanding that ritual activity is where emotional spontaneity comes to be controlled.[11]

Notably, Mona's understanding of prayer belies the neat separation of spontaneous emotions from disciplined behavior which anthropologists have often taken for granted. A close examination of Mona's advice to the young woman reveals that the enactment of conventional gestures and behaviors devolves upon the spontaneous expression of well-rehearsed emotions and individual intentions, thereby directing attention to how one learns to express "spontaneously" the "right attitudes." For women like Mona, ritual (that is, conventional, formal action) is understood as the space par excellence for making their desires act spontaneously in accord with pious Islamic conventions.

Means and End

The piety movement's understanding of prayer may be usefully contrasted with another one espoused by many liberal Muslims for whom the proper aim of *salat* should be not so much the accrual of awards with God or pleasing him, but the cultivation of a modern critical consciousness that is able to serve the demands of a modern society and nation. They often criticize piety activists like Mona for fetishizing the act of *salat* over its ultimate meaning, treating such rituals as ends in themselves rather than as means of becoming a better person who can serve her country and community well. *Salat* in this conception is taken as a means of creating an enlightened citizenry – a project shared by the postcolonial Egyptian state which has made use of Islamic rituals to create a sense of national unity among the country's diverse population. Notably, for the state and other liberal-nationalist Muslims, the goal of creating modern autonomous citizens remains independent of the means they propose (Islamic rituals); indeed, various modern societies, it appears, have accomplished the same goal through other means. In other words, whereas rituals such as *salat* may be usefully enlisted for the project of creating a self-critical citizenry, they are not necessary but contingent acts in the process.

In contrast, for women like Mona, ritual acts of worship are the sole and ineluctable means of forming pious dispositions. A central aspect of ritual prayer, as captured in Mona's discussion above, is that it serves both as a means to pious conduct and as an end. In this logic, ritual prayer is an end in that Muslims believe God requires them to pray, and a means insofar as it transforms daily action, which in turn creates or reinforces the desire for worship. Thus, the desired goal (pious worship) is also one of the means by which that desire is cultivated and gradually made realizable. Moreover, in this worldview, neither consummate worship nor the acquisition of piety are possible without the performance of prayer in the prescribed (that is, codified) manner and attitude. As such, outward bodily gestures and acts (such as *salat* or wearing the veil) are indispensable aspects of the pious self in two senses: first, in the sense that the self can acquire its particular form only through the performance of the precise bodily enactments; and, second, in the sense that the prescribed bodily forms are necessary attributes of the self (see Mahmood 2001).

Notably, the debate about the role of prayer in contemporary Egypt mirrors the debate about the veil. While interpretations of the veil abound in Egyptian society, two main views prevail among its practitioners and its critics: one understands the veil to be a divine command; the other regards it as a symbolic marker, no different from other signifiers (religious and nonreligious) that represent a Muslim woman's identity. In my book *Politics of Piety* (Mahmood 2005), I analyze both these understandings of the veil as speech acts that perform very different kinds of work in the making of a religious subject: not unlike my analysis of prayer above, my argument is that to understand a bodily practice (such as veiling or praying) as a symbolic act presumes a different relationship between the subject's exteriority and interiority than that entailed by an understanding of a bodily act as both an expression of, and a means to, the realization of the subject.

The principle on which the pietists' conception of Islamic rituals is based might be usefully elaborated through Aristotle's conception of habitus and its model of ethical pedagogy, in which external performative behavior is understood to create corresponding inward dispositions.[12] Among a range of ancient Greek concepts adopted by early Christians as well as by Muslims is the Aristotelian formulation of habitus, which is concerned with ethical formation and presupposes a specific pedagogical process by which a moral character is secured.[13] In *Nicomachean Ethics*, Aristotle makes a distinction between intellectual and moral virtues, and it appears that the pedagogical principle of habitus pertains to the latter but not the former:

> Virtue, then, being of two kinds, intellectual and moral, intellectual virtue in the main owes both its birth and its growth to teaching (for which reason it requires experience and time), while moral virtue comes about as a result of habit, whence also its name *ethike* is one that is formed by a slight variation from the word ethos (habit). From this it is also plain that none of the moral virtues arise in you by nature; for nothing that exists by nature can form a habit contrary to nature … For the things we have to learn before we can do them, we learn by doing them, e.g. men become builders by building and lyre players by playing the lyre; so too we become just by doing just acts, temperate by doing temperate acts, brave by doing brave acts … By doing the acts we do in our transactions with other men we become just or unjust, and by doing the acts that we do in the presence of danger, and being habituated to feel fear or confidence, we become brave or cowardly. (Aristotle 1941: 592–593)

While a virtuous habitus is acquired through virtuous habits, the two are not to be confused because habitus – unlike habits – once acquired through assiduous practice, takes root in one's character and is considered largely unchangeable.[14] What is noteworthy is that habitus in this tradition of moral cultivation implies a quality that is acquired through human industry, assiduous practice, and discipline, such that it becomes a permanent feature of a person's character. In other words, "a habitus can be said to exist only when someone has actively formed it" (Nederman 1989–90: 96).[15] Premeditated learning is a teleological process in this sense, aimed at making moral behavior a nondeliberative aspect of one's disposition. Both vices and virtues in this understanding – insofar as they are considered to be products of human endeavor rather than revelatory experience or natural temperament – are acquired through the repeated performance of actions that entail a particular virtue or vice, until all behavior comes to be regulated by the habitus. The appeal of this notion to Christian and Muslim theologians is not hard to understand given its emphasis on human activity and deliberation, rather than divine grace or will, as determinants of moral conduct.

This Aristotelian understanding of moral formation influenced a number of Islamic thinkers, foremost among them the eleventh-century theologian Abu Hamid al-Ghazali (d. 1111), but also al-Miskawayh (d. 1030), Ibn Rushd (d. 1198), and Ibn Khaldun (d. 1406). This Aristotelian legacy continues to live within the practices of the contemporary piety movement in Egypt. It is evident in the frequent invocation of Abu Hamid al-Ghazali's spiritual exercises and techniques of moral cultivation, found in popular instruction booklets on how to become pious, and often referred to in ordinary conversations within the piety/*da'wa* circles (see, for example, Farid 1993; Hawwa 1995).[16]

Foucauldian Ethics

How is this Aristotelian model of ethical pedagogy related to Foucault's work on ethics? While it is clear that neither the Aristotelian concept of virtue nor the behavioral model of pedagogy has any place in Foucault's later work, there are other elements of the Aristotelian tradition that are consequential to Foucault's framework – key among them the distinction between ethics and morality, the conception of telos, and the range of embodied practices through which a particular conception of truth and/or happiness is realized. Foucault posits four elements as central to his analysis of ethics: the substance of ethics, modes of subjectivation, techniques of the self, and telos (Foucault 1997b; 1997c). Importantly, this fourfold scheme is not to be taken as a blueprint for the study of ethics; rather, Foucault's analytical framework raises a series of questions about the relationship between moral codes and ethical conduct which are answerable only through an examination of specific practices and the context in which they reside. The first component, which Foucault calls the "substance of ethics," refers to those aspects of the self that pertain to the domain of ethical judgment and practice. The substance of ethics in medieval Christianity, for example, was flesh and desire, whereas the part of oneself most subject to analysis and labor in the modern period is feelings (Foucault 1997c: 263). The second aspect of ethics, what Foucault calls "modes of subjectivation," refers to the models available "for setting up and developing relationships with the self, for self-reflection, self-knowledge, self-examination, for the decipherment of the self by oneself, for the transformations that one seeks to accomplish with oneself as object" (Foucault 1990: 29). As Nikolas Rose has pointed out, this aspect of ethics draws our attention to the kind of authority through which a subject comes to recognize the truth about herself, and the relationship she establishes between herself and those who are deemed to hold the truth (1998: 27). The third aspect of ethics pertains to the operations one performs on oneself in order to become an ethical subject – what Foucault called "techniques of the self." Finally, the fourth component of ethics is telos: the mode of being one seeks to achieve within a historically specific authoritative model.

For Foucault, the relationship between moral codes and modes of subjectivation is not overdetermined in the sense that the subject simply complies with moral codes (or resists them). Rather, Foucault's framework assumes that there are many different ways of forming a relationship with a moral code, each of which establishes a particular relationship between capacities of the self (will, reason, desire, action, etc.) and a given norm. The precise (embodied) form that obedience to a moral code takes is not a contingent but a necessary element of analysis in that it is a means to describe the specific constitution of the ethical subject. In other words, it is only through an analysis of the specific shape and character of ethical practices that one can apprehend the kind of ethical subject that is formed. These practices are technical practices for Foucault and include corporeal and body techniques, spiritual exercises, and ways of conducting oneself – all of which are "positive" in the sense that they are manifest, and immanent, in everyday life. Notably, the importance of these practices does not reside in the meanings they signify to their practitioners, but in the work they do in constituting the individual; similarly, the body is not a medium of signification but the substance and the necessary tool through which the subject is formed.

Foucault's analysis of ethics is useful for understanding key aspects of the women's piety movement I have described above. The practices of this movement presuppose the existence of a divine plan for human life – embodied in the Quran, the exegetical literature, and the moral codes derived therefrom – that each individual is responsible for following. Participants in the piety movement are summoned to recognize their moral obligations through invocations of divine texts and edificatory literature. This form of morality, however, is not strictly juridical. There is no centralized authority (on the model of the church) that enforces the moral code and penalizes infractions. Rather, the piety movement has a strong individualizing impetus that requires each person to adopt a set of ascetic practices for shaping moral conduct.[17] Each individual must interpret the moral codes in accord with traditional guidelines, in order to discover how she, as an individual, may best realize the divine plan for her life.

As I show above, compared to other Islamic interpretive traditions, the piety movement is notable for the extraordinary degree of pedagogical emphasis it places on outward markers of religiosity – ritual practices, styles of comporting oneself, dress, and so on. The participants in the piety movement regard these practices as the necessary and ineluctable means to realizing the form of religiosity they are cultivating. For them it is the various movements of the body that comprise the material substance of the ethical domain. There exists an elaborate system of techniques by which the body's actions and capacities can be examined and worked upon, both individually and collectively. Women participants learn to analyze the movements of the body and soul in order to establish coordination between inner states (intentions, movements of desire and thought, etc.) and outer conduct (gestures, actions, speech, etc.). Indeed, this distinction between inner and outer aspects of the self provides a central axis around which the panoply of ascetic practices is organized. This principle of coordination has implications for how we might analyze the conceptual relationship the body articulates with the self and with others, and by extension, the self's variable relationships with structures of authority and power.

The teleological model that the participants in the piety movement seek to realize in their lives is predicated on the exemplary conduct of the prophet Muhammad and his companions (*al-rashidun*). It would be easy to dismiss this ideal as a nostalgic desire to emulate a bygone past, a past whose demands can never be met within the exigencies of the present. Yet to do so would be to miss the significance of such a telos for practical ethical conduct. Among mosque participants, individual efforts toward self-realization are aimed not so much at discovering one's "true" desires and feelings, or at establishing a personal relationship with God, as at honing one's rational and emotional capacities so as to approximate the exemplary model of the pious self. The women I worked with did not regard trying to emulate authorized models of behavior as an external social imposition that constrained individual freedom. Rather, they treat socially authorized forms of performance as the potentialities – the ground if you will – through which the self is realized. Given this conception of the subject with its model of interiority and exteriority, a central question that I have tried to address in my work elsewhere is: How do we conceive of individual freedom in a context where the distinction between the subject's own desires and socially prescribed performances cannot be easily presumed, and where submission to certain forms of (external) authority is a condition for achieving its potentiality? To put it another way, how does one make the question of politics integral to the analysis of the architecture of the self?

Ethical Engagements

While the analysis I have presented here is indebted to Talal Asad's critique of the modern concept of religion and the questions it opens up, it is important to underscore that Asad himself does not explicitly propound an Aristotelian-Foucauldian framework for the study of religion or Islam. Yet it is noteworthy that for those influenced by Asad's work, this analytical framing has been a productive and important theme. Among those who have developed this line of thinking is Charles Hirschkind (2006) whose work focuses on questions of ethics, politics, and the sensorium. In his book *The Ethical Soundscape*, Hirschkind analyzes the practice of listening to cassette-recorded sermons that is a signature practice of the Islamic revival not only in Egypt (the locus of his ethnography) but also among Muslims living in other parts of the world. This auditory practice is a displacement of the classical tradition of sermon audition in Islam from the space of the mosque to the context of everyday life (in cabs, homes, cafes, shops, street corners), enabled by the transportability of the cassette form in all of its spatial-temporal dispersions. Hirschkind shows how this auditory practice "inherits and extends [the classical Islamic] practical tradition [of somatic learning] for the formation of a pious sensorium" (2006: 79). Notably, these tapes are not simply edificatory, Hirschkind shows, but also offer practical instruction on how to act morally in a world that is shaped and ruled by secular rationalities and modes of governance. Through various ethnographic accounts of this listening practice, Hirschkind argues that its normative and practical aim is to cultivate "the sensitive heart that allows one to hear and embody in practice the ethical sensibilities undergirding moral action" (2006: 9).While engaging the work of Foucault, Hirschkind builds upon historical and anthropological work on the senses, mimesis, kinesthetics, and audition in order to analyze the rearticulation of Islamic somatic forms to contemporary conditions of piety and media.

Hussein Agrama (2010, in press) engages Foucault's work on technologies of the self in a different manner in his ethnography of the practice of the receiving and giving of *fatwas* (religious advice) in the Fatwa Councils of Egypt. In contrast to Muslim Personal Status (or Family Law) courts, whose judgments are legally binding, *fatwas* are a form of religious advice dispensed by religiously trained scholars (*muftis*) whose implementation is impossible to insure. Agrama shows that, surprisingly, Egyptian Muslims follow these *fatwas* far more closely than the injunctions of Personal Status courts, often going to great lengths to abide by their guidelines. In contrast to existing scholarship that analyzes *fatwas* as the dispensation of correct doctrine, Agrama analyzes it as a form of "techniques of the self" and of ethical self-cultivation. Agrama is closer to the kind of analysis I have offered here than to Hirschkind's in that (unlike the latter) he adheres closely to the distinction between ethics and morality I outlined earlier. *Fatwa* for him is not a moral edict but a technology of self-transformation.

Beyond the work on Islam, scholars working in traditions outside of the Muslim world have also engaged and extended Foucault's work on ethics recently with an emphasis on the model of pedagogy and self-formation embedded in the tradition of Aristotelian ethics. Anand Pandian (2009), for example, extends this conversation about ethical formation beyond religion into the domain of agricultural labor in south India. He treats "ethics of cultivation" as a metaphor not only for the care of the self but also for the cultivation of land and of a moral life among the Piramalai Kallar caste. Through a close ethnographic analysis of how the Kallars work the land and the self in related idioms, Pandian draws on the tradition of Tamil literary poetry which has long treated the rural cultivator as a morally cultivated being. Idioms of virtue and cultivation (both moral and environmental) intertwine in this ethnography, extending the "care of the self" literature to rural registers of life and labor.

Ajay Skaria (2002), in an article based on a forthcoming book on Gandhi's political thought, argues that many of the virtues and practices (*seva*, *swaraj*, *swadeshi*) that Gandhi espoused cannot be adequately understood as simply nationalist or proto-nationalist. Instead he shows that these practices are aimed toward creating a certain kind of self that is quite distinct from a modern secular nationalist subject. Skaria emphasizes the ethical nature of a number of Gandhian concepts, and the means–end relationship they articulate, not dissimilar to the model I discussed earlier, one that is central to the Aristotelian tradition of ethics. Beyond these two works, Michael Lambek's (2010) edited volume *Ordinary Ethics* is a signal contribution that demonstrates the centrality of ethical judgment and practice to social life in a variety of contexts. Moving away from a code-based approach to ethics, the contributors to this volume show that ethical practices saturate ordinary life, speech, and action. While some of the contributors draw upon Foucault's work on ethics, others engage nondualistic philosophers (such as Wittgenstein and Cavell) to think about the ordinariness of ethical reasoning. These and other works point to the productive nature of the ethical debate in anthropology, one which started off with religion as its central object of study and has since expanded to include practices that may normatively be regarded as "secular."

NOTES

1 Scholars working in the field of virtue ethics argue for the reinstatement of the priority of virtue as the central ethical concept over that of "the good" or "the right" in contemporary moral thought.
2 Aristotle called these practices "virtues" – a term that finds no mention in Foucault's work on ethics. Insomuch as the Aristotelian grammar of virtues remains important to Islam, I will return to a discussion of its relevance later in the essay when I discuss my fieldwork with the piety movement in Egypt.
3 It is this conception that makes the project of comparative religion possible in that the phenomenal forms of religion (rituals, scriptures, liturgies, acts of worship) come to be understood as the cultural and temporal representations of the abstract and atemporal truth of the divine.
4 For a discussion of the kinds of politics this form of religiosity facilitates, see Mahmood 2005: chs. 4 and 5.
5 Kant is explicit in his objections to a morality grounded in habituated virtues and acquired through the long process of character formation: "When the firm resolve to comply with one's duty has become a habit, it is called virtue also in a legal sense, in its empirical character (virtus phaenomenon). Virtue here has the abiding maxim of lawful actions ... Virtue, in this sense, is accordingly acquired little by little, and to some it means a long habituation (in the observance of the law), in virtue of which a human being, through gradual reformation of conduct and consolidation of his maxims, passes from a propensity to vice to its opposite. But not the slightest change of heart is necessary for this; only a change of mores ... However,

that a human being should become not merely legally good, but morally good (pleasing to God) that is virtuous according to the intelligible character [of virtue] (virtus noumenon) and thus in need of no other incentive to recognize a duty except the representation of duty itself – that, so long as the foundation of the maxims of the human being remains impure, cannot be effected through gradual reform but must rather be effected through a revolution in the disposition of the human being ... And so a 'new man' can come about only through a kind of rebirth, as it were a new creation ... and a change of heart" (1998: 67–68).

6 This does not mean that for Kant morality was purely an individual matter, guided by personal preference; rather, an act was moral only insofar as it was made in accord with a universally valid form of rationality. As Charles Taylor points out, Kant's moral law combines two features: everyone is obligated to act in accord with reason, and "it is an essential feature of reason that it be valid for everyone, for all rational creatures alike. That is the basis of the first form of Kant's categorical imperative: that I should act only according to a maxim which I could at the same time will as a universal law. For if I am right to will something, then everyone is right to will it, and it must thus be something that could be willed for everybody" (1985: 323).

7 These include verbal attestation to faith (*shahada*), praying five times a day (*salat*), fasting (*saum*), the giving of alms (*zakat*), and pilgrimage to Mecca (*hajj*).

8 Examples of *al-a'mal al-saliha* include doing good deeds for the elderly, treating one's parents with respect, helping the needy, giving charity, and so on.

9 This economy of action and desire reverses the Enlightenment model in which desires (sometimes along with volition) were considered to be the necessary antecedents to action. Susan James (1997) has traced the complex history of the changing status of passions and volition in theories of action within Western philosophical thought. She argues that, following Descartes, the understanding of appetites and passions became more narrow, so that desire came to be regarded as the primary passion leading to action. Locke is interesting in this respect because, in contrast to Hobbes, he reintroduces the Scholastic understanding of volition as a mediating force against passions but retains, nonetheless, the Hobbesian view that actions are explained by beliefs and desires (James 1997: 268–294).

10 See Scheff, who draws on Turner's work to argue that ritual is the "distanced reenactment of situations which evoke collectively held emotional stress" such as fear, grief, anger, and embarrassment (1977: 489). None of the 17 scholars responding to Scheff's argument in *Current Anthropology* take issue with his proposition that ritual facilitates the catharsis of universally valid emotions and produces a distance between the performers and their feelings (Scheff 1977: 490–500).

11 Much of this discussion assumes a particular model of the relation between the inner life of individuals and their outward expressions, a model predicated on a Cartesian understanding of the self as it was developed in early modern and Romantic thought in Europe. As a theatrical mode of self-presentation emerged as a legitimate and necessary form of commercial sociability in eighteenth-century Europe, Romantic thinkers, for example, came to see this development in terms of the need for a necessary detachment between the inner life of individuals and their social performances (see Hundert 1997).

12 For a full elaboration of Aristotle's conception of habitus in this context, see Mahmood 2001.

13 For discussions of the Christian adaptation and reformulation of the Aristotelian notion of habitus, see Nederman 1989–90, Carruthers 1990, and Inglis 1999. For historical discussions of how ancient Greek ideas came to be adopted and developed in the Islamic tradition, see Sherif 1975, Fakhry 1983, and Watt 1985.

14 For a discussion of how the Aristotelian conception of *habitus* is different from that proposed by Bourdieu, see Mahmood 2005: ch. 4.

15 Nederman notes, "Aristotle does not ... construe the permanence and stability of moral character as the product of an in-bred or natural inheritance. Nature bestows upon man only a capacity ... to be good or evil. The capacity must be actualized through moral education" (1989–90: 90).

16 While A. H. al-Ghazali was critical of the neo-Platonist influence on Islam (Fakhry 1983: 217–233), his ethical thought retained a distinctly Aristotelian influence. On this point, see Sherif 1975, and the introduction by T. J. Winter in al-Ghazali (1995: xv–xcii). For al-Ghazali's seminal work on practices of moral self-cultivation, see al-Ghazali 1984, 1992, 1995.

17 For an analysis of this individualizing trend in contemporary Islam, see Mahmood 2005: ch. 3.

REFERENCES

Agrama, Hussein (2010) Ethics, Authority, Tradition: Toward an Anthropology of the Fatwa. *American Ethnologist* 37(1): 2–18.

Agrama, Hussein (in press) *Secular Paradox: Islam, Sovereignty, and the Rule of Law in Modern Egypt.* Chicago: University of Chicago Press.

Anscombe, G. E. M. (1981) Modern Moral Philosophy. In *The Collected Philosophical Papers of G. E. M. Anscombe,* vol. 3: *Ethics, Religion and Politics.* Minneapolis: University of Minnesota Press, pp. 26–42.

Aristotle (1941) *The Basic Works of Aristotle*, ed. R. McKeon. New York: Random House.

Asad, Talal (1993) The Construction of Religion as an Anthropological Category. In *Genealogies of Religion: Discipline and Reasons of Power in Christianity and Islam.* Baltimore: Johns Hopkins University Press, pp. 27–54.

Asad, Talal (2001) Reading a Modern Classic: W. C. Smith's "The Meaning and End of Religion." *History of Religions* 40(3): 205–222.

Bloch, Maurice (ed.) (1975) *Political Language and Oratory in Traditional Society.* New York: Academic Press.

Bourdieu, Pierre (1977) *Outline of a Theory of Practice*, ed. R. Nice. Cambridge: Cambridge University Press.

Bourdieu, Pierre (1990) *The Logic of Practice*, trans. R. Nice. Stanford: Stanford University Press.

Butler, Judith (1997) *The Psychic Life of Power: Theories in Subjection.* Stanford: Stanford University Press.

Butler, Judith and Connolly, William (2000) Politics, Power and Ethics: A Discussion between Judith Butler and William Connolly. *Theory and Event* 24(2). At http://muse.jhu.edu/journals/theory_and_event/v004/4.2butler.html, accessed Mar. 8, 2012 (by subscription).

Carruthers, Mary (1990) *The Book of Memory: A Study of Memory in Medieval Culture.* Cambridge: Cambridge University Press.

Colebrook, Claire (1998) Ethics, Positivity, and Gender: Foucault, Aristotle, and the Care of the Self. *Philosophy Today* 42(1/4): 40–52.

Csordas, Thomas (1994) *Embodiment and Experience.* Cambridge: Cambridge University Press.

Davidson, Arnold (1994) Ethics as Ascetics: Foucault, the History of Ethics, and Ancient Thought. In J. Goldstein (ed.), *Foucault and the Writing of History.* Oxford: Blackwell, pp. 63–80.

Evans-Pritchard, E. E. (1965) *Theories of Primitive Religion.* Oxford: Clarendon.

Fakhry, Majid (1983) *A History of Islamic Philosophy.* New York: Columbia University Press.

Farid, Ahmed (1993) *Tazkyyat al-nufus.* Alexandria: Dar al-'aqida lil-turath.

Foot, Philippa (1978) *Virtues and Vices and Other Essays in Moral Philosophy.* Berkeley: University of California Press.

Foucault, Michel (1990) The Use of Pleasure. In *The History of Sexuality*, vol. 2, trans. Robert Hurley. New York: Vintage.

Foucault, Michel (1997a) *The Essential Works of Michel Foucault, 1954–1984*, vol. 1: *Ethics: Subjectivity and Truth*, ed. Paul Rabinow; trans. Robert Hurley et al. New York: New Press.

Foucault, Michel (1997b) The Ethics of the Concern of the Self as a Practice of Freedom. In Foucault (1997a), pp. 281–301.

Foucault, Michel (1997c) Technologies of the Self. In Foucault (1997a), pp. 223–252.

al-Ghazali, Abu Hamid (1984) *The Recitation and Interpretation of the Qur'ān: Al-Ghazālī's Theory*, trans. Muhammad Abul Quasem. London: KPI.

al-Ghazali, Abu Hamid (1992) *Inner Dimensions of Islamic Worship*, trans. Muhtar Holland. Leicester: Islamic Foundation.

al-Ghazali, Abu Hamid (1995) On Disciplining the Soul (Kitab riya'dat al-nafs) and On Breaking the Two Desires (Kitab kasr al-shahwatayn). In *The Revival of the Religious Sciences (Ihya' 'ulum al-din)*, bks. 22 and 23, trans. T. J. Winter. Cambridge: Islamic Texts Society.

Hadot, Pierre (1995) *Philosophy as a Way of Life: Spiritual Exercises from Socrates to Foucault*, ed. A. Davidson, trans. M. Chase. Oxford: Blackwell.

Hawwa, Said (1995) *Al-Mustakhlas fi tazkiyyat al-anfus*. Cairo: Dar al-salim.

Hirschkind, Charles (2006) *The Ethical Soundscape: Cassette Sermons and Islamic Counterpublics*. New York: Columbia University Press.

Hundert, John (1997) The European Enlightenment and the History of the Self. In Roy Porter (ed.), *Rewriting the Self: Histories from the Renaissance to the Present*. New York: Routledge, pp. 72–83.

Inglis, John (1999) Aquinas's Replication of the Acquired Moral Virtues. *Journal of Religious Ethics* 27(1): 3–27.

Jackson, Michael (2009) *The Palm at the End of the Mind: Relatedness, Religiosity, and the Mind*. Durham, NC: Duke University Press.

James, Susan (1997) *Passion and Action: The Emotions in Seventeenth-Century Philosophy*. Oxford: Clarendon.

Kant, Immanuel (1998) *Religion within the Boundaries of Mere Reason and Other Writings*, ed. and trans. A. Wood and G. Di Giovanni. Cambridge: Cambridge University Press.

Kapferer, Bruce (1979) Emotion and Feeling in Sinhalese Healing Rites. *Social Analysis* 1: 153–176.

Lambek, Michael (2010) *Ordinary Ethics: Anthropology, Language, and Action*. New York: Fordham University Press.

Lovibond, Sabina (2002) *Ethical Formation*. Cambridge, MA: Harvard University Press.

MacIntyre, Alasdair (1966) *A Short History of Ethics: A History of Moral Philosophy from the Homeric to the Twentieth Century*. New York: Macmillan.

MacIntyre, Alasdair (1984) *After Virtue: A Study in Moral Theory*. Notre Dame, IN: University of Notre Dame Press.

Mahmood, Saba (2001) Rehearsed Spontaneity and the Conventionality of Ritual: Disciplines of Salat. *American Ethnologist* 28(4): 827–853.

Mahmood, Saba (2005) *Politics of Piety: The Islamic Revival and the Feminist Subject*. Princeton: Princeton University Press.

Martin, Luther, Gutman, Huck, and Hutton, Patrick (eds.) (1988) *Technologies of the Self: A Seminar with Michel Foucault*. Amherst: University of Massachusetts Press.

Minson, Jeffrey (1993) *Questions of Conduct: Sexual Harassment, Citizenship, Government*. New York: St. Martin's.

Nederman, Cary (1989–90) Nature, Ethics, and the Doctrine of "Habitus": Aristotelian Moral Psychology in the Twelfth Century. *Traditio* 45: 87–110.

Obeyesekere, Gananath (1981) *Medusa's Hair: An Essay on Personal Symbols and Religious Experience*. Chicago: Chicago University Press.

Ortner, Sherry (1984) Theory in Anthropology Since the Sixties. *Comparative Studies in Society and History* 26(1): 126–166.

Pandian, Anand (2009) *Crooked Stalks: Cultivating Virtue in South India*. Durham, NC: Duke University Press.

Radcliffe-Brown, A. R. (1964) *The Andaman Islanders*. New York: Free Press.

Rose, Nikolas (1998) *Inventing Our Selves: Psychology, Power, and Personhood*. Cambridge: Cambridge University Press.

Scheff, Thomas (1977) The Distancing of Emotion in Ritual. *Current Anthropology* 18(3): 483–505.

Schmitt, Carl (2006) *Political Theology: Four Chapters on the Concept of Sovereignty*. Chicago: University of Chicago Press.

Sherif, Mohamed Ahmed (1975) *Ghazali's Theory of Virtue*. Albany, NY: SUNY Press.

Skaria, Ajay (2002) Gandhi's Politics: Liberalism and the Question of the Ashram. *South Atlantic Quarterly* 101(4): 954–956.

Smith, Wilfred Cantwell (1991) "Religion" in the West. In *The Meaning and End of Religion*. New York: Fortress, pp. 15–50.

Tambiah, Stanley (1985) A Performative Approach to Ritual. *In Culture, Thought and Social Action: An Anthropological Perspective*. Cambridge, MA: Harvard University Press, pp. 123–166.

Taylor, Charles (1985) Kant's Theory of Freedom. In *Philosophical Papers, vol. 2: Philosophy and the Human Sciences*. Cambridge: Cambridge University Press, pp. 318–337.

Taylor, Charles (1995) Irreducibly Social Goods. In *Philosophical Arguments*. Cambridge, MA: Harvard University Press, pp. 127–145.

Turner, Victor (1969) *The Ritual Process: Structure and Anti-Structure*. Chicago: Aldine.

Watt, W. Montgomery (1985) *Islamic Philosophy and Theology: An Extended Survey*. Edinburgh: Edinburgh University Press.

CHAPTER 14

Care and Disregard

João Biehl

Home is where one starts from ...
And the end of all exploring
Will be to arrive where we started
And know the place for the first time.
T. S. Eliot, *The Four Quartets*

"Take me home, my little João, take me home." It was the first time I was visiting Vó Manda, my paternal grandmother who, against my long-distance wishes, had been placed in a nursing home in the town of Brochier. I was writing my doctoral dissertation at University of California, Berkeley and was back to visit extended family in southern Brazil in the summer of 1996. Vó Manda, who was in her late seventies, had seen her husband and two children die, including my father two years earlier, and even though she had been in a somewhat fragile state for several years she had managed to live by herself in a working- and lower middle-class district in Novo Hamburgo. She was then cared for by my cousin Tania, her most devoted grandchild who lived next door, and by my widowed mother.

I knew Vó Manda was difficult to care for and to please, but I could not leave her there, I told myself. Her piercing eyes and lucid voice made it clear that the asylum, two hours away from her home and family, was a death sentence. We were all killing her. I couldn't stop crying and feeling guilty as I returned to what had once been home. I pleaded with all parties. While I invoked kin ties and morals – what would our father do if he were alive? – I also had to hear that my being distant in the United States made it easier for me to come up with moral imperatives.

My siblings each had family problems and economic insecurities to deal with and my mother was exhausted. She had cared for my father (who had had both legs amputated due to severe diabetes) for over 10 years and she wanted to move on with life. She did not hide the fact that she disliked Vó Manda. We grew up hearing stories about the immense burden of debt that she and my shrewd grandfather Oscar and their daughter Iva had always placed on our family, earlier in rural life and then after

A Companion to Moral Anthropology, First Edition. Edited by Didier Fassin.

migration to Novo Hamburgo (then known as the shoemaking capital of Brazil). It was as if Vó Manda had not earned the right to be cared for. But after intense shaming and blaming and careful economic calculations, I succeeded in making the case that our family, meaning my mother, should pay for a full-time caregiver and that Tania and her family would oversee.

Vó Manda came back and for one year she was cared for by Solange, a young woman from the interior who badly wanted a job in the city. But after a year, Solange simply moved on. Vó Manda had become increasingly frail and supposedly difficult, so the story goes, and was sent to a *casa de idosos*, a makeshift geriatric clinic in a nearby town, which my mother paid for. We later learned that Vó Manda had in fact never returned "home": my cousin Tania and her husband had secretly taken her to a notary where she had signed over the house, all she had, to them.

The last time I saw Vó Manda was on a hot summer day in January 1997, crying and begging to leave that place full of TV noise, flies, the smell of urine, and abandoned voices. By now she was being medicated to calm her down, to dampen her voice. "Take me home, my little João, take me home." A few months later, she was transferred to another geriatric business, this time closer so that people could visit her more easily. She died soon after, her body so curled up that her legs had to be broken to fit into the coffin.

When Nothing Can Be Done

Vó Manda and her social destiny were in the forefront of my thinking when, just a few months later, I met a young woman named Catarina who had been abandoned in an asylum called Vita in Porto Alegre, the state's capital (Biehl 2005). Her speech was slurred and she had difficulty walking: "Maybe my family still remembers me, but they don't miss me."

In our first conversation, Catarina said that she was also from Novo Hamburgo and that her ex-husband had given their daughter Ana to the family of Urbano, his boss, for adoption. She said that she had been seen by psychiatrists and that medicines had worsened her condition, making her "always dependent." Catarina continued, "My brothers and my brother-in-law brought me here. I exercise, so that I might walk. I must wait for some time." Something had made it impossible for Catarina to return home. But the desire was still there: "It is not that one does not want to."

Even though Catarina insisted that she had a physiological problem – "My legs don't work well" – and that her presence in Vita was the outcome of various relational, domestic, and medical circumstances outside her control, to Vita's volunteer caregivers she spoke "nonsense." They referred to Catarina as "mad" and knew nothing about her life outside Vita, haphazardly treating her – and the more than 100 people who were also waiting *with* death in Vita – with all kinds of psychiatric drugs (donations that by and large had expired).

As I was to find out, Porto Alegre contained more than 200 such grassroots institutions of last resort, most of which were called "geriatric houses." These precarious places housed those cut off from family life, the mentally ill, and the sick in exchange for their welfare pensions. A good number of these institutions also received state funds or philanthropic donations. I began to think of Vita and the like as *zones of social abandonment*. The existence of these zones was intertwined with the realities of changing households and with local forms of the state, medicine, and the economy – they absorbed those individuals, young and old, who had no ties or resources left to sustain themselves, whose bodies were not worth governing. Neither the legal authorities nor welfare and medical institutions intervened directly in these zones of abandonment. Here the unwanted were sure to become unknowables, with no human rights and no one accountable to them.

Even though Vó Manda and Catarina had lived in the same city, their everyday worlds had been separated by distinct social and economic boundaries. Yet, seen from the geriatric house and Vita, each also embodied a reality that was more than her own. To some extent, they shared a story of family abandonment, an abandonment that brought the poor and the middle class together in an emergent care enterprise. And, as I traced Catarina ethnographically back to the medical institutions, neighborhoods, households, relations, and crossroads at which her madness and abandonment had taken form, I discovered a moral ambiguity and fatalism similar to what I had found among my own family. In the face of physical and mental deterioration the spoken common sense was "What else could be done?" And the unconsidered reality was that the verb "to kill" was being conjugated. As Catarina wrote in her notebook with an uneven handwriting that betrayed minimal literacy:

> The pen between my fingers is my work
> I am convicted to death
> I never convicted anyone and I have the power to
> This is the major sin
> A sentence without remedy.

In my efforts to verify the sources of this human destiny, I found that the family was increasingly the medical agent of the state, providing and at times triaging care, and that medication had become a key instrument for such deliberate action. I uncovered an intricate domestic moral economy (Fassin 2008), in which illness was the ground on which experimentation with changes and breaks in intimate household relations occurred and that pharmaceutical care both legitimated disregard and sanctioned abandonment, as if Catarina's condition had ultimately been self-generated. As she elliptically wrote: "To want my body as a medication, my body." Or, as she repeatedly stated: "When my thoughts agreed with my ex-husband and his family, everything was fine. But when I disagreed with them, I was mad. It was like a side of me had to be forgotten. The side of wisdom … Why was it only me who had to be medicated?" The renegotiation over what constituted meaningful social relations and the getting rid of the unsound and undesirable was intimately tied to families operating as proxy psychiatrists, to the dying out of values based on blood ties, and to people's attempts to continue with their own lives amid economic insecurity in wounded cities.

Family Complexes

In one of his earliest texts "Family Complexes in the Formation of the Individual," Jacques Lacan (1938) emphasizes the family as a contingent social phenomenon, always situated in history and in culture. Neither a natural structure that follows from biological instinct nor merely a miniature representation of society, families are plural and complex – they are caught up in conflicts and inertia of their own and they must be studied with care. Throughout the text, Lacan develops the idea of the "complex," which, he insists, "is dominated by cultural factors" (12). He continues:

> As for the individual integration of objectifying forms, this is the work of a dialectical process that makes each new form arise from the conflicts between the preceding one and the real. In this process we must recognize the character that specifies the human order, namely the subversion of every instinctual fixation from which arise the fundamental and infinitely variable forms of culture. (Lacan 1938: 12)

In reviewing this text, Jacques-Alain Miller (2005) argued that the "complex" was in fact a "prestructure" and that Lacan then lacked "the concept of structure." Yet, I would argue that this theoretical/structuralist lack, so to speak, enables the appearance of something altogether different in this early text. For Lacan's insight here is not merely that reality and the psyche that perceives it are given shape by culture, but that the vehicle of this "dialectical process" is the family, which both transcends the sterile rigidity of structuralist "culture" and escapes a narrow biological, evolutionary, or genetic determinism. The father and the mother are not the coordinates of everything that is invested by the unconscious (see Deleuze 1997: 62); rather, Lacan wants us to consider the cross-cultural and transhistorical shifts in the constitution of the family as well as the family's plasticity (like the "intrusion" that comes with the birth of a sibling: Lacan 1938: 23) and the demands that all this places on specific human conditions. While identifying, for example, the "social decline of the paternal imago" (55), Lacan thus creates a productive space in which we can rethink the forms and roles of the family today.

In this essay, I explore how the domestic encroachment of medical commodities affects care and family ties in resource-poor contexts, as well as how these commodities become interwoven in the very fabric of symptoms and identities. What is the fate of social bonds in today's dominant mode of subjectification at the service of medical science and capitalism? I am particularly interested in how psychiatric drugs become part of economies of care and disregard – the ways they open up and relimit family complexes and moral imagination – and the agency that solitary and chemically submerged subjects such as Catarina express and live by, reduced as they are to a failed medication regimen. In her words:

Not slave, but housewife
Wife of the bed
Wife of the room
Wife of the bank
Of the pharmacy
Of the laboratory.

As institutional care becomes increasingly outsourced to entrepreneurs and local communities, and as powerful medications circulate without even a doctor's visit, human relationships with medical technology are increasingly constituted outside the clinical encounter (Biehl with Moran-Thomas 2009). New therapeutic populations and forms of intimacy are now emerging around technology at community and domestic levels, as in the case of the massive and often unregulated dissemination of psychiatric drugs worldwide (Luhrman 2000; Ecks 2005; Petryna et al. 2006; Biehl 2007; Martin 2007; Fischer 2009; Biehl and Petryna 2011; Jenkins 2011).

Rationalities play a part in the reality of which they speak, and this dramaturgy of the real becomes integral to how people value life and relationships and enact the possibilities they envision for themselves and others. Psycho-pharmaceuticals seem to have played a key role in altering Catarina's sense of being and her value for others. And through these changes, family ties, interpersonal relations, morality, and social responsibility were also reworked. Her "ex-family," she insisted, thought of her as a failed medication regimen. And in her writing, global pharmaceuticals were not simply taken as new material for old patterns of self-fashioning: "The dance of science, pain broadcasts sick science, the sick study, brain, illness, Buscopan, Haldol, Neozine, invoked spirit." There was a science to Catarina's symptoms and exclusion, a science that was itself sick, a money-making science. The goods of psychiatry, such as Haldol and Neozine, were now as ordinary as Buscopan (an over-the-counter antispasmodic medication) and had become part of familial practices. Ritual-like, they worked on her brain and her illness. "What I was in the past does not matter."

In *The Divided City*, writes Nicole Loraux, one must "expose the city to what it rejects in its ideological discourse yet lives in the time of the event" (2002: 61). Overall, Loraux is concerned with the denial of historicity in Greek classic democracy: "the denial of conflict as a constitutive principle, in order to construct the generality 'city'" (61). Civil war is at the core of civic life. The historian shows how the citizenry's concealment of war generates an affect that works like "the cement of the community." The crime being concealed has been engendered "in a single family" (33). For Loraux, the city is the subject which makes the symptom through the family. Fratricide, she argues, is "ordinary civil war, because the brother is also the paradigm of the citizen" (209). She thus constructs a scenario in which the household is affectively politicized: "hate would be more ancient than love, in which forgetting can be valued only in terms of the unspeakable joy brought by the wrath that does not forget" (66). The restoration of familial relations becomes paradigmatic of reconciliation in the city. In the end, a false brotherhood conceals the original reality of division (39).

My encounter with Catarina and the events it precipitated made it possible to retrieve a world deemed to be lost. This essay brings out of thoughtlessness the set of symptoms, moral sentiments, domestic relations, and practical calculations by which the marketable and those who are left to die are linked to each other and to the political body via pharmaceuticals. As formal institutions either vanish or become nonfunctional in the wake of the country's fast-paced neoliberalization, the household is further and distinctively politicized. Amid the "pharmaceuticalization of health care" (Biehl 2007) and in the daily rituals of medication and compliance, alternative conceptions of caregiving, moral experience, and ideas of what life is for begin to take shape.

Ethnographic work can break open totalizing assumptions and capture this active embroilment of reason, life, and ethics as human lives are reshaped and lost. An immense parceling out of the specific ways communities, families, and personal lives are assembled and valued and how they are embedded in larger entrepreneurial processes and institutional rearrangements comes with the on-the-ground study of a singular "other." While entering the density and intensity of a locality, the anthropologist is challenged to think with the theories, however articulate or inarticulate they may be, created by those excluded, like Catarina, concerning both their condition and their hope. I say hope for, against all odds, Catarina and so many in Vita and other zones of social abandonment keep searching for ways to endure, for ties and a way home.

Catarina resisted the foreclosures that Vita posed, and, in ways that I could not fully grasp at first, she voiced an intricate ontology in which inner and outer space and self and others were affectively laced together, along with the wish to untie it all: "Science is our consciousness, heavy at times, burdened by a knot that you cannot untie. If we don't study it, the illness in the body worsens … Science … If you have a guilty conscience, you will not be able to discern things." Catarina's spoken accounts and her writing contained the confused sense of something strange happening in the body: "cerebral spasm, corporal spasm, emotional spasm, scared heart." As she moved from house to hospital to other houses to Vita, experiencing both pharmaceutical care and human disregard, it seemed there was a danger of her becoming too many, strange to herself, all the while cementing an estranged social body. "One needs to preserve oneself. I also know that pleasure in one's life is very important, the body of the Other. I think that people fear their bodies."

Such difficult and multifaceted realities and the fundamentally ambiguous nature of people living them gives the anthropologist the opportunity to develop a human (not abstractly philosophical or merely psychological or economic) critique of contemporary machines of social death. Ethnography, I believe, can help us to resituate and rethink social death within various familial, technological, and political economic circuits and concrete struggles over belonging, voice, and care of others and of self (Foucault 1988; Fassin 2007). In contrast to subjects of statistical studies and the figures of philosophy, our ethnographic subjects have a future – and we are a part of that.

Technologies of Care and Disregard

Taking Catarina's spoken and written words at face value led me on a journey into the various medical institutions, communities, and households to which she continually alluded. With her consent, I retrieved her records from psychiatric hospitals and local branches of the universal healthcare system. I was also able to locate her family members – her brothers, ex-husband, in-laws, and children – in nearby Novo Hamburgo. Everything she had told me about the familial and medical pathways that led her into Vita matched the information I found in the archives and in the field.

Catarina was born in 1966, and grew up in a very poor place, in the western region of the state of Rio Grande do Sul. After finishing fourth grade, she was taken out of school and became the housekeeper as her youngest siblings aided their mother in agricultural work. The father had abandoned the family. At the age of 18, Catarina married Nilson Moraes, and a year later she gave birth to her first child. Shady deals, persistent bad harvests, and indebtedness to local vendors forced Nilson and Catarina to sell the land they had inherited to take care of Catarina's ailing mother, and in the mid-1980s the young couple decided to migrate and join two of her brothers who had already migrated and found jobs in the booming shoe industry in Novo Hamburgo. In the coming years, she had two more children and began to have difficulties walking. As her condition progressed, her marriage also disintegrated. Catarina had become too much of a burden for her old and new family, a history tangled by the complications of disease, poverty, and fear, and was frequently hospitalized and overmedicated with powerful antipsychotics. In 1996 she was sent to Vita. Her eldest two children went to her husband's family, and her youngest daughter was given up for adoption.

Had I stayed only with Catarina's utterances in Vita, the whole field of tensions and associations that existed between her family and medical and state institutions, a field that shaped her existence, would have remained invisible. Catarina did not simply fall through the cracks of these various domestic and public systems. Her abandonment was dramatized and realized in the juxtapositions of several social contexts. Scientific assessments of reality (in the form of biological knowledge and psychiatric diagnostics and treatments) were deeply embedded in changing households and institutions, informing colloquial thoughts and actions, an emerging common sense that led to her terminal exclusion.

Following Catarina's words and plot was a way to delineate the powerful, noninstitutionalized ethnographic space in which a family gets rid of its undesirable members. The social production of deaths such as Catarina's cannot ultimately be assigned to any single intention. The fabric of this domestic activity of valuing and deciding which life is worth living remains largely unreflected upon, not only in everyday life, but also in the social science and theory of caregiving. As this study unfolded, I was challenged to devise ways to approach this unconsidered infrastructure of decision-making, which operates, in Catarina's words "out of justice" – that is, in spite of the bounds of law – and which is close to home. I also uncovered that Catarina actually suffered from a rare neurodegenerative disorder that caused her to lose her ability to walk and, over time, shut her down. Reaching this diagnosis took me through a maze of medical hoops and, as the picture of her disease became clearer, I took her to a geneticist and neurologist who finally made the correct diagnosis and provided the best possible care.

In what follows, I engage core debates on the gendered meanings of care vis-à-vis the psychology of moral experience, hoping to shed light on the relevance of the ethnography of illness and medicine in refiguring commonly held assumptions about the economics and moral dimensions of caregiving. Yes, caregiving is an existential quality and means for the good, but it is also intimately bound to the possibility of disregard and evil. By using the terms "disregard" and "evil" together, I want to emphasize two points: (1) disregard can be sanctioned by assumptions that the suffering of the abandoned person is a form of punishment for evil done; and (2) the ways in which clinical medicine and psychiatry – disciplines that pledge to do no harm, at the very least – are made instrumental in blaming victims for their own suffering and disqualifying them from care and human connection. I hope to open up an analytical space to engage the negative space inhabited by Catarina in which people could excuse themselves from her, a space of disregard at the nexus of market rationality, science, and intimacy that points to the limits of care (Stoler 2009: 256).

Social theorists have struggled to find ways to understand these often troubling novel entanglements of care and the markets of medical technology. Drawing inspiration from feminist critics like Carol Gilligan, whose book *In a Different Voice* (1993) argues for the relevance of care as a separate value excluded by masculine rationalities that do not acknowledge the relational nature of morality, some theorists have identified an absolute opposition between care and the market (Hankivsky 2004; Held 2006).

In *The Ethics of Care*, Held asks: "What kinds of activities should or should not be in the market and governed by market norms? How does marketing an activity change its character and what values are served by this transition? On what moral grounds can we make such decisions and where should the limits (if any) of markets be drawn?" (2006: 108) For Held, there is an aspect of care that cannot be valued in terms of market capitalism. She distinguishes between compensating caregivers for their work and transforming care into a market commodity. Thus the core issue is one of a prioritization of values: "not whether the work is paid or not but the norms under which it is done and whether the values that have priority in its doing are market values or some others" (111). In other words, "What might the moral grounds plausibly be for deciding on the limits or boundaries of the market?" (116). In her book *Social Policy and the Ethic of Care*, Hankivsky (2004) draws from Held and makes similar arguments about a fundamental opposition between care and commodity. For her, experiences and values of care are incommensurable with market values (90; see Tronto 2008). Hankivsky cites a troubling study conducted by Phillip Morris that concluded that "smoking is not costing the Czech government money because government costs in treating smoking-related illnesses are offset by the early death of smokers. In fact, the company reported that, in 1999, smoking produced a net gain of approximately $150 million dollars for the government" (99–100). This logic produces a deeply unsettling moral calculus.

Both Held and Hankivsky are concerned with the ever encroaching market in public institutions and social relations, its logic of commodification, and the erasure of other social and moral values as they are replaced with consumer-capitalist ideology. Yet, the mixing of commodity and care *does* happen, and if we cannot explain the moral gravity of caregiving by merely defining good care as a pure, transcendent value and opposing it to the corrupting force of the market, how can we apprehend the ethics of care in today's consumer-capitalist society?

Sociologist Viviana Zelizer's work is a strong critique of an analytic scheme where the intimate world of caregiving occupies a "separate sphere" from the corrupting economic rationality of the market. Writing against a monolithic notion of economic rationality and against binary oppositions, Zelizer sees intimacy and economics intersecting constantly in a dynamic she terms "connected lives." In *The Purchase of Intimacy* (2005), she rejects essentializing theories of care that distinguish it absolutely from market values or that reduce it to economics, culture, or biology. Zelizer argues for a complex dynamic of intersection: "Economic arrangements for the provision of care do not simply call up considerations of cost, convenience, and efficiency. They involve negotiation of the forms, representations, obligations, and rights attached to meaningful interpersonal ties" (2005: 172).

Yet, what is the moral dimension of this vision of care? The idea of "intimate care" (as in Gilligan, for example) too easily "sentimentalizes," Zelizer would say, calling up all the familiar images of altruism, community, and unstinting, noncommercial commitment: "From there it is only a step to a notion of separate spheres of sentiment and rationality, thence to the hostile worlds supposition that contract between the personal and economic spheres corrupts both of them" (2005: 207). Yet Zelizer contends that a close examination of how people actually speak of experiences and relationships of care and intimacy challenges this argument:

> In fact, personal care incessantly mingles economic transactions with the provision of sustained and/or life-enhancing personal attention. Looking meticulously at caring relations reveals that participants themselves do not contend over whether those relations should involve economic transactions. They contend instead over appropriate matches among relations, media, and transactions, taking great pains to distinguish relations providing similar practical forms of care but having significantly different implications for longer-term connections among the people involved. In negotiating economic conditions of care, participants are also defining meaningful social relations. (Zelizer 2005: 207)

Although Zelizer demonstrates the mutual involvement of intimacy and economics and does not dismiss or deny the ethical challenges posed by care and caregiving, her descriptive work leaves space to ask about the experience of moral uncertainty confronted by caregivers living, as she calls them, "connected lives." For Catarina's abandonment was not merely a process of social definition, but a moral choice, an unwillingness by those in her life to be accountable to her words and needs. If, as Zelizer argues, economic decision-making is neither wholly excluded nor in a position of absolute determinism over relationships of care, what new moral dimensions emerge in the actual practice of caregiving?

Arthur Kleinman (2008, 2011) has written reflectively and provocatively about the human dimensions of care. Drawing from his own practice of caring for his wife Joan Kleinman, he argues for the moral gravity and human significance of care:

> To use the close experiential language of actually doing it, caregiving is also a defining moral practice. It is a practice of empathic imagination, responsibility, witnessing, and solidarity with those in great need. It is a moral practice that makes caregivers, and at times even the care-receivers, more present and thereby fully human ... Caregiving is one of those relationships and practices of self-cultivation that make us, even as we experience our limits and failures, more human. (Kleinman 2009: 293)

Another important perspective on the moral dimensions of care is given by Annemarie Mol (2008), who argues for a "logic of care," problematizing what she calls the "logic of choice" which defines patient choice as its chief value. Mol demonstrates that "autonomy" and "choice" can be euphemisms for social practices of neglect, as responsibility is placed on the individual for her own care. In the logic of choice, she argues, it is not only that autonomy is regarded as an ethical good, but also that, "in the logic of choice making normative judgments is the moral activity *par excellence*, and it is this activity that this logic endorses" (2008: 74). But in the logic of care, it is not decisions but practices that carry moral weight: "For care is not a (small or large) product that changes hands, but a matter of various hands working together (over time) to produce a result" (18).

The logic of care, according to Mol, is not a matter of identifying an essence of care or caregiving that works in opposition to the market or to Enlightenment rationality; on the contrary, the logic of care for Mol is precisely a consequence of the deconstruction of the binary opposition between the moral and the impartial or rational: "The logic of care has no separate moral sphere. Because 'values' intertwine with 'facts,' and caring itself is a moral activity, there is no such thing as an (argumentative) ethics that can be disentangled from (practical) doctoring" (Mol 2008: 79). The logic of choice, on the other hand, "comes with guilt. Everything that follows after a choice has to be accepted as following from it ... In the logic of choice, having a choice implies that one is responsible for what follows. In the logic of care this is different" (79). This guilt has profound consequences for health care, particularly as we grapple with the place of new technologies in our lives; as Mol writes, "the expectation that technologies subordinate themselves as obedient means to their valuable ends, makes us all too surprised, time and again, when these technologies come with unexpected, undesired effects" (93). In other words, it is a logic of choice which, precisely by attempting to distill the moral from the neutral, rational, and technological, permanently blocks us from approaching the moral dilemmas that are fundamentally linked to those apparently value-neutral objects.

Both Zelizer and Mol argue against a straightforward opposition of idealized care and the market. Zelizer demonstrates that financial transactions are deeply embedded in the social negotiation of caring relationships. Mol argues that the sense of impending doom about market capitalism corrupting the moral good of caregiving is intelligible only in the discursive terms of market capitalism itself; it is a logic of choice that allows us to separate them and then see them as mutually opposed.

While Mol's theoretical framework provides a fresh perspective on the moral consequences of the economies of care, it cannot identify evil or neglect except as discursive functions of neoliberal capitalism. An ethnographic perspective points to a potential new direction for inquiry: how can we put the ethical person or the moral community at the center of our understanding of the intersection between care and capitalism? How can these theoretical debates be refigured by ethnography and by more attention to the social experience of care or lack thereof?

Ethnography has the potential to illuminate how certain technologies that are named or fall under the category of "care" – psychiatric diagnostics, psychopharmaceuticals, and institutionalization in geriatric houses, for example – actually create the conditions for the possibility of evil, precisely because they are not care at all in the sense that Mol and Kleinman define it, as practice rather than decision or commodity. The practices I chronicle in the following sections substitute momentary decisions for relational practices that extend indefinitely over time. What makes them so insidious is that they masquerade as what they are not, enabling the parties making the decisions to feel that their behavior is within the bounds of acceptable morality. It is Orwellian in its absurdity: society gives something a name – "health care" – that means precisely the opposite of what the thing actually is (social abandonment/disregard) – and everybody is off the hook.

In contexts of poverty, the financial and relational aspects of caregiving are often in extreme tension, placing people in very difficult situations in which they feel they have "no choice." As I will show with Catarina's family, people attempt to resolve this tension by substituting drugs and institutionalization for care as relational practice, a strategy made possible by the fact that the former are mistakenly considered forms of caregiving by modern healthcare science. The consequence of conceiving of care as technological intervention rather than relational practice – the abandonment and death of people in great need – is a kind of evil. Detachment and disregard, not purely psychological but socially situated, relational, and economic, are prescribed and practiced, when in fact people's pain calls for the opposite.

These forms of disregard, disguised as caregiving, transform relationships in family and work, reshape community values and priorities, and alter economic prospects and life chances. Local patterns of caregiving and disregard thus illuminate larger social processes and the fundamental human potential for good and evil. Ethnography can also engage the thinking of those subjected to disregard, and, in so doing, force us to inquire into how such human capacity can be made part and parcel of much-needed efforts to reimagine and redirect both caregiving and the knotty relationship between care of the self and care of others. "Could the activity of thinking," asks Hannah Arendt, "be among the conditions that make men abstain from evil-doing or even actually 'condition' them against it?" (1981:5).

Ex-Home

I followed Catarina's clues into Novo Hamburgo's poorest districts. No, nobody around knew of anyone like Catarina, the Gomes family, or the Moraes family. I had gathered a few addresses from Catarina's medical records. To my surprise, one of them led me into a rich neighborhood. Beyond the dead end of Travessão Street, however, a cluster of wooden shacks sat on a large grassy field – a squatter settlement on city property. A bar connected the cluster of shacks. There was a pink house where (according to hospital records) Catarina had once lived. A neighbor kindly gave me his cell phone number and told me that I could call later. If Catarina's husband came around, he would put me in contact with him.

That night I called. It turned out that the owner of the pink house was not Catarina's husband. "My name is Nilson Maurer. I am the other Nilson," he said, "I am married to Sirlei, Nilson Moraes' sister. You can call me Alemão [German]." He added that Anderson, Catarina's teenage son was visiting them, and that I was welcome to stop by.

A semblance. That was the first thing I heard about Catarina as I entered her former house and the world of her ex-family: "She was so beautiful in the wedding photos," said Catarina's sister-in-law. The first memory was not the person but her apparition: "When Nilson first brought her photo home, I said, 'Father and mother, look, what a beautiful girl he got for himself.' Everybody agreed." Catarina entered the new family unit as an appearance, as the property of a man, and as part of a domestic labor force: "When Nilson brought her home, she helped with everything, and now she is in this situation."

For Sirlei, today's paralysis could not be read in the past: "When I first laid eyes on her, one couldn't see she would have the problem she has today. She was a perfect person like us." Alemão, however, suggested that the Moraes family had known something of Catarina's physical condition early on, recalling that "she was already dragging her legs a bit." This physical sign had not entered the initial recollection of Catarina's sister-in-law: "I didn't know her when she was single, but people say that she limped a bit."

Sirlei associated Catarina with another disintegrating body: "Her mother also lost the legs and the hands." "One had to feed her" – a leftover body at the mercy of an impersonal pronoun and a certain moral obligation. A well-off uncle "is also like this," added Alemão, "I think this is hereditary." The onset of Catarina's limping seemed to be of great relevance, for her sister-in-law returned to it, dating its origin to Anderson's birth. This physiological sign also had an economic side: "She worked in a shoe factory. When she had Alessandra, she was still working, but they fired her because she began to fall there." Catarina was no longer work-able. Anderson entered the conversation: "My uncles also have this problem. They have the legs like that." Nobody knew what the disease actually was, but Alemão had noticed that "it attacked her stronger than it did the brothers." The 15-year-old said that he was living with his father in the Boa Saúde district, that he was studying at night, in the sixth grade, and was looking for a job. Adriana was still living with their grandmother in the Santo Afonso district. Ana, the youngest sibling, was living "with her godparents." As for his father, "he is remarried, and has a son with his new wife." I asked whether he worked. "Yes, he has always worked in shoe factories."

Sirlei again began to discuss Catarina's frequent hospitalizations, and her husband interrupted once more: "But she was not hospitalized only because of the legs. There were other problems. One day, she burned Nilson's clothings and documents." In local slang, the word *documentos* also connotes male genitals. Anderson said that he had witnessed it: "It happened in this house. Father came home, and she burned his things. That was long ago." As far as he could recall, "before suffering the attacks, she was normal. She cooked, she did everything in the house." Alemão added that she seemed to have intelligence. Anderson recollected a caring mother: "She woke me up at the right time to go to school, she helped me with homework. We had a normal life … until the problems began." But the child couldn't recall precisely when it all began to fall apart.

"When Anderson was born we began to see that it damaged her head. When Alessandra was born, *it* got worse," stated Sirlei. "It": something in Catarina, a child, an unknown disease, the experience of motherhood? Something worsened. Sirlei was now synchronizing Catarina's mental disturbances with the first expressions of her physical paralysis, and with the experience of motherhood. It was as if these things couldn't be teased apart. And as I listened to the inconsistencies in Sirlei's account of Catarina's deterioration, I thought that perhaps the human actions that had conflated these various occurrences needed to remain veiled. Catarina's condition had been constructed by the ways these various elements were brought together. In the end, Catarina was the equivalent of "it." The neutral pronoun "it" can stand for the contempt one has for a person.

"She went mad. In the middle of the night, she went to the streets and wandered. She had everybody preoccupied with her," recalled Sirlei. Alemão added that "she did not want to know of her husband. No one could talk to her." The attacks "were not that frequent," he said, but when they happened, Catarina did not behave as she should have. She began to flirt with the other Nilson: "She sat next to me, talked to me, said that she liked me, began to say romantic things. But then, next day, she was normal." "She went to the hospital in bad shape, but came back normal," Sirlei rushed to say, as if trying to defuse Alemão's description of a sexuality with the wrong object. Her husband, however, insisted on bringing dissonance into the conversation: "Normal, so to speak – she still had those problems with walking." "Yeah, but normal in her head," rebuked Sirlei.

Alemão was linking Catarina's hospitalization and banishment from family life with her paralysis. He hinted at what should have remained unsaid: "The last time she was hospitalized she couldn't walk anymore, so she had to stay there." Sirlei fixed his account and insisted that Catarina could stand on her own feet: "The last time we saw her, when we were leaving, she stood up from the chair and bid us farewell." In this image Catarina had let the family go of her own volition. "I thought that it was a family disease, that my grandmother also had it," said Anderson. For the child, "it" was not madness. Sirlei interrupted, saying that Anderson was too little when his grandmother (Catarina's mother) died in 1988, "paralyzed in a wheelchair, here in this house." But Anderson remembered his grandfather, he said, and his mother pregnant: "He slaughtered a pig when we visited Caiçara. My father took us. Mom was pregnant with Ana."

The name Ana brought up a dramatic development in this new family complex. "When Catarina was hospitalized, they took the newborn to Dona Ondina, Nilson's mother. But then there was a fight with Tamara and Urbano, the godparents. They wanted to keep the child. They fought with the grandmother and then Seu Urbano was able to – I don't know, we cannot say exactly how it happened … But as far as we know, Seu Urbano made a deal with Nilson. Nilson is illiterate; he can only sign his name. They made a shady deal, and took a paper there and forced her to sign, the poor woman." Catarina? "Yes. So that they could keep the child." Did she know what she was signing? "We don't know for sure … But she was weak … Now the girl has been legally passed onto them." Sirlei said that Urbano and Tamara did not want the siblings to visit each other. "They didn't let the girl call Catarina 'mom' – only 'auntie.'"

The absent mother had to be praised: "I remember the times Catarina lived alone with the kids, down there, next to my mom's. We could see the love she had for them. The little money she had, it was to go to the market to buy things for them." As the image of a self-sacrificing mother, Catarina still had value. But she had no money of her own, and her body was not working. "She separated from Nilson, she returned from the hospital. Then Nilson left her this house, and she exchanged it with Delvane. Then went to the shack that was set on fire, went to the hospital, and did not return."

"When the house burned down, the family did not provide her with a new place. She lived with my mother. She was getting mad … So many problems, poor thing, one can only go insane," said Sirlei. There was compassion now, even an understanding that there was a material and historical course to Catarina's condition, though contingent on her madness.

Catarina had said she wanted to know what people had written of her and went with me to retrieve her medical records from psychiatric institutions. She wanted me to find her family. These people had responded with hospitality and information to my attempt to understand what had happened. And in the course of our interaction – amid dissonant recollections, dissimulations, hidden judgments, and moralities that protected their lives and interests – a common sense had been cracked open. Many relational, physiological, medical, and economic factors intersected and gave form to a common sense or belief that it would be impossible for Catarina ever to return.

Common Moral Sense

That same night Nilson and Anderson took me to see Altamir, Catarina's eldest brother, who lived nearby. Altamir owned a bike repair shop and, according to Nilson, had "married up" as his wife's family owned a small store. I related what I knew of their family history through Catarina and mentioned that she always spoke very highly of her brothers. Her paralysis was the entry point of discussion.

"This comes from the family," said Altamir, using the expression "it is in the trunk of the tree." Their mother, maternal grandfather, and great-grandfather "also had *it*," he said. "My mother had about 10 siblings, and four or five had *it*. Some cousins have *it*, and others don't." His wife Vania, who worked in a shoe factory, linked *it*s manifestation in Catarina to her labor: "*It* got to her when she had her last daughter." Altamir didn't follow that line of reasoning and mentioned that "*it* develops slowly." The symptoms are always the same: "The legs get shaky, more and more, and you walk as if you were drunk. Speech also gets slurred."

He then suggested something of a broken taboo as the root of the disorder: "People used to say that the root of this old trunk was marriage among cousins or brothers and sisters. I don't know if this is true; this is what I heard." "It's a mystery," added Vania. No one in the family had ever had a genetic exam. And I wondered about the identity of this disorder, its incidence, and the dynamics and strategies, both familial and medical, that had been developed over time to manage it and that kept it unacknowledged.

"When Catarina lived with us," Vania continued, "she was treated by the mental health people. Because there were times that she was very crazy, right? Crazy to run out, to escape and all these things." I asked again about the time of onset of Catarina's problems. Altamir described her as "normal" during their childhood. Vania then reintroduced the semblance of Catarina: "She was *very* normal. I remember the wedding photos." I wondered about this gradation of normality and what in one's life or interests determined its application to another family member.

"Catarina passed through the health post, the general Hospital, the Caridade … The truth of her illness nobody knows." Simply put: the outcome of Catarina's passage through medicine and psychiatry has been *nonknowledge*, on several registers. First, Sirlei spoke as if the family had not known of Catarina's physiological deficiency before she entered their household. Second, Catarina was treated and medicated for something else other than "it" – an "it" that remained unknown. Third, Vania, whose husband is beginning to show similar physical signs, looked back and saw Catarina as embodying something they all feared. And, finally, this family (and perhaps others) did not have medical knowledge of their condition and had devised ways to live with the unknown disease.

Vania was dominating the conversation. She commented that Armando was already limping, like the older brothers: "When they walk, you notice a difference. It's not normal." The immediate association was death: "Their mother died in a wheelchair." I wondered what one had to have, own, or be to avoid the certainty of being cast out: "Catarina's children and our son show no signs. Ademar's kids are also normal. I don't know if with time …" The nonknowledge around this condition was visibly measured and had economic meaning: Vania speculated about whether the brothers would be able to work in a few years from now. Altamir noted that when he stopped doing things, the difficulties with locomotion increased. His mindset, he believed, could help to deter the disease: "One must not lose the will."

Vania brought the conversation back to Catarina, suggesting that some disorder other than the unknown disease had led her away from home: "Do you remember, Altamir, you always told me that she escaped home and that Nilson went after her?" But Altamir refused to attribute Catarina's mental condition to pathology: "This was due to the illness itself," he insisted. "I think that she revolted against the illness. I think that this provoked unhappiness in her." Her mood disorder was not a mental illness, so to speak, but a way to face the biological signs – or, perhaps, the ways they were handled domestically. That's what Vania now speculated, for theories of causation focused on Catarina continued to change: "You are right, afterwards she got even crazier. I shouldn't say crazy, for she knows what she is saying. Her daughter was given away, and she couldn't take care of the children anymore – all this had an impact on her.

As Catarina's ex-family members reasoned about her condition, they freely assembled a bricolage of its etiology, unconcerned by contradictions. In the process, however, a constant theme crystallized: she was isolated and beyond treatment. Vania recalled Catarina's last hospitalization at the São Paulo Hospital. By then, no one was responsible for her: "It's complicated. I don't understand it well. She was hospitalized at the São Pedro. I think that her husband Nilson did it. She got better and came home, alone. When you least expected, she was coming home. She was discharged, obtained money at the bus station, and came home. She was so good in her head, that she came home alone." It seems that nobody expected her to come back. That nonplace she had in her family's mind and the indiscriminate medicating made Catarina crazy all over again, as she wrote in her notebook: *louca da cabeça, louca da casa* (crazy in the head, crazy in the house).

As the conversation went on, they began to displace moral attention from Catarina to what happened to her youngest daughter. Alemão again made the case that giving up Ana for adoption had been the "wrong thing." Altamir and Vania, however, were adamant that the child was now well taken care of and lived a rich life. Blood ties were not as meaningful: "The child is much better off than if she lived with her mother or grandmother. It couldn't be better. The stepmother likes her a lot. Ana has her own room; she has everything." For Vania, the only problem was that they did not take the girl to visit Catarina: "Tamara told me Ana couldn't go in to Vita, for it is a place for mad people. But I told her, if you think this will traumatize the kid, then take Catarina to spend a weekend with you." The most they will consider are temporary measures to expunge the doubt of their morality.

Then the inevitable: how to speak of Catarina in Vita? Without my asking, Vania mentioned that "the last time we visited her in Vita she was content and asked to see Ana." The phrase "the last time" minimizes how much time had passed since anyone visited Catarina. Vita's oldest volunteers recalled only a few visits to her, around 1996, just after she had been left there. But tonight's conversation, it seemed, had occasioned the thought of a brief return: "It's time for us to bring her here to spend a weekend with us," suggested Vania.

Overall, I felt that Catarina's relatives saw me as a kind of emissary of the country's laws. In other words, they knew that by law they were legally liable to care for Catarina. As I learned from the Public Ministry in Porto Alegre, public attorneys have the power to subpoena family members of abandoned people and negotiate care or financial responsibility. But as Vita's history suggests, this happens in only a few cases, which then become emblematic of a supposed democratic state of human rights.

"You grew up with her," I said to Altamir, "Seeing what has happened to her, what comes to mind?" "It's tough, but what to do? If one brings her home, one also cannot do anything. And we have to work."

In subsequent years, I have continued to engage Catarina's family. I have always been welcomed into their homes. And I have always been taken aback by the ease with which they spoke of her. For Catarina, there was nothing to be done, I heard over and over again. That was common sense. The impossibility of doing anything to bring her back to social life was assumed rather than analyzed and acted on, I thought. Each one claimed that he or she had done all that was possible, to the limit.

An ordered realm existed in Catarina's exclusion. Who belonged in the house, who was worth medicine, who made money, and the gradation of acceptable normality – these are all key elements of the household's maintenance. The common sense that Catarina was physically unviable and mentally unsustainable had a value and validity for those who possessed it. And as Clifford Geertz has luminously written: "Here, as elsewhere, things [or humans] are what you make of them" (2000: 76). In this context, marked by economic pressure and violence, how does one speak of the "evil" that is done and the "good" one must do? For Altamir and other family members, it was through a rhetorical question to which the unspoken answer is "nothing": "It's tough, but what to do?"

Evilness

Like the others, Nilson, Catarina's ex-husband, also spoke openly about her. "It's all past," he stated in an interview in 2001, "It is not even in my mind." He then added, "In Porto Alegre, they gave her medication for the head. She didn't want to take it, though – she threw it into the toilet and flushed it down. All that medication. A person must help herself. It was just a matter of taking the medication, but she didn't help herself." "What has passed is over. One must put a stone over it."

I asked Nilson when Catarina's problems began, to which he replied, "After the premature birth of Ana." I told him that, according to the records, Catarina was first hospitalized in 1988, four years before Ana was born. He agreed and said that he had lost track of time. At any rate, she had been escaping home: "I worked as a security guard at the city hall at night and left her at home. Then, once at midnight, people came, saying 'Your woman is on the road.' One day we found her in the nearby town of Estância Velha. So I decided to hospitalize her." And this became routine: "It was a month at home and a month at the hospital." The day Catarina set his clothes and documents on fire, Nilson told himself "this is no longer madness, it is evil" and "I went to the judge to get a separation." "Finally," said Nilson, "the city hall took up the case, picked her up and took her there." To Vita? "I don't know where. The last time I saw her was many years ago." In the end, Catarina was a stray thing, to be picked up by the city's humane services, banished from one's view to a place one does not name.

Nilson explained that when he married Catarina, half of the family's land was in his name, as the couple assumed the care of her mother and her younger brother. Nilson didn't comment any further on what had happened to the land, but mentioned that he had brought the mother and brother-in-law along to the city. "The old lady was in a wheelchair. She lost her legs. We even had to feed her." He described Catarina's fraternal ties as ineffective: "My brothers-in-law never supported me. There was nobody to help. I had to leave my work and run after her. The city hall then pitched in. But the brothers never came to see whether we needed anything, and we had little children. One begins to lose strength, right? They had their houses and cars, but never came to visit, never said we will help to search for our sister … that's what happened."

Catarina's family was to be blamed for her destiny, though she herself was not innocent, since she had refused to take medication, he insisted: "They gave her the best medication in Porto Alegre. The problem was that she only took them while there."

Did she tell you what happened in the hospital? "No, she didn't remember." For Nilson, Catarina had no memory, yet it was Nilson who seemed intent on forgetting Catarina's physical conditions. Again, I brought up her difficulties with walking and again the ex-husband spoke as though these things had no clear history or development: "She walked a bit shaky. I don't recall when this began. This comes from the family, from her grandfather, I think. I don't know what this is." He then traced the onset of Catarina's problems not to the mysterious hereditary disease but to Catarina's mistreatment of her disabled mother. In this account, Catarina's mental disturbance was the result of guilt for domestic violence, for her *ruindade* (evilness). "After her mother died, she began saying things that didn't match with reality. She said that her mother appeared to her. She was very bad to her mom. She struck her mom in the face ...We said don't do that to the old lady, you don't know what will happen to you someday, what you will have to endure ... After her mom died, she began having problems." Are you saying that she should be punished? "Of course, if one does such a thing, it comes back to you. To do this to a sick mother. The spirit comes down. Her mom said that Catarina would pay for her evil."

When I later spoke to Ademar, Catarina's middle brother, he mentioned that their mother had, indeed, been a very strong-willed woman, but he knew nothing of Catarina's violence toward her. He was even more frank than Altamir had been about the economics of the changed family complex: "It was tough. We came to work here. Left everything to Nilson, and then afterwards when Catarina became *ruim* [worse] he left her. I think that when she had things, he was with her – and after she became worse, he abandoned her." Given that Catarina had "'been given away'" to Nilson and that the young couple had squandered the family's land, the brothers felt no obligation to her.

Both the brothers and Nilson referred to Catarina as *ruim*, which means "bad," in the sense of physically degraded or "evil." But the verb used with *ruim* assigns the meaning. For the ex-husband Catarina "was" *ruim*: she was an evil person. For the brothers, she "became" *ruim*: her condition worsened. In the ex-husband's interpretation of Catarina as essentially evil, she was solely responsible for her own abandonment, and not even a utilitarian ethics could be invoked: she was paying for her evil actions (such as hitting her disabled mother and burning her husband's documents), she had failed to adhere to her pharmaceutical regimen, and she was simply outside the domain of rational thought. In the brothers' account of Catarina as gradually becoming worse, there was room for a historicity of the physical signs and for a maternal linkage, though not for ongoing relationships. For instance, the brothers associated mother and sister: "In Catarina, it began earlier than in our mother. We were grown up when our mother stopped walking. But with Catarina, no ... Her kids were very small and she was already much worse [*bem ruim*]." It seemed that as Catarina became increasingly like their deceased mother – read: biology – it became possible to leave her behind. This was the economic and gendered fabric of their moral thinking, beyond the domain of the blood tie.

An unspoken order or economically motivated common sense has developed over time around this unknown disease, making possible the unbinding of the family and informing memory and morality. This was an intricate story. Only by listening to all parties, recurrently and over time, by juxtaposing deceptions with finally revealed thoughts, was it possible to access the underlying plot to cast Catarina out. The fact is that, given certain physical signs, Catarina's husband, her brothers, and their respective families believed that she would become an invalid, as her mother had been. They had no interest in being part of that genetic script. Catarina's "defective" body then became a kind of battlefield in which decisions were made within local family–neighborhood–medical networks about her sanity and, ultimately, about whether "she could or could not behave like a human being," as her mother-in-law put it to me. Depersonalized and overmedicated, something stuck to Catarina's skin – the life determinants she could no longer shed.

"What do you remember of Catarina?" I asked the ex-husband. "Her nonsense." Catarina was outside of familial common sense. The tragedy of her destiny in Vita was not simply the extended family's failure to undertake the necessary work of caregiving; rather, her neglect was achieved through a perversion of the meaning of care itself. People now had a medically legitimated fabulation of the mad or evil woman which stood in place of the family tie. The narrative that formed around Catarina had no evident agents and, after some time, no one was responsible for her any longer. As Clifford Geertz pointed out, "common sense is not what the mind cleared of cant spontaneously apprehends; it is what the mind filled with presuppositions … concludes" (2000: 84). By empirically assessing how common sense is forged and conceptualizing deliberations over it, wrote Geertz, one can see how culture is put together and better understand "the kinds of lives societies support" (93).

Catarina had become a leftover in a domestic world that was disassembling and reassembling in intricate interactions. She was the negative value, the unnecessary component of a migrant and urban poor culture. At the core of common sense are practices and attitudes toward death, real and imaginary. Catarina's abandonment speaks of what ties reality together and the forms of human life that are endorsed these days.

Conclusion: Women, Economic Insecurity, and Social Death

In July 2002 I visited the Novo Hamburgo center for psychosocial attention (CAPS) where Catarina was treated between hospitalizations. "We have at least five hundred Catarinas in the service right now," said psychologist Simone Laux, after I told her about Catarina and my work with her. Laux affirmed the ordinariness of the story I was reassembling: "Exclusion always passes through the family." And by "five hundred Catarinas," she meant most of the adult female clientele of the center, which was treating about 1,500 people a month. About half of the clients got free psychiatric medication at the city's community pharmacy.

"When our CAPS began in the late 1980s, it was meant to deal mainly with schizophrenia and psychosis," reported psychologist Wildson Souza, "but this has changed a lot, both diagnostically and numerically. There is an immense growth of mood disorders." He added, "We don't have statistics, but we see that the social field is breaking down and the population is getting sicker and sicker." He cited "unemployment, harsh struggle to survive, no opportunities for social mobility, urban violence" as contributing to this epidemic of mental suffering. The psychologist suggested that the center had become the vanishing social world, the welfare state, and the social medicine that was no more: "Many factories are closed, people don't have jobs or health plans or family support … They need some form of recognition and help, and they demand it from SUS [Brazil's universal healthcare system]. Nothing is isolated." "We have three women's groups here," continued Laux. "Most of them are not psychotic. But at some points in their lives, they had a crisis or were at risk of committing suicide. All of them have a story that resembles Catarina's." The other health professionals who had gathered for a group discussion then began to tell tales of "women's historical subjugation," female bodies entangled in realities of migration, poverty, and violence. "Once a woman came with a machete cut in her head. The husband of another one had raped all their children. Many report that, according to their husbands, they are always inadequate." The common pattern was that "he is the owner of her life, in all possible ways."

I was again struck by how historically entrenched power relations in heterosexual households were woven together with social death. And, after I briefed the group on Catarina's trajectory, Daniela Justus, the service's psychiatrist, replied: "Catarina is not searching for a diagnosis, but for life." I mentioned that Catarina used to say: "I am allergic to doctors." "She is right," Dr. Justus added, "That's the minimum attitude she could have developed. It is a must to trust the patient. The ideology and politics of a psychiatric hospital are not to trust. Patients are treated like animals. Minimal medical effort and social control through medication."

Catarina's story shows that the patterning of the mass patient and her dying at the crux between abandonment and overmedication are both public and domestic affairs, I noted. "Indeed," replied psychologist Luisa Rückert, "families organize themselves so that they are no longer part of the treatment and care." The major exception is when cash is involved, stated Andreia Miranda, the center's occupational therapist. "Families keep their mentally ill relatives as long as they can manage their disability income." Folding together the economic and intimate, the family produces a moral common sense and an adroit abdication of responsibility.

"I don't think that diagnostics makes the differentiation." Dr. Justus then expanded on the family's role in fostering illness: "When patients improved – and we saw this quite often at the Caridade – families discontinued treatment, and the person had to be hospitalized again." Crisis situations were constantly induced. The relation between the family and mental illness, I was told, is made explicit in the culture of pharmaceuticals: "In our group sessions, we can see that the fragility of a minimal social integration is revealed in everyone's relation to the medication, the fight over its discontinuation, the lack of money to buy it, or the problems with forgetting to take it."

Families, in fact, come into the service demanding medication, Rückert stated: "When I ask them to tell their story, many times they say, 'No, I came here to get a medication for her.'" The psychologist added that during initial group meetings, people often ask her "'Why is the psychiatrist not here?' As if I were not sufficient for a first treatment. They want to leave with a prescription." Medication has become a family tool and the family crystallizes its way of being in the ways it deals with medication. "Bottom line, the type of ethics the family installs," said Rückert, "serves to guarantee its own physical existence." The exclusion of Catarina served also as a form of self-care for the family. Yet just as what was called care for Catarina was actually abandonment, what seems here to be the self-care of the family is actually its negation, as kinship ties and relations are disavowed in favor of the exigencies of material survival and novel self-interests. Fabio Moraes, also a psychologist, agreed that "the family caregiver quite often becomes the state that does not care." The family is thus "*a state within the state.*" Sigmund Freud actually used this expression to reiterate the constraining features of neurotic pathologic processes vis-à-vis "external reality" (cited in Loraux 2002: 84).

I take the interplay of political power and individual psychology to be more than analogic: as Veena Das and Renu Addlakha have argued, the domestic sphere "is always on the verge of becoming the political" (2001: 512). The decision to make persons and things work or to let them die is at the center of family life no less than it is at the center of state politics. And in today's local worlds, science, in the form of medication, brings a certain apparent neutrality to this decision-making process – the psychiatric aura of reality. "In the meetings," Rückert continued, "the patient quite often realizes that given the continuing process of exclusion, she has already structured her own schemes of perception and codification of reality." Rather than psychosis, out of all these processes a para-ontology comes into view – a Being beside itself and standing for the destiny of others. The now "irreversible" condition of the mentally afflicted gives consistency to an altered common sense.

In sum, just as care is made through the contribution of many hands (rather than singular choices), so Catarina's destiny shows that intractability and disregard is a shared (if inconsistent and contradictory) process mediated by the indiscriminate use of pharmaceuticals. Families have become psychiatrists by proxy and the abandonment of unproductive and unwanted family members is facilitated and legitimated by drugs, both through the scientific truth value they bestow and through the chemical alterations they occasion. The one who is medicated within the family is, then, in Catarina's words, "on a path without an exit." Pharmaceuticals thus work as moral technologies – they actually make the loss of social ties irreversible.

Here, bodies, inner lives, and new forms of exclusion are entangled with large-scale processes and shifting grounds of knowledge and power, science and money. And the domestic and public display of these entanglements, the reversal of ties and values, the uncertainty of limits, the instability of characters and roles, and the anxieties created indicate the mutation of mental universes and the emergence of new laws of perception and action toward familial others even in the face of an ingrained sameness.

Catarina struggled to transmit her sense of the world and of herself, and in doing so she revealed the paradox and ambiguity of her abandonment and that of others. The human condition in Vita challenges analytical and political attempts to ground ethics and morality in universal terms, in the exceptions that stand outside the system. "People say that it is better to place us here so that we don't have to be left alone at home, in solitude … that there are more people like us here. And all of us together, we form a society, a society of bodies." And she added: "maybe my family still remembers me, but they don't miss me."

When Simone Laux first opened Catarina's folder, she read aloud an entry by nurse Lilian Mello from December 12, 1994, that left us all speechless:

> I drove Catarina home. But as she now lives alone, I left her at the house of her mother-in-law, called Leonora. Catarina was badly received. The mother-in-law said that Catarina should die, because she was stubborn and aggressive, didn't obey anyone, and

> didn't take the medication. The mother-in-law made clear that she would not be responsible for Catarina. I told her that the family should take Catarina to the General Hospital for a clinical evaluation. Ondina told me to call Nilson, Catarina's ex-husband. I went to talk to him. My impression is that he really wants nothing to do with her. He only said that, like other times, Catarina should be taken to Porto Alegre and hospitalized.

No work, be it clinical or anthropological, can do without an entry into the affective tissue of domestic spaces. And there is much to learn from this responsible health professional as she moved through public institutions and households. She disturbed diagnostic certainties and refused to isolate Catarina's body and voice from her surroundings. She followed her behind the scenes of medicine and model health programs, listened to a multiplicity of voices, and registered the modes of affect and social practices that made Catarina a double of sorts and empty of all concrete possibilities. Her work did not veil what was truly happening, the concreteness of "the truth" Catarina embodied. "She died socially," said Laux. "That is the pain that aches in us … when we realize this: she cannot opt to live."

A machine in which a tie to others and to living are rendered impossible. If it were not for this archival fragment, the explicitness of this medical and domestic operations would remain lost to history. Patricia Barbosa, a psychiatrist, named the line that had been crossed: "She was killed." The ex-human.

Acknowledgments

I want to thank Didier Fassin, Joshua Franklin, Peter Locke, and Ramah McKay for wonderful conversations and for their great editorial help.

REFERENCES

Arendt, Hannah (1981) *The Life of the Mind.* Boston: Harcourt, Brace.

Biehl, João (2005) *Vita: Life in a Zone of Social Abandonment.* Berkeley: University of California Press.

Biehl, João (2007) *Will to Live: AIDS Therapies and the Politics of Survival.* Princeton: Princeton University Press.

Biehl, João with Moran-Thomas, Amy (2009) Symptom: Subjectivities, Social Ills, Technologies. *Annual Review of Anthropology* 38: 267–288.

Biehl, João and Petryna, Adriana (2011) Bodies of Rights and Therapeutic Markets. *Social Research* 78(2): 359–394.

Das, Veena and Addlakha, Renu (2001) Disability and Domestic Citizenship: Voice, Gender, and the Making of the Subject. *Public Culture* 13(3): 511–531.

Deleuze, Gilles (1997) *Essays Critical and Clinical.* Minneapolis: University of Minnesota Press.

Ecks, Stefan (2005) Pharmaceutical Citizenship: Antidepressant Marketing and the Promise of Demarginalization in India. *Anthropology and Medicine* 12(3): 239–254.

Eliot, T. S. (1968) *The Four Quartets.* Orlando, FL: Mariner.

Fassin, Didier (2007) *When Bodies Remember: Experiences and Politics of AIDS in South Africa.* Berkeley: University of California Press.

Fassin, Didier (2008) Beyond Good and Evil? *Anthropological Theory* 8(4): 333–344.

Fischer, Michael (2009) *Anthropological Futures.* Durham, NC: Duke University Press.

Foucault, Michel (1988) *The History of Sexuality*, vol. 3: *The Care of the Self.* New York: Vintage.

Geertz, Clifford (2000) Common Sense as a Cultural System. In *Local Knowledge: Further Essays in Interpretive Anthropology*. New York: Basic Books, pp. 73–93.

Gilligan, Carol (1993) *In a Different Voice: Psychological Theory and Women's Development*. Cambridge, MA: Harvard University Press.

Hankivsky, Olena (2004) *Social Policy and the Ethic of Care*. Vancouver: UBC Press.

Held, Virginia (2006) *The Ethics of Care: Personal, Political, and Global*. Oxford: Oxford University Press.

Jenkins, Janis (ed.) (2011) *Pharmaceutical Self: The Global Shaping of Experience in an Age of Psychopharmacology*. Santa Fe, NM: School for Advanced Research Press.

Kleinman, Arthur (2008) Catastrophe and Caregiving: The Failure of Medicine as an Art. *The Lancet* 371: 22–23.

Kleinman, Arthur (2009) Caregiving: The Odyssey of Becoming More Human. *The Lancet* 373: 292–293.

Kleinman, Arthur (2011) The Divided Self, Hidden Values, and Moral Sensibility in Medicine. *The Lancet* 377(9768): 804–805.

Lacan, Jacques (1938) *Family Complexes in the Formation of the Individual*, trans. Cormac Gallagher. Unpublished Manuscript.

Loraux, Nicole (2002) *The Divided City: On Memory and Forgetting in Ancient Athens*. New York: Zone.

Luhrman, Tania (2000) *Of Two Minds: The Growing Disorder in American Psychiatry*. New York: Knopf.

Martin, Emily (2007) *Biopolar Expeditions: Mania and Depression in American Culture*. Princeton: Princeton University Press.

Miller, Jacques-Alain (2005) A Critical Reading of Jacques Lacan's *Les complexes familiaux*, trans. Thomas Svolos. At http://www.lacan.com/jamfam.htm, accessed Feb. 27, 2012.

Mol, Annemarie (2008) *The Logic of Care: Health and the Problem of Patient Choice*. New York: Routledge.

Petryna, Adriana, Lakoff, Andrew, and Kleinman, Arthur (2006) *Global Pharmaceuticals: Ethics, Markets, Practices*. Durham, NC: Duke University Press.

Stoler, Ann L. (2009) *Along the Archival Grain: Epistemic Anxieties and Colonial Common Sense*. Princeton: Princeton University Press.

Tronto, Joan C. (2008) Review of *The Ethics of Care: Personal, Political, and Global*, by Virginia Held. *Hypatia* 23(1): 211–217.

Zelizer, Viviana (2005) *The Purchase of Intimacy*. Princeton: Princeton University Press.

CHAPTER 15

Mourning

Everett Yuehong Zhang

When I was little, I often heard my grandmother who was in her sixties say that she wanted to leave the city of Chongqing in China to go back to her hometown in Fujian Province for an ultimate reason: to die there. Why did she want to die there? "I want to be buried. In Chongqing, I will be burned." Cremation had indeed become a rule in the city since the 1960s and to her it was an imminent threat.[1] She was serious about her afterlife; it was as if she could feel the fire scorching her body under cremation. Her determination to have a burial conveyed an embodied tradition that had been turned into the "other" of the atheism that was dominant.

During the Cultural Revolution (1966–76), however, the Red Guards and rebels built about 15 graveyards in Chongqing to bury their dead comrades-in-arms in the late 1960s. Answering Mao's call to rebel against the "capitalist roaders in power" within the Party, those Red Guards and rebels, however, split into two factions, even though both factions claimed loyalty to the great leader Chairman Mao. The conflict escalated from quarrels to physical fights. Weapons were used ranging from wooden bars, spears, and eventually modern firearms including anti-aircraft machine guns, cannons, and tanks. Thousands died. Graves were built and tombstones erected, modeled on the Monument to the People's Heroes in Tiananmen Square in Beijing. The designation "martyr," a very high honor in the Chinese communist revolution, was inscribed on the tombstones of the dead, along with "Long live the dead martyr!" in Mao's calligraphic hand. Impressed by the grand graves made of granite in one of those gravesites, my grandmother sighed, "If I could be buried in such a grave!" In the burial ceremonies, red flags were hoisted, the "Internationale" was sung, and mourners clenched their fists to make the pledge to "turn sorrow into strength, avenge the dead comrades, and fight to death in defense of Chairman Mao!"

Years later, my grandmother died in Fujian in the post-Mao reform era, and was buried in a mountain, to her great comfort. Ironically, all the graveyards for the Red

A Companion to Moral Anthropology, First Edition. Edited by Didier Fassin.

Guards but one were demolished, as the dead were turned into infamous icons of chaos, violence, and disaster of the bygone era. The only remaining such graveyard in China – the Graveyard for the Red Guards in Shaping Park – barely escaped demolition in the 1980s, when the administration of the park, under the leadership of the Chongqing Party Committee, sealed it off. With about 130 graves in which more than 400 Red Guards and rebels were buried, this graveyard became a site of disgrace. No mourner would come, and even family members of the dead avoided the place. It was not until the early 2000s that resurging waves of mourning breathed life back into the graveyard. On three occasions – Qingming (Tomb Sweeping Festival), anniversaries, and Chinese New Year's Day, survivors mourned the deaths of their relatives or friends (many in their twenties or even teens) again (Zhang 2009). In 2009 this graveyard was designated a "Chongqing cultural relic," which gave it legitimacy for public mourning. However, in whose name do people mourn now?

Taking this graveyard as a point of departure, this essay discusses the moral implications of mourning. First, I will examine two important models in the studies of mourning – "mourning for social solidarity," developed by Robert Hertz, and the "work of mourning," developed by Sigmund Freud. Then, I will examine the effort to go beyond the two models and bring the moral concern about "bad deaths" into focus. Finally, the "model of life-centered grieving" makes life, instead of death, the focus of grieving.

Two Models for Mourning

Hertz's model: social solidarity

Robert Hertz (2009 [1907]) gives an overview of the rationales behind human practices of burial and mourning based on his documentation and review of indigenous practices in the Pacific region. Caught in between the two moments – after the dead body was first interred and before it decayed to the bone, the living were anxious and vulnerable to the pollution of the corpse. It was not until the flesh had completely decayed and the bones were uncovered by the disinterment in order to be reinterred that mourning came to an end. This second burial fully released the soul from the body so that it departed from this world and entered another.

Hertz's model reflects Durkheim's notion of collective conscience and social integration. Death poses a threat to the social order because the society has lost its member and a social relationship. Mourning is performed to end the uncertainty between the death and the second burial, integrating both the dead into the world of the dead and the living back into the community.[2] One major problem with Hertz's focus on social solidarity, however, is its lack of insight into the impact of death and mourning on the living as individuals.

The Freudian model: the work of mourning

For Freud, mourning is the reaction to the lost object of love, arising out of the continued libidinal attachment of the ego to the lost object. Therefore, the work of mourning is to sever such attachment, amounting to the "respect for reality" (Freud 1999 [1917]: 243) and to "offering the ego the inducement of continuing to live" (256). He inferred:

> Each single one of the memories and situations of expectancy which demonstrate the libido's attachment to the lost object is met by the verdict of reality that the object no longer exists; and the ego, confronted as it were with the question whether it shall share this fate, is persuaded by the sum of the narcissistic satisfactions it derives from being alive to sever its attachment to the object that has been abolished. We may perhaps suppose that this work of severance is so slow and gradual that by the time it has been finished the expenditure of energy necessary for it is also dissipated. (Freud 1999: 255)

Compared to Hertz, Freud focuses on the feelings and well-being of the individual, and aims at the role the work of mourning plays in rebuilding balanced sentiment in the individual. Conversely, when the work of mourning breaks down, there will be social consequences and some psychological impact on the well-being of the individual.

The Freudian and Hertzian models – polarized as they were – complemented each other in laying the foundation for an understanding of mourning for the next century. Since then, efforts have been made to overcome their limits as well.

The dialogue between the two models

Anthropological studies of mourning developed primarily along the line of Hertz's ideas in the Durkheimian tradition.[3] Although dialogue between the Durkheimian tradition and the Freudian tradition was limited, the attention to sorrowful sentiment and its regulation during death rituals left the door open for the dialogue. As Richard Huntington and Peter Metcalf observe:

> In our own society, it is quite permissible to cry at funerals. It is common for some individuals, especially some of those close to the deceased, to be overtaken with emotion and shed tears, sob, or occasionally cry out loud. In many societies, crying at funerals is not merely tolerated, it is required by customs, and at predetermined moments that entire body of mourners will burst into loud and piercing cries. Just as suddenly, the weeping halts and the tears that had just been running so profusely cease. (1979: 24)

Regulations on weeping or articulation of sorrow during death rituals were common. For example, among the Andaman Islanders, the display of feelings focuses on its affirmation not of sorrow but of social bond (Radcliffe-Brown 1964: 117); a girl in a funeral in Java is discouraged from crying too hard because it will give rise to the intrusion of the dead (Geertz 1960: 68–76); among the Hakka villagers, it is problematic if expression of sorrow is not choreographed according to social hierarchy (Johnson 1988); in southeastern India, whether one cries or not had to do with a kind of gendered regulation whereby women cry but men do not (Clark-Decès 2005), and so on. In ancient Chinese classics such as *Yili* (Rituals) (Yang 2004b) and *Liji* (The Book of Rites) (Yang 2004a), profuse cries such as *pi* (beating the breast) and *yong* (stamping the ground) are induced according to closeness to the dead, timing, and space. One condition is the principle of balance between *ai qi zhi zhi* (feel extreme sorrow over the death of parents so as to cry hard) and *jie ai shun bian* (restrain sorrow to adapt to the change), because one should not let sorrow ruin one's body against the wishes of the parents (Yang 2004a: 105).

The constraints on expressing sentiment affirm the influence of the Durkheimian concern about social solidarity, resonating with what Durkheim famously said, "If he weeps and groans, it is not merely to express an individual chagrin; it is to fulfill a duty of which the surrounding society does not fail to remind him" (1915: 400). However, an overemphasis on social solidarity can lead to the failure to notice the suppression of sorrow and social injustice.

Engaging with Life

Inclusion of bad deaths

Hertz documents a number of types of inauspicious deaths (or bad deaths) that were excluded from the double burials and the process of mourning. First, the deaths of infants, younger children, and the elderly were excluded. Infants have not yet entered into the visible society so the society has not yet put anything of itself into the infant and does not feel harmed by its disappearance and remains indifferent (Hertz 2009: 144). There is therefore no point in conducting a second burial. The elderly are also excluded from double burials because they have ceased to take part in social life; their death merely consecrates an exclusion already completed in fact and to which others have become accustomed (144).[4]

In addition, "all those who die violent or accidental deaths, women who die in labor, the drowned or lightning-struck, and suicides are often the object of special rites" (Hertz 2009: 144). It is because "their corpses inspire the most intense horror and are gotten rid of precipitately" (144). Also, it is because the "transitional period [from the land of living to the land of ancestors] is indefinitely prolonged, and death is without end for these victims of a particular curse," as "their souls will wander forever on earth, troubled and wicked" (144).

One clue about this exclusion of bad death is a fundamental aversion to the burden of dealing with the overwhelming emotion resulting from bad deaths. "It is not the weakness of emotion felt by the collectivity, but on the contrary its extreme intensity and the abruptness that opposes the carrying out of normal funeral rites" (Hertz 2009: 145). In the end, social solidarity was achieved through suppressing, instead of articulating, sorrow. It did not come as a surprise that the conflict between achieving social solidarity and articulating grief would intensify, as bad deaths increasingly became registered as the target of intervention under modernity.[5]

The transition from focusing on death to focusing on life

Anthropologists began to subvert the Hertzian model of excluding bad deaths by turning bad deaths into a central target of inquiry. Nancy Scheper-Hughes (1992) opened up a new phase in studies of mourning with her long-term engagement with the phenomenon of frequent deaths of infants in a shantytown in Brazil. What caught her attention were not only the frequent deaths of infants but also the "indifference" of the mothers toward the deaths of their babies. Resonating with the rising global concern about infant deaths, her work targeted the death of babies through the issue of "infant mortality," in the language of public health and governance of life. She identified a number of factors contributing to both phenomena. Poverty made hunger a chronic experience. Scarcity of food and subsistence rendered maternal care inadequate, often directly causing deaths. Infants suffered from transmitted diseases resulting from exposure to unhygienic surroundings. The development model of high dependence resulted in a sharp decline of investment in public health and in poverty reduction during economic growth. Serious gender inequality made women vulnerable to sexual violence and frequent pregnancy. The cultural belief that babies were born as a result of God's will placed the burden of reproduction on women's shoulders. In the end, the high infant mortality had a lot to do with weak governance, reflected at least in the poor registration of vital statistics, including births and deaths.

Scheper-Hughes tried to shed light on the "abnormal" attitude of the mothers toward infant deaths, an important local phenomenon. First, mothers were indifferent to the deaths of babies, believing that they were good for the living. In one case, a mother believed that even if the baby had survived it would have been weak and would not have become a healthy child, because it did not have a knack for life and would have suffered if it had survived. The locals treated the death of an infant as "angel's wake" – an angel waking up to its new journey toward heaven. The casual ritual of burial was common. Babies were put in small boxes and buried by the gravedigger. They did not even bother the Catholic nuns to toll for a baby's death. The way to manage the dying baby was to conduct no more than a ritual that symbolically linked it to the crucifix, to represent the initiation of the angel's wake.

These two facets of infant deaths constituted the phenomenon of "death without weeping." Scheper-Hughes challenged the common understanding of a mother's care as intrinsic and an unconditional maternal trait on the one hand and had difficulty suppressing her disgust at the mothers who showed indifference to the deaths of babies on the other hand. Caught in the predicament, she developed a stronger moral concern than ever, while feeling the pressure to suspend moral and ethical judgment. The result is complex. On the one hand, she made the mother's indifference understandable. On the other, her immersion in everyday life made this indifference more abnormal than ever, reminding the reader of the high infant deaths that had previously been taken for granted and were now, with modernity and globalization, coming under scrutiny.

Two types of ethics clashed here – the ethics that value life and the ethics that suspend moral judgment to respect local practice. According to the former, infant mortality should be reduced, whereas according to the latter, death without weeping does not indicate a lack of maternal love or of human emotion, and argues for sympathy for disadvantaged mothers. Eventually, the author's strong impulse to speak on behalf of the disadvantaged overcame the relativistic impulse to withhold judgment, and she called for a change in social conditions. This ethnography marked a shift in the studies of death rituals and mourning from focusing on death in general to focusing on bad deaths.

The inability to mourn

As the model of social solidarity began to be modified, the moral coherence of death rituals and mourning came under question. The phenomenon of "the inability to mourn" sheds light on the shifting moral ground for mourning, particularly when the work of mourning fails. The Freudian notion of "the work of mourning" reveals a tension between "mourning" and "the work of mourning." "Mourning" is characterized by intense attachment to the lost object through memories and even hallucination. In contrast, "the work of mourning" refers to the effort to sever the ego from the lost object. Through repeated confrontations with the reality from which the loved object has departed, the ego is absolved from the attachment and is able to turn its libidinal energy into detachment or dissipation. But, "mourning" (a reaction) and "the work of mourning" (an intentional attempt to detach) are not always distinguishable. This is where I would like to evoke a distinction between "mourning" and "grieving."

"Mourning" and "grieving" are synonyms in English that share the connotation of feeling grief, but "mourning" covers more ground than "grieving" and emphasizes a ritualistic arrangement of lamenting. In this essay, the term "mourning" is used to focus on the action and the structure in coping with the loss of a member in a community, whereas "grieving" is used to focus on articulating the feelings associated with loss of life. Referring to "the work of mourning" as "grieving" instead of "mourning" can shed light on the impairment of the "work of mourning" seen in the situation of "the inability to mourn."

"The inability to mourn" refers to the state of collective psychology in which mourning loses its moral justification when the loved object loses its moral legitimacy. It derived from the context of postwar Germany (Mitscherlich and Mitscherlich 1975). In this context, Hitler, who had been a loved object for the Germans, lost his moral legitimacy to be mourned. When the loved object is lost not as a result of his or her death but as a result of moral rejection of him or her, it poses a huge problem for the ego, because the ego identified so much with the lost object that it has internalized the object to form a narcissistic relationship with the ego, making ego and the dead inseparable. The normal reaction – mourning – becomes problematic. Melancholia, a comparable phenomenon to mourning, now accounts for the impairment of the ability to mourn. A normal state of mourning can become an abnormal state of melancholia. As a result, "the inability to mourn" occurs.

What is also often seen is the change in political climate that deems the mourning impossible, however heroic or glorious the dead has been considered before. As in the case of the graveyard for the Red Guards mentioned at the beginning of this essay, the changing political climate post-Mao negated the cause they died for – the Cultural Revolution – but diverted the responsibility for the deaths away from the top leader of the Cultural Revolution toward his followers in the party as well as the dead themselves. Because mourning their deaths in public would vent not only grief but also grievances relating to their stigmatization, it would pose a challenge to the power that sacrificed the Red Guards in the Cultural Revolution and the power that gave rise to their "second deaths" afterward. Such a challenge results in "the impossibility of mourning."[6]

To overcome "the inability to mourn," a different way of doing the work of mourning has to be developed. Instead of telling that the dead does not exist anymore, it requires telling the truth that the dead is not worth mourning; instead of making amends to the ego, which is consumed by the narcissistic and self-blaming complex, and severing the ego from the lost object, it is necessary to show that it ought to be the ego that rejects the lost object. In contrast, to overcome "the impossibility of mourning," the work of mourning often becomes the political action of protest, or simply takes the form of protest to break down the boundaries between the symbolic space of the death ritual and the broad setting of everyday life, between private and public spaces. Instead of detaching the ego from the dead, the desire to win the entitlement to mourn in public intensifies attachment to the dead and motivates the mourner to change reality. Instead of a psychological symptom, the attachment to the loved object becomes a political identity.

In the face of bad deaths, analyses of psychodynamics could no longer stand outside of moral and political engagement. Skepticism about Hertz's model of solidarity as the highest, amoral merit had already emerged, early on, from the notion of "the work of mourning." The situations of "the inability to mourn" and "the impossibility of mourning" deepen that skepticism. An understanding of mourning was forced to search for a moral ground beyond social solidarity because social solidarity had to be redefined in light of its moral and political implications. In the final analysis, the question of "Who is mourned and why?" turns into the question "Who died and why?"[7]

Mourning as protesting

One of the most serious inadequacies of the Hertzian model is its blindness to the difficulty in carrying out the death ritual because of the disappearance of the body of the dead as a result of exigencies (Lifton 1991). In the case of bad deaths caused by exigencies such as natural disasters, violence, and wars, the missing of the dead bodies was common. Under such circumstances, the burial could not be carried out and cremation could not be done, not to mention disinterment. Survivors could suffer from the syndrome of denial – refusal to accept the fact of death. Death rituals have to deal with sorrowful, troubled emotions of the survivors who have lost not only the loved objects but also their bodies. Any attempt to maintain order and to reintegrate the survivors has to be based on the effort to create ample opportunities for the survivors to articulate sorrow without the bodies.

Veena Das (2006) described vividly the huge difficulty the mourners had to overcome in the absence of the dead body in the aftermath of the riots in India in the 1980s. Shanti lost her husband and two sons when rioters set fire to the house in which the three were hiding. Like many victims, she was trapped in the torrents of guilt and self-blame:

> Shanti would often get up in the middle of the night and wander to the park opposite their house, where she would gather sticks and make them into little piles, which she would proceed to burn. She was unable to explain what she was doing, but some neighbors believed that she was trying to cremate the bodies of the dead. They said, "They burned them alive, but the dead bodies were not cremated. They must wander around as ghosts and spirits. What peace will they get? What peace will we get?" This was always asked, although the ceremony of *antim ardas* for the placation of the dead was held and the *prasad* for peace was taken by a pious congregation. Shanti felt that they were deceiving themselves with these rituals. As long as the dead bodies had not been properly cremated, the souls of the dead could not be appeased. (Das 2006: 190–191)

Shanti eventually hanged herself. Leaving aside all the social and cultural contexts (including the patriarchal tradition that had deprived her of the sense of self-value as a result of the deaths of her sons), we can see the extreme agony of mourning without the dead bodies. It is one thing to see the life burned in violence, and it is entirely another to cremate the dead body to ashes in the due ritual of mourning.

Because the absence of the dead body and the harsh circumstances rendered the death rites hollow, refusal to participate in reintegration could also become a way to mourn. The women like Shanti who had lost husbands would not go into their houses, would not light the cooking hearths, and would not change their clothes, refusing to bring mourning to an end. Their refusal became a potent sign that mourning and protest were the same event (Das 2006: 195).

Like "the inability to mourn," "the refusal to end mourning" intensifies the resistance to the imposed, routinized reintegration through mourning. Like "the impossibility of mourning," "the refusal to end mourning" becomes a political action of protest against the social injustice responsible for the loss of life. In this light, death is no longer accepted as the end of a life, but is scrutinized as the beginning of the pursuit for justice. The gravity of mourning moved away from death toward life along the axis of moral responsibility for the loss.

Secularization and its Discontents

If life continues in a soul, why mourn?

One of the ways for the survivors to obtain some comfort was to think that the dead did not disappear altogether but existed in another form. This is where the notion of "soul" figures prominently in mourning under most religions, because mourning articulates the attachment of the mourner to the dead, who is now an existing soul.[8] Georg Simmel, a German sociologist, points out immortality as the underlying assumption for the creation of the soul: "Our narrow reality is … equipped with the intimation of an intensive endlessness that is projected in the time-dimension as immortality" (2010 [1918]: 76). However, immortality has to be grounded in a form imaginable to the living. Several tensions between immortality and imaginable ways of existence underlie the irresolvable contradictions. The first is that if the dead continue to live as a soul, what is the form of the soul's existence if it is not life again? Simmel described it thus:

> In the thought of immortality, we always bump into something no longer properly thinkable. This surely arises among other things from the fact that we imagine it as a life of the soul beyond the moment of bodily death; yet this is probably just an anthropomorphism, which even the most sublime speculations include no less than do the more childish primitive thoughts. It is not at all settled, though, that life is the only form in which the soul can exist. The soul may have yet other, nonconstruable forms at its disposal than just life, and the fact that it can think of timeless, life-transcendent contents is perhaps a kind of proof for this. (2010: 75)

Simmel calls our attention to the fact that immortality comes closest to comfort for people in mourning only under the condition that this immortality has to settle in the form in which a soul could be imagined to be alive. Most likely, that form is nothing other than life. This is where the contradiction between the boundlessness of the immortal and the boundedness of the mortal becomes acute. On the one hand, if a soul can continue to live a life, there is nothing to be mourned in death; on the other hand, if there is nothing imaginable concerning the continued existence of the dead, loss would become absolute, so absolute that mourning is useless. In the former case sorrow does not exist, whereas in the latter sorrow is too heavy to articulate.

Mourning emerged as a major activity of human beings precisely at the juncture of the destiny of a second life (afterlife) and its unfeasibility, because of its nature of imagination. An imagination of the existence of the soul in a form of life – nothing could really go beyond life – makes mourning a meaningful communication between the living and the dead, between mortality and immortality, and between the mortality present in the dead and the mortality imminent to the mourner.

It is common to hear mourners speaking with the dead in an authentic way in many sites of mourning in China – for example, in Tangshan, Chongqing, and Sichuan, where I have been doing fieldwork. The mourners knew that their loved ones were gone forever, but they could not help but want to speak with them as if they were alive. Whether or not there was a soul did not matter that much anymore.[9] They imagined and felt the dead in front of them (Zhang 2011b). Ms. Qin, a woman in her fifties had lost her parents in the Tangshan earthquake in 1976. After speaking to the inscribed names of her parents on the huge memorial wall, she said to me, with tears streaming down her face, "We all are doing very well, and living a good life. Their [her dead parents'] grandchild is even studying for a PhD. I just want to tell them so that they could know that we are doing well." To tell them as if they could hear was an important part of mourning. If there were not a negotiation between immortality and mortality, mourning would have been much less vivid and less meaningful. The common practice of *shaozhi* – burning "paper money" made of yellowish paper with the cutout or stamped image of a coin on it, to send currency to the dead in *yin* residence – confirmed the same genuine desire to communicate with the dead, despite the many years of radical political hostility toward superstition under Maoism and the atheism that now dominates China.

Hun (soul-like entity) and ancestor worship

The anthropomorphic scheme of the afterworld in Chinese folk beliefs (Wolf 1974) consists of three key figures – god, ghost, and ancestor – which indicate the three different potential forms of destiny of a dead person. First, if everything goes well ritualistically, a dead person is to join his or her ancestors and become a part of the collective target of ancestor worship. Second, if the proper rituals are not performed, however, this person would turn into a ghost after they have died a violent death. Third, an ordinary person is not eligible to become a god; only a few special persons are.[10] The three possibilities attach some kind of social distinction in the mundane world to *hun* or *linghun* (soul-like entity) in the *yin* realm, in contrast to the transcendental nature of the saved soul in the heaven of Christianity (Harrell 1979; Cohen 1988). *Hun* is pacified by proper death rituals and prevented from becoming a ghost to haunt people. The pacified soul is still anthropomorphic and not too far removed from the mundane world, making it imaginable for the mourner to have communication with the dead.[11]

This communicability between the living and the dead in afterlife is a cultural invention. It is different from the melancholic state of obsessive attachment, even though sometimes they are not distinguishable. For example, an old lady said to the inscribed name of the dead on the Tangshan earthquake memorial wall, "Your youngest sister is here to see you," some 30 years later, while touching the name. She spoke to the dead not as a transcended soul in heaven, but as a *hun* close to the mundane world. The mourning ritual of *shaozhi* (burning spirit money) has the connotation of making sure that the dead have money to spend in the *yin* dwelling. I asked the mourners whether they believed the paper money they burned could be delivered to the dead. The most common answer was, "I do this as my sincere offering. It makes me feel good." At first glance, it seems to be done only to comfort the mourner. But this comfort often lies in the mourner's imagined communication with the dead in which the image of the dead appears lively. Many mourners told me how they saw their dead relatives in dreams around the time of important occasions (Tomb Sweeping Festival and anniversary). After they burned paper money to make their offering, the images faded away from their dreams. Seen from the perspective of psychology, this kind of communicability might be a kind of psychological suggestion addressing anxiety in the mourner. Seen from the perspective of cultural practice, it confirms the collective imagination of the ethical responsibility of the living toward the dead. I often overheard mourners say to the dead: "You take care of yourself, and stay well with [somebody, be it a brother or sister, or someone else who is also dead]." Often the words were said with sincerity, tenderness, and emotion as a public affirmation of their continuing care for the dead.

In local practices of folk religion in Sichuan, the mourners took care of *hun* ritualistically.[12] For example, in death rituals I observed in villages in Sichuan, on the way to the grave site for burial, the mourners needed to send *hun* off along with the procession of the dead body in the coffin. Participants in the ritual lit firecrackers to contain the ghosts or made offerings in the form of food or paper money, to prevent the ghosts from harassing the procession of *hun* toward its destiny.

The impact of secularization of death on grieving

It is clear that the process of secularization has changed the practice of mourning and grieving today. Tony Walter (1997) has shown how, in the United Kingdom and in many other Western countries within the Christian tradition, death has changed its meaning over time even among those who claim to be Christians.

As a result of changes in social conditions, the church has lost control of the dying and the dead. For example, cremation has replaced burial to become the primary form of disposal of the body: crematoria are not owned by the church, most burial grounds have been commercialized, public health concerns have taken priority over religious considerations, and so on. Clergymen have been edged to the periphery as a result of death occurring predominantly in hospitals. Dying is no longer seen as a preparation for the passage of the soul to God. A good death is no longer where one prepares for the next life and meets one's Maker, but has now become the final stage of a life cycle. And death rituals are no longer a formal rendering of the spiritual passage of the soul to God. The grief of the survivors, rather than the journey of the soul, has become the issue to be managed, and the "life-centered" funeral has become the norm. Grief over the loss of life has become more important than Christian concerns such as the fear of hell and anxiety about judgment for sin. Even though funeral and memorial services are still predominantly conducted in church, such changes have resulted in the transformation of the mourning process into a more personalized, human-centered, individually tailored, and this-worldly oriented way of grieving[13]

(Walter 1997). It is no wonder that the articulation of personal feelings has taken its place in the death ritual.

> Whereas once the emotions of the dying and bereaved were judged in terms of whether they demonstrated faith and assisted passage to heaven (the Puritans, for example, feared that certain emotional outbursts on the deathbed could damage your chances of getting to heaven), now religious beliefs are judged in terms of whether they assist "the grief process." (Walter 1997: 181)

There has been a growing concern about abnormal expressions of grief under secularization and medicalization, so much so that "grief pathology," a cluster of abnormal phenomena relating to grieving, came into being in psychology and psychiatry (Kleinman 2012). "Grief pathology" is concerned with "grief that is never expressed, grief that goes on too intensely for too long, grief that is delayed, grief that involves delusions, grief that involves threats to others, grief that involves self-injury" (Rosenblatt 1997: 41). Even though the notion of proper grieving is not a recent one and is not confined to medicalized modern societies (Wellenkamp 1988; Yang 2004a, 2004b), its central place in death rituals and in the management of death is a modern development.

One recent development in the medicalization of grief, or "grief pathology," is the emergence of the category of trauma. Bad deaths resulting from war, natural disasters, and accidents have given rise to reactions now categorized as symptoms of post-traumatic stress disorder (PTSD). Studies of trauma have developed tremendously over the past two decades (Krimayer et al. 2007). The moral implications of this development on mourning are complex. First, it unpacks the melancholic reaction perceived by Freud into a whole set of symptoms, and has expanded the "work of mourning" into collective intervention in disaster situations and into careful management of the well-being of the survivors. For example, the avoidance of scenes reminiscent of the deaths and disasters among the mourners was taken for granted pre-PTSD, but PTSD has become a condition to be managed, if not completely cured, because it might hinder a citizen's ability to work and social relationship in modern society.

Second, the medicalization or "psychiatrization" of grief has provided medical categories, as well as evidence, for survivors of disasters to pursue compensation for the trauma they have suffered (Fassin and Rechtman 2009). This development has put more pressure on the state to develop a sophisticated apparatus to cope not only with the material destruction but also with the psychological impact in the aftermath of deaths, particularly as a result of disasters. However, while it may enhance the means of managing grief, the category of trauma could also conceal instead of disclosing the source of suffering because of its focus on the immediate influence of the disastrous event and its blindness to the long-term historical and social roots of the suffering and the chain of events (Zhang 2011a). There is a need to integrate the medicalized management of trauma with the cultural tradition of mourning.

The destruction of mourning rituals and their conditional revival

Secularization in China over the past century (particularly in the second half of the twentieth century) had dramatic twists. The decline of traditional mourning has not followed a lineal trajectory but a process of interactions between decline and revival. This can be seen in the story of the "age of wild ghosts" told by Erik Mueggler (2001).

In the village of Zhizuo in Yunnan Province, sacrificial and mourning rituals were an integral part of the *huotou* system (a self-governing system) in this community of Yi ethnicity. The most prominent ritual was the ten months of sacrifice required for all who had died the previous year. Even though it was criticized as superstition in the early 1950s by the cadres under the socialist state, it continued to be performed because the cadres too had to deal with deaths in their own families. Its primary function was to insure the transition of the dead from this world to the next world, to separate the dead from the living, and to complete the process of mourning. It was supposed to last eight hours and involved making offerings to the dead, ranging from rice cakes to sacrificial goats. However, the Great Leap Forward in 1958 made it difficult to carry on the ritual. After the People's Commune was established, commune members had to give up all privately owned resources, including any animals, and to eat in the commune mess halls. This collectivization deprived the villagers of the resources they needed to conduct the ritual. The Great Leap Forward also greatly increased the workload of each villager, who was turned into a member of the People's Commune. Many had to work more than 12 hours a day, both day and night. At the same time, they did not have much to eat because the food quickly ran out in the mess halls after several months of unrestrained consumption of food, allegedly to reflect the advent of a "communist society." Commune members were also too exhausted to climb up to the mountain top where the ten-month sacrifice ritual was supposed to be held.

The change in the social body – the collectivization of ownership, the change in space for eating from households to mess halls – and the change in the physical body from exhaustion due to overwork destroyed the ritual. Furthermore, when famine started to result in abnormal deaths, conducting any death rituals (even two small related rituals, the night vigil and the day vigil) became politically dangerous.

Ironically, the death ritual was destroyed around a time that saw an increase in abnormal deaths. As a result, people were not able to cope with death properly. The consequence was the arrival of what the locals called the "age of wild ghosts." According to local interpretation, the dead who had not had proper mourning and burial now came back to haunt the living, demanding food and care. People started to experience possession, whereby they would speak in the voice of a dead relative. Such speeches often included an insatiable demand from the dead for food. Interestingly, most of the bad deaths had happened to the cadres involved in carrying out orders from above in the Great Leap Forward and the Socialist Education Movement. That they became ghosts was evidence of the power of the local symbolic system to punish those who destroyed the death rituals, arguing loudly for the restoration of the cultural order after Maoism declined.

As the political atmosphere relaxed, particularly after the disbanding of the People's Commune, villagers started to perform the ritual of exorcism. The ritual set up a time and space for the living to make offerings to the dead who had turned into ghosts. Chants were read, mourning songs sung, and food offered to urge the dead souls to go to the place where other souls of the dead were congregated. The space was arranged so that the living had the chance to engage and then disengage with the dead, thus unraveling the entanglement of the dead with the living. The ritual was frequently performed in the age of wild ghosts, as a way to stop the social chaos, to put away the threat of the dead, and to heal the wounds.

At first glance, the story of the age of wild ghosts reinforces the Hertzian idea of solidarity built upon proper death and burial rituals, the absence of which had led to the age of wild ghosts. However, the reconstruction of the ritual could not restore the death rituals completely, because the old self-governing system was gone. Furthermore, death rituals such as exorcism and night vigils were already in decline because mourners in a secular society could not, as before, draw moral lessons from avenging the grieved souls. Secularization, however twisted, is a reality.

Life-Centered Grieving

Lessened control over grieving

The trend observed in studies of mourning reflects either an increasing concern about the well-being of individual survivors or a desire to articulate a personal grief over the loss of life. These have developed at the expense of the collective concern about social integration. More accurately, they have developed under the condition of redefining the moral foundation of social solidarity. Diane O'Rourke's (2007) work on the ritual of disinterment in Greece over the past decades shows the increasing articulation of grief and the weakened ritualistic and self-control of public display of emotions, confirming the trend. The changing social conditions – the decline in agricultural production, the increasing population, and the development of transportation – account for the decline of communities' control over ritual processes and therefore over the articulation of grief. As a result, participation in grieving is more an individual affair than a communal matter. Public grieving does not seem to matter much.

However, in many other contexts (particularly contexts of war, natural disasters, and intense conflicts), grievability – the eligibility of the dead to be grieved in public – has become acute.

Grievability

Judith Butler (2010) raises the notion of "grievability," based on her reflections on terrorist attacks, anti-terrorist wars, and the conflict in the Middle East. She argues: "Only under the conditions in which the loss matters did the value of life appear. So grievability is the presupposition for life that matters" (Butler 2010: 14). This argument is extremely insightful. First, instead of arguing for the human right to live (and not to die a bad death), "grievability" highlights the eligibility to grieve – both the dead person's right to be grieved over and the mourner's right to grieve – as a crucial way to realize one's rights. Grieving gives a cultural form and capacity to that eligibility. Second, "grievability" substantiates the value of life by emphasizing the common practice of grieving, as if the value of life were produced through grieving. It is revealing that the significance of death rituals lies in that the value of life is evident only when the loss of life is taken seriously. The crucial way to make the loss of life matter is to gain access to public grieving.

It is not new to argue that mourning is not about the dead but about the living. Even the Hertzian model testifies to this, for social solidarity is about resuming order for the living. However, it is entirely new to say that mourning is not about death but about life, because to elaborate on Butler's argument, grievability – the eligibility to mourn in public – is about the worthiness of life – for the dead as well as for the living.

The notion of grievability arose out of the precariousness and vulnerability of life in the contemporary world, and the unequal distribution of the worthiness of life under globalization.[14] In recent decades, anthropological explorations have intensified on human conditions crucial to the issue of life and death, such as human suffering (e.g., Kleinman et al. 1997), structural violence (e.g., Farmer 2004), necropolitics (Mbembe 2003), abandonment and social death (e.g., Biehl 2005), and so on. The studies of biopolitics intensified inquiries into the struggle for equal distribution of value of life through notions such as "biological citizenship" (Rose 2001; Petryna 2002; Rose and Novas 2005) and "biolegitimacy" (Fassin 2005, 2009). That the Great Leap Famine in China between 1959 and 1961 killed peasants exclusively is now the best example of the unequal distribution of the value of life (Dikötter 2010; Zhang 2011c). At the same time, those inquiries sharpened concerns about the relationship between life and power – namely, how death is accounted for by the state, and how conscionable struggles for entitlement to be mourned in public around the globe confirmed grievability as a measure of life.[15] Grieving for the loss of life in public is not just to bring mourning to an end, but to raise questions about life – whether life is valued, partially valued, or not valued at all.

Grievability is also a measure of the state's orientation. In the traditional view of death, a death in a remote mountainous village might have little to do with the governing power. From this perspective about grieving, any death, particularly a bad death, could in one way or another implicate the state whose role is to extend life. Mourning has therefore become a more and more important space for making inquiries into the responsibility of the state. Moreover, the progress from the inclusion of bad deaths to life-centered grieving raises the question of who should be mourned by whom. Answers to this question will put the practice of life-centered grieving to the test: How far should and can mourning reach beyond the deaths of one's kinsmen to form inclusive moral communities of mourning? In practice, we cannot help but notice exclusion upon exclusion of "others" from joining the moral community of mourning and from gaining grievability, when the rifts in human society prevail. The issue of inclusion is not about how every death should be mourned by everyone; it is about how the moral community of mourning led by the state and the nation should not exclude those citizens because of their status of otherness.

This is where I want to offer a reinterpretation of one episode in the story of the age of wild ghosts (Mueggler 2001). The villagers conducted a ritual of exorcism for the ghosts who had emerged in local folklore as a result of the destruction of death rituals in the Great Leap Forward. They read chants, followed the map detailing a route of exorcism moving beyond the village, along the Yangzi River, to reach Beijing. Beijing was where the emperor and empress of ghosts resided. They turned out to be Lin Biao and Jiang Qing. Lin Biao was vice chairman of the Chinese Communist Party and Mao's hand-picked successor who had turned against him. He died in an air crash in a flight from China in 1971. Jiang Qing was Mao's wife, one of the members of the Gang of Four who was put on trial after Mao's death. In this exorcism,

Mao was replaced by Lin Biao and thus spared the exorcizing curse. But village ritual specialists could not be so insensitive as to misstate the spousal relationship by assigning Lin Biao and Jiang Qing to the roles of emperor and empress. In the surface script they displaced Mao with Lin but in the deep script they implicated Mao in the lack of grievability for the deaths of villagers and for several tens of millions of lost peasant lives around the country. Unlike the dead Red Guards in Chongqing who were finally given the entitlement to be mourned, no tombs have been publicly erected for the peasants who died. That one more group of the dead was included for grieving only calls our attention to the exclusion of more groups of the dead from grieving.

Conclusion: The Moral Ground for Grieving

Studies of mourning have moved far beyond Hertz's model, but we still owe a debt to Hertz's insights in the irony that has not gone away. Hertz stated: "In the final analysis, death as a social phenomenon consists of a dual and painful labor of mental disintegration and synthesis; it is only when this labor is completed that society, returned to a state of peace, can triumph over death" (2009: 145). In his view, only the society, and not the individual, could triumph over death through the reintegration of individuals. If "triumph" means the continuation of a vital force after death, no individual can triumph over death. But what is at stake is the kind of society to which Hertz is referring.

This essay has reviewed important developments in anthropological studies of mourning and their moral implications. Redefining the moral foundation of social solidarity and the moral nature of the work of mourning, the perspective of life-centered grieving has come to prominence and become a central perspective on the study of mourning. Social solidarity is no longer achieved primarily through sending off the soul peacefully, but is best achieved through accounting for deaths equally. What concerns the society in mourning should not be only social stability, without taking into account what kind of solidarity is maintained, whose grief is articulated or suppressed, in whose interests, and at whose expense. Moreover, deaths – particularly bad deaths – have become critical events subject to scrutiny as to what causes them and who are responsible for them. How death is mourned is crucial to how the death is accounted for; how death is accounted for is crucial to how life is valued. Ultimately, life takes priority over social solidarity. In this sense, the anthropological scope of mourning has been acutely moralized since Hertz's time.

Secularization demystifies death and contributes to the prolonging of life but, ironically, only to leave mourners facing the increased power of death, because the idea of death has become more threatening. In contrast, believing in the impermanence of life but in cyclical rebirth, Buddhists commonly have a lower anxiety about death.[16] Recent evidence shows that, under the influence of Buddhism, survivors of the Yushu earthquake in China were significantly less anxious and had a lower rate of PTSD than those in the Wenchuan quake. This is where life-centered grieving reveals an ethical predicament: while life is enhanced, death is empowered.

To sum up, in coping with death, life continues through mourning, but grieving expands further and further beyond mourning, to chase and cover every trace of mortality in hope of its reduction for all.

NOTES

1 About the simplification of death rituals in socialist China, see Whyte 1988.
2 In his famous studies of rites of passage including death rituals, van Gennep (1960 [1909]) shared with Hertz the Durkheimian idea of social solidarity, through differentiating the ritual process into several phases toward reintegration.
3 Social solidarity affirmed by death rituals has many effects, including affirming hierarchy – by generation, blood, and gender (Martin 1988; Naquin 1988; J. L. Watson 2004), symbolic regeneration of life (Humphreys and King 1981; Bloch and Parry 1982;), communal mobilization (R. S. Watson 2004) or reciprocity (Yan 1996; Chau 2006), etc.
4 The notion of bad death is common around the world (Robben 2004), but practice in China contradicts Hertz's point concerning the elderly. The higher the age of the dead, the stronger the impulse to celebrate it as *xishang* (auspicious death).
5 Xu Jijun (2004) shares the discovery of the exclusion of inauspicious deaths in death rituals in China. Because inauspicious deaths were thought to be caused by evil ghosts or possession, they were believed to bring bad luck to the living, and were to be avoided at all costs. Quick burials, their exclusion from the primary space of the household, and so on were believed to prevent the inauspiciousness from harming the living. As Huo and Huang point out, early on the death of soldiers in battlefields were treated as *xiongsi* (inauspicious deaths) and excluded from public grave sites. The state started to glorify the deaths of its warriors by building grand graves for well-known warriors such as Huo Qubing in the Han period (Huo and Huang 1992: 44). This transformation had a profound influence on the practice of mourning for dead soldiers later on. The religious notion of a good death shaped the management of deaths in the American Civil War in the nineteenth century and helped turn horror into good deaths under modern governance (Faust 2008).
6 I thank Didier Fassin for offering this phrase.
7 The Civil War, along with the management of the large-scale deaths, advanced the solidarity of the American nation on the moral ground of emerging modern citizenship (Faust 2008). The distinction between mourning for life and mourning for solidarity in the case of war, particularly international wars, complicates the argument and requires much more space to engage a discussion than is allowed here.
8 An afterlife, or its variations, is central to religious belief around the world and became the basis for the idea of the "soul."
9 This is yet another characteristic of folk religion in Chinese practice.
10 The process of becoming a god varies across Chinese society. For example, Lin, a dead woman in Fujian, became a local goddess, Mazu, only after a legendary story of how she had saved the lives of seafarers became widespread. This deity was later officially granted the title of Tianhou (Empress of Heaven) by the imperial state (Watson 1985). She has been worshipped in many places along the coast of southeastern China and in Taiwan. Such deities number in the thousands in Chinese history.
11 The spirit of *qi* is *hun*. *Hun* was considered a spirit riding on or attached to *qi* (vital energy) in ancient Chinese understanding (Kong 1965).
12 *Yili* (Rituals) records how this was done. A man climbed up to the roof of the house from the east, called the name of the dead, and then threw down the cloth of the dead to someone on the ground who caught it. The caller then went down to the west. The cloth was then used to cover the body of the dead. The dead person's *hun* leaves the body and wanders to the dark place that remind us of the *yin* realm. Calling *hun* means trying to call the *hun* back from the dark place, so that it can re-enter the body and reside there so that the dead can be reborn. Only after the *hun* calling fails to recover the dead can the death ritual proceed (Yang 2004b). However, different interpretations of this practice exist, for

example, calling the *hun* can be seen as trying to prevent it from doing harm to the living. This interpretation resembles the practice Hertz documented among the Dayaks of Borneo. De Groot (1964 [1892]) noticed that this practice had already disappeared, but its variations continued to exist, for example, sending *hun* is popular in many death rituals (Xu 2004).

13 "In the rubric of the 1662 Prayer Book, a funeral could be conducted without even mentioning the name of the departed" (Walter 1997: 171). I attended a memorial service in a church in Buffalo in 2009 for a female historian who had died in an air crash, at which her husband delivered a speech that included intimate memories of how they had dated in college.

14 I would add the notions of "bare life" of the *homo sacer*, biopower, and governmentality to the list of inspiration (Agamben 1998; Foucault 2007).

15 Reburial after political rehabilitation became a way to win back grievability (Verdery 1999; Robben 2000; Kwon 2008). A panel devoted to grieving in Annual Meetings of the Association for Asian Studies in 2011 contained presentations about building a database of dead soldiers from Australia in the Vietnam War, building graves for Vietnamese refugees who had died at sea, the grave sites of Vietnamese recruited by French colonists to fight World War I in Europe, and the participation of a US Vietnam War veteran in the reburial of a villager who had been killed under his fire some 40 years earlier. I saw the author of the last-mentioned presentation weeping and heard the audience sobbing.

16 See Desjarlais 2003.

REFERENCES

Agamben, Giorgio (1998) *Homo Sacer*. Stanford: Stanford University Press.

Biehl, João (2005) *Vita*. Berkeley: University of California Press.

Bloch, Maurice and Parry, Jonathan (eds.) (1982) *Death and the Regeneration of Life*. New York: Cambridge University Press.

Butler, Judith (2010) *Frames of War: When is Life Grievable?* New York: Verso.

Chau, Adam Yuet (2006) *Miraculous Response*. Stanford: Stanford University Press.

Clark-Decès, Isabelle (2005) *No One Cries for the Dead*. Berkeley: University of California Press.

Cohen, Myron (1988) *Soul and Salvation: Conflicting Themes in Chinese Popular Religion*. In James L. Watson and Evelyn S. Rawski (eds.), *Death Ritual in Late Imperial and Modern China*. Berkeley: University of California Press, pp. 180–202.

Das, Veena (2006) Three Portraits of Grief and Mourning. In *Life and Words: Violence and the Descents into the Ordinary*. Berkeley: University of California Press, pp. 184–204.

De Groot, Jan Jakob Maria (1964 [1892]) *The Religious System of China*. 6 vols. Taipei: Literature House.

Desjarlais, Robert (2003) *Sensory Biographies*. Berkeley: University of California Press.

Dikötter, Frank (2010) *Mao's Great Famine*. New York: Walker.

Durkheim, Emile (1915) *The Elementary Forms of the Religious Life*. London: Allen & Unwin.

Farmer, Paul (2004) *Pathologies of Power*. Berkeley: University of California Press.

Fassin, Didier (2005) Compassion and Repression: The Moral Economy of Immigration Policies in France. *Cultural Anthropology* 20(3): 362–387.

Fassin, Didier (2009) Another Politics of Life is Possible. *Theory, Culture and Society* 26(5):44–60.

Fassin, Didier and Rechtman, Richard (2009) *The Empire of Trauma*. Princeton: Princeton University Press.

Faust, Drew Gilpin (2008) *This Republic of Suffering*. New York: Knopf.

Foucault, Michel (2007) *Security, Territory, Population: Lectures at the Collège de France 1977–1978*. New York: Palgrave Macmillan.

Freud, Sigmund (1999 [1917]) Mourning and Melancholia. In *The Standard Edition of the Complete Psychological Works of Sigmund Freud*, vol. 14: 1914–1916. New York: Vintage, pp. 237–258.

Geertz, Clifford (1960) *The Religion of Java*. Glencoe, IL: Free Press.

Harrell, Stevan (1979) The Concept of Soul in Chinese Folk Religion. *Journal of Asian Studies* 38(3): 519–528.

Hertz, Robert (2009[1907]) A Contribution to the Study of the Collective Representation of Death. In Alexander Riley et al. (eds.), *Saints, Heroes, Myths, and Rites*. London: Paradigm, pp. 109–181.

Humphreys, S. C. and King, Helen (eds.) (1981) *Mortality and Immortality: The Anthropology and Archaeology of Death*. London: Academic Press.

Huntington, Richard and Metcalf, Peter (1979) *Celebrations of Death*. New York: Cambridge University Press.

Huo Wei and Huang Wei (1992) *Sichuan Sangzang Wenhua* [The Culture of Death and Mourning in Sichuan]. Chengdu: Sichuan renmin chubanshe.

Johnson, Elizabeth L. (1988) Grieving for the Dead, Grieving for the Living: Funeral Laments of Hakka Women. In James L. Watson and Evelyn S. Rawski (eds.), *Death Ritual in Late Imperial and Modern China*. Berkeley: University of California Press, pp. 135–163.

Kleinman, Arthur (2012) Art of Medicine: Culture, Bereavement and Psychiatry. *The Lancet* 379: 608–609.

Kleinman, Arthur, Das, Veena, and Lock, Margaret (eds.) (1997) *Social Suffering*. Berkeley: University of California Press.

Kong Yingda (1965) *Zuozhuan zhu shu* [Annotations of the History of Spring and Autumn]. Taipei: Taiwan Zhonghua shuju.

Krimayer, Laurence J., Lemelson, Robert, and Barad, Mark (eds.) (2007) *Understanding Trauma*. New York: Cambridge University Press.

Kwon, Heonik (2008) *Ghosts of War in Vietnam*. New York: Cambridge University Press.

Lifton, Robert (1991) *Death in Life*. Chapel Hill: University of North Carolina Press.

Martin, Emily (1988) Gender and Ideological Differences in Representations of Life and Death. In James L. Watson and Evelyn S. Rawski (eds.), *Death Ritual in Late Imperial and Modern China*. Berkeley: University of California Press, pp. 164–179.

Mbembe, Achille (2003) Necropolitics. *Public Culture* 15(1): 11–40.

Mitscherlich, Alexander and Mitscherlich, Margarete (1975) *The Inability to Mourn*. New York: Grover.

Mueggler, Erik (2001) *The Age of Wild Ghosts*. Berkeley: University of California Press.

Naquin, Susan (1988) Funerals in North China. In James L. Watson and Evelyn S. Rawski (eds.), *Death Ritual in Late Imperial and Modern China*. Berkeley: University of California Press, pp. 37–70.

O'Rourke, Diane (2007) Mourning Becomes Eclectic: Death of Communal Practice in a Greek Cemetery. *American Ethnologist* 34(2): 387–402.

Petryna, Adriana (2002) *Life Exposed*. Princeton: Princeton University Press.

Radcliffe-Brown, A. R. (1964) *The Andaman Islanders*. New York: Free Press.

Robben, Antonius C. G. M. (2000) State Terror in the Netherworld: Disappearance and Reburial in Argentina. In Jeffrey A. Sluka (ed.), *Death Squad: The Anthropology of State Terror*. Philadelphia: University of Pennsylvania Press.

Robben, Antonius C. G. M. (ed.) (2004) *Death, Mourning, and Burial: A Cross-Cultural Reader*. Oxford: Wiley-Blackwell.

Rose, Nikolas (2001) The Politics of Life Itself. *Theory, Culture and Society* 18(2): 1–30.

Rose, Nikolas and Novas, Carlos (2005) Biological Citizenship. In Aihwa Ong and Stephen Collier (eds.), *Global Assemblages*. Malden, MA: Blackwell, pp. 439–463.

Rosenblatt, Paul C. (1997) Grief in Small Scale Societies. In Colin Murray Parkes et al. (eds.), *Death and Bereavement across Cultures*. London: Routledge, pp. 28–51.

Scheper-Hughes, Nancy (1992) *Death without Weeping*. Berkeley: University of California Press.

Simmel, Georg (2010[1918]) *The View of Life*. Chicago: University of Chicago Press.
van Gennep, Arnold (1960[1909]) *The Rites of Passage*. Chicago: University of Chicago Press.
Verdery, Katherine (1999) *The Political Lives of Dead Bodies: Reburial and Postsocialist Change*. New York: Columbia University Press.
Walter, Tony (1997) Secularization. In Colin Murray Parkes et al. (eds.), *Death and Bereavement across Cultures*. London: Routledge, pp. 166–187.
Watson, James L. (1985) Standardizing the Gods: The Promotion of T'ien Hou (Empress of Heaven) along the South China Coast, 960–1960. In David Johnson et al. (eds.), *Popular Culture in Late Imperial China*. Berkeley: University of California Press, pp. 292–324.
Watson, James L. (2004) Funeral Specialists in Cantonese Society: Pollution, Performance and Social Hierarchy. In James L. Watson and Rubie S. Watson, *Village Life in Hong Kong*. Hong Kong: Chinese University Press, pp. 391–422.
Watson, Rubie S. (2004) Remembering the Dead: Graves and Politics in Southeastern China. In James L. Watson and Rubie S. Watson, *Village Life in Hong Kong*. Hong Kong: Chinese University Press, pp. 325–354.
Wellenkamp, Jane C. (1988) The Notion of Grief and Catharsis among the Toraja. *American Ethnologist* 15(3): 486–500.
Whyte, Martin K. (1988) Death in the People's Republic of China. In James L. Watson and Evelyn S. Rawski (eds.), *Death Ritual in Late Imperial and Modern China*. Berkeley: University of California Press, pp. 289–316.
Wolf, Arthur (1974) Gods, Ancestors, and Ghosts. In Arthur Wolf (ed.), *Religion and Ritual in Chinese Society*. Stanford: Stanford University Press, pp. 131–182.
Xu Jijun (2004) *Changjiang Liuyu de Sangzang* [Death Rituals along the Yangzi River]. Wuhan: Hubei jiaoyu chubanshe.
Yan, Yunxiang (1996) *The Flow of Gifts*. Stanford: Stanford University Press.
Yang Tianyu (2004a) *Liji yizhu* [The Book of Rites and its Annotation and Translation]. Shanghai: Shanghai guji chubanshe.
Yang Tianyu (2004b) *Yili yizhu* [Rituals and its Annotation and Translation]. Shanghai: Shanghai guji chubanshe.
Zhang, Everett (2009) Grieving at the Graveyard for the Red Guards in China: In the Name of Life Itself. Paper presented at Department of East Asian Studies, Princeton University, Jan. 20.
Zhang, Everett (2011a) Grieving from the Tangshan Earthquake to the Wenchuan Earthquake: The Emergence of the Category of "Trauma" in China. Paper presented at the Annual Meetings of the Association for Asian Studies, Hawaii, Apr. 1.
Zhang, Everett (2011b) How Life Became Grievable: Three Decades after the Tangshan Earthquake. Paper presented at the Department of East Asian Studies, Princeton University, Feb. 9.
Zhang, Everett (2011c) The Truth about the Death Toll in the Great Leap Famine in Sichuan: An Analysis of Maoist Sovereignty. In Everett Zhang et al. (eds.), *Governance of Life in Chinese Moral Experience*. London: Routledge, pp. 62–80.

CHAPTER 16 Poverty

Harri Englund

"What would the world look like," Kwame Anthony Appiah (2006: 166) exclaims, "if people always spent their money to alleviate diarrhea in the Third World and never on a ticket to the opera?" The question goes to the heart of the choices self-styled cosmopolitans in affluent Northern countries are likely to pose themselves. In a world where the values guiding decisions are multiple and the scale of economic and political problems often overwhelms, what is the relationship between choice and obligation, between ethical discretion and moral imperative? The kind of cosmopolitanism Appiah espouses represents a turn toward value pluralism in much moral and political philosophy since the late twentieth century.[1] Cosmopolitans, Appiah states, "hope and expect that different people and different societies will embody different values" (2006: 144). At the same time, they believe that "every human being has obligations to every other. Everybody matters" (144). Here the predicament of world poverty raises its ugly head, a test of consistency in cosmopolitan moral philosophy. Appiah asserts the special value that the nearest and dearest embody even in the cosmopolitan lifeworld: "Whatever my basic obligations are to the poor far away, they cannot be enough, I believe, to trump my concerns for my family, my friends, my country" (165). Even the most monied of cosmopolitans can do no more than his or her "fair share" (164), and the plurality of values cannot be reduced to a single principle of goodness and badness. "You are not killing anyone by going to the opera" (167). The drift of Appiah's argument is to associate obligations with ethical choices. The white man's burden becomes the cosmopolitan's burden.

Appiah's is a lenient response to the moral dilemma that the distant needy have posed to liberal theory since the late twentieth century. One of the earliest definitions of this dilemma also had the most demanding conclusion. "It makes no moral difference," Peter Singer argued, "whether the person I help is a neighbor's child ten yards from me or a Bengali whose name I shall never know, ten thousand miles away"

A Companion to Moral Anthropology, First Edition. Edited by Didier Fassin.

(1972: 231–232). Not only did the argument insist that the obligation to help a stranger was as compelling as the obligation to help a neighbor's child, it also rejected the idea that physical distance would play a role in moral obligations. Although this demanding thesis continues to have its adherents, urging the well-off to contribute most of their present and future earnings and property to organizations fighting world poverty (Unger 1996; see also Singer 2009), the liberal debate is enlivened by a subtle sense of complexity. Claims to cosmopolitanism are common, albeit not always in harmony with Appiah's particular position.

Renewed interest in economic rights is another source of fresh reflections on involuntary poverty and obligation in liberal political and moral theory (see, e.g., Pogge 2002; Hertel and Minkler 2007; Sengupta 2007). Against the conventional liberal view that the scope of economic rights should be confined to insuring that individuals and companies can engage in productive activities with minimal interference, economic rights focus attention on the provision of adequate resources and opportunities as a matter of justice (Kimenyi 2007). This approach recognizes that severe poverty in the contemporary world is not a natural calamity but an avoidable predicament. The issue of obligation arises, because economic rights require a degree of specificity about the link between rights violations and those capable of rectifying them. As such, liberal theorists debate not only states as the expected guarantors of rights but also the role various other actors from individual human beings to multinational corporations ought to play in alleviating world poverty.

Obligation as duty or responsibility exercises liberal theorists, because it can entail both the negative duty of not to deprive persons of access to basic necessities and the positive duty of protecting their opportunity to earn a subsistence income (Ashford 2007). What might exercise anthropologists, on the other hand, is the way in which the moral argument about world poverty in liberal theory evokes the liberal ideas of personhood, freedom, and autonomy. The philosophical and sociological antecedents of this moral argument are, of course, complex enough to undermine any simple contrast between liberal theory and anthropology. While often mindful of the ideological individualism inherent in efforts to view one person's duty as the corollary of another person's right, those anthropologists who want their discipline to change its focus from morality to ethics have much in common with liberal cosmopolitans.[2] Obligation is, however, a classic topic in anthropology, particularly in studies of kinship and gift exchange (see, e.g., Fortes 1949; Mauss 1974 [1925]; Shipton 2007), but the liberal debate on world poverty draws it into an altogether fresh philosophical territory. Here anthropologists' distinction between ethics and morality may prove unproductive. The challenge is to engage that debate with conceptual and ethnographic resources that liberal cosmopolitans rarely have at their disposal.

In this essay, world poverty comes to be inflected through the single case of Malawi, not as an argument for keeping the debate confined to specific localities, even less for taking Malawi to stand for all the poverty in the world, but as a way of asserting anthropology's particular attention to the difference a *perspective* makes. Rather than allowing the debate on world poverty to proceed as though the concepts of obligation, autonomy, and the individual had the self-evident value liberal cosmopolitans attribute to them, anthropology can deploy the single-case approach to suggest that their uses by liberal cosmopolitans might be highly specific. The approach requires, first, awareness of the extent to which some cosmopolitan positions represent innovations within the liberal tradition. It also requires ethnographic and linguistic consideration of the ways in which the poor might themselves describe their condition and the obligations it entails. The essay then proceeds to examine targeted aid as one recent instance in which contrasting perspectives on morality and poverty have collided.

Threats, Obligations, and Autonomy

Although no one country should be taken as the paradigm of African poverty, Malawi tends to assume iconic qualities in Western concerns. With its predominantly rural economy and lack of significant mineral and oil resources, coupled with its avoidance of large-scale civil strife throughout its independence since 1964, Malawi may seem to offer a conveniently pure case of African poverty. Both *The End of Poverty* by Jeffrey Sachs (2005) and *The Bottom Billion* by Paul Collier (2007), published at the height of one of the West's periodic panics over African poverty, begin their narratives with their authors' reminiscences of visits to Malawi. Sachs describes passing through a village devastated by HIV/AIDS and the "dying chamber" (2005: 8) of a major hospital. Collier, in turn, recalls his early days as a development economist in Malawi in the 1960s and reports that "Malawi hasn't changed much in the last thirty-five years" (2007: ix). The jump from the scale of one country to that of world poverty is effortless. "There are," Sachs explains, "roughly one billion people around the world, one sixth of humanity, who live as the Malawians do" (2005: 18). He is referring to the same one billion people who, according to Collier, "are living and dying in fourteenth-century conditions" (2007: 3).

The idea of change, however, is what drives the two books. For both authors, despite the differences in their approach to foreign aid, Malawi serves a rhetorical purpose to define not only the nature of world poverty but also the threat it poses to the West. Their portrayals of Malawi might be expected to evoke pity in the minds of their readers, with moral agency invested in *us* rather than *them*. Threats to the security and affluence of the West are what issue a call to action in both books. For Sachs, "the question isn't whether the rich can afford to help the poor, but whether they can afford not to" (2005: 288). "If we let this continue," Collier warns with regard to the fourteenth-century conditions in a twenty-first century world, "our children will face an alarmingly divided world and all its consequences" (2007: 191).

Threats to *our* children and *our* security and affluence may well be necessary to spur Western governments and citizens into action. However, the need for action should not cloud other ways in which world poverty presents an intellectual, moral, and pragmatic challenge. By making Malawi an unchanging, timeless template for the condition of poverty, Collier and Sachs leave that predicament unspecified, in its abstraction a condition that no one really inhabits. Perhaps they are not interested, or able, to attend to the specifics of claims and aspirations that inform the variable experiences of being poor, a methodological oversight apparent in Sachs's consistent misspelling of Malawi's then vice president's name.[3] One consequence is their failure to envision any other method than the use of threat to capture the attention of affluent Westerners. It becomes all but impossible to consider mutual dependence as a positive rather than a negative condition.

Collier and Sachs stand apart from liberal cosmopolitans, who draw on political and moral philosophy in their efforts to explore obligation and autonomy instead of threat as the key to confronting world poverty. Many liberal cosmopolitans distinguish themselves from the argument in John Rawls's *The Law of Peoples* (1999).[4] The disagreement derives from Rawls's concept of peoples as the basic units of a theory of global justice. This choice to highlight peoples rather than individuals separates Rawls from the Kantian notion of cosmopolitan citizens who are members of a world society (compare Bohman and Lutz-Bachmann 1997).[5] Not only is Rawls's view incompatible with the historical and contemporary significance of migration (Benhabib 2004: 74–94) and with a critique of hierarchy and subordination within societies that undermine, for example, women's capabilities (Nussbaum 2004). It also justifies, in Thomas Pogge's words, "inequality by appeal to group autonomy" (2002: 234), a position akin to "explanatory nationalism," which diverts attention from "how we ourselves might be involved, causally and morally," in the perpetuation of world poverty (Pogge 2002: 49).

It is here that the issue of obligation appears in its specific cosmopolitan guise. Tormented by their awareness of a world that is as interdependent as it is unequal, liberal cosmopolitans debate institutional, moral, and legal interventions to ameliorate, if not to eradicate, severe poverty. Despite their consensus on many important moral and political issues, these liberal authors begin to differ when the possibility of global redistribution of wealth is raised. Rawls's viewpoint serves, again, as a useful foil. While admitting that affluent peoples have a duty to assist less fortunate ones, he denies that "the only way, or the best way, to carry out this duty of assistance is by following a principle of global distributive justice" (Rawls 1999: 106). His cosmopolitan critics agree that obligations go beyond Rawls's natural duty of assistance. Indeed, some point out that terms such as "assistance" and "aid" suggest "charity and optionality rather than justice and obligation" (Lichtenberg 2004: 95). However, in response to the common objection against distributive justice that no person or institution can possibly control all the world's resources and decide how they are to be redistributed (see, e.g., Nozick 1974: 149), Pogge proposes a different concept of distributive justice. He calls for "economic ground rules that regulate property, cooperation, and exchange and thereby condition production and distribution" (Pogge 2002: 176). This concept of distributive justice is, therefore, less about deciding how existing resources are to be redistributed than about making moral and political interventions prior to production and distribution.[6]

Much as these debates indicate liberal cosmopolitans' penchant for both philosophical and policy-oriented work, they should not conceal their most consequential shared feature. Whatever their awareness of transnational and institutional conditions, it is poverty's assault on personal autonomy that spurs liberal cosmopolitans into a critique. Poverty provokes, in other words, their theoretical and moral sensibilities because of its adverse effects on the individual's capacity to make choices and to lead an independent life (see, e.g., Sen 1999; Fleurbaye 2007; Kreide 2007). Pogge identifies individualism as an aspect of all liberal cosmopolitanism, with individuals as "the ultimate units of concern" (2002: 169) instead of families, ethnic and religious communities, nations, and so on. Martha Nussbaum endorses this view by insisting that "the separate person should be the basic unit for political distribution" and that women, rather than be seen as "parts of an organic entity, such as the family is supposed to be," are to be regarded as "political subjects in their own right" (2000: 247). Crucial to this view is the principle of each person as end, their separateness thought to be evident not only on theoretical grounds but also in poor people's subjective experience of hunger and hard physical labor (57) and in "the empirical fact of bodily separateness" (60). While liberal cosmopolitans may disagree on the exact scope of structural reform, they are in no doubt about personal autonomy as both the means and end of alleviating poverty.[7]

Individualism also informs the cosmopolitan critique of Rawls's (1999) theory of global justice. Seyla Benhabib (2004: 92–93), for example, points out how his reliance on the category of peoples represents an unfortunate diversion from the Kantian principle of individuals as moral and political agents in a world society. Benhabib's own argument, however, is a good example of how classic liberal concerns both enable and constrain moral and political theory. Her interest in the contemporary processes of migration and citizenship brings her not only to Kantian cosmopolitanism but also to the idea of membership, famously expressed in Hannah Arendt's insight that "we are not born equal; we become equal as members of a group on the strength of our decision to guarantee ourselves mutually equal rights" (1951: 301). This insight, along with the exclusionary policies that many nation-states inflict on migrants and asylum-seekers who wish to become their members, makes Benhabib skeptical about both world society and nation-state as an institutional framework for membership. The "cosmopolitan federalism" she advances is not an argument for automatic membership in democratic polities but a call for using cosmopolitan norms to guide the rules of membership. Yet behind the urge to decouple "the right to have rights from one's nationality status" (Benhabib 2004: 68) lies little else than the individual human being, no matter how much this entity is said to possess "the dignity of moral personhood" (177).

These liberal cosmopolitans subscribe to individualism with an appreciation of the objections that this doctrine has encountered over a long period of time. Individualism here is ethical and normative, the foundation on which liberal egalitarianism is erected, and not a denial of the "constitutive attachments" (Kelly 2005: 9) that make up individual identities everywhere. Banal arguments and counterarguments between liberals and communitarians, incited by statements such as "communitarians often champion culturally embedded social identities that are highly paternalistic" (Talbott 2005: 12), are thereby replaced by a good deal more sophisticated analysis.[8] However, from an anthropological point of view, liberal cosmopolitanism still refuses to properly open up the question of personhood.[9] Nussbaum's "empirical fact of bodily separateness" (2000: 60), for example, flies in the face of ethnographic work on how bodies can be repositories of human relationships, such as in the experiences of affliction and healing, or the very means by which persons come to know their involvement with other beings, human and nonhuman (see, e.g., Turner 1968; Csordas 1994). The refusal to dispense with the notion that persons are, or ought to be, autonomous individuals is no accident, of course. It betrays a commitment to that other linchpin of liberal thought: liberty. Nussbaum wishes every life to have "the preconditions of liberty and self-determination" (2000: 60), while Pogge's goal is to free the poor from "bondage and other relations of personal dependence" (2002: 197).

Liberal cosmopolitans may well dismiss the ethnographic record as a collection of so much culturally determined obfuscation. But they do so at the expense of allowing, as cosmopolitans probably should, the full variety of human experience to enter the debate on morality and poverty. Consider, for example, the argument for individualism as an ethical ideal. The inalienable worth of human beings qua human beings, irrespective of their constitutive attachments, is surely one of the most powerful moral notions of our time, and in many contexts quite indispensable. Yet as the above discussion on political membership indicates, it can also be an extraordinarily inconsequential notion. It is particularly weak in explaining what would compel individuals to meet their moral obligations after they have been stripped of all existential, religious, or legal necessity to do so (compare Lichtenberg 2004: 80–81). The autonomous individual can only be *persuaded* to take others into account, all too often resulting in some form of contractualism by which distinct parties reach a mutually beneficial agreement.[10] If the autonomous individual is a liberal cosmopolitan of Appiah's (2006) variety, moral obligation becomes a matter of ethical choice, a weighing of options to justify, among other things, a visit to the opera.

Lost from view is the possibility that moral concerns are entwined with existential ones (Englund 2008). Human relationships do not simply attach identities to individuals as though individuals' existence predated relationships, nor are relationships optional, because human lives can be sustained only in relationships with others.[11] The liberal cosmopolitan's burden to assist the distant needy indicates not so much moral obligation as the extent to which the unequal world has made it possible for some to consider themselves separate from others. The challenge of ethnography on Malawi is to recover a sense of relatedness from the quagmire of communitarian culturalism and to convey ways in which human beings, including mutual strangers, come to have obligations toward each other.

Varieties of African Poverty

One immediate difficulty with liberal cosmopolitans' concerns over world poverty is that they sidestep the question of how those classified as poor have themselves made distinctions between different kinds of poverty and hardship, thereby suggesting variation in moral conditions and practical needs. In Chichewa, Malawi's most commonly spoken language and a lingua franca in south-central Africa, the standard concept for poverty is *umphawi*. It refers to all manner of deprivation and physical want in the basic requirements of decent life, such as food, medicine, housing, and clothing.[12] It is closely related to *usiwa*, which summons up shabbiness in appearance and dwelling. A range of verbs are in frequent daily use to describe how poor people experience their condition, such as *kuvutika* and *kuvutikira* for "having problems" and "struggling," and *kusauka* and *kusaukira* for "being needy" and "lacking." These verbs come with gradations of intensity, but they all connote the struggle and discomfort that *umphawi* is thought to entail.

It is essential to recognize that Chichewa has conceptual resources to distinguish poverty from destitution. The intensification of the experience conveyed by the verb *kusaukitsa*, "to impoverish," produces *kusaukitsitsa*, to depict impoverishment taking hold of the person to the extent that he or she is a destitute, devoid of all possessions and relationships. *Masikini*, a word introduced into Chichewa from Arabic probably through Kiswahili, is the noun for a destitute, usually deployed in reference to beggars. *Kuzunzika* contributes to envisioning this state of being by evoking "suffering" and "affliction" as its corollaries. Malawian poverty is, in other words, severe by

Euro-American standards, but it is not necessarily destitution. Much of the moral debate about poverty carried in Chichewa explores the thin line that separates the two conditions. It contrasts with the current policy preference for targeting that assumes a fixed stock of poor people (see below).

Conceptual distinctions in African languages were also what John Iliffe (1987: 2) put forward as means to nuance the concept of African poverty in his foundational overview of the subject. Moreover, his comparison of conjunctural poverty and structural poverty over a long period of time was precisely the kind of historical analysis that is lacking in more prescriptive works such as Sachs's and Collier's. During the colonial period, it was conjunctural poverty, largely associated with great famines, that changed more than structural poverty by which the very poor were often those who lacked the support of family ties in the event of incapacity and adversity (Iliffe 1987: 143). By the 1930s, large-scale famines became less common, apparently as a result of changes both in rainfall and in governance, transport, and markets (157–158). Drought had been only one of the disasters leading to famines in the early colonial period, with locusts and cattle plague no less fatal to human lives that came to be decimated by disease as much as by starvation.[13]

Within the enduring patterns of structural poverty, however, new types of rural poverty emerged during the colonial period. Taxation made cash as scarce as it was needed, while European settlement and land alienation pushed Africans into less productive land or made them impoverished and exploited tenants on large estates, particularly in southern and east Africa. Variations across time and space, ably handled by Iliffe, are far greater than can be considered here, but what is important to the moral debate about poverty is the pattern by which destitution was often a result of social breakdown. Even after the independence of African nations, kin relationships remained the foremost institution for the care of the poor, with the nature and extent of obligations varying according to environment, personal circumstances, and local notions of relatedness.

New forms of poverty heralded by migration to Africa's growing towns and cities threw into relief the ways in which obligations could become a burden rather than a blessing. Although many urban dwellers in Africa, whether impoverished or well-off, continue to attach moral and spiritual value to their rural areas of origin (see, e.g., Geschiere and Nyamnjoh 1998; Englund 2002), Iliffe (1987: 260–277) identified in South Africa's historical trajectory a plausible trend for the rest of the continent. At the heart of the trend was a shift from the abundance of land and the scarcity of labor to a condition in which able-bodied men and women could no longer compensate for their lack of resources by working for others, because no such work existed. The nature of poverty changed when labor was abundant, land and work scarce. Wealth in people (Guyer 1993) could give way to a situation in which newcomers to town quickly overstayed their welcome in their urban relatives' households.

The Making of a Poor Country

A similar scenario for rural poverty has been identified in Malawi, where disputes over land and property are reported to be turning kin into strangers in densely populated areas (Peters 2002).[14] The feminization of poverty in these predominantly matrilineal areas can be an important aspect of this trend, but it is not new. During the colonial period, land shortage and increasing dependence on male earnings created a category of the new poor: women who lived alone with their young children and relied on casual labor and other insecure income-generating activities (see Vaughan 1987). Significant variations in both farm sizes and kin relationships obtain across Malawi's three administrative regions (southern, central, and northern regions), but it is worth noting that an apparent shift toward the narrowing of obligations by no means makes those obligations obsolete in Malawians' moral debate on poverty. On the contrary, precisely by experiencing an acute discrepancy between their resources and the number of people expecting assistance, those who have avoided destitution are drawn into debating the nature and extent of obligations.

Malawi, then known as Nyasaland, became a British protectorate in 1891 but was, as one historian puts it, "a child that Britain never wanted" (Sindima 2002: 34). Initially established as a buffer against Portuguese expansion into British territories, Malawi saw negligible investment and infrastructural development virtually throughout its colonial period (Vail 1983). European tobacco, tea, and coffee planters did settle in parts of the country, but it was largely seen as a labor reserve for the mines and plantations elsewhere in southern and central Africa. A development strategy based on large-scale estate agriculture gained momentum after independence in 1964, with estate ownership becoming subject to President Kamuzu Banda's patronage and his increasingly autocratic ways (Kydd and Christiansen 1982; Mhone 1992; Mkandawire 1992). A distinction between smallholder and estate agriculture was buttressed by legal and institutional measures that stipulated crop production, land tenure, and marketing. Estate farmers were allowed to cultivate any crop they wished and opted for high-value cash crops such as tobacco. The export market was never directly accessible to smallholders who, if they were tenants on estates, had to sell their crop to estate owners at a low price. The cultivation of maize, the main food crop, received few official incentives throughout the three decades of Banda's rule.

At a time when the topic of poverty reduction dominates policies in and on Africa, it is easy to forget that many African countries, Malawi included, pursued economic growth after their independence. The suggestion that many Malawians were poor was anathema to Malawi's government which regarded the term "needy" as more acceptable than "poor." Malawi's macroeconomic indicators did register growth until 1979, but its benefits were not equitably distributed. In 1981, always seemingly willing to pursue a capitalist path to development, Malawi's government was the first in the region to enter a Structural Adjustment Programme with the World Bank. Its operations within sectors such as fiscal policy, agriculture, and institutional development had yielded so few rewards in initiating economic recovery by 1990 that a strategy to address its adverse social consequences was added to the program. The Social Dimension of Adjustment represented a strategy that, with its intention to enhance social sector expenditure and smallholder farming, brought poverty reduction to the government's agenda. Ever since then, no political leader in Malawi has failed to mention poverty alleviation as his or her main preoccupation.

Apart from featuring in politicians' rhetoric, the topic of poverty is also subject to constant surveying, measuring, monitoring, and reporting by a variety of actors.

Local and transnational organizations, some of them faith-based, are engaged in their own poverty research and charitable acts, distributing food and other aid, providing training, and dispensing microcredit in particular localities. Ever since poverty alleviation entered the rhetoric of Malawi's political elite, an array of governmental programs and strategies have been introduced. The Structural Adjustment Programme was followed by the Poverty Alleviation Programme, launched in 1994, which was replaced by the Malawi Poverty Reduction Strategy from 2002 until 2005, which was in turn taken over by the Malawi Growth and Development Strategy, launched in 2007. A close analysis of each program would no doubt uncover significant changes in policy, but external demands and national political obstacles to implementation would cast some doubt over substantial results in practice. Much as international financial institutions and foreign-aid agencies have sought to move from government-driven poverty alleviation to the concepts of "civil society participation" and "country ownership," externally imposed priorities and measures have not declined in significance (Gould 2005).

Following the country's transition to multiparty democracy in 1993–94, private entrepreneurship was all the rage in the new government's rhetoric, accompanied by a range of microcredit facilities and the president's own flamboyant, if mysterious, wealth creation (see Chinsinga 2002). A Starter Pack Programme was introduced in 1998 to soothe the distress caused by the removal of agricultural subsidies, but its free rations of fertilizer and seeds were too small to have a significant impact on smallholder productivity. Seasonal hunger, as opposed to outright famine, had already become a feature of rural life in many parts of Malawi before independence (Mandala 2005), but mismanagement in the government made the chronic food insecurity reach its apotheosis in the 2001–2 famine. Climatic causes assumed fatal consequences after a delay in the delivery of relief aid, caused by donor agencies' qualms about high-level corruption in the country and the government's own belated declaration of a state of disaster. Also crucial to the onset of the crisis was the manipulation of parastatal and commercial maize markets by elements in the political and business elites (Dorwald and Kydd 2004; Devereux and Tiba 2006).[15]

Malawi's third president was sworn into office in 2004. Initially sponsored by the United Democratic Front, the party that had won the right to govern during the democratic transition, Bingu wa Mutharika soon abandoned it in order to establish his own party. One of the policies that distinguished his government was the reintroduction of subsidized fertilizer. Agricultural subsidies had remained a politically volatile issue after their abandonment by the democratically elected government in 1994. Aid agencies, still influenced by international lending organizations' hostility toward anything that was considered to interfere with the market, were reluctant to commit funds to Mutharika's policy. His government did launch a targeted Agricultural Input Subsidy Programme in 2005, followed by refined and expanded versions in subsequent years (Dorwald et al. 2008; Ellis et al. 2009). Far better resourced than the Starter Pack Programme of the United Democratic Front, it involved distributing coupons which could be used to purchase fertilizer and improved maize seeds at roughly 28 percent of the full price. Backed by sufficient rains, the program appeared to restore basic food security among many smallholders. It may have been one reason for Mutharika's landslide victory across the country in the 2009 elections.

Targeted Aid

Despite its initial status as a challenge to the prevailing donor emphasis on liberalized markets, the Agricultural Input Subsidy Programme did resonate with current trends in aid by targeting only a section of the poor. Targeting appeals to policymakers and development economists because of its promise of cost efficiency, with the same amount of poverty reduction expected to be achieved with fewer resources than in more universal programs (Krishna 2007). Although the farm input subsidy program could not target the very poorest of the poor – the beneficiaries were supposed to have access to land and enough cash to meet the minimum payment – it certainly evoked the idea of vulnerability that is integral to targeted aid (Ellis 2007; Ellis et al. 2009: 23–39). It thereby fell under the general rubric of social transfers in the view of aid practitioners, comparable to the programs of direct cash transfers, social pensions, and school feeding which all target those who are considered particularly vulnerable to hunger and other consequences of poverty. In aggregate terms, crucial to targeting the vulnerable is the distinction between the ordinary poor and the ultra-poor. The government of Malawi (2008: 7) has reported that the proportion of the ultra-poor dropped from 22 percent of the population in 2003 to 17 percent in 2006 and to 15 percent in 2007. The positive results have been corroborated by more independent sources (see ODI 2010), but the achievements remain precarious. The poverty gap ratio – the average distance separating the poor from the poverty line – has changed little, suggesting that some of the ordinary poor are never far from the condition of the ultra-poor (Government of Malawi 2008: 4).

From an anthropological point of view, the rhetoric of vulnerability and the practice of targeting gloss over major conceptual and ethnographic issues. One reason why the assumption about a fixed stock of vulnerable people runs into difficulties is empirical. The incomes of poor people are often variable, undocumented, and not directly verifiable, and decisions on including and excluding them in social transfers raise difficult questions about power relations between donors and recipients and among the vast populations who can claim the status of being poor. Whether targeting takes the form of geographical targeting, community-based targeting, or self-targeting, these difficulties are likely to arise because of the sheer impossibility of isolating the vulnerable from those who may be less vulnerable to the effects of severe poverty. Here the value of autonomy advocated by liberal cosmopolitans comes to be associated with the beneficiaries of targeted aid. A philosophical justification calls for "the targeted support of others if people for whatever reason are unable to develop [capacities] by themselves" (Kreide 2007: 163; emphasis omitted). In a related formulation, development is about human capabilities, understood as "substantive freedoms … to choose a life one has reason to value" (Sen 1999: 74). Note again the cosmopolitan's appreciation of value pluralism. While poverty is defined as capability deprivation, the cosmopolitan does not prescribe the lifestyle enhanced capabilities should support. Autonomy stands out as the supreme value that makes value pluralism possible.

The difficulty of separating those who are vulnerable to the risks associated with severe poverty from those who are not became clear during the input subsidy program in Dedza district, where I have carried out fieldwork since the early 1990s. "We are all poor here" (*tonsefe ndife amphawi kuno*), many villagers commented on the official policy to single out about a third of farming households for the subsidies. Although in this district, as elsewhere in Malawi, problems with fraud and secondary markets made the government experiment with different methods of distribution in different years, chiefs and village headmen remained its local partners. Entrusted with the task of identifying those who deserved the subsidies, they were frequently embroiled in controversies over exclusion and inclusion. A remarkable trend was for villages to split when these controversies threw up longstanding grievances about headmen's conduct. New headmen emerged to lead new villages, not by physically relocating their subjects but by seeking recognition from more senior chiefs for their authority. While the district commissioner, the highest-ranking civil servant in the district, would dismiss this trend as villagers' effort to gain access to more subsidies, the villagers' own justifications often evoked both grievances and loyalties that predated the program. Above all, the most vociferous demands for a village of their own often came from the poorest villagers, the ones who were entitled to the targeted aid anyway.

Communitarianism does not capture the ways in which chiefs and headmen have long been integral to local government in Malawi. Shaped by the attentions of colonial and postcolonial regimes, their authority has been circumscribed by the various state-driven interventions to which they have been drawn, from taxation to mobilizing support for public works and political parties.[16] At the same time, they have, particularly at the level of village headmen, remained subject to popular demands and expectations that have made their positions unstable under the conditions of severe poverty. Far from answering a communitarian call to duty, most nominees for the new headmanships were reluctant to assume the position. A common reason was the exposure to envy (*nsanje*) and hatred (*udani*) that it was felt to entail, largely because of headmen's involvement in complex negotiations over family disputes and the distribution of aid. A corollary was the association of headmanship with powers to harm others and to protect oneself through witchcraft (*ufiti*). "You have joined the club of witches" (*munalowa mugulu la afiti*) is a common phrase when new headmen are being instructed on their duties during installation ceremonies, alluding to their vulnerability to other villagers' occult methods even if they themselves want to avoid those methods. The candidates who did become new headmen often regarded themselves as fortified by the Christian God against the immoral and potentially lethal methods employed by those who envied or hated them.

The role played by headmen in distributing targeted aid, therefore, illustrates vulnerability in a different sense than what was mentioned above. Vulnerability here is not so much proneness to an acute loss in the capability to acquire food or fertilizer (Ellis 2007: 671) as exposure to other people's passions, whether destructive or generative.[17] On the one hand, headmen who keep themselves aloof from their subjects by seeking favors and recognition from the government often face challenge, either through the emergence of rivals to lead villagers or through the less public methods of witchcraft. On the other hand, the example of targeted aid in Dedza district shows how those deemed vulnerable by policymakers can experience vulnerability of a different kind, such as unease over their being singled out for subsidies when their neighbors and relatives are not. It was this unease, again expressed as fear of envy and hatred culminating in occult attacks, that made the subjects of targeted aid active in demanding village headmen of their own.

These observations oblige the anthropologist to resist the temptation to replace the emphasis on individual choice in targeted aid and liberal cosmopolitanism with a notion of obligation as a matter of communal solidarity and ascribed statutes. Consider, in this regard, the actual way in which coupons were distributed in villages. Those headmen who felt vulnerable to their subjects had the obligation to cut (*kudula*) the coupons into half or even smaller portions to include more villagers as beneficiaries.[18] At the same time, what distinguished the new villages was their practice of holding public meetings when their headmen received the coupons. It was during these meetings that the headman was asked to distribute them, but while the relatively small size of the new villages made it possible to share the coupons with virtually all adults, deliberation took place on who should receive more. The elderly and the less fortunate tended to be given more fertilizer than others, not with reference to the government policy of targeted aid but after eloquent speeches describing their propensity to work hard and their relationships with other villagers.

The speeches were rarely made by these beneficiaries themselves but by their children or sisters' children or their grandchildren.[19] Rather than evoking pity as the justification for access to more fertilizer, they elaborated on the burden the elderly and the subjects of misfortune placed on their able-bodied relatives who themselves faced all manner of hardship. Communal solidarity, in other words, was as alien to these deliberations as was the liberal-cosmopolitan emphasis on autonomy. Those who deserved more were subjects to specific, defined relationships within the village, productive members in their own right as well as potential burdens to others. Yet it was by having a headman they could influence and by having others to speak for them that their productive membership could be ascertained.

The Anthropology of Morality

A single-case approach, as argued above, distinguishes anthropology from both philosophical and technocratic perspectives on world poverty. It does so not by denying the importance of global inequalities but by being explicit about the vantage point from which world poverty is viewed. To their credit, the liberal cosmopolitans mentioned in this essay recognize their own vantage point when they contemplate the extent to which they ought to assist the distant needy. It is an approach that contrasts us and them, but precisely because it revolves around this most abstract of contrasts, it fails to specify any of the multiple ways in which severe poverty is a moral as much as an economic predicament. For liberal cosmopolitans, the poor appear undifferentiated in their misery, and they pose only one moral dilemma: how to help them in a way that is fair to both them and us. As has been seen, this dilemma occasions lively debate among liberal cosmopolitans, the pendulum of their moral argument swinging between personal and corporate responsibility. One of the contributions anthropology can make to this debate is not simply to insist on finding out how the poor themselves make distinctions between various gradations of poverty and the moral dilemmas they pose. It is also to enrich the debate on world poverty with a concept of obligation that is attuned to this complexity of moral predicament.

How does the study of poverty, on the other hand, enrich the anthropology of morality? I have elsewhere identified, with some regret, a parallel between liberal cosmopolitans' preoccupation with personal ethics and recent anthropological calls to rethink the disciplinary legacy of theorizing morality (see Englund 2008). Those anthropologists who emphasize Émile Durkheim's influence on this legacy not only tend to lament the association of morality with rules and norms but also find it necessary to invent an entirely new subfield of anthropology to address the subtleties of morality (Robbins 2007; Zigon 2007; compare Parkin 1985). To the extent that Durkheim's influence has been to conflate the moral with the social, these anthropologists have a point. The assumption that society is a moral totality precludes investigation of the diverse situations in which contradictory desires and principles operate (Zigon 2010). However, while the problems with structural functionalism are well known, this critique runs the risk of caricaturing mid-twentieth-century social anthropology, especially as it was practiced by UK-based scholars working in Africa. Surely, for instance, Max Gluckman's (1955) portrayal of the Reasonable Man juggling with multiple loyalties and conflicts went far beyond a preoccupation with "principles of social control" he has been accused of (Howell 1997: 7). Both judges and defendants in the Barotseland of present-day Zambia employed a concept of reasonableness to assess conduct and to determine the level of compensation for wrongdoings. Barotse law, "not trammeled by writing or recording of precedent or procedural device," was "elastic" in that it could be "stretched to cover new types of behaviour, new institutions, new customs, new ranges of leeway" (Gluckman 1955: 160). Reasonableness, as formulated by Gluckman on the basis of his Barotse ethnography, may have saved some current anthropologists the trouble of having to address the impossibility "to speak of morality as either obligatory or normative in a strict sense" (Zigon 2010: 5). Intellectual resources in their own discipline have tended to escape them when current anthropologists have declared the need for a new subdiscipline to study morality.

It is important to be clear about the conceptual and methodological implications of such intellectual resources in anthropology. The focus on specific, observable instances of moral argument is undoubtedly the first of them, at present no less than in the period when Gluckman wrote (see also Fassin 2008). More prone to disciplinary amnesia is the way in which concepts such as reasonableness have undermined the distinction between ethical discretion and moral imperative, or between freedom and obligation. The Foucault-inspired examination of ethical self-formation may have run its course when it is observed that even the most paradigmatic instances in this literature, such as the cultivation of pious dispositions, involve transaction as much as worship (Anderson 2011).[20] The methodological implication is obvious: the anthropologist must attend to a range of everyday practices in order to observe moral argument in a variety of settings. The conceptual implication, on the other hand, requires special consideration lest obligation comes again to be distinguished from discretion and reasonableness, as rules and norms are distinguished from choice and manipulation. The case of village headmen and targeted aid presented here has given some grounds for rethinking such apparent opposites in describing moral argument. The existential sense of vulnerability obliged headmen and their subjects to be attentive to relationships as they unfolded well beyond any abstract set of customs or norms.

Conclusion

What the anthropological engagement with world poverty brings to the study of morality is a renewed interest in obligation that qualifies the recent trend to regard ethical self-formation as the key topic in the anthropology of morality. The interest in the ethics of the self, as this essay has suggested, finds a parallel in liberal cosmopolitans' debates about the extent of personal and institutional responsibility in an unequal world. It would be a pity if anthropology had little else to offer to such debates than versions of a similar preoccupation with ethics. A consideration of poverty compels a fresh look at anthropology's intellectual resources, particularly at its conceptualizations of obligation as moral argument that necessarily exceeds the parameters of law and codified custom. Far from reducing obligation to a matter of communal solidarity or rule-bound behavior, the observations presented here on targeted aid in Malawi serve to shift the locus of freedom from autonomy to relationships.

NOTES

1 This work, including Appiah's, has found its impetus in the perceived pluralism of established liberal democracies. Ethnic, religious, and linguistic diversity has raised doubts about classic liberal concepts of universal values, most notably within the liberal tradition itself, in communitarian critiques (see Sandel 1982). Forging a way beyond communitarianism and libertarianism, a great number of liberal theorists have offered various revisions that seek to address so-called multiculturalism (for overviews, see Kymlicka 1995; Gray 2000). It is in this intellectual climate that liberal discussions on obligations and world poverty have to be understood.

2 On the anthropological turn to ethics, see Zigon 2008. I return to this shift in emphasis at the end of this essay, but it is worth noting that, apart from the distinction between positive and negative duties, liberal theory has long advocated a focus on personal ethics too through the distinction between imperfect and perfect duties. While the domain of imperfect duties is justice that lies beyond that of strict justice, perfect duties are those that correspond to perfect rights, such as right to life and therefore duty not to kill (Schneewind 1998: 132–133). The Kantian interest in imperfect duties has tended to contrast the ethical considerations of merit, happiness, and virtue with obligation, understood to be lawlike and enforceable (Schneewind 1998: 526–527). Another antecedent to the study of obligation can be found in sociology, where Georg Simmel's (1994 [1908]) argument about charitable giving and the poor situated obligation in processes of differentiation and inequality. It is this notion of obligation as constitutive of relationships and subjectivities that appears to be de-emphasized in the recent turn to ethics in anthropology.

3 Justin Malewezi becomes Justin Mulawesi in Sachs's account.

4 Rawls's (1999) work on global justice extended the arguments about justice, fairness, and the arbitration between rival claims put forward in his influential *A Theory of Justice* (1971). It re-established the link between egalitarian justice and liberal political thought. The arguments that these works have generated are too varied and, with the proliferation of "micro-debates" (Kelly 2005: 6) about aspects of Rawls's work, often too specialized to detain discussion here. However, certain responses to Rawls's work on global justice are pertinent to the present discussion.

5 For a debate on whether Rawls's choice can be defended on ethical or sociological grounds, see Beitz 2000, Buchanan 2000, and Kuper 2000.

6 The debate continues, with Seyla Benhabib (2004: 106–114), for example, raising concerns about democratic processes and misplaced concreteness that can obscure complex moral and epistemic issues in the world economic system. She points out, among other things, that apart from redistribution, other measures to achieve a more equal world would include debt amnesty, democratizing the governance of international lending institutions, and controlling and penalizing financial speculation that endangers weak economies. The crux of her argument is to warn against assuming that a globally shared standard for measuring well-being exists.

7 Further insight into the sophistication with which these liberal theorists defend autonomy can be gauged by considering the capabilities approach to poverty alleviation that both Nussbaum and Amartya Sen have advocated, albeit with somewhat different emphases (see Nussbaum 2000: 11–15). Both theorists stress the ability of people "to choose to function in certain ways, not simply their actual functionings" (Nussbaum 2000: 101) and "to choose a life one has reason to value" (Sen 1999: 74). As is discussed later in the context of targeted aid, the value pluralism underlying these subtleties does little to displace personal autonomy as the principal value.

8 Indeed, Benhabib (1992) has elsewhere offered a subtle argument for moral individuation by highlighting the importance of the distinction between self and other.

9 Even so, ethical individualism does have its anthropological advocates (see, e.g., Cohen 1994; Rapport 1997).

10 It is necessary to distance my critical remark on persuasion from Conor Gearty's complaint that Amartya Sen's (2004) notion of human rights – a notion congenial to liberal cosmopolitanism – is "rooted in discourse, dialogue and discussion rather than the delivery of objective truth" (2006: 36). It is not the loss of "objective truth" that I regret in liberal cosmopolitans' views on persuasion but their axiomatic stress on personal autonomy as a condition of deliberation.

11 Certain forms of feminist theory have taken liberal thought forward by making a distinction between autonomy and freedom (see, e.g., Hirschmann 2003).

12 The monolingual Chichewa dictionary defines *umphawi* as a loanword from Shona and its scope as "to lack many essential things in a person's life such as food, medicine, place, and clothes" (*kukhala osowa pazinthu zambiri zofunika pamoyo wa munthu monga chakudya, mankhwala, malo ndi zovala*: Centre for Language Studies 2000: 349).

13 Elias Mandala, contending that every famine is "a social and political crisis," has complained that "all one sees" in Iliffe's thesis "is the triumphant hand of colonial capitalism defeating 'famine' … and brightening the 'dark' continent" (2005: 52).

14 Although a discernible trend, particularly in some parts of Malawi's southern region, the use of land disputes in turning kin into strangers faces its limits in the ambiguities of land tenure in much of rural Malawi. Eyolf Jul-Larsen and Peter Mvula (2009) have suggested that these ambiguities underpin egalitarian norms that can be recognized by courts and chiefs.

15 While admitting that the question of how many people died during the 2001–2 famine is controversial and will probably never be answered with any certainty, Devereux and Tiba (2006) extrapolate from localized surveys a range of 46,000 to 85,000 famine-related deaths in the country as a whole, a much higher figure than the official estimate of between 300 and 500 deaths.

16 For comparative perspectives on so-called traditional authority in the region, see Nyamnjoh 2003; Oomen 2005.

17 A parallel could be drawn to certain aspects of Emmanuel Levinas's ethics in which vulnerability is understood as the exposure of self to the other and "true freedom requires an absolutely Other if it is not to be imprisoned in the same, if it is not a determinism, if it can actually cocreate something new" (Harold 2009: 190). Freedom, in this sense, is a relation to that other.

18 Such a strategy of sharing subsidies was hardly conducive to increased productivity. However, the assessment of the input subsidy program that noted this strategy in many parts of Malawi did not dismiss it as an example of irrationality (Dorward et al. 2008: 66–67). According to this assessment, the contrast between "concentration" and "dilution" is one between increased productivity in aggregate terms and the more modest but immediate concern with household food security. These economic considerations were, as the present essay indicates, inseparable from the moral question of who should have access to the subsidies, and on what basis.

19 The role sisters' children play in villagers' lives accords with certain matrilineal features that are characteristic of this region.
20 The number of anthropological works devoted to the study of ethical self-formation has increased rapidly in recent years, but representative examples include Mahmood 2005, Heyes 2007, and Cook 2010. One parallel with liberal cosmopolitanism inheres in these authors' sophisticated critique of individualism.

REFERENCES

Anderson, Paul (2011) "The Piety of the Gift": Selfhood and Sociality in the Egyptian Mosque Movement. *Anthropological Theory* 11(1): 3–21.

Appiah, Kwame Anthony (2006) *Cosmopolitanism: Ethics in a World of Strangers*. New York: Norton.

Arendt, Hannah (1951) *The Origins of Totalitarianism*. New York: Harcourt, Brace, Jovanovich.

Ashford, Elizabeth (2007) The Duties Imposed by the Human Right to Basic Necessities. In Thomas Pogge (ed.), *Freedom from Poverty as a Human Right: Who Owes What to the Very Poor?* Oxford: Oxford University Press, pp. 183–218.

Beitz, Charles (2000) Rawls's Law of Peoples. *Ethics* 110(4): 669–696.

Benhabib, Seyla (1992) *Situating the Self: Gender, Community, and Postmodernism in Contemporary Ethics*. New York: Routledge.

Benhabib, Seyla (2004) *The Rights of Others: Aliens, Residents, and Citizens*. Cambridge: Cambridge University Press.

Bohman, James and Lutz-Bachmann, Matthias (eds.) (1997) *Perpetual Peace: Essays on Kant's Cosmopolitan Ideal*. Cambridge, MA: MIT Press.

Buchanan, Allen (2000) Rawls's Law of Peoples: Rules for a Vanished Westphalian World. *Ethics* 110(4): 697–721.

Centre for Language Studies (2000) *Mtanthauziramawu Wa Chinyanja/Chichewa*. Blantyre: Dzuka.

Chinsinga, Blessings (2002) The Politics of Poverty Alleviation in Malawi: A Critical Review. In Harri Englund (ed.), *A Democracy of Chameleons: Politics and Culture in the New Malawi*. Uppsala: Nordic Africa Institute, pp. 25–42.

Cohen, Anthony P. (1994) *Self Consciousness: An Alternative Anthropology of Identity*. New York: Routledge.

Collier, Paul (2007) *The Bottom Billion: Why the Poorest Countries are Failing and What Can Be Done about It*. Oxford: Oxford University Press.

Cook, Joanna (2010) *Meditation and Monasticism: Making the Ascetic Self in Thailand*. Cambridge: Cambridge University Press.

Csordas, Thomas J. (ed.) (1994) *Embodiment and Experience: The Existential Ground of Culture and Self*. Cambridge: Cambridge University Press.

Devereux, Stephen and Tiba, Zoltan (2006) Malawi's First Famine, 2001–2002. In Stephen Devereux (ed.), *The New Famines*. New York: Routledge, pp. 143–177.

Dorwald, Andrew and Kydd, Jonathan (2004) The Malawi 2002 Food Crisis: The Rural Development Challenge. *Journal of Modern African Studies* 42(3): 343–361.

Dorwald, Andrew, Ephraim Chirwa, Valerie Kelly, et al. (2008) *Evaluation of the 2006/7 Agricultural Input Subsidy Programme, Malawi*. Lilongwe: Ministry of Agriculture and Food Security.

Ellis, Frank (2007) Vulnerability and Coping. In *The Elgar Companion to Development Studies*. Northampton, MA: Edward Elgar, pp. 671–675.

Ellis, Frank, Stephen Devereux, and Philip White (2009) *Social Protection in Africa*. Northampton, MA: Edward Elgar.

Englund, Harri (2002) The Village in the City, the City in the Village: Migrants in Lilongwe. *Journal of Southern African Studies* 28(1): 137–154.

Englund, Harri (2008) Extreme Poverty and Existential Obligations: Beyond Morality in the Anthropology of Africa? *Social Analysis* 52(3): 33–50.

Fassin, Didier (2008) Beyond Good and Evil? Questioning the Anthropological Discomfort with Morals. *Anthropological Theory* 8(4): 333–344.

Fleurbaye, Marc (2007) Poverty as a Form of Oppression. In Thomas Pogge (ed.), *Freedom from Poverty as a Human Right: Who Owes What to the Very Poor?* Oxford: Oxford University Press, pp. 133–154.

Fortes, Meyer (1949) *The Web of Kinship among the Tallensi*. London: Oxford University Press.

Gearty, Conor (2006) *Can Human Rights Survive?* Cambridge: Cambridge University Press.

Geschiere, Peter and Nyamnjoh, Francis B. (1998) Witchcraft as an Issue in the "Politics of Belonging": Democratization and Urban Migrants' Involvement with the Home Village. *African Studies Review* 41(1): 69–91.

Gluckman, Max (1955) *The Judicial Process among the Barotse of Northern Rhodesia*. Manchester: Manchester University Press.

Gould, Jeremy (ed.) (2005) *The New Conditionality: The Politics of Poverty Reduction*. London: Zed.

Government of Malawi (2008) *2008 Malawi Millennium Development Goals Report*. Lilongwe: Ministry of Economic Planning and Development.

Gray, John (2000) *Two Faces of Liberalism*. Cambridge: Polity.

Guyer, Jane I. (1993) Wealth in People and Self-Realization in Equatorial Africa. *Man* 28(2): 243–265.

Harold, Philip J. (2009) *Prophetic Politics: Emmanuel Levinas and the Sanctification of Suffering*. Athens: Ohio University Press.

Hertel, Shareen and Minkler, Lanse (2007) Economic Rights: The Terrain. In Shareen Hertel and Lanse Minkler (ed.), *Economic Rights: Conceptual, Measurement and Policy Issues*. Cambridge: Cambridge University Press, pp. 1–35.

Heyes, Cressida J. (2007) *Self-Transformations: Foucault, Ethics, and Normalized Bodies*. Oxford: Oxford University Press.

Hirschmann, Nancy J. (2003) *The Subject of Liberty: Toward a Feminist Theory of Freedom*. Princeton: Princeton University Press.

Howell, Signe (1997) Introduction. In Signe Howell (ed.), *The Ethnography of Moralities*. London: Routledge, pp. 1–22.

Iliffe, John (1987) *The African Poor: A History*. Cambridge: Cambridge University Press.

Jul-Larsen, Eyolf and Mvula, Peter (2009) Security for Many or Surplus for the Few? Customary Tenure and Social Differentiation in Southern Malawi. *Journal of Southern African Studies* 35(1): 175–190.

Kelly, Paul (2005) *Liberalism*. Cambridge: Polity.

Kimenyi, Mwangi S. (2007) Economic Rights, Human Development Effort, and Institutions. In Shareen Hertel and Lanse Minkler (ed.), *Economic Rights: Conceptual, Measurement and Policy Issues*. Cambridge: Cambridge University Press, pp. 182–213.

Kreide, Regina (2007) Neglected Injustice: Poverty as a Violation of Social Autonomy. In Thomas Pogge (ed.), *Freedom from Poverty as a Human Right: Who Owes What to the Very Poor?* Oxford: Oxford University Press, pp. 155–181.

Krishna, Anirudh (2007) For Reducing Poverty Faster: Target Reasons before People. *World Development* 35(11): 1947–1960.

Kuper, Andrew (2000) Rawlsian Global Justice: Beyond *The Law of Peoples* to a Cosmopolitan Law of Persons. *Political Theory* 28(4): 640–674.

Kydd, Jonathan and Christiansen, Robert E. (1982) Structural Change in Malawi since Independence: Consequences of a Development Strategy based on Large-Scale Agriculture. *World Development* 10(5): 355–375.

Kymlicka, Will (1995) *Multicultural Citizenship: A Liberal Theory of Minority Rights.* Oxford: Oxford University Press.

Lichtenberg, Judith (2004) Absence and the Unfond Heart: Why People are Less Giving than They Might Be. In Deen K. Chatterjee (ed.), *The Ethics of Assistance: Morality and the Distant Needy.* Cambridge: Cambridge University Press, pp. 75–97.

Mahmood, Saba (2005) *Politics of Piety: The Islamic Revival and the Feminist Subject.* Princeton: Princeton University Press.

Mandala, Elias C. (2005) *The End of Chidyerano: A History of Food and Everyday Life in Malawi, 1860–2004.* Portsmouth, NH: Heinemann.

Mauss, Marcel (1974 [1925]) *The Gift.* London: Routledge & Kegan Paul.

Mhone, Guy C. Z. (1992) The Political Economy of Malawi: An Overview. In Guy C. Z. Mhone (ed.), *Malawi at the Crossroads: The Post-Colonial Political Economy.* Harare: SAPES, pp. 1–33.

Mkandawire, Richard (1992) The Land Question and Agrarian Change in Malawi. In Guy C. Z. Mhone (ed.), *Malawi at the Crossroads: The Post-Colonial Political Economy.* Harare: SAPES, pp. 171–187.

Nozick, Robert (1974) *Anarchy, State, and Utopia.* New York: Basic Books.

Nussbaum, Martha C. (2000) *Women and Human Development: The Capabilities Approach.* Cambridge: Cambridge University Press.

Nussbaum, Martha C. (2004) Women and Theories of Global Justice: Our Need for New Paradigms. In Deen K. Chatterjee (ed.), *The Ethics of Assistance: Morality and the Distant Needy.* Cambridge: Cambridge University Press, pp. 147–176.

Nyamnjoh, Francis B. (2003) Chieftaincy and the Negotiation of Might and Right in Botswana Democracy. *Journal of Contemporary African Studies* 21(2): 233–250.

ODI (Overseas Development Institute) (2010) *Millennium Development Goals Report Card: Measuring Progress across Countries.* London: ODI Publications.

Oomen, Barbara (2005) *Chiefs in South Africa: Law, Power and Culture in the Post-Apartheid Era.* Oxford: James Currey.

Parkin, David (1985) Introduction. In David Parkin (ed.), *The Anthropology of Evil.* Oxford: Blackwell, pp. 1–25.

Peters, Pauline E. (2002) Bewitching Land: The Role of Land Disputes in Converting Kin to Strangers and in Class Formation in Malawi. *Journal of Southern African Studies* 28(1): 155–178.

Pogge, Thomas W. (2002) *World Poverty and Human Rights: Cosmopolitan Responsibilities and Reforms.* Cambridge: Polity.

Rapport, Nigel (1997) *Transcendent Individual: Towards a Literary and Liberal Anthropology.* New York: Routledge.

Rawls, John (1971) *A Theory of Justice.* Cambridge, MA: Harvard University Press.

Rawls, John (1999) *The Law of Peoples.* Cambridge, MA: Harvard University Press.

Robbins, Joel (2007) Between Reproduction and Freedom: Morality, Value, and Radical Cultural Change. *Ethnos* 72(3): 293–314.

Sachs, Jeffrey D. (2005) *The End of Poverty: How We Can Make It Happen in Our Lifetime.* London: Penguin.

Sandel, Michael (1982) *Liberalism and the Limits of Justice.* Cambridge: Cambridge University Press.

Schneewind, J. B. (1998) *The Invention of Autonomy: A History of Modern Moral Philosophy.* Cambridge: Cambridge University Press.

Sen, Amartya (1999) *Development as Freedom.* New York: Knopf.

Sen, Amartya (2004) Elements of a Theory of Human Rights. *Philosophy and Public Affairs* 32(4): 315–356.

Sengupta, Arjun (2007) Poverty Eradication and Human Rights. In Thomas Pogge (ed.), *Freedom from Poverty as a Human Right: Who Owes What to the Very Poor?* Oxford: Oxford University Press, pp. 323–344.

Shipton, Parker (2007) *The Nature of Entrustment: Intimacy, Exchange, and the Sacred in Africa*. New Haven: Yale University Press.

Simmel, Georg (1994 [1908]) The Poor. In D. N. Levine (ed.), *On Individuality and Social Forms*. Chicago: University of Chicago Press.

Sindima, Harvey J. (2002) *Malawi's First Republic: An Economic and Political Analysis*. Lanham, MD: University Press of America.

Singer, Peter (1972) Famine, Affluence and Morality. *Philosophy & Public Affairs* 1(3): 229–243.

Singer, Peter (2009) *The Life You Can Save: Acting Now to End World Poverty*. New York: Picador.

Talbott, William J. (2005) *Which Rights Should Be Universal?* Oxford: Oxford University Press.

Turner, Victor W. (1968) *The Drums of Affliction: A Study of Religious Processes among the Ndembu of Zambia*. Oxford: Clarendon.

Unger, Peter (1996) *Living High and Letting Die: Our Illusion of Innocence*. Oxford: Oxford University Press.

Vail, Leroy (1983) The State and the Creation of Colonial Malawi's Agricultural Economy. In Robert I. Rotberg (ed.), *Imperialism, Colonialism, and Hunger: East and Central Africa*. Boston: Lexington, pp. 39–87.

Vaughan, Megan (1987) *The Story of an African Famine: Gender and Famine in Twentieth-Century Malawi*. Cambridge: Cambridge University Press.

Zigon, Jarrett (2007) Moral Breakdown and the Ethical Demand: A Theoretical Framework for an Anthropology of Moralities. *Anthropological Theory* 7(2): 131–150.

Zigon, Jarrett (2008) *Morality: An Anthropological Perspective*. Oxford: Berg.

Zigon, Jarrett (2010) Moral and Ethical Assemblages: A Response to Fassin and Stoczkowski. *Anthropological Theory* 10(1–2): 3–15.

CHAPTER 17

Inequality

Caroline Humphrey

The great majority of ethical arguments about inequality in the contemporary world take it for granted that inequality is a wrong done to people that should be righted. How then should we think about the fact that radical equality once put into practice is by no means seen by actors on the ground as an unqualified good? There is a disequilibrium between the two views, seemingly one another's opposites, that I propose to analyze by investigating the ethnographic salience of fairness. Here I have in mind not fairness as a generalized object of consensus (Rawls 1971), but the variable judgments invoked by people in actual situations. Of course such a theme can deal with only an aspect of inequality, but it does provide a key to penetrate its intersection with morality, ethics, and subjectivity. One advantage of studying fairness (and its equivalents in other languages) rather than the more commonly invoked justice is that it has a broad social applicability and avoids association with the instituted law. Fairness is like a joker in the pack, uncertain in content. Analytically and comparatively, fairness has little content except what is given it in some particular situation by the actors. Two neighbors may disagree about what is fair; husbands and wives frequently do. Fairness is a swaying ethical compass steeped in emotion and perhaps indeed it is an emotion first of all. Yet from perceptions of inequality it can be a mover in the potentiality of politics: in Russia, at least during times of change such as 1989–91, powerful trade union movements and a political party were created under its name (*spravedlivost'*), and in many countries and circumstances people call for fairness against the prevailing order and the justice meted out by judges. But we cannot avoid observing that fairness is always spoken from a point of view; therefore it can also be invoked as a justification for the status quo, and in objections to *too much equality*, the failure to reward differences in merit. In exposing such paradoxes, ethnographic analysis of fairness can draw attention to the moral dimension of inequality, in particular to clarify the values at play in constructions of difference, inequality, discrimination, and inequity (if we take the latter word to imply moral condemnation of inequality).

This essay proposes to reach considerations of inequity through a roundabout route, by first discussing incommensurability. For it would seem logical that

A Companion to Moral Anthropology, First Edition. Edited by Didier Fassin.

inequality can be judged to be such only according to some criterion – the most obvious one in the contemporary world being wealth – demonstrating that group X and group Y are not equal in that respect. Incommensurability by contrast would imply the presence of difference but the suspension or inapplicability of the idea of inequality. I shall argue, however, that inequality is not a logical but a pragmatic matter. Commensurability, or more correctly comparability (Chang 1997: 2–4), produces distinct regimes of serial value, precedence, and hierarchy. These provide a conceptual spine for ranking difference; but they radically underdetermine inequality, for while measuring one or more qualities they do not account for the co-presence of a myriad of other uncounted actualities. The practice of commensurability makes certain inequalities visible, but it seems always incomplete; it tends to advance and retreat in accordance with the degree of penetration by governmental, centralizing regimes. Yet there always remains some space of the unmeasured which, I shall suggest, should not be seen only as a residue of unexamined actualities but is very often set up precisely *as* "incommensurable." A creator of separate "worlds," incommensurability can be seen as a curtain drawn across reality. I shall argue, however, that it generates different kinds of subjectification and works to different effect depending on whether the incompatibility is affirmed from a dominant or, alternatively, a subaltern point of view. Thus certain "totemic" orders can be seen as subaltern creations, setting up intergroup relations that are deliberately noncommensurable and hence nonhierarchical, in the midst of imperial, colonial, and capitalist realities. In this case incommensurability acts not as a self-serving cloak over inequality but to sidestep hierarchy and create a space that refuses it. From the perspective of dominant social formations on the other hand, incommensurability generates a known "unknown," a category that can be manipulated and legislated for, while ignoring its *substance* as inequality (Fassin 2009). The most grim inequality is felt and experienced while its subjects exist in the constructed limbo of those we do not even want truly to know.

Inequality, it will be suggested here, is made up of an agglomeration of elements that are not related to one another in an obvious way – such as health, gender, geographical position, material possessions, political disparities, religious status, (lack of) social esteem or a sense of belonging – and it consolidates when these separate elements are made to coincide, are meshed together by social practices that concentrate and rigidify different kinds of disadvantage. Such inequality can be reproduced systemically over long periods of time and this is where fairness re-enters my argument. For this peremptory, almost childish notion ("It's not fair!") opens a space of contradictory dynamics. On the one hand, the ranks in hierarchical systems wield their own positional notions of fairness that – by riding over unfortunate "unknowns" – justify the status quo, and this practice tends not only to support but in some cases also to generate inequality. On the other hand, as I will show later in the case of postsocialist Russia, this same notion of fairness has wider and deeper dimensions that are invoked in the ethical calls for equal treatment that also fundamentally question the system. It is not that the positioned subject who calls for fairness has disappeared; but that for this subject to be counted an ethical actor requires that she realize that projects, purposes, and needs are not necessarily made discursively *for* me: rather, I must deliberate *from* what I am, on behalf of a wider truth (Williams 1985: 200). In the conclusion to this essay I hope to be able to show that this kind of ethical thinking about inequality has import in very different social and political environments. Such thinking has diverse idioms, but proceeding always from a position it reaches out to general principles that are nurtured in the recesses of a given culture.

I shall first discuss the character of models that maintain incommensurability in the context of hierarchy and inequality, move to consider social exclusion in relation to incommensurability, and then begin the ethnography of fairness by showing how an institutionalized practice of *spravedlivost'* (fairness, justice) is a driving force in reproducing inequality in contemporary Russia. Finally, ethnographic accounts of situated actors' use of this same word "fairness" will show how the idea may be used alternatively as an ethical and critical practice.

Difference and Incommensurability

Béteille's classic paper makes the point that the crucial problem is to understand how social acknowledgment of human difference is transformed into inequality (1983: 29). Let us therefore begin with difference as such, by taking another look at those "totemic" societies where social segments are conceptualized on a model of *nonranked* difference, often the discontinuity between biological species. Lévi-Strauss argues (1963: 2) that it is not the perceived utilitarian properties of such species that matter, but their logical properties, the ability of selected animals, plants, and so on to serve as symbols expressing contrasts that then become a means to express differences between social groups. This "totemic" practice we could think of as a game with incommensurability. Yet if the contrast between the Mushroom clan and the Tailless Cow clan of the Baganda is difficult to conceive as anything other than pure difference, in some of the cases described the character ascribed to the animal species had import: a definite physical and psychological resemblance was postulated for the humans and animals. Thus the Haddon–Rivers Expedition at Mabuiag reported that clansmen were constrained to live up to the traditional character of their respective clans. The Cassowary, Crocodile, Snake, and Shark clans were reputed to love fighting, while the Shovel-Nosed Skate, Ray, and Sucker-Fish clans were said to be peaceable, and the Dog clan was said to be sometimes pugnacious and sometimes pacific, like dogs (Lévi-Strauss 1963: 4–5). Lévi-Strauss argued that this latter case – where instead of a homology of relationships there is a homology between terms (i.e., the clan and the species) – is comparable theoretically to a "caste" system of differentiated hereditary occupational groups, and he went on to demonstrate that "totemic" and "caste" systems are in theory mutually transformable one into the other. Focusing on such structures, he ignored the fact that since such systems operate only on one plane incipient difference of degree (whether this be fierceness/peacefulness, purity/pollution, etc.) may lurk within them.

Yet such systems – even "caste" – do not inevitably transform into hierarchies but may stand out as fragile pockets of parity against already present asymmetries. "Totemic" or "caste" ways of thinking do not belong to a never-never land, a prelapsarian time dreamed up by anthropologists. Recent anthropology has rightly observed that "nonmodern" forms through which people uphold parity by virtue of the interdependence of unlike social groups are different in kind from the equality valued in Euro-American individualism (Robbins 1994; Rio and Smedal 2009);

yet they remain our coevals and their ancient forms have inspired modern thinkers such as Gandhi.[1] Orders that refuse to rank social groups have to be chosen and actively upheld. This is not just the activity of reproducing a form that somehow happens to exist, as might have been imagined in an earlier anthropology, but that of self-maintenance in the context of differently organized and usually far more powerful formations (religious, imperial, colonial, national, or capitalist). Few societies can have experienced such a massive increase of wealth differentials than Russia in the last 20 years, but it is from that world that a young Buryat woman told me recently about her village in southern Siberia. Now free to choose where to live, the villagers clustered in "clan" groups[2] on either side of a central road. These groups are typified in "caste" or alternatively "totemic" fashion as the Shamans, the Hunters, the Herders, the former Lords,[3] the Artisans, and the Incomers (migrants from Mongolia in the nineteenth century). Normatively exogamous, holding their own rituals, the clans intermarry and are counted as equal to one another – they are seen as the components of "a people" (*ulus*). Their occupational characters refer to a subjective feeling of difference, even if very few, or even no, living members pursue the given profession.[4]

It seems to me that Lévi-Strauss's semiotic conception of difference is less apt here than the Deleuzian notion of ontological difference.[5] The "totemic" mode proposes a distinctive *being* proper to each group, and this way of being has its language: clan groups are known by the name of the relevant ancestor, time is reckoned by generations rather than calendrical dates, and the holistic settlement as "a people" (Buryat *ulus*) not a village (Russian *derevnya*). Assigning occupations to the various clan groups in the village is not done merely to mark them off from one another but to register that they are somehow actually different. To agree with this point, we have to be able to conceive of an ontological difference that is not through and through, not fixed, and does not obtain in all circumstances. Rather, these are regimes of thought that become manifest in ordinary experience only as assemblages counterposed to other assemblages.

For such "totemic" patterns are not an original state but a way of thinking about relations historically adopted. When in the seventeenth century certain small groups of Halha Mongols fled over the border into Buryat lands from civil war, they had no clans and were categorized according to the all-embracing hierarchical military organization that remained from the days of the Mongol empire. Once across the frontier, the refugees abandoned their regimental statuses and went over to totemism. They formed "clans" and the shamans of each group took to wearing, as tassels on their hats, the skin of a distinctive wild animal: black squirrel, white squirrel, hare, and gray wolf (Baldaev 1970: 23–24). Not only does this show that hierarchy is reversible, but it also turns out that Lévi-Strauss's cold societies have actually been hot enough to absorb others into their mold.

In this light we can see that positional strategies are compatible with ontological thinking. Many Torguud Mongols think of ethnic groups as if they were species – born into one group, one cannot acquire the abilities proper to another (Gil-White 2001: 527). We should understand such an essentialist way of thinking not as an evolutionary adaptive mechanism (Gil-White 2001), nor as due to cognitive hard-wiring (Atran 1990), but as an example of a social philosophy, in this case one of parity amid hierarchy, which has been well honed through the history of Asia. It creates a "deterritorialized milieu" (Yurchak 2006: 126–157) or a "nonpolitical" space (Candea 2011) that can be flipped into politics when the "totemic" way of thinking is consciously opposed to other modes of thought. Conceptualizing human groups or individuals as innately different from one another has to be the ultimate weapon against any ideology that would hierarchize all groups in relation to a quality they hold in common.

There are reasons why "totemic" systems are unstable: as hinted earlier, they not only abstract themselves from, or run counter to, external political hierarchies but also need to suppress or discount internal ordering of an asymmetric kind. There is, for example, the well-cited case of the Chewong hunters and gatherers whose egalitarian individuation relegates shamanic hierarchical notions to a subordinate level (Howell 1985; Rio and Smedal 2009: 29–31). Disjunctive in the opposite direction is the case described by Simon Harrison (1985) for the Avatip in Papua New Guinea where a secretive male ritual hierarchy perches above the egalitarian relations of domestic life of both men and women. An important conclusion has to be that while social incommensurability appears to actors to be found and not made, from an anthropological point of view this situation is a matter of the creation of forms of knowledge of relations. As Harrison writes about the Avatip:

> Social inequality will tend to manifest itself only in those contexts in which ritual knowledge is relevant, and in which the institutionalized exclusion of particular social categories from this knowledge is salient: that is primarily in the setting of ritual itself. In contexts to which mundane knowledge applies … social inequalities will tend contextually to "dissolve" because these forms of knowledge are not subject to, and therefore do not "register" the structures of exclusion on which inequality is based. (1985: 435)

Precedence and Hierarchy

Let me continue, however, with Inner Asia, as considering the political environment in which "totemic" modes had their precarious existence in this region enables me to clarify a distinction between precedence and hierarchy. The "caste"/"totemic" notion of complementary clans always had to cut across the internal system of seniority generated by agnatic kinship itself. In Inner Asia, birth order insures that there is no equal position; every person, male or female, is born senior or junior to others, a binary switch that is extended to groups of siblings and clusters of relatives. In Mongolian languages the pair *ah* (senior) and *degü* (junior) is in some ways similar to the far more resonant *mori/mora* pair found in Proto-Oceanic languages. *Mori/mora*, denoting back/front, past/future, base/top, and senior/junior, has been called a key conceptual device for ranking, "a complete parameter for ranging all important substances such as food and social relations between juniors and seniors and men and women" (Rio and Smedal 2009: 40–41). However, *ah/degü* is not as "totalizing" as *mori/mora*, since it is not the language categorizing many relationships (gender, military, patronage, employment). *Ah/degü* can be seen as the kernel of precedence, but not of hierarchy. A recent anthropological collection on southeast Asia has discussed the difference between these concepts: precedence, it is argued, is defined as a recursive or sequential mode of establishing asymmetry, and it can operate in various contexts and at different scales; but, invoking Dumont (1980), the authors affirm that hierarchy involves something more, a totality within which the ranked statuses are related (Fox 2009: 1–12).

In Buryat Mongol areas, local "totemic" arrangements had to deny, cut off, and flatten the ever present potentiality for the emergence of genealogical orders of precedence that would rank clans.[6] In the same historical period (nineteenth to twentieth century) both "totemic" and precedence modes encountered massive *hierarchies*, the Manchu empire of the Qing dynasty and the tsarist Russian empire. Each was centered on, and given unity by, the ideologies surrounding their respective sovereigns. These governments, in different ways, made use of their subjects' genealogical ranking systems. But what made the edifices hierarchical was the top-down referencing of all political appointments to the center, rather than being generated from below by kinship (for debate, see Sneath 2007: 93–120). Hierarchy, we can see, can be imagined in different shapes. It need not appear like a ladder of pure/impure castes as implied in Dumont, but may be likened to concentric circles (the circles of ever greater secrecy of Avatip men), or a branching tree using the botanic idiom of "trunk" and "tip" (McWilliam 2009: 111–132), or a pyramid with the emperor at its apex as in the Qing and tsarist empires.

I have mentioned that the equality implicit in "totemic" systems is contingent – after all, in the Mabuaig case the Shark could be thought of not just as different from the Skate and the Ray, but as *better* (stronger, fiercer, a winner). However, some constructions of parity seem set up to be impervious to inequalities, and furthermore not to be localizing in scope but universalizing. I am thinking here of ancient Indic concepts that spread through Inner Asia with Buddhism. "Flat" cosmologies on the model of the mandala were present for centuries in India in the same complex lived space as hierarchies of purity/pollution, patrons/clients, and kingly rule. The mandala is a structure of spatial occupation whereby gods, ethnic groups, colors, and physical elements (fire, water, air, etc.) are arranged in symmetrical patterns around a center, all interrelated and yet none having priority over any other. Such a vision of the known world is mentioned in many Tibetan and Mongolian Buddhist sources, but we may note one in particular, the *Altan Tobchi* written by Mergen Gegen from the Urad region of Inner Mongolia in 1760. This book is notable because it is not a theological work, but a history of the Mongols that discusses the political situation in which it was written, the Manchu Qing empire at the height of its power (Baldanzhapov 1979). Urging his readers to embrace his philosophy of balance, Mergen Gegen criticizes those who bow obsequiously to imperial might to further their own advantage. His own cosmological geography, in which the Chinese, the Tibetans, and other peoples are pictured as equivalent elements grouped in a flat mandala formation around the Mongols, has no "front" or "top" and hence there can be no possibility of ranking its components. This is a political statement ("our space as we conceive it") which addresses the peripheral status of Mongols in the Manchu–Chinese empire and it can also be seen as a refutation of the very validity of hierarchy.

These were alternative cosmological visions of space, but the word "cosmology," which perhaps seems redolent of an anthropological never-never land should not mislead us into thinking that spatial allocations do not matter to people. Anyone who has attended a banquet in China knows that people really mind – they can be wounded to the quick – about seating round the table, which visibly demonstrates their rank.

Spatial discrimination, especially as geographical exclusion (Sibley 1995), is a way in which precedence and hierarchy produce an important substantive content of inequality.

Incommensurability and Exclusion

So far incommensurability has appeared as a social imaginary of refusal of hierarchy, but there is a completely different argument that requires discussion. Verena Stolcke's (1995) influential article on rhetorics of exclusion from Europe suggests the reverse: that incommensurability is crucial in generating inequality. She argues that cultural fundamentalism of the political right postulates a multiplicity of distinct and bounded cultures and that their supposed incommensurability produces a radical opposition between nationals and immigrants. The incapacity of cultures to communicate, together with an alleged human universal – people's natural propensity to reject strangers – means that alien incomers are seen as threatening and therefore, through a range of policies, they are excluded and treated as nonequals (Stolcke 1995: 7–8).

Interestingly, in France, where the language of exclusion started in the late 1980s, the term did not refer to immigrants but to poverty and unemployment, with Alain Touraine among others claiming that contemporary societies are no longer vertical (composed of hierarchies of classes) but horizontal (the included versus the excluded). Didier Fassin discusses how this rhetoric of exclusion can be compared with the language of underclass in the United States and *marginalidad* in Latin America, in each case referring to a "symbolic topology" founded on spatial oppositions such as inside/outside, above/below, or center/periphery (1996: 38).

If we have a topology, what does it mean to say some part of it is incommensurable? Peter Fitzpatrick's ironic comment on Stolcke points out that the rightists' rhetoric of absolute incommensurability between cultures postulates something that is actually unknowable: being bounded by a particular culture we cannot know that we know, or do not know, other cultures – "and, what is particularly delicious, we cannot know that people of other cultures do not know us" (1995: 14). The implication is that really not knowing offers no grounds for exclusion, or anything else. This is a conclusion one may take from Tom Boellstorff's illuminating account of people suspended in "the silence of incommensurability" (2005: 575). He argues that in Indonesia social norms render being gay and being Muslim "ungrammatical" with one another in the public sphere. Religion and desire are incommensurable, but this does not result in the exclusion of gay men. Rather, homosexuality is not even debated among Islamic clerics in Indonesia; unlike heterosexual infringements, which are heavily criticized, it is a sin beyond the public discourse of Islam.

Thus incommensurability can be understood in several ways. One would be the chasm created by an alternative, dissenting vision, such as the "totemic" village. Another is what exists in a hiatus, an absence in a dominant discourse, as with the gays in Indonesia. Yet another appears as the creation within a would-be hegemonic discourse of a specific category of the "known to be other." This can be made visible as a problem to the social order (the people of the *banlieues*, the sink estates), a mysterious irritant requiring investigation, or as the danger to it posed by morally and/or politically divergent groups. Povinelli observes that such groups can always in fact be made commensurable. She notes the *pragmatic* approaches taken by many anthropologists that have revealed ways in which supposed nonintelligibility is in practice "worked around" in encounters (2001: 324). But she argues that in liberal democracies the best public action that can be hoped for is the self-adjusting function of continuously realigning the law to accommodate divergent moral worlds. Even this horizon of good intentions does not result in shared epistemic and moral values; rather, "these discursive and institutional gaps could be seen as always already allowing repressive acts" (327). Fassin clarifies how this happens in the case of the urban poor: the very categories used to bracket off groups as other (exclusion, underclass, etc.) both define but also occult the actual conditions they purport to represent, above all the existence and experience of inequality (1996: 42).

This hiatus is itself fundamentally perceived and constructed as moral, or as essential to a political teleology. The more tightly organized the ideology the more dire the effects on the excluded, for moral condemnation serves to excuse exceptional regimes of brutality. In the Soviet Union, for example, "internal enemies" in many different guises, and to which various morally negative adjectives were attached, were systematically expelled from their collectives to the gulag and then exiled to distant places, where they were subject to extreme impoverishment and deprived of normal rights (Humphrey 2001). Today, state practices of exclusion on political grounds have been greatly curtailed, though not altogether renounced as can be seen in the Khodorkovsky trials; but the remains of the old system are not difficult to find, such as people stuck in some God-forsaken place because their parents happened to be exiled there. This place could well be the "totemic" Buryat village – southeast Siberia was a well-established region of labor camps and exile.

We now need to return to broad disparities in how hierarchy and inequality are imagined. For a start, the Buryat village – though one could cite virtually any town anywhere in the world – exists within the jurisdiction of a large and elaborately ranked state. In what follows I shall again move the discussion away from the classic grounds of India, Polynesia, and southeast Asia to contemporary Russia, where two great systems coexist that seem on the face of it to be incommensurable: the state-organized system of ranked estates[7] and the buccaneering capitalist relations introduced in the 1990s. I have already suggested that the state does not in fact eliminate totemic thinking – Deleuze and Guattari's vision of the rigid, concentric, compartmentalized macro-face displacing primitive society's multiplicity of "subtle micro-heads with animal faces" (1987: 211) has not quite been achieved here. Rather, we find several kinds of noncorrespondence in coexistence, and I shall argue that the ostensible incommensurability between them serves to disguise their empirical intergearing and that it is precisely this enmeshing that consolidates inequality. I will also show how invoking "fairness" is an engine that reproduces this situation.

Fairness Rhetoric as an Engine of Inequality

Until the 1917 Bolshevik revolution Russian society was officially organized by its own peculiar politico-legal system of estates (sing. *sosloviya*, pl. *soslovie*). This was an imperial vision, a legal categorization that set aside nationalities and religions and instead designated "layers" of subjects ranked according to their services to the empire. The hierarchy was given by the value accorded each estate in relation to the sovereign (the tsar or his state). The estates were not equal before the law. Until the early twentieth century, despite the patchy development of capitalism and class identities, "the strong hereditary patterns, the persisting legal distinctions, the segregation of groups in administration and law, the deeply rooted cultural differences among various groups, and the conscious effort of the state to preserve the *soslovie* separation – all acted to maintain the old social structure" (Freeze 1986: 36).

Although the estates were abolished in 1917 in the name of equality, the radicalism proclaimed by the revolutionaries lasted only a few years. Leveling (*uravnilovka*), it turned out, was unpopular with the very people the state relied upon most. The rebellion against it came from factory workers, not on grounds of differing natural abilities (see Béteille 1983) but so that higher productivity and qualifications could be rewarded. They organized themselves into separate cooperatives, and before long Stalin was denouncing out-and-out egalitarianism as "primitive, the product of the peasant type of sharing mentality" (Kuromiya 1988: 284). Thereafter the Soviet Union came to construct a comprehensive and tightly organized system of political-legal ranks that – although their broad categories were confusingly called classes – can be understood as "estates"[8] (S. Fitzpatrick 1999: 12; Kordonskii 2008: 44–56). The Buryat village to which I have referred would have been part of a collective farm in which practically all the inhabitants bar a few officials were classed as "peasants," a lowly estate with severely limited rights.

It is conventionally imagined that the "revolution" of 1991 got rid of the entire soviet system, replacing it, to be sure, with far greater economic inequalities but bringing at least some form of democracy, social mobility, and equality before the law. However, Simon Kordonskii, a biologist turned political adviser to Vladimir Putin and latterly sociologist, argues that a new estate system has re-established itself in Russia and is expanding (Kordonskii 2008). There is no space here to assess Kordonskii's theory as empirical sociology, nor to discuss his seeming approval of the notion that Russia is somehow fated to come up with such social forms as estates, but let us use his ideas to think with. Kordonskii argues that the new system is not a deliberate recreation of the Soviet system, for the government has consciously set itself on a state-managed *market* course, reflected in its language and categories. Rather, it is Russian people who have created – unawares, and because they are comfortable with it – an agglomeration of estates. Without thinking of their activities in these terms, lawmakers have set in place regulations that underpin the existence and ranking of estates. At the top are the groups performing direct state duties (*sluzhba*): administration, military service, external and internal security, policing, legal, and law-creating services; second are the groups that provide services for the above, such as accountants, a vast number of auditing institutions, doctors, teachers, or hired workers; and third are the groups who "service" (*usluzhenie*) the others (food producers, cleaners, guards, nurses, etc.). Even groups one might not intuitively think of as estates are part of the system inasmuch as they actually service other groups: private suppliers (*kommersanty*), prisoners and those with limited rights, and pensioners who work in various ways. What makes all these groups "estates" is that they are *not* equal before the law, and that they have corporate interests, which they sedulously follow.

This is where "fairness" re-enters the picture – as a generator of further de facto inequality. An estate's interest lies in obtaining resources in return for services. Initially this comes from the state or its proxies in the form of salaries, allocated housing, and other benefits. But Kordonskii (2008: 88–94) argues that an immeasurably larger income is taken by estates as "rent" – resources acquired from other less powerful estates for services rendered, an income that is seen as "our due." Some of this is legal – a fascinating appendix details the federal laws entitling members of the FSB (the security service) to commandeer goods, transport, tax benefits, and so on from any state or nonstate institution (Kordonskii 2008: 170–174). But estates also obtain resources by means that are alegal. Often these methods are called "corruption." Actually, in estate thinking they are simply the normal activity of acquiring what the members see as their "fair" (*spravedlivoe*) share of the limited total amount of resources. This income then should be distributed equally within the estate, or allocated according to its interior ranks. Overwhelmingly people assume that "fair" is more than they receive in wages. At the same time, it is "unfair" if some other group seems to have more than what is appropriate for their standing and therefore it is legitimate to appropriate anything they possess above that level. In the case of business people and firms outside the estate system, that is those working in the market, their entire enterprise is fair game.

If each group is in competition for fairness on their own behalf the system can only intensify. A "service" is usually given, but this often takes a strange form, as in the following vivid case. An agricultural enterprise located far from any lake or river was visited – rendered a service – by the Fishery Department of Rusprirodnadzor (the environmental inspectorate) and ordered to pay a substantial fine: "You have manure, which means you must transport it; so some of it must fall on the ground and it must pollute the drainage system; so pay up, or it will be the worse for you." The farm manager paid; he knew it would be worse, even really bad, and lead to a court case if he did not (Kordonskii 2008: 93). Estates acquire rent in many upward-flowing forms: bribes, fines, tribute (*dan'*), supplementary "taxes," kickbacks, gifts, and of course unpaid labor of various kinds. No less important is rent in the form of an agreement that the subordinate will not pay up to some other estate, thus protecting a constant resource for one side and limiting outgoings on the other. This is an asymmetrical relation, called the "roof" (*krysha*, "protection, patronage"), and it creates local disparities of power that nestle within the far broader Federation-wide "intuitive hierarchy" whereby it is generally acknowledged that the military and security services rank above law enforcement, and the latter above municipal administrations or local Cossack militias. Members of high estates mark their status by visible signs (clothing, types and number of their cars, etc.) that warn off predatory estates – such as the traffic police – from collecting dues from them as they do from other, "lower" people (Kordonskii 2008: 88–89).

It is noticeable that there is little *ideological-moral* basis in Kordonskii's vision of estate ranking in post-Soviet Russia. No longer is there a Christian tsar (the representative of God on earth), nor a communist party to guide society to a bright future. In this respect, distant as the comparison may seem, the present-day Russian case may be contrasted with that of the Etoro of Papua New Guinea, where Raymond Kelly (1993) describes an all-encompassing and unitary moral hierarchy based on cosmological beliefs about the contribution different social groups make to the perpetuation or depletion of life forces.

The estate system is an agglomeration of segments and sectional interests. Yet Kordonskii argues that it is an ontology in two senses: it tells people who they are, to which kind they belong, and it provides a doxic rationale of relations:

> Estates are reproduced in part because people are socialized from birth into the system of mutual service and servicing that is led by the state, either by tradition or policy. They do not conceptualize the organization of the social world in any other way – they not only unreflectively serve someone or another, but they understand other people serving them as a natural phenomenon. (2008: 27)

This ontology is why the quite differently organized world of the market, which coexists with the estates, can be seen as "incommensurable," even though in many cases the very same people operate both systems. Kordonskii observes that market behavior is not based on mutual services, with all its concomitants of personalized deals, currying favor, bullying, and so on, but on individual rights, equality before the law, pay for work, making profits, and the resulting wealth and poverty. Markets generate the factual existence of economic classes, but Russians do not tend to think of themselves in class categories. In the estate mode, by contrast, people know where they belong. Here rightful income does not depend on ability and diligence or producing things that other people need and are willing to pay for, but on what you *are* – in other words your status according to the service your estate is supposed to render. Market individualism is "outside the boundaries of this picture of the world" and striving to become wealthy for the sake of it is morally condemned (Kordonskii 2008: 27). In this perspective "rich" and "poor" are not applicable to estates, for each receives what it deserves, that is, the satisfaction (*udovletvorenie*) appropriate to the service it provides: 2,000 roubles for the street-sweeper, 200,000 roubles for the boss of the tax inspectorate.

Now there is no complex society without something like "estates," such as unionized workers, doctors, police, and so on, but Kordonskii argues (perhaps rhetorically and certainly unrealistically) that in democracies they have a harmonious coexistence with capitalism, whereas in Russia the relations are confused, bewildering, and antagonistic. The majority of people belong simultaneously to two different systems of stratification, that of service and that of market wealth and poverty – for example, the teacher who provides honest service in a state school for a very low salary and also sells her expertise by giving private lessons for the highest possible commercial price. Many people find this ambivalence of identity troubling, incomprehensible. The irresolvable "ontological bifurcation" of social organization generates inner conflict, anomie, and alienation (Kordonskii 2008: 133).

The nature of the articulation of incompatibles is thought of in different ways by diverse disciplines. If analytical philosophers argue that incommensurables are never truly such but can always be made comparable *in practical reason* by a third term, parity (Chang 1997: 25–27), the very subject of economics is based on the fact that people in real life make choices between "incommensurable" things all the time; the freedom to achieve the very disparate functions that a person values, via choice, is indeed a way to assess equality/inequality (Sen 1992: 4–5; see, however, Lambek 2008, who opposes choice in economics with the ethical *judgment* required by the presence of numerous and inevitable incommensurables in society). But surely the most important point is that the same actors, collective as well as individual, work – and are worked upon – by what would seem unconnected systems; yet these modes are linked in unforeseen ways. Buryat villagers, for example, who refuse to labor for one another because that would be demeaning to their status as equals in estate or "totemic" clan-type thinking, *will* work for outsiders (operating with a capitalist rationale) and for this very reason are liable to exploitation by employers who have no reason not to act only for their own profit. The villagers' exploitability is deepened by their lowly situation as the prey of numerous predatory estates and their lack of economic alternatives, which is underpinned by their geographical isolation from markets.

The piling up of dissimilar disadvantages and the nonrecognition of connections between them, of course, also occurs in many societies. A longitudinal study of some 8,000 British civil servants over the period 1967–88 established a previously unsuspected steep inverse association between social class, as assessed by grade of employment, and mortality from a wide range of diseases (Marmot et al. 1991). These were all people in stable employment without the obvious disadvantages of poverty, bad housing, unsanitary conditions, and so on, usually thought to cause illness. Yet for a series of internal and communicable diseases the study found systematic and lasting differences in rates of disease experienced by people in different employment grades. The conclusion was that differential social standing *in itself* affects health and longevity. Such findings have now begun to be discussed worldwide, but even so it is not clear what corrective measures (see Povinelli 2001) might be taken, for health and employment ranking still seem to most people "incommensurable" things.

Marmot's work on the social determinants of health inequalities across the world not only points to different health effects of absolute and relative deprivation in both richer and poorer countries; it also forcefully makes the point that since so many diverse factors (education, sense of security, stress, social exclusion, food, lack of transport, esteem, spiritual resources) are among the social determinants of disease and morbidity, "the health of a population is important precisely because it is a measure of whether, in the end, a population is benefiting as a result of a set of social arrangements" (Marmot 2005: 1103). Health is thus perhaps the most fundamental indicator of inequality; it can be measured and is therefore an empirical matter. Considering their manifold disadvantages, we should not be surprised to find that deprived and disdained Buryat villagers have several years' lower life expectancy than the (already low) Russian average.[9] Fassin (2009: 53–54) observes in his critique of Foucault that biopolitics is not just about normalization but has consequences for life, in other words for inequality; the issue is the recognition – or not – of the lives of others.

Fairness and Recognition of Inequality

Spravedlivost' ("fairness, justice") is a word omnipresent in Russian public life, yet ethnography suggests that ordinary people regard it with suspicion. When bureaucrats in the town of Ul'yanovsk set up a Fairness Chamber to combat corruption the project was greeted with scorn – "How can a Chamber created by power and dependent on it influence the quality of work of those very powers?"[10] Indeed, to judge from contemporary blogs, the whole idea of fairness is a mirage. Either it is pure demagoguery, or it is an invention of "naive idealists who paint pretty worlds for themselves and do not understand that in the real, harsh world, everything exists by a different understanding, that of the plunderer and the victim … Everyone has their own idea of fairness, but no one is interested in fairness as such, because it brings nothing that any single person or group would want."[11] This reaction chimes with Olga Shevchenko's (2009) description of post-Soviet Moscow, where people retreat to protective domesticity, avoiding public life in favor of a self-sufficiency that minimizes the vulnerability of the immediate lifeworld. Oleg Kharkhordin (2005) makes a similar point. But whereas for Shevchenko (2009: 166–167) this move can engender a certain ethical unease – some people recognize that their fierce defense of their private property and desire to increase it makes certain of their own practices look suspiciously similar to those of the much-criticized wealthy – Kharkhordin conceptualizes the circle of mutual support as one of friendship, the persistence of a Soviet era notion of fraternity, where fairness is a virtue built into the very nature of the group (2005: 158). Even he remarks, however, on the danger that such personalized relations of trust could morph into mafias or the plethora of "noncivil" entities that occupy niches within the weak state (2005: 57–58). Amid widespread indications that wealth is attributed to sheer luck or fate (Khakhulina and Stevenson 1998: 42), it is not surprising that neither author even mentions *spravedlivost'* as a discourse of general and public good among ordinary people.

Some reasons for this may be found in recent ethnographies of homelessness and humiliation. Morally condemned ("it is their own fault"), vagrants are completely excluded from state systems of distribution of public rights and goods, which are based on territorial registration. "Their treatment is not so much discrimination as excommunication. The main agency dealing with homeless people – through segregation and expulsion – is therefore the militia, with whom the social services essentially join forces" (Stephenson 2006: 145). Respectable folk are not expected to assist the homeless, only to call the police to remove them. But these unfortunate ones, who in principle might see their desperate situation as unfair, have no stable position from which to make any such statement. Höjdestrand describes a characteristic switchback of perspectives: they use the very adjectives that humiliate them (*neliudi*, "monsters," "non-people") to describe the police; after some matey encounter over a bottle they swiftly redefine the officials as semi-reasonable people, only to revert to idioms of "unpredictable sadism" in a few minutes. "Masha, Vora and the others seemed to understand that their explanations regarding police violence could never be more than makeshift attempts to make sense of a reality that was beyond their control." Constant inconsistency was a form of subjectivity as a survival strategy. Coherence in the shape of enduring opinions and lasting models of reality was a luxury item (Höjdestrand 2005: 123–124). This is an example of the inequality that is felt before it can be expressed mentioned at the beginning of this essay.

Why then have I focused on fairness if it is an idea that so few people use in a non-self-interested way in Russia? It is because in some form or another it is *potentially available* (even for Russia's homeless) as an ethical means of questioning inequality. Anthropological accounts like Kelly's (1993) can sometimes give the impression that ethics emerges seamlessly from social arrangements, which are saturated with the given culture so that ethics is simply the way that system works. This, however, cannot be the case, for people think sideways, contrariwise, or out of history when they see through the justifications of precedence and hierarchy given by a current morality (here I distinguish the broad span of ethical thinking from the closed subsystems of "morality" along the lines proposed by Bernard Williams (1985: 195)). To conclude, I would like to address two occurrences, located in different kinds of symbolic topology mentioned earlier, where the dominant mode of thought is interrupted by ethical thinking derived from somewhere else – and one could think of this "somewhere else" as a human propensity like compassion or alternatively as a recess, a wellspring, in the given culture.

There is plenty of evidence that fairness was a preoccupation of ordinary Mongols during the quasi-feudal rule of the Manchu-Qing. Most of the petitions of grievances submitted by herders to ruling princes during the eighteenth century concerned wrongful tax appropriations by lower aristocrats. It was frequently argued that taxes and duties should be imposed equally for all households of a given status, and in the context it is clear that "equally" (*niigem tegsh*) functioned to mean "fairly" (Natsagdorj 1966: 15–18). Significantly, however, Mongol ideas of fairness were not limited to sectional collective rights (as in Kordonskii's account of the Russian estates) for, while all the documents are authored and speak on behalf of particular groups, some petitions recognized absolute poverty, which could happen among the people of any estate. We begin to see how fairness can be invoked in relation to a wider ethical horizon. For example, in 1788 a minor official Janggi Ashig submitted a complaint that the higher officers of the Banner had confiscated the people's livestock and enslaved many of them. He wrote:

> Although I am a Janggi by position I am also at the same time just an ordinary person of the place. If the taxation continues in this way many people will not be able to endure it. Is this the norm (*jirum*) of our Banner? Is this the norm of many Banners? Although my complaint is the complaint of many other people they do not bring it out because they are afraid. The suffering of the many is my suffering, and when it comes to miserable me, I can do no more than bear my head in my hands[12] and send [this petition] upward. Therefore, I beg all of you, my great caring lords and superiors, to tell me what to do and I will follow your orders. (Natsagdorj 1966: 12)

An ethical stance toward inequality shines from this document. It goes beyond the fairness that would concede that others should have their due. Janggi Ashig puts himself in their position. He invokes not law (*hauli*) but "norm" (*jirum*).[13] Writing "*from* himself" (Williams 1985: 200) he identifies with the suffering (*gomdol*) of people in the serf ranks and he also presumes a common diapason of humanity when he makes an appeal to the caring (*asaragch*) of those on high.

My second example returns to Russia, where anyone who knows the language will agree that *spravedlivost'* is not confined to the sectional role it plays in Kordonskii's account. The word derives from *pravda*, which originally combined the notions of justice and truth. Olga Inkova argues that *pravyi*, much like the adjective *juste* in French, referred not only to a simple conformity with reality but to an ideal norm. *Pravda* is absolute, ultimate, God-given truth (*istina*) that is carried out on earth (Inkova 2006: 80–81). It came to diverge from the law (*zakon*) and legal justice (*yustitsia*), which tsarist codes had made into an ideological weapon and came to be seen by the mass of people as unjust, arbitrary, and "external" – opposed to the moral, "inner" law that was identified with *spravedlivost'*.

So what then is the source of the inner law? Inkova argues that *pravda* and fairness can be traced to fraternity, or more concretely to a familial notion of one's brothers, one's own people. But such fairness/rightness is not necessarily turned inward. It is given a wider ambit, an active life in society, by its distinction from *istina*, the truth of contemplative life – it is always practical, personalized, among the people. The familial can be spun out, distributed, and this is how we can understand Dostoevsky's words about Pushkin: "To be Russian, perfectly Russian, is perhaps nothing other than being brother to all men" (quoted in Inkova 2006: 91). It is in this light that we can understand the statement of Marina Khodorkovskaya, the mother of the imprisoned oligarch, who in a newspaper interview called for a trial that would be both lawful *and* fair.[14] Speaking after the second punitive decision against her son, her account of their family life makes clear that she was conscious both of the empirical singularity and of the historical contingency of the moment. Her son had behaved no differently from other businessmen in the early 1990s. From this position, to mention *spravedlivost'* was implicitly to reach out to a multitude of unknown sympathizers, coevals, and brothers who would share her understanding of equal treatment.

While it is true that "fairness" can be used to legitimate self-interest on behalf of some collective group, we can see that this use is a limiting (self-)deception. The same word with its full wealth of association is not confined to a given political discourse, such as that of the system of estates – it can cut across the incommensurables and can accuse of being unfair both public justice and the structures that generate inequality.

Conclusion

I have tried to describe different systems of both parity and asymmetry, to show that they almost always coexist with other systems of power and rank, and to discuss in what ways these modes of thinking about difference can be considered "incommensurable" ontologies. This essay has shown how a subaltern ontology can be a strategy of non-assent to hierarchy and power. But from a position of strength assertions of essential difference enable the emergence of self-interested positional discourses of fairness and thus become a means of misrecognition that both masks and deepens inequality. Such a discourse hides the fact that ostensibly separate modes of creating politico-economic differentiation can lock into one another and consolidate empirical inequality. If we are considering inequality, we have to see incommensurability for what it is, a use of difference to construct nonintelligibility, and to notice that it can be punctured in many ways, both practical and ethical.

Acknowledgments

I am very grateful to Didier Fassin, Matei Candea, and Martin Holbraad, whose helpful comments have contributed to the ideas in this essay.

NOTES

1 Gandhi maintained that the broad caste categories of the *varnas* are based on an idea of naturally different abilities and social functions that are interdependent and not hierarchical. He considered that feelings of superiority/inferiority were a perversion of *varnadharma* and he condemned actual castes (*jati*) as "artificial" man-made constructs of competition and discrimination (Béteille 1983: 18–19, 51–52).

2 Groups claiming descent from a common ancestor and linked to other such groups through agnatic ties in more distant generations (Baldaev 1970: 18).
3 The Lords (*noyod*) were a kin group whose ancestors had occupied administrative positions in pre-revolutionary times, but the name was understood currently to refer to the "nature" of the group rather than a position of power.
4 Olga Shaglanova, personal communication (Mar. 2011) describing the village of Tory in the Tunka district of Buryatia in the Russian Federation.
5 See Bogue (2007: 143) on Deleuze's explanation of ontological difference, in which he contrasts the abstract notion of color (a genus in relation to the species, the individual colors) with colors that are no longer objects *under* a concept but the nuances or degrees of the concept itself – the concept itself has become a thing.
6 In some regions, notably where shamanism was thoroughly replaced by Buddhism, totemic identities altogether gave way to genealogical ranking at local level, for example among the sprawling migratory kinship groups linked together in the Hori Buryat "tribe." However, totemic thinking reappeared even here, scaled up to the tribal level: the three major groups of Buryats were made equivalent to one another by their association with different species, the Hori with the swan, the Ekhirit with the burbot fish, and the Bulagat with a bull (Baldaev 1970: 9–11; see ethnography of contemporary Hori identification with the swan in Empson 2011: 216–217). See also Pedersen (2001: 417–420), who argues that "the Mongolian (totemic) episteme" does not counter but is proper to a vertically organized shamanic society. To make this argument, however, Pedersen envisages not clans but other kinds of social entities (elders, shamans, women, etc.) related by homologous (totemic) differences. He identifies horizontal continuity between human and nonhumans with the animism (Descola 1996: 89) found more in north Asia than in Mongolian regions.
7 According to a commonly accepted definition, an estate is a social group occupying a defined position in a hierarchically organized society in accordance with its duties and privileges fixed in law and/or passed on in inheritance (Kordonskii 2008: 26).
8 I use inverted commas as Soviet social segments would on no account have been recognized as *soslovie* at the time.
9 Agin-Buryat statistics for 2007–10 at http://statinfo.biz/HTML/M112F0S0L2.aspx, accessed Feb. 29, 2012.
10 At http://www.gazeta.ru/social/2011/04/13/3583165.shtml, accessed Feb. 29, 2012.
11 At http://otvety.google.ru/otvety/thread?tid=0772dd429fe2b077, accessed Feb. 29, 2012.
12 He means "my head is all I can offer," his head being his life.
13 *Jirum* originally meant a line and came to mean norm, line of action, established order, policy. The idea of "line" links it with *sidurgu*, straight, honest, faithful.
14 At http://khodorkovsky.ru/news/2011/02/01/15865.html, accessed Feb. 29, 2012.

REFERENCES

Atran, Scott (1990) *Cognitive Foundations of Natural History*. Cambridge: Cambridge University Press.

Baldaev, S. P. (1970) *Rodoslovnye predaniya i legendy Buriad. Chast' pervaya: Bulagaty i Ekhirity [Genealogical stories and legends of the Buryat]*. Ulan-Ude: Buriadskoe Knizhnoe Izdatel'stvo.

Baldanzhapov, P. B. (ed.) (1979) *Altan Tobchi: Mongol'skaya Letopis' XVIIIv* [Altan Tobchi: A Mongolian chronicle of the 18th century]. Facsimile of the text by Mergen Gegen Lubsangdambijalsan written in 1765, with translation into Russian, notes and commentary. Ulan-Ude: Akademiya Nauk SSSR.

Béteille, André (1983) *The Idea of Natural Inequality and Other Essays.* New Delhi: Oxford University Press.

Boellstorff, Tom (2005) Between Religion and Desire: Being Muslim and Gay in Indonesia. *American Anthropologist* 107(4): 575–585.

Bogue, Ronald (2007) *Deleuze's Way: Essays in Transverse Ethics and Aesthetics.* Aldershot: Ashgate.

Candea, Matei (2011) "Our Division of the Universe": Making a Space for the Nonpolitical in the Anthropology of Politics. *Current Anthropology* 53(3), 1–26.

Chang, Ruth (1997) Introduction. In Ruth Chang (ed.), *Incommensurability, Incomparability, and Practical Reason.* Cambridge, MA: Harvard University Press.

Deleuze, Gilles and Guattari, Felix (1987) *A Thousand Plateaus: Capitalism and Schizophrenia.* London: Athlone.

Descola, Philippe (1996) Constructing Natures: Symbolic Ecology and Social Practice. In P. Descola and G. Palsson (eds.), *Nature and Society: Anthropological Perspectives.* London: Routledge, pp. 82–102.

Dumont, Louis (1980) *Homo Hierarchicus: The Caste System and Its Implications.* Chicago: University of Chicago Press.

Empson, Rebecca (2011) *Harnessing Fortune: Personhood, Memory and Place in Mongolia.* Oxford: Oxford University Press for British Academy.

Fassin, Didier (1996) Exclusion, underclass, *marginalidad*: figures contemporaines de la pauvreté urbaine en France, aux États-Unis et en Amérique Latine [Exclusion, underclass, *marginalidad*: contemporary images of urban poverty in France, the United States and Latin America]. *Revue française de sociologie* 37(1): 37–75.

Fassin, Didier (2009) Another Politics of Life is Possible. *Theory, Culture and Society* 26(5): 44–60.

Fitzpatrick, Peter (1995) Comment on "Talking Culture: New Boundaries, New Rhetorics of Exclusion in Europe," by Verena Stolcke. *Current Anthropology* 36(1): 14–15.

Fitzpatrick, Sheila (1999) *Everyday Stalinism: Ordinary Life in Extraordinary Times: Soviet Russia in the 1930s.* Oxford: Oxford University Press.

Fox, James J. (2009) The Discourse and Practice of Precedence. In Michael P. Vischer (ed.), *Precedence: Social Differentiation in the Austronesian World.* Canberra: ANU E Press, pp. 1–13.

Freeze, Gregory (1986) The Soslovie (Estate) Paradigm and Russian Social History. *American Historical Review* 91(1): 11–36.

Gil-White, Francisco J. (2001) Are Ethnic Groups Biological "Species" to the Human Brain? Essentialism in Our Cognition of Some Social Categories. *Current Anthropology* 42(4): 515–553.

Harrison, Simon J. (1985) Ritual Hierarchy and Secular Equality in a Sepik River Village. *American Ethnologist* 12(3): 413–426.

Höjdestrand, Tova (2005) *Needed by Nobody: Homelessness, Humiliation and Humanness in Post-Socialist Russia.* Stockholm: Department of Social Anthropology, Stockholm University.

Howell, Signe (1985) Equality and Hierarchy in Chewong Classification. In R. H. Barnes et al. (eds.), *Contexts and Levels: Anthropological Essays on Hierarchy. JASO Occasional Papers in Anthropology 4.* Oxford: JASO, pp. 167–180.

Humphrey, Caroline (2001) Inequality and Exclusion: A Russian Case-Study of Emotion in Politics. *Anthropological Theory* 1(3): 331–353.

Inkova, Olga (2006) La notion de justice dans la culture russe [The notion of justice in Russian culture]. In O. Inkova (ed.), *Justice, liberté, égalité, fraternité: sur quelques valeurs fondamentales de la démocratie européenne* [Justice, liberty, equality and fraternity: on some fundamental values of European democracy]. Geneva: Institut Européen de l'Université de Genève, pp. 71–93.

Kelly, Raymond (1993) *Constructing Inequality: The Fabrication of a Hierarchy of Virtue among the Etoro.* Ann Arbor: Michigan University Press.

Kharkhordin, Oleg (2005) *Main Concepts of Russian Politics.* Lanham, MD: University Press of America.

Khakhulina, Ludmila A. and Stevenson, Svetlana A. (1998) Inequality and Justice. *Sociological Research* 17(2): 38–49.

Kordonskii, Simon (2008) *Soslovnaya struktura postsovetskoi rossii* [The estate structure of post-Soviet Russia]. Moscow: Institut Fonda "Obshchestvennoe mnenie."

Kuromiya, Hiroaki (1988) *Stalin's Industrial Revolution: Politics and Workers, 1928–1932.* Cambridge: Cambridge University Press.

Lambek, Michael (2008) Value and Virtue. *Anthropological Theory* 8(2): 133–157.

Lévi-Strauss, Claude (1963) The Bear and the Barber. *Journal of the Royal Anthropological Institute* 93(1): 1–11.

Marmot, Michael (2005) Social Determinants of Health Inequalities. *The Lancet* 365: 1099–1104.

Marmot, Michael et al. (1991) Health Inequalities among British Civil Servants: The Whitehall II Study. *The Lancet* 337: 1387–1393.

McWilliam, Andrew (2009) Trunk and Tip in West Timor: Precedence in a Botanical Idiom. In Michael P. Vischer (ed.), *Precedence: Social Differentiation in the Austronesian World.* Canberra: ANU E Press, pp. 111–133.

Natsagdorj, Sh. (1966) *Ardyn Zargyn Bichig (XVIII–XX zuuny ehen)* [Ordinary citizens' litigation documents, 18th–20th centuries]. Ulan Bator: Shinjleh Uhaany Akademiin Hevleh Üildver.

Pedersen, Morten A. (2001) Totemism, Animism and North Asian Indigenous Ontologies. *Journal of the Royal Anthropological Institute* 7: 411–427.

Povinelli, Elizabeth A. (2001) The Anthropology of Incommensurability and Inconceivability. *Annual Review of Anthropology* 30: 319–334.

Rawls, John (1971) *A Theory of Justice.* Cambridge, MA: Harvard University Press.

Rio, Knut M. and Smedal, Olaf H. (2009) Hierarchy and Its Alternatives: An Introduction to Movements of Totalization and Detotalization. In Knut M. Rio and Olaf H. Smedal (eds.), *Hierarchy: Persistence and Transformation in Social Formations.* New York: Berghahn, pp. 1–63.

Robbins, Joel (1994) Equality as a Value: Ideology in Dumont, Melanesia and the West. *Social Analysis* 36: 21–70.

Sen, Amartya (1992) *Inequality Reexamined.* New York: Russell Sage Foundation; Oxford: Clarendon Press.

Shevchenko, Olga (2009) *Crisis and the Everyday in Postsocialist Moscow.* Bloomington: Indiana University Press.

Sibley, David (1995) *Geographies of Exclusion: Society and Difference in the West.* London: Routledge.

Sneath, David (2007) *The Headless State: Aristocratic Orders, Kinship Society, and Misrepresentations of Nomadic Inner Asia.* New York: Columbia University Press.

Stephenson, Svetlana (2006) *Crossing the Line: Vagrancy, Homelessness and Social Displacement in Russia.* Aldershot: Ashgate.

Stolcke, Verena (1995) Talking Culture: New Boundaries, New Rhetorics of Exclusion in Europe. *Current Anthropology* 36(1): 1–24.

Williams, Bernard (1985) *Ethics and the Limits of Philosophy.* Cambridge, MA: Harvard University Press.

Yurchak, Alexei (2006) *Everything was Forever, Until It was No More.* Princeton: Princeton University Press.

CHAPTER 18 Sexuality

Stacy Leigh Pigg

Consider this: Nepal's 2011 census is reputed to be the first in the world to offer respondents the option to identify themselves as third gender. The Nepali Supreme Court had ruled in 2007 to eliminate discrimination of third gender persons, making it possible for a citizenship document to register an alternative other than male and female. How – and why – did the Nepali state come to break with entrenched, internationally standardized conventions of gender binarism? What does the addition of another tickable box on a form signify? And why is it considered to have something to do with sex? So far only a handful of Nepalis have sought citizenship papers as third-gender persons. Dila Buduju's quote appears in multiple news stories on the Web: "I was born as a girl, but as I grew up I felt I was a boy. Today I feel totally like a man." For some, the new gender category represents a potential moral threat, and for many in Nepal and the Nepali diaspora, it indicates a particularly "Western" sensibility they would like to reject in defense of traditional values. Others (or the same people, but in a different mood) laugh: it is one small, and to them not especially consequential, event among many occurring in a recent period of astonishing, fluid, frustrating, and possibly productive social and political change. By contrast, the Nepali activists who mobilized newly available legal mechanisms to protect the rights of sexual minorities describe their efforts firmly within values of liberation, truth to self, recognition, and empowerment. Previously illegible claims to desire and identity are affirmed through the mechanism of state recognition. International gay rights movements and Internet news feeds made it possible to publicize and frame the event in Nepal so that it could carry significance across contexts. The Nepali activists were also able to form their organizational base in part through the opening created by well-funded, donor-led AIDS prevention, and gender-oriented activities begun in the 1990s. This is why for UNAIDS, Nepal's recognition of the "third gender" is a laudable "best practice" in the service of AIDS prevention; this is why it appears as a news item on the web page of the International Planned Parenthood Federation for its relevance to that organization's mandate to work for sexual and reproductive

A Companion to Moral Anthropology, First Edition. Edited by Didier Fassin.

health; this is why the World Bank supported a beauty contest in Nepal for third gender persons as a way to counter stigma and discrimination of people with HIV. Meanwhile, CNN, using temporal metaphors of progressive enlightenment, reported that the "move [was] seen as a major victory for equality in a country that only decriminalized homosexual relationships three years ago," quoting an official who stated that "the new categorization was an attempt to open up the traditionally conservative country to different points of view."[1]

Although the new census and citizenship category is ostensibly about identity, it is understood also to be about sexual orientation. Its international newsworthiness stands as a reminder of how embedded the gender binary and heterosexual presumption is within the prosaic mechanics of modern states. That this occurred in Nepal, no less, startles assumptions that the West is and must be the vanguard of progressive legal reforms. However, the official recognition was not the outcome of a large-scale social movement leading to a shift of public opinion in support of nonnormative genders/sexualities. Much less can it be construed as an expression of some kind of cultural "tolerance" inherent in Nepali "traditions." Far from it: Nepali citizens who identify themselves as homosexual apply for refugee status in the United States, Canada, and Australia with credible claims of life-threatening persecution by police and sometimes by family members. Divergent, complementary masculine and feminine social roles are strongly entrenched in Nepal, and the expectation for a proper life is that adult men and women marry and have children. In short, the newly official third gender is not a reflection of an existing social norm, or of a widely validated self-identification. It is an anticipatorily imagined future norm/identity placed anachronistically into a present that is cross-cut by numerous partial contextualizing frames. It occupies this position between what is and what could be because it is variously caught up in, and refracted through, kinship structures, state power, post-Enlightenment liberal concepts of rights, the rewriting of a constitution, fears of Western cultural imperialism, international flows of money for global health disease prevention, political parties in post-monarchy Nepal, routinized governmental technologies of enumeration and documentation, identity politics, global media imaginaries, concepts of citizenship, global solidarity movements for gays and lesbians, public health philosophies, the real and metaphorical control of borders, and transnational travels of a variety of people that cross those borders or at least imagine themselves against the horizons of what Arjun Appadurai has evoked as different "scapes." And somewhere within this tangle, people like Dila are conceiving of themselves as subjects, and as national and international citizens, in ways that activate both a new ethical mode of being within themselves, as well as a call to moral accountability in others.

This unwieldy example provides a starting point for a discussion of sexuality and morality because it immediately – and usefully – confounds ready assumptions about how and why sexuality is an object of moral attention. This event is only *sort of* about sexuality. It thus forces us to (re)consider what we mean by sexuality and how and why sexuality can be evident as a recognizable domain. Similarly, third-gender recognition is also only in *some frames* a moral issue. To the extent that it has moral significance it acquires it by being transected by a number of value regimes. It is only partly a matter of moral regulation. A third gender is both a claimed identity to be judged by society, and a space for the formation of a new kind of subject, one whose self (*pace* Foucault) acquires ethical responsibility for self-regulation and self-fulfillment via its sexuality.

I thus use this example to draw attention to the sorts of complicated relationships between values, contexts, and modes of being that must be addressed in an anthropology of morality. Simplistic scalar terms like "local" and "global" fit poorly when superimposed on multiply directional, historically structured, and ambiguously emergent processes. Terms like "traditional" and "modern" are equally inadequate. Configurations of values are discernible, but not so easily placed "in" or "outside" of the nexus of sociality and meaning we like to call local culture. Dominant moral norms and values can be described at any moment of time, but they are not necessarily stable. Values can be the object of explicit political claims that either shore up, or resist, a given order. When is an assertion about values an expression of culturally accepted moral norm, and when is it a vested political claim disguised as a cultural claim? The ethnographic research tradition would direct us to look to what people do and say, how their context is structured, which forms of action are possible, and why these actions hold the meaning they do. Anthropological research on sexuality shows that forms of personhood, agency, and subjectivity are drifting, shifting, and reconfiguring as contexts also change. In that ambiguity between truth regimes constituted as cultural common sense and the political shoring up of possibly weakening orders, people live, engage others, and reformulate themselves as subjects. Importantly, as organized international projects of sexual reform – that is, promotion of sexual rights, sexual health, and sexual identity – have become more extensive and influential, anthropologists need to find ways to conceptualize how these projects operate and how people engage them.

My reflections, presented here, have a very mundane ethnographic origin: watching Nepali health educators in 1997 equivocate over the best wording for the first wave of public health messages about AIDS. I had not at the time conceived my research in terms of "sexuality." But I began to attend to what was hard and what was easy about creating public informational statements about the sexual transmission of disease. I noticed that international public health had already framed its explanation: the problem is that the "moral approach" to sex in "cultures like Nepal" makes sex "taboo" and therefore "hidden," and the solution is to bring sex into "open and frank" discussion that emphasizes "facts" over "values." These oft-repeated statements made me wonder about the way the term "moral" was being used in this discourse. It suggested that the "morals" of some cultures are at odds with the ethical high ground of responsible global citizenship. It was not hard to see that the well-consolidated international AIDS prevention wisdom fell short of anthropological standards of relativism and contextualization. It was equally obvious that the self-styled "nonjudgmental" approach to AIDS was perceived by many in Nepal as an imposition of a foreign set of values. In the midst of my research, I found it tempting to simply reach for the most well-known passages of Foucault's *History of Sexuality* (1990 [1978]) to narrate an encroaching modernization of sexual subjectivity. When I attempted to explain (in my adequate but flawed Nepali) to a few of my trusted interlocutors in Nepali NGOs the social history of the sexual sciences and Foucault's thesis about the "incitement to discourse," the reaction was complex. By reframing what NGO educators had encountered until then as an authoritatively backed, normative script about the true and best way to view sex, gender, and sexuality, I had validated for them the sense of friction they felt in the process of translation. In particular, educators had been telling me that they felt "odd" when they executed the required, foundational component of AIDS awareness education called "the sexual words exercise." In this exercise, facilitators elicited from trainees many "formal" and "slang" terms for body parts and sexual acts, in an activity that was meant to illuminate the values attached to things sexual. Educators were ambivalent about this exercise and often discussed whether it really worked as intended "in the Nepali context." When I participated in these discussions, I suggested that the sexual words exercise was based not on neutral, universal "facts" (as the international templates for AIDS education stated) but rather on a historically constructed cultural frame that conceived of a domain of "sexuality" that could be broken down into decontextualized pieces, such as body parts (penis), acts (oral sex), and orientations (homosexual). This relativizing move, however, sat at an awkward juncture. AIDS prevention work in Nepal was already struggling against detractors who argued that AIDS was a Western disease spread by Western sexual immorality, and that NGOs were profiting from externally driven priorities. There was an emerging politics of stigmatization of the so-called risk groups that also fed off a discourse asserting a singular, authentic, and traditional Nepali sexual morality. And it was obvious that the modern sexual subject Foucault discerned was for some in Kathmandu already a common sense reality, not so much introduced by sex education as elicited by it. No matter how many historians had described the emergence of the modern sexual subject in the West, this subject also had a history in Nepal that could not be said to be entirely new, but was strangely overshadowed by reference to the Kama Sutra and uncomfortable allusions to the so-called erotic carvings on Kathmandu's temples. My interlocutors in Nepal prompted me to attend to the vexed, heterogeneous, and changing realities in Nepal and also to read the social history of the cultural construction of sexuality in the West with more care. This project led also to reflection on forms of international expertise, cosmopolitan sensibilities, and political solidarities and the ways they include, exclude, and call to account different constituencies organized around values and truths (for instance, Pigg 2005).

Anthropological research on sexuality has long wrestled with the tension between universalizing and particularizing gestures. These gestures themselves have potent moral meanings *within* the discipline. The relativist impulses of anthropology direct us to locate values, idioms, and practices in specific contexts, supporting the idea that there are different moral values attached to things sexual. Our relativist habits also lead us to seek to avoid ethnocentrism by not imposing inappropriate analytical categories. It has thus been possible to describe cultural variation in norms governing gender and sexuality, as well as to question the extent to which we can recognize the "sexual" across diverse cultures (Elliston 1995; Clark 1997; Manderson et al. 1999). At the same time, anthropology has had, since the mid-nineteenth century, a commitment to some kind of idea of the unity of humankind and a strong sense of higher social purposes to be served by anthropological research on human diversity. These commitments have given purpose to several distinctive modes of narrating sexuality in culture. I take the current moment in anthropology to be one in which we are in the midst of working out how to bring the two hallmark approaches from twentieth-century anthropology – holistic contextualization and relativization – into an adequate relationship with an analytics of interconnection and influence at larger scales. In this essay, I sketch some of the ways in which morality intersects with sexuality, with an eye to clarifying the complexities that current international sexual reform projects pose to the most ready-to-hand forms of anthropological relativism and universalist moral commitments.

At the very least, recent anthropological research on sexuality can be summed up as a call for a more sophisticated analysis of "context." It has been argued that the concept of the social construction of sexuality has had a profound impact by stressing that all sexualities are local. Constructionist interpretations have indeed worked well for explaining the complicated histories of sexualness in society within the space of certain stable framing devices (for instance, a nation, a social class, or a given time period). But when used unreflectively, the relativizing, contextualizing habits of constructivist analysis serve less well in the task of dealing with the multiple, intersecting temporalities of historically shaped and dynamically emergent "global" sexualities – much less in the task of the multiple moral worlds, and the politics anthropologists might wish to engage. In other words, the world today demands an anthropology that envisions more moving parts in relation to each other, and does so while also attending to multiple perspectives on these relations.

Here, to unpack what is involved in this kind of anthropological project, I first explain an accepted delineation between two major anthropological approaches to sexuality. In the wake of Foucault's thesis that biopower is characteristic of both modern forms of governance and the production of the ethically self-regulating subject, the very obviousness of a domain of "sexuality" becomes at once more significant, and more problematic, for cross-cultural research. I suggest that it is productive to leave open the question of the conditions under which a domain of sexuality can be said to exist, and nonetheless ask about the moral investments that accrue to sexuality. To this end, I go on to provide a brief overview of moralized sexuality in kinship, colonialism, nationalism, and international development. In these and other forms of social relations, the explicit moral coding of sex also induces modes of self-knowledge and subjectivity, such that conduct and even identity can acquire significance (Butler 2002). Morality and sexuality intersect at the production of collectivities and the making and remaking of self and other.

Models of Nature, Culture, and Self in Anthropological Studies of Sexuality

Anthropological studies of sexuality can be read as an elaboration of the question of culture's relation to nature, by way of the theorization of the body, subjectivity, and sociality. Carole Vance, in a landmark article, distinguished two approaches in the conceptualization of the sexual body's relationship to collective patterns of meaning and action. The first approach, which Vance (1991: 878) dubbed "cultural influence theories," posits sexuality as an already existing, self-evident, biologically set raw material ("a kind of universal Play-Doh") that is molded through socialization. Anthropological studies working from this assumption have been able to document cross-cultural variability in both sexual activities and social attitudes toward sex. These sorts of studies stand as an empirical challenge to strong forms of biological essentialism. Research framed within the social influence model work as a liberal call for respect for difference against the totalizing moral conclusions about human nature that essentialism supports. Nonetheless, cultural influence theories – however much they might emphasize the enormous role of culture as an influence – do not regard sexuality itself as analyzable. Sexuality is so accepted as a given that no pause to define it is required. It is considered to be grounded in a transcultural, transhistorical body that is conceived as purely biological where biology stands for the ultimate human universal and ground of sameness. This is a body that has urges that can be channeled and dispositions that can be shaped, but a body whose impulses and forms always precede the action of the social upon it.

The second approach outlined by Vance, cultural constructionist theory, posits that sexuality comes into being in and through social forms, as these exist not only in social structures, institutions, discourses, and practices, but also in the embodiments of gender, in the subjectivity of expectation and desire, and in the aesthetics of pleasure. In contrast to the presocial body that is the premise for influence theory, constructionist theory imagines a body that is – quite literally and materially – built. As Vance put it, biology does not explain "a culture's sexual schema any more than the auditory range of the human ear explains its music" (1991: 879). The longings, pleasures, fecundities, aesthetics, and sensualities that our physiology can yield are not only variable, but also require a calling forth in and through already existing socialities and intelligibilities. This is not a body whose organic grid contains an ontological teleology of sexuality, but a known, felt, lived, and interpreted body. It is a body of relationality and meaning. Constructionist theories pull to the fore the processes that establish the social significance and subjective meanings of sexual acts, such that identical acts can *be* quite different things, thereby introducing cautions against inappropriate assumptions about the transhistorical character of categories used in comparative analysis.

Although the difference between these approaches is now well known, I review the contrast here at the outset because the question of a so-called human nature, and its malleability, is interlaced with the questions of universality and specificity through conceptualizations of context. Whereas society in the influence model is something that either encourages or restricts sexual actions, society in constructionist theory is itself polymorphous, contradictory, dynamic, and fractured. Importantly, this plurality makes sexuality imaginable as a contested terrain on which political and symbolic struggles are fought and where dominant and marginalized constructions can coexist. Thus, in addition to providing a conceptualization of sexuality, each of these frameworks imply corollary ideas about morality by way of their theorization of both body and society.

To add another layer of complexity, both models are actively taken up by positioned social actors in various kinds of global projects, often around the promotion of rights, of emancipation, of health, or of cultural autonomy. Poor women in many parts of the world are being instructed to distinguish between fixed biological "sex" and culturally constructed "gender" as part of empowerment projects run by international nongovernmental organizations. Gay and lesbian philanthropists from the United States organize to catalyze political mobilization based on sexual identity in the global South, sometimes citing the statistic that 10 percent of all people are homosexual. In the movement to repeal the law criminalizing "unnatural sex" in India, activists disagreed on whether a paradigm of queerness or of gayness would provide the best political strategy to both overturn the law and create space for nonnormative sex/genders. In these and many other examples, we see a looping effect. Theoretical models of sexuality are out there in the world doing cultural work, even as we as anthropologists attempt to empirically document a changing world through the lens of these models. This has implications for the question of the relationship between so-called local moral worlds and forms of translocality.

The Modernity of the Sexual Subject

We come up against Western modernity: is it ubiquitous and if so in what forms? Although anthropologists flatly reject the simplistic idea that a unidirectional, singular process of "Westernization"/"modernization" is homogenizing a previously diverse world according to patterns predicted in Western social theory, we also recognize that certain historically distinctive orientations and logics are in fact being internationalized via influential political forms associated with global capitalism, albeit in complex, multidirectional, and contradictory ways. Sexuality itself is one such distinctively modern concept. The ability to discern a domain of sexuality arose gradually out of a series of shifts in social organization associated with industrialization and urbanization and that coalesced, over time, from public debates under these changing conditions. Social history shows, in short, that

> the separation, with industrial capitalism, of family life from work, of consumption from production, of leisure from labor, of personal life from political life, has completely reorganized the context in which we experience sexuality ... Modern consciousness permits, as earlier systems of thought did not, the positing of "sex" for perhaps the first time as having an "independent" existence. (Ross and Rapp 1997[1981]: 164)

Writing of nineteenth- and twentieth-century Britain, historian Jeffrey Weeks notes that "sexuality has assumed major symbolic importance as a target of social intervention and organization, to a degree that differentiates this period from those preceding it" (1989 [1981]: 11). In line with the delineation of an "incitement to discourse" provided by Foucault in *The History of Sexuality*, Weeks lays out core cultural assumptions:

> In our society sex has become the supreme secret ("the mystery of sex") and the general substratum of our existence. Since the nineteenth century it has been seen as the cause and "truth" of our being. It defines us socially and morally; its release or proper functioning can be a factor in health, energy, activity; its frustration is a cause of ill health, social unorthodoxy, even madness. (1989: 12)

The "our" in this passage is interesting for anthropologists to ponder. It implies a polite acknowledgment of the existence of "others" – outside the modern West, not caught up in its history – who attach different meanings to sex. Yet anthropologists – mindful of alternative global modernities and the complicated legacies we call postcoloniality – might want, instead, to query the means by which more and more people in the world might have come or be coming (at least some of the time, and in some ways) to see sex, and themselves, in these terms (see, for instance, Stoler 1995; Boyce 2006; Boelstorff 2007; Srivastava 2007; Boyce and Khanna 2011).

In *The Care of the Self*, Foucault turned his attention to the ethical regimes within ancient Greek and Roman philosophy as a means to query the very relationship between a self and the body that is the basis for the communication of values through actions. What Foucault calls "the cultivation of the self" emerged through an ethics of pleasure, whereby the very practice of modulation and self-control could give rise to a way of conceiving the self in relation to others. Foucault saw this as "a different way of considering oneself as the subject of one's pleasures" such that "the individual could form himself as the ethical subject of his actions" and therefore make efforts "to find in devotion to self that which could enable him to submit to rules that give a purpose to his existence" (1988 [1986]: 71, 91). In this way, the sexual body (or, more accurately, the self's body in its sexualness) can become an object for regimes of moderation, of control, or of indulgence. The self becomes self-regulating by internalizing a social logic of subjectivity that is prior to moral norms, a condition Foucault termed "ethics."

Foucault argues that morality can inhere in sex not solely (or even mainly) through the valuations (moral norms) attached to specific sexual acts in specific relationships, but rather via subjectification, that is, the constitution of a subject that regards its forms of living in the body to be ethical acts. Butler describes this as "a self-transformation prompted by a form of knowledge that is foreign to one's own. And this form of moral experience will be different from the submission to a command" (2004: 308). This is a line of reasoning that pushes us past the common tendency (evident in international public health, for instance) to provide mere inventories of value stances toward things sexual. It directs us instead to problematize the conditions under which a sexual way of being in a body becomes known to itself as a subjectivity, in part through the not quite reiteration of already existing logics of intelligibility and normativity in society.[2]

In Euro-American modernities, the sexual domain has been a magnet for the expression of moral concerns. In the essay "Thinking Sex: Notes for a Radical Theory of the Politics of Sexuality," Gayle Rubin calls for a political, rather than a moral, interpretation of sexuality. Rubin begins by noting that "contemporary concerns over sexual conduct and erotic values … acquire immense symbolic weight. Disputes over sexual behavior often become vehicles for displacing social anxieties and discharging their attendant emotional intensity" (2007 [1984]: 150). She traces a historical line from nineteenth-century morality campaigns against vices (such as prostitution, masturbation, obscenity, and lewd behavior) to preoccupations with a purported "homosexual menace" and "sex offenders" in the 1950s through today's preoccupations with, for instance, child pornography or the sex scandals of elected leaders. She draws attention to the "persecution" of particular "erotic communities" through law, medicine, economic penalties, and social sanctions, arguing that "a radical theory of sex must identify, describe, explain and *denounce* erotic injustice and oppression" (157; emphasis added). This theory begins, she says, by recognizing a hierarchical system of sexual value, a system that "draw[s] and maintain[s] an imaginary line between good and bad sex, creating a 'charmed circle' of sexual acceptability with 'outer limits' forms of sexual expression that are coded as bad, abnormal, dangerous, or damned." "This kind of sexual morality," says Rubin, "has more in common with ideologies of racism than with true ethics. It grants virtue to the dominant groups and relegates vices to the underprivileged" (160).

If sexuality is a moral issue, then anthropologists should analyze it within systems of values and meanings, and through an ethics of relativism. If sexuality is a political issue, then anthropologists should analyze it within systems of resources and power, and within an ethics that tracks and fights oppression. It is both. Critical interpretive anthropology therefore must grapple with the challenge of this duality.

Moral Investments in Sex

How is it that values come to inhere in sexuality? Why is it that the sexual dimension of social/bodily being-in-the-world holds a social significance for self or for others? How are moralities themselves dislodged and attached, eliminated and reclaimed, in domains and practices that become configured as sexual? Anthropological research is clear: sexuality is experienced – even formed – in social matrices, through organizing sets of public meaning, and within a history. Sexuality manifests not (just) as personal experience but also as a set of public, shared cultural beliefs about the practices and consequences of sexual behavior. Until the last two decades or so, anthropologists rarely posed "sexuality" per se as a central research problem. If we look at much ethnographic work through the lens of an anthropology of morality, we find that a great deal is said about sexuality (though, to be sure, often in an indirect manner). A strategy for reading the ethnographic literature would be to ask two questions: (1) What moral investments are attached to sexuality in a given context? (2) What are the multiple arenas in which specific claims about sexuality operate? These two questions can build an analytics of both meaning and power, as well as of subjectivity.

To begin, then, studies of kinship – the core of the classical anthropological canon – can be reread with an eye to these two questions. Various analyses of kinship propose different ways of understanding the relationship between morality and sexuality, depending on the foundational theoretical assumptions about what kinship "is" and how it "makes" society. Victorian anthropologists understood the family to be the most basic social institution and gender to be the foundational social difference. Considering sex (that is, heterosexual copulation) to be the node that linked family and gender into the building blocks of society, investigation of the patterns of sexual partnership was a means to understanding the scope of human variation, including the very capacity for sociality. Victorian anthropologists narrated an evolution from chaotic sociality evidenced (as they thought) in "primitive promiscuity" through progressive stages of ever more organized systems of recognizing, legitimizing, and regulating passion, sexual intercourse, affinal bonds, and relations of descent. (In other words, sorting people out into neat lines of male–female sexual pairs and their children.) As is well known, Victorian evolutionary anthropologists often grossly misinterpreted the social arrangements of peoples around the world in their quest to trace the origin of the family. With equal ethnocentrism, they also, paradoxically, took the Anglo-European bourgeois nuclear family as at once the most true-to-nature and yet most culturally refined way of regulating affinity and descent. For the Victorian anthropologist, the bringing of sexuality under moral control was the definition of civilization.

Structural functionalism, in contrast, put forward the idea that morals derived from the investment people make in the social order itself. Structural-functionalist assumptions about the unifying centrality of social structure, the cohesion of society, and the natural equilibrium of social reproduction made the moral investments in sex in each society a matter only to be described, not to be interrogated, because it could be taken as a given that a community will value social reproduction. If kinship was social structure, and if social structure was society, and if kinship was a regularization and structuring of sexual pairings and reproduction, then (by implication) the moral investment in sexuality was a moral investment in the social order itself.

To take an ethnographic example familiar to most anthropologists, Evans-Pritchard's three books on the Nuer explore the larger question of how a socio-moral order is sustained in the absence of formal political institutions and despite a cultural ethos of individual autonomy. In *The Nuer* – a book not commonly understood to have much to say about sex – Evans-Pritchard famously laments that "I never discussed anything with the young men but livestock and girls, and even the subject of girls led inevitably to that of cattle" (1969b [1940]: 19). The custom of bridewealth, of course, was what linked girls and cattle so obviously in the minds of those young men in the 1930s, but in developing the thesis that "the kinship idiom is a bovine idiom" Evans-Pritchard considered exchanges of cattle to be that which gave form and substance to social ties. Hence, as Evans-Pritchard describes in *Kinship and Family among the Nuer* (1969a [1951]) sexual relationships between men and women become a matter of community attention mainly to the extent that such liaisons might have the potential to create situations that could confound bridewealth exchanges. Practices such as ghost marriage and woman marriage (a woman becoming a social male and marrying another woman), and the rituals to reverse the life-threatening consequences of incestuous sexual intercourse, were interpreted to show that it was not sex but procreation, however it might be achieved, that mattered morally, that is to say, what mattered socially. Structural-functionalist studies of kinship found "systems" that allocated social rights, duties, and obligations according to role. So although anthropologists working in this vein were not interested in the analysis of erotic desire or sexual subjectivity, they clearly described normative values contained within expected social roles organized through kinship.

Strathern has extended this insight, extrapolating from it an abstraction that is mathematical in its purity: that which we call kinship in any given society is actually a formative cultural ideology of "how relationships *as such* are held to be constituted" (1992: 5; emphasis added). Of course, kinship and sexuality cannot be collapsed into each other: not everything to be said about sexuality falls under kinship, and not everything that matters in kinship has to do with sexuality. Nonetheless, sexuality can be a means – perhaps as affect, perhaps as a catalyst to conception and reproduction, perhaps in the service of groups such as patrilines, perhaps in the enactment of desired forms of personhood – by which many types of relationships may be constituted. A new wave of anthropological research no longer takes kinship as the key that unlocks "the system" of a society, but instead reformulates the study of kinship as the tracing of "the production of relatedness" (Franklin and McKinnon 2001), an "ethics of care" (Borneman 2001), and a society's "theory about the past, present, and future" (Strathern 1992). Kinship, then, is ethical praxis.

Making Social Orders: Empires, Nations, and Moderns

If sexuality is embedded in social institutions that far exceed those pertaining to biological and social reproduction, it is necessary to ask how various visions of sexuality circulate in and through value regimes not only in the family or the community but also in imperialism, in nation-building, in globalized economic systems and class relations, in international humanitarianism, in identity-based movements, and in forms of modern administration such as law and medicine. Concepts of freedom, of rights, of individuality, of collective governance, and of social order spill out of the pages of political philosophy and social theory into a messy historicity of dynamic social transformation. Political agendas restructure worlds; hybrid imaginaries reach out for new futures. Models of sexuality can be advanced by variously positioned, and variously constituted, actors in the name of different value-infused projects.

Under colonialism, gendered sexuality has functioned as a site for the elaboration of group boundaries and differences. Stoler (2002: 42) argues that "the very categories of 'colonizer' and 'colonized' were secured through forms of sexual control." Marriage, concubinage, and prostitution were matters of explicit policy, but when "European identity and supremacy … was thought to be vulnerable, in jeopardy, or less than convincing … colonial elites responded by clarifying the cultural criteria of privilege and the moral premises of their unity" (51). It is evident from changing colonial debates, fears, postures, fantasies, and justifications that moral positions vacillated: concubinage was lauded when this domestic arrangement helped establish long-term settlement and secure profits, but when sharpening and securing racial categories was politically necessary, these same arrangements were recast as a threat to respectability and therefore also a danger to imperial rule. According to Stoler, colonial regimes of sexual access, reproduction, and domesticity organized not just the racial ideology of rule, but also the politics of class and gender through which power and profit were secured. Morality here – even when articulated around what kinds of sexual relationships were appropriate, what kinds of domestic and child-rearing practices would guard against "degeneracy" and "turpitude" – was very much about a moral vision of colonial authority itself: "how empires should be run, how agents of empire should rule, and where, how, and with whom they should live" (77).

Beyond the values the colonial elite applied to their own, rule was also exerted through direct interventions into the sexual, familial, and reproductive practices of those positioned as natives. Many researchers of colonial history have documented the unmistakable diction and tone of colonial writings, which were so often obsessed with documenting exactly how the sexuality of the native other was closer to nature, unrestrained, animal-like, impulsive, excessive, licentious, unregulated, or improperly masculine or feminine. Such characterizations were often interwoven into technocratic documents in which colonial officials considered how best to address, for instance, the perceived problems of low fertility and decline in workers' vigor. In the Trobriand Islands of the early twentieth century, missionaries and officials used medicine, law, and fiscal pressures to induce natives to behave as responsibly procreative monogamous couples, and to raise children who would be shielded from knowledge of or pursuit of eroticism (Reed 1997). British crusades against infibulation in Sudan emerged as officials tackled the problem of securing a large, compliant proletariat labor force (Boddy 2007). Female circumcision was constructed as a problem insofar as it was pinpointed as the cause of infant and maternal mortality. The new administrative interest in the operations fostered detailed discussions of genital forms, the aesthetics governing male desire, sources of male and female sexual pleasure, and the social mechanisms needed to keep women's sexual behaviors in line. The 1936 comments of one official show how the problem of the health of populations flows smoothly into considerations of character that index the position of races in an evolutionary hierarchy:

> The chastity of a virgin in cultured races means much more than the mere anatomical condition of virgo intacta. It implies strength of character and high moral development … When we find the conception of virginity has dwindled to the dimensions of a crude surgical operation we must assume that the moral fiber of the race is no longer what … it must have been. (Quoted in Boddy 2007: 264.)

Studies of colonial and neocolonial rule draw our attention to the racialized, class-inflected, and gendered social divides that make the sexual actions of particular types of people an object of control within specific structures of stratification (for instance, Butt 2005). Sexuality can operate as the pivot around which valued/devalued forms of difference are not only identified but also managed.

What, then, is the role of a broader rhetoric of modernization in shaping social relations by way of sexuality? Efforts to reform and modernize the nation have often linked sexual conduct to national progress. In Brazil in the 1920s and 1930s, for instance, intellectuals like anthropologist Gilberto Freyre saw the pattern of (coerced) sexual relations between white masters and black slaves as the foundation of Brazilian national character. Influenced by international eugenic sentiments, Brazilian leaders saw in a future, rational miscegenation the gradual whitening of the population as a key to modernization (Larvie 1999). Around the same time, in Republican era China, popular scientific and medical treatises on sexual and reproductive matters reflected the view among educated groups in the country that control of sexual desire would restore strength to the nation and help it achieve modernity (Dikötter 1995). These cases highlight how historically specific constructions of vitality and group purity emerge to articulate concerns not just about the form and character of the nation itself, but also its place in an international order and the hierarchies that would govern an imagined global future.

Sexual practices can also be quite purposively framed as a form of activism within social movements, as means of large-scale social reform, even revolution. Utopian communities of nineteenth-century America, such as the Oneida colony, held the reworking of sexual relations to be essential to the making of a new society. In another instance, Mahdavi (2007) reports that in Iran of the early 2000s, young adults of the secular middle class saw themselves as challenging the repressive political regime by challenging its morality by participating in secret parties and sexual encounters. While the state polices morality in the public sphere, enforcing sexual and social modesty by patrolling, apprehending, and punishing offenders, an urban youth subculture revolved around flaunting state-enforced versions of Islamic norms of the modest body by means of their private parties (drinking, making out, dancing, wearing prohibited provocative clothing). Youth speak of this as a "sexual revolution," that is, a political revolution that is being purposively enacted through transgressive sexual activity. This is a case where the state exercises overt social control specifically to regulate sexuality. The Islamic revolution in Iran invested its political order with moral meanings (linking a view of Islamic modesty and lifestyle to both a resistance to Western influence and a larger project of rule). The body, the sexual body, is an object of state control, and so it becomes a tool for the assertion of a critique of the regime.

Fertility, more than any other aspect of sexuality, has been made to carry nationalist meanings. How – for instance – have ideals of rational sexuality and moderated fertility come to form, via nation-building projects and international technocratic programs, a common-sense morality invested in the two-child family and the contracepting couple? Women citizens are in some circumstances asked to bear children for the sake of the nation, while in others their fertility comes to be construed as a threat to social order, economic productivity, and national security. In these cases sexuality becomes the subtext for a far-reaching set of concerns about shared values and the health of the nation. For both health planners and contraceptive users, investments in reproductive behavior have forced a new kind of imagining about sexual relations. Where national population-control projects have reigned, men and women are encouraged to think of their sexuality as nonreproductive and as an object for self-improvement (Pigg and Adams 2005). Organized international and national population control efforts have been and continue to be framed as key to other ethical projects, such as reducing poverty, improving quality of life, promoting choice, empowering women, or saving the planet from environmental destruction. These efforts have also been passionately criticized for the ethical breaches to health, autonomy, and rights that have been justified in the name of the greater good. For instance, Ram (2001) dissects the contradictory logic by which the Indian state upholds principles of liberal democratic citizenship but deems the potential overfecundity of some categories of women to be a site of crisis, occurring outside the space of modern rationality on which the concept of citizenship rests, that justifies overriding normal rights. Both family-planning programs and pronatalist policies contain implicit moral assumptions about the purpose of sexual relations, the nature of persons, and the meaning of social bonds, and these assumptions uphold particular political orders.

Subjectification and Recognition

In much of the world, today's efforts at sexual reform occur through reproductive health and disease prevention programs organized along the lines of "best practices" established by professional international experts and promulgated through donor aid to national health programs. These programs foster dynamic, but often conflicted, spaces of social action. In public health, epidemiology and intervention strategies work in tandem to promote the neoliberal virtues of risk reduction whereby the self-regulating subject is responsible for optimized health. As Pigg and Adams have pointed out, "little notice is given to the extraordinary degree to which these efforts not only assume but also create and attempt to enforce a certain definition of the sexual dimension of body and experience" (2005: 20). Currently, both economic and health development programs are organized around tutelary strategies to educate recipients into new subjectivities, such as "loving couples" and "empowered women" (Bedford 2009). What kind of moral object does sex become in development- and public health-oriented programs? What kind of sexual subject is induced into being by these programs?

A stance of scientific detachment toward sexuality took shape from the late nineteenth century onward in modern cosmopolitanism, and through these changes the very idea that there could be an objective view on sexual matters became plausible. Consequently, at present, scientific, medical, and biological claims about sex and sexuality are put forth with a certainty of both their universality and their status as neutral truths outside culture and history. The idea that aspects of sexuality can be removed from the realm of moral debate altogether, however, is an "objectification of sex" that is itself often perceived as a moral act (Adams and Pigg 2005). As I noticed in Nepal, the correct execution of AIDS prevention programs requires a strict separation between "the facts" of disease transmission and "moral approaches" to sex. The discourse of public health positions its "science" as rational, nondiscriminatory, efficacious, and fair, against "cultural beliefs" that are assumed to be arbitrary, prejudicial, and misguided. The mainstream public health position derives its conviction from twentieth-century Euro-American historical experiences where medicalization replaced moral reform campaigns, sometimes in ways that allowed sufferers to reformulate social identities that subverted stigma or allowed socially marginalized categories of people access to basic conditions for health. Nonetheless, public health rationalism can itself be the vehicle for politicized moral agendas. Some would argue that the much-touted "ABC" approach ("Abstain, Be Faithful, use Condoms") of US-led AIDS prevention reflects not only an individualistic ethos of a Western neoliberal common sense, but also the particular local politics of a certain Christian morality in the United States that acquires international influence through both US funding for AIDS and through US-led evangelical movements.

Yet, seen from the receiving end of this internationally validated expertise, most debates among metropolitan commentators are obscure, if not irrelevant. Both AIDS (as a sexually transmitted disease) and AIDS interventions (as a kind of public management of citizens' sexual lives) accrue social meaning within the particular, often contested, history of a place, even as globally coordinated public health strategies lay claim to a transcendent virtue of saving lives. In 1990s Nepal, for instance, AIDS awareness activity was backed entirely by massive international funding put in place before an actual epidemic registered in the public consciousness. AIDS messaging coincided with political and economic liberalization. In urban areas consumerism, democracy, youth culture, and an expanded media landscape, together with noticeable social trends toward love marriage and the formation of nuclear households conjoined in a heightened public attention to sex. When an AIDS donor quietly launched an FM radio show inviting listeners to call in with their questions about sex, the unexpectedly enthusiastic live listener response to the show disturbed many defenders of the social and political status quo (Pigg 2002). Critics questioned whether it was "appropriate" material "for Nepal" and represented it as inauthentic: "Do they want to make us into Americans?" "We are not that 'free' yet!" "No Nepali girl would ever say that!" Critics framed listener questions as distasteful (young men worried about wet dreams and masturbation), or irrelevant to the health education objectives (questions about orgasm in women). It disturbed these critics that young adults wrote in to confess that they were deeply attached to a partner of the same sex, seeking advice on how to evade the social requirement to marry. A few distressed young women called in to talk about sexual abuse they had experienced from a male relative. Husbands worried about how best to excite their wives. The show violated a middle-class sense of decorous, respectful, and well-ordered families, yet it appealed to precisely this class. It also pulled back the curtain to reveal a population of people already at least partially defining themselves as subjects whose truth to self was to be found in a sexuality – an "education of desire" (see Stoler 1995) – that coalesced at the intersection of medicalization, consumer culture, and class. The donor-supplied international public health expertise that had heretofore organized AIDS interventions had always asserted that it was a "problem" that "in Nepal no one talks about sex." In the shortlived controversy around this radio show, the "problem" became "cultural appropriateness." Holding both a moral and technocratic high ground, donor organizations have insisted that AIDS prevention initiatives both follow a global standard of fact and openness *and* at the same time be "culturally appropriate." At the actual interface at which health education occurred, no such clarity could be maintained, leaving Nepali health educators to mediate contradictory calls to accountability. In a heterogeneous society, undergoing rapid cultural change during an era of political questioning and heightened mobilization around differing visions of the future, who decides – and who enforces – what is deemed culturally appropriate? Interventions contain hopes of change and visions of achieving a goal. These hopes and visions enter into complex social fields, in which the stakes for different actors may be divergent, fragmentary, or contradictory.

Ethical or political orientations – contained (as Butler argues) within concepts of gendered personhood – can be built into concepts and arguments that are then ossified and dispersed, whether through transnational organizing or through the social scientific grounds of technocratic interventions. The concept of sex work is a case in point. Prostitution has long been a focus for activist, feminist, and public health concern, in relation to both the AIDS pandemic (disease) and exploitative labor trafficking (gender-based economic violence). The terms "sex work" and "survival sex" have displaced the word "prostitution" because they shift the discussion of sexual exchanges from the moral to the economic. Although the term "sex work" is viewed as neutral in contrast to prostitution, these terms reflect the same Western anxiety about the commodification of human relationships. Prostitution/sex work troubles the modern separation of a private domain of affect from a public domain of impersonal, monetized relationships, such that the decoupling of sex and love comes to be figured as either a betrayal of self (prostitution) or a form of labor (sex work). As Holly Wardlow (2004: 1028) shows in her work on Huli "passenger women" in Papua New Guinea, neither concept translates well:

> two of the pivotal concepts that "make sense" of prostitution in a Western context – women as sexually desirable objects and sex as a compensable kind of labor – are confounded by Huli logics that assert that women are not necessarily the desirable ones and sex is not work … Western pseudobiologistic and pseudo economistic assumptions about desire, and its supply and demand, carry little weight in this context.

Instead, she argues, Huli passenger women she met transacted sex not because they must resort to this to survive, but because they felt deeply betrayed by their kin. A means to express anger against a wrong of magnitude is to withdraw their sexuality from the clan-based systems of bridewealth exchange. Passenger women, according to Wardlow, "are women who refuse to cooperate" (2004: 1034). At the intersection of a moral logic of kinship built on the exchange of women and the economic transformations that turn men into paid laborers, passenger women find means to make a moral claim against wrongs: "in their eyes, their kin have forfeited their 'ownership' of women's sexuality by engaging in actions as selfish – if not more selfish than – passenger women's exchange of sex for money" (Wardlow 2004: 1036).

In refusing the position structured for them by marriage exchanges, passenger women suffer from stigmatization, violent attacks, and risk of disease; their situation might well be improved through common cause with international movements supporting sex workers. Organizing and interventions that can occur by means of the category of sex work reject one kind of moralization of sexuality in service of one sort of political aim, potentially producing new forms of solidarity, but as Wardlow notes, the seemingly value-neutral concept of sex work "is potentially problematic because it assumes particular kinds of subject positions, motivations, and gendered identifications that may not be accurate for all women" (2004: 1038). At issue in the mobilization around the concept of sex work is not simply whether or not "other" cultural logics might be "understood," but rather how social science concepts activated within advocacy and public health globalize particular models of sexual personhood and sexual sociality.

Conclusion

Modernizing and emancipatory projects that claim that they supplant so-called moral views of sexuality with frameworks that are neutral, objective, and universally ethical pose an interesting challenge for an anthropology of the global contemporary. These sorts of projects – found in disease prevention, population control, sex education, rights advocacy, sexual identity-based solidarity networks, activism against persecution – rest on common sense ideas about the sexual body as an object or means for ethical action. Although anthropologists have no trouble mustering a reflexive recognition of the historical and cultural specificity of this common sense, for critically oriented analysts the question of political and moral commitments in an actually existing interconnected world remains. Anthropology in the twentieth century took on the task of providing a ground of commensurability in its relativist efforts of cross-cultural translation. This task vested in anthropologists a moral authority to arbitrate between universals and particulars. Today, most anthropologists eschew this Archimedean position and instead grapple with a complicated ethnographic and ethical positionality in the midst of multiple points of view and diverse calls to accountability, in a world where our own anthropological theories and descriptions of sexualities loop back into the ethnographic arenas we occupy. Considering this situation to be one in which commensurability itself is at stake can be an analytical way forward (for instance, Pigg 2001). What are the conditions under which actors (including anthropologists, humanitarians, technocrats, and activists) assume, propose, or seek commensurability? What common measures, standards, facts, or frames are proposed, by whom, and what are the processes by which actors seek to establish them? What are the consequences of the routinization of certain paths of connection?

Historians of anthropology (such as Henrika Kuklick and George Stocking) argue that anthropologists' efforts to explain others have been a prolonged project of engagement with social and political conditions "at home." This thesis is explored in relation to sexuality in Andrew and Harriet Lyons's book *Irregular Connections* (2004). Victorian anthropologists advanced narratives of progressively more organized and regulated sexual activity, such that the scope of global cultural history could be read as a necessary movement to the greater social complexity of civilizational/moral refinement in which sexual customs and attitudes indexed the passage from a state of nature to a state of culture. Mid-twentieth-century anthropology, in contrast, used relativism to stress difference by emphasizing local systems of value and social reproduction, while at the same time commenting on Western social theory. Malinowski's *The Sexual Life of Savages* (1929) and Mead's *Coming of Age in Samoa* (1928) self-consciously portrayed non-Western others in order to comment both on the (misplaced) values of modern society and on inappropriately universalized theories of the person. Much subsequent work on sexuality has followed this path by producing what Kath Weston (1993) dubbed "the ethnocartography" of sex/gender system differences. However ethnographically compelling such accounts might be, this approach maintains the allochronic view exposed in Fabian's thesis in *Time and the Other* (1983). Fabian criticized theoretical paradigms in anthropology on ethical grounds, arguing against modes of analysis that demarcate distinctive cultural others whose worlds appear not only self-contained but also removed from any claim to a shared present and future. In current anthropology, spatial tropes are more evident than temporal ones: the terms "local" and "global" allude to a problematic of difference and historical world systems but do not in themselves account for the vexed (re)production of local moral worlds in, through, and sometimes against universalizing ethical projects. Sexuality has long been a pivot around which anthropology stakes out explanatory claims about cultural difference and universal values. If "culture is the conceptual and discursive space we reserve to struggle to refine our understandings of social differences and similarities,"[3] then anthropologists' analyses of the values invested in sexualness also stake out claims about separation and interconnection.

Acknowledgments

This essay owes much to my collaboration with Vincanne Adams, as well as the other contributors to *Sex in Development* (Adams and Pigg 2005). My research in Nepal was supported by the Joint Committee of South Asia of the Social Science Research Council and the American Council of Learned Societies (with funds from the National Endowment for the Humanities and the Ford Foundation) and the Social Sciences and Humanities Research Council Small Grants Program at Simon Fraser University.

NOTES

1 This account, including quotations, comes from an Internet search through Google, using the simple search term "Nepal third gender," conducted in May, July, and September of 2011. The same narrative and quotations appear across numerous press releases, news feeds, and blogs, though there is some difference between the English-language Nepali and international accounts.

2 In *Bodies that Matter*, philosopher Judith Butler (1993) further develops the implications of this ambivalent duality whereby the subject constructs the conditions of its possibility within the ongoing performance of itself under the conditions set by a hegemonic cultural order (see also Butler 2002). Clark (1997) is an excellent example of how these analytical paths might be translated into an empirical ethnographic analysis of non-Western gendered

personhood under colonialism. Stoler (1995) analyzes how race and sexuality converge in bourgeois sensibilities, providing the bridge between Foucault's suggestive theorization and the historiography of colonial subject formation.

3 Sylvia Yanagisako, quoted in Delaney 2004.

REFERENCES

Adams, Vincanne and Pigg, Stacy Leigh (eds.) (2005) *Sex in Development: Science, Sexuality, and Morality in Global Perspective*. Durham, NC: Duke University Press.

Bedford, Kate (2009) *Developing Partnerships: Gender, Sexuality, and the Reformed World Bank*. Minneapolis: University of Minnesota Press.

Boddy, Janice (2007) *Civilizing Women: British Crusades in Colonial Sudan*. Princeton: Princeton University Press.

Boelstorff, Tom (2007) *A Coincidence of Desires: Anthropology, Queer Studies, Indonesia*. Durham, NC: Duke University Press.

Borneman, John (2001) Caring and Being Cared For: Displacing Marriage, Kinship, Gender, and Sexuality. In James D. Faubion (ed.), *The Ethics of Kinship: Ethnographic Inquiries*. Oxford: Rowman & Littlefield, pp. 29–46.

Boyce, Paul (2006) Moral Ambivalence and Irregular Practices: Contextualizing Male-to-Male Sexualities in Calcutta/India. *Feminist Review* [special issue: "Sexual Moralities"] 83: 76–98.

Boyce, Paul and Khanna, Askay (2011) Rights and Representations: Querying the Male-to-Male Sexual Subject in India. *Culture, Health and Sexuality* 13(1): 89–100.

Butler, Judith (1993) *Bodies that Matter: On the Discursive Limitations of "Sex."* New York: Routledge.

Butler, Judith (2002) What is Critique? An Essay on Foucault's Virtue. In Sara Salih with Judith Butler (eds.), *The Judith Butler Reader*. Oxford: Blackwell, pp. 302–322.

Butt, Leslie (2005) Sexuality, the State, and the Runaway Wives of Highlands Papua New Guinea. In Adams and Pigg (2005), pp. 163–185.

Clark, Jeffrey (1997) Sites of Desire: Transformations of Huli Sexuality. In Lenore Madnerson and Margaret Jolly (eds.), *Sites of Desire, Economies of Pleasure: Sexualities in Asia and the Pacific*. Chicago: University of Chicago Press, pp. 191–211.

Delaney, Carol (2004) *Investigating Culture: An Experiential Introduction to Anthropology*. Malden, MA: Blackwell.

Dikötter, Frank (1995) *Sex, Culture, and Modernity in China: Medical Science and the Construction of Sexual Identities in the Early Republican Period*. Honolulu: University of Hawaii Press.

Elliston, Deborah (1995) Erotic Anthropology: "Ritualized Homosexuality" in Melanesia and Beyond. *American Ethnologist* 22(4): 848–867.

Evans-Pritchard, E. E. (1969a [1951]) *Kinship and Family among the Nuer*. Oxford: Clarendon.

Evans-Pritchard, E. E. (1969b [1940]) *The Nuer: A Description of the Modes of Livelihood and Political Institutions of a Nilotic People*. Oxford: Clarendon.

Fabian, Johannes (1983) *Time and the Other: How Anthropology Makes Its Other*. New York: Columbia University Press.

Foucault, Michel (1988 [1986]) *The History of Sexuality*, vol. 3: *The Care of the Self*, trans. Robert Hurley. New York: Vintage.

Foucault, Michel (1990 [1978]) *The History of Sexuality*, vol. 1: *An Introduction*, trans. Robert Hurley. New York: Vintage.

Franklin, Sarah and McKinnon, Susan (eds.) (2001) *Relative Values: Reconfiguring Kinship Studies*. Durham, NC: Duke University Press.

Larvie, Sean (1999) Queerness and the Spector of Brazilian Nation Ruin. *GLQ: Gay and Lesbian Quarterly* [special issue: "Thinking Sexuality Transnationally"] 5(4): 527–558.

Lyons, Andrew P. and Lyons, Harriet D. (2004) *Irregular Connections: A History of Anthropology and Sexuality*. Lincoln: University of Nebraska Press.

Mahdavi, Pardis (2007) Passionate Uprisings: Young People, Sexuality, and Politics in Post-Revolutionary Iran. *Culture, Health & Sexuality* 9(5): 445–457.

Malinowski, Bronislaw (1929) *The Sexual Life of Savages in North-Western Melanesia: An Ethnographic Account of Courtship, Marriage, and Family Life among the Natives of the Trobriand Islands, British New Guinea*. London: Routledge.

Manderson, Lenore, Bennett, Linda Rae, and Sheldrake, Michelle (1999) Sex, Social Institutions, and Social Structure: Anthropological Contributions to the Study of Sexuality. *Annual Review of Sex Research* 10: 184–209.

Mead, Margaret (1928) *The Coming of Age in Samoa: A Psychological Study of Primitive Youth for Western Civilization*. New York: William Morrow.

Pigg, Stacy Leigh (2001) Languages of Sex and AIDS in Nepal: Notes of the Social Production of Commensurability. *Cultural Anthropology* 11(2): 160–201.

Pigg, Stacy Leigh (2002) Too Bold, Too Hot: Crossing "Culture" in AIDS Prevention in Nepal. In Mark Nichter and Margaret Lock (eds.), *New Horizons in Medical Anthropology: Essays in Honor of Charles Leslie*. London: Routledge, pp. 58–80.

Pigg, Stacy Leigh (2005) Globalizing the Facts of Life. In Adams and Pigg (2005), pp. 39–65.

Pigg, Stacy Leigh and Adams, Vincanne (2005) Introduction: The Moral Object of Sex. In Adams and Pigg (2005), pp. 1–38.

Ram, Kalpana (2001) Rationalizing Fecund Bodies: Family Planning Policy and the Modern Indian State. In Margaret Jolly and Kalpana Ram (eds.), *Borders of Being: Citizenship, Fertility, and Sexuality in Asia and the Pacific*. Ann Arbor: University of Michigan Press, pp. 82–117.

Reed, Adam (1997) Contested Images and Common Strategies: Early Colonial Sexual Politics in the Massim. In Lenore Manderson and Margaret Jolly (eds.), *Sites of Desires, Economies of Pleasure: Sexualities in Asia and the Pacific*. Chicago: University of Chicago Press, pp. 48–71.

Ross, Ellen and Rapp, Rayna (1997 [1981]) Sex and Society: A Research Note for Social History and Anthropology. In Roger N. Lancaster and Micaela di Leonardo (eds.), *The Gender/Sexuality Reader: Culture, History, Political Economy*. New York: Routledge, pp. 153–168.

Rubin, Gayle (2007 [1984]) Thinking Sex: Notes for a Radical Theory of the Politics of Sexuality. In Richard Parker and Peter Aggleton (eds.), *Culture, Society, and Sexuality: A Reader*, 2nd edn. New York: Routledge, pp. 150–187.

Srivastava, Sanjay (2007) *Passionate Modernity: Sexuality, Class, and Consumption in India*. New Delhi: Routledge.

Stoler, Ann Laura (1995) *Race and the Education of Desire: Foucault's "History of Sexuality" and the Colonial Order of Things*. Durham, NC: Duke University Press.

Stoler, Ann Laura (2002) *Carnal Knowledge and Imperial Power: Race and the Intimate in Colonial Rule*. Berkeley: University of California Press.

Strathern, Marilyn (1992) *Reproducing the Future: Anthropology, Kinship, and the New Reproductive Technologies*. New York: Routledge.

Vance, Carole (1991) Anthropology Rediscovers Sexuality: A Theoretical Comment. *Social Science and Medicine* 33: 867–884.

Wardlow, Holly (2004) Anger, Economy, and Female Agency: Problematizing "Prostitution" and "Sex Work" among the Huli of Papua New Guinea. *Signs* 29(4): 1017–1040.

Weeks, Jeffrey (1989 [1981]) *Sex, Politics, and Society: The Regulation of Sexuality Since 1800*, 2nd edn. London: Longman.

Weston, Kath (1993) Lesbian/Gay Studies in the House of Anthropology. *Annual Review of Anthropology* 22: 339–367.

PART IV Worlds

CHAPTER 19

Religion and Morality

Michael Lambek

The relationship of religion to ethics (or morality – I do not distinguish between these terms) is complex, entailing such matters as whether religion is intrinsic to or necessary for ethics and whether ethics is one of the necessary features or criteria by which one establishes a set of practices as "religion." Regarding the first point, in much of the world one can easily be deemed unethical or ethically suspect if one stands outside the majority religion or outside the Abrahamic, "God-fearing" religions entirely; to declare oneself an atheist or a practitioner of animism, for example, could place one under considerable suspicion. In Europe, the Enlightenment and post-Enlightenment intelligentsia have had the task of constituting and legitimating ethics on nontheological grounds; this is surely one of the achievements of Kant and a continuing project of ethics in the analytic tradition. Regarding the second point, the late nineteenth-century evolutionists used ethics as a criterion to distinguish between so-called "magic" and "religion" and it was one of the achievements of later twentieth-century anthropology, in the work of people like Mary Douglas (1966; see also Lambek 1992), to demonstrate the ethical in such unlikely places as food taboos and hygienic practices. One of the central implications of this work is that ethics can be implicit, embedded in forms of practice no less than in explicit codes.

The entire discussion is embedded within two large historical processes. The first of these is the curtailment or retrenchment of religion, especially Christianity and Judaism in Europe, by forces or developments one could lump together as "secularist," especially in law, science, and philosophy. To this general picture one can highlight attempts to suppress or eradicate religion within communist regimes. The second historical process is one which, viewed from certain locations, appears to be a worldwide attempt to defeat animism or polytheism, especially by the two main competing traditions of monotheism, Christianity and Islam, which are hence placed in further competition with each other, and which argue their respective positions in

A Companion to Moral Anthropology, First Edition. Edited by Didier Fassin.

part on moral grounds. This is a kind of religious rationalization but it is hardly the disenchantment that Weber depicted. There are also "counter-reformations" to both these historical processes, in which forms of purificatory "fundamentalism," in response to the first, but also of animism, if not polytheism, and religious pluralism, in response to both, return, resurge, or simply quietly perdure. If the former response entails an ethics, if not a politics, of social reform (often beginning with the family), the latter is sometimes associated with an ethics of personal self-fashioning.[1] In both these large historical processes, constituted as they are partly through debate, scholars of religion and ethics, including anthropologists, are not simply neutral observers, but writers whose choice of words and perspective has effects. Explicitly or implicitly we participate in these processes.

As these remarks suggest, the analytic ground is complicated by the fact that no agreement exists on what constitutes either "religion" or "ethics" and that the various definitions proffered for one often have direct implications for discerning or defining the other, leading to circular arguments about their "relationship."[2] Moreover, it is by no means clear that ostensibly secular and objective systems of thought like philosophy or anthropology can escape their intellectual inheritance from specific religious traditions and hence may implicitly work within their terms (Cannell 2006). In what follows I will not claim the authority to adjudicate which definitions are correct in some objectivist sense (assuming any could be). I will try to combine a rational account based on an anthropological tradition of abstraction, comparison, and deduction with a practical, inductive, historical, and ethnographical appreciation of how things play out on the ground, that is, in actual life, in human experience, and over time. This requires taking a rigorous and generous approach to (cultural) difference and coming to some kind of terms with the essential tension between relativism and universalism. In the end, what this essay can do is simply review some of the arguments to which thinking about the relation of religion to ethics gives rise.

Religion and Morality Are Not Isomorphic or Commensurable

A problem with the response to Frazer that ethics can be found in the seemingly most unlikely places is that it may leave unquestioned the association between ethics and religion, merely expanding the reach of both. But religion – in the sense of the ideas, and especially the practices, that go under its name – has no more claim to be ethical than many other fields of human activity. Indeed, it could be argued that ethics, understood as the recurrent establishment of criteria for evaluating practice (as good, just, correct, etc.), as well as subsequent practice enacted in light of such criteria, is intrinsic to all human action (Lambek 2010b). But even when ethics is understood simply as good behavior (or the profession, clarification, advocacy, or cultivation of such behavior) or as recognition of its limits, it is certainly not restricted to religion and it is questionable whether it is more prevalent there than elsewhere (despite claims by certain religious authorities to the contrary). For example, in his exemplary and courageous account of mid-twentieth-century North American Roman Catholicism, Robert Orsi (2005) demonstrates the cruelty as well as good that religion can incite.

While religion is often understood as providing traditions of ethical certainty and self-formation, Orsi's is also but one of many scholarly accounts to show that a given religious tradition can be riven with internal ethical debate and uneven consequences. Thus, for example, the Muslim piety movement could not substantiate any claims (should it want to) that its adherents are morally superior to other Muslims or that they act ethically all the time. Moreover, the call to be ethical or to act ethically, the rewards and punishments associated with it, the dangers and fantasies – these are not to be equated with acting ethically. Ethics must surely entail self-questioning, not only about one's own claims or behavior, but about the limits of what is possible with respect to such matters as human well-being, comprehending suffering, or providing justice. Indeed, that it must not only have a theodicy, but also bear responsibility for acknowledging its limits, is a key point in Geertz's (1973) famous essay on religion.

One might add to this the tension between ethical persons, practice, or insight and the authority or power to make or enforce ethical judgment or to lay claim to the ethical high ground that is found in all religious hierarchies. This is not to deny that at certain moments religion can provoke or inspire people to particular ethical feats, and many religious figures ("saints') can be understood as ethical exemplars, as can ordinary people using "religious" means to extend their ethical reach (e.g., Lambek 2002a). At the same time, religion can pursue and punish witches, heretics, and immodest persons in ways that outsiders would consider unethical, and it often celebrates ethically ambiguous figures – wandering ascetics, holy fools, trickster figures, and the like. Indeed, myth has been repeatedly noted for its ethical ambiguity and this ambiguity can also be found in various forms of mythopraxis, notably in the range of practices and figures associated with "liminality," carnival, and the like (Turner 1969). A final point here is that the ethical acts and insights of ordinary people may be "religiously" informed yet outside and even counter to the precepts of "official" religion, as in popular attempts in Vietnam to appease and release the ghosts of the dead (Kwon 2008).

Anthropological circumscriptions of "religion" have shifted over time, from relatively narrow objectivist accounts in which belief in God or other "supernatural" beings was simply asserted as a definition, to broader accounts characteristic of symbolic and structural anthropology, and more recently again to narrower genealogical and skeptical ones based on the emergence into public discourse of the category or subject of "religion" and the rise to scholarly consciousness of the ferment within Christianity and Islam. One of the reasons some anthropologists painted the field broadly was to show that practices outside the Abrahamic traditions or the "axial religions" were not thereby beyond the ethical pale and hence deserving of the same intellectual and practical respect as those within them. The structural–symbolic synthesis of the 1960s and 1970s enabled such practices to be understood as being as meaningful and as ethically informed as those within the Abrahamic traditions. Indeed, it was the success of this work that gave anthropologists the means and courage to tackle the Abrahamic traditions themselves, hitherto left to scholars within those traditions. Not only that, the Abrahamic religions could be seen to be characterized by structures, relations, and tropes that were found in the culture at large no less than within the official boundaries as characterized by their respective gatekeepers. "Sacrifice" in its various formulations from head-hunting to Hindu temple offerings, rules for butchering and consuming animals, alms and charity, or Faustian bargains sealed with innocent victims is a salient example of an analytical (not "natural") category, that enables fruitful comparison across cultural, religious, and institutional lines and encourages anthropological work within Old Testament, Christian, and Muslim contexts (though the subject of Jesus continues to be treated with some circumspection).

Sacrifice, in turn, links up to the ethical side of the literature on the gift and the various questions raised and debated about the relative and absolute values and virtues of giving and receiving, reciprocity and altruism (Lambek 2008b). Philosophical responses to Mauss (1990 [1925]) are sometimes marked by a Christian bias in which the idea of "grace" may underlie arguments concerning the "pure gift." Similar ideas of ostensibly selfless giving recur in the work and lives of missionaries and religious martyrs and their contemporary descendants, activists in philanthropy, international development, and humanitarian relief (Fassin 2011), echoing Weber's formulation of the calling.[3] Yet we know that one-sided ethical formulations of the pure gift or fully disinterested acts need to be treated with some skepticism, at the very least offset by the sense of balance characteristic of Mauss (and which he drew from both Aristotle on virtuous practice and Kant and Durkheim on obligation). The balance of interest and disinterest (and freedom and obligation) in the gift has been well explicated by Parry (1986) who derives the attraction of the pure gift less from the Christian idea of grace than as a kind of idealized dialectical opposition to the idea of the capitalist pure commodity. Moreover, in Mauss, and as taken up by Lévi-Strauss, circulation is widely seen as a social good in itself, as is reciprocity; however, these are understood as the ways in which precapitalist societies ("naturally") work rather than as exemplary acts or as explicit religious ideals impossible of achievement in this world by ordinary mortals. Finally, Mauss viewed acts of gift or sacrifice as "total social facts" rather than abstracting them as "religion" or "ethics," let alone discussing them with respect to the "relationship" between such reified abstractions. This suggests in turn that the very subject of this (my) essay is a historically particular one, possible of formulation and debate only in this manner in a secular modern epoch.

In a different kind of abstraction, human sacrifice has provided a significant religious source for reflection on the ethical. The Akedah (the story of Abraham's sacrifice of Isaac) has done so for generations of thinkers, not only for religious practitioners but for philosophers and anthropologists engaged in understanding the meaning of sacrifice (e.g., Evens 2008).[4] Interpretation of this religious event or story may lead eventually to a distinction between the religious and the ethical. Notably for Kierkegaard (1985) the Akedah demonstrates that religion is a teleological suspension of the ethical. To have religious faith and to exhibit it moves radically beyond the ethical – a father ready to kill his son – at least, beyond the ethics of the ordinary. This intention to kill his offspring, to make a human sacrifice, is not selfish or ethically utilitarian (as may be the Greek sacrifice of Iphigenia by her father, Agamemnon, as depicted by Euripides), not infra-ethical, as it were, but supra-ethical; it serves no calculable ends.[5] And it is true that much of what falls under the rubric of religion pushes humans to violent extremes that may be considered beyond the ethical in any ordinary sense: head-hunting in Southeast Asia, slicing off the foreskins of Muslim and Jewish babies or children, penitential flagellation in Roman Catholicism and Shi'ism, the Hindu widow who jumps into the funeral pyre, the Buddhist protester who sets himself alight, perhaps the suicide bomber.[6] At the least, religion offers an image of the hero or martyr who sacrifices the ordinary for something higher or beyond. More broadly and less dramatically, Victor Turner argued that the liminal phase of ritual was a time when social rules and categories are done away with, hence when anything and everything is possible, hence beyond ethics understood in most senses except the existential one of pure freedom (cf. Faubion 2010). In sum, religion is sometimes able to contextualize or circumscribe ethics, but conversely, religion itself may sometimes be circumscribed or contextualized out of ethical concerns, whether by a quiet "descent into the ordinary" (Das 2007) or by a radical overturning.

In sum, from an anthropological perspective religion and ethics are not fully isomorphic and cannot be fully identified with one another. Yet an account of religion and ethics must address the historical consequences of abstracting them from the rest of social and cultural life as distinct contemporary regimes and hence the ostensible liberation of the ethical from the religious. Here, one of the more interesting moves would surely be the replacement of a simple binary pair with the triangulation characteristic in contemporary society of religion, ethics, and law. For example, in providing justice, the law should be (conceived as) ethical; but what happens when it comes to be seen, from a religious perspective, as violating basic ethical principles, whether in admitting or prohibiting capital punishment, abortion, blood transfusion, or same-sex marriage? How does a liberal legal language of rights translate into a religious language of obligation, devotion, love, obedience, etc., and conversely? On which side of this debate does "ethics" sit, or how can or does it serve to mediate or increase conflict?

Conversely, an anthropological account of ostensibly disembedded institutions must be equally wary of the ethnocentric assumption that our context (call it "modernity" or "postmodernity" or the (neo)liberal state) is a special case, unique in its radical difference from all the other cultural and historical differences that precede it and that continue to be found more or less hidden alongside it or within its makeup. Are not relative tensions between religion, ethics, and law found everywhere? Was it not, for example, an ethical queasiness in the face of religious injunction that led Igbo mothers of twins (considered polluting and destined for immediate death) to be among the first to convert to Christianity (Achebe 1996 [1959])?[7] Tensions between Rujia (Confucian) ethical ritualism and Legalism go back to ancient China (Yang 1994). Finally, rather than taking literally the institutionalization of religion and ethics in a historical context in a manner that presumes their commensurability with one another, it might be more interesting to think of "religion" and "ethics" as different, incommensurable ways to analytically transect the social whole or the human condition.[8]

Roughly speaking, there are two major streams or themes in anthropological accounts of the relationship between religion and ethics that may avoid some of the aporias I have described. I call these streams Durkheimian and Weberian (with their respective philosophical predecessors, Kant and Aristotle), while acknowledging that in practice there is a good deal of diversity within and crossover between them. The Durkheimian stream emphasizes submission to the authority of a single social or liturgical order while the Weberian concerns the practical juxtaposition of alternative models for living.[9]

The Durkheimian Stream: Obligation, Commitment, and Ritual Performance

In the Durkheimian stream, religion or ritual forms the foundation for ethics and ethics is foundational for, or intrinsic to, society or social life. Durkheimian models are structural, locating ethics at arm's length from individual intention, although Durkheim (1973) begins by arguing that ethics entails the transcendence of the biological individual, characterized by primal needs and desires, by the social person who lives and acts on behalf of rules and ideals that come to him or her from the outside, that is, from society, but that become internalized. In this, Durkheim's perspective is rather similar to Freud's argument that healthy socialization entails the constitution of the superego or conscience, such that a proper balance is developed between social repression and ideals and narcissistic engagement in love, work, and play. In both authors there is the assumption that "natural" man (or human "nature") is itself amoral, if not actively immoral. At the same time, it is an intrinsic feature of the human condition that such biological nature gets transcended by humanity's social nature. In Durkheim, society, especially as it represents itself to itself as religion, and as it comes to a kind of self-understanding, enables humans to transcend themselves – to become better people. Turner's (1967) ethnographic accounts of Ndembu ritual are among the most successful illustrations of this part of the Durkheimian paradigm in the way he shows how ritual brings together "the necessary and the desirable." Through ritual people come to want to do what society (and possibly the social theorist) says is right and necessary. The good is confirmed as the social good. Voilà ethics! In Freud social transcendence (sublimation) is offset by the simpler notion of repression; internalization remains partial and conflict is central to the picture. One of the best anthropological accounts of this tension between Durkheimian and Freudian versions remains Robert Murphy's *Dialectics of Social Life* (1971).

More recently, Roy Rappaport makes explicit claims for the close connection between ritual and morality. In a complex exposition whose stages I cannot rehearse here, he argues that ritual offsets the possibilities that language provides to lie and to propose alternatives (or waver between them) by demonstrating – and indeed producing – commitment by participants to the particular acts and utterances established therein, and moreover, acceptance of the order that makes such particular ritual enactments possible, that defines, legitimates, and sanctifies them as particular instances of a given kind, affirming not only that this wedding or this blessing has particular effects on its participants but that such effects can be produced only by enacting wedding or blessing rituals of this kind (see Rappaport 1999, especially ch. 4). Ritual is thus simultaneously both performative and meta-performative. Ritual enactment establishes moral order and direction for those who engage in it. Ultimately, ritual not only founds morality and is thus intrinsic to society, but each instance of ritual exemplifies it. "In enunciating, accepting, and making conventions moral," Rappaport concludes, "ritual contains within itself not simply a symbolic representation of social contract, but tacit social contract itself. As such, ritual … is *the* basic social act (1999: 138; emphasis original).

Performative acts and effects need not be described specifically, exclusively, or unilaterally as "religious," and they are not even all specifically or explicitly "ritual" acts (though they all contain what for Rappaport are the two main features of ritual, namely a degree of formality and embodied performance). However, as noted, ritual acts are not only performative but meta-performative and thus establish the grounds for morality more generally. Rituals are embedded in, and manifestations of, what Rappaport calls liturgical orders, which is an analytically precise way of conceptualizing something central to religion. Liturgical orders are generally enacted in temporal sequences and cycles, but consist also in a hierarchy of entailment. You cannot meaningfully swear to God as a Christian unless the existence of God and your acceptance of that fact and identity as a Christian have been established in temporally but also foundationally prior rituals. A key feature of ritual is what Rappaport calls ultimate sacred postulates. These are often the primary tenets of what from a Christian perspective (or Christian-influenced anthropology) could be called religious belief. They are established in the most formal rituals, characterized by invariance and certainty (like the Mass), but then used to sanctify other, more contingent performative acts such as jural proceedings or a family meal. Ultimate sacred postulates are not themselves ethical precepts, since they are relatively informationless. To say "There is no God but God" is semantically and pragmatically quite different from saying "Thou shall not kill." For Rappaport, however, it is the former utterance that grounds, sanctifies, and legitimates the latter. In other words, insofar as ritual is metaperformative it is also metaethical. Put another way, the relationship of ritual to ethics is primarily one of formal entailment rather than of substance (specific content). Once grounded in religious sanctification ethics can develop at arm's length from religion.

Rappaport's approach can be compared with that of Maurice Bloch (1989, 1992; cf 2007), who also approaches religion by means of its constitution in ritual. Neither author retains the model of the socially transcended amoral natural man although, interestingly, both thinkers are naturalists, interested less in distinguishing the level of social facts from the biological, as in Durkheim's project, than in understanding them as part of a single order. Bloch does describe the seizing and even ostensible taming of vitality and the "wild" (including sex and aggression) in and through ritual, but he does not moralize about it. Indeed, he critiques rather than celebrates repression, which he sees carried out less for the needs of society or for ethics writ large than for the imposition of an alienating transcendent world on ordinary human life and for the legitimation of social hierarchy. If the product of ritual is a transcendent world, for Bloch this is not identified with society but, on the contrary, at arm's length from it. Implicitly the ethical subsists outside the transcendent or in the attempts to escape from its shadow. Indeed in his later work Bloch is explicit that morality is a matter of "innate predispositions (the product of evolution) and the nature of social interaction" rather than of religion.[10]

Although both Bloch and Rappaport draw from Austin's (1962) concept of performativity, they differ sharply in how they evaluate illocutionary effects. Whereas Bloch sees ritual language as imposing constraints on action, a vehicle of power, and a means to construct a transcendental world that is somehow antihuman, for Rappaport, as for Durkheim, ritual founds society and completes the human rather than preying upon or opposing itself to it. As I have elaborated the argument (Lambek 2010b), the performative acts and effects of ritual are closer to those of ordinary language than to metaphysics; speech act theory illustrates the ordinariness of ritual rather than its distinction from, or transcendence of, the human.

Bloch and Rappaport partially rejoin each other insofar as Rappaport recognizes (though perhaps does not sufficiently emphasize) the mystification of performative acts. If ritual achieves its conventional effects through human action, these effects can be considerably enhanced if that mechanism is concealed, and particularly if participants' own roles in the process are mystified to them. The effects are then said to be caused by the acts of the gods, spirits, or other forces that are actually the product of the ritual. The mystification of human agency in ritual action has a strong kinship with Marx's analysis of the mystification of the value of human labor and the fetishism of capital and commodities. This raises then another kind of question about the relationship between ethics and religion, namely the ethics of both mystification and demystification, whether to perform the masquerade or unmask the performers, so to speak. The ethics of mystification is of concern to priests and healers,[11] while the ethics of demystification is a feature of purifying movements, whether they come from within religion or from outside it. The question of where anthropologists are to stand is ambiguous. What is surely ethically problematic is to unmask the mystification of others without stopping to consider the sources and effects of one's own mystification. It is one of the features of Rappaport's approach, in contrast to Marx, that some form of mystified performativeness is intrinsic to the human condition; life would be unbearable and unworkable without it. A corollary of this view is that neither natural or social scientists nor genealogists or deconstructionists necessarily hold the ethical higher ground in comparison with religious subjects (but, conversely, this is not to romanticize the pious and religiously adept either).

Neither Bloch nor Rappaport claim that ritual produces hegemony; both leave open the possibility for skepticism or resistance. Although Rappaport argues that in performing or submitting to a ritual a person intrinsically accepts the order of which it is a part and even becomes a part of that order herself, he also claims both that ritual does not directly shape subsequent behavior and that the effects of ritual are quite distinct from whatever the participant may be thinking or feeling (that is, irrespective of subjective "belief"). What ritual produces is less specific (moral) behavior or consciousness, or even constraints on behavior, than the criteria for construing behavior as being of one kind rather than another and for evaluating its quality and appropriateness. In other words, it is ritual that makes value – and specifically ethical value – possible, and less for repressing the biological or psychological individual or the everyday social world than for defining specific kinds of persons, acts, and conditions integral to that world, hence for establishing the distinctions of social life and enabling the ethical evaluation of behavior. In defining the criteria for judgment and delineating and discriminating between actors and acts, ritual does not preclude ethical judgment or constrain human freedom (as it might seem to do from Bloch's perspective, where it clashes with ordinary cognition, morality, and common sense) but rather sets up the conditions for them.

Rappaport departs from previous Durkheimian analyses of ritual as asserting, idealizing, and internalizing the obligatory to understanding ritual as establishing the criteria by which ethical judgment can take place. What Rappaport shows, in effect, is how the performance of ritual produces the criteria by which practice is defined and evaluated (Lambek 2010b). It puts behavior or practice, as philosophers say, "under a description," such that the persons who have undergone a given ritual are now persons of a certain kind, bearing specific commitments: as wives, priests, converts, Christians, devotees of a particular Hindu god, and so on, whose subsequent comportment is to be evaluated with respect to the criteria associated with the respective descriptions.

Rappaport draws out the implications of Austin's discussion of truth to show that the relation of words to world is reversed between the locutionary and illocutionary functions of speaking. In the locutionary aspect, if my words do not conform to what they purport to describe or refer to, the words are false and I am mistaken or lying. But in the illocutionary aspect, if my words have been correctly ("felicitously") performed, it is subsequent events or behavior that are at fault if they do not conform to the utterance (Rappaport 1999: 133). Insofar as discriminations of truth and falsity or fault are at the heart of ethics, the argument is deeply significant. Performance of specific illocutionary acts shapes subsequent practice not by producing good or bad behavior but by establishing the criteria by which we know the difference, and hence the standards to which people commit themselves and to which most people will try to conform. However, the analysis does not explain the intervention of subsequent performances, especially ones that might shift the relevant criteria. By what values or concerns, with what judgment, are new illocutionary acts instantiated, promises made (or broken), particular commitments taken up (or abandoned) or preferred over others? What is their timing and how are they to be evaluated? For this we need to turn to practice theory.[12]

The Weberian Stream: Practice and Religious Values

The second major stream is broadly Aristotelian, in which the ethical is posited as providing horizons and goals for living and is realized in practice and social action. Thinkers located within this stream include Foucault and MacIntyre but insofar as this essay is focused on religion rather than other forms of virtue or practice, I take as the exemplar Max Weber.[13] In contrast to Durkheim, Weber emphasizes the intentional rather than the obligatory dimension of action, hence thought (or meaning) over ritual. The discussion of alternative means and ends (and means–ends relationships), and hence of specific cultural values, becomes critical; these values are located by various analysts within or overlapping with religion and certainly with theodicy and eschatology. Weber also replaces Durkheimian functionalism and his assumption of a relatively homogeneous social order with historical causality, social heterogeneity, and elective affinity.[14]

A central component of Weber's argument in *The Protestant Ethic* (1958 [1904–5]) is psychological, namely the role of anxiety and its relation to anomie. Weber is unusual among anxiety theorists insofar as instead of arguing for religion as a product of anxiety (including ethical anxiety) or as primarily a means to alleviate it, he sees religious formulations or religious worlds as generating their own specific forms of anxiety, which then get alleviated in particular kinds of social action and their accompanying ethical formulations or rationalizations. Weber's famous example is the way that Calvinism created a context generative of a certain work ethic and capital accumulation. This has the historical irony that ethical and religious concerns lie at the root of the essentially nonreligious and amoral or immoral system of capitalism and the "iron cage" of bureaucracy. Theories of religious change or renewal (revitalization, millenarianism) also often start from ideas of ethical anxiety generated by particular historical circumstances, like subjection to colonial rule. Similarly, it can be argued that religion forms a creative means to address or transform guilt, whether understood as an intrinsic part of psychological maturation or as the "secondary guilt" that some individuals experience more than others (Obeyesekere 1981).

Obeyesekere's conjunction of Weber and Freud was elaborated in a mixed Hindu and Buddhist context, but anxiety is also central to Christian ideas of sin, expiation, and redemption (Ricoeur 1967; Burridge 1969; Robbins 2004). Nevertheless,

Weber's point was that Christian ethics are themselves internally diverse. In Calvinism there is no chance of absolution by means of intentional human action, undergoing confession, taking the sacraments, showing devotion to Mary, and the like. Divine grace is direct, absolute, and unreachable. This provides a quite particular context for ethics (and politics: Walzer 1965). Compare it to Ethiopian orthodoxy as recounted by Tom Boylston:

> The power of begging in the name of a saint is illustrated by the story of Belay the Cannibal, which is known across Orthodox Ethiopia, and which is painted in episodic form on the door to the inner sanctum of Ura Kidane Mihret church. The story has it that Belay ate every person he met including his parents, amounting to seventy-five, or seventy-five thousand depending on which version you hear. The exception was one leprous beggar who was begging by the roadside for water, in the name of Mary. Belay, hearing the name, takes pity and gives the beggar a single handful of water. The final, largest panel of the mural depicts Belay's final judgement. St Gabriel weighs the seventy-five murdered people against the single handful of water. In the panel Mary can be seen casting her shadow over the side of the scale containing the water, causing it to outweigh the murdered people, and so by having answered one request in the name of Mary, Belay is saved. (2012: 232)

A central feature of an Aristotelian approach is that in practice ethics entails not simply following one's obligations or values, but choosing or judging between alternative means and ends and cultivating the capacity to do so wisely.[15] Life entails difficult decisions (to whom or what I should commit, how far to follow through with a calling, how to balance my needs with those of others, etc.). A Weberian approach might show how a certain set of religious practices settles among a certain segment of society into a kind of habitus of moral commitment and conformity, but also how practical judgments are made in the face of minor contingencies and major issues, and equally how the conservative complacency of the mainstream, the middle or priestly class, comes to be challenged, overturned, or otherwise got around.

Religion can also be seen as providing a sort of archive, tradition, or primary resource for ethical thought and understanding. Religion from this perspective has been, virtually by definition, the heart of ethics, conceived as wisdom. Some notable examples aside (Radin 1957; James 1988), the repository of ethical wisdom is generally understood by scholars of religion to lie in the written texts of specific religious traditions, so that one can speak of Buddhist or Jewish or Islamic ethics (and so on) and an ethical pedagogy based on reading and recitation. Ethnographers of non- or partially literate societies have generally located ethical pedagogy and cultivation in ritual, most explicitly in so-called initiation rituals (e.g., Richards 1995 [1956]), but also in divination, proverbs, oratory, and in ritual understood more broadly as the formal dimension of practice and hence embedded in such things as the articulation of persons by means of gender, age, generation, and kinship categories and relations (Fortes 1987), in sum, by means of respect and dignity. For both literate and nonliterate societies ethnographers have come to locate ethics in religiously shaped bodily disciplines and dispositions (Asad 1993; Mahmood 2005). Ethics in this sense shifts between foreground and background. Once cultivated as disposition, it becomes part of the habitus, where, for Aristotle, to "go without saying," in the sense of being able to do what is right in the circumstances without first standing back and thinking about it, is understood as a singular achievement of excellence, not simply a manifestation of social status or the blind following of a rule. Yet in some contexts people do reflect on what otherwise goes without saying and perhaps challenge convention on what they consider ethical grounds. Indeed, some would argue that ethics entails the giving of reasons for one's acts, and that religion is one place, at least in modernity, where this is expected (Keane 2010).

Society is frequently characterized by a tension between an ethics of tradition ("it is right to do as our parents and grandparents did"; "what our parents and grandparents did is right and good") and an ethics of reform ("it is right and good to question authority, to improve, to correct past mistakes"). In the course of history this can emerge more strongly as a conflict between what has come to be seen as empty ritualism or as obedience and more direct social engagement. This was the case periodically in the course of Chinese history (Yang 1994) and in the Protestant Reformation, as well as in the emergence of a body of thought distinct from religion in Western philosophy, perhaps most acutely in the crisis expressed by existentialism over the death or absence of God. Analytically speaking, the tension here is between, on the one hand, the urgency to maintain a firm (metaethical) foundation for ethics, which perhaps only ritual or theology can provide and which often draws upon mythic acts of violence and the mystification of performativeness to legitimate social and political conservatism, and on the other hand, the need to enable and articulate a practical reform of ethics that responds to contingency, disquiet, skepticism, contradiction, and new social events or conditions (witness the successive challenges of events in biology and biomedicine), as well as human freedom, political activism, social dissension, and personal transformation.[16] Religious traditions are never static but always entail intergenerational conversation and sometimes transformation. These may be sharply articulated or go relatively unmarked. Thus, within south Asia David Pocock observed some time ago that "'The all-pervading relativism of the traditional Indian universe' was giving way to a 'more authoritarian moral absolutism.' It was a 'radical innovation' that amounted to a 'revolutionary' change in mentality" (1973; quoted in Parry and Simpson 2010: 348). Similarly, Jain understandings of the ethics of nonviolence shift substantially between south Asia and the diaspora (Vallely 2008 Laidlaw 2010).

There are also periods of social crisis in which the anchoring functions of religion appear to be discredited, dissolved, or unavailable, leading to heightened anxiety that is not readily discharged in positive directions. Articulated and abetted by charismatic Christian discourse, the epidemics of witchcraft diagnoses and accusations in parts of Africa are one expression.[17] Evans-Pritchard's (1937) argument about the rationality of witchcraft at an earlier phase of African life is intrinsically also about its ethical basis. Anthropologists have spent less time on witchcraft's irrationality and unethical qualities. This has partly to do with the ethics of anthropology itself, which is to help make sense of what we see, to understand it, and hence often to keep our personal disapproval in check. (This is not the same as the argument for cultural relativism.) In any case, witchcraft forms a field in which to think about ethics. As the imagination of the immoral, witchcraft serves an ethical function. But when the imagination is overwhelmed by actual accusations, interrogations, and punishments of suspected "witches," the situation is one in which ethical judgment is submerged in a kind of moral panic. As a form of social breakdown, such a setting forms the exception that proves the Durkheimian rule. A particularly compelling case is the epidemic of violence against children suspected of witchcraft in Kinshasa (De Boeck 2004).

It can be argued that highly disruptive and exploitative historical experience leads to the sense that a chain has been broken; ancestors have withdrawn their protection and witches can now reign freely. Where, for a variety of social reasons, family relations have also broken down, access to positive figures with whom not simply to identify but to introject (as mediated by strong, positive "religious" figures, like spirits, saints, mythical heroes, and apical ancestors, but also public figures like politicians, musicians, healers, and athletes, as well as fictional characters) may be restricted, leaving the field open to excessive projection, the introjection of negative (weak or destructive) figures, and hence further anxiety and ethical and epistemic murk. In other words, where religion, kinship, and the political order fail to provide figures for positive intergenerational introjection, ethical worlds may break down and the cultivation of ethically positive selves rendered more difficult.[18] These anomic situations can be contrasted with those characterized by the cultivation of an ethics of memory (Lambek 1996, 2002a, 2002b; Kwon 2008), itself often given religious form and doubtless as cognizant of human tragedy as of comedy.

A Brief Ethnographic Invitation

Because so many of the arguments about religion and ethics have been caught up in discourses generated by or about the Abrahamic or other religions of the book, I invite consideration of the embodied practice of spirit possession in the western Indian Ocean. Traditions of Malagasy and African spirit possession subsist alongside Islam and Christianity, in practical and imaginative relations with but distinct from them. While it is questionable whether to define possession as "religion," and ostensibly counterintuitive to see it as ethical, I have seen it as replete with ethical opportunity and insight, providing a means for ethical self-formation and enlarging the context for the exercise of, and reflection upon, ethical capacity.

I mention three general features. First, the healing and initiation rituals of spirit possession performatively constitute spirits as persons with the ethical obligations intrinsic to personhood and focus on moving each particular spirit from exploiting the host to engaging in a commitment to help the host and her family. During the course of treatment moral injunctions are clearly specified and all parties could be said to realize and cultivate a moral disposition in the process. Yet, the explicitly amoral nature of spirits, whether expressed in public spectacle or in private pain, forces people to confront the limits of the ethical. Overall, possession could be said to be constituted by a tension between the progressive move to socializing or humanizing each manifest spirit and the recognition of a contrast between spirits and humans that can never be resolved, a contrast between social obligation, confirmed criteria, and caring for others – and the power and freedom to do otherwise. When, after a ceremony at which the spirits had blessed the assembled humans, I asked what had been said, a spirit chuckled in response that I could hardly expect them to wish that people remain healthy and untroubled by spirits when that was how they drew their sustenance … Thus, whether observing the performance of spirits in public festivities or supplicating them in relatively private contexts, ethics is always in practice yet also in question (Lambek 1981).

Second, as spirit mediums, healers engage in ethical practice and develop an extended scope and means for ethical action. Which spirits one comes to be possessed by over the life course entails tacit ethical judgments concerning identification with and separation from others as well as the acceptance of a calling. Mediums are faced with demands by kin and clients that cannot be adequately met or compensated, suffer in their craft, become vulnerable to suspicion as sorcerers, are privy to personal secrets, need to develop empathy, manage the transference, and so forth – all these challenges and contingencies both require ethical integrity and help to reflect upon and produce it. Being a healer requires continuous practical judgment, including such implicit judgments as when to enter trance and speak as a particular spirit rather than as another spirit or as oneself, and what to say or do differently, so as to produce a distributed yet forceful and consistent polyphony. The Aristotelian concept of phronesis is indispensable to elucidate all this and to offset arguments that attempt to explain possession instrumentally, mechanically, or pathologically. The management of extremes is itself a form of phronesis in the sense of forging a virtuous balance and developing and enacting maturity, insight, and wisdom in personal relations (Lambek 1993; cf. Boddy 1989).

Third, strong mediums display virtuosity in deploying and extending the imaginative, communicative, and performative means that spirit possession provides and can thereby become ethical exemplars in their communities. In particular, they exemplify both a consciousness and a conscience of history; in speaking in and for particular voices, they offer an appropriate or provocative balance of remembering and forgetting, acknowledging the past, addressing the present, and looking to the future (Lambek 2002a, 2002b).

Overall then, spirit possession provides an enlarged field of play, in which ethical disposition can be cultivated, ethical concerns expressed and possibly satisfied, and in which the human capacity for ethical judgment and practice (Macpherson 1973) can be given full exercise. Similar developments can be found within other religious traditions and the practices they establish and legitimate but one of the central features of possession is the highlighting of irony (Lambek 2003b). The facts of multiple personhood and multiple voicing have the effect of acknowledging uncertainty and ambiguity, hence of privileging continuous contextual judgment over absolute rule-following, modesty over self-righteousness, and the ordinary and this-worldly over the transcendental and otherworldly. In the inspired performances of the spirits, Islam and Christianity themselves are not rejected but gently ironized.

Conclusion

In distinguishing between Durkheimian and Weberian traditions it has not been my intention to suggest it is necessary to choose between them. On the contrary, fruitful approaches to the articulation of religion and ethics will draw judiciously upon each. From the former perspective, ritual is the foundation of the ethical; it establishes, validates, and sanctifies the criteria by which ethical judgments are made and founds the basis of value. From the latter perspective, religion specifies and substantiates distinctive values, fields, and forms a field of moral practice, in which means and ends inform historical action and, conversely, the exercise of the virtues is informed by social and historical circumstances.

Ritual and religion support the constitution of ethical persons characterized by the dignity they are owed and the respect they owe others. Personal dignity and responsibility are anchored in the performance of rituals (from ordinary greetings to the correct disposal of the dead), in the cultivation of the virtues and virtuous practice, and in the introjection of strong figures. Where the conditions for dignity break down, whether at the collective or individual level, an ethical crisis ensues. The situation may either unravel further in witchcraft accusations, racism, and other self- or socially destructive forms of behavior or be resolved by healing, pastoral, and disciplinary forms of religious activity, the rise of ethical prophets, conversions to new forms of religious practice, and the establishment of new criteria.

While in some respects ethics is a human universal, there is also a dialectical movement in human social life and history between ethics conceived and practiced as submission to, and judicious action within, a given order understood as originating outside the individual and even outside society, and ethics understood as the freedom and initiative to escape the constraints, criteria, routines, and negative effects of such order. Presumably at some historical moments it will feel to the majority of adherents that a good balance has been achieved, in which some set of practices (call them "religion") provide the means for both certainty and restraint *and* creative hopeful action (call them "ethics"). But social life does not stand still and debate over the good life for human beings will never be fully resolved (were it to be resolved, the quality of life would be lesser for the loss of debate). Therefore one might add that ethics always needs to provide a space for argument, if not simply conversation, which religion may sometimes appear to enhance and at other times to close down.

Ethics in the tradition of ordinary language philosophy entails the linguistic means for fine discriminations between actors, acts, reasons, excuses, character, and interpretations. To add a more dynamic component, one could include the social possibilities for making and following through on these discriminations. One could say that human beings thrive when this field is rich, variegated, and accessible, but experience dissatisfaction when the means for the full exercise of their ethical capacity is limited, constrained, or denied. Religion in its various social and historical formations can be examined with respect to how it both enables and frustrates ethical exercise. Ethical practice in this sense concerns judgment between valued means and ends, generally conjoined, rather than either strict rules and their observance or strategies and their calculation. It includes space for contemplation or reflection as well as for the virtuous practice that "goes without saying." And it entails the establishment of a range of criteria that produce original kinds of persons, relations, contexts, and actions, hence specific possibilities for judgment, acknowledgment, recognition, and engagement; the enlargement and refinement of discriminations and commitments and the means for their fulfillment; and the movement between the passionate, the extraordinary, and the calling – and the ordinary work of daily action, observation, and care.

Acknowledgments

Thanks to Maurice Bloch and Didier Fassin and to the Canada Research Chairs program.

NOTES

1 Consider the expansion of "new age" practices in North America or the United Kingdom, the resurgence of spirit possession in Vietnam (Fjelstad and Nguyễn 2011) and of Daoism in China, and the thriving forms of spirit possession in Brazil and the western Indian Ocean. However, possession is on the retreat or defensive in parts of Africa (Masquelier 2001, for Niger; Boddy, personal communication, for Sudan), as is shamanism from Buddhism in north Asia (Bernstein 2011). The case of Hinduism is different yet again, as proliferating Hindu deities nevertheless occlude or destroy tribal ones (Nandy 2001).
2 On defining religion from multidisciplinary perspectives see De Vries 2008. On ethics from anthropology see Lambek 2010a.
3 On the politics of "sacrifice" and violent "sacrificial" acts there is now a burgeoning literature (e.g., Kahn 2008).
4 For culturally distinct examples of sacrifice see Lambek (2007, 2008a) and Obeyesekere (1984).
5 Sacrifice might also be said to establish the foundation or ultimate standard of value (Lambek 2008b) and self-sacrifice to catch people in unfulfillable obligation (Lambek 2007).
6 On the ethical limits of this argument, see Hasan-Rokem 2003.
7 Although Achebe's portrait is fictional, he offers an explanation for the first Igbo conversions to Christianity. This is not to argue that Christianity is ethically superior to Igbo ancestral practice.
8 By "incommensurable" I do not mean contradictory but simply not mapping fully onto or alongside each other (Lambek 1991; 1993: ch. 12).
9 For full discussion of Durkheim and Weber see Chapters 1 and 2 in this volume.
10 Personal communication, Mar. 14 and 16, 2011. Bloch is equally clear that this is not a matter of unmediated instincts. See also Bloch 2007.
11 See, for example, Lévi-Strauss (1963) on the shaman or my account of a healer who removes sorcery (Lambek 1993: ch. 9). Famous examples are the strategic deception of initiates (e.g., Barth 1975) and of women by men in Melanesia, Amazonia, and elsewhere.
12 For a more extensive attempt to integrate them in a dialectic of performance and practice, see Lambek 2010b.
13 On Foucauldian ideas of discipline and self-formation, see Chapters 4 and 13 in this volume.
14 Ruth Benedict and those she influenced draw, like Weber, from the German idealist tradition and share an interest in values, but they lack a strong sense of social differentiation; hence their portraits tend to be homogeneous and ahistorical (like some Durkheimians').
15 For an attempt to distinguish between simple "choice" and ethical "judgment," see Lambek 2008b.
16 These positions can be marked, respectively, by Weber's ideal types of priest and prophet, understood not as characteristic of different kinds of societies or different kinds of religion but as the most vocal or visible proponents of distinct ethical stances under specific historical conditions.
17 Racist and anti-Muslim hysteria in North America and Europe may be another.
18 This model has been briefly proposed in Lambek and Solway (2001) and Lambek (2003a) and draws on our reflection on accounts of witchcraft by Ashforth (2000) and others as filtered through psychoanalytic models of Loewald (1980) and Mitchell (1988). It seems superior to the simple invocation of "trauma."

REFERENCES

Achebe, Chinua (1996 [1959]) *Things Fall Apart*. Portsmouth, NH: Heinemann.

Asad, Talal (1993) *Genealogies of Religion: Discipline and Reasons of Power in Christianity and Islam*. Baltimore: Johns Hopkins University Press.

Ashforth, Adam (2000) *Madumo: A Man Bewitched*. Chicago: University of Chicago Press.

Austin, J. L. (1962) *How to Do Things with Words*. Oxford: Oxford University Press.

Barth, Fredrik (1975) *Ritual and Knowledge among the Baktaman of New Guinea*. New Haven: Yale University Press.

Bernstein, Anya (2011) The Post-Soviet Treasure Hunt: Time, Space, and Necropolitics in Siberian Buddhism. *Comparative Studies in Society and History* 53(3): 623–653.

Bloch, Maurice (1989) *Ritual, History, and Power: Selected Papers in Anthropology*. London: Athlone.

Bloch, Maurice (1992) *Prey into Hunter: The Politics of Religious Experience*. Cambridge: Cambridge University Press.

Bloch, Maurice (2007) Durkheimian Anthropology and Religion: Going In and Out of Each Other's Bodies. In Harvey Whitehouse and James Laidlaw (eds.), *Religion, Anthropology and Cognitive Science*. Durham, NC: Carolina Academic Press.

Boddy, Janice (1989) *Wombs and Alien Spirits: Women, Men, and the Zar Cult in Northern Sudan*. Madison: University of Wisconsin Press.

Boylston, Tom (2012) The Shade of the Divine: Orthodox Christian Time and History in Zege, Ethiopia. PhD dissertation, Department of Anthropology, London School of Economics.

Burridge, Kenelm (1969) *New Heaven New Earth: A Study of Millenarian Activities*. Oxford: Blackwell.

Cannell, Fenella (2006) Introduction to *The Anthropology of Christianity*. Durham, NC: Duke University Press.

Das, Veena (2007) *Life and Words: Violence and the Descent into the Ordinary*. Berkeley: University of California Press.

De Boeck, Filip (2004) *Kinshasa: Tales of the Invisible City*. Antwerp: Ludion.

De Vries, Hent (ed.) (2008) *Religion: Beyond a Concept*. New York: Fordham University Press.

Douglas, Mary (1966) *Purity and Danger: An Analysis of the Concepts of Pollution and Taboo*. Harmondsworth: Penguin.

Durkheim, Emile (1973) *Emile Durkheim on Morality and Society: Selected Writings*, intro. R. Bellah. Chicago: University of Chicago Press.

Evans-Pritchard, E. E. (1937) *Witchcraft, Oracles, and Magic among the Azande*. Oxford: Clarendon.

Evens, T. M. S. (2008) *Anthropology as Ethics: Nondualism and the Conduct of Sacrifice*. New York: Berghahn.

Fassin, Didier (2011) *Humanitarian Reason: A Moral History of the Present*. Berkeley: University of California Press.

Faubion, James (2010) From the Ethical to the Themitical (and Back). In Lambek (2010a), pp. 84–101.

Fjelstad, Karen and Nguyễn Thị Hiền (2011) *Spirits without Borders: Vietnamese Spirit Mediums in a Transnational Age*. New York: Palgrave Macmillan.

Fortes, Meyer (1987) *Religion, Morality and the Person: Essays on Tallensi Religion*. Cambridge: Cambridge University Press.

Geertz, Clifford (1973) Religion as a Cultural System. In *The Interpretation of Cultures*. New York: Basic Books.

Hasan-Rokem, Galit (2003) Martyr vs. Martyr: The Sacred Language of Violence. *Ethnologia Europaea* 33(2): 99–104.Repr. in Michael Lambek (ed.), *A Reader in the Anthropology of Religion*, 2nd edn. Malden, MA: Blackwell, 2008, pp. 590–595.

James, Wendy (1988) *The Listening Ebony: Moral Knowledge, Religion and Power among the Uduk of Sudan*. Oxford: Clarendon.

Kahn, Paul (2008) *Sacred Violence: Torture, Terror, and Sovereignty*. Ann Arbor: University of Michigan Press.

Keane, Webb (2010) Minds, Surfaces, and Reasons in the Anthropology of Ethics. In Lambek (2010a), pp. 64–83.

Kierkegaard, Søren (1985) *Fear and Trembling*, trans. Alastair Hannay. New York: Penguin.

Kwon, Heonik (2008) *Ghosts of War in Vietnam*. Cambridge: Cambridge University Press.

Laidlaw, James (2010) Ethical Traditions in Question: Diaspora Jainism and the Environmental and Animal Liberation Movements. In Anand Pandian and Daud Ali (eds.), *Ethical Life in South Asia*. Bloomington: Indiana University Press, pp. 61–80.

Lambek, Michael (1981) *Human Spirits: A Cultural Account of Trance in Mayotte*. New York: Cambridge University Press.

Lambek, Michael (1991) Tryin' to Make It Real But Compared to What? *Culture* [special issue, "From Method to Modesty: Essays on Thinking and Making Ethnography Now"] 11(1–2): 29–38.

Lambek, Michael (1992) Taboo as Cultural Practice among Malagasy Speakers. *Man* 27: 245–266.

Lambek, Michael (1993) *Knowledge and Practice in Mayotte: Local Discourses of Islam, Sorcery, and Spirit Possession*. Toronto: University of Toronto Press.

Lambek, Michael (1996) The Past Imperfect: Remembering as Moral Practice. In P. Antze and M. Lambek (eds.), *Tense Past: Cultural Essays in Trauma and Memory*. New York: Routledge.

Lambek, Michael (2002a) Nuriaty, the Saint, and the Sultan: Virtuous Subject and Subjective Virtuoso of the Post-Modern Colony. In Richard Werbner (ed.), *Post-Colonial Subjectivities*. London: Zed, pp. 25–43.

Lambek, Michael (2002b) *The Weight of the Past: Living with History in Mahajanga, Madagascar*. New York: Palgrave Macmillan.

Lambek, Michael (2003a) Fantasy in Practice: Projection and Introjection, or The Witch and the Spirit-Medium. In Bruce Kapferer (ed.), *Beyond Rationalism: Rethinking Magic, Witchcraft and Sorcery*. New York: Berghahn, pp. 198–214.

Lambek, Michael (2003b) Rheumatic Irony: Questions of Agency and Self-Deception as Refracted through the Art of Living with Spirits. In Michael Lambek and Paul Antze (eds.), *Illness and Irony*. New York: Berghahn, pp. 40–59.

Lambek, Michael (2007) Sacrifice and the Problem of Beginning: Reflections from Sakalava Mythopraxis. *Journal of the Royal Anthropological Institute* 13(1): 19–38.

Lambek, Michael (2008a) Provincializing God? Provocations from an Anthropology of Religion. In de Vries (2008), pp. 120–138.

Lambek, Michael (2008b) Value and Virtue. *Anthropological Theory* 8(2): 133–157.

Lambek, Michael (ed.) (2010a) *Ordinary Ethics: Anthropology, Language, and Action*. New York: Fordham University Press.

Lambek, Michael (2010b) Towards an Ethics of the Act. In Lambek (2010a), pp. 39–63.

Lambek, Michael and Solway, Jacqueline (2001) Just Anger: Scenarios of Indignation in Botswana and Madagascar. *Ethnos* 66(1): 1–23.

Lévi-Strauss, Claude (1963) The Sorcerer and His Magic. In *Structural Anthropology*, vol. 1. New York: Basic Books.

Loewald, Hans (1980) *Papers on Psychoanalysis*. New Haven: Yale University Press.

Macpherson, C. B. (1973) *Democratic Theory: Essays in Retrieval*. Oxford: Clarendon.

Mahmood, Saba (2005) *Politics of Piety*. Princeton: Princeton University Press.

Masquelier, Adeline (2001) *Prayer Has Spoiled Everything*. Durham, NC: Duke University Press.

Mauss, Marcel (1990 [1925]) *The Gift*, trans. W. D. Halls. London: Routledge.

Mitchell, Stephen (1988) *Relational Concepts in Psychoanalysis*. Cambridge, MA: Harvard University Press.

Murphy, Robert (1971) *The Dialectics of Social Life.* New York: Basic Books.
Nandy, Ashis (2001) A Report on the Present State of Health of the Gods and Goddesses in South Asia. *Postcolonial Studies* 4(2): 125–141.
Obeyesekere, Gananath (1981) *Medusa's Hair: An Essay on Personal Symbols and Religious Experience.* Chicago: University of Chicago Press.
Obeyesekere, Gananath (1984) *The Cult of the Goddess Pattini.* Chicago: University of Chicago Press.
Orsi, Robert (2005) *Between Heaven and Earth: The Religious Worlds People Make and the Scholars Who Study Them.* Princeton: Princeton University Press.
Parry, Jonathan (1986) *The Gift*, the Indian Gift, and the "Indian Gift." *Man* 21: 453–473.
Parry, Jonathan and Simpson, Edward (2010) David Pock's *Contributions* and the Legacy of Leavis. *Contributions to Indian Sociology* 44(3): 331–359.
Pocock, David (1973) *Mind, Body, and Wealth.* Oxford: Blackwell.
Radin, Paul (1957) *Primitive Man as Philosopher.* Mineola, NY: Dover.
Rappaport, Roy (1999) *Ritual and Religion in the Making of Humanity.* Cambridge: Cambridge University Press.
Richards, Audrey (1995 [1956]) *Chisungu.* London: Routledge.
Ricoeur, Paul (1967) *The Symbolism of Evil.* New York: Harper & Row.
Robbins, Joel (2004) *Becoming Sinners: Christianity and Moral Torment in a Papua New Guinea Society.* Berkeley: University of California Press.
Turner, Victor (1967) *The Forest of Symbols.* Ithaca, NY: Cornell University Press.
Turner, Victor (1969) *The Ritual Process: Structure and Anti-Structure.* Chicago: Aldine.
Vallely, Anne (2008) Moral Landscapes: Ethical Discourses among Orthodox and Diaspora Jains. In Michael Lambek (ed.), *A Reader in the Anthropology of Religion*, 2nd edn. Malden, MA: Blackwell, pp. 560–572.
Walzer, Michael (1965) *The Revolution of the Saints.* Cambridge, MA: Harvard University Press.
Weber, Max (1958 [1904–5]) *The Protestant Ethic and the Spirit of Capitalism*, trans. T. Parsons. New York: Scribner's.
Yang, Mayfair Mei-hui (1994) *Gifts, Favors, and Banquets: The Art of Social Relationships in China.* Ithaca, NY: Cornell University Press.

CHAPTER 20 Charity

Jonathan Benthall

No anthropologist has published a global comparison of charitable traditions since the chapter on "charity and generosity" in Edward Westermarck's *The Origin and Development of the Moral Ideas* (1909: 526–569). This Frazerian collage of historical and ethnographic snippets, much less substantial than his monograph *Ritual and Belief in Morocco* (1926), is bound to alienate readers a century later with its assumptions – part of the intellectual currency of his day – about a hierarchy of savage and civilized "races." But if we disregard this, the inferences he arrives at are a starting point for reflection.

Westermarck adduces obligations within the family as the source for "such conduct as positively promotes the existence and material comfort of a fellow-creature" (1909: 526) – some of them too generalized in the light of modern ethnography. A mother's caring for her children is universal, a father's nearly so. Second to this obligation, he says, are a married man's obligation to provide for his family, and the marital bond. The duty to look after aging parents is nearly universal: Christianity was exceptional in preaching that duty to parents was subordinate to duty to God. Duty to parents is grounded not merely in gratitude and affection but in fear: parents are able to curse and to take revenge posthumously, as ghosts, on neglectful children. Siblings are owed greater care than more distant relatives. Westermarck proceeds to give examples of groups that show kindness not only to their own members, but less commonly to strangers too. Charity and mutual aid may, however, be influenced by egoistic motives. He concludes with a more arresting claim: that the importance ascribed to charity in all the "higher religions" cannot be understood unless we understand its association with sacrifice:

> When food is offered as a tribute to a god, the god is supposed to enjoy its spiritual part only, whilst the substance of it is left behind and is eaten by the poor. And when the offering is continued in ceremonial survival in spite of the growing conviction that, after all, the deity does not need and cannot profit by it, the poor become the natural heirs of the god, and the almsgiver inherits the merit of the sacrificer. (Westermarck 1909: 565)

A Companion to Moral Anthropology, First Edition. Edited by Didier Fassin.

The only other early anthropologist with a sustained interest in the theme of charity was R. R. Marett, author of the aphorism "Real progress is progress in charity, all other advance being secondary thereto" (1935: 40). Like Westermarck, he saw maternal nurturing as the fountainhead of charity: "charity is the mother's, while Justice is the father's, contribution to the moral life of mankind … However estimable public philanthropy may be, the cold compassion that it doles out is a poor substitute for the warmth of the nursing mother's bosom" (Marett 1939: 141, 147). Westermarck, free from Marett's sentimentality, offers a still provocative insight. He was able to show that, in Jewish and Christian teaching alike, almsgiving came to be a substitute for sacrificial offerings to God. Ilana Silber (2000) has argued for the need to distinguish three kinds of religious giving – gifts to the gods, to religious officials, and to the needy – which seems to apply broadly to the Hebraic or Old Testament pattern. Yet Jesus, in the parable of the sheep and the goats, assured his followers that anything they did to benefit the hungry, thirsty, homeless, naked, sick, or imprisoned was equivalent to performing the same service for God (Matthew 25: 31–46).

Jesus never abrogated the Jewish doctrine of tithing, which is still practiced by some Christian churches, but it was generally replaced in Christianity by an emphasis on free-will offerings. Since the sixteenth century, European almsgiving has been overlaid with the spiritual connotations of "charity" in the sense of the highest Christian virtue, spiritual love. This was one of the words used to translate into English, via the Latin *caritas*, the Greek New Testament word *agapē* – as in the famous passage from 1 Corinthians 13 that extols it: "Though I speak with the tongues of men and of Angels, and have not charity, I am become as sounding brass or a tinkling cymbal." In modern translations, "charity" is always replaced by "love," which the first English translators may have used sparingly because of its sexual connotations.[1] At about the same time in England, "charity" began to acquire a restrictive legal definition as a result of a decision by Parliament in 1601 to regulate the system of private funds devoted to good causes. "Charity," over four centuries since, retains a Christian aura – to the extent that some Christian apologists are happy to conflate the two senses of the word.[2]

Westermarck quotes from the Acts of the Apostles 10: 4, where an angel says to Cornelius, the God-fearing centurion of Caesarea who was to be the first Gentile to be converted to Christianity, "Your prayers and almsgiving have gone up [like smoke of a sacrifice] for a memorial [burnt offering] to God."[3] But Westermarck also draws attention to the spiritual merit that almsgiving acquires, citing the third-century St. Cyprian of Carthage's eloquent treatise *Works and Alms.* "Divide your returns with the Lord your God," wrote St. Cyprian, deviating slightly from the Abrahamic principle that all wealth belongs to God anyway; "share your gains with Christ; make Christ a partner with you in your earthly possessions, that He also may make you a fellow-heir with Him in His heavenly kingdom." This brings us to the vexed question of reciprocity.

The principal focus of this essay will be the relationship between charity and scripturalist cultures. But before digging deeper we must first consider a more fundamental question for anthropologists, that of sharing and exchange. In passing, we will see that charity received little serious scholarly attention for some 50 years after Marett, and that the revival of interest was led by historians – though it has now become a topic of increasing importance for studies of relief and development. After a review of Islamic charity, I will finally suggest some pointers toward more rigorous cross-cultural comparison of the charitable field.

Reciprocity, Sharing, and Giving

All anthropologists agree that reciprocity and exchange are one of the most important elements in human interaction. There is no doubt that charitable giving can reap recompense: whether in recipients' gratitude and blessings, or in the "symbolic capital" of prestige, or in the celestial economy that St. Cyprian outlined – which has an analogue in the karmic principle of the south Asian religions, whereby merit gained by good actions can be carried forward to a subsequent incarnation. But if we think of the nurturing mother advanced by Westermarck and Marett as the archetype of amity, any expectation of reciprocity is surely indirect and uncertain. Support in her eventual old age? Perpetuation of her genes?[4] Maybe, but it is hard to distinguish the element of "instinct" from that of "obligation."

James Woodburn (1998 and personal communication), an authority on hunter-gatherer societies, is convinced that reciprocity is not universal to all human groups. The Hadza of Tanzania, according to him, would not understand the concepts of generosity or charity, being profoundly and assertively egalitarian, with strong prohibitions against clientelage or accumulation of goods. Sharing is focused on the distribution of large game animals: the killer of an animal has no special claim on the meat. Woodburn calls these and other similar groups "immediate returners" in that there is no concept of investment for future consumption, as opposed to "delayed return" hunter-gatherers who have investments such as beehives or storehouses (and may hence be able to make an easier transition to agriculture). Woodburn maintains that the Hadza lifestyle – though now under intense external pressure with the loss of 90 percent of their land – was well adapted to a habitat unsuitable for most other types of subsistence.[5] We may conclude from his findings that, however powerful the principle of reciprocity has proved in human history, the principle of mutuality or sharing is like a countersubject in music.

Most anthropological discussions of charity since Marett have focused on Marcel Mauss's study in reciprocity and social solidarity, *The Gift* (1990 [1925]). The interpretation of this work, dazzlingly innovative but sometimes opaque in the original French, with added problems in English translations, has attracted some fine minds, touching on the relationships between persons and things that are at the heart of anthropology. One of them has written that "[Mauss] was right where anthropologists have generally thought him wrong, and wrong where anthropologists have generally thought him right" (Parry 1986: 453), another that Mauss "never tells us what a gift is" (Testart 1998: 97). Maussology has become a specialty of its own.

Two linked suggestions in Mauss's essay are especially important for our purpose here. The first is that when a gift cannot be reciprocated, moral credit accrues to the donor but the recipient suffers a wound. Hence the reputation for "coldness" that organized charity in Europe has acquired since the nineteenth century.[6] Social reformers sought to replace it with the welfare state, in which citizens have entitlements. Some Indian ethnography reveals an interpretation of charitable giving as especially sinister: unreciprocated gifts, known as *dān*, when made to priests and renouncers, can bring misfortune which migrates from donor to recipient unless careful precautions are taken (Laidlaw 2000).

The second point is that, as several commentators on *The Gift* have argued, a "free" gift cannot admit that it has a dimension of reciprocity. When I make a gift I must do it in such a way as to deny to others that it has an economic aspect or that I will be rewarded, in this world or in the hereafter. To be credible, I must also believe this myself. The paradox is confronted in the teaching of all the world religions. In Maimonides's code of Jewish law, the section entitled "The laws of giving to the poor" states that the second highest degree in the giving of charity (exceeded only by the merit of enabling a recipient to be self-supporting) is an anonymous gift without knowing to whom one gives. Both Christian and Islamic scriptures enjoin that alms are best given in secret: "do not let your left hand know what your right is doing" (Matthew 6: 3).[7] Islam stresses the importance of *niyyah*, or intention: giving should come straight from the heart, and its merit is negated by ulterior motives.

But it is in India that we find perhaps the most sophisticated working through of the paradox, suggesting that all the founders of great religions must – whatever privileged revelations may be ascribed to them – have also been accomplished anthropologists. The Bhagavad Gita distinguishes charity "in the mode of goodness" (given without expectation of reward), "charity in the mode of passion" (with intent of recompense, or given grudgingly), and "charity in the mode of darkness" (given at the wrong place or time, to an unworthy recipient, or with disrespect).[8]

James Laidlaw describes how in the Shvetambar sect of Indian Jainism, itinerant celibate renouncers depend on lay families. They collect alms along random routes as Jain families finish preparing their lunch, not asking for their rule-restricted vegetarian food but waiting to be invited in – which is called *gocari*, or grazing. Before they have lunch themselves, family members place small amounts of food in the renouncers' alms bowls, pressing them to accept more, but they respond by saying "No! Less of that! Stop!" They offer no thanks or appreciation, except for a brief benediction. "The renouncer's surly indifference encourages the importunate generosity of the donor" (Laidlaw 2000: 626). They proceed to another house: the food collected is mixed with that brought by other members of the group into a single mass, and eaten out of public view. Those who make the *dān*, an act of good karma, have their spiritual reward, but if the act is motivated by the desire for merit, then none will result. "A good gift is given 'without desire,' and even self-congratulation invalidates the gift." Laidlaw concludes that this determined effort in Jainism not to create social relations is due to the renouncers' overriding aim of achieving a timeless spiritual perfection. He concludes (as part of a more complex argument) that "religious charity and philanthropy in all the great religions have repeatedly rediscovered the supreme value of the anonymous donation, only to find that time again donors have been more attracted to the benefits of the socially entangling Maussian gift, which does make friends" (Laidlaw 2000: 632). Laidlaw's insights have been carried forward in Erica Bornstein's study of charity in India, where the beliefs and practices aggregated as modern "Hinduism" interact with Buddhist, Islamic, Christian, and secular traditions (Bornstein 2012).

A Scholarly Hiatus

Jonathan Parry's (1986) analysis of Mauss's *The Gift* stimulated a number of anthropologists, such as those cited above, to turn their attention to charity. But there was a nearly 50-year hiatus in the anthropological endeavor between Marett and Parry. During this period many supporters of social reform disliked the notion of charity, on the grounds that it tended to address symptoms rather than causes, forgetting that William Beveridge, the architect of Britain's welfare state, also devoted substantial study to pluralism in welfare, striving for a compromise between the two models. Many socialists actually opposed charity as a ploy to legitimate the privileges of the rich and reduce the pressure on politicians to promote redistribution – hence, in strict Marxist doctrine, to slow down the inevitable proletarian revolution.

It is strange, after all the convulsions of the first half of the twentieth century, to read the following words by a luminary of the London School of Economics, Morris Ginsberg, in an address to anthropologists in 1953: "The duty of charity … loses its primacy in an age in which the abolition of poverty by organized effort has become possible. The giving of charity to individuals may even come to be deprecated as likely to divert attention from the need of a radical reconstruction of the system of poverty" (1953: 123). Quite apart from the question of practicability, the likely conclusion of such a policy is to place all power in the hands of the state. Such was the policy of the former Soviet bloc since the earliest days of the Bolshevik revolution. The extensive networks of Russian charitable organizations were as far as possible abolished by the Soviets as inimical to the principles governing human relations in a socialist state. Serious welfare crises and famines later forced the communist regime to call on Russian and foreign philanthropic organizations for help; and after Stalin's death in 1953 official hostility somewhat abated. The socialist government of Algeria followed a similar statist policy for some 20 years after it won its independence. Today, only a few resolute believers in state socialism and world government still dispute the necessity of charity as an adjunct to entitlements paid for by taxation.

One important contribution to academic research on charity during the latter part of the twentieth century was Paul Veyne's brilliant but idiosyncratic *Bread and Circuses: Historical Sociology and Political Pluralism* (1990 [1976]), which explored the public munificence of private individuals in the Greco-Roman period (from c.300 BCE). This he called "euergetism" from the Greek for "good works." Veyne is vigorously opposed to catchall explanations, insisting on the "singularity" of his material. Euergetism was the provision by notables of public buildings, entertainments, and military campaigns for the citizenry as a whole: it could be either free and voluntary or *ob honorem*, that is to say coinciding with the assumption of a public office. Euergetism had something in common with the American northwest coast potlatch, and may have been motivated by the desire to be famous after death. But as for piety, redistributive taxation, depoliticization, clientelage, a reaction to pressure from the lower classes, conspicuous consumption – none of these possible explanations satisfied Veyne. His key argument is that this was a system of apolitical paternalism, inseparable from the Greco-Roman idea of the city as a showcase where the people had a right to receive presents. We may hesitantly suggest that the present-day United States' highly developed system of personal and corporate sponsorship of opera, orchestras, and museums, facilitated by a sympathetic tax regime, has a Veynian aspect.

Other historians gave their attention to Renaissance Venice and Tudor England. In a different genre, we may single out Ellen Condliffe Lagemann's (1989) study of one of the great American philanthropic foundations, the Carnegie Corporation, moving beyond conventional institutional history to explore its liberal-progressivist influence on education and society in the United States during the twentieth century. Covering the opposite end of the social scale, Frank Prochaska (1988) acknowledged the "philanthropy of the poor to the poor" in Britain, which was earlier appreciated by Engels as a mechanism of solidarity and which was probably more extensive, before the advent of the welfare state, than the relative shortage of historical documentation might suggest. Prochaska has also published monographs on women philanthropists in nineteenth-century England, and on the "royal bounty" that enables a modern monarchy such as Britain's to compensate for its loss of political power by devoting itself to good causes.

A distinction is often made in European languages between "charity" and "philanthropy." *Philanthrōpia*, for the ancient Greeks, was "love of the principle of humanity." Sir Francis Bacon revived the term in his essay "Of Goodness, and Goodness of Nature" (1612), which begins: "I Take Goodness in this sense, the affecting of the weal of Men, which is that the Grecians call *Philanthropia*; and the *Word Humanity* (as it is used) is a little too light to express it" (Bacon 1696: 31–31). Later, in the century of the Enlightenment and the Rights of Man, this concept was fused with the idea of public benefactions – no doubt with the aim of establishing a philosophical basis for "charity" in humanism, shorn of religious connotations. However, even in the United States, where the concept of philanthropy was especially important to the thought of Alexander Hamilton, one of the founding fathers, it never replaced "charity." It came, however, to be associated in particular with the munificence of the rich, monumental benefactions, and patronage of high culture. All attempts so far to study our topic comparatively have dispensed with the charity/philanthropy distinction (as in Ilchman et al. 1998: x–xi), one good reason being that it has no parallels in major non-European languages such as Arabic or Hindi.

Anthropology lagged behind history. The first collection of comparative essays on charity to be published (Ilchman et al. 1998) included not a single anthropologist among its 22 authors.[9] Interest was slowly picking up, however, from the mid-1980s. We may single out in retrospect two landmarks, each pointing to productive fields of research: Parry's lecture, cited above, which turned attention à la Westermarck to non-Western charitable systems, and Barbara Harrell-Bond's (1986) iconoclastic monograph on the work of international humanitarian agencies, based on her fieldwork with Ugandan refugees in southern Sudan in the early 1980s, an early exercise in appraising institutions whose high charitable ideals had hitherto largely immunized them from criticism (see also Colson 2011). The more recent study of Islamic charity integrates both these concerns. Through the classic anthropological maneuver of decentering, this research is able to unsettle prior assumptions about the West's supposedly unique vocation to charity.

Islamic Charity

The connection between giving to God and giving to the needy is physically salient throughout the Muslim world, in many parts of which, to this day, animal sacrifice is still routinely practiced, with the meat given to the needy. This includes Morocco, where Westermarck had already undertaken four years of fieldwork before 1906. Silber (2000) argues that subtle "echoes" of sacrificial ideologies and practices still reverberate across long stretches of time. Charity in general is habitually either praised as an expression of empathy or else disparaged as appeasing the conscience of donors, but anthropology suggests a third way of conceiving it: as an act of devotion.

In the Quran itself, the major sacrifices of camels and cattle that were retained in Islam, especially to celebrate the annual Great Feast, Eid al-Kabir (*'īd al-kabīr*), are clearly not only ceremonies but also a practical means of providing for the needy. The Quranic tithe, or *zakat*, is instituted mainly to benefit the poor. Both animal sacrifice and *zakat* are associated with prayer, and *zakat* has lexical connotations of both productivity and purification. *Zakat* overlaps with another Quranic term, *ṣadaqa* – optional almsgiving, above what is obligatory – which has connotations of rectitude, hence affirmation of the oneness of God and Islam. The practice of *zakat* has undergone many variations during the history of Islam, as we will see later in this essay, but the discursive field to which it belongs remains a reality for devout Muslims, especially because the Quran is considered to be the unmediated word of God.

Studying Islamic traditions presents a different intellectual problem from the familiar worries about cultural relativism. Much of the distinctiveness of anthropology in the past lay in the respectful attention it gave to small-scale societies and subcultures. Judaism, from which both Christianity and Islam emerged, became an ethno-religion and abstained from an agenda of conversion. But the intentions of Islam are no less universalistic than those of Christianity or its successor, post-Enlightenment secularism. Christianity and Islam both set out to transcend ethnic limitations – one way of doing this being to adapt to local folkways, but with frequent outbursts of rigorism.

Studying Islamic charitable traditions is of interest for two particular reasons. First, they may be found today among all populations that include either Muslim donors or Muslim beneficiaries or both – which covers a large part of the world and reveals as much variety of religious practice as can be found within Christendom. This is of practical relevance to aid and development policies. What is distinctive about Islamic charity, we may ask, both from the viewpoint of Muslims themselves and from that of outsiders? How important are the distinguishing features?

The second reason is more intellectual. An intriguing question for our time is to what extent Judeo-Christian assumptions underlie Western claims to secular universalism. How deep-seated is the heritage of implicit religious values that cultures are left with, when religious doctrine has ceased to dominate? Imagine that the Muslims had repelled the Crusades and the Reconquista and successfully colonized medieval Europe. A kind of post-Islamic humanism might have eventually emerged in the modern West rather than the post-Christian humanism that we actually have. (Classical Islamic scholars such as Al-Biruni and Averroes belonged to the same line of thought as Aquinas and Maimonides in facing the problem of harmonizing religion with revelation.) *Zakat* rather than Christian charity might have become the dominant idiom of "good works" in Europe. The lexical association between Christian "good works" and *agapē* is historically contingent. Both Christian and Islamic "good works" have been closely linked to religion, as counterbalances to selfish accumulation of wealth; but it evidently disturbs some Westerners to find that humanitarian concern is not a Western monopoly. Another question arises: How secure will be the survival of these traditions of "good works" if we accept the proposition that further secularization will set in (unless reversed by apocalyptic catastrophes) as a by-product of scientific and technological advance?

Zakat and allied principles

We may think of the essence of charity as a bodily act, such as reaching out with a hand like the Good Samaritan to a traveler in distress, or in the Islamic tradition even smiling at a neighbor. All acts of charity imply an inequality between benefactor and recipient. This opens the way to political activity as soon as actions coalesce into institutions. We may tend to diagnose politicization more readily in unfamiliar charitable traditions than in our own, since the importance of a charitable sphere purified from political interests – sometimes nowadays under the name of "humanitarian space" – amounts, for liberal Western society, to what the anthropologist Roy A. Rappaport (1999) called an "ultimate sacred postulate."

By giving part of their wealth in *zakat*, Muslims can purify that which remains, and also themselves – through a restraint on their selfishness and indifference to others' privations. The beneficiary too is purified – from being jealous of the well-off. *Sadaqa* – almost equally important in practical Islamic teaching – is so closely associated with *zakat* in the Quran that the key verse defining the purposes of *sadaqa* (9.60) is treated as referring to *zakat*. Prayer is dismissed as ineffective if the *zakat* obligation is not met.

Zakat is the third of the five pillars of Islam – the others being the religious affirmation (*shahada*), prayer, fasting during Ramadan, and performance of the *hajj* if practicable. Muslims should donate a proportion of their assets (normally one-fortieth), after deducting the value of their home and working necessities, to a specified list of eight categories of people. These are – to borrow the most usual descriptions: the poor, the destitute, those employed to administer the *zakat*; those who might be converted to Islam or assist in the cause; slaves; debtors; those engaged in the "way of God"; and finally, travelers in need. Treatises have been published on the interpretation of this list. For instance, "slaves" may include prisoners of war or the victims of oppressive regimes. The "way of God" is taken to mean the same as *jihad* – a term that must always be understood in its context.

Jihad, or "striving," can mean an exertion of spiritual effort to master one's baser instincts and to lead a better life, of which one outcome is effective compassion for the disadvantaged. The nearest equivalent in English is the idea of the church militant resisting the powers of evil. But frequently in the history of Islam it has referred to a more aggressive or military type of campaign. In 1968 a fatwa was issued in Saudi Arabia by the General Mufti authorizing the use of *zakat* funds to purchase weapons for the Palestinian struggle, provided that the Saudi government authorized the expenditure. But a ruling of this kind would be repudiated by nearly all Islamic charities today.

The Quran enjoins Muslims not only to be generous themselves – the emulous piling up of wealth is denounced – but to encourage other people to be generous. One Maussian sociologist, Thierry Kochuyt (2009), has ingeniously extended the theory of reciprocity by means of a triadic model of *zakat* in which the third party is God. God gives well-off believers the wherewithal to live, and recompense to all for their good deeds in the hereafter. The well-off reciprocate by their prayers to God but also by paying *zakat* to the needy (who are exempted from almsgiving if their wealth is below a fixed threshold). The needy reciprocate, too, by their prayers to God, and specifically for the donor. By accepting charity, "those at the margin of society agree that they are brought back to the community of faith. Poor people are rescued by pious ones, possible skeptics are reintegrated, those under non-Muslim authority are liberated by fellow believers, and by accepting the *zakat* they align themselves with the *Ummah* [community of believers]" (Kochuyt 2009: 109–110).

Giving earns special merit, or *baraka*, during the annual holy month of Ramadan, at the end of which a small additional payment to the needy is required – a rule more scrupulously observed in many present-day Muslim communities than the annual levy on assets. Despite the importance ascribed in the Quran to *zakat*, no sanctions for enforcing it are specified. *Zakat* has inspired a body of didactic texts that set out how the original prescriptions should be interpreted in response to economic realities. The principle observed is that the less the amount of labor exerted and capital invested, the greater should be the levy. Thus the *zakat* on treasure trove should be as much as one-fifth, whereas the product of land watered only by wells is one-twentieth.

Another major Islamic institution is the *waqf* (plural *awqaf*), also known in North Africa as *hubs*, which has much in common with the European charitable foundation. Though not grounded in the Quran, *waqf* is based on the tradition that the Prophet Muhammad bequeathed almost nothing except a small plot of land for public use. *Waqf* in Arabic means "stopping," that is, the property is barred from any other ownership (as in the European mortmain, or "dead hand"). It spread over all the Muslim world except west Africa: at the beginning of the nineteenth century, over half the land in the Ottoman empire was legally tied up in this way, either for use or for investment. Fountains, roads, hospitals, schools, or animal refuges could be designated as *waqf*. Like European charitable foundations, this institution met not only social needs, but also the need of donors for prestige and spiritual merit. As in English law, it was possible to endow a "private" *waqf* and keep some benefits for one's own family. Most Muslim countries nationalized their *awqaf* over the last two centuries, and Ministries of Awqaf are now often limited to supervising mosques and religious schools. The principle of *waqf* has been revived in several countries as a framework for charitable activity with an Islamic face.

The malleability of *zakat*

At various points in the history of Islam, *zakat* has been reduced to a vehicle for extracting taxes. This was the case in medieval Cairo, before the Mamluk dynasty decided to make it a private matter for individuals; and in the nineteenth century, under the Ibadite imamate of Oman, it was the only tax levied by the government. In Malaysia in the 1970s, the state's attempt to monopolize *zakat* collection was obstructed by peasants. Today, the Taliban in Afghanistan have reportedly levied a *zakat* tax on the value of opium consignments.

Some historians give credit to *zakat* for anticipating by many centuries the development of the welfare state; but the imposition of taxes has always and everywhere run the risk of being resented as exploitative. *Zakat*'s taxative capacity is balanced by a long tradition wherein it has been extolled as a form of "financial worship." Al-Ghazali, the great medieval Persian philosopher (d. 1111), wrote a chapter on *zakat* in his *Revival of the Religious Sciences*, which integrated legal doctrines with a Sufi concern for the spiritual obligations of both donors and recipients (Singer 2008: 33–34, 147). In the very different idiom of the late twentieth-century Muslim Brothers, the Egyptian Islamist Sayyid Qutb maintained that *zakat*, as "the outstanding social pillar of Islam," was superior to Western ideas of charity (Carré 1984: 151). He reiterated a fundamental tenet of Islam, that whenever an individual is destitute blame should fall on the community as a whole. *Zakat* is often presented as the opposite of *riba*, that is to say usurious lending. One of the sources of funding for Islamic charities today is "halalization" by Islamic financial institutions, whereby money deriving from bank interest is diverted into *zakat* contributions and so purified. *Zakat* is a major resource in the standard Islamic case against both capitalism and communism (Benthall and Bellion-Jourdan 2009: 6–28, 37–44).

Amy Singer (2008) has shown that *zakat* has always been a flexible principle throughout its history. Today, no state in the world has organized it as Islamic teaching prescribes. At one extreme, in Oman, *zakat* is hardly institutionalized, but is left for individuals to pay to individuals of their choice through informal channels. In Saudi-Arabia, by contrast, a centralized Zakat Office distributes to quasi-governmental charities such as orphan programs – which are an almost universal feature of Islamic charities. Among Muslim majority countries, Jordan has found an intermediate solution. The Ministry of Awqaf oversees a directorate of *zakat*, but local committees are also allowed to raise and distribute funds. Such is the weakness of pan-Arabism, however, that calls by Prince Hassan of Jordan and others for the foundation of an international *zakat* fund for relief and development within the Muslim world have not been taken up by Jordan's richer neighbors.

Alms are still collected locally, in many conservative mosques throughout the world, for the benefit of local Muslims in need, following the classical interpretations that restricted the benefits to Muslims only. Religious traditions of charity have always displayed a marked exclusionary aspect in tension with a more inclusive commitment to fellow humans. A more liberal interpretation has gained ground: that "the poor" means all the poor. In an industrial country such as Britain, the dominant opinion among Muslims is that real poverty does not exist in a country with welfare safety nets, and they accept that most of their charitable gifts should be spent overseas.

Islamic charities are increasingly adapted to the international aid system. Historically, Arab societies were grounded in networks of kinship and clientelage – though it is worth remembering that the Arabic word *wasta* ("pull" or "clout") has equivalents in every language. The duty of *nafaqa* – the provision of food, clothing, and shelter to one's dependents – shaded into acts of charity. According to one traditional text, interceding on behalf of an inferior is "*sadaqa* of the tongue," so that whoever does such a favor becomes a donor (Singer 2008: 88). Patron–client relations are still especially strong in conservative Arab societies. A tendency in charitable institutions to replace them by impersonal bureaucratic procedures has been led from Europe and from jurisdictions such as Jordan influenced by European example.

The Islamic charity sector today

Some major Islamic voluntary associations date back a century. The largest voluntary association in Egypt, Gam'iyya Shar'iyya, founded in Egypt in 1912, is a conservative Islamic organization with some 6,000 mosques and about three million loosely affiliated members who pay small subscriptions. It aims to be totally nonpolitical, supported by big private donors who have funded three medical centers. It seeks no publicity and is almost completely unknown outside Egypt. In the same year, the

Muhammadiyah was founded in Indonesia – a reformist Islamic association supported today by 29 million members, responsible for hundreds of clinics and thousands of schools. It played a major part in coordinating relief after the Indian Ocean tsunami in 2004; but this was barely recognized in the voluminous evaluations of international aid published in the West, which followed the usual practice of underestimating the importance of local response systems (Benthall 2012).

Islamic charities working at an international level began to be founded in the late 1970s and 1980s. They represent a confluence of two historical movements. One was the general rise and diversification of nongovernmental organizations (NGOs) during this period: the 1980s were named "the NGO decade," as the funds transferred through NGOs from the industrial countries increased at twice the rate for international aid as a whole. The second was the Islamic resurgence. This had much older roots, and was also strong in south Asia; but in the Arab world the victory of Israel in the Six Day War of 1967 was a turning point. Islamism began to succeed socialism and pan-Arabism in the region, partly because Zionism was interpreted locally as an effective mobilization of religion, against which pan-Arabism would provide a defense. Islam was co-opted by authoritarian states as a source of legitimacy, but it also provided the most attractive idiom for political opposition – since socialism and communism failed to gain traction in the region, and Christianity was tainted by its historical status as a second-class minority under Islam and by its later association with the colonial period.

One of the difficulties holding back most of the Muslim world is that, for understandable reasons, it is preoccupied with politics. Humanitarian politics, that is to say dissension and power play between and within the aid agencies, is an arena of its own, heightened by tensions concerning some of the world's most troubled regions. Hence the Islamic charity sector today is steeped in controversy. In Saudi Arabia, for instance, the immemorial custom of raising charitable funds through collection boxes in mosques has been banned, and some once mighty charities such as the International Islamic Relief Organization (IIRO) have been forced to downsize.

Such controversies may be traced back at least as far back as the foundation in 1928 of the Muslim Brotherhood of Egypt, which later became a loose-knit international movement, for it has always combined welfare, religious, and political goals – the weighting of these three elements varying in different geopolitical contexts. One type of Islamic charity today is associated with opposition movements. Hezbollah in Lebanon controls an important network of Shi'a welfare organizations quite openly.

The case of the *zakat* committees in the Palestinian Territories is more open to question. These committees, over 100 in number, used to work from towns all over the Territories, providing basic services such as food and health aid, and care of orphans and families, until the takeover of Gaza by Hamas in 2007 – which was followed by radical reorganization of the committees in both sections of the Territories, so that by 2011 they were tightly controlled in the West Bank by Fatah and in Gaza by Hamas. The settled view of the Israeli and US governments in 2011 was that these committees were (before 2007) simply adjuncts or departments of Hamas: hence, under antiterrorist legislation, anyone giving or raising funds for them was guilty of providing "material support" for Hamas – which was equivalent to committing acts of terrorism and punishable in the United States by long prison sentences.

The alternative view of these pre-2007 *zakat* committees, supported by a number of researchers, is that they were "social coalitions" representing a cross-section of

Palestinian opinion – including inevitably a fair proportion that did not submit to the Oslo peace process – working transparently and honestly with minimal overheads to help those most in need in their localities, and thus earning considerable trust and legitimacy (Schaeublin 2009). By contrast, corruption and cronyism had infected the Fatah-dominated Palestinian Authority since its inauguration in 1994. Western-style civil society organizations in the Territories, despite presenting themselves as professional NGOs, have often been accused of dubious financial management, tarnishing the local image of many Western donors by the process of association. Many of the Islamic charities remained closer to the poorer segments of the population, providing alternative channels for the distribution of aid and responding to locally defined needs rather than the agendas of international donors.

Charitable organizations are always vulnerable to abuse because they rely on trust. Accusations that Islamic charities were acting as conduits for terrorist finance date back to the 1990s. It seems that during the Afghan conflict of the 1980s and the Balkan conflict of the early 1990s certain Islamic charities, deriving especially from the petrodollar states, engaged in activities that pursued a mixture of humanitarian, religious, political, and sometimes military aims. But the American government agency USAID made use during the 1980s of the US charity regime, which was then comparatively permissive, as a supplement to direct government support for the mujahideen in Afghanistan through propaganda and medical services. Some Islamic charities continued to support Afghan and Bosnian militants into the 1990s, when the United States had reclassified them as terrorists.

After the terrorist attacks of September 11, 2001, the US government intensified its efforts to purge the Islamic charity sector of abuse, publishing a blacklist of Specially Designated Terrorist groups, closing charities in the United States and punishing their organizers under wide-ranging legislation against "material support" for terrorism. The fact that money is "fungible," that is transferable, leads to the conclusion that if a donation is sent to a clinic deemed to be linked to a designated entity, this frees up funds for that organization to buy weapons – even if it can be shown that the clinic is providing its services according to accepted humanitarian and medical ethics. Indeed, optimizing its service to the community on the basis of need does not let such a clinic off the hook, since it is then accused of "winning hearts and minds" for terrorism.

The result of these measures, broadly followed by several other governments, has been to inhibit the growth of international Islamic charities in the United States. In the period following September 2001, the mainstream non-Muslim charities in the United States did not react immediately, but by the end of the decade they were coming to the view that draconian counterterrorist measures might actually have the opposite effect from that intended: not only reducing the flow of aid to beneficiaries, but also aggravating feelings of resentment in the Muslim world, and leaving a "humanitarian vacuum" for violent extremists to penetrate (Benthall 2010). It is believed that Osama bin Laden had personally funded relief and development programs in Sudan and Afghanistan in the 1980s. In Pakistan, after the Kashmir earthquake in 2005 and the floods in 2010, welfare groups closely associated with the extremist group Lashkar-e-Taiba were successful in bringing effective relief aid (in common with many moderate Islamic aid agencies); and on each occasion, statements attributed to Ayman al-Zawahiri and bin Laden respectively called on Muslims and Arab governments to do more for humanitarian causes.

The future of Islamic charities

The healthy record of Islamic Relief Worldwide, founded in 1984 in Birmingham, England and now the largest international Islamic aid agency, shows that the turbulence within the sector in the United States, recorded above, was not inevitable or irreversible. The supportive policies of the British government and its Charity Commission were helpful. Like Christian Aid 30 years earlier, Islamic Relief decided to eschew proselytism and concentrate on relief and development. It also accepted the principles of nondiscrimination and administrative transparency, which opened the door to government funding and cooperation with non-Muslim NGOs. It developed the traditions of *zakat*, *Qurbani* (the annual festive sacrifice), and Ramadan as professional fund-raising vehicles. In 2005 it was elected a member of the Disasters Emergency Committee, the elite of British overseas aid agencies which coordinates joint fund-raising through the media after major emergencies. Moreover, Islamic Relief, like the Aga Khan Foundation, founded in 1967, has set a standard for other Islamic charities to engage with current debates about aid and development.

But the wider Islamic charity sector outside Europe has remained somewhat paternalistic. Conservative Islamic teaching on *zakat* is still donor-oriented, as if the poor were necessary for the spiritual well-being of the wealthy. For instance, an ethnographic study of Islamic gift practices in the Sahel concludes that, as a "pathway to God" for the donor, they entrench a hierarchy based on wealth differences (de Bruijn and van Dijk 2009) – a familiar charge against "good works" in all social contexts.[10] But current interest in the role of faith-based organizations in general, with their access to huge civil society networks, is likely to stimulate rapid innovation (De Cordier 2009).

Charity that Dares Not Speak Its Name

We have so far dealt with whatever goes explicitly by the name of charity or its near synonyms such as "good works." Most international NGOs constituted as private charities now derive substantial income from official sources, effectively acting as contractual middlemen between donor governments and beneficiaries. Are there actions which may be regarded analytically as forms of charity, but which those undertaking them insist on calling something else? Médecins Sans Frontières has always insisted that it is not a charity, but this is part of the distinctive ideology that has earned it a high degree of secular sanctity (Benthall 2008).

It is almost a shibboleth in enlightened aid circles to declare that international development is not a form of charity. The politicians and administrators who dispense state aid try to distance themselves from the idiom of charity in favor of norms such as the Millennium Development Goals or the "right to development." But when beneficiaries have no enforceable entitlements – they have "uninsured life," by contrast with citizens in most industrial countries, who have "insured life" (Duffield 2008) – any aid that flows to them is voluntarily given, and relies by necessity on the same moral basis as personal charity, albeit with salaried administrators. Even when Western aid workers in danger zones make the supreme gift of sacrificial charity, that of their lives, it tends to be classed as more heroic than that of local staff (Fassin 2011: 236–242). Admittedly, governments have treaty obligations to provide financial support to intergovernmental institutions; but overall volumes of aid funding remain at the discretion of governments, and can be increased or reduced in response to domestic priorities and pressures. To deny that overseas aid ministries are engaged in a form of collective charity is surely an illusion. The revival of Russia as an international development donor, 16 years after the collapse of the Soviet Union, has been well interpreted by Patty A. Gray (2011) in Maussian terms "at least partly as a defence mechanism against the demeaning experience of being treated as a perpetual recipient on the world stage, and an effort to be seen as a global player with prestige and influence." Africa remains "the world's most iconic perpetual recipient" and is a favored recipient of Russian largesse (Gray 2011).[11]

Constructs for Cross-Cultural Analysis

Anthropological reflections on the nature of charity as a system of exchange, with minor variants in different cultural traditions, could make for clearer thinking on the reality of international aid. Global aid flows may be broadly conceived as belonging to a cyclical system, whereby representations of misery are exported northward as media consumables to be "paid for" by voluntary prestations to the South (Benthall 2009). If this is a correct analysis, the same paradox of individual charity – that it must not be admitted as having an element of reciprocity, otherwise its moral worth is negated – applies too at the level of donor agencies.

A fruitful though demanding approach for social science, where the fieldwork skills of anthropologists have a clear advantage, is to try to gain access to the perspective of aid recipients as well as that of providers. The comparative ethnography of charity will need to adopt this mode of analysis more assiduously if it is not to remain weighted toward the donors' side of the equation. Moreover, the need for material and spiritual security is universal. It is catered for by a wide variety of risk-mitigating networks and caring institutions, some based on legal entitlements and others on customary obligation, but with increasing vulnerability in most regions because of the widespread withdrawal of the state from welfare commitments. An expanded concept of social security, as "the dimension of social organization dealing with the provision of security not considered to be an exclusive matter of individual responsibility", as defined by Franz and Keebet von Benda-Beckmann (Thelen et al. 2009: 2), may offer a framework for comparative etic analysis, to supplement emic constructs such as "charity," "*zakat*," "aid," and their lexical congeners, each of which is deeply embedded in an *idéologique*.

Acknowledgments

Erica Bornstein, Simon Coleman, Didier Fassin, David Lewis, Filippo Osella, Peter Redfield, and Emanuel Schaeublin helped in various ways with ideas and information.

I owe a longer-term debt to several colleagues associated with the Islamic Charities Project, sponsored by the Swiss Federal Department of Foreign Affairs.

NOTES

1 According to a biographer of William Tyndale, the English Protestant scholar and martyr, one reason why he offended the Catholic authorities in 1526 was that he translated *agapē* as "love" rather than "charity." It was arguably in the interests of the Catholics, as later for the Anglican committee responsible for the King James Bible (Authorized Version), to promote good works and donations, whereas Tyndale, influenced by Luther, believed that good works unaccompanied by faith had no merit (Moynahan 2002: 104–106).

2 See "Charity and Charities," *Catholic Encyclopedia*: at http://www.newadvent.org/cathen/03592a.htm, accessed Mar. 6, 2012.

3 For more on the connections between charity and sacrifice (including first fruits) in the Abrahamic traditions, see Benthall and Bellion-Jourdan 2009: 21–28, 164.

4 The problem of altruism is critical to neo-Darwinian evolutionary biology. For relevant texts, see Oren Harman's (2010) biography of the mid-twentieth-century eccentric genius George Price, who formulated an equation to distinguish selective processes at different levels – in genes, in individuals, and in groups; and Fuentes's (2009) overview article explaining some of the problems of arriving at an interdisciplinary synthesis of social-cultural and evolutionary anthropology.

5 Some "hunter-gatherer revisionists" have criticized the model of immediate return, suggesting that groups such as the Hadza and the !Kung of the Kalahari desert are marginals dependent on regional agricultural economies. Woodburn contends that societies of this type have, in fact, been too widely spread geographically for the revisionist case to be generally convincing (personal communication).

6 Emerson and Dickens both eloquently questioned the motives of organized philanthropy, as did Anatole France and Octave Mirbeau later, at the beginning of the twentieth century. Yet a skeptical view of charity and philanthropy goes back much further. In ancient Rome, Cicero and Seneca both warned against the risks of indiscriminate charity. In Cervantes's novel *Don Quixote* (1605) the ludicrous knight-errant hero sees the dust raised by two flocks of sheep and concludes that they are two opposed armies, so he must "favor and assist the weaker side."

7 Among a number of hadiths, see the collection *Sahih al-Bukhari* 11.629. Discretion in charitable giving is also enjoined in the Quran, e.g., 2.271.

8 Bhagavad Gita 17.20–22. See also Bornstein 2009: 624–625, 644.

9 Among the contributors to this groundbreaking collection, Joanna Handlin Smith has expanded her findings on charity on late Ming China (c.1580–1644) in a monograph (Handlin Smith 2009). She shows that during this period some members of an educated elite took an interest in charitable activities as vehicles for the transformation of society, drawing on an amalgam of Confucian, Daoist, and Buddhist beliefs stiffened by legalist texts espousing behavioral conditioning through rewards and punishments.

10 This was also largely true of the medieval church in Europe. God could have made all men rich, but he wanted there to be poor people in this world, that the rich might be able to redeem their sins (Geremek 1994: 15–36).

11 Other sources of charity, in this expanded sense, that would be candidates for further anthropological study – especially because they disturb conventional stereotypes of donor–recipient relationships – include "non-DAC [Development Assistance Committee] donors" such as China and Iran, various diaspora communities such as Hindu caste associations, commercial corporations, and military organizations that engage in humanitarian aid.

REFERENCES

Bacon, Francis (1696) *The Essays; or, Councils, Civil and Moral*. London: H. Herringman et al.

Benthall, Jonathan (2008) The Humanitarian Movement. In *Returning to Religion: Why a Secular Age is Haunted by Faith*. London: I. B. Tauris, pp. 76–107.

Benthall, Jonathan (2009) Preface. In *Disasters, Relief and the Media*. Wantage: S. Kingston, pp. ix–xxvii.

Benthall, Jonathan (2010) Islamic Humanitarianism in Adversarial Context. In Erica Bornstein and Peter Redfield (eds.), *Forces of Compassion: Humanitarianism between Ethics and Politics*. Santa Fe, NM: SAR, pp. 91–121.

Benthall, Jonathan (2012) "Cultural Proximity" and the Conjunction of Islam with Modern Humanitarianism. In Michael Barnett and Janice Stein (eds.), *Faith and Humanitarianism*. Oxford: Oxford University Press, pp. 65–89.

Benthall, Jonathan and Bellion-Jourdan, Jérôme (2009) *The Charitable Crescent: Politics of Aid in the Muslim World*. London: I. B. Tauris.

Bornstein, Erica (2009) The Impulse of Philanthropy. *Cultural Anthropology* 24(4): 622–651.

Bornstein, Erica (2012) *Disquieting Gifts: Humanitarianism in New Delhi*. Palo Alto, CA: Stanford University Press.

Carré, Olivier (1984) *Mystique et politique: lecture révolutionnaire du Coran par Sayyid Qutb, Frère musulman radical*. Paris: Editions du Cerf.

Colson, Elizabeth (2011) Imposing Aid: The Ethnography of Displacement and its Aftermath. *Kroeber Anthropological Society Papers* 99–100: 154–167.

de Bruijn, Mirjam and van Dijk, Rijk (2009) Questioning Social Security in the Study of Religion in Africa: The Ambiguous Meaning of the Gift in African Pentecostalism and Islam. In Carolin Leutloff-Grandits et al. (eds.), *Social Security in Religious Networks*. Oxford: Berghahn, pp. 105–27.

De Cordier, Bruno (2009) Faith-Based Aid, Globalisation and the Humanitarian Frontline: An Analysis of Western-Based Muslim Aid Organizations. *Disasters: The Journal of Disaster Studies, Policy and Management* 33(4): 608–628.

Duffield, Mark (2008) Global Civil War: The Non-Insured, Intellectual Containment and Post-Interventionary Society. *Journal of Refugee Studies* 21(2): 145–165.

Fassin, Didier (2011) *Humanitarian Reason: A Moral History of the Present*. Berkeley: University of California Press.

Fuentes, Agustín (2009) A New Synthesis: Resituating Approaches to the Evolution of Human Behaviour. *Anthropology Today* 25(3): 12–17.

Geremek, Bronislaw (1994) *Poverty: A History*. Oxford: Blackwell.

Ginsberg, Morris (1953) On the diversity of morals. *Journal of the Royal Anthropological Institute* 83(2): 117–135.

Gray, Patty A. (2011) Looking "The Gift" in the Mouth: Russia as Donor. *Anthropology Today* 27(2): 5–8. At http://eprints.nuim.ie/3028/1/PG_Gift.pdf, accessed Mar. 12, 2012.

Handlin Smith, Joanna (2009) *The Art of Doing Good: Charity in Late Ming China*. Berkeley: University of California Press.

Harman, Oren (2010) *The Price of Altruism: George Price and the Search for the Origins of Kindness*. London: Bodley Head.

Harrell-Bond, Barbara (1986) *Imposing Aid: Emergency Assistance to Refugees*. Oxford: Oxford University Press.

Ilchman, Warren F., Katz, Stanley N., and Queen, Edward L., II (eds.) (1998) *Philanthropy in the World's Traditions*. Bloomington: Indiana University Press.

Kochuyt, Thierry (2009) God, Gifts and Poor People: On Charity in Islam. *Social Compass* 56(1): 98–116.

Lagemann, Ellen Condliffe (1989) *The Politics of Knowledge: The Carnegie Corporation, Philanthropy, and Public Policy*. Middletown, CT: Wesleyan University Press.

Laidlaw, James (2000) A Free Gift Makes No Friends. *Journal of the Royal Anthropological Institute* 6(4): 617–634.

Leutloff-Grandits, Caroline, Peleikis, Anya, and Thelen, Tatjana (eds.) (2009) *Social Security in Religious Networks.* Oxford: Berghahn.

Marett, R. R. (1935) *Head, Heart and Hand in Human Evolution.* London: Hutchinson.

Marett, R. R. (1939) Charity and the Struggle for Existence. *Journal of the Royal Anthropological Institute* 69(2): 137–149.

Mauss, Marcel (1990 [1925]) *The Gift: The Form and Reason for Exchange in Archaic Societies.* New York: Norton.

Moynahan, Brian (2002) *If God Spare My Life: William Tyndale, the English Bible and Sir Thomas More: A Story of Martyrdom and Betrayal.* London: Little, Brown.

Parry, Jonathan (1986) *The Gift*, the Indian Gift and the "Indian Gift." *Man* 21(3): 453–473.

Prochaska, Frank (1988) *The Voluntary Impulse.* London: Faber & Faber.

Rappaport, Roy A. (1999) *Ritual and Religion in the Making of Humanity.* Cambridge: Cambridge University Press.

Schaeublin, Emanuel (2009) *Role and Governance of Islamic Charitable Institutions: The West Bank Zakat Committees (1977–2009) in the Local Context.* CCDP Working Paper No. 5. Geneva: Centre on Conflict, Development and Peacebuilding. At http://graduateinstitute.ch/webdav/site/ccdp/shared/6305/WP5_2_engl.pdf, accessed Mar. 5, 2012.

Silber, Ilana (2000) Echoes of Sacrifice? Repertoires of Giving in the Great Religions. In Albert A. Baumgarten (ed.), *Sacrifice in Religious Experience.* Leiden: Brill, pp. 291–312.

Singer, Amy (2008) *Charity in Islamic Societies.* Cambridge: Cambridge University Press.

Testart, Alain (1998) Uncertainties of the "Obligation to Reciprocate": A Critique of Mauss. In Wendy James and N. J. Allen (eds.), *Marcel Mauss: A Centenary Tribute.* Oxford: Berghahn, pp. 97–110.

Thelen, Tatjana et al. (2009) Social Security in Religious Networks: An Introduction. In Carolin Leutloff-Grandits et al. (eds.), *Social Security in Religious Networks.* Oxford: Berghahn, pp. 1–19.

Veyne, Paul (1990 [1976]) *Bread and Circuses: Historical Sociology and Political Pluralism*, abridged translation. London: Allen Lane.

Westermarck, Edward (1909) *The Origin and Development of the Moral Ideas*, vol. 1. London: Macmillan.

Woodburn, James (1998) "Sharing Is Not a Mode of Exchange": An Analysis of Property-Sharing in Immediate-Return Hunter-Gatherer Societies. In C. M. Hann (ed.), *Property Relations: Renewing the Anthropological Tradition.* Cambridge: Cambridge University Press, pp. 48–63.

CHAPTER 21

Medicine

Adriana Petryna

In this essay I explore what the study of medicine as a set of cultural values can bring to the anthropological study of morality more generally. I combine a broad view on the anthropological and sociological literature on the topic with a more ethnographic approach based in my fieldwork in post-Chernobyl Ukraine, in the US privatized health system, and in emergent economies such as Brazil where a right to health is constitutionally guaranteed. In each setting, we see sick individuals desperately struggling to understand new medical diagnostics and to access treatments. Healing has progressively been displaced from the clinic and the patient–doctor relationship to precarious social institutions and domestic spaces as well as experimental settings. Regardless of where we live, no one can bear the full cost of her health care and recovery alone (see Das 1996; Kleinman 2008; Mol 2008). This essay takes this unbearability as a social fact and a starting point to explore practical and conceptual shifts in the sick role: from the sick role understood as "social deviance" (Parsons 1951) to a medically neglected, but powerfully informative, people-centered science of survival. This science of survival, I argue, is grounds for a moral right to health, and the keystone for a new politics of recovery.

Philosopher of science Georges Canguilhem once noted that the "measure of health is a certain capacity to overcome crises and to establish a new physiological order, different from the old. *Health is the luxury of being able to fall ill and recover*" (2008: 132; emphasis added). This essay juxtaposes health as luxury with the unbearable cost of survival in a variety of industrialized medical settings. It asks: What has become of health in settings where there is often no right to exit from one's disease? Where disease may lead to capitalizable data in for-profit research (as in clinical trials), or where it may become an instrumental political resource used by a state (as in the aftermath of a nuclear crisis), what insures that right of exit from one's disease? What new physiological as well as political orders are at stake in recovery?

The sick role is an idea that describes sickness as a socially sanctioned behavioral role and as potential deviance to be controlled. In what follows, I consider this concept

A Companion to Moral Anthropology, First Edition. Edited by Didier Fassin.

alongside anthropological findings and question the political, medical, and cultural availability of the sick role for patients and families today. I draw from my research into the Chernobyl nuclear disaster's aftermath, the globalization of clinical trials, the right to health litigation, as well as a family experience with cancer treatment to show how societal moralities and political responsibilities with respect to the sick role have led to non-optimal health care.

The non-optimality of health care has led, for example, to healthcare reform in the United States. The Patient Protection and Affordable Care Act signed into law in 2010 focuses on the *quality* of patient outcomes rather than the *quantity* of care. Yet the meaning and definition of "quality outcome" is hard to gauge, in part, because we lack a meaningful narrative of the morality of medical recovery. In the Parsonian account, there is such a narrative. The sick, excused from normal obligations, are obligated to seek appropriate medical resources to try to get well. The sick role locates the project of health in a contract between a doctor and patient and the hope of getting better is predicated on a reciprocal moral obligation: a physician's duty to treat is complemented by a patient's good-faith effort to try to get better and subsequently reintegrate into a normal, functioning social world. The sick not only should place their trust in physicians' competencies but should also master a social interaction attached to being sick. The locus of therapeutic engagement is limited to the doctor–patient relation (which is also a locus of social control), and the event structure of sickness–recovery is well defined and plays out accordingly through medicalized interactions.

Today, access to the sick role and a health-optimizing morality of medicine are limited in the new contexts of global medicine. Moreover, the afflictions, conditions, needs, and desires of patients and their families on the ground are constantly exceeding the medico-scientific and healthcare frameworks they are cast into. As sick roles are being undone or overturned, patients are finding themselves in new paramedical spaces of authority. These spaces – related to courts, health insurance, or clinical trials – are better characterized as arenas where patients and state, market, and scientific actors face off against each other and perform one-by-one rescue missions.

For the judge in a rights-oriented Brazil the concern is: Have I fulfilled a right to health? For the state bureaucrat in post-disaster Ukraine the question is: Have I compensated enough people to keep my state legitimate? And the clinical trialist asks: Have I gathered the optimum data to make sure this drug can be approved? There is no *predefined* population to treat or adequately articulated ethics or expertise to insure patienthood in these new upside-down paramedical worlds. Where judges become pharmacists and state agents emergency care providers, often there are no norms informing action. Patients have the double burden of enacting new roles to counteract a hidden calculus of triage or to struggle for a reliable physiological and political order of health.

As assemblages of life, survival, and sacrifice are being reconceptualized, I am also interested in the unique capacities that patients develop in the face of disease. What is the social and political fabric of rescued lives? How do sufferers themselves "recapture" the sick role within non-optimal medical settings and deploy it to make public and private institutions responsive? Which moral practices underpin care (or its lack) and how do these realities impinge on recovery? By attending to the moral dimensions of healing, we can imagine the agency of the sick person and affirm the social fabric of rescued lives.

Sick Role Unmade

Sociologist Talcott Parsons introduced the idea of the sick role at a time of postwar scientific and economic optimism, when the power of biomedicine was becoming palpable. New vaccines were preventing deadly childhood scourges. Novel chemical agents like penicillin had dramatically reduced rates of infectious disease. The notion of the sick role also arose, perhaps not coincidentally, in a critical moment in US healthcare reform efforts. Governmental efforts to put into place a single-payer universal health care system were opposed by, among others, the American Medical Association, and the United States ended up with a two-tiered system of private health insurance for those who could afford it and public services for other qualified groups.

In this postwar context, the concept of the sick role was as much a sociological category of deviance control as it was a prescription for society's moral obligation to the sick (and vice versa). The work of health service agencies involved distributing medicines but therapeutics, according to Parsons, was predominantly a reintegrative process. In this rendition, the social and the medical colluded to, ideally, reintegrate the sick. A kind of moral efficacy was ascribed to this social-medical nexus in which patients not only were cast or could cast themselves into the sick role, but could actually *recover*. The inequality underpinning access to health care as well as the lack of a sound public debate about health as a right rather than a commodity is largely unaddressed in this rendering. Over time, an idealized ability of society and a medical marketplace to take up the complexity of recovery has run its course.

Deviations from the sick role are writ large in the diverse global medical worlds I have engaged over the past 15 years. In my work on the scientific, political, and social aftermath of the Chernobyl disaster (Petryna 2002), I charted how rational-technical interventions, both selective and strategic, altered the language of accountability and human rights in postsocialist Ukraine, contributing to the open-endedness of the crisis. In Kiev, I observed countless scenes in which individual accounts of disease, if they were to be acted on medically at all, had to be transmogrified through criteria and codes fitting standard medical categories and hidden economic rationales. "They are alive," a biologist told me who took care of injured clean-up workers, "but we don't know how they survived." Their experiences spoke of a heterogeneous and largely unaccounted-for social science and politics of survival that exceeded the logistical capacities of the state or its medical organs.

In my study of the global clinical trials industry (Petryna 2009), I documented the complex ways that commercial medical research is being integrated into struggling health systems in Brazil and Poland. Clinical trials are placed in host communities that often lack access to the best proven treatment, relying on the untreated to generate information that is relevant to planned consumers elsewhere. Or trials are used as marketing tools to create specific medical demands. The words of one clinical trial scientist, "I don't see patients, I see data," reflect the recasting of the patient role as data to be captured, transferred, and even manipulated. For the patients who become trial subjects in this expanding global research enterprise, questions of post-trial treatment access are often left unaddressed. Bioethical approaches have by and large focused on human subject protection in research to the exclusion of actual patient protection.

Arguably, today, we have lost that space of "efficacious collusion" in a social-medical nexus of health. My last research trip to Ukraine in 2000 was cut short by news that my father was diagnosed with lung cancer. Documenting how patients in Ukraine engaged a constant "work of illness" in order to receive state medical care, I now faced the challenge of a family member who was actively being divested of his sick role possibility at home. Medics affiliated with a health-maintenance organization assured us that there was nothing to be done medically. We resisted such claims and learned to navigate labyrinthine triage systems so as to insure treatment for the patient on the basis that he was a healthy man, able to withstand aggressive treatment. Eleven years on, this individual has outlived all other patients with the same disease, young and old, who underwent the same procedure. His survival outcome speaks of a specific, physical wherewithal as well as the role of family control and intervention that led to a reinstatement of the sick role against cost-effective insurance measures. A hard-won patienthood re-established the terms of therapeutic engagement and opened up possibilities for recovery, a fact that has to be accounted for both politically and medically.

Today, patients in the United States also enter in trials of sorts. All too aware of the prohibitive cost of health care, they may postpone or never receive it, and insurance companies have discriminated against people with preexisting conditions (though the Patient Protection and Affordable Care Act now requires insurers to offer the same premiums without consideration of preexisting conditions, excluding tobacco use). Health outcomes in the United States continue to get worse, no matter how much money is spent on medicines, tests, and diagnostics (Porter and Teisberg 2006). By the same token, there are no "markets" in medical recovery. Health systems do not calculate outcomes or profits by how well people get, but by the volume of services and technologies delivered. My concern lies with the patient's role in recovery in spite of these limits as recovery itself may be viewed as the consummate idiosyncratic side of medicine today. My experiences have also taught me to appreciate the potentially wide-ranging nature of recovery processes and their nonmedical loci.

In what follows, I trace an intellectual geography of the sick through various registers of my fieldwork. At stake is how patients make sense of their trajectories and engage new infrastructures to create and enact a politics of recovery (or to avoid harm). Not only clinical, but also post-disaster, juridical and experimental settings make up key sites in a global political economy of health in which suffering and patient needs are acknowledged or made invisible. Bureaucrats, judges, and trialists make up a curious world of paramedical officialdom through which a moral economy of sacrifice burrows itself into survival.[1] They by and large do not work with a biomedical concept of health, but with social and political criteria related to compensation, rights to health, or cost-effectiveness. The focus of this set of political health actors is not on recovery from disease but on the political and economic exploitation of disease. Indicators of success have nothing to do with an individual right to exit from a disease, but with the enumeration and perpetuation of disease as a political category.

"The Diagnosis We Write is Money"

When the Chernobyl nuclear reactor exploded in 1986, it blasted a radioactive plume as high as eight kilometers into the sky. Winds carried a radioactive cloud over Belarus, Ukraine, Russia, and Europe and set off alarms at a nuclear facility in Sweden.

Chernobyl is widely acknowledged as the world's worst peacetime nuclear disaster. At the time, though, it took the Soviet government 18 days to acknowledge that anything out of the ordinary had transpired. For five years (1992–97), I worked in a convoluted world of science, statistics, and bureaucracy in which international scientists were adjudicating the validity of citizens' claims to Chernobyl-related suffering. How did some kinds of suffering become acknowledged and visible, and why, while others remained invisible? Given the open-endedness of the catastrophe, what roles did people take on in order to insure accountability and health? These questions about the everyday lived aspects of the Chernobyl aftermath led me to extended conversations with key scientific and political actors in Kiev and Moscow, comparing scientific standards that informed changing concepts of biological risk and safety in the Soviet and post-Soviet administrations of the aftermath.

Meanwhile, across the region, the Soviet industrial framework fell apart. Household financial savings were wiped out by hyperinflation. Social protection systems were overburdened and inadequate to address fast-paced changes in which a core group of long-term poor emerged. What I discovered was that the very framing of biomedical injury was now intimately linked with the region's economic restructuring: "There are a lot of people out of work," an administrator who ruled on claims, told me. "People don't have enough money to eat. The state doesn't give medicines for free anymore. Drugs stores are commercialized." He likened his work to that of a bank. "The diagnosis we write is money." Workers in the so-called "Chernobyl zone" realized they faced fewer job prospects outside the Zone and continued working there, hiding their illnesses until they could no longer do so. For evacuees and those still living on contaminated territories, illness became a "form of work." I joined patients' families in their journeys through a maze of legal and medical bureaucracies and institutions. Together, these institutions mediated an informal economy of illness and claims to compensation rooted in what I call *biological citizenship*, that is, a demand for a form of social welfare based on scientific and legal criteria that both acknowledge injury and compensate for it. The demand for compensation centered on a right of entry *to a sick role*. Patients burdened with radiological exposure were caught in a long-term bureaucratic cycle; they carried the burden of proof of their physical damage while experiencing the risk of being delegitimated as patients in legal, welfare, and medical institutional contexts.

In 1997 I spent one month in the office (located in a major research center in Kiev) of an administrator adjudicating compensation claims, taking notes and asking questions of patients or pre-patients entering the room. Around this time, amendments to compensation laws were being enacted to rein in the number of Chernobyl claims. The World Bank, promoting drastic reductions of the state's social welfare coffers, called the Chernobyl compensation system a "dead weight" on Ukraine's less than ideal market transition. The following interactions capture the sense and flow of desperate appeals linked to a right of entry to a state-protected sick role.

A rural woman walks in. She has been evacuated from her village in the Zone. When she says how her daughter was pregnant at the time of the disaster, she starts to cry. "The little girl," she says, "now 10 years old, has a dry mouth, she's weak, her thinking is slow, her thyroid is swollen. Her legs hurt. Her blood indicators are poor." She works hard to elicit sympathy from the administrator, who will eventually decide whether the girl will become state-protected. He interrupts the grandmother and tells her that she is in the wrong place and should go to the Chernobyl children's hospital for evaluation of the child's status.

A man in his mid-fifties enters. He says that he has worked at the reactor site since 1978, and that he regularly checks in at the local clinic of the Chernobyl plant for monitoring and treatment. The man makes a reasonably good salary working in the Zone but he also keeps careful records of his illnesses. He shows evidence of his dose, a high 73 rem. When I ask him why he is seeing the state official only now he says, "I'm sick." The administrator then asks him, "And before?" The man answers that he was sick, but that he "hid it." When I ask him why, he answers, "So I could work in the Zone. I'm used to working." He did not want to be seen as sick so that he could continue his well-paid but highly dangerous work.

A middle-aged urban woman enters the office. She says that her husband died three days ago and that she is seeking additional state protections. Her husband, a driver by profession, worked in the Zone in two-week shifts, transporting contaminated building materials from the reactor to "burial pits" scattered throughout the Zone. She lives on a pension of US$26.00. He collected a pension of US$75 before his cancer-related death. "Was there a Chernobyl pension already calculated in his regular pension?" the state official asks her.

"Yes, an added $16 a month for work in the Zone," she answers.

"Did you get compensation for his death?" he asks.

"Just for his funeral," she says.

"What do you want here?" the official asks.

The woman answers, "My husband said to me, 'When I die, get the Chernobyl privileges.'"

Faced with unbearable physical and economic burdens, patients and families were increasingly called upon to set a price on their survival, to create assets out of sickness, which could be used to leverage the state for compensation. In this case, the deceased calculated in advance the benefits to his family of his Chernobyl-related death. His wife "inherited" his medical documents, using them to push for greater social protection from the state.

Another man enters the room. He shows the Chernobyl administrator documents from a specialized examination. The man worked at the nuclear plant for eight months. He alleges that he has acute radiation dermatitis, "diagnosed in Moscow." The official tells him that there are no disability privileges associated with acute radiation dermatitis. The diagnosis he needs is skin cancer. After the man leaves, the official explains to me that "in general, disability is no longer given for acute radiation sickness. However, if a person shows complications from the effects of acute radiation sickness, he would be entitled to consideration. Skin cancer would count."

What these vignettes tell us is that who has the right of entry to the sick role, and who has the right of recovery from disease, are never settled and are subject to a variety of constraints. Denials were often based on poorly documented evidence of exposure or on the principle that the patients' illnesses had developed beyond the accepted time limits. Spurious diagnostics were also applied that did not match the disease or symptomatology in question. Overall, few formal rules guided the allocation of privileges. Some individuals pleaded for them; others were given advice about informal clinical procedures to expedite their applications. The new Ukrainian state, faced with too many people claiming to have been made sick by Chernobyl, conceded that it could not afford to compensate everyone, even if they *were* sick, while other claimants, even if they were sick, preferred not to be identified as such for fear of losing a lucrative job in the Chernobyl Zone. The effects of this government approach to the allocation of the sick role played out almost daily in this research center where I conducted fieldwork.

"We Don't See Patients, We See Data"

Just across the border from Ukraine, in Poland and the Czech Republic, other stories, other banishments from a sick role were taking form in the context of a growing global clinical trial industry. Physicians I knew who tended to Chernobyl sufferers routinely expressed eagerness to learn how to conduct clinical trials and to attract clinical trial contracts from multinational pharmaceutical sponsors owing to the abundance of various untreated diseases. They were also eager because the scientific infrastructures on which they were dependent were quickly deteriorating without state funding. The combination of local public health crises and commercial and scientific interest led to the sudden revaluing of patients who themselves had lost state protection in the form of guaranteed health care. Particular characteristics of populations would make these patient resources visible not only to the state, but to capital as well. A new global economy of experimentation was being formalized without adequate regard to its underlying insecurities. It was not quite the dream "of Neel, Chagnon, and their gold-rush, tourist-hunting allies 'to turn the Yanomami's homeland into the world's largest private reserve,' a six-thousand square-mile research station and 'biosphere' administered by themselves" (Geertz 2001: 21). But scientists' rush to reconceptualize their object of study "not as a people but as a population" (21) to be brokered as valued research subjects on the pharmaceutical world scene was certainly there.

Trials moved to Poland because of available professional expertise, English-language proficiency, and especially high rates of certain untreated diseases. Given the collapse of basic health care there, patient enrollment in clinical trials is said to be quick. Postsocialist healthcare systems are conducive to running efficient trials because they remain centralized. High literacy rates in this region mean that subjects offer more "meaningful" informed consent, thus smoothing potential regulatory problems in the future. Patients enrolled in trials, promised the same proton-pump inhibitors, serotonin boosters, antipsychotics, and beta-blockers that have now become a permanent feature of many human bloodstreams in the United States.

One former public health specialist and Czech physician turned clinical trial professional recounted to me in 2006 how he spent two decades transforming what he calls "non-competitive health infrastructures" (ailing postsocialist centralized health systems) into competitive "clinical trial markets" in central eastern Europe. Dr. Stanek saw the presence of clinical research as an indicator of his country's move from political collapse to economic competitiveness: "There was a quiet and chaotic transition at all levels of societies, including the public health services and its privatization, restructuring, and of course, research. State-governed research had collapsed. Of course, I am not saying everything was bad, just that our society was not competitive." A regulatory void was crucial in providing a foothold for this emergent competition for patients and political economy of research.

Stanek spoke of phases in the life cycle of clinical trial markets. Between the lines of his description one can hear how patients are dislodged from a sick role as they enter into a new and intricate system of standardized drug-testing. The first stage is the gold rush period: "For companies it was cheap. They got good data quick," according to Stanek. He continued: "There was a need for services, and all of a sudden Western companies realized the huge potential here. The people were not being treated by medicines that were available in the West, so it was quite attractive. We had many untreated populations, people you could hardly find in the US or western Europe. We had extremely high recruitment rates." Stanek's narrative leaves no doubt regarding clinical research as a social good. Being part of a trial for Western medicines is equated with an act of self-rescue because it is better than nothing. This first stage of reframing patients as subjects was "the opportune moment," he said, when most central eastern Europeans could barely afford new Western medications and the state was not willing or able to pay for them either.

The second stage of this experimental life cycle – the peak moment – arrives when patients see clinical trials, according to this professional, as a "normal part of health delivery." The identity of patient and subject folds into one: "People no longer view trial participation in terms of being examined, like rabbits." At this stage, clinical trials supplement or become a surrogate to public health needs. With the flow of trials and human and financial capital, governments foster a culture of regulation and compliance – however soft or simulated that culture may be – but with all the means of supporting commercial work. The same monitoring that led to "robust" data is also a thin veil for otherwise weak legal and medical infrastructures and, ultimately, conceals emergent voids in patient protection. It is interesting to observe the kind of agency Stanek ascribes to patients. They chase elusive medicines that aren't there; there is a calculative structure to the madness of finding subjects, and to the madness of finding care.

In my fieldwork in Poland, for example, I learned that some physicians who were considered "too sympathetic" toward their patients and public health needs could not be trusted to carry out industry-sponsored research. Their recruiters branded them as potential "protocol violators" who had a tendency to overenroll patients for medicinal purposes. Arguably, there and elsewhere, physician-investigators were valued to the extent that they can privatize patient–doctor relations and re-embed them in global experimental networks aimed at data capture, all the while distancing themselves from the long-term public health implications of their work. During the first two stages, professionals are very careful "not to mix up clinical trials with clinical care. We don't see patients, we see data."

Then the moment comes when these trial markets become exhausted, the third stage. At this stage, "trials start to migrate eastward, to Ukraine, Russia, Uzbekistan, and Kazakhstan." According to Stanek, there are too many firms competing for investigators, who begin to get "too choosy" and charge the equivalent of western European prices for their expertise. This trials expert conceived of subjects as being temporarily loyal and after a while "they no longer see advantage in trial participation. They leave the trials," he said. People begin to access drugs from state institutions or to pay for them out of pocket. At a point of increased competitiveness for the right kind of patients, and when regulations start to be less flexible, he said, "It simply becomes too expensive for us, just like in the US, western Europe, and Canada." In the end, the globalized clinical trial seemingly floats away, transforming public health care into an ever greater mosaic of private sector involvement and mounting patient demand for new drugs.

Indeed, some of the dysfunction of the US system has been globalized by a transnational pharmaceutical industry, in part, by "manufacturing demand by marketing expensive and unaffordable drugs to developing countries in the guise of research trials" (Annas 2010).[2] In the United States, health is presented as if it were a homogeneous product like a car or a bar of soap to be bought and sold at some optimum price by rational actors whose actions are not limited by any external influence: no messy politics of access, insurance, or gatekeeping practices in the march toward "first best outcomes."[3] Over the course of my research in central eastern Europe, I observed how ideas and ideals of (coming) health markets in transitioning countries such as Poland were imagined and deployed by the professionals involved. I also saw how some people with rare disorders who would never normally have access to needed medicines enrolled in trials. They began to understand their own contribution to the logic of value, cost, and sacrifice in research in particular terms. One lets go of the sick role when one becomes a trial subject. But when the trial was over, the patients with rare disorders had no sick role to return to, in part because of the overwhelming burden of paying for the medicines they were first tested with.

From Patients to Subjects

In the meantime, debate over the ethics of the provision of less than standard care in clinical trials in treatment-scarce settings continues. In an earlier essay (Petryna 2005), I took the controversy over placebo use in Africa in 1994 during trials of short-course AZT treatment to halt perinatal transmission of HIV as a focal point in the debate over ethical standards in global clinical research and of the role of ethical variability in constructing global subjects. I traced the relation between regulation and the evolution of ethical standards in human research, and how subject populations are created at the intersection of regulatory deliberation, commercial interest, and crisis (upon crisis) of public health. The impact of the debate over the ethics of placebo use on actual practice was not what bioethicists might have predicted.

Recent debates over the content of ethical guidelines such as the Helsinki Declaration have focused on the ethics of making exceptions to the provision of best treatment (specifically around the ethics of placebo control) in clinical trials. Are researchers obligated to provide the best treatment in a resource- or infrastructure-poor setting? The debate has not been resolved. The lack of consensus on the issue is indicative of a broader confusion that persists around the Declaration's intent and audience – does it stand for the care and "dignity" of the patient, or is it ever more strictly about the ethics of research? Is the Declaration written for doctors or for researchers? Who makes up the medical community that the Declaration, written almost 50 years ago, seeks to address?

I participated in a recent (2011) World Medical Association expert conference on the ethics of the placebo control in clinical trials. When I raised these issues, the secretary-general was adamant that the Helsinki Declaration, originally adopted in 1964, was written by doctors for doctors ("for world physicians") and aimed at "raising the general standards of professional conduct."[4] My concern was that any further move toward creating exceptions, which the World Medical Association is considering, continues to overinvest physician-researchers with the moral power to decide who *is* and who *is not* a patient. The Declaration was never meant to give physicians legitimate reason to unfasten patients from their sick role.

What follows is an example from Poland of how an ethical document (the Helsinki Declaration) "allows" for this unfastening to take place. It is generally known that the clinical trials industry searches for patients for whom refusing trial participation would be less of an option. The language of subject coercion or of rational choice, however, does not fully capture the processes that turn patients into subjects, placebo subjects in this case. No matter how important some regulators say a placebo trial is from a scientific standpoint (Petryna 2009), there is nothing obvious or easy about recruiting patients, especially untreated ones, for a placebo-control study. The promise of an incipient consumer-patienthood is part of a carrot-and-stick method that makes experimental scenarios possible.

An experienced human subjects recruiter in eastern Europe gave me insights into how ideas of incipient consumer-patienthood can help drive subject recruitment – while rendering concerns over subject coercion obsolete. A key factor driving trial globalization is a US regulatory requirement to test new drugs using a placebo control. A placebo is an inactive treatment made to appear like real treatment; it amounts to no treatment. (In some cases it may be better to be on a placebo rather than on an experimental drug.) US Food and Drug Administration (FDA) drug regulators remain very committed to the placebo for scientific reasons (Petryna 2005), but most people who are sick generally don't want to be on the placebo arm of the study. This means that many trial protocols originating in the United States will "float" to other countries where there are people willing to be on a placebo-controlled study. While US regulators require placebo studies for drug approval, it is not at all obvious how people in the world become placebo subjects.

Dr. Król, whom I met in Warsaw in 2005, led his firm's expansion in eastern Europe and oversees the activities of its clinical trial monitors. Very polite and austere, Król was known for his pinpoint accuracy in identifying and fixing potential errors in the clinical trial documentation process. He told me of an "enterprising" way in which to enlist untreated patients who could not afford their medications for a placebo-control study, *but to do so in an ethical way.* "We all know," he told me, "that it is unethical to withdraw treatment from patients during a trial. If a patient can get the required treatment where they live, then we certainly cannot withhold treatment or use the placebo." But for a patient with a newly diagnosed condition, say hypertension, withholding treatment is ethically justified. That is because you cannot put the second patient immediately on the medication anyway. It is totally acceptable to wait and see if, say, the patient's hypertension can be controlled by nonpharmaceutical means." A patient can be treated "through diet, less salt, exercise," Król added.

This lifestyle treatment approach – potentially positive in its own right – was a mere stepping stone to turn this hypothetical and treatment-needy hypertension patient into an untreated placebo subject. The recruiter's task here is to identify people who are in a "window" of nontreatment. But that window, as Król suggests, must be engineered. In this window, patients will be diagnosed and told about their condition. They will learn about a new treatment that is available elsewhere but is unaffordable for them. Lastly, they will be told that they would have a 50 percent chance of getting the treatment if they sign up for the placebo-controlled trial. Here consent is culturally reoriented toward the pharmaceutical and toward a consumer-patienthood that is yet to be realized. For Król, the moment of informed consent is when patients are fully informed and fully exposed to the realities of the pharmaceutical market which excludes them. The sick role is bypassed and, as with Franz Kafka's wounded patient who whispers into the ear of the country doctor who visits him – "You make my deathbed more narrow" (1997: 36) – the intriguing process through which a person comes to "voluntarily" consent to participate in a trial is not easily observed in this ethical transparency.

I have written about this recruitment process as a consequence of organized regulatory and ethical processes in which populations, either by intention or by default, can be reworked as objects of experiments ("experimentality"). While ethical rules are designed to protect *subjects*, they do not always protect *patients*. Clinical trials come and go, and their contractual aspects do not always spell out clearly how patients will be protected (i.e., treated) after the trial ends. But those ethics, as I show in the next case, can also be partly undone via a hard-won patienthood that re-establishes the terms of therapeutic engagement and opens up possibilities for recovery. In the following case I am interested in how a patient recreates structures of care and asserts not only a right to be protected or a right to health, but also a right to recovery.

Entrar No Justice: Patient-Litigants

In Brazil for example, where I conducted research on access to high-cost genetic therapies, I encountered people and problems that made the postclinical trial experience much messier and less easy to leave than this professional's narrative suggested. The trial became a public health trial; many issues, such as post-trial access to medications, were left unresolved.

From 2007–8, I followed a case in which both trial subjects and investigators had no way of protecting patients after a clinical trial. Brazilian physicians were testing a new therapy for a rare inherited disorder. Advanced-stage patients who had never received any treatment were recruited, according to the study protocol's requirements. Their director wanted the trial because of the needed resources it would bring. Without his colleagues' knowledge, he agreed to the biotech company's demand to reserve the right to withdraw the drug at any time – this was written into the consent forms that the patients signed. Informally, however, the company agreed to provide medication for two years, and it continued to do so for a third year. The drug worked well. But, without notice, the company withdrew the study drug. A company representative hinted to the clinicians that Brazil was too slow in registering the drug. Company lawyers had contacted the patients to form a patient activist group to pressure the government to buy these drugs (which can cost up to US$200,000 per patient annually). This effort failed. Later, I learned that the company running the trial had been sold. Whatever had led to the withdrawal, clinicians had no institutional recourse. Their advanced-stage patients would suffer immensely because of the lack of the drug.

A middle-aged man, Inacio Santos, had had symptoms of the disease since adolescence. He came from the country's interior to take part in the trial, but was now trying to make sense of the new medical and legal challenge of how to access the drug after the trial abruptly ended. "Most people with the disease at my age," he said, "were already dead or had killed themselves." I asked him if the treatment had extended his life. "I have survived," he answered, "I chose to participate. I could have chosen not to do anything, and maybe I would not be talking to you today. But there is no way I can know the actual impact of the study." And investigators were bound by protocol to not tell him whether or not it was worthwhile for him to go home and live out his remaining days.

Inacio's deliberations took place within a complicated web of expectations and abiding medical trust. "The only document I remember signing said that I was not responsible for paying the bill for anything. For two years they even provided me with a full tank of gas." In case the treatment worked, "those patients who were willing to continue were told they were going to have continued treatment until they died." Inacio and other patients couldn't understand how a company had been allowed to begin a trial and could now be exempt from the legal responsibility to continue providing the treatment. "We exposed ourselves to the drug without knowing if it was or was not going to work. Some benefits the company had. We didn't die." Inacio's life was precariously tethered to a new medical commodity, but who would be responsible for his treatment access? Who would pay? How was he actually doing medically? All were open questions.

Meanwhile, the "judicialization of the right to health" – or the recent swell of access-oriented and rights-based judicial demands – has become the public arena in which public and private health actors and sectors confront each other and where patient-litigants press for their right to health, understood as medication. All this happens in the context of an uncontested market and acquiescent regulatory state while questions of health systems reform, sustainability, and the social determinants of health are not addressed (Biehl et al. 2009; Petryna 2009).

Inacio resisted becoming a patient-litigant at first, but finally joined a class action suit against the state. The question of Inacio's treatment was temporarily settled when the highest court in the state of Rio Grande do Sul, through majority opinion, required the drug-maker to continue providing the treatment to those who did not have the means. The drug-maker, sensing an impending media scandal around these patients, finally conceded and provided treatment for some patients.

When I spoke to him recently, Inacio was hard of hearing and had experienced five ministrokes in the past three years. His physician was helping to organize his medical paperwork to obtain back taxes that were owed to him due to his disabled status. His disease had progressed far more rapidly than those in his cohort of clinical trial subjects. Of the five patients on the trial three were obtaining their medicines through direct provision by the manufacturer, and two were receiving them through the government. What he wanted me to understand about his treatment odyssey was that he and the other patients compelled the chief of the service to "take care of us." As a trial subject, Inacio contributed to the remaking of biomedical science and markets around an unprecedented high-cost treatment for a rare disease. "You agreed to this trial, you took on this responsibility for us, now act like a doctor," he told me, recounting what he had said to the chief. Inacio challenged the doctor-researcher to become a doctor and to recognize Inacio as *his* patient. As for the cost of the drug, he said, "I don't know the cost of the drug." He was now a patient; he didn't need to know it. His awareness of the full cost of his survival was much more palpable to him as a patient (and to me).

Implicated in the right of recovery is a series of other empirical questions such as: How do patients gain a sense of value of their own participation in the broad political economy of health? How do they resist sacrifice (of themselves or of others) as a predominant political strategy of healthcare access? In the hybrid structures of transnational medicine, economic trickle-down theories of technology access are being challenged (Cutler et al. 2006). And in the lives of these very sick patients, we learn what is at stake (health, a future, dignity, family, and political belonging) in the struggle for the sick role.

The New Nature of Medical Deviance

Inês kept saying to me, "I am a number, I am just a number there." She is a 55-year-old Brazilian mother of four daughters who for the last decade has suffered from an untreatable and often fatal lung disorder (a type of pulmonary hypertension) that is resistant to current treatments. Once she learned that her breathing difficulties were linked to this particular rare disorder, she was able to find a specialist through a network of family and friends. Inês tried the standard plan of medical care, but it did not work for her. To help with her symptoms, she took five other medications. In 2008 her pulmonologist invited Inês to participate in a trial for a new medicine for someone with her exact medical condition. Knowing that Inês was a "good" patient – reliable, compliant – the doctor pressed hard for her to join the trial, which he thought would be of benefit to her medically. The trial had a placebo arm. After much discussion in her family, Inês decided to join the trial because she "trusted the doctor," she told me.

For the first three months, the study was double-blind, meaning that no one, including the patient-subject and the physician-researcher, would know who was on the placebo and who was on the active arm. After three months, patients would learn who was getting what. Complications, however, began to arise. Inês, the trusted patient, stopped taking the experimental pills that she had been given. "The doctor chastized me. He told me that I couldn't come back to the clinic with all these extra, leftover pills." Every pill Inês took or didn't take was counted, monitored. "I told my doctor that I am taking too many pills already, a diuretic, a heart pill, a high blood pressure pill, I can't take any more pills!" Her doctor responded, "If you are going to skip any medicines, *skip the ones you are taking now*, not the experimental one!" Inês continued to be a noncompliant subject, but when she realized (given her palpable physical improvements) that she was probably not on the placebo arm, she initiated a different sort of conversation with her physician: "I asked the doctor, 'What happens to me afterwards? Who is going to take care of me? I will take your pill only if you guarantee that I will have this treatment after the trial.'" I realized in the course of our discussion over unconsumed pills that she was using her noncompliance as a way of leveraging the doctor's care and commitment to her well-being.

Importantly, Inês did not want to become a "patient-litigant" like Inacio; she didn't want to sue the state for treatment access (Biehl and Petryna 2011). Indeed, many physician-researchers in Brazil encourage patient-subjects who lack access to newly tested technologies to "judicialize"; Inês used the expression *entrar na justiça*, "to enter the judiciary" (or, literally, "to enter justice") to refer to this process. However, cases can take years to reach a verdict. Most defendants ask for temporary court injunctions and if these are granted, they can receive treatment immediately.[5] But patients can also be trapped in an endless cycle of requesting new court injunctions, depending on the judge.[6] Already in the third stage of her disease, Inês said, "Judicializing would surely take me into stage 4."

As Inês's case shows, access to new medical technologies opens up tenuous spaces not only between treatment and research, but also research and recovery. As people's counterknowledge becomes integral to the structure of the trials themselves, it has the potential to protect patients from the consumer-patient fantasy of the health market or the vagaries of suing the state, a process that they may never have the conditions (or in Inês's and Inacio's case, time and physical stamina) to truly attend to. Inês's sense of a *right to recovery*, like Inacio's, was linked to her keen awareness of her individual contribution as a clinical trial subject and what, therefore, was owed to her: continued care. Inês told me that throughout this trial she "almost lost her future." Now she has recovered it, "now I am living in the present."

In my long-term engagement with trial entrepreneurs and researchers, I encountered concrete and trackable sources of failure in systems of human subject protection, but I also found stories of how those failures (particularly with regard to recurrent failures to provide treatment after a trial for very sick patients) could be potentially addressed. While clinical trials may have become a surrogate to public health in some countries where research is carried out, reasonable estimates of how much drug companies actually invest in terms of treatments and experimental medicines is not available. For patients, being in a clinical trial has become a reasonable part of a set of health-seeking practices, but there continues to be a general absence of sustained debate over the politics of clinical research and specifically about the nature of pro-patient policies. Participation in trials may exacerbate the uncertainties of disease. And what I found consistently true in my work is that getting treatment after the trial was never easy.

Sick Role Rejoinders

Within mid-century medical sociology, Parsons's structural-functionalist approach to healthcare systems and his theory of the sick role were the subjects of considerable debate. The work of several scholars shifted the field's gaze from the macro-level "social system" to micro-level individual social interactions (Hafferty and Castellani 2006; Conrad 2007), and developed complex notions of patienthood that can partly account for the novel illness experiences above. In particular, Anselm Strauss, Erving Goffman, and Eliot Freidson – three prominent mid-century sociologists trained at the University of Chicago in the school of symbolic interactionism (Conrad 2007: 141) – each took day-to-day interactions between individuals as a point of departure for their sociological work on patienthood, but remained locked in the doctor–patient dyad as the classic therapeutic locus.

Anselm Strauss (with Barney Glaser) nuanced Parson's analysis of the sick role by attending to the event structures of illness. Studying terminal patients and later patients with chronic illnesses, Strauss proposed the idea of a variable "illness trajectory" which captures how the contingencies of individual illness experiences and the possibilities opened up by new medical technologies determine the kinds of medical work that surround the patient, particularly with respect to end-of-life care (Strauss and Glaser 1970). Clearly this idea of a trajectory has relevance today. "The illness, treatment, other pertinent social conditions," and the temporalities of illness or "*trajectory phases*" can alter the "schemas of the physician and of the patient" (Baszanger 1998: 364; emphasis original). Strauss's focus on daily interaction also opened up analytical room for thinking about "the *patient as an actor* in the medical work and analysis of the different components of patients' work" (365; emphasis original).

Freidson and Goffman's analyses further nuanced the event structure of the illness experience as well as to patienthood as a form of work. Both explored divergent notions of the "career" as a more useful analytic than a discrete social "role" when thinking about patienthood (Freidson 1970a: 224–243; see also Goffman 1961; Freidson 1970b: 14). Goffman, for example, does not take the likelihood of the patient's acceptance of the sick role for granted. In his notion of "prepatients" (which he described as the stage of alienation and medical labeling), class and culture inform whether the patient will accept his label. The self is socially (re)constructed in light of one's becoming/having become mentally ill. Unlike the emphasis in anthropology on agentive self-making, the patient's "moral career" is a trajectory in which, ultimately, social relations and institutions of control through which the patient passes begin to constitute the patient's self (Goffman 1961: 127–169; see esp. 168).

Of these three sociologists, Freidson most directly engages with Parsons's specific formulation of the sick role. In his seminal book *Profession of Medicine* (1970a), he draws insights from other sociologists, particularly Goffman, to deconstruct elements of Parsons's sick role – particularly around the notion of deviance. Specifically, Freidson theorizes that the (involuntary) social deviance caused by illness can come in a *range of forms* and that these forms vary with the physiological severity of the illness, the temporality of the illness (i.e., whether it is acute or chronic) and the level of Goffmanian stigmatization of that illness. Freidson rethought illness trajectories in terms of the variety of potential interactions which might yield a variety of sick roles, of which Parsons's is only one. In Goffman's and Freidson's accounts, patients move through multiple roles in the course of the same illness and through multiple agents of social control as relief from illness is sought.

Be it in the realm of fragmented illness trajectories, of patienthood conceptualized as work, or in the new varieties of potential deviance, these sociological critiques of the sick role pinpoint problems in the conceptualization of disease and recovery that are still relevant today. Suing the state for medicines as a patient-litigant, "working" to be sick so as to guarantee care, or being noncompliant in a clinical trial to attract a doctor's care and attention are all new types of patient "social deviance" that challenge medical institutions and a current ethics of care. While the doctor–patient relationship is often viewed as the "prototypical" healing relationship, specific doctor–patient relationships can vary considerably, as can the relationships between patients and the range of nonprofessional healers they may consult (Freidson 1970b: 14–15). As the nature of the doctor–patient relationship shifts with changes in the medical marketplace (i.e., the rise of prepaid insurance contracts), for Freidson, conflict between doctors and patients becomes a more useful analytic (Freidson 1980: 41–54).[7]

In the view of Strauss, Goffman, and Freidson, the fact of being ill and its outcome is a function of contingencies that operate throughout the disease and recovery process and that shape different patient "roles" beyond the sick role.[8] In spite of their relevance, these critics still assume optimality as a normal biomedical function. High treatment costs, for example, disinvest the patient/sick role in multiple ways, a process that neither Parsons nor his critics seriously anticipated. As I have shown in this essay, the *locus classicus* of health has moved beyond the doctor–patient relationship. Yet, in light of other paramedical authorities, a new ethic of patient care and a politics of recovery is still to be worked out.

A Right to Recovery

What I have conveyed from my own fieldwork is that in different settings health, or the experience of sickness and the work of recovery, has progressively been displaced from the clinic and the doctor–patient relationship to precarious social institutions, domestic spaces, and experimental settings that themselves enact distinct moralities that may or may not insure patients' access to the sick role, but indeed to some other role (such as trial subject, activist, litigant, sufferer). And the sick role has become a precarious vehicle at best for patients to obligate doctors to *doctor*. That is because in recent years, doctors have become governed by various externalities (for-profit research agendas, insurance company algorithms, court orders, evidence-based medical protocols, for example), introducing conflicting values regulating their behavior and the amount and quality of care that is doled out. At stake is how patients make sense of these moralities to create and enact a politics of recovery (or to avoid harm) – not only in clinical but also in juridical and experimental settings – all the obvious and not so obvious settings of recovery that are part of a global political economy of health.

Whether they are biological citizens, placebo subjects, patient-consumers or patient-litigants, the sick, perhaps like never before, are being confronted with the full cost of their survivorship. Claims about "more technology equaling better health outcomes" (Cutler et al. 2006) must be tempered by the on-the-ground realities and struggles of patients in Ukraine, Brazil, Poland and in US health care to address the *demise* of the sick role. This essay traced the intellectual geography of the sick role and the new anthropological realities that have dislodged patients from that role. The medical and cultural availability of the sick role is limited for many patients today. Recovery has become much more idiosyncratic and unpredictable or much less guaranteed or even calculable. Recovery from disease, *actual* recovery – involving continued access to proper medicines say, in the context of clinical trials; or access to state health guarantees, say in the aftermath of a nuclear disaster – are new problems that are beyond biomedicine but that also pose challenges to its ethics and expertise.

What I have also tracked in this essay is how the sick themselves "recapture" the sick role within non-optimal medical settings, recreating some form of "efficacious collusion" that the concept of the sick role generally aspires to. The fine-grained social realities of patients on whom the burden of recovery lies and their subjacent sociopolitical worlds beg for analytic attention that would allow for people-centered evidence to add up and matter publicly – beyond the rhetoric of rights, access, economic trickle-down, or individual consumer choice.

How patients – be they in a clinical trial, an insurance pool, a struggling household, or a litigant and activist group – gain a sense of value of their own participation in the broad political economy of health must be further explored. How they apply self- and social knowledge to resist sacrifice as a political strategy of healthcare access must also be addressed. Anthropology's close attentiveness to patients' visions of themselves creates holes in dominant theories and modi operandi. How ordinary people gather together resources in non-optimal or overburdened health and legal systems to assert their rights to health and thus to survive is part of a neglected social science of survival. By attending to moral dimensions of recovery, we can reimagine the agency of the afflicted and affirm a social fabric of recoverable life in transnational medicine.

NOTES

1 In the context of humanitarianism, Fassin writes of these bureaucratic relations in terms of an inequality between those who have the freedom to sacrifice versus those who have the fate of being sacrificed. He notes: "In contemporary society this inequality is perhaps both the most ethically intolerable, in that it concerns the meaning of life itself, and the most morally tolerated, since it forms the basis for the principle of altruism" (2007a: 507).

2 In other words, high costs disinvest the patient/sick role in multiple ways, a process that Parsons did not anticipate in his sociological scheme.

3 Such "perfectly competitive" images of health rarely give any hint of true outcomes. For example, there is a long-running newspaper advertisement some of us may have seen. It is for a premier cancer hospital on the east coast of the United States in which a patient holds a handwritten note to the camera. "Nice try, cancer," one note reads. "Cancer, you said I'd never bear children," reads another. The message is that we can outwit the fate of terrible diseases by exercising the power of our consumer choice: choosing wisely in the health market will yield "first best outcomes" for patients, that outcome being survival in these cases. "Where you're treated first can make all the difference." Meanwhile, economists readily concede that this idea of health violates almost all of the requirements for markets to yield first best (health) outcomes (Brief Amici Curiae 2010: 4).

4 At http://www.wma.net/en/60about/70history/index.html, accessed Mar. 6, 2012. The text continues: "It noted that in those years the custom of medical schools to administer an oath to its doctors upon graduation or receiving a license to practice medicine had fallen into disuse or become a mere formality."

5 The injunction prevents irreparable harm and works as a safety net for the judge's conscience.

6 We have also found that treatments distributions can be stalled. As a result, treatments are interrupted, compromising adherence and health outcomes. Some people die before a final decision is reached.

7 In an article memorializing Freidson's life, Charles Bosk (2006) points to the democratic project in Freidson's work: Freidson was concerned about the power imbalance between experts and laymen in a modern democracy, the inability of professionals (especially physicians) to regulate themselves ethically, and the freedom (or lack thereof) of the patient to make choices about his own treatment.

8 In their analyses of the day-to-day work of practicing medicine, medical anthropologists have also shown how moralities of medicine and health do not exist in a vacuum but co-construct distinct patient roles and health outcomes. Medical anthropological studies indicate an array of difference with respect to the metaphors and meanings that signify health. More recently, they have been particularly concerned with the transformations in health as those transformations express differences in power, social position, and social

inequality, particularly as experienced by marginal groups and individuals. The very economic, technical, and industrial development that has benefited so many coexists with ongoing massive societal disruptions. A production of suffering and death comes via inadequate public health measures, violence, demographic changes, travel, and other human actions that intensify the flows and resistance of pathogens. Anthropological studies have emphasized the importance of understanding patterns of everyday life experience, local knowledge, and social networks that influence personal agency and access to health care, as well as modes of transmission of diseases. Where they first focused on illness whose event structure was relatively defined, today it is hard to find a disease experience or trajectory that is not shaped by interactions with social, political, or transnational institutions (see, among many others, Scheper-Hughes 1992; Kleinman and Petryna 2002; Farmer 2004; Kaufman 2005; Das and Das 2006; Biehl 2007; Fassin 2007b; Adams et al. 2008; Nichter 2008; Whitmarsh 2008; Rouse 2009; Rylko-Bauer et al. 2009; James 2010; Nguyen 2010; Whyte et al. 2010; Inhorn and Wentzell 2012).

REFERENCES

Adams, Vincanne, Novotny, Thomas, and Leslie, Hannah (2008) Global Health Diplomacy. *Medical Anthropology* 12(4): 315–323.

Annas, George (2010) Globalizing Pharmaceutical Trials. *Nature Medicine* 16: 262.

Baszanger, Isabelle (1998) The Work Sites of an American Interactionist: Anselm L. Strauss, 1917–1996. *Symbolic Interaction* 21(4): 353–377.

Biehl, João (2007) *Will to Live: AIDS Therapies and the Politics of Survival*. Princeton: Princeton University Press.

Biehl, João and Petryna, Adriana (2011) Bodies of Rights and Therapeutic Markets. *Social Research* 78(2): 359–394.

Biehl, João, Petryna, Adriana, Gertner, Alex, et al. (2009) Judicialization of the Right to Health in Brazil. *The Lancet* 373: 2182–2184.

Bosk, Charles (2006) Avoiding Conventional Understandings: The Enduring Legacy of Eliot Freidson. *Sociology of Health and Illness* 28(5): 637–653.

Brief Amici Curiae of Economic Scholars in Support of Defendants (2010) State of Florida, by and through Bill McCollum, et al., Plaintiffs, v. United States Department of Health and Human Services, et al., Defendants. Case No. 3:10-cv-91-RV/EMT. At http://www.justice.gov/healthcare/docs/florida-mccollum-v-hhs-summary-judgment-support.pdf, accessed Mar. 6, 2012.

Canguilhem, Georges (1978) The Normal and the Pathological. In *Knowledge of Life*, trans. Stefanos Geroulanos and Daniela Ginsburg; intro. Paola Marrati and Todd Meyers. New York: Fordham University Press, pp. 121–134.

Conrad, Peter (2007) Eliot Freidson's Revolution in Medical Sociology. *Health* 11(2): 141–144.

Cutler, David, Deaton, Angus, and Lleras-Muney, Adriana (2006) The Determinants of Mortality. *Journal of Economic Perspectives* 20(3): 97–120.

Das, Veena (1996) Language and Body: Transactions in the Construction of Pain. *Daedalus* 125(1): 67–91.

Das, Veena and Das, Ranendra K. (2006) Pharmaceuticals in Urban Ecologies: The Register of the Local. In Adriana Petryna et al. (eds.), *Global Pharmaceuticals: Ethics, Markets, Practices*. Durham, NC: Duke University Press, pp. 171–205.

Farmer, Paul (2004) *Pathologies of Power: Health, Human Rights, and the New War on the Poor*. Berkeley: University of California Press.

Fassin, Didier (2007a) Humanitarianism as a Politics of Life. *Public Culture* 19(3): 499–520.

Fassin, Didier (2007b) *When Bodies Remember: Experiences and Politics of AIDS in South Africa*. Berkeley: University of California Press.

Freidson, Eliot (1970a) *Profession of Medicine: A Study of the Sociology of Applied Knowledge*. New York: Harper & Row.

Freidson, Eliot (1970b) *Professional Dominance: The Social Structure of Medical Care*. Chicago: Aldine.

Freidson, Eliot (1980) *Doctoring Together: A Study of Professional Social Control*. Chicago: University of Chicago Press.

Geertz, Clifford (2001) Life among the Anthros. *New York Review of Books* 48(2): 18–22.

Goffman, Erving (1961) *Asylums: Essays on the Social Situation of Mental Patients and Other Inmates*. New York: Anchor.

Hafferty, Frederic and Castellani, Brian (2006) Medical Sociology. In Clifton Bryant and Dennis L. Peck (eds.), *21st Century Sociology: A Reference Handbook*, vol 1. Thousand Oaks, CA: Sage, pp. 331–338.

Inhorn, Marcia and Wentzell Emily A. (eds.) (2012) *Medical Anthropology at the Intersections*. Durham, NC: Duke University Press.

James, Erica (2010) *Democratic Insecurities: Violence, Trauma, and Intervention in Haiti*. Berkeley: University of California Press.

Kafka, Franz (1997) *A Country Doctor*. Prague: Twisted Spoon.

Kaufman, Sharon (2005) *… And a Time to Die: How American Hospitals Shape the End of Life*. New York: Scribner.

Kleinman, Arthur (2008) Catastrophe and Caregiving: The Failure of Medicine as an Art. *The Lancet*, 371: 22–23.

Kleinman, Arthur and Petryna, Adriana (2002) Health: Anthropological Perspectives. In *International Encyclopedia of the Social and Behavioral Sciences*. London: Elsevier Science, pp. 6495–6499.

Mol, Annemarie (2008) *The Logic of Care: Health and the Problem of Patient Choice*. New York: Routledge.

Nguyen, Vinh-Kim (2010) *The Republic of Therapy: Triage and Sovereignty in West Africa's Time of AIDS*. Durham, NC: Duke University Press.

Nichter, Mark (2008) *Global Health: Why Cultural Perceptions, Social Representations and Biopolitics Matter*. Tucson: University of Arizona Press.

Parsons, Talcott (1951) *The Social System*. Glencoe, IL: Free Press.

Petryna, Adriana (2002) *Life Exposed: Biological Citizens after Chernobyl*. Princeton: Princeton University Press.

Petryna, Adriana (2005) Ethical Variability: Drug Development and the Globalization of Clinical Trials. *American Ethnologist* 32(2): 183–197.

Petryna, Adriana (2009) *When Experiments Travel: Clinical Trials and the Global Search for Human Subjects*. Princeton: Princeton University Press.

Porter, Michael and Teisberg, Elizabeth (2006) *Redefining Health Care: Creating Value-Based Competition on Results*. Cambridge, MA: Harvard Business Press.

Rouse, Carolyn (2009) *Uncertain Suffering: Racial Health Disparities and Sickle Cell Disease*. Berkeley: University of California Press.

Rylko-Bauer, Barbara, Whiteford, Linda, and Farmer, Paul (eds.) (2009) *Global Health in Times of Violence*. Santa Fe, NM: SAR.

Scheper-Hughes, Nancy (1992) *Death without Weeping: The Violence of Everyday Life in Brazil*. Berkeley: University of California Press.

Strauss, Anselm and Glaser, Barney (1970) *Anguish: A Case History of a Dying Trajectory*. London: Martin Robertson.

Whitmarsh, Ian (2008) *Biomedical Ambiguity: Race, Asthma, and the Contested Meaning of Genetic Research in the Caribbean*. Ithaca, NY: Cornell University Press.

Whyte, Susan Reynolds, Whyte, Michael A., and Kyaddondo, David (2010) Health Workers Entangled: Confidentiality and Certification. In Hansjörg Dilger and Ute Luig (eds.), *Morality, Hope and Grief: Anthropologies of AIDS in Africa*. New York: Berghahn, pp. 80–101.

CHAPTER 22 Science

Michael M. J. Fischer

In Memoriam, Fritz Bach
b. Vienna, April 5, 1934,[1] d. Manchester-by-the-Sea, MA, August 14, 2011

Fritz had a donor: US$200 million to start an Institute for Ethics. Harvard was not interested, so I introduced Fritz to the MIT administration. President Charles Vest, Provost Bob Brown, and Chancellor Lawrence Bacow were interested. For several months we were on an exhilarating quest, including a visit to a penthouse with 360-degree views in New York City to meet the donor. Then came the dot.com stock market crash of 2000–2 and the donor decided to return to running his company rather than pursuing his interest in the Institute. MIT, a few years later, started some anemic programs in "ethics." But in the meantime Fritz's quest was a global effort to experiment with forms of civic decision-making about the incalculable risks of xenotransplantation.

Dr. Fritz Bach, a pioneer in immunology, was the inventor of the mixed leukocyte culture (MLC) test for selecting a best match for bone marrow transplant donors, a test that transformed the field, and proved to be a lifesaver for thousands of patients. He described the human leukocyte antigen Class II locus and its antigens, part of the major histocompatibility complex of the immune system, and made seminal discoveries in the immunogenetics of T cell immune responses. Fritz performed the world's first bone marrow transplant in the fall of 1968, published in *The Lancet* back to back with the paper by Robert Good at Minnesota who had concurrently successfully performed a BMT using Fritz's MLC test. In 1975 Fritz dramatically improved the speed with which the test could be performed. At Fritz's funeral, Dr. Paul Sondel, a close pediatrics colleague at Wisconsin with Fritz, spoke of a 14-year-old girl, a leukemia patient who had received a lifesaving bone marrow transplant at the University of Wisconsin. As it happened, she had just written to Fritz a few days

A Companion to Moral Anthropology, First Edition. Edited by Didier Fassin.

before his sudden heart attack, on the twenty-fifth anniversary of her 1986 operation, to report that she was healthy, married, and happy.

No nay-sayer to technology, Fritz loved the latest gadgets of all kinds, and delightedly showed me his voice-activated phone built into the dashboard of his Mercedes: "Call Peter," "Call home"). Fritz's quest in ethics when I got to know him was to warn against premature xenotransplantation of animal, in particular porcine, organs into humans. Fritz himself was a pioneer in the early research into xenotransplantation and its promise to make organs available to thousands of desperate human patients. Fritz's lab at Harvard's Beth Israel Deaconess Medical Center was working on the mysteries of long-term versus acute rejection of tissue or organs transplanted from one body to another and on the clinical application of the genetics of stress and inflammation. It was one of the first labs to which I had access, and among the first lab meetings that I attended. Fritz's infectious enthusiasm for the research process was palpable as he ran the lab meeting. He was worried, however, by reports he had heard of colleagues in Britain and elsewhere jumping the gun and voicing interest in experimenting with organ transplantation before fully understanding the risks involved. One of the key unknowns was the risk of retroviral infection across species. Pigs, in particular, are reservoirs of retroviruses different from those harbored by the human genome, some of which we know about and can test for. If there are others about which we are unaware, we would have no tests to screen for them. We might raise pigs in antiseptic environments, selecting for, or genetically engineering, pigs that carry none of the known retroviruses deleterious to humans, and still not be certain that living tissue from these animals might not cause pandemic disease in humans once they crossed the species barrier.

This was, Fritz liked to point out, an ethical problem quite unlike that of traditional medical ethics (decisions between doctors and patients about risks only to the patient) or even hospital ethics (decisions about family demands to provide extraordinary care versus physician ethics of not creating or extending suffering under futile circumstance or versus hospital and community concerns not to waste money on heroic but futile procedures at the expense of the care of other patients). This potentially involved the fate of human populations at large. After all, this was the age of the HIV-AIDS pandemic, thought to be caused by a species transfer of retrovirus from simians to humans, a much smaller species jump. It was, in addition, an opportunity, Fritz thought, for broad training in public understanding, and public decision-making about risks that might affect the public at large. At a simple level, Fritz would say, this is not a decision that should be left to doctors or research scientists. The risk of such unknown retroviruses jumping the species barrier might be, as many of his colleagues claimed, very small. And yet, were a very small probability to eventuate in virulent disease, the effect could be devastating. If it was a risk to the population at large, only the population at large could decide if the risk was worth the experimentation. Fritz, to be clear, was not opposed to the experimentation. He wanted the public to make the decision in a form of real, not just formal, informed consent.

How to go about such a process of education to allow for real informed consent was the challenge he set himself, and it would have been a topic for his projected Institute of Ethics.[2] After all, both the patients waiting for organs, and the need to fend off "cowboy" surgeons only too willing to experiment, were circumstances of urgency. China was widely mentioned in the press reports on xenotransplantation as one of the countries eager for the prestige of medical breakthrough, where regulatory structures were weak or nonexistent, and where "cowboy" surgeons might try such procedures. But even in Europe there were reports of shipping experimental animals from England to Holland or Italy to take advantage of differences in regulatory rules.

Fritz's campaign was not well received by many of his colleagues in xenotransplantation research. They argued that, whatever other merits Fritz's arguments might have, the effect of his public campaign was to make funding for their work, even under the tightest of regulatory controls, more difficult. But for Fritz, the stakes were higher than just funding, higher in two different registers.

First of all, there was the real, if probabilistically small, threat to human health if experimentation should go wrong. In this regard, such experimentation was not the only line of research available. Basic immunological work was advancing along several fronts: stem cell research, ethically contested on other grounds, was another advancing frontier of basic biology and immunology. If regenerative medicine could be made to work, the need for xenotransplantation would be much reduced, and the knowledge gained from stem cell regulation (dedifferentiation, redifferentiation, and epigenetic processes) might help provide tests and screens for xenotransplantation.

Second, this was an opportunity to learn how to create more informed publics upon which the legitimacy of medical research would depend and through which informed consent for risk could be made more realistic. Fritz envisioned, and implemented, a multipronged set of experiments in "reflexive social institution" building (Beck 1992 [1986]; Fischer 2003 2009; the term was not native to Fritz).[3] From the top, he convinced national parliaments in both the Third World and the First World (from Egypt and the Philippines to Holland and Canada) to establish parliamentary committees to discuss whether xenotransplantation should be pursued, and if so how it should be regulated, approached, or precautionarily staged (as for instance, had happened in the 1970s with recombinant DNA techniques, through the temporary moratorium, the Asilomar Conference of 1975, and the rules developed under the United States National Institutes of Health, with gradually relaxed rules as experience with the technique accumulated). From the bottom, Fritz organized high school multiweek short courses in immunology and the challenges of xenotransplantation, with role-playing exercises by patients, doctors, researchers, politicians, and regulators, visits to parliamentary committees, and ending with voting exercises. The idea was that these high school students would serve as ambassadors to organize similar exercises in other schools or community venues. At the meso level, Fritz and colleagues, such as former surgeon and now Toronto bioethics professor Abdullah Daar, held meetings at venues such as the Hastings Center (for medical ethics) in New York state, as a way to mobilize professionals both in medicine and medical ethics. These were exhilarating meetings involving student liaisons to the high school experiments as well as some parliamentarians, professional ethicists such as Daar, and importantly also some science journalists and former publishers from the Nature Publishing Group.

At our Health, Science, and Technology (HST) class at the Harvard Medical School, which Professors Mary-Jo DelVecchio Good and Byron Good and I have been teaching over the past decade and a half, I was privileged to bring Fritz for a number of years to engage first- and second-year medical students to begin thinking about these issues. Always available to dive into the technical details of the immunology and the mysteries of our increasing ability to control acute rejection of transplanted organs but not the longer-term processes of rejection, Fritz seemed much more engaged with the social questions of how to pioneer a broad, informed engagement of the public in matters that concern and affect everyone if not through disease, then at least through the proper direction and funding of research endeavors, legitimation of biomedical research on firm grounds, and institutions for pragmatic, exploratory, but not reckless, experimental science.[4]

The Bach example illustrates the various levels at which ethical decisions and moral sensibilities play out – from the level of science at the bench to institutional structures. "Bench-level ethics" involves not cheating (keeping proper lab notebooks, not falsifying data, giving proper credit, and so on), but also keeping one's moral and ethical equilibrium in efforts to game international journal and project reviewers in worlds where reviewers are often competitors and cannot always be expected to behave ethically. Credit and reputation, funding and institutional clout, are at stake. And so in these mid-level scientific tournaments one can track the switching points between individual ethics and how institutional legacies are created, as well as switching points in the macro level, for which Bach was striving, how public policy at the highest ethical and moral level can be institutionally constructed with broad legitimacy and understanding of the risks involved.

As biological and ecological sensibilities grow in the twenty-first century away from (or subsuming) the cultural dominance of the physics-based engineering of the twentieth century, a parallel recognition of the need for nonplebiscite modes of participatory decision-making are also being fostered. In the next section, examples from the twentieth-century International Biological Programs of the US National Institutes of Health are used to briefly sketch the shifting moralities of the quite different scientific enterprises of the 1960s and the 1990s along three axes: the ethics and institutional contexts of science (institutional review boards, codes of ethics, norms of informed consent, return of benefit, do no harm); the ways in which scientists, as well as many other actors in the scientific enterprise, become media players, complicating questions of who speaks for whom; and the palimpsest continuities and differences between, in this case, the human biology research projects (population genetics, sociobiology, human genome diversity project, health and epidemiological transition) of the 1960s and 1990s. In the third section, I then turn to a set of twenty-first-century crucibles, hieroglyphs or ethical plateaus of contested ethical and moral decision-making, before concluding with a brief reflection on the anthropological voice in these contemporary stakes, and a brief update of the biological research programs as they have morphed into twenty-first-century genomics and infectious disease programs.

Twentieth-Century Tools of Analysis

The US National Institutes of Health (NIH)'s International Biological Programs of the 1960s is one venue for seeing the changes in moral sensibilities and moral institutional structures over the course of late twentieth-century science, and for estimating changes as thought in the twenty-first century moves toward ever greater biological and ecological sensibilities and more holistic decision-making platforms. In the field of STS (science, technology, and society) these latter are signaled by such heuristic terms as "reflexive" or "second-order modernity" social institutions for decision-making

(Beck 1986; Fischer 2003, 2009), enunciatory communities (Fortun 2001), civic epistemologies that differ between similar advanced industrial societies producing different policy outcomes (Jasanoff 2007), parliaments of things that turn from matters of fact to matters of concern (Latour 2005), and more generally a concern in political theory for methods of participatory or deliberative politics using formats such as the interest in the Danish consensus conference model in the 1990s, and the interest in crowd sourcing in media theory, YouTube citizen journalism, and open-source web platforms, and recursive public spheres (Kelty 2008).

The International Biological Programs of the 1960s were a multiperson decades-long research endeavor, involving geneticists and anthropologists, and famously including the Yanomami and other groups in Amazonian Brazil, and the Fore and other groups in New Guinea. Many of these projects have long afterlives and successor projects. As one Brazilian anthropologist notes, the Yanomami in the 1960s watched physical samples (feces, saliva, urine) moving to Penn State and the University of Michigan, and in the 1990s a repeat of the movement, this time of DNA.

More dramatically, the solving of the kuru disease among the Fore by Carleton Gadjusek and colleagues (which gained him a Nobel Prize) was a precursor to contemporary concerns with mad cow disease, Creutzfeld-Jakob disease, and other prion-based encephalopathies, as well as the concern with the mechanisms of "slow viruses" and normal versus pathology-causing prions.

Indeed, as argued elsewhere (Anderson 2008; Fischer 2011) the kuru-encaphalopathy story encapsulates at least 10 key issues and dimensions for thinking about how to account for the changing moralities of scientific institutions: (1) historical epistemology (what did we know, when, in relation to what other knowledges and frames?); (2) testing terrains (how to model complex interactions); (3) scientific imperialisms and subimperialisms, or turfs, and control over information flow; (4) medical research institution building in independent Papua New Guinea (since 1975); (5) the sequence of genetics-behavioral-ecological projects (population genetics and sociobiology to genomics, biomics, and syndemics) from, as revealed by the Yanomami debates, watching blood, feces, and urine samples flow from the Brazilian Amazon to Penn State and the University of Michigan in the 1960s and watching the flow repeated in the 1990s, only now for DNA; (6) the development of institutions of ethical accounting (IRBs, formal consent protocols); (7) the use of comparative animal models (sheep scrapie, mice, hamsters, mink, monkeys, chimpanzees, yeast, and today comparative genomics); (8) anthropological methods, archives, and perspectives (genealogies, story elicitation and interpretation, attention to belief and local cultural frames for clinical effectiveness); (9) the role of the media (who speaks for whom, public relations, exoticizing moral panics, representations of science); (10) shifting logics of exchange in various spheres (gift economies; commodity exchange and capital accumulation in symbolic, power, or economic currencies; cosmological exchange cycles).

These high-profile, occasionally also highly ethically contested, science research programs reveal over time the changing nature of the scientific enterprise along three axes: the ethics and institutional contexts of science; the way in which actors of all sorts, including scientists, become media players, complicating questions of who speaks for whom; and the palimpsest continuities and differences between the human biology research projects (population genetics, sociobiology, human genome diversity project, health and epidemiological transition) of the 1960s and 1990s. The differences between the 1960s and 1990s also have to do with the increasing pressure for the participation of publics in decision-making about scientific research that affects their welfare, a pressure toward accountability if not transparency. The ethics of science and the representation of science in both the epistemological sense (accuracy, reference, completeness) and in the political or stakeholders' sense are no longer marginal issues left to the sensibility of the researcher or expert. Across the sciences these are becoming matters for institutional review, and subjects of efforts toward transparency and negotiations between publics and researchers over the propriety of research that involves peoples and publics.

Contrary to accounts of logically coherent, often rule-defined, schools of ethics and morals – Stoic, Epicurean, hedonistic, Cyrenaican hedonistic, consequentialist, deontological (*deon*, "duty, obligation"), pragmatic, utilitarian, bioethics, business ethics, robot ethics (Asimov) – anthropology has developed a series of sociological and cultural tools of analysis attuned to shifts (1) toward the increasing necessity to attend to, rather than exoticize, the interaction of disparate cultures, including cultures of expertise, local biologies and ecologies; (2) from agrarian and industrial to information, or code, forms of political dominance or social formations; and (3) in changing notions of the *bios*, or goals of the good life.

Among these tools are moral conflicts, third spaces, and ethical plateaus. Moral conflicts between different evaluative cultures tend to be the most obvious frames of choosing between binary options: should one do *x* or *y*. But ethical choices for individuals often happen in third spaces, in the ambiguous zones between clearly defined options, in repeated tournaments of decision-making, where slight shifts in circumstances undo efforts at consistency, routine, or rule-following. In these spaces, cultural frames for evaluation are resources but not scripts, drawn upon for testing options but not followed as templates. It is the location in ever novel, recursively challenging, ambiguous spaces that turns these into moral tests of an individual's ethics. Ethical plateaus are complex decision-making terrains in which multiple technologies intersect with their conflicting logics and social momentums, creating ambiguous moral spaces that defy simple binary choices, that thus require flexibility and mindful attentiveness, and whose resolution however temporary creates an emotional feeling of achievement of good outcomes, of appropriate and justified tradeoffs, under the circumstances, and for longer than a momentary instant.

Anthropology has a rich tradition both of presenting ethnographic crucibles of moral conflict and ethical choice, and of articulating the social-institutional and cultural-semiotic systematicities that produce these ethical plateaus of temporary resolution and emotional climaxes of feeling a sense of "rightness." The call of anthropology to always involve a healthy inquiry into the performative social and cultural grounds – the poetics and politics – of ethics and morality is itself an ethics and a moral vocation.

Twenty-First-Century Crucibles, Third Spaces, and Ethical Plateaus

Several recent dissertations by Aslihan Sanal (2011), Candis Callison (2010), Sara Wylie, (2011), and Orkideh Behrouzan (2010) provide ethical crucibles for thinking about contemporary third spaces and ethical plateaus at all four registers of our natures: first nature, or acts of God; second nature, or lives within our industrialized worlds; third nature, or reworking our bodies inside-out; and fourth nature, or living with our companionate others (companionate species, but also radically other belief systems within our own polities) (Fischer 2009: ch. 3).

Organs and infrastructures: slippery slopes and unstable plateaus

The ethics of kidney transplants can be posed as a series of moral conflicts and medical tradeoffs ranging from the illegal sale of organs to moral pressures on kin to donate.[5] Some of these can be posed as slippery slopes in which grey areas can easily turn black. Markets for organs can be created by the provision of transplant facilities and the existence of poor and indebted populations, under conditions where doctors do not want to be policemen and are motivated by both their calling and the satisfaction of saving a life.[6] Individual ethics of the patient in desperate need, the physician called to help, the committee allocating available organs, and the rule-maker drawing the line between what is legal and what is not, of how to properly solicit organs from families of dying or deceased patients, of the pressure to obtain organs while they are still viable – all these can be posed as moral conflicts, regulated and policed, and subject to slippery slopes.

There is, however, a more systemic set of issues to be considered: how policy conflicts are worked out between public versus private organ networks (and supply), reforms relating to who may be legitimate living donors, models of allowable compensation for donors,[7] rules of anonymity to moderate the tyrannies of the gift,[8] technologies of extending the viability of less than perfect organs,[9] physician obligations for aftercare, provision of and payment for transplant clinics, dealing with motivations for donation and psychologies of undergoing transplant, psychologies of being on dialysis, gender dynamics, work and health implications for donors as well as recipients, stimulation of new markets, inequities in access and care, oversight of regulations, use of media panics and public scandal to change public opinion,[10] relation between policy choices and theodicies.

In short there are many moving parts, and when one part changes there are implications for other parts of the system. These include changing laws, media swings between hysteria and cynicism (or mafia hunts and less blunt means of minimizing black markets), traditional attitudes toward life and death (sometimes accepting as a moral test or means of teaching what God has provided as one's lot rather than asking others to place themselves at risk that one might live: see Hamdy 2012), prestige of the modern in new understandings of the biotechnical and the symbolic place of lifesaving surgery, trading one kind of medicalization (dialysis) for another (immunosuppression), psychosis and mutation of sense of personhood or identity in the transplant process as well as afterward in perceiving the world with an awareness of "new organs within us."

These multiple intersecting technologies, legalities, rationales, values, and so on constitute unstable ethical plateaus, moments of stabilization by a particular set of legal guidelines, or by a particular state of the art of transplantation or sensibilities about public valorizing of lives being given new meaning by donation or public fear of organ snatching and illegal trade as functions of arbitrage across transnational borders. Plateau, in the usage drawn from Deleuze and Guattari, here alludes not merely to a geomorphic temporary stabilization of contending dynamic forces, but also a feeling of rightness when one has negotiated the multiple moral conflicts appropriately. It also alludes to the fact that is what are slippery slopes at one time may become common sense at another, as in the furor over *in vitro* fertilization (IVF), "test tube" babies, or now standard recombinant DNA technology. Black markets in organs are evils not to be viewed with indifference (Scheper-Hughes 2000), but new organs within us are metaphors and realities of the multiple infrastructures of our emergent forms of life.

Climate and ethical vernaculars: articulations, motivations, infrastructures

Ethical decisions populate not just our organs within, and their social medical relations without, but our external habitats and global connections. In matters of climate change four enunciatory communities – shifting and evolving coalitions – speak for the facts, for policy interventions, and for the four major levers of policy formation: law, market, church (mobilizing norms and morality), and science (generation of facts from instrumentation, models, simulations, probabilistic scenario-building).[11] The four enunciatory communities play upon newly developing media platforms, often fragmented and targeted media environments different from the imagined communities of earlier mass media.

That ethics is often strongly mediated by the vernaculars of local communities rather than recognized in terms of universalizing mainstream media, elite science, or political hegemonic discourses is brought home by an anecdote from Candis Callison's (2011) fieldwork among the Inuit. Coming down to breakfast at a conference, she noted the television on and some elders sitting quietly talking. Saying good morning, she mentioned something about the agenda item on climate change, only to be told that climate change was just something talked about on CNN, not a local concern. Given the softening tundra, change in whale and caribou migrations, and northward move of southerly vegetation, and given the role of the Inuit Circumpolar Conference (ICC) in mobilizing an experientially based case for the damages of climate change, with a possible international law suit in the offing, Callison was surprised. Talking to a leader of the ICC, she was reminded that while the Inuit do not talk about climate change in the terms that CNN or the *New York Times* do, if you take an elder out into the environment and ask him about what he sees, he will talk for hours about the climate change he sees.

The Arctic and sub-Arctic are key sites where climate change indicators press on everyday life the most dramatically. Data have been collected at a ring of sites around the Arctic (Barrow's Point, Alaska is perhaps the best known) since the late nineteenth century. While scientists have both worked with and ignored local Inuit and other First Nations' environmental knowledge, in recent years these on-the-ground knowledge systems have become more and more integrated with scientific databases. In recent years, the Inuit have joined with environmental lawyers to experiment with filing violation of human rights lawsuits, that is, that the United States and large corporations are liable for environmental degradation, which is a violation of cultural and human rights. There is some legal precedent within the Organization of American States conventions (the Inter-American Commission on Human Rights) for this kind of suit. But it also works as a highly visible alliance and public awareness strategy, and focuses attention on the experiential level of climate change where it is happening visibly first, affecting livelihoods and fauna and flora behavior, and rearranging winners and losers, who in the near future may, and indeed already do, involve new legal claims on territory and waterways in the Arctic.[12] (It turns out, unsurprisingly but with quite interesting differential dynamics between different Inuit groups, that this mode of intervention is associated especially with Canadian Inuit leaders – the Alaskan, Greenland, and Russian Inuit have different configurations from those of the Canadians.) In any case, while the Inuit, together with environment protection legal organizations, may leverage some legal protections for rights against the degradation of culture and ways of life, their primary legal claims are likely rather to rest on their demand for a seat at the table for determination of the futures of the Arctic, to be players rather than afterthought recipients of restitution, remediation, resettlement, or reservation.

Church mobilization of moral normative claims have been an important component of climate change debates, in the past two decades primarily on the side of neoliberal laissez-faire skepticism, but in the past decade the Evangelical Climate Initiative and similar Christian environmental initiatives have become publicly prominent in reasserting Christian social justice and stewardship traditions. Here, Callison's fieldwork again makes clear that what is at issue is an ethical vernacular that does not fold easily into mainstream environmentalist discourses. Environmentalism and science are not seen as authoritative, but as parts of "the enemy." For issues of this sort to be made acceptable, the "facts must be blessed," must come through believable Christian leadership. The struggle to provide this has not been seamless or conflict-free.

Similarly, the ethics of the now 17-year-old Ceres network of investors, entrepreneurs, and corporations is always under suspicion of "green washing." It is associated with the Chicago Climate Exchange and is organized to use market levers to move to new green economies. The network negotiates with large corporations to adopt, initially if only for better public relations, tools such as audits of their waste, emissions, and carbon footprints. These can be used then as tools by the public to keep up the pressure on them to do better. The ethical balance of dealing with companies whose greenness is not very good leads purists to view the network as selling out, while other voices see it as incremental pressure toward good goals.

Finally, the facts themselves, and the scientists who speak for the facts they produce, are constantly under ethical, political, and media pressure. Scientists who wish to contribute to public discussions are perforce being drawn into developing media strategies to protect their own credibility and legitimacy. Callison reports on the egregious, and hilariously comic (were it not also serious), charades of Congressional public hearings as political theater in which politicians ensnare scientists, making them appear to agree to conclusions diametrically opposed to the ones they are asserting. Scientists must learn how to operate in public with a view of science that invokes (does not hide) the instrumentation and modeling involved. They must show how relatively certain, versus relatively uncertain, knowledge is achieved. They must do this in the face of politicians and media who wish to use degree of certainty to dismiss the need for concern, or of those who would jump to short-term projects that might benefit some businesses among their constituents. Rather than argue the merits of anthropogenic causes of climate change, scientists have been able to gradually move the debate toward questions of remediation, adaptation, and prudence. In areas where there is increasing intensity of storms or other obvious climate changes, scientists need not reach consensus on all the details of causation and modeling in order to agree that coastal areas, for instance, have been dangerously overbuilt, or that the state should not be insuring wealthy homeowners along coasts whose houses are uninsurable by private insurers because the actuarial and other models show the risks to be unsustainable. The latter might be seen as public policy that is not only inequitable (taxpayers subsidizing the rich), but also ethically questionable insofar as it is hidden in state accounts that are rarely exposed to scrutiny or horse-traded for other kinds of legislative votes.

In short, the ethical vernaculars of which Callison writes require addressing in their own terms. Translation is never easy and never one-way. Mainstream journalism cannot use its own idiom and expect local idioms to be simply encompassed, rather than according local idioms their own implications that need not always agree with mainstream journalist presuppositions, and that need to be engaged in their own terms. Translation frequently, especially in politial terrains, must be (at least) two-way. In Levinas's terms, perhaps, the sin of universalizing discourse is reducing the other to the same, that is, not really paying attention to the face of the other, not thinking with the other in mind.

Fracking and fuming: testosterone shafts, estrogen wells

In between the ethics and morals of dealing with body and habitat there is the shadowy world of industrial and chemical toxic waste that has the potential for causing illness and death. In the history of this shadow world, information is sequestered, corporations deny citizens' claims of systematic illness (suggesting that they have neither the tools of perception, the instrumentation to register the emissions, nor the statistical expertise, the claim that cancer clusters are statistically meaningless), and governments are captured by corporations and the need for energy or economic growth. The pattern is repetitive (Love Canal, Louisiana Chemical Corridor, Woburn, Minimata, Bhopal, Chernobyl, Fukushima, and many others): people become aware of illness patterns and ask for epidemiological surveys, which are denied; corporations and governments deny any role in the alleged problems and, more importantly, sequester information behind proprietary walls; citizens are forced to conduct their own epidemiology and to make it robust enough to stand up in court, at which point corporations attempt to settle and gag claimants, and continue as before; civil mobilization occurs and a decades-long struggle ensues (Reich 1991; Crawford 1996; Harr 1996; Mikkelsen and Brown 1996; Bullard 1997, 2006; Fortun 2001; Petryna 2001; Allan 2003; Onishi and Fackler 2011). Richard Powers's novel *Gain* (1999) provides one of the most exquisite accounts of ethical tradeoffs in the long-term growth of an American corporation whose employees and neighbors also suspect them of poisoning them.

The contemporary natural gas "gold rush" in Colorado, Texas, and elsewhere renews the story and its dramaturgical tragic form, with a few new more hopeful elements. Two of these new elements are the creation of new fields of science and new tools of informed citizen science for mobilization in the service of both health and democratic oversight. As chronicled by anthropologist Sara Wylie (2011) from participant-observation ethnography inside both developments, the new field of endocrine disruptors, established by the extraordinarily dedicated work of Theo Colburn was a response both to findings of congenital abnormalities and skewed sex ratios among wildlife surrounding the Great Lakes of North America, and to the inability of traditional toxicology, testing one chemical at a time for linear causality, to deal with simultaneous interactions of multiple chemicals. Colburn managed to collate enough information on enough species to convince enough specialists in various biological fields to entertain seriously the hypothesis that industrial chemical release into the environment was causing endocrine disruption. This was apparently not an innocent scientific endeavor, as her files were invaded and security had to be tightened. This became even more necessary as the gold rush for natural gas extraction intensified in Colorado in the areas surrounding Colburn, and ranchers began to come to her with complaints of illness (as well as smells, unsightly waste pools, and fast-talking landmen who gained control of subsurface mineral rights). The hard-sell tactics of the "here today, gone tomorrow" landmen working on contract for large companies, who could deny responsibility for the unethical behavior of these contractors, repeated the amoral Wild West of the nineteenth-century landmen of the gold rushes. Proprietary rights over the chemical formulas used in the injection fluids to force the natural gas in shale deposits to the surface allowed companies to withhold from citizens (and even emergency room personnel dealing with seriously ill patients) information as to what was being put into the land. This meant that Colburn and others had to begin forensic tracking and collating information. Local and national governments were incentivized to look the other way. Most egregious was the stonewalling by Vice President Dick Cheney in the face of demands that he make public his dealings with oil and gas lobbyists when formulating US national energy policies in the Bush administration. Today, with the rapid spread of the "fracking" process of natural gas exploration including to the edge of the watershed of New York City, Energy Secretary Steven Chu and President Barack Obama asked former CIA director and MIT professor John Deutsch to form a commission to see if fracking could be done in safer ways. The "90 day" report, written in Washington-speak, supports the release of more information to the public, but has no teeth, and is generally dismissive of worries about the procedure.

In response, the MIT Center for Future Civic Media, in a project directed by Wylie and Chris Csikszentmihalyi, began to design web-based platforms to allow citizens to map the incidence of illness, chart experiences with landmen, and track wells and disposal sites. As it turned out, they were not the only ones to begin doing such work, and it proved to be possible to ally with some of these other efforts. In 2011 Josh Fox produced an HBO documentary, *Gasland*, which was promptly disputed by the natural gas industry.

The natural gas fracking debate is filled with ethical quandaries pursued under the legal provisions of the state and the self-organizing capacities of civil society. Like the debates over intellectual property and the Internet and biotechnology, there are moral conflicts, third spaces, and unstable ethical plateaus to be traversed by citizens, patients, corporate lawyers, engineers, company executives, politicians, bureaucrats, and others. A few Environmental Protection Agency scientists have turned whistle-blowers, and persons in other positions must individually make their own calls. But just as community morals guide traditional religious or event elicited "enunciatory communities," so too there are social stakes in these issues beyond good intentions or behavior proper to interests and loyalties.

At issue is democratic governance in high tech societies. Democratic societies are based upon the promise of citizen oversight of all matters that affect the commonweal. The strength of American representative democracy has resided in its ability to self-correct problems that sometimes arise from imbalances of power and decision-making through open information processes as guaranteed under the Article I, Section 8, Clause 8 of the *United States Constitution* (regarding the limitation of proprietary rights over patents, copyright, and trademarks, which should be for the public good rather than only for private ownership), the First Amendment of the U.S. Constitution (regarding free speech and the rights of investigation), and various legislative actions such as the Freedom of Information laws (regarding activities in which government decisions are involved). Each of these matters of constitutional law are disputed and subject to constant testing in this case and others. Thus the drift has swung too far in recent years toward claims that patent rights are individual property rights rather than mechanisms to make inventions and processes public and available for the public good, with only temporary protection for inventors as incentives and means to recoup investments. Likewise the extraordinary ability of Vice President Cheney's office to sequester information that should be public, even from the Congress. At issue, after all, are matters of public health, the ability of representative democracy to engage in meaningful urban and regional planning, protection of citizens' private property and homes, rights to clean air and water, and to provide oversight of properly functioning energy and resource market allocations.

These are matters of public ethics and American civic morals that require not just legal and political redress, but also reclarification of the presuppositions on which a feeling of "rightness" depends.

Negotiating moral vernaculars to acquire a national HIV-AIDS program

Iran provides an interesting example of negotiating ethics and morals under the threat of an AIDS crisis to eventually achieve a national HIV-AIDS and addiction prevention and treatment program that received the World Health Organization's Regional Best Practices certification. Like a number of other countries, Iran denied and downplayed the existence of AIDS as a Western disease. Two young doctors who were also brothers, Arash and Kamran Alae'i, graduates of Tehran University's Medical School, began an innovative program to address the AIDS epidemic in their hometown Kermanshah. They were able not only to set up clinics and obtain therapy, but eventually to gain access inside prisons (an incubator of the epidemic) to create "triangular clinics" across the country that provided other care as well. Provision of general care avoided the stigmatization of those who were seen going into the clinics. Orkideh Behrouzan, in a superb paper detailing the minefields in the negotiations to get a government progam in place, tells the complicated story of getting local mullahs on board, slowly finding contacts for isolated and stigmatized victims of the disease, quietly encouraging them to come to an unmarked clinic and eventually to start therapy, gaining access to the local prison, expanding their clinics to treat for other diseases so that no one seen entering the clinic would be stigmatized by being identified with AIDS, using addiction as a cover to downplay homosexuality and the secondary epidemic spreading among and by (former) wives of infected men, and gradually working the bureaucracy to get permission to open such clinics and services across the country. Behrouzan also explores a different and more public strategy led by a woman physician and professor whose purchase was on a different class and political nexus. She was among the first to be willing and allowed to go on radio and television in Tehran to speak about safe sex, as well as to pay attention to the shadow epidemic among women. In both settings, or both class strata, delicate negotiations operated and continue to operate over such issues as homosexuality. One of the lessons of Behrouzan's account, thus, is a detailing of how "one size fits all" policies can become counterproductive, rather than promoting medical moral neutrality or standardized best standards of care, as intended and desirable goals. In Iran, the triangular clinic model could work because it was sold publicly as about addiction and not about sexual practices. A domestic or international gay rights campaign, as is popular in the United States and internationally, would have been counterproductive. Similarly, in the prisons, where conjugal visits are allowed, wardens and other officials, once educated, could allow condoms in and turn a blind eye. Attention to the quite different languages required for policy-speak in the public arena as opposed to private discussion with the ill and stigmatized is another important strand of her argument. Different models, practices, formulations, and terminologies have different consequences in a highly conflicted and complex set of social arenas, including those of policy-makers walking ambiguous, politically fraught, and changeable lines between political correctness in an Islamic republic and good public health policy, or between conservatives and reformers jockeying for space and influence within the government ministries. Complications and negotiations do not stop here: having helped the country forge a national program, the Alae'i brothers were jailed for allegedly pursuing too many international contacts and hence potentially encouraging a velvet revolution, for terms of three and six years. (The younger brother was released, as is often done, after serving half his term; the elder brother was eventually also released later in 2011 after beginning his fourth year in jail.)

And yet, one more complication is that of the international "humanitarian" and "human rights" level itself. Behrouzan's paper, produced for an international UNESCO conference and accompanying volume, was repeatedly re-edited to a standardized international language, which erased cultural specificities that are part of the "take home" message and demonstration as to how to negotiate fraught political and cultural sensitivities and yet accomplish public health goals. Such highly offensive terms as "MSM" (men having sex with men) was insisted upon as the correct term for an array of Persian terms that carefully nuance different modes of homosociality in a society that criminalizes homosexuality.

In the end, despite an agreed-upon text, Behrouzan's paper remained the only paper not to be included in the published volume, online or off, with no explanation provided in two years of inquiry. It is, as they say, turtles all the way down, whether in politics, morals, or ethics – of the written about, as well as of the writers, editors, and publishers who write, publish, and establish hegemonic discourses about the former. The essay has now finally been published (Behrouzan 2011).

Conclusions

I have proposed three heuristics and four natures to think with as we keep the other in mind. The three heuristics (and they are merely that) – crucibles, third spaces, ethical plateaus – are meant to signal degrees of complexity and topologies of reason and affect folding back upon themselves, from simple dyadic and binary decision-making, to more complex arenas of mapping three or more contending commitments, to multiplicities of simultaneous moral and ethical contention and commitments whose resolutions are often temporary moments in continuing tournaments of engagements. When good temporary resolutions are achieved, "plateaus" offer or express a sense of achievement and "rightness" at least for the moment. The four natures are: first nature, or "acts of God," or the fantasies of nature untouched by human determinism; "second nature," or agriculturally reworked, and even more industrially and, as we now say, technologically (including informationally or cyborgian) reworked habitats and environments; "third nature" or redesigning ourselves inside-out with new biotechnologies; and "fourth nature," or learning to live with companionate species and radical cultural others as in the Iranian domestic struggles alluded to above, all Iranian but ethically and morally quite at odds over many things. These four natures constitute challenges for moralities to come, forms of emergent life, and ethics that have few satisfactory models in our pasts, but that maintain legacies from those pasts.

In 2003, as the SARS (severe acute respiratory syndrome) crisis terrified the world, Dr. Edison Liu, the new director of the then two-year-old Genome Institute of Singapore, offered to use GIS to identify, by genomic sequencing, the SARS coronavirus (Vancouver was first to publish a sequence, Atlanta second, but GIS identified five strains needed for the comparative analysis to develop the diagnostic kits). It was a proof of concept for genomics and global health monitoring, and the beginnings of building more robust global biosecurity systems, constructed through collaborative competitions under emergency conditions despite deep and principled distrust across national borders.

Distrust: in 1996–97, during the spread of the fast-mutating, highly pathogenic H5N1 avian flu, Indonesia refused to share samples with Singapore's effort to isolate the strain on the principled grounds that while it was expected to provide samples to the world, vaccines and drugs developed were rarely made available at prices affordable to its population. And, as it turned out, the culling of backyard chickens, which international agencies insisted on, was a misdirected and much resented effort, since the virus most probably came from large industrial chicken farming and not household chickens. Trust needs to be built and maintained; it is not established by moral proclamations of sharing for the good of all.

Following the completion of the initial Human Genome Project in 2003, a series of new technological innovations – SNPs (single nucleotide polymorphisms), GWAS (genome-wide association studies), and now whole genomes – began to provide new ways of using comparative genomics to find disease targets, and equally importantly to foster the trust on which regional collaborative projects might be platformed. This was pioneered by GIS with the early Pan-Asian SNPs Project, and is now to be furthered through a more disease-focused and denser array phase 2 of the project.

When Edison Liu moved the Human Genome Organization headquarters to the Genome Institute of Singapore, he suggested that the HGO could help foster collaborative scientific relations across southeast Asia and the Pacific rim by making available genomics technology and inviting collaboration in an SNPs-based genomics project. Scientists from resource- and technology-poor countries would maintain physical custody of their samples, but be invited to work on the machines in more resourced countries. It was decided to work on a migration study to help build up trust and working relations among scientists. Everyone, it was said, was interested in "origins," and this might avoid countries feeling stigmatized if they were found to have a particularly high incidence of some disease.

The initial Pan-Asian SNPs project was relatively small-scale, and was intended to start building a network of people who trusted one another based on past collaborative work experience, as well as providing a model for protecting national sovereignty and scientific credit by insuring that local scientists maintain chain of custody over samples, but are enabled to use, think with, and contribute to state-of-the-art technology and research platforms. It also explored models of ethical engagement with indigenous and minority communities to avoid the sorts of problems that derailed the Human Genetic Diversity Project. In India, for example, labs were opened to children to see what was going on, and to explain to their parents what they had seen, as part of a longer-term engagement and not as a single collecting event. Discussions and experiences were exchanged about the ways in which indigenous and minority communities, who are suspicious of their known national governments and majority communities, and not just international scientists, might be made to feel empowered by access to and perhaps some sort of ownership in the scientific process. The research produced a *Science* paper as a demonstration of what could be done with SNPs analysis, although the results are based on too few samples and array density. It is, as Edison Liu puts it, like a low-resolution map; and phase 2 will expand the sampling and density of arrays. Phase 2 will not use SNPs but pioneer new whole-genome technological platforms, and sampling in the thousands for stronger scientific breadth and depth than the original pilot SNPs project.

But while the scale and focus will be different, the networking goals remain in place. It will also begin an effort to build Asian reference sets and to diversify biomedical data sets. The basis of the Illumina arrays widely used in genomic studies are based on patient information and genome sequencing from Caucasian populations, useful but not optimal for Asian populations, a case of bias possibly being built into the technology. So it is time to be building localized arrays at various levels of spread across populations and down to the individual genome to control for drug-metabolizing enzymes, for different dosage levels, and to achieve more detail on and identification of the genes involved in the metabolism of drugs.

At the HUGO meeting in Dubai in March 2010 informal meetings were organized to help formalize the design, publicize the effort, and stimulate interest among potential collaborators. This was also the occasion for a preliminary discussion of such issues as privacy and informed consent, with some, like biotechnology leader George Church, arguing for developing future-oriented protocols that recognize the difficulty of keeping any information private and circulating at the same time (issues of anonymization and reidentification, but also the desire to link genomic data with medical records, to be able to follow the course of diseases, and so on), and those (in this case from the south Asian subcontinent) arguing for updatable pragmatic protocols and supplementary communication needs (such as bringing school children into the labs) in societies with limited literacy or scientific understanding.

I cite the two phases of the Pan-Asian SNPs Consortium as an example of how the scientific enterprise is being used, like the International Geophysical Year (IGY) in the 1950s, to experiment with not just networks of, but also models for, cross-national mutual help. Genomics technologies are useful to think with because they cross all four natures – understanding ourselves inside-out, across species, as we have modified our habitat, and as we encounter the effects, say, of malarial spread as a result of climate change – and involve a constantly shifting scaffold of decision-making crucibles, third spaces, and ethical plateaus.

NOTES

1 We enjoyed speculating that our grandfathers, both prominent rabbis in Vienna, would have had to know each other. Fritz was evacuated from Vienna after Kristalnacht (November 1938) to England on a Kindertransport (which saved some 10,000 children and placed them with British families), and was later reunited with his parents in England. Later in his career Fritz spent five years in Vienna, a time he described with affection.

2 With startup funds from his donor, Fritz rented space in Harvard Square and started the work of the Institute. MIT's negotiations with the donor and Fritz in the middle continued mainly over governance issues until the financial crisis and the donor's withdrawal. Provost Brown was anxious that the new Institute not be as separated from MIT as the Whitehead (with its own board of governors), or worse the Dibner Institute for the History of Science, whose relations with MIT fell apart as a result of the donor family's repeated ignoring of academic ethics, such as gender nondiscrimination (in the process of selecting a new director), insistence on selecting the director and requiring that it be an MIT faculty position, and ignoring the consortium of universities whose participation in the selection of fellows was stipulated in the contract with MIT.

3 I introduced him to Ulrich Beck's *Risk Society*, a text he happily incorporated into his talks.

4 For one of many public discussion, see a PBS transcript of an interview with Fritz, at http://www.pbs.org/wgbh/pages/frontline/shows/organfarm/interviews/bach.html, accessed Mar. 7, 2012.

5 This section draws upon the work of Aslihan Sanal (2011). Her remarkable case studies in Turkey go far beyond what can be alluded to here, involving medical modernity, anxieties about life and death, psychosis as a passage point of transplantation, ritualization of the social personas of cadavers for medical training, media mobilization for transplant donation, media panics and myth-making of the unknown (sources of osteomatrices, earthquakes, and disappeared bodies), competition between philosophies of social versus private medicine, legal reforms, transnational technologies and markets, and the politics and poetics of religious, national, and regional identities.

6 On India, see the superb essay by Lawrence Cohen (1999) describing the unintended consequences of laws outlawing organ sales, the return of physicians from the United States and Europe who establish elite clinics, and the stimulation of a market for organs in the triangle between Chennai, Hyderabad, and Bangalore. Cohen also pays attention to the gender dynamics within families of donors, the aftermath of surgery on ability to work, and the temporary nature of the bailout from debt by being paid for organs.

7 Iran has experimented with flat fee payments to donors and the provision of free organs to patients in need. Some European countries have presumed consent for taking organs from beating-heart cadavers (families must opt out if they wish donation not to happen).

8 See Fox and Swazey (1992) for a discussion of the introduction of anonymity rules for heart transplants to counter the unbearable pressures of the tyranny of the gift both on the recipient to the donor, and on the donor's family's lingering sense of connection to the donor's heart in another person.

9 Mehmet Habermal, who performed the first living-related kidney transplant and later the first cadaveric kidney transplant in Turkey, is also the inventor of a technique to extend the time an organ can be kept viable for transplant. This became ethically controversial within the European Organ Share Network, within which he worked, for using organs no longer considered for transplant by many. Known for establishing one of the two major organ share networks in Turkey, he was also a major figure in the drafting of legal rules for living-related donors. For his national role as leader of the private network of hospitals and clinics for transplantation, dialysis, and burns, see Sanal 2011.

10 On the use of "public scandal" see Cohen 1999; for further examples and discussion, see Sanal 2011.

11 On "enunciatory communities" see Fortun (2001); on the analogy of law, market, science, and church to those Lawrence Lessig (1999) identifies as key tools for creating the Internet: coding or engineering the hardware and software; laws of intellectual property rights (copyleft, commons, patents, copyright, trademark, First and Fourth Amendment decisions in the United States, international trade law); market (incentives and barriers); and norms.

12 In 2001 Russia submitted a first claim to the Lomonosov Ridge and was told by the UN Commission on the Limits of the Continental Shelf to come back with better evidence. Since then the Russian nuclear research submarine *Akademik Fyodorov*, under the expeditionary lead of Artur Chillingarov and cartographer Valery Kuznetzov, has been assiduously mapping the ridge during the summers, and Russia plans to submit its claim in 2013. Canada expects to submit its claim then too. In 2007 Russia planted its flag under the North Pole. At issue are oil, fish stocks, coal, and minerals. Denmark, Norway, and Britain also have indicated claims to parts of the Arctic, and the United States has been mapping the Chuckchi Cap north of the Bering Strait.

REFERENCES

Allan, Barbara (2003) *Uneasy Alchemy: Citizens and Experts in Louisiana's Chemical Corridor Disputes*. Cambridge, MA: MIT Press.

Anderson, Warwick (2008) *The Collectors of Lost Souls: Turning Kuru Scientists into Whitemen*. Baltimore: Johns Hopkins University Press.

Beck, Ulrich (1992 [1986]) *Risk Society: Towards a New Modernity*. New York: Sage.

Behrouzan, Orkideh (2010) Prozak Diaries: Post-Rupture Subjectivities and Psychiatric Futures. PhD dissertation, Massachusetts Institute of Technology, Cambridge.

Behrouzan, Orkideh (2011) An Epidemic of Meanings: HIV and AIDS in Iran and the Significance of History, Language and Gender. In Jennifer E. Klot and Vinh-Kim Nguyen (eds.), *The Fourth Wave: Violence, Gender, Culture and HIV in the 21st Century*. Paris: UNESCO.

Bullard, Robert D. (1997) *Unequal Protection: Environmental Justice and Communities of Color*. San Francisco: Sierra Club.

Bullard, Robert D. (2006) *The Quest for Environmental Justice: Human Rights and the Politics of Pollution*. San Francisco: Sierra Club.

Callison, Candis (2010) More Information is Not the Problem: Spinning Climate Change, Vernaculars, and Emergent Forms of Life. PhD dissertation, Massachusetts Institute of Technology.

Cohen, Lawrence (1999) Where It Hurts: Indian Material for an Ethics of Organ Transplantation. *Daedalus* 128(4): 135–166.

Crawford, Colin (1996) *Uproar at Dancing Rabbit Creek: The Battle over Race, Class and the Environment in the New South.* New York: Perseus.

Fischer, Michael M. J. (2003) *Emergent Forms of Life and the Anthropological Voice.* Durham, NC: Duke University Press.

Fischer, Michael M. J. (2009) *Anthropological Futures.* Durham, NC: Duke University Press.

Fischer, Michael M. J. (2011) Galactic Polities, Radical Egalitarianism, and the Practice of Anthropology: Tambiah on Logical Paradoxes, Social Contradictions, and Cultural Oscillations. In F. Aulino, M. Goheen, and S. J. Tambiah (eds.), *Radical Egalitarianism.* New York: Fordham University Press.

Fortun, Kim (2001) Advocacy after Bhopal: Environmentalism, Disaster, New Global Orders. Chicago: University of Chicago Press.

Fox, Rene and Swazey, Judith (1992) *Spare Parts: Organ Replacement in American Society.* New York: Oxford University Press.

Hamdy, Sherine (2012) *Our Bodies Belong to God: Organ Transplants, Islam, and the Struggle for Human Dignity in Egypt.* Berkeley: University of California Press.

Harr, Jonathan (1996) *A Civil Action.* New York: Vintage.

Jasanoff, Sheila (2007) *Designs on Nature: Science and Democracy in Europe and the United States.* Princeton: Princeton University Press.

Kelty, Christopher (2008) *Two Bits: The Cultural Significance of Free Software.* Durham, NC: Duke University Press.

Latour, Bruno (2005) *Making Things Public: Atmospheres of Democracy.* Cambridge, MA: MIT Press.

Lessig, Lawrence (1999) *Code and Other Laws of Cyberspace.* New York: Basic Books.

Mikkelsen, Edwin J. and Brown, Phil (1996) *No Safe Place: Toxic Waste, Leukemia and Community Action.* Berkeley: University of California Press.

Onishi, Narimitsu and Fackler, Martin (2011) Japan Hid Nuclear Radiation Path, Leaving Evacuees in Peril. *New York Times* (Aug. 9), A1, 8.

Petryna, Adriana (2001) *Life Exposed: Biological Citizens after Chernobyl.* Princeton: Princeton University Press.

Powers, Richard (1999) *Gain.* New York: Picador.

Reich, Michael (1991) *Toxic Politics: Responding to Chemical Disasters.* Ithaca, NY: Cornell University Press.

Sanal, Aslihan (2011) *New Organs within Us: Transplants and the Moral Economy.* Durham, NC: Duke University Press.

Scheper-Hughes, Nancy (2000) The Global Traffic in Organs. *Current Anthropology* 41(2): 191–224.

Wylie, Sara (2011) *Corporate Bodies and Chemical Bonds: An STS Analysis of Natural Gas Development in the United States.* PhD dissertation, Massachusetts Institute of Technology.

CHAPTER 23

Finance

Karen Ho

The current devastating global economic recession was instigated largely by the cultural practices of elite financial actors empowered by fundamental shifts in the process of wealth accumulation and in the relationship between finance and production. While the meltdown has produced an impetus to analyze, blame, and repair Wall Street, little has been accomplished in the way of large-scale structural changes in the values and practices of key actors and institutions that undergird our financial system. The sheer scale of the bailout and the subsequent elision of finance's dependence on government aid have puzzled critical observers who assumed that perhaps, this time, Wall Street's crisis-producing culture would be curbed.

Given the resurgence of business as usual in Wall Street financial institutions after such a massive challenge to their place in the world, this essay attempts to think through why investment bankers issued no mea culpas in the wake of the crisis, instead sticking to claims that they do "God's work."[1] Whereas most social critics presumed that major financial institutions were centrally and obviously responsible and should thus be held accountable, many Wall Street leaders and bankers, even in the face of their own institutional near demise, resisted substantive changes in their organizational structures and practices. Their core beliefs about their own abilities, importance, and proper place in the capitalist order remained almost completely intact. To explain the crisis, they pointed away from fundamental failures in dominant models, and placed the blame instead on the carelessness and excess of individuals caught up in a bubble mentality.

Clearly the subject of morality in high finance has not received its due. On the one hand, social scientists and critics have either largely avoided an interrogation of financial moralities, *or* have presumed the activities of the financial sector to be already predefined as immoral or amoral. On the other hand, Wall Streeters continue to articulate deeply moral claims to explain their actions and ground their socioeconomic validity. What has gone missing in critical accounts of financial values and

A Companion to Moral Anthropology, First Edition. Edited by Didier Fassin.

practices is an interrogation of the actual discourse of morality – the strong moral beliefs, defenses, and hierarchies – that imbues and rationalizes the ideologies and interests of Wall Street and financialization.

In this essay, I make the argument that to comprehend fully how finance has continued to command the authority and legitimacy to solve the problems of the American economy, it is crucial to understand capitalism as an explicitly moral order, as well as finance capital's particular, meritocratic place within this order. The inability of key decision-makers, business leaders, and government officials to shake their faith and confidence in Wall Street as savior begins with the fact that over the past 30 years, the management, security, and stability of the American social welfare system, that is the "safety net," have been outsourced from state and more stable corporate institutions to financial markets and Wall Street actors. In other words, while it is true that 401K retirement accounts, insurance policies, and all kinds of state, university, and corporate pensions and investment funds demanded alignment to (and bailout of) Wall Street, it is Wall Street's moral imbrication with larger American understandings of what constitutes economic righteousness that has enabled the financial sector to fight back challenges to its power.

An in-depth ethnographic examination of Wall Street moralities necessitates a manifold approach that recognizes their "assemblages," their multiple aspects and layers, and the interrelatedness between them. We must recognize that moralities, like taken-for-granted cultural norms and ideologies, are both conscious and unconscious, official and unofficial – and one key way to access some of their most normative aspects is to investigate their habitus. In my previous research (Ho 2009a, 2009b) I demonstrated that one way to complexify the official discourses of shareholder value was to investigate the habitus of investment bankers through their individual biographies, school and workplace experiences, and institutional milieus. Similarly, an important way into Wall Street's moral order is to investigate "morality as habitus." As anthropologist Jarrett Zigon observes, drawing from Saba Mahmood's work, morality is produced through human practice, "acquired through the repeated performance of actions that entail a particular virtue or vice," and not only "obligatory rule-following or conscious reflection on a problem or dilemma" (2010: 8). By examining Wall Street morality as "embodied dispositions," however, my point is not to trump or counter Wall Street's official representations of morality, but rather to demonstrate how they co-produce and often legitimate the moral order of finance.

I begin this essay with a brief tour and analysis of contemporary interpretations of financial morality, comparing and examining multiple (popular, financial, and social scientific) approaches and discourses in order to apprehend the current landscape. I demonstrate how these understandings often misunderstand and bypass one another. I then contextualize these representations and assumptions with an in-depth ethnographic investigation of Wall Street's moral subjectivities and investments in order to explicate the contours of their moral order and how such an order shapes capitalist practice and direction. By putting fine-grained ethnography side by side with other etic and emic accounts, I hope to show the potential of field research to shed light on obfuscating and taken-for-granted discourses from both Wall Street "insiders" and social scientists. In this vein, I also use ethnography to reflect on a variety of academic knowledge production, including my own.

Contemporary Representations of Financial Morality

While social critics often skewer Wall Street for its apparent lack of morals, I make the contrary argument that major Wall Street financial institutions actually have a highly distilled sense of morality framed as social purpose. When *Liquidated: An Ethnography of Wall Street* (Ho 2009b) was first published, during the darkest days of the financial meltdown, one question I almost always received from audiences of social scientists and social critics was, "How do investment bankers sleep at night?" I usually answered that most of my informants had a fairly well-honed sense of the social goodness of their work and their place in the capitalist order. Above all, it was their sense of Wall Street as an unparalleled meritocracy, dovetailing as it did with official discourses of the general social and economic importance of investment banking, that strengthened their economic rectitude and moral resolve while under fire.

Many simply shook their heads in disbelief at my response. It was difficult to understand how morals, social good, and Wall Street could be uttered in the same breath, much less believe that for Wall Street Gordon Gekkos, such associations were common, even taken for granted. Now, while there could certainly be an element of moral marketing and gamesmanship involved, for the most part my informants imbibed and internalized these moral discourses, and espoused them unironically. And herein lies one of the key analytical problems I pose: what accounts for the limits in our anthropological and sociological imaginations such that we often substitute the results of our analyses for a considered engagement with the moral cosmology of financiers? Why are we more apt either to presume Wall Street amorality or immorality, or to distance our analyses from engaging with morality at all, than to substantively confront the morality of traders and bankers as an object of serious analysis? Why would it surprise us to find that Wall Street financial capitalists and advocates in fact have a well-developed discourse of morality and sense of moral purpose?

To engage with these questions, let us continue with two ethnographic examples from popular culture and mainstream business culture that illustrate this misapprehension of financial morality: the transformation of Oliver Stone's Gordon Gekko into heroic cultural icon, and the recent contestation surrounding the MBA Oath at Harvard Business School. One of the reasons why Oliver Stone, director and co-writer of *Wall Street*, long delayed the production of a sequel was his continued surprise and consternation that the character Gordon Gekko, whom he created "as a monster" and "cautionary tale" to critique financial culture, became a "heroic figure," "glamorous archetype," and glorifying recruitment tool on the Street (Broughton 2009; Popper 2010). Actor Michael Douglas, who won an Oscar portraying the infamous Gekko, was similarly shocked:

> The continued resonance of Gekko, Mr. Douglas said, has "probably been the biggest surprise of my career, that people say that this seductive villain has motivated me to go into this business." To this day, Mr. Douglas said, it is a usual occurrence to finish dinner out and have "a well-lubricated Wall Street businessman come up to me and say, 'You're the man.'" Mr. Douglas added, "There's an absurdity to it." (Arango 2009)

In a similar vein, in MBA ethics courses, Gordon Gekko's "greed is good" speech is often shown as a "morality lesson," and yet "ends up feeling more like a pep talk," for the students already accept the argument and make the causal linkages that the character does, viewing Gekko as a "liberator," not a "destroyer," of companies."[2] I would argue that Gekko's reclamation as symbol of Wall Street's intense culture comes as a surprise because it is not always well understood that notions of greed, excess, and (creative) destruction are already incorporated into Wall Street's moral philosophy as central elements (Arango 2009; Broughton 2009).[3] The failure of Oliver Stone's critique stems from the misplaced presumption that finance is either immoral or amoral, in which case exposing greed as the primary motivation might induce moral reflection – when in fact Gekko already hits a chord as an (admittedly excessive) exemplar of the moral order of American capitalism.

The other ethnographic example is the debate over signing the MBA Oath at Harvard Business School (HBS). In the wake of the financial meltdown, the business professors Nitin Nohria and Rakesh Khurana joined a group of students to propose that MBA students make a formal pledge to practice what the official website of the MBA Oath (www.mbaoath.org) calls "responsible value creation." Khurana, for example, has long advocated for the reform of American business education to teach management as a profession charged with the long-term responsibility for the interests of multiple stakeholders as well as society at large. Modeled on the Hippocratic oath, the pledge charges students to manage enterprises ethically and to safeguard not only the well-being of "shareholders" but also "co-workers," "customers," and the world in which their enterprises are embedded. While the oath has garnered much attention at many well-known business schools and many students signed it, it has also been hotly contested, in large part because almost half of Harvard's MBA students reasoned that, like Gordon Gekko, they already have a morality and an ethics. Taking the oath would support the presumption that Wall Street lacks ethics or is inherently immoral, when for those protesting the oath, the point was that there was a clash of competing ethics. Below is an excerpt from an MBA student refusing to sign the oath:

> But I assure you that your best contribution to society will be if you work for your self-interest. Less people are hungry today and living better lives because of "greed." Planes, trains, medicines, and the Internet would be nothing without it. Most of society would be jobless without the "profiteers." If you really care about those who need electricity or those who are jobless, then pursue your own ambitions aggressively, for the profit motive is the true engine of prosperity. Follow the law and your personal ethics, but resist the urgings to "play fairly." Rather, compete doggedly. If you see excessive costs, cut them. If you have an invention, see it through to fruition. Do not settle for second place. Take risks. Compete. Strive. Until you have nothing left. And when the fruits of your ingenuity and hard labor redound to your reward, do not apologize to the people who will both demonize your "immorality" when you fail and criticize your "materialism" when you succeed, those who hitchhike on the wings of capitalists. For you will have done your community and your world a greater service than you will ever know. (Sridhar 2009)

It is thus not a huge leap to consider how Wall Street financial institutions and their executives responded, in moral terms, to the devastating critiques leveled at them in the wake of the great recession of 2008. The whole financial industry was attacked for its greed and selfishness, mocked for its hubris, and even vilified for its "evil," degraded immorality (Farrell 2010; Johnson and Kwak 2010; Lewis 2010;

McGee 2010). News of exorbitant bonuses in the wake of massive foreclosures crystallized and exacerbated this sentiment. In response to growing public outrage, however, Wall Street leaders drew from longstanding, sedimented moral rationales. While these justifications seemed jarring at the time because the bankers' claims to moral righteousness did not match general opinion, their very articulation in the face of massive anti-Wall Street sentiment demonstrates their sturdy underpinnings.[4]

Perhaps the most pivotal example is the much-quoted interview with Lloyd Blankfein, CEO of Goldman Sachs, in which he restated his case for investment banking to *The Times* of London a year after September 2008:

> I know I could slit my wrists and people would cheer, [but] [w]e're very important … We help companies to grow by helping them to raise capital. Companies that grow create wealth. This, in turn, allows people to have jobs that create more growth and more wealth. It's a virtuous cycle … We have a social purpose. (Arlidge 2009)

When the interviewer then asked him if it was possible to make too much money, Blankfein replied:

> Is it possible to have too much ambition? Is it possible to be too successful? … I don't want people in this firm to think that they have accomplished as much for themselves as they can and go on vacation. As the guardian of the interests of the shareholders and, by the way, for the purposes of society, I'd like them to continue to do what they are doing. I don't want to put a cap on their ambition. It's hard for me to argue for a cap on their compensation. (Arlidge 2009)

To this, he added, seemingly facetiously, that as an investment banker, he was "doing God's work."

While Blankfein's "God's work" comment sparked immediate and wide-ranging mockery, disbelief, and charges of hypocritical delusion, it was in line with deeply ingrained Wall Street sensibilities and longstanding rationalizations of finance capitalism. Notice, for example, how quickly and seamlessly Blankfein transitioned from tacitly acknowledging public anger directed at bankers to reclaiming his industry's ultimate worth and virtuousness, boldly reasserting his social importance and purpose. Even a leading critical question about the social consequences and implicit immorality of "making too much money" was swiftly reframed as indefatigable ambition *in the interests* of both shareholders and society. Brian Griffith, a Goldman Sachs international vice chairman, in a speech at St. Paul's Cathedral in London for a panel discussion "What is the Place of Morality in the Marketplace?" hit Blankfein's point home: "We have to tolerate the inequality [of record pay for Wall Street] as a way to achieve greater prosperity and opportunity for all" (Binham 2009).

Wall Street Moralities: A Decade Retrospective

Throughout the late 1990s and into the new millennium, these same assurances were made by many of my informants as well.[5] It was not only when faced with their own possible demise that investment bankers began to cloak themselves in "radiant robes of ethical purity"; they have long done so. Over the past 30 years, Wall Street has cultivated "an audacious sense of personal worth and entitlement," which comes in part from the cultural assumption that global improvement occurs only through their labors (Hightower 2009). During my research at the time of the bull market, when stock market populism and America as an investor nation saturated the airwaves as well as the psyches of the middle classes and the well-to-do, Wall Street arguably felt that its place in the global capitalist moral order had been vindicated after its contested rise in the 1980s "decade of greed." Even though the bull market, of course, was also characterized by continual upheavals (such as the Asian and Russian financial crises and the demise of Long-Term Capital Management), massive insecurity, and heightened inequality, Wall Street – through governmental reregulation in its favor, the belief in the myth that investment banks were the originary sources of capital for corporate America, and the reframing of financial accumulation as the strategy to create a true "ownership society" – captured and solidified its role as poster child for the singular success of American-style capitalism. It is instructive to remember that 30 years ago, "the best and the brightest" did not flock to Wall Street, indicating how historically contingent this construction of finance as capitalist pinnacle is. As one informant reminded me, "Coming out of college [in the late 1970s], nobody went to Wall Street … Everybody, even Wharton, was telling you – go work for Johnson and Johnson, or IBM, or Proctor and Gamble."[6]

Thus I should not have been surprised that in 1998 and 1999, when I asked about Wall Street's social impact, almost all of my informants gave immediate, heartfelt answers about the beneficial effects of their industry. While they accessed the social by way of the financial, their defenses of Wall Street as a force for social good and prosperity were fluid and emphatic (though not without nuance), and coalesced around the themes of efficiency, creativity, and the belief that finance is the inevitable, exemplary model for the success of all corporations and nations globally. While they allowed that Wall Street does not explicitly set out with the goal of making the world a better place, the financial markets, in their view, almost always succeeded in doing just that. Most also recognized the problems of social dislocation, short-termism, even wealth inequality, yet still concluded that there was no other, better way toward socioeconomic prosperity. I remember being struck by how effortless their responses were, demonstrating that my informants had long ruminated on and often discussed these matters. They had been exposed to an explicitly articulated, even official, set of local moralities in universities, business schools, and across Wall Street institutions over a sustained period of time.

"We make the world more efficient," Michael Williams, a vice president of Emerging Market Sales and Trading at Lehman Brothers, earnestly stated. "That really is true, I think," he added, "not just the standard line. There is not another way to do it that is any better." He then described in detail how one "justified [one's] life in terms of what one is adding to it by being in the business." I was surprised by his self-reflexivity, how he had obviously mulled over how Wall Street's representations of its own social purpose matched up with his own experiences in the workplace.

> I think the only way to do it is to say, "I am part of a process and this is what the process adds to the world." What I am doing on a day-to-day basis is very short-term oriented and selfish, but what is interesting is that a selfish process actually brings out a lot of what

> are traditionally known as good behaviors, not always … You are in a process that is, in fact, positive for the world, good for the world … the process of creative destruction where you need to get rid of things that don't work or focus on things that do work … The interesting thing is that you could have people who are very selfish and evil and immoral and who succeed very much in a system that still, paradoxically, is beneficial to the whole.

His combination of multiple strands of dominant representations and justifications, from "creative destruction" to "greed is good" demonstrated, for me, how deeply informed he was by these local ways of making sense of the world. There were, of course, fissures. He punctuated his claims with questions and sidebar caveats ("This does not mean that financiers should get paid what they do"; "Maybe Wall Street demands too much change from people and that is not good"), but concluded that, "in general, Wall Street is a good thing" that makes people more "free," "flexible," and adaptive.

Many informants emphasized Wall Street's unique status as the only socioeconomic model that could bring about social progress on a world stage. They all structured their belief in Wall Street as the only path to global economic success through comparative contrast with the following straw men: Japan's prolonged recession, the Asian and Russian financial crises, "stagnant" welfare capitalism in Europe, and the demise of socialism as an alternative. As Roy Allen, a managing director at Fidelity Investments who had previously worked at Lehman and Salomon Brothers, explained:

> Part of the United States' prosperity is the result that it has the best financial system in the world, if not the best, certainly then the most liquid and the most creative. Why do we have the ability to make sub-prime mortgages? A lot of that has been a result of Wall Street's creativity … [O]ur ability to own property or finance things in the United States far exceeds what a lot of other countries in the world have, so I guess arguably you could suggest that over time our financial engineering expertise should and could help other parts of the world modernize, develop, securitize, invest and structure corporations. It's horrible what's going on in a lot of southeast Asia, but a lot of why it happened is that they didn't stick to standards that are similar to what we have had in the UK and the United States. And today if you look at every one of these countries, their advisers are US firms. Thailand has two US firms advising them. Indonesia has two US firms advising them on everything from debt restructuring to how they should even set up their banking system. So part of me wants to say that we are not sure how much good we've been, but certainly [we're creating] a platform for pretty good things to happen socially.

Part of what allows the financial sector to imagine itself as possessing a moral vision of the economy is how Wall Street positions itself in a global context, telling a story of American-led capitalist triumph, which in itself becomes proof that financially dominant capitalism is the best possible version of social economy. The vision of American global superiority in contradistinction to "other economies" *and* the understanding that Wall Street is *the* inevitable, rational catalyzer of such dreams go hand in hand. According to Peter Lucas, an investment banking research analyst who has worked at Merrill Lynch, Bankers Trust, and Dresdner Bank:

> Wall Street's capitalistic model has been shown to function much more efficiently than any other. Whereas five years ago, Japan was going to take over the world, now Japan

> needs to become like America and basically, all the prescriptions for Japan are to be more like us. It is basically what is happening in Europe. I mean, the U.S. has that [advantage] over all the countries in the world: efficient capital markets, especially for small businesses, entrepreneurs, venture capital, all of that stuff where Europe is still very much lacking. For an entrepreneur in France, you can't get any money to support your ideas.

To achieve Wall Street's model of success both at home and elsewhere, "the breaking of eggs" is a "necessary evil." As Lucas continued:

> Inefficiency requires reallocation of assets. That includes people, and that can be painful, especially if you are one of the people. But society as a whole is still, without question, better off. So if society has an obligation or a business has an obligation, or anyway if there is an obligation, it is to provide people with the means to adapt – funding sound education, providing for retraining – the point being to reallocate some of this extra to the people that lost out. So you shouldn't focus on the fact that some people lost out. It's a necessary evil. Because the alternative is for people to stay in jobs that are not productive and then ultimately you turn into the Soviet Union.

The specter of the "evil empire," the Soviet Union, is a central metaphor that links Wall Street practices promoting constant liquidity (from employment to capital movements) to the global moral order. According to Paul Flanagan, a mergers and acquisitions associate at Goldman Sachs, he worked on Wall Street because "Wall Street really makes the world go round. Which I do truly believe":

> Companies can borrow money very cheaply because America has the best banking facilities, financial markets. [L]ook at American growth in light of the whole world's falling apart and America is doing fine right now. You go back to the entrepreneurial system. We are allocating capital. Looking at corporate America versus the rest of the world – everyone's daily life and quality of life in the rest of the world – in America things have been better because of the Wall Street system.

What makes Wall Street "awesome" and "great for the country as a whole and for the economy" is that we are a "great value trader for our country." Because Wall Street mandates liquidity, we "force inefficient companies to get efficient or to get out." As Christine Chang, a vice president at Bankers Trust in the late 1990s, echoed, "In the US, strong companies have a chance to access capital and grow in a way that companies in other countries without strong capital markets don't. Companies which are bleeding are not attractive to investors and therefore are closed down and stop using the resources of society."[7]

Taken together, these discourses demonstrate that investment bankers are socialized into a very particular understanding of the world that is grounded in explicit judgments about moral worth, legitimacy, and order. Wall Street morality is about hierarchy and classification, making value judgments about the worth of groups of people, industries, and nations. Their values and practices, as well as financial markets writ large, are not simply moral projects but moralizing systems of hierarchical classification.

Yet, in order to fully understand just how intensely moralized and moralizing Wall Street's conception of its role in reacting to and shaping markets is, it is crucial to investigate how these moral discourses come alive, get catalyzed, and become fiercely defended and enacted (Fourcade and Healy 2007: 286). Given the widespread condemnation of Wall Street in the wake of September 2008, it is easy to presume that

Wall Street moral articulations are simply ideological justifications to make bankers feel better.

The quandry is why claims of truth and market expertise by those on Wall Street have largely been undamaged by financialization having liquidated corporations, undermined productive assets, and created new, attendant risks; i.e., despite their models being proven "wrong," major financial institutions have maintained their status as engines for growth, investment allocators, and risk hedgers. I hope to make the case that for financiers it is precisely the presumed unassailability and uniqueness of their particular brand of meritocracy, not the lack of contradictions in their worldview, that propel their discourses forward. Their pinnacle status (both self-nominated and appointed) both gives them the agency and wherewithal to lay claim to social purpose despite failures, and serves as proof that the capitalist moral hierarchy and sense of relational self are correct.

Two intersecting characteristics form the pillars of Wall Street's moral standing. One is the supposed "smartness" of individual bankers – their intelligence and perspicacity. The other is the necessary accompaniment to smartness, the characteristic that catalyzes their meritocratic subjectivity – a combination of aggression, "drivenness," and speed.[8] This "catalyzed smartness" generates an innovative agility and a no-holds-barred attitude that constantly searches for and executes new approaches, permutations, and solutions in financial markets, constantly finding or manufacturing opportunity. It is not so much a particular technical expertise or knowledge that renders bankers superior; rather, it is the ability to swiftly mobilize innate smartness to exploit and solve new uncertainties and opportunities. In this context, furthermore, exorbitant banker bonuses also serve as evidence of Wall Street's moral abilities. Being empowered with the ability to literally make a fortune in a short amount of time, elite financial actors are socialized into a certain structure of feeling, one characterized by drive and a sense of something approaching omnipotence. This potent structure of feeling works hand in hand with "catalyzed smartness" to create the environment of competitive meritocracy in which Wall Street actors feel justifiably compelled to undertake the enormous project of remaking business practices at large in its own image. In this ideal universe, anything is possible, "things get done" immediately, and stagnancy is obliterated. In stark contrast, most other industries in the United States – what Wall Streeters understand to be "run-of-the-mill" corporate America – are literally understood to be "dumb," "slow," "fat." Such a schema, grounded in a hierarchy of superiority and inferiority, is buttressed, energized, and sealed in by moral righteousness, making it highly resistant to challenge and critique.

The consensus among Wall Street investment bankers (as well as most of the traders and financial consultants I have spoken with) is that what distinguishes and differentiates them from most other groups and industries is their smartness. With the exception of two informants, every elite employee, from managing directors to analysts, talked about pinnacle smartness. Wall Street places a "premium on having smart people … as opposed to the medium-quality students." Almost without fail, what investment bankers find the most rewarding about their jobs is being surrounded by "really smart and intelligent and really quick" people. "You can't be dumb and do this." "I like the most the fact that [we] are really smart people and you know, when you work in finance, you feel like your job is the center of the universe. And to a large degree, it has a lot of influence." As Jason Kedd, a mergers and acquisitions specialist at Donaldson, Lufkin, and Jenrette (now part of Credit Suisse First Boston), described the work environment, "It's very dynamic; it tends to be very fast-paced. You are working with a lot of very smart people … it is a stepping stone to a lot of different other things … [It's] a fairly aggressive culture, with high-grade personalities, generally." This rank ordering of smartness is so pervasive – within every organization in the financial world – that Wall Street employees who work in less prestigious, "back-office" departments (operations, internal auditing, risk management) will describe themselves as "not that smart" or "run of the mill," while marveling at the "innovation" and "creativity" of the fast-paced front office. These are employees who would, by most standards, be considered well qualified and able people, successful managers who hold JD and MBA degrees.[9] One high-level employee, who worked in "market surveillance" of insider trading in the New York Stock Exchange before investigating trading inconsistencies for an investment bank, remarked that unlike most of the people she attempts to watch over, she was "not innately smart": "I am not a genius. I'm just like this girl from New Jersey, you know. Really. My undergraduate degree is in special education from Glassburg State College, which is now known as Roland University. I am not innately smart. I mean, I'm not *dumb*. I have good people skills and I'm a good observer and I work hard."

In light of this hierarchical ranking, Wall Street's visceral distaste of institutions and actors they understand as "controlling" (i.e., regulatory and ratings agencies) gains clarity. Every graduate from business school, it seems, knows that it is only "the bottom of the heap" from their MBA class that goes to work at the ratings and regulatory agencies. As Peter Felsenthal, a bond trader at Saloman Smith Barney, told me, bankers and traders can "just figure how to beat the system. The whole thing is a kind of accounting game and there are a lot of ways that you can really, pretty easily get away with it for a number of years. What happens is that the people who are doing these things are a lot smarter than the people who risk-manage." The assumption is that no one wants to go into risk management; that is mainly for the MBAs who did not make the cut, could not get into front-office investment banking or trading. "In the big picture," this means that when you pit "bank regulator versus investment banker," the regulator will almost never be the "smarter" one. Thus "you can fool the other guy" every time.

Crucially, in Wall Street's view (though it resides in the realm of the taken-for-granted and is thus not explicitly articulated as such), smartness becomes fully kindled only when partnered with aggression, competition, and drive. As Jason Kedd further explains, investment bankers and traders are "very cynical and insecure … very smart," with a "fairly aggressive culture," who tend to have what he calls "high-grade personalities." Chris Logan, a high-yield analyst at Bankers Trust, immediately noticed that everyone "has to be smart, hardworking, and aggressive. Everything else is sort of considered tangential."

There is perhaps no better explicator of this specific combination than a 30-year veteran of Wall Street, Lou George, a retired managing director at Salomon Smith Barney; he explains it in terms of a "meritocratic contradiction":

> there is something at once very contemporary, very modern, very highly developed about Wall Street, and there are some things that are very *primitive* about it … *It's a very meritocratic place but also has a contradiction within.* On one hand, they sift through the best business schools. [On the other hand], the thing that is uniform and homogeneous

> about the population is the fact that they are all driven and aggressive … You always wind up with these interesting sort of dualities, these *interesting juxtapositions of opposites, [creating] something that's highly creative, highly intellectual, highly technical on one hand, and sort of primitive behaviors that go along with the execution.* [emphases mine]

It is precisely this mixture of meritocracy and primitivity, the smartness and the aggression, the moral and the immoral, which enables and produces economic, social, and moral achievement. Their "predatory aggression" allows them to execute and spread their meritocracy writ large.[10]

To put a finer point on it, in this imagined hierarchy of the business world, as articulated by Lou George, "by and large, the people on the Street are superior to their clients – in an almost evolutionary sense." And, it is precisely Wall Street's "willingness to compromise" mainstream codes of conduct, cut corners, and "play fast and loose" with normal barriers that we must *appreciate and credit* for innovation and socioeconomic betterment. Such vices, from taking advantage to unfair play, from cheating to trickery, are routinely understood as part and parcel of the rule-breaking, competitive drive needed to *make* new markets and create financial innovation. Competitive meritocracy, smartness combined with drive and competition, is the secret ingredient that forges an ethos that moves and creates markets. Moreover, Wall Street's morality is considered a higher morality than the usual sort: bankers are allowed to break the rules because they're superior beings. In Wall Street's moral understanding, then, the duality of morality and immorality is not a contradiction, but rather the very *condition* though which their moral achievements are made. Moreover, if Wall Street culture rewards, expects, and heightens individual and institutional "fast and looseness," does not full-scale fraud become the result? And yet, because such practices are seen less as deception than as competitive, edgy meritocracy, Wall Streeters are socialized to misunderstand the effects of their own industry. Many bankers were genuinely surprised that the totality of their actions led to global financial meltdown.

Finally, it is crucial to connect this cultivation of extralegal meritocracy, or rather, an exceptional smartness that transcends the normative, rule-bound world, to Wall Street's global imaginings. Finance renders fundamental its status as capitalist vanguard through the linking of meritocracy to the hierarchical differentiations between countries. Again, Lou George encapsulated the point: Wall Street is global, but "the technology and practices of investment and finance and capital markets really are American inventions that have been exported around the world." It is, therefore, New York finance that leads global economic achievement. George continued:

> The character of this overall enterprise is probably best [exemplified] by the big firms in New York and by what goes on there. It's at once a very intellectual and dynamic kind of enterprise – full of new and wonderful inventions … all these fancy, securitized financing vehicles. And it's also a very primitive, prototypical human enterprise in its emotions and in the aggression. It is the very pinnacle of achievement, very courageous in the sense of risk-taking, not in an ill-considered kind of sense, but they were better risk-takers than other people.

In a similar vein, Peter Felsenthal, a trader at Salomon Smith Barney, observed that in London,

> Things are much slower, they really are. It's not the sort of American work ethic. They kid around ... We had the luxurious lunch, [we didn't] sit at our desks every day like Americans do. In general, things tend to be a lot slower. [There] isn't this "things have to be done right away" attitude in London ... [But] at least London is pretty on top of things versus France.

Perhaps the bluntest distillation of this sensibility occurred when one Wall Street investment banker from now defunct Lehman Brothers told me, "Yes, there are smart and dumb countries. Greece, for example, is one of the dumb ones."[11]

Wall Street, then, structures and legitimates its moral position through the twin constitution of both a competitive and an imperial meritocracy. The broader understandings of "free market," "American exceptionalism," and evolutionary development grounded in colonial, global hierarchies and measures all inform Wall Street's moral culture. It is thus a mistake to presume that the following narrative – how financial "necessary evils" (from selfishness to creative destruction), when combined with Wall Street's particular institutional culture of liquidity and primitive meritocracy, produce the most efficient and best economic system in the world – is a mono-causal formation that is constructed inside an abstract financial bubble. Rather, Wall Street's moral order and practices, though particular, also intersect with longstanding, mainstream American cultural assumptions, which, it turns out, are complicit with, not antithetical to, financial morality.

Academic Interventions

By way of a coda, I wish to pose a provocative question: To what extent do social scientific representations of market moralities parallel official and mainstream understandings of finance? I make the argument that not only do these two fields of discourse unwittingly intersect, but the particular way in which social critics' understandings of financial morality articulate with the imaginings of key financial actors and institutions reinforces a circular logic that sidesteps the interrogation of existing, substantive moral subjectivities of elite financial actors. By pointing out these convergences and pitfalls, my point is not to oversimplify the multiplicity and contested nature of scholarly literatures on the sociality of financial markets, but rather to urge us, following Didier Fassin's plea for an "anthropology which has morals for its object," to continue to rethink and reframe why morality might be an effective tool for understanding financial markets and how we might best proceed (Fassin 2008: 334).

Sociologists Marion Fourcade and Kieran Healy make the important observation that for much of the social scientific history of analyses on markets, "intellectuals have variously praised, reviled, or downplayed the moral consequences of market capitalism" (Fourcade and Healy 2007: 305). Recent scholarship in such disciplines as economic sociology has gone beyond these three categories of moral, immoral, and amoral by "opening the black box of morality," understanding markets as "intensely moralized, and moralizing entities," and "dissecting the cultural and technical work necessary to produce, to sustain, or – conversely – to constrain the market" (286). While it is precisely this methodology that has influenced the present essay, it is instructive to understand why certain approaches to markets and morality have not provided the necessary tools to more critically comprehend contemporary practices and ideologies of finance.

Social scientific scholarly inquiry has predominantly categorized and approached markets as "civilizing," "destructive," or "feeble" (that is, amoral), such that they must be re-embedded into stronger social relations (Hirschman 1982). These approaches match the dominant discursive repertoires of financial advocates and spokespeople as well as the popular and critical media, where markets are predictably depicted as moral (as in the "doux commerce" view of free markets generating the fruits of civilization), immoral (greedy, destructive), or amoral (i.e., autonomous and characterized by naturalized logics of efficiency, rationality, and neutrality). In the argument that follows, I make the case that such parallelism detracts from an inquiry into how and why finance maintains a relatively robust social status despite the empirics of colossal failures.

Let us begin with the conceptual scheme that Albert O. Hirschman charted 30 years ago and the recent updating by Fourcade and Healy that is most applicable to critical social scientific scholarship: Hirschman's "destructive" thesis (which Fourcade and Healy reframed as the "commodified nightmare") as well as the "embeddedness" paradigm, which presumes markets to be abstract, amoral, empty, or, as Hirschman characterized them, "feeble." In the latter "embeddedness" approach, the character, form, and direction of markets depend upon their particular entanglements and ties to larger social institutions and cultural concerns (Fourcade and Healy 2007: 286, 291, 295–296). And yet, it is this conceptualization, which privileges amorality and presumes "culture" to be the external context that grounds essential and abstract markets, that is quite entrenched among social scientists. As Fourcade and Healy observe:

> The dominant paradigm of embeddedness implies that culture and institutions mediate, and often trump, the moral implications (good or bad) of capitalist markets. In this view, markets do not have a moral nature outside the particular social and cognitive arrangements from which they emerge and that sustain them. (2007: 286)

I argue that both the destructive, commodified thesis and the embeddedness approach are unsatisfactory for engaging with financial morality, in particular, because both are easily conflated with either the "greed is good," immoral-finance-as-moral paradigm or the popular view of rational, free markets as essentially amoral. That despite divergent social purposes, powerful advocates of finance and their critics can produce nearly identical interpretations blunts the very possibility of critique, and opens the way for critical work on finance to be mistaken for justification, or conscripted for use in Wall Street's rhetoric.

For example, in historical sociologist Greta Krippner's influential and trenchant critique of the embeddedness paradigm, she argues that "quite paradoxically, the basic intuition that markets are socially embedded – while containing an important insight – has led economic sociologists to take the market itself for granted" (2001: 776). Instead of exploding the constructed disciplinary and social boundaries between "economy" and "society," the embeddedness concept "was used to envelope and submerge the *asocial* market construct in social relations, all the while preserving intact the notion that somewhere there was a hard core of market behavior existing outside of social life (and hence that needed to be 'embedded')" (778; emphasis added). Adding to this binary is what might be dubbed a hierarchy of sociality or embeddedness, where instantaneous, transaction-oriented market practices are presumed to be further away and more disembedded from society, whereas class struggles, human resources, and organizational hierarchies are understood to be more closely imbricated in complex social relationships. Such an assumption allows "'social' factors" to "enter into the analysis only as one moves away from the market end of the continuum," thus reproducing the underlying notion of markets as asocial (784–785). This schema further reinforces finance – often understood as the most rarefied, temporally truncated, and abstract portion of markets – as outside the parameters of sociality, and by extension, as amoral. The dual construction of finance as both asocial and amoral reinforces its hold on the academic imagination as abstract, instrumental logics, and such a categorization, however inadvertent, complements mainstream notions of rational and efficient markets as neutral, natural, and self-regulating.

The "markets as destruction and commodification" thesis, which is strongly grounded in Marxist thought, also leads to an impasse in apprehending financial morality. While it goes without saying that critical, social scientific analyses of capitalism as alienation and exploitation, which "carries within itself 'the seeds of its own destruction,'" are indebted to Marx, it is important to also query the ramifications of this same scholarly legacy's avoidance of questions of morality (Hirschman 1982: 1467; Fourcade and Healy 2007: 291). Let us begin with what political and social theorist Steven Lukes has, importantly, called the fundamental moral paradox of Marxism. The paradox is this: On the one hand, Marxism invoked ethical and moral precepts in its advocacy for socialism, believing that such a society would be markedly better for humanity, with broad emancipatory effects. On the other hand, Marxism also attempted to transcend morality and ethical standpoints, mistrusting, even disdaining, moral judgments and authority as "bourgeois prejudice," ideology that is "social in origin, illusory in content, and serving class interests" (Lukes 1985: 3; Soper 1987: 103). "In short, what is striking about Marxism is its apparent commitment to both the rejection and the adoption of moral criticism and exhortation" (Lukes 1985: 4). This paradoxical ambivalence toward morality has set the stage for much debate, contestation, and a particular legacy of approaching capitalist markets. Some critics, for example, argue that the Marxist stance toward morality is ethically disabled and disabling, paving the way for dangerous policy and political consequences. In other words, the attempts to avoid all morality as biased, idealistic, and hierarchical renders Marxism not only less able to condemn atrocities committed in its name, but also allows it to "evade … crucial tasks" such as articulating what might constitute justice, "justifying the 'higher' or more emancipated nature of the coming future," and "detailing the types of institutions and forms of social intercourse essential to the realization of that future" (Soper 1987: 106; Majoribanks 2009).

While recognizing these pitfalls, many scholars also importantly sought to qualify these criticisms, emphasizing, for example, that Marx sought to historicize morality, to render it contingent, and to emphasize its potential for misuse.[12] "The moral critic," in Marjoribanks's view, seeks to "moralize history," and "imagines himself … outside of history, a spectator, able to pass judgment on history unconstrained by facts," which Marx assiduously avoided (2009: 3–4). In a sense, Marx's critical distrust of moralism was prescient: finance explicitly uses moral discourses to uphold powerful interests and redirect dissent. And, while I would agree that Marxism's important disavowal of ideological abstraction and moral advocacy as reproductive of ruling class interests continues to be an important challenge to contemporary capitalist practices, its simultaneous avoidance of morality has contributed to a *moral vacuum*, a legacy of privileging *amorality* and transcendence that has discouraged directly investigating moral cosmologies and how they are used. I make this observation in light of our complicated social context. As I have argued above, finance, like other powerful social systems, is often characterized by essentialist, self-evident, and teleological arguments and representations. Financial approaches to morality do *not* shy away from universal moral principles, moral righteousness, or moral superiority, precisely the kinds of ahistorical, naturalizing, and ruling-class-legitimating "truths" that Marx sought to avoid. Herein lies the rub: given our neglect of morality, how does one counter and resist a financial apparatus that not only flexibly inhabits multiple positions of morality, but also claims moral superiority, achievement, even truth?

For example, let us revisit how, in Wall Street self-understandings and representations, finance not only inhabits multiple properties of a moral spectrum (immoral, moral, and amoral), but also morphs from and into these three moral states, allowing finance to counter and move away from attempts to singularly locate or critique its practices. As the ideology goes, investment bankers, through their selfish greed for gain and corresponding exploitation of resources, ideas, and institutions (i.e., *the immoral*), create highly efficient, neutral markets (i.e., *the amoral)*, which in turn generate moral social purpose through higher standards of living, streamlined access to goods and services, and actualizations of the best ideas (i.e., *the moral)*. It is worth noting that these interrelated justifications are precisely what eighteenth-century defenders of capitalism utilized: private vice (paradoxically) functions as public virtue. Here we see that capitalist morality, immorality, and amorality are not only sutured together in a tightly knit ideological narrative, but also ventriloquize and stand in for one another in such a way that avoids targeted interrogation.

In this light, consider again the embeddedness paradigm and "destructive" thesis critiques of Wall Street. First, the "commodified destruction" scholarly critique is largely ineffective in the face of finance precisely because destruction is already built into finance's moral understanding of social purpose, virtue, progress, wealth creation, and entrepreneurial spirit. There is an already existing Wall Street antidote to anti-banker sentiment: immorality begets their moral universe. Financial morality, then, not only deflects Marxist criticism of capitalist "immorality," but its flexible structure also allows it to narrate moral inevitability and incorporate multiple moral states. Similarly, the "embeddedness" argument is no more effective in its critique of finance because it reinforces market amorality, which is finance's enduring normative position or baseline. In dominant finance, the amoral, for example, functions as part of a triadic feedback loop between immoral bankers, amoral markets, and good moral consequence. As such, unlike the empty scholarly notion of "feeble" and amoral finance, which needs to be embedded in society, Wall Street's notion of amorality is still deeply moral, and more flexibly resistant to challenge. I juxtapose these official "insider" and mainstream financial discourses of morality with their academic critiques to demonstrate that narrow scholarly interrogations of finance that do not pay attention to its larger epistemological and substantive structure are unable to fully challenge its powerful claims. In fact, I would argue that the triadic configuration of financial morality is actually quite empowering to Wall Street interests, practices, and institutions precisely because of its representational fluidity and multiplicity.

The epistemological structure of official financial understandings of morality gives powerful financial institutions and actors the flexibility to increase their points of connection with larger American cultural narratives of economy and society, while also offering a compelling, enveloping, and justificatory causal narrative. Importantly, of course, the conviction through which these discourses are articulated on Wall Street, not to mention "the proof" that these moral arguments are self-evident, is supported and grounded in the moral meritocracy and pinnacle status of elite financial actors (not the robust logic of their moral articulations). And yet the scholarly legacies and binary approaches of many social scientists and critics inadvertently dovetail with (and reinforce) official and mainstream financial moralities while rendering the local moralities of major Wall Street financial institutions and investment bankers difficult to investigate. Too often we ignore the morality of finance in general and, in particular, refuse to engage with Wall Street conceptualizations and practices of morality as *real*, preferring to dismiss them as misguided delusions, false consciousness, or self-serving justifications. What we do not get from such a refusal is a grounded, detailed, and everyday understanding of financial morality. And it is precisely a substantive and ethnographic understanding of financial morality – one that highlights the extent to which their moral habitus of "proto-meritocracy" undergirds their special sense of self, their superior placement in the hierarchy of economy, and their fluid articulation of social purpose – that can challenge their firmly integrated and socially sedimented moral representations to themselves and to the world. Given the exigencies of our contemporary moment, it is time for the anthropology of economy and finance to follow the lead of the Occupy Wall Street movements, who have centrally mobilized moral discourse – one that directly pivots on inequality – to challenge and critique dominant finance on moral grounds. Given that Wall Street itself has long used moral hierarchy to legitimate its own claims and practices, it is perhaps through an equally intense engagement with morality – one grounded in social and economic justice – that we can dislodge finance from its dominant place in our economic imagination.

NOTES

1 CEO of Goldman Sachs Lloyd Blankfein famously employed the term "God's work" in *The Times* with reference to the social importance and purpose of Wall Street a year after the "official" meltdown in September 2008 (Arlidge and Beresford 2009).

2 A transcription of the central lines of the speech is as follows: "The point is, ladies and gentlemen, that greed – for lack of a better word – is good. Greed is right. Greed works. Greed clarifies, cuts through and captures the essence of evolutionary spirit. Greed in all of its forms – greed for life, for money, for love, [for] knowledge, has marked the upward surge of mankind and greed – you mark my words – will not only save Teldar Paper but that other malfunctioning corporation called the USA. Thank you very much" (*Wall Street* 1987).

3 Interestingly enough, Oliver Stone articulated that, given his previous experience of "glorifying pigs," "he never would have made a second version if it didn't appear that the system, and high finance, had finally been brought to its knees." The irony here, of course, is that Wall Street has been reinvigorated, bailed out as it was, and deemed to be systemically necessary (Arango 2009).

4 The historical legacy has been forged through the complex imbrication of ahistorical myth-making and decontextualized appropriation: from particular interpretations of Adam Smith's self-interest precept to Milton Friedman's ideological intertwining of maximization and liberty, from Ayn Rand's contention that capitalism is the world's only true moral system to Reaganomics and Thatcherism, from evolutionary approaches in the development project to libertarianism.

5 Although I engaged with and interviewed a wide variety of financial actors (from traders to investment managers), my main informants were investment bankers who worked in corporate finance and mergers and acquisitions departments at major investment banks such as Merrill Lynch and Lehman Brothers. While my research has demonstrated that a focus on investment bankers as a central site can serve as a proxy for understanding Wall Street moralities more generally, it is important to note that trading, sales, research, and investment management units might also have divergent moral discourses and justifications. Large financial institutions, after all, are composed of multiple departments with specific organizational histories, recruitment practices, and incentives.

6 In this section, all the extended quotations from investment bankers, traders, and investment managers are taken from my interviews with front-office financial actors throughout most of the major Wall Street financial institutions during the time of my ethnographic field research (1997–99). Although all of my informants have been given pseudonyms, the investment banks in which they worked have not. Bankers Trust, for example, is not a pseudonym; it is the name of the bank where I worked. I changed the name of bankers' Wall Street affiliations only when their confidentiality could be compromised. It is important to remember that most of my informants are no longer working at the same banks and that most of the financial institutions have merged, gone bankrupt, or changed their names since the late 1990s.

7 Though such values were by in large accepted and imbibed by most of my informants, a few differences are important to note. One is that a few informants did not subscribe to the notion that Wall Street practices would always lead to social good (i.e., if companies simply focused on shareholder value, if Wall Street simply practiced its version of efficient, rational, free markets, all of society would benefit). For example, while John Carlton, a managing director at Bankers Trust, believed that Wall Street epitomizes efficient capital markets, which "increase innovation" and thus "prosperity," he stated that it is "not the conscience of society" and thus does not directly address issues of "distribution," "fairness," "employees," "environment." Second, while Wall Street's mainline moral arguments and beliefs were espoused by most of my informants, marked investment bankers (by race, gender, etc.) were less likely to frame their pinnacle status through grand evolutionary terms that were explicitly couched in the histories of moral imperialism.

8 As I have demonstrated (Ho 2009a, 2009b), Wall Street's workplace culture, based on worship of smartness and the cultivation of privileged biographies and networks, produces institutional structures that thrive on liquidity and real-time market identity, which are in turn writ large to restructure corporate America. The moral habitus that is cultivated in this context is that of investment bankers assuming self-imagined roles as the heroes of corporate America and guardians of the moral order of American capitalism.

9 Even in the face of failure, smartness is unquestioned. Referring to Long-Term Capital Management, the bankrupt hedge fund that almost brought down the global financial markets in 1998 before receiving a bailout, one banker still proclaimed, "What an amazing firm. You are talking about the smartest people in the world. You are. They are the smartest people in the world. If you don't know anything, why wouldn't I invest with the smartest people in the world. They must know what they are doing. And I mean it is just the [a panic] – they have no control over that."

10 In fact, what differentiates Wall Street's smartness from the sorts of smartness valued by non-Wall Street people and institutions is its extraordinary, rule-bending speed and decisiveness. Investment bankers often like to compare themselves favorably to plodding bureaucracies mired in red tape and internal rivalries. According to John Carlton, a managing director at Bankers Trust, "In comparison with other corporate entities and even compared with universities, [Wall Street] is not very bureaucratic. I spent a lot of years at universities. Universities are pretty bureaucratic. They have a lot of smart people, but they have problems with this, problems with that. There is infighting and politics and that sort of thing. We are, in comparison, pretty efficient."

11 While many European countries and Japan are understood to be close competitors, (as opposed to entire spaces which are rendered virtually invisible, such as Africa), they are commonly denigrated as incapable of global economic mastery because they are stymied by regulation, bureaucracy, and a lack of aggression.

12 While it makes little sense to blame Marxism for either the fetishization of historical materialism such that the inevitable ends justify the means, or the explicitly moral utilization of good and evil to justify the dominance of finance capital, Marxism's ambivalent approaches to morality does leave a theoretical gap. The hope, of course, was that the proletarian revolution could transcend morality: it would happen through practice, propelled by the unsustainable conditions of historical materialism, not through the powerful articulation of ideology and holier-than-thou moral legitimation.

REFERENCES

Arango, Tim (2009) Greed is Bad, Gekko. So is a Meltdown. *New York Times* (Sept. 7). At http://www.nytimes.com/2009/09/08/movies/08stone.html?_r=1&dbk, accessed Mar. 21, 2012.

Arlidge, John and Beresford, Philip (2009) Inside the Goldmine. *Sunday Times* (Nov. 8).

Binham, Caroline (2009) Goldman Sach's Griffiths Says Inequality Helps All (Update 1). Bloomberg. Oct. 21. At http://www.bloomberg.com/apps/news?pid=newsarchive&sid=a8upOpH5Q3Tw, accessed Mar. 21, 2012.

Broughton, Philip Delves (2009) Wall Street 2: Gordon Gekko is Back. *London Evening Standard* (Sept. 14). At http://www.thisislondon.co.uk/lifestyle/wall-street-2-gordon-gekko-is-back-6751551.html, accessed Mar. 21, 2012.

Farrell, Greg (2010) *Crash of the Titans: Greed, Hubris, the Fall of Merrill Lynch, and the Near-Collapse of Bank of America.* New York: Crown Business.

Fassin, Didier (2008) Beyond Good and Evil? Questioning the Anthropological Discomfort with Morals. *Anthropological Theory* 8: 333–344.

Fourcade, Marion, and Healy, Kieran (2007) Moral Views of Market Society. *Annual Review of Sociology* 33: 285–311.

Hightower, Jim (2009) The Worthiness of Banker Charity. Nov. 18. At http://www.creators.com/opinion/jim-hightower/the-worthiness-of-banker-charity.html, accessed 15 September 2011.

Hirschman, Albert O. (1982) Rival Interpretations of Market Society: Civilizing, Destructive, or Feeble? *Journal of Economic Literature* 20: 1463–1484.

Ho, Karen (2009a) Disciplining Investment Bankers, Disciplining the Economy: Wall Street's Institutional Culture of Crisis and the Downsizing of American Corporations. *American Anthropologist* 111: 177–189.

Ho, Karen (2009b) *Liquidated: An Ethnography of Wall Street.* Durham, NC: Duke University Press.

Johnson, Simon and Kwak, James (2010) *13 Bankers: The Wall Street Takeover and the Next Financial Meltdown.* New York: Pantheon.

Krippner, Greta (2001) The Elusive Market: Embeddedness and the Paradigm of Economic Sociology. *Theory and Society* 30: 775–810.

Lewis, Michael (2010) *The Big Short: Inside the Doomsday Machine*. New York: Norton.

Lukes, Steven (1985) *Marxism and Morality*. Oxford: Oxford University Press.

Majoribanks, David (2009) Marxism and Morality: Out of the "Moral Wilderness"? Paper presented at the Marx and Philosophy Society Annual Conference, University of London. June 6.

Popper, Nathaniel (2010) Wall Street Insiders Open Up for "Money Never Sleeps." *Los Angeles Times* (Sept. 24). At http://articles.latimes.com/2010/sep/24/business/la-fi-ct-wall-street-20100924, accessed Mar. 21, 2012.

McGee, Suzanne (2010) *Chasing Goldman Sachs: How the Masters of the Universe Melted Wall Street Down … And Why They'll Take Us to the Brink Again*. New York: Crown Business.

Soper, Kate (1987) Review of *Marxism and Morality*, by Steven Lukes. *New Left Review* 163: 101–113.

Sridhar, Andrew (2009) MBA Oath: An Oath and Its Flaws. *The Harbus* (Sept. 28.). At http://www.harbus.org/2009/MBA-Oath-An-Oath-4645/, accessed Mar. 21, 2012.

Wall Street (1987) [Film] Dir. Oliver Stone; prod. Edward Pressman. 20th Century Fox.

Zigon, Jarrett (2010) Moral and Ethical Assemblages: A Response to Fassin and Stoczkowski. *Anthropological Theory* 10: 3–15.

CHAPTER 24 Law

Carol J. Greenhouse

Law is not a legal category; its generality belongs to the human sciences – and with it, the question of law's morality. Today, the morality of law is acutely in question in the anthropology of law, as a point of theoretical renewal and critical recuperation. Readers familiar with legal anthropology's traditions at mid-century will know that one major interpretive tradition was an emphasis on the continuity between legal rules and social norms, reading the one as evidence of the other. Once this formulation was called into question in the 1980s, it yielded to a second interpretive focus on questions of power, and the entwinements of power, social knowledge, discourse, and identity (for synoptic reviews, see Nader 1965; Moore 1970; Collier 1975; Merry 1992; and Mertz 1994).

The starting point of this essay is in the observation that most recent work pursues neither of these routes. Contemporary ethnographers make evident their deep concerns with the morality of law in their attention to it as an interpretive issue, but just as evidently they seek neither a continuity of law and social norms nor a unifying theory of power. Instead, their moral critiques of law are performed as ethnographic practice itself, as ethnographers draw attention by the very pragmatics of their craft to a break between the interests and values of legal institutions and the communities they serve. Moral community emerges ethnographically from these studies in relational terms, embedded in (and as) the social.[1] In this sense, while current work departs from a vision of law and society as a continuous cultural field, it does so in ways that situate *social science* as a theoretical check on the legitimation claims of legal institutions.

In interesting ways, the break between law and society, and the explicit rendering of the social as moral community, return us to the classic formulations of a social science rationale for the ethnography of law as developed by Emile Durkheim and Bronislaw Malinowski at the turn of the twentieth century – another time of unsteady nationalisms and unsettled discourses of state legitimation. Today, those formulations invite fresh reading, as present circumstances illuminate hesitations in those foundational works that the main reception traditions – born of liberal state nationalisms in

A Companion to Moral Anthropology, First Edition. Edited by Didier Fassin.

a more confident age – have tended to overlook. In what follows, I begin with a rereading of the conversation between Durkheim and Malinowski, as preface and reader's guide of sorts, to a synthesis of current work in terms of its implications for anthropologies of morality in our own times.

"Pictures of Nothing"

By the time Malinowski gave the lectures that appeared as *Crime and Custom in Savage Society*, Durkheim was dead, his ideas about law recast and resorbed into the generalized notions of collectivity, structure, and function then current in British social anthropology. Malinowski caricatures the notion of collective conscience as "the assumption that in primitive societies the individual is completely dominated by the group ... he obeys the commands of his community, its traditions, its public opinion, its decrees, with a slavish, fascinated, passive obedience" (1985 [1926]: 3–4) – ascribing this view to "the French school of Durkheim" among others. Later in *Crime and Custom*, he cautions against the "exaggerated views" of Durkheim along with Rivers, Sidney Hartland "and others" (55), ascribing to "the great French sociologists Durkheim and Mauss" the view that "responsibility, revenge, in fact all legal reactions are founded in the psychology of the group and not of the individual" (57).

This is unfair to Durkheim (and to Mauss, to whom Malinowski offers an olive branch in a footnote: 1985: 41 n. 1). For Durkheim, mechanical solidarity was not some sort of group thinking but a symbolic order that gives precedence to adherence over recognition as the basis for identity. The symbolic order of mechanical solidarity makes the leader and the criminal alike the embodiment of the collectivity – an operation made visible in criminal sanctions. Similarly, for Durkheim, under conditions of organic solidarity, the leader and the criminal are alike in making visible a symbolic order based on mutual recognition. Mechanical and organic solidarity are the two broad routes to Durkheim's formulation of "conscience" as the active principle of morality constituted in "society": "Society does not find the bases on which it rests fully laid out in consciences; it puts them there itself" (1933: 350). Read in context, that statement does not negate the individual, but rather calls into sharp question the moral legitimacy claimed by the state and other powerful institutions (Durkheim 1933, 1992 [1957]; Jones 2001, 2002; Rawls 2003; Greenhouse 2011b). That formulation is a broader version of his famous antithesis: "we must not say that an action shocks the common conscience because it is criminal, but rather that it is criminal because it shocks the common conscience" (Durkheim 1933: 81). As I argue at length elsewhere (Greenhouse 2011b), Durkheim's formulation of law in *Division of Labor in Society* and *Professional Ethics and Civic Morals* calls into question the very assumption often ascribed to him by his sharpest critics – that is, a communitarianism that would make law the de facto expression of collective values.

Malinowski distances himself from Durkheim on that critical ground. He derides "the old 'shocker' interest in the over-emphasis of criminal justice, in the attention devoted to the breaches of the law and their punishment" (1985: 72) and shifts his focus to what he terms civil law (73–84). But for Malinowski, too, law's main function in the text is as a keyword that makes visible the "binding force" of social relations (1985: 29, 55, 67). If people obey legal rules, it is not because they are incapable of breaking them, or because it is in their interest to do what is expected of them. He tells us that legal norms have no binding force of their own; it is other social forces that align norms with feelings, such that acting in accordance with norms takes on a positive valence – when it does. Malinowski is insistent on a break between law and anything that could be called an inherent moral force: "reciprocity, systematic incidence, publicity and ambition will be found to be the main factors in the binding machinery of primitive law" (1985: 68). On this point, Malinowski's reception – which tends to conflate his idea of legal norms with social norms (for discussion of such traditions, see Moore 1970: 256–261; Nader 2002: 85) – has perhaps been as unfair to his subtlety as he was to that of Durkheim.

Malinowski seems to be drawn to the very element in Durkheim that he resists. That he refers to his project as *law* at all suggests this. Since Trobrianders had neither jural or legislative institutions as such, nor a definite category "law" (Malinowski 1985: 58–59), there was no inherent need for Malinowski to refer to his subject matter as law except that Durkheim (et al.) had done so. He could have called it economics, or exchange – and sometimes did. Significantly, Malinowski's law is not empirically accessible; it is an inference he draws from the disparities between normative discourse and the actualities of everyday life. Law neither describes nor explains behavior, he insists throughout *Crime and Custom*; rather, legal rules swim in a normative soup with other rules, norms, and commandments (Malinowski 1985: 54). For Malinowski, law is a particular register of social cohesion, but not the only one: "though in my survey attention has naturally been mainly focused on the legal machinery, *I was not intent on proving that all social rules are legal, but on the contrary, I wanted to show that the rules of law form but one well-defined category within the body of custom*" (54; emphasis added). Rules of law "stand out" by their being supported "by a definite social machinery of binding force, based … upon mutual dependence, and realized in the equivalent arrangement of reciprocal services, as well as in the combination of such claims into strands of multiple relationship" (1985: 55). In short, "law" is an interpretive category for Malinowski – a choice he makes, at once theoretically based on his observations of the slippage between enunciated norms and everyday practice, and critically trenchant in reflexive terms: "The heathen can be as self-seeking and self-interested as any Christian" (1985: ix).

Importantly, then, legal rules are not moral rules for Malinowski; rather, he tells his readers that morality enters law through norms attached to "legal statuses." These appear to be norms that maintain asymmetrical relationships as reciprocal ones: "the whole structure of Trobriand society is founded on the principle of *legal status*. By this I mean that the claims of chief over commoners, husband over wife, parent over child, and vice versa, are not exercised arbitrarily and one-sidedly, but according to definite rules, and arranged into well-balanced chains of reciprocal services" (1985: 46; emphasis original). The specificity of this point helps account for what could otherwise be taken as a paradoxical rendering of law as both general ("The rules of their law … are maintained by social forces": 74) and, at the same time, pervasively subject to doubt ("It would be a very one-sided picture indeed of the law in the Trobriands, if the rules were shown only in good working order, … in equilibrium": 74). The paradox disappears once we read Malinowski as formulating the principal domain of law not in reciprocity in general, but in the specificities of a normative association of legal statuses and what he frequently refers to as "clan solidarity" – itself subject to fissures and reformulations in practice (112).

In this respect, too, Malinowski approaches Durkheim even as he opposes him, in constructing law as the visibility of social structure – a dubious visibility from an empirical or pragmatic standpoint. For Durkheim, it is criminal sanctions that – under the terms of his thought experiment in *Division of Labor* – make the "collective conscience" visible. Malinowski is at pains to connect law to sanctions, as in his claim that the violation of a moral norm has no consequences unless and until they are mobilized by an active social response (notably shaming). Where Durkheim is (largely) silent on law, Malinowski is (largely) silent on collective conscience, but not completely so:

> The unity of the clan is a legal fiction in that it demands – in all native doctrine, that is in all their professions, and statements, sayings, overt rules and patterns of conduct – an absolute subordination of all other interests and duties to the claims of clan solidarity, while, in fact, this solidarity is almost constantly sinned against and practically non-existent in the daily run of ordinary life. (1985: 119)

Where Durkheim is ironic with regard to an association of organic solidarity with modernity, Malinowski, too, demurs from the notion that solidarity is an empirical fact. For Malinowski, narrative may produce an idealization of law; however, real life is another matter: "This [i.e., the complexity of real life], like everything else in human cultural reality is not a consistent logical scheme, but rather a seething mixture of conflicting principles" (1985: 121).

Law has no clear boundaries for Malinowski. It is not social *rules* but social *relations* that give law its "binding force" – when it has force at all (1985: 29, 55, 67). While "the commandments of law and custom are always organically connected and not isolated … they only exist in the chain of social transactions in which they are but a link" (125). Still, the organic quality of these "chains of reciprocal services" does not make law a system: "Primitive law is not a homogeneous, perfectly unified body of rules, based upon one principle developed into a consistent system" (100; see also 79). The society as a whole "is founded on the principle of *legal status*" (46; emphasis added). In sum, Trobriand law is about the relational qualities of legal statuses – and morality enters law, if it does, only through the feelings associated with norms of reciprocity as these are lived outside of law. Recall, again, that "law" was an optional term.

Over the decades since its reception, this formulation of Malinowski's tends to be overwritten by the very equations he resists: rules of law = social rules; law's function = maximizing interests. The reception tradition surrounding *Crime and Custom* reduces Malinowski's concerns to the form of a social contract just as Durkheim's hermeneutics of legitimacy in *Division of Labor* has been recast as a definition of law. Law, though visible in punishment (for Durkheim) and exchange (for Malinowski), is a "picture of nothing" – in Varnedoe's (2006) sense of modernist abstraction, the ethnographer sustaining for the observer an experience of law's moral arbitrariness and emptiness. Moral meaning is social; law is something else. Malinowski, like Durkheim before him, works law in relation to the social through an ethnographic practice conceived as a "recurrent push for the temporarily meaningless" (Varnedoe 2006: 271) – and in this sense, in retrospect, suspending the ordinary meanings of law, committing law to alien moralities, and reframing law *through social science* as an interpretive and critical project that bears directly on the moral self-legitimation of contemporary states.

What is at stake in mending relations between Malinowski and Durkheim is a sharper understanding of the anthropological investment in legal institutions as the locations of a particular sort of accountability – the moral accountability of those whose mutual expectations (per Malinowski) are particularly visible as emblematic of the social (per Durkheim). Their missing conversation is particularly relevant in our own moment, in aid of tracking the emergence of a new anthropology of law that takes its critical force from the moral claims of people who seek relief or revindication against state actors under the law, and thus giving ethnography itself a particular critical burden. That law is a critical vantage point inscribed in the very notion of the social is evident in ethnographers' concerns with law's failures or with its absence as a sign of larger social deficits, and a source of demoralizing effects. It seems we (anthropologists, citizens, strangers) are taking the measure of our times when we align law against the social in these ways, in effect setting law against what may be its own claims to moral legitimacy, through an ethnographic practice that doubles as moral critique. Where anthropological scholarship on law once treated it as self-evidently moral by virtue of its social embeddedness, we now know that nothing of law's morality can be assumed in advance. In pursuit of their own interests, legal institutions cannot be presumed to be either innocent of conniving nor immune to a calculus of indifference (see Clastres 1989: 43).

Re-engaging that classic dialogue also lends clarity to the conceptual location of law in relation to the relativity principle that animated ethnology before World War II, as distinct from the relativism that entered anthropological parlance in the war's aftermath. Law was not a "total social fact" for Durkheim; it was the visible product of particular institutions at work. For Malinowski, law was his term for the binding effect of particular reciprocal relations. In neither case did law feature as an empirical project – but only and always as an interpretive project, reflexively turned back on familiar Western institutions that wind legality around claims of moral legitimacy. Thus, their cultural relativity entails no particular claims for a relativity of law as moral or cultural practice; again – their association of law and morality is an interpretive venture, not an empirical finding. In this sense, both Durkheim and Malinowski set law outside of any universalist–particularist paradigm. As we shall see, these clarifications are relevant to current anthropological debates over international human rights law – seen by some as a universalist, antirelativist project.

Law in/as the Social, I: The Legal as Moral Irony

> *It must be remembered that those who invent the world are not fully autonomous beings.*
>
> Gananath Obeyesekere, *Imagining Karma*, 2002 (p. 348)

Let us turn now to current landscapes. Contemporary legal ethnographers, though working in settings that might have been unknown or unimaginable at the beginning of the twentieth century, continue to limn the morality of law through their attention to legal processes, legal statuses, and institutional *techne* as the far side of a break between law and the social. The idea of such a break is not in itself new: it is as old as the is/ought distinction that animated much early work in sociolegal studies, and it is familiar, too, as a horizon of political tension and hegemonic effect. Those issues remain, but what is striking in the current work is the range and variety of settings in which that break is formulated theoretically as a *moral* break – in the process reinstantiating a vision of solidarity as a moral or ethical bond accessible to ethnography and in relation to which ethnographic practice is an active form of participation. In what follows, I review a selection of current literature that suggests both the enduring legacy of legal anthropology's attachment to the social as a locus of moral constitution, and its currency in resisting any a priori construction of law as a consolidation of moral concerns. To be sure, there is more than the unfinished business between Durkheim and Malinowski that moves today's legal anthropologists to take up their ethnographic and critical positions – but Malinowski's ironic sensibility is suggestive in relation to current anthropological concerns with the status of the state relative to moral community, and with the status of relativism relative to legal pluralism.

The universalist–particularist debate appears to have entered anthropology from the legal profession (see Latour 2004 [2002]: 267), questions of local legality arriving into anthropology precoded as a question of cultural relativity. The traces of universalist–relativist (or universalist–pluralist) debates are evident in the new ethnographic accounts, but current anthropological studies of human rights law in action suggest that that polarity errs twice – both in its construction of human rights as a global or universal legal field and in its misreading of local practices as ruptures of that field (Dembour 2006; Merry 2006; F. von Benda-Beckmann 2009; Clarke 2009; Goodale 2009; Goodale and Clarke 2010; Wilson 2010).

Here, too, Malinowski's formulation of the ethnography of law has a salutary relevance, as his claim is not that law is everywhere, or locally relative – only that it features centrally among the cherished notions the European scholars of his own time offer in defense of their claims to cultural superiority. Malinowski bends this prejudice back, never relativizing, but detailing the sense in which "the 'savages' [note his scare quotes] do not differ from the members of any self-contained community with a limited horizon, whether this be an Eastern European ghetto, an Oxford college, or a Fundamentalist Middle West community" (1985: 52).

In this context, new ethnographic studies of international tribunals offer novel reprises of anthropology's classic concerns with trouble cases and the normative work of jural institutions (Kelly and Dembour 2007: 2). Those questions are now turned the other way, to focus on the ways the universalist premises of international criminal tribunals (ICTs) and human rights tribunals are themselves potentially disabling of those very institutions, producing new forms of disjuncture and differential. Barkan refers to the "incoherence of human rights" in this regard (2011: 180; see also Wilson 2010).[2] Legal anthropology's classic postcolonial formulation of legal pluralism also faces new challenges, at least to the extent that it translated cultural relativism into a subsidiarity principle favoring a universalistic notion of state-made law (see Clarke 2009; Goodale and Clarke 2010).

Malinowski deploys ethnography to ironize both the claims of legal institutions as to their self-evident moral vindication *and* any proclaimed universality of law. That double voice resonates throughout anthropology's current projects with law, particularly in transnational social fields. Novel ethnographic locations have emerged from tribunals with transnational mandates. In recent years, anthropologists have studied ICTs in Rwanda, Guatemala, Peru, South Africa, the former Yugoslavia, and the United States (Greensboro, NC), as well as the European Court of Human Rights (Dembour 2006; Theidon 2006; Magarrell and Wesley 2008; Clarke 2009; Wilson 2010). Courts are increasingly used for political ends ("lawfare" in the phrase of Comaroff and Comaroff 2006: 22) and, in the international arena, as legal "antidotes to impunity" (Macedo 2004: 6).

Domestic criminal courts are also increasingly faced with parties who are themselves transnationally mobile. For example, Susan Hirsch gives a remarkable first-person account – as survivor, witness, and ethnographer – of the New York City federal criminal trial of the men charged with the bombing of the United States embassy in Nairobi (Hirsch 2006: on the negotiations of survivor status, see especially ch. 2). Coutin's study of asylum hearings for Salvadoran refugees in California gives a nuanced account of the intricate cross-border interconnections of legal pragmatics, personal subjectivity, and social policy (2000; see also Coutin 2007). These accounts illustrate with particular vividness how the anthropological sensibility to moral force is associated with intimacy (ethnographic and otherwise), against the depersonalizing effects of law.

Indeed, the critical thrust of current ethnographic practice with respect to law is indicated in the way *opposition* itself is rendered as evidence of a subject's moral or ethical agency in relation to the state's interested hold on sovereignty, redress, and channels of humanitarian relief. For example, an ethnographic account of a prison strike in Ecuador is taken as evidence of the prisoners' subjectivity: "the quickening power of political theology as an ethical foundation for contesting sovereign violence" (Garces 2010: 491). Cultural tradition is proposed as evidence of a jurisdictional claim: "Hopi cultural politics might be productively rethought as expressions of Hopi jurisdiction that orient to the limits of Hopi sovereign authority, even as they presuppose its power" (Richland 2011: 205). Failures of "clinical continuity" in AIDS treatment reveal a critical gap between "state and citizen" (Biehl 2010: 188). On its largest scale, that critical gap is the conceptual space of a highly contemporary vision of humanitarianism as both a "moral discourse (based on responsibility toward victims) and a political resource (serving specific interests)" (Fassin 2010b: 239). The critical implication of that vision is inherent in the formulation of humanitarianism as a commitment to reconciling political interests around "life in its multiple forms" (Fassin 2010a: 94).

Anthropological critiques of law also echo claimants' protests against state actors. In this vein, one important new literature tracks indigenous claims to sovereignty, increasingly reliant on "native legalities" as well as human rights law (Buchanan and Darian-Smith 2011: 116; see also Comaroff and Comaroff 2009; Biesaw 2010; McMillan 2011; Nesper 2011; van Krieken 2011). Another new area of sociolegal research examines the prosecution of state actors, including heads of state – some 67 of whom have been prosecuted between 1990 and 2008 (Macedo 2004; Lutz and Reiger 2009). The narrative voice in these accounts implicitly resonates with the discourse of universal jurisdiction, as in Mary Robinson's assessment that "certain crimes are too heinous to go unpunished" (2004: 17) – a neat rhetorical inversion of Durkheim's formulation of collective conscience, in that the idea of *impunity* is shocking. This is a comment not just on the mood of the moment, but also on the contemporary legal apparatus of impunity: sovereign immunity, selective prosecutions, failures of the administration of justice, political evasions of culpability, or the risk of prosecution.

Law in/as the Social, II: Legal Status as Moral Bond

The law needs the company of other virtues.

Nasser Hussain and Austin Sarat, "Toward New Theoretical Perspectives on Forgiveness, Mercy and Clemency: An Introduction," 2007 (p. 1)

There is a a Durkheimian side to these current ethnographic projects in the way they mobilize the social to sustain their critical ironies – the social understood as the location, or implication, of moral relations outside the state. As noted earlier with respect to the "gap" of care between states and citizens, or between politics and "the human," contemporary scholars formulate that difference as moral distance – implicitly locating moral community where Durkheim does: in mutual recognition, and in the felt obligations and intimate exchanges of everyday life. By virtue of its attention to everyday practices, ethnography by its very nature heightens the differentiation between formal law and the felt force of mutual expectation in the Durkheimian sense.

Importantly in this regard, the moral implication of the social emerges through the ethnography itself – not as metanarrative. In his ethnographic study among West Bank Palestinians, Kelly tracks the moral implication of the social through local debates over rights and the "jurisdictional politics" of the West Bank (2009 [2006]: 78). He explores the discursive contingencies that derive individual rights from collective rights based largely on ethnonationalist principles – which in turn "potentially undermine" individual rights (14–15). The ethnography does not stop with a statement of law's incompleteness or the conundrums of rights; these are thrown into relief ethnographically, especially when observation is conducted at check points on the Green Line – where rights, identities, legality, illegality, autonomy, and contingency are daily scrambled in real time (ch. 4).[3]

Such moral distancing is an analytic as well as an ethnographic object in current ethnographies from war zones, postconflict situations, and other sites of radical insecurity – sometimes explicitly so. For example, in her ethnographic study of everyday practices of security in Israel, Ochs finds that self-protection merges with security practices of state. Such practices and the fantasies that sustain them are bound up in rationales for a certain kind of state while also constructing security and fear as "beyond politics" (2011: 4); one of her main conclusions is that the "illusion of normalization" precludes popular engagement with possibilities for ameliorating the conflict (18). In Ochs's study and others (Goldstein 2004; Peteet 2005; Maček 2009; Feldman 2010; Greenberg 2011), the ethnographic project does not rest with the irony that policing and other security practices fail to achieve their ends; rather, they examine in detail how those very practices materially contribute to insecurity – even if they also offer selective and transitory moments of relief or redress.

The experiential effects of a moral inversion of sovereignty and security are explicit in recent ethnographic work on treason and liberation movements (Kelly and

Thiranagama 2010a). Such ethnographies are legible against a more general state of affairs in which the very notion of ethnic, subaltern, or minoritarian "identity" has been drawn into the meaning of citizenship through the hegemonies of modern governing as both an affirmation of inclusion in an encompassing state and a threat of alienation. In the United States, the political mainstreaming of neoliberalism in the 1990s was accomplished in part through an explicit critique of antidiscrimination protections in law as reverse racism – and as the infrastructure of a culture of dependency (Greenhouse 2011a).

Property (as capital, land, sovereign territory, and in other forms) is central to the materialization of the social as it emerges in ethnography through anthropologists' current engagements with law (Cattelino 2008; K. von Benda-Beckmann 2009; Braverman 2009; Clemmer 2009; Comaroff and Comaroff 2009; Li 2009). To some extent, property has displaced *identity* as anthropologists' primary opening to law through the social – reflecting liberalism's shift from rights discourse (in the United States, specifically civil rights) toward markets, as well as the prominence of property claims attendant on revindications of sovereignty (Comaroff and Comaroff 2009). Such reformulations challenge the conventions of scale, even as the geopolitics of scale come under revision (as in the creation of the European Union and other transnational arrangements: Abélès 1996) – profoundly unsettling the localizing conventions that gave anthropology its traditional associations (still current in some quarters outside the discipline) with remoteness and traditionalism. Contemplating the potential for an anthropology of globalization, Abélès notes the role of anthropology in the "de-reification" and "de-sacralization" of the state (2008: ch. 3). He envisions an "anthropology of globalization" as a space for diverse anthropologies to address each other – suspending the discourse of center and periphery (2008: 102–105). Transnationalism, he argues, is not the cause of the displacement of politics, but its effect – politics increasingly drawn toward survival (notably but not only in the context of terrorism) and irreducible to institutions (124, 152, 158 and passim; Abélès 2010).

The "rupture with the idea of the bright future" (Abélès 2010: 20) signals the eruption of broad questions – in anthropology as elsewhere – with respect to the relationship of *the human* to *power* (124). For Abélès and others (including some discussed above), the politics of life – of survival – is a theoretical re-engagement with a Foucauldian notion of the capillary circulation of power, challenging any convention that would limit sovereignty to containment around a vertical axis that culminates in "the" state (Abélès 2008: 130). This is an imaginative recalibration of politics itself – its institutions and forms of agency not yet known.

Such visions of a politics of the future are, for now, located critically and ethnographically in studies of the practices of legal institutions, NGOs, and state regulation – where the *human* doubles as the keyword of anthropology's widest embrace of the social, and its most fundamental critical discourse. Feldman and Ticktin open their edited volume with the question: "What does it mean to claim 'humanity' as your political constituency?" (2010b: 1) – drawing out contradictions ("sentiment and threat": 6; see also Hirsch 2006 and Malkki 2010) and ambivalances ("the peril of imperial expansion": 25; see also Fassin 2010b: 239). Fassin explores these tensions in his interrogation of humanitarianism as moral discourse and political resource, as well as the pervasive contradictions between the universalism of that discourse and the practicalities that create inequalities and exclusions (2010b: 239). But if humanity is an emergent "political fact" (Fassin 2010b: 255; 2010a), there is a political project of "enlarging the circle of moral inclusion … [and the] obligation to treat fellow humans as connected" (Feldman and Ticktin 2010b: 2). Law, ethnographically, marks critical locations where those connections emerge in and as an ongoing "politics of presence" (Anne Phillips, quoted in Ritter 2006: 297–325).

Law as *Techne*

A poem itself is something that happens.

Michael Wood, *Yeats and Violence*, 2010 (p. 137)

In the works cited above, law's concreteness is critical (literally and figuratively) to its theoretical salience as ethnographic object and its ethical salience as a register of moral critique. The moral critique targets the depoliticization of the state and the dehumanization of citizenship; the "state of emergency" is compelling as both an actual state of affairs and critical synecdoche (Calhoun 2010: 30, 55). In this context, for anthropologists, the concreteness of the legal as subject matter is the other side of its epistemic availability for the ethical transformation of social relationships.[4] Understanding law as *techne* (practical knowledge) is thus a critical foil to the concept of agency – the intentional specificity of agency ethnographically countering the generality of a legal field that is "everywhere" and "nowhere" – to borrow from Clastres (1989: 18) in a related context – particularly within the social fields of legal practice.

The technologies of law are emergent ethnographic concerns – for example, in studies of the social relations of technical expertise in legal education (Mertz 2007), legal reasoning (Riles 2011) and law-making (Latour 2004). Anthropologists prepared to manage the legal profession's internal knowledge demands (gaining fluency through a law degree, for example, in addition to their ethnographic work) are increasingly engaged on terrains of "collateral knowledge" (to borrow from the title – and spirit – of Riles 2011). These ethnographic accounts of legal practices are major ethnographies of knowledge that remind us that legal authority claims the monopoly not only of legitimate violence but also certain forms of writing and speech (Clastres 1989: 151–155; see also Latour 2004: 298–299). In these studies, in other words, law's forms of knowledge are "duplex" – that is, forms of knowledge drawn and reworked from other social fields: including formulations of subjectivity, agency, hierarchy, purpose, and personal fate (Strathern 2005: 83–91; see also Jain 2006).

In some contexts, legal practices are shown in their capacity to empty the social of its political implication. From that perspective, Coles examines the technology of the ballot box in her ethnography of an international inspection team in Bosnia, finding that the reduction of the election to "political techne" reworks the very meaning of the election – "depoliticiz[ing] and naturaliz[ing] the constructed and contested ideas of representation, participation and trust" (2007: 245).[5] That said, the technicalities of politics do not automatically cancel strong subjective involvement. Abélès's (2005) study of electoral defeat opens with an account of the deep visceral responses of candidates and supporters alike, as they register an unthinkable defeat in terms shared with powerful social experiences such as illness, mourning, and shock.

The technical aspects of law are reminders that law, like governing more generally, involves multiple materialities, including the materiality of labor. In this regard, Harney's formulation of "a phenomenology of government work" is at once an ethnographic and ethical incitement, envisioning "a labor that is not a displacement of society but a practice of it, a practice of society on society" (2002: 5). The idea of government being ideally "a practice of society on society" echoes the classic rendering of the social as a theoretical check on the moral legitimacy of state power (Durkheim 1992) and accordingly remote as an empirical state of affairs.

Conclusions

Like tears in rain.

Roy Batty in *Blade Runner*, quoted in Kirk Varnedoe, *Pictures of Nothing*, 2006 (p. 239)

Through their engagements with law, ethnographers illuminate the current status of the state, as well as connecting anthropology dialectically to other "knowledges of the contemporary" (Boyer 2005) – including other anthropological domains. In that spirit, it is relevant to wonder how it is that law has emerged so strongly in fresh terms, in recent years, as an ethnographic domain. The historical context for current anthropological scholarship on law is shaped in part by the militarization of security that followed the attacks of September 11, 2001, including a series of developments that – in theoretical terms – pointed up some of the limitations of legal anthropology's classic communitarian paradigm: its conflation of discourse and consensus, its equivalencing of states and countries, its categorical hierarchical distinction between state power and private forms of power, and its rendering of hegemony as nonagentive.

Most prominent among the post-9/11 circumstances in this regard were the unilateralism of the so-called Bush Doctrine (justifying preemptive war); the failures of the US Congress and British Parliament to sustain legislative checks on executive claims to war powers; the commencement of military operations against Iraq by the US-led coalition over popular protest against the war policy in Europe and the United States; deliberate actions on the part of the executive branch to evade the jurisdiction of the judiciary; and – in all the main countries of the coalition – unprecedented consolidations of executive power in the name of security. That these developments could take place in the United States and elsewhere through the normal institutions of government and partisan politics starkly illuminated the extent to which democratic discourse – including its social science extensions – failed to account for such accumulations of state power and answer to that breach (Greenhouse 2005a, 2005b, 2009a, 2009b).

The moralizing discourse of the Bush administration was calculated to fracture political opposition to the war, sometimes inserting wedge issues drawn from superficially remote connections (such as abortion, gay marriage, and multiculturalism). From across those surfaces, however, emerged a tactical essentialism aimed at evacuating the political from the social in favor of a universalistic construction of moral order – a literal and figurative fundamentalism that was crucial to the administration's self-legitimation and electoral appeal (Greenhouse 2006a, 2009a). It is not surprising, then, that the discursivity of legitimacy drew the attention of anthropologists and academic lawyers (Greenhouse 2006b), forcing the issue of how to assess the moral legitimacy of states. Schooled by recent events to be suspicious of claims to moral and political representation on the part of government, they took up analytical positions simultaneously outside and inside the "performativity of power" (Caton and Zacka 2010), that is, as its observers and its objects.

That reflexive doubling back of ethnographic practice on and as moral solidarity extends well beyond the politics of power in the United States or other countries of the coalition. The ethnographic contexts covered in this essay include zones of pervasive conflict in the Middle East, sub-Saharan Africa, and eastern Europe and, in western Europe and the United States, policies of exclusion and containment, particularly for migrants.[6] Where an earlier generation might have attached law to these developments via a generalized notion of norms in crisis, this generation of scholars offers no such vision. In these studies – as in the circumstances they examine – identity ceases to be a neutral keyword or category, and becomes instead a rubric of contingency and instability, as citizenship slides unpredictably in and out of gear in relation to subsistence, subject positioning, self-knowledge, and the politics of insecurity.

In its critical break with the presumed legitimacy of law, its performative turn to the social, and the specificity of its pragmatic accounts, contemporary ethnography of law is distinct from the "law and" engagements of other disciplines. The significance of anthropology's moral critique does not emanate from some unified program or moral scale, but rather from its assertion – more than that, its enactment, through ethnography's very methods – of the irreducible authority of men and women in determining their mutual moral demands. That their authority should be in doubt is the story of society; that it is a tenet of ethnographic practice testifies to the conviction inscribed in our discipline that modern life should improve the prospects for life – and that this is not some idle dream. However, this aspect of anthropology – its subjunctive quality – is also what makes it arcane, necessarily "in/disciplined" (Comaroff 2010), even when the ethnographic ground is as familiar as anyone's home, neighborhood, or workplace. The studies referenced here are remarkably silent, theoretically speaking, on issues of ideology and power; that very suspension of a search for some unifying theory of power is the essence of their ethnographic acumen and moral critique. Regarding the presumptive legitimacy of law, they insistently proceed from a null assumption – "nothing" in Varnedoe's modernist sense. Law's power is what it does, exposing the ambiguity of its moral legitimacy.

These anthropological accounts belie at least two commonplace assessments of the state: that it exists primarily as an interiorized discourse, and that it has been displaced by the institutions of transnational capitalism and international human rights. Based on the current state of the anthropology of law, then, it seems that if Foucault's idea of power is (for some) too open, Agamben's forecloses too quickly what is actually ethnographically promising in a state of exception (see Agamben 2005). An executive's legal declaration of a state of exception is precisely an explicit acknowledgment of a moral gamble. In this, it is not a lie, even if its rationalization involves a lie – since the lie (by its very recognition as such) points to the social conditions of its making and unmasking. In this sense, recent history puts the ethnography of law into productive contradiction to Derrida's claim that a lie "cannot become an object of knowledge" (2002: 70); a political lie may pretend to a continuous field of sociolegal knowledge that ethnography exposes as illusory or broken. The contemporary anthropology of law registers something of this tragic decade's illuminations in this regard. Looking at law heterogeneously, it records the shock of a moral break within the law as a truth lived diversely, not as an event, but as a condition of inquiry – yielding diverse new questions and new knowledges.

NOTES

1 "The social" was Durkheim's phrase for the aggregate effect of social relationships experienced as entailing moral or ethical obligations (see Durkheim 1933 [1893]).
2 Stover's (2005) study of witnesses returning home after testifying before the International Criminal Tribunal for the former Yugoslavia – including extensive first-person testimony drawn from his interviews – charts the complexities of the process and their transit from certainty to ambivalence in relation to their own participation in the prosecutions.
3 Sovereign borders are simultaneously legal and ethnographic locations from which ethnographers demarcate the space of the social, literally and figuratively, in novel projects – for example, on "deportation regimes" (De Genova and Peutz 2010), transnational adoption (Yngvesson 2010), language politics (Gustafson 2009), and improvised channels of transit (Coutin 2000, 2007; Spener 2009; Gomberg-Munoz 2010).
4 I am borrowing key terms (as a deliberate juxtaposition of knowledge frames) from Obeyesekere (2002).
5 Pollock's (2008) ethnography of the US Department of Education's Office for Civil Rights relates the technologization of law to depoliticization from a different angle – showing how staff members' cynicism with respect to the efficacy of law disables federal power at a critical location (race discrimination in public schools).
6 My thanks to Didier Fassin for his observation about the civil applications of repressive law.

REFERENCES

Abélès, Marc (1996) *En attente d'Europe* [Waiting for Europe]. Paris: Hachette.

Abélès, Marc (2005) *L'Echec en politique* [Failure in politics]. Belval: Circe.

Abélès, Marc (2008) *Anthropologie de la globalization* [Anthropology and globalization]. Paris: Payot.

Abélès, Marc (2010) *The Politics of Survival.* Durham, NC: Duke University Press.

Agamben, Giorgio (2005) *State of Exception*, trans. Kevin Attell. Chicago: University of Chicago Press.

Barkan, Elazar (2011) Ethnic Cleansing, Genocide, and Gross Violations of Human Rights: The State versus Humanitarian Law. In Austin Sarat et al. (eds.), *Law without Nations.* Stanford: Stanford University Press, pp. 157–184.

Benda-Beckmann, Franz von (2009) Human Rights, Cultural Relativism and Legal Pluralism. In Franz von Benda-Beckmann et al. (eds.), *The Power of Law in a Transnational World.* New York: Berghahn, pp. 115–134.

Benda-Beckmann, Keebet von (2009) Anthropological Perspectives on Law and Geography. *Political and Legal Anthropology Review* 32(2): 265–278.

Biehl, João (2010) "Medication is Me Now": Human Values and Political Life in the Wake of Global AIDS Treatment. In Feldman and Ticktin (2010a), pp. 151–189.

Biesaw, April A. (2010) Memory, Identity, and NAGPRA in the Northeastern United States. *American Anthropology* 112(2): 244–256.

Boyer, Dominic (2005) *Spirit and System: Media, Intellectuals, and the Dialectic in Modern German Culture.* Chicago: University of Chicago Press.

Braverman, Irus (2009) Uprooting Identities: The Regulation of Olive Trees in the Occupied West Bank. *Political and Legal Anthropology Review* 32(2): 237–264.

Buchanan, Nicholas and Darian-Smith, Eve (2011) Introduction: Law and the Problematics of Indigenous Authenticities. *Law and Social Inquiry* 36(1): 115–124.

Calhoun, Craig (2010) The Idea of Emergency: Humanitarian Action and Global (Dis)Order. In Didier Fassin and Mariella Pandolfi (eds.), *Contemporary States of Emergency: The Politics of Military and Humanitarian Intervention*. New York: Zone, pp. 29–58.

Caton, Steven C. and Zacka, Bernardo (2010) Abu Ghraib, the Security Apparatus, and the Performativity of Power. *American Ethnologist* 37(2): 203–211.

Cattelino, Jessica (2008) *High Stakes: Florida Seminole Gaming and Sovereignty*. Durham, NC: Duke University Press.

Clarke, Maxine Kamari (2009) *Fictions of Justice: The International Criminal Court and the Challenge of Legal Pluralism in Sub-Saharan Africa*. Cambridge: Cambridge University Press.

Clastres, Pierre (1989) *Society against the State: Essays in Political Anthropology*, trans. Robert Hurley. New York: Zone.

Clemmer, Richard O. (2009) Land Rights, Claims, and Western Shoshones: The Ideology of Loss and the Bureaucracy of Enforcement. *Political and Legal Anthropology Review* 32(2): 279–311.

Coles, Kimberley (2007) *Democratic Designs: International Intervention and Electoral Processes in Postwar Bosnia-Herzegovina*. Ann Arbor: University of Michigan Press.

Collier, Jane F. (1975) Legal Processes. *Annual Review of Anthropology* 4: 121–144.

Comaroff, John L. (2010) The End of Anthropology, Again: On the Future of an In/Discipline. *American Anthropologist* 112(4): 524–538.

Comaroff, John L. and Comaroff, Jean (2006) Law and Disorder in the Postcolony: An Introduction. In Jean Comaroff and John Comaroff (eds.), *Law and Disorder in the Postcolony*. Chicago: University of Chicago Press, pp. 1–56.

Comaroff, John L. and Comaroff, Jean (2009) *Ethnicity, Inc.* Chicago: University of Chicago Press.

Coutin, Susan Bibler (2000) *Legalizing Moves: Salvadoran Immigrants' Struggle for United States Residence*. Ann Arbor: University of Michigan Press.

Coutin, Susan Bibler (2007) *Nations of Emigrants: Shifting Boundaries of Citizenship in El Salvador and the United States*. Ithaca, NY: Cornell University Press.

De Genova, Nicholas and Peutz, Nathalie (eds.) (2010) *The Deportation Regime: Sovereignty, Space, and the Freedom of Movement*. Durham, NC: Duke University Press.

Dembour, Marie-Bénédicte (2006) *Who Believes in Human Rights? Reflections on the European Convention*. Cambridge: Cambridge University Press.

Derrida, Jacques (2002) History of the Lie: Prolegomena. In *Without Alibi*, ed. and trans. Peggy Kamuf. Stanford: Stanford University Press, pp. 20–70.

Durkheim, Emile (1933 [1893]) *The Division of Labor in Society*, trans. George Simpson. New York: Free Press.

Durkheim, Emile (1992 [1957]) *Professional Ethics and Civic Morals*, trans. C. Brookfield. London: Routledge.

Fassin, Didier (2010a) Ethics of Survival: A Democratic Approach to the Politics of Life. *Humanity* 1(1): 81–95.

Fassin, Didier (2010b) Inequality of Lives, Hierarchies of Humanity: Moral Commitments and Ethical Dilemmas of Humanitarianism. In Feldman and Ticktin (2010a), pp. 238–255.

Feldman, Ilana (2010) Ad Hoc Humanity: UN Peacekeeping and the Limits of Internal Community in Gaza. *American Anthropologist* 112(3): 416–429.

Feldman, Ilana and Ticktin, Miriam (eds.) (2010a) *In the Name of Humanity: The Government of Threat and Care*. Durham, NC: Duke University Press.

Feldman, Ilana and Ticktin, Miriam (2010b) Introduction: Government and Humanity. In Feldman and Ticktin (2010a), pp. 1–26.

Garces, Chris (2010) The Cross Politics of Ecuador's Penal State. *Cultural Anthropology* 25(3): 459–496.

Goldstein, Daniel (2004) *The Spectacular City: Violence and Performance in Urban Bolivia*. Durham, NC: Duke University Press.

Gomberg-Munoz, Ruth (2010) Willing to Work: Agency and Vulnerability in an Undocumented Immigrant Network. *American Anthropologist* 112(2): 295–307.

Goodale, Mark (2009) *Surrendering to Utopia: An Anthropology of Human Rights*. Stanford: Stanford University Press.

Goodale, Mark and Clarke, Maxine Kamari (eds.) (2010) *Mirrors of Justice: Law and Power in the Post-Cold War Era*. Cambridge: Cambridge University Press.

Greenberg, Jessica (2011) On the Road to Normal: Negotiating Agency and State Sovereignty in Postsocialist Serbia. *American Anthropologist* 113(1): 88–100.

Greenhouse, Carol J. (2005a) Hegemony and Hidden Transcripts. *American Anthropologist* 107(3): 356–368.

Greenhouse, Carol J. (2005b) Nationalizing the Local: Comparative Notes on the Recent Restructuring of Political Space. In Richard Wilson (ed.), *Human Rights in an Age of Terror*. Cambridge: Cambridge University Press, pp. 184–208.

Greenhouse, Carol J. (2006a) Fieldwork in Law. *Annual Review of Law and Social Science* 2: 184–208.

Greenhouse, Carol J. (2006b) Lear and Law's Doubles: Identity and Meaning in a Time of Crisis. *Law, Culture and the Humanities* 2(2): 239–258.

Greenhouse, Carol J. (2009a) Fractured Discourse: Rethinking the Discursivity of States. In Julia Paley (ed.), *Anthropology and Democracy*. Albuquerque, NM: School of American Research Press, pp. 193–218.

Greenhouse, Carol J. (2009b) The Military Order of 13 November 2001: An Ethnographic Reading. In Franz von Benda-Beckmann et al. (eds.), *The Power of Law in a Transnational World*. Oxford: Berghahn, pp. 33–53.

Greenhouse, Carol J. (2011a) Durkheim and Law: Divided Readings Over *Division of Labor*. *Annual Review of Law and Social Science* 7: 165–185.

Greenhouse, Carol J. (2011b) *The Paradox of Relevance: Citizenship and Ethnography in the United States*. Philadelphia: University of Pennsylvania Press.

Gustafson, Bret (2009) *New Languages of the State: Indigenous Resurgence and the Politics of Knowledge in Bolivia*. Durham, NC: Duke University Press.

Harney, Stefano (2002) *State Work: Public Administration and Mass Intellectuality*. Durham, NC: Duke University Press.

Hirsch, Susan F. (2006) *In the Moment of Greatest Calamity: Terrorism, Grief, and a Victim's Quest for Justice*. Princeton: Princeton University Press.

Hussain, Nasser and Sarat, Austin (2007) Toward New Theoretical Perspectives on Forgiveness, Mercy and Clemency: An Introduction. In Austin Sarat and Nasser Hussain (eds.), *Forgiveness, Mercy, and Clemency*. Stanford: Stanford University Press, pp. 1–15.

Jain, Sarah S. Lochlann (2006) *Injury: The Politics of Product Design and Safety Law in the United States*. Princeton: Princeton University Press.

Jones, Susan Stedman (2001) *Durkheim Reconsidered*. Cambridge: Polity.

Jones, Susan Stedman (2002) Reflections on the Interpretation of Durkheim in the Sociological Tradition. In W. S. F. Pickering (ed.), *Durkheim Today*. New York: Berghahn, pp. 117–141.

Kelly, Tobias (2009 [2006]) *Law, Violence and Sovereignty among West Bank Palestinians*. Cambridge: Cambridge University Press.

Kelly, Tobias and Dembour, Marie-Bénédicte (eds.) (2007) Introduction: The Social Lives of International Justice. In M.-B. Dembour and T. Kelly (eds.), *Paths to International Justice: Social and Legal Perspectives*. Cambridge: Cambridge University Press, pp. 1–28.

Kelly, Tobias and Thiranagama, Sharika (2010a) Introduction: Specters of Treason. In Kelly and Thiranagama (2010b), pp. 1–23.

Kelly, Tobias and Thiranagama, Sharika (eds.) (2010b) *Traitors: Suspicion, Intimacy, and the Ethics of State-Building*. Philadelphia: University of Pennsylvania Press.

Latour, Bruno (2004 [2002]) La fabrique du droit [The making of law]. Paris: Editions La Decouverte.

Li, Fabiana (2009) Documenting Accountability: Environmental Impact Assessment in a Peruvian Mining Project. *Political and Legal Anthropology Review* 32(2): 218–236.

Lutz, Ellen L. and Reiger, Caitlin (eds.) (2009) *Prosecuting Heads of State*. Cambridge: Cambridge University Press.

Malkki, Liisa (2010) Children, Humanity, and the Infantilization of Peace. In Feldman and Ticktin (2010a), pp. 58–85.

Macedo, Stephen (ed.) (2004) *Universal Jurisdiction: National Courts and the Prosecution of Serious Crimes under International Law*. Philadelphia: University of Pennsylvania Press.

Maček, Ivana (2009) *Sarajevo under Siege: Anthropology in Wartime*. Philadelphia: University of Pennsylvania Press.

Magarrell, Lisa and Wesley, Joya (2008) *Learning from Greensboro: Truth and Reconciliation in the United States*. Philadelphia: University of Pennsylvania Press.

Malinowski, Bronislaw (1985 [1926]) *Crime and Custom in Savage Society*. Totowa, NJ: Rowman & Littlefield.

McMillan, L. Jane (2011) Colonial Traditions, Co-optations, and *Mi'kmaq* Legal Consciousness. *Law and Society Inquiry* 36(1): 171–200.

Merry, Sally Engle (1992) Anthropology, Law, and Transnational Processes. *Annual Review of Anthropology* 21: 357–377.

Merry, Sally Engle (2006) *Human Rights and Gender Violence: Translating International Law into Local Justice*. Chicago: University of Chicago Press.

Mertz, Elizabeth (1994) Legal Language: Pragmatics, Poetics, and Social Power. *Annual Review of Anthropology* 23: 435–455.

Mertz, Elizabeth (2007) *The Language of Law School: Learning to Think Like a Lawyer*. Oxford: Oxford University Press.

Moore, Sally Falk (1970) Law and Anthropology. In Bernard Siegel (ed.), *Biennial Review of Anthropology 1969*. Stanford: Stanford University Press, pp. 252–300.

Nader, Laura (ed.) (1965) The Ethnography of law [special issue]. *American Anthropologist* 67(6): part 2.

Nader, Laura (2002) *The Life of the Law: Anthropological Projects*. Berkeley: University of California Press.

Nesper, Larry (2011) Law and Ojibwe Indian "Traditional Cultural Property" in the Organized Resistance to the Crandon Mine in Wisconsin. *Law and Social Inquiry* 26(1): 151–169.

Obeyesekere, Gananath (2002) *Imagining Karma: Ethical Transformation in Amerindian, Buddhist, and Greek Rebirth*. Berkeley: University of California Press.

Ochs, Juliana (2011) *Security and Suspicion: An Ethnography of Everyday Life in Israel*. Philadelphia: University of Pennsylvania Press.

Peteet, Julie (2005) *Landscape of Hope and Despair: Palestinian Refugee Camps*. Philadelphia: University of Pennsylvania Press.

Pollock, Mica (2008) *Because of Race: How Americans Debate Harm and Opportunity in Our Schools*. Princeton: Princeton University Press.

Rawls, Anne (2003) Conflict as a Foundation for Consensus: Contradictions of Industrial Capitalism in Book III of Durkheim's *Division of Labor*. *Critical Sociology* 29: 295–335.

Richland, Justin (2011) Hopi Tradition as Jurisdiction: On the Potentializing Limits of Hopi Sovereignty. *Law & Social Inquiry* 36(1): 201–234.

Riles, Annelise (2011) *Collateral Knowledge: Legal Reasoning in the Global Financial Markets*. Chicago: University of Chicago Press.

Ritter, Gretchen (2006) *The Constitution as Social Design: Gender and Civic Membership in the American Constitutional Order*. Stanford: Stanford University Press.

Robinson, Mary (2004) Preface to Part I: The Princeton Principles. In Macedo (2004), pp. 15–17.

Spener, David (2009) *Clandestine Crossings: Migrants and Coyotes on the Texas–Mexico Border*. Ithaca, NY: Cornell University Press.

Stover, Eric (2005) *The Witnesses: War Crimes and the Promise of Justice in The Hague*. Philadelphia: University of Pennsylvania Press.

Strathern, Marilyn (2005) *Kinship, Law and the Unexpected: Relatives are Always a Surprise*. Cambridge: Cambridge University Press.

Theidon, Kimberly (2006) The Mask and the Mirror: Facing up to the Past in Post-War Peru. *Anthropologica* 48: 87–100.

van Krieken, Robert (2011) *Kumarangk* (Hindmarsh Island) and the Politics of Natural Justice Under Settler-Colonialism. *Law & Social Inquiry* 36(1): 125–149.

Varnedoe, Kirk (2006) *Pictures of Nothing: Abstract Art Since Pollock*. Princeton: Princeton University Press.

Wilson, Richard Ashby (2010) Crimes against Humanity and the Conundrum of Race and Ethnicity at the International Criminal Tribunal for Rwanda. In Feldman and Ticktin (2010a), pp. 27–57.

Wood, Michael (2010) *Yeats and Violence*. Oxford: Oxford University Press.

Yngvesson, Barbara (2010) *Belonging in an Adopted World: Race, Identity, and Transnational Adoption*. Chicago: University of Chicago Press.

PART V Politics

CHAPTER 25 Humanitarianism

Peter Redfield

What, if anything, distinguishes humanitarianism from charity? The question arises from an observation: many contemporary aid organizations do not define themselves as "charities" and indeed their workers actively avoid the term. Their heartfelt, emotional appeals for funds, however, clearly echo a much longer, plural lineage of solicitation extending from religious alms. Likewise their activities – feeding the hungry, caring for the ill, advocating mercy – are surely charitable in the large sense, if cast on a new scale and directed through novel forms. Nonetheless, these organizations generally prefer to cast themselves in other idioms, distinguishing their efforts from the longer lineage upon which they clearly draw. While an outsider might underscore continuities and dwell on familiar patterns of effects, those dedicated to these endeavors assert some degree of rupture from the past. What should an analyst do, in the face of such native insistence?

The ethnographic tradition suggests that such points of emphasis often prove revealing, indicating a specific architecture of anxiety and certainty. This essay pursues this perceived distinction between humanitarianism and charity as another opening into the contradictory logic of this contemporary form. My larger ambition is to examine the problem of situating moral action amid secular politics. In particular, I am interested in the suspect nature of action that does not claim a political rationale, or indeed opposes overt political status. "Antipolitics" is a thoroughly vexed term.[1] Framed negatively, it often arrives to discussion in an already deceased state, thoroughly buried by repudiation. Here I would excavate one corner long enough to consider what the term might look like when alive, and what it would reveal to an anthropology of secular morality. From the perspective of secular critical analysis, any apolitical – let alone antipolitical – stance may appear a mystified fiction. Nonetheless, it displays surprising resilience in actual human practice, where, like neutrality, it names a lively and unsettling knot of contradiction (Redfield 2011). For that reason my use of the term here will remain resolutely literal. By antipolitics I simply mean to recognize the inchoate and shifting claim that the realm of politics has a limit, beyond

A Companion to Moral Anthropology, First Edition. Edited by Didier Fassin.

which one should refuse political language and logic. Although rule-generating bureaucratic expertise can certainly work against political action, here I also want to acknowledge more passionate claims to moral value, as well as abiding tensions between ethics and politics in secular reason.

The line between charity and humanitarianism may indeed prove revealing, I suggest, inasmuch as the shift in vocabulary reflects an altered perception of what might legitimately claim to lie "beyond" politics. Contemporary international discourse recognizes "humanitarianism" as a justifiable form of moral concern, allowing it to serve as a point of reference and negotiation for a remarkable range of actors: NGOs, social movements, corporations, states, and military forces. While they may pursue different goals and exhibit different levels of sincerity, they share a common vocabulary of apprehension over human life and suffering. Claims of good and evil now find their measure in body counts, and the real or potential harms of ordinary people. Whatever the political question, bystanders should not suffer. A humanitarian sensibility thus both defines the proper mode of political conduct and suggests a limit to it.

The humanitarian view also proves particularly unsettling for anthropological sensibilities. Like anthropology, humanitarianism claims the human, but universally and in an expressly moral fashion. The discipline's general discomfort with morality (Fassin 2008) here arrives home, as most anthropologists share a secular concern about human life and suffering. At the same time they remain dedicated to principles of difference as well as of equality and prefer to frame their statements about good and evil in the political language of social justice. Whether or not this ambivalence bears on the discipline's belated recognition of humanitarianism as a force in the world (as opposed to its relatively long and varied engagement with development), it remains a significant and potentially revealing factor for present consideration. In recent years humanitarian action, like related topics of disaster, emergency, war, and the aftermath of violence, has appeared on the disciplinary horizon. Matters related to human movement, in the form of both individual asylum-seekers and huddled masses of refugees, elicit renewed attention (e.g., Malkki 1996; Ticktin 2006; Feldman 2007). With the rise of both global health as a primary area for international engagement as well as security concerns (Lakoff 2010), and expanded military operations "other than war" (Lutz 2000; Duffield 2007), humanitarianism frames both positive and negative poles of moral possibility. Although each may offer ample opportunity for denunciation, the larger whole has grown hard to escape.

If we do inhabit an era increasingly marked by humanitarian government at the level of state policy as well as international affairs (Fassin 2012), it would be incumbent on us to investigate the moral sensibilities informing it with greater care. The matter may not prove as simple as it might first appear. In contrast to views that presume a simple distinction between humanitarianism and politics, often denouncing the erosion of the former by the latter, Didier Fassin proposes a different problematic: "We should consider humanitarianism as a new repertoire for public action at both the international and local levels – in other words, not as something external to politics, but as something that reformulates what is at stake in politics. To paraphrase Clausewitz, one could say that humanitarianism is nothing but the continuation of politics by other means" (2010: 274). The point is well taken, adroitly bypassing the now familiar lament of "depoliticization" common in academic critique. Surely there is more to say about contemporary forms than what they are not. Surely humanitarianism – like war – deserves recognition as a complex intersection of human discourse and practice, however unsettling. But even Fassin's artful formulation ultimately leaves the category of "politics" itself comfortably secure. If focused less on the practice of government (in the broad sense of attempts to direct human affairs) and more on the architecture of sentiment and judgment (as the motive force and expression of deeply held values), then the wording requires further disruption. The "other means" for politics offered by humanitarianism presents a fundamentally apolitical face, after all. Humanitarians assert the primacy of moral concern above and beyond other interests, presenting their values of life and care as fundamental, elementary matters of human conscience. In doing so they recall not only the general legacy of belief beyond the secular domestication of religion, but also the ever unsettling root question of ethics: how best to live?

Approaching humanitarianism as a moral form of antipolitics as well as politics, then, brings the larger problem of secularism momentarily into view (Cannell 2010). Anthropology, of all disciplines, might recall the tenuous nature of any line dividing categories of politics and religion. Given that the human sciences emerged firmly on the side of Enlightenment reason, their analyses will inevitably apply the language of the polis to all phenomena. But when confronting the actions that display traces of other logics, the ethnographic gesture of hesitation serves to recall that the secular perspective too is an assertion of value, and a claim to truth and the real. The variety of love expressed by traditional acts of charity, or the deliverance of alms, explicitly extends into the divine. To the extent that humanitarian action echoes such practices, identifying something approaching the sacred in the form of a suffering human, it recalls the historical and conceptual possibility of not subscribing to secularism, or the "concepts, practices and sensibilities" that coalesce in secular sovereign self (Asad 2003: 14).

Nevertheless, contemporary humanitarianism operates in a world of secular reference. This is precisely how its moral claim acquires a sense of political negation, and where its conceptual terrain grows contradictory. For, as Fassin rightly notes, humanitarianism has indeed emerged as "a new repertoire for public action," infusing state policies and offering another form of legitimation. Functioning as politics, amid political expectations, its moral force frequently erodes into reactive moralism, in the sense suggested by Wendy Brown (2001: 22). Tellingly, even the most pure of humanitarian actors, organizations self-designated through that cause, exhibit a desire for their actions as something other than – or more than – charity. Their antipolitics expects to touch the human world, and in some sense, however modestly, to improve it.

Over the ensuing pages I approach humanitarianism from the perspective of its most passionate adherents: transnational NGOs who explicitly define themselves through the term. They are far from the only entities to deploy humanitarian moral reasoning, given that states and military forces have invoked it to legitimate both foreign adventures (Bass 2008; Fassin and Pandolfi 2010a) and domestic policy (Fassin 2012). Nor are they the only contemporary inheritors of charitable work, given that Islamic aid networks now also extend worldwide and in some settings claim greater legitimacy (Benthall and Bellion-Jourdan 2009; Benthall, Ch. 20 in this volume). The history of humanitarian concern likewise extends into an older and broader tableau of sentiment about human suffering, stretching well beyond emergency aid (Barnett 2011). Within this contested terrain, however, nongovernmental organizations face the problem of humanitarian identity most acutely. The term not only describes their action but also defines their essence; they have no other *raison d'être*. As a consequence, their claim to transcend or limit politics proves most central, and their resistance to charity most curious.

This essay emphasizes the aid world's current identification of humanitarianism with states of emergency, recalling the longer, heterogeneous use of the term primarily as a point of contrast. Focusing on a particularly fundamentalist sect of contemporary actors – Médecins Sans Frontières (Doctors Without Borders, or MSF) – it describes the group's back-and-forth trajectory around the fraught question of intervention and a full embrace of the surviving utopian ideal of human rights (Moyn 2010). How best to speak in the name of antipolitical moral values, and yet still signal political desire? My argument in a nutshell is that humanitarianism outlines a revealing frontier between modern conceptions of politics and secular morality. Within this moral structure of feeling (Williams 1977) good deeds must always affect the world; thus even antipolitics faces political judgment, under which mere charity can never be enough. Before expanding on this theme, however, I will first elaborate on the opening observation in order to lend it greater force of detail.

"Not a Relief Organization"

Like all specialists, aid practitioners have elaborated their own dialects, thick with acronyms and sensitive to residue of past debates. Just as in academic settings, apparent synonyms ring differently than they would in common speech. I became aware of the significance of such distinctions during one of my first forays into the aid world, at the Amsterdam office of the Dutch branch of MSF in 2001.[2] When I arrived at the director's office for an appointed interview, I found him with his latest cup of coffee in hand, studying my research proposal. To my surprise he had already gone through much of it, and continued to scribble marginal notes and impatiently cross out offending terms as we spoke. To start with, he asserted emphatically, MSF was "not a relief organization." The comment baffled me, as it seemed thoroughly counterintuitive given their operational history. It soon became clear, however, that the director associated the term both with arguments in the now distant 1970s and 1980s, as well as with politically naive efforts to do good. "Relief is a dirty word," he told me, "we don't do charity; we're here to foment radical change, not to keep the status quo." Still recovering from the shock that he was actually reading the document with care, I dutifully nodded. I found the remark revealing and yet still puzzling, particularly given that he also stressed that the group could hardly oppose political sovereignty in any simple sense, since it was not in a position to "offer an alternative solution." MSF's task, rather, was strictly to respond to the failures of the existing international system, providing people in crisis settings with medical care. Noting the organization's history of irritating ideologues on both political left and right with some relish, he assured me that "morality comes from action." The group found legitimacy less in pure principles than in messy engagement. It conceived this engagement as simultaneously rebellious and politically attenuated. But whatever it was, it was not charity.

MSF represents a distinctive and extreme humanitarian perspective. Indeed, its position may prove ultimately revealing for this reason, given that the group balances on the edge of politics while focusing on issues of global health. With respect to its general dissatisfaction with the limitations of traditional charity, however, the organization has plenty of company. Indeed, many other major agencies proclaim far more ambitious goals. Oxfam, for example, may have begun modestly fighting famine during World War II, but subsequently embraced development. It describes itself as "an international confederation of 15 organizations working together in over 90 countries and with partners and allies around the world to find lasting solutions to poverty and injustice."[3] Save the Children, an even older alliance with roots in combatting hunger after World War I, now sees its mission as "working together to inspire breakthroughs in the way the world treats children, and achieving real and lasting change in their lives."[4] The American branch of Doctors of the World (which tellingly renamed itself HealthRight International in 2009) intends to "build lasting access to health for excluded communities."[5] The International Rescue Committee claims to offer not just lifesaving care, but also "life-changing assistance."[6] This pattern extends even beyond the secular quadrant of the aid sector. World Vision, a massive and explicitly Christian organization, embraces the term "relief," but matches it with endeavors in "development" and "advocacy," seeking to work "with children, families and communities to overcome poverty and injustice."[7] For all these groups, charity alone does not seem enough. Even the president of the Catholic alliance Caritas – named for the very virtue itself – proclaims "Poverty and social injustice are the real weapons of mass destruction."[8]

How to read such assertions? In light of the continuing state of the world and the projects such organizations sponsor, they appear poignantly aspirational rather than reflecting realizable ambitions. A dismissive critic might even call them delusional. Nonetheless the pattern runs deeply enough to raise a more fundamental question: Why is charity no longer enough? Why not accept the simple value of a "bed for the night" in Bertolt Brecht's telling phrase (Rieff 2002)? I suggest that if we treat these self-descriptions as symptomatic of secular expectation, then an answer may lie partly in the very symptom itself. To the extent that charity accepts the status quo as given, then a humanitarianism operating within a secular, modernist ethos of progress *must* be something more. Without claiming politics – indeed, while expressly asserting moral values – its practitioners retain a social conscience. The particularities of this conscience vary considerably, to be sure, as do the visions associated with it; to describe it as "social" holds true only in the widest sense. But even the conservative religious framing of World Vision is hardly quiescent about the current state of international affairs. The group's actions determinedly recall the possibility of another world in this one, whether or not they actually help achieve it.

As a point of partial contrast, one can turn to the venerable International Committee of the Red Cross (ICRC). Established in 1863 as a part of wave of reform in the conduct of warfare and treatment of wounded soldiers, the ICRC has greatly expanded its scope and reach, just like the Geneva Conventions with which it remains intertwined. Unlike the NGOs mentioned above, it occupies an official position within international law, and operates under a more formal mandate: "to provide humanitarian help for people affected by conflict and armed violence and to promote the laws that protect victims of war."[9] The association with war is telling, since it demarcates a clear boundary for action, and places humanitarianism within a state of exception. If a state of war suspends laws and norms, then the ICRC operates beyond ordinary conditions, reintroducing humanity into inhumane settings. To the extent that it ventures beyond such exceptional moments it does so through the promotion of laws that might affect them, preemptively responding to future ruptures. The Red Cross humanitarian legacy is clearly delimited, and stands strictly apart from political struggles. For this reason, and the fact that the organization follows a coherent and rigorous set of principles in its operation (famously including impartiality and neutrality), political scientists routinely position it as a classic form to calibrate other humanitarianisms (Barnett and Weiss 2008). Moreover, the group's location at the border between religious and medical symbolism – its iconic cross, crescent, and neutral crystal seeking to mediate universal appeal through historical difference – can serve as a watershed for the emergence of contemporary secular order.

The Red Cross position is indeed rigorously focused. Its concern very much remains a matter of compassionate relief, if usually channeled in highly specific and attenuated ways around conflict and disaster. The ICRC, at least, is not likely to throw itself headlong into development projects or embrace human rights, let alone to disrupt the established order of nation states. Indeed, as early critics feared, by eschewing pacifism and spawning national societies that effectively served as medical auxiliaries, the wider Red Cross movement may have ultimately helped to normalize modern warfare (Hutchinson 1996). Yet the ICRC does display occasional traces of a "will to improve" (Li 2007), particularly in its patient nurturing of the evolving Geneva Conventions as the "core" of international humanitarian law.[10] The addition of civilian protection in the extensive 1949 revision serves as a watershed of sorts, recognizing the concerns of war beyond formal battle, and reaffirming noncombatant populations as third-party bystanders. The ICRC might not assert pacifism, but it does discretely dream of minimal civility.

With the emergence of Médecins Sans Frontières as the Red Cross's unruly offspring, this staid legacy acquired new passion. Part of a revivalist wave that swept through the aid world at the end of the 1960s and beginning of the 1970s, the group asserted an oppositional ethos and rapidly embraced a public role. Emphatically secular in the French republican tradition, it also incorporated legacies of Catholic activism and colonial medicine alongside post-Holocaust and postrevolutionary sensibilities (Taithe 2004). Indeed, during the 1980s the original French branch defined itself expressly against Third Worldist solidarity, accusing Parisian intellectuals of ignoring suffering in the name of Marxist doctrine. A number of its early champions had spent time as political activists, and a few would emerge as influential politicians. Nonetheless, MSF balanced at the edge of politics, defining itself through the figure of the ethically committed biomedical doctor. It stood for simple virtues: life, health, and – in an oft-repeated summation – the sense that people "people shouldn't die of stupid things" (see also Farmer 2003: 144). Rony Brauman, the influential former head of the original French section, once provocatively went further to define the human as "a being who is not made to suffer" (1996: 7). MSF would both claim its moral legitimacy and judge the actions of others in the name of such humanitarian virtues (Fassin 2010: 279). It thus recognized and articulated a limit to political justification. At the same time it loudly and repeatedly opposed any state of affairs it deemed undesirable. Contentious and contradictory, it saw itself as the antithesis of a model charity, politically apolitical, if you will, or apolitically political.[11] No matter how much it might have defined itself around emergency care, MSF could never simply be a "relief" organization.

Humanitarianism beyond Emergency

Both the contemporary, professionalized aid world and its division into discrete sectors are relatively recent phenomena. So too is the association of humanitarianism with emergency relief. As Craig Calhoun points out, the term emerged prior to the Red Cross, and only later shifted meaning: "Humanitarianism took root in the modern world not as a response to war or 'emergencies' but as part of an effort to remake the world so that it better served the interests of humanity" (2008: 76). The end of the eighteenth century in Europe, historians suggest, saw a revolution in sentiment as well as politics. Alongside liberalism and the new revolutionary vocabulary of political left and right, a transnational wave of reform sought to address the slave trade and slavery, to establish more humane punishments, and to improve the general human condition. Amid new conditions of market exchange and practices such as novel reading, both individual experience and relations with strangers acquired greater currency and value (Haskell 1995; Hunt 2007; Wilson and Brown 2009; Festa 2010). Humanitarianism, like philanthropy, designated grander attempts at promoting welfare, a more ambitious form of charity that sought to reach beyond the contingencies of particular individuals. Simply put, it acted in the name of humanity (Feldman and Ticktin 2010).

Such historical observations matter less for simply complicating definitions than for suggesting that current moral desires may draw on deeper roots. Both the Red Cross emphasis on emergencies, and its model of operational restraint appear to be as much anomalies as sure foundations. Indeed, the long nineteenth century, and the vast complex of concepts and institutions inherited from it may represent a detour rather than a straight line of progress. Like modern states and their formalization of warfare, the categorical sense of neutrality may be a relative aberration amid the longer sweep of human history (Nordstrom 2004; Redfield 2011). Medical conceptions of emergencies and accidents may prove more durable, but even they are hardly timeless (Cooter and Luckin 1997; Nurok 2003). From a historical perspective, then, it should be no surprise if anxieties over the value of good deeds waxed and waned not only with political affiliation, but also with shifting conceptions of what might constitute a proper sphere of political action.

Calhoun, we should not forget, situates humanitarianism firmly in what he calls the "modern world." Like most analysts, he recognizes specificities of conjuncture, the reweaving of antecedent threads such as charity and cosmopolitanism into a novel formation and project, if not an epochal transition. As a term "humanitarianism" is etymologically recent to be sure, appearing in English only in the early nineteenth century (Calhoun 2008: 77). Forms of feeling and action we might now identify as humanitarian likewise emerged rather suddenly, finding disparate expression as pious opposition to slavery and military intervention to support Greek independence (Haskell 1995; Bass 2008). Adam Smith (2009 [1759]) famously announced a natural theory not only of market reason but also of moral sentiment and benevolence. But with regard to the sensibilities of the aid world, taking the designation "modern" to be a description of an attitude (Foucault 1984; Rabinow 2008) may ultimately prove more revealing. Whether or not those invested in it have ever *been* modern (Latour 1993), they have clearly thought themselves so in perceiving a break with traditional charity. Moreover, their desire to act on the world, and even more the language they use to express it, invokes progressive sensibilities. Whether or not the future actually yields a better world, those who allude to development believe their role includes attempting to make it so. Recognizing the larger historical arc of humanitarianism, then, highlights that its troubled relation to charity in the eyes of practitioners is a categorically modern problem.

A similar point can be made about politics. Although secularism and modernity are not synonymous, a modern attitude entails a particular emphasis on action as opposed to contemplation, and highlights tangible, material effects. The secular conceptual distinction between religion and politics thus resonated profoundly. To quote Calhoun again, "The increasing emphasis on the secular world did not imply irreligion, and indeed it was produced largely as a transformation within religious life and thought" (2008: 78). Efforts to affect human welfare should attend to the fate of bodies and the conditions that affected them. Even the overtly Christian aid of missionary medicine walked a line between sacred and secular care, removing tumors and cataracts in a public flourish, mixing treatment with prayer, and constructing clinics and hospitals (Vaughn 1991). To the extent that religion appeared a private matter, then, politics designated the legitimate space of public action. As a result, charitable deeds increasingly faced political judgment.

Liberalism (understood in the large sense) expects fundamental equality, as announced in its key assertions about natural rights (Asad 2003: 56–62). Liberal moral logic can therefore only accept inequality as either a temporary state or the results of an individual's private failure, never as a natural condition. Permanent disparities such as a hierarchical ranking remain anathema, and even structural problems like multigenerational poverty fit uncomfortably into the framework of liberal sensibilities. This is not to suggest that liberalism worked against inequality in historical experience, any more than it did violence. Rather, the point is that the naturalization of a liberal subject – a self-governing person, born to equality – changed the terms through which inequities might be explained or justified. The moral reasoning of politics had altered. To the extent that charity addressed suffering without holding out the prospect of eventual change, or accepted nonfamilial relationships of open dependency, it would now appear "damaging to human dignity" (Calhoun 2010: 35). Just as liberalism developed rival strains, more radical or conservative in orientation, so too did modern efforts to undertake good works. But even lineages that derive from conservative paternalism rather than a vision of social equality, or that advocate spiritual development rather than material liberation still invest in a rhetoric of transformation (Pupavac 2010).

Amid this modernist sense of political evaluation, emergency can constitute an exception in more than one sense. Since a state of emergency, like a state of war, recognizes the suspension of political norms, it offers the comforting justification that any inequality is only temporary. For the duration of unusual circumstances urgent needs take precedence; once the moment of crisis has passed then one can return to the political project of remaking the world. As Calhoun notes: "'Emergency' thus is a way of grasping problematic events, a way of imagining them that emphasizes their apparent unpredictability, abnormality, and brevity and that carries the corollary that response – intervention – is necessary" (Calhoun 2010: 55). Thus the Red Cross, defined in response to the graphic carnage of modern weaponry, could establish a humanitarian tradition defined narrowly around rupture and exhibit only minimal ambitions of progress. It is precisely this tradition out of which MSF emerges, and its subsequent trajectory along the moral edge of politics renders it a particularly interesting case. In addition the group enjoys an unusual condition of relative financial autonomy, deriving the bulk of its funds from private contributions rather than state allocations. Unlike the largely state-subsidized ICRC, or its rivals who work largely on donor contracts, MSF reflects something closer to a truly "nongovernmental" expression of civil society, and its moral response to emergency.

The Double Edge of Intervention

Médecins Sans Frontières began as an effort to create an independent form of medical humanitarianism, answerable to the conscience of private citizens rather than states. Although it would quickly acquire a reputation for publicity and subsequently a tradition of witnessing, the group's founding dream was one of intervention: the provision of urgent care without regard to race, religion, or political belief. Its charter largely mirrored that of the Red Cross, but it sought to free itself from the unwieldy, cautious apparatus of older organization (Vallaeys 2004). The founding generation, a loose coalition of doctors and journalists running a medical publication, drew their immediate inspiration from two defining events: the Nigerian civil war around the breakaway province of Biafra at the end of the 1960s, and the bloody birth of Bangladesh out of bifurcated Pakistan in 1971. Both were watershed moments for humanitarianism in general. Biafra marked a new intensity of media involvement and manipulation, the fertile mix of mass suffering and visceral imagery that would become a hallmark of the "humanitarian crisis." The Red Cross responded with its largest relief operation to that point, counting some of the future founders of MSF among its volunteers. Oxfam likewise threw itself into the effort to feed the Biafran civilians, only to emerge deeply shaken. Bangladesh – where the foundations of MSF never actually arrived – saw both a military intervention by India justified on humanitarian grounds as well as a pioneering benefit concert (Fassin and Pandolfi 2010b: 11). In the wake of these events a second wave of media-friendly humanitarian organizations emerged, most famously MSF.

As indicated by its name, the new group carried with it an expansive suggestion of superseding sovereignty. It must be stressed that this was a suggestion rather than a practice; in the earliest days MSF remained emphatically French in personnel and language. Moreover, its members initially volunteered for other organizations and – on their first "independent" mission responding to the Nicaraguan earthquake in 1972 – even joined an effort from the French defense department, hitching a ride on a military plane (Vallaeys 2004: 136). The implications of operating "without borders" only emerged later, in fits and starts amid a cycle of action and reaction. From the outset, however, the group faced a tension between the Red Cross tradition of emergency and the slower dream of development common to "Third Worldist" solidarity movements of the time. Although urgency emphatically carried the day, the lure of development would remain as a persistent temptation even in this purist organization, surfacing every now and then in counter initiatives and alternative projects. At the level of practice, the collective trajectory proved rather more complicated than its official narration.[12] The individuals who joined MSF shared a medical orientation and a fierce desire to intervene in the world; they did not always agree how best to do so.

By the middle 1970s MSF was well on its way to notoriety, if not yet making much material impact. It launched a publicity campaign and began to make a habit of public agitation over humanitarian causes. The driving force during this period was Bernard Kouchner, who would become a charismatic force in international humanitarianism and French political life. Passionate and telegenic, he had already emerged as something of a public figure at the time. Although far from alone, he spoke the early vision most grandly and left an abiding mark. Decades after he angrily parted ways with the organization his name has remained attached to it, much to the frustration of his successors when their positions diverge.[13] Moreover – as one of these very skeptics admitted to me in 2003 – Kouchner displays the virtue of remaining remarkably consistent, a valuable characteristic for any project of analysis. Thus I will use his particular background and perspective to mark a more general point of possibility.

The child of Jewish doctor and a Catholic nurse, Kouchner entered the world during the uncertain lull at the onset of World War II. He grew up in a France shadowed by that conflict and infused with the cult of the Resistance. Haunted by the Holocaust, particularly after learning about the death of his own grandparents in Auschwitz, Kouchner easily gravitated into leftist politics, joining the communist student union, opposing the Algerian War and visiting Yugoslavia and Cuba. While studying to be a physician he nursed journalistic aspirations, writing, editing, and keeping an eye firmly planted on the public arena. Amid the tumult of May 1968 in Paris, he heard a different call to arms and departed for Biafra. The experience clearly consumed him. Kouchner would ultimately travel there three times, growing increasingly passionate. Back in Paris he campaigned for the Biafran cause, and together with other colleagues signed an open letter to diplomats attesting to the suffering they had seen, as well a testimonial in the French newspaper *Le Monde*. Although this was perhaps a more modest beginning than later myth might have it, his actions departed from Red Cross discretion in an echo of student activism. For Kouchner, humanitarianism was a naturally "militant" endeavor, to the extent that he announced himself as "a mercenary of emergency medicine" (Vallaeys 2004: 46, 61, 75, 116). Politics and morality ran together. MSF would be the perfect vehicle for their union, personified by the figure of a crusading doctor. The medical student and journalist had found his calling: to intervene and speak loudly.

Kouchner's stint with the organization he helped found lasted less than a decade. The moment of rupture is telling in several ways. The precipitating event came after Malaysia denied entry to a boatload of Vietnamese refugees in full view of the media. The image of thousands suffering aboard inspired a project in 1979 to create and equip a "Boat for Vietnam" to demonstrate solidarity. This appeal engendered a remarkable display of solidarity across France's own political divides: most notably long-time opponents Jean-Paul Sartre and Raymond Aron both signed on, joined by a host of other intellectual luminaries such as Roland Barthes, Simone de Beauvoir, and Michel Foucault. Such glaring human suffering appeared to stand beyond ordinary politics; humanitarianism offered the proper moral response. Naturally Kouchner played a leading role. To his surprise and outrage, the plan met with strident criticism from within MSF. Younger members, including those who had spent time working in refugee camps in Thailand, were skeptical, seeing the mission as more of a publicity stunt than an effective aid project. The disagreement precipitated an angry showdown, where Kouchner's faction found itself outvoted. Announcing that MSF was now effectively dead, killed by "technocrats of assistance," he left to begin a rival organization (Vallaeys 2004: 299). This latter group, called Médecins du Monde (Doctors of the World, or MDM), would remain a smaller, purer embodiment of Kouchner's vision, moving over time into a warm embrace of human rights. MSF, by contrast, invested more heavily in developing technical capacity, and continued to insist on a more strictly humanitarian identity.

This well-known episode displays a number of competing moral claims: suffering should surpass ideological divisions; a response should be materially effective; humanitarian aid should remain an organic gesture. It thus suggests different variations of antipolitics as well as politics. A concern for human life stirs secular intellectuals beyond their political habits, even as a political struggle of sorts breaks out among agents of moral response. The latter accuse each other of false action in the name of competing priorities, even as they agree on the general humanitarian goal. From one position, public gestures in isolation risk empty conceit and political moralism. From the other, a focus on efficiency risks dehumanization and soulless bureaucracy. But in either case, intervention was a moral as much as a political matter. As a later president of MSF France put it, a humanitarian should always reject "the logic that divides humanity into those who may live and those who must die" (Bradol 2004: 4)

Despite personal animosities on the part of the protagonists and their shifting emphases, MSF and MDM would undergo a largely parallel evolution in their shared prioritization of suffering over other considerations. Shortly after the schism both famously intervened in Afghanistan's civil war on the side of the mujahideen. The clandestine project was in this sense openly political. It was also a dramatic realization of action "without borders," authorized by the moral conscience of citizens rather than states. For all that MSF remained a stricter humanitarian sect, in practice it retained a sharp public edge. Over time it retreated from open violations of state sovereignty, and avoided strong alignments with one side in a conflict, but it remained fiercely committed to independence. One defining moment came with the eviction of the French section from Ethiopia in 1985, after it denounced government resettlement policies amid the famine. Another came a decade later, when MSF called for military intervention amid its helpless frustration during the Rwandan genocide, and then, amid internal debate, withdrew from refugee camps in Zaire when it perceived blatant manipulation of its attempts to offer aid. Although the group may have retreated behind Red Cross insignia during the Rwandan crisis, its reputation for public speech was by now secure (Orbinski 2008: 193). At the same time it had greatly increased in size and amplified its technical capacity, while working to wean itself off state funding to realize financial independence.

Meanwhile, Kouchner had gone through his own evolution, becoming a significant, if unorthodox French politician. In 1988 he entered the cabinet of the then Socialist government, taking charge of social affairs and employment, followed by a novel portfolio in humanitarian affairs. In 1992 he became minister of health before going on to serve in the European Parliament. Along the way he found a principle to champion: the *droit d'ingérence*, a sense of right or duty to intervene on humanitarian grounds (Allen and Styan 2000). The declaration of this right formalized the supremacy of moral concern over political sovereignty. Suffering was a human affair, and consequently a matter of responsibility that exceeded the authority of states. Should they fail to care for their citizens, then others had both license and obligation to intervene. Although implicit in the formulation of MSF, and a sometime article of faith for MDM, the principle now followed Kouchner into the sphere of formal politics. A vigorous advocate of intervention, he drew little distinction between governmental and nongovernmental actors when lives were at stake, pressing for United Nations recognition of such a principle and encouraging French actions abroad. In 1999 he headed the UN mission in Kosovo, and in 2007 crossed the political divide to become minister of foreign affairs in the new conservative government in France.

MSF, by contrast, never warmed to idea of a general "right to intervene," and as the concept took on an increasingly political cast Kouchner's former compatriots recoiled. Instead of asserting a positive right of intervention they defined their humanitarian approach around an "ethic of refusal," as they put it when accepting the Nobel Peace Prize in 1999 (Orbinski 1999). As "a citizen's response to political failure," humanitarianism should remain distinct from any state policy, free to protest and "push the political to assume its inescapable responsibility." Nonetheless, such distinctions grew murky on the ground. MSF found itself alongside Kouchner in the Kosovo adventure, and however much it endeavored to distinguish between political and humanitarian rationales, the group struggled within a "gray zone" of converging military and aid objectives (Pandolfi 2008). Following the events of September 11, 2001 and the subsequent declaration of a "war on terror" by the United States, MSF pivoted even further away from political invocations of humanitarianism and back toward the Red Cross tradition. Denouncing such "just" wars waged on behalf of states, the group distanced itself from any calls for violence (Weissman 2004). True humanitarianism should stand beyond politics, or at least at its very edge, saving lives and opposing any justification for civilian death.

I retell this familiar story in order to emphasize the degree to which humanitarian intervention tangles political and moral logic, as well as states and voluntary organizations. By the turn of the millennium both MSF and MDM had evolved into large, established international NGOs, running a wide range of projects worldwide. Only a few provoked dramatic contest or controversy. But in those that did, the question of political status arose in multiple ways, sometimes contradictory and frequently discomforting. Kouchner's version of humanitarian reason offered clarity, consistently endorsing intervention in the name of life. The price, however, was an association with power that not everyone was willing to pay. Amid contemporary states of emergency, any sense of humanitarian moral purity grew harder to maintain (Fassin and Pandolfi 2010a). At the same time, aid organizations had found other engagements with the world. Even MSF devoted more time and attention to significant nonemergency projects; by moving considerable resources into long-term HIV–AIDS projects and launching a pharmaceutical advocacy campaign, it flirted anew with versions of development and human rights. Amid its own larger economy of morals, the retreat from politics in one domain balanced an expansion in others (Redfield 2008; Fassin 2010).

Conclusion: The Secular Discomfort of Antipolitics

For keen and casual observers alike, contemporary efforts to provide humanitarian aid summon up the specter of religion (e.g., Benthall, Ch. 20 in this volume; McFalls 2010). Certainly the devout desire of volunteers to engage in good works expresses something like faith, and contemporary concern for human life reaches spiritual intensity. Surely the regular outpouring of funds in response to natural disaster (particularly those featuring putatively innocent and photogenic victims) signals a desire to display virtue in the impulse of philanthropy (Bornstein 2009), and even the material donations of states and corporations – however riddled with self-interest – suggest something like charitable alms. The potential value of this allusion lies less in the question of whether this secular morality really counts as "religion," or indeed, whether it is altruistic or always fully sincere.[14] Rather, its contribution stems from recognizing a key form of public morality in secular society. To participate in the good, one expresses concern for suffering, and acts to save lives. This is not the only value, to be sure – beyond appeals to classic goods such as justice or truth, environmentalism clearly demarcates a fertile arena of contemporary conscience. But humanitarianism falls so close to the sacred as to appear untouchable (Fassin 2011).

When approaching aid as a form of "secular religion," we would do well to recall that the primary religious heritage in question is Christianity. This is not to ignore the charitable traditions of other religions, but simply to recognize the particular historical associations that frame dominant definitions of both aid and secularism (Benthall, Ch. 20 in this volume; Bornstein and Redfield 2011). As Hannah Arendt noted long ago, a Christian conception of the sacredness of life echoes in the modern tenet that life represents "the highest good," even without the promise of immortality, and amid a world of emphatically material values (1998 [1958]: 319). Similarly, contemporary humanitarianism retains a language of sacrifice and salvation, as well as an egalitarian sense of human worth and potential redemption. Medical care offers particularly suggestive resonances; although the biomedical body is emphatically not the Christian soul, both are individuated, noninterchangeable objects of value, and thus a point of focus for ethical concern. The pain and suffering of ordinary people matters. Absent spiritual benefit – or acceptable political rationalization – it demands physical rescue.

Humanitarianism identifies a fundamentally moral standpoint. At the same time, however, it prescribes instrumental action, and expects its practice of value ethics to be consequential. For contemporary humanitarians the defense of life remains a categorical good, anchoring a deontological logic of associated principles and duties. Without it charitable action cannot express virtue in and of itself (even if so registered in public evaluation), nor can one accept any utilitarian rationale that justifies death. At the same time, however, humanitarians retain a consequentialist conscience born of secular politics. From such a perspective it becomes harder to act on faith alone, without affirmation that one's actions have beneficial effects, or contribute to a larger form of improvement. In this sense it should come as no great surprise that the rhetoric deployed by aid organizations mixes transformational ambition into expressions of moral outrage. Modernist in orientation, NGOs express their particular versions of "organized goodness" (Heins 2008: 159) amid historically liberal expectations of personhood, biopolitical norms of health, and secular understandings of the frame of moral action. An "antipolitics," after all, takes shape within a world that is politically defined. The case of MSF proves particularly acute in this regard. Moving along the sharp edge of morality, it confronts politics at every turn while seeking to stand against it. Frustrated by enduring conditions within which it works, the organization describes its endeavor as "not a contented action" and ultimately demands "change, not charity" (Orbinski 1999). Even this purist stance wants more, just like its academic critics.

If we are to consider our own "anthropological discomfort with morals as heuristic rather than paralyzing" (Fassin 2008: 342), then a reflexive start would be to acknowledge the deep commitment of social science to a secular perspective, in which political analysis defines moral – as well as an ontological and epistemological – truth.[15] In discussing the problem of moral standing and aid amid war, Hugo Slim (1997: 342) notes that Dante's vision of hell included a vestibule of sorts, reserved for the uncommitted. There the souls of those who never choose between good and evil mingle with angels who followed neither God nor Satan, chasing a fickle banner while being stung by hornets. Writing for an audience of aid practitioners, Slim presents this sin of moral vacillation in terms of political neutrality. The translation of categories, however, is even more apt than the author suggests. Viewed from the perspective of an anthropology of secular morality, it becomes clear that the primary judgment faced by aid agencies is a political one. When good and evil present themselves in terms of the politics of commitment, solidarity, and measurable outcomes, it grows uncomfortable to stand to one side. Even when resisting politics in the form of justifications of suffering, those invested in aid face their own political expectations and desires. The political quiescence associated with traditional charity – its implication that poverty and suffering may be an inevitable feature of human experience, its acceptance of inequality – disturbs modern, liberal sensibilities, including those of both aid workers and anthropologists. Within a secular cosmology one must claim political good or risk the torments of near damnation.

NOTES

1 A full review of "antipolitics" lies beyond this essay. I would simply note that some authors (including Nietzsche) have claimed it as a field of open possibility, while others have deployed the term variously to indicate duplicity, technocratic rationalization, or reactionary closed mindedness (see, e.g., Konrád 1984; Bergmann 1987; Ferguson 1990; Brown 2001; Moyn 2007).

2 In organizational terms MSF is actually a federation of 19 national sections, plus several branch and international offices. Historically, five of these have been independently operational (France, Belgium, Holland, Switzerland, and Spain), and have not always seen eye to eye. Recent years have seen a greater degree of international harmony and involvement of "partner" sections in running operations. For the purposes of this essay I will generally treat the wider group as a single entity, in keeping with its public profile. For more on humanitarianism see Wilson and Brown (2009), Feldman and Ticktin (2010), and Bornstein and Redfield (2011).

3 At http://www.oxfam.org/en/about, accessed Mar. 21, 2011.

4 At http://www.savethechildren.net/alliance/index.html, accessed Mar. 21, 2012.

5 At http://www.healthright.org/who-we-are, accessed Mar. 21, 2012.
6 At http://www.rescue.org/about, accessed Mar. 21, 2012.
7 At http://www.wvi.org/wvi/wviweb.nsf/maindocs/3F50B250D66B76298825736400663F21?opendocument, accessed Mar. 21, 2012.
8 At http://www.caritas.org/about/Caritas_Internationalis.html, accessed Mar. 21, 2012.
9 At http://www.icrc.org/eng/who-we-are/index.jsp, accessed Mar. 21, 2012.
10 See http://www.icrc.org/eng/war-and-law/treaties-customary-law/geneva-conventions/index.jsp, last accessed Apr. 27, 2011.
11 See Renée Fox's (1995: 1609) gloss of the French humanitarian position as "nonideological ideology." As Fassin (2010: 277) observes, one must attend to the factions and divisions that open within it in practice.
12 The point is also true at the level of national sections. For example, the branch of MSF that emerged in Belgium in 1980 remained more enamored with development than their French cousins. The two quarreled bitterly over a number of key issues in the ensuing years, to the extent that Paris sued Brussels over the use of their common name.
13 Although consistently popular with the French public, Kouchner has long been a controversial figure. For a caustic assessment of his trajectory as a generational icon – as well as a dismissal of "ambulance politics" – see Ross (2002: 147–169). See also Taithe (2004) and Bourg (2007) for wider context, as well as Caldwell (2009), for an account of recent controversy. Within MSF, his public legacy has proved a source of continued frustration, such as when the organization won the Nobel Peace Prize in 1999 and found itself misidentified in the press with his positions (Vallaeys 2004: 749–750).
14 See Hans Blumenberg's (1983) emphasis on "reoccupation" rather than transposition when comparing secularism with Christian theology.
15 As Talal Asad notes, whereas the opposition between sacred and profane may have found "no place in premodern writing," it became foundational in social science (2003: 32).

REFERENCES

Allen, Tim and Styan, David (2000) A Right to Interfere? Bernard Kouchner and the New Humanitarianism. *Journal of International Development* 12: 825–842.

Arendt, Hannah (1998 [1958]) *The Human Condition*. Chicago: University of Chicago Press.

Asad, Talal (2003) *Formations of the Secular: Christianity, Islam, Modernity*. Stanford: Stanford University Press.

Barnett, Michael (2011) *Empire of Humanity: A History of Humanitarianism*. Ithaca, NY: Cornell University Press.

Barnett, Michael and Weiss, Thomas (2008) Humanitarianism: A Brief History of the Present. In Michael Barnett and Thomas Weiss (eds.), *Humanitarianism in Question: Power, Politics, Ethics*. Ithaca, NY: Cornell University Press, pp. 1–48.

Bass, Gary (2008) *Freedom's Battle: The Origins of Humanitarian Intervention*. New York: Knopf.

Benthall, Jonathan and Bellion-Jourdan, Jérôme (2009) *The Charitable Crescent: Politics of Aid in the Muslim World*. London: I. B. Tauris.

Bergmann, Peter (1987) *Nietzsche, "the Last Antipolitical German."* Bloomington: Indiana University Press.

Blumenberg, Hans (1983) *The Legitimacy of the Modern Age*, trans. R. Wallace. Cambridge, MA: MIT Press.

Bornstein, Erica (2009) The Impulse of Philanthropy. *Cultural Anthropology* 24(4): 622–651.

Bornstein, Erica and Redfield, Peter (eds.) (2011) *Forces of Compassion: Humanitarianism between Ethics and Politics*. Santa Fe, NM: School of Advanced Research Press.

Bourg, Julian (2007) *From Revolution to Ethics: May 1968 and Contemporary French Thought.* Montreal: McGill-Queens University Press.

Bradol, Jean-Hervé (2004) The Sacrificial International Order and Humanitarian Action. In Weissman (2004), pp. 1–22.

Brauman, Rony (1996) *Humanitaire, le dilemme.* Paris: Textuel.

Brown, Wendy (2001) *Politics Out of History.* Princeton: Princeton University Press.

Caldwell, Christopher (2009) Communiste et Rastignac. *London Review of Books* 31(13): 7–10.

Calhoun, Craig (2008) The Imperative to Reduce Suffering: Charity, Progress and Emergencies in the Field of Humanitarian Action. In Michael Barnett and Thomas G. Weiss (eds.), *Humanitarianism in Question: Power, Politics, Ethics.* Ithaca, NY: Cornell University Press, pp. 73–97.

Calhoun, Craig (2010) The Idea of Emergency: Humanitarian Action and Global (Dis)Order. In Fassin and Pandolfi (2010a), pp. 29–58.

Cannell, Fenella (2010) The Anthropology of Secularism. *Annual Review of Anthropology* 39: 85–100.

Cooter, Roger and Luckin, Bill (eds.) (1997) *Accidents in History: Injuries, Fatalities and Social Relations.* Amsterdam: Rodopi.

Duffield, Mark R. (2007) *Development, Security and Unending War: Governing the World of Peoples.* Cambridge: Polity.

Farmer, Paul (2003) *Pathologies of Power: Health, Human Rights, and the New War on the Poor.* Berkeley: University of California Press.

Fassin, Didier (2008) Beyond Good and Evil? Questioning the Anthropological Discomfort with Morals. *Anthropological Theory* 8(4): 333–344.

Fassin, Didier (2010) Heart of Humaneness: The Moral Economy of Humanitarian Intervention. In Fassin and Pandolfi (2010a), pp. 269–293.

Fassin, Didier (2011) Noli Me Tangere: The Moral Untouchability of Humanitarianism. In Bornstein and Redfield (2011), pp. 35–52.

Fassin, Didier (2012) *Humanitarian Reason: A Moral History of the Present.* Berkeley: University of California Press.

Fassin, Didier and Pandolfi, Mariella (eds.) (2010a) *Contemporary States of Emergency: The Politics of Military and Humanitarian Interventions.* New York: Zone.

Fassin, Didier and Pandolfi, Mariella (2010b) Introduction: Military and Humanitarian Government in the Age of Intervention. In Fassin and Pandolfi (2010a), pp. 9–25.

Feldman, Ilana (2007) Difficult Distinctions: Refugee Law, Humanitarian Practice and Political Identification in Gaza. *Cultural Anthropology* 22(1): 129–169.

Feldman, Ilana and Ticktin, Miriam (eds.) (2010) *In the Name of Humanity: The Government of Threat and Care.* Durham, NC: Duke University Press.

Ferguson, James (1990) *The Anti-Politics Machine: "Development," Depoliticization, and Bureaucratic Power in Lesotho.* Cambridge: Cambridge University Press.

Festa, Lynn (2010) Humanity without Feathers. *Humanity* 1(1): 3–27.

Foucault, Michel (1984) "What is Enlightenment?" In *The Foucault Reader*, ed. Paul Rabinow. New York: Pantheon, pp. 32–50.

Fox, Renée C. (1995) Medical Humanitarianism and Human Rights: Reflections on Doctors Without Borders and Doctors of the World. *Social Science and Medicine* 41(12): 1607–1626.

Haskell, Thomas (1995) Capitalism and the Origins of Humanitarian Sensibility. In Thomas Bender (ed.), *The Antislavery Debate.* Berkeley: University of California Press, pp. 107–160.

Heins, Volker (2008) *Nongovernmental Organizations in International Society: Struggles over Recognition.* New York: Palgrave Macmillan.

Hunt, Lynn (2007) *Inventing Human Rights: A History.* New York: Norton.

Hutchinson, John F. (1996) *Champions of Charity: War and the Rise of the Red Cross.* Boulder, CO: Westview.

Konrád, György (1984) *Antipolitics: An Essay.* Boston: Harcourt, Brace, Jovanovich.

Lakoff, Andrew (2010) Two Regimes of Global Health. *Humanity* 1(1): 59–79.

Latour, Bruno (1993) *We Have Never Been Modern.* Cambridge, MA: Harvard University Press.

Li, Tania (2007) *The Will to Improve: Governmentality, Development, and the Practice of Politics.* Durham, NC: Duke University Press.

Lutz, Cathy (2000) *Homefront: A Military City and the American Twentieth Century.* Boston: Beacon.

Malkki, Liisa H. (1996) Speechless Emissaries: Refugees, Humanitarianism, and Dehistoricization. *Cultural Anthropology* 11(3): 377–404.

McFalls, Lawrence (2010) Benevolent Dictatorship: The Formal Logic of Humanitarian Government. In Fassin and Pandolfi (2010a), pp. 317–333.

Moyn, Samuel (2007) On the Genealogy of Morals. *The Nation* (Apr. 16), 25–31.

Moyn, Samuel (2010) *The Last Utopia: Human Rights in History.* Cambridge, MA: Harvard University Press.

Nordstrom, Carolyn (2004) *Shadows of War: Violence, Power, and International Profiteering in the Twenty-First Century.* Berkeley: University of California Press.

Nurok, Michael (2003) Elements of the Medical Emergency's Epistemological Alignment: 18th to 20th Century Perspectives. *Social Studies of Science* 33(4): 563–579.

Orbinski, James (1999) Nobel Lecture. Dec. 10. At http://nobelprize.org/nobel_prizes/peace/laureates/1999/msf-lecture.html, accessed Mar. 9, 2012.

Orbinski, James (2008) *An Imperfect Offering: Humanitarian Action for the Twenty-First Century.* New York: Walker.

Pandolfi, Mariella (2008) Laboratory of Intervention: The Humanitarian Governance of the Postcommunist Balkan Terroritories. In Mary-Jo DelVecchio Good et al. (eds.), *Postcolonial Disorders.* Berkeley: University of California Press, pp. 157–186.

Pupavac, Vanessa (2010) Between Compassion and Conservatism: A Genealogy of Humanitarian Sensibility. In Fassin and Pandolfi (2010a), pp. 129–149.

Rabinow, Paul (2008) *Marking Time: On the Anthropology of the Contemporary.* Princeton: Princeton University Press.

Redfield, Peter (2008) Doctors Without Borders and the Moral Economy of Pharmaceuticals. In A. Bullard (ed.), *Human Rights in Crisis.* Aldershot: Ashgate, pp. 129–144.

Redfield, Peter (2011) The Impossible Problem of Neutrality. In Bornstein and Redfield (2011), pp. 53–70.

Rieff, David (2002) *A Bed for the Night: Humanitarianism in Crisis.* New York: Simon & Schuster.

Ross, Kristin (2002) *May '68 and Its Afterlives.* Chicago: University of Chicago Press.

Slim, Hugo (1997) Relief Agencies and Moral Standing in War: Principles of Humanity, Neutrality, Impartiality and Solidarity. *Development in Practice* 7(4): 342–352.

Smith, Adam (2009 [1759]) *The Theory of Moral Sentiments.* New York: Penguin.

Taithe, Bertrand (2004) Reinventing (French) Universalism: Religion, Humanitarianism and the "French Doctors." *Modern and Contemporary France* 12(2): 147–158.

Ticktin, Miriam. (2006) Where Ethics and Politics Meet: the Violence of Humanitarianism in France. *American Ethnologist* 33(1): 33–49.

Vallaeys, Anne (2004) *Médecins Sans Frontières: la biographie.* Paris: Fayard.

Vaughn, Megan (1991) *Curing Their Ills: Colonial Power and African Illness.* Stanford: Stanford University Press.

Weissman, Fabrice (ed.) (2004) *In the Shadow of "Just Wars": Violence, Politics and Humanitarian Action.* Ithaca, NY: Cornell University Press.

Williams, Raymond (1977) *Marxism and Literature.* Oxford: Oxford University Press.

Wilson, Richard and Brown, Richard (eds.) (2009) *Humanitarianism and Suffering: The Mobilization of Empathy.* Cambridge: Cambridge University Press.

CHAPTER 26

Human Rights

Mark Goodale

A theory free from illusions can only conceive of human purpose negatively.
Max Horkheimer, "Remarks on Philosophical Anthropology," 1993 [1935]

How does the recent anthropology of human rights contribute to both the anthropology of morality and the broader understanding of morality itself? This is the question I will address. Anthropologists have found the ethnography of human rights practices to be a fertile source of new ideas about the relationships between normativity, agency, and social and political intentionality, in particular, and this essay examines the implications of one of these ideas: that the practice of human rights has become a new sphere of contested *moral* practice in the contemporary world, one that is essentially creative, contingent, and shadowed by the specter of tragedy.

The essay is structured as follows. In the next section, I locate the anthropology of human rights within just enough historical context to make the observations in the essay meaningful. Although the essay is not intended to survey the full history of and ambiguities in the fraught relationship between anthropology and the postwar project of human rights, it is necessary to say something about the temporality through which human rights has become a dominant contemporary logic of personhood and social and political change. I then establish the theoretical underpinnings of the chapter by describing several conventional categories of moral understanding that are undermined by the anthropology of human rights, which leads to a radically alternative account of normative self-making. Finally, I draw selectively from several signal ethnographies to illustrate how a poetics of human rights as moral practice reveals tragedy and possibility to be intimately connected within the processes of human rights diffusion and consolidation that anthropologists have been tracking over the last 20 years.

A Companion to Moral Anthropology, First Edition. Edited by Didier Fassin.

Anthropology and the Neoliberal World Order

After the end of the cold war, the institutions and rhetorics of human rights expanded with urgency. In the absence of alternative frameworks for social and political change and moral renewal with equal global reach and legitimacy, those of human rights underwent something of an apotheosis. The promulgation of new international human rights instruments like ILO 169 (1989) – the international indigenous peoples' bill of rights – and the creation of new human rights judicial bodies like the International Criminal Court (1995), were important signs of the emerging relevance of human rights within the post-cold war transition. But the real transformative work of human rights took place when the institutions of international and transnational development were reconfigured as moral agents of neoliberal subject-making.

If the eventual coalescence of the "neoliberal world order" (Ferguson 2006) was marked by increasing disparities in global capital distribution, the retreat of the state from political economy, and the imposition by the mandarins of Bretton Woods of shock doctrine social policies on the "newly emerging democracies," its reach and scope were also visible every time another alphabet soup NGO held a human rights workshop in a village at what Hardt and Negri call the "capillary ends of … contemporary networks of power" (2000: 313). Here is where human rights was reinscribed as a moral vernacular par excellence for social and political action just at that moment when material conditions were worsening for many, especially in the global South, and the obligations of the welfare state were being replaced by policies that promoted economic self-reliance, social autonomy, and skepticism about the public sphere.

The anthropology of human rights – that is, the ethnography of the emergence of human rights as the moral language of neoliberalism – was less an intentional methodology than a kind of halting recognition that a political and legal project that began its life as "the last utopia" (Moyn 2010) was becoming something else entirely: an unpredictable logic for moral practice in times of disenchantment. That anthropologists observed this shift taking place in the midst of neoliberal crises was not surprising. The liminal period after the end of the cold war was marked by a particular kind of anxiety around the disjunctures between the promises of (neo)liberalism and the pervasiveness of enduring vulnerabilities.

The ethnographic encounter with the "anxiety of incompleteness" (Appadurai 2006) captured the ways in which the rhetoric of human rights was reorienting the relationship between moral identity, social action, and politics. At the same time that moral subjects increasingly came to see themselves as part of the "collective subject over itself" (Cheah 2012) – that is, as part of "humanity" – they were confronting deepening material insecurities and the loss of traditional forums for legal and political redress. Much of the anthropology of human rights has examined this growing gap between what might be called "expectations of universality" and the lived reality of violence, ethnic discrimination, and political exclusion.[1]

And although the ethnographic account of disenchantment has challenged a dominant narrative in the post-cold war about the triumph of international law and neoliberal governmentality, the implications for an anthropology of moral practice have been less obvious. This is in part due to the pervasive influence of several conventional assumptions about the relationship between morality and creative action.

Legacies of Moral Misunderstanding

Among its many unacknowledged implications, the recent anthropology of human rights has provided empirical evidence for one of the more profound arguments in Charles Taylor's seminal 1989 *Sources of the Self*: that the legacy of much of Western philosophy has left us with a narrow, cramped, and ultimately wrong-headed account of morality by defining it in terms of "what it is right to do" rather than "what it is good to be" (1989: 3). For Taylor, "morality" is more productively deployed as way to characterize and ideally understand the intersections of subject-making (and unmaking) and normativity – those processes by which culturally flexible and often ambiguous social categories both constrain and enable social action. This is not to say that in Taylor's view the practices of morality are entirely disconnected from outcome, political action, or the instrumental development of standards of right conduct. But for Taylor the key revision is to pull morality away from its historical linkages to *both* rules and consequences and reattach it – as both a framework of analysis and description of human agency – to what he describes as "modern identity," the processes through which the self emerges in relation to the social within particular historical moments.

The essential insight here is the notion that morality itself should be understood as a kind of social practice – rather than a description of one of several categories for evaluating social practice – and that it is a form of practice through which, and in terms of which, the subject is shaped, framed, and reframed. "Subjectivity," in this sense, is neither entirely a social construct nor the outcome of any number of internal conflicts over the nature and meaning of being (or, perhaps, being-there). Rather, it is constituted by the tenuous inter linkages that connect the self with a matrix of contested norms that make claims on people *as such* and not as actors committed to a particular course of action. As ethnographies have demonstrated, human rights have become a significant category of contested norms and the practice of human rights has become the means through which these norms articulate a particular way of being, not doing.

But if the practice of human rights has become a consequential type of moral practice, this fact must be reconciled with another rooted and pervasive bias in Western intellectual and political history. In the classical division of labor, human action is understood as rationally purposive in relation to one of several Aristotelian virtues, the most important of which for my purposes here is *phronesis* (Greek φρόνησις). Phronesis is the capability and the willingness to self-evaluate action – or, we might say, practice – in terms of both prevailing social norms and desired ends. What makes an archaeology of phronesis so critical as an ancestral influence on dominant conceptions of morality is that the vast range of everyday kinds of practice that it encompasses share one important thing in common: they do not, and cannot, produce anything new. The essence of phronesis as a conception of modes of human action – one that grounds the full spectrum of purposive social practices (legal, political, economic, and, most important here, moral) – is the relationship between the norm, rule, standard, social expectation, or principle and intentionality, which, for Aristotle (in the *Nicomachean Ethics*), is not a given trait of human nature but a result of a lifetime of experience in the world. In other words, for Aristotle (and thus for all later theories shaped in one way or another by these foundational ethics), a person performs – rather than embodies – phronesis over the course of a lifetime by shaping action to structure in increasingly more sophisticated ways and with increasingly more consequential results.

Phronesis is the gold standard of ancient intellectual virtues – and thus an important (if unacknowledged) part of the wellspring of many later theories of social, political, and moral action – precisely because it is a conception of modes of human action that encompass so much of the range of practices that are understood to be essential to a well-functioning political and moral community. But phronesis is not a virtue that is meant to encompass all modes of human action, especially those that *are* generative, capable of producing something new, something that lies beyond the rules, norms, and principles that provide the templates for practical action. For this we are given – and thus must confront – another ancestral category: that of *poiesis.*

Poiesis is the root virtue that gives birth to a legacy of assumptions about the social role and dangers of human action that creates, that brings forth (whether from nothing or otherwise), that instantiates. Poiesis encompasses a much narrower range of human action. In fact, the scope of poetic action can become so narrow that generativity, creativity, and real production come to be seen as the domains of isolated geniuses or outcasts, those who are incapable of living within the constraining logics of existing categories and who must therefore act *de novo*, with results that can span the range from the revolutionary to the destructive, from the flowering of transcendent art to the creation of ideologies of human suffering. But as we will see below, a poetic conception of human action is necessary for understanding the practice of human rights as a creative – that is, unpredictable, generative, potentially transformative – practice of self-making.

Human Rights and the Poetic Self

The anthropology of human rights challenges the classic distinction between poiesis and phronesis as models of human action and suggests an alternative one that assumes that *all* human action is capable of both real generativity and practical wisdom. A cross-section of anthropological research on different aspects of contemporary human rights practices (see note 1) reveals the ways in which people self-(re)constitute within ongoing struggles, conflicts, and moments of reparation in terms of norms that demand both creative self-reflection and practical deployment. That the ideas and institutional structures of human rights have become increasingly hegemonic in relation to existing and often opposing alternatives makes this essential creativity all the more significant. And if it is true that the rhetoric of human rights has also become the “archetypal language of democratic transition” (Wilson 2001: 1), then the fact that this language is *poetic* in this sense has profound implications for political reorganization after conflict, resistance and the articulation of dissent, and the possibilities for radical social change.

Indeed, it is here that I recover, in a sense, the usefulness of certain aspects of poiesis as a framework for understanding moral practice, but without returning to the basic distinction between creativity and purposive practical action that has obscured the full implications of the growing body of ethnographic research on human rights.

This reconditioned use of poiesis as an analytical device for understanding the practice of human rights draws from the work of the ethical and social theorist John Wall, whose critical study (2005) of Paul Ricoeur likewise examines the problem of the relationship between creativity and normativity. Although Wall's purposes are quite different – his study is both an intellectual history and philosophy of dominant understandings of moral practice from what he calls the "high Enlightenment" onward – his re-examination of Ricoeur's "poetics of the will" provides several key insights for a poetics of human rights as moral practice.

First, if for Wall "some … human capability for creativity is ultimately presupposed in moral life" (2005: 5), this capability is realized in ways that are crucially nonteleological – again, as against the "biased origins" of centuries of moral theory that assumed that the essence of moral practice was the linkage between norm and outcome. As we will see, the practice of human rights reveals itself as a kind of moral practice that is indeed purposive, but in a quite different way. This is particularly significant given that the formal institutional, discursive, and legal frameworks of human rights in the contemporary world – transnational, international, and national, if not "local" (see Goodale and Merry 2007) – are intensely, and multiply, teleological.[2]

Second, as Wall explains, Ricoeur's poetics of the will "imagines a moral world of large and generous proportions," in part because creativity itself is so "large and generous," indeed, excessive. So if a poetic account of human rights as moral practice takes up Wall's observation that "we *must* create our moral world, even if we wish we didn't have to" (2005: 14; emphasis original), one implication is that this particular moral world is marked by different forms of excess: of rhetoric, of ambiguity, of moments of critical self-reflection, and of meaning. (Wall emphasizes the "excessive creation of social meaning" through moral practice, but the anthropology of human rights uncovers practices that create and shape a broader range of forms of meaning.)

And finally, a poetics of human rights-as-moral practice that is inspired, in part, by Wall's reconfiguration of Ricoeur's poetics of the will sees moral creativity as both the capacity for, and practice of, self-redescription (see also Robinson and Rundell 1994). That is to say, the kind of creativity revealed by the anthropology of human rights is of a very specific kind, one that is itself quite at odds with the broader relevant intellectual histories. Instead of creativity as a kind of *sui generis* fount from which issues ideas, self-expressions, models of practice, etc., without precedent or even explanation – a dominant account of creativity that is easy to caricature – human rights-as-moral practice is characterized by moments of critical self-engagement in relation to (but *not* in terms of) moral expectations within existing social, religious, and political contexts.

The process of redescription within the practice of human rights is also, necessarily (and quite anthropologically), a critical reflection on the social, but as Ágnes Heller has observed, "the starting point of the moral attitude … is 'monological'" (1994: 58). That is, although moral practice – including the practice of human rights – is also obviously concerned with conditions of vulnerability in the world (Heller's particular interest), it is important to distinguish between the social uses of moral practice and moral practice itself. Again, as Heller argues, the "non-reciprocal character of the initial moral gesture needs to be emphatically underlined" (58). As the anthropology of human rights demonstrates, this "gesture," which redescribes the self and thus creates something critically new, is at the heart of human rights practice in the contemporary world.

To summarize to this point: the ethnography of the practice of human rights over the last 20 years has documented the contradictions and possibilities within what is an emergent domain of moral practice. This is a type of moral practice that is marked by self-(re)constitution in relation to – but not necessarily in terms of – what can loosely be described as norms: the rules, expectations, principles, and implicit understandings that have classically preoccupied anthropologists of law, politics, and morality as much as moral and political philosophers. In the post-cold war era, this normative mélange has in many places been profoundly altered by the rapid transmission of human rights discourse within new networks of institutions, legal forums, and what Keck and Sikkink (1998) have described as "activists beyond borders." As I have also suggested, the bias toward the distinction between (potentially creative) practice on the one hand, and, on the other, the practical wisdom that matches norms with desired outcomes, has obscured what is in fact a much more interesting set of relationships between subject-making (and unmaking), norms, and purposeful action. Within the practice of human rights-as-moral practice, these relationships are shaped by tensions that are particular to this key domain of the moral present. As the examples from the ethnography of human rights in the next two sections reveal, tragedy and contingency are key among them.

Human Rights and the Three Tragedies

The practice of human rights-as-moral practice is shaped by tragedy in at least three ways. If it is true that moral practice is a fraught process of self-reflection through which the self is configured and reconfigured in socially and historically relevant ways, then what happens if there is a failure to create moral meaning? I don't mean a failure as such, because the very nature of moral practice means that some meaning will be created. But the broader logic and culture of human rights create something like a moral imperative – not the demand to think or act in terms of specific moral rules directed toward specific ends, but the demand to self-constitute as a specific kind of moral person.

In Malawi, this failure to self-constitute within the rigid expectations of prevailing conceptions of human rights norms – and thus this tragedy – was the result of the politics of translation, or mistranslation. Malawian elites pushed for "human rights" to be translated in the Chichewa language as *ufulu wachibadwidwe*, which Harri Englund renders as "the freedom one is born with" (2006: 51). The problem with this politicized rendering is that it excludes a fuller range of meanings of human rights, including, ironically, meanings that are meant to express the basic fact that human rights are specific kinds of entitlements that people have simply by virtue of being. So the moral practices of Malawians in the era of human rights led to a kind of misbegotten self-constitution through which people came to see themselves as bearers of an amorphous but also unrestrained "freedom" that was expressed in ways that elites and transnational aid workers constructed as un-Malawian, from unruly behavior toward teachers in schools to the introduction of new clothing styles for women that were more revealing. And this tragic failure to create the kind of moral meaning demanded by a more expansive rendering of "human rights" had other consequences. In what Englund describes as "disempowerment through translation," poor

Malawians – newly self-constituted as vaguely and unpredictably "free" – were as a result not able to confront their conditions of vulnerability as moral actors entitled to specific forms of redress and social reallocation by the state.

The second sense of tragedy that hovers over the practice of human rights-as-moral practice is what might be described as the "tragic sense of self." This is an analytical paraphrase from the work of the Basque intellectual Miguel de Unamuno, who explored in his *Tragic Sense of Life* (1954 [1913]) the implications of what he argued was the central dilemma of our time: the struggle between a wisdom that intuits – but does not know – that there is something beyond the individual (whether immortality, or, better for my purposes, a global community interconnected by a faith in human rights), and knowledge, which is what is left behind after the methodological skepticism of the rationalist "takes away our fever by taking away our life" (110). And what is particularly tragic about this struggle is that it brings together two opposing forces that are forever joined in battle, a battle that is itself the definition of life for human beings now and thus inescapable. To paraphrase Unamuno again, faith and skeptical rationality are enemies, and because they are enemies they have need of one another.[3]

The ethnography of the practice of human rights reveals an isomorphic struggle, one that takes place at the interface between the actually existing (re)constituting moral self and the ideology of self that is intensely normative within human rights. This tragic sense of self is the result of the impossibility to reconstitute morally in terms of the entirely abstract conception of personhood that appears throughout international law, but which is devoid of what Unamuno would call "vitality." This is the cosmopolitan self who "for a few spells during the day … is [morally virtuous] but, for the rest, … has nothing in common with man" (1954: 116). Among other implications, this struggle between the cosmopolitan self of human rights, and the creative and thus unpredictable reconstituting self within actual moral practice, establishes a sort of outer limit to the kinds of transformations that are possible through the forms of human rights advocacy that emphasizes moral consciousness-raising rather than direct political or legal action.

This tragic sense of self comes into particularly sharp relief through encounters with human rights that take place on a normative landscape in which collective identity and practice are firmly rooted. Shannon Speed's (2008) ethnography of this struggle over the meaning of the self – including what we might call the "collective self" – in the small villages of Chiapas during the Zapatista uprising reveals the ways in which it is also shaped by the changing politicization of selfhood within different historical moments. She describes a deeply contested period in the late 1990s in which multiple politicized and often ambiguous narratives of the self were in play against a backdrop of the unpredictability of creative moral practice. Narratives derived from existing workers and Mexican revolutionary ideology, early 1990s human rights discourse (which emphasized individual autonomy and empowerment), and mid- to late-1990s indigenous rights discourse (which emphasized the experience of historical marginalization for abstract collectivities – the "indigenous"), were combined in new and not always socially productive ways within a more organic and local "shift in self-identification" through which people sought to recover yet another sense of self – a cultural one rooted in place and expressed through language (Speed 2008: 109–110). In the end, the neoliberal rendering of human rights – which acknowledges the collective but only as a bracketed category of morally and legally autonomous individuals – eventually either displaced, or incorporated, these other narratives of self and social action. The result was that despite the fact that villagers in Chiapas had "beg[un] to get oriented" and be aware of a new kind of "[moral] consciousness" (111), their actual poetic moral practice within this era of human rights was framed against what might be called (paraphrasing James Ferguson) "expectations of selfhood" that were both disciplinary and radically disconnected – as are all cosmopolitanisms – from the local.

The final sense of tragedy uncovered by the recent anthropology of human rights is perhaps more obvious: the tragedy of human destruction that is a consequence of the denial of humanness. The generative practice of human rights-as-moral practice is shaped in particular ways when it takes place within a wider history that is riven by the traumas of conflict that touch on the very meaning of what Giorgio Agamben (1998) described in a different context as "bare life" – life before, or excluded from, the "qualified" categories of politics, cultural belonging, law. And this sense of tragedy is in many ways coextensive with modern human rights itself: as I have explored elsewhere (Goodale 2009), the origins of postwar human rights law, politics, and cultural practice in the ashes of genocide continues to inflect everything from monitoring and measurement strategies (Merry 2009) to the search by international criminal courts for what Clarke (2009) has called "fictions of justice."

But what I emphasize here is something different: the struggle to define, celebrate, or destroy the broadest category of belonging – the "human" – in the face of what Martha Nussbaum (2001) has called the "fragility of goodness." This was Nussbaum's description for her own resolution of the contradictions underlying the ancestral distinction between poiesis and phronesis. As Wall explains, Nussbaum wanted to disentangle our understanding of moral life from its rigid association with both normative expectations and outcomes by tempering the classical "sense of rationalistic self-mastery with a poetic moral wisdom about human vulnerability, passivity, and dependence" (Wall 2005: 70). For Nussbaum, in other words, a poetical conception of moral practice was not just a way of recognizing that creativity was in the very fiber of moral life and therefore fundamental to the (re)constitution of the self. Even more, it was an acknowledgment of the fragile balance between the demand to create meaning through moral practice and the possibility of a destructive unraveling when the grounds of moral practice become unsustainable.

As Richard A. Wilson (2001) demonstrates in his ethnography of trauma and reconstruction in South Africa, the tragedy of the Truth and Reconciliation Commission (TRC) was not so much that it became a technocratic "truth-making machine" bureaucratically divorced from the lived experiences of political transition and social reckoning; and nor was it even that the TRC took place before the post-apartheid state could fully ripen its legitimacy through a well-functioning regime of law. Rather, the tragedy of the TRC was that, as the principal means through which the "moral accounting of apartheid" (2001: 56) took place, it was institutionally and perhaps historically incapable of accounting for the very thing that justified and perpetuated apartheid: the social denial of humanness that is the precondition for (mutual) moral comprehension across categories of difference. So even if the TRC managed to establish at least some basic normative bright lines going forward, it did nothing – or very little – to either confront the moral unraveling that apartheid represented or establish what Habermas called the "web of moral feelings" (1990: 47), that "community of moral subjects in dialogue" (McCarthy in Habermas 1990: viii) that was a bulwark against the dark side of moral practice, a moral practice that has succumbed to its own fragility.

Contingency and Neoliberal Self-Making

As we have seen, the classical account of morality (and normativity more generally) that is shaped by the bias toward phronesis as the gold standard of moral virtues suggests a specific relationship between norm and outcome and thus norm and practice. To understand this relationship, and to be able to act in terms of it in the face of dilemmas both mundane and extraordinary, was, for Aristotle, the essence of the particular type of wisdom that was the sine qua non of a rational and well-functioning moral community. But as Wall (2005) explains, in his critique of both the distinction between poiesis and phronesis and its multiple legacies, the end of moral practice for Aristotle was no more specific than the support of a well-ordered society. Within what might be described as this vague teleology, multiple outcomes of moral decisions were to be expected, as long as they, taken together, reflected in practice the collective search for the best possible outcome under the circumstances given prevailing standards.

But the ethnography of human rights-as-moral practice has found something quite at odds with this conventional framework for understanding the ways and means of what Habermas called the "sphere of everyday moral intuitions" (1990: 55). The practice of human rights is a kind of moral practice that is essentially creative, but creative in a very specific way: what is created is both the capacity to reflect in new ways on the self *and* what emerges through this process of self-(re)constitution. Yet if we return to Charles Taylor's (1989) suggestion that the relationship between moral practice and selfhood should be understood in terms of "what it is good to be" rather than "what it is good to do," we are left with an account of human rights practice (again, as moral practice) that is radically contingent. Of course, as Kirsten Hastrup (2007) has argued about creativity more generally, to reflect generatively – and thus contingently – on the self is also to reflect on society.[4] Yet what results cannot be measured in terms of specific forms of social or political action but rather in terms of new understandings of the self – "what it is good to be" – within particular historical moments that are themselves defined, in part, by forms of social and political action.

The contingency of human rights-as-moral practice creates two lines of tension. First, this kind of essential indeterminacy does not merely problematize what might be called the ideology of human rights. It runs precisely counter to it. As I have argued at length elsewhere (Goodale 2009), both the conceptual and the political modes of human rights are intensely teleological: the idea of human rights opens up axiomatically from one or more unproven/unprovable first principles and moves through a set of ever more refined corollaries, all teetering on the tip of an inverted analytical pyramid; and as a political and legal framework that is fundamentally utopian, human rights implies a narrow line of progress from the chaos of war and genocide to the Kantian tranquility of a world marked by perpetual peace (see also Winter 2006; Hunt 2008; Moyn 2010). And second, the contingency of human rights practice complicates even the most sophisticated forms of human rights advocacy and implementation, despite the fact that in all of its social, political, and legal dimensions, human rights is calculated to shape action – if not thought and feeling – in almost baroquely articulated ways.

This is no more apparent than in the legal provisions and monitoring networks that were created to realize the dream of women's rights through the Convention on the Elimination of All Forms of Discrimination against Women (CEDAW). Among the entire corpus of international law, CEDAW best represents the elaborated disciplinarity of human rights taken to its logical conclusion. Its various articles require states parties to the convention to "take all appropriate measures" at all levels of society, public and private, to transform both gender norms and gender practices to "ensure the full development and advancement of women, for the purpose of guaranteeing them the exercise and enjoyment of human rights and fundamental freedoms on a basis of equality with men" (Art. 3). Article 5(a) outlines the breadth and intent of the convention in a slightly different way: state parties *shall* "modify the social and cultural *patterns of conduct* of men and women, with a view to achieving the elimination of prejudices and customary and *all other practices* which are based on the idea of the inferiority or the superiority of either of the sexes or on stereotyped roles for men and women" (emphases mine).[5]

But as Sally Engle Merry's (2006) study of the practices of CEDAW demonstrates so clearly, the encounter with CEDAW's various provisions is permeated by moments of indeterminacy, confusion, and the vagaries of perceived interest. Her case study of the controversy over the Fijian customary practice of *bulubulu* within the CEDAW monitoring system provides a sharp illustration of how the essential contingency at the heart of the practice of human rights creates a space for what might be called moral liberty at the same time as it frustrates the programmatic aspirations of human rights advocates and institutions. *Bulubulu* is a way of describing a complicated social process for transforming conflicts in Fiji through a series of ritualized encounters between parties to the conflict and the exchange of gifts. As Merry describes its various manifestations, *bulubulu* is:

> a formal ceremony of apology in which the offender offers gifts such as a whale's tooth and kerosene along with an apology and seeks reconciliation with the victim … It provides reconciliation between equals or when an inferior has offended a superior … it is still frequently used to negotiate a peaceful relationship between kin groups after a marriage by elopement … [It] is a practice of renegotiating relationships of inequality. (2006: 118–119)

The traditions, narratives, and debates around *bulubulu* emerged as symbols of the contingency of human rights practice when Fiji's first report to CEDAW's monitoring committee was presented in 2002. In the report, the government criticized its own legal system for accepting the reconciliation of *bulubulu* in cases of rape in particular, in which fathers of victims were able to reach an accord with the families of perpetrators before legal cases could even proceed. During the oral hearing on the country report, the CEDAW committee focused on this part of the country report's self-critique and made it the basis for its evaluation of Fiji's progress in a later set of "concluding comments" (Merry 2006: 116). But in its response to the CEDAW committee's rejection of *bulubulu* as a form of conflict resolution and, a fortiori, a social mechanism for reconciling parties affected by the crime of rape (which include the fathers of victims and perpetrators as much as the victims and perpetrators themselves), the Fijian government mounted a spirited defense of *bulubulu* as a "vital custom of the Fijian community for reconciliation and cementing kinship ties" (115).

And while the government acknowledged that *bulubulu* was not an appropriate response to cases of rape, its assistant minister for women, in follow-up interviews with Merry, argued that *bulubulu* was more than anything a window into a cultural universe in which reconciliation was an essential part of moral life. Without *bulubulu*, "society will fall apart"; and "eliminating bulubulu was impossible since it was the basis of village life" (Merry 2006: 116). Echoing the response to the shaping intentions of human rights in Malawi that we have already seen, the assistant minister went further and assailed the way that the focus on freedoms in women's rights legislation has "persuaded women that they can do whatever they want, including dressing and acting without sexual modesty," as Merry describes the minister's critique of the "individualist human rights system" (117).

Merry's subsequent research revealed that the controversy over *bulubulu* and the CEDAW reporting process took place within a wider historical moment in which ethnic relations had been politicized in particular ways and the multiple practices of *bulubulu* had undergone shifts with the demise of rural life. This knowledge of the broader social and political contexts in which the practice of human rights in Fiji and within the transnational monitoring networks of CEDAW took place merely deepens the ethnographic insight into the contingency of human rights-as-moral practice.

The point is *not* that the moral lives of Fijians in rural villages would be any less contingent were *bulubulu* the only normative game in town; rather, it is that the disciplinary ways and means of human rights are simply frustrated in ways that those of *bulubulu* – in whatever historical form – are not. To make this point another way: the ethnographic revelation that human rights-as-moral practice is essentially contingent allows us to bracket the wider, and arguably neo-imperialist, aspirations of human rights by recognizing their structural limitations. Of course not all such aspirations are equal, and we might very well regret the fact that the universalizing morality of human rights is destined to go off the rails when confronted with the "transformational creativity" (Parkin 2001) of moral practice. But as the great symbolic anthropologist Roy Wagner might have put it, creative moral practice is something we *must* do "if we are to live and preserve our mysteries" (1975: 75).

Conclusion: Human Rights and the Anthropology of the Moral Present

By way of conclusion, let me briefly restate the essay's main arguments and then make a plea for the importance of an anthropology of the moral present. The anthropology of human rights over the last 20 years has documented the ways in which human rights has become the principal moral mode of neoliberalism. At the same time, the globalization of the "collective self over itself" has taken place amid the deepening of a range of structural vulnerabilities, including economic inequality, ethnic antipathies, and the pervasiveness of neoliberal antipolitics. It has been within these contradictions that anthropologists have confronted the unpredictable moments of self-constitution that characterize the practice of human rights-as-moral practice.

But the full implications of the anthropology of human rights for the broader understanding of moral practice have been obscured by the legacies of several longstanding conventional assumptions about the relationship between morality and political and social action on the one hand, and between morality and creativity, on the other. Recent critical scholarship in social and ethical theory forms the basis for an alternative account of these relationships. Drawing on John Wall's reappraisal of Ricoeur's poetics of the will, I made the argument for a poetical approach to the practice of human rights-as-moral practice that reorients self-making in relation to purposive social and political action. By recasting moral practice in terms of categories of "what it is good to be" rather than "what it is good to do," it becomes possible to appreciate the ways in which creative (and thus unpredictable) self-making, and not instrumental action, is at the heart of the practice of human rights in the contemporary world.

With what might be called a "poetics of the impossible" as a theoretical lens, I surveyed from the recent ethnography of human rights, which reveals the growing gap between the ideology of human rights within international institutions and discourse and the lived realities of people who are caught within spirals of despair and misunderstanding. Anthropological studies of human rights further show that these disjunctures are marked by tensions – which I describe as "tragedy" and "contingency" – that are particular to these domains of moral practice.

The anthropology of the moral present has become more vital than ever. The close ethnographic encounter with modes of moral practice (such as the practice of human rights) in the post-cold war reveals a troubling divergence: at the same time that dominant logics of self-making are becoming both more narrow and more triumphalist, the possibilities for structural change and the redistribution of power are also narrowing as the "neoliberal world order" matures and encompasses new regions and political regimes. This makes it all the more necessary to pay close attention to the micro-practices of self-making and moral agency, even if this kind of anthropology does not temper the prevailing mood of disenchantment.

NOTES

1 See, e.g., Wilson 2001; Slyomovics 2005; Englund 2006; Merry 2006; Goodale and Merry 2007; Tate 2007; Speed 2008; Clarke 2009; Goodale 2009, n.d.*b*; Deal 2010; Shaw et al. 2010; Bornstein 2012.

2 Just take the Preamble to the Universal Declaration of Human Rights (1948), which makes the international human rights system the instrumental foundation for achieving the interrelated, but distinct, ends of "freedom, justice and peace in the world."

3 Unamuno's elegant description of this existential conflict is worth quoting *in extenso*: "Every position of permanent agreement or harmony between reason and life, between philosophy and religion, becomes impossible. And the tragic history of human thought is simply the history of a struggle between reason and life – reason bent on rationalizing life and forcing it to submit to the inevitable, to mortality; life bent on vitalizing reason and forcing it to serve as a support for its own vital desires" (1954: 115).

4 Hastrup's piece is included in an important volume in the anthropological study of creativity (Hallam and Ingold 2007) which bears significantly on the wider study of human rights

and moral creativity (Goodale n.d.*a*). In this longer work, I depart critically, but appreciatively, from the main underlying theoretical assumption of the volume, namely, that creativity characterizes forms of practice that take place apart from those "codes, rules, and norms" that constitute the static backdrop of the social.

5 At http://www.un.org/womenwatch/daw/cedaw/text/econvention.htm, accessed Mar. 23, 2012.

REFERENCES

Agamben, Giorgio (1998) *Homo Sacer: Sovereign Power and Bare Life*. Stanford: Stanford University Press.

Appadurai, Arjun (2006) *Fear of Small Numbers: An Essay on the Geography of Anger*. Durham, NC: Duke University Press.

Bornstein, Erica (2012) *Disquieting Gifts: Humanitarianism in New Delhi*. Stanford: Stanford University Press.

Cheah, Pheng (2012) Acceptable Uses of People. In Mark Goodale (ed.), *Human Rights at the Crossroads*. New York: Oxford University Press.

Clarke, Kamari Maxine (2009) *Fictions of Justice: The International Criminal Court and the Challenge of Legal Pluralism in Sub-Saharan Africa*. Cambridge: Cambridge University Press.

Deal, Jeffrey L. (2010) Torture by *Cieng*: Ethical Theory Meets Social Practice among the Dinka Agaar of South Sudan. *American Anthropologist* 112(4): 563–575.

Englund, Harri (2006) *Prisoners of Freedom: Human Rights and the African Poor*. Berkeley: University of California Press.

Ferguson, James (2006) *Global Shadows: African in the Neoliberal World Order*. Durham, NC: Duke University Press.

Goodale, Mark (2009) *Surrendering to Utopia: An Anthropology of Human Rights*. Stanford: Stanford University Press.

Goodale, Mark (n.d.*a*) Human Rights and Moral Creativity: Essays on Power, Agency, and Ethical Practice. Unpublished manuscript.

Goodale, Mark (n.d.*b*) The Violence of Ambiguity: Constitutional Revolution and the Problem of Radical Social Change in Bolivia. Unpublished manuscript.

Goodale, Mark and Merry, Sally Engle (eds.) (2007) *The Practice of Human Rights: Tracking Law between the Global and the Local*. Cambridge: Cambridge University Press.

Habermas, Jürgen (1990) *Moral Consciousness and Communicative Action*. Cambridge, MA: MIT Press.

Hallam, Elizabeth and Ingold, Tim (eds.) (2007) *Creativity and Cultural Improvisation*. London: Berg.

Hardt, Michael and Negri, Antonio (2000) *Empire*. Cambridge, MA: Harvard University Press.

Hastrup, Kirsten (2007) Performing the World: The Imaginative Link between Action and History. In Hallam and Ingold (2007), pp. 193–206.

Heller, Ágnes (1994) The Elementary Ethics of Everyday Life. In Robinson and Rundell (1994), pp. 48–64.

Horkheimer, Max (1993 [1935]) Remarks on Philosophical Anthropology. In *Between Philosophy and Social Science: Selected Early Writings*. Cambridge, MA: MIT Press, pp. 151–176.

Hunt, Lynne (2008) *Inventing Human Rights: A History*. New York: Norton.

Keck, Margaret and Sikkink, Kathryn (1998) *Activists beyond Borders: Advocacy Networks in International Politics*. Ithaca, NY: Cornell University Press.

Merry, Sally Engle (2006) *Human Rights and Gender Violence: Translating International Law into Local Justice*. Chicago: University of Chicago Press.

Merry, Sally Engle (2009) Measuring the World: Indicators, Human Rights, and Global Governance. *Proceedings of the Annual Meeting of the American Society of International Law* 103: 239–243.
Moyn, Samuel (2010) *The Last Utopia: Human Rights in History*. Cambridge, MA: Belknap Press of Harvard University Press.
Nussbaum, Martha (2001) *The Fragility of Goodness: Luck and Ethics in Greek Tragedy*. New York: Cambridge University Press.
Parkin, David (2001) The Paradox of Cultural Creativity. In John Liep (ed.), *Locating Cultural Creativity*. London: Pluto, pp. 133–143.
Robinson, Gillian and Rundell, John (eds.) (1994) *Rethinking Imagination: Culture and Creativity*. London: Routledge.
Shaw, Rosalind and Waldorf, Lars, with Hazan, Pierre (eds.) (2010) *Localizing Transitional Justice: Interventions and Priorities after Mass Violence*. Stanford: Stanford University Press.
Slyomovics, Susan (2005) *The Performance of Human Rights in Morocco*. Philadelphia: University of Pennsylvania Press.
Speed, Shannon (2008) *Rights in Rebellion: Indigenous Struggle and Human Rights in Chiapas*. Stanford: Stanford University Press.
Tate, Winifred (2007) *Counting the Dead: The Culture and Politics of Human Rights Activism in Colombia*. Berkeley: University of California Press.
Taylor, Charles (1989) *Sources of the Self: The Making of the Modern Identity*. Cambridge, MA: Harvard University Press.
Unamuno, Miguel de (1954 [1913]) *Tragic Sense of Life* [*Del Sentimiento Trágico de la Vida*], trans. J. E. Crawford Flitch. New York: Dover.
Wall, John (2005) *Moral Creativity: Paul Ricoeur and the Poetics of Possibility*. Oxford: Oxford University Press.
Wilson, Richard A. (2001) *The Politics of Truth and Reconciliation in South Africa: Legitimizing the Post-Apartheid State*. Cambridge: Cambridge University Press.
Wagner, Roy (1975) *The Invention of Culture*. Chicago: University of Chicago Press.
Winter, Jay (2006) *Dreams of Peace and Freedom: Utopian Moments in the Twentieth Century*. New Haven: Yale University Press.

CHAPTER 27

War

Catherine Lutz and Kathleen Millar

At once paradoxically and predictably, morality lies at the center of the human institution of warfare. War has been, for modern states, the ultimate moral arbiter of who counts as a citizen and what counts as a national purpose. It has stood as the ultimate sign of what the state does for its members: war is often claimed to be *the* moral endeavor of states. In a fundamental sense, war and moral claims co-constitute each other via the question of when it is required that human life be taken for a larger purpose. Even as realists claim that morality has no place in statecraft, including war-making, public pronouncements by political leaders, military recruiters, and the public at large make large moral claims for war. And morality is increasingly defined *by* war, as something which is most in evidence in the willingness to die (and, sometimes, sotto voce, to kill) to protect others, in service to the nation.

In this essay, we explore war as a privileged site of morality production. By considering war a *privileged* site, we seek to draw attention to war's distinctiveness as a social institution that makes value and values out of the obliteration of human lives. By conceptualizing war as morality *production*, we focus our analysis on the intense moral work done to legitimate or condemn particular forms and elements of war, while leaving the war paradigm itself unquestioned.

We have organized our discussion into three parts. The first provides a brief overview of how the anthropology of war has engaged and critiqued dominant moral models of war in the United States. Anthropologists interested in questions of morality and war have often turned to war actors and sites that fall beyond the bounds of a Clausewitzian view of war as the rational and legitimate use of violence by states. In doing so, ethnographies, such as Cynthia Mahmood's (1996) study of Sikh militants and Emiko Ohnuki-Tierney's (2002) account of kamikaze pilots during World War II, have made significant contributions to understanding local meanings and the moral sensibilities of those who have committed seemingly inexplicable, horrific acts of violence. This work, while specifically attempting to undermine certainties in readers

A Companion to Moral Anthropology, First Edition. Edited by Didier Fassin.

about the morality of the normative Western way of war, retains a focus on the moral margins of war, and leaves the moralities invoked and produced at the center of that way of war – the Pentagon, high-lethality weapons production, military contractors, and the international security system – relatively unexamined.

The second part of this essay presents our overarching argument that the morality of war in the West has been policed at a shifting margin. At different historical moments in the past century, particular war agents (e.g., child soldiers, mercenaries, terrorists), instruments (e.g., nuclear weapons, landmines), and goals (e.g., strategic resource access, human rights protections) have drawn overwhelming attention in moral debates on war. This fixation on a limited number of often marginally significant war elements has mobilized enormous resources and efforts that include the establishment and enforcement of national and international laws of war; the creation of NGOs or NGO programs targeting some aspects of war, like child soldiering, that evoke moral outrage; and academic research, international conferences, and extensive media coverage that focus on issues such as these. Through our analysis of the extensive moral work devoted to some aspects of war and not others, we ask why the moral examination of war itself remains at the near invisible edges of contemporary life and how the limitations of debate implicitly sanction the globally pervasive militarism of everyday life.

In a third section, we turn to three professions which have worked to evaluate or regulate war or to rescue its victims. There we argue that law, medicine, and military or militarized social science have had the effect of limiting the moral and political framing of the idea of war, managing and facilitating rather than critiquing or combating it. Their work and discourses have helped form part of the now dominant public understandings of war and its future.

Anthropology's Engagement with War's Dominant Moral Models

Euro-American anthropology has a long, intimate relationship to war, first emerging as a professional field of study in the context of colonial conquest and administration. Yet anthropologists in the early twentieth century largely ignored the wars that paved the way to their field sites or the colonial struggles raging in the midst of their fieldwork. Evans-Pritchard, for example, hardly mentioned in his extensive ethnographic work on the Nuer the ongoing armed attacks by the Anglo-Egyptian government on Nuer cattle camps (Hutchinson 1996). Furthermore, the anthropological literature on war that did emerge in the latter half of the twentieth century rarely made moralities and ethical systems concerning war an explicit object of study.

That said, the underlying questions driving ethnographic research on war have often been shaped by dominant moral understandings of war at particular historical moments. World War II recruited the majority of US anthropologists to war work in a conflict widely defined as just and moral. During the cold war, nuclear weapons and the arms race between the United States and the Soviet Union made the complete annihilation of human life a possibility, while political campaigns against dissent in the university made moral discrimination around issues of war and peace dangerous (Price 2004). Questions about war in this period were restricted to identifying modes and meanings of warfare in preindustrial societies. The Vietnam War brought killing on a grand scale in what was considered a modern conflict in a postcolonial society; it instigated stronger moral debate about contemporary war in a discipline that was forging a more historicized and overtly political approach to its subject and doing so in a new social context of free speech and social justice movements. Finally, the attacks of 9/11 and the US wars that followed for over a decade created a greatly expanded war system and a social science turn in the military's counterinsurgency doctrine that, among other things, foregrounded the problem and moralities of war for anthropologists.

For many years, anthropologists interested in understanding war had focused on the question of human nature and the origins of organized violence. They asked: What are the reasons for which human groups went and go to war? What are the ecological constraints and facilitators of war-making? What are the political forms of organization that make it more likely and what is its role in the evolution of social and political forms? These questions steered ethnographic inquiry toward the study of "primitive war," that is, toward cases of organized violence in cultural groups taken to be representations of an essentialized human nature. The study of the Yanomami in the Amazon basin is perhaps the best-known example of such anthropological work, generating an extensive amount of debate on its causes and its potential evolutionary benefits (see Chagnon 1968; Harris 1974; Gross 1975). The warring practices of the Yanomami might have seemed far removed from the nuclear arms production of the United States and USSR. Yet, cold war realism – the view of state interest as the only criterion by which to judge wars' merits, and of war as a mechanism that produces the survival of the fittest among states in the international system – permeated the anthropological debate on the Yanomami and other cases of nonindustrial warfare.[1] In the process, anthropology continued to miss the contemporary war system including the peasant and proxy wars then occurring around the world (Wolf 1969; Starn 1991).

In the post-cold war political context, many anthropologists turned their attention to local moralities of war in contemporary states. This shift paralleled a resurgence of just war theory and its amendment in humanitarian war following the end of the cold war, as a variety of primarily Northern countries and alliances, as well as the United Nations, engaged in multiple wars and military operations termed "humanitarian interventions." Such operations in Somalia (1992–94), Bosnia (1993–95), Haiti (1994; 2004–5), Kosovo (1999), Liberia (2003), Libya (2011), and to a certain degree, Afghanistan (from 2001) and Iraq (2003–11),[2] have been justified on the grounds that they serve humanitarian goals. Humanitarian intervention departs from the just war tradition in that the defense of rights and values (democracy, lasting peace, human rights), rather than self-defense, constitutes the justification for using force. Nonetheless, humanitarian intervention can be seen as a reformulation of just war theory in that moral values (versus strategic self-interests in the realist paradigm) are considered grounds for going to war.

Yet, just as anthropologists during the cold war engaged realism obliquely through their study of primitive war, many of the anthropologists who began studying questions of morality and war in the 1990s chose wars, war actors, and war effects that failed to conform to the just war model or that pushed beyond the parameters of just war theory. Anthropologists produced extensive and eloquent ethnographic work on the meaning-making and moral reasoning of such war actors as perpetrators of genocide in Rwanda (Taylor 1999); Sikh militants who set off bombs in crowded marketplaces (Mahmood 1996); *tokkotai* (kamikaze) pilots who crashed their planes or submarines into US ships at the end of World War II (Ohnuki-Tierney 2002); and Khmer Rouge who performed executions of prisoners in Cambodia (Hinton 2005). Others focused on the long and deep consequences of war unaccounted for in the just war model and its calculations of proportionality including displacement, ruptured communities, and persistent fear in everyday life (Hoffman 2011; Nordstrom 1997, 2004). In postwar contexts ranging from a Hutu refugee camp (Malkki 1995) to widow-headed households in Guatemala (Green 1999), anthropologists asked: What moral work is entailed in the reconstitution of community and social world in the aftermath of war?

Following in a long anthropological tradition of working to make the strange familiar, many of these ethnographies sought an understanding of perpetrators of violence as deeply moral actors. For example, Mahmood (1996) and Ohnuki-Tierney (2002) explore the search for meaning, the inner lifeworlds, and the processes through which Sikh militants and young *tokkotai* pilots, respectively, made painful decisions in difficult and extraordinary circumstances. "My task here, then," writes Mahmood, "is to convey the sense of meaningful striving, the sense of being at the peak of one's humanity in spite of the hellish conditions around one, that animates Sikh militants as they fight and die for a sovereign Sikh nation" (1996: 21). For Ohnuki-Tierney, a sense of personal "moral obligation" led her to write for a non-Japanese audience about the contradictions and ambivalent decisions that resulted in the tragic deaths of hundreds of young Japanese pilots, "known outside Japan only as ultra-nationalistic zealots" (2002: xi). In both ethnographies, the reader comes to understand the political, cultural, and symbolic worlds in which the fighters live and in which they make moral sense of their acts of violence.

Mahmood's and Ohnuki-Tierney's ethnographies, among others, approach war from its putative moral margins, through the lived experiences of fighters who stand in an ambivalent relationship to what standard Western models of war consider to be the legitimate use of violence. The next step – to make explicit the moralities invoked and produced at the center of those models of war – is left to be taken. Some ethnographic work has begun to do so, most notably ethnographic studies of the locations of nuclear weapons production (Gusterson 2004; Masco 2006), military bases (Lutz 2001; Vine 2009), and military training (Gill 2004; Fruhstuck 2007).

The Emergent Moral Margins of War and the Legitimated Center

To see the morality of war in these more central and modern Western contexts and in the process of production, we can turn to history and to specific debates about war that have taken place over the last century both in the United States and in what has come to be known as the international community. Contemporary discourses on war have been characterized by acceptance of the premises of just war theory, succinctly defined by Crawford:

> War is just if the cause and intention are just: namely, self-defense and the promotion of peace. War should be a last resort; it should be undertaken by competent authorities only

> if there is a possibility of success and if the overall good of the war will outweigh the harm it does. War must also be conducted justly: unnecessary violence should be avoided, and non-combatants should not be deliberately targeted. (2003: 3)

The widespread acceptance of these criteria for evaluating the morality of war has structured the sometimes tacit debates about which aspects of warfare are beyond the moral pale. The idea of war as immoral or amoral in and of itself has garnered almost no traction. The debates that have occurred usually assume that the warrior status and ethos are heightened moral ones and they take up war elements that are at the margin of acceptability rather than the question of the morality of the war paradigm or war economies themselves. The debates often erase the violently damaged body at war's center, focusing instead on war's putative cause, strategic progress, and outcomes (Scarry 1985) and on the moral validity of the competing parties' aims and methods. When those debates do bring the body into view, they often focus on precisely how the body was injured, how old the body was, whether it wore the uniform of a state or not, and so on.

Moreover, in centering debate around the moral margins of war, the result has been not so much to move inexorably toward a critique of the center of the institution, but to implicitly accept and to confer moral legitimacy on war's core actors and practices themselves. And despite the assumption that international law and the international community have developed more and more morally civilized ways of and responses to war over time – the standard progressive narrative of modernity in all of its elements, including this – the labor of moralizing and legislating about war has as often led to determinations that greater lethality, wider definitions of appropriate targets and agents of war, and expanded goals are warranted.

The moral center on which legitimacy has been conferred is this: state warfare and in particular that of democratic states, waged with a certain range of weapons by uniformed actors over the age of 18, with only a small percentage of total deaths occurring to those categorized as civilians. These are what are considered civilized, normative forms of war. Debate has focused on whether particular weapons, actors, and goals are morally proper (as well as pragmatic or utile) in the pursuit of war and whether the actors waging war have moral standing to do so. So there has been intense and explicitly moral scrutiny of nuclear weapons and landmines, but not of Tomahawk missiles or AK-47s. In recent decades, there has been a virtual moral panic about the figures of the child soldier and the suicide bomber, but not about the contemporary German conscript or US volunteer enlisted man (although the contradictory concept of the "poverty draft" volunteer has raised some moral queries about who carries the burden of soldiering and whether the choice to do so is unfree). There has been strong condemnation, particularly since the period leading up to the Third Geneva Convention, of degrading or torturing prisoners of war and elaborate efforts to enforce these moral injunctions. The war refugee, on the other hand, has moral standing as a victim but no universal protections against garnering that status or small protections once in it. Rescue narratives confer moral standing on the rescuer but little opprobrium for failure to do so. Finally, certain goals have been judged morally proper, such as defending the borders of a state or fighting for the human rights of others, while wars with other goals, for example, instilling fear in the civilian populace to achieve political ends or going to war to gain access to essential resources are now generally condemned. The outcomes of these moral debates have increasingly been codified in the laws of war at the international level and in legal and ethical regulation at the national and military institutional levels. The labor of making this morality is prodigious and the struggle over the moral high ground is ongoing in every case.

The morally marginal war agent

The contemporary moral condemnation of certain war actors at the margins, such as child soldiers, is simultaneously the moral legitimation of the soldier 18 years and older. Beyond the child's vulnerability and innocence, many critics of child soldiering point to the lack of moral discrimination in the young, which includes a greater readiness to follow orders and to be manipulated (United Nations 1996). These discourses suggest that the moral maturity of the 18-year-old is required for the decision about whether to participate in war and to be properly moral in engaging in war activities. By contrast, many other moral decisions are considered ones children are able to and should make, most notably religious affiliation and commitments, by the ages of 7, 13, or 16.

The moral condemnation of the child soldier is a recent development in the West, however, running parallel to the reformulation of childhood more generally as a period for protection and segregation from adults. Rosen (2005) notes the common participation of children in all major US wars through World War II (in the Civil War, 10–20% of recruits were younger than 18, by a conservative estimate). These "boy soldiers" were not merely perceived as unproblematic, but were actively celebrated. They were praised at their funerals as valiant contributors to transcendent causes, their impulsivity and lack of maturity recognized, but "recast as grand and heroic" (Rosen 2005: 6). The war experience is seen not as damaging but as ennobling them.

The expansion in the use of contractors in warfare has been accompanied by moral anxiety. Condemnation or distinct ambivalence about the soldier for hire stems from the notion that the soldier takes life in a moral exchange with the state and in selfless service to the protected citizenry, while the contractor makes his or her exchange only indirectly with the state via the corporate form and through market exchange. As an ideal type, the soldier, like a religious figure, has a mission and a calling; the contractor, like an office worker, merely has a job and a profit motive. The morality of war at its core depends fundamentally on the notion of the elevated moral character of the uniformed soldier, whose work is "sacrifice" and whose motive is love of community. Within this category then, as well, the volunteer accrues more moral weight than the draftee because the volunteer is seen as entering war of his or her own free will, the latter a necessity for proper moral agency.

Certain moral dilemmas have arisen as contractors have become an ever larger proportion of the military labor force in the United States in tandem with the rise of neoliberal visions and practices of statecraft. Viewing the state increasingly via the model of the marketplace has led to the outsourcing of much security work to the private sector. Whereas contracting has long been the centerpiece of weapons production, until fairly recently civilian workers have been kept away from combat zones. That zone is the location of the central machinery of morality production through war, and therefore the source of the greatest anxiety about the moral propriety of those actors. As a consequence, contractors' labor and their deaths and injuries have been deeply invisible to the general public: most are not aware that US contractors working in Iraq and Afghanistan have sometimes outnumbered uniformed soldiers, or that over 2,300 have died there.

The adult soldier is not only legitimated in contrast to these other kinds of less moral or amoral actors (the child soldier and the contractor) but is positively celebrated as a moral exemplar in comparison with the civilian. The soldier comes to embody the heroic and virtuous while the civilian becomes seen as a moral bystander, morally inert and even deficient. A set of values have come to be called military values (e.g., discipline, loyalty, honor, integrity, courage, and selflessness) and a set of (dis)values have come to be associated with civilian life (e.g., consumerism, individualism, selfishness, and moral permissiveness). There is little discussion of a phenomenon noted by some soldier critics themselves (Goff 2003), which is that nihilism is a common consequence for soldiers returning from war as the result of the contradiction they experience between what counts as acceptable behavior in war and the morality of everyday life with which they were raised.

Feminist analysis has pointed out that full moral agency has been highly gendered in large measure through the long-time restriction of warrior status to heterosexual (and white) males. The military creates and functions via a militarized masculinity, in which the male is identified as the protector of "womenandchildren" (Enloe 1990) and as a "Just Warrior" and the female as innocent, peaceful, and in need of protection (Elshtain 1987). War becomes and remains a central mechanism by which moral agency itself is defined: the men of the US military, for example, are construed as those who create a just outcome for the victimized if ethically inert Afghan woman. The vision of the protector male is a benevolent one of pastoral power – power "masked by virtue and love" (I. M. Young 2006: 122) – and it depends on the two images: of threat from an outside dominating male intent on doing harm and of the women and children at home who need protection and whose agency in any moral sphere outside the home is muted.

The struggle for moral status through soldiering has also contributed to an expansion in recent years of who counts as a moral agent of war. In the mass mobilization, and through the massive labor needs of World War II, black men struggled for moral/warrior status, and in the wake of the labor needs of the more affluent, expanding economy and political conditions that produced the all-volunteer force, women, gays and lesbians have, through long struggle, been increasingly included in Western militaries and allowed the most valued identity within the institution, that of the combat soldier.

The morally marginal war instrument

A social history of the machine gun (Ellis 1986) provides an extended example of the confluence of cultural moralities and particular weapons. The machine gun, which was first widely used in the colonial campaigns of the nineteenth century, passed with little moral comment when used against "savages." In intra-European use, however, it would come to stand for all that was morally right or wrong with the machine age itself. Most particularly, it stood as a challenge, in the minds of many, to the development and centrality of valor and individual courage on the battlefield. The slaughter it produced would eventually seem to pale in comparison with later weaponry, and its modern version (whether light, heavy, or submachine gun) is today accepted as the central tool of the infantryman.

Between 1945 and 1991, debates about the morality of weaponry overwhelmingly centered on the ethics of nuclearism. In the first years of the atomic bomb's existence, the US public responded with fear and a desire to control or abolish the weapon. Within five years, however, there was widespread resignation to the nuclear bomb as a result of government and other elite efforts to emphasize the positive benefits of the atom, and to sell the ideas of nuclear self-defense and of the necessity for prevailing in an inevitable arms race and "death struggle" with the Soviets (Boyer 1985). In Japan, official efforts to erase the memory of the nuclear explosions of Hiroshima and Nagasaki were countered by popular efforts to document the suffering of the dead and the survivors, particularly women, both through and against hegemonic notions of maternalism and timeless Japaneseness (Todeschini 2001). Arising out of a variety of culturally distinctive antinuclear movements, a global taboo on the use of this war technology (rather than simply deterrence itself, as claimed by its adherents) came to account for nonuse of nuclear weapons. The emerging moral discourse in this movement (along with notions of self-interest and rationalism) was taken up by state discourses on nonuse (Tannenwald 2008). This was the case even as testing, stockpiles, investments, and suffering on account of them (Masco 2006; Johnson 2007) grew exponentially.

Other weapons which have instigated moral debate and the evolution of legal constraints on use include chemical and biological agents, landmines, cluster munitions, and unmanned drone fighter planes. Complex confluences of factors have created the moralities around each. During World War I, all parties to the conflict used chemical weapons. They were commonly distinguished from the use of "poisons" in war, with some Europeans arguing that the latter was a morally degraded practice of savage peoples (while also drawing on a medieval tradition of opprobrium toward the use of poison in war, on the basis that it allowed the weak to subvert the heavy investments in regular armed warriors), while chemical weapons were, by contrast, a mark of the civilized: "if the German Army achieved such great successes in gas battles and gas defence, so this speaks only for its intellectual superiority, but has nothing whatsoever to do with customs and morals" (Hanslian and Bergendorff, quoted in Zanders 2003: 407). The negation in the last clause indexes the existence of an emerging condemnation of these weapons as indiscriminate and causing unnecessary suffering. Eventual international treaties banning the use of chemical and biological weapons were also, however, the result of judgments by the US military that biological weapons would have limited military utility.

Paradoxically, weapons against which an army or a people could defend themselves have been seen as more moral than those which allowed secret attack. Chemical weapons could be defended, then, after the invention of gas masks. This was also one basis on which bombs that tore soldiers limb from limb were made more acceptable than biological agents that corroded them insidiously and defenselessly from within. War's individual weapons, ironically, have been deemed acceptable to the degree that one might possibly evade or survive their effects.

Landmines and cluster munitions (because they consist of a number of dispersed bomblets, many of which remain unexploded on impact, and wreak havoc later) have come only recently to be judged immoral because they have no long-term human operator to make moral discriminations on whom they may target once they are on or in the ground. Cluster munitions, however, have been vigorously defended by the United States and Britain, not simply as *not immoral* but as *more humane* than others because they belong to the category of "smart weapons," weapons which, it is claimed, exhibit "a morally exact intelligence" (Nixon 2007: 163). They discriminate and protect civilians in a way that the landmine, also labeled barbarous, does not. A 2003 treaty, however, required nations to clean up unexploded cluster bomblets after a conflict. The United States went on to claim moral high ground because it had invested research and development dollars in reducing the "dud rate" for those bombs, insuring that more of the bomblets do their killing on impact rather than months or years later. Such are the dark turns in contemporary work around the morality of modern weapons.

Just war theory, government public relations work, and resulting popular sentiment continue to allow a vast modern arsenal of other weaponry to be accepted and often actively celebrated as the righteous tools of self-protection, democracy promotion, or justice. The US arsenal includes, by official moniker, the Peacemaker nuclear bomber and the Patriot missile, as well as such bureaucratic and opaquely named weapons as the CBU-72 FAE, a fuel air explosive which produces an aerosol cloud 60 feet across and 8 feet high that detonates and ignites just above ground (264 of which were used in the first Gulf War against Iraqi personnel). This weaponry has been normalized in a variety of ways, not least of which involve techniques of gendering and racial erasure (Cohn 1987; Gusterson 2004; Masco 2006).

Changes in the nature of warfare, many connected with new technologies of warfare but not restricted to them, have helped shape the debate about and centrality of the idea of individual soldier morality in warfare. The use of more lethal weaponry from the nineteenth century onward led to the use of more dispersed military formations and so soldiers who once operated under close mass-coordinated supervision began to operate in smaller more autonomous units, where moral discrimination came to be seen as an issue in ways it had not before. The Victorian military emphasis on the moral qualities of the individual combat soldier was not simply a cultural lament in an era of new mass industrial warfare (Ellis 1986) but a response to the need for line soldiers to operate with less immediate control from above (Phillips 2011).

Morally marginal goals and targets

Just war theory and the related international conventions that have emerged from it in the twentieth century made the self-defense of sovereign states the only morally acceptable goal of warfare and armed combatants the only acceptable intentional target of violence. The extreme moral malleability of notions of self-defense have made this a much more limited constraint than it first appears, allowing for many wars through the twentieth century fought far from a military's national borders.

The end of the cold war led to expanded efforts to redefine the morality of war to include violence whose primary goal is the protection of human rights and welfare. The notion of a responsibility to intervene militarily in order to pursue the moral goals of protection has introduced the humanitarian expert as someone who can pronounce on the necessity for and conduct of war and the fuller deployment of the idea of the soldier as a humanitarian worker as much or more than a security worker. While moral criteria have long been invoked in explaining and justifying offensive wars, what is new is that "the politics of military intervention are now played out in the name of humanitarian morality" and that arguments for war are made less in terms of legality and law and more in terms of legitimacy and humanitarianism (Fassin and Pandolfi 2010: 12). The new humanitarian military operations take place under the new historical conditions of more intense media coverage and accompanying international moral judgment. They also take place, inversely, in space cleared of some moral judgment: many humanitarian agents construct the war's violence as an unpredictable and uncontrollable event to which neutral parties bring their humane services (Fassin and Pandolfi 2010).

This humanitarian turn in war rationales creates moral debates about the responsibility of the West (qua international community) to intervene, usually in the global South, to prevent harm. The identity work that is done for the West through these moral debates and claims is a gendered one of masculine heroics, and one reminiscent of colonialism's discourse of a militarized civilizing mission (Orford 2003). It hinges on erasure of the moral questions involved in the West's prior actions that helped create the problems in those same places.

The last decade has also seen attempts by the United States to revise the moral consensus about self-defense to encompass a broad notion of preemption. The United States claims that the revolution in warfare (the rise of asymmetry as a central principle, for example, and the use of terror tactics) makes preemption (the seeking out and destroying of an enemy who has the intention of doing violent harm to the nation) morally acceptable because it is the only effective form of self-defense under these new conditions in which attack will come surreptitiously and without warning. In so doing, the United States has violated what scholars and practitioners see as the tenets of just war theory (Crawford 2003).

Conversely, and despite the low lethality and frequency of nonstate terror violence, terrorism has become the center of the main moral discourse around targeting. Universal moral arguments are common, in which all people are said to have the right to live in particular ways or to be free from intentional targeting, with the Western states as arbiters of what those rights and goals are. The extreme moralism of the debate around terrorism can be seen as more dangerous than geostrategic arguments for particular war goals and targets (Barker 2008).[3] As has been pointed out, this debate also tends strongly if tacitly to legitimate state violence (in which the civilian death toll – direct and indirect – is often much higher than that for nonstate violence).

After 10 years of war in Iraq, Afghanistan, and Pakistan, the moral condemnation of terrorist attacks by nonstate actors in the United States has contributed to the widespread invisibility and ignorance of and indifference to the extensive civilian death toll in those and other wars. Those deaths are widely accepted as necessary in pursuit of protection from nonstate terror and with consequentialist reasoning about why they have occurred (Barker 2008; Crawford, in press). Those civilian deaths – their graphic reality and their numbers – are rarely disseminated as a result of state campaigns to control information flow about the battlefields in which they occur. Searching for photographs of injured civilians is more likely to produce widely posted Pentagon photographs of US military medics treating children wounded in suicide bomb attacks in Iraq than photographs of children shot at US checkpoints or birth defects as a result of toxic exposures in Fallujah. In the end, this public relations work and the often repeated notion that the omelet of war requires some regrettably broken civilians means these deaths are now widely ignored and widely accepted (Crawford, in press).

The US military has rewritten its codes of warfare to substantially broaden the field of morally acceptable targets. The increased reliance on smart weaponry has led military strategists to argue that this ability to precisely target and avoid civilians means that attacking dual-use targets such as power plants or water purification systems is acceptable. The reasoning is that such bombing will undermine the civilian economy without killing, by incentivizing a disgruntled populace to rise up against their rulers (Shue 2010). Air Force Doctrine Document 2–1.2, *Strategic Attack*, edited and reissued in 2003, deleted language that for years had disallowed air attack for purposes of degrading civilian morale on grounds of both international legality and proven lack of efficacy (cited in Shue 2010: 3). So, too, did the US Navy's main handbook interpreting the laws of war issued in 1995 expand the definition of an acceptable military objective to include a broader range of civilian infrastructure. The moral imperative of sheltering civilian life from war is explicitly rejected while the goal of avoiding civilian direct death is elevated ever more explicitly and fervently. The range of exception expands in many directions.

The Demoralization and Management of War

Despite the increasingly moralistic language with which war's goals are identified and pursued by states and their citizens and its margins monitored, aspects of the conduct of war have been increasingly managed by a variety of professions beyond the warrior and outside the terms of moral discourse. This work includes especially the use of the powerful institutions and discourses of law, medicine, humanitarianism, and social science to prosecute, limit, or attempt repair of war's damages. These institutions do so in ways that mimic moral judgment around war, lay claim to be equivalent to or to substitute for it, or sidestep it altogether.

Law

The laws of war have effloresced from the late nineteenth century onward, both internationally and nationally, and within military institutions. From the Hague and Geneva Conventions to the Anti-Personnel Mine Ban Convention to rules of engagement for ground units to the squads of military lawyers passing judgment on targeting, laws and legal experts have emerged which are commonly seen as devices that impose restraints on the launching and conduct of war. In common belief, those laws have gradually civilized war and made it less likely and less vicious. These laws are treated as congruent with morality, even as it is clear that they are not; the protection afforded all combatants, just or unjust, by laws regarding treatment of POWs, for example, is one clear instance where questions of morality take a back seat to other more pragmatic considerations (McMahan 2007). Critical legal scholars have pointed out, moreover, that legal mechanisms in fact facilitate war by providing legal immunity for most of the violence of armies (Berman 2004), and that the law itself is more commonly used as an implement of war than as an apolitical and technical guide to waging war justly or to eliminating it, so much so as to make "lawfare" an apt descriptor (Orford 2003; Kennedy 2006).

Contract law is used to bring McDonald's to US bases in Korea recently expropriated from rice farmers, and the laws of war guide Air Force lawyers in approving bombing runs over Afghanistan with acceptable levels of civilian death, wounding, and displacement. Law is increasingly confused with legitimacy and with moral progress. When claims about adherence to the laws of war are needed to legitimate state violence, public relations become ever larger components of war labor and war spending. The Department of Defense spent US$1.1 billion on contracts with image and sales experts, including advertisers, public relations firms, and media outlets, to promote the Iraq War in the first three years after the 2003 invasion. Images of the unjust outcomes of war have been increasingly censored.

Legal rules have been steeped and enmeshed in moral narratives about the conduct of soldiers, obscuring fundamental moral questions about killing; about the interests, histories, and political economies that drive the pursuit of military campaigns; and about the injustices produced both via the preparation for and the aftermath of the period of most intense violence. Focus remains on a small number of cases of "war crime," while everyday atrocity is rendered morally acceptable: contemporary international law allows states to burn, explode, or mutilate women, men, and children in their beds and to create massive refugee flows so long as they do so unintentionally and with some care to keep the numbers of dead and injured smaller rather than larger. In less spectacular ways, the law is used to legitimize ongoing systems of military power and institutional reproduction, such as US military basing in 46 countries and territories (Lutz 2009). Ethnographic work shows how anti-base activists in many of those contexts have used primarily legal rhetoric over the post-World War II years in countering the negative social and environmental effects of those bases. Arguments centered around national sovereignty have had much cultural purchase in some locations in which those activists work, while human rights and feminist arguments have come to dominate in others.

Medicine

Allan Young's (1995) well-regarded analysis of the emergence of post-traumatic stress disorder (PTSD) as an entity out of the complex of war experience, military history, and biomedical aspiration first alerted the field to the notion that the political and moral dilemmas entailed by the combat experience were being handed over to psychiatry in a package that required only management by medication and other therapeutic interventions rather than political and moral reflection and adjustment. The anxiety, depression, mood swings, startle response, nightmares, insomnia, addiction, and memory problems suffered by many soldiers returning from war are discussed as symptoms of PTSD, a medical and psychological disorder, rather than as a normal and moral human response to the types of atrocities experienced and witnessed in modern warfare. The problem of what happens to the soldier and what the soldier is trained to do in war is redefined in medical, not moral terms. Public debate revolves around issues of how to recognize, treat, and support soldiers returning from war with symptoms of PTSD without raising deeper questions of why it is that participation in armed conflict often leads to long-term trauma and whether it is therefore morally acceptable to send men and women into war.

The moral duty to care for wounded veterans of war is one of the most widely accepted aspects of contemporary political life. Deep investments have been made in battlefield medicine and in post-combat medical care, leading both to unusually high survival rates for the severely wounded and unprecedented financial costs for the decades of care they then require. The privileging of the combat zone as the arbiter of the moral valence of wounds has also structured how medicine participates in the making of war's moralities, with political struggles ensuing over the recognition of suicide, war-zone-acquired disease, and military-industrial accidents. Medical care for wounded soldiers has been a large component of the political economy of most modern national security states, with corresponding enlarged and enhanced roles and rewards for medical professionals.

The heroic ideal of military medicine has also performed the work of moral repair of contentious military missions themselves. This occurs through the focusing of attention on the wounded soldier as victim rather than perpetrator, and the foregrounding of life and resilience over death. So a 2010 CBS News piece on the "The Medical Frontlines of War" begins with this portrait of war's doctors and patients: "They are the wounded who survive, living, breathing testaments to 21st century military medicine, [and they are the medical personnel] who work on the front lines of ground-breaking advancements, giving America's wounded a chance of survival like never before in warfare" (Alfano 2010). Especially crucial has been the marriage of a narrative of technological progress with a moral medicine, evident in the iconic image of the prosthesis-repaired 20-year-old amputee veteran. The heroic ideal and its intentional deployment toward moral renovation of military invasion and occupation are also evident in the heavy circulation on the Web and elsewhere of images of US medics treating indigenous civilian victims.

Finally, the moral task of assessing and treating victims of violence in many contemporary contexts has expanded considerably beyond the soldier and the battlefield. All who witness violence, even if only remotely via televised image, may be treated for trauma; political judgment and subjectivity are reduced to concepts of pain, healers, and healing (Fassin 2008). In these ways, it has come to be even more difficult than it has been over the course of the twentieth century to make adequate moral, affective, and political determinations about the war paradigm itself.

Social science

Social science has been increasingly identified by military institutions as a technique for producing more humane warfare. In particular, morality, anthropology, and war have come together most recently through a cultural turn within the US military. The Pentagon's renewed interest in counterinsurgency warfare, newly framed and energized by resistance to the US occupations of Afghanistan and Iraq, has led it to recruit anthropologists and other cultural experts for its prosecution. The debate about whether anthropologists and anthropology should be deployed in counterinsurgency warfare first emerged in response to advertising by security agencies in the *Anthropology Newsletter* in 2006 and then in response to awareness of recruitment for the military's Human Terrain System teams in 2007. The debate within anthropological circles about the nature of this work and its appropriateness has focused on the question of professional ethics, or the morality of participating as a scientist and/or citizen, in the work of counterinsurgency. Can such work, it has most commonly been asked within the profession, "do no harm" or conform to the moral imperative to allow for informed consent to participate in war zone research? Some critics (Gonzalez 2009; Network of Concerned Anthropologists 2009; Price 2011) have also pointed to the pragmatics and inanities of the vision of human life that emerges from the military's engineering and contractor-outsourced context of knowledge production (where the seller of cultural services helps to shape the Pentagon buyer's desires for particular kinds of knowledge). They question not just whether the work is ethical, but whether it is efficient or effective in pursuit of its goals.

The separation of the question of the morality of war or particular wars themselves from the question of the morality of anthropological or other social scientific participation is problematic. The question of whether professional ethics preclude participation cannot be separated from the question of whether morality more generally precludes it. The debate has been impoverished in just this way, however, in part because academia remains deeply embedded in liberal national modes of thinking about what the US military mission and methods are. Reasoning has often begun from the moral necessity to help US soldiers (regardless of what they are tasked with doing) or the moral necessity to help US soldiers help the Iraqi or Afghan people, reasoning which rests on acceptance of the imperial premise that this empire is beneficent. A concerted campaign to silence alternative visions of war among intellectuals has been conducted by groups such as the American Council of Trustees and Alumni, and a narrowly diminished range of voice have been aired by a corporatized media. The ethics debate has been impoverished to the extent that it has been divorced from these political questions and larger moral issues around organized violence.

The debate over the morality of anthropology in US war fighting has been responding to that aspect of the professional zeitgeist which imagines us as a part of the cosmopolitan, international community which decides to act on behalf of justice through international or transnational organizations, rather than one interested and enculturated actor or nation among many. The debate picks up on the notion that we might be experts in purveying the voices of, and therefore representing the interests of, others. Finally, the moral anger that has emerged in this debate is also implicated in the problem of fetishizing our methodological tools, thereby attributing more power to them than they actually have (i.e., the belief that those ethnographic tools can reduce casualties in Afghanistan or that they can facilitate military domination of the occupied territories).

To these three kinds of experts should be added the military trainers, publicists, and chaplains who work each day toward the moral education of soldiers. In their practice, one can see the fraught and incomplete process of moral education and moral management in the US military, something evident in basic and advanced training, which includes both explicit and hidden curricula for understanding proper soldiering. It is evident in small unit work on rules of engagement, laws of warfare, and proper moral attitudes to one's comrades, and in broader exposures to intense public relations work within and without the military, suggesting the centrality of moral (and ultimately masculine) character and of moral sacrifice to soldier identities.

For six dissident soldiers interviewed in Gutmann and Lutz (2010), it is in part professed moral ideals that lead them to either suffer a breakdown of moral certainty or reverse a process of moral construction when they observe amoral or immoral behavior, particularly toward Iraqi civilians. During their crises of conscience, the professional chaplain corps is called on repeatedly to take the questioning soldiers through biblical verses that suggest their mission is just. Despite the deployment of a variety of experts from law, psychiatry, and medicine, as well as the chaplaincy, to narrow the existential complaints of soldiers about their war experience to a singular diagnosis of PTSD and to shore up ethical certainty, it is clear that moral doubt, political dissent, and suffering remain common.

The contradictions within the moral universe of the US military are evident in the case of one soldier who came into the military from evangelical missionary work in Thailand. He found his moral uncertainty emerging among a variety of experiences, including seeing a panicked civilian riddled with gunfire at a checkpoint for backing his car quickly away from the Americans manning it, being interrogated on the definition of terrorism by an imprisoned Iraqi he was managing, and, as importantly, having the discursive authority of his commanders and chaplains in matters of war ethics come into question. The chaplains were less knowledgeable about Christian scripture in some ways than he, but more than this, he said, "The chaplain was praying before missions that we would be God's hand of justice, and all the guys around me were bowing their heads and praying for this when forty minutes before they were watching porno on their computers and laughing about shooting animals. I was like, 'You guys are praying, you're Christians, are you kidding me?'"

Conclusion

As the rich ethnographic work on local moralities of war above has illustrated, anthropology has the potential to show how political realism masks the moral thinking that informs and shapes military actions. This work examines the moralities of those fighting wars, making its weaponry, or wading through it as civilians. It examines how they make sense of and evaluate the violence and their own roles in it. What this essay attempts is an understanding of the moral, ideological, and political labor that goes into the legitimation and prosecution of war.

The examples given here of the production of moral understandings of war illustrate how the aspects of war that are considered morally acceptable or repugnant have changed in different historical contexts. The nuclear bomb, an object of great moral anxiety at first, comes to be accepted or at least tolerated in the United States after a few short years of state information campaigns immediately after World War II and is raised again as a major moral question only decades later. The child soldier, celebrated at one time, generates a moral panic at another. These shifts in the moral margins of war call for more ethnohistorical work that could analyze this evolution in moralities and war, thereby drawing into question what is taken for granted as beyond ethical debate today. This critical anthropology could pay special attention to the labor of producing these shifting moral understandings of war: what institutions are involved, what resources are used in this effort, and what struggles push them forward. An ethnographic effort is surely needed to understand the ways in which political rhetoric and commitment – to nationalism, imperialism, masculinism, or humanitarianism, for example – develop their power to define the good in war and each of its elements.

As moralities produce wars, so wars produce moralities. From the actual moment of violence comes both nihilism and the search for moral grounding to justify the killing and to explain the suffering. War is a site of morality production that extends as far beyond that battlefield as the institution itself does, informing how nuclear scientists or military psychiatrists build their identities as professionals producing virtuous outcomes for the nation and how citizens understand their empathetic response to the victims of another state's repression and their state's military response to it. While the soldiers' and other war workers' situations create moral dilemmas that have been explored, less examined has been the question of how the civilian – in the home front and in the line of fire – develops a moral imagination in the midst of war.

Debates over who is properly a soldier have done this work of allocating moral values across a social field: at the moral high ground, at least of contemporary US society, the soldier identity as heroic protector has produced values for society at large, valorizing certain forms of masculinity while also being used to make claims for full moral agency by those with degraded racial and sexual statuses. So, too, has the heroic ideal forged by the soldier in battle shaped the professional discourses and identities of law, medicine, and social sciences deployed for war. A moral anthropology of war will examine how war produces not only moralities of war but wider notions of what is right, wrong, good, and bad in society. It will show how principles such as hierarchy and force become viewed as virtues rather than vices or simple efficacies. And it will ask how the moralities of war work to create profit and redistribute suffering so unevenly across the contemporary world.

NOTES

1 The emergence of a more historicized view of the problem of war that also questioned the primacy of state interest was signaled by Ferguson's (1995) account of Yanomami warfare.

2 Many scholars have argued that the 9/11 attacks ended the era of humanitarian intervention (MacFarlane et al. 2004). The US military operations in Afghanistan and Iraq have explicitly stated goals of furthering the "war on terror" and enhancing US security. However, the emphasis on bringing democracy and human rights to Afghanistan and Iraq and the "hearts and minds" campaign still frame these operations, at least in part, as moral interventions with humanitarian goals.

3 This includes a particular contemporary Western horror with the suicide bomber, Asad (2007) argues, because that act reminds us too sharply of the West's own impulse and history of sacrificial violence.

REFERENCES

Alfano, Sean (2010) The Medical Frontlines of War. CBS News. Feb. 10. At http://www.cbsnews.com/2100-3445_162-1680075.html, accessed Mar. 12, 2012.

Asad, Talal (2007) *On Suicide Bombing*. New York: Columbia University Press.

Barker, Jonathan (2008) *The No-Nonsense Guide to Global Terrorism*, 2nd edn. Oxford: New Internationalist.

Berman, Nathaniel (2004) Privileging Combat? Contemporary Conflict and the Legal Construction of War. *Columbia Journal of Transnational Law* 43(1): 1–71.

Boyer, Paul (1985) *By the Bomb's Early Light: American Thought and Culture at the Dawn of the Atomic Age*. Chapel Hill: University of North Carolina Press.

Chagnon, Napoleon (1968) Yanomamö: The Fierce People. New York: Holt, Rinehart & Winston.

Cohn, Carol (1987) Sex and Death in the Rational World of Defense Intellectuals. *Signs* 12: 687–718.

Crawford, Neta (2003) Just War Theory and the U.S. Counterterror War. *Perspectives on Politics* 1(1): 5–25.

Crawford, Neta (in press) *Collateral Damage*. Oxford: Oxford University Press.

Elshtain, Jean Bethke (1987) *Women and War*. Chicago: University of Chicago Press.

Ellis, John (1986) *The Social History of the Machine Gun*. Baltimore: Johns Hopkins University Press.

Enloe, Cynthia (1990) Women and children: Making Feminist Sense of the Persian Gulf Crisis. *Village Voice* (Sept. 25), 29ff.

Fassin, Didier (2008) The Humanitarian Politics of Testimony: Subjectification through Trauma in the Israeli–Palestinian Conflict. *Cultural Anthropology* 23(3): 531–558.

Fassin, Didier and Pandolfi, Mariella (2010) Introduction: Military and Humanitarian Government in the Age of Intervention. In Didier Fassin and Mariella Pandolfi (eds.), *Contemporary States of Emergency: The Politics of Military and Humanitarian Interventions*. New York: Zone, pp. 9–25.

Ferguson, Brian (1995) *Yanomami Warfare: A Political History*. Santa Fe, NM: SAR.

Fruhstuck, Sabine (2007) *Uneasy Warriors: Gender, Memory, and Popular Culture in the Japanese Army*. Berkeley: University of California Press.

Gill, Lesley (2004) *The School of the Americas: Military Training and Political Violence in the Americas*. Durham, NC: Duke University Press.

Gonzalez, Roberto (2009) *American Counterinsurgency: Human Science and the Human Terrain*. Chicago: Prickly Paradigm.

Goff, Stan (2003) Hold On to Your Humanity: An Open Letter to GIs in Iraq. *Counterpunch* (Nov. 13). At http://www.counterpunch.org/2003/11/13/an-open-letter-to-gis-in-iraq/, accessed Mar. 12, 2012.

Green, Linda (1999) *Fear as a Way of Life: Mayan Widows in Rural Guatemala*. New York: Columbia University Press.

Gross, Daniel R. (1975) Protein Capture and Cultural Development in the Amazon Basin. *American Anthropologist* 77(3): 526–549.

Gusterson, Hugh (2004) *People of the Bomb: Portraits of America's Nuclear Complex*. Minneapolis: University of Minnesota Press.

Gutmann, Matthew and Lutz, Catherine (2010) *Breaking Ranks: Iraq Veterans Speak Out against the War*. Berkeley: University of California Press.

Harris, Marvin (1974) *Cows, Pigs, Wars and Witches: The Riddle of Culture*. New York: Random House.

Hinton, Alexander Laban (2005) *Why Did They Kill? Cambodia in the Shadow of Genocide*. Berkeley: University of California Press.

Hoffman, Danny (2011) *The War Machines: Young Men and Violence in Sierra Leone and Liberia*. Durham, NC: Duke University Press.

Hutchinson, Sharon (1996) *Nuer Dilemmas*. Berkeley: University of California Press.

Johnston, Barbara Rose (2007) *Half-Lives and Half-Truths: Confronting the Radioactive Legacies of the Cold War*. Santa Fe, NM: SAR.

Kennedy, David (2006) *Of War and Law*. Princeton: Princeton University Press.

Lutz, Catherine (2001) *Homefront: A Military City and the American 20th Century*. Boston: Beacon.

Lutz, Catherine (2009) *The Bases of Empire: The Global Struggle against U.S. Military Posts*. New York: New York University Press.

Mahmood, Cynthia (1996) *Fighting for Faith and Nation: Dialogues with Sikh Militants*. Philadelphia: University of Pennsylvania Press.

Malkki, Liisa (1995) *Purity and Exile: Violence, Memory, and National Cosmology among Hutu Refugees in Tanzania*. Chicago: University of Chicago Press.
MacFarlane, S. Neil, Thielking, Carolin J., and Weiss, Thomas G. (2004) The Responsibility to Protect: Is Anyone Interested in Humanitarian Intervention? *Third World Quarterly* 25(5): 977–992.
Masco, Joseph (2006) *The Nuclear Borderlands: The Manhattan Project in Post-Cold War New Mexico*. Princeton: Princeton University Press.
McMahan, Jeff (2007) The Morality of War and the Law of War. Unpublished MS. At http://www.law.upenn.edu/academics/institutes/ilp/200708papers/mcMahanMoralityofWar.pdf, accessed Mar. 12, 2012.
Network of Concerned Anthropologists (2009) *The Counter-Counterinsurgency Manual, or, Notes on Demilitarizing American Society*. Chicago: Prickly Paradigm.
Nixon, Rob (2007) Of Land Mines and Cluster Bombs. *Cultural Critique* 67: 160–174.
Nordstrom, Carolyn (1997) *A Different Kind of War Story*. Philadelphia: University of Pennyslvania Press.
Nordstrom, Carolyn (2004) *Shadows of War: Violence, Power, and International Profiteering in the Twenty-First Century*. Berkeley: University of California Press.
Ohnuki-Tierney, Emiko (2002) *Kamikaze, Cherry Blossoms, and Nationalisms: The Militarization of Aesthetics in Japanese History*. Chicago: University of Chicago Press.
Orford, Anne (2003) *Reading Humanitarian Intervention: Human Rights and the Use of Force in International Law*. Cambridge: Cambridge University Press.
Phillips, Gervase (2011) Military Morality Transformed: Weapons and Soldiers on the Nineteenth-Century Battlefield. *Journal of Interdisciplinary History* 41(4): 565–590.
Price, David (2004) *Threatening Anthropology: McCarthyism and the FBI's Surveillance of Activist Anthropologists*. Durham, NC: Duke University Press.
Price, David (2011) *Weaponizing Anthropology: Social Science in Service of the Militarized State*. Oakland, CA: AK Press.
Rosen, David (2005) *Armies of the Young: Child Soldiers in War and Terrorism*. New Brunswick, NJ: Rutgers University Press.
Scarry, Elaine (1985) *The Body in Pain: The Making and Unmaking of the World*. Oxford: Oxford University Press.
Shue, Henry (2010) Targeting Civilian Infrastructure with Smart Bombs: The New Permissiveness. *Philosophy and Public Policy Quarterly* 30(3–4): 2–8.
Starn, Orin (1991) Missing the Revolution: Anthropologists and the War in Peru. *Cultural Anthropology* 6(1): 63–91.
Tannenwald, Nina (2008) *The Nuclear Taboo: The United States and the Non-Use of Nuclear Weapons Since 1945*. Cambridge: Cambridge University Press.
Taylor, Christopher (1999) *Sacrifice as Terror: The Rwandan Genocide of 1994*. New York: Berg.
Todeschini, Maya (2001) The Bomb's Womb? Women and the Atom Bomb. In Veena Das et al. (eds.), *Remaking a World: Violence, Social Suffering, and Recovery*. Berkeley: University of California Press, pp. 102–156.
United Nations (1996) *Impact of Armed Conflict on Children: Report of Graça Machel, expert of the Secretary-General of the United Nations* (A/51/306). New York: United Nations.
Vine, David S. (2009) *Island of Shame: The Secret History of the U.S. Military Base on Diego Garcia*. Princeton: Princeton University Press.
Wolf, Eric (1969) *Peasant Wars of the 20th Century*. New York: Harper & Row.
Young, Allan (1995) *The Harmony of Illusions: Inventing Post-Traumatic Stress Disorder*. Princeton: Princeton University Press.
Young, Iris Marion (2006) *Global Challenges: War, Self Determination and Responsibility for Justice*. Cambridge: Polity.
Zanders, Jean Pascal (2003) International Norms against Chemical and Biological Warfare: An Ambiguous Legacy. *Journal of Conflict and Security Law* 8(2): 391–410.

CHAPTER 28 Violence

Alexander Hinton

Violence and morality are deeply intertwined, a warp and woof in the fabric of time, place, and understanding. While there are many points at which this relationship is manifest, some stand out as more significant, at least from our current perspective. The late 1940s constitutes such a moment, as the world looked back at the extreme brutality of World War II and forward toward making sure such atrocities would never happen again.

At Nuremberg, many of the former leaders of the Nazi regime were tried and convicted from 1945 to 1946. Instead of proceeding with their summary execution, the victors decided to "stay the hand of vengeance" and seek justice through an international court of law (Bass 2000). Meanwhile, during the legal proceedings, the notion of "crimes against humanity" began to take shape as a major principle of international law (see Douglas 2001). Two years later, in December 1948, in Paris and New York, the United Nations General Assembly passed the Universal Declaration of Human Rights (UDHR) and the Convention on the Prevention and Punishment of the Crime of Genocide, which asserted a set of universal human rights protections ("the inalienable rights of all members of the human family") and outlawed mass murder. The next year in Geneva, delegates passed the 1949 Geneva Conventions, which explicitly extended protections to civilians, the wounded, and prisoners of war in the course of conflict.

Other groups and organizations also spoke out during this period. For example, the World Medical Association, confronted with the atrocities perpetrated by the Nazi doctors, passed the 1948 Declaration of Geneva, which created a Physician's Oath that included a promise not to use "medical knowledge contrary to the laws of humanity" (WMA 1948). Academic schools and disciplines responded differently. Some, like the Frankfurt school of critical theory, grappled with the significance of World War II and the Holocaust directly, leading to the publication of works like Fromm's *Escape from Freedom* (1994 [1941]) and Horkheimer and Adorno's (2007 [1944]) *Dialectic of Enlightenment.*

A Companion to Moral Anthropology, First Edition. Edited by Didier Fassin.

Even as other disciplines took up such questions about genocide, violence, and the nature of evil, others, like anthropology, remained largely silent about such issues, a silence that was somewhat disconcerting given the role played by anthropologists in the Holocaust (see Proctor 1988; Schafft 2004). This essay traces out the story of how violence and morality came to be foregrounded as topics of anthropological concern toward the end of the cold war. Like all such narratives, this one involves certain inclusions and exclusions. I focus largely upon political and structural violence, while touching less upon topics like domestic and family violence in the United States, which have been less studied by anthropologists and perhaps even ignored as something more suitable to sociology. My hope is that other scholars will help fill in the inevitable gaps in my account.

The essay begins with a discussion of the 1947 American Anthropological Association statement on human rights, which foregrounds the issue of cultural relativism. If human rights activists and scholars working in other fields could discuss the "nature" of violence and evil with an underlying assumption of unambiguous moral condemnation, anthropologists had a harder time doing so. One of the foundational principles of anthropology is cultural relativism, which requires the suspension of judgment, at least temporarily during the ethnographic encounter, for the sake of understanding. Any attempt to judge the cultural practices of other societies, even ones that violate our norms of propriety, risks ethnocentrism. If these fundamental anthropological principles may have led anthropologists to shy away from engaging with issues like political violence, the discipline nevertheless had much to say about the sets of moral understandings that underpin and even legitimate violent behaviors in diverse societies. Scholars who dealt with violence often did so within the frame of social order, illustrating how seemingly irrational social practices like witchcraft fulfilled basic functions in society, such as regulating and diffusing structural tensions linked to issues like kinship and religion. Even if they studied violence in "primitive" societies, anthropologists often overlooked state-level and colonial practices of violence, including civil war, state oppression, and revolutionary struggles.

The first part of this essay, then, explores some of the ways that violence and morality intersected until an anthropology of political violence began to more fully engage such issues in the 1980s, a literature that has matured into the present. In the second part, I discuss some of the issues with which a moral anthropology of violence might be concerned, in part through a discussion of the trial of a former perpetrator at the Khmer Rouge Tribunal in Cambodia.

Anthropology, Morality, and Violence after World War II

Anthropology's response to the newly forming human rights regime of the late 1940s was fraught with ambivalence. In fact, the American Anthropological Association more or less rejected the notion in an official statement, made in 1947 in response to the deliberations about the UDHR, arguing that such a declaration was ethnocentric since "ideas of right and wrong, good and evil, are found in all societies" and since the "individual realizes his personality through his culture" (American Anthropological Association 1947: 541–542). In doing so, the statement sought to affirm another key anthropological precept, a basic "respect for differences between cultures." There was no mention of Nazi Germany.

The following year, in a comment on the AAA Statement on Human Rights, Julian Steward noted the tension at the heart of this relativist assertion. On the one hand, the Statement asserts an ideal of respecting alternative value systems, through which individuals constitute their personality and understand the world. On the other hand, Nazi Germany had just such an alternative set of "ideas about right and wrong, good and evil," and had committed mass murder. While the AAA Statement had tried to provide a loophole by suggesting that alternative, nonviolent values existed in all societies, including Nazi Germany, Steward argued that this tension was "the fatal breach in the dyke. Either we tolerate everything, and keep hands off, or we fight intolerance and conquest – political and economic as well as military – in all their forms" (1948: 351). Because of these contradictions, Steward states, the AAA, since it is a scientific organization, "has no business dealing with the rights of man" and, by so doing, comes "perilously close to advocacy of American ideological imperialism" (352).

Besides highlighting a moral conundrum at the heart of anthropology's response to violence, and perhaps part of the reason it failed to grapple in any significant way with the Holocaust and political violence in the years that followed, Steward's reply, as well as the AAA Statement itself, are revealing about several other dimensions of how violence and morality intersect in anthropology.

First, anthropology had an uneasy and even contradictory relationship with violence. Like other social scientists, many anthropologists operated within a prevalent Hobbesian paradigm that assumed social life was premised upon order and a sort of escape from violence (Didier Fassin, personal communication; see also van Binsbergen 2002). Violence remained on the periphery as an exception, a threat to order that had to be controlled or even incorporated into the larger social system itself. Not surprisingly, some of the earliest anthropological accounts of violence and morality were framed in this manner, such as in structural-functionalist accounts of how violent practices were functionally linked to the larger social system in which they were embedded (e.g., Evans-Pritchard 1937; Gluckman 1955). If anthropologists sought to confine violence in these sorts of ways, they often found themselves grappling with it in other contexts. In some cases, this might involve an awareness of colonial oppression or revolutionary struggle and how it was impacting upon the "traditional" societies they were studying (e.g., Gluckman 1955). In others, anthropologists sometimes immersed themselves directly into global conflict and wars, sometimes going as far as to work as spies (Price 2000).

During World War II, Steward notes, anthropologists "gladly used our professional techniques and knowledge to advance a cause" (1948: 352). Indeed, some of the leading anthropologists of the day, including Gregory Bateson, Clyde Kluckhohn, Margaret Mead, and Ruth Benedict, had worked for government agencies such as the Office of Strategic Services and the Office of War Information (Price 2000). As illustrated by the AAA Statement on Human Rights, which began with the premise that the "individual realizes his personality through culture," anthropology was at this time heavily influenced by culture and personality theory, which correlated group behavior with socialization. At times, this school focused on violence, such as Ruth Benedict's (1934) study of three Native American groups, each of which, she argued, was characterized by a different sort of personality structure – a view of culture as "personality write large." Each of these configurations, like a person's temperament, were characterized by certain tendencies, including aggression in the case of the more volatile Dobu, which were linked to related moral values and imperatives in that society. Among other things, during World War II, anthropologists conducted studies of the "national character" of the war adversaries, as exemplified by Benedict's postwar account of Japan, *The Chrysanthemum and the Sword*.

This line of thinking, which divides different societies into "peaceful" or "aggressive" types resulting from socialization practices and related moral codes, persisted after the war, even after culture and personality had diminished as an anthropological paradigm. Examples include Dentan's (1968) sociocultural analysis of the "nonviolent" Semai in Malaysia, Chagnon's (1968) sociobiological arguments about Yanomami aggression, and Harris's (1984) ecological materialist take on the Yanomami and other groups. A number of debates have ensued about the aggressivity of peoples such as the Semai, the Samoans, the !Kung, the Balinese, the Fore, the people of Tepoztlan, and the Tahitians. Such discussion sometimes mirrored cold war realities, with hopes and fears about the intrinsic peacefulness or aggression of human societies paralleling discussions of superpower conflict and the threat of nuclear destruction (see Gusterson 2007). Here, as with anthropological studies of World War II, anthropological analysis of violence became bound up with the pressing political and moral issues of the time. Similar conflict broke out over the involvement of anthropologists in the Vietnam War and, most recently, the post-9/11 US military Human Terrain teams, a project that drew a rebuke from the Executive Board of the American Anthropological Association in 2007 (see also Price 2000; Forte 2011).

These protests highlight another strong current that runs through anthropological work on violence and morality. This sort of anthropology as political critique of violent practice was evident in the AAA Resolution on Human Rights, which notes, in passing, Western European and US economic and military practices, legitimated by the doctrine of the "white man's burden" and related conceptions of primitivism, progress/savagery, and civilization, had led to "economic exploitation" and denying "the right to control their own affairs to millions of peoples all over the world" (AAA 1947: 540). It was precisely this Pandora's box of potential struggle against all sorts of forms of "intolerance and conquest – political and economic as well as military" that led Steward to say that "As a scientific organization, the Association has no business dealing with the rights of man" (1948: 352). Doing so risked coming "perilously close to advocacy of American ideological imperialism."

Here, again, we find a key tension in anthropological practice emerging, the split between the anthropologist as scientist and as activist. This duality was embodied by Boas (1995), whose studies of race were based on scientific methods yet accomplished a social purpose. More broadly, the Boasian school of American historical particularism conducted research that struck at the core of precisely the sorts of pseudo-evolutionary stage theories that had been used to justify colonial conquest and exploitation. In doing so, they engaged at times in "salvage anthropology," which sought to preserve and record the languages and cultural traditions of groups, like Native Americans, who were being crushed by the colonial project. This endeavor was perhaps the first sustained effort by anthropologists to respond to genocide.

If, at the time, it seemed clear to Steward and others that science should be divorced from activism, this distinction increasingly broke down over time, particularly when a closer examination revealed, as Boas's work suggested, that even scientific work was often highly normative (thus Boas's political critiques of race and stage theory and project of salvaging disappearing cultures). We see this normative dimension of anthropology not just in the context of US foreign policy and war, but on the peripheries where anthropologists often lived and work among marginalized populations, including various indigenous peoples.

In many cases, anthropologists have felt compelled to speak out for the victims, whose voices, especially prior to post-cold war global flows, were largely muted even as they began to mobilize more effectively. Here we find yet another stream of work in which violence and morality converge as anthropologists conducted research linked to advocacy on behalf of indigenous peoples. The Maybury-Lewises' founding of Cultural Survival in the 1970s serves as a marker of this renewed concern with this issue, one coinciding with the mobilization of domestic indigenous rights groups and the research and activism of people like Colin Turnbull (1972), Marc Munzel (1973), John Bodley (1975), Pierre Clastres (1994), and others (see Totten and Hitchcock 2010).

The Anthropology of Political Violence

Emergence

This emerging body of scholarship and activism on indigenous peoples converged with a number of other trends to lay the ground for the emergence of an anthropology of political violence in the 1980s. Some of the scholars who later began working on issues of political violence had been involved in social protests in the 1960s and early 1970s, such as the antiwar movement in the United States, the 1968 student riots in France, and the protests about Biafra in the late 1960s. Many were also influenced by at least three streams of theory that rose to prominence during this period.

First, a revitalized Marxist anthropology dropped its evolutionist assumptions while drawing inspiration from world system theory and dependency theory (e.g., Wallerstein 1976; Frank 1979) to explore issues like global capitalism, political economy, imperialism, and power. At the same time, French social theorists Michel Foucault (1977) and Pierre Bourdieu (1977) published groundbreaking works on the intersection of violence, power, knowledge, and sociopolitical structure, issues that were also manifest in Pierre Clastres's (1994) research on tribal warfare in South America. And finally, while it more rarely addressed the topic of violence, symbolic anthropology examined the public manifestations and layers of meaning of ritual and cultural knowledge (Turner 1970; Geertz 1973; Bloch 1991).

Drawing on these and others streams of theory in creative ways, anthropologists began to grapple more directly with the issue of political violence in the 1980s and early 1990s, often in the context of Latin American state terror (see, e.g., Taussig 1984; Manz 1987; Suárez-Orozco 1990; Coronil and Skurski 1991) or other situations of ethnic strife in places like India, Ireland, and Sri Lanka (e.g., Das 1991; Feldman 1991; Tambiah 1992). Issues of violence and morality converged in such accounts, where the death and suffering called for, at a minimum, recognition and understanding. Conditions were ready for the publication of a book on "the anthropology of violence" (Riches 1986; see also Nagengast 1994 for a review of this early literature), which included an influential introduction mapping out a perpetrator–victim–bystander triad and various aspects of the violent encounter.

These trends only increased with the end of the cold war and the intensification of time–space compression in the new world order of the 1990s. On an academic level, these events catalyzed the study of globalization in all its many permutations, including ones that directly intersected with issues of violence and its aftermaths. Meanwhile, the United Nations set out to launch postconflict operations in a variety of locales even as political violence erupted in different areas of the globe, including genocide in Bosnia and Rwanda and, toward the end of the decade, the perceived threat of Islamic terror, culminating in 9/11, the global "war on terror," and the invasion and subsequent (counter)insurgencies in Afghanistan and Iraq. As these events unfolded, the human rights infrastructures that had been laid down in the late 1940s contributed to the proliferation of a post-cold war human rights regime that demanded action in response to atrocity and accountability for culprits.

This was the context in which the American Anthropological Association passed the 1999 Declaration on Anthropology and Human Rights,[1] which had been drafted by the AAA Committee for Human Rights, established in 1995 to "promote and protect human rights."[2] In sharp contrast to the 1947 Statement, the 1999 Declaration fully embraced the UN Universal Declaration of Human Rights, referring to it as a "base line" and noting that the 1999 Statement built on both this document and related international human rights law, including the 1948 Genocide Convention. The preamble of the 1999 Declaration begins with the assertion that the "capacity for culture is tantamount to the capacity for humanity" and therefore, "peoples and groups have a generic right to realize their capacity for culture."

The Preamble explicitly notes that "the global environment is fraught with violence" that limits this capacity. In such situations, anthropologists have "an ethical responsibility to protest and oppose such deprivation." The potential pitfalls of an argument that might support the right of groups to choose to harm others was elided by the limiting condition that group activities must not "diminish the same capacities in others." If the tensions of cultural relativism were not fully resolved by this caveat, the 1999 Declaration clearly advocated for an ethics of action in the face of human rights violations, including an obligation to protest such abuses. Violence and morality were fully intertwined.

Recent directions

By the time of the statement, the anthropology of political violence was rapidly growing. While any parsing of complex, overlapping literatures necessarily oversimplifies, we can make out some broad trends that have emerged within the more recent literature on the anthropology of political violence. First, a number of anthropologists have explicitly taken up an ethics of action and protest in response to structural violence, focusing on issues such as poverty, addiction, inadequate health care, the drug trade, war, profiteering, the arms trade, state repression, and discrimination (e.g., Scheper-Hughes 1993; Bourgois 2002; Farmer 2004; Nordstrom 2004; Bourgois and Schonberg 2009). A number of these books were published by the University of California Press's new series on Public Anthropology, which also marked the rise of a politically engaged or public anthropology that fully emerged in at the turn of the millennium.

Two of my own books on genocide appeared in this series (Hinton 2002a, 2005). I attended graduate school in the 1990s, just as the anthropology of political violence was emerging. After conducting fieldwork in Cambodia on the genocide that took place there from 1975 to 1979, I quickly realized that it would be necessary to read widely on the literature on the Holocaust and other genocides. I was somewhat stunned to find that there was virtually no mention of the Holocaust or Armenian genocide in anthropology. Indeed, when I attended a meeting of the newly founded Association of Genocide Scholars, I found that anthropology was more or less absent from the conversation. Meanwhile, new genocides were taking place in Bosnia and Rwanda, which helped catalyze anthropological interest in genocide.

Much of my subsequent work has been devoted to trying to help bring anthropology into the conversation on this critical issue, something I continue to through scholarship, founding/running a Center on the Study of Genocide, Conflict Resolution, and Human Rights at Rutgers University, and becoming actively involved in the interdisciplinary International Association of Genocide Scholars (IAGS), of which I am currently president. Like many colleagues, I often feel the tension between an obligation to speak out and the need to maintain a scholarly perspective, a tension that has been foregrounded in IAGS debates over whether to pass resolutions affirming past genocides as historical fact (thereby asserting a truth that may diminish academic debate but otherwise saying nothing in the face of genocides about which few people care or politically orchestrated campaigns of denial, such as Turkey's campaign to avoid recognition of the Armenian genocide) or whether or not intervention is warranted to prevent potential genocides in the making, an issue that has sharpened with the promulgation of the "responsibility to protect" doctrine and an emerging global genocide prevention movement.

During this time, an anthropology of genocide has emerged (e.g., Bringa 1995; Malkki 1995; Linke 1999; Wolf 1999; Maybury-Lewis 2001; Taylor 2001; Hinton 2002a, 2002b, 2005; Sanford 2003; Robben 2007; Schafft 2004; Hinton and O'Neill 2009; Mamdani 2010; Totten and Hitchcock 2010), one that has been paralleled by a growing anthropology of human rights (see Goodale 2006). Even if anthropology continues to remain largely silent on the Holocaust, this body of work provides a number of points of entry into this topic for future research.

Another stream of recent work on anthropology and violence, one that intersects frequently with the other strands mentioned above, deals with social suffering. Early work in this literature argued for the medical establishment to take into account local understandings and responses to illness and mental health, including local idioms of distress that emerge in contexts of political and structural violence (e.g., Kleinman 1980; Nichter 1981). In the early 1990s, Arthur Kleinman and Veena Das, who were members of a SSRC Committee on Culture, Health, and Human Development, planned the publication of three volumes "on the relation of violence to states, local communities, and individuals" (2000: 1). The first book to emerge from this initiative was Kleinman, Das, and Lock's *Social Suffering* (1997), which argued that there was an urgent need to recognize how human suffering and social adversity are directly related to issues of politics, morality, and health issues that vary across often vastly different, if globally interconnected, sociocultural terrains.

The topics covered were diverse, ranging from media representations of suffering to the genealogy of torture and victimhood. Such themes have become part of a growing literature on the anthropology of social suffering, particularly in relation to mental health issues like trauma and post-traumatic stress disorder (Young 1995; Kirmayer et al. 2008; Fassin and Rechtman 2009) and public health crises such as AIDS (e.g., Fassin 2007; Biehl 2009; Zigon 2011). A politics of critique operates in many of these works, which speak out against spaces of structural violence in which people remain unseen, ignored, misunderstood, or abused within given regimes of power such as the biomedical establishment.

The two other volumes that followed *Social Suffering* suggest other ways in which violence and morality intersect in the anthropology of social suffering. Das and colleagues' *Violence and Subjectivity* (2000) explored the felt experience of people living in contexts of violence and power. Many of the contributors had made early contributions to the anthropology of political violence, sometimes focusing on the limits of language in the face of terror and violence (Daniel 1996; Argenti-Pillen 2002; Das 2006), the production of subjectivity in the context of violence (e.g., Feldman 1991; Das 2006), and the ways in people experience and navigate terrains of fear and terror (e.g., Green 1999; Sluka 1999), themes that continue to be influential in this literature (e.g., Aretxaga 1997; Argenti 2007; Das 2008).

The last volume, Das and colleagues' *Remaking a World: Violence, Social Suffering, and Recovery* (2001) converges more directly with another recent thread in the anthropology of political violence, studies of postconflict identity, redress, and recovery. If much of the recent anthropological literature on political violence has been inflected by global processes and the rapid rise of global studies (which provides yet another key theoretical current that has shaped the anthropology of political violence), studies of postconflict social suffering are particularly enmeshed with it. Violence and memory provide one illustration of this point, as anthropologists have looked at the ways in which people have negotiated violent pasts through narrative, ritual, forms of resistance, and institutional mechanisms (e.g., Malkki 1995; Kwon 2006; Shaw 2007; Hinton 2009).

Over the last decade, a small but growing literature on transitional justice has begun to emerge in anthropology, one which approaches these postconflict attempts to deal with the past with a somewhat critical eye, perhaps in part because of the teleology and universalism implicit in the project (Hinton 2011; Shaw and Waldorf 2010). If this literature initially focused on memory and reconciliation in post-cold war eastern Europe (Borneman 1997; Verdery 2000) and the South African truth and reconciliation commission (e.g., Wilson 2001; Ross 2002), it has rapidly expanded to consider truth and reconciliation commissions in other contexts (e.g., Shaw 2007; Rojas-Perez 2010; Silber 2010) and issues ranging from the identification of the dead (e.g., Sanford 2004; Wagner 2008) and disarmament (Theidon 2009) to the dynamics of international courts (Clarke 2009; Eltringham 2009; Wilson 2011). In all of these situations, violence and morality intersect dramatically in attempts to determine right and wrong, assess innocence and guilt, and find a path to peace and reconciliation after mass violence and genocide. Gender is an emerging theme in this literature, which also looks at how women, in particular, negotiate life in such postconflict moments (Ross 2002; Moran 2010), which may erase aspects of gendered experience while simultaneously providing them with new opportunities (Das 2008).

If an anthropologically informed "critical transitional justice studies" (Hinton 2011) began to take shape in the first decade of the twenty-first century, a revitalized anthropology of militarism also emerged in the aftermath of 9/11 (see Gusterson 2007). Most immediately, anthropologists sought to reflect upon what had happened (see, e.g., the 2002 special issue of *Anthropological Quarterly* on 9/11). In the longer term, they had to grapple with a host of other issues related to the "war on terror" and the invasions of Iraq and Afghanistan, including Abu Ghraib, depictions of Muslims, anthropological involvement in counterinsurgency, trauma, and military life (e.g., Lutz 2001; Mamdani 2005; Hirsch 2008; Forte 2011; Robben 2011).

This issue of violence and morality has also converged sharply in critiques of militarized humanitarian interventions (e.g., Fassin and Pandolfi 2010; Mamdani 2010), where violence has been legitimated in the name of averting crisis and bloodshed. These recent works emerged out of a larger body of work on humanitarianism that had proliferated after the end of the cold war with a spate of new conflicts, a rise in UN peacekeeping efforts, and a growing NGO presence in various localities (e.g., Fisher 1997; Redfield 2005).

The Anthropology of Violence and Morality

General approach

As this brief discussion has illustrated, anthropologists have approached the intersection of violence and morality from a variety of cross-cutting theoretical approaches and ethical stances. In doing so, they have often engaged in an anthropology of morality, as conceptualized in this volume (see also Fassin 2008, 2011), even if it was not always labeled as such. This sort of science of parsing the moral world, as exemplified by Nietzsche's (1996 [1886]) analysis of good and evil, manifested itself early in the anthropology of violence, in works ranging from Benedict's expositions of Apollonian and Dionysian moral systems in *Patterns of Culture* (2006) to the Durkheimian notion of collective conscience to British structural-functionalist conceptions of social institutions and local understandings related to things like witchcraft.

One of the key contributions of this literature has been a critical approach to a topic, violence, which is readily naturalized, thereby obscuring the politics at stake. One of the most simplistic, yet tenacious forms of naturalization is linked to Enlightenment notions of rationality, which closet off our understanding of phenomena like violence by placing them into the black box of irrationality and superstition. To understand how Azande witchcraft (Evans-Pritchard 1937) works is to demystify a practice that had been fetishized and used to demean this more "primitive" group. A related set of dichotomies groups rationality with civilization, progress, and order in contrast to the irrational primitives living in a regressive state of savagery, with all of its Hobbesian connotations of anarchy and violence.

This sort of naturalization of violence is particularly common in genocide. One of the reasons the Holocaust seemed so confounding is that it took place in the heart of "civilized" Europe, a paradox that led some to portray the Nazis as atavistic, a regression to a more primitive, emotional mode of being. Popular depictions of the savage Nazi interfaced with this idea, even if a variety of works, including Horkheimer and

Adorno's (2007 [1944]) early critical theory on the *Dialectic of Enlightenment*, Hilberg's (1961) and Arendt's (1964) accounts of the bureaucratic structures of Nazi Germany, and Bauman's (1989) more recent work focused on the modernity of the Holocaust. But the trope endures, having found recent expression in dismissals of the conflicts in Bosnia, Rwanda, and Darfur as the result of tribal warfare or ethnic primordialism. The war on terror was legitimated in similar terms as a conflict between (rational) civilization and (irrational) terrorist barbarians.

It is precisely by unpacking the sets of moral understandings that undergird the depiction of those dismissed as irrational savages that anthropology may make a critical contribution to our understanding of violence and morality. A number of texts in the recent literature on the anthropology of violence have argued this point. Examples include such important works as Michael Taussig's (1984) unpacking of how the different understandings of rubber traders and indigenous Putumayo Indians structured seemingly irrational violence on the borders of civilization, Liisa Malkki's (1995) discussion of the understandings that motivate refugee behaviors linked to identity and genocide but readily dismissed by outsiders, Begona Aretxaga's (1995) discussion of the moral protest leading female prisoners in Ireland to smear excrement and menstrual blood on the walls of their cells, acts explained away as "uncivilized" by some British officials, and Christopher Taylor's (2001) explication of the complex, embodied understandings that motivated seemingly incomprehensible acts of genocide in Rwanda such as evisceration and the stuffing of people in latrines.

The Cambodian genocide

My own research on the Cambodian genocide fits into this body of research on violence and moral anthropology and provides an illustration of some of the points noted above. Most recently, I have been conducting research on the first case at the Extraordinary Chambers in the Courts of Cambodia, where a former Khmer Rouge prison commandant, Duch, was tried for crimes against humanity and war crimes. Duch ran S-21, an interrogation and torture center where almost all of the over 12,000 prisoners who passed through its gates were killed. More broadly in Cambodia, perhaps 1.7 to 2.2 million of Cambodia's 8 million inhabitants perished from disease, starvation, overwork, and execution under Khmer Rouge rule (1975–79).

S-21 has come to stand as a domestic and international symbol of the Khmer Rouge atrocities and Duch, as its head, has become notorious. He, like other Khmer Rouge leaders, have been described as savages by Cambodians, the media, and tourists. Indeed, one day while visiting S-21, which has been converted into a Museum of Genocidal Crimes, I saw a black-and-white portrait of Duch's face, which graffiti artists had transformed into a demonic-like visage. (Other Khmer Rouge leaders, like Pol Pot, were similarly graffitied/defaced.)

One of the difficulties in the ethnographic encounter is to grapple with one's own unease at engaging with such individuals. One of my most memorable meetings with an alleged mass murder was with Lor, a KR cadre who had worked under Duch and had been depicted by one of the only survivors of S-21 as a "savage" who had murdered over 2,000 people. When I first met Lor, I expected to meet a monster but instead found an ordinary person whose path to involvement in the genocide was complicated even if in the end he also made choices and acted in abusive ways (Hinton 2005). Pol Pot himself played upon this trope when interviewed by a foreign journalist shortly before his death, asking him "Am I a savage?" – a question that later ran as a newspaper headline.

In such encounters, it is critical to try to make sure one is not falling into "ethnographic seduction," to use a phrase Tony Robben (1996) coined to describe the transference and projection that may go on between an interviewer and interviewees. What makes this all the more complicated is an ambiguity that often runs through such encounters, as pasts are hidden and revealed and positionings as victim or perpetrator are often never fully clear. Primo Levi's (1988) notion of the "gray zone" captures a sense of this moral fuzziness that permeates the roles people play within violent spaces, such as when perpetrators become victims or victims become spies or even abusers of other victims. It was certainly true of S-21, where many of the inmates were former Khmer Rouge who had been purged, including former S-21 personnel and interrogators.

If Duch is clearly guilty and bears moral and criminal responsibility for the crimes he committed, as he admitted on numerous occasions during his trial, his story is also more complicated and certainly can't be understood simply by dismissing him as a "savage" or a "monster." In a sense, maybe we want him to be a monster since this makes him other than us and pushes away the frightening possibility that we, too, might have made poor choices in a similar situation. This is a discomforting thought and, understandably, an almost outrageous one for the families of victims. All of these dynamics were at play during the Duch trial.

By the time Duch was arrested, he had converted to evangelical Christianity and stated that he would be a cooperative witness. Indeed, on the third day of his trial, he issued a long apology to his former victims and their relatives, many of whom were civil parties and seated in the court. Some said that they might be able to forgive him eventually. But for many of the victims, no apology from Duch was acceptable. He had to go to jail, hopefully for the rest of his life. He had killed their relatives and was still savage, apologizing only to get a reduced sentence. Any observation Duch offered that contradicted incriminating evidence or testimony was taken as yet further proof of his guilt and inner nature. Such apologies and the victim response raise a whole host of other questions about violence, morality, and reconciliation as victims and perpetrators seek some sort of way to coexist in the postconflict society, an issue that, as noted earlier, anthropologists have recently begun to explore.

Before concluding, I would like to briefly discuss the story of Duch's life that emerged during the trial and the moral claims related to violence implicit within it. Duch was born in 1942 in the midst of World War II and just before the promulgation of the human rights institutions and laws that would later ensnare him and bring him to face justice before a UN-backed tribunal. This period was also an important time in Cambodian history, marking the rise of nationalism, the path to independence from French colonial rule in 1953, and, by the end of the decade, the beginnings of the Cambodian communist movement.

Duch was an ideal recruit. His family was poor and ethnic Chinese, which may have contributed to a sense of devaluation, disempowerment, and humiliation.[3] He eventually became aware of his father's financial problems and indebtedness to a usurious uncle, precisely the sort of class contradiction upon which the Khmer Rogue sought to play.[4] By the age of 15, Duch was starting to be drawn to discussions of class exploitation and the communist alternative, sentiments that were amplified by one of his first mentors and teachers, Kae Kim Huot, who spoke about social injustice and later joined the Khmer Rouge. Kae Kim Huot would later pass through the gates of S-21 and be forced to eat excrement while being tortured into confession.[5] Like almost all of the prisoners at S-21, he was subsequently executed.

By the mid 1960s, Duch himself had become a teacher and joined the revolutionary movement. His formal induction into the Khmer Rouge took place on December 5, 1967, when he "stood before the party's flag. I raised my hand to respect and to swear to be sincere to the party, the class and the people of Kampuchea for my entire life and to serve the party … [to be willing to] sacrifice anything for the party."[6] He explained that he had joined "to liberate the nation, my own people from any oppression. I did not have any intention to do criminal activities."[7]

This was basically the moral line he took throughout his trial and the implicit explanation for all he did. Duch claimed that he had joined the revolution to help liberate his country from US imperialism and his compatriots from capitalist oppression. When he was later asked to run M-13 (an interrogation and torture center operating during the civil war) and S-21 after the war, Duch claimed that he tried to refuse but ultimately did so out of a sense of duty. He told the French anthropologist François Bizot, who was imprisoned at M-13, as much one evening, saying that "he considered that this was something that he had to do and he had to force himself to do it. He had to make this into some form of duty" even if "it was something he disliked."[8] Indeed, Duch's defense was built upon the notion that he was an almost noble figure who had performed terrible duties out of a sense of obligation and commitment to a larger cause. "I came to hate the excrement," he would say, "but I had to walk in it."[9] If he had disobeyed orders, he explained, he and his family would have been executed.

As this brief discussion suggests (and even if we must bear in mind that the moral line Duch asserted might vary dramatically from the realities during the Khmer Rouge regime), it is only through a set of historical events and personal decisions that Duch arrived at a point at which he oversaw an institution at which acts of extreme brutality took place. He made the choice to participate in mass murder and is responsible for his actions, to be sure. But what does it mean that many of us want to explain away such human complexity by invoking the trope of savagery or barbarism? This move reduces explanation to a naturalized set of understandings holding that perpetrators are like savages, occupying a more "primitive" and "less developed" state of being, or sadists, whose psyches are pathological and twisted. On the one hand, such explanations assert an opposing status, that of the "civilized" and psychologically "normal" person who could never do such things. We thereby construct our own state of moral goodness through the violence of the other. It is much more difficult to accept that people like Duch are not so different from us and that the potential for horrible acts of violence lies within each of us and the societies in which we live.

François Bizot struggled with this very issue after Duch told him that he had disliked his work but had had to fulfill his duty to the revolution. "I had expected to encounter a monster, and inhumane person, but I realized then that things were much more tragic, much more frightening," Bizot explained during his testimony. "I realized that in front of me there was a man who looked very much like many friends of mine, a Marxist, a human being who was a Marxist who was prepared to surrender his life for his country [and] for the revolution. He believed in this cause and the ultimate goal of his commitment and … the wellbeing of the inhabitants of Cambodia. He was fighting against injustice."[10]

While recognizing that Duch was fully responsible for the acts of violence he had perpetrated – and indeed he was ultimately convicted and sentenced to life imprisonment – Bizot realized that it "would be the greatest possible mistake to turn such monsters into a different category of people, a different species … It is necessary to make a distinction between what humans do from what humans are."[11] This is precisely the point at which violence and morality intersect and critical anthropological analysis can shed light on matters that are obscured by naturalized discourses such as the savagery explanation. In doing so, it can make an important contribution to the study of violence, including the extremes of the Holocaust.

Conclusion

Anthropology has a long and complicated relationship with the study of violence and morality. If in the face of the Holocaust and other forms of political violence, scholars in other disciplines were more easily able to grapple with the topic with an underlying normative assumption that such behaviors are bad or even evil, anthropologists were placed in a more tricky position. Cultural relativism called for the suspension of moral judgment to understand local systems of meaning. Meanwhile, the predominant anthropological focus both on holistic, small-scale societies and on social order and coherence meant that violence, as a topic of independent study, was not of primary relevance: it usually mattered only insofar as it was functionally related to the overall social system. This meant that, even if anthropologists joined the war effort or took an activist stance at times, they by and large missed the larger-scale political violence that was taking place around them, including numerous revolutionary struggles against colonial regimes. On the more rare occasions when anthropologists did grapple with such issues, they often did so through recourse to more universalizing discourses, ranging from Chagnon's sociobiological perspective to Colin Turnbull's Hobbesian assumptions.

In the 1970s and 1980s, this situation began to change due to a variety of factors, ranging from an intensification of global interconnectedness to the radicalization of a generation of scholars who grew up in shadow of the civil rights movement, Cambodia, Biafra, riots in France, the threat of nuclear conflict, Bangladesh, and the Vietnam War. Violence that had been long pushed out of sight began to come into the anthropological view. Some of the engagement led to calls for the "primacy of the ethical" and a more "morally engaged anthropology" (Scheper-Hughes 1995).

As part of this engagement, and in the midst of political violence and genocide in the post-cold war era, a number of scholars began to grapple directly with the topic of violence. If earlier anthropologists had shied away from such issues because of the slippery ground of moral relativism, this new generation of scholars directly took up the issue of violence and morality as they unpacked the logics of violence, ranging from the ways in which communities remake their lives after atrocity to the sets of local moral understandings that underlie and motivate violence. Here, at last, anthropology had come to a point at which it was able to begin to respond to the host of questions about violence that emerged in the aftermath of the Holocaust. While some anthropological work emerged that addressed the Holocaust directly, much more of this work focused on post-cold war contexts of political violence. Moral issues, ranging from the ethical choices anthropologists make and the moral imperatives they follow to the analysis of how local moral understandings are mobilized and negotiated before, during, and after violence, remain at the forefront of this literature.

There are other related issues that are less discussed, such as the dangers and ethical challenges we face when we do "fieldwork under fire" (Nordstrom and Robben 1995). In some situations, these choices may have major consequences on the group under study, as the recent controversies about the Yanomami and the Human Terrain Systems illustrate (see Borofsky 2005; Forte 2011). Less discussed are issues such as the ways in which we write and teach about violence. What effect does teaching about a very difficult and discomforting subject like violence have on our students? And what does it mean to communicate in clear prose as opposed to abstract "insider" language to which many people do not have access? And, finally, beyond the dangers of "ethnographic seduction," what effect does studying and writing about violence have upon the researcher? These are all critical questions related to violence and morality that also call for our attention.

Acknowledgments

I would like to thank Didier Fassin and Nicole Cooley for their insightful comments on this essay. I would also like to thank the Institute for Advanced Study at Princeton for providing support and an institutional space in which this essay could be written and the United States Institute of Peace and the Rutgers Research Council for providing support for my research on the Khmer Rouge Tribunal.

NOTES

1 For a related call for moral engagement by anthropologists, see Scheper-Hughes 1995.
2 At http://www.aaanet.org/cmtes/cfhr/index.cfm, accessed Mar. 13, 2012.
3 Transcript of Proceedings – "Duch" Trial, Aug. 31, 2009, Trial Day 67. Phnom Penh, Cambodia: Extraordinary Chambers in the Courts of Cambodia, pp. 67–68. (Hereafter "Duch Trial, Day 67.")
4 "Closing Order indicting Kaing Guek Eav alias Duch (Public Redacted Version)." Phnom Penh, Cambodia: Extraordinary Chambers in the Courts of Cambodia, p. 40. Aug. 8, 2008. (Hereafter "Duch Closing Order.")
5 Duch Verdict, p. 87.
6 Transcript of Proceedings – "Duch" Trial, Apr. 6, 2009, Trial Day 4. Phnom Penh, Cambodia: Extraordinary Chambers in the Courts of Cambodia, p. 18. (Hereafter "Duch Trial, Day 4.")
7 Duch Trial, Day 4, pp. 49–50.
8 Duch Trial, Day 5, p. 10.
9 Duch Trial, Day 4, p. 79.
10 Duch Trial, Day 5, p. 72.
11 Duch Trial, Day 5, p. 73.

REFERENCES

American Anthropological Association (1947) Statement on Human Rights. *American Anthropologist* 49(4): 539–543.

American Anthropological Association (2007) American Anthropological Association Executive Board Statement on the Human Terrain System Project. Oct. 31. At http://www.aaanet.org/issues/policy-advocacy/Statement-on-HTS.cfm, accessed Mar. 13, 2012.

American Anthropological Association (1999) Declaration on Anthropology and Human Rights. At http://www.aaanet.org/stmts/humanrts.htm, accessed Mar. 13, 2012.

Arendt, Hannah (1964) *Eichmann in Jerusalem: A Report on the Banality of Evil.* New York: Viking.

Aretxaga, Begona (1995) Dirty Protest: Symbolic Overdetermination and Gender in Northern Ireland Ethnic Violence. *Ethos* 23(2): 123–148.

Aretxaga, Begona (1997) *Shattering Silence.* Princeton: Princeton University Press.

Argenti, Nicolas (2007) *The Intestines of the State: Youth, Violence, and Belated Histories in the Cameroon Grassfields.* Chicago: University of Chicago Press.

Argenti-Pillen, Alex (2002) *Masking Terror: How Women Contain Violence in Southern Sri Lanka.* Philadelphia: University of Pennsylvania Press.

Bass, Gary Jonathan (2000) *Stay the Hand of Vengeance: The Politics of War Crimes Tribunals.* Princeton: Princeton University Press.

Bauman, Zygmunt (1989) *Modernity and the Holocaust.* Cambridge: Polity.

Benedict, Ruth (2006) *Patterns of Culture.* New York: Mariner.

Biehl, João (2009) *Will to Live: AIDS Therapies and the Politics of Survival.* Princeton: Princeton University Press.

Bloch, Maurice (1991) *Prey into Hunter: The Politics of Religious Experience.* New York: Cambridge University Press.

Boas, Franz (1995) *Race, Language, and Culture.* Chicago: University Of Chicago Press.

Bodley, John H. (1975) *Victims of Progress.* Menlo Park, CA: Cummings.

Borneman, John (1997) *Settling Accounts.* Princeton: Princeton University Press.

Borofsky, Robert (2005) *Yanomami: The Fierce Controversy and What We Can Learn from It.* Berkeley: University of California Press.

Bourdieu, Pierre (1977) *Outline of a Theory of Practice.* New York: Cambridge University Press.

Bourgois, Philippe (2002) *In Search of Respect: Selling Crack in El Barrio.* New York: Cambridge University Press.

Bourgois, Philippe and Schonberg, Jeffrey (2009) *Righteous Dopefiend.* Berkeley: University of California Press.

Bringa, Tone (1995) *Being Muslim the Bosnian Way.* Princeton: Princeton University Press.

Chagnon, Napoleon A. (1968) *Yanomamö, the Fierce People.* New York: Holt, Rinehart & Winston.

Clarke, Kamari Maxine (2009) *Fictions of Justice: The International Criminal Court and the Challenge of Legal Pluralism in Sub-Saharan Africa.* New York: Cambridge University Press.

Clastres, Pierre (2000) *Chronicle of the Guayaki Indians*; trans. Paul Auster. New York: Zone.

Clastres, Pierre (1994) *Archeology of Violence*, trans. Jeanine Herman. New York, Semiotext(e).

Coronil, Fernando and Skurski, Julie (1991) Dismembering and Remembering the Nation: The Semantics of Political Violence in Venezuela. *Comparative Studies in Society and History* 33(2): 288–337.

Daniel, E. Valentine (1996) *Charred Lullabies: Chapters in an Anthropography of Violence.* Princeton: Princeton University Press.

Das, Veena (ed.) (1991) *Mirrors of Violence: Communities, Riots and Survivors in South Asia.* New York: Oxford University Press.

Das, Veena (2006) *Life and Words: Violence and the Descent into the Ordinary.* Berkeley: University of California Press.

Das, Veena (2008) Violence, Gender, and Subjectivity. *Annual Review of Anthropology* 37: 283–299.

Das, Veena and Kleinman, Arthur (2000) Introduction. In Das et al. (2000), pp. 1–18.

Das, Veena, Kleinman, Arthur, Ramphele, Mamphela, and Reynolds, Pamela (eds.) (2000) *Violence and Subjectivity*. Berkeley: University of California Press.

Das, Veena, Kleinman, Arthur, Lock, Margaret, et al. (eds.) (2001) *Remaking a World: Violence, Social Suffering, and Recovery*. Berkeley: University of California Press.

Dentan, Robert Knox (1968) The Semai: A Nonviolent People of Malaya. New York: Holt, Rinehart & Winston.

Douglas, Lawrence (2001) *The Memory of Judgment: Making Law and History in the Trials of the Holocaust*. New Haven: Yale University Press.

Eltringham, Nigel (2009) "We Are Not a Truth Commission": Fragmented Narratives and the Historical Record at the International Criminal Tribunal for Rwanda. *Journal of Genocide Research* 11(1): 55–79.

Evans-Pritchard, E. E. (1937) *Witchcraft, Oracles and Magic among the Azande*. Oxford: Clarendon.

Farmer, Paul (2004) *Pathologies of Power: Health, Human Rights, and the New War on the Poor*. Berkeley: University of California Press.

Fassin, Didier (2007) *When Bodies Remember: Experiences and Politics of AIDS in South Africa*. Berkeley: University of California Press.

Fassin, Didier (2008) Beyond Good and Evil? Questioning the Anthropological Discomfort with Morals. *Anthropological Theory* 8(4): 222–244.

Fassin, Didier (2011) *Humanitarian Reason: A Moral History of the Present*. Berkeley: University of California Press.

Fassin, Didier and Pandolfi, Mariella (eds.) (2010) *Contemporary States of Emergency: The Politics of Military and Humanitarian Interventions*. New York: Zone.

Fassin, Didier and Rechtman, Richard (2009) *The Empire of Trauma: An Inquiry into the Condition of Victimhood*. Princeton: Princeton University Press.

Feldman, Allen (1991) *Formations of Violence: The Narrative of the Body and Political Terror in Northern Ireland*. Chicago: University of Chicago Press.

Fisher, William F. (1997) Doing Good? The Politics and Antipolitics of NGO Practices. *Annual Review of Anthropology* 26: 439–464.

Forte, Maximilian C. (2011) The Human Terrain System and Anthropology: A Review of Ongoing Public Debates. *American Anthropologist* 113(1): 149–153.

Foucault, Michel (1977) *Discipline and Punish: The Birth of the Prison*, trans. Alan Sheridan. New York: Vintage.

Frank, Andre (1979) *Dependent Accumulation*. New York: Monthly Review Press.

Fromm, Erich (1994 [1941]) *Escape from Freedom*. New York: Holt.

Geertz, Clifford (1973) *The Interpretation Of Cultures*. New York: Basic Books.

Gluckman, Max (1955) *Custom and Conflict in Africa*. Oxford: Blackwell.

Goodale, Mark (2006) Toward a Critical Anthropology of Human Rights. *Current Anthropology* 47(3): 485–498.

Green, Linda (1999) *Fear as a Way of Life*. New York: Columbia University Press.

Gusterson, Hugh (2007) Anthropology and Militarism. *Annual Review of Anthropology* 36: 155–175.

Harris, Marvin (1984) *Cultural Materialism: The Struggle for a Science of Culture*. Lanham, MD: AltaMira.

Hilberg, Raul (1961) *The Destruction of the European Jews*. New York: Harper & Row.

Hinton, Alexander (ed.) (1999) *Biocultural Approaches to the Emotions*. New York: Cambridge University Press.

Hinton, Alexander (2002a) *Annihilating Difference: The Anthropology of Genocide*. Berkeley: University of California Press.

Hinton, Alexander (ed.) (2002b) *Genocide: An Anthropological Reader*. Malden, MA: Wiley-Blackwell.

Hinton, Alexander Laban (2005) *Why Did They Kill? Cambodia in the Shadow of Genocide.* Berkeley: University of California Press.

Hinton, Alexander Laban (2011) *Transitional Justice: Global Mechanisms and Local Realities After Genocide and Mass Violence.* New Brunswick, NJ: Rutgers University Press.

Hinton, Alexander Laban and O'Neill, Kevin Lewis (eds.) (2009) *Genocide: Truth, Memory, and Representation.* Durham, NC: Duke University Press.

Hirsch, Susan F. (2008) *In the Moment of Greatest Calamity: Terrorism, Grief, and a Victim's Quest for Justice.* Princeton: Princeton University Press.

Horkheimer, Max and Adorno, Theodor W. (2007 [1944]) *Dialectic of Enlightenment.* Stanford: Stanford University Press.

Kirmayer, Laurence J., Lemelson, Robert, and Barad, Mark (2008) *Understanding Trauma: Integrating Biological, Clinical, and Cultural Perspectives.* New York: Cambridge University Press.

Kleinman, Arthur (1980) *Patients and Healers in the Context of Culture: An Exploration of the Borderland between Anthropology, Medicine, and Psychiatry.* Berkeley: University of California Press.

Kleinman, Arthur, Das, Veena, and Lock, Margaret (1997) *Social Suffering.* Berkeley: University of California Press.

Kwon, Heonik (2006) *After the Massacre: Commemoration and Consolation in Ha My and My Lai.* Berkeley: University of California Press.

Levi, Primo (1988) *The Drowned and the Saved.* New York: Summit.

Linke, Uli (1999) *Blood and Nation: The European Aesthetics of Race.* Philadelphia: University of Pennsylvania Press.

Lutz, Catherine (2001) *Homefront: A Military City and the American Twentieth Century.* Boston: Beacon.

Malkki, Liisa H. (1995) *Purity and Exile: Violence, Memory, and National Cosmology among Hutu Refugees in Tanzania.* Chicago: University Of Chicago Press.

Mamdani, Mahmood (2005) *Good Muslim, Bad Muslim: America, the Cold War, and the Roots of Terror.* New York: Three Rivers.

Mamdani, Mahmood (2010) *Saviors and Survivors: Darfur, Politics, and the War on Terror.* New York: Three Rivers.

Manz, Beatriz (1987) *Refugees of a Hidden War: The Aftermath of Counterinsurgency in Guatemala.* Albany, NY: SUNY Press.

Maybury-Lewis, David (2001) *Indigenous Peoples, Ethnic Groups, and the State.* Upper Saddle River, NJ: Allyn & Bacon.

Moran, Mary H. (2010) Gender, Militarism, and Peace-Building: Projects of the Postconflict Moment. *Annual Review of Anthropology* 39: 261–274.

Munzel, Mark (1973) *The Aché Indians: Genocide in Paraguay.* Copenhagen: IWGIA.

Nagengast, Carole (1994) Violence, Terror, and the Crisis of the State. *Annual Review of Anthropology* 23: 109–136.

Nichter, M. (1981) Idioms of Distress: Alternatives in the Expression of Psychosocial Distress: A Case Study from South India. *Culture, Medicine and Psychiatry* 5(4): 379–408.

Nietzsche, Friedrich Wilhelm (1996 [1886]) *On the Genealogy of Morals.* New York: Oxford University Press.

Nordstrom, Carolyn (2004) *Shadows of War: Violence, Power, and International Profiteering in the Twenty-First Century.* Berkeley: University of California Press.

Nordstrom, Carolyn and Robben, Antonius C. G. M. (eds.) (1995) *Fieldwork under Fire: Contemporary Studies of Violence and Survival.* Berkeley: University of California Press.

Price, David (2000) Anthropologists as Spies. The Nation. Nov. 2. At http://www.thenation.com/article/anthropologists-spies, accessed Mar. 13, 2012.

Proctor, Robert (1988) *Racial Hygiene: Medicine under the Nazis.* Cambridge, MA: Harvard University Press.

Redfield, Peter (2005) Doctors, Borders, and Life in Crisis. *Cultural Anthropology* 20(3): 328–361.

Riches, David (1986) *The Anthropology of Violence*. Oxford: Blackwell.

Robben, Antonius C. G. M. (1996) Ethnographic Seduction, Transference, and Resistance in Dialogues about Terror and Violence in Argentina. *Ethos* 24(1): 71–106.

Robben, Antonius C. G. M. (2007) *Political Violence and Trauma in Argentina*. Philadelphia: University of Pennsylvania Press.

Robben, Antonius C. G. M. (ed.) (2011) *Iraq at a Distance: What Anthropologists Can Teach Us about the War*. Philadelphia: University of Pennsylvania Press.

Rojas-Perez, Isaias (2010) Fragments of Soul: Law, Transitional Justice, and Mourning in Post-War Peru. PhD dissertation, Johns Hopkins University, Baltimore.

Ross, Fiona C. (2002) *Bearing Witness: Women and the Truth and Reconciliation Commission*. London: Pluto.

Sanford, Victoria (2003) *Buried Secrets: Truth and Human Rights in Guatemala*. New York: Palgrave Macmillan.

Schafft, Gretchen E. (2004) *From Racism to Genocide: Anthropology in the Third Reich*. Urbana: University of Illinois Press.

Scheper-Hughes, Nancy (1993) *Death without Weeping: The Violence of Everyday Life in Brazil*. Berkeley: University of California Press.

Scheper-Hughes, Nancy (1995) The Primacy of the Ethical. *Current Anthropology* 36(3): 409–440.

Shaw, Rosalind (2007) Displacing Violence: Making Pentecostal Memory in Postwar Sierra Leone. *Cultural Anthropology* 22(1): 66–93.

Shaw, Rosalind and Waldorf, Lars (eds.) (2010) *Localizing Transitional Justice: Interventions and Priorities after Mass Violence*. Stanford: Stanford University Press.

Silber, Irina Carlota (2010) *Everyday Revolutionaries: Gender, Violence, and Disillusionment in Postwar El Salvador*. New Brunswick, NJ: Rutgers University Press.

Sluka, Jeffrey A. (1999) *Death Squad: The Anthropology of State Terror*. Philadelphia: University of Pennsylvania Press.

Steward, Julian H. (1948) Brief Communications. *American Anthropologist* 50(2): 351–352.

Suárez-Orozco, Marcelo M. (1990) Speaking of the Unspeakable: Toward a Psychosocial Understanding of Responses to Terror. *Ethos* 18(3): 353–383.

Tambiah, Stanley J. (1992) *Buddhism Betrayed? Religion, Politics, and Violence in Sri Lanka*. Chicago: University Of Chicago Press.

Taussig, Michael (1984) Culture of Terror – Space of Death. Roger Casement's Putumayo Report and the Explanation of Torture. *Comparative Studies in Society and History* 26(3): 467–497.

Taylor, Christopher C. (2001) *Sacrifice as Terror: The Rwandan Genocide of 1994*. London: Berg.

Theidon, Kimberly (2009) Reconstructing Masculinities: The Disarmament, Demobilization, and Reintegration of Former Combatants in Colombia. *Human Rights Quarterly* 31(1): 1–34.

Totten, Samuel and Hitchcock, Robert (eds.) (2010) *Genocide of Indigenous Peoples: A Critical Bibliographic Review*. New Brunswick, NJ: Transaction.

Turnbull, Colin M. (1972) *The Mountain People*. New York: Simon & Schuster.

Turner, Victor (1970) *The Forest of Symbols: Aspects of Ndembu Ritual*. Ithaca, NY: Cornell University Press.

van Binsbergen, Wim (2002) Violence in Anthropology: Theoretical and Personal Remarks. At http://www.shikanda.net/ethnicity/violence.htm, accessed Mar. 13, 2012.

Verdery, Katherine (2000) *The Political Lives of Dead Bodies*. New York: Columbia University Press.

Wagner, Sarah (2008) *To Know Where He Lies: DNA Technology and the Search for Srebrenica's Missing*. Berkeley: University of California Press.

Wallerstein, Immanuel (1976) *The Modern World-System I: Capitalist Agriculture and the Origins of the European World-Economy in the Sixteenth Century*. New York: Academic Press.

Wilson, Richard (2001) *The Politics of Truth and Reconciliation in South Africa: Legitimizing the Post-Apartheid State.* Cambridge: Cambridge University Press.
Wilson, Richard Ashby (2011) *Writing History in International Criminal Trials.* New York: Cambridge University Press.
WMA (1948) WMA Declaration of Geneva. At http://www.wma.net/en/30publications/10policies/g1/index.html, accessed Mar. 13, 2012.
Wolf, Eric R. (1999) *Envisioning Power: Ideologies of Dominance and Crisis.* Berkeley: University of California Press.
Young, Allan (1995) *The Harmony of Illusions: Inventing Post-Traumatic Stress Disorder.* Princeton: Princeton University Press.
Zigon, Jarrett (2011) *HIV is God's Blessing: Rehabilitating Morality in Neoliberal Russia.* Berkeley: University of California Press.

CHAPTER 29

Punishment

Roger Lancaster

Beware of those in whom the will to punish is strong.

Friedrich Nietzsche, *Thus Spake Zarathustra*

If a monster is wandering in the world, we need to catch him, imprison him, cage him … There are, however, different ways – none certain – of catching the monster.

Antonio Negri, "The Political Monster: Power and Naked Life"

There is something vexing about punishment, and this difficulty emerges as soon as one turns away from moral and legal models based on retribution: "an eye for an eye, a tooth for a tooth." In most versions of the classical canon, both law and morality[1] have less to do with a settling of scores than with protection from injury, the establishment of balance or equity, and the promotion of well-being. That is to say, these versions are consequentialist (they look forward to future effects) rather than deontological (looking backward to the event of the crime, as defined by absolute moral or legal codes, sometimes given by divine command). Yet on such reckonings, punishment is precisely that part of legal morality that deliberately aims to inflict injury – that is, to deprive the sanctioned person of freedom, goods, well-being, or life – either to cure an ill or to deter future lawbreaking. Theoretically, such injuries are to be inflicted in a just, calibrated, and lawful manner.

Plato, whose legal framework was curative ("the best kind of purification is painful, like similar cures in medicine": 2000: 104), was well aware of the problem: a cycle of vengeance does little to "cure" the lawbreaker of his illness or to promote well-ordered social relations. Much of *Laws* is thus concerned with restraining punishment as vengeance (*timōria*). Punishment as justice (*dikē*) should be measured, and never more than necessary either to instruct the lawbreaker or to serve as an object lesson. "Not that he is punished because he did wrong, for that which is done can never be undone, but in order that in future times, he, and those who see him corrected, may utterly hate injustice, or at any rate abate much of their evil-doing" (Plato 2000: 274).

A Companion to Moral Anthropology, First Edition. Edited by Didier Fassin.

And so the rub: moral philosophers since Plato have seldom imagined a system of morality or law without a place for punishment. Yet they have generally held the urge to punish in low esteem: the visceral satisfaction taken from vengeance stirs the baser instincts, clouds judgment, and incites mobs. It attaches, in ways that demean or diminish, to the character of those in whom the will to punish is strong. For such reasons, vindictiveness generally has not been regarded as a defensible foundation upon which to build a rational system of justice. Indeed, it has been viewed as contrary to the basic intent of reasoned law. But still it remains: the starting point, the origin to be renounced, the temptation to be transcended. Edward Westermarck commented on the paradoxical place of retribution in moral systems this way: "moral consciousness … in vain condemns the gratification of the very desire from which it sprang" (1906: 93).

In this essay, I sketch how classical distinctions and the tensions they produce are taken up in Enlightenment ideas and modern social theories. Using the United States as my field, I then show how such models fail to predict American trends in the late twentieth century. Drawing on political, psychological, and social approaches, I try to understand the surge of a vengeance orientation in US culture, and I venture some generalizations about the social form that has developed in its wake.

Civilizing Punishment

Seventeenth- and eighteenth-century thinkers put the classical distinctions between repressive and instructive punishments on a new footing. "Revenge," wrote Francis Bacon, "is a kind of wild justice; which the more man's nature runs to, the more ought law to weed it out" (2002: 347). Jeremy Bentham went further. "All punishment is mischief," he declared (2000: 249), showing how harsh punishments debased the condition of both the punishers and the punished. Lest the necessary evil of punishment be barbaric, it should only be enough to outweigh the pleasure of the crime. And Voltaire mocked the brutality of corporeal punishments, religious intolerance, and secret accusations: "shall the law delight in barbarity?" (in Beccaria 1872 [1764]). Enlightenment and progressive theories thus reinscribed deontological and consequentialist approaches as distinctions between the primitive and the civilized: vengeance, retribution, and unreason, as opposed to rehabilitation, prevention, or restitution. Such oppositions carry over into the sociological cannon and remain with us.

Reasoned, calibrated law

Emile Durkheim draws the following distinctions: "repressive law" is associated with the "mechanical solidarity" of small-scale societies. Under this arrangement, people go along and get along because they are similar to each other: they perform the same labors, live the same routines, and think in much the same ways. Accordingly, primitive law aims to repress differences and to punish nonconformity. Examples of this type of law include penal law, sanctions that damage or kill the lawbreaker, and punishments for blasphemy, defilement, or other offenses against the group. In contrast, nuanced sanctions that have the effect of restoring disrupted social relations ("restitutive law") are associated with the "organic solidarity" of complex, cosmopolitan societies. Under this latter arrangement, goodwill and fellow feeling are negotiated between people who perform different kinds of labor, have different styles of life, and express different ways of thinking. Under organic conditions, law thus aims not to enforce conformity but to regulate ordered differences, to structure diversity, and to maintain an equilibrium. The calibration of penalties is a key feature of restitutive law, which includes contract law, civil law, and constitutional law (Durkheim 1984 [1893]: 31–87).

Durkheim thus roots different kinds of moral facts in social facts: when modes of social solidarity change, the basis for rule-making shifts from sanction to regulation. But the supposedly temporal dimension of his model masks a problem, or perhaps expresses a wish. If it can be said that for Durkheim what originally defines the moral fact is the sanction – in other words, that punishment founds morality – then the shift to restitutive law with its very different orientation and forms comes as something of a surprise.

Similar ideas about social progress leave their mark in American thinking, albeit in distinctly American ways. By the early twentieth century, US philosophers and sociologists were posing a distinction between "punitive justice," which was associated with communal violence, especially race lynchings, and other variants of justice: reformative justice, and sometimes social justice (e.g., Willoughby 1910; Knight 1911). On all accountings, punitive justice expresses base anger, resentment, or vindictiveness, in contrast to preventive, reformative, or restorative ideals. It also tends toward "summary" forms: abbreviated adjudication procedures, if any at all, stand between accusation and punishment. But perhaps what is most striking about the American scholarly essays of the period is the pessimism they express, a pessimism that reads jarringly against the backdrop of lynch law. George H. Mead takes lynch law as paradigmatic: "Lynch law is the very essence of retribution and is inspired with the grim assurance that such summary justice must strike terror into the heart of the prospective criminal … What, then, are the values evidenced in and maintained by the laws of punitive justice? The most patent value is the theoretically impartial enforcement of the common will" (1918: 584). He goes on to depict punitive acts, because of their primitive nature, as essential to the designation and marginalization of outsiders – and thus as essential to the dynamics of group solidarity and social order. "The social worker in the court is the sentimentalist, and the legalist in the social settlement despite his learned doctrine is the ignoramus" (Mead 1918: 592). Still, even Mead expresses a wish. He tries to imagine how agonal impulses might be channeled and domesticated by evolving social institutions that keep hostility in check: "The energy that expressed itself in burning witches as the causes of plagues expends itself at present in medical research and sanitary regulations and may still be called a fight with disease" (602).

The regimes of power described by Michel Foucault in *Discipline and Punish* (1978), *The History of Sexuality* (1980 [1976]: 135–145) and other works, echo the familiar dichotomy between deontology and consequentialism while introducing a third term. The form of power Foucault designates as "sovereign" is essentially the brute right of the ruler to seize things: time, property, or bodies. By the classical age, this right of the king to punish, torture, or kill had been constrained, at least theoretically, to states of emergency – to instances when the sovereign or the state was imperiled by enemies from within or without. By contrast, the regime of "discipline" aims to correct or rehabilitate. The "gentle punishments" of Enlightenment law aim to induce the miscreant to mend his or her ways. "Bio-power" follows suit. As Foucault sketches it, this mode of power is neither deductive (in the sense of subtracting life or enjoyment) nor correctional (in the usual sense of straightening out crooked ways) but productive: it aims to "invest" in life. Biomedicine, psychology, and other disciplines that promote well-being intervene in life, not from "without," but from within. Obviously, state actors and other authorities utilize the life sciences to secure the integration of individuals into economic systems, and they use demographic techniques to manage populations; more subtly, biopower induces individuals to "work on themselves" through various forms of self-care, self-improvement, fitness schemes, and so on. And this work of self-care is precisely what makes biopolitical subjects governable in new ways.[2]

Is punishment "primitive"?

In Enlightenment doctrines and in classical social theory, it is understood that brute punishment is "primitive" or archaic, and that reformative, restitutive, or preventive approaches are "modern." Such is the beginning of a misunderstanding of the problem. Ethnographic studies of small-scale societies give little support to the idea that "primitive" law invariably tends toward abbreviated forms and punitive, as opposed to restorative or harmonizing, practices, nor do they sustain the idea that the natives of such societies cringe before the majesty of the law. Quite the contrary. Bronislaw Malinowski (1926) shows that Trobriand Islanders take a practical, even cynical, approach to the laws and rules they observe or break. Laura Nader (1990) describes how Zapotec legal practices seek balance and try to establish harmony rather than trying to assert guilt. Claude Levi-Strauss (1992 [1955]: 388) describes how instead of severing social ties between lawbreakers and society – the penal model – Plains Amerindians temporarily deprived offenders of their goods in order to bind them more tightly into a reciprocal relationship with society. Empirical studies reveal the common occurrence of restitutive practices in small-scale, homogeneous societies and punitive practices in large-scale, cosmopolitan societies; they show that the familiar dichotomies mark coexisting types or modes, not epochs.

However, the use of such terms as "archaic," "atavistic," and "primitive" does perform a certain other work. We fling the label "primitive" at practices we do not like in order to convince ourselves that we, and practices we do like, are modern. This conviction that we are civilized propels assorted missions of amelioration, advancement, progress, hygiene, justice. It also prepares the way for the unleashing of violence in the name of civilization. Thus Levi-Strauss's famous quip: "The barbarian is, first and foremost, the man who believes in barbarism" (1952: 12). But even this proposition trades in the prejudice it purports to criticize.

Now on all accounts, certain trends should manifest. On Durkheim's reading, punitive law should diminish in proportion to restitutive law as civilization "advances." A similar process of amelioration logically should occur under Norbert Elias's (1994 [1939]) conception of the civilizing process. As civilizational standards associated with self-restraint and shame rise, cruel punishments should decline (Elias 1994; see also Pratt 2004). Perhaps especially under the model Foucault sketches, the modern state logically should continue developing forms of power that are more invasive but also gentler and more rational, that are more effective but also kinder and more nuanced.

The Punitive Turn

This has not happened, at least not in the United States. Or rather, this process *was* happening, over a long period of time, but it then suddenly reversed course. In the 1960s and 1970s laws and penal codes were being submitted to a process of rational revision. Victimless crimes were being progressively decriminalized, incarceration rates were declining, and the goal of law enforcement was generally conceived in terms of "correction," or rehabilitation. After the 1972 Supreme Court decision ruling the death penalty, as then practiced, "cruel and unusual," capital punishment was on hiatus – presumably to be abolished at a later date. These and other reforms were grounded in decades of research by criminologists and sociologists; they were also motivated by the desire for a more just system of justice. Little remains of these progressive legacies today, and the received theories seem ill equipped to explain the sudden reversal. Indeed, as late as 1979 Michel Foucault was heralding the advent of a tolerant biopolitics quite different from what actually developed. Neoliberal penal policy in the United States, Foucault elaborated, "does not aim at the extinction of crime, but at a balance between the curves of the supply of crime and negative demand … This amounts to posing as the essential question of penal policy, not, how should crimes be punished, nor even, what actions should be seen as crimes, but, what crimes should we tolerate?" (Foucault 2008: 258–259, 256).

The surge of punishment in the United States

Today, by contrast, punishment looms large. The United States is one of the leading practitioners of judicial murder – quite a bit behind China but not far behind Iran. Reversing trends, successive revisions of the criminal code have mandated ever longer periods of incarceration for ever lesser offenses. State and local governments invest in prisons, not schools. Punishment has replaced rehabilitation as the dominant rationale for the justice system, and incarceration rates have soared.

A few comparative statistics will throw light on what has happened in US society. In the 1960s rates of incarceration in Western democracies generally ranged from 60 to 120 per 100,000 inhabitants. These rates tended to decline until about 1990 and then posted modest to substantial increases thereafter, depending on the country. For example, in post-fascist Italy incarceration rates declined from 79 per 100,000 in 1960 to 57 in 1990, before climbing again to 112 in recent estimates.[3] Similar patterns have been posted in other western European countries. The decline was especially steep in Finland, which began with high crime rates and a penal system built on the Russian model, and, after decades of humanitarian and social-democratic reforms, now posts one of the lowest incarceration rates in Europe. Not coincidentally, since its prison system is correctional in the best sense of the term, not dehumanizing, it provides no breeding ground for anger, resentment, and recidivism. Finland posts one of the lowest rates of serious crime in Europe. Even after slight increases in recent years, its rate of imprisonment is 61 per 100,000.

Britain followed a different course. Under Tony Blair's Labourites, even more so than under Margaret Thatcher's Tories, the state pursued an ever more punitive approach to crime. An obvious measure of this punitiveness is the passage of more laws with more exacting punishments. Nick Cohen (2003) derisively described New Labour's overhaul of the criminal code in the *New Statesman*: under Blair the government found 661 new reasons to lock people up. As a result the rate of imprisonment for England and Wales doubled, from 70 per 100,000 in 1966 to 153 per 100,000 in 2010.

But the United States stands out even in comparison to the British model. In 40 years the United States more than quadrupled its total prison population. The rate of imprisonment has soared from 166 per 100,000 in 1970 to 730 per 100,000 in 2010. The United States thus imprisons five to ten times more people per capita than other developed democracies. The country now ranks first in the world in both the rate of imprisonment (1 in every 99 adult residents is behind bars) and the absolute number of people imprisoned (2.27 million). That is more prisoners than China (1.65 million, or 122 per 100,000), a strong-arm state with more than four times the population of the United States. It is more than Russia (749,600, or 525 per 100,000), once the gendarme of Europe, a culture whose fondness for locking people up both predates and postdates the Stalinist period. With only 5 percent of the world's population, the United States claims about 25 percent of the world's prisoners.[4]

The carceral state

Perhaps the most impressive social trend in post-1960s America has been surge of a vengeance orientation and the rise of what academic critics have called the "carceral state."[5] In plain English the carceral state is a type of political organization in which three conditions obtain. First, incarceration becomes the preferred sanction for a growing number of infractions. Second, official bureaucracies and civil society collude to intensify enforcement, enhance penalties, and keep the prison system growing. Third, a bloated prison system begins to supply norms for other institutions of government: surveillance becomes routine, and a crime-centered approach shapes the activities of functionaries working in offices unrelated to the penitentiary.

The most basic facts call to mind the gauge Maurice Merleau-Ponty – endorsed by Jean-Paul Sartre – applied to the loftier claims of Soviet socialism in 1950: "There is no socialism when one out of every 20 citizens is in a camp" (Merleau-Ponty 1964 [1950]: 264).[6] If we take the French existentialists' measure as a general guide, then what might be said of the state of American democracy under prevailing conditions? If recent incarceration rates remain unchanged, 1 in every 15 Americans will serve time in a prison during his or her lifetime. For men the rate is more than 1 in 9. The weight of these numbers falls disproportionately on black and brown men. For African American men the expected lifetime rate is roughly 1 in 3: 32 percent of black men will spend some portion of their lives incarcerated, compared to 17 percent of Latino males and 5.9 percent of white males. Twelve percent of African American men aged 20–34 are currently behind bars. Such figures have no precedent, not even in the post-slavery period, when Southern states first organized systems of compulsory prison labor as a substitute for slavery, or during Jim Crow (Bonczar 2003; see also Egan 1999; Dyer 2000; Garland 2001; Bruner 2003; Alexander 2010).

The US criminal justice system metes out stiffer sentences, longer incarcerations, and more onerous terms of release and surveillance to far, far more people than any of the nations Americans like to think of as their peers. As a result a large percentage of people in US prisons today – even many inmates serving extremely long sentences – were not convicted of a violent crime. Many were convicted for offenses against public order or morality: they are drug offenders of one sort or another. Others serve long sentences for property crimes that once would have drawn a short term, a fine, or a suspended sentence. Another expanding class of criminals has been created by states that have raised the age of consent. (Many of the resulting criminals – statutory rapists – are themselves young men, barely adult.) The image of the "repeat offender" has been exploited by politicians and victims' rights advocates who campaigned for tougher sentencing provisions, but data from the Bureau of Justice Statistics show that the great run-up in the prison population is the result of an increase in first-time incarcerations (Bonczar 2003: 3).

The criminologist David Garland describes this system of control in the bleakest of terms. The present prison system "serves as a kind of reservation system, a quarantine zone," where "purportedly dangerous individuals are segregated in the name of public safety" (2001: 178). In form, number, and arbitrariness it "resembles nothing so much as the Soviet gulag – a string of work camps and prisons strung across a vast country, housing [more than] two million people most of whom are drawn from classes and racial groups that have become politically and economically problematic … Like the pre-modern sanctions of transportation or banishment, the prison now functions as a form of exile" (178). Remarkably, this unprecedented expansion of the prison system, which is inimical to the spirit of a free society, occurred under formally democratic conditions – indeed, it was prodded by electoral pressures to "get tough on crime."

And once the system gets its hooks into a person, it is loath to let him go. Nearly five million Americans are on probation or parole. Added to the 2.3 million behind bars, this means that 1 in every 32 adults – 3.2 percent of the adult population – is actively caught up in the long reach of the penal state. (This figure does not account for all 740,000 registered sex offenders, most of whom are no longer on parole or probation, and many of whom are registered for nonviolent, noncoercive first offenses.) Extended periods of parole, with their mandatory meetings, reporting conditions, and drug tests, virtually assure future infractions. As a result the number of people in prison today for parole violations alone is the same as the total US prison population in 1980. This is not how the parole system was intended to work, but it is a gauge of the growing punitiveness of all procedures associated with law enforcement, even those formerly conceived as having a rehabilitative effect (Urban Institute 2002; Gonnerman 2004; *Washington Post* 2006).

Only two states, Vermont and Maine, allow prisoners to vote. Thirteen more states allow all ex-convicts to vote as soon as they set foot outside prison. In the rest of the states some form of felony disenfranchisement is the norm. Most states strip ex-cons of the right to vote and bar them from holding work-related business licenses while on parole or probation. Some states extend this effective loss of citizenship beyond parole or probation – and in a shrinking handful of states this disenfranchisement remains in effect for life, thus creating a more or less permanent caste of criminal outcasts. More than five million Americans (1 in 41 adults) have temporarily or permanently lost their right to vote; black men (roughly 6 percent of the adult population) represent more than a quarter of this figure (Staples 2004; Sentencing Project 2011).

Such numbers have stark implications for the integrity of the political process. In many states where closely contested elections are common, Republicans have used felon disenfranchisement to purge the voter rolls of minority voters (and to intimidate or confuse other minority voters). Even assuming a clean count of ballots, this disenfranchisement of black citizens likely made all the difference in the 2000 presidential elections and in other close races. Consider: If 2.3 percent of the adult population is barred from voting by law, and if a similar number of voters stay away from the polls because they mistakenly believe that they have been disenfranchised – for example, for a misdemeanor conviction or not realizing that their probationary period has ended – then a considerable portion of the public has been excluded from democracy (Uggen and Manza 2002).

The penal system churns the poor and marginal, rendering them all but unemployable, thus poorer and ever more marginal. This approach can only be understood as vindictive. This spirit of vindictiveness – the idea that law exists not to correct or balance but to punish – obviously animates the continuing popularity of capital punishment in the United States. Until the 5–4 Supreme Court decision in *Roper v. Simmons* in 2005, the United States even allowed the execution of minors. And although the Supreme Court has barred states from executing the mentally disabled, nothing prevents pro-death penalty states from defining mental disability more narrowly than less vindictive states.

Spectacles of punishment

At the beginning of *Discipline and Punish*, Foucault (1978: 7–17) contrasts sovereign with disciplinary power: under the old regime, executions and punishments were gruesome public spectacles; under the new regime, they generally will be increasingly painless, invisible affairs. Elias, too, contrasts premodern with modern sensibilities by noting that "sentence, execution, death" are progressively withdrawn from public view, "removed behind the scenes"; the arousal of pleasure in sadistic spectacles is said to be "abnormal" today (1994: 175, 172). Trends of the past 40 years would seem to complicate if not confound such observations. What has happened in the United States involves an intensification of both incarceration (the hidden, less visible part of punishment) and spectacularization: visible, public punishments, sometimes presented as news, sometimes as mass entertainment, sometimes imbricated with ideas about informed citizenship and "the need to know."

Americans, it would appear, adore punishment; they have become obsessed with it, addicted to it. Politically ambitious prosecutors have long relished the theatrical staging of "perp walks" for the evening news: unnecessarily manacled defendants are paraded like captured quarry before a crowd of photographers and videographers. Such values have leached into the broader world of commercial entertainment. Network police dramas, afternoon programs devoted to courtroom scenarios, and an entire cable channel, Court TV (now rechristened TruTV), put the "show" in "show trial" and reinforce the image of law as a punitive spectacle. Much of what reality television programs serve up is the spectacle of punishment, gratuitous humiliation: *Cops* and *Judge Judy*, obviously, but less obviously, judged competitions like *American Idol* and *Survivor* – "The tribe has spoken."

Among the images endlessly circulated on the Web are sex offender registries and police mug shots of celebrities, arrestees, or convicts. These fire the public's appetite for ever more public, ever more humiliating, and ever more stigmatizing forms of retribution. Some judges make convicts wear signs, post notices in their front yards, or perform some other public ritual as part of their punishment. Such forms of humiliation, in excess of fines paid or time served, are usually associated with "archaic" legal practices, but their application is growing, not diminishing, in the modern state.

Nowhere is the spectacle of crime and punishment more extravagantly enacted than in the case of sex crime, and on *Dateline NBC*'s "To Catch a Predator" series, a sweeps week staple, journalists partnered with cops to push the theater of cruelty to new lows. In 2006 Louis William Conradt, Jr., a 56-year-old district attorney living in Texas, was accused of making online advances to an adult decoy pretending to be a 13-year-old boy. The decoy attempted to lure Conradt to the "sting house" where, in the usual sequence of events, a certain ritual is enacted: the show's host, Chris Hansen, confronts and humiliates the suspect. Then, after Hansen tells the suspect he can leave, the cops move in to make a dramatic arrest. Even arrestees who offer no resistance are tackled, thrown to the ground, and violently subdued by swarming officers. But when Conradt did not show up at the designated house, the producers instead arranged a police raid on the district attorney's home. As police and the television crew stormed the house, Conradt shot and killed himself. One of the participating police officers is reported to have told the NBC producer, "That'll make good TV." In fact, the episode aired in 2007, and the series continued through 2008 (Cohen 2008; Stelter 2008). In the guise of producing public service exposes and undertaking investigative journalism, NBC has not blurred but erased distinctions between journalism, law enforcement, and the gratuitous arousal of its audience's baser instincts.

There is no direct relationship between Americans' fascination with the police blotter and real-world conditions of crime and depravity. This disconnect describes not only the tabloid world of infotainment, but also what passes for news in the serious public sphere. Although crime rates have fallen dramatically since the early 1990s, crime reportage has actually risen in inverse proportion. Half the lead stories on local news broadcasts are crime stories. As much as 50 percent of local news airtime in some locales is now devoted to crime reportage: prurient stories about sex abuse, lurid tales of gang violence, breathless accounts of callous predation (Hamilton 1998: 248–249; Macek 2006: 152–153; Trend 2007: 67). While the news media have profited from sensational coverage of the overblown crime beat, right-wing political interests have manipulated it, stoking fear of crime and predation to win elections – and, more enduringly, to reshape the social contract. This new social contract involves ever more sticks and ever fewer carrots.

Framings

How, then, to frame the surge of a punitive orientation in the justice system, along with the spread of a monitory, preemptive approach throughout other areas of social life? It is tempting to rehearse the familiar analyses of American exceptionalism, looking for the roots of present-day institutions in Puritanism, slave society, or rural and small-town values. Such analyses tend to reproduce the red/blue state divide, pitting "archaic" forms of coercion in Southern and Midwestern regions against the cosmopolitan and progressive norms of coastal urban cities. Such tropes can be invoked to explain certain features of the system, for example, comparatively higher incarceration rates in the South. But they cannot explain other features of the system, for example, comparatively more racialized patterns of incarceration in the North.

A scrupulous look at social trends does not support the reflexive notion that provincial or rustic components of US society are really the primary sources of punitive justice, either historically or today. Puritan witch hunters, Ku Klux Klansmen, intrusive social uplifters, and modern moral entrepreneurs who launch careers off crusades to get tough on crime are invariably middle-class townsfolk or suburbanites with a patina of education. Moreover, urban coastal states have been at the vanguard of the punitive turn. New York's Rockefeller drug laws, passed in 1973, set the stage for the passage of draconian drug laws in other states and at the federal level. (Such laws, with their minimum mandatory sentences for possession or distribution of small quantities of drugs, underpinned policies of mass incarceration.)

In any event, what was once "exceptional" about American legal practices was their aversion to punitive sanctions. The US Constitution has always prohibited torture ("cruel and unusual punishment"). As James Q. Whitman (2007: 251; see also Whitman 2003) reminds readers, once upon a time Europeans viewed the US prison system as a model of humane and enlightened practices, not as the scandal of the Western world. Foreign governments sent visiting delegations on tours of US penitentiaries to learn how to better manage their own penal systems. De Tocqueville extolled the mildness of punishment in America.

Victims and monsters

In opposition to authors who view excessive punitiveness as an essential, entrenched feature of US culture, I have stressed the recent nature of what Michael Sherry (2005) calls "the punitive turn" and I have tried to show how a series of contingencies sustained that turn. The social upheavals of the 1960s, which correlated with spiking crime rates, stirred fear of lawlessness in broad sectors of the working and middle class. Social conservatives targeted consequentialist approaches to punishment and legal protections that safeguarded the rights of the accused as *causes* of criminality; the resulting resentments against rule-breakers were institutionalized in the 1970s and 1980s. But what set trends in motion – varied forms of white backlash – is not necessarily what keeps them in motion, and waxing punitiveness has attached to various sorts of perils at various times: street crime, drug dealers, sex offenders, gangs, terrorism (Lancaster 2011: 139, 191–194, 219–222, 238–239). In other words, a brisk sequence of moral panics (Cohen 2002 [1972]) has stoked public anxieties – has defined the public in terms of such anxieties – and consolidated what sociologists have glossed a "culture of fear" (Glassner 1999). Species of monsters have populated the political landscape in rapid succession, and as against their monstrosity, variants of victimized innocents who cry out for retribution.

The mass media played an important role in these developments. By the 1970s television dramas, news reportage, and politicians all were focusing on the plight of the victim; these approaches reinforced visceral emotional responses and gave everyone a sense of personal vulnerability to criminal predation. Paul Virilio (2007: 28) has described such orchestrations of public affect, which "cripple the world with grief" and pave the way for revenge, as "emotional pollution." So primed, the white middle classes turned away from educated ideas about rehabilitation and humane punishment ("penal welfarism") to embrace harsh penalties and long prison sentences ("expressive punishment") (see Garland 2001: 3, 139–165).

Meanwhile, a continuous ratcheting up of punishment was prodded by a new social movement: the victims' rights movement. Didier Fassin and Richard Rechtman (2009) have analyzed the emergence of trauma as a master metaphor for collective suffering and an international foregrounding of victimhood as a basis for recognition and reparation. In the United States, these developments follow a distinctive trajectory. Born in the welfare state of the 1960s, subsequently transformed by moral panics of the 1970s, and eventually "Reaganized" (allied with conservative causes) in the 1980s, the victims' rights movement represents a curious blend of liberal and conservative forms (Lancaster 2011: 194–206). As discussions by Barbara Nelson (1984) and Wendy Brown (1995) might suggest, liberal political conventions – which tend to define government action narrowly, as intervention on behalf of the weakest and most vulnerable – set the stage for the promulgation of victimhood as a durable political identity, for attempts to "outlaw" injury, and for a punitive approach to crime. Marie Gottschalk (2006: 115–164) meticulously describes how American feminism contributed to the development of a specific sort of victims' rights movement in the United States: mainstream feminists made common cause with law-and-order conservatives, and some in the women's movement assisted with the promulgation of increasingly punitive laws. Submitted to certain types of pressure under certain conditions, liberal forms were bent into increasingly illiberal shape (Lancaster 2011: 178, 215).

Over time, the resulting carceral state has put down deep economic roots. Imprisoning millions of Americans for long periods of time succinctly accomplishes two feats: it creates "guard labor" (secure work for police and prison guards) to contain and control what Marx called "surplus labor" at a time when the unionized industrial sector was in steep decline. Reversing the usual arguments, I have tried to show that the distinctly American variant of deregulated, privatized capitalism (neoliberalism) is less a cause than a consequence of the punitive turn in US culture (Lancaster 2011: 220–224).

Form and norm

It is not then the brute, the instinctive, or the primitive that should concern us here, but rather, the production of monsters and monstrosity, the deliberate stoking of fear and rage, which is accomplished by an elaborate and sophisticated institutional apparatus spanning advocacy groups, media, law enforcement, political actors, and segments of the state. In this context, the urge to punish is less a "natural" or "instinctual" phenomenon than a systematically cultivated response.

And what happens to a morality ruled by fear, to legal codes driven by panic, to a public culture keyed to the emotional register of rage? In this curious space, a much darker sociology might be planted than what obtains in the classical literature – at least on its brighter, sunnier side. Even Durkheim allowed that the march of civilization is beset by crises, breakdowns, or losses of meaning (anomie), and Elias understood all too well that the banishment of unpleasant topics from polite society, which is part of the civilization process, opens up spaces out of sight and out of mind where civilization runs in reverse. Exaggerated fear of crime produces just this boomerang effect: the savagery of "primitive" violence solicits "civilized" brutality. The sex panics about which I have written would seem a paradigmatic example of this paradoxical process: a more "civilized" sensitivity to child maltreatment unleashes the "barbarism" of current sex offender laws.

Nietzsche's riffs on *ressentiment* tell us much of what we need to know about the psychological reverb effect between fear and loathing in the rage to punish:

> For every sufferer instinctively seeks a cause for his suffering, more exactly, an agent; still more specifically, a *guilty* agent who is susceptible to suffering – in short, some living thing upon which he can, on some pretext or other, vent his affects, actually or in effigy ... This ... constitutes the actual physiological cause of *ressentiment*, vengefulness, and the like: a desire to *deaden pain by means of affects*, ... to *deaden*, by means of a more violent emotion of any kind, a tormenting, secret pain that is becoming unendurable, and to drive it out of consciousness at least for the moment: for that one requires an affect, as savage an affect as possible, and, in order to excite that, any pretext at all. (1969: 127; see also Brown 1995: 7, 26, 68)

But more than that – when fear becomes the normative condition, I suggest, it inaugurates a broken social order based on mistrust, resentment, and ill will. The pervasive assumption that anonymous, lurking others cannot be trusted undermines goodwill and feeds a sort of poisoned solidarity: We shall all be diligent in monitoring each other for signs of transgression.[7] This compulsion to surveil reverberates, internalized, in the psyche. It predicates an authoritarian, fear-based ethics that Vygotsky (1997 [1929]: 227) once glossed the "policeman of the soul." Of course this worldview mandates preemption, intense punishments. Coercion is the only language the bad man will understand.

Fear induces a dread of the other, a tear in the social fabric, and a propensity toward violence. Violence, masked as retribution, cannot be seen as aggression, nor can the harm it inflicts ever be acknowledged. The emergent republic of fear thus constructs an essentially negative sense of community, nation, and social good. Once established, this negativity becomes self-perpetuating (thus its ability to attach to different objects at different moments in a sped-up history of the present). Citizenship becomes tantamount to vigilant surveillance, a conception Americans once ridiculed as a defining feature of totalitarian societies. Law becomes an obsessive-compulsive process: the closing of imaginary "loopholes," the proscription of ever more closely circumscribed behaviors. Procedures once deemed anathema to democratic governance become first thinkable, then necessary, and at last unavoidable.

Exception or rule?

The Italian philosopher Giorgio Agamben gives some insight into law in an anomic condition. In *State of Exception* (2004), Agamben theorizes executive power in modern states as the power of exception: the power, in an emergency, to bypass normal legal procedures, to suspend constitutional rights, and to issue impromptu laws. In the immediate context of the USA Patriot Act and the war on terror, and against a wider backdrop framed by domestic and international crises, Agamben ominously notes "a continuing tendency in all of the Western democracies": "The declaration of the state of exception has gradually been replaced by an unprecedented generalization of the paradigm of security as the normal technique of government." By degrees the norm is replaced by the exception. Modern democracies are becoming "protected democracies" (Agamben 2004: 6–7, 14–16). Perpetual punishment looms large in the resulting state apparatus, and preventive measures become the order of the day.

Much of what happens in the realm of governance today is premised on the existence of this or that emergency, some state of affairs so menacing that measures at once protective, preemptive, and punitive are said to be in order. These measures may be called "exceptional" in the sense that they depart from classical traditions of law, perhaps especially guarantees against excessive punishment and *ex post facto* provisions. But *State of Exception* is marred by gaps. Curiously absent from Agamben's analysis is any reckoning with irrational, imaginative, or phantasmic elements in the developments he describes. This, it seems to me, makes the exceptional state seem far more rational than it is. Agamben's depiction of law as an abstract, self-generating system subject to periodic perturbations tends to remove law from its historical contexts. The notion that the exceptional state both exceeds and lies at the perpetual font of law poses a conundrum of the sort that invariably amuses structuralists and poststructuralists. But it is difficult to see how placing the exception at the "threshold" or "edge" of normative law sheds light on how any particular set of laws works as a system or how it breaks down during a crisis. Ahistorical thinking has other consequences: the implicit equation of Guantánamo with Auschwitz, as an instance of sovereign power over "bare life," is too broad to be useful for purposes other than rhetorical ones.

What Agamben's textual study of legal documents and political theory ultimately fails to disclose is how deeply embedded undemocratic trends are in both government *and* civil society and how these trends are involved with deeper institutional and political-economic shifts. Far from being restricted to the presidency, the "security paradigm" and its associated forms of action are distributed across executive, legislative, and judicial functions of government. Far from being confined to organs of government proper, the state of panic (as I dub it) is spread across a style of journalism, a mode of activism, a kind of civic ideal, and a way of thinking. Precisely what goes missing in Agamben's analysis, then, is the connection between democracy and repression, such that the public is driven by outrage or fear to support undemocratic policies. Perhaps the most pernicious effect of these pressures on legal norms is not that they entail a suspension of law or rule by decree, but that they subject the law itself to a slow, constant revision; they lodge exceptionality inside the rule, where it remains in force long after any panic or crisis has passed.

Sex crime panics seem to me paradigmatic of this process. A modern sequence of agitations begins with the satanic ritual abuse day-care panics of the 1980s; similar themes are taken up in the 1990s by true crime stories of outrages against helpless children, and these continue into the present. No doubt these panics, with their exaggerated fears for the safety of children, were fueled by pervasive anxieties about the condition of the heterosexual nuclear family, perceived by many as being "in decline."

They were also significantly buttressed by variants of liberal rhetoric and progressive narratives of rescue. These moral panics involve coordinated efforts among organized civil society, mass media, and the state; they blur distinctions between the real and the delusional, statistically common and statistically anomalous events – and they show how fear of outsized monsters stokes the will to punish and undermines democratic legal norms. The resulting laws codify exceptional horrors and make once exceptional conditions the rule. What seems most characteristic about Megan's Law (which mandated public registries for a wide variety of sex offenders), variants of Jessica's Law (which expel sex offenders from homes and workplaces in broadly designated child safety zones), civil confinement procedures (which allow for the indefinite detention of some sex offenders after their criminal sentences have been served), and the Adam Walsh Act (which empowers the attorney general to apply new, harsher provisions retroactively) is first that they turn certain types of offenders into demonized objects of perpetual punishment and supervision, and second that these techniques apply to ever broader categories of miscreants (including offenders whose crimes involved no coercion and sometimes no sex or physical contact) (Lancaster 2011: 78–81, 89–91).

Now few would argue that American sex crime laws have been as toxic to democratic legal norms as the signing of statements issued by President George W. Bush, which produced a legal netherworld populated by "unlawful enemy combatants" subject to policies of indefinite detention and torture. I point out only that sex crime laws have circumscribed the lives of far larger numbers of people who "cannot be integrated into the political [or social] system" (Agamben 2004: 2). This process of making the law into something that appears unlawful by classical standards has happened over a much longer period of time, and it continues to intensify. In this process, sex offenders are progressively stripped of rights not because they are "unclassifiable" and thus relegated to the lacunae of normal law but by dint of the development of a classification system that lodges them in closely written definitions of law. In other words, the production of categories of people who have diminished rights has happened not by undemocratic or unlawful means but by means of a process that is effectively poisoned while remaining democratic and lawful. The state of exception passes when crises end and edicts are retired. But the state of panic, which is abnormal, comes to be written at the heart of law, which provides norms.

Anxiety (dis)order

Engin Isin (2004) has traced the emergence of what he calls "the neurotic citizen." His brisk paper asserts that the prevailing models of governance and governability are marred by a central weakness: what if the subject who stands at the center of governance is not well balanced or clear-headed? In contrast to Foucault's biopolitical subject, who is governable because he or she is rational, calculating, and seeks self-improvement, or the subject of risk theory, who is informed, competent, and seeks to reduce or manage exposure to risk, Isin poses the neurotic citizen, who is defined by irrational fears and impossible wants. This neurotic citizen is "anxious, under stress and increasingly insecure"; he or she governs himself/herself "through responses to anxieties and uncertainties" (Isin 2004: 225, 223). Isin lays out a set of useful shorthand terms: "governing through neurosis" (as opposed to governing through risk), and neuropolitics (as opposed to biopolitics).

There is much that is useful here. But Isin's lodging of the neurotic citizen within the regime of neoliberalism fails to draw out an obvious and important ideological connection between the naturalization of economic insecurity and the politicization of personal insecurity. Although the punitive turn began before the neoliberal turn, its ideas about victimization now have the effect of calling attention to criminal micropredation at a time of untrammeled economic macropredation. Surely this is an important part of the picture.

And I wonder whether Isin's reliance on neurosis as master-trope misses the mark. In neurosis, the ego tries to manage conflict between the superego and the id by repressing a desire from the id, and this abnegation produces a symptom (distress, anxiety, obsessive-compulsive disorders, hysteria, or depression, but also art, science, and other forms of sublimation) (Isin 2004: 223–224). Neurotic symptoms are evident enough in the present political landscape, but many of the symptoms of collective disturbance register in the psychotic range. In psychosis, the ego resolves a conflict between the id and the superego by detaching from a part of reality, or by projecting around itself a delusional world. A great many of the moral panics of the past 40 years clearly have taken paranoid or delusional form. The satanic ritual abuse day-care panics, which fostered irrational anxieties, stimulated an expansion of child protective services, and initiated the drafting of new laws and procedures, were most clearly of this type (Lancaster 2011: 46–56).

Pace Isin, *The History of Sexuality* provides useful conceptual tools for thinking about modern moral panics and social anxieties. This is especially the case in connection with race and class relations. Recall how Foucault (1980: 122–127) periodizes biopolitics in terms of class contests: He treats the role played by sex in class definitions and class struggles at the outset of European modernity. Aristocratic rulers of the old feudal regime had based their right to rule on kinship, descent, *blood*. In contrast, the rising bourgeoisie contested blood right and asserted its right to rule based on fitness, life force, *vitality*. The nascent class cultivated this vitality in myriad eighteenth- and nineteenth-century hygienic practices, and in those practices two methods repeatedly recur: one involves sexual abstention, prohibition, the repression of sex; the other involves the control, use, and productive disciplining of sex.

The entrenched bourgeoisie, whose power today derives from its ownership of capital and the domination of capital over every sphere of economic activity, no longer relies on these procedures, but not so the striving middle class (broadly defined to include the stable working class). And when bourgeois values crossed the Atlantic, they gained an especially durable purchase. Because the United States lacks both an aristocratic tradition and a strong socialist movement, bourgeois values and identities are stamped indelibly everywhere. The white middle class has repeatedly asserted its claim to be the universal class, the class whose values are life-sustaining, by keeping vigil against moral lassitude and by undergoing periodic purifications, renewals, and moral renovations. In these undertakings it has occasionally tilted against the "bluebloods," whose refined tastes and work-free money the middle class equates with sexual decadence, but the main adversaries of the middle class are the nonwhite lower classes (whose profligate sexuality and implicit criminality are held to threaten the social order from without) and white sexual deviants (who threaten the order from within). Such definitions have much to do with the domestication and pacification of the working class historically; remain centrally ingredient to the manufacture of whiteness and middle-classness today; they are deeply embedded in contemporary political neuroses; and they have everything to do with the elaboration of the modern carceral state.

Imbalanced subjects and irrational citizens of the emergent system might be productively mapped against Foucault's basic gridwork. Contemporary sex and crime panics typically revolve around a distinctly nonrational concept that might be deemed biopolitical, in the sense that it corresponds to a theory of health: the *innocence* of the victim. Foucault's old saw about nineteenth-century campaigns against masturbation, a linchpin of that century's sexual hygienics, is instructive here. The modern imagination of innocence, like the antecedent prohibition of acts that are not really susceptible to eradication, seems illogical on the face of it but nonetheless produces logical effects: it facilitates the development of new webs of authority, new forms of expertise; it leads to the elaboration of new suspicions, new disciplining institutions, and new subjectivities. The secrecy it forces stimulates the laying of traps and the application of surveillance technologies at new sites. The production of new demonologies, the conjuring of outsized risks and harms – which are not distinguished from actual risks and real harms – is part of this work, but the prohibited act is not so much the enemy of as the support for these procedures (Foucault 1980: 41–42). And so less than rational ideas come to define the operational logic of far-flung practices.

Lastly, Foucault acknowledged that biopower is sometimes organized in terms of racisms and sexual phobias. Many of these biopolitical moments have taken the form of what we might call "moral panics." Biological criminals, sexual perverts, and racial degenerates were among the earliest inventions of the emergent disciplines, and the hunt for the biopolitical monster is a recurring feature of biopower. Perhaps what has happened in US culture is, in part, a retrogression to an earlier mode of biopower; the hunt for the monster has become a perpetual condition. The result is a curious admixture of social forms. The middle term in Foucault's three-part suit – the correctional approach – all but disappears. Restraints on power associated with "disciplining" give way to "punishment" and the rage for more and more of it. But the punitive state is not simply a retreat to premodern practices. Today the role of the sovereign is not played by the king; rather, ongoing social crusades are undertaken on behalf of the population, its biopolitical health and well-being. Today, it is the populace – or a segment of it speaking on behalf of the rest – who claims that society is in peril and who thus assumes the right (democratically expressed by elected officials, lawmakers, and judges) to inflict increasingly public and spectacularized punishments on a variety of enemies within and without.

Should we, then, name a fourth regime of power – after the sovereign, the disciplinary, and the biopolitical – "panic"? If so, this regime would be the mutant offspring of sovereign power and biopower.[8] Its practices would tether technical advances in biopower and cyber-technology to increasingly irrational undertakings, twenty-first-century technologies to nineteenth-century concepts. I emphasize the uniqueness of this regime. Archaic tyrannies and antecedent totalitarianisms, of course, also were based on fear, but in a different fashion. Elites terrorized the masses directly, to extort their acquiescence. And ancient regimes sometimes directed pogroms against witches, Jews, perverts, and others – but these horrors, too, seem different from the present orchestrations of anxiety. The modern state of panic traffics in fear, not as a special effect, nor to stand down adversaries, nor as a safety valve for the release of pent-up social pressures, nor even to terrorize subjugated peoples, but as the justification for its own existence, as ballast and support for its rule, as the very definition of its democracy, and as the social cement that holds things together. Power flows through the nervous system of a body politic paralyzed by dread. Ruled and rulers alike are equally trapped in fear.

Panics and hysterias have broken out from time immemorial, wherever humans have lived under conditions that allow for rumor. And in the past, those who would intimidate opposition, unseat authority, or ride fear into power have manipulated gossip, scandal, and collective disturbances. But that is to say that panic is power in an abnormal condition, in a process of siege, crisis, mischief, or instability. Panic was the wild card of the ancient regimes: an instrument to be selectively applied, but also the prospect of systemic breakdown. It could never before constitute a steady state, a durable regime of power, a universal tendency toward hypochondria, obsessive-compulsive behaviors, and deliriums, because reliable techniques for its communication and perpetuation did not exist. Not so today. Never before have so many mechanisms existed for panic's stoking, democratization, modulation, and institutionalization. The present system's normative operational mode does not correspond to power in any previously existing normative mode.

Risks remain to this twitchy, mass-mediated system, of course, and not only for all the usual suspects: scapegoats, whipping boys, objects of unmodulated dread and perpetual punishment. One risk, as Paul Virilio notes, is that the besieged will be "buried alive … behind their protective enclosures" (2007: 58). Another is the accidental release of a "terror that is unspeakable and counterproductive" for its anonymous managers (16). Yet another outcome, perhaps, was foreseen by Franz Kafka, whose protagonist in "The Penal Colony" has come to masochistically adore, to mystically crave punishment: he straps himself into the discombobulating contraption, yet is in the end deprived of the exquisite sentence to be written on the body of the condemned.

Conclusion

What is vexing about punishment – which cannot quite be got rid of in consequentialist approaches – remains in the founding violence of the terms: a disowned violence attributed to the primitive. And so the history of enlightened reforms is littered with spectacles of cruelty: Bentham's whipping machine, frontal lobotomies, and shock therapies: a succession of practices undertaken in the name of civilization then subsequently renounced as barbaric. It might be said that penal modernism never could fully acknowledge its own quotidian forms of violence and coercion. It might also be said that the Enlightenment project of discipline always harbors within it the potential for its own breakdown, its relapse into the very modes of savagery it attributes to the primitive, the archaic, or the provincial. This is Critique of Enlightenment 101.

Critique of the present should go beyond these terms, but it is difficult to see just how. No tidy theory can quite explain the surge of a punitive culture in the United States. We cannot say yet what will be the outcome of present trends: whether they will continue another 40 years. There are signs that prison rates are topping out and may be poised for a decline – but the use of electronic monitoring, which offloads the costs of imprisonment onto offenders and their families, is growing. We cannot even yet be sure that excessive punishment is entirely a US phenomenon; there are signs that the punitive approach is spreading across the Atlantic (Wacquant 2012).

We must instead tell what happened and try to describe how it happened. I have thus kept to a rigorously historicist approach, describing how a sequence of shocks and crises were metabolized in certain manners, and how these came to be articulated into a new institutional nexus. No doubt this new nexus connects not only the state, laws, social movements, and mass media but also a personality type, modes of subjectivity, a new concept of citizenship.

If no one theory can quite adequately describe these interconnections, a critical approach can at least describe the gaps in existing theories. I have tried to do just that. And if the resulting dispensation cannot be readily mapped onto oppositions between progress and reaction, liberal and conservative, then it might be better to say that there is a tension, a push and pull, at work in decades-long trends, and that both liberals and conservatives have played their roles. Just as sex panics of the period correlate to the rise of gay visibility and a loosening of other sexual strictures, the mass incarceration of black and brown men takes off in the post-civil rights era and correlates with the growth of a minority middle class (Lancaster 2011: 233–235). Finally, if what has happened is that a certain social order has been erected in the name of morality and justice, then surely the resulting apparatus demands not simply social analysis, in the usual sense, but also moral criticism. Gauged by the civilizational clock – the only measure US culture has ever consistently applied to itself – Americans have been marching in reverse for 40 years. I have thus used a certain language of decay, breakage, or discombobulation: ordinary solidarity has been "poisoned"; the law has been "hollowed out"; norms have become distorted; biopower has retrogressed to an early mode. The forms of power on display were once associated with crisis and breakdown; these have become institutionalized today. The point, of course, is to view these not as signs of loss but as new productive conditions.

Brecht's old maxim seems apposite: Start not from the good old days but from the bad new ones.

Acknowledgments

Some passages contained in this essay appeared in *Sex Panic and the Punitive State* (Berkeley: University of California Press, 2011). These are used by permission of the press.

NOTES

1 I leave aside long-running debates over the relationship between morality and law in theories of jurisprudence. See, for instance, Hart 1958.

2 For an overview of biopower, see Rabinow and Rose 2006.

3 I draw current incarceration rates come from the website maintained by the International Centre for Prison Studies at King's College London, at http://www.prisonstudies.org/info/worldbrief/wpb_country.php?country=147, accessed Mar. 21, 2012. On the fall and rise of rates over time, see Bruner 2003: 44–46.

4 See International Centre for Prison Studies, and the Sentencing Project's website at www.sentencingproject.org, as well as the Pew Center on the States 2008.
5 I draw the phrase "carceral state" from Foucault's (1978) "carceral system," which is frequently glossed as "carceral society." See also Gottschalk 2006: 1–17; 2008.
6 The piece, drafted by Merleau-Ponty and endorsed by Sartre, was originally published as an editorial in *Les temps modernes.*
7 My argument here goes beyond conventional sociological work on trust. The attitude I am describing resonates more with the sort of social paranoia that produces lynchings and witchcraft accusations. See, e.g., Lewis and Weigert 1985: 968–969, 979.
8 For a different tack on the admixture of forms of power, see Deleuze 1992.

REFERENCES

Agamben, Giorgio (2004) *State of Exception.* Chicago: University of Chicago Press.

Alexander, Michelle (2010) *The New Jim Crow: Mass Incarceration in the Age of Colorblindness.* New York: New Press.

Bacon, Francis (2002) *The Major Works*, ed. Brian Vickers. Oxford: Oxford University Press.

Beccaria of Milan, Marquis (1872 [1764]) *An Essay on Crimes and Punishments ... with a commentary by M. de Voltaire. A New Edition Corrected.* Albany, NY: W. C. Little. At http://oll.libertyfund.org/index.php?option=com_staticxt&staticfile=show.php%3Ftitle=2193&Itemid=27, accessed Mar. 13, 2012.

Bentham, Jeremy (2000) *Selected Writings on Utilitarianism.* Ware: Wordsworth.

Bonczar, Thomas P. (2003) *Prevalence of Imprisonment in the U.S. Population, 1974–2001.* Bureau of Justice Statistics Special Report. Washington, DC: US Department of Justice. National Criminal Justice Reference Service no. 197976. At http://bjs.ojp.usdoj.gov/content/pub/pdf/piusp01.pdf, accessed Mar. 13, 2012.

Brown, Wendy (1995) *States of Injury: Power and Freedom in Late Modernity.* Princeton: Princeton University Press.

Bruner, Jerome S. (2003) Do Not Pass Go. *New York Review of Books* (Sept. 25), 44–46.

Cohen, Adam (2008) What's on TV Tonight? Humiliation to the Point of Suicide. *New York Times* (Mar. 10), A16.

Cohen, Nick (2003) 661 New Crimes and Counting. *New Statesman* 16(764): 18.

Cohen, Stanley (2002 [1972]) *Folk Devils and Moral Panics*, 30th anniversary edn. New York: Routledge.

Deleuze, Gilles (1992) Postscript on the Societies of Control. *October* 59: 3–7.

Durkheim, Emile (1984 [1893]) *The Division of Labor in Society*, intro. Lewis Coser. New York: Free Press.

Dyer, Joel (2000) *The Perpetual Prisoner Machine: How America Profits from Crime.* Boulder, CO: Westview.

Egan, Timothy (1999) Hard Time: Less Crime, More Criminals. *New York Times* (Mar. 7), 4 (Week in Review), 1.

Elias, Norbert (1994 [1939]) *The Civilizing Process: Sociogenetic and Psychogenetic Investigations*, rev. edn., trans. Edmund Jephcott. Oxford: Blackwell.

Fassin, Didier and Rechtman, Richard (2009) *The Empire of Trauma: An Inquiry into the Condition of Victimhood*, trans. Rachel Gomme. Princeton: Princeton University Press.

Foucault, Michel (1978) *Discipline and Punish: The Birth of the Prison*, trans. Alan Sheridan. New York: Pantheon.

Foucault, Michel (1980) *The History of Sexuality*, vol. 1: *An Introduction*, trans. Robert Hurley. New York: Vintage.

Foucault, Michel (2008) *The Birth of Biopolitics: Lectures at the College de France, 1978–1979*, ed. Michel Senellart; trans. Graham Burchell. New York: Palgrave Macmillan.

Garland, David (2001) *The Culture of Control: Crime and Social Order in Contemporary Society.* Chicago: University of Chicago Press.

Glassner, Barry (1999) *The Culture of Fear: Why Americans Are Afraid of the Wrong Things: Crime, Drugs, Minorities, Teen Moms, Killer Kids, Mutant Microbes, Plane Crashes, Road Rage, & So Much More.* New York: Basic Books.

Gonnerman, Jennifer (2004) A Beaten Path Back to Prison. *New York Times* (May 8), A17 (Op-Ed).

Gottschalk, Marie (2006) *The Prison and the Gallows: The Politics of Mass Incarceration in America.* Cambridge: Cambridge University Press.

Gottschalk, Marie (2008) Hiding in Plain Sight: American Politics and the Carceral State. *Annual Review of Political Science* 11: 235–260.

Hamilton, James T. (1998) *Channeling Violence: The Economic Market for Violent Television Programming.* Princeton: Princeton University Press.

Hart, H. L. A. (1958) Positivism and the Separation of Law and Morals. *Harvard Law Review* 71(4): 593–629.

Isin, Engin F. (2004) The Neurotic Citizen. *Citizenship Studies* 8(3): 217–235.

Knight, William K. (1911) The Psychology of Punitive Justice. *Philosophical Review* 20(6): 622–635.

Lancaster, Roger N. (2011) *Sex Panic and the Punitive State.* Berkeley: University of California Press.

Lévi-Strauss, Claude (1952) *Race and History.* Paris: UNESCO.

Lévi-Strauss, Claude (1992 [1955]) *Tristes Tropiques*, trans. John Weightman and Doreen Weightman. New York: Penguin.

Lewis, J. David and Weigert, Andrew (1985) Trust as a Social Reality. *Social Forces* 63(4): 967–985.

Macek, Steve (2006) *Urban Nightmares: The Media, the Right, and the Moral Panic over the City.* Minneapolis: University of Minnesota Press.

Malinowski, Bronislaw (1926) *Crime and Custom in Savage Society.* London: Kegan Paul, Trench, Trübner.

Mead, George H. (1918) The Psychology of Punitive Justice. *American Journal of Sociology* 23(5): 577–602.

Merleau-Ponty, Maurice (1964 [1950]) The USSR and the Camps. In *Signs*, trans. Richard C. McCleary. Evanston, IL: Northwestern University Press, pp. 263–273.

Nader, Laura (1990) *Harmony Ideology: Justice and Control in a Zapotec Mountain Village.* Stanford: Stanford University Press.

Nelson, Barbara J. (1984) *Making an Issue of Child Abuse: Political Agenda Setting for Social Problems.* Chicago: University of Chicago Press.

Nietzsche, Friedrich (1969) *On the Genealogy of Morals*, trans. Walter Kaufmann and R. J. Hollingdale. New York: Vintage.

Pew Center on the States (2008) *One in 100: Behind Bars in America 2008.* Washington, DC: PewCharitableTrusts.Athttp://www.pewcenteronthestates.org/uploadedFiles/8015PCTS_Prison08_FINAL_2-1-1_FORWEB.pdf, accessed Mar. 13, 2012.

Plato (2000) *Laws*, trans. Benjamin Jowett. Amherst, MA: Prometheus.

Pratt, John (2004) Elias and Modern Penal Development. In Steven Loyal and Stephen Quilly (eds.), *The Sociology of Norbert Elias.* Cambridge: Cambridge University Press, pp. 212–228.

Rabinow, Paul and Rose, Nikolas (2006) Biopower Today. *BioSocieties* 1: 195–217.

Sentencing Project (2011) Felony Disenfranchisement Laws in the United States. At http://www.sentencingproject.org/doc/publications/fd_bs_fdlawsinusDec11.pdf, accessed Mar. 21, 2012.

Sherry, Michael (2005) Dead or Alive: American Vengeance Goes Global. *Review of International Relations* [special issue, "Force and Diplomacy"] 31: 245–263.

Staples, Brent (2004) How Denying the Vote to Ex-Offenders Undermines Democracy. *New York Times* (Sept. 17): A26 (Opinion).

Stelter, Brian (2008) NBC Settles with Family That Blamed a TV Investigation for a Man's Suicide. *New York Times* (June 26), C03.

Trend, David (2007) *The Myth of Media Violence: A Critical Introduction*. Oxford: Blackwell.

Uggen, Christopher and Manza, Jeff (2002) Democratic Contraction? Political Consequences of Felon Disenfranchisement in the United States. *American Sociological Review* 67(6): 777–803.

Urban Institute (2002) Beyond the Prison Gates: The State of Parole in America. Nov. 5. At http://www.urban.org/url.cfm?ID=900567, accessed Mar. 13, 2012.

Virilio, Paul (2007) *The Original Accident*, trans. Julie Rose. Cambridge: Polity.

Vygotsky, Lev (1997 [1929]) Ethical Behavior. In *Educational Psychology*, trans. Robert Silverman. Boca Raton, FL: St. Lucie.

Wacquant, Loic (2012) The Prison is an Outlaw Institution. *Howard Journal of Criminal Justice* 51(1): 1–15.

Washington Post (2006) U.S. Prison Population Sets Record. *Washington Post* (Dec. 1), A03.

Westermarck, Edward (1906) *The Origin and Development of the Moral Ideas*. New York: Macmillan.

Whitman, James Q. (2003) *Harsh Justice: Criminal Punishment and the Widening Divide Between America and Europe*. Oxford: Oxford University Press.

Whitman, James Q. (2007) What Happened to Tocqueville's America? *Social Research* 74(2): 251–268.

Willoughby, Westel W. (1910) *Social Justice: A Critical Essay*. New York: Macmillan.

CHAPTER 30

Borders

Josiah M. Heyman and John Symons

The policies and practices found at international borders result from a tangled and often conflicting variety of normative and pragmatic factors. In this essay we work to clarify the moral status of international borders and discuss the kinds of moral reasoning and related actions that people engage in relative to borders. While there are many different activities at borders, we focus on migration, due to the existence of a well-defined debate in moral philosophy and the wealth of anthropological evidence on the topic. We examine two absolute positions commonly found in moral and political philosophy, national sovereignty, and moral universalism, and then we explore the presence of more complex alternatives found in everyday border practices of border crossing and connections. From this, we develop the view that the current system of migration from poor to prosperous countries creates new kinds of relationships between people and thereby involves new patterns of moral obligation. A proper understanding of these obligations requires more attention to empirical phenomena at borders than is common in moral philosophy and political theory, bringing anthropology and related fields to the fore. We focus on the United States–Mexico border, the region where we work, but we bring in relevant material from other world regions; we believe that general implications can be drawn concerning the moral status of international borders more broadly. While we focus on ideas and practices about international borders, we place that in the wider moral economy of migration and group boundaries within and across societies (Fassin 2011).

We begin with a brief introduction to the existing literature on borders and migration in moral and political philosophy before turning to the social scientific evidence concerning moral views of various border issues. Through this, we offer a useful distinction between empirical border regions and the "border" imagined in the national interior. We then explore more deeply the various moral frameworks, sentiments, and practices by dwellers in national interiors toward migrants and border issues, activists drawn toward

A Companion to Moral Anthropology, First Edition. Edited by Didier Fassin.

the international border, long-distance migrants and migration law enforcers, and finally established border-region dwellers. We conclude by stating our own moral analysis that differs in important respects from the existing literature in philosophy and political theory, and that builds on various empirical observations in the preceding survey.

A Dilemma at the Heart of Liberal Democracy: Moral and Political Philosophers on International Borders

Although our inquiry centers on anthropology and related social sciences, it is helpful to survey the main positions in moral and political philosophy, and relatedly political theory, so as not to reinvent the wheel. These positions are not limited to scholars, but partially capture aspects of moral thinking and practice in various communities.

Territorially bounded geographical spaces in which people can legitimately exercise political agency have long been understood as a condition for the possibility of modern citizenship. However, transnational migration has posed a basic challenge to the idea of citizenship as a nonarbitrary and morally legitimate institution. Most obviously, the presence of migrants challenges egalitarian conceptions of citizenship and civil rights insofar as migrants are persons within the territory of some community who are to some extent or other not permitted to participate in the political decisions of that community. Seyla Benhabib aptly describes the philosophical problem as follows: "From a philosophical point of view, transnational migrations bring to the fore the constitutive dilemma at the heart of liberal democracies: between sovereign self-determination claims on the one hand and adherence to universal human rights principles on the other" (2004: 2).

Migrants have a more pressing stake in the future of their host countries than tourists or other temporary visitors. However, like tourists and other aliens, migrants are excluded, to varying degrees, from participation in political decision-making. The exclusion of migrants happens in virtue of their being born beyond the territorial boundaries of the state or by virtue of not having the specified kind of putative coethnic or familial relation to existing citizens. Thus, the border plays a central role in the system of exclusion and self-determination that Benhabib identifies as the constitutive dilemma at the heart of liberal democracy.

While not logically bound to political self-determination, and perhaps more variable for that reason, borders that enclose territories also affect various legal statuses, rights, and claims to societally distributed resources. Cara Nine (2008), for example, has argued for a Lockean defense of international borders, arguing that political communities have the right to exclude others from access to their resources. Open border policies, in her view, undermine the possibility for community self-determination. Her argument emphasizes the importance of sovereign self-determination, in particular the right to exclusion (thus justifying border and interior migration enforcement) by contrast with arguments for universal rights to transit and access.

By contrast, for philosophers who adopt some version of cosmopolitanism, the arbitrariness of international borders undermines their role in legitimizing exclusion. Charles Beitz (1999 [1979]) challenged the view that the sovereignty of states, as expressed in existing borders, trumps considerations of the universality of human rights. Later, Joseph Carens (1987) extended the argument from critiquing the moral arbitrariness of borders to the view that we are obligated to have a system of open borders. Carens argued that freedom of movement is a more significant right than the right of a political community to exclude outsiders. We will refer to this strong position as "univeralism." In a more nuanced position, Benhabib (2004) and other cosmopolitans have argued against strict exclusion of migrants from membership in political communities and more specifically argued for a right to citizenship for aliens who have fulfilled certain conditions.

Arguments like Nine's derive from assumptions concerning the effects of immigrants on the existing capacity for self-determination among natives. Whether it is the case that the rights of native populations are overridden in any significant way by a growing population of immigrants is, at least partly, an empirical question; indeed, perhaps the various effects of migration actually strengthen real capabilities for self-determination. Establishing the precise nature in which a member of the native population is harmed by the arrival of an immigrant might involve, for example, an understanding of the economic impact of migration, the advantages (if any) conferred on natives in a society that has a mix of citizens and immigrants, the emergent ties to the new society, and so on. The philosophical arguments concerning borders have, perhaps of necessity, been abstract and not directly engaged with the kind of empirical data that would settle such questions. Nevertheless, as we shall see, the anthropological study of borders is attuned to what Benhabib called a dilemma at the heart of liberal democracy.

The philosophical debate concerning the moral status of borders exhibits a variety of sophisticated variations on universalism and sovereigntism. These two poles form relatively clean conceptual opposites. Naturally, matters are not so simple in the daily lives of border people. Given that people do not act according to pure versions of sovereigntism or universalism, their moral reasoning around decision-making is a complicated matter. As we will see, folk cosmopolitanism and folk sovereigntism are often present and in tension simultaneously. Beyond that, we find in border life complex patterns of moral sentiments and reasoning that do not fit either model well, because they are more contextual than absolute; they emerge from relations between host society residents, migrants, and other border crossers. The important point is not just that such phenomena are complex, but that they derive from activities of creating and maintaining relations among persons that cross political borders and social boundaries. The existing universalist and sovereigntist philosophical and political-theoretical positions are in their nature too absolute, and thus discard the subtlety of moral ties and duties based on interactions within and across borders. We propose a sophisticated and powerful moral approach, as much of interest to philosophers and political theorists as social scientists, which arises from attending to how people connect to each other – which admittedly is varied and contradictory – and then generalizing a moral framework from this relational view. We find particularly suggestive evidence in the subtle quality of borderlanders' reasoning about the realities of their home region, rather than the absolutes of the border imagined from a distance.

Borders, the US–Mexico border, and *the Border*

International borders play a variety of roles in political, economic, and social life. The multivalent quality of borders means that for some, borders are becoming more rigid and salient, while others are finding them more permeable and less important. The North American Free Trade Agreement (NAFTA), for example, helped to create a US–Mexico border that is easier to traverse for privileged travelers, such as transnational managers, as well as for investments and commodities; while at the same time – and probably for connected reasons – it became harder to cross for Mexican workers and their families (Heyman 1999b; Nevins 2010). By reference to borders, then, some people inside the national territory are still envisioned and treated as outsiders, such as Mexican migrants within the United States or Africans in Europe, while others are envisioned and treated as unbounded, even though they have also crossed borders, such as prosperous white Europeans (Sasse and Thielemann 2005; Fassin 2011). Yet couching the matter in terms of wealthy and poor or white and nonwhite people is an oversimplification, given how a variety of nationalities, immigration statuses, and life experiences affect actual abilities to cross various international boundaries (e.g., Heyman 2004). Mobility is a key axis of social inequality in the contemporary world (Heyman 2009, 2010; Pallitto and Heyman 2008). As part of this, border regimes treat people differentially, a diversity that is shaped by and affects moral thinking about borders.

Likewise, there are multiple moral registers concerning the border, depending on just which specific border-crossing practice is involved. The anthropology of the morality of borders will thus differ depending on whether the matter at hand is cooperative management of a binational baseball team (Klein 1997), importing foreign consumer goods (Heyman 1997), used clothing smuggling (Gauthier 2007), and so forth. The distinction made by Abraham and Van Schendel (2005) between legal and illegal, and legitimate and illegitimate, is useful in untangling views of multiple border phenomena. Smuggling of certain consumer goods (e.g., fruits and vegetables or unprescribed medicines to the United States and household electronics and used clothing to Mexico) is illegal – and people are arrested or fined for it – but it is widely practiced and morally accepted by most borderlanders. Even human and drug smuggling are legitimate, in certain ways and in certain circles (Campbell 2009; Spener 2009). For example, Howard Campbell finds that many nonviolent roles in the drug-smuggling business are understood, with ambivalence, as morally acceptable forms of normal work aimed at livelihood for self and family. As Hastings Donnan and Thomas Wilson (1999) point out, borderlands often have "subversive economies" that challenge not only national economic regulations and monopolies, but also raise morally charged questions of sovereignty, legality, and legitimacy.

The variety of people and topics themselves are interesting, but we point to the wider fact that subtlety and diversity of experiences tend to emerge from border life. Much of this complexity and the moral recognition of it is local to border sites, reflecting the varied and deep ways that geographic proximity encourages intensity and multiplicity of border-crossing practices. This contributes to a borderlander perspective that tends to recognize, both in personal experience and in the experience of nearby others, a certain flexibility, diversity, ambiguity, subtlety, and depth to moral issues (Donnan and Wilson 1999; Long 2011). This proximal view contrasts with a commonly found distant one of borders as essentially simple. In this situation, people who live or work far from the border and have little or no direct contact with it, address it morally as an idea – often, a simple, unambiguous one – rather than as a messy and quotidian site of experiences and activities, which we call "the border."

A wider generalization of this idea would extend to people with experience with border-crossing processes of various sorts, such as immigrant community relationships or international residence in personal backgrounds, even while having a current location deep in the national interior. The point is not just the geography, then, but the implication of boundary-crossing experiences and practices on moral imagination.

This proximate–distant contrast overlaps with – but is not identical to – a distinction between the border as a practice and the border as a symbol. Border practices are diverse, as illustrated just above, and border settings also are diverse. An unauthorized laborer, violating a temporary border-shopping card to clean houses in El Paso, is likely to be looked on as more licit by borderlanders than an unauthorized migrant in a remote desert setting, but both are viewed with more suspicion than a documented, wealthy Mexican doing business at an El Paso bank. As a result, proximal practices are morally plural and often shaded.

By contrast, the border as a symbol of the sovereign, territorial polity and its role in various public imaginaries of outside versus inside (again, *the border*) tends toward the singular and unified. In this view, border crossings are either legal and right or illegal and wrong. Or more strongly – in symbolic reasoning above and beyond formal legalism – the inside of a border is good and safe, the exterior bad and threatening. The symbolic view still entails major differences of moral evaluation (e.g., the border may symbolize either sovereignty or universal human rights) but it leaves less space for recognition of diversity of persons and activities, and ambiguity and subtlety of moral issues on the ground. It is more reified, in keeping with the simplification process of state logic (Scott 1998). *The border* operates as a powerfully evocative, highly condensed, singular symbol, while border-crossing experiences and persons act and think in morally diverse ways.

Border symbolism is more prominent at a distance from actual international borders. Nevertheless, it exists in border regions also. Furthermore, border symbolization helps shape immediate border practices. For example, it drives US boundary enforcement operations. In turn, this creates practices that are enacted at immediate border sites by a socially significant group, central government employees. Distant border symbolism also forms a point of reference and response by local borderlanders, either using such symbols in their own moral discourses and practices, or reacting against what they see as oversimplification and misunderstandings by interior dwellers.

In this essay, we focus primarily on the US–Mexico border and related interior processes in the United States, due to the richness of the material and our personal expertise. However, related phenomena occur throughout the world of migration and border control, such as Europe's "Schengenland" zone of free internal movement and heavily controlled external entry (Andreas and Snyder 2000; Houtum and Pijpers 2007; Houtum 2010), and we make reference to this work as appropriate. Likewise, our key US–Mexico border theme of differences in moral evaluation between borderlanders and interior dwellers is paralleled throughout the world, where borderlanders sometimes identify more with the border region than the core, and more generally by borderlanders' incomplete regard for national institutions, rules, and categorizations (Flynn 1997; Wilson and Donnan 1998; Ishikawa 2010; but see Grimson and Vila 2002). Similarly worldwide is the use of borders as symbols of moral distinction and the us-versus-them comparison (Donnan and Wilson 1999). Many, though not all, border-related moral phenomena are captured in our case material.[1]

We proceed in the subsequent sections by characterizing, first, some moral attitudes and practices among geographically distant groups, then groups that move from the interior to act directly at the border, and finally border-near groups. We seek to use cases where there is anthropological research, but also include some items that are insightful if not ethnographic. We conclude by suggesting that cross-border practices, including migration, challenge narrow definitions of membership in favor of more complex, multistranded notions of relationship and membership in the contemporary world. This is a different sort of pro-migrant moral stance than universalism, and is something that rises out of the anthropological engagement with ideas and practices on the ground.

Borders and Interiors

Broadly, we argue that the moral reasoning about borders by residents of interior locations tends toward externalization and simplification of complex debates over national membership brought about by transnational migration, intertwined with internal racial-ethnic inequalities. Positions tend toward absolutes, mainly restrictive sovereignty but, among dissenting voices, also strong universalism. However, border sites and actors are scattered throughout national interiors, not just found at land and sea margins, and we will consider these important hybrid sites.

Untangling interior US perspectives on external borders, in particular the US–Mexico one, is difficult. The anthropological source material is uneven, emphasizing arm's-length analyses of commodified discourses (media and political), and there are few ethnographic case studies that touch on this subject, despite its clear societal prominence. Leo Chavez (2001), for example, analyses US magazine covers addressing the topic of immigration, and relies similarly on media discourse evidence in a more general book of essays (Chavez 2008; also see Santa Ana 2002). He finds that images of immigration in general include positive as well as fearful evaluations; in particular, he notes the persistence of the US tradition of seeing immigrants as striving for a better life (ideologically, an "American" one). However, this positive discourse is receding in favor of a fearful image of poor and culturally strange invaders, racialized as Mexicans. Images of the US–Mexico border mainly show threats, such as long columns of Mexican-appearing male figures penetrating like arrows into the United States, crowds of impoverished families surging northward (emphasizing the reproductive symbol of women with children), and the region as fractured or chaotic. He also suggests, and Dorsey and Díaz-Barriga (2010) confirm, that visual media images represent the border as empty, remote, and inhuman terrain, with lonely enforcers and surreptitious violators, by contrast with how borderlanders experience and envision it as a populated, diverse, and often urbanized, landscape.

Interwoven with these themes about Mexican migrants is a "security" discourse about borders, especially the Mexican border: that is, borders are the prime passage through which threats to security come from outside in, and thus key locations for defeating these threats (Heyman 2008). Huysmans (2006) and Pratt (2005) cover parallel material on securitization and risk discourses applied to migration and borders in Europe and Canada respectively. While there are indeed, internationally and domestically, genuine human security threats, their moral framing in the wealthy countries of the world displaces the security agenda away from empirical causes and sites of occurrence (e.g., postcolonial, geopolitical struggles) and toward laboring, culturally "othered" migrants (e.g., for the US–Mexico border, see Heyman and Ackleson 2009). This expansive and slippery notion of security – in particular, the notion of a purely safe inside and a distinctly threatening outside (including outsiders within) – is crucial to sovereigntist reasoning that denies the moral weight of actual flows, connections, and relations.

As provocative as discursive analyses are, they decode isolated representations (e.g., Chavez's magazine covers), and there is a notable lack of ethnography directed toward the production and reception of such discourses (Heyman 2001a). This is a major need in the anthropology of moralities about borders. There is little ethnographic study of a variety of sectors involved in framing discourses and moral evaluations: media producers, security bureaucracies, politicians, business organizations, labor unions, funders, religious hierarchies, national level advocacy organizations, and migrants themselves. Of course, we have reams of their public products (e.g., in Nevins 2010); what is missing is ethnographic study of the processes within and between these sectors (however, concerning the US–Mexico border wall, see Maril 2011, and for European migration control, Feldman 2011). Moral attitudes from a distance do not just exist as such, but are produced, reproduced, challenged, and transformed.

Interior site case studies of reception of migrants and tensions between migrants and hosts do offer provocative hints about how moral displacements of local migrant–host interactions to *the border* occur. Heyman (1998) argues that immigration presents a moral challenge of mutual interaction between hosts and migrants (often, however, complex and indirect). He suggests that it can either grow into mutual recognition and obligation or be "bordered" through social and moral mechanisms of distance and othering. He then proposes that distancing responses have not only an interactional and discursive component, but also a spatial one: keeping out the envisioned risky, bad, or different others, through the use of sovereignty at borders, both national and local. As plausible as this analysis seems, ethnographies of host–immigrant relations in the United States do not touch on how people talk about and act politically on borders and migration policy beyond the local setting (see, e.g., Lamphere 1992; Millard and Chapa 2004; Zúñiga and Hernández-León 2005; Massey 2008). Yet the broader policy analysis literature and public opinion literature suggests that such displacements are indeed important (see Gilot 2007; Nevins 2010; Segovia and Defever 2010).

Host populations often have reduced contact with new migrants outside of the commodity relation (employment). Often, even employment is indirect (purchase of services from a local business that in turn uses migrant labor). In this reduced contact situation, the focus often is on large groups of single male laborers, or to a lesser but still important extent, women with young children. This is by contrast with richer, more multidimensional relations with individuals and families who have established longer-term residence and have to some extent climbed the occupational status and income hierarchies, that result in favorable or at least ambivalent moral evaluations. The former migrants (single males, new families, occupationally lower groups) in fact may be crucial to the local economy, but they are often seen as outsiders allowed to enter through a failed border. This is supported by Inda's (2006) nonethnographic discourse analysis of Latino migrants as antisocial beings in the US postsocial formation. This morality, it is important to say, contains within itself a contradiction that has not been explored by scholars, between the positive evaluation of hard work and economic contribution and the moralized fear of the laborers themselves (criminal, dirty, diseased, etc.).

In the current US racial hierarchy, Latino migrants are the most stigmatized group in reports of local immigrant–host relations. The diversity of Latino migration, in terms of source countries and legal status, is reduced to an image of illegal Mexican aliens, as evidenced by several instances of violent attacks on non-Mexicans by persons shouting anti-Mexican phrases. Chavez (2008) refers to this as the "Latino threat narrative." Its roots lie in enduring US imperialist relations with Mexico (and to a smaller extent, the Caribbean), defending the symbolism of domination (involving the southwest border, of course), as well as skin color racism. It draws on the salience of Mexicans as the largest and thus most representative group of new immigrants to the United States. *The border* then becomes a dominant trope in the United States for new Latin American migration, and then for migration issues in general. Borders are not in imagination and practice (e.g., the US wall is only on the Mexican line) posed equally against all groups, but rather according to specific societal boundaries of race, class, and gender (Lamont and Molnár 2002; Fassin 2011).[2]

This is seen in the profusion of border-like sites in the national interior, as well as at outer frontiers. Characteristic locations include international airports (which are, of course, borders and sites of sovereignty), other transportation sites, and various aspects of interior policing, especially when interconnected with national immigration policing. While increasingly studied in the United States (see especially Coleman 2007, 2009), the literature most attentive to the moral dimensions of these sites and practices comes from Europe, and especially France (Fassin 2001, 2005; Fassin and d'Halluin 2005; Ticktin 2006; Kobelinsky and Makaremi 2008; Richard and Fischer 2008; Makaremi 2009). Two themes emerge in this work. One is the complex and changing moral agenda of exclusion and inclusion, shifting for example from positive moral evaluation of strong, mostly male working bodies to negative evaluation of them. Relatedly, there has been a change toward a positive evaluation of suffering (ill, injured, persecuted) bodies but an exclusion of other bonds, such as residence, work, marriage, parenthood, and so forth. The other, connected to the re-evaluation of suffering, is involvement of humanitarian advocates and measures in the overall process of migrant exclusion and expulsion. Despite the ambivalent presence of formal legality and humanitarian exceptionalism, the overall trend is toward more intensive and more widely distributed systems of exclusion.

So why do we witness these widely distributed policies of exclusion, the so-called "wall around the West," which occurs in other settings as well (Andreas and Snyder 2000)? A particular kind of symbolic and moral reasoning separates members from outsiders in various performances of the border. We start with Mary Douglas's (1966) classic work on the symbolism of external boundaries. External boundaries of many kinds (bodies, homes, nation-states, etc.) represent who and what are understood to belong, in various roles and spaces. Items (people, substances, ideas, and symbols) that cross boundaries are unusual in some way, either symbolically powerful or dangerous, or both. Impurity and pollution are conceptualized as elements belonging properly to one side of a symbolic-spatial boundary. Having crossed over to the other side, they violate the proper categorical order. However, this sort of reasoning can be applied to many boundaries in social life, and it has many potential valences. Boundary crossers can have unusual sacredness and power, not just danger and risk.

Unquestionably, an important factor focusing boundary symbolism on international border sites is the pervasive and powerful territorial frame, both discursive and material, of the modern state (including its recent reworkings, such as immigration zones in the European Union), whose rise to centrality is diagnosed by Nevins (2010). It reinforces extremes in moral thought: most notably, borders are a strong symbol of the outer limits of membership, citizenship versus outsiders, of safety inside a womb-like arrangement, as seen in the US–Mexico border wall. But the simplifying logic of border symbolism can be reversed; smaller constituencies see borders as symbolic gateways outward, expressions of moral universalism.

Chavez (2008: 10–15) convincingly argues that border and migration discourses address membership: who is contained inside, and who is outside; who is a citizen (and in what senses: legal, practical, cultural, and so forth); what is a national identity and what is not; and who is and should be a member of the collectivity (for European parallels, see Anthias and Yuval-Davis 1992; Silverstein 2005; Fassin 2011; Palidda 2011). The ethnographic literature reports these moral membership debates from sites in national interiors, concerning issues such as schools, housing codes, police stops, and so forth. In these sites, however, such lines are made ambiguous by the dense web of interactions between migrants and hosts. *The border* then, imagined and politically practiced at a distance (the boundary with Mexico) or in isolated detention and removal sites, is a crucial simplifying move, giving "order" to ambiguous membership. In fact, ongoing relations cut across actual borders just as much–they are transnational – and thus such sites are also morally complex, but this not what largely occurs in interior opinion formation, mass media representations, or politics and policy.

From Distance to Proximity: Activists at the Land Border

Here, we focus on people (other than agents of the state) who act primarily and directly on their moral convictions about the border: "Minutemen" and border humanitarians. The Minutemen are volunteers who act as if they were border guards, placing themselves near the border, detecting people on the move, and placing calls to the Border Patrol, though they have no powers of arrest. The humanitarians carry out varied activities to aid migrants, an example of which is stocking water in the desert to help unauthorized entrants from dying of hyperthermia on their dangerous hike northward. Both groups thus go beyond imagining the border to practical action on it. But at the same time, the moral reasoning involved is relatively simple and pure: the border is in one case a location threatened by illegitimate invasion of nonmembers; in the other, it is an illegitimate barrier to universalism. They are also transitional geographically: many of their members come from the national interior to the border – some do originate in the border region – with the goal of acting at this specific moral site (more humanitarian activists are long-term border residents while more Minutemen are outsiders).

Accounts of the Minutemen are not ethnographic; they are based on documentary research on key members (e.g., Holthouse 2005), secondary analysis of journalistic accounts (Chavez 2008: 132–151) and an interesting opinion survey of both

Minutemen and humanitarian activists (Cabrera and Glavac 2010). From these reports, they have a strongly felt, highly distilled sense of threat to enclosed membership. The US government has, in their view, failed to protect the territorial boundary adequately, the entity that delineates and guards this membership from unauthorized claimants. Their degree of racism is debated (in a politically correct society, racism can be displaced onto criticisms of the migrants' lack of legal status), but the Latino threat narrative is certainly present. We have seen these themes in a more diffuse way in the US interior; what is striking in this case is the drive to purist moral rectification, and the entrepreneurial moral volunteerism involved.

There are a number of ethnographic studies of border humanitarian activists, many of whom, though not all, are religiously motivated (Cunningham 1995; Doty 2006; Hondagneu-Sotelo 2007, 2008; Dunn 2009; Heyman et al. 2009). Broadly, the activists express and act on a moral skepticism of borders.[3] A telling example is Hondagneu-Sotelo's (2008: 133–169) description of a religious ritual (the Posada sin Fronteras) which protests against deaths in unauthorized border crossing. This uses the border precisely as the setting of ritual negation of current migration policies. She terms this "Christian antiborderism"; it could also be termed Christian universalism, with a sacred vision of the human in God's image set against the nation-state. Likewise, Doty's (2006) study of Humane Borders, a coalition with both religious and secular members, identifies their moral action, helping migrants survive the desert, as acting precisely against the normalized, deadly political-social order. Secular forms of universalism also motivate some activists; Dunn's (2009) study of El Paso, Texas activism in the 1990s identifies in the Border Rights Coalition a philosophy of universal human rights that broke with citizenship viewed as strong but bounded rights.

Interestingly, the Minutemen and humanitarian activists both hold critical attitudes toward dominant patterns of globalization (Cabrera and Glavac 2010). Both are critical of the North American Free Trade Agreement, for example, and further proposals to create a Free Trade Agreement of the Americas. Both insist on a moral vision against the amoral, power- and profit-driven agenda of the dominant political-economic order. That dominant agenda values specific capital, commodities, and people who are free to cross borders, denies the value of others, and ignores alternative visions of either national or global communities. The two groups differ, however, in that humanitarians favor free trade agreements with cross-border labor and environmental protections, as well as arrangements for the free mobility of labor, while the Minutemen disapprove of such measures. The Minutemen target the border in order to reinforce national unity and closure; the humanitarians target it in order to move toward globalization of human membership and related rights.

In both cases, the borderline becomes the physical symbol for moral positions and actions. These issues – migration, free trade, and so on – are, after all, matters of whole societies and indeed transnational orders. The border is merely a passageway; it does not cause those phenomena.[4] Borders help to delineate relevant entities – in this case, the sovereign territorial state, and its patterns of membership – but relevant entities are only part of the interconnected totality. But in the moral imagination, *the border* stands in for the totality. This is a problematic simplification of borders and their relation to wider processes and places.[5]

From Distance to Proximity: Migrants and Enforcers

Processes of vast scale such as transnational migration bring face to face, in the border setting, people with contrasting moral perspectives on the same activity, such as unauthorized migrants and border enforcers (Heyman 2000). Unauthorized migrants, going from the interior of Mexico to the interior of the United States, experience border crossing as a passage of considerable uncertainty, danger, and expense. They are aware of their categorization in the United States as "illegal" (though they may understand little of the actual laws and penalties), but also as desired by US employers as well as by friends and families. In this context, Sandell (2009, 2010) sensitively elicits migrant and migrant family perspectives. They recognize as an external reality the various categorizations, barriers, and risks, but give this no moral recognition as orderly, right, or meaningful. They view migration as a practical necessity, part of a lifeway centered on crafts of survival;[6] their own local moral orders build on age, gender, kin relations, religion, land, house, and so forth. The practical logic of migration thus impels people into morally incomprehensible and tragic encounters with domination, including border crossing.

Heyman's (2000) ethnography with US border enforcement officers addressed both those who had grown up in proximity to the border and those from the US interior who moved to the border region because of this employment. He examines their immediate reasoning within a wider public policy context driven in part by distant moral frameworks discussed above. Unsurprisingly, he found that bureaucratic legality and orderliness was a central value, which unauthorized migrants violated, but also found a paradoxical identification with the needs of migrants to seek to work in the United States. This poses a key moral dilemma, the distillation at the point of action of the society's wider moral contradictions. One solution is to distinguish among unauthorized migrants between "good" (but still arrested) workers and a smaller group of dangerous border crossers (e.g., criminals, drug smugglers). The latter serve to justify the contradictory treatment of the former, as "you never know who you will catch." Otherwise "innocent" (in this view) labor and family migrants are admitted to be human (they are largely not dehumanized), but are considered a lower order of people, outsiders who are now out of place. Higher kinds of people are insiders, citizens, among whom border officers counted themselves. Insiders have complex abilities to choose and act, and deserve respect; migrant-outsiders are one-dimensional beings, with simple motivations and moral characters, who upon being apprehended and processed should abandon their volition and obediently follow the imprisonment and expulsion process. While this moral stance broadly justifies the practical needs on the part of a police force, it is also a moral model for construing the border as a line between members and outsiders, dominant and subordinate (parallels can be found in Europe: see Spire 2008; Hall 2012).

Borderlanders

Our central argument is that the kernel of a new moral framework for migration and other boundary-crossing flows emerges from observing border experiences. The border material (Martínez 1994; Vila 2000; 2005; Heyman 2001b, 2010) is varied and contradictory; that complexity and fluidity is, in fact, part of our argument. First, borderlanders are diverse. There are both Mexican and US-side borderlanders, although there is a substantial population of transnationals (Mexican citizens, say, living in the United States, but commuting to Mexico to work, etc.). Likewise, there are many lines of division within these broad categories: citizenship and legal status, race, class, gender, age, and personal value choices. This makes generalization more difficult, but points to the penetrability and ambiguity of the boundary line to borderlanders.

Mexican borderlanders, following Vila (2005),[7] identify themselves by a series of contrasts. They consider themselves morally superior to North Americans, as having human values, caring family bonds, and so forth. Mexicans, border and otherwise, regard their northern border as essentially illegitimate (stolen territory) and US border enforcement as unjust and hypocritical with respect to US use of migrant labor (e.g., Heyman 1999a: 304). But they also view the border positively as a site of connection with US public safety, prosperity, and modernity. Mexicans, then, have a subtle and complex moral evaluation of cross-border relations.

Vila divides US borderlanders into several ethnoracial groups, and then subdivides people of Mexican origin into recent immigrants and generationally deep Mexican Americans. The latter are a useful example for our purposes, making up the majority of US border communities except San Diego. They tend to offer negative narratives about the present-day Mexico side – it is corrupt, it is poor, it is dirty – mixed with positive narratives about an idealized Mexican past. This draws strong moral boundaries, with Mexican Americans self-identifying as US members, not transnational Mexicans. But it also resists dominant Anglo-American stigmas viewing them as permanent outsiders (the Latino threat narrative). At the same time, such Mexican American borderlanders (and some, but fewer, Anglo- and African American borderlanders) frequently cross the border, including legal visiting and shopping, and in some cases petty smuggling. Employment of unauthorized workers (domestics, gardeners, etc.) who commute from Mexico is widespread and morally tolerated by all ethnoracial groups (Heyman 2009). All of these border-crossing relations are regionally legitimate. US borderlander evaluations, then, are complex, ambivalent, and situational.

Fundamentally, borderlanders from both sides have practices, personal and official/business relationships, and broader sorts of knowledge (i.e., storytelling and listening) that bring the geographic proximity of the boundary to bear on moral evaluation of *the border* (also see Long 2011). The border is, first off, intimate, a part of the self-identity, which includes to some extent the nation on the other side, even when people are critical of it. Second, it is recognized as complex, nuanced, and ambiguous: not a single divider of inside/outside but a locus of many different possible people and acts, with diverse evaluations. Third, sentiments in the region oscillate constantly between sympathy with borderlanders of the other side and tension with them; even tensions and differences are not permanent and absolute. Fourth, borderlanders often feel alienated from the national interior, even when they broadly identify as members of the nation state. They criticize reductive discourses from the interior for their lack of subtlety. Finally, borderlanders often view crossing and penetration of the boundary as normal, offering complex and situational evaluations depending on particular circumstances. Borders are reasonable and acceptable – theirs is not moral universalism – but the morally reasonable version of borders is that they are places for interaction and transit, as well as some regulation and closure. Membership is understood to involve complex, transnational gradations, widely encountered in this region. Membership, then, is not absolute, but interactive and situational.

Conclusion

Whether in moral philosophy, or in the public discourse of national interiors, borders are often treated in reductive and absolute manners. In moral and political philosophy, cosmopolitans critique borders as barriers to shared humanity, while for sovereigntists, borders are fundamental to defining membership in delimited political collectivities. However, the practices and ideas of borderlanders, admittedly incoherent, point to a different approach.

The borderlands setting focuses attention on activities and interactions that occur because of the personal and collective uses of moving, cutting across, and combining differences. At the same time, borderlanders recognize distinctions and conflicts. Our view is that moral decision-making with respect to border-related phenomena, such as transnational migration, should start with relationships in practice, and then build toward mutual moral recognition (Heyman 1998). The kinds of interactions include work/employment, trade, education, family and friendship relations, and so forth. Such relationships often emerge by historical accident, but over time they form general webs of connectedness. Being tied to other persons does and should impose a set of correlated obligations on their participants. While arguably all humans should have fundamental moral equivalence, in practical terms the persons to whom we owe moral equivalence are the ones with whom we have active relations. This is particularly the case in transnational migration, where morally important interactions occur between migrant and host. This is neither bounded by preexisting nation-state membership nor is it just a theoretical global equivalence between people who do not actually have relations. Seen as an emergent moral framework, relevant agents, duties, and moral goods begin to be defined.

Our ethical stance, then, turns away from absolutes. We begin with observations on the moral relationality and sensitivity to context often found empirically in borderlands ethnographies, but seek to develop out of that a more generalizable framework. We are not advocating complete flexibility. Instead, we argue that moral obligations are grounded in close analysis of relationships, and that if we create relationships (as prosperous societies do with transnational migrants), we cannot escape moral obligations. Likewise, we build on the border experience, where crossing, interactions, and bonds occur across lines of social differentiation, such as international boundaries. Such emergent relations should be recognized and valued, and should entail steps toward inclusion in membership.

Such a view does not entail the rejection of international borders as such. Borders have a place in the contemporary world, as ways to conduct collective activities and regulatory mechanisms. Concretely, for example, borders are helpful places to intercept international gun smugglers or terrorists. However, we resist the move from this sort of modest practical value toward morally arbitrary conceptions of absolute group membership. Instead, discourse on international borders requires the interplay between clear moral principles and careful empirical consideration of transnational relations that emerge over time. To do that requires thinking on the border between moral and political philosophy and the social sciences.

NOTES

1 One important theme that we capture only partially is borders as morally loaded symbols of lost or stolen lands, sovereignties, and identities, as represented by Ireland (Donnan and Wilson 2010) and Israel–Palestine (Bornstein 2002). Such issues in fact have happened at the US–Mexico border. On the US side of the border, ethnonational irredentism by Mexicans in territories seized by the United States in the Mexican–American War of 1845–48 declined after the failure of several attempted revolts at the end of the nineteenth century, in favor of internal US struggles for immigrant and racial civil rights. On the Mexican side of the border, this moral meaning is still alive, partly because of nationalistic education in schools (of course, US education is equally nationalistic: Rippberger and Staudt 2003). While this topic informs our understanding of Mexican migrants and borderlander views of the United States, its role at the present is modest.

2 For reasons of space, we have skipped over important elements of variability, including the geographic site of host–immigrant relations, race and ethnicity, class, gender, and personal moral perspectives (discussed later in the essay).

3 Not all activists fit these generalizations; the more pragmatic political wing discussed by Heyman et al. (2009) holds similar values but engages in different moral practices, working within the existing nation state and border frame.

4 The border enforcement system does, however, contribute to the death of unauthorized migrants. Direct action (Doty 2006) addresses this issue.

5 We do not view the humanitarians as morally equivalent to the Minutemen, since they hold very different views of and actions toward their fellow humans. We just point out some structurally parallel features of their moral thinking and practice.

6 This view is supported by David Spener's (2010) interpretation of the migration/smuggling (*coyotaje*) process as *movidas rascuaches*, a difficult term to translate but approximately "creatively absurd manuevers." *Rascuache* points to tacky or strange bricolages done by the poor and powerless. *Movida* is a hustle, a way of surviving and thriving.

7 Vila's work was done before the terrible outbreak of widespread violence in Mexican northern border cities. We do not have an account comparable to his for the contemporary situation.

REFERENCES

Abraham, Itty and Van Schendel, Willem (2005) Introduction: The Making of Illicitness. In *Illicit Flows and Criminal Things: States, Borders, and the Other Side of Globalization*. Bloomington: Indiana University Press, pp. 1–37.

Andreas, Peter and Snyder, Timothy (eds.) (2000) *The Wall around the West: State Borders and Immigration Controls in North America and Europe*. Lanham, MD: Rowman & Littlefield.

Anthias, Floya and Yuval-Davis, Nira (1992) *Racialized Boundaries: Race, Nation, Gender, Colour, and Class and the Anti-Racist Struggle*. London: Routledge.

Beitz, Charles (1999 [1979]) *Political Theory and International Relations*, rev. edn. Princeton: Princeton University Press.

Benhabib, Seyla (2004) *The Rights of Others*. Cambridge: Cambridge University Press.

Bornstein, Avram S. (2002) *Crossing the Green Line between the West Bank and Israel.* Philadelphia: University of Pennsylvania Press.

Cabrera, Luis and Glavac, Sonya (2010) Minutemen and Desert Samaritans: Mapping the Attitudes of Activists on the United States' Immigration Front Lines. *Journal of Ethnic and Migration Studies* 36: 673–695.

Campbell, Howard (2009) *Drug War Zone: Frontline Dispatches from the Streets of El Paso and Juárez.* Austin: University of Texas Press.

Carens, Joseph H. (1987) Aliens and Citizens: The Case for Open Borders. *Review of Politics* 49: 251–273.

Chavez, Leo R. (2001) *Covering Immigration: Popular Images and the Politics of the Nation.* Berkeley: University of California Press.

Chavez, Leo R. (2008) *The Latino Threat: Constructing Immigrants, Citizens, and the Nation.* Stanford: Stanford University Press.

Coleman, Mathew (2007) Immigration Geopolitics beyond the Mexico–US Border. *Antipode* 39: 54–76.

Coleman, Mathew (2009) What Counts as the Politics and Practice of Security, and Where? Devolution and Immigrant Insecurity after 9/11. *Annals of the Association of American Geographers* 99: 904–913.

Cunningham, Hilary (1995) *God and Caesar at the Rio Grande: Sanctuary and the Politics of Religion.* Minneapolis: University of Minnesota Press.

Donnan, Hastings and Wilson, Thomas M. (1999) *Borders: Frontiers of Identity, Nation and State.* Oxford: Berg.

Donnan, Hastings and Wilson, Thomas M. (2010) Symbols of Security and Contest along the Irish Border. In Hastings Donnan and Thomas M. Wilson (eds.), *Borderlands: Ethnographic Approaches to Security, Power, and Identity.* Lanham, MD: University Press of America, pp. 73–91.

Dorsey, Margaret E. and Díaz-Barriga, Miguel (2010) Beyond Surveillance and Moonscapes: An Alternative Imaginary of the U.S.–Mexico Border Wall. *Visual Anthropology Review* 26: 128–135.

Doty, Roxanne Lynn (2006) Fronteras Compasivas and the Ethics of Unconditional Hospitality. *Millennium: Journal of International Studies* 35: 53–74.

Douglas, Mary (1966) *Purity and Danger: An Analysis of Concepts of Pollution and Taboo.* London: Routledge & Kegan Paul.

Dunn, Timothy J. (2009) *Blockading the Border and Human Rights: The El Paso Operation that Remade Immigration Enforcement.* Austin: University of Texas Press.

Fassin, Didier (2001) The Biopolitics of Otherness: Undocumented Immigrants and Racial Discrimination in the French Public Debate. *Anthropology Today* 17(1): 1, 3–7.

Fassin, Didier (2005) Compassion and Repression: The Moral Economy of Immigration Policies in France. *Cultural Anthropology* 20: 362–387.

Fassin, Didier (2011) Policing Borders, Producing Boundaries: The Governmentality of Immigration in Dark Times. *Annual Review of Anthropology* 40: 213–226.

Fassin, Didier and d'Halluin, Estelle (2005) The Truth from the Body: Medical Certificates as Ultimate Evidence for Asylum-Seekers. *American Anthropologist* 107: 597–608.

Feldman, Gregory (2011) *The Migration Apparatus: Security, Labor, and Policymaking in the European Union.* Stanford: Stanford University Press.

Flynn, Donna K. (1997) "We are the Border": Identity, Exchange, and the State along the Bénin–Nigeria Border. *American Ethnologist* 24: 311–330.

Gauthier, Mélissa (2007) Fayuca Hormiga: The Cross-border Trade of Used Clothing between the United States and Mexico. In Emmanuel Brunet-Jailly (ed.), *Borderlands: Comparing Border Security in North America and Europe.* Ottawa: University of Ottawa Press, pp. 95–116.

Gilot, Marie (2007) Believe the Hype: The Symbolic Tendencies of Immigration Legislation in the United States, 1980–2005. MA dissertation, University of Texas, El Paso.

Grimson, Alejandro and Vila, Pablo (2002) Forgotten Border Actors: The Border Reinforcers. A Comparison Between the U.S.–Mexico Border and South American Borders. *Journal of Political Ecology* 9: 69–88.

Hall, Alexandra (2012) *Border Watch: Cultures of Immigration, Detention and Control.* London: Pluto.

Heyman, Josiah M. (1997) Imports and Standards of Justice on the Mexico–United States Border. In Benjamin S. Orlove (ed.), *The Allure of the Foreign: Post-Colonial Goods in Latin America.* Ann Arbor: University of Michigan Press, pp. 151–184.

Heyman, Josiah M. (1998) *Finding a Moral Heart for U.S. Immigration Policy: An Anthropological Perspective.* Washington, DC: American Anthropological Association.

Heyman, Josiah M. (1999a) State Escalation of Force: A Vietnam/US-Mexico Border Analogy. In Josiah M. Heyman (ed.), *States and Illegal Practices.* Oxford: Berg, pp. 285–314.

Heyman, Josiah M. (1999b) Why Interdiction? Immigration Law Enforcement at the United States–Mexico Border. *Regional Studies* 33: 619–630.

Heyman, Josiah M. (2000) Respect for Outsiders? Respect for the Law? The Moral Evaluation of High-Scale Issues by US Immigration Officers. *Journal of the Royal Anthropological Institute* 6: 635–652.

Heyman, Josiah M. (2001a) Class and Classification on the U.S.–Mexico Border. *Human Organization* 60: 128–140.

Heyman, Josiah M. (2001b) On U.S.–Mexico Border Culture. *Journal of the West* 40(2): 50–59.

Heyman, Josiah M. (2004) Ports of Entry as Nodes in the World System. *Identities: Global Studies in Culture and Power* 11: 303–327.

Heyman, Josiah M. (2008) Constructing a Virtual Wall: Race and Citizenship in U.S.–Mexico Border Policing. *Journal of the Southwest* 50: 305–334.

Heyman, Josiah M. (2009) Risque et confiance dans le contrôle des frontières américaines. *Politix* 22(87): 21–46.

Heyman, Josiah M. (2010) U.S.–Mexico Border Cultures and the Challenge of Asymmetrical Interpenetration. In Hastings Donnan and Thomas M. Wilson (eds.), *Borderlands: Ethnographic Approaches to Security, Power, and Identity.* Lanham, MD: University Press of America, pp. 21–34.

Heyman, Josiah M. and Ackleson, Jason (2009) United States Border Security after September 11. In John Winterdyk and Kelly Sundberg (eds.), *Border Security in the Al-Qaeda Era.* Boca Raton, FL: CRC, pp. 37–74.

Heyman, Josiah M., Morales, Maria Cristina, and Núñez, Guillermina Gina (2009) Engaging with the Immigrant Human Rights Movement in a Besieged Border Region: What Do Applied Social Scientists Bring to the Policy Process? *NAPA Bulletin* 31: 13–29.

Holthouse, David (2005) Arizona Showdown: High-Powered Firearms, Militia Maneuvers and Racism at the Minuteman Project. Intelligence Report No. 118. Southern Poverty Law Center. At http://www.splcenter.org/intel/intelreport/article.jsp?aid=557, accessed Mar. 14, 2012.

Hondagneu-Sotelo, Pierrette (ed.) (2007) *Religion and Social Justice for Immigrants.* New Brunswick, NJ: Rutgers University Press.

Hondagneu-Sotelo, Pierrette (2008) *God's Heart Has No Borders: How Religious Activists are Working for Immigrant Rights.* Berkeley: University of California Press.

Houtum, Henk van (2010) Human Blacklisting: The Global Apartheid of the EU's External Border Regime. *Environment and Planning D: Society and Space* 28: 957–976.

Houtum, H. van and Pijpers, R. (2007) The European Union as a Gated Community: The Two-Faced Border and Immigration Regime of the EU. *Antipode* 39(2): 291–309.

Huysmans, Jef (2006) *The Politics of Insecurity: Fear, Migration and Asylum in the EU.* London: Routledge.

Inda, Jonathan Xavier (2006) *Targeting Immigrants: Government, Technology, and Ethics.* Oxford: Blackwell.

Ishikawa, Noboru (2010) *Between Frontiers: Nation and Identity in a Southeast Asian Borderland*. Athens: Ohio University Press.

Klein, Alan M. (1997) *Baseball on the Border: A Tale of Two Laredos*. Princeton: Princeton University Press.

Kobelinsky, Carolina and Makaremi, Chowra (eds.) (2008) Alien Exclusion: Between Circulation and Confinement [special issue]. *Cultures & Conflits* 71.

Lamont, Michéle and Molnár, Virág (2002) The Study of Boundaries in the Social Sciences. *Annual Review of Sociology* 28: 167–195.

Lamphere, Louise (1992) *Structuring Diversity: Ethnographic Perspectives on the New Immigration*. Chicago: University of Chicago Press.

Long, Nicholas (2011) Bordering on Immoral: Piracy, Education, and the Ethics of Cross-Border Cooperation in the Indonesia–Malaysia–Singapore Growth Triangle. *Anthropological Theory* 11: 441–464.

Makaremi, Chowra (2009) Governing Borders in France: From Extraterritorial to Humanitarian Confinement. *Canadian Journal of Law and Society/Revue Canadienne Droit et Société* 24: 411–432.

Maril, Robert Lee (2011) *The Fence: National Security, Public Safety, and Illegal Immigration along the U.S.–Mexico Border*. Lubbock: Texas Tech University Press.

Martínez, Oscar J. (1994) *Border People: Life and Society in the U.S.–Mexico Borderlands*. Tucson: University of Arizona Press.

Massey, Douglas S. (ed.) (2008) *New Faces in New Places: The Changing Geography of American Immigration*. New York: Russell Sage Foundation.

Millard, Ann V. and Chapa, Jorge (2004) *Apple Pie and Enchiladas: Latino Newcomers in the Rural Midwest*. Austin: University of Texas Press.

Nevins, Joseph (2010) *Operation Gatekeeper and Beyond: The War on "Illegals" and the Remaking of the U.S.–Mexico Boundary*, 2nd edn. New York: Routledge.

Nine, Cara (2008) A Lockean Theory of Territory. *Political Studies* 56: 148–165.

Palidda, Salvatore (ed.) (2011) *Racial Criminalization of Migrants in the 21st Century*. Farnham: Ashgate.

Pallitto, Robert and Heyman, Josiah M. (2008) Theorizing Cross-Border Mobility: Surveillance, Security and Identity. *Surveillance & Society* 5: 315–333. At: http://www.surveillance-and-society.org/articles5(3)/mobility.pdf, accessed Mar. 14, 2012.

Pratt, Anna (2005) Securing Borders: Detention and Deportation in Canada. Vancouver: University of British Columbia Press.

Richard, Clémence and Fischer, Nicholas (2008) A Legal Disgrace? The Retention of Deported Migrants in Contemporary France. *Social Science Information* 47: 581–603.

Rippberger, Susan J. and Staudt, Kathleen A. (2003) *Pledging Allegiance: Learning Nationalism at the El Paso–Juárez Border*. New York: Routledge.

Sandell, David P. (2009) A Space of Their Own: Stories about Work and Migration from Mexico. *Urban Anthropology* 38: 203–233.

Sandell, David P. (2010) Where Mourning Takes Them: Migrants, Borders, and an Alternative Reality. *Ethos* 38: 179–204.

Santa Ana, Otto (2002) *Brown Tide Rising: Metaphors of Latinos in Contemporary American Public Discourse*. Austin: University of Texas Press.

Sasse, Gwendolyn and Thielemann, Eiko R. (2005) A Research Agenda for the Study of Migrants and Minorities in Europe. *Journal of Common Market Studies* 43: 655–671.

Scott, James C. (1998) *Seeing Like a State: How Certain Schemes to Improve the Human Condition Have Failed*. New Haven: Yale University Press.

Segovia, Francine and Defever, Renatta (2010) The Polls – Trends: American Public Opinion in Immigrants and Immigration Policy. *Public Opinion Quarterly* 74: 375–394.

Silverstein, Paul A. (2005) Immigrant Racialization and the New Savage Slot: Race, Migration, and Immigration in the New Europe. *Annual Review of Anthropology* 34: 363–384.

Spener, David (2009) *Clandestine Crossings: Migrants and Coyotes on the Texas–Mexico Border*. Ithaca, NY: Cornell University Press.

Spener, David (2010) *Movidas Rascuaches*: Strategies of Migrant Resistance at the Mexico–U.S. Border. *Aztlán: A Journal of Chicano Studies* 35: 9–36.

Spire, Alexis (2008) *Accueillir ou reconduire: enquête sur les guichets de l'immigration* [Welcome or return home: a study of immigration front offices]. Paris: Raisons d'Agir.

Ticktin, Miriam (2006) Where Ethics and Politics Meet: The Violence of Humanitarianism in France. *American Ethnologist* 33: 33–49.

Vila, Pablo (2000) *Crossing Borders, Reinforcing Borders: Social Categories, Metaphors, and Narrative Identities on the U.S.–Mexico Frontier*. Austin: University of Texas Press.

Vila, Pablo (2005) *Border Identifications: Narratives of Religion, Gender, and Class on the U.S.–Mexico Border*. Austin: University of Texas Press.

Wilson, Thomas M. and Donnan, Hastings (1998) *Border Identities: Nation and State at International Frontiers*. Cambridge: Cambridge University Press.

Zúñiga, Víctor and Hernández-León, Rubén (eds.) (2005) *New Destinations: Mexican Immigration in the United States*. New York: Russell Sage Foundation.

PART VI Dialogues

CHAPTER 31

Moral Philosophy

Kwame Anthony Appiah

Moral philosophy and anthropology are each wide-ranging and diverse; and there are surely many ways in which each can illuminate the other's concerns. In the last half-century or so, in particular, there have been many philosophical discussions in which evidence and arguments from anthropology have played a significant role. An essay that aims, from a philosophical perspective, to engage with anthropological thinking, cannot adequately address all of these discussions, or even all the most important ones. Nevertheless, I shall try, at the start, to sketch the main ways philosophers writing in English over the last half-century or so have engaged with anthropology. That way you will see the broad background against which the issues I focus on are arrayed.

I shall then take up in more detail just one area – the discussion of moral relativism. In part, as you will imagine, this is because it is the discussion that I find most *interesting*. It is also, I think, the most *obvious* point of disciplinary intersection, one that arises again and again (as we shall see) in many of the other debates. And it is, finally, an especially *important* issue because it is one where these two fields can usefully enrich public reflection. In debates about foreign policy – in discussions, say, of the issue of what role a concern for human rights should play in framing relations between nations – assumptions about moral universality and relativity are sometimes in the foreground and almost always in the background. There are similar ways in which questions of relativism arise in debates about multiculturalism (Taylor 1994). If there is to be progress in discussion of these questions, I think lessons from both fields will be helpful.

I begin the paper by offering, in the first section, a sketch of the five areas, where philosophical discussions have been powerfully enriched by an engagement with anthropology. They are in the literatures on:

A Companion to Moral Anthropology, First Edition. Edited by Didier Fassin.

1 cultural relativism in general, and moral relativism in particular;
2 the universality of standards of rationality, including an important debate about this issue in recent African philosophy;
3 ethno-philosophy and the cultural specificity of key concepts, such as person or human rights;
4 the post-independence critique of colonial anthropology;
5 the question whether there is a fundamental neuropsychological basis to the normative systems of all human societies.

In the second section, I discuss a broadly Humean philosophical background that shapes (including by opposition) much recent philosophical discussion of the metaphysics and epistemology of the normative and especially the metaphysics of the fact/value distinction. I aim to show how, despite the fact that major figures in the history of European philosophy – including Kant and Hegel – were not (or not obviously) moral relativists, their fundamental ideas were open to relativist interpretations; and that these relativist interpretations fed into the intellectual background of modern anthropology through Dilthey – who influenced Franz Boas – among others.

In the third and longest section, I suggest ways of thinking about what might be true in Boas's claim that "civilization is relative," and argue that this could be right even if the forms of relativism that mostly interest philosophers were not. My aim is not to defend any – let alone all – of the relativisms I discuss, but to explore the relationships between them.

Conversations between Philosophy and Anthropology

First, and perhaps most obviously, philosophers have responded to the advocacy of some sort of cultural relativism by some anthropologists; prominently, in American anthropology, by Melville Herskovitz (1972), though he was following a path also taken by others, such as Franz Boas, Ruth Benedict, and Margaret Mead (Stocking 1968). The debates of central philosophical importance here, and to which I will return, have been about *moral* relativism.

Cognitive relativism (relativism about truth) has been a central topic in modern Anglo-American thought and some of the major figures in that tradition – W. V. O. Quine and Nelson Goodman (1978) prominent among them – have endorsed cognitive relativism of some kind. This was in part because they took concepts to be individuated by their relations to each other in conceptual schemes – what Quine and Ullian (1978) called "the web of belief," using a metaphor long before offered by Evans-Pritchard, writing in *Witchcraft, Oracles and Magic among the Azande*: "In this web of belief every strand depends upon every other strand, and a Zande cannot get out of its meshes because it is the only world he knows" (1937: 195).

But despite this echo, these philosophers' arguments were essentially abstract and did not rely on ethnographic specifics about actual (or purported) cases where truth about nonmoral matters was relative to some specific cultural background. Clearly, though, *holism* of this kind, which identifies the meaning of a sentence (or the content of a belief) with its place in a total network of sentences (or beliefs) makes meaning (or content) relative, in an obvious way, to a system. (The system might, of course, be the beliefs of an individual person: but I am not going to discuss forms of relativism that make truth relative to individuals rather than cultural or social groups, since this is an issue that anthropologists have for obvious reasons not taken up.)

In the debates about moral relativism, on the other hand, the actual existence of moral disagreement across cultures – the fact of moral disagreement – has often been supposed to be established by anthropological data and analysis. Indeed, many philosophers have accepted on ethnographic evidence what philosophers call "descriptive cultural relativism" (Brandt 1967) – the thesis that "the moral practices of diverse social groups generate 'ultimate' or 'fundamental' moral disputes, disputes that are neither reducible to non-moral disagreement nor susceptible of rational resolution – disputes, that is, that are in principle irresolvable" (Moody-Adams 1997: 15).

A second point of intersection has been in the literature on the universality of standards of rationality. One line of debate here grew out of the works of some of Wittgenstein's followers – most prominently Peter Winch – who argued that we could see in the ethnographic accounts of traditional modes of thought that standards of truth and rationality were internal to forms of life (Winch 1964). Winch discusses Evans-Pritchard's (1937) classic *Witchcraft, Oracles and Magic among the Azande*, and took himself to be exemplifying in the ethnographic materials a thesis that was itself founded in a philosophical argument, namely that "the relation between idea and context is an internal one." The idea gets its sense from the role it plays in the system. It is nonsensical to take several systems of ideas, find an element in each which can be expressed in the same verbal form, and then claim to have discovered an idea common to all systems (Winch 1990 [1958]: 107).

The holism here is shared with Quine (Quine and Ullian 1951), who had defended the related view (which Michael Dummett called the "inextricability thesis") that "convention and experience cannot be disentangled as determinants of our linguistic dispositions" (Dummett 1990 [1978]: 387). But it is put to specific use in arguing that Evans-Pritchard had been wrong to seek to apply standards or rationality from his own culture to Zande practices of witchcraft and magic. The standards for epistemic rationality – which addresses what is evidence for a proposition or what evidence makes it rational to accept it – and for practical rationality – which tells us what is grounds for an action or what grounds make it rational to undertake it – are both, Winch argues, internal to a culture. The application of different standards from outside is therefore always inappropriate.

In another discussion, philosophers and philosophically inclined anthropologists mined ethnographic case studies to see how social practices of inquiry affected the content of traditional modes of thought, in part as a contribution to thinking about what (if anything) was distinctive about the modes of thought that began in the West with the scientific revolution of the seventeenth century. The most important starting point for this literature was a two-part paper by the philosopher-anthropologist Robin Horton in *Africa* entitled "African Traditional Religion and Western Science" (1967) (Appiah 1992: 107–136). A useful survey of these debates in African philosophy is found in two chapters in Barry Hallen's introduction to modern African philosophy: "Rationality as Culturally Universal" (Hallen 2009: 30–47) and "Rationality as Culturally Relative" (Hallen 2009: 48–67). These discussions raise issues in the philosophy of action, in epistemology, and in the philosophy of science. Since rationality is a normative concept, though not centrally a moral one, these discussions are relevant not just to what is but also to what ought to be, but in the realm of judgment rather than of action.

A third line of philosophical inquiry inspired by anthropology has been in the field of ethno-philosophy, where philosophers have inquired into the conceptual structures of particular non-Western traditions, arguing sometimes that concepts that European philosophers had taken to be universal – for example, mind, person, human rights and knowledge – were in fact specific to a particular intellectual context (Appiah 1992: 85–106). Gyekye (1978) exemplifies this for mind, Wiredu and Gyekye (1992) and Carrithers et al. (1985) for person, in each case in Akan languages; Bauer and Bell (1999) discuss this issue for human rights in a Chinese Confucian context; Hallen and Sodipo (1997) explore knowledge; and Hallen (2000) examines a wide range of evaluative concepts in Yoruba. Debates about the universality of the particular psychological and social concepts – like person – that we use in our assessment and evaluation of agents are, of course, of special relevance to moral philosophy.

Indeed, as Hallen's work argues, the very idea of a separation between cognitive and moral domains (which, as I shall argue below, has a particular centrality in modern Western philosophical writings) is itself not obviously universal. Hallen (2000) shows that concerns that have to do with the source and the reliability of the information that people act on and share – concerns that would be canonically epistemological in European traditions – are central to the evaluation of people and their utterances in Yoruba society. He shows, too, that the distinction between moral and aesthetic evaluation is, at best, quite fluid in Yoruba evaluations of people, exploring the significance of the idea (expressed in a Yoruba saying) that "true beauty is a good moral character" (Hallen 2009: 54).

What we are to make of accounts such as this one, depends, in the end, on our answer to the questions about moral universality and relativity that I shall take up later. For clearly, if there is a single, correct, universally valid, understanding of the relationship between cognitive, moral, and aesthetic concerns, then the issue raised by Hallen's work is whether the Yoruba account is (approximately) correct. Of course, if this is the right question, then ethnographic evidence about the range of views on this question will presumably be part of what we have to bear in mind in answering it.

Fourth, philosophers in the postcolonial world have joined with contemporary anthropologists in critiques or various ways in which earlier ethnography and anthropological theory were ethnocentric in their evaluation of traditions from elsewhere; (e.g., Wiredu 1984; Mudimbe 1988, 1994). Mudimbe, in particular, has conducted a powerful critique of what he has called the "colonial library" (1994: xii). "Only from the eighteenth century on," he writes, "is there, thanks to the Enlightenment, a 'science' of difference: anthropology. It 'invents' an idea of Africa. Colonialism will elaborate upon the idea" (Mudimbe 1994: 30). While there is a vast literature now in postcolonial studies, much of which shares Mudimbe's skepticism about older anthropological discourses, it is important to bear in mind that much of this critique came from within the discipline itself. The methodological self-consciousness of a great deal of "postmodern" anthropology is not simply the result of the introduction of ideas from philosophy (see Ashcroft et al. 2007).

Finally, as new work in the social and biological sciences has suggested a common set of fundamental psychological mechanisms and an evolutionary narrative of their development, philosophers and others in the behavioral and brain sciences have looked to anthropology to provide evidence about the range of actually existing normative systems. (These discussions are exemplified in the essays on neuroethics and moral psychology, Chapters 33 and 32, respectively, in this volume. My own view of these matters can be found in Appiah 2008.)

Each of these literatures can be seen as raising issues about the universality of certain norms and concepts, and thus as related broadly to the question of relativism. In this essay, as I said at the start, I shall focus on some of the debates about moral relativism because they are, as I suggested, the most obvious – and I think one of the most important – points of engagement between the two fields.

A Philosophical Background

But it helps, I think, to start with a sketch of a philosophical background. In modern philosophy, there is always the looming power of a picture of the human self and the human situation that is broadly visible for the first time in the work of David Hume. (Whether Hume himself held this view is a disputed question, but it is often ascribed to him.) This Humean picture is at the root of the ways of thought that shaped the empiricism of the Vienna Circle in general and Wittgenstein in particular, as well as of figures like Alfred Ayer in England and Carnap and Quine in the United States. But I think – more controversially, perhaps – that it is in the background to German idealism as well.

Here is the picture: What people do is driven by two fundamentally different kinds of psychological states. *Beliefs* – the first kind – are supposed to reflect how the world is. *Desires*, by contrast, reflect how we'd like it to be. Beliefs are meant to fit the world; the world is meant to fit desires. So beliefs can be true or false, reasonable or unreasonable. Desires, on the other hand, are satisfied or unsatisfied.

Beliefs are supposed to be formed on the basis of evidence, and there are principles of reasoning that determine what it is rational to believe on the basis of what evidence. Desires are just facts about us. Because they are just things that happen to (or in) us, no evidence determines which ones are right. When we act, we use our beliefs about the world to figure out how to get what we desire. Reason, as Hume famously put it in his *Treatise of Human Nature*, "is, and ought only to be the slave of the passions" (Hume 1896 [1739]: 415). If our passion is for apples, we go to where our beliefs suggest the apples are. And, once we go looking for the apples we're after, we'll find out whether our beliefs were right.

Because beliefs are about the world, on the other hand, and there's only one world, they can be either right or wrong, and we can criticize other people's beliefs for being unreasonable or simply false. But desires can't be right or wrong, in this sense. Desires are simply not responses to the world; they're aimed at changing it, not at reflecting how it is.

There's a complication to the story, because much of what we ordinarily desire has beliefs, so to speak, built into it. I want the glass because I believe it has the soda in it. No soda, and the desire loses its point. So the desire for the glass is dependent on the belief that there's soda in it. If the belief is wrong, there's a basis for criticizing the desire. On the Humean picture, this is the only way desires can be criticized: by criticizing beliefs they presuppose. Once you remove the conditional element from the specification of a desire, you get to what we might call your *basic desires*. And since these depend on *no* assumptions about how the world is, you can't criticize them for getting the world wrong.

Hume himself drew the distinction, in a famous passage, between judgments about how things are and judgments about how things ought to be. Normative judgments naturally come with views about what one ought to think, do, or feel. And the positivist picture is often thought to be Humean in part because Hume insisted that the distinction between *is* and *ought* was, as he said, "of the last consequence" (1896: 469). Like desires, *oughts* are intrinsically action-guiding, in a way that *is* isn't. And so, according to the familiar slogan, "you can't get an *ought* from an *is*." Since we are often tempted to move from what is to what ought to be, this move, like many moves philosophers think illicit, has a disparaging name: we call it (following G. E. Moore) the *naturalistic fallacy* (Moore 1993: 12).

Such a distinction between the way beliefs and desires result in action is the key to the Humean picture of how human beings work. Desires – or, more precisely, basic desires – set the ends we aim for; beliefs specify the means for getting to them. Since these desires can't be wrong or right, you can criticize only the means people adopt, not their ends. Finally, the Humean identifies the truths that beliefs aim at with the facts. If you believe something and your belief is true, it gets one of the facts in the world right.

If that's what facts are on the Humean view, what are values? You could say the Humean thinks that, strictly speaking, there aren't any values. Not at least in the world. "The world," the young Ludwig Wittgenstein said, "is the totality of facts" (1991: 5). The world can force us to believe in facts, because if we don't they'll bump into us anyhow, get in our way. But reality can't force us to desire anything. Where, after all, would one look in the world for the wrongness of a basic desire? What science would demonstrate it? A science may be able to explain why you desire something, but it can't explain that you should – or shouldn't – desire it. Normativity is never reducible to facts alone.

Talk of values, then, is really a way of talking about certain of our desires. Which ones? Well, when we appeal to what we take to be universal values in our discussions with one another – the value of art or of democracy or of philosophy – we're talking about things we want everyone to want. If we think exposure to art is valuable, then, roughly, we'd like everyone to want to experience it. If we say democracy is valuable, then, roughly again, we want everyone to want to live in a democracy. We might say, as a *façon de parler*, that someone who wants everyone to want X "believes that X is valuable," but that is still just, in reality, a way of talking about a complex desire. Again, some values will subsist upon certain facts. I could value universal vaccination for smallpox, because I want to make everyone safer – but I may give up this "value" once I learn that smallpox has been eradicated. If a value reflects unconditional desires, however, since these basic desires can't be criticized, values can't either. I value kindness. I want to be kind. I want me to want to be kind. I want all of us to want to be kind. As a matter of fact, I want *you* to want everyone to want to be kind. But I don't want this because I believe that all these kindnesses will lead to something else. I value kindness intrinsically, unconditionally. Even if you showed me that some acts of kindness would have effects I didn't want, that wouldn't persuade me to give up kindness as a value. It would only show me that kindness can sometimes conflict with other things I care about.

It may be that there are basic desires like this that everyone has. So it may turn out that there are things that everyone values. Those values will be *contingently* universal; that is, it will turn out that, while there could have been rational people who valued different things from the rest of us, there are, in fact, none. This is a claim to universality that is grounded in human nature: it is the kind of universality claimed by many contemporary defenders of the idea of the "ethical brain." Still, on the Humean view, there remains no rational basis on which to establish that they're correct. If someone who lacked such a desire came along, there would be nothing we could say that would provide her with a rational ground for acquiring it.

Against this background something like relative truth looks like the best we can hope for. When I say that kindness is good, we can take this as a reflection of my desires, so that, in that sense it is "true for me." Or we could suppose, as the philosopher Gilbert Harman (1975) did, that such remarks are always implicitly relative to a shared commitment; and then it will be true for the group whose shared commitment it is, reflecting desires they have in common. That will give you a form of moral relativism that is quite recognizable to anthropologists: indeed many American anthropologists will regard this as a truism.

And yet, though there are philosophers, like Gilbert Harman (1975), who have endorsed and defended this view – and claimed for it the virtue that it explains the alleged fact of descriptive moral relativism – there is, in fact a great resistance to relativism of this sort in modern moral philosophy. In a recent poll for the website PhilPapers, professional philosophers were twice as likely to favor realism as opposed to antirealism about morality (PhilPapers 2010). (By "realism," in this context, we mean the position that moral propositions, like factual ones, express claims about how things are, claims that are either true or false.) But, as Maria Baghramian (2004, 2010) has pointed out, while relativism in modern (Western) philosophy has multiple roots in the Enlightenment and the counter-Enlightenment, the major figures are broadly convinced of the universality of standards, even if their heirs often found a way to some form of relativism.

So, for example, Kant's idea that our experience of the world is mediated by our concepts – or, as he puts it, that our perceptions might be "a composite of that which we receive through impressions and that which our own cognitive faculty … provides out of itself" (1998: 136) – opens up the possibility that, in a sense, the reality we experience is, in part, dependent on our concepts. Kant himself thought that reason supplied the same basic conceptual resources to all of us; but by the nineteenth century scientists like Wundt and Helmholtz had "psychologized" the Kantian categories, thus opening up the possibility that people with different concepts might experience different "realities." An Enlightenment idea that was not at all intended to encourage the "irrationality" of multiple competing standards was opened to a relativist interpretation.

As for the counter-Enlightenment, a second line of argument, stretching back at least to Johann Gottfried von Herder and Wilhelm von Humboldt, holds that each person has a distinctive spirit, its *Geist*, which is expressed above all in its language. Different language, different *Geist* and, potentially at least, a different – and equally justified – vision of the world. Herder wrote in a 1766 essay "On the Change of Taste" that "ruling customs, … favorite concepts of honor, of moiety, of what is useful can blind an age with a magical light … and yet all this dies with the century"

(2002: 256). This historicism feeds into Hegel in the nineteenth century, once more opening up the possibility that history shapes judgment, which leads eventually to the idea – which Hegel himself would not have supported – that different local histories make for different local forms of reason. There is a line that leads, that is, from Hegel at the beginning of the nineteenth century to the historical relativism of Wilhelm Dilthey at its end. (This line is literal as well as metaphorical: in 1883 Dilthey assumed the chair at the University of Berlin that Hegel had held.)

Dilthey claimed that the metaphysical and religious ideas of a society – including, of course, its normative claims – were shaped by their historical origins. Each worldview, though complete and coherent in itself, was to some degree in conflict with the others. And, by implication at least, the proper attitude to this diversity of fundamental beliefs and values is a kind of acceptance. "With historical consciousness human beings attain the sovereignty to enjoy every experience to the full, to surrender themselves to it completely and unencumbered, as if there were no system of philosophy or faith that could bind them" (Dilthey 2002: 310). This truth – the truth of the historical relativity of values – is itself absolute. It is a notable fact about the relationship between the histories of philosophy and of anthropology that Franz Boas was one of the many students at Dilthey's lectures in Berlin.

Finally, with Nietzsche, we reach a figure who seems, at least sometimes, to be committed to a view that looks like much contemporary relativism. His perspectivism insists that every theoretical claim – even in physics – is, as he puts it in *Beyond Good and Evil*, "an interpretation and arrangement of the world" (Nietzsche 1977: 63). Not surprisingly, therefore, he has been taken to have a relativist view about normative questions as well. And, however we are to understand his relativism, Nietzsche is engaged, by the end of his philosophical career, in a radical critique of conventional ideas about morality. Because that critique was expressed in a genealogy of morality – an account of how morality was created by human beings – it seems to be committed to antirealism from the start.

Moral Relativism: The Dialogue between Anthropology and Philosophy

a. Suppose cultural relativism were to be defined as the thesis that truth is relative to a culture. Then many anthropologists have taken some form of cultural relativism to be evident. In an 1887 letter to the journal *Science* about ethnological museums Franz Boas, one of the founding fathers of anthropology in the United States, wrote: "It is my opinion that the main object of ethnological collections should be the dissemination of the fact that civilization is not something absolute, but that it is relative, and that our ideas and conceptions are true only so far as our civilization goes" (1887: 589).

Many philosophers, on the other hand, say they regard this as a serious error; though, as we have seen, if one associates a culture with a "web of belief" (including, we may assume, beliefs about values), there is a strong philosophical tradition, encompassing philosophers as diverse as Nietzsche, Wittgenstein, and Quine, that agrees. But there are reasons, against the complex background I have just sketched, for wondering whether the relativism of the anthropologist is the same as the relativism of the philosophers. Indeed, there are reasons for supposing that there is more than one anthropological relativism; and philosophers themselves have identified many forms of philosophical relativism.

I want to suggest in this final discussion, that there is a great variety of ways of interpreting a claim like Boas's, and that the main line of philosophical critique, in focusing on some of these interpretations, loses sight of the plausibility of others. And so, for the rest of this essay, my aim will be to identify a number of distinct ways in which moral "ideas and conceptions" might be "true only so far as" a "civilization goes."

b. It will help to have an actual example of moral belief to illustrate various ways in which its truth might be relative to a culture. Here, then, is one:

> G: Other things being equal, fathers ought to play a central role in securing the welfare of their dependent children.

One has to say "other things being equal" – introducing one of those famous philosophers' *ceteris paribus* clauses – because there are circumstances in which it is not possible for a man to look out for his children. He may be too ill, too poor, too far away from them. He may have given them up for adoption. They may have betrayed him. He may have something much more important to be doing – like saving the village from marauders. We can think of many ways in which a particular father may reasonably rebut this presumption. And we should not be confident that we could anticipate in advance all the possibilities. Still, this looks as though it is a completely general claim about all fathers everywhere.

Beliefs like G are, of course, usually expressed in the context of particular societies. Questions about what is owed to whom across all places and times arise only in a certain kind of theoretical discussion. But many people who make such claims would be quite happy to apply them across all societies. What grounds could there be for accepting Boas's cultural relativism about G?

There seem to be at least four points where some sort of cultural relativity might be identified. First, there might be cultural variation in the sorts of things that excuse a father from carrying out his duties, so that the "other things being equal" might vary in its effect across societies. In Asante, for example, a man may be called into the service of an *obosom* (a local god) by a sign – such as the discovery of a "flaming stone" in the forest (Busia 1999:193). If he accepts the call, he must then take up the long-drawn-out process of training for the priesthood. In that society, this new commitment might well be thought to be a basis for withdrawing from worrying about his children. A man who announced that he could no longer care for his children in New Jersey because he had found a flaming stone and was taking up service to a shrine for it would probably not be so sympathetically received. What a normal member of the society takes to be an excuse clearly varies as a matter of fact across societies. And we might think that a traditional Asante person, given her beliefs, reasonably accepts the excuse, while a reasonable New Jerseyan should not.

So we might conclude, that is, that

> E: The discovery of a flaming stone that leads a person to believe that a god is calling you to his service excuses that person from looking after his children

is true for Asante people and false for New Jerseyans.

This is not a very helpful way of putting things, though, because the suggestion that something can be true for one person and false for another suggests that they occupy different realities. Whereas all that is going on here is that the very same reality that demands one response from an Asante demands a different response from a New Jerseyan. Notice that the New Jerseyan can concede that it would be reasonable for an Asante to respond with these priorities but unreasonable for her to do so, because of their different cultural assumptions.

c. You could, thus, "de-relativize" the situation and make it clearer, by explicitly recording the cultural background in your claim:

> D: The discovery of a flaming stone that leads you to believe that a god is calling you to his service excuses you from looking after your children *if you have the religious beliefs of a traditional Asante.*

But now it is clear that the excuse for the father depends on his subjective attitudes, on the beliefs he happens to have. This is not very surprising, since whether you are excused for what you do or fail to do often depends on your interpretation of the situation. You are especially likely to be excused if your beliefs are reasonable (or, if you like, normal) for a person in your situation.

D is no more surprising, in other words, than the fact that you might be excused for shooting someone if you reasonably believed him to be attacking you, even if he was not. That is, the excuse depends on the *fact* of your belief and on its *reasonableness*, not on its *truth*. And many of us will think that, against the background of traditional Asante life and belief, responding in this way to evidence that a god has called you is reasonable, whether or not we ourselves believe in gods that call people in this way.

Some philosophers, though, will not take the truth of D as having established an example of true cultural relativism about morality. To see why, consider a useful distinction drawn by the philosopher David Lyons between two kinds of relativism. One, which he calls *agent's-group* relativism, says that "an act is right if, and only if, it accords with the norms of the agent's group." The other, which is *appraiser's-group* relativism, holds that an appraiser's moral judgment "is valid if, and only if, it accords with the norms of the appraiser's social group" (Lyons 1976: 109). D establishes a form of agent's-group relativism. It says that whether it is right for someone to do something depends on what the norms are that govern his group. But, as I said, D is supposed to be something that anyone, Asante or not, can see to be true. And so it is not just true *for* Asantes or those who share their cultural assumptions. It is true, if true, for all of us. D, in other words, is not supposed to be an instance of appraiser's-group relativism. (An instance of appraiser's-group relativism would be the claim, which I suggested at the end of the last section was unhelpful, that the sentence E is true for an Asante and false for a New Jerseyan.)

Now why should a philosopher think that appraiser's-group relativism is the really interesting and important claim? Because it is that thesis that undermines the idea that people in all human cultures share a single moral reality. And the philosophical interest lies in the idea that there is no universal moral reality – which fits, of course, with the

Humean picture I sketched at the start. Remember that on that picture, to speak of moral truth or moral reality is only a (potentially misleading) *façon de parler*, because each of these "moral realities" is defined by a set of basic desires. But the agent's-group relativist claim is a claim about what the moral world is like *for everyone*: namely, a moral world in which what it is right for each person to do sometimes depends on facts about his cultural background. It is consistent with a rejection of the Humean picture.

That is why the philosopher thinks D less interesting than this claim, which I discussed a little while ago:

R: E is true for an Asante and false for a New Jerseyan.

("True for" here means "as appraised by," of course. It doesn't mean that E is true when the person who finds the stone is Asante and false when the person who finds it is New Jerseyan. That would make it more or less equivalent to D.)

d. If a philosopher finds R more interesting, that should not distract us from the interest of D, or from the fact that D is much more likely to be what the anthropologist who supported it had in mind. Cultural relativism was proposed, in part, by Boas and his heirs, as an alternative to ethnocentrism: and D teaches us (in New Jersey) that we may be wrong to think that the Asante's abandonment of his children was a moral error. Once we see why he did it, once we understand the cultural context, we see him as reasonable, in light of the beliefs he has, beliefs that his cultural context makes it natural for him to have. Even if the beliefs are false (because there are no *abosom*, say), we can hold it to be reasonable for anyone who has those beliefs to act in the way that he did. And to get to that conclusion we do not need to accept R.

We can still think there's a sense in which what a father who neglects his children after a call to serve a god did was wrong, even if it is excusable. It's wrong because there are no gods, so that taking up service to them is pointless. But this draws attention to another way in which a broader nonmoral cultural relativism may be relevant to the moral evaluation of the acts of people in other societies. For if you thought that the question *whether there were any gods* could be settled only within a cultural frame – if you thought that the claim that there were gods was true for some and not for others – then you could suppose that D was true because if you have the beliefs of a traditional Asante it is true-for-you that there are gods.

I have great difficulty in understanding this last claim. It seems to me obvious that a person can reasonably believe what is not, in fact, true. It seems to me obvious too that what it is reasonable for you to believe can depend on your cultural background and the beliefs and values you inherit from it. And from this it follows, I think, that it can be reasonable, faced with a certain body of evidence, to believe something if you have one cultural background that it would be unreasonable to believe, faced with the same evidence, if you had a different cultural background. I take it that most anthropologists and philosophers would accept all this.

But I do not find it easy to make sense of the thought that the *abosom* exist-for-the-Asante while not existing-for-the-New-Jerseyan. I suppose this may be a – somewhat misleading – way of formulating what I said seemed obvious in the last paragraph. I can also see why someone might think that, in these circumstances, there is nothing either party can do to rationally require the other to change her mind. But taken literally it strikes me as just nonsense to suppose that the Asante lives in a world where there really are *abosom* and the New Jerseyan exists in a world where there really are none. Nevertheless, I think the truth of D, and claims of that form, would establish a kind of relativism of the sort that I think Boas aimed to disseminate.

There is another way in which someone might think you could make sense of the idea of something being true for the Asante but not for the New Jerseyan. It would be to adopt the sort of holism about meaning that I mentioned at the start, which holds that a concept's content is fixed by its place in a whole system of belief. From that starting point, you might conclude that you could only understand talk of the *abosom* if you shared all or (more modestly) many Asante beliefs. That is, in essence, what Peter Winch thought about Zande witchcraft, oracles, and magic. He thought you could not assess them if you did not inhabit the Zande world of thought; and conversely, if you did inhabit it, you would be bound to find them reasonable. If that were true, then our situation with respect to the father who thinks he is called by an *obosom* would be different: we would literally not have any idea what he was thinking. To say that there was something that was true-for-him, though you could make no sense of it would be rather less generous than at first appeared. But most ethnographers have not been tempted by this line of thought. They have thought that their task was to make alien forms of thought intelligible to us, not to prove them unintelligible.

e. Someone might reasonably hold D to be true, I claim, but R makes little sense. Accepting D, however, is not the same as agreeing that agent's-group relativism is true in every case. I could accept D while denying a different agent's-group relativist claim:

> M: If your culture has a norm that allows fathers not to take care of their children (and you accept the norm), then you are not blameworthy if you do not take care of your children (in circumstances where the norm permits you not to do so).

M looks like it expresses a moral idea: namely that what matters most in assessing blame is something like integrity, acting consistently with moral principles you (reasonably) hold to be right. It suggests, too, that someone can never be blameworthy if they act out of a sincere but mistaken moral belief. It is a matter of current philosophical controversy whether this is so (Rosen 2004; Harman 2010).

But you could hold M to be true while still thinking that, in allowing fathers to evade responsibility for their offspring, a culture would be propagating the false moral belief that there is nothing wrong with acts of that kind. M, that is, could be accepted *either* by someone who was an agent's-group relativist – someone who really thought that the fact that your society holds something permissible makes doing it right for you – *or* by someone who held that, in those circumstances, not supporting your children was still wrong but was nevertheless not blameworthy. We can distinguish, that is, between the moral status of the act and the moral status of the agent. Saying the agent is okay does not require us to think the act is.

If you are not an agent's-group relativist, but you believe things like M, you will be very concerned with whether descriptive moral relativism is true. You will want to know whether there is any way of rationally demonstrating to people in such a society that their sincere belief is wrong. Even if you think there are a priori arguments to be made about this, you might want to look at ethnographic and historical evidence about encounters between people with conflicting moral beliefs in order to decide whether, even if there is no a priori guarantee that such arguments are available, certain basic human norms are – as Donald Brown (1991) among others, has argued – contingently universal. (As I said at the start, recent work in moral psychology suggests that there might be neuropsychological reasons why this was so.) Of course, even if there are contingently universal moral starting points, it is a further question whether, starting from them, reasonable people could reach consensus in the long run on every question. But surely anthropology has a great deal of information on these topics that is of great relevance to this important moral question.

f. I said there were at least four points at which cultural relativity might get a grip on G. We have considered the way in which the *ceteris paribus* clause at the start might work in a way that depends on the culture of the father in question. Two further places where culture might make a difference are through the concept of fatherhood and the concept of a dependent child.

So far as dependency goes, there are surely very different views in different societies about when a child reaches the age at which he or she ceases to be subject to the management of adults. In many places, too, the answer is different for female and male children, and perhaps for children of different castes or classes. G gains its generality by ignoring these distinctions, through using the culturally variable idea of a dependent.

A similar difficulty applies to the concept "father." Not only are there many differences between the ways in which the obligations of social fatherhood and biological fatherhood are defined, but there are societies where the primary adult male concerned for a child's welfare is neither the mother's husband nor the genitor but the mother's senior brother, as in Asante (Busia 1999); and there are a few, like the Na (Hua 2001), where men play a role in caring for their children without formal marriage to their mothers. These are not, of course, the only possibilities. More than this, whether or not the genitor of a child has a central role, societies differ enormously in the roles they allocate in socialization by gender.

For example, in Warlpiri communities in Australia a "negligent father (who is indeed rare) receives little more than scoldings from his wife and diffuse censure from the rest of the camp. The negligent mother, on the other hand, is sure to be beaten by her husband and very probably by her own mother as well" (Meggitt 1962: 93). Central African Aka Pygmy men spend 85 percent of the day within earshot of their infant children when they are living in the forest and 54 percent when they are in the village (Hewlett 1992: 81); they sleep with their infants and hold them for more than a fifth of their waking hours. Most contemporary New Jerseyans would think demanding this level of attention from a father was simply absurd.

Consider now the complex allocation of responsibilities between a father and a maternal uncle (*wofase*) in Asante. Here are three passages from an account by Meyer Fortes (1950), based on fieldwork in Asante in the mid twentieth century.

> About half of the children under 15 live with their fathers, a large proportion because their parents are living together, and the other half live in households presided over by their mothers' brothers. (262)

> An Ashanti father has no legal authority over his children. He cannot even compel them to live with him or, if he has divorced their mother, claim their custody as a right. Ashanti say that children should grow up in their father's house, but investigation shows that not more than 50 per cent. of pre-adolescent children are found living with their fathers at a given time. Nevertheless, it is regarded as the duty and the pride of a father to bring up his children, that is, to feed, clothe, and educate them, and, later, set them up in life ... This applies especially to sons. Their moral and civic training, in particular, is his responsibility. (268)
>
> A person's oldest living mother's brother (*wofa*) ... within the lineage segment sprung from his mother's grandmother is the male of the parental generation in whom is vested sole legal authority over him. A *wofa* cannot discipline his sister's child (*wofase*) unless she or her husband asks him to; but he can command, and in former times had the power to pawn, his *wofase*. (270)

(To pawn someone is to transfer his or her labor to another person as security for a loan.)

Against this background, it is unclear whether we should say that the Asante (as described by Fortes) accepted the truth of G, since they might also have said:

> W: Other things being equal, the *wofa* ought to play a central role in securing the welfare of his sister's children.

My fourth and final point of difficulty is attendant on the fact that G invokes the idea of a child's welfare. An anthropologist might remind us that a father who arranges the female genital cutting of his daughter no doubt sees himself as looking after her welfare, as does a father who arranges a "good" marriage for a son who wants to marry someone else. Is this evidence that he accepts G? Or, since, in my view, neither of these decisions is actually good for the child, should I say that he does not understand it?

g. How should we take these sorts of problems into account in facing the question whether they establish that cultural relativism is correct about paternal obligations? Before we answer this question, I think we should agree that a large part of what Boas was after in insisting that anthropology teaches the relativity of civilization was just that ethnography shows that *we have to ask this question*. There are then a variety of ways you can go in giving a theoretical account.

One would be to deny that G was anything other than a rough and ready summary of a very complex situation. What any particular father should do rightly depends on what his expectations are about what will happen to his children if he fails to take care of them. That will naturally depend on how the local institutions of family and community are arranged. Of course, there are other relevant factors. What commitments did he enter into in having them in the first place? (Was he a sperm donor, for example, who offered to contribute his semen but nothing else?) If you have a child in the standard way in the context of a standard family in a society that regards fathers as responsible in some particular way for the children they sire, you are, no doubt, *ceteris paribus*, responsible in those ways. But this will also depend on the local institution's meeting certain broad moral conditions: I think, for example, that the moral arguments against slavery mean that an Asante father ought not to have permitted a *wofa* to pawn his children, even if the uncle had a legal right to do so. But I also think that most Asante fathers in the precolonial past were not culpable for failing to see that they had this responsibility. As we have seen, it is perfectly coherent both to say that there is something they ought to have done and that they were not culpable for not doing it, provided they reasonably believed that they were free not do so. It is perfectly coherent, too, to think that the cultural circumstances of Asante life made that belief reasonable.

Another way to go, then, would be to refine G to say something like this:

> G': Other things being equal, fathers ought to play the role in securing the welfare of their dependent children that the local institutions of the family require of them, provided (or to the extent) that those institutions are morally acceptable.

Though the *ceteris paribus* clause here is something whose content would, as we have seen, be the subject of much cross-cultural disagreement, and it remains an open question whether these disagreements are rationally resolvable.

Or you could say, with moral particularists, that there are no general truths of this sort and that one must make one's judgment as to what a particular father ought to do in a particular culture and time (Dancy 2004). And, of course, Kantians will ask what the universalizable maxims are that govern the behavior of fathers; consequentialists will examine the consequences of adopting various practices for human welfare; and virtue ethicists will ask what character traits are distinctive of a good father.

But all of these philosophical strategies, so it seems to me, must proceed with an acute awareness of exactly the range of normative practices that anthropologists report. Even those who think that the fundamental moral principles are a priori and discoverable by reasoning (Smith 2004), must surely show that their conclusions deal plausibly with these human variations. Boas thought that the ethnographic museum ought to teach us that truth was relative to our civilization. I have argued that there are ways of interpreting this view that are philosophically plausible. I hope I have shown too that some of the distinctions of the philosophers allow us to see what is helpful and unhelpful in various ways of formulating cultural relativism about morality.

Envoi

I aim to have accomplished two tasks. One is to sketch a perspective on the territory over which moral philosophers and anthropologists travel together; the second is to show, by way of an exploration of some specific issues in debates about moral relativism, that there is much to be gained from conversing with one another as we travel these common conceptual spaces. It has always seemed to me that philosophy is most vital when it is open to debates with other disciplines; I hope it is not presumptuous for a friendly outsider to declare that it seems to him that the same is true of anthropology.

REFERENCES

Appiah, Kwame Anthony (1992) *In My Father's House: Africa in the Philosophy of Culture.* New York: Oxford University Press.

Appiah, Kwame Anthony (2008) *Experiments in Ethics.* Cambridge, MA: Harvard University Press.

Ashcroft, Bill, Griffiths, Gareth, and Tiffin, Helen (2007) *Post-Colonial Studies: The Key Concepts*, 2nd edn. New York: Routledge.

Baghramian, Maria (2004) *Relativism*. New York: Routledge.

Baghramian, Maria (2010) A Brief History of Relativism. In Michael Krausz (ed.), *Relativism: A Contemporary Anthology*. New York: Columbia University Press, pp. 31–50.

Bauer, J. R. and Bell, D. A. (eds.) (1999) *The East Asian Challenge for Human Rights*. Cambridge: Cambridge University Press.

Boas, Franz (1887) Museums of Ethnology and their Classification. *Science* 9(228): 587–589.

Brandt, Richard (1967) Ethical Relativism. In Paul Edwards (ed.), *Encyclopedia of Philosophy*, vol 3. Englewood Cliffs, NJ: Prentice Hall, pp. 75–78.

Brown, Donald E. (1991) *Human Universals*. New York: McGraw-Hill.

Busia, K. A. (1999) The Ashanti of the Gold Coast. In Darryl Forde (ed.), *African Worlds*. Oxford: James Currey, pp. 190–209.

Carrithers, Michael, Collins, Steven, and Lukes, Steven (eds.) (1985) *The Category of the Person: Anthropology, Philosophy, History*. Cambridge: Cambridge University Press.

Dancy, Jonathan (2004) *Ethics without Principles*. Oxford: Clarendon.

Dilthey, Wilhelm (2002) *The Formation of the Historical World in the Human Sciences*. Princeton: Princeton University Press.

Dummett, Michael (1990 [1978]) The Significance of Quine's Indeterminacy Thesis. In *Truth and Other Enigmas*. London: Duckworth, pp. 375–419.

Evans-Pritchard, E. E. (1937) *Witchcraft, Oracles and Magic among the Azande*. Oxford: Clarendon.

Fortes, Meyer (1950) Kinship and Marriage among the Ashanti. In A. R. Radcliffe-Brown and D. Forde (eds.), *African Systems of Kinship and Marriage*. London: International African Institute, pp. 252–284.

Goodman, Nelson (1978) *Ways of Worldmaking*. Indianapolis: Hackett.

Gyekye, Kwame (1978) Akan Concept of a Person. *International Philosophical Quarterly* 18(3): 277–287.

Hallen, Barry (2000) *The Good, the Bad, and the Beautiful: Discourse about Values in Yoruba Culture*. Bloomington: Indiana University Press.

Hallen, Barry (2009) *A Short History of African Philosophy*. Bloomington: Indiana University Press.

Hallen, Barry and Sodipo, J. O. (1997) *Knowledge, Belief and Witchcraft: Analytic Experiments in African Philosophy*. Stanford: Stanford University Press.

Harman, Elizabeth (2010) Does Moral Ignorance Exculpate? Unpublished MS. At http://www.princeton.edu/~eharman/Blame101310.pdf, accessed Mar. 14, 2012.

Harman, Gilbert (1975) Moral Relativism Defended. *Philosophical Review* 84(1): 3–22.

Herder, Johann Gottfried von (2002) *Philosophical Writings*, ed. Michael N. Forster. Cambridge: Cambridge University Press.

Herskovitz, Melville J. (1972) *Cultural Relativism: Perspectives in Cultural Pluralism*. New York: Random House.

Hewlett, Barry S. (1992) *Intimate Fathers: The Nature and Context of Aka Pygmy Paternal Infant Care*. Ann Arbor: University of Michigan Press.

Horton, Robin (1967) African Traditional Religion and Western Science. *Africa* 37(1): 50–71; 37(2): 155–187.

Hua, Cai (2001) *A Society without Fathers or Husbands: The Na of China*, trans. Asti Hustvedt. New York: Zone.

Hume, David (1896 [1739]) *A Treatise of Human Nature*, ed. L. A. Selby-Bigge. Oxford: Clarendon.

Kant, Immanuel (1998) *The Critique of Pure Reason*, trans. and ed. Paul Guyer and Allen W. Wood. Cambridge: Cambridge University Press.

Lyons, David (1976) Ethical Relativism and the Problem of Incoherence. *Ethics* 86(2): 107–121.

Meggitt, Mervyn J. (1962) *Desert People: A Study of the Walbiri Aborigines of Central Australia.* Sydney: Angus & Robertson.

Moody-Adams, Michele M. (1997) *Fieldwork in Familiar Places: Morality, Culture, and Philosophy.* Cambridge, MA: Harvard University Press.

Moore, G. E. (1993) *Principia Ethica.* Cambridge: Cambridge University Press.

Mudimbe, V. Y. (1988) *The Invention of Africa: Gnosis, Philosophy, and the Order of Knowledge.* Bloomington: Indiana University Press.

Mudimbe, V. Y. (1994) *The Idea of Africa.* Bloomington: Indiana University Press.

Nietzsche, Friedrich (1977) *The Nietzsche Reader*, ed. R. J. Hollingdale. New York: Penguin.

PhilPapers (2010) PhilPapers Surveys. At http://philpapers.org/surveys/results.pl, accessed Mar. 14, 2012.

Quine, W. V. O. and Ullian, J. S. (1951) Two Dogmas of Empiricism. *Philosophical Review* 60: 20–43.

Quine, W. V. O. and Ullian, J. S. (1978) *The Web of Belief.* New York: McGraw-Hill.

Rosen, Gideon (2004) Skepticism about Moral Responsibility. *Philosophical Perspectives* 18(1): 295–313.

Smith, Michael (2004) *Ethics and the A Priori: Selected Essays on Moral Psychology and Meta-Ethics.* New York: Cambridge University Press.

Stocking, George (1968) *Race, Culture and Evolution: Essays in the History of Anthropology.* New York: Free Press.

Taylor, Charles (1994) *Multiculturalism: Examining the Politics of Recognition.* Princeton: Princeton University Press.

Winch, Peter (1964) Understanding a Primitive Society. *American Philosophical Quarterly* 1(4): 307–324.

Winch, Peter (1990 [1958]) *The Idea of a Social Science and its Relation to Philosophy.* London: Routledge.

Wiredu, Kwasi (1984) How Not to Compare African Thought with Western Thought. In Richard A. Wright (ed.), *African Philosophy: An Introduction.* Washington, DC: University Press of America, pp. 159–171.

Wiredu, Kwasi and Gyekye, Kwame (eds.) (1992) *Person and Community: Ghanaian Philosophical Studies.* Washington, DC: Council for Research in Values and Philosophy.

Wittgenstein, Ludwig (1991) *Tractatus Logico-Philosophicus.* London: Routledge.

CHAPTER 32

Moral Psychology

James Dungan and Liane Young

One goal of moral psychologists is to understand the cognitive processes that support and influence human moral judgment. Perhaps unsurprisingly, this task has proven to be quite daunting. Moral psychology, as well as moral philosophy and anthropology, have revealed great diversity in human moral judgment. Moral philosophers have debated ethics for centuries, yet to this day display a wide diversity of opinion on what a correct solution is. Anthropologists have also documented diversity in moral judgment, only across different cultures – what is moral in some cultures is seen as extremely impermissible in others. Still further, psychologists have used the tools of cognitive neuroscience (such as functional magnetic resonance imaging) to show that individual differences in cognitive processes greatly affect moral judgment.

Historically, psychologists have dealt with this diversity by focusing on the unifying aspects of morality, studying commonalities in moral judgment across individuals and cultures. Many moral judgments are robust to different demographic factors such as gender, age, ethnicity, and religion. For example, intent plays a consistent role in the moral judgment of people of all ages (e.g., intending to harm someone is worse than accidentally harming someone). Also, in the trolley dilemma (a popular philosophical scenario), an overwhelming majority of participants judge turning a runaway trolley away from a track with five people on it to a track with one person on it to be permissible, but pushing a man off a bridge onto the tracks to stop the trolley to be impermissible (even though both cases trade one life to save five).

While these approaches have rendered understanding moral judgment a tractable problem, many complexities in moral judgment are left unresolved. No comprehensive model or taxonomy of moral judgment thus far has accounted for its full diversity. Some models call for a division of the moral space based on the content or kind of moral violation. We judge those who harm others, those who cheat and steal, those who betray their family, friends, and country, those who are disrespectful and disobey

A Companion to Moral Anthropology, First Edition. Edited by Didier Fassin.

authorities, and even those whose actions do not necessarily affect others but instead render themselves "impure," such as consuming taboo foods. Each of these acts may represent a distinct area of moral judgment. Other models carve up morality in terms of the nature or structure of the relationships affected by the violation. For example, how one should act toward another depends on whether the target is a friend, a stranger, an equal, a subordinate, or an authority.

How should we divide up the moral space? Settling on a good taxonomy represents a crucial step toward understanding moral psychology, allowing us to determine through experimentation how different kinds of moral judgment are influenced by psychological, emotional, social, and cultural factors. Here, we discuss the limitations of existing act-based and relationship-based divisions and offer a compromise between these existing divisions. We propose a two-type model of morality, wherein both the moral act and the relationship it affects are taken into account. We suggest this model reflects a real psychological distinction with evidence from emotional, behavioral, and cognitive processes.

Do Different Kinds of Moral Acts Define Different Moral Domains?

When faced with the substantive task of dividing up the space of morality, the specific content of moral actions emerges as an obvious starting point. That is, moral boundaries may serve to separate actions that cause harm to others, from actions that show disrespect, from actions that offend God, and so on. To its credit, this approach explains much of moral diversity across cultures. For example, Shweder and colleagues (1997) surveyed Hindu Indians and compared their explanations of moral actions to explanations delivered by Westerners. By and large, Westerners presented a restricted conception of moral action, defining immoral actions as primarily those that violate the "ethic of autonomy." In this case, an action is wrong because it directly harms someone or violates his or her individual freedom and rights. By contrast, Indians, as well as many other Eastern cultures, additionally moralize actions concerning disobedience and impurity, the "ethic of community" and "ethic of divinity," respectively. These ethics include additional moral concerns of doing one's duty to the community and respecting social hierarchy as well as respecting the sacredness of God and the sanctity of the human body. Shweder and his colleagues propose that variation in human moral psychology across cultures around the world can be explained by differing adherence to these three distinct ethics, community, autonomy, and divinity, nicknamed the CAD triad hypothesis (Rozin et al. 1999).

This content-based approach also proves fruitful in explaining different emotional responses to different kinds of moral violations. In particular, Shweder and colleagues' (1997) three ethics map well onto three kinds of emotional reactions to moral violations. In one study (Rozin et al. 1999), students in Japan and the United States read descriptions of moral violations and indicated their emotional response by selecting an appropriate facial expression or emotion word. As this study found, violations of community evoke contempt, violations of autonomy evoke anger, and violations of divinity evoke disgust, supporting the CAD triad hypothesis, and more generally Shweder and colleagues' content-based division of morality.

A more recent content-based approach supports even further division in the moral space. Haidt and Joseph (2004) surveyed the anthropological literature for actions commonly governed by moral codes across cultures, but divided the moral space into five domains, not three. According to the latest version of their moral foundations theory (MFT), these domains are harm/care, fairness/reciprocity, in-group/loyalty, authority/respect, and purity/sanctity (Haidt and Graham, 2007). In many respects, MFT represents a culmination of content-based divisions of morality, offering precise predictions about many levels of moral psychology. At a mechanistic level, the five moral domains correspond to specific evolved psychological mechanisms that explain the intuitive, emotional basis of many moral judgments (Haidt et al. 1993; Greene 2001). For example, purity norms stem from evolutionary concerns of disgust (Rozin et al. 2000), thereby explaining the disgust response across many cultures to purity violations such as incest. At the level of social and cultural considerations, MFT explains cultural and political differences in moral judgment. Consistent with other content-based approaches, people from different cultures or of different political orientations vary in how they value different moral domains.

While MFT, like its content-based predecessors, has clear predictive power for moral psychology, it may suffer from being too limited or too infinitely divisible. For example, MFT has been said to be limited in failing to account for the full range of moral values, including moral valuations of modesty and industriousness (Suhler and Churchland 2011). Content-based theories can, of course, be extended to accommodate additional divisions. Indeed, even now the MFT is being extended to include a domain related to liberty/constraint and a domain related to wastefulness (Haidt and Joseph 2011). However, the flexibility of content-based approaches may also be a weakness, that is, infinite divisibility. Content can be divided (depending on the individual or the culture) to fit any possible behavior, leading to three, five, eleven, or more moral foundations. On what basis do we decide that one kind of behavior deserves its own domain? What principles that operate over moral content ought to guide moral psychologists to lump versus split? Though these questions aren't impossible to answer, they prompt careful consideration of content-based approaches to carving up moral psychology. Indeed, these questions center on a broader one: Are content-based approaches capturing qualitative differences in moral psychology as opposed to differences in the mere content of different actions (e.g., kick versus hit versus cut)?

Do Different Moral Relationships Define Different Moral Domains?

On March 16, 2008, 17-year-old Rand Abdel-Qader was beaten, strangled, and stabbed to death by her father, Abdel-Qader Ali, in Basra, Iraq. What was the reason for this violent attack? Rand had been seen in public conversing with a Christian British soldier, considered by her family to be the enemy. Abdel-Qader was held for only two hours before being released without charge and reportedly congratulated by the local police for restoring honor to his family (Sarhan and Davies 2008). Though many people would emphatically denounce this action as unambiguously abhorrent, honor killings are permitted in the penal codes of a number of countries around the globe – Argentina, Venezuela, Israel, Jordan, Syria, Egypt, and Iran, to name a few.

For instance, according to Article 460 of the Islamic Penal Code, a man who finds his wife committing adultery may kill her and the man she is with.

Suppose, however, that Abdel-Qader Ali had murdered not his daughter but a police officer. Surely the other officers would not have offered him praise. This hypothetical case and the actual event present a problem for content-based divisions of morality, as surveyed in the previous section. Within the same culture, and for the same people, the same act (in this case, murder) may be judged moral or immoral, right or wrong, depending on its target (or victim). Observations about an action's content (e.g., whether the action is harmful, unfair, impure) appear to be insufficient to account for complex moral judgments. What theory of moral psychology can account for such moral judgments that a content-based approach fails to accommodate?

One solution is to divide up the space of morality not by content but rather by the nature of the social relationship that provides the context for the action. Rai and Fiske (2011) propose that morality consists of specific motives to preserve different kinds of relationships. This model of moral psychology is completely content-neutral – the kind of action does not matter; what matters is the relationship that is primarily affected by the action. This approach has the advantage of being able to explain how an action may be judged quite differently depending on the relationship context. Specifically, Rai and Fiske (2011) describe four distinct relationship schemas: unity, hierarchy, equality, and proportionality. *Unity* relationships are close-knit in-groups that share a common fate, such as relationships between family members or close friends. In unity relationships, people can freely take from one another; indeed, active accounting to keep things objectively fair is counterproductive and often undermines the relationship. By contrast, in *equality* relationships, balance, fairness, and reciprocity must be maintained. Equality emerges in justice systems where the punishment is equal to the crime (i.e., the death penalty for murder or more extreme cases in the Middle East, where a victim who was paralyzed by his attacker asked the Saudi Arabian courts in turn to medically sever his attacker's spinal cord: CNN News 2010). *Hierarchy* relationships maintain a linear ranking where people at the top, the leaders, are entitled to more than people at the bottom. In exchange, people expect their leaders to provide protection and guidance. The balance differs further in *proportionality* relationships, where interactions are based on proportional cost and benefit, not equality (i.e., paying a fine that is proportional to the severity of a committed crime). On this theory, then, even fairness cannot be defined by the content of any single action – what is considered fair varies depending on the relationship of the interacting agents.

We suggest that while Rai and Fiske's model explains the variability of moral judgments of the same acts across different moral relationships, this model may go too far in abandoning considerations of content. A father murdering his daughter may be worse than his murdering a stranger (or better, as in the view of Abdel-Qader Ali); however, a father murdering his daughter is still qualitatively different from, for example, his lying to his daughter. Because Rai and Fiske's model is completely content-neutral, it does not adequately account for differences between acts targeting the same relationship.

On a different account, the *kind* of relationship may not actually matter. Instead, what matters for morality is simply the presence of (at least) two interacting agents – independent of their relationship. Gray and Wegner (2011) propose that the moral dyad defines all of morality. More specifically, dyadic morality requires two different people – the moral agent who performs a moral action, and the moral patient whom the action affects. Critically, an act is perceived to be in the domain of morality whenever a moral agent helps or harms a moral patient.

Gray and colleagues provide the clever example of stealing to support the dyadic nature of morality – you can't steal from yourself. Yet, what about moral cases where there is no dyad? Self-harms, for instance, are often seen as immoral (e.g., eating taboo foods, committing incest or suicide), but involve no clear dyad – the moral agent and moral patient may be one and the same. Furthermore, by restricting the realm of moral acts to a single positive/negative dimension of help/harm, dyadic morality may sacrifice the strength of content-based approaches – namely, explaining how different kinds of moral acts may be viewed so differently.

A Compromise: Content and Relationship Matter

Cultural views of self-harm vary substantially. Suicide is expressly forbidden in Abrahamic religions and often carries negative connotations in Hinduism and Buddhism, since it is seen as an affront to God's will or a desecration of the soul and its spiritual journey. Meanwhile, self-cutting is seen in Western cultures as desecrating the body, God's temple, or is otherwise highly stigmatized (Synnott 1992). By contrast, more positive associations with self-harms can be found in other cultures. Seppuku, a form of Japanese ritual suicide, is performed to preserve honor or in response to committing a deeply shameful act. Many religious cults such as Peoples Temple or the Order of the Solar Temple endorse mass suicides as a purifying escape for the soul to a better world. Finally, throughout history, self-harms such as self-flagellation have been practiced in order to purify the flesh (see also Bastian et al. 2011).

A striking similarity across these self-harms, whether permissible or forbidden, is their association with purity. An important determinant of their association with purity seems to be that they affect the self. Performing precisely these acts – killing, cutting, whipping – on another person, is seen as obviously harmful, but not at all impure. This dichotomy lays bare the problem with theories of morality that separate content and relationship – content and relationship are not absolutely orthogonal. Both the content of an action and the relationship the action affects matter for how the moral violation is judged. Put concretely in terms of harm and purity, morals of purity are not simply concerned with preventing disgusting impure acts – but impure acts that *defile the self*. Meanwhile, harm morals are not simply about preventing hitting, cutting, or other harmful acts – but acts that *harm another person*.

To test this theory, we conducted a series of pilot studies aimed at testing people's willingness to commit purity and harm violations against themselves or others (Dungan et al., forthcoming). We presented people with a list of 10 purity violations and 10 harm violations varying in severity (e.g., picking up a dirty Kleenex, drinking cow's blood, being pinched on the arm, being whipped with a belt). Subjects ranked these violations from 1 to 20 from what they would most "prefer" to what they would least prefer. Critically, half the subjects ranked what they would prefer to happen to themselves while the other half ranked what they would prefer to happen to a close friend. We predicted that people would prefer the option most consistent with the adaptive function of the particular moral at stake – not hurting others, not contaminating the self. Consistent with this prediction, when participants chose for themselves, most preferred to be harmed rather than rendered impure; however, when choosing for a friend, the pattern reversed – most people preferred to render impure rather than to harm their friend.

Do people's preferences also accord with their moral judgments? We conducted a second study where we presented subjects with a hypothetical situation in which they were standing in front of two buckets with a friend (Dungan et al., forthcoming). One bucket is filled with painfully hot water and the other with a stranger's sterile urine. In this scenario, subjects had to choose either for themselves or for their friend to dunk their hand in one of the buckets for three seconds. Subjects were told to imagine choosing one of the options for themselves or for a friend and to answer three questions: how gross, how harmful, and how wrong their choice was. As predicted, subjects judged dunking a hand in the stranger's sterile urine as more gross, regardless of whether it was their own hand or their friend's. Subjects also rated the painfully hot water as more harmful for themselves and their friend. Importantly, though, both the act (purity versus harm) and its target (self versus friend) affected judgments of moral wrongness. Subjects rated choosing the urine for themselves as more morally wrong than choosing urine for their friend. Subjects made the opposite judgments about the hot water – choosing hot water for their friend versus themselves was more wrong. This overall pattern supports our theory, that harms are most immoral when directed toward another person, while purity violations are most immoral when directed toward the self.

Preliminary evidence is therefore consistent with the need for a theory that represents a compromise between content-based and relationship-based divisions of morality, a theory that takes both content and relationship into account. We propose that morality can be defined by two types of moral rules:

1 Morals that govern how one should treat the self: these morals dictate how we should and should not treat the self or highly similar others that are seen as connected to the self.
2 Morals that govern how one should treat other people: these morals dictate how we should and should not treat other people, including people we see as independent and unrelated to self-identity.

So far, we have only described how harm and purity fit into the model. Can a two-type model of morality account for other moral concerns such as loyalty, hierarchy, and fairness? In the remainder of this essay, we argue that this two-type model of morality is a useful taxonomy of the full range of moral actions.

Beyond Harm and Purity

Purity norms dictate what acts are appropriate or inappropriate when the self is the target. The same may be true for the domain of loyalty. Indeed, loyalty and devotion can be seen as a blending of self and other – the weaker the distinction between self and other, the stronger the ties of loyalty. This is quite literally true at the genetic level for family members, and at the cognitive level for strong relationship pairs, as in transactive memory – where couples operate using the same shared system of encoding and retrieving information (Wegner et al. 1991). Even less extreme instances of loyalty, including loyalty to one's friends or to one's country, often define who a person is. People experience loyalty and affinity to a group to the extent that a violation against the group threatens their own self-identity. This is seen in group members' reactions to an outside force that threatens the value of the group. Members who show low loyalty react by distancing themselves from the group to protect their individual identity, whereas members who display high loyalty aggress toward the threat, defending the group and by proxy their own identities (Branscombe et al. 1999; Ellemers et al. 2002). In this way, actions against one's own in-group often feel the same as actions against one's self.

Violations of hierarchy and respect are similar in that they also impact self-identity. Hierarchy constitutes the structure of a group, defining the specific duties and responsibilities of each member, importantly, in relation to the other members. The relationship between each member and the group, and of all the members with each other, means that the entire group may experience the impact of any individual member's action – a staff sergeant's transgression reflects poorly on the entire platoon he represents just as the transgression of a platoon reflects poorly on the staff sergeant who leads it. Disrespect undermines the cohesiveness of the group, and thus affects every member. To the extent that what's good for the self is tied to what's good for the group, it makes sense that another group member's disrespectful actions are seen and felt as impacting the self.

As in loyalty and respect, fairness also requires an entity besides the self (i.e., you cannot steal from yourself: see Gray and Wegner 2011). However, whereas loyalty and hierarchy necessarily entail special obligations and connections, fairness does not. In its purest sense, fairness means treating everyone equally, unbiased by relationship commitments. Family and friends are treated no differently from strangers (and even enemies). Fairness, like harm, operates independently of groups or shared identities, honoring notions of autonomy, independence, and freedom. With the absence of any connection between people, unfairness directed toward another person does not necessarily affect the self. As such, fairness morals govern how one should treat other people – not one's own self.

The five domains of morality, as posited by moral foundations theory (Haidt and Graham 2007), seem to fit quite well into a two-type model of morality. Loyalty, hierarchy and purity morals govern acts aimed at the self (or others who are intimately tied to the self-identity, by group membership or relationship status), whereas harm and fairness morals govern acts aimed at others (strangers or people unrelated to the self-identity). Of course, these five "domains" may not constitute an exhaustive list of all moral concerns, but it is reasonable to believe that the two-type model can accommodate other concerns as well (modesty/boasting, industry, equity) (Suhler and Churchland 2011). Indeed, the unique strength of the two-type model is that it is not based solely on content and therefore does not require an amendment for every new moral concern that may arise.

It is worth noting that grouping loyalty, hierarchy, and purity together to make up one type of morality, and harm and fairness another, matches Haidt's grouping of binding versus individualizing morals (Graham et al. 2009; Wright 2011). We emphasize that our model does not rely on the binding–individualizing dimension to distinguish between the two types of moral rules. Nevertheless, this dimension usefully describes the consequences of these morals on a society. For instance, since the function of purity norms is to keep a person's body and soul free from physical and perhaps spiritual contaminants, it may be assumed that one person shouldn't care about another's impurity (barring fear that another's impurity might spread to contaminate others). However, the way that one interacts with his or her environment (e.g., the avoiding or not avoiding of specific contaminants, body modification, or cleanliness) may serve as an overt signal as to whom should be avoided and who would make for a compatible group member. Purity norms may thus reinforce group boundaries and bind groups together (or break them apart) (Sosis and Bressler 2003) without specifically governing interaction between individuals.

Also worth mentioning is the factor analysis of Haidt's Moral Foundations Questionnaire – a scale of the extent to which people care about different moral concerns. Though the model that this questionnaire is designed to test (moral foundations theory) is different from the proposed two-type model, it is significant that an exploratory factor analysis of the data, free from any imposed theoretical constraints, supported a single distinction between two types, that is between binding and individualizing moral concerns (Graham et al. 2011).[1] It is significant that a factor analysis divides moral domains into two types.

The two-type model of morality succeeds in accommodating various types of moral transgressions. We argue that dividing morals into those that govern actions toward the self and those that govern actions toward others is the best taxonomy for moral judgment. Though we have shown how this model works in theory, it is important that the division into two types of morals is not simply an abstract categorization. Rather, this division should reflect a real difference in our moral psychology, each type giving rise to different emotions, different behaviors, and judged according to different cognitive rules. We devote the rest of the essay to outlining three types of evidence that suggest it does.

Evidence from Emotions

Cicero famously said: "Study carefully, the character of the one you recommend, lest their misconduct bring you shame." This exhortation highlights a crucial aspect of shame: it involves expectations, or more precisely the failure to meet them. In particular, shame arises when a person fails to live up to the expectations of others – when a person fails in his or her duties or responsibilities. Shame signals a threat to a person's social bonds. Importantly, a person's negative evaluation is directed at the self, taking into account others' opinions and impressions as well (Lewis 1971; Niedenthal et al. 1994). By contrast, in the case of guilt, a person's negative evaluation is directed not at the self, but rather at his or her specific immoral actions. Guilt arises when a person's behavior is out of line with his or her *own* conscience or moral standards. Consequently, feelings of guilt are found to rely relatively less on whether there happened to be an audience for the action – guilt can arise independently of external observers (Tangney et al. 1996; Smith et al. 2002).

The distinction between shame and guilt raises an opportunity for testing the two-type model of morality. Since shame represents a negative evaluation of the self, then violations of loyalty, hierarchy, and purity – actions that violate the self, so to speak – should be more effective at evoking shame than violations of harm and fairness. Since guilt can arise regardless of whom immoral behavior targets (immoral behavior is immoral whether it affects the self or someone else), the difference between self and other type violations should be diminished. If anything, one might expect actions that negatively affect another person to evoke a guiltier conscience than actions that affect one's self. Therefore, violations of harm and fairness – which impact autonomous agents, free from group concerns – may be more effective at evoking guilt than loyalty, hierarchy, and purity violations. Evidence confirming the prediction that shame is associated with one type of morality while guilt is associated with the other would provide significant support for the two-type model.

Anthropological work provides preliminary evidence. For instance, many traditionalist Eastern cultures such as those of the Middle East, India and Pakistan, and Japan are often described as shame cultures. In shame cultures, shame is used as a primary deterrent of immoral behavior. Not by coincidence, these cultures are the very cultures that emphasize loyalty, hierarchy, and purity as important moral values. Shweder and his colleagues (1997) described these cultures as "holistic cultures," where the concept of a person is role-embedded or bound to context. In this view, an individual is conceptualized as a node in a network. Consequently, people are expected to do what others expect of them, as opposed to simply what is objectively right or wrong. By contrast, Western cultures conceptualize individuals as more independent (Nisbett 2003). Of course, people are still connected to others, but these connections are less fundamental to self-identity. These cultures, including ours in the United States, are often described as guilt cultures. In tune with the proposed distinction between the two types of morals, these cultures overwhelmingly emphasize concerns of harm and fairness – freedom, autonomy, and equality are valued highly (Haidt 2007).

The difference between shame and guilt cultures leads to reliable, measurable differences in behavior such as punishment. In Japan, more people endorsed restitution as a sanction for moral transgressions – with the goal of repairing the damaged social bond. Other work shows that apology has a bigger impact on subsequent punishment in Japan than it does in America (Haley 1986). Apology significantly reduces punishment in Japan, but plays little role in punishment in America. Furthermore, Americans are more likely to endorse retribution and punishment as sanctions for immoral behavior – reflecting a focus on the individual agent. Indeed, punishments in America often result in intentional isolation of the offender from society; reintegration appears to be secondary (Hamilton et al. 1983, 1988). Future work should move from the level of cultures to the level of individuals to provide a more complete psychological characterization of the relationship between guilt and shame and the two types of morality.

These findings concerning shame and guilt offer indirect support for the two-type model. Evidence from other emotions is also consistent with the model. For instance, violations of hierarchy and purity often evoke contempt and disgust, respectively (Rozin et al. 1999). In the two-type model, hierarchy and purity violations represent violations of the self; thus, the function of these emotions is to distance the violator from the self. When the violator is a person, contempt and disgust sever ties, removing the person from the in-group. In contrast, emotions such as compassion, pity, and empathy draw a person into the in-group. When a person meets a stranger in need, one of the strongest predictors of an empathetic response is whether the person perceives the stranger as being similar (Stotland 1969; Krebs 1975). Furthermore, when subjects responded to hypothetical vignettes, empathy increased helping behavior only when subjects felt connected to the victims (Cialdini et al. 1997).

Of course, these emotions can be taken too far in either direction. Disgust and contempt can lead to pushing people completely outside the moral circle, dehumanizing them (Waytz et al. 2010). Likewise, too much empathy and compassion for others comes at a cost to the self. The bi-directional aspect to these emotions fits well with the two-type model of morality. Enemies may be harmed, but not mere strangers. As emotional attachment forms for a stranger, so forms friendship. With friendship comes loyalty. Emotions impact moral judgment in many ways, but certain types of emotions may have a privileged role in determining what types of morals should apply.

Evidence from Behavioral Tensions

Army Warrant Officer Hugh Thompson Jr. ordered M60 machine guns to be turned on his fellow American troops. Though they were never fired, many congressmen were infuriated by Thompson's actions. Beyond Congress, the general public sent him hate mail, death threats, and even mutilated animals. On this description, Hugh Thompson Jr. appears to be violently disloyal and anti-American. And on this description, anyone would seem to be justified in judging him as criminally immoral. But from another perspective, the same man appears much more complicated. Hugh Thompson Jr. famously ordered his men to turn their machine guns on American soldiers who were mercilessly killing dozens of unarmed civilians, mostly women and children, in what would become known as the My Lai massacre. In total, 347–504 unarmed civilians died in the massacre. Surely many more would have perished if it were not for Thompson's brave actions, for which he would receive the Soldier's Medal, albeit not until a full 30 years later.

Though this case seems extraordinary, many people find themselves in high-stakes environments where they are forced to choose between following the orders of an authority and doing what is best for a group versus doing what is just and fair and in the interest of everyone, not simply for the good of one's own group or leadership. Whistleblowers – people who publically expose immoral or illegal acts – illustrate this tension dramatically, as in the case of Joseph Darby, who blew the whistle on the prisoner abuse at Abu Ghraib; and Cynthia Cooper, who exposed phony bookkeeping at WorldCom, which aimed to hide US$3.8 billion in losses – at the time, the largest incident of accounting fraud in US history. Unfortunately, just as common is the violent backlash from a community against those who speak out against wrongdoing. Consider the case of Michael Brewer, who reported a classmate to the police for stealing his father's bicycle. In response, the classmate and two others doused Brewer in alcohol and set him on fire for being a "snitch" (CNN Justice 2009).

A two-type model of morality may explain this backlash against people who are nevertheless acting in the name of morality. Being devoted and loyal to one's group will by definition require favoritism or bias – in other words, not treating everyone equally or being at least a little bit unfair. Similarly, moral action taken for one's own self-interest (or the interest of one's in-group) would naturally come into conflict with the proper action to take for unrelated others (or even the out-group).

With Adam Waytz, we conducted a pilot study to determine whether the type of morals people cared most about predicted how they would behave when given the chance to blow the whistle on immoral behavior. We first presented subjects with the Moral Foundations Questionnaire (Graham et al. 2009) to determine the extent to which considerations of loyalty and fairness mattered to them. Subjects then responded to a series of events in which someone they knew (varying in relationship closeness) committed a crime (varying in severity). Subjects were asked what they would do if they had the opportunity to report the crime to the police. The results show that the difference in how much people cared about loyalty versus fairness, not either loyalty or fairness alone, predicted the likelihood of their blowing the whistle and reporting the crime to authorities.

The tension between loyalty and fairness appears in children too. For instance, reactions to tattling change over development. Infants as young as 10 months old possess a rudimentary sense of fairness and justice, distinguishing helpers from hinderers (Hamlin et al. 2007) and even preferring a character that punishes a hinderer as opposed to someone who rewards them, effectively endorsing third-party punishment and thereby showing an early sense of justice (Hamlin et al. 2011). Toddlers' tattling behavior also reflects similar sensibilities, signaling cases of injustice, like one child taking another's toy (Ingram and Bering 2010). Importantly, these tattles are almost always truthful and result in positive actions on the part of adults to fix problems. Yet in adolescence, when social groups, group membership, and group loyalties become highly salient, tattling is seen extremely negatively. The more an adolescent is perceived as tattling, the less he or she is liked and the more he or she is socially rejected, as measured by both peer and caregiver ratings (Friman et al. 2004).

Thus, the evidence suggests that both the young and the old experience a strong tension between acting loyally and acting fairly. People seem to be forced to favor one or the other, as indicated by their image of the ideal moral person. When people are asked to describe the prototypical moral exemplar, different conceptions emerge (Walker and Hennig 2004). One conception is of a *caring* exemplar – the ultimate moral person is someone who is loving, empathetic, and altruistic. The caring person is agreeable, generous, and selfless to those around them. But another conception is that of the *just* exemplar – someone who is fair and objective, principled, rational, and open-minded. These divergent conceptions of moral excellence are in line with the idea that people are guided by different sets of morals when acting on the behalf of their loved ones and acting in spite of relationships in the name of fairness; consequently, the two may conflict.

Perhaps the most obvious example of conflicting moral values can be seen in the so-called culture war between liberals and conservatives in the United States (Graham et al. 2009). Anthony Giddens writes, "The left favors greater equality, while the right sees society as inevitably hierarchical" (1988: 40). A meta-analysis of 88 studies conducted in 12 different countries confirms that a reliable difference between conservatives and liberals is conservatives' acceptance of inequality (Jost et al. 2003). In exchange, conservatives care more about social order and the familiar. This tension between liberals and conservatives is not limited to a tension between fairness and loyalty, but is found in the full spectrum of moral concerns, clustered in a way that is consistent with the two-type model. Liberals care more about morals of harm and fairness, while conservatives care more about loyalty, hierarchy, and purity (Graham et al. 2009).

Evidence from Cognitive Processes

On the night of October 2, 1996 a piece of masking tape caused the death of 70 people. During a routine cleaning of a Boeing 757 airliner, Eleuterio Chacaliaza left a piece of tape over the static ports just prior to Aeroperú Flight 603's departure. The static ports are pressure-sensitive sensors that send vital information to the pilot about an aircraft's airspeed and elevation. The tape interfered with these instruments, causing the plane to crash into the ocean, killing all nine crew members and 61 passengers. Eleuterio Chacaliaza was charged with negligent homicide and was sentenced to a two-year suspension from his job (Seattle Times 1998). Compare this to the case of Angelica Ortiz who was also charged with negligent homicide but was sentenced to two years in prison for the death of a single person (KZTV10 2011). Why did Ms. Ortiz receive a harsher punishment than Mr. Chacaliaza when her crime, also accidental, resulted in the loss of only a single life? Perhaps because the death she caused was that of her 11-month-old daughter. The 11-month-old was left in a hot car for at least half an hour, where she died of heat stroke, while Ms. Ortiz shopped for groceries.

Relationships between mother and child, husband and wife, are special in that they come with certain responsibilities. Parents have a duty to care and to provide for their children. Friends have a duty to be devoted and faithful to each other. Leaders must insure the well-being of their followers. These obligations, though they aren't necessarily defined or explicitly stated, are intrinsic to the nature of close-knit or hierarchical relationships. Accordingly, qualitatively different standards may be applied to transgressions of loyalty or hierarchy, where people have a duty to protect, as opposed to transgressions of harm and fairness, where "extra" relationship-defined duties are absent.

One way to show this is by examining the difference between actions and omissions. People show a robust tendency to judge harmful and unfair actions to be worse than omissions or failures to act to prevent harm and injustice. This remains true even when the consequences of the action or omission and the intent of the actor are held constant (DeScioli et al. 2011a, 2011b). However, this is not the case when people are bound by certain relationships, as in the case of mother and daughter. Subjects were less sensitive to the moral difference between actions and omissions when the perpetrator was an authority figure or in a relationship with the victim compared to when the perpetrator was a subordinate or in an anonymous relationship with the victim (Haidt and Baron 1996). In other words, a mother failing to protect her child is judged just as harshly as if she had taken positive action to harm her child – since she should have foreseen the danger and was thus responsible for preventing it.

This difference in moral judgment has important implications for divisions in the moral space. Further evidence for a distinction between loyalty, hierarchy, and purity as one type of morality and harm and fairness as another type would be different cognitive inputs to these two different types of moral judgment. This is precisely what Haidt and Baron's (1996) study suggests. In tight-knit relationships where loyalty and hierarchy play a large role, people are judged based on the consequences of the actions rather than on whether or not they intended for the action to occur. By contrast, intent plays a significant role in judgments of harm and fairness. Specifically, people who accidentally cause harm or injustice are judged more leniently than those who cause harm or injustice intentionally (Young and Saxe 2009), as in the difference between murder and manslaughter.

To test this idea, we presented subjects with stories depicting harmful actions (e.g., physical and psychological harm) and purity violations (e.g., committing incest and eating taboo foods). Subjects' judgments of moral wrongness reflected a large difference between accidental and intentional harms and a significantly smaller difference between accidental and intentional purity violations (Young and Saxe 2011). In particular, accidental purity violations were judged especially harshly whereas accidental harms were judged relatively leniently. Purity violations, like loyalty and hierarchy violations, appear to depend less on intent than violations of harm and fairness. To insure that this behavioral difference was not due to specific features of the intent information provided in the stimuli (e.g., the possibility that participants are simply unwilling to accept that people could truly unknowingly sleep with their own siblings), but due to fundamental differences in the cognitive processing for different moral types, we conducted a version of this experiment in the brain scanner. Subjects delivered their moral judgments while undergoing functional magnetic resonance imaging (fMRI). Functional magnetic resonance imaging measures blood oxygenation levels, a proxy for brain activity, allowing us to determine if the neural response to different kinds of moral violations is consistent with the observed behavioral response. Indeed, consistent with the behavioral evidence, brain regions for reasoning about mental states like intentions (including the right and left temporo-parietal junction, precuneus, and medial prefrontal cortex) showed reduced activity in response to purity violations compared to harm violations (Young et al., forthcoming). Intent information, whether measured behaviorally or neurally, matters less for moral judgments of purity versus harm.

The findings that cognitive inputs like intent matter to moral judgments concerning loyalty, hierarchy, and purity less than judgments of harm and fairness provide further support for the two-type model of morality. Actions affecting strangers or other people rely more on mental states, since intention serves as a reliable indicator of a person's future actions – if he or she is friend or foe, to be trusted or to be avoided. For actions affecting the self, however, we are usually aware of our own mental states. The focus is simply on avoiding bad outcomes.

Research investigating the cognitive differences across moral domains is in its infancy. Nevertheless, the findings so far corroborate the two-type model of morality. For instance, a cross-cultural survey has found that in Japan (an interconnected society with strong concerns of loyalty, hierarchy, and purity) people use mental state information significantly less for judgments of wrongdoing than people in America do (an independent, autonomous society concerned primarily with harm and fairness) (Hamilton et al. 1983). Furthermore, new research shows that increasing cognitive load, interfering with the ability to regulate moral responses, causes conservatives to de-prioritize loyalty, hierarchy, and purity in favor of harm and fairness (Wright 2011). Accordingly, it is plausible that adherence to one type of morality, whereby everyone is treated as a stranger, not to be harmed or treated unfairly, is the baseline. It may require extra cognitive resources to adhere to the second type of morality, whereby people are seen as relating to the self and connections are formed. Taken together, these emerging results provide further evidence that the divide suggested by the two-type model reflects a real difference in cognitive processing and not simply content. We suggest that the two-type model of morality succeeds best at explaining these differences.

Conclusion

Morality is complex. It makes sense then that the space of morality can be divided up in many ways. Past theories have suggested divisions by content to explain cultural variability. Newer theories have suggested divisions by relationship, accounting for differences in judgments of the same act across different relationships. We suggest that neither approach suffices. A compromise is needed to fully explain human moral psychology – a theory that takes into account both the content of a violation and the relationship the violation affects. We have proposed how a two-type model of morality divides the space of morality into morals that govern how we treat our selves and morals that govern how we treat others. Based on three types of evidence (emotion, behavior, cognition), we suggest that the two-type model reflects a real psychological difference, rather than simply an intuitive taxonomy.

While we believe this taxonomy can guide future experiments in moral psychology, we emphasize the importance of openness to compromise as new findings emerge. Morality pervades many aspects of our lives. It is inevitable that a full understanding of moral judgment will require perspective and insight from multiple fields of research. Psychology, as well as philosophy, anthropology, and evolutionary biology all have relevant findings for researchers interested in morality. Just as the two-type model of morality represents a compromise between competing theories, so will compromise through dialogue between these fields lead to fruitful results.

NOTE

1 A subsequent confirmatory factor analysis, performed to see if the data conformed to their pre-established theory, supported a breakdown of the moral space into the five domains posited by moral foundations theory (harm, fairness, loyalty, respect, and purity); however, there are reasons to be skeptical of this support. It is trivial that dividing into more factors explains more variance in the data. As it is unclear how parsimony was weighed in the confirmatory factor analysis, it is possible that this analysis was subject to overfitting. Furthermore, the Moral Foundations Questionnaire was designed specifically to emphasize five different domains. This could artificially bias the data toward favoring the five-domain breakdown. The confirmatory factor analysis should be trusted only if a less constrained survey of a broader range of moral values still supports a five-domain model over a two-domain model.

REFERENCES

Bastian, B., Jetten, J., and Fasoli, F. (2011) Cleansing the Soul by Hurting the Flesh: The Guilt-Reducing Effect of Pain. *Psychological Science* 22(3): 334–335.

Branscombe, N. R., Ellemers, N., Spears, R., and Doosje, B. (1999) The Context and Content of Social Identity Threat. In N. Ellemers et al. (eds.), *Social Identity*. Oxford: Blackwell, pp. 35–58.

Cialdini, R. B., Brown, S. L., Lewis, B. P., et al. (1997) Reinterpreting the Empathy–Altruism Relationship: When One into One Equals Oneness. *Journal of Personality and Social Psychology* 73(3): 481–494.

CNN Justice (2009) Police: Juveniles Laughed after Setting 15-Year-Old on Fire. Oct. 13. At http://articles.cnn.com/2009-10-13/justice/florida.teen.burned_1_malissa-durkee-suspect-michael-brewer?_s=PM:CRIME, accessed Mar. 14, 2012.

CNN News (2010) Saudi Judge Mulls Spinal Paralysis Sentence. Aug. 20. At http://www.cbsnews.com/stories/2010/08/20/world/main6789603.shtml, accessed Mar. 14, 2012.

DeScioli, P., Bruening, R., and Kurzban, R. (2011a) The Omission Effect in Moral Cognition: Toward a Functional Explanation. *Evolution and Human Behavior* 32: 204–215.

DeScioli, P., Christner, J., and Kurzban, R. (2011b) The Omission Strategy. *Psychological Science* 22(4): 442–446.

Dungan, J., Chakroff, A., and Young, L. (forthcoming) Purity versus Pain: Distinct Moral Concerns for Self versus Other.

Ellemers, N., Spears, R., and Doosje, B. (2002) Self and Social Identity. *Annual Review of Psychology*, 53: 161–186.

Friman, P. C., Woods, D. W., Freeman, K. A., et al. (2004) Relationships between Tattling, Likeability, and Social Classification: A Preliminary Investigation of Adolescents in Residential Care. *Behavior Modification* 28(3): 331–348.

Giddens, A. (1998) *The Third Way: The Renewal of Social Democracy*. Cambridge: Polity.

Graham, J., Haidt, J., and Nosek, B. A. (2009) Liberals and Conservatives Rely on Different Sets of Moral Foundations. *Journal of Personality and Social Psychology* 96(5): 1029–1046.

Graham, J., Nosek, B. A., Haidt, J., et al. (2011) Mapping the Moral Domain. *Journal of Personality and Social Psychology* 101(2): 366–385.

Gray, K. & Wegner, D. M. (2011) Morality Takes Two: Dyadic Morality and Mind Perception. In P. Shaver and M. Mikulincer (eds.), *The Social Psychology of Morality: Exploring the Causes of Good and Evil*. New York: APA.

Greene, J. D., Sommerville, R. B., Nystrom, L. E., et al. (2001) An fMRI Investigation of Emotional Engagement in Moral Judgment. *Science* 293(5537): 2105–2108.

Haidt, J. and Baron, J. (1996) Social Roles and the Moral Judgment of Acts and Omissions. *European Journal of Social Psychology* 26: 201–218.

Haidt, J. and Graham, J. (2007) When Morality Opposes Justice: Conservatives Have Moral Intuitions that Liberals May Not Recognize. *Social Justice Research* 20: 98–116.

Haidt, J. and Joseph, C. (2004) Intuitive Ethics: How Innately Prepared Intuitions Generate Culturally Variable Virtues. *Daedalus* [special issue, "Human Nature"] 133(4): 55–66.

Haidt, J. and Joseph, C. (2011) How Moral Foundations Theory Succeeded in Building on Sand: A Response to Suhler and Churchland. *Journal of Cognitive Neuroscience* 23(9): 2117–2122.

Haidt, J., Koller, S. H., and Dias, M. G. (1993) Affect, Culture and Morality, or, Is It Wrong to Eat Your Dog? *Journal of Personality and Social Psychology* 65: 613–628.

Haley, J. O. (1986) Comment: The Implications of Apology. *Law & Society Review* 20: 499–505.

Hamilton, V. L., Sanders, J., Hosoi, Y., et al. (1983) Universals in Judging Wrongdoing: Japanese and Americans Compared. *American Sociological Review* 48(2): 199–211.

Hamilton, V. L., Sanders, J., Hosoi, Y., et al. (1988) Punishment and the Individual in the United States and Japan. *Law & Society Review* 22(2): 301–328.

Hamlin, J. K., Wynn, K., and Bloom, P. (2007) Social Evaluation by Preverbal Infants. *Nature* 450: 557–559.

Hamlin, J. K., Wynn, K., Bloom, P., and Mahajan, N. (2011) Third-Party Reward and Punishment in Infants and Toddlers. *Proceedings of the National Academy of Sciences, USA* 108(50): 19931–19936.

Ingram, G. P. D. and Bering, J. M. (2010) Children's Tattling: The Reporting of Everyday Norm Violations in Preschool Settings. *Child Development* 81(3): 945–957.

Jost, J. T., Glaser, J., Kruglanski, A. W., and Sulloway, F. J. (2003) Political Conservatism as Motivated Social Cognition. *Psychological Bulletin* 129(3): 339–375.

Krebs, D. L. (1975) Empathy and Altruism. *Journal of Personality and Social Psychology* 32: 1134–1146.

KZTV10 (2011) Kingsville Mother Pleads Guilty To Negligent Homicide. Apr. 14. At http://www.kztv10.com/news/kingsville-mother-pleads-guilty-to-negligent-homicide/, accessed Mar. 14, 2012.

Lewis, H. B. (1971) *Shame and Guilt in Neurosis.* New York: International Universities Press.

Niedenthal, P., Tangney, J. P., and Gavinski, I. (1994) "If Only I Weren't" versus "If Only I Hadn't": Distinguishing Shame and Guilt in Counterfactual Thinking. *Journal of Personality and Social Psychology* 67: 585–595.

Nisbett, R. E. (2003) *The Geography of Thought: How Asians and Westerners Think Differently … and Why.* New York: Free Press.

Rai, T. S. and Fiske, A. P. (2011) Moral Psychology is Relationship Regulation: Moral Motives for Unity, Hierarchy, Equality, and Proportionality. *Psychological Review* 118(1): 57–75.

Rozin, P., Haidt, J., and McCauley, C. (2000). Disgust. In M. Lewis and J. M. Haviland (eds.), *Handbook of Emotions*, 2nd edn. New York: Guilford, pp. 637–653.

Rozin, P., Lowery, L., Imada, S., and Haidt, J. (1999) The CAD Triad Hypothesis: A Mapping between Three Moral Emotions (Contempt, Anger, Disgust) and Three Moral Codes (Community, Autonomy, Divinity). *Journal of Personality and Social Psychology* 76(4): 574–586.

Sarhan, A. and Davies, C. (2008) "My Daughter Deserved to Die for Falling in Love." The Observer/The Guardian. May 11. At http://www.guardian.co.uk/world/2008/may/11/iraq.humanrights, accessed Mar. 14, 2012.

Seattle Times (1998) Peru Orders $29 Million Payment For Crash Victims. Jan. 21 At http://community.seattletimes.nwsource.com/archive/?date=19980121&slug=2729869, accessed Mar. 14, 2012.

Shweder, R. A., Much, N. C., Mahapatra, M., and Park, L. (1997) The "Big Three" of Morality (Autonomy, Community, and Divinity), and the "Big Three" Explanations of Suffering. In A. Brandt and P. Rozin (eds.), *Morality and Health.* New York: Routledge, pp. 119–169.

Smith, R. H., Webster, J. M., Parrott, W. G., and Eyre, H. L. (2002) The Role of Public Exposure in Moral and Nonmoral Shame and Guilt. *Journal of Personality and Social Psychology* 83(1): 138–159.

Sosis, R. and Bressler, E. R. (2003) Cooperation and Commune Longevity: A Test of the Costly Signaling Theory of Religion. *Cross-Cultural Research* 37: 211–239.

Stotland, E. (1969) Exploratory Investigations of Empathy. In L. Berkowitz (ed.), *Advances in Experimental Social Psychology*, vol. 4. New York: Academic Press, pp. 271–313.

Suhler, C. L. and Churchland, P. (2011) Can Innate, Modular "Foundations" Explain Morality? Challenges for Haidt's Moral Foundations Theory. *Journal of Cognitive Neuroscience* 23: 2103–2116.

Synnott, A. (1992) Tomb, Temple, Machine and Self: The Social Construction of the Body. *British Journal of Sociobiology* 43(1): 79–110.

Tangney, J. P., Miller, R. S., Flicker, L., and Barlow, D. H. (1996) Are Shame, Guilt, and Embarrassment Distinct Emotions? *Journal of Personality and Social Psychology* 70: 1256–1269.

Walker, L. J. and Hennig, K. H. (2004) Differing Conceptions of Moral Exemplarity: Just, Brave, and Caring. *Journal of Personality and Social Psychology* 86: 629–647.

Waytz, A., Epley, N., and Cacioppo, J. T. (2010) Social Cognition Unbound: Psychological Insights into Anthropomorphism and Dehumanization. *Current Directions in Psychological Science* 19: 58–62.

Wegner, D. M., Erber, R., and Raymond, P. (1991) Transactive Memory in Close Relationships. *Journal of Personality and Social Psychology* 61: 923–929.

Wright, J. C. (2011) The Role of Cognitive Resources in Determining Our Moral Intuitions: Are We All Liberals at Heart? *Journal of Experimental Social Psychology* 47: 1007–1012.

Young, L. and Saxe, R. (2009) Innocent Intentions: A Correlation between Forgiveness for Accidental Harm and Neural Activity. *Neuropsychologia* 47: 2065–2072.

Young, L. and Saxe, R. (2011) When Ignorance is No Excuse: Different Roles for Intent across Moral Domains. *Cognition* 120: 202–214.

Young, L., Chakroff, A., Dungan, J., et al. (forthcoming) Neural Evidence for When the Thought Counts Less.

CHAPTER 33 Neuroethics

Massimo Reichlin

The word "neuroethics" entered the vocabulary at the turn of the century.[1] In slightly more than a decade, it has become very fashionable – as perhaps is the case with terms prefixed with "neuro." It is now a respectable field of research, with its own journals and textbooks,[2] attracting researchers from many fields of expertise – neuroscience, psychology, developmental biology, evolutionary theory, philosophy, and legal studies. The breadth of interest generated by this field of research is clearly understandable. As witnessed by 40 years of bioethical controversies, ethics is one of the few areas of philosophical research that has a direct and practical impact on everyday life; but there are almost as many theories of ethics, and as many views on specific bioethical issues, as there are philosophers. The promise of neuroethics is to offer – thanks to the investigation of the biological bases of moral judgments – the definitive word on ethics, that is, the explanation of moral differences and possibly the "treatment" of these differences by direct manipulation of brain processes. While this promise may be rejected outright as mere folly or nonsense, the very hypothesis of such a radical "naturalization" obviously deserves discussion and careful attention.

It is commonly agreed that neuroethics can be divided in two different strands (Roskies 2002; Farah 2005): on the one hand, studies dealing with the ethical implications and applications of neuroscientific research and findings; on the other, studies dealing with the neurobiological processes involved in moral judgment and decision-making. Accordingly, the first part of this essay will discuss the ethics of neuroscience and the second the neuroscience of ethics; the last section will give a closer look to some of the more philosophical questions that arise in these two domains.

The Ethics of Neuroscience

The establishment of fixed correlations between the activation of certain areas of the brain and the performance of certain mental operations was suggested by

A Companion to Moral Anthropology, First Edition. Edited by Didier Fassin.

evidence of changes in a person's mental life and capacities following selective lesions in certain areas of the brain. This research received a very strong impulse with the development of neuroimaging techniques such as PET and fMRI, which provide images of the brain showing the activation of different areas.[3] The increasing body of knowledge concerning brain–mind correlations suggests that mental states may, at the deepest level, be *identical to* neural states, or at least essentially *constituted by* states of the brain. Should this prove true, we could, on the one hand, use neuroscientific techniques to obtain knowledge of people's mental states, and on the other, induce changes in the neural hardware by pharmacological or mechanical means, in order to favor the accomplishment of certain tasks or, more generally, to enhance human well-being.

Ethics and some neuroscientific applications

Several applications have been explored. One relevant area of research concerns the legal arena. Several systems were tested with the aim of revealing the subject's inclination to lie, as evidence of the credibility of witnesses in trials. Such research has been much criticized, mainly because of the difficulty of extrapolating laboratory findings to real life testimony in courtrooms, and because of the difference between instructed lies in a laboratory and authentic lies in real life (Farewell and Smith 2001; Wolpe et al. 2005; Buller 2006; Sip et al. 2008; Bizzi and Hyman 2009). However, it has also been argued that these methods, though they may not be able to support scientific conclusions, may yet prove useful for defendants in trials, where only the reasonable possibility of innocence has to be proved (Schauer 2010). Moreover, it must be noted that the alternative is simply to trust the subjective impressions of judges and juries and the testimonies of witnesses which are notoriously scarcely reliable. As a matter of fact, some such methods of proving the credibility of testimonies and obtaining evidence for the defense have been accepted as evidence in criminal trials. In one case, the court accepted the testimonies of two neuroscientists who stated that genetic testing of the defendant's DNA showed the presence of such polymorphisms as to increase the risk of developing aggressive and impulsive behavior at the phenotypic level; the defendant was acknowledged as suffering from partial mental incapacity, and obtained a significant reduction of punishment on appeal.[4]

More applications in other areas of human life are forthcoming. Several studies aimed to explain the political choices of potential voters by performing fMRI scans of their brains while they were presented with photos and videos of prospective candidates (Iacoboni 2007; *Nature* 2007). It is suggested that the study of emotional reactions, as revealed by the activation of particular brain areas such as the amygdala, may help predict undecided voters' behavior. Furthermore, it may be used as an effective way to identify prospective political candidates who are more likely to win the public's consensus. Likely future projects include the realization of population screenings in order to detect socially undesirable behavioral traits, such as the predisposition to violence or to racist attitudes (Phelps et al. 2000; Phelps and Thomas 2003). The hypothesis of a sort of "neural fingerprint" promises to help predict and possibly counter antisocial behavior. More ambitious projects may go so far as to attempt neurophysiologic explanations of such processes as falling in love or sexual attraction (Esch and Stefano 2005; Young 2009).

Several problems are raised by these actual or prospective applications (or better by their implicit assumptions). For one thing, it must be questioned whether the results of these neurophysiologic investigations can in fact be taken as reliable forms of "mind reading." In fact, although certain associations between the activation of some brain areas and the performance of some mental operations are established, they do not display any kind of necessity, and even less any bi-uniqueness: the results of neuroimaging techniques basically have a statistical value, and nothing excludes that different subjects, or the same subject at different times, should show slightly different brain activations correlated to the same mental operations; conversely, nothing unequivocally ties the activation of a certain area to the performance of one specific type of mental operation. That certain brain activations are detected, for example in regions connected to the emotional sphere, cannot always be simply interpreted as the decision to undertake a specific action, or even as a settled disposition to undertake any such action. Human decision-making is a very complex process; brain activations are part of the story we need to reconstruct in order to reach an explanation, but they cannot be the whole story. To single out a particular brain factor as a determinant is always risky, since many brain processes, with many reciprocal interactions, are being performed at any time.

Moreover, though we should accept the possibility of detecting relatively stable patterns of brain activation in an individual, sufficient to establish the existence of a settled disposition, this could not mean that the individual will inevitably react in a certain way if certain conditions are met; nor will it justify any preemptive intervention on the part of society. In fact, any brain activation may be consistent with more than one interpretation. For example, if people react with certain emotions on being shown the faces of people whose skin color is different from theirs, this may mean that they have racist thoughts and dispositions; however, it may also simply reflect a surprise connected with any relationship with people of a different language, culture, or way of thinking, or even just a vague uneasiness connected with what is different from us. Further, it may well be that the unconscious processes of the brain display a wealth of bad thoughts and immoral dispositions. However, just as the process of civilization consists, in Freudian terms, in restraining the wild impulses of the id through the constraints of the superego, so the building of a mature personality may consist in the cultivation of the capacity to inhibit one's spontaneous reactions through calm reflection. The realization of any program of "mind reading" is not only problematic in principle, as it seems to represent a violation of "brain privacy"; it may also lead to overall bad consequences, because negative emotions and dispositions that would never have been implemented in observable behavior may be unduly revealed to cause undesired social effects. In short, the results of brain scans seriously underdetermine mental operations and intentional behavior, and their interpretation cannot be accomplished with any particular confidence (Farah 2005; Gazzaniga 2005).

One more observation bears on the underlying assumption that, in any case where some correlation between brain activation and mental state holds, the causal process must go from the biological to the cultural level. Actually, it seems very likely that, on some occasions, this cannot be the case. Take, for example, the studies on undecided political voters: no one can really believe that the brain activations generated in the subjects' emotional areas are the causal factor that accounts for the formation of their political opinions and therefore explains their voting decision. Common sense suggests that the causal story must be the other way around. It is not that certain configurations of the brain explain a person's conservative or leftist political outlook; rather much broader cultural, sociological, economical, and biographical factors explain his or her political viewpoint, and account for the reactions he or she has when looking at the prospective candidates' faces (Lavazza and De Caro 2010). If this is so, it is also possible that, on other occasions, certain mental factors of the individual's history and personality cause certain brain activations and not the other way around.

The ethics of cognitive and mood enhancement

The detection of stable correlations between brain and mental states also opens up the possibility of modifying the former in order to improve the latter, that is, using neuroscientific knowledge to enhance the well-being of people. Contemporary debate on enhancement is very complex, and much of it has nothing to do with neuroethics (see Parens 1998; President's Council on Bioethics 2003; Savulescu and Bostrom 2009). However, at least two sectors in enhancement research are directly relevant to it: the research aiming to improve cognitive performance and that devoted to improving a person's mood.

In the first kind of intervention, so-called "smart drugs" are now widely used to enhance cognitive functions such as memory, attention, and the ability to concentrate on a task, to resist mental stress, and to work for long periods of time. Some of these drugs have been used for many years on school children, in order to improve their scholastic performance (Diller 1996; Diller 1998; Rose 2002; Farah et al. 2004). Of course, pharmacology is not the only means through which cognitive enhancement may be accomplished. Other more or less realistic interventions include gene therapy, the use of stem cells, and even direct manipulations such as transcranial magnetic stimulation or deep brain stimulation. The situation is very much the same with reference to the enhancement of mood. Here the pharmacology of enhancement has already gone a long way, thanks in particular to selective serotonin reuptake inhibitors (SSRI), effective and safe antidepressants that are believed to have some positive effect on the mood of people not affected by any psychological or psychiatric disease (Knutson et al. 1998; Braun 2000; Elliot and Chambers 2004). And here again it is possible to speculate that genetic intervention, the use of stem cells, or direct manipulation may contribute to this end in the future.

The ethical problems raised by these technologies are many (Farah and Wolpe 2004). Prominent considerations include, of course, questions of safety, as with any other biomedical research on human beings; but there are also much more complex and controversial objections. One such objection – admittedly, not original in kind, since it can also be raised with reference to the pharmacological treatment of many psychological or psychiatric conditions – focuses on the notion of authenticity. The worry is that altering our memory, consciousness, and emotions may threaten our sense of identity, generating an artificial well-being that is far from true happiness. Moreover, the existential value of accomplishing certain cognitive tasks may be lessened by their being the mechanical output of smart drugs, instead of being the effect of one's efforts and capacity to work. As noted by the President's Council on Bioethics, the pharmacological management of our mental lives threatens to confer upon us a "fraudulent happiness": "by disconnecting our mood and memory from what we do and experience, the new drugs could jeopardize the fitness and truthfulness of how we live and what we feel, as well as our ability to confront responsibly and with dignity the imperfections and limits of our lives and those of others" (2003: 213). This worry seems pertinent with reference to the erasure of memory. While interventions to lessen the impact of terrible memories in particular conditions such as post-traumatic stress disorder may seem appropriate, interventions in ordinary conditions pose a high risk of destroying the continuity and meaningfulness of a subject's life history and are very unlikely to promote happiness (Erler 2010). However, the objection is much less telling against basic forms of cognitive enhancement, such as improving the working memory, the capacity to compute, or the ability to concentrate. These basic, all-purpose cognitive abilities are instrumental to much higher and more complex cognitive efforts which may be genuine sources of existential value.

The objection of lack of authenticity has real force with reference to mood enhancement as well. In fact, an increased dependence on drugs in order to cope with the difficulties of our lives may extinguish our capacity to tackle our problems effectively, to develop and strengthen our character so as not to surrender to despair and depression. The active involvement of the patient in the treatment of the psychological uneasiness that is promoted by traditional interventions, such as psychotherapy, seems to preserve the conditions of human identity and of an authentic and lasting psychological well-being better (Levy 2007; Schermer 2011). However, the two kinds of intervention need not be conceived of as in opposition, but may also be jointly pursued. In any case, the worry concerning authenticity does not seem to justify a downright rejection of such technology, rather a presumption in favor of more traditional, noninvasive technologies for the enhancement of mood.[5]

A related consideration focuses on the ideas of autonomy and liberty. Does the desire to enhance certain capacities really express the subject's autonomy? Is it not the expression of some kind of pressure to conform oneself to the implicit standards of an ever more competitive society? (Elliott 1998; Elliott and Chambers 2004). Questions such as these can be pressed against both cognitive and mood enhancers. It seems likely that part of this drive toward bettering one's performance answers not to informed, thought out, and freely made decisions of the subjects, but to desires that are externally induced. This may be particularly so in competitive contexts, such as work or education, where there is an additional worry that the use of cognitive enhancers may alter the conditions of fair competition between people. Many fear a sort of arms race that may be set in motion by the positional advantages that certain enhancers could provide to their users. This is an important ethical consideration, even though hardly a decisive one, as far as the permissibility of cognitive enhancement is concerned. It may justify some kind of regulation in order to avoid situations of unfair competition, for example the provision of equal access to such technologies, along with a ban on interventions for which questions of safety have not been answered. However, it does not seem to justify a blanket prohibition.

One last ethical consideration that is very often voiced against enhancement is the worry that such technological interventions fall prey to the temptation of playing God. It is urged that we abandon the pretension to shape and project our identity and performances, and that we accept the limitations of the human condition as a necessary element of our happiness and well-being. Whatever the value of this objection in other areas of the enhancement debate, it seems very weak with reference to cognitive and mood enhancement. Unlike the hypothesis of radically altering the boundaries of human life – for example, allowing everyone to live for 150 years – the idea of extending our mnemonic capacities, or of bettering the control of our emotions by pharmacological and other interventions, does not amount to a radical change in the human condition. There seems to be no reasonable sense in which we could say that these projects would significantly alter human nature, or be charged with a Promethean usurpation of God's rights or, more prosaically, of nature's "evolutionary wisdom."

In conclusion, while we can be skeptical about the actual capacity of any such intervention to significantly increase our cognitive or psychological performance, and while we have reasons to fear some possible adverse effects, it seems reasonable to believe that cognitive and mood enhancement should be carefully monitored and implemented with great attention, and not that it should be considered morally suspect.

The Neuroscience of Ethics

The second area of neuroethics, and perhaps the one better known to the public and more often discussed, has to do with the study of the neural correlates of ethical judgments. This is a fascinating field of study, which has attracted much attention in recent years because it promises to provide the definitive naturalized view of ethics – the underlying idea being that the complex mental operations in which ethical decision-making and judgment are alleged to consist can be reduced to complex biochemical processes in the brain, and that the observable ethical output is the causal effect of biological mechanisms. If this is so, manipulating these mechanisms could in principle bring about parallel modifications in observable behavior.

Moral dilemmas

Research on the neural correlates of ethical judgments was stimulated by the evidence of the relative roles played by different areas of the brain in generating moral responses; evidence about the functional roles of different brain areas was obtained by the study of the alterations of behavioral patterns in patients with selective brain damage. The most famous patient studied was Phineas Gage, the celebrated nineteenth-century American railroad construction foreman, who, amazingly, survived the passing of an iron rod through his head caused by the accidental explosion of blasting powder. The accident destroyed a large part of his frontal lobe and led to a dramatic change in his personality and behavior, particularly the loss of "normal" social behavior and of the capacity for serious and hard work that had previously characterized him. Neurologist Antonio Damasio used this, as well as recent cases of severe damage in the ventromedial cortex, to stress the interplay of reason and emotion in the ordinary processes of social interaction and moral decision-making, and to criticize traditional views describing moral judgment as a process of conscious reasoning from explicit principles (Damasio 1994; Damasio et al. 1994).

The evidence concerning the basic role of emotions in moral judgment was then tested by analyzing the neural activations of subjects who were asked to respond to situations presenting an ethical dilemma. The most famous of these situations was a mental experiment originally proposed by Philippa Foot (1967) whose aim was to test our intuitions concerning positive and negative moral duties. Suppose that a trolley is riding on a track and the driver is unable to halt it because of its faulty brakes. If she does nothing, five men who are working on the track ahead will be killed. However, if she chooses to steer the trolley to another track, only one man will be killed. This predicament is typically contrasted with another, imagined by Judith Thomson (1976), in which your intervention does not involve simply pulling a switch, but pushing a man from a footbridge onto the track (supposing the man to be sufficiently fat to halt the trolley). This less realistic situation is identical to the former in consequentialist terms, but generates much more problematic reactions in the people interviewed. This intuitive judgment received wide support in recent neuroscientific investigations: most people come to the conclusion that any responsible person has a moral duty to pull the switch in order to spare the five people on the track in the first case, while a large majority of respondents deny that any such duty exists with reference to the pushing onto the track of the fat man; indeed, most people believe it would be *wrong* to push the fat man.

The proposed psychological explanation of the different judgments in the two scenarios is that pulling the switch and pushing the man involve different emotional engagements. The latter is much more emotionally salient, and it is the prominence of this emotional response that accounts for the different judgments in two situations which, on the basis of mere rational considerations (one dead and five spared in each case), are on a par. One famous neuroscientific experiment tested this hypothesis by presenting to the subjects 60 practical dilemmas, divided into "moral" and "nonmoral" categories (Greene et al. 2001); the moral ones were further distinguished into "personal" and "nonpersonal," the former being constructed on the pattern of the pushing of the man, the latter on the pattern of the pulling of the switch. The results showed that the pattern of neural activations in the nonpersonal moral dilemmas were much more similar to those in the nonmoral ones than to those in the personal moral ones. In other words, the areas associated with the emotions – such as the medial frontal gyrus, the posterior cingulated gyrus, and the angular gyrus – were much more involved in the latter, while the first two groups showed greater activity in the areas associated with higher-order cognition – such as the dorsolateral prefrontal cortex (see also Greene et al. 2004). Moreover, as had been predicted by the investigators, the responses of those who approved of pushing the man were significantly slower than those of the people who judged it inappropriate, the explanation being that in these cases the rational, "utilitarian" response had to beat the interference of a countervailing emotional response to assert itself.

Of course, the demonstration of the role played by emotional processes in moral cognition, per se, does not establish the existence of a definite causal link between the emotions and judgment. It does not show that the emotions are necessary for moral judgment, nor that moral judgment is the effect of activation in the brain areas associated with emotional response. Some studies tried to provide just this piece of evidence, by studying moral judgment in individuals with focal damage to the ventromedial prefrontal cortex (VMPC) (Koenigs et al. 2007). These patients exhibit diminished emotional responsiveness – in particular, very scarce empathy, compassion, and guilt – while their capacity for general intelligence, logical reasoning, and even declarative knowledge of social and moral norms are preserved. Compared to neurologically normal and brain-damaged subjects, these patients show a normal pattern of judgment as far as nonmoral, or impersonal moral scenarios are concerned, but they exhibit an abnormally high rate of endorsement of utilitarian responses in the emotionally salient, personal moral scenarios. In particular, the higher the conflict and the emotional involvement generated by the situations presented, the higher the difference observed between the VMPC patients and both the neurologically normal and the brain-damaged ones. These findings are consistent with the abovementioned interpretation of the respective role of emotions and reason in the generation of moral judgments: rational, utilitarian judgments are generally inhibited by the existence of fixed patterns of emotional response, and can find their way only by overcoming such inhibitions, a process which prolongs the reaction time. Patients whose brain injury weakens or annihilates the emotional response rely on the maximization of aggregate welfare, as suggested by the "rational," calculative areas of the brain; since they do not have to overcome the negative emotion generated by the direct infliction of harm on others, VMPC patients treat the high-conflict moral dilemmas just as they treat all other cases (Ciaramelli et al. 2007; Greene et al. 2008). According to the researchers, this shows that emotions play a causal role in the generation of moral judgments, and cannot be regarded as mere consequences of the judgments themselves; moreover, the emotions seem decisive not only in order to put into effect the moral knowledge already possessed, but also in order to acquire such moral knowledge in the first place. In fact, VMPC subjects who were injured early in their childhood did not even possess the declarative knowledge of moral norms (Anderson et al. 1999).

Interpretations of the moral mind

These findings suggested new interpretations of our moral nature, all of which share a critical stance toward the traditional rationalistic view of morality, and an insistence on the role of emotions. The basic idea is that a large part of our moral behavior is shaped by the existence of a coherent set of undeliberate responses that are somehow wired into our brains and automatically generated in the presence of certain conditions. In most situations, we do not reflect rationally on the pros and cons, on the normative reasons in favor of one or the other moral judgment and course of action: we simply respond in a predetermined fashion, appealing to the deposit of moral reactions developed in the course of evolution.

Two general interpretations of the nature of morality have been proposed. In one view, proposed by Joshua Greene and Jonathan Haidt, morality can be reconstructed in a dual-process framework, in which emotional processes are clearly distinguished from rational ones (Haidt 2001; Greene and Haidt 2002; Greene et al. 2004). The moral response is triggered by emotions spontaneously generated by morally loaded situations, just as reactions of disgust are generated by olfactory sensations (Schnall et al. 2008; Chapman et al. 2009). Higher-order cognitive processes, such as computations of the cost–benefit ratio, may intervene, mainly with a view to supporting already-reached conclusions, when time for more reflexive operations is allowed. In this picture, conscious moral reasoning is not decisive for morality; automatic, mainly emotive[6] responses are dominant, for these processes are loaded with a motivational force that deliberate ones lack. Therefore, in cases of conflict between the two systems, it is very likely that the emotions trump the conclusions of the rational system. In other words, this view conceives of our moral nature as based on a moral sense, viewed in a Humean fashion;

ethics is a matter of feeling, "an innate preparedness to feel flashes of approval or disapproval toward certain patterns of events involving other human beings" (Haidt and Joseph 2004: 56), and particularly toward patterns involving (1) suffering and compassion; (2) reciprocity and fairness; (3) in-group and loyalty; (4) authority and respect; (5) purity and sanctity (Haidt and Graham 2007). This position is nativist, in that it assumes that the basic intuitions that shape our moral landscape are not the result of a process of learning in childhood, but are built into our minds by evolution. The basic moral intuitions are like "social receptors" that shape our moral sense just as a few receptors in our skin give us the sense of touch, and those in our tongue the great variety of tasting experiences. This view is also morally noncognitivist in that it relies on the analogy between perceiving a moral quality and perceiving "secondary qualities," such as smells or colors: moral properties are not real properties in the world. These ways of feeling may display some sort of universality, due to the adaptive utility of certain responses, but they may also change in different circumstances. In this view, reason is but *post factum* rationalization, and to explain moral judgments by concentrating on moral reasons is to confuse the cause with its effect.

A partly different interpretation was proposed by Marc Hauser (2006), who developed a close analogy between the development of language, as accounted for by Chomsky's theory of generative grammar, and moral development in human babies. According to Hauser, we should acknowledge the existence of a moral module in the human brain. This module provides a set of innate moral principles that are mainly not accessible to consciousness, but that structure our emotional responses to the facts. Just as the principles of generative grammar do not generate a single natural language but define the structural borders of any possible natural language, so the principles of universal moral grammar do not univocally determine a moral code, but set the borders of any moral code; the variety of human moralities is linked to the determination of certain parameters that are partial variations on the principles (Mikahil 2007). According to this approach, emotions are not enough to make up our moral sense; innate principles are needed to help develop our moral competence by putting to work unconscious specific mechanisms that are sensitive to the deep structure of the situations. In this view, we have developed a moral faculty that is not simply a set of moral emotions; it is a specific mechanism of computation that recognizes the peculiar structure of moral situations and activates the corresponding emotions. For example, as far as directly harming other people is concerned, most people's moral judgments are guided by three principles that are sensitive to the formal structure of the relationship: (1) harm caused by action is worse than harm caused by omission; (2) harm intended as the means to a goal is worse than harm foreseen as the side effect of a goal; and (3) harm involving physical contact with the victim is worse than harm involving no physical contact (Cushman et al. 2006). This structure of innate principles guides the development of our moral experience, just as the principles of universal grammar guide our acquisition of linguistic expertise. The universality of this "moral module" is allegedly confirmed by the large cross-cultural agreement observed in the responses given to the Moral Sense Test, a test that can be performed on the Internet, which gathers responses from all over the world to moral dilemmas such as those presented above.

Both general interpretations of the data available by now are highly revisionist with reference to traditional views of moral judgment and moral decision-making.

They see morality as being mainly concerned not with the weighing of normative reasons for or against certain judgments, or with the reasoned application of certain consciously believed principles, but with the automatic activation of certain emotions of approval and disapproval with regard to the treatment of other human beings, or with the unconscious appeal to the principles embodied in our emotional reactions. In both cases, the Kantian idea of moral agency as practical reason is rejected in favor of some other view, in which the conscious appeal to reason plays a much more limited role, if any. The tenability of these images of moral agency depends on the tenability of some more or less explicit philosophical conclusions concerning the self and the concepts of free will and responsibility.

Philosophical Puzzles

Personal identity

As noted earlier, questions of personal identity have been raised particularly in the context of the enhancement debate. One traditional theory of human identity centers on the continuity between the subject's mental states at different times: in this view, the individual A at t_1 is the same individual as B at t_2 if there is continuity of mental contents between A and B. Now, should cognitive enhancement significantly alter the individual's capacity for storing information, and should it modify the individual's ways of thinking as well, a real break in the person's identity may occur: in a philosophically relevant sense, we could say that the enhanced individual would no longer be the same as the one who chose to be enhanced in the first place. From a moral viewpoint this may or may not be considered decisive; however, it poses a serious challenge to the desirability of cognitive enhancement. If the individual B at t_2 is no longer who she was at t_1, it is not clear what the benefit is for A to undergo cognitive enhancement; in order to accept that cognitive enhancement will really benefit A, we should accept such puzzling notions as that B is A's "closest continuer" (Nozick 1981), or that our egoistic concerns extend not only to ourselves, but also to individuals who – while not being *us* – show a sufficient relation of psychological connectedness with us (Parfit 1984).

This problem may be solved by accepting a biological or physical conception of identity, according to which it is the continuity of our body, or of physical conditions such as the existence of the same brain, irrespective of any mental content, that accounts for the continuity of ourselves (Olson 1997; DeGrazia 2005). However, a greater problem is posed by the study of patients with split brains, who have undergone commissurotomy as a therapy for severe epilepsy. The existence of two streams of consciousness in the experience of these patients suggests that the traditional view of the self, as the central organizer of mental representations and the ultimate controller of decision-making, is hardly tenable. On the basis of this evidence, Michael Gazzaniga (1998) argued that the brain is a physical entity, whose different parts work in an independent and parallel way, lacking any central governing authority: our beliefs are the product of our left hemisphere, interpreting the inputs received from the environment, and the unity of consciousness is not a propriety of a Cartesian *cogito*, but the conferral of an *a posteriori* unity to the reports of the various independent cerebral modules. In short, the self is an idea artificially created by the brain for the purposes of our subjective experience, without any real causal powers (Gazzaniga 2005). This means that a conscious person's beliefs and explanations are very partial and largely questionable versions of the observable events. Our conscious beliefs and decisions, of which we believe we are the authors, are nothing but our belatedly becoming aware of what has happened in our brain, and often a largely unreliable rationalization of those events. This view emphasizes the importance of our brain up to the point of denying that an individual with a very severely damaged brain, such as someone suffering from an advanced stage of dementia, can be considered a human being any longer. It entirely reduces our mind to our brain, at least as far as causal explanations are concerned: our mind is merely epiphenomenic, and the true causes of our actions are to be found in the "neural unconscious," that is, in the neural mechanisms acting behind our consciousness.

However, this picture is far from being the only possible account of the facts. The modularity of our brain, and the importance that its different areas have for the correct performance of our cognitive functions, does not show the illusory character of our ordinary notions of rational decision-making and moral agency: the fact that we cannot perform certain tasks without the support of our brain functions does not imply that it is the brain itself that performs those tasks. And that individuals with split brains experience two streams of consciousness does not demonstrate that conscious decision-making by the self plays no role in healthy patients. The discussion of the questions of free will and moral responsibility will help us to see why.

Free will and responsibility

The view of our moral nature emerging from neuroethical research is one according to which our mental states are the product, or the subjective coin, of states of our brain; this, together with the ideas that our brain is a physical entity, governed by the laws of physics, and that the world of physics is deterministic – that is, every event in it is caused by prior events and conditions, according to the laws of nature – produces the inevitable conclusion that the notion of free will must be jettisoned (Smilansky 2000; Walter 2001). Our decisions and intentions to act must then be understood as functions of the state of our brain at the time, which in turn is determined by the biochemical and electric processes going on in our head; our brain is a causal machine that, in the presence of certain inputs, such as increased blood flow or increased quantity of certain neurotransmitters, produces outputs such as decisions and intentions. Accordingly, it would be wrong to say that people are responsible for what they have done because they might have chosen to do otherwise or because different futures were open before them. This notion, grounded in the idea that the subject's consciousness of her states has causal powers in producing her decisions, incorporates the illusion of free will, and must be abandoned.

One possible objection to this emerging view is that neuroscience cannot corroborate either determinism or indeterminism at a fundamental level. What neuroscience reveals is not only that the brain is organized in a mechanistic fashion, but also that its processes are stochastic and largely unpredictable: "However, whether the unpredictability we perceive is really due to fundamentally indeterministic processes, or to complex deterministic ones beyond our present understanding is something neuroscience cannot tell us" (Roskies 2006: 420). In other words, the objection urges that it is up to physics to decide whether our universe is deterministic or not; neuroscience describes the laws regulating the high-level operations of the brain, but has nothing to say on the low-level interactions of atoms and molecules. Moreover, even if neuroscience should undermine some traditional idea of the free will as a sort of lawless, uncaused cause of our choices, this would not do away with the notion of responsibility. In fact, in order to reasonably attribute moral responsibility for action to a person, there is no need to commit ourselves to an indeterministic worldview, or to accept counterfactual claims about the possibility to do otherwise. It would be enough to say that an action was not performed involuntarily, or accidentally, but knowingly and while in control of one's mental state (Churchland 2006). Neuroscience can help us construct a compatibilist view of moral responsibility, which accepts being in control of one's actions as the central idea of responsibility, while acknowledging that the ultimate cause of our mental states is to be found in the deterministic processes of our brains. Such compatibilism may allow that different choices are possible, provided we have different preferences: that we decide in some way in this case does not mean that our choice will be the same in a similar future case, because our desires and preferences may alter. In any case, the concept of agency, and the related mental concepts of folk psychology, are so profoundly embedded in our ways of thinking to ourselves that we cannot do without them; accepting neuroscientific explanations of the deeper causes of our intentions and decisions will not have a very serious impact on our ethical outlook, and ordinary judgments of moral responsibility are not likely to be altered (Roskies and Nichols 2008). At most, accepting a neuroscientific account of responsibility may imply a shift from a retributive to a consequentialist account of punishment, according to which misdeeds are punished in order to deter future crimes (Greene and Cohen 2004).

However, this account seems to embody a much too radically reductive view of the mind, according to which mental states are fully explained by their brain causes. To say that no action can be performed unless there has been some brain activation, though, is not the same as saying that our choosing to perform an action is caused by such activation. That undeliberate mechanistic processes play a much larger part in our behavior than people commonly believe does not demonstrate that no decisions are caused by the free choice of the subject. I am not thinking of decisions to perform simple motor tasks – which were the object of the most relevant neuroscientific studies on this issue (Libet et al. 1983; Libet 1985; Soon et al. 2008) – but of existentially salient decisions in which more complex and long series of factors are involved. It is not that these choices are uncaused, or that free moral agency should be conceived of as arbitrary and purely fortuitous; rather, some of these choices can be considered free in that the chooser retains the power to attribute decisive weight to one or the other consideration, to let herself be influenced by one or the other element in the motivational field. Moreover, the subjective motivational set itself – that is, the set of considerations that are potential motives for the subject – is the result of causes in which prior "free" decisions of the subject play an important role. When an individual takes a decision in a situation, it is partly because her past choices have contributed to shape her character in a particular way and to make herself inclined to be influenced by certain kinds of motives. For example, the fact that some of the neurologically normal people who perform the Moral Sense Test give utilitarian responses to dilemmas such as that of the fat man shows that they have overwritten evolutionary preselected responses in the light of a more "rational" theoretical approach. This is not intended to show that there are "uncaused" choices, but that the agent herself can be the cause of some of her choices. That is, while many brain events do cause mental events, some mental events may also cause brain events; or free decisions and intentions to act may alter a person's brain configuration, thus predisposing her to particular kinds of behavior and reaction.

Conclusion

Biological and evolutionary mechanisms are the foundations of what we are, as social and moral, as well as physical, beings; but they are constantly being altered by the environment and by the life history of the living subject. Culture and the processes of socialization play a very relevant part in determining a person's character, a process in which the subject's decisions are also an element in a very complex causal field. It is the very complexity of the physical basis from which this subjective activity emerges that enables the performance of even more complex cultural processes, which are ultimately irreducible to their physical conditions. In short, free action cannot be conceived of as uncaused action, but as action in which agent causation plays a role, along with other causal factors (see O'Connor 1995). If this is right, the revisionist views of moral agency emerging from several areas of neuroethics must be partly reconsidered, not in order to reinstate the traditional ethical rationalism or some Cartesian view of human identity, but in order to provide more complex accounts of the subtle interplay between the physical and the mental, the emotions and reason, that accounts for our decision-making. This larger picture seems necessary in order to give a plausible explanation of such a complex phenomenon as human morality.

NOTES

1 Particularly, after the first Dana Conference, which was held in San Francisco in May 2002 (Marcus 2002). The word had already been used in two papers by the Harvard physician A. A. Pontius (1973, 1993).

2 The journal *Neuroethics* started publication in 2008. The first comprehensive textbooks on neuroethics are Farah 2010, Glannon 2011, and Illes and Sahakian 2011.

3 Positron emission tomography (PET) measures the consumption of glucose by the brain following the injection into the blood of a sugar marked by an isotope emitting positrons; functional magnetic resonance imaging (fMRI) measures the local increase in the blood flow in relation to the performance of some cognitive task. Both techniques are useful in locating specific cognitive functions in the human brain.

4 This was an Italian case; the ruling was issued by the Tribunal in Trieste on Sept. 18, 2009. Relevant works on the relationship between neuroscience and the law include Garland 2004 and Uttal 2008.

5 It must be added that a recent meta-analysis of the data showed that SSRIs have little or no effect on moderate depression, compared to a placebo, which suggests that their use in normal individuals may have no more than a placebo effect (see Fournier et al. 2010).

6 In fact, the distinction between so-called System 1 and System 2 is not a distinction between the emotive and the cognitive, but between two different modes of cognitive function; emotions, as well as intuitions, are viewed by many as modes of automatic cognition. See Kahneman 2003 and Moll et al. 2005.

REFERENCES

Anderson, S. et al. (1999) Impairment of Social and Moral Behaviour Related to Early Damage in Human Prefrontal Cortex. *Nature Neuroscience* 2: 1032–1037.

Bizzi, E. and Hyman, S. E. (eds.) (2009) *Using Imaging to Identify Deceit: Scientific and Ethical Questions.* Cambridge, MA: American Academy of Arts and Sciences.

Braun, S. (2000) *The Science of Happiness: Unlocking the Mysteries of Mood.* New York: Wiley.

Buller, T. (2006) Brains, Lies, and Psychological Explanations. In J. Illes (ed.), *Neuroethics: Defining the Issues in Theory, Practice, and Policy.* Oxford: Oxford University Press, pp. 51–60.

Chapman, H. A., Kim, D. A., Susskind, J. M., and Anderson, A. K. (2009) In Bad Taste: Evidence for the Oral Origins of Moral Disgust. *Science* 323: 1222–1226.

Churchland, P. S. (2006) Moral Decision-Making and the Brain. In J. Illes (ed.), *Neuroethics: Defining the Issues in Theory, Practice, and Policy.* Oxford: Oxford University Press, pp. 3–16.

Ciaramelli, E., Miccioli, M., Làdavas, E., et al. (2007) Selective Deficit in Personal Moral Judgment Following Damage to Ventromedial Prefrontal Cortex. *Social Cognitive and Affective Neuroscience* 2(2): 84–92.

Cushman, F., Young, L., and Hauser, M. (2006) The Role of Conscious Reasoning and Intuition in Moral Judgments: Testing Three Principles of Harm. *Psychological Science* 17: 1082–1089.

Damasio, A. (1994) *Descartes' Error: Emotion, Reason, and the Human Brain.* New York: Putnam.

Damasio, H., Grabowski, T., Frank, R., et al. (1994) The Return of Phineas Gage: Clues about the Brain from the Skull of a Famous Patient. *Science* 264: 1102–1105.

DeGrazia, D. (2005) *Human Identity and Bioethics.* Cambridge: Cambridge University Press.

Diller, L. H. (1996) The Run on Ritalin: Attention Deficit Disorder and Stimulant Treatment in the 1990s. *Hastings Center Report* 26(2): 12–14.

Diller, L. H. (1998) *Running on Ritalin: A Physician Reflects on Children, Society and Performance on a Pill.* New York: Bantam.

Elliott, C. (1998) The Tyranny of Happiness: Ethics and Cosmetic Psychopharmacology. In E. Parens (ed.), *Enhancing Human Traits: Ethical and Social Implications.* Washington, DC: Georgetown University Press, pp. 177–188.

Elliott, C. and Chambers, T. (2004) *Prozac as a Way of Life.* Chapel Hill: University of North Carolina Press.

Erler, A. (2010) Does Memory Modification Threaten Our Authenticity? *Neuroethics* 4: 235–249.

Esch, T. and Stefano, G. B. (2005) The Neurobiology of Love. *Neuroendocrinology Letters* 26(3): 175–192.

Farah, M. J. (2005) Neuroethics: The Practical and the Philosophical. *Trends in Cognitive Sciences* 9(1): 34–40.

Farah, M. J. (ed.) (2010) *Neuroethics: An Introduction with Readings.* Cambridge, MA: MIT Press.

Farah, M. J. and Wolpe, P. R. (2004) Monitoring and Manipulating Brain Function: New Neuroscience Technologies and their Ethical Implications. *Hastings Center Report* 34(3): 35–45.

Farah, M. J., Illes, J., Cook-Deegan, R., et al. (2004) Neurocognitive Enhancement: What Can We Do? What Should We Do? *Nature Reviews Neuroscience* 5: 421–425.

Farewell, L. A. and Smith, S. S. (2001) Using Brain MERMER Testing to Detect Concealed Knowledge Despite Efforts to Conceal. *Journal of Forensic Science* 46: 1–9.

Foot, P. (1967) The Problem of Abortion and the Doctrine of Double Effect. *Oxford Review* 5: 5–15.

Fournier, J. C., DeRubeis, R. J., Hollon, S. D., et al. (2010) Antidepressant Drug Effects and Depression Severity: A Patient-Level Meta-Analysis. *JAMA* 303(1): 47–53.

Garland, B. (ed.) (2004) *Neuroscience and the Law.* New York: Dana; Washington, DC: AAAS.

Gazzaniga, M. S. (1998) *The Mind's Past.* Berkeley: University of California Press.

Gazzaniga, M. S. (2005) *The Ethical Brain.* New York: Dana.

Glannon, W. (2011) *Brain, Body, and Mind: Neuroethics with a Human Face.* New York: Oxford University Press.

Greene, J. D. and Cohen, J. (2004) For the Law, Neuroscience Changes Nothing and Everything. *Philosophical Transactions of the Royal Society B* 359: 1775–1785.

Greene, J. D. and Haidt, J. (2002) How (and Where) Does Moral Judgment Work? *Trends in Cognitive Science* 6: 517–523.

Greene, J. D., Sommerville, R. B., Nystrom, L. E., et al. (2001) An fMRI Investigation of Emotional Engagement in Moral Judgment. *Science* 293: 2105–2108.

Greene, J. D., Nystrom, L. E., Engell, A. D., et al. (2004) The Neural Basis of Cognitive Conflict and Control in Moral Judgment. *Neuron* 44: 389–400.

Greene, J. D., Morelli, S. A., Lowenberg, K., et al. (2008) Cognitive Load Selectively Interferes with Utilitarian Moral Judgment. *Cognition* 7: 1144–1154.

Haidt, J. (2001) The Emotional Dog and its Emotional Tail: A Social Intuitionist Approach to Moral Judgment. *Psychological Review* 108: 814–834.

Haidt, J. and Graham, J. (2007) When Morality Opposes Justice: Conservatives Have Moral Intuitions that Liberals May Not Recognize. *Social Justice Research* 20: 98–116.

Haidt, J. and Joseph, C. (2004) Intuitive Ethics: How Innately Prepared Intuitions Generate Culturally Variable Virtues. *Daedalus* 133: 55–66.

Hauser, M. (2006) *Moral Minds: How Nature Designed Our Universal Sense of Right and Wrong.* New York: Ecco.

Iacoboni, M. (2007) This is Your Brain on Politics. *New York Times* (Nov. 11). At http://www.nytimes.com/2007/11/11/opinion/11freedman.html?pagewanted=all, accessed Mar. 21, 2012.

Illes, J. and Sahakian, B. J. (2011) *The Oxford Handbook of Neuroethics.* Oxford: Oxford University Press.

Kahneman, D. (2003) A Perspective on Judgment and Choice: Mapping Bounded Rationality. *American Psychologist* 58: 697–720.

Knutson, B., Wolkowitz, O. M., Cole, S. W., et al. (1998) Selective Alteration of Personality and Social Behavior by Serotoninergic Intervention. *American Journal of Psychiatry* 155: 373–379.

Koenigs, M., Young, L., Adolphs, R., et al. (2007) Damage to the Prefrontal Cortex Increases Utilitarian Moral Judgements. *Nature* 446: 908–911.

Lavazza, A. and De Caro, M. (2010) Not So Fast: On Some Bold Neuroscientific Claims concerning Human Agency. *Neuroethics* 3: 23–41.

Levy, N. (2007) *Neuroethics: Challenges for the 21st Century.* Cambridge: Cambridge University Press.

Libet, B. (1985) Unconscious Cerebral Initiative and the Role of Conscious Will in Voluntary Action. *Behavioral and Brain Sciences* 8: 529–566.

Libet, B., Gleason, C. A., Wright, E. W., and Pearl, D. K. (1983) Time of Conscious Intention to Act in Relation to Onset of Cerebral Activity (Readiness-Potential): The Unconscious Initiation of a Freely Voluntary Act. *Brain* 106: 623–642.

Marcus, D. (ed.) (2002) *Neuroethics: Mapping the Field: Proceedings of the Dana Foundation Conference.* Chicago: University of Chicago Press.

Mikahil, J. (2007) Universal Moral Grammar: Theory, Evidence, and the Future. *Trends in Cognitive Science* 11(4): 143–152.

Moll, J., Zahn, R., de Oliveira-Souza, R., et al. (2005) The Neural Basis of Human Moral Cognition. *Nature Reviews Neuroscience* 6: 799–809.

Nature (2007) Mind Games: How Not to Mix Science and Politics [editorial]. *Nature* 450: 457.

Nozick, R. (1981) *Philosophical Explanations.* Cambridge, MA: Belknap Press of Harvard University Press.

O'Connor, T. (ed.) (1995) *Agents, Causes, Events: Essays on Free Will and Indeterminism.* Oxford: Oxford University Press.

Olson, E. T. (1997) *The Human Animal: Personal Identity without Psychology.* New York: Oxford University Press.

Parens, E. (ed.) (1998) *Enhancing Human Traits: Ethical and Social Implications.* Washington, DC: Georgetown University Press.

Parfit, D. (1984) *Reasons and Persons.* Oxford: Clarendon.

Phelps, E. A. and Thomas, L. A. (2003) Race, Behavior, and the Brain: The Role of Neuroimaging in Understanding Complex Social Behaviors. *Political Psychology* 24: 747–758.

Phelps, E. A., O'Connor, K. J., Cunningham, W. A., et al. (2000) Performance on Indirect Measures of Race Evaluation Predicts Amygdala Activation. *Journal of Cognitive Neuroscience* 12: 729–738.

Pontius, A. A. (1973) Neuro-Ethics of "Walking" in the Newborn. *Perceptual and Motor Skills* 37: 235–245.

Pontius, A. A. (1993) Neuroethics vs Neurophysiologically and Neuropsychologically Uninformed Influences in Child-Rearing, Education, Emerging Hunter-Gatherers, and Artificial Intelligence Models of the Brain. *Psychology Report* 72: 451–458.

President's Council on Bioethics (2003) *Beyond Therapy: Biotechnology and the Pursuit of Happiness.* New York: Regan.

Rose, S. P. R. (2002) "Smart Drugs": Do They Work? Are They Ethical? Will They be Legal? *Nature Reviews Neuroscience* 3: 975–979.

Roskies, A. (2002) Neuroethics for the New Millennium. *Neuron* 35: 21–23.

Roskies, A. (2006) Neuroscientific Challenges to Free Will and Responsibility. *Trends in Cognitive Sciences* 10: 419–423.

Roskies, A. and Nichols, S. (2008) Bringing Moral Responsibility Down to Earth. *Journal of Philosophy* 105: 1–15.

Savulescu, J. and Bostrom, N. (eds.) (2009) *Human Enhancement.* Oxford: Oxford University Press.

Schauer, F. (2010) Neuroscience, Lie-Detection, and the Law. *Trends in Cognitive Science* 14(3): 101–103.

Schermer, M. (2011) Health, Happiness and Human Enhancement: Dealing with Unexpected Effects of Deep Brain Stimulation. *Neuroethics.* doi 10.1007/s12152-011-9097-5.

Schnall, S., Haidt, J., Clore, G. L., and Jordan, A. H. (2008) Disgust as Embodied Moral Judgment. *Personality and Social Psychology Bulletin* 34: 1096–1109.

Sip, K. E., Roepstorff, A., McGregor, W., and Frith, C. D. (2008) Detecting Deception: The Scope and Limits. *Trends in Cognitive Science* 12: 48–53.

Smilansky, S. (2000) *Free Will and Illusion.* Oxford: Clarendon.

Soon, C. S., Brass, M., Heinze, H. J., and Haynes, J.-D. (2008) Unconscious Determinants of Free Decisions in the Human Brain. *Nature Neuroscience* 11: 543–545.

Thomson, J. J. (1976) Killing, Letting Die, and the Trolley Problem. *The Monist* 59: 204–217.

Uttal, W. R. (2008) *Neuroscience in the Courtroom: What Every Lawyer Should Know about the Mind and the Brain.* Tucson: Lawyers & Judges.

Walter, H. (2001) *Neurophilosophy of Free Will: From Libertarian Illusions to a Concept of Natural Autonomy.* Cambridge, MA: MIT Press.

Wolpe, P. R., Foster, K., and Langleben, D. D. (2005) Emerging Neurotechnologies for Lie-Detection: Promises and Perils. *American Journal of Bioethics* 5: 39–49.

Young, L. J. (2009) Love: Neuroscience Reveals All. *Nature* 457: 148.

CHAPTER 34

Evolutionary and Cognitive Anthropology

Nicolas Baumard and Dan Sperber

When interpreting the actions of people from other societies from a moral point of view, we often err. Two types of errors are of particular relevance here. One consists in overestimating the similarity across cultures of the moral judgments that guide people's actions and interactions. The other consists in underestimating this similarity. Arguably, the first kind of error is common among psychologists who, since Piaget (1932) and Kohlberg (1981), have studied the stages through which children acquire moral competencies and tried to identify basic principles and components of human morality. Although psychologists do not entirely ignore cultural diversity, they, as a matter of course, approach morality as a general human disposition and competence. The bulk of their evidence is experimental and most of their experiments are carried out with Western or at least Westernized participants. Anthropologists object to these theoretical, methodological, and sampling biases (Westermarck 1906; Benedict 1934; Shweder et al. 1987). Anthropological studies of morality based on participant observation in a great variety of societies show how much moral judgments can vary across cultures, casting doubt, most anthropologists think (but see Laidlaw 2002; Lambek 2010), on the existence of universal moral norms, or even on the very existence of morality as a universal trait of the human mind. After all, "morality" might just be one of these "family resemblance" categories – a notion that Wittgenstein (1953) introduced and illustrated with the category of games – where items are lumped together because each resembles some of the others, without there being any characteristic trait shared by every item in the category. Still, while the richness and relevance of anthropological evidence is clear, its interpretation is not. Moreover, anthropologists' focus on cultural differences

A Companion to Moral Anthropology, First Edition. Edited by Didier Fassin.

and local idiosyncrasies may result in errors of the second type, that is, in underestimating similarity of moral judgments across cultures.

In this essay, we do three things. In the first section, we highlight from a cognitive perspective some of the issues raised by the interpretation of anthropological evidence. We suggest that, when properly interpreted, this evidence leaves open the possibility that, notwithstanding important cultural differences, there may well be universal foundations to human morality. In the second section, we outline an evolutionary account of what such a foundation might be. More specifically, we argue that humans have an evolved moral sense based on fairness, that is, a disposition to take others' interests into consideration and to expect others to do likewise. Finally, in the last section, we suggest how such a hypothesis not only is compatible with the recognition of cultural differences in morality but may even contribute to explaining them.

Issues in Interpreting Anthropological Evidence

The diversity of moral judgments has attracted the attention of students of morality since antiquity. In a well-known passage, Montaigne, for instance, wrote: "Here they live on human flesh; there it is an act of piety to kill one's father at a certain age; elsewhere, the father decides, when the children are in the womb, which will be kept and brought up, and which will be killed and abandoned" (1580: 134). From such examples, Montaigne concluded: "The laws of conscience, which we pretend to be derived from nature, proceed from custom; every one, having an inward veneration for the opinions and manners approved and received among his own people, cannot, without very great reluctance, depart from them, nor apply himself to them without applause" (135). A problem with such early relativistic reflections about morality is that there is no attempt at situating, let alone explaining cultural practices. Anthropologists, by contextualizing these practices, have made them more intelligible and relevant.

That killing one's parent should be seen as an act of piety may seem to be based on moral values incommensurable with those of Western societies. However, in situations found in nomadic foraging societies where finding food may involve walking long distances, the practice is not so hard to understand. As Redfield notes:

> The Eskimo who walled up an aged parent in a snow house and left him to die, did so because in their hard, migratory life the old person could no longer travel, endangered his close kinsmen by his presence, and perhaps himself endured an almost unbearable existence. Furthermore, good reporters of actual cases of these assisted suicides – for that they were, rather than homicides – show the tenderness, even the filial respect, with which the thing was done. (1959: 10)

Redfield goes on to conclude that "seen in context, most customs then showed a reasonableness, a fitness with much of the life, that allowed the outsider more easily to understand and more reluctantly to condemn" (10).

Anthropologists themselves have shown in countless cases how practices that seemed to reveal radically different moral values could be interpreted in a more ordinary manner when the range of options available was taken into consideration. Allowing one's parent to age in comfortable conditions – the "moral" thing to do when possible – may not be an available option. Still, not all cultural norms lend themselves to this type of commonsense explanation. Ethnographic contextualization may, for instance, help one understand how in some societies, people may see it as their moral obligation to kill a daughter or a sister who has been raped in order to save the honor of the family. Still, the moral sentiments involved are likely, for most readers, to remain quite alien or even abhorrent. In the end, it might be argued, ethnographic interpretation replaces Montaigne's superficial moral relativism with serious and compelling evidence of the cultural character and hence the variability of moral values.

What does a cognitive perspective contribute? It leads to questioning not the validity or relevance of ethnographic evidence, but the specific uses that can be made of it in evaluating theoretical claims of a general anthropological nature about what all humans have in common.

Public norms and mental attitudes

At the collective level, anthropologists and historians are particularly interested in norms that are publicly expressed in a given society, either as integrated doctrines such as the Dao or the Talmud, or in a less integrated manner but not less forcefully, as for instance (in Mediterranean rural societies) norms about honor, or (in Polynesia) norms about taboo. These explicit norms vary greatly across cultures, and in many cases are mutually contradictory: in Jainism for instance any killing is forbidden, whereas in many religions bloody sacrifices are mandatory.

Does such cross-cultural incompatibility of explicit norms provide clear evidence against the hypothesis that human morality has universal foundations? To answer, one should consider the place of such normative statements in the cognitive processes of the people who produce or accept them. From a cognitive perspective, what people say is an output of complex mental processes aimed at communicative goals, rather than a simple reflection of their thoughts and attitudes (Sperber 1985; Bloch and Sperber 2002). This is true in general, and particularly so when, in their statements, people quote or at least echo culturally transmitted discourse. Culturally explicit norms are objects of thought as much as or more than contents of thought. Of course, these public representations affect people's moral ideas and sentiments; and, of course, they are in part the collective output of the thought and sentiments of many generations of individuals. Still, it is quite conceivable that such cultural constructions have a rigid and often hyperbolic character that makes them seem to diverge more across societies than the mental states of the people who produce and endorse them. It is conceivable also that, inside a given society, the mental states of individuals differ more than their shared endorsement of the same explicit norms might suggest. In other terms, there might be less cross-cultural variation and more intracultural variation than commonly assumed.

A good historical illustration of the relative disconnect between public norms and moral attitudes is provided by the case of the early Roman Empire. Some Romans endorsed ancient pagan traditions, others had embraced the new Christian religion, and yet others defined themselves as Stoics. Despite this diversity of explicit doctrines appealing to very different principles (the traditional Roman ethos for pagans, the gospel and the divine commandments for Christians, the idea of a natural order for Stoics), Romans had very similar moral opinions on specific practices such as slavery, gladiature, paternal authority, and so on (Veyne 2005).

A good ethnographic illustration of the complex relationship between public acceptance of norms and personal sentiments is provided by Christine Walley's (1997) discussion of so-called "female circumcision" among the Sabaot of Kenya (for other illustrations, see for instance Briggs 1970 about the Inuits; or Wikan 1987 about Bali). Young women, Walley notes, had little choice but to embrace the practice: "For them, to criticize circumcision publicly or to reject it would have led to accusations of cowardice, to social ostracism and perhaps to physical violence" (1997: 411). Girls, but also their families, were trapped in a web of constraints in which circumcision appears to be a necessary condition to get a husband.

Walley, however, wanted to know what the girls "really thought," but the answer proved elusive. In a conversation with some of the young women whom she had seen undergoing the ritual, for instance, Walley elicited mixed reactions. One of them "who had a look of religious ecstasy on her face that startled me argued that it was something that a person had to accept with her 'whole being' and when one did so, one did not feel the pain." Would they, Walley asked, regret the ceremony later? They replied "in a light but serious tone 'but we are already regretting it'":

> there was no delusion among these adolescent girls … about how it would affect their sexual pleasure. I asked whether they wanted their daughters to be "circumcised." One said she would because it was an important custom to continue; a second, after some thought, said she would not; and Mary, whose initiations photos we were perusing, looked uncomfortable and refused to comment. (Walley 1997: 411)

Walley describes this variety of reactions as a shifting of voice according to context. She sees her initial goal to find out what the girls "really thought" as naive. From a cognitive point of view, we would agree, and we would also argue that it would be naive to view the expression of different attitudes according to context as a mere ability to do what is expected of you in different contexts. The young women interviewed by Walley were not mere conformists. They could express acceptance of cultural norms and at the same time think and talk critically about them, drawing on implicit considerations and preferences that have greater cross-cultural relevance. The expression and acceptance of highly culture-specific explicit norms does not imply that the underlying attitudes are equally culture-specific: that much may be commonsensical. Still, the challenge is then to identify and explain these underlying attitudes.

Moral intuitions and moral justifications

At the individual level, under the influence of Piaget and of Kohlberg, psychologists studying morality have long focused much of their attention on the way in which people justify their moral judgments (as, for instance, the young women interviewed by Walley did). These justifications vary with age (which was of particular interest to developmental psychologists) and also with culture. More specifically, moral judgments can be justified by invoking the risk of punishment, respect for authority (that of specific individuals or institutions, or that of public opinion), personal commitment, or by applying general moral principle to the case at hand.

From a normative point of view, these different types of justification are not on par. Basing one's moral judgments, for instance, on a principled reasoning may seem morally different from (and better than) basing them on fear of punishment. These differences in justification are also of anthropological interest. Some societies demand that one's judgments be based on respect for authority whereas other societies encourage personal deliberation, yielding what might be called quite diverse moral styles.

Still, these differences in the style of justification are not specifically moral. Appeal to authority, or on the contrary to personal deliberation, is found in a variety of domains: choice of a spouse, economic decisions, political commitments, factual beliefs, and so on. Moreover, apparently quite different forms of justification may point back implicitly to the same ultimate foundation of empirical or normative judgments. A layperson's deference to scientists may come not from the view that scientific truths are of a different order from ordinary everyday knowledge but from a sensible cognitive modesty. Religious believers who rely for moral guidance on spiritual advisers may attribute to them a special competence to reason from possibly God-given universal principles. Similarly, public opinion or socially accepted norms may be invoked because they are considered as indicative of the good, without for all that conceiving the good as that which is sanctioned by public opinion or social norms. Hence recourse to different forms of justification does not by itself provide evidence of differences in moral values.

Recent work, moreover, suggests that justifications of moral choices are to a large extent *ex post facto* rationalizations of moral intuitions (Haidt 2001; Hauser et al. 2007; Mercier, in press). Jonathan Haidt and his collaborators (2004) for instance have found that people commonly hold strong moral opinions even though they are hard put to justify them. Participants in a now famous experiment found consensual incest between adult brother and sister happening only once, in secrecy, and with adequate precaution against pregnancy morally objectionable but could offer as justification only rationalizations that contradicted the premises of the story (e.g., the risk of genetic defect of offspring). When the inadequacy of their justifications was pointed out to them by the experimenter, they recognized it but maintained their moral condemnation and were dumbfounded by their inability to justify it.

Like collective moral doctrines, individual moral justifications (which often appeal to these doctrines) and the way they vary across culture are of great anthropological interest. They do not, however, provide direct evidence or even strong indirect evidence regarding the existence and character of universal moral dispositions among humans (see also Sperber 1993).

FAIRNESS: EVOLUTIONARY, COGNITIVE AND ANTHROPOLOGICAL ASPECTS

Fairness and the evolution of human cooperation

Since the 1980s, cognitive psychology has taken an evolutionary turn. In discussing specific psychological mechanisms, it has been found more and more relevant to ask whether they are biologically evolved adaptations (as has been claimed of face recognition), or an outcome of a specific acquisition process governed by some specialized adaptation (as has been claimed of linguistic competence), or a side effect of one or several adaptations (as has been claimed, in cognitive anthropology, of religious thinking). To the extent that anthropology is about the human species across time and space, an evolutionary perspective on psychological mechanisms should be of particular anthropological relevance. Morality provides in this respect an excellent illustration.

Homo sapiens is a uniquely cooperative species (Tomasello 2009). Human foraging in particular involves a variety of cooperative activities. Humans share goods and information. They help each other not only in joint action but also when one is disabled by, for instance, illness or injury. Contrary to other primates, humans obtain most of their resources through social interactions (Hill and Kaplan 1999). Although cooperative interactions are mutually advantageous, they also create conflicts of interest. In many cases, individuals are in a position to take advantage of others. For instance, they could accept help offered by others and yet not help others themselves. They could enjoy the benefits of living in a group where people warn others in case of danger or keep an eye on children, but not contribute to these benefits. They could take a larger share of resources produced through collective actions than their own contribution justifies. Of course, if everybody aimed at taking the benefits of cooperation without incurring the costs, cooperation itself would collapse.

How come humans do not take advantage of others to a degree that would undermine cooperation altogether? Understanding cooperation in general, and the uniquely developed forms it takes among humans, has been a major focus of evolutionary thinking in the past 40 years. Several approaches have been developed that may all have something to contribute to an integrated understanding of human cooperation. Since Hamilton (1964), cooperation among close kin is well explained in terms of the advantages it brings to carriers of the same genes. Trivers (1971) has shown how in principle reciprocal relationships could evolve among non-kin. The conditions for such an evolution are, however, rarely found. The idea that group selection could favor groups of individuals disposed to interact altruistically with one another has been vigorously developed and discussed in the past 30 years (e.g., Sober and Wilson 1998; Gintis et al. 2003; Haidt 2007). More recently, the idea of reciprocity has been revised and expanded into a mutualistic approach. According to this approach, there is a "social selection" for reliable partners that favors the evolution of a genuinely moral disposition to value fairness in others and in oneself. For lack of space, we do not compare these different approaches to human cooperation but focus on the last, mutualistic approach (Barclay and Willer 2007; Baumard 2010; Chiang 2010; André and Baumard 2011) and on some of its psychological and anthropological consequences.

In the ancestral environment, as strongly suggested by the study of contemporary foraging groups, individuals could to a large extent choose with whom to cooperate. When individuals can choose their partners, they are also in a competition to be chosen. In this competition, the long-term reputational cost of taking advantage of others is higher than the short-term benefits of doing so: having a bad reputation as a cooperator results in lost opportunities to cooperate (Trivers 1971; Bull and Rice 1991; Noë et al. 1991; Roberts 1998). In the long run, the dynamics of such social selection of good partners are likely to have selected for the psychological foundations of what had been described (with Mauss's *Essai sur le Don* in the background) as "generalized reciprocity" (Lévi-Strauss 1969; Sahlins 1972) and that is now better understood in terms of mutualism (reciprocity being just a mutual relationship between two individuals). What is needed in order to be recognized by others as a mutualistic cooperator and hence desirable partner is a sense of fairness, that is, a disposition to take into account the others' interests, to expect them to recognize one's own interests, and to act accordingly in a mutually advantageous way (Baumard 2010) This sense of fairness is a cognitive mechanism aiming at balancing the burden and benefits of social interactions.

When we say the sense of fairness is a cognitive mechanism, we do not mean to contrast cognition and emotion. On the contrary, in keeping with much recent work on emotion, we see emotions as strongly embodied cognitive states with motivating power. We agree with, for instance, Haidt et al. (1993) that moral cognition is largely intuitive and emotional, a matter of "gut feelings" rather than ratiocination. We agree that emotions that are not exclusively moral, disgust or empathy in particular, may play an important role in moral interactions. But is it that people find behavior that elicits in them a feeling of disgust morally objectionable, or that they find behavior that they judge morally objectionable on other grounds disgusting (as when people say that they are disgusted by treason or corruption)? We favor this second hypothesis and maintain that a sense of fairness plays a central role in morality whereas other emotions play a mere biasing or an enhancing role. Still, there is much cultural variability in the way these other emotions are deployed in issues of morality, contributing to making it hard to ascertain whether there is a universal moral core and, if so, what it consists of.

Fairness across cultures

Moral judgments have often been characterized in contractual terms. We act, defenders of this "contractualist" view argue, as if we had entered into an agreement with others to behave in mutually beneficial ways (Rawls 1971; Scanlon 1998) – or, as the "golden rule" has it, to treat others as we would like them to treat us. To what extent are the "golden rule" and the contract-like interactions it dictates culture-specific Western traits? Isn't it the case that, in most non-Western societies, the group has priority over the individual? As Malinowski (1926) noted in his classic study of morality in the Trobriand Islands, this was indeed the main impression one might gain from the outside when looking at economic interactions in small-scale societies, for instance at the way Trobrianders shared resources such as canoes: "To an observer who does not grasp all the details, and does not follow all the intricacies of each transaction, such a state of affairs looks very much like communism: the canoe appears to be owned jointly by a group and used indiscriminately by the whole community." However, on a closer look, it emerges that relationships between Trobriand fishermen are actually based on mutual advantage:

> In using the craft, every joint owner has a right to a certain place in it and to certain duties, privileges, and benefits associated with it. He has his post in the canoe, he has his task to perform, and enjoys the corresponding title, either of "master" or "steersman," or "keeper of the nets," or "watcher for fish." … Each canoe also has its place in the fleet and its part to play in the maneuvers of joint fishing. Thus on a close inquiry we discover in this pursuit a definite system of division of functions and a rigid system of mutual obligations, into which a sense of duty and the recognition of the need of co-operation enter side by side with a realization of self-interest, privileges and benefits … It is the sum of duties, privileges and mutualities which bind the joint owners to the object and to each other.

In line with Malinowski's early study, much modern ethnography has revealed a comparable pattern in other forms of collective action. Among the Ache, for instance, a semi-nomadic hunter-gatherer population in Paraguay, resources are shared in two different ways: big game is shared equally between all the members of the group, while small game, plants, and fruit are kept by each family (Kaplan and Hill 1985). This different treatment results from the way these kinds of resources are obtained. Small game and vegetables are predictable resources: the longer you spend gathering and hunting, the more of them you end up with. If individuals do not spend the same amount of time hunting and gathering, it is not mutually advantageous to share them equally. Doing so would amount to favoring those who work less than others. Big game, by contrast, is highly unpredictable. Luck plays a much greater role in the killing of a large animal, and hunters thus have an interest in sharing each animal equally: this creates a form of mutually advantageous insurance against bad luck and respects everyone's contribution (see also Bailey 1991, Winterhalder 1997, Alvard and Nolin 2002, and Gurven 2004 on mutualistic relationships in hunter-gatherers societies).

Like resource distribution, punishment had long been seen as an instrument that serves the interests of the whole group (Durkheim 1893). Many studies have, however, shown how, in stateless societies as in most ancient societies, punishment is mainly restorative. Its aim is to rebuild mutually advantageous relationships (for a review, see Baumard 2011). The level of compensation is therefore directly proportional to the harm done: for example, a wrongdoer owes more to the victim if he has killed a member of his family or eloped with his wife than if he has stolen his animals or destroyed his crops (Malinowski 1926; Hoebel 1954; Howell 1954). This restorative logic was quite manifest in the system of punishment for adultery among the Ifugao, a Philippine group observed by Barton in the early twentieth century. An adulterer had to pay compensation in two ways:

> to the in-laws of his partner in adultery and also to his own wife's kinsmen as a penalty for the breach of his own marital contract. The same holds for a married adulteress as well. Adultery is, as noted, a ground for divorce, but it need not be so used. However, if the marriage is to be continued, the offender must then put up a "general welfare" feast at which he regales both his wife's and his own kinsmen. Eating together restores and renews the equable relations of the two groups. (Hoebel 1954: 119)

The same logic held for rape:

> Rape of a married woman by a married man offends both her own and her husband's kin group. Each collect damages equivalent to those paid in a case of aggravated adultery. And then, if the rapist is married, he pays not only to the woman's, her husband's, but also his wife's kin damages that go with aggravated adultery. (Hoebel 1954: 120)

This example clearly shows that punishing rape is about compensating the victims. The greater the harm, the greater the compensation that is required.

Compensation is not always enough to restore justice, however. In some cases, such as murder, it may not be possible to fully compensate victims for the harm that has been done to them. This may explain why, in these kinds of cases, people turn to punishment: since it is not possible to reduce the gap between the wrongdoer and victim by compensating the victim, people may judge that inflicting a cost on the wrongdoer is the only way to fully restore fairness. In line with this idea, experimental studies suggest that as the seriousness of crimes increases, people tend to feel that a retributive component (e.g., a prison sentence) should be added to restorative justice (i.e., compensation) (Gromet and Darley 2006). In the same vein, a range of studies in the United States have consistently shown that the judgments of both juries and judges are based on the idea that the punishment should be proportional to the crime (Baron and Ritov 1993; Sunstein et al. 1998; Carlsmith et al. 2002). If, on the other hand, the function of punishment was to serve the interest of the group through, in particular, dissuasion (as in group-based theories of morality: see for instance Boyd et al. 2003), then, *ceteris paribus*, crimes that are easier to commit should be more harshly punished. Although such a principle has been argued for by utilitarian philosophers of law, it has very limited application in modern law and does not seem to be evidenced in the anthropological literature.

Finally, although mutual help may seem to exhibit the characteristics of an unbounded generosity, it is actually regulated by the same mutualistic requirements that we see elsewhere. In foraging societies, for instance, where mutual help may be rendered vital by the unpredictable availability of resources and the impossibility of stockpiling, individuals expect others to share the costs as well as the benefits of solidarity, and if they fail to do so, they simply end the relationship (see for instance Henry 1951; Price 1975; Aspelin 1979).

More generally, this mutualistic logic pervades social interactions and regulates all kinds of mutual help. Among the Yuroks of northwestern California, for instance, it was the duty of a canoe owner to ferry any traveler across a river when called upon. However, as Hoebel notes:

> in balance with this duty of the canoe owner he enjoyed a … right against the traveler for any injury he (the canoe owner) suffered in consequences of service rendered. A boat-owner whose house caught fire and burned while he was engaged in ferrying a passenger enjoyed a … right for full damages by his passenger on the presumption that he could have brought the fire under control if he had not been engaged on the river. (1954: 57)

This is an example of how the actual workings of help offered on mutualistic terms are carefully monitored, to insure that its terms do not favor one of the parties over the others.

These are just a few illustrations of the commonality of mutualistic arrangements and of the idea of fairness to which they conform. It would take a systematic survey to assess its true generality, but these illustrations are enough to raise a fundamental question: How are such mutualistic norms of fairness maintained generation after generation? The commonality of such norms in societies where they are not imposed by judicial institutions, police support, and systematic teaching suggest that norms of fairness are intuitive enough to be easily acquired and deployed and for departure from these norms to meet spontaneous resistance. This in turn suggests that the acquisition of these norms by children recruits evolved psychological dispositions that somehow "look for" the specific way in which these norms are locally implemented, just as there may be evolved psychological dispositions that cause young children to attend to linguistic inputs and to "look for" the underlying regularity of the local language. This of course, is rather speculative, but it is a speculation that suggests precise cognitive anthropology questions. For instance, do children acquire and deploy cultural norms of fairness with particular ease and do they have any problem in acquiring norms that override fairness? Do people, including young children, invoke considerations of fairness (for instance, in defending their own interests) even when doing so is not a culturally approved practice? Do people attribute fairness-based sentiments or motivations to others even in cases where they are not culturally appropriate (for instance, do they imagine that someone who is harmed in a culturally sanctioned way may nevertheless feel that this is unfair)? These are questions which could be fruitfully addressed by a cognitive anthropology approach mixing sophisticated ethnographic and experimental method (well illustrated in the work of Rita Astuti among the Vezo of Madagascar: Astuti 1995, 2008).

How Far Can the Mutualistic Framework Be Extended?

So far, we have considered only a restricted number of moral situations where considerations of fairness are obviously relevant and indeed central: distributive justice, mutual help, reciprocal relationships, and retributive punishment. Moral judgments, however, apply to a much wider range of cases (Shweder et al. 1987; Haidt et al. 1993) and biologists (de Waal 1996), psychologists (Haidt and Joseph 2007), and social scientists (Wilson 1993) have in consequence proposed to regard morality as the product of diverse emotions such as disgust, empathy, or in-group loyalty that need not be moral in and of themselves. Here we consider just two types of cases where, it seems, norms other than that of fairness play a central role: hierarchical relationships and sexual morality. We will ask whether the norms involved in these cases are (1) independent of, and in contradiction with, norms of fairness, (2) independent of, but nevertheless compatible with, norms of fairness, or (3) at least partly dependent on norms of fairness.

Morality in hierarchical relationships

Since the Neolithic revolution, most societies have been characterized by hierarchy and inequality. People are hierarchically ranked and have unequal access to resources (Johnson and Earle 2000). Most of the time, people seem to accept these unequal allocations of resources and to endorse hierarchical relationships. India with its caste system provides the best-known illustration of this very widespread phenomenon (Dumont 1970). It may seem that, if social interactions were based on mutual advantage, hierarchy ought to be rejected, and that therefore such social arrangements must be based on nonmutualistic value systems.

Still, before drawing such a conclusion, one should ask to what extent acceptance of hierarchy is based on beliefs about matters of fact as opposed to values and preferences. In all human societies for instance, there are hierarchical relationships between parents and children. This is commonly based on the belief that adults' authority over children is, rather than a value in itself, a necessary means to maintain social order through the passage of generation and to help children become competent adults. Not only is such a view quite compatible with mutualism: it follows from mutualism, given these beliefs. Other forms of hierarchy might be based on much more questionable beliefs, but still on *beliefs* regarding the usefulness or the unavoidability of hierarchy rather than on a *preference* for hierarchy in itself. Before the feminist revolution, for instance, most people in the West could not seriously imagine that men and women might share the household chores equally, or that men could have paternal leave to take care of their children. In the absence of an alternative, there was, for the vast majority, no injustice in the fact that women did most of the work. Although people's morality was truly based on mutual advantage, it also took into account what individuals thought were intangible constraints such as the intrinsically feminine character of household chores and child-rearing.

Similarly, as Shweder et al. (1987) suggest, Oriyas believe that a husband's control over his wife's behavior is essential to the working of the family. Allowing wives to be independent would be like organizing an army on a democratic basis: it would simply not work. For the Oriyas,

> beating a wife who goes to the movies without permission is roughly equivalent to corporal punishment for a private in the army who leaves the military base without permission. For Oriyas there are rationally appealing analogical mappings between the family unit and military units (differentiated role and status obligations in the service of the whole, hierarchical control, drafting and induction). (Shweder et al. 1987: 71)

If this parallel is justified, then, for the Oriyas, hierarchical relationships are not incompatible with a principle of fairness, for they are the only possible interactions inside a family. Moreover, just as hierarchy is believed to benefit everyone in the army because it makes it collectively functional and successful, hierarchy within the family is seen as mutually beneficial because both wife and husband benefit from this arrangement. Actually, the Oriyas clearly emphasize mutual advantage: "Wives should be obedient to their husbands, and husbands should be sensitive and responsive to the needs, desires and inclinations of their wives" (Shweder et al. 1997: 145) In this situation, social interactions have a clear mutualistic interpretation: "The person in the hierarchical position is obligated to protect and satisfy the wants of the subordinate person in a specified way. The subordinate person is also obligated to look after the interests and 'well-being' of the superordinate person" (Shweder et al. 1997: 145)

In traditional societies where social mobility is low, statuses are relatively rigid, and institutions seem static, individuals who occupy subordinate positions entertain little hope of changing their situation and may find it hard to imagine that another kind of social arrangement might be possible. In the Roman Empire, for instance, the existence of slavery was considered a natural fact: neither laypeople nor philosophers envisaged that a society could work without slaves. Even rebel slaves who fought against their owners did not have the abolition of slavery as their aim (Veyne 1992). To be born a slave or to become one was commonly seen as a matter of bad luck, not injustice (in the same way that we view the unequal allocation of beauty or talent).

So, just as in the case of relationships between parents and children, various forms of hierarchical relationships may be conceived by the people involved as mutually beneficial. It is too hasty to conclude from a social arrangement that we see as unfair that the values on which it is based are incompatible with fairness. In principle, such an arrangement might even be based on the application of fairness considerations to the necessities of the social world as seen by the people involved. But is it so? To decide whether and when such is indeed the case, what is needed are ethnographic accounts that understand the cognitive complexity of such a question, really aim at addressing it, and are not driven by interpretive biases that prejudge the issue.

Sexual morality

Students of morality have sometimes observed that moral judgments on sexual practices or personal behaviors are difficult to account for in terms of fairness (Shweder et al. 1987; Haidt and Joseph 2007). Indeed, when we speak of social interactions and mutual advantage, we often think of economic exchanges between buyers and sellers, workers and companies, taxpayers and the state, and so on. But a society involves a much greater diversity of interactions, and fairness concerns can be applied to much more than just resource transfers. People are not only consumers, workers, and taxpayers; they are also parents and children, wives and husbands, teachers and pupils, and so on. If, instead of playing their role in each of these interactions, they favor their own interests at the expense of those of others, they behave no less unfairly than they would shortchanging others in economic interactions.

From this perspective, a vast array of normative expectations can be understood in terms of fairness. If we think that a nurse is committed to being compassionate and caring, then we may think he is behaving unfairly to the hospital and to the patients if he were to perform his duties in a cold and indifferent manner. If we think that a school-bus driver must be particularly prudent, we will feel that she does not deserve her job if she does not behave in a prudent way. In the same way, it may be thought that a friend must be loyal, a child respectful, or a partner faithful in order for friendship, family, or marriage to be mutually beneficial. Loyalty, respect, and faithfulness may be valued not in the absolute, but because they are seen as necessary to fair relationships between friends, parents and children, and partners.

More generally, every kind of behavior that is seen as necessary to performing a task of mutual interest in a cooperative interaction is likely to be so moralized. Consider the Christian "capital sins": wrath, greed, sloth, pride, lust, envy, and gluttony. These behaviors can be seen as threatening the actual working of social interactions. If your neighbor is greedy, he won't help you as much as neighbors should help each other. If your colleague is lazy, she won't do her proper share of the work. If your friend is envious, he will ask more and more of you. And so on. Of course, from a theological point of view, what makes these behaviors sins is their effect on grace rather than on social interactions. But from a cognitive anthropological point of view, the question is: what made this list of capital sins such a cultural success? At least part of the answer may be that, in the context of popular Christianity, they are easily interpretable as immoral, not on arcane theological grounds, but on the basis of intuitions of fairness.

Of course, the same behavior may be looked at differently depending on contextual constraints. Passive homosexuality, for instance, has been reviled both by the ancient Greeks and Romans and by the Christians albeit for different reasons. In the Greco-Roman world, passive homosexuality was a sign of weakness. Among the aristocracy, displaying masculine dominance was an essential quality, both in politics and in war. A man who practiced passive homosexuality was displaying personal preferences incompatible with the conduct of a career in service of the common good. Note that, in contrast, passive homosexuality was acceptable and even required of slaves and adolescents whose part in the Greco-Roman social contract was to serve and obey their master and elders (Veyne 1992).

Among Christians, on the other hand, both passive and active homosexuality are condemned. Homosexuality is condemned, in particular, as a threat to the marriage institution. From a religious point of view, marriage is intrinsically linked to procreation and is "sacred," which, intuitively, may be understood as meaning that it is an unbreakable social contract, creating inalienable mutual rights and duties. In the same way, any sexual behavior that is not strictly related to procreation (masturbation, oral sex, etc.), is condemned, as well as any practice that reduces the cost of cheating (prostitution, abortion, etc.) or that encourages sexual promiscuity (drug usage, cohabitation, sexual education, premarital sex) (for experimental evidence, see Weeden et al. 2008; Kurzban et al. 2010). Even for Christians who understand and accept the dogma behind these rules, mutualistic intuitions may govern their everyday sentiments about their implementation and may play a crucial role in the cultural success of the institution of Christian marriage. They may feel that married couples who obey the rules and procreate do their fair share in society whereas people who "fornicate," that is, have sexual relationships not aimed at procreation within the framework of the Christian marriage – and particularly those who fornicate with people of the same sex, excluding the possibility of transforming the union into a Christian marriage – are free-riders or parasites.

In spite of this radical opposition, both opponents and advocates of homosexual marriage may share a deep concern for fairness. Advocates of the right of homosexuals to marry, in particular, are moved by considerations both of fairness vis-à-vis heterosexuals, who are seen as having an unfair advantage in being the only ones allowed to enter into a matrimonial relationship, and of fairness between homosexual would-be spouses: mutual respect, mutual assistance, reciprocal commitment, common property, and so on. We are not denying, of course, that there is a deep moral disagreement between the two sides; we are just suggesting that at the deepest level there may well be major commonalities.

Even for Christians whose strongest emotion toward homosexuality – an "abomination" – is disgust, it could be that disgust is not the primary moral intuition at play but, rather, is an emotion culturally recruited in the service of a fairness intuition without which moral disgust would not "stick." Alas, we lack crucial evidence to decide between this possibility and Haidt and Joseph's (2007) argument that disgust is a basic rather than a derived moral emotion.

This brief survey suggests that humans may moralize sexual practices not because sexual purity is seen as a value in itself, but rather because sexual relationships carry high social stakes and naturally generate conflicts of interest. Indeed, the moralization of sexual practices follows the general line of conflicts of interest. When social forces are favorable to men's interests, women's chastity tends to be moralized and sexual promiscuity condemned. When women gain some leeway in their interactions with their husband and their own kin, sexual promiscuity becomes more acceptable and chastity less praised (on the social determinants of matrimonial arrangements, see Marlowe 2000; Scheidel 2009). Given beliefs about the social necessity of specific matrimonial arrangements, threats to these arrangements may be seen as contrary to the mutual interests of the people involved, and preventing these threats may be seen as a just thing to do. As in the case of hierarchy, we are not asserting of sexual morality that it is, after all, just a matter of fairness. We are arguing that, for all the evidence we have, it may well be a matter of fairness combined with factual beliefs about what is possible and impossible. To go beyond a theoretical argument based on evolutionary considerations and reinterpretation of evidence that has been gathered with different theoretical aims (if any), both psychological and anthropological evidence has to be gathered with the aim of testing these and other evolutionary hypotheses, and therefore without prejudging what the results of the test should be.

Conclusion

At first sight, moral judgments greatly differ across cultures, suggesting that human morality may be based on radically different systems of values. Evolutionary considerations on the bases of human cooperation suggest, however, that there must be evolved dispositions that make this cooperation sustainable. There are competing views regarding what these dispositions might be, an altruistic disposition to act for the benefit of the group even at an irredeemable cost to oneself, a mutualistic disposition to act and to expect others to act fairly, or some combination of both. Here we have explored the hypothesis that among the dispositions involved a sense of fairness is paramount. How then should we interpret differences of moral judgment? We suggested that much can be done by paying attention to people's beliefs about the range of their actual choices – beliefs that may be true (as in the case of Inuits who see themselves as no longer able to take care of their aged parents) or false (as in the case of Romans who see slavery as part of a natural order). Taking into consideration such beliefs, what had looked like cruelty may come to appear charitable, and what had looked like blatant disregard for fairness may appear compatible with considerations of fairness in a situation perceived quite differently. But speculative reconstructions of people's beliefs and inferences are not good enough. Appropriate cognitive anthropological evidence is needed to further our understanding of human morality.

REFERENCES

Alvard, M. and Nolin, D. (2002) Rousseau's Whale Hunt? Coordination among Big Game Hunters. *Current Anthropology* 43: 533.

André, J. B. and Baumard, N. (2011) Social Opportunities and the Evolution of Fairness. *Journal of Theoretical Biology* 289: 128–135.

Aspelin, P. (1979) Food Distribution and Social Bonding among the Mamainde of Mato Grosso, Brazil. *Journal of Anthropological Research, J* 35: 309–327.

Astuti, R. (1995) "The Vezo Are Not a Kind of People": Identity, Difference, and "Ethnicity" among a Fishing People of Western Madagascar. *American Ethnologist* 22(3): 464–482.

Astuti, R. (2008) What Happens After Death? In R. Astuti, J. Parry, and Ch. Stafford (eds.), *Questions of Anthropology*. Oxford: Berg, pp. 227–247.

Bailey, R. C. (1991) *The Behavioral Ecology of Efe Pygmy Men in the Ituri Forest, Zaire.* Ann Arbor: Museum of Anthropology, University of Michigan.

Barclay, P. and Willer, R. (2007) Partner Choice Creates Competitive Altruism in Humans. *Proceedings of the Royal Society B: Biological Sciences* 274: 749–753.

Baron, J. and Ritov, I. (1993) Intuitions about Penalties and Compensation in the Context of Tort Law. *Making Decisions about Liability and Insurance* 7(1): 7–33.

Baumard, N. (2010) *Comment nous sommes devenus moraux: une histoire naturelle du bien et du mal.* Paris: Odile Jacob.

Baumard, N. (2011) Punishment is a Not Group Adaptation: Humans Punish to Restore Fairness Rather than to Help the Group. *Mind and Society* 10(1): 1–26.

Benedict, R. (1934) *Patterns of Culture.* Boston: Houghton Mifflin.

Bloch, M. and Sperber, D. (2002) Kinship and Evolved Psychological Dispositions: The Mother's Brother Controversy Reconsidered. *Current Anthropology* 43(4): 723–748.

Boyd, R., Gintis, H., Bowles, S., and Richerson, P. (2003) The Evolution of Altruistic Punishment. *Proceedings of the National Academy of Sciences of the United States of America* 100(6): 3531–3535.

Briggs, J. L. (1970) *Never in Anger: Portrait of an Eskimo Family.* Cambridge, MA: Harvard University Press.

Bull, J. and Rice, W. (1991) Distinguishing Mechanisms for the Evolution of Co-Operation. *Journal of Theoretical Biology* 149(1): 63–74.

Carlsmith, K., Darley, J., and Robinson, P. (2002) Why Do We Punish? Deterrence and Just Deserts as Motives for Punishment. *Journal of Personality and Social Psychology* 83(2): 284–299.

Chiang, Y. (2010) Self-interested partner selection can lead to the emergence of fairness. *Evolution and Human Behavior* 31(4): 265–270.

de Waal, F. (1996) *Good Natured: The Origins of Right and Wrong in Humans and Other Animals.* Cambridge, MA: Harvard University Press.

Dumont, L. (1970) *Homo Hierarchicus: An Essay on the Caste System.* Chicago: University of Chicago Press.

Durkheim, É. (1893) *De la division du travail social.* Paris: F. Alcan.

Gintis, H., Bowles, S., Boyd, R., and Fehr, E. (2003) Explaining Altruistic Behavior in Humans. *Evolution and Human Behavior* 24(3): 153–172.

Gromet, D. and Darley, J. (2006) Restoration and Retribution: How Including Retributive Components Affects the Acceptability of Restorative Justice Procedures. *Social Justice Research* 19(4): 395–432.

Gurven, M. (2004) To Give and to Give Not: The Behavioral Ecology of Human Food Transfers. *Behavioral and Brain Sciences* 27: 543–583.

Haidt, J. (2001) The Emotional Dog and its Rational Tail: A Social Intuitionist Approach to Moral Judgment. *Psychological Review* 108: 814–834.

Haidt, J. (2007) The New Synthesis in Moral Psychology. *Science* 316: 998–1002.

Haidt, J. and Joseph, C. (2007) The Moral Mind: How Five Sets of Innate Intuitions Guide the Development of Many Culture-Specific Virtues, and Perhaps Even Modules. In P. Carruthers et al. (eds.), *The Innate Mind*, vol. 3. New York: Oxford University Press, pp. 367–391.

Haidt, J., Koller, S., and Dias, M. (1993) Affect, Culture, and Morality, or, Is It Wrong to Eat Your Dog? *Journal of Personality and Social Psychology* 65: 613–628.

Haidt, J., Bjorklund, F., and Murphy, S. (2004) Moral Dumbfounding: When Intuition Finds No Reason. Unpublished MS, University of Virginia.

Hamilton, W. (1964) The Genetical Evolution of Social Behaviour I and II. *Journal of Theoretical Biology* 7: 1–16; 17–52.

Hauser, M., Cushman, F., Young, L., and Jin, R. (2007) A Dissociation Between Moral Judgments and Justifications. *Mind & Language* 22(1): 1–21.

Henry, J. (1951) The Economics of Pilagá Food Distribution 1. *American Anthropologist* 53(2): 187–219.

Hill, K. and Kaplan, H. (1999) Life History Traits in Humans: Theory and Empirical Studies. *Annual Review of Anthropology* 28: 397–430.

Hoebel, E. A. (1954) *The Law of Primitive Man: A Study in Comparative Legal Dynamics.* Cambridge, MA: Harvard University Press.

Howell, P. (1954) *A Manual of Nuer Law: Being an Account of Customary Law, Its Evolution and Development in the Courts Established by the Sudan Government.* Oxford: Oxford University Press for International African Institute.

Johnson, A. W. and Earle, T. K. (2000) *The Evolution of Human Societies: From Foraging Group to Agrarian State*, 2nd edn. Stanford: Stanford University Press.

Kaplan, H. and Hill, K. (1985) Food Sharing among Ache Foragers: Tests of Explanatory Hypotheses. *Current Anthropology* 26(2): 223–246.

Kohlberg, L. (1981) *Essays on Moral Development*. San Francisco: Harper & Row.

Kurzban, R., Dukes, A., and Weeden, J. (2010) Sex, Drugs and Moral Goals: Reproductive Strategies and Views about Recreational Drugs. *Proceedings of the Royal Society B: Biological Sciences* 277: 3501–3508.

Laidlaw, J. (2002) For an Anthropology of Ethics and Freedom. *Journal of the Royal Anthropological Institute* 311–332.

Lambek, M. (2010) *Ordinary Ethics: Anthropology, Language, and Action*. New York: Fordham University Press.

Lévi-Strauss, C. (1969) *The Elementary Structures of Kinship* [*Les structures élémentaires de la parenté*], trans. J. H. Bell and J. R. von Sturmer ; ed. R. Needham. Boston : Beacon.

Malinowski, B. (1926) *Crime and Custom in Savage Society*. New York: Harcourt, Brace.

Marlowe, F. (2000) Paternal Investment and the Human Mating System. *Behavioural Processes* 51(1–3): 45–61.

Mercier, H.(in press) What Good is Moral Reasoning? *Mind & Society*.

Montaigne, M. de (1580) *Essais*. Paris: Arléas.

Noë, R., van Schaik, C., and Van Hooff, J. (1991) The Market Effect: An Explanation for Pay-Off Asymmetries among Collaborating Animals. *Ethology* 87(1–2): 97–118.

Piaget, J. (1932) *Le jugement moral chez l'enfant*. Paris: Presses Universitaires de France.

Price, J. A. (1975) Sharing: The Integration of Intimate Economies. *Anthropologica* 17: 3–27.

Rawls, J. (1971) *A Theory of Justice*. Cambridge, MA: Belknap Press of Harvard University Press.

Redfield, R. (1959) Anthropological Understanding of Man. *Anthropological Quarterly* 32(1): 3–21.

Roberts, G. (1998) Competitive Altruism: From Reciprocity to the Handicap Principle. *Proceedings of the Royal Society B: Biological Sciences* 265: 427–431.

Sahlins, M. D. (1972) *Stone Age Economics*. Chicago: Aldine-Atherton.

Scanlon, T. (1998) *What We Owe to Each Other*. Cambridge, MA: Belknap Press of Harvard University Press.

Scheidel, W. (2009) A Peculiar Institution? Greco-Roman Monogamy in Global Context. *History of the Family* 14(3): 280–291.

Shweder, R., Mahapatra, M., and Miller, J. (1987) Culture and Moral Development. In J. Kagan and S. Lamb (eds.), *The Emergence of Moral Concepts in Young Children*. Chicago: University of Chicago Press, pp. 1–83.

Shweder, R., Much, N. C., Mahapatra, M., and Park, L. (1997) The "Big Three" of Morality (Autonomy, Community, Divinity), and the "Big Three" Explanations of Suffering. In A. Brandt and P. Rozin (eds.), *Morality and Health*. New York: Routledge, pp. 119–169.

Sober, E. and Wilson, D. (1998) *Unto Others: The Evolution and Psychology of Unselfish Behavior*. Cambridge, MA: Harvard University Press.

Sperber, D. (1985) Anthropology and Psychology: Towards an Epidemiology of Representations. *Man* 20(1): 73–89.

Sperber, D. (1993) Remarques anthropologiques sur le relativisme moral. In J.-P. Changeux (ed.), *Fondements naturels de l'éthique*. Paris: Odile Jacob, pp. 319–334.

Sunstein, C., Kahneman, D., and Schkade, D. (1998) Assessing Punitive Damages (with Notes on Cognition and Valuation in Law). *Yale Law Journal* 107(7): 2071–2153.

Tomasello, M. (2009) *Why We Cooperate*. Cambridge, MA: MIT Press.

Trivers, R. (1971) Evolution of Reciprocal Altruism. *Quarterly Review of Biology* 46: 35–57.

Veyne, P. (1992) *A History of Private Life: From Pagan Rome to Byzantium*. Cambridge, MA: Belknap Press of Harvard University Press.

Veyne, P. (2005) *L'empire gréco-romain*. Paris: Seuil.

Walley, C. J. (1997) Searching for "Voices": Feminism, Anthropology, and the Global Debate over Female Genital Operations. *Cultural Anthropology* 12(3): 405–438.

Weeden, J., Cohen, A. B., and Kenrick, D. T. (2008) Religious Attendance As Reproductive Support. *Evolution and Human Behavior* 29(5): 327–334.

Westermarck, E. (1906) *The Origin and Development of the Moral Ideas.* London: Macmillan.

Wikan, U. (1987) Public Grace and Private Fears: Gaiety, Offense, and Sorcery in Northern Bali. *Ethos* 15(4): 337–365.

Wilson, J. (1993) *The Moral Sense.* New York: Free Press.

Winterhalder, B. (1997) Gifts Given, Gifts Taken: The Behavioral Ecology of Non-Market, Intragroup Exchange. *Journal of Archaeological Research* 5: 121–168.

Wittgenstein, L. (1953) *Philosophical Investigations,* trans. G. E. M. Anscombe. Oxford: Blackwell.

Index of Names

A Companion to Moral Anthropology, First Edition. Edited by Didier Fassin.

Subject Index